Also by A. M. Rosenthal and Arthur Gelb

The World of New York
The Sophisticated Traveler: Beloved Cities
The Sophisticated Traveler: Winter, Love It or Leave It
The Sophisticated Traveler: Great Tours and Detours
The Sophisticated Traveler: Enchanting Places and How to Find Them: From Pleasant Hill to Katmandu

The New York Times

GREAT LIVES

OF THE TWENTIETH CENTURY

The New York Times

GREAT LIVES

OF THE TWENTIETH CENTURY

EDITED BY

ARTHUR GELB

A.M. ROSENTHAL

AND

MARVIN SIEGEL

Times
BOOKS

Published in the United States by Times Books, a division of Random House, Inc., New York, and simultaneously in Canada by Random House of Canada Limited, Toronto.

Library of Congress Cataloging-in-Publication Data
New York times great lives of the twentieth century.
Includes index.
1. Biography—20th century. 2. Obituaries.
3. Celebrities—Biography. I. Rosenthal, A. M. (Abraham Michael), 1922– . II. Gelb, Arthur, 1924– .
III. New York times.
CT120.N46 1988 920'.009'04 [B] 88-2263
ISBN 0-8129-1625-5

Interior Design by Robert Bull Design

Manufactured in the United States of America

9 8 7 6 5 4 3 2

First Edition

Since all the permissions cannot legibly appear on this page, *they are begun on this page and continue on page vii.*

Grateful acknowledgment is also made to the following for permission to reprint previously published material:

Stella Adler: "Poet and Puritan" by Harold Clurman from *The New York Times Magazine* of March 29, 1970. Reprinted by permission of Miss Stella Adler.

American Foundation for the Blind: Excerpt from a letter of Helen Keller dated February 17, 1956. Reprinted with permission from American Foundation for the Blind, 15 W. 16th St., N.Y., N.Y. 10011.

The Associated Press: "Le Corbusier, Pioneering Architect, Is Dead." Reprinted by permission of The Associated Press.

Georges Borchardt, Inc.: "The World of Edward Hopper" by James Mellow from *The New York Times Magazine* of September 5, 1971. Reprinted by permission of Georges Borchardt, Inc., and the author. Copyright © 1971 by James Mellow.

Curtis Brown, Ltd.: "A Memoir" by Herbert Gold from *The New York Times Book Review* of July 31, 1977. Reprinted by permission of Curtis Brown, Ltd. Copyright © 1977 by Herbert Gold.

Joan Daves: "The Time for Freedom Has Come" by Martin Luther King, Jr., from *The New York Times Magazine* of September 10, 1961. Reprinted by permission of Joan Daves. Copyright © 1961 by Martin Luther King, Jr.

Faber and Faber Ltd: Excerpts from *The English Auden: Poems, Essays and Dramatic Writings, 1927–1939,* and *Look Stranger* by W. H. Auden. Reprinted by permission of Faber and Faber Ltd.

Juan Hamilton: Excerpts from *Georgia O'Keeffe* by Georgia O'Keeffe. © Juan Hamilton. Published by Viking Press.

Harcourt Brace Jovanovich, Inc.: Excerpts from: "The Dry Salvages" and "Little Gidding" in *Four Quartets,* copyright 1943 by T. S. Eliot, renewed 1971 by Esme Valerie Eliot; "The Naming of Cats" in *Old Possum's Book of Practical Cats,* copyright 1939 by T. S. Eliot, renewed 1967 by Esme Valerie Eliot; "Five Finger Exercise," "The Love Song of J. Alfred Prufrock," "The Hippopotamus," and "The Waste Land" in *Collected Poems 1909–1962* by T. S. Eliot, copyright © 1963, 1964 by T. S. Eliot. Rights in the U.S. administered by Harcourt Brace Jovanovich, Inc. Rights in all other territories administered by Faber and Faber Ltd. Reprinted by permission of Harcourt Brace Jovanovich, Inc., and Faber and Faber Ltd.

Alan Levy: "In the Autumn of the Age of Anxiety" by Alan Levy. © 1971, 1983 by Alan Levy, in whose book, *W. H. Auden: In the Autumn of the Age of Anxiety* (Permanent Press, Sag Harbor, N.J., 1983), this article was incorporated.

Ludlow Music, Inc.: Excerpts from the lyrics to "We Shall Overcome." Words and musical arrangement by Zilphia Horton, Frank Hamilton, Guy Carawan and Pete Seeger. TRO © Copyright 1960 (renewed 1988) and 1963 Ludlow Music, Inc., New York, N.Y. Used by permission.

McGraw-Hill Book Company: Excerpts from *Life with Picasso* by Francoise Gilot and Carlton Lake. Copyright © 1964 by McGraw-Hill, Inc. Reprinted by permission of McGraw-Hill Book Company.

Oxford University Press: Excerpts from "Clerihew" by Eric Bentley. Reprinted from *The Complete Clerihews of E. Clerihew Bentley* (1981) by permission of Oxford University Press.

Random House, Inc.: Excerpts from *W. H. Auden: Collected Poems* edited by Edward Mendelson. Copyright © 1976 by Edward Mendelson, William Meredith and Monroe K. Spears, Executors of the Estate of W. H. Auden. Rights in the U.S. administered by Random House, Inc. Rights in all other territories administered by Faber and Faber Ltd. Reprinted by permission of Random House, Inc. and Faber and Faber Ltd.

Bertrand Russell Estate: Excerpts from five letters of Bertrand Russell. © The Bertrand Russell Estate.

Simon & Schuster, Inc.: Excerpts from *The Complete War Memoirs of Charles de Gaulle,* Vols. I and II by Charles de Gaulle. Vol. I copyright © 1955 by Viking Press, Inc., Copyright renewed 1985 by Simon & Schuster, Inc. Vol. II copyright © 1959 by Simon & Schuster, Inc., Copyright renewed 1987 by Simon & Schuster, Inc. Reprinted by permission of Simon & Schuster, Inc.

Sterling Lord Literistic, Inc.: "The Ordeal of Picasso's Heirs" by Deborah Trustman from *The New York Times Magazine.* Copyright © 1980. "Our Mr. Eliot Grows Younger" by V. S. Pritchett from *The New York Times Magazine* of September 21, 1958. Copyright © 1958. Reprinted by permission of Sterling Lord Literistic, Inc.

Time Inc.: "Vigorous and Decisive Leader" by Dean Acheson. *Life* Magazine © Time Inc.

A. P. Watt Ltd: Excerpts from *Memoirs of Field Marshal Montgomery* by Viscount Montgomery. Reprinted by permission of A. P. Watt Ltd. on behalf of Viscount Montgomery of Alamein.

'Tis an old well-known proverb of mankind,
"You cannot tell men's fortunes till they die,
In any case, if they be good or bad."

—Sophocles, *Trachiniae*

CONTENTS

INTRODUCTION

The reporter from *The New York Times* was walking near her Manhattan home when she saw the elderly playwright she had interviewed a few weeks earlier.

"Well, how are you these days?" she asked brightly.

The playwright looked at her, laughed a small and mirthless laugh, and said: "Obviously better than you think I am."

It was not the cheeriest way to begin a conversation in the street but there seemed no point in denying it. The reporter had been assigned to the interview because she and her editors considered the playwright a likely candidate for death in the not-too-distant future; otherwise they would not have bothered sending her over. Happily, the playwright lives at this writing, several years later, but then you cannot win them all.

Still, he will no doubt die one day, and his obituary will be ready in a special file at *The Times*—carefully written, facts checked, appraisals of peers and pithy quotations from his works included, and the total space devoted to his time on earth generous by any reasonable measure.

The playwright knew perfectly well that the reporter was working in a fairly new specialty in journalism—she was a skilled practitioner of writing obituaries in advance of the subject's death. He consented to the interview because he wanted the newspaper to do him justice in the edition he would miss. He preferred the reminder of his age and infirmity that the visit implied—never stated, of course—to having to put up, even in absentia, with a slipshod, hastily prepared final review of his life. He was convinced that if there was an afterlife, the irritation of a poorly done obituary in *The New York Times* would follow him.

And he was fully aware that the very fact that *The Times* had selected his life story to be included in the file of "advance obituaries" was a substantial compliment, however somber.

Not all advance obituaries are written by journalists who devote themselves to that craft. On *The Times,* which pays high professional respect to advance obituary writers, most obituaries written before a subject's death are still turned out by experts in the fields in which the honored subjects spent their own lives. Alden Whitman and Albin Krebs, talented advance obit writers, produced about a dozen of the biographies in this book. But the paper's editors also call upon the special knowledge gained through years, sometimes decades, of endeavor by other members of the staff.

For example, Anna Kisselgoff, dance critic of *The Times,* was asked to write the obituary of George Balanchine. The famous foreign correspondent Homer Bigart wrote of David Ben-Gurion. Hanson Baldwin, long the *Times*'s military correspondent, contributed to the obituary of Eisenhower, and the paper's jazz critic, John Wilson, wrote Duke Ellington's.

Often, when the obituary itself is not written by a specialist in the field, that person is asked to contribute a separate appraisal—for example, Anthony Lewis on Felix Frankfurter, Max Frankel on Lyndon Johnson and Dwight David Eisenhower, Hilton Kramer on Picasso.

The creativity in this book comes, of course, from the writers. At the same time, it is a very personal book as far as the editors are concerned.

Arthur Gelb and I started our editing careers together, after almost two decades each as reporters. Arthur was headed toward being the drama critic of *The Times* and I was quite content to go on being a foreign correspondent. However, Fate, otherwise known as Turner Catledge, the Mississippian who was managing editor of *The Times,* decided in 1963 that I would be of more use to the paper as metropolitan editor in New York than spending my time in Tokyo, just writing and being happy. I persuaded Arthur Gelb to join me. In time, we both rose in the newspaper hierarchy to the point where we, too, could devote our energies to looking for correspondents happy in their jobs so we could drag them out and make them editors.

As new editors, we quickly discovered that God came under the jurisdiction of the metropolitan desk. We were responsible for the religious coverage of the paper, so we were not too surprised when we discovered that death also came under our aegis as well.

It was our task to assign preparation of advance obituaries. We also dealt with reports on the deaths of those people who died before the newspaper staff could get around to them—those who passed away while the daily deadline approached. This often caused stress among reporters assigned to turn out the obituary quickly. Therefore, unless an advance obituary is written, it is best to die before noon, 2 P.M. at the latest, so that there will be decent time for justice to be done before the early-evening deadline of the first edition—and less inconvenience to the staff. All those interested in having *The Times* sum up their lives, even briefly, should avoid dying on Saturday, when the deadline is very early.

Early on we had to deal with the question of relativity. How much is a person's life worth, in inches of type, or columns? One of the first obituaries I assigned was that of a fine *Times* foreign correspondent. I ordered about three columns in total, including quotes from his dispatches, a considerable amount of space.

The next day Clifton Daniel, then assistant managing editor, told me he thought I had overplayed the story out of sentiment. I did not agree at first, but Mr. Daniel convinced me when he said that he doubted he would give me three columns were I to die on the spot.

It was Mr. Daniel, incidentally, who first took the leadership in convincing other editors on the paper, particularly the two new men on the metropolitan desk, that obituaries should be handled as matters of special importance deserving of the best talent available to the paper. It was our last chance to do justice not only to the subject, but also to the reader in terms of that person's life, by presenting a rich, thoughtful biography with attention to detail and context.

When it was decided to prepare this book of *Times* biographies, our publisher selected a time frame running from the beginning of our careers as editors in 1963 to the present. The obituaries would be ones in which we had a particular professional interest or involvement. We asked Marvin Siegel, an editor on the *Times* who had worked with us on the metropolitan desk, to join us in the work. He suggested opening the scope of the book, not limiting it to the obituaries themselves. So, in addition to the obituaries, he selected appraisals, news stories, selections from the subjects' work. The book became more than a compilation of biographies; it became a piece of contemporary history.

Lists of *Times* obituaries of people in politics, science, art, entertainment and literature were drawn up. There were hundreds of interesting names, and it was obvious that it was impossible to winnow them down to a final fifty, the number of subjects to which one book had to be limited to present them properly.

So it was decided that this was to be the first of a series of books of *Times* biographies. That removed from us the necessity of immediately presenting the biographies of some obvious choices, like President Kennedy. It enables us to answer complaints about why we left out one person or another: just wait. And, more important, the fact that this was to be the first of a series allowed us to make it more varied than if we limited ourselves to subjects with strictly historic importance.

We learned a great deal from the selection process—about the lives involved, about our own values and about judgments made by history. We learned that many people once considered individuals of power seemed to have little real significance soon after their deaths. (Management seems to be the fastest road to historical oblivion, by the way. On the first lists were names of men who headed huge companies; later they were all removed; they just did not seem to matter much anymore.)

What did matter, looking back? Creativity, mostly. It is possible to leave out, or defer for another book, prime ministers, dictators, kings. It is impossible to leave out Charles Chaplin or Louis Armstrong.

It was a special kind of creativity that kept a person on the list—a talent never matched, like Fred Astaire's, or one that opened new fields, like Walt Disney's.

In addition to creativity of performance there was creativity of intellect: Felix Frankfurter. And there is a kind of creativity of character, a sense that here is a life whose very living will always have meaning: Helen Keller, Martin Luther King, Jr.

Political power sustained an importance second only to creative power. But almost always the deciding factor turned out to be something more than high office. It was the person's role in an event of lasting moment—victory in war for Churchill, de Gaulle and Eisenhower; defeat for Haile Selassie and Lyndon Johnson; revolution for Ho Chi Minh; the building of a nation for Ben-Gurion.

Sometimes it was the field of achievement that led to the choice. Who do we want to represent poetry? Architecture? Painting? We could have done without T. S. Eliot, say, and included another political leader, but then it would not have been our book at all.

There is historical bias in this book: relatively few women. Georgia O'Keeffe and Margaret Sanger and Coco Chanel seemed more interesting to us than Indira Gandhi. That is a reflection of taste and choice. It may tell something about *The Times* that there were comparatively few women given major attention. It tells more about the restricted roles of women in the early and middle decades of this century.

There is also bias in the selection, since it was done by three individuals, not three machines. It is heavier on the arts than three other editors might have decided. And it should be stated that a certain amount of horse trading was involved: I will give you Joe Louis if you will give me John L. Lewis. Give me Groucho Marx and I will give you any other two.

The editors thank the reporters and writers who created the stories of these lives and, at least in most cases, the people who lived them. The editors promise to take readers' choices into account in future volumes, perhaps.

And, of course, our thanks to the hundreds of prominent people still living who have sat for interviews knowing full well they would never see them in print. We appreciate the time you have given our obituary writers just as we know you appreciate the dour honor.

—A. M. Rosenthal
June 1988

The New York Times

GREAT LIVES

OF THE TWENTIETH CENTURY

LOUIS ARMSTRONG

1900–1971

By Albin Krebs

Louis Armstrong, the celebrated jazz trumpeter and singer, died in his sleep July 6, 1971, at his home in the Corona section of Queens. He had observed his 71st birthday two days earlier.

Tributes to Mr. Armstrong came from a number of leading musicians, including Duke Ellington, Gene Krupa, Benny Goodman, Al Hirt, Earl (Fatha) Hines, Tyree Glenn and Eddie Condon.

Mr. Ellington commented: "If anybody was Mr. Jazz it was Louis Armstrong. He was the epitome of jazz and always will be. He is what I call an American standard, an American original."

"He could play a trumpet like nobody else," Mr. Condon said, "then put it down and sing a song like no one else could."

Mr. Hines, who frequently said he had taken his piano style from Mr. Armstrong's trumpet style, remarked: "We were almost like brothers. I'm so heartbroken over this. The world has lost a champion."

In Washington, the State Department, noting that Mr. Armstrong had toured Africa, the Middle East and Latin America on its behalf, said: "His memory will be enshrined in the archives of effective international communications. The Department of State, for which he traveled on tours to almost every corner of the globe, mourns the passing of this great American."

A master showman known to millions as Satchmo, Mr. Armstrong lived by a simple credo. Putting it into words a couple of years ago, he said: "I never tried to prove nothing, just always wanted to give a good show. My life has been my music, it's always come first, but the music ain't worth nothing if you can't lay it on the public. The main thing is to live for that audience, 'cause what you're there for is to please the people."

Mr. Armstrong was first and most importantly a jazz trumpet player without peer, a virtuoso soloist who was one of the most vivid and influential forces in the development of American music.

But he was also known to delighted millions around the world for his ebulliently sandpapery singing voice, his merry mangling of the English language and his great, wide, grand-piano keyboard of a smile.

Jazz music, probably the only art form ever originated wholly in America, and Louis Armstrong grew up together in New Orleans. It was in a seamy slum there that Mr. Armstrong learned to love and play jazz in the company of gamblers, pimps and prostitutes.

But in time he was to play his trumpet and sing in command performances before royalty and, through his numerous worldwide tours, to become known unofficially as "America's ambassador of goodwill."

Jazz experts, even the purists who criticized Mr.

AP/WIDE WORLD

Armstrong for his mugging and showmanship, more often than not agreed that it was he, more than any other individual, who took the raw, gutsy Negro folk music of the New Orleans funeral parades and honky-tonks and built it into a unique art form.

Over the years, his life and his artistry changed radically. He left New Orleans for Chicago in the early 1920s, when he was still playing the cornet, and before 1930 made some of his most memorable recordings—with his Hot Five or Hot Seven groups.

Mr. Armstrong won his initial fame playing an endless grind of one-night stands. Under constant pressure to put on a show that made the customers tap their feet and cry for more, he did not hesitate to exploit a remarkable flair for showmanship. His mugging, his wisecracking and most of all his willingness to constantly repeat programs that had gone over well in the past won him the cheers of his audiences, along with the disapproving clucks of some of his fellow musicians and jazz specialists.

The criticism that he no longer improvised enough or innovated enough mattered little to Mr. Armstrong. He dismissed the more "progressive" jazz approved of by some leading critics as "jujitsu music."

He did not mind being called "commercial" because he followed popular music trends, and he deliberately introduced into his repertory crowd pleasers such as "Mack the Knife" and "Hello, Dolly!" which put his recordings on the best-seller charts when he was in his sixties.

As his ability to play his horn exceptionally well waned with the years, Mr. Armstrong supplanted his trumpet solos with his singing voice. An almost phenomenal instrument in its own right, it has been compared to iron filings and to "a piece of sandpaper calling to its mate."

Just watching an Armstrong performance could be an exhilarating experience. The man radiated a jollity that was infectious. Onstage he would bend back his stocky frame, point his trumpet to the heavens and joyfully blast out high C's. When he sang, he fairly bubbled with pleasure. And as he swabbed away at the perspiration stirred up by his performing exertions, Satchmo grinned his famous toothy smile so incandescently that it seemed to light up the auditorium.

"I never did want to be no big star," Mr. Armstrong said in 1969, in an interview for this article. "It's been hard goddamn work, man. Feel like I spent 20,000 years on the planes and railroads, like I blowed my chops off. Sure, Pops, I like the ovation, but when I'm low, beat down, I wonder if maybe I hadn't of been better off staying home in New Orleans."

Mr. Armstrong's early years, spent in New Orleans, were marked by extreme poverty and squalor, but he emerged able to recall them without self-pity and even with good humor.

"I was a Southern Doodle Dandy, born on the Fourth of July, 1900," said Daniel Louis Armstrong. "My mother, Mary Ann—we called her Mayann—was living in a two-room shack in James Alley, in the Back O' Town colored section of New Orleans. It was in a tough block, all them hustlers and their pimps and gamblers with their knives, between Gravier and Perdido streets."

Mr. Armstrong's father, Willie Armstrong, who stoked furnaces in a turpentine factory, left Mrs. Armstrong when the boy was an infant. Leaving the child with his paternal grandmother, Mrs. Armstrong went to live in the Perdido–Liberty Street area, which was lined with prostitutes' cribs.

"Whether my mother did any hustling I can't say," Mr. Armstrong said. "If she did, she kept it out of my sight."

However, Louis, who rejoined his mother when he was 6 years old, recalled that for many years afterward there was always a "stepfather" on the premises and that before his mother "got religion and gave up men" around 1915, "I couldn't keep track of the stepdaddies; there must have been a dozen or so, 'cause all I had to do was turn my back and a new pappy would appear." Some of them, he added, "liked to beat on little Louis."

However, Mr. Armstrong was always intensely

fond of his mother, and he cared for her until her death in the early 1940s.

Dippermouth, as he was called as a child, and his friends often sang for pennies on the streets. To help support his mother and a sister, Barbara, Louis delivered coal to prostitutes' cribs and sold food plucked from hotel garbage cans.

The night of Dec. 31, 1913, Louis celebrated the New Year by running out on the street and firing a .38-caliber pistol that belonged to one of his "stepfathers." He was arrested and sent to the Colored Waifs Home for Boys.

"Pops, it sure was the greatest thing that ever happened to me," Mr. Armstrong said. "Me and music got married at the home."

Peter Davis, an instructor at the home, taught Louis to play the bugle and the cornet. Soon the boy became a member of the home's brass band, which played at socials, picnics and funerals for a small fee. Louis was in the fifth grade when he was released from the home after spending 18 months there. He had no other formal education.

The youth worked as a junkman and sold coal, while grabbing every chance he could to play cornet in honky-tonk bands. The great jazz cornetist Joe (King) Oliver befriended him, gave him a cornet and tutored him.

"I was foolin' around with some tough ones," Mr. Armstrong recalled in 1969. "Get paid a little money, and made a beeline for one of them gambling houses. Two hours, man, and I was a broke cat, broker than the Ten Commandments. Needed money so bad I even tried pimping, but my first client got jealous of me and we got to fussing about it and she stabbed me in the shoulder. Them was wild times."

In 1918, Mr. Armstrong married a 21-year-old prostitute named Daisy Parker. Since Daisy "wouldn't give up her line of work," Mr. Armstrong said, the marriage was both stormy and short-lived.

The same year he was married, Mr. Armstrong joined the Kid Ory band, replacing King Oliver, who had moved to Chicago. In the next three years he marched with Papa Celestin's brass band and worked on the riverboat *Sidney* with Fate Marable's band. Dave Jones, a mellophone player with the Marable band, gave him his first lessons in reading music.

By then Mr. Armstrong's fame was spreading among New Orleans musicians, many of whom were moving to Chicago. In 1922 King Oliver sent for his protégé. Mr. Armstrong became second cornetist in Mr. Oliver's by-then-famous Creole Jazz Band. The two-cornet team had one of the most formidably brilliant attacks ever heard in a jazz group. Mr. Armstrong's first recordings were made with the Oliver band in 1923.

The pianist in the band was Lilian Hardin, whom Mr. Armstrong married in 1924. Miss Hardin had had training as a classical musician, and she gave him some formal musical education.

Mrs. Armstrong, convinced that as long as her husband stayed in the Oliver band he would remain in the shadow of his popular mentor, persuaded him to leave the band in 1924 to play first cornet at the Dreamland Cafe. The same year he joined Fletcher Henderson's orchestra at the Roseland Ballroom in New York.

For the first time, Mr. Armstrong found himself in the company of musicians of an entirely different stripe from those he had known in New Orleans and Chicago, who, like himself, had fought their way up out of the back alleys and were largely unschooled in music. From these New York men, many of whom had conservatory educations, he learned considerable musical discipline.

Moving back to Chicago in 1925, Mr. Armstrong again played at the Dreamland Cafe, where his wife, Lil, had her own band, and with Erskine Tate's "symphonic jazz" orchestra at the Vendome Theater. It was at that point that he gave up the cornet for the trumpet.

"I was hired to play them hot choruses when the curtain went up," Mr. Armstrong recalled. "They put a spotlight on me. Used to hit 40 or 50 high C's—go wild, screamin' on my horn. I was crazy, Pops, plain nuts."

During his second Chicago period, Mr. Armstrong doubled in Carroll Dickerson's Sunset Cabaret orchestra, with billing as the "World's Greatest Trumpeter." The proprietor of the Sunset was Joe Glaser, who became Mr. Armstrong's personal manager and acted in that capacity for the rest of his life. Mr. Glaser died on June 6, 1969.

In that Chicago period, Mr. Armstrong began to make records under his own name, the first being "My Heart," which was recorded on Nov. 12, 1925. Louis Armstrong's Hot Five (and later Hot Seven) recorded, over a three-year span, a series of jazz classics, with Earl (Fatha) Hines on the piano. These records earned Mr. Armstrong a worldwide reputation, and by 1929, when he returned to New York, he had become an idol in the jazz world.

While playing at Connie's Inn in Harlem, Mr. Armstrong also appeared on Broadway in the all-Negro review *Hot Chocolates*, in which he introduced Fats Waller's "Ain't Misbehavin,'" his first popular song hit. (He later appeared as Bottom in *Swingin' the Dream*, a short-lived travesty on *A Midsummer Night's Dream*. Over the years he appeared in many movies, including *Pennies from Heaven*, *A Song Is Born*, *The Glenn Miller Story* and *High Society*.)

For several years, Mr. Armstrong "fronted" big bands assembled for him by others. By 1932, the year he was divorced from Lil Hardin Armstrong, he had become so popular in Europe, via recordings, that he finally agreed to tour the Continent.

It was while he was starring at the London Palladium that Mr. Armstrong acquired the nickname Satchmo. A London music magazine's editor inadvertently invented the name by garbling an earlier nickname, Satchelmouth.

While he was in London, Mr. Armstrong demonstrated memorably that he had little use for the niceties of diplomatic protocol.

During a command performance for King George V, Mr. Armstrong ignored the rule that performers are not supposed to refer to members of the Royal Family while playing before them, and announced on the brink of a hot trumpet break, "This one's for you, Rex."

(Many years later, in 1956, Satchmo played before King George's granddaughter, Princess Margaret. "We're really gonna lay this one on for the princess," he said, grinning, and launched into "Mahogany Hall Stomp," a sort of jazz elegy to a New Orleans bordello. The princess loved it.)

One of Mr. Armstrong's pre-World War II European tours lasted 18 months. Over the years, his tours took him to the Middle East and the Far East, to Africa and to South America. In Accra, Ghana, 100,000 people went into a frenzied demonstration when he started to blow his horn, and in Léopoldville (now Kinshasa Zaire), tribesmen painted themselves ocher and violet and carried him into the city stadium on a canvas throne.

His 1960 African tour was denounced by Moscow radio as a "capitalist distraction," which made Mr. Armstrong laugh.

"I feel at home in Africa," he said during the tour. "I'm African-descended down to the bone, and I dig the friendly ways these people go about things. I got quite a bit of African blood in me from my grandmammy on my mammy's side and from my grandpappy on my pappy's side."

Before World War II, Mr. Armstrong worked with several big bands, including the Guy Lombardo orchestra, concentrating on New Orleans standards such as "Muskrat Ramble" and "When the Saints Go Marchin' In" and on novelties such as "I'll Be Glad When You're Dead, You Rascal You." He did duets with Ella Fitzgerald and he accompanied Bessie Smith.

After 1947 he usually performed as leader of a sextet, working with such musicians as Jack Teagarden, Earl Hines, Joe Bushkin and Cozy Cole. He was a favorite at all the jazz festivals, in this country and abroad.

Mr. Armstrong lost track of the number of recordings he made, but it has been estimated there were as many as 1,500. Dozens have become collectors' items.

The jolly Mr. Armstrong was quite inured to his fame as a jazz immortal. Not too many years ago, he was interviewed backstage by a disk jockey, who began with the announcement "And now we bring you a man who came all the way from New Orleans, the Crescent City, to become a Living American Legend." The Living American Legend, who was changing his clothes, dropped his trousers and began the interview with the observation "Tee hee!"

"Tee hee" was part of a uniquely Armstrong vocabulary, which included Satchmo-coined words such as *commercified* and *humanitarily*. In his speech he arbitrarily inserted hyphens in the middle of words (*ar-tis-try* and *en-ta-TAIN-uh*) and, unable to remember names too well, peppered his conversations with friends and interviewers with salutations such as *Daddy* and *Pops*.

Despite the hard life he led—traveling most of the time, sleeping too little, living out of suitcases, eating and drinking too much or not enough—Mr. Armstrong, even into his sixties, was still going strong. His chest was broad and powerful, and his 5-foot-8-inch frame carried a weight that varied between 170 and 230 pounds.

He was, however, keenly aware of his health. "I'm one of them hy-po-CHON-dree-acs," he would say with a delighted laugh. He was afraid of germs and always carried his trumpet mouthpiece in a carefully folded handkerchief in his back pocket. He liked to talk at length about his physic, a herbal mixture called Swiss Kriss, while at the same time he recounted how unwisely he sometimes ate, especially when his favorite food, New Orleans–style red beans and rice, was set before him.

Although in later years he suffered from a kidney ailment, Mr. Armstrong's greatest worry was chronic leukoplakia of the lips, what amounted to a tough corn that resulted from blowing his horn. He used a special, imported salve to soothe his lips.

"If you don't look out for your chops and pipes," he said, "you can't blow the horn and sing. Anything that'll get in my way doin' that, out it goes. That trumpet comes first, before everything, even my wife. Got to be that way. I love Lucille, man, but she understands about me and my music."

He was referring to the former Lucille Wilson, whom he married in 1942.

He loved all forms of music. When asked what he thought of the country-and-western and folk music so favored by the young, he replied, "Pops, music is music. All music is folk music. I ain't never heard no horse sing a song."

Some Negro militants criticized Mr. Armstrong for his earthy speech and his habit of rolling his eyes and flashing his toothy grin while performing. They said he was using stereotyped characteristics of the happy-go-lucky Negro and playing the Uncle Tom. Mr. Armstrong ignored the charges.

Nevertheless, Mr. Armstrong, on learning in 1965 that the police in Selma, Ala., had taken violent action against freedom-marching Negroes in that city, told an interviewer: "They would beat Jesus if he was black and marched. Maybe I'm not in the front line, but I support them with my donations. My life is my music. They would beat me on the mouth if I marched, and without my mouth I wouldn't be able to blow my horn."

For many years, Mr. Armstrong refused to perform in New Orleans, his hometown, because of segregation there. He did not return until 1965, after passage of the Civil Rights Act. On that occasion he triumphantly played with an integrated band in the city's Jazz Museum.

Reflecting on his more than 50 years as a musician, Mr. Armstrong said, "There ain't going to be no more cats in this music game that long."

There was no doubt that he was the most durable of the great jazzmen, nor that millions of people held him in great affection. His fellow musicians, many of whom were influenced by his artistry, looked upon him with awe.

Miles Davis, a contemporary jazz star, has asserted that "you can't play anything on a horn that Louis hasn't played." Teddy Wilson, who played piano with Mr. Armstrong in 1933, has called him "the greatest jazz musician that's ever been."

And Leonard Feather, the jazz critic and author of *The Encyclopedia of Jazz*, wrote of Mr. Armstrong:

"It is difficult . . . to see in correct perspective Armstrong's contribution as the first vital jazz soloist to attain worldwide influence as trumpeter, singer, entertainer, dynamic show business personality and strong force in stimulating interest in jazz.

"His style, melodically and harmonically simple by the standards of later jazz trends, achieved in his early records an unprecedented warmth and beauty. His singing, lacking most of the traditional vocal qualities accepted outside the jazz world, had a rhythmic intensity and guttural charm that induced literally thousands of other vocalists to imitate him, just as countless trumpeters through the years reflected the impact of his style.

"By 1960, Armstrong, set in his ways, improvised comparatively little; but he retained vocally and instrumentally many of the qualities that had established him, even though entertainment values, by his own admission, meant more to him than the reaction of a minority of musicians and specialists."

As for Mr. Armstrong, it was pleasing his listeners that really mattered.

"There's three generations Satchmo has witnessed," he said, "the old cats, their children and their children's children, and they still all walk up and say, 'Ol' Satch, how do you do!' I love my audience and they love me and we just have one good time whenever I get up on the stage. It's such a lovely pleasure."

Mr. Armstrong is survived by his widow, the former Lucille Wilson, and by an adopted son, Clarence Hatfield of New York. He also leaves a sister, Mrs. Beatrice Collins of New Orleans, and two half brothers, Henry and William Armstrong, both of New Orleans. The Armstrongs' home in Corona was at 34-56 107th Street.

NEW ORLEANS BIDS FAREWELL

JAMES T. WOOTEN

THE BOYS from Bourbon Street blew a big, brassy good-bye to Louis Armstrong on July 11, 1971.

Thousands turned out in New Orleans to pay tribute to a native son. The event was billed as a memorial to the celebrated trumpeter, who died on July 6 at the age of 71, but there were only fleeting moments of sadness.

"We don't need a body for a funeral," said Matthew (Fats) Houston, honorary leader of the Olympia Brass Band. "All we need's for the man to be gone—and he's gone, Lord keeps him, he's gone."

With that, he put a whistle in his mouth, blew it violently and turned at the head of his band toward City Hall, where clergymen, municipal officials and jazz buffs were waiting to offer formal eulogies to Mr. Armstrong.

The bandsmen had gathered at Basin and Canal streets as they waited for Mr. Houston's signal. They were nearly crushed in the press of the thousands who came to join them in the march to the formal ceremonies.

"We were going to dirge it on up to the place," said the leader, a retired drummer, "but none of these folks are in a dirging mood."

At Mr. Houston's signal, two trumpeters—a black man and a white man—blasted out a fanfare. From the beginning, the beat of the parade was quick and the music was loud.

The marchers twirled umbrellas above them as they danced—swirling, jerking, sliding—toward City Hall.

They were black and white, too, and they followed behind with beer cans wrapped in paper napkins and bottles of wine in brown paper bags.

At City Hall, the Basin Street parade merged with one led down Loyola Street by the Onward Brass Band. The music grew in its bouncing intensity. It was Dixieland, or New Orleans jazz, the kind that Mr. Armstrong had learned to play as a boy in this city.

Like the squirming crowds around them, both bands were fully integrated, an arrangement that was banned by city law from 1955 until the late 1960s. Mr. Armstrong boycotted the city after the ban on integrated bands was put into effect.

After the formal statements of tribute, Teddy Riley, a 47-year-old trumpeter at a bistro known as Crazy Shirley's, sounded taps on a cornet that once belonged to Mr. Armstrong.

The instrument will not be played again, officials at the New Orleans Jazz Museum said.

While Mr. Armstrong cherished his roots in New Orleans, he found its racial customs and segregation laws abhorrent and did not return to play an engagement until a few years ago after close friends persuaded him that the city had changed.

He declined to take part in public demonstrations for civil rights; instead, he contributed substantial sums to various black-oriented organizations, including the National Association for the Advancement of Colored People and the National Urban League, both of which played major roles in the transformation of his hometown's posture on race.

"Pops was very impressed when he came back," recalled Jack Jackson, a bass player who knew Mr. Armstrong. "He saw colored folks doing about what they pleased. He gave me his card and said, 'Jack, you write me every once in a while and tell me how the people is doing.' "

But, according to Mr. Jackson and other New Orleans musicians, Mr. Armstrong was never able to erase completely his distasteful memories of New Orleans, and his appearances here were rare.

Nevertheless, it seemed appropriate that the final notes from his old horn should be sounded in a city that thrives on bits and pieces of yesterday.

Like the instrument itself, its bright, spirited music has tarnished a bit over the years until now, here and across the country, it is primarily an artifact—a fragment of American history, to be remembered like spats, the rumble seat and the Charleston.

The moods and tastes of the nation transformed the rough-hewn but sparkling jazz of New Orleans into the better-organized styles that Mr. Armstrong played with King Oliver's Creole Jazz Band in Chicago in the 1920s. Those styles also faded, into the big-band arrangements called swing, and, ultimately, the world of jazz became a many-splintered community that included bebop and various forms of "progressive" music.

Even Mr. Armstrong changed with the times, leaving behind him the music he had helped make immensely popular and, with his prodigious talents, moving easily into new avenues of expression.

Still, in all of his music there was the obvious flavor of his New Orleans beginnings—a sense of his Dixieland roots faithfully preserved today in a few bistros, clubs and halls regarded as the haunts of the purists.

"Really, that's what this memorial could be for today—our music," lamented Mr. Riley. "We're going to put this horn on a little pillow in the museum and nobody's gonna play it again. They've already laid Pops down up there in New York and it ain't going to be long before the whole thing's dead and gone."

THE ROOT SOURCE OF JAZZ

JOHN S. WILSON

LOUIS ARMSTRONG was more than a great jazz virtuoso. He was the root source that moved jazz onto the path along which it has developed for more than 45 years. Through the sheer power of his musical imagination and personality, he reshaped the relatively limited urban folk music in which he grew up, opening up the possibilities that have made it part of a global culture.

When young Louis Armstrong left his home in New Orleans to join King Oliver's Creole Jazz Band in Chicago in 1922, jazz was still a music of ensemble improvisation.

But this form was being shaken up in the active jazz world that Mr. Armstrong found in Chicago. Soloists were breaking through the ensemble pattern. It was Mr. Armstrong who gave the solo stature by showing such steadily developing virtuosity in the series of records made by his Hot Five and Hot Seven that his solos soon became the focal points of the recordings.

"Cornet Chop Suey," "Potato Head Blues" and, in deeper and more deliberate fashion, "West End Blues" and "Tight Like That" contained jazz solos of such compelling brilliance that the emphasis in jazz performance was changed from the ensemble to the soloist.

And it was Mr. Armstrong, too, who provided the spark that made the big jazz band viable. His presence in Fletcher Henderson's orchestra in 1924 changed a dance band that was not unlike other dance bands of the period into a jazz band, the first of its kind.

Because he made these essential contributions to the development of jazz in the 1920s, when jazz—the real thing, as opposed to the popularly accepted "jazz" of such bandleaders as Paul Whiteman—was still largely an underground music, most of Mr. Armstrong's career was, in a sense, an anticlimax.

But, fortunately, he had a second string to his bow as a singer and entertainer, and through this, in his later years, he reaped the fame and rewards that too often have eluded the influential creators in jazz. To gain these, he became known to a generation or two primarily for his toothy grin and his singing of pop ballads. But that was just a surface. Underneath bubbled that same spirit and expressiveness that had made possible the jazz that musicians were playing 30 and 40 years ago, the jazz they are playing today and whatever they may play tomorrow. Wherever they are, they're playing Louis's music.

A SELECTED DISCOGRAPHY

The 1920s

The Great Louis Armstrong. Orpheum 105

King Oliver. Epic 16003

Young Louis "The Sideman." Decca 9233

The Louis Armstrong Story. Columbia CL 851–854

The 1930s and Early 1940s

V.S.O.P. (Very Special Old Phonography). Epic 22019

A Rare Batch of Satch. Victor 2322

In the 30's and 40's. Victor 2971

Louis Armstrong. Up Front 143

Since World War II

Town Hall Concert Plus. Victor 1443

Satchmo at Symphony Hall. Decca DX 108

Satchmo at Pasadena. Decca 8041

Plays W. C. Handy. Columbia CL 591

Satch Plays Fats. Columbia CL 708

Greatest Hits. Columbia CS 9438

With Duke Ellington: *Echoes of an Era*. Roulette RE-108

With Ella Fitzgerald: *Ella and Louis*. Verve 4003

FRED ASTAIRE

1899–1987

By Richard F. Shepard

Fred Astaire's flashing feet and limber legs not only made him America's most popular dancer but also set standards for motion picture musical comedies that have rarely been met and never exceeded.

Mr. Astaire blithely danced his way into the heart of an America tormented by the Depression and edging toward World War II. His deceptively easy-looking light-footedness, warm smile, top hat, cane, charm and talent helped people to forget the real world that nagged at them outside the movie house.

The Astaire legend, which spanned more than six performing decades on stage, screen and television, began before he was 10 years old when his mother paired him as a dancer with his sister, Adele, the partner with whom he first found success.

Mr. Astaire starred in more than 30 film musicals between 1933 and 1968. Ten of these co-starred Ginger Rogers, his most durable dancing partner. The music they danced to was written by the cream of the popular music world, including Cole Porter, Irving Berlin, Jerome Kern and George and Ira Gershwin.

There were other famous dancers, but few could match the sophistication and inventiveness of Mr. Astaire in such films as *Flying Down to Rio*, *The Gay Divorcée*, *Top Hat*, *Swing Time*, *Follow the Fleet*, *Blue Skies* and *Easter Parade*.

For all the lushness of his films, often in settings of splendor and champagne, Mr. Astaire projected a down-to-earth personality, that of a good-hearted fellow whose effortless steps, even at their most dazzling, matched his casual demeanor.

His dance numbers fit neatly within the bounds of a movie screen, but they gave the illusion of being boundless, without regard for the laws of gravity or the limitations of a set.

He danced with Rita Hayworth atop a wedding cake (*You'll Never Get Rich*, 1941), danced on roller skates (*Shall We Dance?*, 1937), danced while hitting golf balls off a tee (*Carefree*, 1938) and danced up the walls and on the ceiling (*Royal Wedding*, 1951). He danced while airborne, aboard ships and in countless ballrooms where he glided flawlessly across wide-open spaces. It was the kind of dancing that caught the imagination, even of those who disdained the thought of witnessing any dancing at all.

He was popular and beloved, a thin, sandy-haired man 5 feet 9 inches tall, who fretted and sweated off-camera and offstage to make his dance come across with a spontaneity that few could equal. During a long career in which he went from vaudeville to Broadway to Hollywood and later to triumph in television—his own special, "An Evening with Fred Astaire," won nine Emmy Awards in 1957—he never failed to delight mass audiences.

He was also a paragon among his professional peers. George Balanchine, the artistic director of the

Fred Astaire and Ginger Rogers in Roberta *in 1935*

New York City Ballet and a man whose supreme standards rarely allowed for superlatives, called him, simply, "the greatest dancer in the world."

Irving Berlin, in whose musical *Top Hat* Mr. Astaire wore the topper and tails that became the dancer's working hallmark, said: "He's not just a great dancer; he's a great singer of songs. He's as good as any of them—as good as Jolson or Crosby or Sinatra. He's just as good a singer as he is a dancer—not necessarily because of his voice but by his conception of projecting a song." On learning of Mr. Astaire's death, Mr. Berlin told the Associated Press that "there hasn't been such a talent as his."

"He was an international star," Mr. Berlin added.

Anna Kisselgoff, dance critic of *The New York Times*, gave this description of the Astaire genius: "At its most basic, Mr. Astaire's technique has three elements—tap, ballet and ballroom dancing. The ballet training, by his account, was brief but came at a crucial, early age. He has sometimes been classed as a tap dancer, but he was never the hoofer he has jokingly called himself. Much of the choreographic outline of his dancing with his ladies—be it Miss Rogers or Miss Hayworth—is ballroom. But of course, no ballroom dancer could dance like this."

The Astaire seen in performance was a different Astaire from the one who lived out of the spotlight. He detested formal dress, although his personal wardrobe was stylish, and frequently told interviewers how he regarded top hat and tails as no more than working dress, certainly nothing to be worn on his own time.

The easygoing air that surrounded his own performance was developed by a dancer who was extremely serious and painstaking about his work. He was frequently described as a perfectionist, and the evidence seems to leave little doubt that he worked with more than average diligence to bring his production numbers to final gloss.

"Dancing is a sweat job," he said in a *Life* magazine interview when he was 66. "You can't just sit down and do it, you have to get up on your feet. When you're experimenting you have to try so many things before you choose what you want, that you may go days getting nothing but exhaustion. This search for what you want is like tracking something that doesn't want to be tracked."

"It takes time to get a dance right, to create something memorable," he continued. "There must be a certain amount of polish to it. I don't want it to look anything but accomplished and if I can't make it look that way, then I'm not ready yet. I always try to get to know my routine so well that I don't have to think, 'What comes next?' Everything should fall right into line and then I know I've got control of the bloody floor."

As the years went by, Mr. Astaire kept himself and his own ability in perspective with his capacity for agonizing self-appraisal. He stopped dancing professionally about 1970, when he was already more than 70 years old.

"I don't want to be the oldest performer in captivity," he said nearly a decade later. "I don't know why anybody should expect a dancer to go on forever. I don't want to be a professional octogenarian. I feel very much the same as I have always felt, but I couldn't attempt to do the physical exertion now without being a damn fool. At this age, it's ridiculous. I don't want to look like a little old man dancing out there."

The Astaire dance story did not start at birth, but was begun not long after that event, which took place in Omaha on May 10, 1899. His name was Frederick Austerlitz, the same as his father's; his father was a brewery worker and an emigrant from Austria who during World War I Anglicized the family name to Astaire.

As soon as the boy could toddle, he toddled along with his mother to pick up his sister Adele, who was 18 months older than Fred, at dancing school. She was outstanding as a dancer at the age of 6, and it wasn't long before their mother, Ann Geilus Austerlitz, had Fred studying ballet there, too, at the age of 4.

A few years later, Mrs. Austerlitz took the children to New York, where they were enrolled in the performing-arts school run by Ned Wayburn, a pioneer in modern tap dancing. By the time Fred was 7, they had an act called Juvenile Artists Presenting an Electric Musical Toe-Dancing Novelty.

When Fred was 10, he and Adele—who were to become one of the best-known dance teams in the country—made their first professional appearance, in vaudeville, in a Keyport, N.J., theater where they earned $50 for a split-week date.

The teenage brother and sister hoofed their way through the Midwest but climbed to the first rung of success and critical attention in a Shubert Broadway revue, *Over the Top*, in 1917. The show was not a hit, but the Astaires were and they were immediately booked into *The Passing Show of 1918*, in which a critic called Fred "an agile youth, and apparently boneless."

There followed more theater engagements and, finally, stardom in 1922 in *For Goodness' Sake*, which had several songs by George and Ira Gershwin. In the New York production, the Astaires had sixth billing, but they stole the show.

The Astaires danced their way to Broadway triumphs in the 1920s, starring in 11 musicals, among them *Funny Face*, *Lady, Be Good!* and *The Band Wagon*, their last big hit together in 1931. Adele married Lord Cavendish in 1932 and retired from the stage. At her retirement, Mr. Astaire said, "She was a great artist and inimitable, and the grandest sister anybody could have." She died in 1981.

Mr. Astaire found a new partner, Claire Luce, and in 1932 they starred in Cole Porter's *Gay Divorce*—later filmed as *The Gay Divorcée*—in which he introduced the song "Night and Day." It was his last stage musical. In that year he took a screen test and was approved by David O. Selznick of RKO Pictures, who found that the dancer's charm was tremendous, even though he had "enormous ears and a bad chin line."

His first movie was *Dancing Lady* (1933), with Joan Crawford and Clark Gable. This was followed the same year by *Flying Down to Rio*, in which he appeared with Ginger Rogers. The hit of the movie was their performance of Vincent Youmans's "Carioca," and although they did not have top billing they danced off with the laurels.

From that point on, they were the uncontestable stars of their films. Their string of successes at RKO included such hits as *Top Hat*, *Roberta* and *Swing Time*, ending in 1939 with *The Story of Vernon and Irene Castle*.

The only film he made without Miss Rogers during that time was the 1937 *Damsel in Distress*, which co-starred Joan Fontaine. Mr. Astaire and Miss Rogers were later reunited for a last time in MGM's *Barkleys of Broadway* in 1949.

From 1940 on, Mr. Astaire made movies for many studios with many dancing partners, among them Miss Hayworth (*You Were Never Lovelier*, 1942), Lucille Bremer (*Yolanda and the Thief*, 1945), Judy Garland and Ann Miller (*Easter Parade*, 1948), Cyd Charisse (*The Band Wagon*, 1953, and *Silk Stockings*, 1957) and Audrey Hepburn (*Funny Face*, 1957).

Mr. Astaire's later years saw him adapting to other assignments. His role as a scientist in *On the Beach* (1959) was called his first nonmusical, dramatic part, and drew critical praise, although in 1948 he had appeared in a comedy, *On Our Merry Way*. In 1975 he was nominated for an Oscar for his supporting role in *The Towering Inferno*. Mr. Astaire had never been nominated for an Oscar as an actor when he was a musical star, although he received an honorary Oscar in 1949 for his musical contributions to movies.

He again drew critical praise, with Gene Kelly, in 1976 when the two served as lively hosts of the film *That's Entertainment, Part 2*. His autobiography, *Steps in Time*, which, he emphasized, he wrote himself, was published in 1959.

In later years, his daily routine was little changed from the life he had always led: He woke up at 5 A.M. and breakfasted on a single boiled egg that kept his weight at a perpetual 134 pounds. Addicted to television serials such as "The Guiding Light" and

"As the World Turns," he would telephone his housekeeper if he could not watch the soap operas to find out what had happened.

In 1973, the Film Society of Lincoln Center, along with the Museum of Modern Art and the City Center of Music and Drama, co-sponsored a tribute to Mr. Astaire at Philharmonic (now Avery Fisher) Hall in a two-and-a-half-hour gala for which he selected 40 dance excerpts from 200 he reviewed in his films. In 1981, he was honored at a dinner, attended by many stars in the entertainment world, given for him by the American Film Institute, which presented him with its ninth Life Achievement Award.

Mr. Astaire died of pneumonia on June 22, 1987, at Century City Hospital in Los Angeles at the age of 88.

Mr. Astaire's first wife, Phyllis Livingston Potter, whom he had married in 1933, died in 1954. In 1980, at the age of 81, he married Robyn Smith, then 35 years old. A catalyst for this romance was a shared interest in horses; she was a jockey and Mr. Astaire had for more than 30 years been a stable owner and a serious student of the turf.

In addition to his wife, Mr. Astaire is survived by three children: Fred and Ava, from his first marriage, and Peter, a son of his first wife's previous marriage.

FRED ASTAIRE PERFECTED A NEW ART FORM

ANNA KISSELGOFF

THERE WAS a time when every American boy wanted to be Fred Astaire—even Fred Astaire. The magnitude of his achievement is as great a social phenomenon as it is a chapter in the history of art and entertainment.

Mr. Astaire made dancing more than respectable in a country with a Puritan heritage. He became a national symbol: Ask any foreigner to name one of the great movie stars of all time and "Fred Astaire," more often than not, will be the reply.

The point is that this image is a dancer's image. Should Fred Astaire be appraised specifically from the "dance" point of view? What other point of view is there? Would we be honoring him today for his singing, for his acting—that is, if he had never danced or choreographed the brilliant set pieces that fortunately film has preserved for posterity?

Fred Astaire entertained through his art. The continual inanity of commentators who claim he made it all look easy never ceases to amaze. A professional dance watcher can testify to the complexity of attempting to analyze the phrases and steps of every Astaire solo and duet. As Ginger Rogers has remarked, she and Mr. Astaire would rehearse for six weeks straight *before* the filming of any of their movies would even begin.

At a time when Anna Pavlova and Martina Graham toured in vaudeville, it was natural that Mr. Astaire's viewpoint on dance would be shaped by a variety of influences. By his own account, these included John Bubbles, the tap dancer, Adeline Genée, the Danish ballerina, and the dance teams of Vernon and Irene Castle and Bert Kalmar and Jessie Brown, as well as Rita Hayworth's parents, Eduardo and Elisa Cansino.

Mr. Astaire came to film prominence in the 1930s—the era of the ballroom teams. The astoundingly inventive and virtuosic Astaire solos remain in the mind's eye—jumping around the furniture ("Needle in a Haystack") in *The Gay Divorcée*; the tap brilliance ("I Won't Dance") in *Roberta*; the unsurpassed class act of "Top Hat, White Tie and Tails" in *Top Hat*; the fantasy and whimsy of the clothes-tree number ("Sunday Jump") in *Royal Wedding*.

The irony of the dancer's career is that this exceptional soloist, a polished technician in every sense, achieved his success as a member of a team—first with his sister Adele and then with Miss Rogers. There is no doubt that Rogers and Astaire captured the public imagination because they acted out a continuing romance in chapters. The world they inhabited in their best duets consisted almost always of empty ballrooms and empty stages. Two special people, nothing real about them, a pair whose keynote was Mr. Astaire's super-real dancing.

The ballroom team as a genre fell out of favor in the 1940s. Gene Kelly was among the first to profit from this shift and to emerge as a soloist, attached to no specific partner. It was no surprise, however, that Mr. Astaire still gave a younger generation a run for its money.

His technique, incorporating tap, ballet and ballroom, was impeccable in terms of the dance image he invented for himself. *Top Hat* and *Swing Time*, the quintessential Astaire films, define his special contribution: Mr. Astaire never lost sight of the fact that he was dancing on film.

His movies should be seen, then, as dance films with plots—not as story films that contain dances. Merce Cunningham once made a telling point when he said it didn't matter whether one had seen Mr. Astaire live on stage: "I'm not sorry that I saw him only on film," he said. Mr. Astaire's use of the film medium cannot be divorced from the dancing and choreography. He perfected "film dance" as a new art form.

What of Mr. Astaire's influence on the dance world? It was chiefly one of inspiration. Imitating the inimitable was impossible, although in recent years there have been many overt tributes to him. The most recent is Rudolf Nureyev's clothes-tree number in the Paris Opera Ballet's *Cinderella*, seen recently in New York. Jerome Robbins's *I'm Old Fashioned* starts out with an actual film clip of Mr. Astaire and Rita Hayworth before the New York City Ballet swings into variations on their duet.

It might be fitting to close with one dancer's appraisal of another. Mr. Cunningham singled out some special Astaire qualities—"his wit and play with steps, going slightly ahead of the beat and again delaying to stretch something a fraction . . . the sheer pleasure of his dancing—a quality that makes us lose track of mental gymnastics. It gives the mind a rest and the spirit a big boost."

THE ASTAIRE PERSONA: Urbane Wit and Grace

VINCENT CANBY

IN MUCH the same way that Evelyn Waugh's great comic novels blend together to form a single, brilliantly funny work, the individual films of Fred Astaire are not as important as the entire career they ultimately defined. Mr. Astaire never played down to the needs of even the tackiest librettos for his musical-comedy films. Instead, he threw himself into these playboy roles with such elegance that their deficiencies never affected him.

When one thinks of *The Gay Divorcée* or *Top Hat*, one remembers not the tedium of dated musical-comedy books. The memory, rather, is of the urbane wit and grace of the Astaire personality, which was only fully expressed through music and dance, as well as through the soft, slightly raspy voice of a singer whose phrasing is as singularly knowing and sophisticated as Frank Sinatra's or Mabel Mercer's.

The extent to which Mr. Astaire soared above his films was dramatically demonstrated here in 1973, when the Film Society of Lincoln Center honored the performer with, among other things, a dazzling anthology film composed of musical numbers from several dozen of his films. The collection was a revelation to someone who'd more or less grown up during the 1930s, when Mr. Astaire's name seemed forever connected to that of Ginger Rogers.

As a boy, I'd never sighed at the start of an Astaire-Rogers number, as I did when Harpo Marx sat down beside a harp or Chico lunged toward a piano, but I enjoyed the comedy of Helen Broderick, Eric Blore and Edward Everett Horton as much as I did "The Continental" from *The Gay Divorcée* or "The Carioca" from *Flying Down to Rio*.

Most anthology films obscure the career of a performer by smashing it into fragments. The Astaire film had the opposite effect. It suddenly liberated Mr. Astaire's genius from its obligations to conventional narrative. These extraordinary dance-and-song numbers have lives of their own. They're short, ecstatic, romantic fictions with beginnings, middles and ends. Witness Mr. Astaire doing a rueful solo, contemplating his (temporarily) single status in the "By Myself" number from *The Band Wagon* (possibly his best film), or courting Miss Rogers in a Central Park gazebo to "Isn't This a Lovely Day?" from *Top Hat*.

Remember, too, "A Foggy Day" from *A Damsel in Distress*, "All of You" from *Silk Stockings*, "Something's Got to Give" from *Daddy Long Legs*, "Let's Face the Music" from *Follow the Fleet*. The movies are good, bad and all right, but the numbers slide effortlessly together to portray a romantic sensibility impossible to define without music and the movement of dance.

Mr. Astaire worked with the best composers and choreographers in the business, but he was his own auteur. He was almost alone among movie choreographers in understanding the importance of expressing himself through the use of the full figure. Not for him were cutaways to close-ups of feet or face during a production number.

Never before Fred Astaire, nor since his retirement, has dancing on film been more thoroughly understood and realized. We attend to his later performances as a dramatic actor with respect, but watching the nondancing, nonsinging Astaire is like watching a grounded skylark.

TOP HAT REVIEW [1935]

ANDRÉ SENNWALD

FRED ASTAIRE, the dancing master, and Miss Rogers, his ideal partner, bring all their joyous gifts to the new song-and-dance show at the Radio City Music Hall. Irving Berlin has written some charming melodies for the photoplay and the best of the current cinema teams does them agile justice on the dance floor. When *Top Hat* is letting Mr. Astaire perform his incomparable magic or teaming him with the increasingly dexterous Miss Rogers it is providing the most urbane fun that you will find anywhere on the screen. If the comedy itself is a little on the thin side, it is sprightly enough to plug those inevitable gaps between the shimmeringly gay dances.

Last year this column suggested that Miss Jessie Matthews would make a better partner for the debonair star than our own home girl. Please consider the matter dropped. Miss Rogers, improving magnificently from picture to picture, collaborates perfectly with Mr. Astaire in *Top Hat* and is entitled to keep the job for life. Their comic duet in the bandstand, danced to the lyric music of "Isn't This a Lovely Day?", and their romantic adagio in the beautiful "Cheek to Cheek" song are among the major contributions of the show. In his solo flights, when he is abandoning his feet to the strains of "Fancy Free" or lulling Miss Rogers to sleep with the overpowering opiate of his sandman arrangement, Mr. Astaire is at his impeccable best. Then there is the "Top Hat, White Tie and Tails" number, which fortifies the star with a chorus of gentlemen of the evening and makes for a highly satisfying time.

The narrative complication that keeps the lovers apart for 90 minutes will have to go down as one of the most flimsily prolonged romantic misunderstandings of the season. Mr. Astaire, star of a London show, is occupying a hotel suite with his manager, the jittery Edward Everett Horton, at the time he falls in love with Miss Rogers. Somehow the lady becomes convinced, as ladies will, that Mr. Astaire is the one who is married to her friend, Helen Broderick, when all the time it is Mr. Horton. By a miracle of attenuation this mistaken identity persists in complicating matters all through the picture, causing Miss Rogers to slap Mr. Astaire's face vigorously every time he catches up with her, Miss Broderick to poke the unfortunate Mr. Horton in the eye, and the passionate Latin, Erik Rhodes, to make terrifying lunges in all directions with a bared rapier. An amusing but largely undeveloped secondary theme in the film concerns Mr. Horton's feud with his manservant, Erik Rhodes, whereby the two manage not to be on speaking terms despite the intimacy of their life.

All the minor players are such skilled comedians that they are able to extract merriment from this none-too-original comedy of errors. Miss Broderick, that infamously funny lady, has too little support, though, from the script. *Top Hat*, after running almost its entire course with admirable restraint, collapses into one of those mammoth choral arrangements toward the end. It isn't worth 10 seconds of the delightful Astaire-Rogers duet during the thunderstorm. Anyway, *Top Hat* is worth standing in line for. From the appearance of the lobby yesterday afternoon, you probably will have to.

IRVING BERLIN TIPS HIS TOP HAT TO FRED ASTAIRE [1976]

JOHN S. WILSON

IRVING BERLIN's personal favorite among the multitude of musical scores he has written since 1914 is his score for *Top Hat*.

"It's as favorite as I can get," the 88-year-old songwriter said. "I love it. And 'Top Hat, White Tie and Tails' is the best of the songs I wrote for the Astaire films."

The mere mention of Mr. Astaire "touches a soft spot," Mr. Berlin acknowledged. He speaks of the dancer as "my closest and best friend."

But Mr. Berlin's deep admiration for Mr. Astaire goes well beyond personal ties, pointing up not only Mr. Astaire's peerless dancing, but also the fact that Mr. Astaire was a particularly affecting singer who attracted America's leading composers—the Gershwins, Cole Porter, Jerome Kern and Dorothy Fields and Johnny Mercer—who wrote film songs especially for him.

"He's a perfectionist—and that's why he's so good," Mr. Berlin declared. "I've never seen anyone work as hard as he did to get a certain step. He'd get mad at himself on the set—not at other people, but at himself—when he couldn't get a step to work. . . .

"You gave Astaire a song, and you could forget about it. He knew the song. He sang it the way you wrote it. He didn't change anything.

"And if he did change anything"—Mr. Berlin's sly chuckle rattled over the telephone line—"he made it better. He might put a different emphasis on the lyric. He'd do things that you hoped other singers wouldn't do."

Top Hat, which was released in 1935, was Mr. Berlin's first experience in writing for Mr. Astaire. There were only five songs in the score and, Mr. Berlin proudly points out, every one was a hit—"No Strings," "Isn't This a Lovely Day?", "Top Hat, White Tie and Tails," "The Piccolino" and "Cheek to Cheek."

"Writing for him was different from writing for

other singers," Mr. Berlin recalled. "If I was writing songs for a picture with Bing Crosby or a show with Jolson or Ethel Merman, I just wrote songs and they sang them. But with Fred, I wrote the songs with him in mind. Once I started writing for the Astaire-Rogers films, I was writing dance music. Even the lyrics were about dancing—'Cheek to Cheek,' 'Change Partners,' 'Let's Face the Music and Dance.' This was not true of other singers I wrote for."

Despite Mr. Astaire's thin, reedy voice and the effort that seemed evident in his facial contortions as he tried to reach certain notes, Mr. Berlin was not conscious of any limitations in writing for him.

"He actually had a very long range," he insisted. "Take 'Cheek to Cheek.' The melody line keeps going up and up and up, he *crept* up there. It didn't make a damned bit of difference. He made it."

In *Top Hat*, Mr. Astaire, as always seemed to happen, plays a young man with chronically itchy feet. Everything eventually turns into a dance, which in most cases is adroitly developed to make a point or advance the plot. But Mr. Berlin says that he was never conscious of how his songs were going to be used in the film.

"Take 'Isn't This a Lovely Day to Be Caught in the Rain?'," he suggested. "It was written. Then they had a scene in London, and they made it rain in order to put the song in."

Although Mr. Berlin may settle on "Top Hat, White Tie and Tails" as the best of the songs he wrote for the Astaire-Rogers films, the one that is closest to his heart is "The Piccolino." This was a follow-up to the big production numbers that Mr. Astaire and Miss Rogers had done in two earlier films—"The Carioca" in *Flying Down to Rio* and "The Continental" in *The Gay Divorcée*.

"I wrote it because it was a tradition," Mr. Berlin explained. "It was the thing to do for an Astaire-Rogers production. I hadn't done a tune like that since the Music Box Revues in the 1920s. I think it's one of my best, both as an instrumental and for the lyric. Go over it sometime. Look at it, measure by measure. Go over the lyric, and you'll find the phrases are very carefully worked out. I love it, the way you love a child that you've had trouble with. I worked harder on 'Piccolino' than I did on the whole score."

Jerome Kern, who wrote the music for *Swing Time*, also had one particularly difficult assignment in that film. The rhythmic "Bojangles of Harlem" was a far cry from the gracefully melodic tunes that were Mr. Kern's specialty. He found it impossible to get the right beat for this tribute to Bill (Bojangles) Robinson in his hotel suite improvising tap routines while Mr. Kern composed.

The score that Mr. Kern eventually wrote for *Swing Time*, with lyrics by Dorothy Fields, includes, in addition to "Bojangles of Harlem," "Pick Yourself Up," "Never Gonna Dance," "The Way You Look Tonight" and "A Fine Romance."

W. H. AUDEN

1907–1973

By Israel Shenker

The singular voice of W. H. Auden gave resonance to a troubled age. He was often called the greatest living poet of the English language; much honored in his lifetime, he was quickly eulogized at his death.

When he took American citizenship in 1946, he lost his chance to be poet laureate of his native country. But so great was his fame, so strong his accomplishment, that he was proposed for the title nonetheless, as though the republic of letters knew no boundaries. He did win the Pulitzer Prize for poetry in 1948, as well as the British King's Gold Medal of Poetry, the Merit Medal of the American Academy of Arts and Letters, the Bollingen Prize in Poetry and the Gold Medal for Poetry of the National Institute of Arts and Letters.

At home with classical no less than with modern verse, he was a man of lucid style and engaging artistry. Essayist and reviewer, he wrote pithily about abstruse science and airily about the dross of every day.

Auden spent half of each year sharing a house in Kirschstätten, Austria, with his good friend and collaborator, the poet Chester Kallman. Up until 1972 he spent each winter in Manhattan in a wildly cluttered, seedy bachelor's apartment on St. Mark's Place, living alone and fearing the worst. "At my age it's not good to be alone," he told an interviewer in February 1972. "Supposing I had a coronary. It might be days before I was found."

And so he left New York for his old school, Christ Church College, Oxford, which had offered him a delightfully sylvan cottage at a rent of about three pounds (roughly $7.50) a week. His duties were simply to do what the late E. M. Forster had done as a writer in residence at Cambridge—give counsel to callers. But his delight remained the same, to go on writing—essays, book reviews, but above all poetry—as though his life depended on it.

"I always have two things in my head—I always have a theme and the form," he said. "The form looks for the theme, theme looks for the form, and when they come together you're able to write."

Wystan Hugh Auden was born in York, England, on Feb. 21, 1907, the son of a professor of public health and a nurse. Both his grandfathers were Anglican ministers, and to the very end there was something of the divine about Auden. His sermons to modern man were artfully concealed within the forms of rhyme; he was too civilized to force his views on any audience, and he did not always preach what he practiced.

He grew up in Birmingham, and later even wrote lines to the machinery: "When I was a child, I / Loved a pumping-engine, / Thought it every bit as / Beautiful as you."

Auden was shipped off to a boarding school that wore a thin cloak of progressivism over the full body

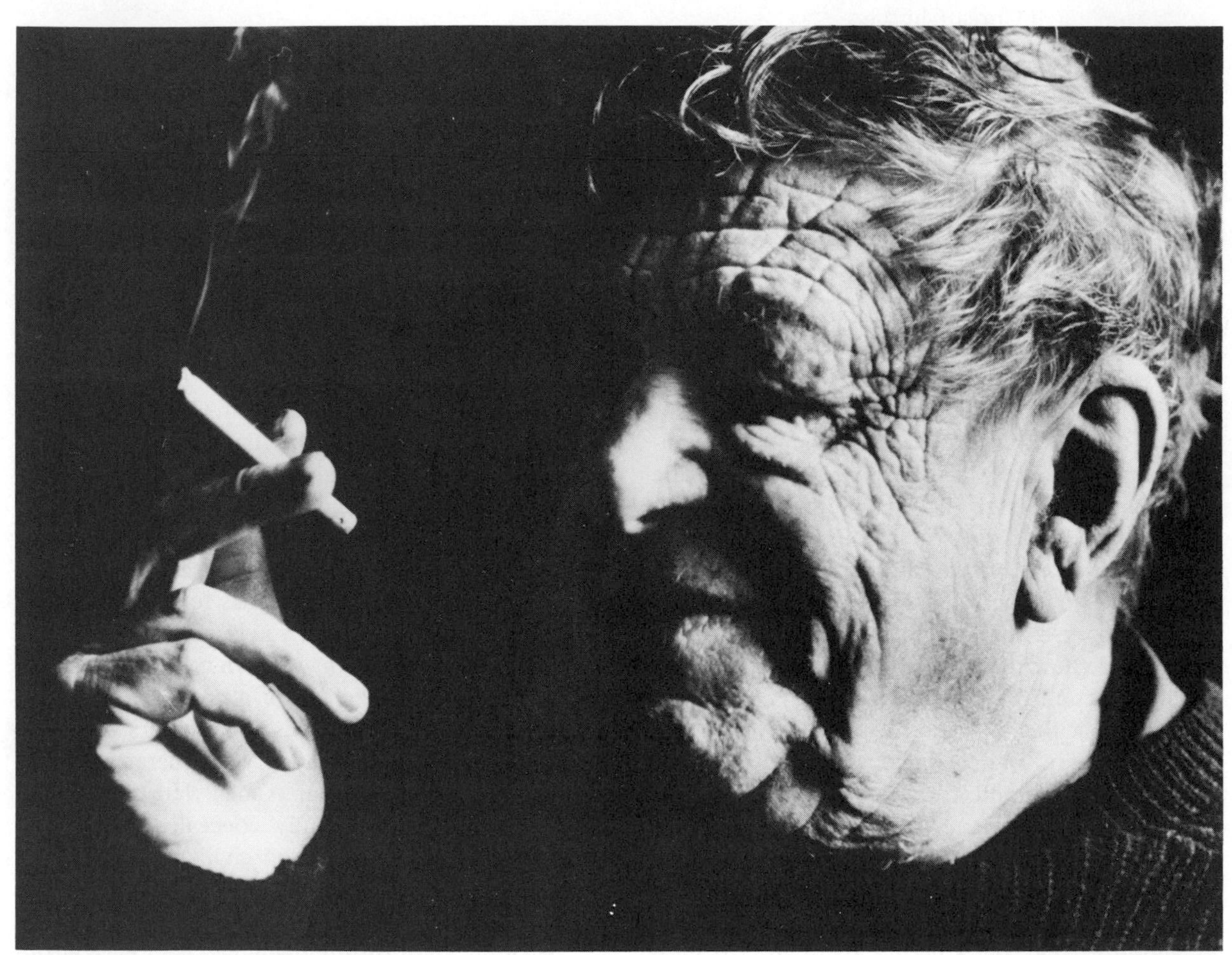

Neil Libbert/The New York Times

of tradition. This meant cold baths, which were supposed to inhibit the sexual drive and strengthen the soul—ineffective on both counts, Auden decided.

When he was 15, he turned to poetry almost casually, at the offhand suggestion of a friend. But he was already sensitive to the nuances of language and had great curiosity about the natural world concealed beneath fine letters.

Auden entered Christ Church College in 1925 as a science student, but was soon devoting himself to the great range of English poetry, and writing his own to fill the blank spaces. Stephen Spender, his friend and fellow poet, printed an edition of 30 copies of Auden's poems on a handpress.

Auden, Spender, Cecil Day Lewis and Christopher Isherwood formed a group that became known as the Auden Circle—and they collaborated on poetry and enjoyed similar interests. All were beneficiaries of the emancipating influence of T. S. Eliot, whose poetry spoke colloquially, yet with stately rhythms.

For five years after leaving Oxford, Auden earned a living as a schoolmaster. *Poems*, his first volume of verse to be commercially published, came out in 1930. Two years later came *The Orators: An English Study*, a difficult work of prose and poetry dealing with the culture of his day.

Spender wrote of his friend's early poetry: "Auden was a highly intellectual poet, an arranger of his world into intellectual patterns, illustrated with the brilliant imagery of his experience and observation. His special achievement was that he seized on the crude material of the unconscious mind which had been made bare by psychoanalysts, and transformed it into a powerful poetic imagery."

Auden was a founder of the Group Theater, in 1932, and wrote for it his first produced play, *The Dance of Death* (1933). With Isherwood he collaborated on *The Dog Beneath the Skin* (1935), *The Ascent of F-6* (1936) and *On the Frontier* (1938).

Earlier, Auden and his friends had traveled to Weimar, Germany, and been fascinated by the hedonism and culture and tensions of the place. With the rise of Nazism, Auden and his friends turned to left-wing politics. Auden probably never joined the Communist party, but he shared the enthusiasm of young Communists who opposed the triumphs of fascism in Abyssinia and Spain; he even went to Spain to drive an ambulance for the Loyalists and to write a long poem on the cause.

Above them, expensive, shiny as a rich boy's bike,
Aeroplanes drone through the new European air
On the edge of a sky that makes England of minor importance;
And tides warn bronzing bathers of a cooling star
With half its history done.

Later he disowned the poem. He was forever dismissing certain of his poems as unworthy or unripe, and several years ago he wrote:

"A dishonest poem is one which expresses, no matter how well, feelings or beliefs which its author never felt or entertained . . . and one must be honest even about one's prejudices. . . . I once wrote: 'History to the defeated / may say alas but cannot help nor pardon.'

"To say this is to equate goodness with success. It would have been bad enough if I had ever held this wicked doctrine, but that I should have stated it simply because it sounded to me rhetorically effective is quite inexcusable."

In 1937 he collaborated with the poet Louis MacNeice on *Letters from Iceland*, a travel book of prose and poetry, and in 1938 he went to China and with Isherwood wrote *Journey to a War*.

The next year he composed an elegy for W. B. Yeats. It dealt briskly with some fellow poets and feelingly with political portents:

In the nightmare of the dark
All the dogs of Europe bark,
And the living nations wait,
Each sequestered in its hate.

"When I went to Berlin," he told an interviewer in 1971, "I realized that the foundations were shaking."

One of his best-known works is entitled "The Unknown Citizen" (who has a marble monument erected to him by the state):

Both Producers Research and High-Grade
Living declare
He was fully sensible to the advantages of
the Installment Plan
And had everything necessary to the Modern
Man,
A phonograph, a radio, a car and a
Frigidaire.
Our researchers into Public Opinion are
content
That he held the proper opinions for the time
of year;
When there was peace, he was for peace;
when there was war, he went.

But Auden never really studied politics. Indeed, he cheerfully admitted that none of his close friends at Oxford read newspapers.

Early in 1939 he left for the United States, and George Orwell called him "the kind of person who is always somewhere else when the trigger is pulled." Auden had grown bored with his home country and with the English, and when World War II erupted he was in New York.

He became skeptical about the power of poetry to affect men's political destinies. "You can write an anti-Hitler poem," he said, "but you don't stop Hitler."

In 1934, Auden married Erika Mann, a daughter of the great writer Thomas Mann. It was a marriage of convenience—arranged so that Miss Mann would have British nationality and not be stateless when the Nazis canceled her German citizenship.

Auden had never met her before she came here from the Netherlands for the wedding, and they signed an agreement not to make financial claims on each other. Upon their marriage, Mrs. Auden returned to the Netherlands, and husband and wife remained good, though distant, friends. Mrs. Auden died in 1969.

Auden protested that a writer's "private life is, or should be, of no concern to anybody except himself, his family and his friends." But he wrote himself large in his poems, examining places where he lived, beliefs he cherished, friends he appreciated and the future he feared. After his early enthusiasm for Freud and Marx he turned to religion and to a concern for freedom of the will.

He never lost his pleasure in humor or his willingness to try his hand at new delights. He became a renowned librettist, beginning with Benjamin Britten's *Paul Bunyan*. In collaboration with Mr. Kallman he wrote the words for Igor Stravinsky's *The Rake's Progress* and for Hans Werner Henze's *Elegy for Young Lovers*.

As Isherwood explained: "You could say to him: 'Please write me a double ballade on the virtues of a certain brand of toothpaste, which also contains at least 10 anagrams on the names of well-known politicians, and of which the refrain is as follows . . .' Within 24 hours, your ballade would be ready—and it would be good."

Auden supported himself in America by his poetry and by lecturing and reading his poetry at colleges. He became that rarest of poets who made an excellent living, and one who wrote prolifically. His reviews appeared in *The New Yorker* and in *The New York Review of Books*, and it was always hard to predict what subject would catch his fancy and spur his praise. He wrote as engagingly to praise a volume dealing with migraine as to commend another that dealt with a 19th-century English novelist.

From 1956 to 1961, he was Professor of Poetry at Oxford, and his lectures in fulfillment of his appointment were at once rambling and aphoristic. Auden boasted that his purpose in life was to defend the English language against assaults, and in Austria as well as in Oxford he steeled his aim with the unabridged Oxford English Dictionary. He delighted in obscure words used exactly. This made his poetry occasionally trying for those who lacked his lexical aids, but he also knew when to leave well enough alone and speak poet-to-man.

Auden was a Stakhanovite of literature, moving constantly from the longhand of a new poem to the typewriter for a new review. He could not understand what he called the besetting vice of the English—idleness.

"The wish to make something, always perhaps the greatest conscious preoccupation of the artist himself, is a constant, independent of time," he wrote.

Marianne Moore, the poet, called Auden's prose and verse "stature in diversity," and the critic Edmund Wilson called him "a great English poet who is also—in the not *mondain* sense—one of the great English men of the world."

Though he never liked the unadorned confessional—in religion he much preferred dead languages to living ones—Auden came in his last years to speak openly of his homosexuality and suggested that his own acceptance of his state had given him an easier time on a restless earth.

"In a world of prayer," he wrote, "we are all equal in the sense that each of us is a unique person, with a unique perspective on the world, a member of a class of one."

Auden had worked hard to emancipate himself from earlier models, and the voice that issued from his seared and craggy face was like no other on earth. It could sing lyrically and it could speak plain. Auden delivered his lines from a perspective unmatched, a member of a class of one. Auden died of a heart attack in Vienna on Sept. 28, 1973.

POET OF CIVILIZATION

HILTON KRAMER

VIRTUALLY FROM the publication of his first book of poems in 1930, W. H. Auden was regarded—first by other young poets in England, then by the literary public of the English-speaking world—as the most important poet of his generation. At his death, he was universally considered one of the preeminent masters of modern English verse, and posterity is unlikely to challenge that judgment. He was not, however, the kind of poet we tend to think of as characteristically modern. There was nothing shocking or outrageous in the content of his verse, and no suggestion of experimental high jinks in its form. He had a positive horror of exploiting, or even revealing, the details of his private life in his poetry and a comparable distaste for relaxing the traditional disciplines of English versification.

His style changed, of course, but without venturing into the symbolist, confessional or hermetic modes that have otherwise dominated so much of modern poetry. The intense, elliptical compression of Auden's early poems, which brought him a reputation for being "difficult," gave way to a more ruminative idiom in his later writings. The assertive modernist syntax of the 1930s was abandoned for the more speculative poetic discourse that, in his middle and late periods, permitted the poet to speak with clarity and wit on the fate of civilization itself.

For Auden was, above all, the poet of civilization rather than of the private self. His voice was the voice of cultivated intelligence—erudite, amused, paradoxical and deeply concerned with matters of faith, manners, politics and civility. He was, in this sense, primarily a social poet even in those poems, which he came increasingly to write in his later years, addressed to his closest friends. He wrote poems about his own household, about the cities in which he lived, the writers he admired, the meals he enjoyed and the general corruption of culture, but always with an eye to their general rather than to their personal significance.

Auden's poetry thus represents, in some respects, a reaction against the syntactical and subjective lib-

A SAMPLING OF AUDEN'S VERSE

"September 1, 1939"

I sit in one of the dives
On Fifty-second Street
Uncertain and afraid
As the clever hopes expire
Of a low dishonest decade:
Waves of anger and fear
Circulate over the bright
And darkened lands of the earth,
Obsessing our private lives;
The unmentionable odour of death
Offends the September night.

"In Memory of W. B. Yeats"

He disappeared in the dead of winter:
The brooks were frozen, the air-ports almost deserted,
And snow disfigured the public statues;
The mercury sank in the mouth of the dying day.
O all the instruments agree
The day of his death was a dark cold day.
. . . .
Earth, receive an honoured guest;
William Yeats is laid to rest:
Let the Irish vessel lie
Emptied of its poetry.

"Under Which Lyre:
A Reactionary Tract for the Times"

Thou shalt not answer questionnaires
Or quizzes upon World-Affairs,
Nor with compliance
Take any test. Thou shalt not sit
With statisticians nor commit
A social science.

Thou shalt not be on friendly terms
With guys in advertising firms,
Nor speak with such
As read the Bible for its prose,
Nor, above all, make love to those
Who wash too much.

"Musée des Beaux Arts"

About suffering they were never wrong,
The Old Masters: how well they understood
Its human position; how it takes place
While someone else is eating or opening a window or just walking dully along. . . .

In Brueghel's Icarus, *for instance: how everything turns away*
Quite leisurely from the disaster; the ploughman may
Have heard the splash, the forsaken cry . . .
. . . and the expensive delicate
ship that must have seen
Something amazing, a boy falling out of the sky,
Had somewhere to get to and sailed calmly on.

"On the Circuit"

Another morning comes: I see,
Dwindling below me on the plane,
The roofs of one more audience
I shall not see again.

God bless the lot of them, although
I don't remember which was which:
God bless the U.S.A., so large,
So friendly, and so rich.

"Song: Stop All the Clocks"

Stop all the clocks, cut off the telephone,
Prevent the dog from barking with a juicy bone.
Silence the pianos and with muffled drum
Bring out the coffin, let the mourners come.

He was my North, my South, my East and West,
My working week and my Sunday rest,
My noon, my midnight, my talk, my song;
I thought that love would last for ever: I was wrong.
The stars are not wanted now; put out every one;
Pack up the moon and dismantle the sun;
Pour away the ocean and sweep up the woods:
For nothing now can ever come to any good.

erties of modern verse, including his own early poems, which in later years he diligently revised and in some cases suppressed. And just as he came to reject his own early style, he likewise repudiated the political ideology that informed that style—a mixture of Marxism and rebelliousness that influenced an entire generation of English poets.

He could be extremely amusing even when he was being most propagandistic—Delmore Schwartz once spoke of one aspect of Auden's early poetry as being the work of "the Noël Coward of literary Marxism"—and he was at all times a didactic poet, instructing his readers in the etiquette of intelligence.

Though he was deeply influenced by psychoanalysis, his poetry never allowed the deeper sexual passions to agitate or influence the detachment of his style. He called ours the Age of Anxiety, yet his poems often left an impression that the ills of the age might be cured if only we observed a higher standard of civility and a more rigorous use of language.

In one of his finest poems, "At the Grave of Henry James," Auden wrote:

All will be judged. Master of nuance and
scruple,
Pray for me and for all writers living or
dead;
Because there are many whose works
Are in better taste than their lives; because
there is no end
To the vanity of our calling: make
intercession
For the treason of all clerks.

Auden, too, is certain to be judged a "master of nuance and scruple," one of the truly virtuoso practitioners of English verse. Will he also be judged a great poet for the ages? There is at least some reason to doubt it. The poet of civilization is rarely a poet who touches the heart. He instructs us—often magnificently. He amuses us—with tremendous intelligence. He warns and discriminates and offers affectionate sermons. But beyond the generalizations and classifications in his verse, there was a world of emotion that eluded his civilized meters.

IN THE AUTUMN OF THE AGE OF ANXIETY [1971]

ALAN LEVY

THE LOCAL train from Vienna—a rickety, green Third Avenue El retread with iron-grated open platforms—hews to its schedule: precisely 54 minutes from the Wien Westbahnhof to Kirchstetten. Red roofs glisten in the noonday sun; neat green-and-brown fields stretch out from this village of 800. Squatting on the station platform's lone bench, the tall man in the red sport shirt, worn loose and flowing like a body bandanna over baggy khakis, checks the train's arrival against his wristwatch and nods approvingly. Then his creased face—which has been described as "grooved and rutted like a relief map of the Balkans"—furrows further while his watery eyes canvass the train to ascertain if the visitor who invited himself down is indeed aboard. Only when the sole disembarking passenger in city clothes marches directly toward him does the face refold itself into a smile and W. H. Auden rise to extend a brisk handshake of welcome.

"We have to hurry because lunch is in 15 minutes," he says, ushering his guest toward a creamy Volkswagen. This slave to the clock needs no further introduction on the station platform, for the world recognizes him as the bard who named our times "The Age of Anxiety" and won a Pulitzer Prize for his long 1946 poem of the same name set in a New York bar. This is the poet who pleaded—in a poem called "September 1, 1939," which he later withdrew from circulation—that "we must love one another or die." This is the heir who wears, somewhat reticently, the mantle of Yeats and Eliot; Jacques Barzun says he is "the greatest living poet in English" and the *New York Daily News* touts him as "a classic in his own lifetime."

This is also the British-born, naturalized American son-in-law of Thomas Mann and casual widower of Mann's dark-haired, dark-eyed daughter Erika. This is the former partner of the novelist Christopher Isherwood and, for a good two decades now, part-time partner of the opera librettist Chester Simon Kallman. But right now, this is Wystan Hugh Auden, 64, long-time resident of St. Mark's Place in the East Village, who spends April through October in rural Austria. He calls Kirchstetten "a chapter in my life which is not yet finished," and so what follows must be an interim report on Auden the way he is now.

I first beheld Kirchstetten
on a pouring wet
October day in a year
that changed our cosmos,
the annus mirabilis
when Parity fell.

"That was 1957," Auden explains, "a rather important year in the history of physics—when it was discovered that all physical reactions are not symmetrical." He came here more than a decade after the end of the war freed him from Fire Island summers—when the shabby, volcanic Italian isle of Ischia grew "altogether too expensive and too touristy. That will never happen here: Kirchstetten has no beaches, no skiing, no hotels and no tourists."

Speaking in British cadences (though occasional Americanisms creep in: "I was brought up to say *grahss,* but now I say *graass*"), Auden's bass voice resonates with Oxonian certainty even though the rumble of the Autobahn a half mile away means anything can yet happen.

For now, however, he is secure in the two-story, shingled, two-tone green farmhouse that, along with three acres of land, he bought for $10,000 "soon after the Russians had left, when everything was cheap and very run-down and hardly anybody here had cash. I had dollars, so I was able to beat out a theater director who was after the same property."

It is a quiet life that Auden lives here once he puts the anarchy of the city and the publishing world behind him. In insular, caste-conscious Austrian provincial society, Auden is an *Ausländer,* a *Herr Professor* (Oxford, Smith, etc.) and sometimes *Herr Dichter* (Mr. Poet). This, by definition, means that the only Kirchstetten *Inländer* with whom he can associate socially, he says, are "the schoolmaster and his wife, the doctor and his wife, and the new priest—a young man whose name is Schickelgruber! I've recently introduced Father Schickelgruber to his first martini. It was a huge success. . . . Some Viennese friends briefed us on the system soon after we arrived here. For example, I'm on very good terms with the local *Bürgermeister* [mayor], but I've never invited him over for dinner. For all his qualifications, he doesn't have a degree, and one doesn't know whether or not he'd accept, but one does know he'd be embarrassed."

A steady, careful driver, Auden follows the direction of a varnished, rustic wooden marker pointing toward Weinheberplatz, named after a poet who collaborated with the Nazis and took an overdose of sleeping pills when the Russians came. In a poem of his own called "Joseph Weinheber (1892–1945)," Auden has written:

Reaching my gate, a narrow
lane from the village
passes on into a wood:
when I walk that way
it seems befitting to stop
and look through the fence
of your garden where (under
the circumstances they had to)
they buried you like a loved
old family dog.

And now Weinheber's grave is covered with weeds, but Auden is still affected by the tangible presence of "a poet I'd never heard of until I came here." For the 20th anniversary of Weinheber's death, Auden wrote:

Categorized enemies
twenty years ago,
now next-door neighbors,
we might have become
good friends sharing a
common ambit and
love of the Word,
over a golden Kremser
had many a long
language on syntax,
commas, versification.

Near Weinheberplatz, Auden swerves off down a side road with a smaller marker that says Audenstrasse. Only when the visitor remarks on it does Auden say, with unfeigned embarrassment: "The *Gemeinde* [township] really shouldn't have done it. I don't have the bad manners to tell them how much I detest it, but I don't have the nerve to thank them for it either. The name Hinterholz is so much better." The sign on his garden gate and the print on his stationery both identify Hinterholz, not Audenstrasse, as the street where he lives.

It is seconds before 1 P.M. when Auden drives inside a square concrete garage. Then, wheezing slightly from exertion, he leads his visitor up a steep footpath to the set-back farmhouse that is almost invisible from below. Metal garden furniture is arranged informally (and, thus, in a highly un-Austrian manner) on the front lawn. Auden seats his guest before going inside "to tell Chester we're here and to fetch the Bloody Marys." The host returns, after a few minutes, with a dish of pistachio nuts and a crossword puzzle, which he will fill in during lulls in the cocktail conversation.

Not that Auden is anything less than an ardent conversationalist. He listens attentively and, sometimes much later, will take you up on something you said to him before. He anticipates what you're going to say and even mouths your lines, usually quite accurately, but he doesn't speak them. If your punch line comes out all right—that is, the way he anticipates—his eyes flash an unspoken signal of *well done!* But when you cross him up, he either crinkles with delighted surprise or puckers with disappointment.

"The drinks will be out shortly. Chester is still preparing lunch," Auden reports, looking relieved at not having disrupted a schedule. "And do you happen to know a four-letter word . . . 'first names of Swoboda and Hunt'?" This guest supplies "Rons." Auden asks: "What are they? Statesmen?" "No, ballplayers." Auden moans over American crosswords; he prefers London's Sunday puzzles and, besides, "the Americans are so inaccurate—for example, a five-letter word for 'irreligious person'; answer 'pagan'! But if the pagans were anything, they were overreligious."

Auden is indeed a lover of the Word—but of the written Word and of the Word that is spoken face-to-face. In Kirchstetten, he lives without telephone or television: "I do have a phone in New York. One night—at 1 in the morning!—I was awakened by Miss Bette Davis, the actress, calling from California to tell me how much she admired something of mine. She had no idea that it was anything later than 10 o'clock at night where *I* was.

"I didn't mind that, but in March, just before I left, the phone rang and a voice said, 'We are going to castrate you and then kill you.' All I could say to that was, 'I think you have the wrong number.' I'm quite sure he did. . . .

"When you live in the city, you have to have a phone for making arrangements. And the mail is so terrible there. New York is the richest city in the world and I don't get my mail until 12 or 1; but here in a little Austrian village I always have it before 9 A.M. I can take care of everything by correspondence—and, if I have to phone Vienna or Munich, I place a call at the *Gasthaus* or the post office when I'm down there shopping.

"And here my mail reaches me in decent condition. One hears about American 'know-how,' but New York mailboxes are so small that they're clearly designed for people with no friends and no business. Besides, they have little hooks to gaff whatever mail does squeeze in."

As for television, Auden won't swallow Marshall

McLuhan's concepts of a "cool medium" and the end of the Gutenberg era. "People still buy books," says the author of more than 20 volumes of poetry. "The one good thing I think McLuhan said is that if TV had been invented earlier, Hitler would not have come to power."

A purring voice interjects: "Of course, since TV, peace hasn't broken out all over." Enter Chester Kallman, bearing a pitcher of Bloody Marys. Even in farmers' blues on an Austrian hillside, Kallman remains a very *heimisch* 50-year-old Chester from Brooklyn: a Jewish opera lover who wound up adapting Mozart and Shakespeare and collaborating with "not only the most eloquent and influential but the most impressive poet of his generation" (Auden described by Louis Untermeyer).

Frog-faced, friendly and fond of an occasional "cutesy-poo" or "my dear," Kallman is a man who rarely says "hello" or "good-bye"; he just includes you in or sees you out without so much as a nod or a word. He winters in Greece while Auden braves New York, but when they come together in Kirchstetten, the household roles are clearly delineated: Auden shops; sets the table and clears it off; and mixes the evening martinis. Kallman presides over the gardening, cooking, eating and nonmartini drinking.

Whetting the appetite for the lunch to come, Kallman reveals that it will start with a cold cucumber-and-sour-grass soup. The sour grass is homegrown. Kallman refers to it as "spicy sorrel," but Auden—who is particularly fascinated by German, Yiddish and Jewish usages—presses him: "You call it something else, Chester, when we don't have company."

"Well, Wystan," replies Kallman, "you can buy it at the *Naschmarkt* [central market of Vienna] by asking for *schav,* which is what we used to call it when we picked it in the back lots of Brooklyn. Of course, I'm no longer sure I'd eat *anything* that grew in Brooklyn."

Auden asks his guest, "Do you know the frightening thing about the dandelions?" The guest, bracing himself for a riddle, confesses that he doesn't. Auden says, "The dandelions originally were sexual plants. We don't know when, but in the course of evolution they gave it up. They go on, though, with the same genes."

(The guest recalls an interview in which Webster Schott quoted Auden thus: "I have no complaints. Good genes and a good education. Published early in the right places. . . . No trouble after I learned I was queer.")

The conversation turns from dandelions and *schav* to marijuana and LSD. Auden is relating his lone adventure with LSD: "I would take it only under medical supervision [as an experiment, not for any medicinal reason]. My physician came around to St. Mark's Place at 7 A.M. and administered it. All I felt was a slight schizoid dissociation of my body—as though my body didn't quite belong to me, but to somebody else.

"Around 10 o'clock, when the influence was supposed to be at its peak, we went out to a corner luncheonette for ham and eggs. And then it happened! I thought I saw my mailman doing a strange dance with his arms and legs and mail sack. Well, I *never* see my mailman before noon—so I was very impressed by the results of LSD.

"But the next day, at noon, my mailman showed up very angry. 'What's the matter with you?' he wanted to know. 'I saw you in the coffee shop yesterday and I waved at you and jumped up and down to catch your eye, but you looked right at me and didn't even give me a nod.' "

Auden, a prodigious smoker—who boasts that "like all heavy smokers, I smoke only half a cigarette; apparently, the last half is the most dangerous"—has also "tried pot. It gave me a distortion that was the exact opposite of alcohol's. I'd start a sentence and wouldn't remember how I began it. This wasn't for me. I belong to the cigarette-alcohol culture, not the drug culture."

The drinks are drained and it is time to go in to lunch. Auden parts with his crossword, but not before asking, "What kind of seven-letter butterfly ends in 'roy'?" and entering Kallman's succinct answer: "vice."

Thus does the dialogue flit to Vladimir Nabokov. Whenever Auden has harsh words for a fellow author, he puts them off the record. Thus, one can only suggest that the Anglican wordsmith might find the Slavic punnologist a trifle show-offish in too many tongues. But Auden will confess publicly to a liking for *Lolita*, which he finds "not in the least pornographic. It's a very funny book of anagrams."

"It's a very sad book," says Kallman.

"But there are no scenes in it that are pornographic," says Auden.

"Oh, well, Wystan, there *are.*"

"No, not really," Auden argues. "It's all a game of words." Auden's definition of pornography is "any material that will give a male an erection. I would give it to a jury to read and then I would say: 'Will the male members please stand up?'

"What I object to is that you can plead artistic intention; that seems quite irrelevant. Had I been called to give evidence, I'd have had to say that *Lady Chatterley's Lover* is pornographic—no matter what Lawrence's intention was. The moment you get into intention, you can say that pornography is realism. And one can't help wondering if, after everything that's written has been justified by intention, we'll have a reaction so prudish that we won't be able to refer to the legs of a piano."

Lunch is served on a sturdy wood table in a corner room with flowered farm furniture that American visitors find "kitschy" and Europeans call "life-enhancing." In a poem dedicated to Chester Kallman, Auden once wrote:

> . . . *I'm glad the builder gave*
> *our common-room small windows*
> *through which no observed outsider can*
> *observe us;*
> *every house should be a*
> *fortress.*

Kallman's soup would put Jennie Grossinger to shame; his ham steak, cooked in a currant jelly sauce, defies comparison; and the fresh-picked strawberries and homemade *espresso* help to explain why life on Audenstrasse revolves around mealtimes. The conversation over food and drink (Austrian beer with lunch) is almost exclusively about food and drink. Martinis will be served precisely at 6:30; the vodka is already on ice; the glasses, too, will be iced; and the vermouth (Noilly Prat; Auden favors a "not extravagant ratio" of 3 to 1) must be added an hour before cocktail time. Auden wonders whether he'll be back from the station in time to add the vermouth, and thus does the visitor learn he's leaving on the 5:18 P.M. train.

With one meal out of the way and the next already in the works, Auden removes the plates and sweeps the crumbs—and now the talk can turn to poetry.

"I have never been prouder of my profession," he remarks, "than when my friend Dorothy Day [the Catholic pacifist] told me of something that happened when she did some time in New York's Women's House of Detention. Each prisoner was taken out to be bathed once a week. Dorothy shared a cell with a whore and, when the time came, Dorothy's cellmate was led off toward the shower chanting a line from Auden: 'Thousands have lived without love, not one without water.' "

Auden's guest had not known that another famous line, "We must love one another or die," was no more. When he learns this, he asks: "But why did you withdraw it?"

"I didn't withdraw it. I scrapped the whole poem," Auden replies. "Even at the time, I tried to alter it to 'and die,' because it's obvious we all die—but later I decided the whole poem just won't do. It's omitted from my *Collected Poems* and, as long as I'm alive, I'm in a position to prevent its being reprinted anywhere. . . . One can never tell whether a poem one writes is good or bad. All one can tell is whether it is *you.* It may be a quite good poem, but *I* should never have written it."

Another Auden one-liner crops up in the conversation: "Lord, teach me to write so well, that I shall no longer want to." Auden flinches and protests: "I never wrote that!"

Kallman says, "Oh yes, you did."

"Well, then, I wouldn't agree with it now," Auden snaps. "It just doesn't seem to be true. You just have to think about someone like Mozart; he wanted to go on writing all his life."

Kallman is busy checking sources in a British paperback bibliography. "You said it," he announces, "in the 'Poet's Prayer' in the notes of *New Year Letter*" (1941).

"No matter who said it," Auden bristles, "it doesn't have any bearing on anything."

To one who is not Auden, however, the quotation is relevant. Webster Schott wrote in 1969, when Auden published *City Without Walls*: "W. H. Auden tried and succeeded at everything—sonnets, sestinas, villanelles, ballads, oratorios. Now he builds smaller. *City Without Walls* is often an aging cleverness. The words are there, the passion spent . . . Auden's forms have slackened with time and his poetry has drifted to the occasional."

Even earlier, the English poet and critic William Empson suggested on a BBC television program that Auden has entered a rather sterile period in middle life, but "will write again magnificently before he dies."

"It's no use asking me to comment about *that,*" Auden says with a sigh. "*That's* for other people to worry about. . . . The chief problem for a writer is being one's age. The moment you've learned to do something is when you should do something else. The public always wants you to go on doing what you've done well.

"My own definition of a minor writer has nothing to do with his work. If you take two poems written by the same poet at different times and you can't tell which was written first, then he's a minor poet. Housman wrote quite beautifully, but to me he's a minor poet because you can't date him.

"When I get an idea for a poem, I can reject it for two reasons: 'I'm sorry. No longer,' and 'I'm sorry. Not yet.' "

The excuse has more often been "no longer," because, for three decades, Auden's audacity rivaled his technical virtuosity and literary versatility. Essayist, critic, playwright, librettist, book club judge and polemicist as well as poet, he has amused many, amazed some and angered a few. Around the time of "September 1, 1939" (and Auden's emigration to America that year), George Orwell flayed him as "the kind of person who is always somewhere else when the trigger is pulled." (Auden recently delivered a favorable review of Orwell's collected journalism: "I never write a review of a book if I dislike it. . . . No, I never met Orwell, but his widow is a great friend of mine.") But even the critic who, in the 1940s, called Auden "the Freudian's Noël Coward" had to concede that "the combination of acridity and banality is unsurpassably his own." And, writing in the *Virginia Quarterly Review* in 1945, Daniel S. Norton said, "When we compare the Auden of the *Collected Poetry* with the Eliot of *The Waste Land*, we find in Auden more vigor, more scope, greater tension, but less fulfillment. This is natural enough, for Auden is in the middle of the arena riding a wildly bucking horse, whereas Eliot, on the sidelines, has just completed the examination of his horse's broken leg and has shot the horse neatly through the head."

And, 10 years later, Anthony Hartley wrote in the *Spectator* that "it is Mr. Auden's readiness to risk a thoroughly bad poem that makes him a far greater poet than Mr. Empson, the most original poet, in fact, to appear during the last 30 years."

Every morning and most afternoons in Kirchstetten, Auden mounts an outside staircase to his cluttered study—a small room adjacent to a larger empty loft set off by a warning sign in German: BE CAREFUL! RAT POISON!—though Auden has seen neither rats nor rat poison there. (In New York, he works in his small, windowless living room.) Here he writes poetry in longhand and revises on a portable typewriter; he writes reviews directly on the machine. At 62, Auden told Webster Schott: "Some days nothing happens, but that's all right. . . . One begins to slow down a little, but I wouldn't say it's more difficult. One tries not to repeat oneself. One may fall flat on one's face, but it's more fun. . . . Do the best you can."

Now, two years later, Auden will add only that aging is "purely physiological." When asked if nowadays he writes for himself or for a specific audience, he admits that "all you can think of is the dead looking over your shoulder" and that "critics are no help at all." Then, with an eye to the future, he declares: "Every poet also likes to think that some people will read him who are not yet born." Even in composing a toast to be delivered at a banquet, Auden takes care that "while it may be appreciated by a specific audience, it should not necessarily be obscure to all others"; his 1946 Harvard Phi Beta Kappa poem is a good example:

Thou shalt not be on friendly terms
With guys in advertising firms,
Nor speak with such
As read the Bible for its prose,
Nor, above all, make love to those
Who wash too much.

In 1969, Schott found "Auden and Kallman in Austria . . . structuring time like Eric Berne's people playing games because the more structured the time the less threatening its passage" and growing old "under control and, if possible, gracefully, in the autumn of the Age of Anxiety." And a scholar of Auden's recent work says her "dominant impression . . . is that of a willed, or accepted, stabilization." Published words and lines and whole poems are being dropped, altered, or retired ("On Installing an American Kitchen in Lower Austria" becomes a Brechtian "Grub First, Then Ethics") to meet Auden's changing poetic and moral standards—or to make the local and ephemeral truth more universal and lasting.

Auden is definitely putting his career in order—with remarkable precision and detachment. Handed any edition of his poetry for autographing, he goes first, unfailingly, to the typographical errors and dropped lines. After correcting them with pen, he says, "I think it's all right now," turns back to the title page, crosses out his name and signs it with best wishes.

"Whenever I see my name in print," he explains, "I feel it's someone else's."

Auden and Kallman have collaborated on the libretto for Igor Stravinsky's *The Rake's Progress*, English adaptations of *Don Giovanni* and *The Magic Flute*, and an *Elizabethan Song Book*. Now their latest joint effort—*Love's Labour's Lost*, an opera with music by Nicholas Nabokov, Vladimir's cousin—is awaiting its world premiere next season at Berlin's Deutsche Oper.

"We stamped Shakespeare to bits and then put it together again," Kallman recalls.

"We threw out characters you couldn't imagine singing," says Auden. "Then Chester got the brilliant idea of making Moth into a cupid who deliberately misdirects a letter—and gives us more variety of voices. . . . *Love's Labour's Lost* is one of the few Shakespeare plays which, if English is your mother tongue, you have no qualms about changing words around. And I *enjoy* the freedom of writing a libretto. Opera is one of the last refuges of high style."

"Only," says Kallman, "you're lucky if it gets done at all." Their opera *had* been scheduled for this August's Edinburgh Festival, but then it was deferred—apparently because of internal festival politics.

"Collaboration is enormous fun, too," Auden goes on. "People don't realize what it's like. If you collaborate with someone at all, you form a third person who is entirely different. Critics like to play the game of what is by me and what is by him with a collaboration and they're wrong 75 percent of the time. Anyway, no critic can help you once you've published or had your premiere. But, to have someone who says *before* you've published, 'Now look here, that won't do at all!'—well, *that* is a blessing of collaboration."

At moments of disagreement, though, are even a cozy farmhouse and five acres (Auden the country squire has added two acres of territory over the years) big enough for both collaborators?

Auden dismisses the question: "One can stay in a bad temper for just a few hours."

And Kallman says: "Of course, you can't collaborate with someone you're not speaking to."

More recently, Auden has collaborated long-distance with an Italian draftsman, Filippo Sanjust, on *Academic Graffiti*, an illustrated volume of clerihews that they hope to have out for Christmas. Clerihew was the middle name of E. C. Bentley (1875–1956), better known as the author of *Trent's Last Case* than as the inventor of this verse form: four lines, preferably irregular in length, rhymed a a b b and always having a first line that ends with a proper name. Perhaps the most famous of Bentley's clerihews was:

George the Third
Ought never to have occurred.
One can only wonder
At so grotesque a blunder.

Two of Auden's forthcoming clerihews are:

St. Thomas Aquinas
Always regarded wine as
A medicinal juice
That helped him to deduce.

and, more autobiographically:

My first name is Wystan,
Rhymes with Tristan,
But—O dear!—I do hope
I'm not such a dope!

"Now," says the wistful Wystan (named after an Anglo-Saxon saint martyred for opposing his mother's uncanonical marriage to his godfather), "we can, alas, dedicate this book to the memory of Ogden Nash [who had just died]. I expected him to have written clerihews, but he never did."

It is teatime: 4 P.M. While Auden takes charge of serving, his guest asks him, "Is there any good *factual* biography of you?"

"Oh dear, I hope not!" Auden replies.

His guest has noted a number of *critical* biographies and studies, but wonders if, to help chronicle his life, Auden can provide any research suggestions.

Auden has just one: "Don't do research. You'll only compound inaccuracies that are in print. I'll tell you anything you want to know."

"And anything *he* won't, *I* will," Kallman chimes in.

There are the landmarks: boyhood in the Midlands of Britain as the son of a medical officer and a nurse . . . the birth of the poet at 15 ("At 3:30 P.M. on a Sunday afternoon in March 1922, I was walking with a friend—the painter Robert Medley—and he asked, 'Do you ever write poetry?' 'I never have. Never cared to.' 'Why don't you?' I decided this was what I would do") . . . Oxford, where he abandoned a biology scholarship to plunge into a budding, post-Eliot generation of poets and writers including Isherwood, Stephen Spender, Louis MacNeice and C. Day Lewis: lifelong friends and sometime collaborators . . . and then Berlin.

"After I went down from Oxford, my parents said I could have a year abroad. To the previous generation, this meant France and French culture, but to me it meant Berlin—even though I knew no German at all. [Today, Auden speaks German rapidly, fluently and wittily, if not perfectly grammatically.] And 1928 happened to be a very exciting time in Berlin.

"Back in England, we hadn't had social revolution or inflation. At Oxford, I wouldn't have dreamed of reading a newspaper! The only undergraduates who did were the [Hugh] Gaitskells and [Richard] Crossmans and, for them, it was professional preparation. But England seemed incredibly safe to the rest of our Oxford generation. We'd been too young for the First World War. True, my father had been at it, but I was sure he hadn't been in any real danger.

"When I went to Berlin, I realized that the foundations were shaking."

It has been written that the thirties were the decade when "Auden searched for God and found Freud" (upon whose death he wrote: "To us he is no more a person / Now but a whole climate of opinion"), but this oversimplifies. Perhaps it would be fairer to remember the thirties as Auden's flirtation with Marxism:

The judge enforcing the obsolete law,
The banker making the loan for the war,
The expert designing the long-range gun
To exterminate everyone under the sun,
Would like to get out but can only mutter—
"What can I do? It's my bread and butter."

Entries like this one have been expunged from the Auden anthologies. And perhaps their glibness implies a certain distance from events that wasn't the case—for Auden went to Spain as a Loyalist in 1937 ("I just wandered in Barcelona and Valencia. They didn't give me anything to do—perhaps because I wasn't a party member") and to China with Isherwood to collaborate on *Journey to a War*.

"One read Marx and one read Freud," Auden says now, "but that didn't make one a Marxist or a Freudian." Whatever Auden was in those days, he caught the spirit of the age. Robert Lowell said of him: "He's made the period immortal, of waiting for the war."

In the last months of the thirties (and first months of World War II), Auden discovered America and rediscovered God. Although four of his uncles and both his grandfathers were Anglican clerics, he had given up religion "when I was 16 and decided it was all nonsense." Soon after emigrating ("England was a small place. One knew everybody. It was like a family; I loved my family, but I didn't want to live with it"), he found faith at a movie house in Yorkville in November 1939. The German-language film on display was particularly brutal Nazi propaganda. When Poles were shown, the author of "September 1, 1939" was shocked to hear some people in the audience scream "Kill them!"

"There was no hypocrisy. I wondered, then, why I reacted as I did against this denial of every humanistic value. The answer brought me back to the Church." For the concerned political poet of the thirties, this revelation coincided with the dawn of a gradual realization that he articulated later: "Nothing I wrote saved a single Jew from being gassed . . . it's perfectly all right to be an *engagé* writer as long as you don't think you're changing things. Art is our chief means of breaking bread with the dead . . . but the social and political history of Europe would be exactly the same if Dante and Shakespeare and Mozart had never lived.

"Oh, I suppose that if Hitler had been a better writer, people might have become alarmed earlier. It's all there in *Mein Kampf*, but it's so boring." Asked about his marriage of convenience to the actress (also writer, journalist and auto racer) Erika Mann, Auden replies: "The facts are perfectly simple. In 1934, Erika was in Holland and I was asked to marry her because some mutual friends feared that Goebbels might take away her German citizenship and she would become a stateless person. They were quite right. On the very day we were married, Goebbels *did* remove Erika's citizenship.

"I had never met her before she came to England to marry me. Of course, I knew who her Pa*pa* was. And we signed an agreement to make no financial claims on each other.

"These marriages were not uncommon in England then. I attended one where the bridegroom forgot the bride's name. You see, under British law, the bride automatically becomes a citizen."

Erika Mann Auden thereupon returned to the Netherlands as a proper Englishwoman. Auden opened his 1936 volume, *Look, Stranger!*, with a short dedicatory poem to her that reflected the times he and she traveled in:

Since the external disorder, and extravagant
lies,
The baroque frontiers, the surrealist police;
What can truth treasure, or heart bless,
But a narrow strictness?

Mr. and Mrs. Auden saw each other occasionally and remained good friends. The *Celebrity Register* and *Contemporary Authors* referred to the Audens as "divorced" and the *Columbia Encyclopedia* described Thomas Mann's daughter as "formerly the wife of the poet W. H. Auden." But, if Erika ever divorced Wystan, he still knew nothing about it "when she died in 1969."

"Last year, not 1969," Kallman corrects.

"No, 1969," says Auden, "I know because when I took out my passport in 1970, I had to say I was a widower." Then he reminisces about a visit to his father-in-law in Switzerland. "I would tease him that the greatest modern German writer was Kafka. He took it very well; he admired Kafka."

Auden now uses Kafka to put the conversation back on the landmark trail: "I thought of Kafka when I was in the Pentagon briefly during World War II. I wandered down 800 corridors and, just as I went through a turnstile, I saw a guard and asked him, 'How do I get out?' And he said, 'You *are* out.' "

Auden served the Pentagon as a civilian with assimilated rank of major, "which meant I could walk around with carpet slippers." He was part of a team, headed by John Kenneth Galbraith, that studied the effect of Allied bombing on German war production.

According to Auden: "Our report showed that German war production didn't go down until December 1944, when the war was already lost. The bombing didn't seriously affect it. The Pentagon didn't like the report, of course, but it was what makes the bombing of Vietnam so senseless to me. How could they expect mass bombing to achieve this result in a country like Vietnam when it didn't even work in a highly industrial country like Germany?"

(Auden himself may have been a casualty of Vietnam. Although he was mentioned often for the Nobel Prize, there was some feeling that no American writer, even a Briton who was naturalized in 1946, could win while the war continued. Auden said he would "prefer not to discuss this.")

He was in Darmstadt on V-E Day: "How easy it is—quite normal—to turn people out of their house and just move in. Oh, we had assurances that the homes we took over belonged to Nazis, but even so! The house we used in Darmstadt *had* belonged to a Nazi couple. They had gone into hiding and left their children with the grandparents.

"When the couple came home, I was the one who had to tell them that the grandparents had killed themselves—and taken it upon themselves to kill their grandchildren, too."

The good weather in Austria brings four religious holidays when the whole nation shuts up shop: Christi Himmelfahrt (Ascension Day), Whitmonday, Corpus Christi, and Marie Himmelfahrt (Assumption of the Virgin) on August 15. With apologies to Father Schickelgruber, however, the Anglo-Catholic Auden objects to both "the Immaculate Conception and the Marie Himmelfahrt. I just won't swallow this."

On the way to the station, he tells a favorite story involving Marie Himmelfahrt and T. S. Eliot: "I wrote to Eliot one August 15 and dated my letter 'Marie Himmelfahrt.' He had a secretary who answered his mail. One day, my postlady brought around a letter from Eliot in England and asked if it was for me. It was addressed to Frau Marie Himmelfahrt on Hinterholz in Kirchstetten."

Although Auden was personally fond of Eliot and his second wife ("If you had them over to dinner, you had to seat them together and they held hands"), he disdains the critical biographer's pronouncement that "as an undergraduate at Oxford, Auden had discovered the work of T. S. Eliot, which immediately and lastingly influenced his own."

Auden says: "I think you will find that Eliot was a peculiar, very idiosyncratic poet. For all his fame, he had surprisingly little influence on other people's writing."

Auden was a Ford Foundation cultural-lion-in-residence in West Berlin at the time of Eliot's death in

January 1965. When the end was near, the BBC asked Auden to tape a talk for use after Eliot's death. Auden obliged, but "I have never felt more ghoulish in my life. It's bad enough when you have to *write* something like that—but to *speak* in the past tense of someone who's living is much too much."

Now, seated on the station bench where his afternoon started, Auden fills the silences until the train to Vienna can be heard approaching. He deplores the regional medical custom of not telling a patient when he is dying. Auden recalls, admiringly, his final visit to "my father when he was on his deathbed, writhing in pain and plucking at the bedsheets. I said, 'You know, father, you're dying,' and he said, 'I know I am,' and went off into his final coma. Ah, here's your train—a little more modern than the one you came out on and perhaps a few minutes faster. After the first five or six stations, it's practically nonstop."

And, as the blue-and-cream local-express gathers speed into the Age of Anxiety, the visitor who will write about his host will think of Auden breaking bread with the dead who look over his shoulder: his father, Eliot, Ogden Nash, Housman, the Manns and Weinheber. But the words that come to mind are, inevitably, Auden's—"At the Grave of Henry James":

All will be judged. Master of nuance and
scruple,
Pray for me and for all writers living or
dead;
Because there are many whose works
Are in better taste than their lives; because
there is no end
To the vanity of our calling: make
intercession
For the treason of all clerks.

GEORGE BALANCHINE

1904–1983

By Anna Kisselgoff

George Balanchine, one of the greatest choreographers in the history of ballet and the co-founder and artistic director of the New York City Ballet, died April 30, 1983. In guiding the New York City Ballet to international preeminence, Mr. Balanchine established one of the foremost artistic enterprises the United States has called its own. As a 20th-century master, his personal contribution loomed even larger.

More than anyone else, he elevated choreography in ballet to an independent art. The plotless ballet became a synonym for Balanchine ballet. In an age when ballet had been dependent on a synthesis of spectacle, storytelling, decor, mime, acting and music, and only partly on dancing, George Balanchine insisted that the dance element come first.

In his dictum that the material of dance is dance itself, he taught dancers and the public to look at ballet in a new way. In his attraction to the very essence of dance—movement, steps and combinations of steps—he enlarged the ballet vocabulary as had no other 20th-century choreographer.

And because his choreography was so closely related to the music, a Balanchine work, in his words, became an invitation to "see the music and hear the dancing."

Like Stravinsky and Picasso, the 20th-century modern artists with whom he has been ranked, Mr. Balanchine was an innovator who came out of a classical tradition.

The hallmark of the Balanchine style was, indeed, its conscious use of tradition as a base. The idiom in which Mr. Balanchine chose to work was the 400-year-old academic movement vocabulary he had learned as a child in his native Russia at the Maryinsky Theater.

It was at this imperial theater in St. Petersburg that the 19th-century French-Russian choreographer Marius Petipa created his greatest works, including *The Sleeping Beauty*.

Because of his return to Petipa's classical idiom at a time when ballet borrowed from freer-style movement, and because of his own foremost role in the development of a 20th-century neoclassical style, Mr. Balanchine was often called Petipa's heir. Willingly and "very definitely," as he said, he was flattered by the attribution. He called Petipa his "spiritual father."

Yet, as he made abundantly clear, the Petipa heritage was to be used as a springboard for expanding the ballet vocabulary and the capacities of dancers in 20th-century terms.

In every sense, George Balanchine was a modern artist. Balanchine dancers danced the same steps as Petipa's, but they were partnered at perilous angles undreamed of by Petipa and at a speed that could exist only in the 20th century.

Tradition was the base for renewal, and radical innovation could come only from those steeped in tradition. This belief was central to Mr. Balanchine's

Photograph by Martha Swope

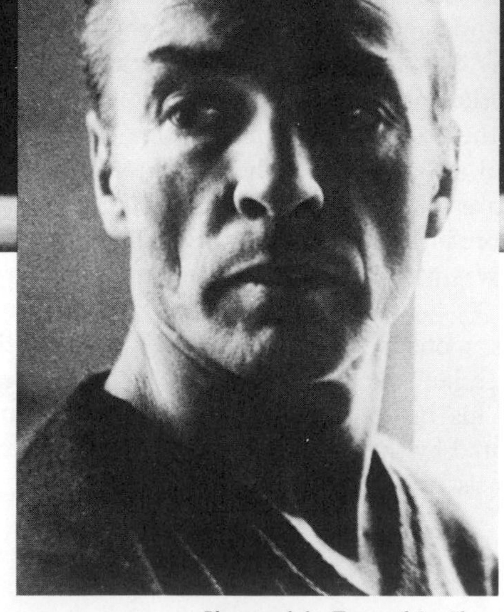

Photograph by Tanaquil Le Clercq

work, and it was reiterated in print by Lincoln Kirstein, the distinguished dance scholar who became Mr. Balanchine's patron and co-founder of the City Ballet and its precursor companies.

Together they established the School of American Ballet in 1934 and embarked on a venture that helped raise ballet to the highest status it has ever enjoyed in the performing arts.

It is very likely that Mr. Balanchine's genius—undisputed even by those opposed to his formalist esthetic—would have eventually flourished in any situation. But there is no doubt that Mr. Kirstein's invitation to Mr. Balanchine to come to the United States in 1933 made it easier.

The result was a creative output that raised the total of major Balanchine ballets to more than 200, only a few of them dating from the choreographer's years in Russia or in Serge Diaghilev's Ballets Russes and other European companies.

Throughout his career in the United States, the clarity of Mr. Balanchine's artistic vision remained remarkably consistent. The goal was a school and an American classical company with its own new works rather than 19th-century classics and revivals. The museum concept was ruled out. Spectacle would be subordinate to dancing.

Distinguished musical collaboration—illustrated by Mr. Balanchine's association with Stravinsky—was a priority.

"Whether a ballet has a story or none, the controlling image for me comes from the music," was the way Mr. Balanchine explained his own work, and he then proved it in ballets that not only "visualized" the structures of their scores but also contributed a dimension of their own to the music.

Above all, a Balanchine ballet, the work itself, was more important than the individual dancer. The result was Mr. Balanchine's celebrated no-star policy.

"As soon as you start selling a person, that's commercial," he once explained. A deeper reason lay in his insistence on the purity of movement, uncolored by the idiosyncrasies of a star performer.

Consistently, however, Mr. Balanchine used dancers of star quality who helped create the image of a new kind of dancer. The speed and sharp attack with which City Ballet dancers performed were singular.

Yet none of this virtuosity—usually concealed rather than overt in a show-stopping number—was limited to the leading dancers. More than any other ballet choreographer, Mr. Balanchine made the ensemble the star, using the corps de ballet on the same level as the ballerina. The interplay between the two was constant.

To those who could not share Mr. Balanchine's formalist aesthetic—that movement alone was interesting in itself—the Balanchine vision offered a very limited range of ballet. It was not for those who looked for the dance-drama of the 20th-century psychological ballet or for those who looked for spectacle.

At the same time, the strong artistic profile established by Mr. Balanchine concealed the apparent contradictions of man and artist. Considered the great anti-Romantic, he produced a sizable number of ballets with Romantic motifs. The theme of love thwarted by fate wove in and out of *Serenade*, *La Sonnambula*, *La Valse* and other works.

In the same way, the choreographer for whom Stravinsky composed four ballets because he considered him a fellow musician would also feel free to turn to the marches of John Philip Sousa and to cowboy tunes for his ballets.

For many years, in fact, Mr. Balanchine favored a western style of dress, appearing often in denim outfits, with a Texas string tie or a Zuni Indian bracelet. Nonetheless, he kept his Russian accent and his fondness for Russian Easter cake, which he made himself.

He could also mimic any television commercial. American popular culture was thoroughly familiar to him. He choreographed more than 19 Broadway shows and 4 Hollywood films. It was this experience as well as the Stravinsky collaboration that, in Mr. Kirstein's view, shaped the Balanchine style in the United States.

George Balanchine, whose original name was

Georgi Melitonovitch Balanchivadze, was born in St. Petersburg, Russia, on Jan. 22, 1904. The Georgian surname of Balanchivadze was simplified for Western ears by Serge Diaghilev in 1924, when the young dancer-choreographer, fresh from Russia, joined Diaghilev's Ballets Russes.

In later years, Mr. Balanchine would proudly refer to his non-Slavic ancestry. His mother, Maria Vasilyeva, a bank employee, was Russian. But his father, Meliton Balanchivadze, was a well-known Georgian composer who moved with his wife; daughter, Tamara; and younger son, Andrei—later a well-known Soviet composer—to Tiflis (now Tbilisi) in 1918 to be part of the short-lived Socialist government of the independent Menshevik Georgian Republic. Andrei Balanchivadze, who still lives in Tbilisi, is Mr. Balanchine's sole survivor.

Young Georgi was left behind in the Russian capital at the Maryinsky Theater's ballet school, where he had been enrolled in 1914 as a boarder by his parents.

Mr. Balanchine's subsequent performing career never showed him to be in the mold of a danseur noble. But he was seen in character parts and some solo roles in the classics at the State Academic Theater, as the Maryinsky was known after the Russian Revolution in 1917. In the Diaghilev company, a knee injury in 1927 sidelined him and then led him to give up dancing, except to fill in on an emergency basis, by 1930.

Shortly before he graduated in 1921 from the ballet school, the young student entered the Petrograd State Conservatory of Music, toying with the idea of becoming a pianist. Although he did not finish the conservatory, his three years of studies gave him a training in music that was singular among choreographers.

Mr. Balanchine also became involved in the staging of avant-garde theatrical productions that were part of the artistic ferment swept in by the Russian Revolution.

The old Maryinsky school had changed. Night classes were begun for students who were not in the regular divisions. One of these evening ballet students was Tamara Gevergeyeva, who became known later, as Tamara Geva, as an actress in America. In 1936, Mr. Balanchine would create his celebrated dance sequence "Slaughter on Tenth Avenue" for Miss Geva and Ray Bolger in the Broadway musical *On Your Toes*.

In 1922, he and Tamara were married. He was 18; she was almost 16. At the insistence of Mr. Balanchine, who remained a lifelong member of the Russian Orthodox Church, they followed a civil ceremony with a religious one.

Together they became part of a nucleus of young dancers from the ballet school that Mr. Balanchine used to present his first pieces of choreography. "I loved music and suddenly I wanted to move people to music, to arrange dances," he said in 1954.

Like other young artists, he was in revolt against the past. A chief influence at the time was Kasyan Goleizovsky, whose choreography revealed to Mr. Balanchine the use of the unadorned human body in a fluent plastique of movement.

The message that dance could be a self-sufficient art was impressed on him even more strongly through the choreographer Fyodor Lopukhov. Mr. Lopukhov invited Mr. Balanchine and his friends, including Alexandra Danilova, to perform his *Dance Symphony*. The ballet was given on May 7, 1923.

As a plotless work that drew its inspiration from the music, it was very much the kind of work Mr. Balanchine would make his own emblem in the future. For Mr. Kirstein, Mr. Lopukhov's ballet was the "prototype for the work Balanchine produced in America 12 years later, notably *Serenade*."

In 1923, Mr. Balanchine presented the first of several concerts under the name "Evenings of the Young Ballet." Armed with the confidence and arrogance of the young, he entitled the first program *The Evolution of Ballet from Petipa to Fokine to Balanchivadze*.

Speaking of his youthful rejection of Petipa and his subsequent return to classicism, he later declared: "Now you discover that what stays with you are the essential things. You discover what you are doing is really Petipa."

In 1923, Mr. Balanchine was named a balletmaster at Petrograd's more experimental Maly Theater. He also continued to dance in the State Academic Theater's ballet and opera productions.

Yet by that time he had agreed to a proposal by Vladimir Dimitriev, a former singer, to be part of a small concert group that would tour Germany during the summer. The Soviet authorities allowed the group out in June 1924 under the name Soviet State Dancers. It included as dancers Mr. Balanchine, Miss Geva, Miss Danilova and Nicholas Efimov. A few weeks later, when they were ordered home, Mr. Balanchine, Mr. Dimitriev and the dancers remained in the West.

Within a few weeks they had been hired by Diaghilev's Ballets Russes. Mr. Balanchine was taken on to dance and choreograph the ballets the famed impresario had promised to provide the opera company at Monte Carlo.

Impressed with his new find and bereft of a choreographer after the departure of Bronislava Nijinska, Diaghilev then appointed the 21-year-old Mr. Balanchine to be choreographer of the most famous ballet company in the world. As Diaghilev's last balletmaster, Mr. Balanchine choreographed 10 ballets as well as one in collaboration with Nijinska.

By the time Diaghilev died suddenly in August 1929, the 25-year-old choreographer had made an international name for himself. Yet, choreographically, he was still in search of a personal style. Typically, his last ballet for Diaghilev, the 1929 Prokofiev *Prodigal Son*, was a far remove from the plotless, streamlined neoclassicism with which he is now identified.

"There are no hidden meanings in my ballets now," Mr. Balanchine said in 1978. "But in *Prodigal Son* I did use symbols."

Actually, as he and his admirers would see in retrospect, he had found his true self in the 1928 Stravinsky *Apollo*, whose uncluttered neoclassic style pointed to the direction Mr. Balanchine's work would take in the future. "I regard this ballet as the crucial turning point in my artistic life," he said.

With Diaghilev's death, the members of the Ballets Russes faced an uncertain future. There were also changes in Mr. Balanchine's personal life. His marriage to Miss Geva had broken up in 1927, and she had gone to the United States. She was replaced in Mr. Balanchine's affections by the ballerina Alexandra Danilova, but for such stateless Russian refugees, the paperwork involving divorce and marriage was out of the question.

The fact that Mr. Balanchine did eventually marry four times—each time to a dancer for whom he created ballets—became a part of ballet lore. After he came to the United States, he married Vera Zorina in 1938, and later the City Ballet's Maria Tallchief, and then Tanaquil LeClercq, from whom he was divorced in 1969.

In earlier years, Mr. Balanchine was quoted as saying it was his wives who had left him. Outwardly, his personality emitted the same lack of overt emotionalism that he preferred in ballet.

"Some people think that you have to cry to have emotions," he once said. "Suppose you don't—then people believe you're cold and have no heart. Some people are hot, some cold. Which is better? I prefer cold. I have never cried at a ballet. I never cry anytime."

The years between 1929 and Mr. Balanchine's immigration to the United States in October 1933 were rootless ones, but there is every sign he relished the creative opportunities that came his way. In 1930 he created several "ballets" for Charles Cochrane's sophisticated musical revues in London. After serving as guest balletmaster in 1930–31 for the Royal Danish Ballet, he returned to London to stage dances for another English producer, Oswald Stoll.

London is where Mr. Balanchine would have liked to settle, but the British government refused him a residence permit. The immediate future brightened when he was asked to become balletmaster of a new company organized by René Blum in

Monte Carlo that became known as the Ballets Russes de Monte Carlo.

Mr. Balanchine choreographed three ballets in 1932, including the notable *Cotillon* and *La Concurrence*. Policy differences with the company's new manager, Vassily Voskresensky, known as Colonel de Basil, led to his dismissal. In 1933, Mr. Balanchine organized his own small company to create new works of his own. Its name, Les Ballets 1933, underscored its contemporaneity.

The troupe folded, but not before the all-Balanchine repertory had convinced Mr. Kirstein that he would like to invite Mr. Balanchine to the United States to found a school and a company. Mr. Balanchine accepted, but asked that Vladimir Dimitriev be the school's administrator. Mr. Kirstein, who had not yet come into his inheritance, had persuaded a classmate, Edward Warburg, to finance the venture.

A. Everett Austin, director of the Wadsworth Atheneum, a museum in Hartford, offered the institutional sponsorship for the school, but Mr. Balanchine and Mr. Dimitriev refused to work in Hartford. On Jan. 2, 1934, the School of American Ballet opened in Manhattan on East 59th Street at Madison Avenue.

The first Balanchine-Kirstein company was named the American Ballet in 1935. Its repertory included *Serenade*, the first Balanchine ballet choreographed in America and one that remained consistently in the City Ballet repertory.

In a few months, however, the American Ballet's first tour suffered a financial collapse. To stabilize their fledgling company, the two men accepted an invitation to make the American Ballet part of the Metropolitan Opera. It was an unhappy association, ending in 1938 with Mr. Balanchine denouncing the Met's management for what he considered its conservatism and philistinism.

Faced with the failure of his company, Mr. Balanchine spent the next eight years mostly choreographing for Broadway shows and films.

In 1941, Nelson A. Rockefeller, coordinator of the Office of Inter-American Affairs, sent the American Ballet Caravan, an amalgamation of the American Ballet and Ballet Caravan, on a goodwill tour to South America. For this occasion Mr. Balanchine created two of his most enduring ballets, the Tchaikovsky *Ballet Imperial* and the beautiful Bach *Concerto Barocco*.

Faced again with having no company of his own, Mr. Balanchine made several new ballets for the Ballet Russes de Monte Carlo in 1944 and 1946. He created *Waltz Academy* and *Theme and Variations* for Ballet Theater in the same period. In 1947, he was guest balletmaster for the Paris Opera Ballet, where he choreographed *Symphony in C*.

Meanwhile, in 1946, Mr. Kirstein, back from army service, had established a new organization, Ballet Society.

For this small group, drawn from the School of American Ballet and which made its debut on Nov. 20, 1946, in the Central High School of Needle Trades, Mr. Balanchine created two of his finest ballets—both to commissioned scores by distinguished contemporary composers. One was *The Four Temperaments* to Paul Hindemith's score of the same title, and the other was the Stravinsky *Orpheus*. The latter had its premiere in October 1948 at the City Center, rented by Ballet Society for a brief engagement.

Morton Baum, chairman of the City Center, invited Ballet Society to become a constituent of the center, which operated the old Mecca Auditorium on West 55th Street and functioned as a nonprofit, popular-price arts sponsor. Ballet Society was renamed the New York City Ballet. For many of the City Ballet's original fans, Mr. Balanchine's years at the City Center from 1948 to 1964 were the ones they most cherished.

Financially pressed, the City Ballet was often obliged to present its ballets without scenery or costumes.

Necessity became a virtue: Mr. Balanchine stripped earlier ballets, such as *The Four Temperaments*, of their elaborate costumes and put his dancers in practice clothes. A whole line of practice clothes ballets developed in the Balanchine repertory. Almost all were identified with his most avant-garde works to contemporary music. Among these were *Agon*, *Episodes*, *Ivesiana*, *Kammermusik No. 2* and the entire cluster of Stravinsky ballets created by Mr. Balanchine in the 1960s and for the City Ballet's 1972 Stravinsky Festival.

In these stark, sparse or highly concentrated ballets, Mr. Balanchine created some of his greatest works. Yet the City Ballet was hardly a popular company. Critical reception was mixed or cool in the early years. Psychological ballet was then in fashion, and it would be years before a larger public could accept the pure-dance ballets of which Mr. Balanchine was the master. It was in the mid-1950s, 20 years after his arrival in the United States, that he began to achieve wider recognition.

For the first time, Mr. Balanchine had found a permanent company that could serve as his creative instrument.

An astonishing number of ballets from the City Center period remained long or permanently in the repertory. These included *La Valse*, a one-act *Swan Lake*, *Scotch Symphony*, *The Nutcracker*, *Western Symphony*, *Ivesiana*, *Allegro Brillante*, *Divertimento No. 15*, *Agon*, *Stars and Stripes*, *Episodes*, *Liebeslieder Walzer*, *Raymonda Variations*, *A Midsummer Night's Dream*, *Bugaku*, *Tarantella* and *Monumentum Pro Gesualdo—Movements for Piano and Orchestra*.

When it moved to its new home in the New York State Theater at Lincoln Center in 1964, the City Ballet reached a wider audience, and the Balanchine reputation was at its peak.

To the surprise of some of his most devoted followers, but not to those who knew that he had always envisioned a company like the Maryinsky, Mr. Balanchine began to create elaborate works long on spectacle and even on story. These included *Harlequinade*, *Don Quixote*, a new staging of *Coppélia* and such novelties as *Union Jack* and *Jewels*.

Nevertheless, the choreographer's range was as wide as ever, going from the 1966 Stravinsky *Variations*, in which the same music was played three times, to his 1980 Romantic masterpiece, *Robert Schumann's "Davidsbündlertänze,"* and the popular *Vienna Waltzes*. A second Stravinsky Festival was held in 1982, following the 1981 Tchaikovsky and 1975 Ravel festivals.

It was a commonplace to say that Mr. Balanchine choreographed better for women than for men. But, as he pointed out, *Apollo* and *Prodigal Son* were created for Serge Lifar.

In the early 1970s, when Edward Villella and Jacques d'Amboise were joined in the City Ballet by a new generation of superb classical dancers such as Helgi Tomasson, Peter Martins and Jean-Pierre Bonnefous, Mr. Balanchine proved that he could create some of his best work for men. Twenty years apart, he accepted two male stars with international reputations into his company—André Eglevsky and Mikhail Baryshnikov.

Yet there was no doubt that he believed his own often-repeated remark that "ballet is woman." Whether they were trained by him or not, a galaxy of ballerinas would always be identified with his works or the City Ballet. Among them were Miss Tallchief, Marie-Jeanne, Miss LeClercq, Melissa Hayden, Patricia Wilde, Diana Adams, Allegra Kent, Violette Verdy, Patricia McBride, Kay Mazzo and Suzanne Farrell.

In a remarkable summation of his beliefs in this matter and of his attitude toward life, Mr. Balanchine gave the following interpretation of his *Don Quixote*, in which he had once cast himself as the Don and Miss Farrell as Dulcinea: "My interest in *Don Quixote* has always been the hero's finding something to live for and sacrifice for and serve. Every man wants an inspiration. For the Don, it was Dulcinea. I myself think that the same is true in life, that everything a man does he does for his ideal woman. You live only one life and you believe in something, and I believe in that."

Mr. Balanchine died on April 30, 1983, of pneumonia, a complication that arose from the rare progressive neurological disorder Creutzfeldt-Jakob disease.

BALANCHINE CREATES: A 1972 New York City Ballet Rehearsal

JOHN CORRY

GEORGE BALANCHINE is creating, which in his case is a highly visible and sometimes even audible thing. "Now we go like this," he says, or, "Maybe we should do this." Sometimes, however, he just stands and stares at nothing while his dancers stare at him. "All right," he says after a while, "we will try it this way."

At 68 years of age, Balanchine is deep in what is probably the most furiously creative spasm of his life, choreographing eight new ballets and revising a few others for the Stravinsky Festival that the New York City Ballet opens on Sunday.

In all, the company will do 24 new productions in a week, and one way or another Balanchine is involved in every one of them.

For one thing, he wanted to celebrate the music of Stravinsky, an old friend and collaborator, and so the festival itself was his idea.

For another, he has trained the dancers; they are his, and indeed he has touched and shaped most things at the New York City Ballet. For years he was the company's artistic director. Now he prefers to be called a balletmaster, which is what Jerome Robbins and John Taras are also called, but the company is still unmistakably his.

"There are no words in dancing," Balanchine keeps saying about his work, and in truth he does not so much talk to his dancers as he does enter into a kind of reverie with them.

Sometimes Balanchine, who still moves with great style, dances for them himself; sometimes he counts their steps aloud while they dance for him, and sometimes he even sings to them.

"Ya-ta-ta-ta-tum," he sings, and if it is a good day in the rehearsal studio it will mean something to the dancers it can hardly mean to anyone else. After all, Balanchine has known nearly all of them since they were children, and together they have a vocabulary of their own.

"I think he's God," a girl said solemnly, thereby capturing an elusive but apparently pervasive feeling in the company. This was after he had shown up unexpectedly at a performance of the *Donizetti Variations*.

He had stood where he always does, in the first wing on stage right. He had cupped his chin in his right hand, hooked his other hand in a pocket, and stared, utterly immobile and without expression.

Consequently, the girls on stage became undone, suddenly possessed of a dark fear that they would fall over their own feet.

"It was terrible," a dancer said. "You look up and he's practically on stage with you. It's terrifying. But later we joked about it and said that after he goes we'll put up a big picture of him so that we could always see him.

"But that was even worse. After he goes! We couldn't even think of being without him. It would be awful."

In turn, Balanchine sometimes thinks of the dancers as angels. He means this literally, and he will say they are agents of heaven sent to his company.

Balanchine, in fact, is a mystical man, a pious communicant in the Russian Orthodox Church and a believer in things unseen.

"There are other things," he says, "but people don't understand them. It's about what's above. People on earth, scientists with their computers, don't understand it."

Balanchine moves his hands, one above the other, conjuring.

"I feel, like how do you feel about music? It's when I feel this thing inside me, but you cannot explain it. This strange thing, it's a little beyond the three dimensions.

"Maybe the big, great monks in Tibet know what it is, but we all have it. People always want to name it, pin it down, but they cannot.

"You hear a certain sound and there's a feeling in the air, but you cannot talk about it. Even eating—how can you explain how something tastes?

"It is also like the dancers, when they put their training, their techniques, to work. It is a different life, but who knows what it is?"

Sometimes, touched by whimsy, Balanchine thinks of the dancers as animals. There is a girl he calls a snake, another a frog, and another a monkey. There is a girl he calls a piglet, although he says he once thought of her as a duck, and another he calls his Clydesdale, which is a draft horse.

Balanchine says that he himself is an eagle, or maybe a rat. Being an eagle presumably refers to a gift of spirit, while being a rat seems to have something to do with the way he looks, or perhaps his taste for sunflower seeds.

He is, nonetheless, a slender, attractive man, with high cheekbones, a chiseled face and a slight scimitar of a nose. Most often he looks as if he were about to be surprised, and if a caricature were to be done of him it could very well look like a bemused chipmunk.

As he rehearsed Karin von Aroldingen and Peter Martins in the *Choral Variations on Bach's "Vom Himmel Hoch"* he was, as he seems to be most of the time, in a high good humor, amused by himself and the things about him, and as he showed the dancers their parts his instructions went like this: "No, you don't do 1, 2, 3; you do 1, 2, 3, 4 . . . Just once through because I don't even know what it is, I forgot . . . Slow, slow, slow . . . It's easy, chata-chata-cha . . . You know, like shish kebab when you put it on a spit, you want to see every side. . . .

"Now you walk this way, da-da-da . . . The man needs the woman, or else how does he know what to do? . . . And now I have to go left . . . AH, THAT'S GOOD, GOOOOOD."

Precisely then, Kay Mazzo, another principal dancer, walked in, unaccountably carrying a very small kitten. Balanchine was at her instantly.

"Where you get the pussy?" he said. "Kitty, kitteeee. Animals are good. People are lonely. But you should give it to a kennel. You like it now. It's so soft. It feels good. Then it grows up. It scratches. It does things in your apartment. You should give it to a kennel now.

"I know people in the country. They take in cats and keep them two months and then get rid of them. The cats go wild. They become wildcats."

Balanchine screwed up his face, made claws of his fingers and pressed his hands to his face. He hissed and snarled, bewildering his dancers, and perfectly mimed an enraged cat.

The temptation, of course, is to think of Balanchine as an eccentric, as a mad Russian, or anyway a Georgian, which is what he is. He is hardly mad, although he is certainly more of a public mystery than, say, Leonard Bernstein, who is perhaps equally celebrated in the arts.

Mr. Bernstein, for example, goes everywhere. He lends his name. He escorts Mrs. Onassis. He is Lennie. Balanchine goes nowhere. He does his own laundry. A big evening is to have some people from the company over for dinner. He cooks them lentil soup.

"Why should I meet people?" Balanchine says. "My métier, you know, what I have to do—it's associated with music, sounds. Also, I have known many famous people. When I was young in Europe I lived with painters. They were famous—Matisse, Utrillo, Rouault, many of them.

"But they're all gone and here it is different. Here I decided to show that dancing is important. Nobody before us dared to eliminate the surroundings, to show that dancing could exist not in the opera house, where they use a little and then throw it away, but exist alone.

"Who should I meet? Painters? I remember Kurt Seligmann, the painter. Just after the war we commissioned him to do the scenery and costumes for a ballet. It was lousy. He dressed up the dancers and nobody could see their bodies.

"So I said, 'Seligmann, could we take out the sleeves, the neck, a little here, a little there, so people can see the dancers?'

"He said, 'If you do that, where is Seligmann?' OK, I understood, but a few years later we threw out the costumes and did the ballet in leotards.

"Ballet is a peculiar art. It's visual, but it's not for the brain. It's not logical, but we have our own logic. Who could I explain it to?"

Who would he need to explain it to? The New York City Ballet is as democratic as the court of Czar Nicholas II. It has its own school, the School of American Ballet, where Balanchine is director of the faculty, and children enroll there at the age of 8.

At 15, any number of them may be fine dancers; at 17, any number may look brilliant; at 19, any number may have failed. Balanchine, meanwhile, will have chosen the dancers he wants, and they will have chosen him, swearing themselves to a kind of fealty.

A colleague of Balanchine's observed: "They must say, 'Here is my small talent. I place it in your hands. Do with it what you will.' "

Or, as Balanchine said at a rehearsal, "I don't want soul," meaning he didn't want mannerisms; his choreography was enough.

Ballet is relentlessly physical, and dancers who are as graceful as flowers on stage leap off it shaking off great drops of sweat and sobbing sobs of exhaustion. It is a cruel art, and Balanchine must know what a dancer is able to do with it.

"I'd love to be able to do this," Patricia McBride said to Balanchine after failing several times in a movement he wanted. Dancers often giggle when something goes wrong. Miss McBride, however, was close to tears.

Very slowly, Balanchine said, "You will do it," which, of course, is what she did.

Then, deeper into the rehearsal, in a spectacularly impossible pose, on point and entwined with Helgi Tomasson, Miss McBride said in a small voice: "I feel uncomfortable."

Balanchine hardly paused.

"Then we'll change it," he said.

Balanchine choreographs for bodies, which is what any choreographer is supposed to do, but Balanchine does it more meaningfully than others.

"The land of lovely bodies," he once called America, and long ago Serge Diaghilev, the impresario of the Ballets Russes, said sulkily that Balanchine "had a morbid interest in women."

In fact, Balanchine has been married four or five times, the figure being imprecise because he has declined to say whether a wedding ceremony accompanied one of the relationships.

All of his wives, however—Tamara Geva, Alexandra Danilova, Vera Zorina, Maria Tallchief and Tanaquil LeClercq—were ballerinas. He has been attracted to other ballerinas, too.

When one of them left the company, plunging him into deep gloom, he said, "I have lost my muse," which seemed to catch the point of it nicely.

Certain women inspire him, which the company understands, and even applauds. Sometimes, however, there are resentments. One dancer, for example, announced that she intended to be the next Mrs. Balanchine, and in the intensely competitive world of the company this was considered presumptuous.

"He will always have someone around," a dancer said. "She will always be the same girl. She will look 18, and no matter who she is, she will help his work."

One day recently, Balanchine summoned the full cast of *Choral Variations on Bach's "Vom Himmel Hoch"* for its first rehearsal together. For days he had been muttering, "If I can only finish 'Vom Himmel Hoch,' if I can only finish 'Vom Himmel Hoch,' " and this was to be a great step forward.

He looked at the cast—28 dancers from the company and 12 little girls from the school—milling about in no order, and said: "All right, we begin."

He did not look worried in the slightest. He had said that for this ballet he was under the protection of the shades of both Bach and Stravinsky, and he had sounded absolutely sure of it.

He took the children first, waving them about,

leading them by the hand, and making up the steps as he went along. He had begun it all weeks before with an absolute knowledge of the music and a sure instinct of what his dancers could do. The rest he would do in the rehearsal hall.

"Now, little girls," he said, "we go 1, 2, 3, 4, turn and so."

His other dancers, meanwhile, lined the wall of the studio, looking respectful. Probably not one of them had any idea of what he was up to.

"Now," he said, "we make it more complicated. It is better. Yes?"

Then he summoned the other dancers, arranging them first in a square and then in something that looked like a fan. Presumably he knew how they would look on stage, not only from the orchestra, but from the balcony, too.

He put the dancers into groups of three. He put them into four lines, into five lines. He had the children running in and out of moving circles of the other dancers. He sang.

"Ah," he said with satisfaction, "that's never been done before."

Then the children became baffled; so did the other dancers. Balanchine counted aloud for a while, and then he turned his back on everyone, regarded himself in the mirror, and stretched his arms in supplication.

Soon he was looking pleased again. "How many boys are here?" he asked, and was told 13.

"Oh, good, my lucky number. I got married Friday the 13th, and if I'd stayed married to the same person," he said, and paused, "I'd be married 50 years."

Balanchine looked up at the clock. "I have 4 minutes left," he said, "and they're all mine."

He waved at the pianist.

"Now," he said, "I have a new idea."

KARL BARTH

1886–1968

By Edward B. Fiske

In 1919 an unknown Swiss country pastor gave the world a rather unpretentious-sounding book titled *The Epistle to the Romans*. He had had difficulty finding a publisher, but, as a fellow theologian later put it, the volume "landed like a bombshell in the playground of the theologians."

The young pastor was Karl Barth, and his commentary on Romans was one of those events that happen only rarely in a discipline such as theology—when a revolutionary idea falls into the hands of a giant who possesses the powers not only to utter it but also to control its destiny.

In this case the idea was the radical transcendence of God. At a time when theologians had reduced God to little more than a projection of man's highest impulses, Dr. Barth rejected all that human disciplines such as history or philosophy could say about God and man. He spoke of God as the "whole other" who entered human history at the moments of His own choosing and sat in judgment on any attempt by men to create a God in their own image.

Forty years later Dr. Barth (pronounced to rhyme with "heart") was to apply a "corrective" to this radical distinction between God and man. In the meantime, however, he would produce one of the monuments of 20th-century scholarship, *Church Dogmatics*, and come to be widely regarded as the most important Protestant theologian since John Calvin. He was frequently compared with Augustine, Anselm and Martin Luther.

"One can responsibly disagree with Barth; one cannot responsibly ignore him," said Robert McAfee Brown, the American Presbyterian theologian.

A French Protestant biographer, Georges Casalis, described Dr. Barth as "one of those few men within a given period of history who make such an impact on their own sphere of influence that a new epoch begins with them; even their adversaries are only important in relation to them."

Dr. Barth's conclusions were sometimes radical; but his language was traditional, and it was the classic dogmas of the Church that excited his imagination. His overriding concern was to spell out in large, bold letters the grand Trinitarian themes of the Christian faith.

Largely because of this he came to have as much influence in the Roman Catholic community as any contemporary Protestant thinker.

There was a touch of irony in this, for his distrust of "movements" led him to react coolly to the formation of the World Council of Churches in 1948 and to other ecumenical endeavors.

He soon changed his mind, however, and his writings provided much of the theological foundation on which the worldwide Protestant and Orthodox organization has been built.

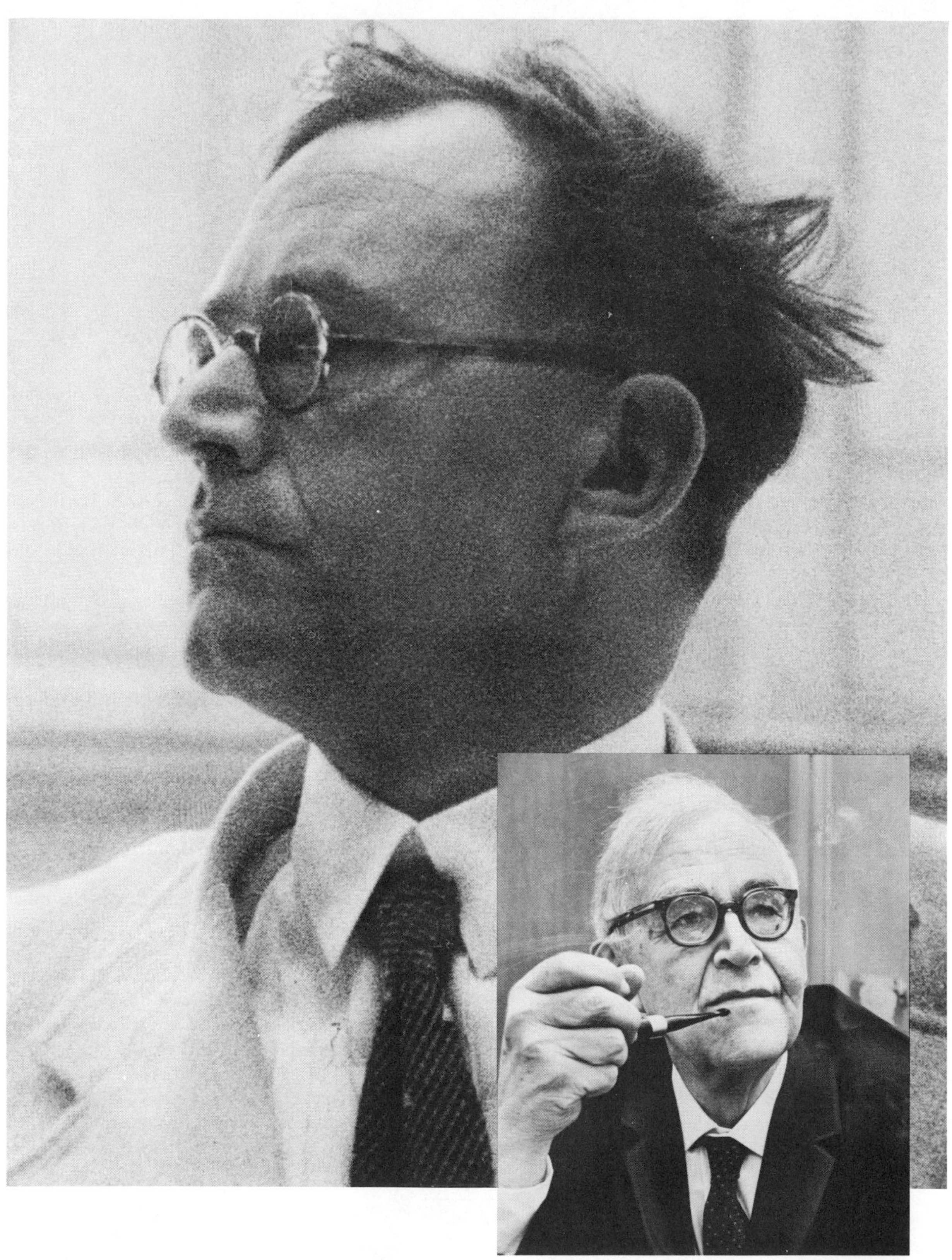

The New York Times

Years after the appearance of the commentary that made him into a major theological figure, Dr. Barth likened himself to "one who, ascending the dark staircase of a church tower and trying to steady himself, reached for the banister, but got hold of the bell rope instead.

"To his horror, he had then to listen to what the great bell has sounded over him and not over him alone."

Liberal theology of the 19th century had started out as a protest against the sterile dogmatism and biblical literalism into which Protestant thought had degenerated in the centuries following the Reformation.

Liberalism was a child of the Enlightenment that attempted to reconcile Christian thought with the burgeoning natural science of the day.

In contrast to Luther, who was preoccupied with the sinfulness and helplessness of man before a just God, liberal theologians emphasized reason, the scientific method and the establishment of the Kingdom of God on earth.

By the turn of the 20th century, however, such thinking had itself become sterile.

Ludwig Feuerbach had reduced theology to anthropology, and the "queen of the sciences" came to be measured not by its own standards but by those of philosophy, natural science and history. Jesus took on all the attributes of a European gentleman.

The man who rang in a new theological era was as Swiss as cheese fondue.

Dr. Barth spent most of his adult life in Basel, with whose citizens he shared a passionate and independent spirit, a curious blend of the provincial and the cosmopolitan and a love of quick repartee.

He was rather tall, with a high forehead and cheekbones, craggy eyebrows and pale blue eyes. In his later years he looked like a casting agency's idea of a German professor—with a shock of wayward gray hair and horn-rimmed glasses that usually sat at the tip of his nose. His physique was rugged and showed the effects of much horseback riding and mountain climbing in his youth.

He was noted for his wit. Once, a man who had been introduced to Dr. Barth (whose name in German means "beard") asked if he knew the great theologian with the same name. "Know him? I shave him every morning," he reportedly replied.

Hearing once that Pope Pius XII had paid tribute to his writing, Dr. Barth remarked, "This proves the infallibility of the Pope."

He had a passion for Mozart, and for years his day began and ended with one or two Mozart records. He once tried in an essay to find a logical reason for this, but was not convincing. Martin E. Marty, Church historian, attributed the infatuation to his "puckish side."

The ideas that led to *The Epistle to the Romans* were formed during a 10-year pastorate in Safenwil, a small village in north central Switzerland that contained a sawmill, a dye factory and a weaving plant.

Along with Eduard Thurneysen, a close friend who was pastor in a neighboring village, Dr. Barth began to entertain doubts about the tradition in which he had been reared.

The critical moments came in 1914, the year that hopes for establishing the Kingdom of God on earth were trampled into the European mud by the heels of marching troops. It was also the year when Ernest Troeltsch, the leader of the most progressive school of systematic theology, abandoned his theological chair for one in philosophy.

The biggest shock occurred on what Dr. Barth later described as a "black day" in August when 93 German intellectuals proclaimed their support of the war policy of Kaiser Wilhelm II.

"Among these intellectuals I discovered to my horror almost all of my theological teachers whom I had greatly venerated," Dr. Barth said. "I suddenly realized that I could not any longer follow either their ethics and dogmatics or their understanding of the Bible and of history."

In *The Epistle to the Romans* in 1919, and in a completely revised second edition three years later, Dr. Barth set out, as he put it, "to turn the rudder [of theology] an angle of exactly 180 degrees."

The marker on which he set his sights can be illustrated by a picture that hung above his desk during this period, Matthias Grunewald's *Crucifixion*. Dominating the darkened landscape is the agonized figure of Jesus on the cross. At the right, John the Baptist is looking at the Virgin Mary, Mary Magdalene and John the Evangelist, but with an elongated finger he is pointing to the crucified figure.

Just as the composition of Grunewald's painting sends the viewer's eyes repeatedly back to the central figure on the cross, so Dr. Barth's theology is built around the revelation of God in Jesus Christ.

Because Dr. Barth regarded this revelation as central to all knowledge of God and man, its record, the Bible, took on central importance for him.

The Scriptures, said Dr. Barth, contain "divine thoughts about men, not human thoughts about God." He saw this as the cure for doctrinal errors that had led to the divisions within Christendom.

His fidelity to the Bible as the Word of God led him to reject Calvin's idea that some men were "predestined" by God to eternal salvation or damnation.

In defense of this and his other modifications of the great Genevan reformer, Dr. Barth once remarked, "Calvin is in Heaven and has had time to ponder where he went wrong. Doubtless he is pleased that I am setting him right."

Dr. Barth's views were the source of much controversy. Zurich-born Emil Bunner, who agreed with him at many points, could not go along with his dismissal of "natural theology." This is the assertion that some knowledge of God is possible from reason and nature apart from revelation in Jesus Christ.

Fundamentalists, on the other hand, charged that despite his emphasis on the Bible, Dr. Barth had actually replaced the Scriptures with Christ as the ultimate authority for faith.

Reinhold Niebuhr maintained that Dr. Barth's radical emphasis on revelation as opposed to human experience made ethics impossible. Niebuhr described him as irresponsible and irrelevant.

Paul Tillich also joined those who charged that Barth was too hasty in rejecting all that human culture and thought could say about reality.

Dr. Barth was also accused of being too rigid, and many maintained that his emphasis on the helplessness of man in the face of evil was too pessimistic.

To Dr. Barth, however, the sinful condition of man was the natural corollary of the infinite goodness and transcendence of God, and he maintained that the act of God in bridging this distance in Jesus Christ made his theology the most optimistic of all. Man, he maintained, is "swamped by grace."

If Dr. Barth was a revolutionary, his ideas were also deeply imbedded in the traditions of the Calvinistic, or Reformed, branch of Protestantism. Many Barths before him, including his father, Fritz, had been Swiss Reformed pastors.

He was born May 10, 1886, in Basel, where his father had a church. When he was 3, the family moved to Bern, where Fritz Barth had accepted a post as professor of New Testament and church history at the university. It was there that Karl, the oldest of five children, was reared and educated and acquired the local Swiss German dialect that caused German purists to shudder.

He began studying theology under his father in 1904, at the age of 18. Two years later he went to Berlin and then, after a summer at Tübingen, to Marburg. He studied there with Wilhelm Herrmann, whom he called the greatest single influence on his theological studies.

Dr. Barth was ordained by his father in 1908 at the Reformed Cathedral in Bern. After a year as assistant to the editor of a liberal theological journal in Marburg, he took his first pastorate, in Geneva, where he was vicar of a German-speaking congregation. Two years later he moved to Safenwil.

It was at Safenwil that Dr. Barth first revealed the penchant for political debate that later led to his confrontation with the Third Reich and an international dispute over his attitude toward Communism.

Both Dr. Barth and his friend Dr. Thurneysen had become religious socialists, and they supported the factory workers in Safenwil in their struggle for higher wages and better working conditions.

Dr. Barth was dubbed the "Red Pastor," and his own congregation became sharply divided over his stand, which was not typical of Reformed pastors at the time. In 1915 he joined the Social Democratic party.

Following the publication of *The Epistle to the Romans*, Dr. Barth accepted, in September 1921, a post as professor of Reformed theology at the University of Göttingen. Thus, at the age of 35, he had made the unusual leap from a small Swiss pastorate to a theological chair in Germany.

He found his relations with the theological faculty at Göttingen less than harmonious, however, and in 1925 he took a post as professor of dogmatics and New Testament exegesis at the University of Münster in Westphalia.

By 1927 Dr. Barth's theological ideas had crystallized sufficiently for him to publish *The Doctrine of the Word of God: Prolegomena to Christian Dogmatics*. He soon came to regard this work as an unsuccessful experiment, however, and repudiated it. He did the same with an unpublished two-volume work on Christian ethics.

In 1930 Dr. Barth became professor of systematic theology at Bonn. It was there, in 1932, that he published the first half volume of *Church Dogmatics*, the massive work on which his reputation is largely based.

This exposition of his theological thinking eventually grew to more than 6 million words on 7,000 pages in 12 volumes. It still lacked several volumes when he retired in 1962 and abandoned the project.

The title was carefully chosen and reflected Dr. Barth's conviction that theology must be deeply rooted in the life of the Christian churches.

He thought of his chosen field as the "most beautiful" of the sciences, and wrote frequently of the dangers of pedantry.

"The theologian who has no joy in his work is not a theologian at all," he said. "Sulky faces, morose thoughts and boring ways of speaking are intolerable in this science."

As he demonstrated in his false start on *Church Dogmatics*, Dr. Barth was willing to reverse himself at times, and he insisted that even his own *Church Dogmatics* was tentative and written only to be revised and refined by his students.

Dr. Barth never lost control of his massive project and never fell into a "system." This was largely because he always remained primarily a preacher.

True to his Reformed tradition, he regarded the proclamation of the Word of God as the sole purpose of the Church, and theology was for him merely a way of clarifying one's thoughts in order to perform this task more effectively.

Dr. Barth's confrontation with the Third Reich began in the summer of 1933, when Hitler started to establish "German Christian" churches in which National Socialist teachings were given dogmatic status.

As a professor in Bonn, Dr. Barth was a civil servant, but he refused to take the oath of allegiance that Hitler required of state employees or to begin his lectures with a salutation to the Führer.

In 1934 about 200 leaders of German Protestantism signed the Barmen Confession, which asserted the freedom of the Church from temporal powers. Dr. Barth was the chief author.

He was soon convicted by a Nazi court of "seducing the minds" of his students and was suspended from his teaching position. In October 1935 he was escorted to the Swiss border at Basel and expelled from Germany.

Dr. Barth was as surprised as anyone that he became a symbol of political resistance to Nazism, for his reasons were characteristically theological. He described German Christianity as "a new heresy strangely blended of Christianity and Germanism" and as a "conscious, radical and systematic transgression of [the] First Commandment."

From Basel, where he accepted a teaching post, Dr. Barth continued to resist Hitler. He wrote letters to Christians in Czechoslovakia, France and elsewhere urging them to defy Nazism, and even attempted to return to Germany to speak. He was arrested by the Gestapo and deported.

Poor eyesight had kept Dr. Barth out of the military until then, but at the age of 54 he volunteered to serve in the Swiss army and spent much of his time as a guard at the German frontier.

After the war the outspoken critic of Nazism became a controversial defender of the German people. He visited Germany in 1945 and in the next two years spent two semesters teaching in Bonn.

He became alarmed at what he regarded as the vindictive spirit of the Western victors and argued in a series of pamphlets for a sympathetic attitude toward the people of the defeated nation.

In 1948 Dr. Barth visited Hungary, and in the years following he drew bitter criticism for his refusal to attack Communism with the same vigor with which he had protested Nazism.

He regarded Communism, too, as idolatrous, but he saw it as the "natural result" of the failure of Western culture to solve some of its human problems. Moreover, he regarded anti-Communism as equally idolatrous and attacked efforts to identify Christianity with Western values.

He urged clergymen behind the Iron Curtain to seek a way of living with the Communist regimes and was one of the few leading Western churchmen who did not denounce the suppression of the 1956 revolt in Hungary.

In 1956 Dr. Barth gave an address to a group of Swiss Reformed pastors in which he modified what he called the "exaggerations" inherent in his previous emphasis on the distance between God and man. He outlined ways in which the "deity" of God also includes a "humanity" by which God becomes for man not an abstract concept but a living force.

After his retirement in 1962 at the age of 75, Dr. Barth surprised everyone by undertaking a trip to the United States, where his son Markus was a professor of New Testament at the University of Chicago. He gave a number of lectures, but the highlights of the visit for him were trips to the Civil War battlefields at Gettysburg and Richmond.

From childhood Dr. Barth's hobby had been military history, and he carried in his head the names of all the generals and battles of the Napoleonic and other wars. In later years he became an American Civil War buff.

Despite an ascetic workday that for years lasted from regular 7 A.M. lectures to post-midnight writing and study, he was always willing to take time out to play tin soldiers with his sons. "Dad had a collection of hundreds of soldiers," Markus said, "and he always insisted on being Napoleon. So he always won."

After his retirement Dr. Barth continued to meet with students in a large room on the second floor of the Bruderhold Restaurant near his home in Basel. Regular sessions were held in French, German and English.

A student would read a paper on a section of the *Dogmatics*, and Dr. Barth, sipping a glass of beer or wine and puffing on his large pipe, would lead the discussion and answer points raised by the student. In contrast to earlier days, his manner was mellowed and patient.

Dr. Barth was proud that two of his sons followed him into the field of theology. Markus, the eldest, now teaches at the Pittsburgh Theological Seminary, while Christop is a professor of Old Testament in Mainz, West Germany. A daughter, Franziska, is married to a businessman in Basel, where the third son, Hans Jakob, is a landscape architect. A fourth son died in a mountain-climbing accident.

Their mother, the former Nell Hoffman, was a violin student whom Dr. Barth married in 1913. She regularly attended his lectures and for years was hostess at a weekly open house for nearly 100 of her husband's students.

Another member of the Barth household was Charlotte von Kirschbaum, a nurse who in 1925 became Dr. Barth's secretary and research assistant and never left. She lived in the Barth home and eventually became a knowledgeable amateur theologian in her own right. She published a study of St. Paul's statements on women.

Two years ago the University of Bonn acted to

erase what it termed a "long-standing debt" and made Dr. Barth an honorary senator.

Dr. Barth died in his sleep at his home in Basel on Dec. 9, 1968.

Karl Barth's theological views led him into becoming a symbol of political resistance to Adolf Hitler. Following are reports from *The New York Times* from 1934 and 1935 that provide some insight into the nature of his defiance.

Prof. Barth Suspended at Bonn; Balked at Prescribed Hitler Oath

(Wireless to *The New York Times*)

BERLIN, Nov. 26, 1934—Dr. Karl Barth, distinguished Swiss theologian of Bonn University, has been suspended from his professorship by Dr. Bernhard Rust, Prussian Minister of Culture, on the ground that he refused as a State servant to take the oath of personal loyalty to Chancellor Hitler as provided in a law of last Aug. 20.

It was also announced that disciplinary proceedings would be instituted against Dr. Barth before a court to be appointed by the Ministry.

Although Dr. Barth still retains his Swiss citizenship, as a professor in a German university he is legally obliged to take the oath of allegiance to the Reichsführer. The Swiss government has informed the German authorities, however, that if Swiss professors in German universities are dismissed for political reasons the Swiss government will reply by dismissing all German professors in Swiss universities. Dr. Barth's suspension, therefore, may have a far-reaching effect.

Dr. Barth was one of the earliest and most active leaders of the opposition to the Nazi German Christian doctrine and the policy of Reich Bishop Ludwig Mueller and his former civil administrator, Dr. August Jaeger. A fundamentalist in theology, Dr. Barth is a liberal in the matter of Church organization and particularly in the question of the relations of Church and State. He is a Calvinist and has stood for a more complete separation of the functions of Church and State than many of his Lutheran associates in the conflict with the Reich Bishop and the present ecclesiastical ministry of the German Evangelical Church.

Plans had been made to have him make an American tour this winter to help reestablish more intimate connections between German and American theology.

His teachings are constantly referred to by the German Christians as "Swiss theology," and the leaders of the swastika movement in the Church insist he represents liberal principles of religious life and thought that are "wholly Occidental and wholly contrary to the present-day German ideal."

Although Dr. Barth's name is closely associated with the present struggle in the Church, and he has written a series of articles and several pamphlets attacking Dr. Mueller, he is best known for his insistence on the prime importance of the "Word of God." In Germany he is spoken of as the founder of the dialectical school of theology.

Dr. Barth has held professorships in German universities since 1921, when he came from Safenwil, Switzerland, to Göttingen, transferring later to Münster and Bonn. He had studied before the war in Bern, Berlin, Tübingen and Marburg. Two other Swiss professors of theology are lecturing at Berlin University.

The faculties of all universities are now being sworn in at ceremonies conducted by the rectors. Each faculty member is required to pledge his oath with his signature.

Explains Position on Oath

(Wireless to *The New York Times*)

BONN, Germany, Nov. 26, 1934—Official notification of his suspension from the theological faculty of Bonn University had not reached Dr. Karl Barth tonight and he was surprised to learn that disciplinary proceedings would be instituted against him for his alleged refusal to swear fealty to Chancellor Hitler.

He told a *New York Times* correspondent he had not refused to take the oath but that three weeks ago he had requested permission to swear a formula of his own choosing. He was prepared to take the regular oath, he said, with the addition of "So far as I can defend it as an Evangelical Christian." This formula was rejected by Minister of Culture Rust.

Dr. Barth has been a member of the Bonn faculty since 1930. He is a naturalized German, but has not renounced his Swiss citizenship. He was obliged to postpone a planned trip to the United States, he said, because of pressure of work in connection with the Church situation in Germany. He declined to discuss this situation.

Professor Karl Barth, the most influential theologian among the younger churchmen of Germany, is the heart of the opposition forces in the German Church controversy. Under his spiritual leadership a group of German clergymen formed the Pastors' Emergency League in the autumn of 1933 and opened a counteroffensive to block the Nazification of the Church. Their opposition led to the retreat of the German Christians, whose leader, the Rev. Dr. Joachim Hossenfelder, was relieved of his duties as Bishop of Berlin.

But then, faced with Reich Bishop Mueller's dictatorial power, the Pastors' Emergency League weakened as the bishop proceeded to suppress recalcitrant pastors.

Dr. Barth, who is 48 years old, has published a bold essay on "Our Present Theological Existence." In it he calls on the Church to resist the demands of the State. He rejects completely the ideals of the Nazis and the German Christians and says that a continuing victory of the German Christians means the end of the Evangelical Church and that the Christians of Germany ought to go down into the catacombs rather than yield.

The principles of the true Church Dr. Barth sets forth as follows: "The church preaches the Gospel in the new State but not under it and not in its spirit. The church must remain independent of any political or social theories. The community of the church is not formed by blood or by race but by the Holy Spirit and by baptism. It would cease to be a Christian church if it excluded Jewish Christians."

Commenting last night on the action taken against Dr. Barth in Germany, Dr. Henry Smith Leiper, American Secretary of the Universal Christian Council and Foreign Secretary of the Federal Council of the Churches of Christ in America, said: "The policy that leads to the dismissal of a man like Professor Barth is based, of course, upon the logical application of the ideas of the totalitarian State. It means an irreparable injury to Germany herself as many friends of Germany have been pointing out.

"There has been through the years a stream of students from other lands going to Germany to study under the great theological professors of their universities. These men are Germany's friends and interpreters. This action will cut off that stream instantly—to mention but one of its ill effects."

Germany Expels Professor Barth

Swiss Theologian Is Arrested at Barmen Conference and Taken to the Border.

(Wireless to *The New York Times*)

BERLIN, Oct. 9, 1935—Professor Karl Barth has been arrested at the theological conference at Barmen in the Rhineland and expelled from Germany. He was accompanied by a German police officer to the Swiss border at Basel after his arrest and released at noon today.

Formerly a professor at the University of Bonn and the most widely known member of its theological faculty, Professor Barth now holds the chair of theology at the University of Basel. He is a Swiss citizen.

Bernhard Rust, Minister of Education, removed him from his professorship at Bonn on the charge that he had refused to take the oath of obedience to Reichsführer Adolf Hitler, required of all German professors and State servants. He later offered to take the oath with reservations, but a disciplinary court in Cologne upheld the Ministry of Education on the ground that Professor Barth was unfriendly to the Hitler regime and had failed to give the Hitler salute in the classroom.

This decision was reversed by a higher court a few weeks ago, but the Minister of Education ignored the decision and forbade the university senate at Bonn to reinstate Professor Barth.

At Barmen the Swiss theologian had been invited to address a group of pastors and theologians of the Confessional Synod in the course of "Theological Week." The secret political police ordered his arrest but refused to explain to conference leaders the reason for it. Professor Barth himself was merely informed that he was regarded as an undesirable alien.

Trained in Swiss traditions of liberty, Professor Barth is opposed to State supremacy over the Church. It is possible that his presence in Germany was regarded as a threat to the plan of Hanns Kerrl, Reich Minister for Church Affairs, for securing the support of the Confessional Synod clergy for the recent State supremacy decree by giving them control of a government-appointed Church directorate with dictatorial powers.

The Prussian Brotherhood Council of the confessional Church closed its sessions in Berlin yesterday. It upheld the decision of the Prussian Confessional Synod a week ago to have nothing to do with the government's offer to give the confessional clergy control of the Church.

The Reich Brotherhood Council is still considering the issue.

The South German Protestant bishops who threw in their lot with the confessional clergy are trying to obtain acceptance of the government's proposal.

DAVID BEN-GURION

1886–1973

By Horace Bigart

David Ben-Gurion, a founding father of modern Israel and its first Premier, symbolized the tough little state of Israel. Short, round, with a nimbus of white hair flaring angrily from a massive head, "B-G," as he was known to many, attained world leadership by firmly concentrating on the achievement of a dream.

That dream, the birth and triumphant survival of a Jewish homeland amid a sea of hostile Arabs, led Mr. Ben-Gurion through a lifetime of turmoil.

He was chairman of the Jewish Agency, the executive body of the World Zionist Organization, through the critical years of rising Arab nationalism, of Nazism, of World War II and of the postwar diplomatic struggle between Britain and the Jews of Palestine. When Britain finally gave up the Palestine mandate, it was Mr. Ben-Gurion who proclaimed the Jewish state.

This was his moment of supreme test. For on that same day, May 14, 1948, the Arab armies began their invasion of the fledgling state. Jerusalem was besieged by Transjordan's Arab Legion. In the Judean hills and in Galilee, Jewish settlements were under attack by Syrian and Iraqi forces, while Egyptians invaded from the south.

Exhilarated by the challenge, the 62-year-old leader put on battle dress and assumed the direction of military operations. He was de facto premier and minister of defense.

Some of his decisions were questionable. He ordered a costly and ineffective attack to drive the Arab Legion from Jerusalem. But he had surrounded himself with young and competent officers such as Yigal Yadin, Yigal Allon and Moshe Dayan. The Arabs, who lacked unity of command, were soon routed.

To Mr. Ben-Gurion fell most of the credit for having won the first Jewish campaign since that of Judas Maccabaeus 2,000 years before.

He became an almost mystical figure to many Zionists: the wise patriarch who embodied all the traditional virtues and who would ultimately lead Israel to triumph over the ring of Arab enemies.

But he embittered millions of others. He alarmed the United Nations and insured the continued hatred of the Arab states by adopting a policy of swift and ruthless retaliation for Arab raids on Israel. Although an armistice was arranged by the United Nations, technically Jordan, Lebanon, Syria and Egypt remained at war with Israel, and border incidents were frequent after the war of 1948–49.

Mr. Ben-Gurion also alienated many American Jews by insisting that all true Zionists must live in Israel. Disturbed by the influx of Oriental Jews, which he feared would transform Israel into "just another Levantine state," Mr. Ben-Gurion dreamed of a vast migration of Jews from the Soviet Union and the United States.

Henry Marco/Camera Press

Ed Hausner/The New York Times

In the early years only 5,000 American Jews were "ingathered," a scant migration that drew scornful reproaches from Mr. Ben-Gurion.

A feud between Mr. Ben-Gurion and a large segment of American Jewry dated from August 1957, when he said at a Zionist ideological conference in Jerusalem that a sound Jewish life was not possible outside Israel.

"There seems to be a general agreement," he said, "that a Jew can live in America, speak and read English and bring up his children in America and still call himself a Zionist. If that is Zionism I want no part of it."

In subsequent speeches Mr. Ben-Gurion reiterated his belief that Jewish life in the outside world had a dim future. His dogmatism alienated potential friends of Israel among both Jews and gentiles. Non-Zionist Jews resented his insistence that Judaism was not a mere religion but a nationalistic ethos. Almost every Zionist faction in the United States joined the mounting protest.

Stubbornly, though, Mr. Ben-Gurion insisted that essentially Judaism was a nationality and Israel was the only sovereign spokesman for the world's Jews.

In June 1962, he again infuriated American Jewish leaders at a Jerusalem conference by equating Judaism with nationality. Stanley H. Lowell, chairman of the New York City Commission on Intergroup Relations, retorted: "You aren't the only answer to Jewish living, Jewish creativity and Jewish survival. This generation and the next generations to come shall and will remain part and parcel of the great American experience of democracy."

In later years, though, with the 1967 and 1973 wars and increased United States aid, the old man's idea of Zionism came to be the accepted one. The anti-Zionist organizations became virtually extinct; by 1970, American immigration to Israel was reaching 10,000 a year.

At home, Mr. Ben-Gurion managed to rule elements of the population, even members of his own Mapai party, by methods that often seemed autocratic. He never enjoyed sharing authority, and he chafed under Israel's system of proportional representation, which assures religious parties of representation in the government. These parties were often in bitter disagreement with Mr. Ben-Gurion, who opposed their dream of a theocracy.

The Mapai party, although dominant, was never able to win a clear majority in the Knesset, or Parliament; this was a cause of the formation of 11 coalition governments in Israel, including the provisional government that was set up in April 1948. In March 1949, Mr. Ben-Gurion became premier in the first regularly constituted government of Israel.

These political marriages into coalitions were usually brief and stormy. The Socialist Mapai had little in common with the small left-wing labor parties and religious groups that were persuaded to join coalitions in exchange for concessions in legislation or for a ministerial post or two.

Sometimes Mr. Ben-Gurion would become so frustrated that he would resign and retire to his four-room cottage in Sde Boker, a kibbutz that was his favorite retreat, in the stony Negev Desert.

Usually the mere threat of resignation was enough to force the concessions Mr. Ben-Gurion demanded. The only Israeli with enough stature to offer alternative leadership was Moshe Sharett, another Mapai stalwart. But Mr. Sharett was considered too cautious, too temporizing. Israelis thought they needed daring leadership to meet the growing threat brought on by Egypt's acquisition of Communist bloc arms, by the nationalization of the Suez Canal and by the military alliance between Egypt and Syria.

Mr. Ben-Gurion resigned several times, but his retirements to Sde Boker were fleeting except for one interval: In December 1953, he turned over his office and leadership to Mr. Sharett, explaining that he felt "tired, tired, tired."

Even in retirement he cast his long shadow over the country; soon, in February 1955, he was called to Jerusalem to resume the post of minister of defense, which he had held throughout his premiership. He also assumed leadership of the Mapai and again became premier in November 1955.

Under Mr. Ben-Gurion, Israel adopted a policy that led to war. There had been a flurry of frontier incidents. Israel complained that the United Nations truce supervision teams were futile instruments for checking Arab commando raids. Mr. Ben-Gurion mounted large-scale retaliatory operations aimed at destroying what he called guerrilla bases across the frontier.

To United Nations observers the border incidents about which the Israelis complained often appeared hardly serious enough to warrant the thunderous retaliation visited upon the Arabs by the Israelis. In balance, at least five or six Arabs died for every Israeli killed.

In December 1955, after Syrians had fired on Israeli fishing craft in the Sea of Galilee, Mr. Ben-Gurion ordered his army into Syrian territory. A network of Syrian coastal positions was blown up, and 50 Syrian soldiers were killed.

The raid was ill-timed politically. On that same day the temperate Mr. Sharett, then foreign minister, was waiting in Washington for an answer to his request for Western arms to offset Communist arms that were reaching Egypt. News of the raid shocked and vexed the State Department. Mr. Sharett returned empty-handed, furious with Mr. Ben-Gurion, whom he accused of having undermined his mission.

Mr. Ben-Gurion not only refused to modify his retaliation policy but also told Mr. Sharett that diplomacy was to be subordinated to security. In June 1956, he ousted Mr. Sharett and chose as his new foreign minister Mrs. Golda Meir, a former Milwaukee teacher, whom he could trust to follow his line.

Tension rose during the summer of 1956, and in September a major retaliatory action led by General Dayan, then chief of the Israeli armed forces, resulted in the death of 37 Jordanians.

Mr. Ben-Gurion defended such actions as "self-defense," and he told his Parliament that the greatest menace to Israel was an impending attack by "the Egyptian Fascist dictator," President Gamal Abdel Nasser. He proclaimed: "We will never start a war. We do not believe that wars provide comprehensive solutions to historic problems."

Two weeks after he had spoken those words Mr. Ben-Gurion, in complicity with France and Britain, launched a "preventive war" to knock out President Nasser's army. Israeli forces overran the Gaza Strip, the tiny corner of the old British Palestine mandate administered by Egypt, and plunged deep into Sinai.

Mr. Ben-Gurion's objective was the fall of President Nasser and the signing of a peace treaty with Egypt.

By prearrangement, Britain and France moved to seize the Suez Canal. Port Said fell to the British and French forces. The invasion by the three nations was on the verge of success.

Then the roof fell in. President Dwight D. Eisenhower was furious at Britain and France for having committed open aggression while the West was reaping moral capital over the Hungarian revolt. So the United States supported United Nations demands that the invading forces vacate Egypt promptly and unconditionally.

Confronted also by threats of Soviet intervention, Britain and France withdrew their forces in 27 days.

Israel balked. Mr. Ben-Gurion wanted to keep the Gaza Strip. He also wanted assurances that the Gulf of Aqaba, the northern arm of the Red Sea, would be open to Israeli shipping. The gulf had been denied to Israeli ships for six years by Egyptian guns commanding the narrow passage at Sharm el Sheik.

President Eisenhower insisted that no nation invading another in the face of United Nations disapproval should set conditions on its withdrawal. Aggression, he said, must not be rewarded.

Mr. Ben-Gurion defied the world for weeks, flouting six successive General Assembly orders to get out of Egypt. His Parliament had approved a defiant resolution committing Israel never to yield either the Gulf or Gaza.

But when President Eisenhower cut short a vacation to warn of "pressure" if Israel failed to cooperate, the tough little premier knew the game was up.

Pale and drawn from pneumonia contracted after a PT-boat ride in the Gulf of Aqaba, Mr. Ben-Gurion went before his cabinet to propose more flexibility in Israel's position. Knesset politicians were insisting on all-out defiance.

"The noose is tightening around our neck," a bearded, skullcapped member cried.

"The devil with this," snapped Mr. Ben-Gurion. "The devil with the coalition." He threatened to quit and form a new government. Finally he got the leeway he needed.

Israel agreed to withdraw from Gaza and Sharm el Sheik on these "assumptions": that freedom of navigation would prevail on the Gulf of Aqaba; that the Gaza Strip would be administered by the United Nations pending a peace settlement between Egypt and Israel; and that Israel had the right, under the self-defense guarantee of the United Nations Charter, to send ships through the Gulf of Aqaba by armed force if there should be interference and to "defend its rights" in the Gaza Strip if raids were renewed.

The collapse of the Sinai adventure was the bleakest moment in Mr. Ben-Gurion's career. That he survived it politically was considered a tribute to his toughness, his resilience, and his ability to persuade most Israelis and a great segment of world Jews that his action was morally sound.

Again in 1960 Mr. Ben-Gurion risked alienating world opinion; he decided to try Adolf Eichmann, the Gestapo colonel who had shipped millions of Jews to death camps in World War II.

There was little or no sympathy for Eichmann, but there was widespread resentment over the way he was brought to justice. The Nazi was kidnapped in Argentina, put aboard an El Al Israel Airlines plane and eventually exposed to a show trial in a Jerusalem theater converted into a courtroom.

There were protests that Eichmann could not possibly have a fair trial in Jerusalem, that the case should be heard by a German court or an international tribunal. Many Jews assailed the "arrogance" of Mr. Ben-Gurion's contention that Israel, as the sovereign Jewish state, was "from a moral point of view" the only place where Eichmann could be tried.

The furor died quickly as the trial unfolded. The Israeli judges seemed impeccable in the hearing during the spring and summer of 1961. After they had condemned Eichmann to the gallows, Robert Servatius, his West German lawyer, conceded that the defendant had had a fairer trial than he would have got in West Germany.

The trial enhanced Mr. Ben-Gurion's exalted status in his own country. By bringing Eichmann to trial he had taught the new generation of Israelis that "Jews are not sheep to be slaughtered, but a people who can hit back—as Jews did in the War of Independence."

Israel's man of decision was born in Plonsk, Poland, on Oct. 16, 1886. His name was David Green, and his father was Avigdor Green, an unlicensed lawyer who wore a silk top hat and a frock coat rather than the fur hat and caftan traditionally worn by the men of his community. David was to adopt the pen name "Ben-Gurion" as a journalist in Jerusalem. He thought it had a resonant Old Testament ring—it was the name of one of the last defenders of Jerusalem against the Roman legions. The Hebrew word *Ben* means "son of," and *Gurion* means "lion cub."

Mr. Ben-Gurion's mother, Sheindal, died during the birth of her 11th child. David, her sixth, was 10 years old at the time.

The tone of the family was vigorously intellectual. There were discussions of Socialism and the newly reemerged Zionism advocated by the Viennese journalist Theodor Herzl at the historic Jewish conference at Basel, Switzerland, in 1897.

Mr. Ben-Gurion's formal education did not go much beyond the Plonsk Jewish schools, but he acquired an excellently stocked mind through wide reading, particularly in history. Possessed of tremendous concentration, he became in his lifetime a keen student of Greek and Eastern philosophies. He achieved a reputation as a brilliant linguist through his mastery of English, Russian, Greek, Yiddish, Turkish, French and German. He read but did not speak Arabic. He also studied Spanish.

In Plonsk he was active in the Poale Zion movement, which combined Zionism and Socialism. Plonsk was in Russian Poland, and the revolutionary movement against the Czars was followed by pogroms there. Many Polish and Russian Jews emigrated. In 1906, kindled by Herzl's aim for a Jewish commonwealth, David Green was one of a group of young Plonsk Jews who went to Palestine.

Of his first night in Palestine he wrote in a letter to his father: "I did not sleep. I was amid the rich smell of corn. I heard the braying of donkeys and the rustle of leaves in the orchards. Above were massed clusters of stars against the deep blue firmament. My heart overflowed with happiness."

But Mr. Ben-Gurion was repelled by the political apathy of the Jewish settlers—there were about 60,000 Jews in Palestine when he arrived. He joined the small workers' party, Poale Zion, which was to emerge as Mapai, and soon became one of its leading organizers and propagandists. Today Mapai is moderately Socialist, probably no more leftist than the British Labor party, and has little in common with doctrinaire Marxism.

Mr. Ben-Gurion worked for a time as a farm laborer for wages just sufficient to provide him with a room and one meal a day. He displayed a natural ability to negotiate in labor disputes, and he soon had considerable prestige among his fellow workers.

Articles signed "Ben-Gurion" began to appear in the Poale Zion party newspaper, and Mr. Ben-Gurion was elected to the three-man administrative presidium of the party at the 1907 Jaffa conference. At that conference he succeeded in having this platform plan adopted: "The party will strive for an independent state for the Jewish people in this country."

In that year, to prevent difficulties for his father in Plonsk, Mr. Ben-Gurion returned to Russia to do his military service. He served for one week, deserted and made his way back to Palestine.

The success of Enver Pasha's "Young Turk" movement in Turkey in 1908 led Mr. Ben-Gurion and many of his associates to believe that reasonable coexistence could be established between the new and supposedly liberal Turkish government and the Jewish community in Palestine, which was in the Ottoman Empire. Mr. Ben-Gurion and several other Zionist leaders went to Constantinople [now Istanbul] to study Turkish law and administration, hoping to enter the Turkish government as representatives of Jewish Palestine.

Early in World War I, Mr. Ben-Gurion wrote articles advocating the creation of a Jewish battalion in the Turkish army. But the Turks suspected his motives and expelled him as a subversive. With his chief collaborator, a young Ukrainian Jew named Itzhak Ben-Zvi, who was to become the second president of Israel, Mr. Ben-Gurion made his way to the United States in 1915.

It was in New York that Mr. Ben-Gurion and Mr. Ben-Zvi founded Hechalutz (the Pioneers), which created Jewish settlements in Palestine between the world wars. And it was here that he met Paula Moonwess, daughter of an immigrant from Minsk. She was a student at the Brooklyn Jewish Training School for Nurses. They were married at City Hall in 1917.

Paula, a direct and uninhibited woman, was to become a legend in Israel. She is said to have startled Dag Hammarskjöld, the secretary general of the United Nations, by saying to him, "Why don't you get married and leave the Jews and Arabs alone?" Mr. Hammarskjöld remained a bachelor.

Until Russia had left the war and the United States had entered it, Mr. Ben-Gurion believed that the best interests of the Palestine Jews lay with Turkey. But by 1917 there were indications that the Turks might not be on the winning side. Mr. Ben-Gurion helped organize two Jewish battalions in the United States and Canada to serve with the British in the Middle East. He served as a corporal in one of the battalions, with the Royal Fusiliers in Egypt, but saw no action.

The Balfour Declaration of 1917 established the principle of a Jewish homeland in Palestine, and in 1922 the British were entrusted by the League of Nations with a mandate for Palestine.

Dr. Chaim Weizmann, the intellectual who was to become the first president of Israel, headed the world Zionist movement mostly from London. Mr. Ben-Gurion preached Jewish working-class solidarity on the scene in Palestine.

To a group of Zionist delegates he once said: "Let me inform you gentlemen that Zionism has no content if you do not constantly bear in mind the building of the Jewish state. And such a state is only possible on the basis of a maximum number of workers, and if you cannot understand that, woe to your Zionism."

The Jewish Legion had been formed too late to contribute much to the defeat of Turkey, but its existence provided Mr. Ben-Gurion with a fine channel for propaganda. He proselytized for the Poale Zion party among the 3,000 legionnaires. It was largely because of his initiative that Histadrut, the General Federation of Labor, was formed in 1920, with Mr. Ben-Gurion as secretary general.

This powerful body, now quartered in a modern Tel Aviv skyscraper that enemies of Mr. Ben-Gurion called the Kremlin, expanded into banking, health plans, contracting, agriculture, marketing, education, insurance, transportation, employment agencies, collectives and cooperatives of every kind.

For the next five years Mr. Ben-Gurion campaigned for the union of Palestine's labor parties, and in 1930 the Mapai was formed. In 1935 he became chairman of the Jewish Agency, the executive body of Zionism.

Mr. Ben-Gurion had many opponents in the general Zionist movement. Vladimir Jabotinsky was one leader of a nationalist movement opposed to what many Zionists believed to be Mr. Ben-Gurion's strong Socialist views.

In 1936 Palestinian Arabs staged a bloody revolt against increasing Jewish influence, and the next year Mr. Ben-Gurion favored a partition of Palestine as recommended by a Royal Commission under Earl Peel. The Arabs rejected the proposal, and the British dropped the plan.

British policy became clearly pro-Arab, and in 1939 the British government issued a White Paper that limited Jewish immigration to Palestine and land purchases there and was aimed at insuring a permanent minority status for the Jews there.

When Britain declared war on Germany, the Jews in Palestine pledged support against the common enemy but continued their resistance to the British policy, which they considered a threat to their existence.

Mr. Ben-Gurion put it this way: "We shall fight in the war against Hitler as if there were no White Paper, but we shall fight the White Paper as if there were no war."

During the war years he was preoccupied with these aims and with internal matters in Palestine. And the mass extermination of European Jews intensified his desire to establish a Jewish homeland.

In 1945 he visited displaced-persons camps in Germany and the next year told a conference of survivors: "We shall not rest until the last one of you who so desires shall join us in the land of Israel to build the Jewish state together with us."

Mr. Ben-Gurion believed that if the Jews in Palestine could not defend themselves they would be driven out by the Arabs. From 1907, when he was with Hashomer, the armed guard movement, while he was a labor leader in Sejera, a small isolated village in Galilee, he acted in the belief that the Palestinian Jews would have to protect themselves.

After the United Nations, on Nov. 29, 1947, resolved to partition Palestine into Jewish and Arab states, Mr. Ben-Gurion assumed the security portfolio of the Jewish Agency Executive.

He planned and supervised the transformation of the Haganah from an illegal underground military arm of the Jewish Agency into the Israel Defense Forces. He sent men to Europe to buy arms, including World War II surplus equipment, and to recruit Jewish war veterans to operate the planes, tanks and artillery with which the Haganah had had no experience.

Volunteers came from the United States, Canada, South Africa, South America and most European countries. Mr. Ben-Gurion obtained funds from Jews in the United States and bought machinery to establish an arms industry.

From time to time Mr. Ben-Gurion cooperated with the British against terrorists, and armed clashes were narrowly averted.

During the mandate the Irgun Zvai Leumi, an extreme nationalist group, had conducted terrorist activities against the British government. Unlike the Haganah, it had spurned the authority of the official Jewish leadership.

During a United Nations truce, the Irgun ran the landing ship *Altalena* ashore at Tel Aviv with weapons and volunteers. Mr. Ben-Gurion ordered Haganah troops to fire at the ship, which blew up. Men were killed and wounded on both sides.

The *Altalena* affair was one of the most controversial events in Mr. Ben-Gurion's career as premier. Many Israelis never forgave his order, which deprived Israel of badly needed weapons and nearly touched off a civil war. Others said it had been one of the most courageous and statesmanlike actions of his career. They believed that by handling the situation firmly in that crucial period Mr. Ben-Gurion had established once and for all that there was no authority in the state but the government of Israel, and had, in fact, averted a civil war.

After the truce, renewed sharp fighting with the Arabs secured the Negev and central Galilee for Israel. Armistice agreements with Egypt, Lebanon, Syria and Jordan in 1949 ended the hot war for the time being.

Because large-scale immigration had nearly doubled the population and it was still necessary to maintain military preparedness, the Israelis by 1951 found it necessary to take drastic steps to bolster the country's economy.

Premier Ben-Gurion came to the United States on a fund-raising drive. He was received with enthusiasm and initiated the sale of $500 million in Israeli bonds.

At this time Israel abandoned her foreign policy of "nonidentification" and openly aligned herself with the United States in the Cold War. Previously, Israel, in her independence struggle, had bought arms from Soviet-bloc countries and had enjoyed good relations with the Soviet Union, one of the first nations to recognize the state of Israel.

At home Mr. Ben-Gurion wrestled with succeeding cabinet crises until the day in 1953 when he decided that he had had enough for a while.

In an article written for *The New York Times* from his retreat at Sde Boker on his retirement, he said: "No single person alone can determine the fate of a nation. No man is indispensable. In war there may be a commander or statesman on whom much or even all depends. Not so in time of peace. The fate of a country depends upon its own character, its ability, its capacity, its faith in itself, its sense of responsibility, both individual and collective. A statesman who sees himself as the determining factor in the fate of his country is harmful and dangerous."

Yet for 15 years Mr. Ben-Gurion made most of the decisions for Israel, and the most fateful were to come after he had returned to Jerusalem in 1955 and had begun leading the nation on a more adventurous path.

Although his country was in reality a ward of the United States, absolutely dependent on financial aid from Washington and from American Jewish groups, Mr. Ben-Gurion refused to permit any outside meddling in her affairs.

He showed his freedom from American controls early by ignoring strong Washington pressure to put Israel's capital in Tel Aviv, rather than in Jerusalem, which the United Nations had proposed as an international city. (The United States has refused to move its embassy from Tel Aviv to Jerusalem.)

In domestic politics, Mr. Ben-Gurion also defied

strong forces, notably the ultra-Orthodox religious groups. Once, during an interminable Knesset debate over whether swine—forbidden to Jews as food—should be bred in Israel, Mr. Ben-Gurion remarked that if the Lord had objected to pigs He wouldn't have led them to Noah's Ark.

At another time he shocked rabbis in the Knesset by announcing that after a study of Exodus he had concluded that only 600 Jews—not 600,000, as the Bible maintained—could have left Egypt and crossed the Sinai Desert.

Mr. Ben-Gurion was a profound student of the Bible. His speeches were enriched with references to the heroes and prophets of the Old Testament. He had had little formal education, but his intellectual curiosity led him, at 56, to learn Greek so he could read the Septuagint, the Greek version of the Old Testament. At 68 his interest turned to the Dialogues of The Buddha, and he began learning Sanskrit to understand them fully.

He already knew enough yoga to stand on his head, and photos of Mr. Ben-Gurion in bathing trunks, inverted on the Mediterranean sands, invoked wry comment. Friends insisted, however, that Hazaken—the Old Man—as he was affectionately called, was sharper-witted upside down than most of his opponents were right side up.

The most serious domestic challenge to Mr. Ben-Gurion's rule came as a result of the celebrated "Lavon affair."

A former protégé of Mr. Ben-Gurion, Pinhas Lavon, had risen in the Histadrut until his political influence was so considerable that he was regarded as a possible heir to the national leadership.

But Mr. Ben-Gurion fell out with Mr. Lavon and sought to destroy his power. A cloak-and-dagger fiasco, involving the collapse of an Israeli spy network in Egypt, gave Mr. Ben-Gurion the chance in 1955 to force Mr. Lavon's resignation as defense minister.

The scandal smoldered for six years. Few Israelis knew what the affair was about. The press was allowed to print only the state censor's approved phrase, "a security disaster in 1954." The Egyptian government charged in 1954 that it had uncovered an Israeli spy ring that planned to blow up British and American consular offices to sabotage relations between Cairo and the Western powers.

Then, in December 1960, the Lavon affair burst into the news again. Mr. Lavon was able to prove at a meeting of the Israeli cabinet that forged papers had been part of the evidence that forced him from office. Mr. Ben-Gurion stormed from the room, but even this did not prevent his cabinet from clearing Mr. Lavon of responsibility for the 1954 fiasco.

Mr. Ben-Gurion followed his usual tactic of bringing down the government by resigning. But this time other members of his six-party coalition were so disturbed that they refused to join him in a new government. Hoping to silence his critics, Mr. Ben-Gurion called for new elections. The results, he conceded, were "a national disaster," for Mapai slipped from 47 seats to 42 in the 120-seat Knesset. After lengthy dickering, however, he formed a new cabinet, and meanwhile the Mapai Central Committee had destroyed Mr. Lavon's base of power by ousting him as secretary general of the Histadrut.

Eventually Mr. Ben-Gurion suffered the bitter fate that overtakes a statesman who has been around too long. He became a bore to his people, and they rejected him.

He resigned as premier in June 1963 because of "personal needs." He said later that he wanted to write a history of the Jews' return to their homeland. But in semiretirement he erupted sporadically, like a cooling volcano. He became increasingly critical of Levi Eshkol, the new premier, and the estrangement between the two grew wider when Mr. Ben-Gurion proclaimed that Mr. Eshkol was "unfit to lead the nation."

He demanded a reopening of the Lavon affair. But the country was bored by the 10-year-old scandal, and Premier Eshkol refused a judicial inquiry into the almost-forgotten fiasco.

Mr. Ben-Gurion's efforts to return to active politics ended in humiliation. The Mapai Central Committee refused to put him on the party's list for the 1965 election. So he formed Rafi, a splinter party, taking with him a handful of younger politicians including General Dayan, the former chief of staff. The new party ran a poor fourth with less than 9 percent of the vote, and won 10 seats in Parliament.

Mr. Ben-Gurion's wife died in 1968, and the old warrior spent much of his time thereafter in solitary contemplation. In 1968, after his small Rafi party decided to join the newly formed Israel Labor party, a number of Rafi members, led by Mr. Ben-Gurion, broke away. They formed the Independent National List and won four Knesset seats in 1969.

He remained in the Knesset until 1970, when he delivered a handwritten resignation note to the speaker, Reuven Barkatt, and, dry-eyed, left the chamber for good.

Soon afterward, he told a visitor to Tel Aviv that he had found farm work more satisfying than politics. And he had this to say about Soviet intentions in the Middle East: "They want to get the two oceans, the Atlantic and the Pacific. So first of all they must have the Mediterranean, and it is not easy to get that without the Arabs. They want the Arabs. I do not think they are interested in destroying Israel, because if they do, the Arabs will not need them."

Concerning the territories that Israel occupied in the 1967 Arab-Israeli war, Mr. Ben-Gurion took a relatively dovish position: "I consider peace more important than territory," he said. "The area we had before the Six-Day War would be enough to take in all the Jews."

He continued: "For peace, I would be for giving back all the captured areas, with the exception of Jerusalem and the Golan Heights."

Turning to his old theme of the need for further immigration, he said Israel still needed "another five or six million" Jews. But he observed wryly, "I don't believe that all Jews will settle in Israel—unless the Messiah comes."

On the sometimes controversial question of what constitutes being a Jew, Mr. Ben-Gurion later told a visitor to Sde Boker, "The essence of being a Jew, in my opinion, is the idea of the Prophets—not the Torah, but the prophets. They have two ideas: You must love one single God and you must lead a moral life. That is all that matters.

"Later on," he continued, "when we Jews lost our independence and we had to live in ghettos and were hated, then our leaders provided other things and rules about things to wear and say. They needed these things to keep Jews together as a nation."

But he said that now that Jews again had a homeland and independence, the rituals and practices had faded in significance against the Prophets' more general messages.

In his last years Mr. Ben-Gurion aged considerably. His nimbus of white hair seemed to grow wispier, and his thoughts sometimes rambled.

He spent much of his time in his cluttered study at Sde Boker, living among his books and in the past. There were a large portrait of his wife, a map of Israel, a vase of desert roses among the awards and mementos. On his desk, there were always a Bible and a bottle of apple juice.

When he was well, he participated in kibbutz activities—dedicating a new garden, leading a Bible-study group, pressing Tel Aviv for a teachers' training institute for the settlement.

His time was devoted to study, reflection, writing and a teeming correspondence with Jews all over the world. He produced three big books in his last years, including the 862-page *Israel: A Personal History*, published here in 1971.

On rare occasions, he made public appearances. In early 1971, he toured the fortifications along the Suez Canal with Gen. Haim Bar-Lev, then the chief of staff, engaging in the banter he loved.

The old man was shown a bunker. "What kind of Hebrew word is *bunker*?" he asked. An escort explained: "We use *bunker* because we have not yet got around to Hebraizing defense terminology. On offense, we have no foreign words."

Mr. Ben-Gurion talked with a soldier. "You're younger than I," he said, "perhaps you can tell me when there will be peace." The soldier replied, "Who knows? It depends on the Arabs."

"And on us!" the patriarch put in.

Later in 1971, on his 85th birthday, he publicly rejected an appeal from Mrs. Meir that he give up his splinter party and rejoin Mapai. Mrs. Meir nonetheless went to the celebration in Sde Boker, and they talked for a bit—after five years of silence.

His last appearance was in May in Tel Aviv for Israel's 25th anniversary. He sat bent over in a grandstand watching the pomp, wearing a farmer's hat.

He had become a symbol of the past, a much-loved grandfather hovering at the edge of the thoughts and aspirations of the embattled nation.

He said little about the October war, though he was quoted as having referred sarcastically to the arguments among Israeli generals following the Egyptian and Syrian surprise attacks: "They think they're generals now."

Sometimes in his last years Mr. Ben-Gurion argued that the Israeli government was not genuinely democratic. Old opponents replied that it was Mr. Ben-Gurion himself who had introduced authoritarian ways into Israel during his years as premier.

But even these opponents conceded that he and his wife had never stood much on ceremony. When Mrs. Ben-Gurion was asked once whether her husband should be addressed as "Prime Minister" or "Mr. Ben-Gurion," she reportedly said, "Call him Ben-Gurion. Anyone can be a prime minister, but not everyone can be a Ben-Gurion."

Mr. Ben-Gurion died on Dec. 1, 1973, in Tel Aviv. He succumbed to a brain hemorrhage that had struck him two weeks earlier.

THE BURIAL SERVICE IN THE NEGEV DESERT

TERENCE SMITH

DAVID BEN-GURION, Israel's first premier, was buried on Dec. 3, 1973, in a starkly simple 45-minute religious service near the Negev Desert kibbutz where he spent the contemplative final years of his life.

A silent group of 300 political and military leaders, representatives of foreign governments, family members and former associates watched as the former premier's body was lowered into the ground.

At Mr. Ben-Gurion's insistence, there were no eulogies—only a few psalms, the traditional prayer for the dead and a mournful burial lament sung by a single military cantor.

The chief chaplain of the Israeli army, Gen. Mordechai Piron, said in a short prayer: "The Lord giveth and the Lord taketh away, blessed be His name. Peace in His heavens, He will make peace upon us and all Israel."

The drama of the ceremony was provided by the memory of the man and by the setting: a breathtaking promontory overlooking the rugged canyons and deep desert valley known in the Bible as the wilderness of Zin. Hundreds of feet below, a ribbon of green trees lined the dry riverbed that snakes along the valley floor. As the cantor sang, his dirge echoed off the canyon walls.

Mr. Ben-Gurion selected the site himself. It is on the edge of the campus of Sde Boker College, which he helped found a dozen years ago. In recent years, Mr. Ben-Gurion frequently worked in the library here, staring out at the desert landscape. Finally he decided it was here he wanted to be buried. In January 1968, his wife, Paula, was laid to rest in a neat green plot beneath a grove of pepper trees on the lip of the promontory. The body of the former premier was set in a grave next to hers.

The private ceremony followed a full-dress state funeral held earlier in the day in Jerusalem on the broad plaza in front of the Knesset, or Parliament.

Mr. Ben-Gurion's family, including his son and

two daughters, Premier Golda Meir and her cabinet, members of the Parliament and foreign and religious delegations faced the coffin on two sides of the plaza beneath a brilliant blue sky.

A one-minute siren sounded on the plaza and throughout the country at the start of the ceremony. Radio news broadcasts early in the morning warned listeners that a steady mourning siren would sound at 11 A.M. It would reflect an emergency, the announcers explained, only if the siren was warbling rather than continuous.

Traffic came to a halt and Israelis in cities and towns all over the country stood at attention in honor of Mr. Ben-Gurion's memory.

After the psalms and kaddish, or prayer for the dead, were said, the traditional petition for mercy for the soul of the departed, "El Moleh Rahamim" ("Lord Filled with Mercy"), was sung.

The cantor addressed it in the name of "David Ben-Gurion, son of Avigdor, first prime minister and defense minister of the state, who effected the redemption of the people of Israel in their land."

The title was the closest expression to a eulogy heard throughout the day's ceremonies.

At the conclusion of the ceremony, the coffin was placed aboard a helicopter that thundered down at a landing field a hundred yards from the plaza. Moments later, Mrs. Meir and an official party of about 80 boarded five other Israeli air force helicopters for the hour-long flight to the Negev.

The flight of helicopters set down here in Sde Boker in a giant cloud of dust at 1:03 P.M. About 200 persons from the college and the kibbutz were already waiting at the gravesite as Mrs. Meir, dressed in a black suit and carrying a black handbag, led the official party into the area.

The psalms and songs of the earlier ceremony were repeated, and Mr. Ben-Gurion's simple coffin was lowered slowly into the ground by a team of military chaplains.

At the end of the ceremony, Amos Ben-Gurion, the former premier's only son, removed a flower from one of the wreaths atop his father's fresh grave and gently placed it on the simple stone marker that covers his mother's.

Then he slowly led the Ben-Gurion family out of the area. Among the grandchildren was Yariv Ben-Gurion, who is in the army and was limping slightly from a wound suffered in the October war.

IN HOMAGE TO BEN-GURION

SHIMON PERES

I FIRST met David Ben-Gurion when I was yet a youth, and he already a legend. I spoke with him for the first time when he took me in his car from Tel Aviv to Haifa, a two-hour trip at that time. He was not a man of small talk, and most of the drive passed in disappointment for me, as he sat in silence. Toward the end of the trip, he suddenly turned to me and said, "You know, Trotsky wasn't a true leader. Lenin was." I was dumbfounded. I did not understand why he had suddenly chosen to raise this subject, but I was curious, and I wanted to start a conversation, so I asked, "Why?" And he, as though waiting for the question, immediately replied, "What is this 'no-peace-and-no-war'? This is a Jewish invention. A leader must know how to decide—either war, with all the risks this involves, or peace, and pay the price. Even though intellectually Lenin was inferior to Trotsky, Lenin became the leader of the Russian people because he knew how to decide."

Being a leader is not a profession. It cannot be learned in a university. In a period that demands decisions, sometimes irrevocable decisions, the character of the man who must meet these challenges is part of the synthesis that may lead either to great historical success or to painful national failure.

The period in which Ben-Gurion led our people,

first as secretary general of Histadrut, then as chairman of the Jewish Agency and finally as prime minister, was unprecedented in the history of the Jewish people, and perhaps in the history of mankind. Never, in the 4,000 years of their existence, did the Jewish people experience anything like that which befell them in the 20th century: the greatest of holocausts, and the greatest of rebirths. Never before has a people matched the achievement of the Jewish people: After 2,000 years of exile, the Jews reassembled anew in their homeland—a land with its own language, its various communities, its teachings, its vitality.

Leading the Jewish people is not an easy task—we are a divided, obstinate, highly individualistic people who have cultivated faith, sharp-wittedness and polemics to a very high level. But it is not only the psychology of the people that makes them so exacting—their geographical situation has been equally problematic. To quote Isaiah Berlin: "This is a people richer in history than in geography."

It is therefore no wonder that Ben-Gurion found himself surrounded by contradictions. The great migration of East European Jewry—the heart of the Jewish people—that began in 1882 proved very disappointing for Zionism. Of the three million Jews who emigrated from Russia and Poland before the outbreak of World War I in 1914, only 50,000 went to Palestine, and even all of those did not remain. The land to which they came, while indeed the Holy Land, was desolate and uninviting; a land that had been laid waste, thirsty for water, filled with swamps and malaria, lacking in natural resources. And in the land itself there lived another people—a people who neglected the land, but who lived on it. Indeed, the return to Zion was accompanied by ceaseless violent clashes with the small Arab population in Israel, and with the Arab states that incited them and fought alongside them.

What, then, did Ben-Gurion have, aside from a broken and exiled people, a poor and unproductive land, a tangible enemy and a world so indifferent that even the survivors of the Holocaust sailing to the shores of Palestine came up against the British fleet?

Ben-Gurion was a realist. But of what use was his realism, when nothing seemed real after the Holocaust, except for faith, prayer and a stubborn obstinacy? Of all the leaders this world has known, none made more strategic use of faith than he.

I worked with him for almost two decades, beginning in the early 1950s, often day and night, when Ben-Gurion was defense minister as well as prime minister. For me, this was a time of celebration and a time of enigma. Even today, I am not sure that I fully understood him, so complex was he.

One contradiction in his nature I perceived immediately—the contradiction between his abilities and his character. He had the traits of a true intellectual: an intense curiosity that was never quenched; a phenomenal memory; an extraordinary ability to learn and to absorb; the ability to express himself orally and in writing; a knowledge of languages; the ability to think in abstract terms; a true love of history and philosophy. But he lacked one intellectual quality: the ability to hesitate; the readiness to remain neutral, or at least objective; the patience to wait before reaching binding decisions. He was incapable of acquiring knowledge on a subject without forming an opinion of his own.

For he had the character of a fighter. He knew that some things were frightening, but he could never be a coward. He knew that some things were permanent, yet refused to believe that they could not be changed. He was always eager for battle. He did not believe there were hopeless battles, only fighters who had lost hope. He was eager for ideological battle, and was not dismayed by physical battle. He respected the time factor: Only one who takes the initiative, who uses the element of surprise, understands the hourglass of history and can adjust it accordingly. The rules of the game must be respected only if they cannot be changed. He believed that change was more important than routine. He had the courage to question all accepted conventions in history, in reality, in philosophy. "All the experts," he used to say, "are experts on what was. There are no experts on what will be."

Thus, he was not afraid of conventions, nor was he intimidated by those who sought to give him advice—Jews and non-Jews alike. On Ben-Gurion's 80th birthday, in 1966, I invited our greatest writer, the Nobel laureate S. Y. Agnon, to come with me to Kibbutz Sde Boker, where Ben-Gurion was then living, to celebrate the occasion. On the way, Agnon said to me, "I thought that Jews are afraid of Gentiles. Ben-Gurion evidently wasn't afraid of them." And, after a pause, he added, "He wasn't afraid of Jews either."

Ben-Gurion questioned everything anew. He formed his own opinions. And once he had formed an opinion there was no one who could make him change his mind.

Yet, without the moral dimension of his nature, his personality would have remained merely dramatic. He was not a leader for the sake of leadership, but was the leader of the Jewish people. He believed with all the fervor of his personality that the greatest contribution of the Jewish people to the world lay in the priority they accorded to morality above all else in the life of the individual and the nation. More than esthetics, more than wealth, more than physical size.

He rejected all the accepted definitions of the Jewish people and the Jewish faith. Judaism is not a religion, he argued, but a belief. It is not a framework, but substance—both national and universal. The national substance requires us to relate to land, language and history; the universal substance requires our dedication to one God, to love for our fellow man, to human equality, justice and truth. These two components are inseparable. They lay the foundations for civilized existence.

For years, Ben-Gurion was prejudiced against Charles de Gaulle. He never reconciled himself to the retreat of the French army before Hitler's invasion. Although he knew that de Gaulle headed the Frenchmen who resisted this defeat, he never forgave him his excessive pride in his relations with the Allies. When de Gaulle published his memoirs, I tried to convince Ben-Gurion to write an introduction to the Hebrew translation. He refused, and I wrote it in his stead. But, in time—and, what is more, with the improvement in de Gaulle's attitude toward Israel—there was a marked shift in Ben-Gurion's assessment of de Gaulle. Nevertheless, I awaited the first meeting between the two in 1960 with trepidation.

It soon became apparent that my fears were unfounded. Each immediately awakened appreciation and respect in the other. Ben-Gurion later told me that de Gaulle was an intellectual giant. De Gaulle told me that he found Ben-Gurion truly "a lion with a lion's countenance."

After lunch at the Elysée, on a wonderfully sunny Paris day, we sat on the lawn to drink tea. Around our table were de Gaulle, Ben-Gurion, Premier Michel Debré and myself, as deputy defense minister. De Gaulle suddenly turned to Ben-Gurion and said, "Mr. Prime Minister, what are your secret dreams? Tell me. I won't tell anyone. Do you covet the waters of Lebanon? The Sinai deserts? The mountains of Moab? After all, yours is such a small country . . ." Ben-Gurion reddened slightly. After reflecting for a moment, he replied, "Had you asked me this question 20 or 30 years ago, I would have sketched my dream on a map, but today my dream is different. Today I dream of more Jews, not more territory."

"More what?" De Gaulle asked, taken aback. "More Jews? Why? Where will they come from?"

"Ours is a land built more on people than on territory," Ben-Gurion said. "The Jews will come from everywhere: from France, from Russia, from America, from Yemen."

"From France?" De Gaulle asked. "They will come from France, and give up everything? From America? Will they give up their Cadillacs and televisions? From Russia, and free themselves from the fetters of ideology? And from Yemen—have they indeed maintained their Jewishness?"

Ben-Gurion raced ahead. "Yes, they will give up

everything, except their faith. Their faith is their passport. Their yearning for their homeland is the greatest force in their lives."

Ben-Gurion's great love affair was with history. "A man can truly be judged only by his record," he said. Ben-Gurion's record is unique. If not for him, the state of Israel would not be what it is today; indeed, it might never have been born. He assembled the scattered fragments of the Jewish people and consolidated them into a nation. He stood at the head of a great enterprise to make the desert bloom. He insisted that the Hebrew language must be revived, and Israel is the only place where a people has returned to its ancient language. He conducted a war even before there was a state. And although the odds were heavily against Israel, he emerged the victor.

He altered the image of the Jew from that of rabbi, merchant, wanderer to that of scientist, farmer and soldier. He restored the Bible to its people; he restored the people to the Bible. In his last years he embarked on an all-out war against what seemed to him the perversion of truth (in the Lavon affair, in which Defense Minister Pinhas Lavon was cleared of wrongdoing by Ben-Gurion's cabinet in a security scandal). Ben-Gurion argued with the fervor of youth that ministers cannot be judges, that government must remain separate from justice, that we must take care that even in times of danger or of bloodshed the democratic principle of the separation of authorities must be maintained.

Did he leave us a satisfied man? I doubt it. I doubt whether he sought satisfaction. I once accompanied him on a visit to a school in Dimona, in the Negev, where a 10-year-old girl asked him, "Mr. Ben-Gurion, what was the day in your life that caused you the most satisfaction?" He looked at her, thought a moment and said, "What is satisfaction? We cannot be satisfied. If you are satisfied, you begin to be pampered, to be lazy; you cease to create, to struggle, to believe."

No. He left us in 1973 still unsatisfied. The Negev, where he was buried, still remains largely vacant. The Jewish people have yet to understand the meaning of statesmanship. Peace has not yet been achieved. Most of the Jewish people still live in the Diaspora. And even in Israel there are signs of self-satisfaction.

Yet the memory of David Ben-Gurion lives within us as a leader who achieved the impossible.

PABLO CASALS

1876–1973

By Alden Whitman

I think it goes like this," a cello student struggling with a Johann Sebastian Bach suite once told Pablo Casals.

"Don't think," the master cellist replied. "It is better to feel."

With this emphasis on an inner sensitivity to a composer's intentions, Casals was able to demonstrate what luminescent and human music could be drawn from the strings of a rather awkward instrument. In concerts and recordings over some 75 years, he provoked awe and applause for the profundity of his insights, the felicity of his playing and, above all, the soaring purity of his interpretations of baroque and classical composers. Bach was his specialty, but he was also at home with Boccherini, Mozart, Brahms, Beethoven, Schumann and Dvořák.

At the same time Casals (he pronounced the name Kaa-SAALS) won much admiration and acclaim as a man of probity and principle for his humanitarianism, his personal musical "crusade for peace" and his one-man stand against the regime of Francisco Franco in his native Spain. Few musicians achieved in their own time the international renown accumulated by Casals.

Part of this fame, in the United States at least, came very late in life and rested on Casals's talents in conducting, which he fancied as his real métier and which he had practiced, mainly in Europe, since 1920. Conducting gave him a sense of fulfillment, he said, because orchestras, with their human teamwork, are "the greatest of all instruments."

Early in his career, on his first American tour in 1901, a falling rock crushed the fingers of his left hand. His first thought, as Casals recalled it, was, "Thank God, I won't have to play the cello anymore." He associated that reaction with his desire to conduct.

After a period of semiactivity in Europe starting in 1945, Casals went to Puerto Rico to live in 1956. He was then 79 years old and seemed spent. The next year, however, he started the Festival Casals, which became an annual springtime program of concerts. He had a heart attack just before the opening of the first festival, but he recovered buoyantly in the following years, using an orchestra brought together by violinist Alexander Schneider, an old friend. The concerts drew thousands of mainlanders to the island and introduced the post–World War II generation of music lovers to Casals.

Then in 1961 he joined Rudolf Serkin's Marlboro Music Festival in Vermont, where each July he conducted the orchestra and gave master classes in the cello. And, beginning in 1962, he conducted a choral work in New York every year. His first presentation was his own oratorio, *El Pesebre* (*The Manger*), a lengthy composition dedicated "to those who have struggled and are still struggling for the cause of peace and democracy."

Horst Tappe/Camera Press

In this period of resurgence, Casals gave a widely publicized cello recital at the United Nations in New York in 1958 to mark that organization's 13th anniversary. Three years later he played to a distinguished gathering at the White House on the invitation of President John F. Kennedy.

The public attention that Casals generated in those years helped also to swell sales of his cello recordings, and this, in turn, created new esteem for his wizardry with the bow. Thousands who never saw him nonetheless came to know him intimately.

Another element of his appeal to the public was his apparent refusal to age or grow stale. "Sometimes I feel like a boy," he told an interviewer in 1964. "Music does that. I can never play the same piece twice in the same way. Each time it is new."

Watching him rehearse an orchestra when he was 89, an astonished student exclaimed: "When the maestro came onto the stage he looked 75. When he stepped on the podium he seemed even 10 years younger. And when he began to conduct he could have been a youngster ready to chase Easter eggs."

In the musical world, Casals's enduring reputation was associated with two accomplishments: his single-handed restoration to the repertory of Bach's cello music, especially the six magnificent unaccompanied suites; and his innovations in bowing and fingering that gave the cello a new and striking personality in orchestral and solo works.

He greatly lightened the work of the left hand, for example, by changes of finger positions, thus adding to its mobility. He also showed that it was possible to attain fresh subtleties in tone by freer bowing.

His own style was aristocratic. He made the most difficult passages seem simple yet luscious, all the while shunning pyrotechnics and gimmicks.

Casals came upon the Bach suites by accident when he was 13 years old and browsing with his father in a Barcelona music shop.

"I forgot entirely the reason of my visit to the shop and could only stare at this music which nobody had told me about," he said years afterward. "Sometimes even now, when I look at the covers of that old music, I see again the interior of that old and musty shop with its faint smell of the sea.

"I took the suites home and read and reread them. For 12 years after that I studied and worked every day at them. I was nearly 25 before I had the courage to play one of them in public."

When he did play them, the suites were disclosed as a transcendent musical experience, not the abstract exercises they had previously been believed to be.

"For me, Bach is like Shakespeare. He has known all and felt all," Casals told Bernard Taper in a profile published in *The New Yorker* in 1961. "He is everything. Everything except a professor. Professor Bach I do not know. When people ask me how I play Bach, I say, 'I play him as the pianist plays Chopin.' There is such fantasy in Bach—but fantasy with order."

Casals was of medium stature—not much taller than his Groffriller cello—and not heavily built. The top of his head had been bald since his early 20s. In repose, his face and his blue-gray eyes (behind round glasses) tended to be somber, but a smile imparted radiance and geniality to his face.

He was direct in his speech, exceedingly polite, a careful dresser (youthful photographs show him to have been quite a dandy in a romantic sort of way) and quietly dignified. He relaxed by reading, playing tennis, chatting with friends, smoking a pipe (he was rarely without one) and, in his late years, by watching westerns on television.

To hear Casals was a moving and memorable experience. He sat with his eyes closed, his head turned sidewise and a little lifted, as though he were communing with some secret muse. His fingering and his bowing were so flawless that they seemed automatic, yet it was evident that they resulted from concentration.

He had superb savoir faire. Once when a loose cuff bothered him, he stopped playing, slowly took off the cuff, put it on the floor and resumed playing where he had left off. When a string broke he would retire from the stage, replace it and, returning to his chair, start the solo from the beginning, such was his drive for perfection.

When Casals played a chamber music program at Perpignan, France, in July 1951, Howard Taubman, then music critic of *The New York Times*, wrote: "As a musician, Casals is all of a piece. Whether he conducts as he did in the second orchestral program of the Bach-Mozart-Beethoven festival . . . or plays the cello, there is a fine-grained consistency running through all his musical labors. . . .

"His work at the cello . . . was remarkable for its modesty and restraint, and if one listened closely one could hear innumerable felicities of technical mastery. As an admiring violinist observed, 'Do you note the four shades of color he got in one bow?' "

Casals was an ardent supporter of the Spanish Republican government. He never reconciled himself to the Franco regime, which he considered tyrannical. With the Franco victory in 1939 he went into self-imposed exile, living until 1956 in Prades, France, some 40 miles from the Spanish frontier.

Up until 1958 he refused to visit the United States because it recognized Franco. "I have great affection for the United States," he said when he moved to Puerto Rico, "but as a refugee from Franco's Spain I cannot condone America's support of a dictator who sided with America's enemies, Hitler and Mussolini. Franco's power would surely collapse without American help."

But Casals bent his attitude sufficiently to play at the United Nations in 1958 because of "the great and perhaps mortal danger [of nuclear war] threatening all humanity."

Then in 1961 he relented further and played at the White House. In subsequent years he came to this country for regular yearly visits.

Pablo Carlos Salvador Defilló de Casals was born in the Catalan town of Vendrell, 40 miles from Barcelona, on Dec. 29, 1876, the second of 11 children of Carles and Pilar Defilló de Casals. His father was the town organist.

"From my earliest days," Casals recalled, "music was for me a natural element, an activity as natural as breathing." He could sing in tune before he could talk clearly, and at the age of 5 he was a soprano in the church choir. His father taught him the piano, violin and organ, and when he was 8 he began substituting for his father as church organist.

Shortly after Pablo's 10th birthday he heard a cello for the first time when José Garcia performed in Vendrell. After some coaxing, the elder Casals bought his son a cello and gave him a few lessons. Pablo was fascinated by the instrument and proved so adept at it that he quickly exhausted his father's pedagogical abilities.

With his mother's backing and against the wishes of his father (who wanted the boy to become a carpenter), Pablo—not quite 12—went with his mother to Barcelona, where he enrolled in the Barcelona Municipal School of Music. To earn his living he played evenings for dances with a trio at the Café Tost, and later he persuaded the owner to devote one night a week to classical music.

That night attracted serious musicians to the bistro, including Isaac Albéniz, the composer and pianist. When Casals was graduated from music school at the age of 17 with first prizes for cello, piano and composition, Albéniz gave him a letter of introduction to Count Guillermo de Morphy, a music patron who was an adviser to Queen Mother Maria Christina in Madrid.

The count, taken with the young cellist, introduced him to Maria Christina, who was also charmed and who granted him a monthly stipend of 250 pesetas (about $50) for his studies.

Casals lived in Madrid from 1894 to 1897, going to school at the Royal Conservatory of Music, playing duets with the Queen Mother (she was a fair pianist), chatting with the child who was to become Alfonso XIII and being guided in his general education by the Count de Morphy.

From Madrid, Casals and his mother went to Brussels, but, miffed by an unfriendly reception at an audition there, he went to Paris, where he played at the Folies-Marigny at a wage barely sufficient to keep him and his mother from starvation. After a short time they returned to Barcelona, where Casals got a job teaching at the music school. For two years he taught cello, played it in the Barcelona Opera orchestra, gave concerts in churches and formed a string quartet, all the while saving money for a return to Paris.

In the fall of 1899, just before his 23d birthday, he arrived in that city again, carrying a letter of introduction to Charles Lamoureux, the eminent conductor, from the Count de Morphy. When Casals presented himself for an audition, the conductor was annoyed by the intrusion. Nonetheless, the cellist sat down and began to play parts of the Lalo cello concerto. With the first notes, Lamoureux hoisted himself up from his desk and stood facing Casals until he finished playing, whereupon he embraced the young man and said, "My boy, you are one of the elect!"

Lamoureux immediately engaged him to play the Lalo concerto with his orchestra, and Casals made his Paris debut Nov. 12, 1899. He created a sensation there, as he did in London shortly afterward. In Britain he also played for Queen Victoria.

From then on his career was made, and he never lacked for engagements or for an audience. He commanded top fees, but lived economically.

For the next 20 years, until 1919, Casals, using Paris as his base, played in the principal cities of Europe and the Americas. He made his New York debut in 1904, playing the Saint-Saëns cello concerto with the orchestra of the Metropolitan Opera and winning a chorus of critical bravos. Later that season he was the cello soloist here in Richard Strauss's *Don Quixote*, with the composer conducting his own tone poem.

Many of Casals's performances in those years were chamber music, which he played with Jacques Thibaud, the violinist, and Alfred Cortot, the pianist. In the United States he also gave chamber music recitals with Harold Bauer, the pianist, and Fritz Kreisler, the violinist, and with Kreisler and Ignace Paderewski, the pianist.

In that period Casals formed intimate friendships with such musicians as Georges Enesco, Maurice Ravel, Camille Saint-Saëns, Sergei Rachmaninoff, Gregor Piatigorsky, Emanuel Feuermann, Artur Schnabel, Eugène Ysaye and Paul Hindemith.

In 1914 Casals married Susan Metcalfe, the American *lieder* singer. It was his second marriage; the first, to Guilhermina Suggia, a Portuguese cellist, in 1906, had ended in divorce six years later. For several years Casals was the piano accompanist for Miss Metcalfe, a soprano, and at one point he considered dropping his career to further hers. However, the couple parted in 1920.

After World War I, and with the breakup of his marriage, the cellist turned his energies to Barcelona, where, in 1920, he founded the Orchestra Pau (Catalan for Pablo) Casals and subsidized it for seven years at a total cost of $320,000 until it became self-supporting. In these years (and afterward) he was its principal conductor.

Early in the 1920s Casals also founded the Workingmen's Concert Association in Barcelona, which gave its members, in return for nominal dues, an opportunity to attend Sunday morning concerts of his orchestra and to set up their own musical groups.

As busy as Casals was in Barcelona, he also found time to give concerts in the United States and in Europe and to appear in what seemed increasingly to be his favorite role, that of a conductor. He led the London Symphony, the New York Symphony and the Vienna Philharmonic.

When the Spanish Republic was proclaimed in 1931, Casals became one of its eager and hardworking supporters, all the more because the republic restored many of his native Catalonia's ancient rights and granted the area a good deal of autonomy. He was president of Catalonia's music council, the Junta de Musica, and, during the Civil War, he gave hundreds of benefit concerts abroad for the Republic and put a large part of his personal savings at its disposal. The Government, in turn, named streets and squares for him and encouraged his exertions to bring great music to the common people.

Casals was in Barcelona in January, 1939, when

the Franco forces burst into the city, but he made good an escape to France, vowing never to return to Spain while Franco was in power. (Apart from a fleeting trip to Spain in 1955 to attend the funeral of his long-time close friend and housekeeper, Mrs. Francesca Vidal de Capdevila, he never did.)

After several demoralizing weeks of despondency in Paris, during which he grieved for his country, he went to live in Prades among the thousands of Spanish exiles. There he helped to organize the care of the Catalans held in French camps and solicited funds for them from his friends all over the world. He continued to live in Prades in World War II.

Toward the end of the war he went on tour again. In the autumn of 1945, however, he cut short a concert trip in Britain and retired to Prades.

In explanation, he said he had assumed that an Allied victory would doom not only Hitler and Mussolini but also Franco. The democracies, he went on, had disillusioned him by not acting to topple Franco. He was therefore suspending his concert career until Spain was freed. He had, he pointed out, ceased playing in Germany with the rise of Hitler, had not played in Italy in the thirties, nor had he appeared in Russia after the Bolshevik Revolution. He said he could not separate his beliefs as a human being from his conduct as an artist.

Casals lived quietly and simply in Prades for close to 12 years. In 1950, however, he was prevailed upon to soften somewhat his vow of musical silence and take part in a Bach bicentenary festival. The event, which attracted hundreds of music lovers from many parts of the world, was held in the big Church of St. Pierre in Prades. The critics found that Casals's bow had lost none of its magic.

In that and subsequent Prades festivals Casals appeared in a triple role—as soloist, as chamber music ensemble player and as conductor. In these concerts he was joined by many internationally famous musicians, including Dame Myra Hess, Rudolf Serkin, Joseph Szigeti and Isaac Stern.

Some indication of a further shift in Casals's thinking came in 1951 in a colloquy with Albert Schweitzer, the humanitarian and philosopher. "It is better to create than to protest," Dr. Schweitzer said in urging the cellist to return to the concert stage. "Why not do both—why not create and protest both?" Casals replied. And he seemed to follow that course in his last years.

After a period of self-examination, Casals went to Mexico in 1956 for his first concert date outside the Prades area. It was there, in 1960, that *El Pesebre* had its premiere. The oratorio became the banner of his peace mission, which he carried to many major cities in the Western world. Discussing this crusade, he said in 1962: "As a man, my first obligation is toward the welfare of my fellow men. I will endeavor to meet that obligation through music, the means which God has given me, since it transcends language, politics and national boundaries."

In August 1957, when he was 80, he married Marta Montañez, one of his cello students, who was then 21. They lived in a cheerful modern house on the beach at Santurce, P.R., where Casals liked to take an early morning stroll before beginning his day by playing a Bach work on the piano. "It is like a benediction on the house," he said.

Casals had the unstinted admiration of his fellow artists. And one of them, Mr. Stern, put their feelings this way: "He has enabled us to realize that a musician can play in a way that is honest, beautiful, masculine, gentle, fierce and tender—all these together, and all with unequivocal respect for the music being played and faith in it."

Appearing in New York last summer for a free Central Park concert with Mr. Stern—it was cut short by rain before the cellist could perform—Casals pronounced what could stand as his epitaph.

"What can I say to you?" he asked the assemblage. "I am perhaps the oldest musician in the world. I am an old man, but in many senses a very young man. And this is what I want you to be, young, young all your life, and to say things to the world that are true."

Casals died in Rio Piedias, Puerto Rico, on Oct. 22, 1973, three weeks after a heart attack.

A MUSICIAN WHO LOOKED BEYOND THE PRINTED NOTE

BY HAROLD C. SCHONBERG

PABLO CASALS represented a type of musicianship that is virtually extinct today—a musicianship that had its roots in the romantic traditions of the 19th century. As such he was a romantic himself, and young musicians today tended to look fondly upon him as a living anachronism. All, especially string players, had nothing but respect for Casals's powers as an instrumentalist. But his ideas of musical interpretation ran counter to many of today's cherished notions. Today's musicians tend to be literalists. The printed note is the ultimate guide. Casals, however, along with other great musicians of his generation, tried to look beyond the printed note. The important thing in music, he kept telling his pupils, is what is *not* in the notes. The important thing is the re-creation of an emotion, a mood, an experience.

Thus when Casals played or conducted Bach, he was not afraid to indulge in certain expressive devices that a stricter age regards as anathema. This did not disturb Casals, who considered Bach a romantic anyway. He would use an intensified scale of dynamics, avoid strict metrics (even to the point of the tempo rubato), phrase with a grand sweep and emphasize the melodic elements. His basic approach to Bach and the other early composers was substantially no different than it was to Brahms and Schumann.

And who is to say that Casals, with his concentration on the expressive elements of music, had the wrong approach? He was no musicologist, but he was able to do what very few musicians can do—play with complete mastery, in a manner that always impressed and moved with its sheer conviction. His approach was so big that it simply negated criticism.

As a conductor he brought the same kind of approach exemplified by his cello playing. At rehearsals he was constantly exhorting his players to sing out, to phrase with beauty, to use a full bow, to avoid dryness. He had the orchestra constantly thinking about dynamics.

Even toward the end, his enthusiasm was as great as ever, his ear seemingly infallible. After a lifetime of living in an area of music that extended, approximately, from Bach through Brahms (he was a conservative, and contemporary music did not interest him), there were few things he did not know about his chosen literature. In addition, he had total recall. He had met everybody and heard everybody, and he was a living encyclopedia of performance practice of the past.

But Casals was not a blind idolator of the past. He was the first to admit that the new school was technically superior to the old, even if he had many reservations about the drier emotional approach of the new school. It was his ambition to take the brilliantly gifted young cellists of today and try to instill into them something of the tradition and the ideals that motivated his own work.

He did not expect imitation from his pupils (in any case, nobody could imitate Casals), but he could help them with technical problems, and he could stimulate them to look upon music in an intensified manner. He could, and he did. To all musicians, even the most cynical, he was an inspiration. For he had devoted his long life to music without expecting any rewards aside from the joy of exploring a piece of music and constantly renewing himself in it.

CATALONIA'S HOMAGE TO CASALS

JAMES M. MARKHAM

BARCELONA, Spain, Dec. 29, 1976—Three years after his death in self-imposed exile in Puerto Rico, the memory of Pablo Casals was honored in his beloved Catalonia.

On the 100th anniversary of the birth of the prodigious cellist and composer, the city of Barcelona restored to Pablo Casals the broad avenue that bore his name before Franco came to power in 1939.

At midday several thousand people appeared for a moving ceremony on Avinguda de Pau Casals to honor a man who became a symbol of conscientious resistance to dictatorship in this century.

The crowd erupted in applause and cheers when reminded that Casals had "never bowed to the Gestapo or any dictatorship"—an allusion to his opposition to Franco and his refusal to play for German officers who appeared at his home at Prades in southern France at the end of World War II.

Under a sprinkling of red-and-orange striped Catalan flags, the crowd listened reverently to a Casals recording of "El Cant dels Ocells," the Catalan folk tune he made famous, and then dispersed after singing their haunting national song, "Els Segadors."

Under Franco, who suppressed Catalan nationalist sentiment, people were jailed and beaten for singing "Els Segadors." But today Barcelona's new, 39-year-old mayor, José María Sosias Humbert, sang along. "We share what Pau Casals felt for Catalonia—the feeling of love and liberty," declared the mayor.

The ceremony today, which was another small step in Catalonia's resurgent quest for its ancient liberties, was the climax of weeks of celebrations and concerts in memory of Casals, who left Spain in 1939, returning only once, secretly, to bury a close friend, Francisa Capdevila, in his family plot in the village of Vendrell.

On Dec. 16 and 17, four renowned friends and disciples of Casals—Alexander Schneider, Isaac Stern, Leonard Rose and Eugene Istomin—gave what one critic called "sublime" concerts in honor of the maestro in Barcelona's ornate Palace of Catalan Music. Mr. Istomin's wife, Marta Casals de Istomin, is the widow of Casals.

Bestowing their own honors, towns and villages in the four provinces of Catalonia have named—or named again—plazas and streets for Casals, who vowed not to live in Spain until Franco died and a popular government was installed.

Some years ago, when he was in exile, Casals declared, "Now everything is gone. But if one day circumstances change and if my physical strength permits me, I will go back and resume my interrupted work with the same enthusiasm as on the first day."

Franco outlasted the cellist by two years.

In the last years of Franco's dictatorship, Casals's works were sometimes permitted on the radio—without being identified—but Franco never made a gesture of reconciliation.

Today the government of King Juan Carlos made a small gesture and issued a 3-peseta stamp in the musician's memory, using the Catalan form of his first name, Pau.

Today, the maestro returned to the avenue in Barcelona that Catalans say was usurped by Gen. Manuel Llopis Goded, one of the officers who plotted the July 18, 1936, revolt against the Second Republic.

General Goded was unsuccessful in Barcelona, a stronghold of the republic's defenders, and he was tried and shot for his role in the revolt.

On the day the 1936 revolt started, Casals was rehearsing Beethoven's Ninth Symphony for a performance scheduled for the next evening at the Greek Theater in Montjuich in Barcelona—not far from the site of General Goded's later execution.

The rehearsal was interrupted by word of the uprising, but Casals suggested to the musicians that they complete the symphony since it might be the last for some time. "What a moving moment," he recalled later. "We were singing the immortal hymn to fraternity, while in the streets of Barcelona—and in so many other cities—a fratricidal struggle was being readied that would leave hundreds of Spanish families in mourning."

By the end of the war, Casals was performing during bombardments in Barcelona. Then followed his legendary exile in Prades, which became the site of the famed Bach festivals from 1950 to 1966. In 1956 Casals moved to the gentler climate of Puerto Rico, his mother's birthplace, where he died on Oct. 22, 1973.

Today was another busy day for Joan Alavedra, who shared the Casals exile in Prades for a decade and wrote the verse for his oratorio, *El Pesebre*, as well as several biographies of his hero.

"I have been giving lectures almost every day for the last three weeks in all of Catalonia," said the sprightly 80-year-old author. "The people adore Pau Casals."

The white-haired confidant of the late maestro was asked whether he thought that Casals would have returned to "predemocratic" Spain were he alive today. "His widow asked me that the other day," he said, "and I told her that I believed he would come back, but that he would not take up residence here—not yet.

"He left an autonomous Catalonia," said Mr. Alavedra, "but we do not have that—not yet."

The body of Pablo Casals, who died in October 1973 at the age of 96 and was buried in Puerto Rico, was returned in 1979 to Spain.

The move was in accordance with his wish that his body be returned to his native Catalonian village of Vendrell as soon as democracy returned to Spain. The return will symbolically be the end of Casals's 40-year self-imposed exile after Generalissimo Francisco Franco established his dictatorship.

Casals's wife, Marta Casals de Istomin, decided "the moment had come," and appropriate arrangements were made with the governments of Puerto Rico and Catalonia.

The body of the cellist lay in state in the State Capitol in Barcelona, after which there was a ceremony in the nearby Monastery of Monserrat. Burial took place at the cemetery outside Vendrell. Casals's father was the organist of the church in the village, and Casals sang in the choir as a boy. His home there is now a museum.

COCO CHANEL

1883–1971

By Enid Nemy

Gabrielle (Coco) Chanel was one of the greatest couturiers of the 20th century.

Chanel dominated the Paris fashion world in the 1920s and at the height of her career was running four business enterprises—a fashion house, a textile business, perfume laboratories and a workshop for costume jewelry—that all together employed 3,500 workers.

It was perhaps her perfume more than her fashions that made the name Chanel famous around the world. Called simply "Chanel No. 5"—she had been told by a fortune-teller that five was her lucky number—it made Coco a millionaire.

An intense woman with a scalding tongue, hair-trigger wit, unbounded immodesty and ineffable charm, Gabrielle Chanel was, throughout her life, a free spirit who used fashion as her pulpit. Her message was carried to millions through the medium of Paris haute couture, a world over which she reigned, with arrogant self-assurance, for long stretches of almost six decades.

The darling of French society, a good friend of dukes and dandies, a confidante of the rich and famous, she was impatient of pretense, intolerant of restrictions, incapable of self-deception.

"There is no time for cut-and-dried monotony," she once said. "There is time for work. And time for love. That leaves no other time."

Chanel was the fashion spirit of the century, a Pied Piper who led women away from complicated, uncomfortable clothes to a bone-simple, uncluttered and casual look that eventually became synonymous with her name.

Without marching in a parade or campaigning for rights, she emancipated her sex from the tyrannies of fashion. Her strong convictions and independent opinions, her unswerving belief in simplicity and elegance, freed women of unnecessary constrictions and what she called "ludicrous trimmings and fussy bits and pieces."

Slim and straight and dark-haired, with piercing black eyes and a generous if uncompromising mouth, Chanel always believed she was right, and often was. She was responsible for many of the timeless fashions that look as current today as they did when she first introduced them, in some cases more than half a century ago.

Among her innovations, most of them considered revolutionary at the time, were jersey dresses and suits, tweed suits with jersey blouses, bell-bottom trousers, trench coats, pea jackets, turtleneck sweaters, sailor hats, bobbed hair, costume jewelry and the little black dress, often collared and cuffed in white.

The omnipresent Chanel suit, with its collarless, braid-trimmed cardigan jacket and graceful skirt, has probably been copied more, in all price ranges, than any other single garment designed by a couturier.

Chanel's handbag—soft, quilted leather with a

Cecil Beaton/Camera Press

chain handle—was copied so widely that it became one of the most universal accessories of the 1960s. Other widespread Chanelisms were ropelike necklaces, sling-back pumps in her special colors—beige and black—and large, flat, tailored hair bows.

The copying of her designs never disturbed her. "Let them copy," she said. "My ideas belong to everyone. I refuse no one."

Perhaps the strongest tribute to her genius was that women of wealth, who took pride in exclusivity of design, did not mind being seen in the same clothes as working girls. Both groups wanted, and were willing to pay for, in varying degrees, the Chanel look.

The customers who went to the House of Chanel, a six-story building at 31 rue Cambon in Paris, included, at one time or another, Marlene Dietrich, Romy Schneider, Juliet Greco, Elsa Martinelli, Anouk Aimée, Bettina, Suzy Parker, Françoise Sagan, Colette, Mrs. Georges Pompidou, Princess Paola (wife of the younger brother of King Baudouin of the Belgians), Mrs. Hélène Gordon-Lazareff (editor of the French fashion magazine *Elle*), Mrs. Diana Vreeland (editor in chief of *Vogue*), the Rothschild baronesses and countless American socialites.

Chanel, who was said to have "a true affection for money," dressed comparatively few members of royalty and nobility.

"Those princesses and duchesses . . . they never pay their bills," she was reported to have said. "Why should I give them something for nothing? No one ever gave me anything."

The well-known names, who could afford to pay her prices—about $1,000 for a suit—frequently added to the original Chanels in their wardrobes with line-for-line copies made by American manufacturers.

Chanel, despite her own taste for luxury and her patrician friends, was the constant democratizer of fashion. Her friend Picasso once said, "She is the most sensible woman in Europe," and her own definition of true luxe as "clothes they can wear for years" confirmed the artist's description.

For Chanel, the great changes in fashion stemmed from significant changes in the manner and requirements of daily life. She explained her philosophy in 1957 when she traveled to the United States to receive, from Neiman-Marcus in Dallas, an award as the most significant designer of the last 50 years.

She told a reporter from *The New Yorker* that she inspired women to take off their bone corsets and to cut their hair, in 1925, because they were just beginning to work in offices.

"Women drive autos, and this you cannot do with a crinoline skirt," she said.

"But the grand problem," she added, "the most important problem, is to rejuvenate women, to make women look young. Then their outlook on life changes. They feel more joyous."

During the period in the sixties when many women were feeling more joyous wearing miniskirts, Chanel never ceased her barrage of verbal thunderclaps against the fashion.

As autocratic and articulate as ever, the aging couturier did not take kindly to youth-oriented pop culture and fashion. "An exhibition of meat," was one of the phrases she used.

"I hate *les vieilles petites filles* [old little girls]," she said, railing against miniskirted women over 30.

"She's got horrible taste and she's responsible for spreading it all over America," Chanel said in 1967 of the then Mrs. John F. Kennedy. She was criticizing the white Courrèges dress that the president's widow had worn to Runnymede, England, at the dedication of a monument to him.

The selective memory Chanel employed on other occasions chose to forget that Mrs. Kennedy had worn a Chanel suit for her visit to Dallas on Nov. 22, 1963. Its raspberry wool was stained with her husband's blood.

When skirts were descending to midcalf in 1970, Chanel's hemlines remained more or less where they had always been, hovering near the knee. Some observers thought they might have been a fraction shorter than usual, a typical Chanel gesture of nonconformity.

In Chanel's 87th year, on Dec. 18, 1969, the name that illuminated fashion went up in lights on Broadway. Coco (Little Pet), the nickname bestowed on the couturier by her father, became the title of a musical show based on her life. Starring Katharine Hepburn, it was produced by Frederick Brisson, a longtime friend of Chanel.

The show, with book and lyrics by Alan Jay Lerner, music by André Previn and Chanel-facsimile costumes by Cecil Beaton (263 in all), was one of the greatest fashion spectaculars ever mounted on a stage.

During her lifetime, Chanel created an empire. In the twenties, at a time when she employed 2,400 people in her workrooms, her personal fortune was rumored to be $15 million.

The financial basis of the empire was Chanel No. 5, a perfume that she introduced in 1922 and named after her lucky number. Created by a chemist on the Riviera, it was an unorthodox blend of fragrances and soon became the most familiar perfume in the world.

"Women are not flowers," she once said, commenting on the scent. "Why should they want to smell like flowers?"

In 1924, Chanel founded Les Parfums Chanel with Pierre and Paul Wertheimer, owners of the Bourjois perfume interests. They became the majority stockholders in the new company.

By 1934, Chanel had been removed as president and the next year the company, in which she had a 10 percent interest, began to cede its rights to subsidiaries and to Bourjois.

Les Parfums Chanel became the parent company of a large perfume empire that operated in France, Britain and the United States.

In 1946, Chanel sued Les Parfums Chanel, charging that it had produced merchandise of an inferior quality. The suit asked that the French parent concern be ordered to cease manufacturing and selling all products and restore to her the ownership and sole rights over products, formulas and manufacturing processes.

The suit was unsuccessful, but the feud apparently healed, because when Chanel returned to the fashion world in 1954, after an absence of about 15 years, she exchanged her substantial stock ownership for another system of compensation that involved royalties and commissions.

A legend in her own time, Chanel became increasingly temperamental, willful and, at times, vitriolic, as she grew older. Her parakeet voice never stopped speaking her mind and, although this was done at considerable length and with unabashed frequency, she left untouched the myths that swirled around her.

"What do I care what people write about me?" she once said. "Each year they will invent a new story. I will never sue."

Chanel herself added yearly, and with somewhat pixyish glee, to the tangle of dates, places and names.

Her age was never proved—"A woman has the age she deserves," she used to say—but it is generally accepted that she was born on Aug. 19, 1883. It is certain that she was born near Issoire in the Auvergne, a dour mountainous region of south-central France. She was baptized Gabrielle Bonheur—Gabrielle Happiness.

When she was 6 years old, her mother died of tuberculosis and her father abandoned his four daughters. She went to live with two aunts, who were relentless disciplinarians. They raised horses to sell to the French army, and Coco became an expert horsewoman at an early age. She also learned how to sew.

Before her 16th birthday, she showed signs of the determination and indomitable spirit that remained with her throughout her life. On a visit to her grandfather, a Vichy blacksmith, she escaped from her aunts by persuading a young cavalry officer to take her away.

The obliging officer provided not only a means of escape but also an entry into another world. Etienne Balsan was a member of a wealthy family of industrialists who owned fine stables, and it was during this liaison that Chanel learned the habits and tastes of the wealthy and rode some of the country's best horses.

It is believed that Chanel and Balsan were inseparable for the next 10 years, living in a family chateau outside Paris or following the horsey set through France. About 1911 she was selling hats in a haphazard fashion in a tiny shop in Paris.

The career that was to make her name began in the summer of 1913 in Deauville. She opened a tiny hat boutique. It was the heyday of elaborate and grotesque hats, and she detested them.

"How can the brain function under those things?" she asked, and went on to provide millinery that offered nothing but simplicity and line. She took a fancy to the turtleneck sweaters worn by English sailors in port, and sold a few of them.

The next year she returned to Paris and opened a shop at 31 rue Cambon, where she sold hats, then sweaters and a few clothes. Within five years, she was a force to be reckoned with in the world of fashion.

She began to impress wealthy, influential women with her originality. She was the first designer to use ordinary jersey for clothes; the September 1917 issue of *Vogue* magazine referred to the Maison Chanel as "the jersey house." A little later, she started the "poor-girl look," and rich women playfully wore clothes based on the garments of the humble.

Despite World War I, her social life was brilliant and hectic. Balsan was succeeded in her life by Arthur Capel, who was nicknamed Boy, an immensely rich, polo-playing Englishman. His lavish presents started her astonishing collection of jewels.

The dashing aristocrat was also credited, perhaps apocryphally, with being the inspiration for one of Chanel's most famous fashions. Her boxy suit jacket, with its practical pockets, was said to have been born after she had borrowed Capel's blazer on chilly days at polo games.

Boy Capel, described by friends later as "the only man she really loved," was killed in an automobile accident.

In the mid-twenties, Chanel's name grew luminous. By 1924, well-dressed women on both sides of the Atlantic were taken with a Chanel costume of a beige jersey blouse worn with a single strand of pearls, and a tweed suit with a cardigan jacket. It is possible to appreciate the revolution she wrought only if one studies the ornate creations of the House of Worth and the pictures of pre–World War I Edwardian elegance.

Chanel's first period of professional preeminence, from the mid-twenties to the late thirties, coincided, in part, with her most famous alliance, with Hugh Richard Arthur Grosvenor, the second Duke of Westminster, one of Europe's wealthiest men, who was married four times and was divorced three times.

The duke's devotion to Chanel was expressed in gifts of remarkably valuable jewels. She often had the gifts copied in fake stones.

"I couldn't wear my own real pearls without being stared at in the street, so I started the vogue of wearing false ones," she said.

She also designed real jewelry and for both she used big, chunky stones at a time when fashion called for small, quieter ones. A typical Chanel touch in the late twenties, still much in evidence, was a long necklace with colored stones forming a medallion.

Although she hated the sea, Chanel frequently accompanied the duke aboard his yachts, one of them a converted destroyer manned by a crew of 180. One winter she came back from Cannes with bronzed skin; other women, who had always considered paleness a mark of a lady, began to imitate her.

On a trip to Venice, Chanel ignited another revolution. She appeared wearing slightly bell-bottomed jersey slacks with a sweater and masses of jewelry. A friend contended later that the designer wore the trousers because she did not wish to show her famous legs to the gondolier. It seems more likely that Chanel bought the pants for the sake of comfort and sensation.

Although there was considerable speculation, in both Europe and the United States, that Chanel might marry the duke, the volatile high priestess of couture preferred to retain her own identity.

"Everyone marries the Duke of Westminster," she reportedly said. "There are a lot of duchesses but only one Coco Chanel."

Chanel's friendship with the duke ended by 1934. Years later, she professed to be nostalgic for Scotland—and especially for the Sundays when she used to ride a horse on his estate.

She remained impressed by the clothes worn by Englishmen. When Randolph Churchill told her one day that he had been assigned to write an article for the *Daily Mail* on what women wore for the Derby, her reply was that the women were not worth writing about, that the men had all the distinction.

"My God," she said. "There is nothing more ugly than the way the women dress."

One of the engineering secrets of the Chanel jacket was its high, tight armhole. It could have been tailored in Savile Row.

"The armhole was never high enough. She'd reset a sleeve six times," recalled Jackie Rogers, a Boston-born mannequin who modeled for Chanel in 1963 and now has her own New York boutique. "The high armhole gave the jacket the cleaner, closer fit she wanted. She wanted a tight sweater look.

"But a suit was never finished to her, even when the day came on which it was to be shown. Her designs were her children, never completed."

Unlike most couturiers, Chanel never made a drawing or toile—a linen prototype—of her clothes. The only way she could work was by taking the material in her hands.

All her instincts and professional knowledge seemed to come from her fingers. She loved working with her hands. A few years ago she told a friend, "If I were not embarrassed to be seen, I would love to shoe a horse."

Chanel at one time entertained frequently at the splendid house she kept on the Faubourg St. Honoré. She also kept a small bedroom suite at the Ritz, where she often slept and dressed. She once said that the reason she slept at the Ritz was to escape the disorder in her house after a party.

The Ritz was the scene of one of the few verified episodes in her life. It resulted in the fashion for bobbed hair.

One night, some gas in the hot water heater exploded, spraying her with soot. An impatient woman, Chanel cut off her long black hair so there would be less to shampoo. She washed it quickly and tied a ribbon around it.

That night she appeared at the opera in a white dress and short hair. The effect was stunning and became an immediate fashion craze.

In her later years, Chanel was almost never seen without a hat. It was as much a part of her face as the false bangs she wore. The bangs were due to her antipathy to hairdressers. The hat was never taken off, she said, so that people she did not like would think she was on her way out.

Chanel's salon embraced the artistic world as well as the social. Jean Cocteau once wrote that she had the head of "a little black swan." And the heart, Colette added, of "a little black bull."

During the thirties, Chanel was reported engaged to Paul Iribe, a painter and decorator. He died while playing tennis at her villa in Roquebrune.

A story that has a choice place in the Chanel legend is that Sergei Diaghilev, desperate for funds for his ballet, got a huge check from Chanel on the day they met. Those who thought she had the flint of a French peasant doubted the story. Others, recalling her comment that the artistic White Russians in Paris "brought me everything I missed in my life," found the tale more believable.

She was a close friend of Grand Duke Dimitri of Russia, first cousin of Czar Nicholas II, and of the composer Stravinsky. Although she sometimes felt insecure in this milieu, she was fascinated by it.

In the late thirties, when the fashionable world deserted Chanel for Elsa Schiaparelli, the Italian designer, and World War II broke out, Chanel shut her couture house and went across the street to hibernate at the Ritz. The Nazis later took many rooms there but they never commandeered the hotel. Chanel remained there, then went on to Vichy and to Switzerland, but the record of her life for 15 years is more blurred than usual.

Chanel's comeback, on Feb. 5, 1954, was a major turning point in the fashion world, although hardly anyone realized it.

She showed a suit in heavy navy jersey with two patch pockets, worn with a white tucked muslin blouse and a sailor hat. The critics' reaction was civil but not ecstatic; however, women bought it. It was the forerunner of a style that evolved year after year with increasing success.

The reception was equally lukewarm after her second collection, in October of that year. Chanel had always been considered a rebel and people expected shocks. Instead, Chanel, as always, was simply extending and developing the shapes that satisfied her.

The suit that was in every city in America by 1964 was an evolution of the navy design of a decade earlier. Her own favorite was a beige tweed trimmed with red and dark-blue braid, with the patch pockets used as purses.

Chanel, in her 80s and perhaps at the peak of her career, continued to rule her salon like a royal court. People jostled for favors, almost fearing success, and braced for reversal.

Anne Chamberlin, writing in the *Ladies Home Journal* in October 1963, said, "The weeks preceding the opening of a new collection are, next to the Bastille Day fireworks, one of the great pyrotechnic spectacles in Paris, witnessed by only a privileged few."

Her account bore out the description: "Mademoiselle takes up her station on one of the gold ballroom chairs in the big showroom, with a pair of scissors hanging from a rope around her neck and a box of straight pins on the chair beside her ('I want every single pin in this house changed, not one is long enough'), asks to see the first dress, and the fun begins.

"She suffers from rheumatism and arthritis. Yet she still literally attacks each fitting with her bare hands, clawing and pushing at the fabric, jamming in pins, tearing out seams, sending seamstresses off in tears behind the fitting screens, where they get revenge by jabbing pins into the models.

"While the pretty doe-eyed models in their white smocks wait on gold chairs for their turn at a fitting and an ancient lady in espadrilles sews the treads back on the stairs, a scene of frenzied activity unfolds, accompanied by a stream of Chanelesque advice. 'Look for the woman in the dress,' goes a constant theme. 'If there is no woman, there is no dress.' "

The mannequins, young and energetic, sagged with fatigue as the fittings went on, frequently up to six or eight hours without a break. Chanel was impervious, indefatigable and seemingly indestructible.

One of the few times that Chanel combined designing with other aspects of the couture business was, as she herself admitted, a disaster. She hired four prostitutes as mannequins, apparently thinking she would reform them. Her zeal was generally unappreciated. The prostitutes attempted to draft the other models into their profession, telling them how much more money they could earn on the streets.

"What a scandal!" Chanel recalled with some relish.

Her private quarters in her couture house—a salon with a wide suede sofa, a dining room, a small library, a kitchen and a huge bathroom—were open to only a few members of the staff, friends and clients who impressed her. For several years, she gave a dinner party in the dining room to mark the end of each couture season. The waiters wore white gloves, the guests drank Scotch and wine, and Chanel made a little speech saying, in effect, that this had been her last collection. Everyone knew better.

Always nourished by feuds, she took obvious delight in baiting her fellow designers. "They consider me a sort of pestilence," she said.

A well-known designer who had once worked for her (the experience was so upsetting that he did not even refer to it in his autobiography) and provoked her achieved fame designing for another house.

Chanel vengefully scheduled her opening one year at exactly the same time that his couture house did. Fashion reporters who peeked quickly at his clothes and then streaked to Chanel found themselves barred.

More recently, she endeared herself to another member of the couture by saying, "Saint-Laurent has excellent taste. The more he copies me, the better taste he displays."

Chanel never reserved her rapierlike tongue for her foes, or even those she disliked. After the war, she expressed scorn for the New Look of her friend Christian Dior. A pinch-waisted silhouette with a long billowing shirt, it scored an enormous success with its rejection of all the limitations of wartime.

"I adore you," Chanel was reported to have said to Dior, "but you dress women like armchairs."

The last years of her life were relatively quiet, dedicated to the couture house (which was often operated at a loss, the deficit paid cheerfully by the parent company because the publicity helped the sales of every other Chanel product) and to acerbic comments and racing horses. Her stables in Chantilly included a well-known mare, Romantica.

Her life story was turned into a musical, *Coco*, which ran on Broadway in 1970 and starred Katharine Hepburn in her first singing-and-dancing role. Miss Hepburn, 60 at the time the show opened, was termed "too old" for the part by the tart-tongued Coco, who was 86.

In addition to the Chanel philosophy, the show featured many models parading in the popular fashions Chanel designed through her long career.

Chanel outlived many of her closest friends and felt separated from others. She had never married, not because she preferred solitude but, according to one quotation, because she "never wanted to weigh more heavily on a man than a bird."

Her weight on fashion was immeasurable.

Chanel died on Jan. 10, 1971, in her apartment in the Ritz Hotel in Paris, at the age of 87.

CHARLES CHAPLIN

1889–1977

By Alden Whitman

No motion picture actor so captured and enthralled the world as did Charles Spencer Chaplin, a London ragamuffin who became an immortal artist for his deft and effective humanization of man's tragicomic conflicts with fate. In more than 80 movies from 1914 to 1967, he either portrayed or elaborated (he was a writer and director as well as an actor) the theme of the little fellow capriciously knocked about by life, but not so utterly battered that he did not pick himself up in the hope that the next encounter would turn out better.

His harassed but gallant Everyman was the Little Tramp, part clown, part social outcast, part philosopher. He was "forever seeking romance, but his feet won't let him," Chaplin once explained, indicating that romance connoted not so much courtship as the fulfillment of fancy.

Stumble Chaplin's Everyman might, but he always managed to maintain his dignity and self-respect. Moreover, he sometimes felled a Goliath through superb agility, a little bit of luck and a touch of pluck. There was pathos to the Little Tramp, yet he really did not want to be pitied.

The essence of Chaplin's humor was satire, sometimes subtle, as in *The Kid* and *The Gold Rush*, sometimes acerbic, as in *The Great Dictator* and *Monsieur Verdoux*. "The human race I prefer to think of as the underworld of the gods," he said. "When the gods go slumming they visit the earth." And what they saw mostly was uncelestial folly.

In ridiculing that folly Chaplin displayed a basic affection for the human race. He was serious and funny at the same time, and it was this blend of attitudes that elevated his comedy beyond film slapstick into the realm of artistry.

A serious theme in *The Gold Rush*, for example, is man's inhumanity to man. The comedy arises from the hero's adversity, illustrated by his boiling and eating of his shoe with the éclat of a gourmet. The element of contrast exemplified by that scene was at the root of Chaplin's comedy. This sense of comedy tickled the fancy of millions in the United States for half a century, despite some notoriety that came to Chaplin through marital and political misadventures.

The Little Tramp, the comedy character that lifted its creator to enduring fame, was neatly accoutered in baggy trousers, outsize shoes, an undersize derby redolent of decayed gentility, a frayed short cutaway and a sporty bamboo cane. A jet-black mustache completed the costume. What made it all fit together was that it complemented Chaplin's slight stature—he was 5 feet 4 inches tall—and his slimness—he weighed about 130 in his prime years.

Although Chaplin often suggested that the costume was a studied contrivance, the fact seems to be that it was arrived at by accident in 1914 when he was breaking into films with Mack Sennett. Sennett,

famous for his Keystone Kops and other comic shorts, sent Chaplin to Venice, Calif., to make a bit of film eventually called *Kid Auto Races at Venice*.

He was told to wear something funny, and he assembled, on a grab-bag basis from other members of the company, pants belonging to Fatty Arbuckle, size 14 shoes each placed on the wrong foot, a tight coat, a colleague's derby, a prop cane and a false mustache that he cut down to fit his face. The splayed shuffle was a touch made up on the spur of the moment.

With a few exceptions Chaplin used the costume for about 25 years, and it was his symbol for a lifetime. The artistry with which it was employed, of course, evolved, so that the Little Tramp of *Modern Times* was a far more complex character than the one in *Kid Auto Races at Venice*.

The explanation for this was the meticulousness with which Chaplin studied the structure of comedy. Desiring to make audiences laugh, he analyzed the ingredients of his approach to comedy and each scene that went into the whole.

"All my pictures are built around the idea of getting me into trouble and so giving me the chance to be desperately serious in my attempt to appear as a normal little gentleman," he wrote early in his Hollywood career, adding: "That is why, no matter how desperate the predicament is, I am always very much in earnest about clutching my cane, straightening my derby hat and fixing my tie, even though I have just landed on my head."

One of Chaplin's basic routines had to do with dignity. "Even funnier than the man who has been made ridiculous is the man who, having had something funny happen to him, refuses to admit that anything out of the way has happened, and attempts to maintain his dignity," he wrote in 1918. He continued: "I am so sure of this point that I not only try to get myself into embarrassing situations, but I also incriminate the other characters in the picture. When I do this, I always aim for economy of means. By that I mean that when one incident can get two big, separate laughs, it is much better than two individual incidents.

"In *The Adventurer* I accomplished this by first placing myself on a balcony, eating ice cream with a girl. On the floor directly underneath the balcony I put a stout, dignified, well-dressed woman at a table. Then, while eating the ice cream, I let a piece drop off my spoon, slip through my baggy trousers and drop from the balcony onto this woman's neck.

"The first laugh came at my embarrassment over my own predicament. The second, and the much greater one, came when the ice cream landed on the woman's neck and she shrieked and started to dance around. Only one incident had been used, but it had got two people into trouble, and had also got two big laughs.

"Simple as this trick seems, there were two real points of human nature involved in it. One was the delight the average person takes in seeing wealth and luxury in trouble. The other was the tendency of the human being to experience within himself the emotions he sees on the stage or screen."

In his early days in Hollywood Chaplin had little say in how his movies were constructed or filmed. Later, though, he achieved artistic control, and he took infinite pains in perfecting each scene, often shooting hundreds of feet of film for a few moments of final screen action.

"With only a rudimentary idea in his head he concocted the story as he went along," Theodore Huff wrote in *The Literature of Cinema*. "Some pictures changed completely in the course of production. He improvised a scene or a series of gags, then discussed the results the next day in the projection room. A bit might be used or all of it might be reshot; or the whole project might be scrapped and some other idea substituted. . . . In *City Lights* the meeting of the blind flower girl and the tramp took months before the variation that satisfied Chaplin was reached."

Some of Chaplin's best comic situations resulted from his keen-eyed observation of life around him. "I watch people inside a theater to see when they laugh, I watch them everywhere to get material which they can laugh at," he explained.

"I was passing a firehouse one day," he went on, "and heard a fire alarm ring. I watched the men sliding down a pole, climbing onto the engine and rushing off to the fire.

"At once a train of comic possibilities occurred to me. I saw myself sleeping in bed, oblivious to the clanging of the fire bell. This point would have universal appeal, because everyone likes to sleep. I saw myself sliding down the pole, playing tricks with the fire horses, rescuing my heroine, falling off the fire engine as it turned a corner, and many other points along the same lines.

"I stored these points away in my mind and some time later, when I made *The Fireman*, I used every one of them.

"Another time, I went up and down a moving staircase in a department store. I got to thinking how this could be utilized for a picture, and I finally made it the basis for *The Floorwalker*.

"Watching a prizefight suggested *The Champion*, in which I, the small man, knocked out a big bruiser by having a horseshoe concealed in my glove."

Added to Chaplin's talent for perceiving the comic potential in everyday occurrences was his skill at using contrast. "Contrast spells interest," he once remarked.

"If I am being chased by a policeman, I always make the policeman seem heavy and clumsy while, by crawling through his legs, I appear light and acrobatic. If I am being treated harshly, it is always a big man who is doing it; so that, by the contrast between the big and the little, I get the sympathy of the audience, and always I try to contrast my seriousness of manner with the ridiculousness of the incident."

Entering motion pictures in what was virtually the medium's infancy—before the advent of feature-length films and, of course, sound—Chaplin was obliged to rely on situational comedy and on pantomime, the use of mute gestures and facial expressions to convey emotion. Transcending linguistic barriers, this form of body language permitted the actor to be readily understood by people everywhere.

"I am known in parts of the world by people who have never heard of Jesus Christ," Chaplin said matter-of-factly early in his career.

Indeed, after only two years on the screen, "he was unquestionably the top figure in the motion picture industry," according to Mr. Huff. Audience demand for his pictures was phenomenal. For example, one New York theater played his films continuously from 1914 to 1923, stopping only because the building burned down.

By 1917 world-renowned performers visited his studios—Ignace Paderewski, Leopold Godowsky, Nellie Melba, Harry Lauder. When the Nijinsky ballet played Los Angeles, its dancers spotted Chaplin in the audience and halted the show for a half hour while they embraced him.

Some notion of the adulation of the actor may be inferred from the response to his bond tours in World War I—crowds of 30,000 in New York, 65,000 in Washington, 40,000 in New Orleans. Going to Europe in 1921—*The Tramp*, *Shoulder Arms* and others of his classics had, of course, preceded him—Chaplin was mobbed in London and Paris. The latter city declared a public holiday for the premiere of *The Kid*. Few men in this century in any field attained his stature with the public. "Charlie," "Charlot," his first name in any language bespoke affection amounting to idolatry.

At the same time, Chaplin widened his intellectual and social world, meeting and becoming friendly with Max Eastman, the radical writer; Upton Sinclair, the Socialist novelist; James M. Barrie, the British playwright; H. G. Wells, the British writer; Waldo Frank, the novelist and critic; Georges Carpentier, the boxer; and St. John Irvine, the British dramatist. Throughout his life, he enjoyed the shuttlecock of wits with bright and learned men and women.

With his success, he was taken up by society figures—Mrs. W. K. Vanderbilt, Elsie de Wolfe,

Princess Xenia of Greece and hundreds of others. Although Chaplin was not generally accounted vain, he was impressed, as the latter portion of *My Autobiography* attests. Written after his forced absence from the United States and perhaps in an understandable mood of irritation, the book concludes with accounts of his reception in Europe after 1952 by socially and governmentally prestigious people, in whose attentions he basked.

Other comic actors of the silent or early sound era—Buster Keaton, Harry Langdon, Harold Lloyd and W. C. Fields—also enjoyed acclaim, and their pictures were often revived; but none, with the possible exception of Fields, created a genre. Even the Marx Brothers, in the opinion of many critics, could not rival Chaplin in creativity and fertility.

One explanation was that Chaplin's command of his pictures after 1917 was complete. He was the author, star, producer, director and chief cutter. Moreover, as Mr. Huff's book noted: "He himself played every character in every one of his pictures, to show the actors, men and women, exactly how he wanted them to do a character or a scene. And he accompanied each actor's miming with a running commentary of suggestions, criticism or encouragement."

In one film, *The Great Dictator*, he served as hairdresser in the belief that he could do a better job than a professional coiffeur of arranging Paulette Goddard's hair to resemble a scrubwoman's. This impulse to perfectionism, costly in terms of time and film exposed, caused Chaplin many moments of anxiety and self-doubt. His usual solution was to spend a couple of days in bed working through his problem.

Over all, however, Chaplin possessed an egotism that did not admit of defeat. "You have to believe in yourself, that's the secret," he once advised his son Charles, Jr. "I had that exuberance that comes from utter confidence in yourself."

Even as a London waif "I thought of myself as the greatest actor in the world," he recalled.

Born April 16, 1889, in south London, Charles Spencer Chaplin was the son of a vaudevillian and a music-hall soubrette whose stage name was Lily Harley. By an earlier union, Chaplin's mother, Hannah, had a son, Sydney, four years the actor's senior. Sydney was to become his half brother's business manager.

The elder Chaplin was a heavy drinker. "I was hardly aware of a father, and do not remember him living with us," Chaplin wrote. The couple separated shortly after Charles was born, and for a time Mrs. Chaplin was able to support herself. But her voice lost its quality, and "it was owing to her vocal condition that at the age of 5 I made my first appearance on the stage.

"I remember standing in the wings when mother's voice cracked and went into a whisper," her son recalled. "The audience began to laugh and sing falsetto and to make catcalls. It was all vague and I did not quite understand what was going on. But the noise increased until mother was obliged to walk off the stage. When she came into the wings she was very upset and argued with the stage manager who, having seen me perform before mother's friends, said something about letting me go on in her place.

"And in the turmoil I remember him leading me by the hand and, after a few explanatory words to the audience, leaving me on the stage alone. And before a glare of footlights and faces in the smoke, I started to sing, accompanied by the orchestra, which fiddled about until it found my key."

The lad captivated his audience, especially when "in all innocence I imitated mother's voice cracking," and he was greeted by laughter and cheers and applause.

Very shortly, however, Mrs. Chaplin's fortunes dwindled, and she and the two children were obliged to enter the Lambeth workhouse. Then the boys were dispatched to an orphanage outside London. "Although we were well looked after, it was a forlorn existence," Chaplin wrote of those years. The institution practiced flogging, and at the age of 7 he received a severe caning. Moreover, for suspected ringworm, his head was shaved and iodined and he was put in an isolation ward.

Sydney went off to sea for a while, and young Charles passed through a succession of workhouses. Meantime, Mrs. Chaplin was committed briefly as insane. When she was released, the small family again lived in penury, relieved slightly when Charles joined a troupe of clog dancers. He never forgot his days of poverty and the struggle for the necessities of life. Nor, when he was wealthy and famous, did he neglect his mother, seeing to it that she was well cared for in her eventual emotional breakdown. Finally, he took her to California, where she died.

Clog dancing lasted only briefly, followed by weeks and months of catch-as-catch-can existence. "I (was) newsvendor, printer, toymaker, doctor's boy, etc., but during these occupational digressions, I never lost sight of my ultimate aim to become an actor," Chaplin recalled. "So, between jobs I would polish my shoes, brush my clothes, put on a clean collar and make periodic calls at a theatrical agency."

At 12½ his persistence was rewarded, and he received a small stage part, then toured the provinces as Billy in William Gillette's *Sherlock Holmes*. Later, he played the part with Mr. Gillette in London, receiving favorable notices. An awkward age followed, however, in which he received several burlesque bookings. Then came a substantial run in *Casey's Court Circus*, in which he impersonated a patent-medicine faker.

In this engagement, according to the Huff biography, Chaplin decided to become a comedian. He also learned the unimportance of the spoken word. "Once, while playing in the Channel Islands," Mr. Huff wrote, "he found that his jokes were not getting over because the natives knew little English. He resorted to pantomime and got the desired laughs."

His success landed him a job with the Fred Karno Company. "With Karno he learned the hard way, traveling all over Britain and going twice to America," according to John Montgomery, a writer on film. "The repertory was varied: there were sketches about drunks, thieves, family relations, billiards champions, boxers, Turkish baths, policemen, singers who prepared to sing but somehow never started, conjurers who spoiled their own tricks and pianists who lost the music . . . a wide variety of subjects, mixed with a little honest vulgarity."

The Karno troupe was Chaplin's polishing school, for it taught him the rich lessons of his trade by which the actor makes an audience laugh. In 1913, Mack Sennett, then the producer of short film comedies for an insatiable public, signed the actor for $150 a week.

"I hated to leave the troupe," he recalled. "How did I know that pictures were going to be a successful medium for pantomime? Suppose I didn't make good?"

Nevertheless, he joined Sennett in Los Angeles and made his debut in *Making a Living*, a one-reeler that appeared in 1914. In those early Sennett comedies there was no scenario. "We get an idea, then follow the natural sequence of events until it leads up to a chase, which is the essence of our comedy," Sennett explained.

Chaplin changed that by adopting an identifiable character—the Little Tramp—which allowed the public to single him out from other comedians.

In his year with Sennett, Chaplin played in 35 films, including *Tillie's Punctured Romance*, a six-reeler that also starred Marie Dressler and Mabel Normand. It was the screen's first feature-length comedy, and it is occasionally shown today in various cut-up versions. Others of the Keystone, or Sennett, films have been mutilated or rearranged, according to the Huff book, which notes, "Rarely does one come across an unmutilated Keystone original."

The originals of these films were shown around the world, and they inspired such songs as "When the Moon Shines Bright on Charlie Chaplin." The renown they brought to Chaplin enabled him to shift to the Essanay Company for the then grand sum of $1,250 a week. For Essanay he made 14 films in 1915, including *The Tramp*, his first generally recognized classic and the first in which he introduced a note of pathos.

In the picture, Chaplin, a tramp, saves a farmer's daughter, played by Edna Purviance, from a robber gang, for which he is rewarded with a job on the farm. Routing the gang again, he is shot in the leg and nursed by the daughter. The tramp's happiness is unbounded until the girl's sweetheart arrives. Realizing his fate, the tramp scribbles a farewell and departs.

In the fadeout, Chaplin's back is to the camera. He walks dejectedly down a long road. Then he pauses, shrugs his shoulders, flips his heels and continues jauntily toward the horizon. Several variations on this theme were used in later Chaplin films, notably in *Limelight*.

After his Essanay period Chaplin went to the Mutual Company for $670,000 a year. He was 26, three years out of vaudeville and perhaps the world's highest paid performer. The sudden advent of wealth had little immediate effect on his life-style. When he signed his Mutual contract he remarked, "Well, I've got this much if they never give me another cent—guess I'll go and buy a whole dozen ties."

He was living at the time in a small hotel room, and he kept away from Hollywood parties, preferring to roam at night through Los Angeles's poorer sections. Shortly, however, he moved to larger quarters, hired a secretary, bought a Locomobile and acquired Toraichi Kono, a combination valet, bodyguard and chauffeur. Kono, as he was generally called, remained with the actor for about 20 years, serving as the keeper of his privacy.

In time Chaplin grew passionately attached to money. Although he was not a tightwad, neither was he a conspicuous spender, save on his own comfort. In the end, his fortune was in the millions.

And he insisted toward the close of his life that he had been actuated all along by money. "I went into the business for money, and the art grew out of it," he said. "If people are disillusioned by that remark, I can't help it. It's the truth."

However, those who were close to Chaplin in his early film years were impressed by his painstaking search for artistry. In doing the two-reel *The Immigrant* in 1917, for instance, he shot 90,000 feet of film to obtain the 1,809 feet of the finished picture. His dozen Mutual films were all two-reelers. They included some ranked among his best—*The Floorwalker*, *The Fireman*, *The Vagabond* and *Easy Street*.

The negatives were not preserved, and the worn and duplicated prints that are sometimes shown at Chaplin festivals, according to critics, bear only a slight relationship to the quality of the original films.

When the Mutual contract was up, Chaplin went to First National for $1 million for eight pictures over 18 months. For the first time he was his own producer in his own studio. Actually he made nine pictures over five years, and these included some of his greatest achievements—*A Dog's Life*, *Shoulder Arms* and *The Kid*.

Sparing of caricature, *A Dog's Life* derives its humor from the parallels between a dog's existence and that of a vagabond. *Shoulder Arms* is Everyman at war, and, according to Jean Cocteau, "it moves like a drumroll." For *The Kid*, Chaplin employed Jackie Coogan, a 5-year-old with mischievous brown eyes. Hailed as "a picture with a smile—perhaps a tear," the movie was a chapter out of Chaplin's own slum life. It contains little horseplay and much emotional intensity. Coogan's tears were real, induced by the sad stories Chaplin spun for him at necessary moments.

During the preparation of *The Kid* for release, Chaplin was embroiled in the first of several marital and extramarital episodes that were to plague him. Good-looking and attractive to women, he was involved in a score or more of dalliances, many with glamorous actresses, but these were usually discreetly handled. Not so with his first two marriages.

In 1918, when the actor was 29, he abruptly married 16-year-old Mildred Harris. They were divorced two years later in a fanfare of publicity. Four years afterward he married Lolita McMurry, also

16, whose stage name was Lita Grey. She was ensconced in her husband's 40-room mansion, from which Chaplin soon fled. Two children, Charles, Jr., and Sydney, were born of the union, which ended in 1927 after a sensational divorce case in the course of which Chaplin pictures were barred in some states at the urging of women's clubs.

The actor's third wife was Pauline Levy, a chorus girl whose film name was Paulette Goddard. The two met in 1931, when Miss Goddard was 20, and according to Chaplin, were married in 1936. They were divorced in 1942 without public fuss.

Meantime, in 1941, the actor met Joan Berry, a 21-year-old aspiring actress known as Joan Barry. She later charged that he was the father of her daughter, and Chaplin was once again the subject of lurid headlines. He was indicted for allegedly taking Miss Barry across state lines for immoral purposes, but this charge was dropped and he was acquitted of three related accusations.

Miss Barry then filed a paternity suit, in which blood tests demonstrated that Chaplin was not her child's father. Nonetheless, a jury found against him and he was ordered to support the infant.

In the midst of these troubles, in 1943, Chaplin, then 54, married 18-year-old Oona O'Neill, the playwright's daughter, over her father's vigorous objections. Their marriage proved happy and lasting, and it produced eight children.

Chaplin's later films were made for United Artists, a company he founded in 1919 with three Hollywood friends: Mary Pickford, Douglas Fairbanks, Sr., and David Wark Griffith. Chaplin's initial picture for this concern was *A Woman of Paris*, a comedy of manners that he produced and directed without starring in it. Considered a milestone in screen history—for its influence on movie style—it was based in part on the life of Peggy Hopkins Joyce, briefly Chaplin's mistress, and it stressed social sophistication. In it Adolphe Menjou made his debut as a suave philanderer.

The Gold Rush—"the picture I want to be remembered by," Chaplin said—came out in 1925 and it once again confirmed his hold on the public. It has been frequently revived and much analyzed.

Less successful with the critics was *The Circus*, which opened in 1928. It seemed to lack the feeling of *The Gold Rush*, and its comedy twists were short on flair. Its shortcomings, however, appeared less evident in revivals.

Starting work on *City Lights* in 1928, the actor faced a crisis: the advent of talkies. He was fearful that spoken dialogue would impair the character of the Tramp, cause difficulties in his reliance on pantomime and cut into foreign sales. Moreover, many of Chaplin's effects had been achieved by undercranking the camera, a feat impossible at the set speed of a motor-driven sound camera. After some thought, Chaplin decided to defy the new technology, and *City Lights* was produced as a silent picture with a musical score.

The story of the blind flower girl, played by Virginia Cherrill, used more than 800,000 feet of film over two years. The tragicomedy was an enormous triumph when it opened in 1931, and outgrossed many slick sound films in revivals over the last 40 years. Many critics rank *City Lights* as among Chaplin's greatest creations.

The picture's appeal was one factor in Chaplin's conquering tour of Europe and the Orient—a whirl of meetings with statesmen, writers, artists and celebrities. Returning to Hollywood, he embarked upon *Modern Times*, a satire on mass production, which at the time gave the actor a reputation as a radical.

"It [the picture] started from an abstract idea, an impulse to say something about the way life is being standardized and channelized, men turned into machines—and the way I felt about it," he said of his witty social parable.

The Little Tramp disappeared with *Modern Times,* and with *The Great Dictator* Chaplin joined the sound-picture ranks. A ferocious ridicule of Hitler and Mussolini, the film has grown in stature over the years as its political implications have been, according to critics, more fully realized. "I want to see the return of decency and kindness," Chaplin said at the time. "I'm just a human being who wants to see this country a real democracy . . ."

Despite *The Great Dictator*, the 1940s were difficult years for Chaplin. His private life provided a headline festival for the tabloid press; he was vexed by income-tax trouble; his wartime speeches calling for a western second front to crush Hitler irked many conservatives; and *Monsieur Verdoux* did poorly at the box office.

This fugue of troubles was intensified by the advent of the Cold War. The actor came under fire for introducing Henry A. Wallace at a rally and for protesting the deportation of Hanns Eisler, the composer and a onetime Communist. Westbrook Pegler, the columnist, denounced Chaplin, and Representative John E. Rankin, a right-wing legislator from Mississippi, demanded his deportation. Chaplin's life "is detrimental to the moral fabric of America," Mr. Rankin asserted, urging that he be kept "off the American screen and his loathsome pictures be kept from the eyes of American youth."

Finally, in 1952, the actor, a British subject, was virtually exiled by the United States. While he was sailing to Britain on vacation, the U.S. attorney general announced that he could not reenter the country unless he could prove his "moral worth." Piqued, Chaplin spent the rest of his life in Europe, settling on a 38-acre estate at Vevey, Switzerland.

In 1972, however, amends of a sort were made to Chaplin. He visited the United States to receive a special Oscar from the Motion Picture Academy and to accept accolades in New York. By this time the once-bubbling actor had aged into senility. He could do little more than bow and smile in response to expressions of affection for him and his art.

Meantime, critical opinion vindicated Chaplin's belief that *Verdoux* was a brilliant picture. Its satire of a business- and war-minded world was more appreciated in the context of opinion in the 1960s and 1970s than it had been in the late 1940s.

Apart from *Limelight*, Chaplin's final films—*A King in New York* and *A Countess from Hong Kong*—were accounted by many critics as lesser works.

In his declining years Chaplin looked back with happiness on his early days in the movies at Keystone and Essanay.

"I was able to try anything in those days," he said. "I was free."

Sir Charles—he was knighted by Queen Elizabeth in 1975—died at 4 A.M. on Dec. 25, 1977, a few hours before his family's traditional Christmas celebration was to begin.

His wife and seven of their children were at the bedside when the comedian died. A daughter, the actress Geraldine Chaplin, was in Madrid making a film, but left immediately to join her family at the Chaplin home at Corsier-sur-Vevey, a village near the eastern tip of the Lake of Geneva.

"All the presents were under the tree," Lady Chaplin told a caller, adding, "Charlie gave so much happiness and, although he had been ill for a long time, it is so sad that he should have passed away on Christmas Day."

"He died of old age," said Dr. Henri Perrier, the Chaplin family physician. "His death was peaceful and calm."

Sir Charles had been in failing health for many years. He was confined to a wheelchair, and his speech, hearing and sight were impaired. During the last year, he left his secluded 20-room villa only for an occasional drive into Vevey with his wife. Local people caught an occasional glimpse of the famous actor waiting in his blue-and-silver Rolls-Royce while his wife, 35 years his junior, purchased English newspapers and magazines, which she read to him later.

His last public appearance took place when he attended a circus performance in Vevey. He wore a soft hat pulled down over his forehead and thick-lensed glasses that hid most of his face. He shook hands with one of the clowns at the end of the performance.

THE CREATOR OF A WORLD PAVED WITH BANANA PEELS

VINCENT CANBY

IN APRIL of 1972 Charlie Chaplin returned to New York to be honored by the Film Society of Lincoln Center and then went on to Hollywood where the Academy of Motion Picture Arts and Sciences presented him with a special award. As returns go, this one was more truly triumphant than most, not because he had been away for so long, in self-imposed exile for more than 20 years, but because he had bided his time, and returned to this country on his own terms. Charlie had both ego and pride, but he made them work for him honorably and productively. He could afford the time and the patience to wait until the proper moment.

Sometimes I think that the thing that has most irked a new generation of film critics about Charlie Chaplin is not his rare sentiment (which includes sentimentality), his love of gags of "vulgarity and coarseness," as they were described by an early *Times* critic, or the occasional moments when inspiration was lacking, but, rather, the man himself, who became more and more aloof as the years passed, more and more aristocratic in his way of living, increasingly happy in private life.

How could such a man have possibly been sincere in the left-wing political views that landed him in such hot water? Wasn't there a contradiction between the Tramp and the handsome, urbane, witty, white-haired man who hobnobbed with painters, poets, novelists, politicians—and enjoyed every minute of it?

Most of the great film artists of his generation—including D. W. Griffith and Buster Keaton—died broke or in some other desperate straits. Chaplin didn't. Along with C. B. DeMille and Gloria Swanson, he was one of the few canny businessmen to survive silent films with his fortunes intact and to continue to work productively in the sound era into late-middle and old age. Charlie's public personality was never a reflection of his private life until near the end, when he made *A King in New York* to express his feelings about the country he felt had been so rotten to him. That Charlie should be so bitter about the United States somehow struck critics as a low blow. Could this be the man who ended his great *Modern Times* with the title card, "Buck up. Never say die. WE'LL GET ALONG"?

It was. He'd never pretended to be anything but what he was, but he had the misfortune to live on into an era when the differences between private and public personalities have dwindled to the near-vanishing point. I suspect Charlie would never have considered making a movie that drew as heavily on the specific details of his private life as Woody Allen did when he made his possibly classic *Annie Hall*.

Things like that simply weren't done in Charlie's time. Yet all of Charlie's films can be seen as some aspect of one great, continuing autobiography of his feelings—personal, political and social.

"The cinema," André Bazin once wrote, "more than any other art is particularly bound up with love. The novelist in his relations to his characters needs intelligence more than love; understanding is his form of loving. If the art of Chaplin were to be transposed into literature, it would tend to lapse into sentimentality. . . . [Chaplin's] heart brings to the cinema the nobility of myth. . . ."

The nobility of myth in his movies, though, embraces not only the sentiment expressed by the Tramp through his love for idealized women and children, but also the monumental cruelties faced by the Tramp. Virtue cannot be virtue if it is safely isolated, hermetically sealed in a vacuum. It's the vice of his world—the cruelty, the meanness, the vulgarity—that makes his best movies so funny. A nearly perfect example of Charlie's method can be seen in his 1921 short, *The Idle Class*, in which Charlie plays a dual role, that of a rich, boozing cad and that of the cad's look-alike, the Tramp. It's one of Charlie's funniest, most exuberant films, but it's also one of the saddest and toughest.

Until *The Great Dictator*, all of Charlie's films were fairy tales set primarily in slums—in flophouses, side streets, garrets. But even when he dropped the Tramp figure, the landscape that Charlie traveled as Monsieur Verdoux, as the old actor in *Limelight* and as the king in *A King in New York* was always paved by banana peels. They overlay everything from golf greens to dance floors and courtrooms, even the private offices of the great dictator, Adenoid Hynkel, known to the world as the Phooey, and the other dictator (the marvelous Jack Oakie), Napaloni, Il Dig-a-ditchy. These names still make me laugh unreasonably, but I'm more and more moved each time I see the extraordinary ballet from *The Great Dictator* in which Charlie imagines Hitler realizing his dream of world conquest with a globelike balloon.

Over the decades styles in moviemaking change as radically as the costumes of the periods. I should hope that future generations won't become so put off by the "look" of his films that they will not be able to see them, and to see especially how funny they are. I think of so many scenes at once—the Tramp in the cage with the lion in *The Circus*, the poor king who can't say his m's and v's after an ad-agency-ordered face-lift in *A King in New York*, the Tramp taking a cigarette butt from his cigarette case (an empty anchovy tin) and lighting it, to start *The Kid*.

Like all great artists Chaplin eventually created his own world as removed from particular time and place as Proust's Paris, and Chandler's Los Angeles and Baum's Oz. It was never an easy world. What with all of those banana peels, it was difficult not to fall. One had to get a careful heel-hold, which is why he always walked so funny.

HOW DID THEY KNOW A GENIUS WAS AT WORK?

WALTER KERR

IT ONLY took from February to June. In the first week of February 1914, Mack Sennett released a very short film—just half a reel long—in which his new and as yet unknown comedian, Charlie Chaplin, mingled freely with the crowds who had come to see the annual Kid Auto Races at Venice, Calif. The auto races were real, though of course the children's peanut-sized cars had to roll down a fairly steep ramp in order to pick up enough momentum to stir any dust along the track. Sennett especially liked sending his clowns and a camera to public exhibitions of this sort because it gave him an event to photograph and a flock of free extras to fill in the sidelines. Chaplin had put together his so-called tramp costume for the very first time that day.

Sennett's actors improvised, of course—the company is said to have spent no more than 45 minutes shooting *Kid Auto Races*—and what Chaplin improvised for himself was a most felicitous bit of cinematic playfulness. He turns up as one member of the assembled crowd who is determined to get his picture taken. He does not, however, wish to *appear* to be trying to get his picture taken—that would be vulgar—so that he is forever strolling nonchalantly within the camera's range, forever being yanked back out of it, forever seeming to be taking a deep interest in the miniature racing cars while actually blotting the cars out because he is smack between them and the camera. He is shooed out of range by, I guess, an assistant director, he is manhandled out of range, he is almost nipped by a racer or two as the racers pick up speed. Each time he agrees to step aside, tipping his hat politely, and then reappears a few yards down the track as though he'd just arrived and was curious to know what was going on. Primitive as the venture is, he is funny.

But I am interested, for the moment, in the crowd that lines the track. There must be several hundred onlookers present, rather a large group for a children's event, and they do—from time to time—glance at the camera. Motion pictures were still very new, and it was natural for the sightseers to be curious. *When* they look at the camera, however, they seem to be looking specifically at the machine and its operators, not so much at Chaplin.

Even when Charlie is doing a quick spin that makes his jacket fly out about him, or demonstrating the soon-to-be-celebrated business of flipping the butt of his cigarette over his shoulder so that he can give it a back-kick with his foot, the assembly pays him relatively little mind. And whenever Charlie, suddenly docile, permits himself to be reabsorbed into the crowd, the crowd simply makes room for him unself-consciously and turns its attention to the kids' autos. The kids' autos are what they came to see. It is plain enough that these people have neither seen nor heard of anyone named Charlie Chaplin before.

Things are very, very different in June. During the second week of June 1914, and just 16 short films after the excursion to Venice, Sennett released another film located at a racetrack, *Mabel's Busy Day*. Whence the title? Comedienne Mabel Normand sells hot dogs at the track and is having a terrible time of it because her customers are all intent upon cheating her. Charlie will leap to her assistance, while doing a little cheating of his own on the side. What racetrack? Unidentified, but we'll touch on that in a moment.

There is a crowd here, too, in just a few scenes. But it is nowhere near Chaplin. It seems to have been roped off about a block away, densely herded, while Charlie mauls a policeman close to the camera. The effect could not be more curious. The crowd is staring this time, focused altogether on Chaplin. And Chaplin is protected from this mob by an enormous open space in which nothing at all is happening. Inevitable conclusion? Chaplin has grown so tremendously popular in a little more than four months that he can no longer work on location, certainly not in public situations. He'd be mobbed by fans and not a foot of film would get shot.

In fact, he is not really on location here. There is an auto race going on somewhere; we see cars whipping about an oval course at high speeds. But these are interpolated shots, stock footage picked up God knows where and inserted into the goings-on to suggest that they are indeed going on *somewhere.*

The filming can't be done in the open any longer, not with hordes of people about. The speed of Chaplin's rise has been breathtaking. The size of his now adoring public has become unbelievably vast and close to uncontrollable. And therein lies the great unresolved mystery. How, in 1914, did the public *know*? How, after 16 very short, very raggle-taggle slapstick improvisations, were these perfectly ordinary customers, often entering the movie house at 5 cents a head, able to detect what would later be described as genius?

It certainly didn't look like genius yet. Chaplin *was* doing some funny bits of business, yes. He used his cane to snare a girl's ankle and draw it toward him amorously, used the same cane later to unscrew, violently, a bully's navel. But from the adulation instantly offered this clown, you'd think he'd already done *City Lights*. During the first months of Chaplin's year-long stay at Keystone, months in which he mostly kicked a man and kicked a woman and kicked them both again, moviegoers somehow saw more than was there, saw a promise beyond a kick or even *in* the kick, saw a future that not even Chaplin could imagine. One reason *I* keep going back to the films whenever a kindly retrospective comes along is to see if I can spot what Chaplin's earliest audiences saw. They were talented, those moviegoers, and I keep trying to track their intuitions down. It's pleasant detective work even if the secret remains elusive, eternally rounding the corner one skip-step ahead of Charlie.

I also make my way to retrospectives in order to

check on the quality of the prints. You see, most of us weren't going to the movies at all regularly in 1914, which means that we had to make Chaplin's acquaintance anywhere from 10 to 70 years later (the introduction is still going on). This also means that we were frequently introduced to the man's work in prints that had been used, abused, badly duplicated, retitled by would-be wags, shown at wrong speeds or otherwise misrepresented. We're so used to tired prints, in fact, that we automatically come to believe that the films must have looked this way in the first place.

The Kino International entrepreneurs have taken a conscientious step in the right direction by giving special attention to the three earliest years—the years of Keystone, of Essanay, of Mutual. Clean and reasonably complete new 35-millimeter prints have been made of five Keystones, of eight Essanays and of all 12 exuberant Mutuals, and your eyes just may pop a little as you pick up the blaze of sharp silver light that seems to come from *within* the faces on screen. It's also gratifying to be reminded that once upon a time every inch of the screen was filled with precisely defined blacks and whites and the "live" gradations between. The screen's surface seems to hum and buzz with the interplay.

There is, regrettably, one area in which caution is in order. Chaplin began to produce independently in 1918, for release through First National, and the eight films he made before joining United Artists constitute the bedrock on which all of the great films will be built. The phrase "first masterpiece" was almost immediately applied to *A Dog's Life*, the successful fusion of comedy and pathos was achieved with *The Kid*, and even the shorter films—most particularly *The Idle Class*—have a fresh comic *certainty* about them. Where a Keystone would have been frantic, an *Idle Class* is serenely firm. And funnier for it.

Unhappily, when the First National films were redistributed in this country within the past 15 years or so, they were heavily doctored, and damaged in the process. Apparently someone—not Chaplin himself—was fearful that some of the silent action, filmed at a rate meant to stylize the comedian's movements, would seem "unnaturally" fast to audiences reared on slower sound-film. To "naturalize" the action, most of the footage was stretch-printed. That is to say, every other frame of film, or perhaps every third frame of film, was repeated. The action was thus extended, though on a move, halt, start-again basis. The technique has the feel of an uncontrollable hiccup, and it not only falsifies the rhythm of the comedy that was photographed, it destroys it.

In *A Dog's Life*, there is a remarkably timed, virtually balletic routine performed by Charlie and six or eight beer-bellied job seekers who are lining up at the three windows of an employment agency. Each time Charlie moves toward an available window, he is intercepted by a beefy rival who can somehow move faster than he, and the pace grows dizzier as the cross-weave of unbudgeable bodies and windows slamming shut intensifies. The sequence sets the film's narrative in motion and serves as its first hilarious routine. Slowed by stretch-printing, it's scarcely worth titters. It has lost its dance to lightness, its original arcs of movement, its fancifulness. The element of fantasy that permeated silent film has disappeared in favor of something plausible but not very interesting. Indeed, since the repeated frames were never a part of the action performed and photographed, they have merely succeeded in making Chaplin's designs *unnatural*.

Some gags survive the misguided interpolation. The passage in which Charlie steals muffins from brother Syd at a lunch wagon holds onto most of its humor. The once joyous moment in which a stolen wallet goes hand-over-hand between Charlie, two thugs, and a bartender, does not. The gag gasps and dies, hard as we try to push it. *The Idle Class* moves so slowly, and so jerkily in its slowness, that I find this jewel of a comedy now painful to watch. Any speed would be better than the falsification imposed on it, and I don't like to think of newcomers to Chaplin meeting him on terms so unlike his own.

THE ROBBING OF CHAPLIN'S GRAVE

SPECIAL TO *THE NEW YORK TIMES*

GENEVA, March 2, 1978—The body of Charlie Chaplin was stolen sometime during the night of March 1, 1978, from the grave where it was buried two years before in a small cemetery in the Swiss village of Corsier-sur-Vevey, overlooking the eastern end of Lake Geneva.

Chaplin, who died Christmas Day, 1976, at the age of 88 and was buried two days later, had spent the last 25 years of his life in a baronial estate on the edge of Corsier-sur-Vevey, where villagers had respected his privacy.

The theft of his body was discovered the morning of March 2 by villagers visiting the neatly kept cemetery, which is at the end of a lane of homes 200 yards from the village's main street. The grave was a small plot near a low stone wall, a serene setting lined with cypress trees and overlooking the lake and the French and Swiss Alps beyond.

"We are completely in the dark as to who stole the coffin and why it was stolen," said a spokesman for the police at Lausanne, about 12 miles west of the village.

They announced the theft in a brief statement that said the actor's heavy coffin had been dug up and removed from the unguarded cemetery after dark. Freshly dug earth surrounded the opened grave but a cross at its head was undamaged and was taken to a laboratory for a fingerprint check, investigators said.

Indentations in the ground indicated that the coffin had been dragged for a short distance. Then it apparently was driven away in a vehicle. A village resident who had helped with the Chaplin burial described the coffin as massive and said it would have taken four men to move it.

The police, who placed a guard at the cemetery and notified the Chaplin family, said there were no apparent witnesses among the people who lived near the cemetery. The closest house is about 50 yards away.

Expressions of shock came from residents and public officials.

"I am appalled by this gruesome and sacrilegious act," said Alan Keith Rothnie, the British Ambassador to Switzerland, who had attended Chaplin's funeral on behalf of Queen Elizabeth II. The Queen had knighted the comedian, a British subject, in 1975.

The police called the incident a desecration and said an investigation had been initiated "on grounds of disturbing the peace of the dead."

Asked about the possibility of ransom, an investigator said: "This is the only motive we can think of for this crime." He emphasized, however, that no ransom demand had been made.

Chaplin bought the estate in January 1953, after being virtually exiled by the United States, where he had lived and worked for 45 years. The London-born actor was sailing home to Britain on vacation in 1952 when the U.S. attorney general announced that his visa had been revoked and that he would not be allowed to reenter the country unless he could prove his "moral worth."

Coming at the height of the Cold War, the incident was widely regarded as a rebuff of the comedian's outspoken, left-of-center political and social views. He later spoke astringently of America's "ingratitude," and settled into the role of country squire in Switzerland.

Chaplin's Body Found

Special to *The New York Times*

The body of Charlie Chaplin was recovered May 17, 1978, in a cornfield about 10 miles from its burial place in the Swiss village cemetery at Corsier-sur-Vevey, at the eastern end of Lake Geneva, after being stolen 11 weeks ago.

Gabriel Cettou, chief of detectives of the state police detachment here, said that two refugees, a 24-year-old Pole and a Bulgarian aged 38, confessed to stealing the body after they were arrested May 16.

The Pole was arrested in a telephone booth here while making a call to Jean-Felix Paschoud, the Chaplin family lawyer, to demand a ransom of $250,000 for the body, Mr. Cettou said at a press conference. The second arrest came soon afterward.

Both men are automobile mechanics who were living in Lausanne after having been granted residents' permits as political refugees, Mr. Cettou said. Their names could not be immediately released, according to Jean-Daniel Tenthorey, the examining magistrate in charge of the investigation.

The coffin was dug up and taken to the cornfield at Noville, a village on the opposite side of Lake Geneva, according to the police. A 40-inch-deep grave was dug in a plowed field near where the Rhône River empties into the lake.

THE FILM SOCIETY OF LINCOLN CENTER SALUTES CHARLIE CHAPLIN

McCANDLISH PHILLIPS

A CAPACITY audience of 2,836 filled Philharmonic Hall in Lincoln Center on April 5, 1972, for a salute to Charlie Chaplin in which the legendary mime of silent films appeared in his two selves—on the screen and in person.

The 82-year-old actor was the guest of honor at "a special gala," as it was called, arranged by the Film Society of Lincoln Center as the highlight of Mr. Chaplin's four-day stay in New York.

Police barriers were set up outside the hall but no great crowd formed there on a raw if rainless night.

Barely 200 were present to watch the flow of celebrities entering, including Paulette Goddard, flashing blue-green eyes in the television lights, Norman Mailer and Douglas Fairbanks, Jr., looking dashing and youthful, as if fresh from a castle duel. He had a bandaged nose that went well with that supposition.

Leonard Garment, Nancy Hanks and Frank Shakespeare came from Washington to represent President Nixon.

The celebrity-watchers were disappointed in their hopes of catching a glimpse of Mr. Chaplin. His limousine swung into the rear entrance, where exactly one spectator stood waiting. He was Mack Martin, 14 years old, of 501 West 123d Street, alone in guessing the arrival correctly.

A little earlier there had been a momentarily affecting scene. Two black boys, about 10, both wearing tennis shoes and blue jeans and one in a visored cap a bit too big for him, stood a few feet from the glass lobby of the hall, gazing in at women in gowns and furs and men in black-tie garb, an acre of privilege that dazzled their young eyes. It was pure Chaplin, up to date.

When Mr. Chaplin entered the First Terrace tier above the orchestra level, he was not immediately seen by the audience. Six seconds went by until somebody said "There he is!" and the entire audience rose to pour out a wave of applause and cheers.

Until it subsided, a beaming Mr. Chaplin went through a montage of responsive and fleetingly comic motions—right-hand waving, both arms upraised, a hand over his heart, a kiss flung out over the audience, another wave. He introduced his wife, Oona, all in white, with an upraised palm and then, for a scant two seconds, he indicated that she was a total stranger, using a shrug of perfect innocence.

The audience applauded Mr. Chaplin repeatedly during the showing of two of his early films—*The Idle Class*, a short, and *The Kid*, with Jackie Coogan.

The white-haired old man, just 12 days short of his 83d birthday on April 16, gazed across half a century of time at the quick-limbed Chaplin on the screen, then near the height of his comedic powers. The gratifying sound of laughter welled up from the audience—the sound that had made the slum boy from London rich and famous and acclaimed.

A roar of approval surged at the end, and Mr. Chaplin broke the silence of his visit. He stood at a microphone at his seat: "First, thank you for your wonderful applause . . . It's so very gratifying to know that I have so many friends . . . It's easy for you but difficult for me to speak tonight as I feel very emotional. I'm glad to be among so many friends. Thank you."

Shouts of "Bravo!" went up, and Mr. Chaplin pointed to his ring finger, then to his wife, to include her in it all.

On the way to a champagne reception downstairs later, Mr. Chaplin got hold of a derby and handled it deftly, aware of its uses as his trademark.

He sat the bowler on his fleecy hair, tilted his chin, rolled his eyes and thrust his hand under his nose in clear signification of his old scrub-brush mustache.

An unruly crowd, composed largely of eager photographers, surged around him as he made his way to a small area reserved for his own party. Six policemen surrounded his table, trying to keep everybody back, not with entire success.

Less than 10 feet away, a crowd of watchers outside pressed to the glass wall. Mr. Chaplin turned and waved to them repeatedly. He was mobbed again 20 minutes later while exiting, but he took it very well, tossing off more kisses.

Mr. Chaplin, a British subject, is paying his first visit to the United States in 20 years after a long intermission that began when the federal government revoked his entry permit in offense at marital difficulties and political proclivities not to its taste. Mr. Chaplin would only be permitted to return, it was said at the time, if he could prove his "moral worth."

Mr. Chaplin elected to wait it out. By last night it was evident that these issues of former controversy were lost in a golden cloud of nostalgia and affection for the creator of the pantomimic Little Tramp.

It was this figure, poised so precariously on a line dividing the illusion of elegance from the immediacy of need, that walked, with a jaunty, open-toed gait, into the hearts of millions 50 years ago.

The fact of his worldwide fame—at its peak Mr. Chaplin's hold on his fans amounted to little less than a craze—was in continuing evidence last night with an outpouring of television and newspaper people from Japan and Australia, South America, Britain, Europe and elsewhere, to cover the event.

All of this, Mr. Chaplin said, made him feel as if he were the object of a complete "renaissance," as if he were being "reborn." Indeed, the entire scene suggested the triumphal final flourish of a motion picture script—reconciliation and rejoicing after long estrangement, with the hero having it all his own way.

SIR WINSTON CHURCHILL

1874–1965

"You have sat here too long for any good you have been doing. Depart, I say, and let us have done with you. In the name of God, go!" The date was May 8, 1940. The words were those Oliver Cromwell used in dismissing the Long Parliament in 1653. The man who repeated them, with an accusatory finger pointed at Prime Minister Neville Chamberlain, was a fellow Conservative, Leopold Amery. The occasion was a bitter debate in Commons over Britain's mounting peril in the faltering, bumbling conduct of the war with Hitler's Germany.

Amery's harsh injunction echoed the country's gloomy frustrations, its demand for vigorous war leadership. For two days Chamberlain, the man who had returned from Munich in 1938 after the rape of Czechoslovakia clutching an umbrella and a piece of paper that he said guaranteed "peace in our time," tried to stave off the inevitable. But events forced his hand.

At dawn May 10, Hitler flung his proud and unbeaten forces against the Low Countries and toward France and the channel ports. At that moment Mussolini joined his Axis partner in the war. The hour of Britain's greatest peril since the Spanish Armada loomed.

Chamberlain stepped down, and King George VI called upon Winston Leonard Spencer Churchill, 66-year-old First Lord of the Admiralty, to prosecute the war he had for so long foreseen, and for which his life, up to that point, might be said to have been but a prelude to the greatness of leadership that carried Britain and her allies to triumph in 1945.

He struck the note of his leadership in his first report to Commons May 13 as the Nazi Panzer divisions were heading into France. It was a note he sustained with his countrymen throughout the war—candor that kindled national unity, inspirited the faltering, inspirited the brave, forged the will to fight, fashioned the certainty of victory.

His theme was, as he put it later, "no one can guarantee success in war, but only deserve it."

"I would say to the House, as I said to those who have joined this Government: 'I have nothing to offer but blood, toil, tears and sweat.'

"We have before us an ordeal of the most grievous kind. We have before us many, many long months of struggle and of suffering.

"You ask, what is our policy? I will say: It is to wage war, by sea, land and air, with all our might and with all the strength that God can give us: to wage war against a monstrous tyranny, never surpassed in the dark, lamentable catalogue of human crime. That is our policy.

"You ask, what is our aim? I can answer in one word: Victory, victory at all costs, victory in spite of all terror, victory, however long and hard the road may be; for without victory, there is no survival. Let that be realized; no survival for the British Empire;

New York Times Photo

New York Times Photo

no survival for all that the British Empire has stood for; no survival for the urge and impulse of the ages, that mankind will move forward towards its goal.

"But I take up my task with buoyancy and hope. I feel sure that our cause will not be suffered to fail among men. At this time I feel entitled to claim the aid of all, and I say, 'Come, then, let us go forward together.' "

For Britain and for Churchill that was the beginning of "their finest hour."

Churchill described his own feelings on becoming prime minister in the first volume of his history of the war: "During these last crowded days of the political crisis my pulse had not quickened at any moment. I took it all as it came. But I cannot conceal from the reader in this truthful account that as I went to bed about 3 A.M. I was conscious of a profound sense of relief.

"At last I had the authority to give directions over the whole scene. I felt as if I were walking with Destiny, and that all my past life had been but a preparation for this hour and for this trial. Eleven years in the political wilderness had freed me from ordinary party antagonisms. My warnings over the last six years had been so numerous, so detailed, and were now so terribly vindicated, that no one could gainsay me. I could not be reproached either for making the war or with want of preparation for it. I thought I knew a good deal about it all, and I was sure I should not fail. Therefore, although impatient for the morning, I slept soundly and had no need for cheering dreams. Facts are better than dreams."

The man through whose mind these confident thoughts flowed knew also that his nation now stood virtually alone and at the mercy of Germany and Italy. Indeed, Britain was not to win her first solid victory until the Battle of El Alamein had ended on Nov. 4, 1942. But to his Herculean tasks Churchill brought Herculean energy, Herculean determination, Herculean tact. With them he fashioned the Grand Alliance of 26 nations.

To his tasks, too, he brought all his imposing gifts as a master of the language of Shakespeare, Milton, Gibbon and Macaulay, his skill and wit as an orator. As the late President Kennedy said, "He mobilized the English language and sent it into battle."

Sometimes in a business suit but more often in black jacket and gray striped trousers, he made an imposing figure whether seated on the Treasury bench in Commons with his chin resting on his chest or standing, gripping the upper lapels of his jacket to address the House.

Portly and solid in appearance, he often seemed like a kindly aging schoolmaster peering over his half spectacles.

His voice lacked volume and he had trouble with the letter *S*, but this gave style to his delivery. He was a master of the tempting pause before the utterance of a noble phrase. Emphasis was added by a rising inflection and a half-growl at the end of his most truculent challenges, which produced a cadenced speech of transcendent rhetorical effect.

Churchill was an aristocrat, an imperialist and a royalist who at the same time trusted the people. It is no contradiction to describe him as a Tory democrat. To the multitudes he was "Winnie."

He was both arrogant and humble, courteous and rude. None could question his courage, yet he was unashamed of tears when deeply moved. He was resourceful, inventive, a master at improvisation, a genius at handling detail.

His many hats, the bow tie, the cigar clenched tightly between his teeth, his walking stick and the V sign became a personification of Britain.

"It was the British that had the lion's heart," he said on his 80th birthday. "I had the luck to be called upon to give the roar." He was too modest: His personality kept the heart beating.

Nonetheless, until he reached the pinnacle of power he had been regarded by some as too clever, too daring to be trusted. The disaster of the Dardanelles, the costly futile attempt to break the deadlock in World War I, dogged his career.

On becoming prime minister, Churchill brought Liberal and Labor members into his cabinet to create a national government. He created a war council of five. With Parliament's approval, he established a ministry of defense with himself as its head. He brought in Gen. Hastings Ismay to advise him. In effect, Churchill became commander in chief.

There was a mood of relief among the British people that now at last they could "get on with it" under a leader who knew his goal and who was determined to attain it. No one but themselves could let them down. The long weekend vanished. People called for harder tasks, greater sacrifices.

Only 16 days after speaking to Parliament, Churchill was confronted by Dunkirk. The British Expeditionary Force in France, faced with envelopment by the Wehrmacht and dive-bombed by the Luftwaffe, was being driven into the sea.

On May 28 Churchill informed the House that King Leopold of the Belgians had surrendered. This melancholy news was followed one week later by his announcement that the bulk of the British Expeditionary Force, driven into the sea, had been brought safely home. Many hailed this as a miracle.

More than 1,000 ships from small to large, he told the House, "carried over 335,000 men, French and British, out of the jaws of death and shame, to their native land and to the tasks which lie ahead."

"We must be very careful not to assign to this deliverance the attributes of a victory," he cautioned. "Wars are not won by evacuations."

The ships were protected by the Royal Air Force, which engaged the main force of the Luftwaffe, inflicting losses of 4 to 1.

To the British, the escape of so many husbands and fathers called for thanksgiving, if not for cheers.

Nevertheless, 30,000 were left behind, dead, wounded or prisoners. The cost in matériel was great.

Indomitable as ever in adversity, Churchill closed his Dunkirk report with these words: "We shall not flag or fail. We shall go on to the end, we shall fight in France, we shall fight on the seas and oceans, we shall fight with growing confidence and growing strength in the air, we shall defend our island, whatever the cost may be, we shall fight on the beaches, we shall fight on the landing grounds, we shall fight in the fields and in the streets, we shall fight in the hills; we shall never surrender, and even if, which I do not for a moment believe, this island or a large part of it were subjugated and starving, then our Empire beyond the seas, armed and guarded by the British Fleet, would carry on the struggle, until, in God's good time, the new world, with all its power and might, steps forth to the rescue and the liberation of the old."

Churchill now realized that Britain alone could never win the war. He aimed at getting help from the most likely source, the United States. Although that country was neutral, President Roosevelt was willing to give "all aid short of war."

Quickly Roosevelt made available to Britain an array of light and heavy weapons, all that could be spared from the leftovers of World War I. There followed the exchange of 50 overage destroyers for 99-year leases on British bases in the Western Hemisphere.

Later, with Roosevelt's prodding, the Lend-Lease Act was passed in 1941. "Give us the tools, and we will finish the job," Churchill said.

After Dunkirk, disaster followed disaster. Churchill made a desperate attempt to keep France in the war by offering a Franco-British union with common citizenship, a joint Parliament and a shared military command. It was too late. France surrendered June 21.

Anticipating the surrender, Churchill had told his people four days earlier: "We have become the sole champions now in arms to defend the world cause. We shall do our best to be worthy of this high honor. We shall defend our island home and with the British Empire we shall fight on unconquerable until the curse of Hitler is lifted from the brows of mankind."

Churchill faced a bitter choice. By his order, commanders of the French naval vessels were given the option of coming over to the British, sailing to ports safe from the enemy, or being sunk by British guns.

The commanders hesitated. So, in an action at the French naval base near Oran, in North Africa, one of two French battle cruisers was damaged and beached and one battleship was sunk. Another was badly damaged and two destroyers and an aircraft carrier were sunk or burned.

As the summer, bright and warm, advanced, fears of invasion rose. Businessmen drilled with wooden guns and pikestaffs. The beaches and coasts bristled with improvised obstacles and antique weapons.

Churchill warned of the coming ordeal: "I expect that the battle of Britain is about to begin. Upon this battle depends the survival of Christian civilization. Upon it depends our own British life, and the long continuity of our institutions and our Empire. The whole fury and might of the enemy must very soon be turned on us.

"Hitler knows that he will have to break us in this island or lose the war. If we can stand up to him, all Europe may be free and the life of the world may move forward into broad, sunlit uplands. But if we fail, then the whole world, including the United States, including all that we have known and cared for, will sink into the abyss of a new dark age made more sinister, and perhaps more protracted, by the lights of perverted science.

"Let us therefore brace ourselves to our duties, and so bear ourselves that, if the British Empire and its Commonwealth last for a thousand years, men will still say, 'This was their finest hour.' "

The "finest hour" became the agony of the Battle of Britain, waged in the splendor of the September skies. Although Churchill neither planned nor supervised the battle, he invoked the nation's fortitude that inspired the airmen to their magnificent and sleepless struggle that eventually saved the island kingdom.

In the early days of the battle hundreds of Hurricanes and Spitfires were put out of action; a fourth of the fighter pilots were killed or wounded; thousands of civilians perished.

The raids went on day and night. The banshee howls of the sirens sent people scuttling in and out of shelters. The terror that struck by night was the worst. Finally, as youngsters in flight training took the place of their dead comrades, the Germans found daylight raids too costly, even on the foggiest days of autumn. Thenceforth the bombers came and went at dusk and dawn.

For days and weeks there was a late afternoon march of weary men, women and children, carrying their bedclothes, trundling baby carriages, heading for the underground stations where thousands slept nightly. But there was no real safety.

For the first nights there was no reply to the rain of bombs. Then, all at once, the antiaircraft batteries in the parks and on the outskirts opened up with a resounding and reassuring roar. Bursts even rattled from a Bofors gun atop the Admiralty Arch.

The fire from the ground did little damage to the Germans. The ammunition could hardly be spared. But it did much good for morale to see a bomber pinpointed by searchlights diving and squirming to avoid, not always successfully, bursts of flak.

The tribute Churchill paid to the Royal Air Force just before the bombardment of London began took on a deeper meaning.

"Never in the field of human conflict," he said, "was so much owed by so many to so few."

The people had been told that the ringing of church bells would signal a German invasion. On Sept. 11, Churchill said in a broadcast that if the invasion were going to be tried at all it would not be long delayed.

But British bombers attacked the invasion fleet gathered in ports from Boulogne to Antwerp. On the 17th Hitler postponed and later canceled Operation Sea Lion, his invasion plan.

During those days Churchill spent much time at 10 Downing Street, or the underground war room, usually in what he called his siren suit, the zipper front of which delighted him. On weekends he went to Chequers, the country home of prime ministers.

It was his custom to awaken at 8 o'clock. For the next couple of hours he read dispatches and sent off memos in all directions, usually beginning with "Pray see to it . . ." or "Pray find out . . . ," to his generals or colleagues. By midmorning he was working full blast in his office.

Luncheon, for which he usually had guests, was followed by an hour's nap. Then came more work. In the evening there were generally dinner guests. The meal was followed by a session of idea swapping that often went far into the early morning, with Churchill pouring out an endless flow of suggestions. His constant companions were General Ismay and Brendan Bracken, minister of information, who were said to be the only ones who could stay the course.

London became the seat of eight governments in exile: Belgium, the Netherlands, Free France, Norway, Czechoslovakia, Poland, Greece and Yugoslavia. The government of the Grand Duchy of Luxembourg was in Canada.

With these governments, Churchill busied himself welding the Grand Alliance, often putting the damper on petty squabbles and adjudicating trivial rivalries and smoothing the easily ruffled feathers of Charles de Gaulle, the Free French leader.

"We all have our crosses to bear," he once said. "Mine was the Cross of Lorraine."

As the war became global after the entry of the Soviet Union and the United States, China and Japan, Churchill's travels in keeping the Alliance glued together were ceaseless. He journeyed to Newfoundland, three times to Washington, twice to Quebec, twice to Moscow, once to Ottawa, to Athens, to Casablanca, to Cairo (to confer with Roosevelt and Chiang Kai-shek), to Teheran and to Yalta (for conferences with Roosevelt and Stalin) and to Potsdam (to meet with Truman and Stalin). In all, he saw Roosevelt nine times and exchanged 1,700 communications with him.

On Aug. 9, 1941, Churchill and Roosevelt had their first rendezvous in Placentia Bay, Newfoundland, the president having arrived aboard the cruiser *Augusta* and the prime minister on the battleship *Prince of Wales*.

Supported by the arm of his son, Elliott, the president received Churchill aboard the *Augusta* while the national anthems of the United States and Britain were played. The next day, Sunday, the president returned Churchill's visit and attended divine services on the battleship's quarterdeck.

Churchill described the scene later: "This service was felt by all of us to be a deeply moving expression of the unity of faith of our two peoples and none who took part in it will forget the spectacle presented that sunlit morning on the crowded quarterdeck—the symbolism of the Union Jack and the Stars and Stripes draped side by side on the pulpit; the American and British chaplains sharing in the reading of the prayers; the highest naval, military and air officers of Britain grouped in one body behind the President and me; the close-packed ranks of British and American sailors completely intermingled, sharing the same books and joining fervently together in the prayers and hymns familiar to both."

Out of that meeting at sea came the Atlantic Charter, a statement of principles that was later, in substance, to be incorporated in the aims of the United Nations.

The charter rejected any aspirations for aggrandizement, territorial or otherwise; declared British and American opposition to territorial changes not in accord with the wishes of the peoples concerned, and affirmed the right of peoples to choose their own form of government.

Of importance, too, were the staff talks that took place and the concord reached on the division of supplies from the United States between Russia and Britain.

Although the United States was still neutral, Roosevelt also agreed that the American navy would take over patrol of the American-Iceland segment of the Atlantic, thus relieving the hard-pressed British of some of their convoy duties.

Held to a standstill against Britain, Hitler turned eastward, striking in June 1941 at the Soviet Union, his partner in the nonaggression pact of August 1939. Churchill had warned Stalin that Hitler was about to strike. Now he pledged aid to the Soviet cause.

In a radio broadcast June 22, 1941, he said: "At 4 o'clock this morning, Hitler attacked and invaded Russia. All his usual formalities of perfidy were observed with scrupulous technique. A nonaggression treaty had been solemnly signed and was in force between the two countries. No complaint had been made by Germany of its nonfulfillment. Under its cloak of false confidence, the German armies drew up in immense strength along a line which stretches from the White Sea to the Black Sea; and their air fleets and armored divisions slowly and methodically took their stations. Then, suddenly, without declaration of war, without even an ultimatum, German bombs rained down from the air upon the Russian cities, the German troops violated the frontiers; and an hour later the German Ambassador, who till the night before was lavishing his assurances of friendship, almost of alliance, upon the Russians, called upon the Russian Foreign Minister to tell him that a state of war existed between Germany and Russia."

Churchill heaped invective on Hitler—"a monster of wickedness," "a bloodthirsty guttersnipe"—and upon his "accomplice and jackal Mussolini.

"But," he said, "all this fades away before the spectacle which is now unfolding. Any man or State who fights on against Nazidom will have our aid. Any man or State who marches with Hitler is our foe."

Throughout the war Churchill's relations with Stalin were blunt and forthright. With Roosevelt they were softened because of friendship. Roosevelt tended to see the war in military terms, whereas Churchill directed his mind as much to political considerations.

It was this that in 1942 caused Churchill to lose his enthusiasm for the planned supporting attack on the south of France in favor of a thrust from Italy to stem the advance of Russia into Europe. Churchill did not have his way, and he argued afterward that had his views been adopted postwar Europe would not have been so dark.

With the Germans gaining in Russia—battering at the gates of Leningrad and Moscow and thrusting into southern Russia—Japan, Hitler's Axis partner in the Far East, entered the war with an air attack on United States air and naval bases at Pearl Harbor on Dec. 7, 1941. This brought the United States into the war in Europe, too, for Germany and Italy, as part of the Axis pact, declared war on the United States. Churchill was quick to see that Pearl Harbor was the beginning of the end for Hitler, Mussolini and Hirohito. As he wrote in his memoirs: "Once again in our long island history we should emerge, however mauled or mutilated, safe and victorious. We should not be wiped out. Our history would not come to an end. We might not even have to die as individuals. Hitler's fate was sealed. Mussolini's fate was sealed. As for the Japanese, they would be ground to powder."

True to a promise given Roosevelt earlier, to declare war "within the hour" if Japan attacked, Churchill called his cabinet and then notified the Japanese ambassador that a state of war existed between his country and Britain.

On the day of Pearl Harbor, the Japanese also landed on the Malayan coast and bombed Singapore and Hong Kong. And before they were driven back, they were to sink the *Prince of Wales* and the *Repulse*, to overrun Malaya, Thailand and Burma, and to cost Churchill challenges in Parliament to his leadership.

At the outset Churchill went to the United States to confer with Roosevelt on the conduct of the war. He had fears, later disclosed, over these conferences: "We feared lest the true proportion of the war as a whole might not be understood. We were conscious of a serious danger that the United States might pursue the war against Japan in the Pacific and leave us to fight Germany and Italy in Europe, Africa, and in the Middle East.

"Hitherto, as a nonbelligerent, the President had been able and willing to divert large supplies of equipment from the American armed forces, since these were not engaged. Should we be able to persuade the President and the American Service chiefs that the defeat of Japan would not spell the defeat of Hitler, but that the defeat of Hitler made the finishing-off of Japan merely a matter of time and trouble?"

It was on this visit, on Dec. 26, that Churchill delivered the first of two wartime speeches to Congress. The second was under happier circumstances on May 19, 1943, when the outlook was brighter.

Meantime, things were going badly for the British in North Africa. In a decision the wisdom of which was later questioned, troops were moved from Africa to Crete and Greece when Germany struck into the Balkans. It was seemingly as a consequence of this step that Rommel and his Afrika Korps were able, in the summer of 1942, to capture Tobruk. The victory, although preceded by severe reverses in the desert, came as a shock. In Commons, it brought on a no-confidence vote, but Churchill survived it, 475–25.

The loss of Tobruk was softened somewhat when Roosevelt offered American tanks for the African front. The tide was eventually reversed and Rommel humbled at El Alamein, but that was not until November 1942. Although winning the Battle of Britain had been a strategic victory of great significance, it was at El Alamein that there was tangible military victory, and that was what, in a dark hour, showed the British people the glimmer on the horizon.

The Soviet Union, too, in this period suffered badly, and in May 1942, Molotov visited London with an urgent request for an Anglo-American second front on the Continent to draw off some of the German forces from the east.

The project, at first supported by Roosevelt, was postponed for a large-scale operation in Africa.

It was Churchill's lot to break the news to Stalin in Moscow. He asked Roosevelt to let W. Averell Harriman accompany him because "I have a somewhat raw job."

As Churchill outlined the change in plans, Stalin "looked very glum and seemed unconvinced." He said there was "not a single German division in France that was of any value."

Churchill replied that there were 25, of which nine were of the first line. He agreed that it would be possible to land six divisions but that it could be more harmful to future operations than helpful for the present.

Stalin, now restless and impatient, declared that "a man who was not prepared to take risks could not win a war."

But he became somewhat mollified as Churchill unfolded the North African plan to "threaten the belly of Hitler's Europe.

"To illustrate my point," Churchill recalled, "I had meanwhile drawn a picture of a crocodile and explained to Stalin with the help of this picture how it was our intention to attack the soft belly of the crocodile as he attacked his hard snout."

Stalin seemed to grasp the idea, but the next day, with Stalin and Molotov, there "began a most unpleasant discussion.

"We argued for about two hours during which he [Stalin] said a great many disagreeable things, especially about our being too much afraid of fighting the Germans and if we tried it like the Russians we should not find it so bad."

On the African front, a British-American force under Eisenhower landed Nov. 7, 1942, at Casablanca, Algiers and Oran.

A jubilant but cautious Churchill proclaimed the good news at the Mansion House Nov. 10. "We have victory—a remarkable and definite victory. The bright gleam has caught the helmets of our soldiers, and warmed and cheered all our hearts. Now this is not the end. It is not even the beginning of the end. But it is, perhaps, the end of the beginning."

It was indeed the end of the beginning. From this point on, Allied pressure on the Axis was relentlessly applied on land and sea and in the air. By May 13, 1943, General Alexander reported that the Tunisian campaign was over, that "we are masters of the North African shores." One continent had been freed of the enemy.

Thenceforth Allied fortunes improved. Using Sicily as a stepping-stone, United States and British troops liberated Italy and regained a foothold in Europe.

The following June the supreme effort, the culmination of all the planning that had gone before, came when the greatest amphibious force ever assembled swarmed ashore on the Normandy beaches and began the long, slow march through France, Belgium, the Netherlands and Germany to the Elbe, where it met the Soviet army advancing from the east.

On May 8 Churchill broadcast the news of Germany's unconditional surrender, but warned that Japan "remains unsubdued."

Churchill recalled that night in his memoirs: "The unconditional surrender of our enemies was the signal for the greatest outburst of joy in the history of mankind. The Second World War had indeed been fought to the bitter end in Europe. The vanquished as well as the victors felt inexpressible relief.

"But for us in Britain and the British Empire, who had alone been in the struggle from the first day to the last and staked our existence on the result, there was a meaning beyond what even our most powerful and valiant Allies could feel. Weary and worn, impoverished but undaunted and now triumphant, we had a moment that was sublime. We gave thanks to God for the noblest of all His blessings, the sense that we had done our duty."

Unconditional surrender, insisted upon by Roosevelt at Casablanca and reluctantly accepted by Churchill, was regarded by some in Britain as an obstacle to an early end of the war. After Roosevelt's death the concept caused some heart-searching at the Potsdam conference when Stalin disclosed that he had received an offer of surrender from the Emperor of Japan through his ambassador in Moscow.

The message indicated that Japan could not accept unconditional surrender but might be prepared to settle on softer terms.

Churchill, in talks with Truman, dwelt upon the enormous loss of life that might be entailed if nothing less than complete surrender was required. He suggested giving the Japanese "some way of saving their military honor and some assurance of their national existence." To this Truman replied that he did not believe the Japanese had any military honor after Pearl Harbor.

It was then agreed to send an ultimatum bidding Japan surrender unconditionally or face total destruction. The ultimatum, published July 26, 1945, was followed by the dropping of leaflets over Japan warning of the impending danger, but not mentioning the nature of the weapon about to be dropped on Hiroshima and Nagasaki.

Churchill had been informed that an atomic device had been detonated in New Mexico. He saw in the weapon a means to speed the end to the war in the Far East and to eliminate the necessity of asking favors from Stalin.

With the ultimate weapon at hand, Churchill wrote in his memoirs, he had never any doubt that Truman would use it, "nor have I ever doubted since that he was right.

"To quell the Japanese resistance man by man and conquer the country yard by yard might well require the loss of a million American lives and half that number of British—or more if we could get them there: for we were resolved to share the agony. Now all this nightmare picture vanished."

Just before Potsdam an election had been scheduled. Churchill hoped to keep his government in power at least until Japan had been defeated, but the Labor party, now that the peril in Europe was over, was impatient for a test of domestic strength.

The campaign was not Churchill's most admirable, filled as it was with invective against his Laborite wartime colleagues. This dismayed many of his admirers.

On election day, July 25, he returned to London for the results, satisfied that "the British people would wish me to continue my work.

"However, just before dawn [of the 26th]," he recalls in his memoirs, "I awoke suddenly with a sudden sharp stab of almost physical pain. A hitherto unconscious conviction that we were beaten broke forth and dominated my mind. All the pressure of great events on and against which I had mentally so long maintained my 'flying speed' would cease and I should fall. The power to shape the future would be denied me."

So it was for almost six years.

AT "THEIR FINEST HOUR"

DREW MIDDLETON

OF ALL the wartime memories of Winston Churchill the most moving is that of June 18, 1940, when, from the last ditch, he sounded the call to attack.

The House of Commons was somber and subdued. Beams of sunlight fell across worried men on the benches. All the news was bad. France had fallen. The British Expeditionary Force, almost weaponless, stood on the beaches. The Royal Navy, badly mauled at Dunkirk, refitted. The Royal Air Force, outnumbered, waited.

Mr. Churchill stood with his hands grasping the lapels of his black jacket. The thick, confident voice began abruptly: "Mishter Shpeaker . . ."

There was a gibe at Mussolini, an offer of safe conduct for the Italian navy if it wanted to come through the Strait of Gibraltar to fight. There was the assurance that he saw "great reasons for vigilance and exertion but none whatever for panic or fear."

His confidence had an electric quality. Men saw hope instead of despair. The picture he painted was dour but challenging. Because he so clearly felt it himself, Churchill communicated the excitement and the nobility of the moment.

Not one of Britain's aims would be abandoned, Churchill said defiantly, not one of her fallen allies forgotten. On the benches M.P.s leaned forward. Each sentence brought fresh cheers as the prime minister moved into his peroration.

"Let us therefore brace ourselves to our duties, and so bear ourselves that, if the British Empire and its Commonwealth last for a thousand years, men will still say 'This was their finest hour.' "

There was an excited roar of cheers. Men felt that, even if they did not see how the war could be won, they were sure it would not be lost.

During that summer and fall, Churchill so personified Britain's spirit that it was slightly disconcerting to encounter him in person. In the mind he was a giant. To the eye he was short, brisk, pugnacious and cheerful.

Early one morning late in November, he emerged from his headquarters after a heavy air raid. A British officer passing with an American friend saluted.

Churchill touched his hat, said "Good morning" and started to enter his car. Then he turned. "Four," he said happily. "We got four of them last night."

Few things moved him more than the bravery of the Londoners who endured the bombing night after night. When he saw tiny Union Jacks stuck in the rubble or heard the people cheer him, his eyes filled.

Once he turned to Herbert Morrison and said, "What a people they are, what a great people! What have we done to deserve them?"

At the Casablanca conference in January 1943, there was a break in that jaunty resolution with which he bore his burdens.

When Franklin D. Roosevelt produced the slogan "unconditional surrender," Churchill was visibly startled and worried. Years later, in the quiet of 10 Downing Street, he growled: "Looked surprised, did I? Well, I was surprised."

Churchill's contacts with his fellow Britons were marked by a curious and endearing simplicity. The tongue that terrorized field marshals and admirals talked of simple things in an easy way. He was a most human being.

Over the years, until the twilight, one found him in many moods—mischievous, resolute, gossipy, emotional. Although he was a great historian, there was little interest in the past in his talk.

Just before he retired in 1955, he sat one evening in 10 Downing Street. His talk was all of the future, what would happen to the trades unions, how would the Soviet-Chinese relationship develop, would Aneurin Bevan become Labor's leader.

What made him a great war leader? To those who were there then, it was Churchill's blind, unswerving faith in his country and its people. He asked much of Britain. And, because the people understood and trusted, he was given much in return.

FROM HIS BIRTH AT BLENHEIM PALACE TO PRIME MINISTERSHIP IN THE CRISIS OF 1940

WINSTON CHURCHILL descended from John Churchill, first Duke of Marlborough (1650–1722), a great captain of history who never fought a battle he did not win nor besieged a city he did not take.

In his four-volume biography of Marlborough, Churchill drew a brilliant portrait of this great but devious character. The statesman and moral man of the world of the 20th century cast a keen but understanding eye on the statesman and amoral man of the world of the 17th and 18th centuries.

Churchill's Marlborough was first of all a military genius and a skillful diplomat. He was handsome, charming, courageous and self-possessed; a loving and dutiful husband after rakish earlier years; a man capable of humanity and kindness. He was also avaricious and politically treacherous, a solicitor and taker of bribes, large and small, who speculated on his soldiers' supplies.

Churchill showed him against the background of his times. For example, he took some of the sting out of the story that John Churchill got his start in the army because his sister, Arabella, was a mistress of the Duke of York.

"In those youthful days," he wrote, "John gained no office or promotion that might not have come to any young gentleman accepted at court. Nor shall we join the meretricious disputing about whether John received his commission before or after Arabella became the Duke's mistress. The Guards gained a good recruit officer in normal course."

Marlborough's most celebrated military victory was over the French at Blenheim, Bavaria, Aug. 13, 1704. A grateful Queen Anne ordered built for him a residence at Woodstock, near Oxford.

This ponderous and gloomy pile, Blenheim Palace, has depressed a long succession of Marlborough women, including Winston Churchill's mother. Marlborough left no male heir; his title passed in the female line through his daughters—first Henriette and then Anne, wife of Charles, Lord Spencer. Winston Churchill's full name was Winston Leonard Spencer Churchill.

Down the years the Spencer Churchill family made certain contributions to British history. But no firm tone was set until the appearance of Lord Randolph Churchill (1849–1895). He was the second surviving son of the seventh Duke of Marlborough, and the father of Winston Churchill.

Lord Randolph was Chancellor of the Exchequer in 1886 and seemed on his way to becoming prime minister. He possessed intuitive knowledge of politics, but his wit left scars.

Lord Randolph was a rugged debater in Commons. There he led a small Conservative party "ginger group." His specialty was baiting the somber Gladstone, leader of the Liberal party opposition and sometimes prime minister.

When Lord Randolph became Chancellor of the Exchequer, it was evident that his views were considerably more advanced in respect to social reform than those of Lord Salisbury, the prime minister.

"The final collision occurred over a comparatively trivial point [the budget's military and naval estimates]. He resigned on the eve of Christmas 1886 at the wrong time, on the wrong issue, and he made no attempt to rally support," his son wrote of the end of his father's political career.

Lord Randolph's political career lay far ahead of him at the moment when, at the age of 24, he met the future mother of Winston Churchill. A scintillating member of London's society (despite one or two disapproving frowns from Queen Victoria and a quarrel with the Prince of Wales), Lord Randolph missed few of the occasions of his day.

He was attending the Royal Yacht Squadron regatta at Cowes in August 1873 when he first saw Jennie Jerome of New York at a ball. A brunette beauty with sparkling dark eyes, she was a daughter of Leonard Walter Jerome, a New York financier and turfman.

Randolph proposed a day or two after the meeting. He was accepted. To his father he wrote that "she is nice, as lovable, and amiable and charming in every way as she is beautiful, and by her education and bringing-up she is in every way qualified to fill any position."

The Duke reacted brusquely: "From what you tell me & what I have heard this Mr. J. seems to be a sporting, and I should think, vulgar sort of man. I hear he & his two brothers are stockbrokers, one of them bears a *bad* reputation in commercial judgment in *this* country. I do not know, but it is evident that he is in a class of speculators; he has been bankrupt once, & may be so again."

Randolph finally won over his father and mother. He agreed to meet his father's stipulation that he would settle down and stand for Parliament. There was a bit of a fuss over the dowry. Although Jerome had run into hard luck on the market, he settled £50,000 (about $250,000) on the couple. All the income was to go to Randolph, who promised to give his wife £1,000 a year.

Winston Churchill wrote in his biography of his father: "On April 15, 1874, the marriage was celebrated at the British Embassy in Paris and after a tour—not too prolonged—upon the Continent, Lord Randolph returned in triumph with his bride to receive the dutiful laudations of the Borough of Woodstock and enjoy the leafy glories of Blenheim in the spring."

On Dec. 3, 1874, the *Times* of London printed the following among its birth announcements: "On 30th November at Blenheim Palace, the Lady Randolph Churchill, prematurely, of a son."

Winston Churchill was already a young man in a hurry. A ball (presumably attended by his mother) was held at Blenheim Nov. 30 and Winston was born in a first-floor room of the palace called Dean Jones's Room, in use at the time as a ladies' cloakroom.

At Blenheim, the child played soldier in the vast and drafty halls. He was undersized, sometimes shy, sometimes overassertive. He seemed to be able to learn nothing at school. He adored his brilliant father, who, however, was convinced by his son's school failures that the boy was retarded.

Few homes of the British aristocracy are child-oriented, and Winston saw little of his mother.

"My mother made a brilliant impression upon my childhood life," he said in his memoirs. "She shone for me like the evening star. I loved her dearly but at a distance. She always seemed to me like a fairy princess."

The boy became deeply attached to his nanny, Mrs. Everest. As he put it, "My nurse was my confidante and nearest and most intimate friend."

When he became one of the grand figures of his age, it was Mrs. Everest's picture that was over his desk.

Churchill's brother, John Strange Spencer-Churchill (the form of the Churchill name that he used) was born in February 1880. He was an amiable figure often known as Jack Churchill. He served with some distinction in South Africa and in World War I.

In 1908 he married Lady Gwendoline Theresa

Mary Bertie, daughter of the seventh Earl of Abingdon. A daughter, Anne Clarissa, was married to Sir Anthony Eden. Spencer-Churchill died in 1947.

At 7 Winston was sent to a school at Ascot. He was a sore trial to his masters. He would neither learn nor behave, and he was caned regularly. Caught stealing sugar from the pantry, he received the usual birching. This was repeated when, in revenge, he kicked the headmaster's straw hat to pieces. Sent to another school at Brighton, he discovered books and read everything he could get his hands on.

In 1888 he entered Harrow. When the boys filed past the headmaster in order of their academic standing, he was often at the end of the line. He became used to hearing visitors exclaim, "Why that's Randolph Churchill's boy and he's last!"

Gradually the more perceptive of his teachers began to sense that Winston was far from stupid. He could not come to grips with Latin and Greek and mathematics but he was the school's star in general knowledge. Nonetheless, he never got out of the lower form.

"However, by being so long in the lowest form, I gained an immense advantage over the cleverer boys," he recalled. "They all went on to learn Latin and Greek and splendid things like that. But I was taught English. I got into my bones the essential structure of an ordinary English sentence—which is a noble thing."

Winston was four and a half years at Harrow, and after three examination failures and prodigious cramming, he was finally admitted, in June 1893, to the Royal Military College, now the Royal Military Academy, at Sandhurst. Once there, he did well. He stood eighth in his class of 150 at the end of the courses.

Two years later he was commissioned a lieutenant and joined the Fourth Hussars at Aldershot. There seemed little immediate prospect of active service.

"All my money had been spent on polo ponies," he wrote. "I searched the world for some scene of adventure or excitement."

His eye lighted on Cuba and the fighting between the independence forces and the Spanish. Family connections helped him get clearance from the Spanish government. Lord Randolph had written for the *Daily Graphic*, and his son made use of this to get an assignment to report on the Cuban fighting. He was to get £5 an article.

In Cuba, near Trocham, on Nov. 29, 1895, the eve of his 21st birthday, Winston Churchill came under fire for the first time.

"On this day when we halted for breakfast every man sat by his horse and ate what he had in his pocket," he wrote later. "I had been provided with half a skinny chicken. I was engaged in gnawing the drumstick when suddenly, close at hand, almost in our faces it seemed, a ragged volley rang out from the edge of the forest. So at any rate I had been under fire. That was something."

After he returned to Britain his regiment was ordered to India and he went into garrison at Bangalore. He played polo and read seriously, stocking his mind by memorizing large sections of Bartlett's *Familiar Quotations*.

But he became restless. Through Gen. Sir Bindon Blood, a family friend, he found his way to the headquarters of the Malakand Field Force on the northwest frontier. There was action, and he wrote of an encounter with a Pathan: "I wore my cavalry sword well sharpened. After all, I had the public school fencing medal. The savage saw me coming. He picked up a big stone and hurled it at me with his left hand, and then awaited me, brandishing his sword. There were others waiting behind him and I changed my mind about the cold steel."

Churchill fired his pistol and took off.

A contemporary described him as "a slight, redheaded, freckled snub-nosed young subaltern, vehement, moody, quickly responsive, easily hurt, taciturn at times and at times quite opinionative with a tumbling flow of argument, confident to the point of complacency, but capable of generous self-sacrifice, proud but no snob."

After writing a book—it was his first—that was less than gently critical of the expedition's management, he turned to fiction. The result was his only novel, *Savrola: A Tale of the Revolution in Laurania*.

Savrola is a dashing young man—an understanding liberal who is nonetheless a traditionalist at heart. He bears a striking resemblance to Churchill's conception of himself.

"Would you rise in the world?" said Savrola. "You must work while others amuse themselves. Are you desirous of a reputation for courage? You must risk your life. Would you be strong morally or physically? You must resist temptations. All this is paying in advance; that is prospective finance. Observe the other side of the picture; the bad things are paid for afterward."

The novel, issued in 1900, was a moderate success and it was reprinted in 1956. The author had second thoughts about its literary merit, however. "I have consistently urged friends not to read it," he wrote later.

Having acquired a taste for battle, Churchill sought more, this time in Egypt, where Kitchener was leading a British force slowly up the Nile into the Sudan. Churchill's reputation for aiming journalistic barbs at generals had preceded him, and Kitchener would have none of him.

Churchill invoked his mother's influence in London. "Many were the pleasant luncheons and dinners attended by the powers in those days which occupied two months of strenuous negotiations."

Finally, Prime Minister Salisbury yielded and asked Kitchener to let Churchill join his force. He was classed as a supernumerary officer and he was also a correspondent for the *Morning Post*.

Having agreed to foot his own hospital and burial expenses, he was assigned to the 21st Lancers in time for the Battle of Omdurman on Sept. 2, 1898. He was up early that day.

"Talk of fun! Where will you beat this! On horseback at daybreak, within shot of an advancing enemy and seeing everything."

He charged with his Lancers, pistol in hand (a shoulder injury prevented his wielding a saber), and went through the slashing, stabbing struggle.

The British victory virtually ended the war.

At loose ends after the Sudan, Churchill considered going to Oxford, but he lacked sufficient Latin and Greek. Instead, he opted for India, where he served briefly. He then resigned his commission and determined to enter politics.

The year was 1899. When he applied to the Conservative party for a Commons seat to contest, he was not widely known and had only about enough spare money to pay his election expenses.

He was assigned to contest a vacancy in Oldham, a dreary Manchester industrial suburb. He lost—the first of five defeats as against 19 victories—but he was not disheartened.

"Live and learn!" he wrote later. "I think I might say without conceit that I was in those days a pretty good candidate. However, when the votes were counted, we were well beaten."

It took another war, however, for Churchill to fix himself firmly in British politics. This was the Boer War, brought on when the Boers in South Africa ordered British troops away from their frontiers and the British refused.

"The Boer ultimatum had not ticked out on the tape machine for an hour when Oliver Borthwick [editor of the *Morning Post*] came to offer me an appointment as principal war correspondent, £250 a month, all expenses paid," he wrote.

Churchill had scarcely reached the South African province of Natal when he suffered the ignominy of being captured on an armored train and put, a prisoner of war, in the State Model Schools in Pretoria. After four weeks, however, he escaped by climbing a wall.

"I said to myself," he recalled, " '*toujours de l'audace,*' put my hat on my head, strode into the middle of the garden, walked past the windows of the house without any attempt at concealment, and so went through the gate. I passed the sentry at less than five yards."

Free with £74 in his pocket and four slabs of chocolate, he hopped a freight train without any notion of where it was heading. In the morning he left it (and the coal sacks on which he had slept) at Witbank, in the Transvaal, to seek food and shelter.

To a householder at whose door he knocked, he said he was a Boer lost from his command, but the tale didn't wash, "so I took the plunge and threw all I had upon the board."

"I am Winston Churchill, war correspondent of the *Morning Post*," he confessed. "I escaped last night from Pretoria. I have plenty of money. Will you help me?"

Fortunately, the man, Frank Howard, manager of the Transvaal Collieries, proved sympathetic. He took Churchill down into a coal mine, leaving him with some candles, a bottle of whiskey and a box of cigars.

Meanwhile, his Pretoria escape was discovered, and the Boers sent out a circular offering £25 for his apprehension. He had, the notice said, "a small, hardly noticeable mustache, talks through his nose and cannot pronounce the letter *S* properly."

After a couple of days in the mine, Howard got the bedraggled correspondent onto another freight train, where he hid between two bales of wool until it reached neutral Portuguese East Africa and the city of Lourenço Marques, whence, after getting help from the British consul, he went to Durban.

An astonishing acclaim greeted him. "I reached Durban to find myself a popular hero. I was received as if I had won a great victory. I was nearly torn to pieces by enthusiastic kindness. Sheaves of telegrams from all parts of the world poured in on me."

However, it was with reluctance that the British military permitted him to continue as a correspondent as well as a temporary lieutenant in the South African Light Horse, an irregular force. He was thus on hand for the relief of Ladysmith, the battles in the Orange Free State and hard skirmishing in the Transvaal. He returned to London in the late summer of 1900.

His plan was to reenter politics, but first there was a quick lecture trip in the United States under the sponsorship of Mark Twain. Churchill and Mark Twain had never met and it was suggested that they should confer in private for an hour or so before dinner to become acquainted. Both men preferred talking to listening and each liked to dominate the conversation. Friends waiting for the Churchill-Mark Twain causerie to end were making bets on which would outtalk the other.

Mark Twain was the first to emerge. He looked bemused and beaten, and Churchill was at his heels with, "As I was saying, sir . . ."

Churchill made $10,000 and expenses on this tour, the first of several in America. He gave most of the $10,000 to his banker friend, Sir Ernest Cassel, to invest for him.

In the election of 1900 a total of 11 Parliamentary constituencies offered Churchill a chance to contest them, but with typical stubbornness he chose Oldham, the scene of his earlier defeat. He was asked by many leaders of his party to speak in their districts.

The campaign in Oldham became so raucous that it attracted national attention. Churchill's Boer War adventures were told and retold. "Soldiers of the Queen" had been a popular song and it became Churchill's theme song. The bands played either this or "See, the Conquering Hero Comes!" Girls wore blue sashes emblazoned "God Bless Churchill, England's Noblest Hero."

T. E. Dunville, the music-hall comedian, reminded audiences:

You've heard of Winston Churchill:
That is all I need to say—
He's the latest and the greatest
Correspondent of the day.

However, despite Churchill's martial allure, he just scraped in; and on June 23, 1901, at the age of 26, he entered the House of Commons, part of the 134-vote majority of the Conservative party.

Great interest centered on the new M.P. His father was well remembered and everyone wondered what his son would do. A fellow M.P. said that "Churchill had not been in the Commons for five minutes until he was seen to lean back, tip his top hat over his forehead, cross his legs, bury his hands in his pockets and survey the scene as if he were the oldest, not the youngest member."

New members were not supposed to speak until they had been on hand at least a month, but Churchill got the Speaker's eye and was on his feet four days after he had been sworn in. The Boer War was still on—it was not to end until June 1902—and reference to it in debate gave Churchill a chance to speak.

He stood, lean and red-haired, in a long frock coat with satin lapels. Whether by design or naturally, his gestures recalled his father's. Like his hero, Savrola, "he showed or perhaps he feigned, some nervousness at first, and here and there in his sentences he paused as if searching for a word."

However, he had prepared his speech and had memorized it.

Early in his speech he made a gallant reference to the men he had fought in South Africa by saying, "If I were a Boer fighting in the field—and if I were a Boer I hope I should be fighting in the field— . . ."

Then he went on: "I earnestly hope that the Colonial Secretary will leave nothing undone to bring home to those brave and unhappy men who are still fighting in the field that whenever they are prepared to recognize that their small independence must be merged in the larger liberties of the British Empire, there will be a full guarantee for the security of their property and religion."

The brisk give-and-take of Commons was the breath of life to Churchill. He once called Aneurin Bevan a "squalid nuisance" and referred to the politically supple Ramsay MacDonald as "the boneless wonder."

One of Churchill's most vigorous and durable feuds was with the American-born Lady Astor. There is a story that the exchange between them once became so sulphurous that Lady Astor burst out: "If you were my husband, I'd put poison in your coffee."

"If you were my wife, I'd drink it," Churchill shot back.

Churchill's speeches in Parliament and elsewhere seemed to many to have been delivered extemporaneously. However, according to Lord Birkenhead, Churchill "spent the best years of his life writing his impromptu speeches."

Never a blind follower, Churchill progressively became a problem to his party leaders. His views on social reform were somewhat advanced, and he was soon a leading light in a "ginger group," called the Hughlighans, after one of their number, Lord Hugh Cecil. He began to take pot shots at Balfour, the prime minister, and his position as a Conservative grew untenable.

In a dramatic scene May 31, 1903, Churchill entered the House, glanced at the Conservative bench, bowed to the Speaker and "crossed the floor" amid Tory catcalls to join the Liberal party amid their cheers.

His reward came in the election of 1905, when the Liberals swept into power with a 356-seat majority and he was appointed Under Secretary for the Colonies. Two years later, at the age of 32, he was made a Privy Councillor.

Characteristically, the new under secretary toured the colonies, arranging to write magazine articles about his travels. Lacking a private fortune, he supported himself by such articles and by lecturing. Indeed, he needed the money, for he liked London's social life, good food, the best brandy and cigars, polo and the turf.

Standing for the first time as a Liberal in the election of 1906, Churchill ran in Manchester Northwest and won, although assailed as a Conservative turncoat. Two years later, however, things went badly for him over the issue of women's suffrage. He opposed it; his opponent was for it. With the lusty help of the suffragettes, including, naturally, Sylvia Pankhurst, Churchill lost.

This was by no means his last encounter with that determined band of women. Later, in 1910, when he was home secretary with general supervision of the London police, he was involved in the suffragette "Black Friday" when a riotous group of women surrounded Prime Minister Asquith near 10 Downing Street, and the police, only with difficulty, hustled him to safety in a taxicab.

Churchill was stationed nearby, watching the fray and ordering the police, at one point, to drive a woman away. On several occasions thereafter he was attacked by women wielding umbrellas, but he managed to escape unscathed, except politically, for the Tories taunted him in the House over "Black Friday."

Meanwhile, after his defeat in Manchester Northwest, Churchill bounced back by winning a by-election in Dundee, which caused his colleagues in Commons to greet him with the cry of "Marmalade!"—the well-known product of that constituency.

Under Asquith, Churchill received a full cabinet post, president of the Board of Trade.

It so happened that the Countess of Airlie, who had made herself useful to Churchill in Dundee, had a very attractive granddaughter, Clementine Ogilvy Hozier. Miss Hozier was a daughter of Sir Henry Montague Hozier and Lady Henrietta Blanche Hozier, daughter of the seventh Earl of Airlie.

Churchill and Miss Hozier were married at St. Margaret's, Westminster, Sept. 12, 1908. He had been a full cabinet minister since April and the wedding was a considerable social event. King Edward VII and Queen Alexandra and members of the cabinet sent presents. Lord Hugh Cecil, Churchill's colleague in the Hughlighans, was his best man.

After a few days at Blenheim and a brief trip to Lake Maggiore, the Churchills took up residence in a house in Queens Gate, London. Churchill called his wife Clemmie, and she was standing at his side at the window of their home on his 90th birthday.

In October 1910, Asquith offered Churchill the post of Secretary for Ireland, but, as more than one politician had ended his career in this job, Churchill neatly sidestepped. Asquith made him home secretary instead. This was one of the key cabinet offices—often a step toward the prime ministership.

A coal miners' strike in Wales posed difficulties. After several incidents Churchill had troops sent before local authorities requested them, a move for which he was widely criticized, although the intervention restored order without casualties.

On the morning of Jan. 3, 1911, Churchill was summoned to the telephone from his bath. Girt with a towel, he heard that suspected anarchists were exchanging shots with the police from a house in Sidney Street.

After ordering a battalion of the Scots Guards and two field guns to the scene, Churchill dressed and appeared in Sidney Street in a silk hat and fur-collared overcoat. Several photographers recorded the scene. A desultory exchange of shots ended when the building caught fire. Two bodies, one of a man killed by bullet wounds and the other of a man who had suffocated, were found inside.

The episode produced laughter from the Opposition in Commons. It was charged that the home secretary had turned a simple police action into something resembling war.

In later years Churchill gained so exalted a position in the admiration and affection of his countrymen that it is hard to remember that he was not always so regarded. At various times in his career, he was widely suspected and disliked. When he was a war correspondent and soldier, for instance, he was called a medal snatcher and glory hunter.

In politics, the Conservatives considered him an opportunist for deserting the party of his father. Some of the Liberals regarded him as a Johnny-come-lately in the cause of social reform. He was also thought of as too facile and glib. Stanley Baldwin once referred to "Winston's 100-horsepower mind."

On Oct. 23, 1911, Churchill became First Lord of the Admiralty, the cabinet head of the navy. Having been acquainted with Britain's naval problems, he took steps to spur the modernization of her ships and organization. His prescience was responsible for the fact that naval units were at their posts and battle-ready when World War I opened.

Recalling the war's beginning, Churchill wrote: "It was 11 o'clock at night—12 by German time [Aug. 4, 1914] when the [British] ultimatum expired. The windows of the Admiralty were thrown wide open in the warm night air. Under the roof from which Nelson had received his orders were gathered a small group of admirals and captains and a cluster of clerks, pencils in hand, waiting.

"Along the Mall from the direction of [Buckingham Palace] the sound of an immense concourse singing 'God Save the King' floated in. On this deep wave there broke the chimes of Big Ben and, as the first stroke of the hour boomed out, a rustle of movement swept across the room. The war telegram, which meant 'Commence hostilities against Germany,' was flashed to the ships and establishments under the White Ensign all over the world.

"I walked across the Horse Guards Parade to the Cabinet Room and reported to the Prime Minister and the Ministers who were assembled there that the deed was done."

When the war began, Churchill was besieged by friends or friends of friends who wanted commissions in the Naval Division. Bernard Freyberg, who had been a dental mechanic in San Francisco, told Churchill a tall tale about having fought in Mexico with Pancho Villa and got a commission. He became one of the best natural military commanders of his day, won a Victoria Cross, became a full general and was elevated to the peerage as Baron Freyberg for his World War II services.

The young Cambridge poet, Rupert Brooke, was also a friend and he was commissioned in the Naval Division. He wrote "The Soldier," which so well summed up British feeling in 1914. It begins:

> *If I should die, think only this of me:*
> *That there's some corner of a foreign field*
> *That is forever England . . .*

When the bugles of battle sounded it was agony for Churchill to be out of the fighting. He accompanied the Naval Division on the expedition to relieve Antwerp, but he was a civilian and had no military uniform. Instead, he wore that of an Elder Brother of Trinity House, a venerable guild of lighthouse inspectors. This gave rise to a report in Antwerp that the elder brother of the Trinity had come to the city's aid. He pleaded for a commission and to command the expedition, but in vain, and he returned to the Admiralty in London.

As a naval strategist, he was convinced that the considerable British sea power reserve could be utilized to relieve pressure on the main ground-war fronts on the Continent while at the same time finding and exploiting the flanks of the Central Powers.

The possibility of action in the Mediterranean, so stimulating to Nelson and Napoleon, caught Churchill's imagination, too. The operation that seemed to offer the greatest possibilities was the forcing of the Dardanelles.

The Strait of the Dardanelles unites the Aegean with the Sea of Marmara and controls the approaches to Istanbul, then called Constantinople, and entrance into the Black Sea. The European side of the strait is formed by the Gallipoli Peninsula, a tongue of land 63 miles long. Its possession assures control of the Dardanelles.

A twofold result might be gained from the opening of the Dardanelles. A helping hand could be extended through the Black Sea to Russia and it might be possible to raise the Balkans in the rear of Austria-Hungary and Germany. As it happened, though, the Dardanelles nearly ended Churchill's political career.

On March 18, 1915, a combined British and French fleet attempted to force the Dardanelles with disastrous results and heavy losses in ships and lives. The first infantry units fought their way onto the Gallipoli Peninsula April 25. Other landings followed, and there were months of desperate fighting. Incompetence and ill luck dogged the British efforts. A British general got his men ashore and, instead of moving immediately to seize commanding heights overlooking the beach, let his men go swimming. The Turks managed to get men on the heights during the night and the British attack the next day failed.

It was moments like this that were anguish to Churchill in the London Admiralty headquarters.

He knew he was right, but the atmosphere about him began to cool.

Soon the Dardanelles campaign reached a sort of befuddled standstill. "From this slough I was not able to lift the operation. All the negative forces began to band themselves together," he wrote. "The 'No' principle had become established in men's minds and nothing could ever eradicate it."

Churchill recalled that a War Council meeting May 14, 1915, was "sulphurous."

The ground was cut from under Churchill on the Dardanelles when he was deserted by his chief technical adviser, Admiral Lord Fisher.

A munitions shortage and general dissatisfaction with the conduct of the war forced Asquith to form a coalition government a few days later. Churchill was succeeded at the Admiralty by Arthur Balfour, a Conservative. It was probably the lowest point in Churchill's career. He was subsequently cleared by a board of inquiry of sole responsibility for the Dardanelles failure but that was much later and the damage had been done.

Churchill remained in the government as Chancellor of the Duchy of Lancaster, a sinecure. Within five months he resigned from the cabinet.

He thereupon got a major's commission and went to the front for a refresher course with a battalion of the Grenadier Guards.

There was little or no fighting in that sector, and after he got his battalion smartened up, Churchill spent some time in his dugout in France in an old blue civilian raincoat listening to classical records on a gramophone.

Meantime, Lloyd George managed to bring down the Asquith government and became prime minister Dec. 6, 1916. He wanted Churchill in his cabinet but dared not include him because of the uproar over the Dardanelles. However, he did manage to get him in as minister of munitions in July 1917.

Churchill was in that post when the Armistice was signed Nov. 11, 1918.

"On the night of the Armistice I dined with the Prime Minister at Downing Street," Churchill wrote. "We were alone in the large room from whose walls the portraits of Pitt and Fox, of Nelson and Wellington, and—perhaps somewhat incongruously—of Washington then looked down. My own mood was divided between anxiety for the future and desire to help the fallen foe. From outside the songs and cheers of the multitudes could be remotely heard like the surf on the shore."

After the general election of 1918 Lloyd George reorganized his cabinet and Churchill became secretary for war. No more thankless task could have been given to anybody at that moment.

There were mutinies in France and Britain. Riding in Hyde Park, King George V was surrounded by a disorderly crowd of soldiers and an attempt was made to pull him from his horse. Churchill had to use detachments of Guards to restore order among the more than 3,000 soldiers on the Horse Guards Parade.

Meantime, the specter that had been haunting Europe since 1848 materialized in Imperial Russia when Lenin's Communists seized power in November 1917. Once the outlines of the new regime became evident, Churchill grew alarmed. Trustful of the common man though he was, he was not prepared to trust Lenin's version of the same abstraction. Of the Russian Revolution, he wrote: "Meanwhile the German hammer broke down the front and Lenin blew up the rear. Could any man have made head at once against this double assault? All broke, all collapsed, all liquefied in the universal bubble and approaching cannonade, and out of this anarchy emerged the one coherent, frightful entity and fact—the Bolshevik punch!"

Churchill was convinced of the need for armed intervention to aid the White Russian counterrevolutionaries. Small forces under British command, composed chiefly of British and American troops, did occupy Murmansk and Archangel, but the Red Army in the end prevailed. These expeditions, and Churchill's role in them, were still sharp in the memories of Soviet leaders 20 years afterward, and they contributed to Russian suspicions of Churchill in World War II.

Politics gave Churchill a breathing spell in 1922.

Lloyd George was toppled by the Conservatives under Bonar Law. For the first time since 1900 Churchill was without a seat in Commons.

Vastly annoyed, he contested the Leicester West Division in 1923, but lost.

A bitter moment in Churchill's career came in 1924. He had been twice beaten for a Commons seat. He then posed his candidature in the Abbey Division of Westminster, in which the Houses of Parliament are situated, and one considered safely Conservative.

Churchill ran as an Independent and exerted himself to the utmost to win. Many of his Tory friends helped him. But when the votes were counted he had lost by 43 votes out of 22,778 cast.

Meantime, he was edging his way back toward the Conservative party and he had run as an Independent.

By 1924 Churchill believed that the Liberal party had become so infiltrated by Socialists that it could no longer afford him a spiritual home. Moreover, it was going into eclipse because of factional strife.

The same year Churchill stood in the general election from the Epping Division of Essex as a Constitutionalist. There was a Conservative sweep and Churchill won. He did not expect to be asked to join the Baldwin government. However, Baldwin called him to his office and said, "Will you take the Chancellor?"

Thinking it was the general utility post of Chancellor of the Duchy of Lancaster, Churchill said: "Of the Duchy?"

"No," Baldwin replied, "Chancellor of the Exchequer."

Churchill was well and truly out of the political wilderness.

He went home and dug out the robes of office worn by his father as Chancellor of the Exchequer in 1886. They did him very well on the rare occasions that he had to wear them.

Churchill obtained the backing of Baldwin in restoring the pound to its prewar value. Britain had gone off the gold standard as a war measure. Churchill's act temporarily strengthened Britain's credit but it hurt the country's export trade.

In the coal-mining industry the return to the gold standard threatened to price coal out of the export market. Prices had to be cut, and the mine owners, in turn, cut wages.

This was one of the chief causes of the great General Strike of 1926. It was touched off when printers of the *Daily Mail* refused to set an editorial headed "For King and Country" condemning the threatened strike. Three million British workers quit their jobs May 3 to protest pay cuts for the miners.

Many of the newspapers were shut down. Churchill was assigned to put out an emergency newspaper, the *British Gazette*. He took over the building of the old *Morning Post* just off the Strand, installed himself as editor and laid hands on as much newsprint as he could find.

It became the fashionable thing to do late at night to go down to the Post Building and watch and listen to Churchill put out the *British Gazette*. The *Gazette* made no pretense of printing anything but the government's side of the strike.

The *British Gazette* ran for seven issues before the general strike was ended. Its circulation reached 1,801,400 before it was discontinued.

The most highly publicized duty of the Chancellor of the Exchequer is to present, or "open," the budget in Commons. Churchill presented five budgets in all. The advice that he followed was from highly orthodox financial and economic sources.

In 1924, Churchill ran and won in Epping as a Conservative. He held to his seat in the same constituency in 1929, 1931 and 1935.

He was never again without a Commons seat until his retirement in 1964. After the election of 1935 he was returned from the nearby Woodford Division in 1945, 1950, 1951, 1955 and 1959.

Churchill and Baldwin reached the parting of the ways in 1929, and in June, Churchill resigned from the cabinet. Baldwin was riding along with what was believed to be the country's mood of pacifism, but this was not Churchill's. His political luck held. If he had stayed with Baldwin, he would have had to share some of the criticism of Baldwin's failure to seek rearmament in the face of the rising Hitler threat.

"But I was neither surprised nor unhappy when I was left out of it," Churchill recalled. "What I should have done if I had been asked to stay I cannot tell. It is superfluous to discuss doubtful temptations that have never existed."

In the Churchill of the early 1930s—portly, middle-aged and at times somewhat pugnacious—dignity joined with a youthful spirit to mold the figure the world was to know in World War II. Someone said of him then that he was "half Pitt and half Puck."

King Edward VIII ascended the throne on Jan. 30, 1936, on the death of his father, George V. It soon became known that Edward wished to marry Mrs. Wallis Warfield Simpson, a divorced American with one former husband living and a second divorce in prospect. Baldwin told the king that attempts to obtain Parliamentary consent to a marriage might result in a general election, with the monarch's private life the main issue. Edward was dismayed and confused.

Churchill had always held the monarchy in great respect and esteem. He championed the king's cause in Commons and sought more time for him to decide, and in one tumultuous session underwent the unusual experience of being shouted down. After Edward had abdicated on Dec. 10, 1936, Churchill recalled that as home secretary he had proclaimed Edward's title as Prince of Wales.

"I should have been ashamed if, in my independent and unofficial position, I had not cast about for every lawful means, even the most forlorn, to keep him on the throne of his fathers."

During this period it was generally assumed that Britain would not be menaced by a major war for years to come. However, by 1932 Hitler was a rising power in Germany, calling for rearmament to reverse the terms of the Versailles Treaty. Churchill said in Commons that year: "The demand is that Germany should be allowed to rearm. Do not let the Government delude themselves by supposing that which Germany is asking for is equal status. All these bands of splendid Teutonic youth marching to and fro in Germany, with the light of desire to suffer for their fatherland in their eyes, are not looking for status. They are looking for weapons."

He went on to predict that their demands would "shake to their foundations every country in the world."

Two years later Churchill attacked the limited funds allowed for increasing Britain's air power.

"We are, it is admitted, the fifth air power only—if that. Germany is arming fast and no one is going to stop her. She is going to arm; she is doing it. I dread the day when the means of threatening the heart of the British Empire should pass into the hands of the present rulers of Germany."

On May 3, 1935, Commons was told that Germany had reached at least theoretical air parity with Britain. Soon after this the Baldwin government proposed increases in the country's air capability. Churchill regarded the proposal as inadequate, and asked, "Why, then, not fight for something that will give us safety? Why, then, not insist that the provision for the air force should be adequate?"

Describing his attitude, he recalled, "Although the House listened to me with close attention, I felt a sensation of despair. To be so entirely convinced and vindicated in a matter of life and death to one's country, and not to be able to make Parliament and the nation heed the warning, or bow to the proof by taking action, was an experience most painful."

Nor did he confine his warnings to his countrymen. In 1937 he had an interview with Ribbentrop, the German ambassador to the Court of St. James. Ribbentrop told him that Germany wanted a free hand in eastern Europe. She must have living space for her increasing population. All that Germany asked of the British Commonwealth and Empire was not to interfere. Churchill made clear his belief that Britain would give no such assurances.

To this Ribbentrop replied, "In that case, war is inevitable."

Churchill retorted: "When you talk of war, which, no doubt, would be a general war, you must not underrate England. She is a curious country and few foreigners can understand her mind. Do not judge by the attitude of the present Administration. Once a great cause is presented to the people, all kinds of unexpected actions might be taken by this very Government and by the British nation."

Meanwhile, Hitler reoccupied the Rhineland in March 1936, and two years later to the month took over Austria.

To Churchill the peril to his country was ever more real.

"All this time the vast degeneration of the forces of Parliamentary democracy will be proceeding throughout Europe. Every six weeks another corps will be added to the German army. All this time important countries, great rail and river communications will pass under the control of the German General Staff.

"All this time populations will be continually reduced to the rigors of Nazi domination and assimilated to that system. All this time the forces of conquest and intimidation will be consolidated, towering up soon in real and not make-believe strength and superiority.

"For five years I have talked to the House on these matters—not with very great success. I have watched this famous island descending incontinently, fecklessly, the stairway which leads to a dark gulf. It is a fine broad stairway at the beginning, but after a bit the carpet ends. A little farther on there are only flagstones, and a little farther on still these break under your feet.

"Look back upon the last five years—since, that is to say, Germany began to rearm in earnest and openly to seek revenge. If we study the history of Rome and Carthage, we can understand what happened and why. It is not difficult to understand and form an intelligent view about the three Punic Wars; but if mortal catastrophe should overtake the British nation and the British Empire, historians a thousand years hence will still be baffled by the mystery of our affairs.

"They will never understand how it was that a victorious nation, with everything in hand, suffered themselves to be brought low, and to cast away all they had gained by measureless sacrifice and absolute victory—'gone with the wind!'

"Now the victors are the vanquished, and those who threw down their arms in the field and sued for an armistice are striding on to world mastery. That is the position—that is the terrible transformation that has taken place bit by bit."

In 1938 British and French appeasement of Hitler resulted in the partition of Czechoslovakia. Churchill was distraught, seeing with frightening clarity the war in its chrysalis: "The partition of Czechoslovakia under pressure from England and France amounts to the complete surrender of the Western democracies to the Nazi threat of force. Such a collapse will bring peace or security neither to England nor to France. On the contrary it will place these two nations in an ever-weaker and more dangerous situation.

"The belief that security can be obtained by throwing a small state to the wolves is a fatal delusion."

In April 1939, with Europe on the brink of war, he sounded one of his final and most eloquent warnings.

"The danger is now very near. A great part of Europe is to a very large extent mobilized. Millions of men are being prepared for war. Everywhere the frontier defenses are manned. Everywhere it is felt that some new stroke is impending. If it should fall, can there be any doubt but that we shall be involved? We are no longer where we were two or three months ago. We have committed ourselves in every direction, rightly in my opinion, having regard to all that has happened.

"Surely then, when we aspire to lead all Europe back from the verge of the abyss on to the uplands of law and peace, we must ourselves set the highest example. We must keep nothing back. How can we bear to continue to lead our comfortable easy life here at home, unwilling even to pronounce the word 'compulsion,' unwilling even to take the necessary measure by which the armies that we have promised can alone be recruited?

"How can we continue—let me say it with particular frankness and sincerity—with less than the full force of the nation incorporated in the governing instrument?"

The world war began Sept. 1, 1939. After some light prodding by Churchill, Chamberlain named him First Lord of the Admiralty, a post he assumed on Sept. 3.

"I therefore sent word to the Admiralty that I would take charge forthwith. On this, the board were kind enough to signal to the Fleet, 'Winston is back.'

"So it was that I came again to the room I had quitted in pain and sorrow almost exactly a quarter of a century before."

His removal from the Admiralty in 1915 over the Gallipoli incident had left such scars that when he was First Lord once more, he had passing moments of self-doubt and fear. Such a moment came when he was returning to London after a visit to the fleet in Scotland. He had just learned that the navy had lost the aircraft carrier *Courageous*.

"We had a picnic lunch on the way by a stream," he wrote later. "I felt oppressed with my memories.

"No one had ever been over such a terrible course twice with such an interval between. No one had felt its dangers and responsibilities from the summit as I had or, to descend to a small point, understood how First Lords of the Admiralty are treated when great ships are sunk and things go wrong. If we were in fact going over the same cycle a second time, should I once again have to endure the pangs of dismissal?"

As First Lord he had the responsibility for dispatching sea and land forces to check the German thrust into Norway. The British undertaking was unsuccessful, a fact made all the more galling because at its beginning Chamberlain had assured the nation that "Hitler has missed the bus."

When the early passive phases of the war ended in the spring of 1940, and the Germans invaded the Netherlands, Belgium and France, Chamberlain submitted his resignation.

In his recollections of that May 10, Churchill wrote: "Presently a message arrived summoning me to [Buckingham] Palace. It only takes two minutes to drive from the Admiralty along the Mall. Although I suppose the evening papers must have been full of the terrific news from the Continent, nothing had been mentioned about a Cabinet crisis. The public had not had time to take in what was happening either abroad or at home, and there was no crowd about the Palace gate.

"I was taken immediately to the King. His Majesty received me most graciously and bade me sit down. He looked at me searchingly and quizzically for some moments, and then said: 'I suppose you don't know why I have sent for you?' Adopting his mood, I replied: 'Sir, I simply couldn't imagine why.' He laughed and said: 'I want to ask you to form a Government.' I said I would certainly do so."

That is how Churchill became prime minister.

IN OPPOSITION: Counselor to the West, Foe of Communism, Historian, Painter

"IN DEFEAT: defiance." This apothegm of his own devising Churchill put to practice when war-weary British voters turned him out of the prime ministership within 80 days of the apotheosis of his career, the surrender of Germany.

Stunned, unbelieving at first, the 71-year-old war leader toyed with retirement from politics to bask as an elder statesman, to paint, to write, to live benignly with his wife at Chartwell, his estate in his beloved Kent. At first, too, he took his defeat with ill humor, declining King George VI's offer of the Order of the Garter and peevishly denouncing

Labor's victory as "one of the greatest disasters that has smitten us in our long and checkered history."

To quit the combat and sulk, however, had never been his characteristic, nor was it now, and in October he was telling his fellow Conservatives: "I have naturally considered very carefully what is my own duty in these times. It would be easy for me to retire gracefully in an odor of civic freedom, and this plan crossed my mind frequently some months ago. I feel now, however, that the situation is so serious and what may have to come so grave that I am resolved to go forward carrying the flag as long as I have the necessary strength and energy and have your confidence."

Domestic politics aside, there was another, and perhaps weightier, reason that impelled him to carry on. Explaining it in 1951, he said: "If I remain in public life at this juncture, it is because, rightly or wrongly, but sincerely, I believe that I may be able to make an important contribution to the prevention of a third world war and to bring nearer that lasting peace settlement which the masses of people of every race and in every land so fervently desire."

Thus, Churchill was soon back in the political fray he loved so much, combating Socialism at home and Communism in the world with an energy scarce diminished by the toll of his wartime exertions.

Less than a year after he became leader of the Opposition, he appeared, as the guest of Truman, at obscure Westminster College in an even obscurer Fulton, Mo., "to give true and faithful counsel" to the West. His words on that budding March 5 spring day exploded around the world, heralding the Arctic chill of the Cold War.

Speaking as the war's Grand Alliance, so painfully carpentered, lay virtually shattered by recrudescent Soviet ambitions and by the unleashing of the universe's basic force at Hiroshima, Churchill's words resembled those of a sibylline oracle.

"From Stettin on the Baltic to Trieste in the Adriatic an iron curtain has descended across the Continent. Behind that line lie all the capitals of the ancient states of Central and Eastern Europe—Warsaw, Berlin, Prague, Vienna, Budapest, Belgrade, Bucharest and Sofia—all these famous cities and the populations around them lie in what I must call the Soviet sphere and are all subject in one form or another not only to Soviet influence but to a very high and in many cases increasing measure of control from Moscow.

"On the other hand I repulse the idea that a new war is inevitable; still more that it is imminent. It is because I am sure that our fortunes are still in our own hands and that we hold the power to save the future that I feel the duty to speak out now that I have the occasion and the opportunity to do so. I do not believe that Soviet Russia desires war. What they desire is the fruits of war and the indefinite expansion of their power and doctrines.

"Our difficulties and dangers will not be removed by closing our eyes to them. They will not be removed by mere waiting to see what happens, nor will they be removed by a policy of appeasement. What is needed is a settlement, and the longer this is delayed, the more difficult it will be, and the greater our dangers will become. . . .

"From what I have seen of our Russian friends and allies during the war, I am convinced there is nothing they admire so much as strength, and there is nothing for which they have less respect than for weakness, especially military weakness."

In place of a "quivering, precarious balance of power to offer its temptation to ambition or adventure," he proposed a partnership of the English-speaking peoples in the United States and the British Commonwealth that would be "an overwhelming assurance of security." If the English-speaking peoples and the European democracies stood together in adherence to the principles of the United Nations, no one was likely to molest them. If they failed or faltered "catastrophe may overwhelm us all."

"Last time I saw it all coming and cried aloud to my own fellow countrymen and to the world, but no one paid any attention. Up till the year 1933 or even 1935 Germany might have been saved from the awful fate which has overtaken her and we might all have been spared the miseries Hitler let loose upon mankind. There never was a war in all history easier to prevent by timely action than the one which has just desolated such great areas of the globe."

The Soviet drive for expansion of Communist power and doctrines that Churchill divined soon came to pass. There was strife in Greece, but she was saved for the West, as was Turkey, by timely American aid. The West began to coalesce, to shape a policy of help for freedom-loving nations, to draw the lines of containment, to concert military plans for the common defense.

Before these were consolidated, however, Czechoslovakia passed into the Muscovite orbit and the teeming millions of China came under Communist rule. The French were tumbled from Indochina, and Korea was only half saved. In less than 10 years after the war the world was riven—East and West. Where peace should have dwelt, armies patrolled; where victory's harmony had hinted goodwill among men, emotions of Armageddon prevailed.

Churchill echoed the fears and feelings of many in the West in those years in a speech in 1949.

"We are now confronted with something quite as wicked but in some ways more formidable than Hitler because Hitler had only the Herrenvolk pride and the anti-Semitic hatred to exploit. He had no fundamental theme. But these 13 men in the Kremlin have their hierarchy and a church of Communist adepts, whose missionaries are in every country as a fifth column, obscure people, but awaiting the day when they hope to be absolute masters of their fellow countrymen and pay off old scores.

"They have their anti-God religion and their Communist doctrine of the absolute subjugation of the individual to the state, and behind this stands the largest army in the world in the hands of a government pursuing imperialist aggression as no Czar or Kaiser has ever done."

Earlier, Churchill placed the force of his prestige behind the creation of a new European unity, with Franco-German amity its cornerstone and with a leading role for Britain. His wartime hate had cooled with the surrender of the Nazis, and, indeed, he chose for the motto of his war memoirs an inscription he once proposed for a monument in France. It was:

In War: Resolution
In Defeat: Defiance
In Victory: Magnanimity
In Peace: Goodwill.

A "kind of United States of Europe" aligned with the English-speaking peoples—Churchill's proposed "sovereign remedy" for the containment of Soviet power—did not come off, save in the form of the North Atlantic Treaty Organization.

In these years, Churchill gave the appearance of youthful vigor. Bald save for a thatch of hair on the back of his head, his rotund, cherubic face was still well fleshed and hardly wrinkled. With his seldom smiling, mostly solemn mien, he moved slowly, as an elephant pushing through underbrush, his massive head with its lowering eyebrows almost resting on his chest from his strong, short neck. Only his natural stoop was more marked.

Voters who turned out to hear him noticed that he often let tears roll down his ruddy cheeks when political meetings wound up with the singing of "Land of Hope and Glory."

He went about as always wearing a bow tie and (mostly) a double-breasted suit and a squarish crowned derby or a homburg. Stretched across his ample middle was a heavy gold watch chain and in his right hand a walking stick, which he shifted to his left on occasion to give his victory sign—the first two fingers of his right hand spread in a V.

All the while, Churchill was busy with his private enterprises, pursuits and amusements. Chartwell was enlarged by 500 acres and he became a gentleman farmer. In 1948 he started a stable of horses, to his profit unlike so many others.

One of his horses, a gray three-year-old named Colonist II, romped in, a winner, at Ascot in 1949 and in 1950 ran up a string of 13 victories. In all, Colonist II won £13,000 for his owner.

Churchill spent much of his time at Chartwell puttering, laying bricks and painting. He painted whenever he had an idle moment; while these were few, canvases were many. Hundreds of his landscapes piled up in spare rooms.

Dominating all of his activities was his writing. In this period he worked on his four-volume *History of the English-Speaking Peoples*.

Even more astounding was his compilation of a six-volume history of World War II as seen through his eyes and recorded in memorandums, letters, cables, diaries and official records.

These volumes were *The Gathering Storm*, *Their Finest Hour*, *The Grand Alliance*, *The Hinge of Fate*, *Closing the Ring*, and *Triumph and Tragedy*. All were published between 1948 and 1954.

For this gargantuan task, Churchill gathered an assemblage of scholars, historians, technical experts, researchers and, of course, enough secretaries to keep up with the endless torrent of words that Churchill poured into recording machines. Sometimes the secretaries worked in shifts so that they could keep going while Churchill slept. He often dictated 8,000 words in a day.

The sorting, selection, the rejection of material, the endless winnowing and typing sometimes went on through the night. The words and the choice of phrase were Churchill's; and, despite the committee method of production of a work of more than 1.5 million words, the style is unmistakably, majestically Churchillian.

This was the crown of his literary achievements. His other books included *The Story of the Matakand Field Force* (1898), *The River War: An Historical Account of the Reconquest of the Soudan* (two volumes, 1899), *Savrola* (1900), *Ian Hamilton's March* (1900), *Mr. Broderick's Army* (1903), *Lord Randolph Churchill* (two volumes, 1906), *My African Journey* (1908), *The World Crisis* (five volumes, 1923–31), *My Early Life* (1930), *Thoughts and Adventures* (1932), *Marlborough: His Life and Times* (four volumes, 1933–38), *Great Contemporaries* (1937), *Painting as a Pastime* (1948), and *A History of the English-Speaking Peoples* (four volumes, 1956).

Throughout the years he was in Opposition, Churchill, while continuing to stress the menace of Communism, found time to give the Socialists little peace at home. He attacked them constantly for policies toward the Empire, for the parlous economic situation in Britain and for nationalization policies in coal mining, railroads and especially steel.

In 1947 and 1948 Churchill delivered 52 major speeches on a variety of subjects from independence—he was against it—to nationalization, to devaluation of the pound from its pegged rate of $4.82 to $2.80. He was also against that.

"When I am abroad I always make it a rule never to criticize or attack the Government of my own country," he told the House in April 1947. "I make up for lost time when I come home."

In July 1949, Churchill made a pronouncement of Conservative intentions before 40,000 at an outdoor gathering in Wolverhampton. His speech was based largely on policy devised by R. A. Butler, who had been entrusted with formulating a campaign program after the Conservative defeat of 1945. It conceded that the welfare state—Churchill had been one of its early authors, with Lloyd George—had come to stay.

Churchill almost made his comeback in the election of 1950, pinning his campaign on opposition to Labor's Socialism, but Attlee squeaked by. Labor maintained its precarious hold until October 1951. In this period, the Conservatives' war of attrition in Parliament harried the Laborites; troubles mounted for the government at home as living costs rose and consumer goods grew scarcer; abroad, the situation was sticky, especially in the ever-troublesome Middle East, where traditional British influence was dwindling with the rise of Nasser of Egypt; and the restiveness of the African colonies did not always remain under the surface.

The campaign was venomous. "Vote Tory and Reach for a Rifle," one handbill read. Weakness and vacillation, retorted the Conservatives. From this Churchill's party emerged with a small, but workable, majority in Commons.

In the early evening of Oct. 26, 1951, Winston Leonard Spencer Churchill, a month from his 77th birthday, was invested by King George VI with the seals of office. Doughty still, he undertook the onerous duties of prime minister for a second time.

PRIME MINISTER FOR SECOND TIME: Containing the Soviet Drive for Expansion

BACK IN power after six years in Opposition, Winston Churchill gave himself with his old-time vigor to the three great tasks he had set himself after the victory in World War II.

These were to remove the shadow of a new tyranny by reaching an accord with the Soviet Union for a just and lasting peace, security of the West through the close association of a united Europe with the British Commonwealth and the United States, and, at home, an unscrambling of the Socialist omelet.

It is a measure of the stature he had attained throughout the world that even when he was merely the leader of a minority in the House his pronouncements on world affairs had been received with the attention reserved usually for the head of a government. Now he spoke as the leader of the British nation, not so great as in the Victorian Age of his youth but still a major power.

This time he had not been called to leadership at a time of crisis and cataclysm but through the deliberate choice of voters who, having given Socialism a six-year trial, had decided they wanted a change in the hope of a better and richer life. In four years Churchill sought to give it to them.

They were years with mixed success and failure, of satisfaction mixed with sorrow and disappointment. He who had said he did not "become the King's First Minister to preside over the liquidation of the British Empire" had to watch the beginning of its disintegration from the sidelines and its further weakening by events that even he could not control.

India was gone, but Churchill found a measure of satisfaction that in granting independence to the great subcontinent, the communal massacres he had feared were averted by a provision for a Muslim Pakistan separate from India. He never had believed that independence was itself a cure for social injustice, but the tides of nationalism were stronger than any man could breast.

His hopes for a United States of Europe—never precisely or clearly defined—did not materialize. A stroke of fate prevented his hoped-for confrontation of Malenkov in the brief period he led the Soviet Union after Stalin's death.

Although he lost no time in attacking Socialism in calling for the repeal of the act nationalizing the steel industry in his first session of Parliament, he never succeeded in entirely undoing the work of the Labor party. Indeed, in the 13 years the Conservatives remained in power after 1951 they embraced the basic principles of the welfare state.

The wit and wry humor that spiced so many of the grimmest of his wartime speeches were still with him through this Indian summer of his life.

Speaking at the rebuilt Guildhall, which had been partly destroyed by German bombs, Churchill said, "When I should have been here as Prime Minister [the first time] the Guildhall was blown up and before it was repaired I was blown out."

Churchill's durability and continued capacity to work hard and relax zestfully were the wonder of his friends. He had not been a robust youth and he had had pneumonia several times, but he recovered quickly from these bouts of illness, as he did from his accidents.

He once told Pearson, the prime minister of Canada, that one of his secrets was "never stand when you can sit down and never sit if you can lie down."

In one of his books he wrote that he "always went to bed at least for one hour as early as possible in the afternoon and exploited to the full my happy gift of falling almost immediately into deep sleep." By "this means I was able to press a day and a half's work into one."

The first Parliamentary sessions after Churchill's return to power were not notable for legislative achievements. It was a time for conciliation of party strife and for the consolidation of a new government. Nevertheless the government was blessed by the end of the conflict in Korea and by a truce in Indochina. Vietnam was partitioned and Laos and Cambodia neutralized. Britain's economic position began to improve.

In a progress report to Parliament Churchill asked that his government's achievements be seen in relation to its inheritance from Labor's "six-year record of extravagance and waste, of overspending and living upon American money."

He declared that at the time of the election Britain was spending £800 million a year more than it was earning from exports. If drastic measures had not been taken by his government and followed by the Commonwealth, he said, "the whole reserve of gold and dollars would have been exhausted by the summer's end." These measures, he noted, had reduced purchases abroad by £600 million.

In that speech he also referred to his call in 1950 for a conference between the heads of government and declared that he and Eden still held to "the idea of a supreme effort to bridge the gulf between the two worlds so that each can live its life, if not in friendship at least without the fear, the hatreds and the frightful waste of the 'cold war.' "

On Feb. 6, 1952, a grief-stricken nation learned that King George VI, who had survived an operation for lung cancer some months before, had died in his sleep at Sandringham, a royal country residence. Churchill, devoted to the Crown as a symbol and to King George as a friend and collaborator, delivered one of his most moving tributes to the institution of monarchy and to the king himself in a radio broadcast the next day.

"The last few months of King George's life with all the pain and physical stresses that he endured—his life hanging by a thread from day to day—and he all the time cheerful and undaunted—stricken in body but quite undisturbed and even unaffected in spirit—these have made a profound and enduring impression and should be a help to all.

"During these last months the King walked with death, as if death were a companion, an acquaintance whom he recognized and did not fear. In the end death came as a friend, and after a happy day of sunshine and sport, and after a 'good night' to those who loved him best, he fell asleep, as every man or woman who strives to fear God and nothing else in the world may do."

He concluded with a tribute to the queens of England, a country now about to have another.

"Famous have been the reigns of our queens. Some of the great periods in our history have unfolded under their scepters. Now that we have the second Queen Elizabeth also ascending the throne in her 26th year our thoughts are carried back nearly 400 years to the magnificent figures who presided over and in many ways embodied and inspired the grandeur and genius of the Elizabethan age.

"I, whose youth was passed in the august, unchallenged and tranquil glories of the Victorian era, may well feel a thrill in invoking once more the prayer and anthem:

"God Save the Queen."

On first learning that Stalin was ill, Churchill had sent a secretary to the Soviet Embassy to ask to be kept informed of Stalin's condition.

On March 5, 1953, the day that Stalin died, Churchill thought the time propitious to repeat his call for a "summit meeting." He wanted to "take the measure of the new man in the Kremlin," he told a friend.

The sole survivor of the three who led the Grand

Alliance sent no personal message of condolence when Stalin died. This was in marked contrast to his action when Roosevelt died April 12, 1945, when Churchill mourned the ending of "a dear and cherished friendship forged in the fires of war."

A spokesman for the prime minister explained that the British government had expressed sympathy "and that is all that is required under normal diplomatic procedure.

"Mr. Churchill will do no more and no less," the spokesman said.

It was not until 1955 that Churchill, who had always maintained that successful negotiations with Russia could be held only by those with equal or superior strength, explained why the opportunity of 1953, for high-level talks with Stalin's successor Malenkov, had been allowed to pass.

It came with the announcement to a stilled House that the government had decided to proceed with the manufacture of a hydrogen bomb.

Before Russia caught up with the United States in atomic weapons Churchill had believed that the secret of this dreadful "deterrent" was best left to the United States.

Now he informed the House of his conviction that only possession of the hydrogen bomb, the means of its delivery and a determination to use it, if necessary, was the prerequisite to a "conference where these matters can be put plainly and bluntly."

Churchill would have liked to have arranged such a conference after Malenkov took power, he said, and intended to try to convince Eisenhower of the desirability of such a meeting.

"However, I was struck down by a very sudden illness which paralyzed me completely physically and I had to put it all off and it was not found possible to persuade President Eisenhower to join in the process."

Churchill was referring to June 10, 1953, when he, then in his 77th year, suffered a paralytic stroke that incapacitated him to some extent for several months.

A month previously, he had spoken of the change of attitude and mood in the Kremlin.

"The dominant problem is, of course, Germany. If our advice had been taken by the United States after the Armistice with Germany the Western Allies would not have withdrawn from the line which their armies had reached to the agreed occupation lines until and unless agreement had been reached with Soviet Russia on the many points of difference about the occupation of enemy territories, of which the occupation of Germany was, of course, only a part. Our view was not accepted and a wide area of Germany was handed over to the Soviet occupation without any general settlement among the three victorious powers."

On April 24 of that year, the queen made Churchill a Knight Companion of the Most Noble Order of the Garter, the highest order of chivalry to which a Briton can attain and still be eligible to sit in the House of Commons. Thus, the child of the House of Commons, who always said that the letters he cherished most after his name were M.P., became Sir Winston.

The same year the Nobel Prize for Literature was awarded him. With it went a citation for his oratory.

Churchill was the first statesman and the seventh of his countrymen to receive the world's highest award for literature.

After expressing the hope that the judges had not erred in their assessment, he said, "I notice that the first Englishman to receive the Nobel Prize was Mr. Rudyard Kipling and that another equally rewarded was Mr. Bernard Shaw. I certainly cannot attempt to compete with either of those. I knew them both quite well and my thought was much more in accord with Mr. Rudyard Kipling than with Mr. Bernard Shaw. On the other hand, Mr. Rudyard Kipling never thought much of me, whereas Mr. Bernard Shaw often expressed himself in most flattering terms."

London in April was already aflutter with bunting, flags and decorations in preparation for the coronation ceremony of June 2. It was a time of jubilation in a city long immersed in the gloom of war and an austere peace. Newspapers picked up the theme of the dawn of a new Elizabethan age, and spirits rose higher than they had been at any time since the German surrender.

When the great day came, however, it was pouring rain and the temperature was in the lower forties. In the old abbey transformed for the ritual, half religious and half secular, Churchill sat in his robes as a Knight of the Garter among the crowned heads of many lands, the peers in their robes trimmed with ermine and their ladies wearing glittering tiaras. He who had served as a soldier of the queen in Victoria's reign saw the Archbishop of Canterbury place the old imperial crown upon the girlish head of her great-granddaughter.

After his stroke there were rumors that Churchill was preparing to retire. He scotched them at a party conference.

"If I stay on for the time being, bearing the burden at my age, it is not because of love of power or office. I have had an ample feast of both. If I stay it is because I have the feeling that I may, through things that have happened, have an influence on what I care about above all else—the building of a sure and lasting peace."

By December, Churchill was well enough to journey to Washington to see Eisenhower just before the latter's inauguration. Again in the summer of 1954 he was in Washington to sign the Potomac Charter reaffirming the principles of the Atlantic Charter.

To a question at a news conference here about when he planned to retire, he replied: "Not until I am a great deal worse and the Empire is a great deal better."

He was asked whether death held any terror for him, and he replied: "I am prepared to meet my Maker. Whether my Maker is prepared for the great ordeal of meeting me is another matter."

Meanwhile, in Commons it was noticed that Churchill showed signs of slowing down. He walked with a more pronounced stoop. His step was less firm. He appeared tired and sometimes did not seem able to follow the proceedings. This was perhaps due to increasing deafness, for he wore his hearing aid only sporadically and reluctantly in public.

Churchill passed his 80th birthday on Nov. 30, 1954, still prime minister and still the master of Britain's destiny. Only Palmerston and Gladstone had held that office beyond that age. To mark the occasion, members of the House of Commons and the House of Lords gathered in Westminster Hall to do him honor.

There were messages of goodwill from the great and lesser peoples of his own and many other lands. Churchill's acknowledgment was perfunctory and brief.

The speech on Britain's nuclear plans was delivered March 1, 1955. Just a month later he and Lady Churchill entertained Queen Elizabeth II and Prince Philip at 10 Downing Street. As it turned out, it was the prime minister's farewell to the sixth monarch he served.

On April 5, 1955, he resigned. Ironically, there was a newspaper strike in London and the event that marked the end of a noble era of British statesmanship went unrecorded immediately in London, but it was carried to people across the land and throughout the world by radio.

Freed of the burdens of office, Churchill now entered the twilight of his life, illumined, however, with honors and distinctions that continued to fall upon him.

Even so, he was not ready to relinquish his membership in that most exclusive club, the House of Commons, of which he had been a member for more than half a century. He stood for his old constituency of Woodford and won in the election of 1955 and again in 1959.

No longer was he seated on the front bench as he had been for years with the members of the government and as leader of the Opposition. Instead, he sat among the backbenchers as a private member.

Serenely benign, and for long periods aloof and withdrawn, he took little part in the debates and none in the thrust and parry of Parliamentary procedure. His appearances in the House and his presence in his favorite corner of the members' lounge became less and less frequent.

Churchill had made two visits to the United states after his retirement as prime minister, one in May 1959, when he visited Eisenhower at the White House, and again in April 1961, when he sailed to Miami and New York aboard a friend's yacht.

His sense of humor did not desert him as the years marched on. On his 82d birthday, when a photographer expressed the hope that he might take another picture of him at the age of 90, Churchill regarded him solemnly and said, "I see no reason why you shouldn't, young man. You look hale and hearty enough."

He spent more and more time at Chartwell, surrounded by his family, his grandchildren, his dogs, his racing stable. He puttered and lived the life of a country squire. Much time was spent in painting.

As a painter—mostly in oils—he favored landscapes and interiors rather than the portraits that Eisenhower seemed to prefer. Hitler had tried to paint, too, but his work was marked by the hard, straight line whereas Churchill's style was softer. His work was characterized by bold colors and an impressionist approach that sought to convey a mood or feeling as well as a pictorial representation. An exhibition of 62 of his paintings at Burlington House in 1959 drew more than 140,000 persons.

"Audacity," he said, "is a very great part of the art of painting."

He never relinquished the idea that at the moment of peace victory was lost, and for this loss he felt that Roosevelt's confidence that he could "handle" Stalin was at fault. In the last volume of his memoirs he wrote: "The United States stood on the scene of victory, master of world fortunes, but without a true and coherent design. Britain, though still very powerful, could not act decisively alone. I could at this stage only warn and plead.

"I moved through cheering crowds or sat at a table adorned with congratulations and blessings with an aching heart and a mind oppressed by forebodings."

As a Knight Companion of the Garter, he was a member, along with those of royal blood and the peerage, of the highest order of chivalry his queen could bestow upon him. It had been offered him in 1945 by King George VI but he declined. At that time selections for membership in the order were made by the sovereign on the recommendation of the prime minister. The fact that Attlee was prime minister may have had something to do with Churchill's decision. Subsequently, the older system was restored, making selection the prerogative of the sovereign.

He also held the Order of Merit, which is limited to 24 members at any one time and is awarded for outstanding excellence in the arts, letters and sciences. He was the first non-American to be given the Freedom Award. De Gaulle decorated him with the Cross of Liberation in 1958.

He was a Freeman of more than 50 towns and cities in his own country and abroad and the holder of honorary degrees from more than 20 universities.

Of all his foreign honors, including the Nobel Prize, Churchill prized most highly his honorary citizenship of the United States conferred upon him by John F. Kennedy on April 9, 1963. The proposal to do what Congress had never done for a foreign national was first offered by Representative Francis B. Walter, Democrat of Pennsylvania, April 1, 1958.

At that time Churchill informed Mr. Walter that "after most careful consideration, I think that I should decline it rather than have an official seal put on the affection and high regard in which I hold your country."

Mr. Walter renewed his proposal in 1963, and on Jan. 24, Kennedy told a news conference that he believed that a declaration of honorary citizenship or high esteem for Churchill "would be a gracious act."

Churchill then informed Mr. Walter through the British Embassy that "due to the changed situation from 1958" he would "be delighted to be so honored." He did not elaborate on the cryptic "the changed situation."

H.R. 4374, the bill to confer citizenship on the Briton whose mother was American-born, was passed by the House of Representatives March 12, 1963, and by the Senate April 2.

The conferral ceremony was held in the White House Rose Garden April 9. Unable to be present, Churchill was represented by his son, Randolph, but he watched and heard it all on a television broadcast carried across the Atlantic by a communications satellite. He was deeply moved.

With his election to Parliament in 1959 Winston Churchill had contested 20 elections and been successful in 15 of them. He had held every cabinet post except that of foreign minister. Having represented Woodford successively since 1924, he was the "father of the House of Commons" from 1959 until the dissolution of Parliament for the election of 1964 when, nearing 90, he announced that he would not stand again for Parliament.

On July 28, just before dissolution, the House adopted a motion putting on record "its unbounded admiration and gratitude for [Churchill's] services to Parliament, to the nation and to the world."

As his 90th birthday drew near, Churchill disengaged himself completely from public affairs and lived at Chartwell and at Hyde Park Gate with his wife. His mind remained clear but his health was frail and he tired easily. He saw only such old and close friends as Gen. Hastings Ismay and Lord Montgomery of Alamein.

Sir Winston and Lady Churchill had five children. The third child, Marigold, died in childhood. Diana, who was the wife of Duncan Sandys, was born in 1909 and died in 1963.

Three of their children are living. Randolph Churchill is a journalist who has edited and published several volumes of his father's speeches. He is working on the collected papers and preparing a biography.

Churchill's hand, at 90, was too unsteady to paint but he could still light his own cigars. He was permitted an occasional nip of brandy.

He lived expansively, however, and insisted on surrounding himself with a retinue of retainers and a larger secretariat than he needed.

In the final period of his life Churchill became more and more withdrawn and uninterested in public affairs. He showed little curiosity, for example, over the outcome of the election of 1964, in which Labor returned to power after 13 years.

Like many other elderly folk, he loved to reminisce about his youth, and this he did with his few visitors and with members of his family.

He had outlived most of his contemporaries and he had seen the world change vastly from the horse-and-carriage era to the age of space vehicles. The old great empires of his youth had fallen and the new world that was emerging could hardly have been attractive to the constitutional traditionalist he was.

Although during the war Churchill held the powers of a dictator with the approval of Parliament, he never forgot, or let others forget, that it was in the province of Parliament to dismiss him at its pleasure. Recalling one of his meetings with Stalin and Roosevelt, he wrote: "It was with some pride that I reminded my two great comrades on more than one occasion that I was the only one of our trinity who could at any moment be dismissed from power by the vote of a House of Commons freely elected on universal franchise, or could be controlled from day to day by the opinion of a war cabinet representing all parties in the State.

"The President's term of office was fixed and his powers not only as President but as Commander in Chief were almost absolute under the American Constitution. Stalin appeared to be, and at this moment certainly was, all-powerful in Russia. They could order; I had to convince and persuade. I was glad that this should be so. The process was laborious, but I had no reason to complain of the way it worked."

At 90 he was photographed with his wife of 56 happy years. He was standing at the window of his home at Hyde Park Gate looking wistfully out and evidently near tears at the crowd gathered to cheer the man who had so gallantly led them with the powers of a wartime autocrat and who had then stepped down, leaving them free citizens of a democratic nation. That itself was not the least of his contributions to his times and to his fellow Britons.

CHURCHILL DIES AT 90 AT HOME IN LONDON

ANTHONY LEWIS

LONDON, Sunday, Jan. 24, 1965—Sir Winston Churchill is dead.

The great figure who embodied man's will to resist tyranny passed into history this morning. He was 90 years old.

His old friend and physician, Lord Moran, gave the news to the world after informing Queen Elizabeth and Prime Minister Harold Wilson.

Lord Moran's announcement said:

> Shortly after 8 A.M., Sir Winston died at his home.
> (Signed) MORAN.

The announcement by Lord Moran was read to reporters near the Churchill home at 8:35 A.M. (3:35 A.M., New York time).

About 30 members of the press were standing in the rain at the entrance to Hyde Park Gate, the small street south of Kensington Gardens where Sir Winston had lived for so long. A reporter for the Press Association read Lord Moran's statement to them.

Lord Moran had come to the house at 7:18. A few minutes earlier Sir Winston's son, Randolph, had driven up. Also there at the end were Lady Churchill and their daughter, Sarah, and Randolph's son, Winston.

Another daughter, Mary, Mrs. Christopher Soames, also survives Sir Winston. Other survivors are 10 grandchildren and three great-grandchildren, the last born just two days ago.

Queen Elizabeth II sent the following message to Lady Churchill: "The whole world is the poorer by the loss of his many-sided genius while the survival of this country and the sister nations of the Commonwealth, in the face of the greatest danger that has ever threatened them, will be a perpetual memorial to his leadership, his vision, and his indomitable courage."

The world had been watching and waiting since Jan. 15, when it was announced that Sir Winston had suffered a stroke. The last authentic giant of world politics in the 20th century was going down.

For nine days the struggle went on. Medical experts said that only phenomenal tenacity and spirit of life could enable a man of 90 to hold off death so long in these circumstances.

But then those were the qualities that had made Winston Churchill a historical figure in his lifetime. His pluck in rallying Britain to victory in World War II saved not only his country but, in all likelihood, free nations everywhere.

Sir Winston will be given a state funeral, the first commoner so to be honored since the death of William Ewart Gladstone in 1898.

The body will lie in state in Westminster Hall for several days. Then, after a long march from Westminster, the services will be held in St. Paul's Cathedral, whose huge dome has so long dominated London.

Today was the anniversary of the death of Sir Winston's father, Lord Randolph Churchill, a somewhat eccentric Tory politician. He died in 1894.

For virtually everyone in Great Britain, Sir Winston's death will be a wrenching personal loss and a symbolic break with a past whose glories seem already faded.

For the world, too, it is the end of an age.

Sir Winston will always be remembered as the great war leader who defied Hitler. But he was more than that—a personality larger than life, an extraordinary man in language and character as well as in war and politics.

THE CHURCHILL FUNERAL

ANTHONY LEWIS

SIR WINSTON CHURCHILL was laid to rest on Jan. 30, 1965, after an extraordinary state funeral. Britain and the world joined in homage to the man who had marshaled the spirit of freedom for his age.

It was a day of ceremony, pride and grief. There was rich pageantry—heralds and muffled drums, royalty and red silks, lines of soldiers in dress uniform.

There was also private sorrow. Sir Winston's body was buried this afternoon in a small village churchyard at Bladon, near his family's ancestral home, Blenheim Palace. So private was the service that the public did not know exactly when it ended.

When visitors began to file through the churchyard this evening, they found at the head of the new grave a wreath of red roses, tulips and carnations from Lady Churchill. It bore this inscription: "To my darling Winston, Clemmie."

The great procession through the streets of London this morning and the service that followed in St. Paul's Cathedral went beyond any funeral ever provided for a commoner in Britain. Queen Elizabeth was in the cathedral—the first reigning British sovereign to attend a commoner's funeral.

The thousands who watched at street corners and the millions who watched on television knew they were seeing a moment of history.

The banners and the trumpets and the robes might have been taken from a scene by Shakespeare.

But it was more than a British occasion.

A hundred and ten nations were represented—six by sovereigns, five by other heads of state, 16 by prime ministers. The commanding figure was that of President de Gaulle of France, tall and somber in a plain khaki uniform.

There was an American thread in the tapestry, as was only appropriate for this child of an American mother and foremost advocate of British-American unity. Sir Winston, who died last Sunday at the age of 90, had called himself "a child of both worlds."

One of the most touching moments of the funeral service was the singing of "The Battle Hymn of the Republic," with its connotations of civil war and the struggle for union. Sir Winston had chosen this hymn, along with three others.

And former President Dwight D. Eisenhower, Sir Winston's colleague in war and peace, made a deep impression with a tribute on television. It was broadcast just after the service in St. Paul's.

Preparations for the cathedral service began at 10 A.M., when the Archbishop of Canterbury, Dr. Michael Ramsey, walked down a side aisle.

He was an impressive figure, with his square face, bushy white eyebrows and a fringe of white hair. He wore a long black cope and a white linen miter.

A few minutes later the golden maces of the House of Commons and the House of Lords were brought in.

They were followed, respectively, by the Commons Speaker, Sir Harry Hylton-Foster, and the Lord Chancellor, Lord Gardiner. They took seats on opposite sides of the circle under the dome.

Prime Minister Harold Wilson was already there, with other party leaders. So were all the foreign representatives save the heads of state.

Television sets at various places in the cathedral showed the audience what was happening outside or at points in the cathedral that they could not see.

The queen, wearing a black Persian lamb coat and a black velvet hat, paid special homage to Sir Winston by arriving before the coffin and before official mourners, not last.

Then came the 12 official pallbearers, among them generals and admirals and three men who followed Sir Winston as prime minister—Earl Attlee, Harold Macmillan and the Earl of Avon, formerly Sir Anthony Eden. Some, notably Earl Attlee, looked drawn and infirm.

Those inside the church could hear the muffled beat of drums outside as the end of the procession from Westminster Hall arrived.

Eight Grenadier Guards doffed their tall bearskin hats and lifted the coffin off the gun carriage. Down the main aisle they carried it, tension showing in their young faces. Behind them came Lady Churchill, veiled in black, on the arm of her son, Randolph, with other family mourners behind.

The coffin was set down over the memorial inscription to Wren, under the dome of his great church. It is an inscription that could have been written for today: "*Si monumentum requiris, circumspice*"—"If you seek his monument, look around."

St. Paul's was damaged by a Nazi bomb during World War II, but it survived, the dome intact. The image of the dome against a reddened war sky goes along with the vision of Sir Winston as the symbol of British defiance.

Heralds in marvelous costumes of red, gold and blue silk with a black sash had carried before the coffin Sir Winston's banners and decorations and "achievements."

The banners were heraldic flags of his family and of the Cinque Ports, of which he was Warden. The numerous decorations, from a score of countries, were ribbons and medals, all placed on black cushions on a table in front of the coffin.

"Achievements" are heraldic devices going back to medieval days. They symbolize his knightly status.

The Windsor herald bore a sword, the Somerset herald a shield showing Sir Winston's coat of arms, the York herald spurs, the symbol of knighthood. The Lancaster herald bore a small figure of a lion, the crest taken from above Sir Winston's stall in the Garter chapel at Windsor Castle.

The first hymn contained these words:

Who would true valor see,
Let him come hither;
One here will constant be,
Come wind, come weather,
Hobgoblin nor foul fiend
Can daunt his spirit;
He knows he at the end
Shall life inherit.

After three other hymns, a few brief prayers and "God Save the Queen," there was silence.

Then, from the Whispering Gallery high in the dome, came the sound of a trumpeter playing the Last Post. He wore a medieval gown, and a banner hung from his trumpet.

From farther away came the sound of Reveille, played by a trumpeter of the Royal Hussars in a plain soldier's uniform, silhouetted against the light of a west window. The service was over.

The cathedral rites were the climax of a day that began with a majestic procession from Westminster Hall to St. Paul's.

The public had begun lining up along the streets well before the lying-in-state in Westminster Hall ended. The doors closed there at 6 A.M., after 321,360 persons had walked through.

In the next few hours the procession gradually assembled in New Palace yard, adjoining the 800-year-old hall. There were soldiers and members of the family and a detachment of cadets from Sir Winston's old school, Harrow, where he had been a failure but which he dearly loved.

The eight Grenadier Guards removed their bearskins to shoulder the coffin. They took it out to the yard and placed it on the polished old gun carriage that would bear it through the city.

At 9:45 Big Ben chimed—for the last time until midnight, in deference to Sir Winston. The procession started exactly on schedule.

There were squadrons of Royal Marines in white helmets, and members of the Queen's Household Cavalry in uniforms of red and gold. There were bearskins and silver helmets and plumes of white and red.

They walked the dead march—slow, painfully slow, to the beat of deep drums shrouded in black.

The Household Cavalry's drum horse, Alexander the Great, bore two more drums, of silver, but they were not played. Behind the horse were the state trumpeters, in Tudor costume.

Toward the rear of the mile-long procession was the gun carriage and its burden, the black coffin covered with the Union Jack and bearing a black cushion with Sir Winston's insignia of the Garter. It was drawn from the front and steadied from behind by 142 sailors of the Royal Navy, which has traditionally had this role since Queen Victoria's funeral.

Ten male mourners, headed by Randolph Churchill, walked behind. Lady Churchill and other women followed in five carriages, each drawn by a pair of Cleveland bays.

As the procession moved along Whitehall, the street of government offices that Sir Winston had often irritated and once governed, a gun fired every minute. It was sounded 90 times before and after the funeral ceremony in St. Paul's to mark his years.

The streets were lined by members of the armed services and policemen, stationed alternately. Behind them were the crowds, five deep here, ten there.

It was bitterly cold, though no rain or snow fell from the gray skies. Newspaper vendors did a brisk trade selling papers to women to wrap around their legs.

Around Trafalgar Square the procession moved, up the Strand and Fleet Street and Ludgate Hill. At the approach to St. Paul's, the crowds were thickest.

Mrs. Dora Paddy was waiting there with her 9-year-old son, Charles. She was asked after the marchers passed what had impressed her most.

"The quietness of it," she said. "No cheering."

It was quiet, almost eerily so. There were only the commands of officers, the hammer of horses' hooves, the beat of drums and the sound of brasses until the coffin was borne inside the cathedral.

After the service the Grenadier Guards carried the coffin down the steps with difficulty. The queen followed, and then the others in their multicolored finery.

There was the Lord Mayor of London, Sir James Miller, in scarlet velvet and white ermine; judges in wigs; morning coats and top hats and uniforms of a dozen hues.

As they stepped outside, the bells of St. Paul's were pealing. The notable guests waited on the steps for their cars. On the other side of St. Paul's a small remainder of the procession walked down the hill to the Tower of London, the pier and the river.

The Earl Marshal, the Duke of Norfolk, dressed in black with a red collar and cuffs and a plumed hat, led the mourners and the coffin over a small wooden bridge to the pier.

There was a moment of special poignancy when Sir Winston's body was placed aboard the launch *Havengore*. It was as if crossing the water had a particular quality of finality.

Many minds, British as well as American, turned to the funeral of President Kennedy in Washington 14 months ago. All felt the sharp contrast.

The Kennedy funeral represented a wrenching break with what had seemed to be the path of history. That was the opposite of ordered ceremony; one of its most powerful scenes was the procession of world statesmen in a disordered group up Connecticut Avenue.

Disorder was the meaning of that funeral; fulfillment was a more evident theme today in an observance of the foreseeable end of a completed lifetime.

As the 85-foot launch cast off, old-fashioned guns along the river embankment fired a 19-gun salute.

Havengore turned to move upriver, framed against the famous silhouette of Tower Bridge.

Four Royal Air Force Lightning jet fighters roared a few hundred feet overhead. The crowd looked up to see a second group, a third, a fourth.

Then, as *Havengore* and accompanying ships went on upstream, there came a tribute so slow and majestic that it might almost have been missed.

The great steam cranes on the wharves dipped

down like ponderous prehistoric creatures. They rose only after *Havengore* had passed.

Upriver on the other bank the coffin was transferred to an ordinary hearse. In Waterloo Station it was put aboard a special train drawn by locomotive 34051, named the *Winston Churchill.*

Along the line hundreds had paid their way into the stations to see the train go by. No television cameras watched the last moment of the journey, in Bladon. The coffin went to earth without being seen again by the public.

Beside Lady Churchill's wreath lay another, all white, with this card: "From the nation and the Commonwealth in grateful remembrance—Elizabeth R."

And in London tonight the bells of St. Paul's still pealed.

LE CORBUSIER

1887–1965

Charles-Edouard Jeanneret-Gris, whose professional name was Le Corbusier, was as contentious in his manner as he was influential in his architectural ideas. "I am like a lightning conductor: I attract storms," he said.

Disputes swirled about him and his conceptions for more than 40 years, and in them he was almost always a temperamental participant, for he regarded himself, especially in his later years, as beset by red tape, politics and underappreciation.

Nevertheless, his influence was so enormous and so persuasive that there are few areas in modern building and city planning in which it is not reflected. Le Corbusier, according to Arthur Drexler of the Museum of Modern Art, was one of the three greats in modern architecture, the others being Ludwig Mies van der Rohe and Frank Lloyd Wright.

Le Corbusier's output was not large—fewer than 100 buildings—yet it was distinctive. Among outstanding examples of his work are the Visual Arts Center at Harvard University in Cambridge, Mass.; the Ronchamp Chapel at Vosges, France; the capitol buildings for the Punjab at Chandigarh, India; an apartment house at Marseilles and another in Berlin; a 10-story glass-walled office building in Moscow; a Salvation Army center in Paris; and the Ministry of Education Building in Rio de Janeiro.

That structure, a honeycomb of sun-shading, breeze-admitting vanes at the windows, was widely copied in South America—notably in Brasilia—and in other tropical regions. There are no examples of pure Le Corbusier in New York. The overall conception of the United Nations Secretariat Building, at 43d Street and the East River, was his, but the bold design was toned down, much to his annoyance. When the structure was finished, he complained: "A new skyscraper, which everyone calls the 'Le Corbusier Building,' has appeared in New York. L-C was stripped of all his rights, without conscience and without pity."

The Lever Building on Park Avenue, which appears to be built on stilts, also incorporates one of Le Corbusier's fundamental notions—that the massive bulk of a big building should be offset by placing it on uprights and that pedestrians should be allowed to pass underneath the main structure.

In his early days, before he saw New York, Le Corbusier praised American skyscrapers, but he took one look at the city's slab buildings and crowded canyons and announced: "Your skyscrapers are too small!"

Not only was Manhattan a jungle of masonry, he said, but the Hudson and East rivers were also hidden and New York Harbor was lost. Nonetheless, Le Corbusier liked some aspects of the United States.

He advised his fellow architects "lost in the sterile backwaters of their foliage, their pilasters and their

AP/WIDE WORLD

lead roofs" to look for inspiration to American grain elevators and silos and factories. These he considered "the magnificent first fruits of the new age."

In the years before World War II, Le Corbusier was an amiable man, with an atelier full of students who worked for him for nothing. He was vain then, but not difficult or bitter.

With the end of the war he expected many commissions from the French government to redesign bombed-out cities, but received only one—to plan an apartment house at Marseilles. Frustrated, he grew increasingly acidulous, aloof and egocentric, and his knack of making enemies became almost a developed art.

"New York is the most beautiful manifestation of man's power, courage, enterprise and force," he said in 1935, "but it is utterly lacking in order and harmony and the comforts of the spirit. The skyscrapers are little needles all crowded together. They should be great obelisks, far apart, so that the city would have space and light and order. Those are the things that men need just as much as they need bread or a place to sleep."

Never a ready man with a franc, he also grew penurious, sometimes to the point where he felt he was being taken advantage of. This trait had been exhibited earlier in a long and complicated dispute with the Museum of Modern Art over the ownership of some items the museum displayed in one of its shows devoted to his work.

The architect was quick to see hostility toward him. In April 1965 he was still berating his critics and reminding them of how mistaken they were.

"For 50 years I have gotten kicks in the rear," he said. "And now Le Corbusier has become Le Corbusier. They are worried about what he's doing. They keep track of his projects. What a laugh!

"I have given them plenty of grief, too. I have taught them that architecture is the play of forms and of volume in light. They didn't know this."

When he first enunciated his architectural credo he was equally didactic. "Architecture has nothing to do with the various 'styles,' " he said in the 1920s. "The styles are to architecture what a feather is on a woman's head; it is something pretty, though not always, and never anything more. Architecture has graver ends. . . . Mass and surface are the elements by which it manifests itself."

Structure, Le Corbusier went on, is what makes a building beautiful, and he singled out the "great primary forms"—cubes, cones, spheres, cylinders and pyramids. These, he said, are always beautiful, and what can be reduced to these basic shapes is good architecture.

Le Corbusier was a slight man, and a slim one in his younger days. His face was long and pale; his lips were thin, and his hair was slicked back without a part over a high forehead. According to the painter Fernand Léger, he was "a very odd specimen" who went bicycling in a derby hat and a dark sack suit. The architect was known to his intimates then and later as Corbu, although he often referred to himself in the third person.

He was at one time a constant smoker. "I used to smoke cigarettes, pipes and cigars all day long," he said once. "I had my suits made with a special pocket to hold a box of 250 kitchen matches; I used up a box a day.

"In 1942 I quit smoking because a friend said I couldn't. I put my 60 pipes in a drawer and have never smoked since. Almost every night I dream that a friend is offering me a cigar. I do not accept it, even in the dream."

In later years Le Corbusier took to being solemn. Describing his work habits, he said last spring, "The birth of a project is for me like the birth of a little dog or a child. There is a long period of gestation; there is a lot of work in the subconscious before I make the first sketch. That lasts for months.

"One fine morning the project has taken form without my knowing it. Each problem provokes in me this interior meditation. I don't say to my collaborators, 'Here's a problem; do your best to solve it.' I seek the solution myself, closed up in a room 3 meters by 3 meters."

The architect was not exaggerating the extent of

his working space at his whitewashed studio at 35 Rue de Sèvres in Paris. It was behind an old wooden door at the top of a winding staircase, and on the door was a big Keep Out sign. Dominating the cramped room was a big photograph of children playing on the roof of the Marseilles apartment house that he had designed.

This building, like so many of his creations, was controversial. Completed in 1952, it is made of blocks of raw concrete on which the marks of the form boards were left visible. Traditionalists denounced it, and a hardware supplier refused to sell locks or hinges for it for fear of tarnishing the company name. However, the tenants liked the 17-story building, and Walter Gropius, the architect, declared: "Any architect who does not find this building beautiful had better lay down his pencil."

In the theories of Le Corbusier, the notion of "machine" has an important place. Just as he considered that, in relation to printing, "the picture is a machine of emotion," so he was the inventor of the phrase "a house is a machine to live in," and it reflected his iconoclastic, experimental attitude. Some critics thought it also represented a too austere and even inhuman view of man.

Yet Le Corbusier had always represented himself as the pioneer of an essentially gracious architecture. Thus, in order of importance, he ranked the "raw materials" of the urbanist: the sky, trees, iron, cement; he wished to bring man the essential joys to which all have right—the sun, space, verdure.

From this state of mind stemmed his principles of architecture: primal importance of the site; its exposure to the sun; the support wall, made useless by the steel framework and replaced by a glass sheet; the street belongs to the pedestrian (automobile and rail traffic go underground or overhead); construction on piles (the house is healthier and the ground disencumbered); pure air, cleansed of the toxic fumes of the city and obtained from a system of ventilation incorporated in the building; etc.

On such principles Le Corbusier, an enthusiastic town planner, drew up plans for Paris, Antwerp, Algiers, Buenos Aires, Montevideo and towns in India.

His masterpiece was his predominant share in making Chandigarh, the new city built from scratch on the plains of the Punjab, India, from 1951 to 1957. In this great work, sponsored by Prime Minister Jawaharlal Nehru, Le Corbusier softened the rigidity of some of his characteristic forms.

He bowed to the Indians' objection that their lack of elevator technicians precluded skyscraper construction. Chandigarh is a sprawling bungalow city.

The buildings for which he was primarily responsible—the government center at its heart—contained numerous innovations to cope with India's scorching sun, and were built in undecorated, rough-finished concrete for reasons of economy.

Charles-Edouard Jeanneret-Gris was born Oct. 6, 1887, in La Chaux-de-Fonds, Switzerland. His father was an enameler of watch faces.

After studying at the School of Fine Arts of his native town from 13 to 18, and being apprenticed to an engraver from 1905, he studied in the ateliers of several eminent architects in Vienna, Paris and Berlin, though he never earned a degree.

His first experimental buildings were erected in La Chaux for his father and for well-to-do watch manufacturers. He moved to Paris in 1917, where he at first could find no architectural work and managed a factory while painting in his spare time.

From 1920 to 1925 he wrote a series of articles in the magazine *L'Esprit Nouveau* that expressed his architectural philosophy and made him famous.

He was co-founder with the painter Amédée Ozenfant of this magazine, which propagated "purist" theories. It was the aim of "purism," which derived from cubism and preached plastic severity, to react against the tendency to decoration, which at that time certain cubists seemed to be slipping into.

One important result was to establish his identity under the name Le Corbusier. He had chosen the pseudonym, the family name of his maternal grandmother, to keep his identity as architectural propagandist separate from that as aspiring painter. But

Le Corbusier the architect eclipsed Jeanneret the artist.

A tireless international lecturer, he was also a trenchant writer. He originated the dictum that design should proceed "from within to without; the exterior is the result of an interior." He also wrote of New York and Chicago as "mighty storms, tornadoes, cataclysms, they are so utterly devoid of harmony."

The titles of the works in which Le Corbusier expressed his ideas reflect his humanistic modernism: "A House—A Palace" (1928), "The Radiant City" (1935), "When Cathedrals Were White" (1937) and "The House of Men" (1942).

Le Corbusier formed an architectural firm with his cousin, Pierre Jeanneret, in 1924. Within a few years, he was involved in a bitter controversy over his plan for the League of Nations Building in Geneva.

It was preferred over all others by a majority of the architectural jury, but was ruled out on the technicality that the papers were drawn not in the China ink specified by the contest rules, but in printer's ink.

A series of appeals brought Le Corbusier a consolation prize, and again his plan was recommended by an architects' jury. But a final committee of ambassadors rejected his plan and commissioned four other architects to collaborate on a new design. Le Corbusier sued, but the league's palace was duly built in monumental style.

The architect received several commissions after World War II, when Europe badly needed rebuilding. His plan was adopted for the reconstruction of La Pallice, the port of La Rochelle. His Maison Radieuse, a 17-story apartment house on stilts at Nantes-Rezé, Marseilles, was constructed after difficulties with planning authorities and a suit by the Society for the Protection of Aesthetic Beauty in France.

Le Corbusier's all-concrete chapel to replace a church destroyed by the war in the tiny town of Ronchamp, in the Vosges Mountains, caused a stir in 1955. The building had not a single straight line; its walls sloped inward or outward and the ceiling seemed to sag.

The strange, swelling roof with flared eaves was designed to catch the winds and create organ tones. It swept down to a spout intended to carry rainwater to a tank.

Instead of the usual formal windows, it had a series of irregular openings, no two of the same dimensions, with stained glass of Le Corbusier's own design. Many critics thought it the most humane and personal of all his creations.

In 1930, Le Corbusier married Yvonne Gallis, a Monagesque. She was reputed to be a splendid cook and a calming influence on her volatile husband, although she was not enthusiastic over the walls of glass he built into their Paris apartment.

"I am tearing my hair out by the roots! All this light is driving me crazy!" she said shortly after they were wed, but she put up with it nonetheless.

The architect was a commander of the Legion of Honor and the recipient of the Gold Medal of Architecture from Queen Elizabeth II of Britain. He also held honorary degrees from Zurich, Cambridge and Columbia universities.

Le Corbusier died of a heart attack while swimming at the Riviera resort of Roquebrune Cap-Martin. He was 77 years old.

He had been vacationing at Roquebrune, not far from the Italian border. He had been swimming at the Plage de la Buse, about four miles from Monaco, shortly before noon, when he suddenly went under.

Another bather saw him go down and alerted rescuers, who brought him to the beach. Firemen from a nearby town, who at first thought that he had drowned, tried to revive him.

The architect is survived by a brother living in Switzerland. His wife died in 1957. They had no children.

AN ARCHITECTURAL GIANT

ADA LOUISE HUXTABLE

A RENAISSANCE man who turned the 20th century into a one-man renaissance, Charles-Edouard Jeanneret-Gris, called Le Corbusier, was one of the major shapers of today's world.

As an architect, his work shocked and influenced three generations and changed the look of cities everywhere. A painter and sculptor, his abstract compositions hang in major museums and collections. An ardent polemicist for the modern movement, his writings reached heights of poetic power that led to a cult of personality rivaled only by professional admiration for the equally poetic power of his trend-setting buildings.

These buildings, spanning half a century, are few in number compared to their far-ranging effect. Each new structure, from the coolly cubistic Villa Savoye built outside of Paris in 1931 to the rough, exposed concrete forms of the High Court Building at Chandigarh, the new Le Corbusier-designed capital of the Punjab, built in the 1950s, has been a bomb exploded in architectural circles, with international repercussions.

Professionally he was a giant, and with two other giants of the same stature, Frank Lloyd Wright and Ludwig Mies van der Rohe, he is credited with the revolution in building known as modern architecture.

Personally, he was a contradictory combination of cool, detached Gallic intellectualism and equally Gallic fussiness over petty details. He faced a public that he always believed misunderstood and undervalued him with a brusque reserve; to his friends he displayed a quick, warm wit.

The slight, irascible architect, his gaze owlishly hypnotic behind circular, horn-rimmed glasses, became legend and prophet in his own time.

His style was intensely personal. Le Corbusier buildings stress strong, sensuous forms, very close to the shapes of abstract sculpture, and each structure is a highly individual concept.

At the same time, he sought universality. He devised a unit of measurement, which he called the Modulor, or Golden Section. It was based on the height of a man with his arm upraised, and according to Le Corbusier, any structure based on multiples of this unit of measure would be beautiful and have a human scale. His own use of the Modulor, however, proved to be as personal as everything else he did.

He defined architecture as the correct play of light and shade on the forms enclosing space, a highly intellectual and aesthetic approach to building that made the product difficult for many to appreciate or understand.

Le Corbusier's uncompromising, unconventional vision was always his own, and each building was a textbook of ideas and a wellspring of the contemporary spirit. No one ever really caught up with him. He was a modern Michelangelo, still far ahead of the field at 77, putting his inimitable stamp on a world already modeled in his own image, but only beginning to grasp his lessons.

For years, few listened. Most of his work before and after World War I consisted of paper schemes or private houses, with a few larger landmark buildings, like the Swiss Pavilion at the Cité Universitaire in Paris.

His largest commissions came in his old age, when the battle for modern architecture was won.

His only building in this country is the Visual Arts Center at Harvard, completed in 1963, a building bursting with new ideas and images, on a site too restricted to hold it. It was a goodwill gesture to a country whose newness and vitality aroused his enthusiasm in the 1920s, but to which he became increasingly hostile in later years.

SIMONE DE BEAUVOIR

1908–1986

When Simone de Beauvoir died on April 14, 1986, French Prime Minister Jacques Chirac said, "Her committed literature was representative of certain movements of ideas that, at one time, had an impact on our society. Her unquestionable talent made her a writer who deserves her place in French literature. In the name of the Government, I salute her memory in respect."

Miss de Beauvoir, who was for many years a central figure in left-wing French intellectual circles, was the author of *The Second Sex*, a provocative and influential polemic on the status of women. She also wrote novels, a play and nonfiction ranging from political commentary to autobiography.

Gloria Steinem said that "if any single human being can be credited with inspiring the current international women's movement, it's Simone de Beauvoir." Betty Friedan yesterday called Miss de Beauvoir an "authentic heroine in the history of womanhood."

Over the years, *The Second Sex* remained the book for which Miss de Beauvoir was known worldwide and which made her an important theorist of militant, radical feminism and a heroine of the women's movement. The book, published in France in 1949 and in the United States in 1953, was her own favorite. It was translated into more than a dozen languages, was honored and excoriated, and sold more than a million copies in a paperback edition in the United States alone. The 1953 Knopf hardcover edition and a paperback edition published in 1974 by Vintage are still in print.

Its basic premise—from which it took off for more than 700 pages of compelling, exasperating indictment—was best summed up in two sentences: "One is not born, but rather becomes, a woman. No biological, psychological or economic fate determines the figure that the human female presents in society; it is civilization as a whole that produces this creature, intermediate between male and eunuch, which is described as feminine."

Throughout her life Miss de Beauvoir was active in causes that advanced or supported her beliefs—from a 1960's international "tribunal" condemning the United States role in Vietnam to the signing of a manifesto with 340 other women in 1971 admitting to having had an abortion in defiance of existing French law.

Her disillusionment with Marxism in practice was recurrent—regime after regime, from the Soviet Union through Algeria to Cuba, disappointed her hopes. But she long advocated what she thought of as the concept of authentic international revolution, and the civil rights even of those with whom she disagreed.

Although she proclaimed at 19 that "I don't want my life to obey any other will but my own," she in fact spent much of her life—from 1929, when she

Elliott Erwitt/Magnum

and existentialist philosopher Jean-Paul Sartre met as students at the Sorbonne, until his death in 1980—as his closest companion. They lived not in the same apartment but always near each other, saw each other daily, spent their annual six-week vacation in Rome together, were completely open about their liaison.

"We have," she said once, "pioneered our own relationship—its freedom, intimacy and frankness." She added, with characteristic candor: "We had also, rather less successfully, thought up the idea of the 'trio.' " She wrote that she turned down Sartre's offer of marriage because she knew he did not want it, but that their relationship was central to both their lives, an "essential love," in Sartre's phrase. They made allowance, at least in theory, for "contingent" relationships of less importance.

As she conceded, this was not always a success, but the relationship with Sartre was always the one that mattered: "I knew that no harm could ever come to me from him—unless he were to die before I did," she said once, and at another time commented that "since I was 21"—when she met Sartre—"I have never been lonely."

Although her major theoretical contributions were to feminism, Miss de Beauvoir's writings, both novels and nonfiction, were also regarded as brilliant expositions of basic existentialist belief: that is, that man is responsible for his own destiny. "Men may make of their own history a hopeless inferno, a junkyard of events, an enduring value," she wrote in 1947, a sentence that itself could be a definition of existentialism.

Sartre encouraged her literary ambitions and was credited by her with pushing her into the investigation of women's oppression that led to the rage and accusation of *Le Seconde Sexe*. The book caused a storm of outrage in France and an equal furor in the United States. Philip Wylie called it "one of the few great books of our era." Dr. Karl A. Menninger described it as a "scholarly and at the same time pretentious and inflated tract on feminism."

In 1954, Miss de Beauvoir's novel *Les Mandarins* (*The Mandarins*) won the Prix Goncourt and stirred scandalized delight with what were regarded as thinly disguised portraits of Sartre, Albert Camus and other leading French intellectuals. The author never admitted that it was a roman à clef, but did concede that the novel included an account of her affair with Nelson Algren, the American writer to whom she dedicated the book. It appeared in the United States in 1956.

Her first novel, *L'Invitée*, published in France in 1943 and in the United States as *She Came to Stay* in 1954, concerned itself with a "trio," with the triangular relationship among a man and a woman long attached and a second, younger woman. Miss de Beauvoir, although criticized for longwindedness, said that she felt she had been influenced by Hemingway, and that she admired the writing of Kafka, Proust and Joyce. She was a slow, meticulous, daily writer.

Her other novels included *The Blood of Others* (1948), *All Men Are Mortal* (1955), *Les Belles Images* (1967) and *The Woman Destroyed* (1968). She also wrote four volumes of autobiography—*Memoirs of a Dutiful Daughter* (1958), *Force of Circumstance* (1963), *The Coming of Age* (1972) and *All Said and Done* (1974)—and a play, *The Useless Mouths* (1954).

A tour of China led to *The Long March* in 1958, just as a tour of the United States had produced—or provoked—*America Day by Day* in 1953. Her attitude toward the United States did not mellow with age, and she wrote in the early 1970s: "The moment a nationalist or a popular movement seems to threaten its interests, the United States crushes it." She went on to say that friends predicted the imminent collapse of the country, adding: "Perhaps this collapse may set off a revolution on a worldwide scale? I do not know whether I shall live long enough to see it, but it is a comforting outlook."

With Sartre, she also engaged in acts of political protest. In 1970, for example, they were arrested for selling a banned Maoist newspaper—which they were doing to protest the ban, not in support of the

EXCERPTS FROM DE BEAUVOIR'S WRITINGS ABOUT WOMEN

A man who is compelled to go on materially and morally supporting a woman feels he is victimized. But if he abandons without resources the woman who has pledged her whole life to him, she will be quite as unjustly victimized. The evil originates in a situation against which all individual action is powerless. Women are "clinging," they are a dead weight, and they suffer for it; the point is that their situation is like that of a parasite sucking out the living strength of another organism. Let them be provided with living strength of their own, let them have the means to attack the world and wrest from it their own subsistence and their dependence will be abolished—that of man also. There is no doubt that both men and women will profit greatly from the new situation.

—*From* The Second Sex

In my family it was always held that the things of the spirit came first. Papa devoted his life to the study of literature and Mama to the practice of the Christian virtues, while Marcelle and Pascal were dedicated to the worship of beauty and the inner life. As soon as I was three years old Marcelle taught me to read, and when I was seven I made my first Communion with an extraordinary degree of piety. I was always very advanced for my age because they paid so much attention to me at home: Papa used to read Pascal and the tragedies of Corneille and Racine after dinner and I was allowed to listen; that forms one's mind—I was always first in examinations, and at the end of term the old ladies of the Institut Ernestine Joliet embraced me more heartily than any of the other pupils. These worthy schoolteachers were not overburdened with diplomas, but as far as devotion and morality were concerned they were second to none: they wore long black skirts and plum-colored silk blouses that caressed my cheeks when they pressed me to their bosoms.

—From "Marguerite," one of several short stories about French women rebelling against their upbringing, in When Things of the Spirit Come First

She passed examinations, attended courses, and she won a certificate that enabled her to work as an assistant librarian in the Red Cross. She learnt to ride a bicycle again to go to her office. She thought of doing dressmaking at home after the war. When that time came I was in a position to help her. But idleness did not suit her. She was eager to live in her own way at last and she discovered a whole mass of activities for herself. She looked after the library in an observation sanatorium just outside Paris as a volunteer, and then the one that belonged to a Catholic club in her neighborhood. She liked handling books, putting wrappers on them, arranging them, dealing with the tickets, giving advice to readers. She studied German and Italian, and kept up her English.

—*From* A Very Easy Death, *a reminiscence, as her mother lay dying of cancer, of the new life her mother began when she was left a penniless widow at 54* paper's positions. In 1960, they were both banned from appearing on France's state-controlled radio or television because they had signed a manifesto supporting the right to refuse military service in Algeria, which was fighting for its independence from France at the time. Only a few years later, in 1967, they were put on a list of boycotted authors by a semiofficial Algerian newspaper because of their support for Israel.

Throughout her life, Miss de Beauvoir continued her political activism, speaking out on issues, heading committees, making speeches, signing manifestos. The condition of women was perhaps her primary "cause," followed some years later by a similar outrage at the conditions of old age. These she wrote about in *The Coming of Age* in 1972, arguing that, for once, women had the advantage: "Old age is better for women than for men," she told an interviewer in 1974. "First of all, they have less far to fall, since their lives are more mediocre than those of most men. And then they still have their homes, their housework, cooking, their children . . . all the 'feminine' culture."

The problems of women in France early in this century figured in a collection of five early stories by Miss de Beauvoir that was published in the United States in 1982 under the title *When Things of the Spirit Come First*.

Earlier, Miss de Beauvoir had written about death, specifically that of her mother, in the ironically titled *A Very Easy Death* (1966). Although she had never been close to her mother, the book was unusually free in its expression of emotion. Her mother had been a devout woman; her father a skeptic and unbeliever. Later, Simone Lucie Ernestine Marie Bertrand de Beauvoir, born in Paris on Jan. 9, 1908, was to say that this "disequilibrium, which condemned me to a perpetual soul-searching, largely explains why I became an intellectual."

After conventional studies she went to the Sorbonne for a degree and diploma in philosophy, which she planned to teach. It was there that she met Sartre, a fellow student three and a half years older than she. "It was the first time in my life," she wrote, "that I felt intellectually inferior to anyone else."

For about two years after leaving the Sorbonne, Miss de Beauvoir remained in Paris. In 1931 she obtained a teaching appointment in Marseilles, and in 1933 in Rouen. By 1938, she was back in Paris, teaching, and in October she began work on what would be her first published novel. By 1943, she had given up teaching to write, and in 1945, she joined Sartre in the editing of *Les Temps Modernes*, a monthly review.

Miss de Beauvoir was somewhat humorless, uncompromising and passionate in her convictions. She remained convinced that, as she wrote in *The Second Sex*, a "totally new society" would be needed, but became increasingly convinced that meaningful change in the status of women would not necessarily evolve from change in the forms of government.

"I think that for the proletariat or a government representing it, to own the means of production is not enough to change the relationship between people," she said in the mid-1970s. "That's what is really important, to change relationships between people."

At about the same time, Miss de Beauvoir acknowledged that "there hasn't been the change I'd hoped for" in women's condition. In 1976, some 25 years after *The Second Sex*, she told an interviewer that she was uncertain about the coming of the hoped-for revolution.

"But the changes that women are struggling for," she said, "yes, that I am certain of, in the long run women will win."

Miss de Beauvoir died at Cochin Hospital in Paris at the age of 78. Her death came the day before the sixth anniversary of the death, on April 15, 1980, of Jean-Paul Sartre.

CHARLES DE GAULLE

1890–1970

By Alden Whitman

"Your reply is going to determine the destiny of France," an intense, solemn, yet aged voice told the French people on April 25, 1969, "because if I am disavowed by the majority of you, my present task as chief of state would obviously become impossible [and] I would immediately stop exercising my functions."

That curiously aloof yet paternal voice, which in 1940 had exhorted a prostrate nation to rise from defeat and fight still against a merciless and omnipresent enemy, and which in the years after 1958 had rallied a country to grandeur and glory beyond her size and resources, had now lost the compelling eloquence that, less than a year earlier, had seemed invincible. Thus it was that two days after his appeal for confidence over a relatively minor issue, Charles de Gaulle was repudiated by 53 percent of the voters. And within 12 hours he departed the splendorous Elysée Palace on the banks of the Seine in Paris, his residence for almost 11 years, for his plain home in the tiny village of Colombey-les-Deux-Eglises. More than the end of a singular political reign, it was the end of an era.

That era started virtually unobserved on June 18, 1940, when an obscure temporary brigadier general, having escaped to London from a battered and disorganized France about to capitulate to Nazi Germany, exhorted his countrymen to continue in a war that he perceived would evolve into a world conflict.

"But has the last word been said?" the 49-year-old officer asked in his pungent speech in a British Broadcasting Corporation studio. "Must we abandon all hope? Is our defeat final and irremediable? To those questions I answer—No!

"For remember this, France is not alone. She is not alone. She is not alone. Behind her is a vast empire, and she can make common cause with the British Empire, which commands the seas and is continuing the struggle."

He concluded with these characteristically self-confident words:

"I, General de Gaulle, now in London, invite French officers and men who are at present on British soil, or may be in the future, with or without their arms; I invite engineers and skilled workmen from the armaments factories who are at present on British soil, or may be in the future, to get in touch with me.

"Whatever happens, the flame of French resistance must not and shall not die."

Very few Frenchmen heard that impromptu broadcast; and at first very few hearkened to it. In Britain, too, de Gaulle was unknown except to a few cabinet ministers and Prime Minister Winston Churchill. Churchill, however, had an intuitive confidence in him, having already addressed him as *"l'homme du destin."*

"He carried with him in his small airplane the

New York Times Photo

honor of France," Churchill wrote later of the general's flight to Britain.

Although it seemed ludicrous to some that de Gaulle, with a mere 100,000 francs and a handful of volunteers, could put together a Free French cause, the general exuded total faith in himself.

"When leaders fail," he wrote, "new leaders are projected upward out of the eternal spirit of France: from Charlemagne to Joan of Arc to Napoleon, Poincaré and Clemenceau. Perhaps this time I am one of those thrust into leadership by the failure of others."

And alluding to his self-conceived mission he wrote in *The Call to Honor*, the first volume of his three-volume war memoirs: "What I was determined to save was the French Nation and the French State. What I had to bring back into the war was not just Frenchmen, but France."

In a tone that appeared to derive from Louis XIV, he added: *"C'était à moi d'assumer la France."* ("It was up to me to take responsibility for France.")

This merger of identities—in which de Gaulle believed himself to be the incarnation of the nation, standing superior to factions—accounted for many of his actions, just as it roiled his critics. His certainty that he was France (*"Je suis la France,"* he declared in 1940) sustained him thorough many mutations of fortune before the country's liberation in mid-1944; and it emboldened him when he was shaping the Fifth Republic, decolonizing the empire, freeing Algeria, creating a nuclear capability and fashioning a foreign policy designed to give France an independent world stature. His certainty, which some saw as hubris, or arrogance, also contributed to his downfall—to his blindness to the domestic economic disaffections that turned public opinion against him.

As he emerged in 1940, de Gaulle appeared tailored to the role of a man of destiny. Describing him after his initial broadcast, Pierre Bourdan wrote: "I saw a man of another age. Very tall [he was 6 feet 4 inches], he was wearing a uniform and leggings and held himself extremely straight. But this erectness, accentuated by his thrown-back head and by his arms, which followed exactly the line of his body, seemed a natural and comfortable position for him.

"The bearing of his head, so very remote, and the expression of his face showed his intransigence.

"The chief characteristic of his eyes was that they were oblivious of the outer world. Their expression could not change to suit the mood of the people around him. Their look seemed preordained!"

It was this hauteur that permitted him to stride into the pantheon of heroes in August 1944, as he led a Paris liberation parade from the Arch of Triumph to Notre Dame. Cheered by two million people in an explosion of national fervor, he experienced his finest hour, his apotheosis.

It was this hauteur, too, that exasperated Allied leaders during the war. "The Cross of Lorraine [de Gaulle's emblem] was the heaviest cross I have ever had to bear," Churchill once bristled, although he conceded in another context, "Never mind, he defied all . . ."

The general's fervid nationalism ("France cannot be France without greatness") impressed Stalin, to whom it seemed that this idiosyncratic conception of France explained de Gaulle. "He is not a complicated man," Stalin remarked at the Yalta Conference in 1945. He thought that giving France an occupation zone in Germany was a courtesy gesture, not a right she had won in the war.

President Franklin D. Roosevelt's relations with de Gaulle were hostile from the outset. Suspicious of the general, Roosevelt saw him as "more and more unbearable," as petty, vainglorious and, potentially, a dictator. These attitudes, reinforced by gossip from French exiles in the United States and by adverse reports from the State Department and from pro-Vichy diplomats, involved the United States in a search for alternatives to de Gaulle up to the liberation of Paris.

"De Gaulle may be a good man," Roosevelt told Churchill in 1943, "but he has a messianic complex." One result of the president's mistrust was to foster in the hypersensitive de Gaulle an animosity toward the United States. He never forgot that the United States tried to maneuver him into turning over Free French leadership to Gen. Henri-Honoré Giraud in 1943; that the United States did not recognize the French National Committee until mid-1944, and then only grudgingly; and that Roosevelt had blackballed him from Yalta.

Although impersonal factors undoubtedly entered into the general's American policy, he was convinced on the basis of his own experience that the United States, in the war and later, was seeking "to settle Europe's future in France's absence." This sentiment hardened, and in the 1960s he believed the evidence of world events showed that the United States was aggressive, was engaging in "a dirty little war in Vietnam" and was a menace of great magnitude to European and world stability.

This estimate undoubtedly underlay his efforts to scuttle the North Atlantic Treaty Organization and American arming of West Germany. It also was in part responsible for his diplomatic initiatives in Latin America, Africa, the Soviet bloc, China and Southeast Asia. Tweaking the eagle's beak was not only a calculated sport; it was also a constituent of French glory.

Although much was made of de Gaulle's aloofness and his sibylline utterances, the founder and first president of the Fifth Republic was less of a mystery to those who had read his philosophy of leadership, as set down in *Le fil de l'epée (The Edge of the Sword)* in 1932.

Doctrine, character and prestige, he wrote, are the indispensable ingredients in a leader. "It is essential that the plan on which the leader has concentrated all his faculties shall bear the mark of grandeur," he wrote. And on another page he said, "First and foremost there can be no prestige without mystery, for familiarity breeds contempt."

As another precept, he spoke of calculating the effect of an action. "The great leaders have always carefully stage-managed their effects," he noted.

Summing up, he said: "The statesman must concentrate all his efforts on captivating men's minds. He has to know when to dissemble, when to be frank. He must pose as the servant of the public in order to be its master. He must outbid his rivals in self-confidence, and only after a thousand intrigues and solemn undertakings will he find himself entrusted with full power."

In the first years of the Fifth Republic de Gaulle did indeed seem to "concentrate all his efforts" on establishing his authority and his personality. In large matters, such as liquidating the Algerian war, he served as a unifier by casting what amounted to a spell over metropolitan France. This was nurtured by episodes of personal courage in hostile crowds: He was shot at but never hit; plots against him failed.

In small matters, too, de Gaulle made certain that he projected perfection. Every detail of a trip, a speech, a news conference was worked out in advance; whatever appeared to be a spur-of-the-moment gesture was a well-rehearsed bit of stage business. For television he took lessons from an actor; he practiced before a mirror; he learned his texts by heart.

Equally carefully prepared were his hand-shaking excursions into crowds. However, because he was nearsighted and disliked to wear glasses, he often shook hands with members of his own security guard along with those of the public. In each case, though, there was a stately personal greeting: *"Bonjour, madame"*; *"Bonjour, monsieur"*; *"Bonjour, mon petit."*

When it came to generating goodwill abroad, de Gaulle was indefatigable. For his 12-day trip to the Soviet Union in 1966, for example, he read up on all the places he was to visit and worked references to them into his speeches. Moreover, he took the trouble to conclude every toast with a few words in Russian, even once using a Pushkin quotation.

Although de Gaulle liked to invest every event with as much pomp as it could wear, he skimped on his state banquets. A rapid eater, he set the pace for his guests, who often had their plates snatched away three-quarters full. These repasts were cheeseless (de

Gaulle did not fancy the smell) and fruitless (he thought fruit took too long to peel). An entire banquet rarely lasted more than an hour.

The fact that de Gaulle stood on his dignity so markedly in public gave rise to reports that he was equally ceremonial in private. One such story had de Gaulle's wife, Yvonne, returning to the Elysée from shopping, slumping into a chair and exclaiming, "God, I am tired." Her husband is supposed to have replied, "I have often told you, my dear, it was sufficient in private if you addressed me as *'Monsieur le Président.'* "

Actually, de Gaulle was quite unformidable in his private moments. After dinner, he and his wife, a self-effacing woman who was popularly known as Tante Yvonne, spent many evenings watching television, especially the light programs. On Thursday afternoons, a school holiday in France, their grandchildren often came to tea at the Elysée. De Gaulle had two surviving children: Philippe, a naval officer on his father's staff; and Elizabeth, the wife of Gen. Alain de Boissieu. Another daughter, Anne, was born with Down's syndrome and died when she was 20.

Of his decision in 1940 to try to build a resistance movement at the bleakest moment of the war, de Gaulle wrote: "I felt within myself a life coming to an end—the life I had lived within the framework of a solid France and an indivisible army." And indeed the first 49 years of his life were solidly conventional.

Charles-André-Marie-Joseph de Gaulle was born Nov. 22, 1890, in Lille. Members of the lesser nobility, conservative and staunchly Roman Catholic, the de Gaulle family had furnished soldiers, lawyers and writers to France since at least 1210.

Henri, Charles's father, was lay headmaster of the Jesuit College of the Immaculate Conception in Paris when his son was born. He also taught Latin, Greek, philosophy and literature there and at his own school after the Society of Jesus was expelled from France in 1907. Charles's mother, Jeanne Maillot-Delannoy, was his father's cousin, and, like her husband, she was intensely patriotic and conservative.

In childhood, Charles was much exposed to family conversations about the Franco-Prussian War of 1870, in which his father had been wounded. Talk centered on France's ignominious loss of Alsace-Lorraine and the abject defeat of the French army.

Indoctrinated to believe that the army was the quintessence of France, the young man had little choice but to be a soldier, and in 1910 he entered Saint-Cyr, the officer-training academy. Graduated two years later, he joined the 33d Infantry Regiment at Arras commanded by Col. Henri-Philippe Pétain.

The lives of the two men became ironically entwined. Early in World War II, when de Gaulle founded the French Resistance, his old Arras colonel, then a Marshal of France and head of the collaborationist Vichy regime, had him condemned to death for desertion. When the tables were turned after the war, Pétain was condemned to death for treason, and de Gaulle, the provisional president-premier of France, commuted his sentence to life imprisonment.

In World War I, de Gaulle, who was wounded three times and captured by the Germans at Verdun, won a Legion of Honor and achieved the rank of captain. Afterward he taught briefly in a Polish military college, then at Saint-Cyr; then, becoming a protégé and close friend of Pétain—who was godfather to de Gaulle's son, Philippe—he spent two years at the army staff college.

In 1925 Pétain attached his friend to his secretariat in the Supreme War Council. Two years later de Gaulle became a major and served for two years in the occupation army in the Rhineland and two years in the Middle East. De Gaulle returned to France in 1932, became a lieutenant colonel and, at Pétain's intervention, was named secretary to the High Council of National Defense, a post that he held for five years and that brought him into everyday touch with the country's military leaders.

The job also gave him his first close-up view of parliamentary politics, by which he was not favorably impressed, for in five years no fewer than 14 cabinets chased one another in and out of the swinging doors of the Chamber of Deputies in the Palais Bourbon.

De Gaulle's career up to this point had not been brilliant, despite Pétain's patronage. One reason was the officer's spit-and-polish personality; another was his scholarly but unorthodox book, *Vers l'armée de métier (Toward a Modern Army),* published in 1934.

Scornful of several pet army doctrines, including conscription, the book also disparaged the Maginot Line, a supposedly impregnable fortress system along the French-German border. Equally upsetting to the reigning military minds was de Gaulle's proposal for a modernized army with an elite mobile tank force at its head. This striking force, he argued, could overrun and disorganize enemy territory, which later could be occupied by foot soldiers.

When World War II broke out, de Gaulle was a colonel in command of a tank regiment in Metz. When Hitler, after chewing up Poland, turned on France, the debacle that de Gaulle had foreseen took place: The Maginot Line was turned and northern France was overrun by Nazi tanks. In the sweep de Gaulle, with his meager force, gave a good account of himself and was made a temporary brigadier general—the youngest in the army at that time. Premier Paul Reynaud brought him into the cabinet June 5, 1940, as Under Secretary of Defense. In this capacity he met Churchill for the first time on a visit to London June 9.

It was about then that he came to his momentous decision—that events made it evident that Britain would remain in the war, that the war would become worldwide and that he would try to organize French resistance based on the colonies. A few days afterward, in France, he sat next to Churchill at dinner. "Our conversation confirmed in me my confidence in Churchill," de Gaulle recalled. "And no doubt he also grasped that de Gaulle, though helpless at the moment, was as full of resolve as himself."

After the discomfited French government fled to Bordeaux and prepared to sue for an armistice, de Gaulle took flight to London. Assuming there the epic task of organizing a resistance force, he was recognized June 28 by the British government "as the leader of all the Free French, wherever they may be, who will rally to him in defense of the Allied cause."

With a mystique already sprouting around him, de Gaulle was able, by claiming to embody France (and no one challenged him then), to draw into his cause the governors of French Equatorial Africa, Chad and the French Cameroons. This gave de Gaulle a territorial base that, however far removed from the war theaters, was at least more imposing than his office in Carlton Gardens.

Some of the edge was taken off his first successes when his small naval expedition to Dakar was easily repulsed by the Vichy garrison. Although he set up a Council for the Defense of the Empire in Brazzaville, the French Congo, and raised the Cross of Lorraine there, the Dakar failure made American recognition of the Vichy regime seem plausible.

The setback also held down his following inside France. A further setback in Syria in May 1941, when Free French troops failed to win over Vichyite soldiers, almost made de Gaulle a chanticleer without a flock.

But a month later, in June 1941, the Soviet Union's entrance into the war dramatically altered de Gaulle's fortunes by producing two important developments: direct Free French contact with the Russians and the start of an active resistance in France, now organized by the energetic French Communist party. Ultimately, in July 1942, the Soviet Union set its seal upon de Gaulle as the French Resistance leader. By then the underground war in France was a flourishing armed enterprise of men and women of many political convictions.

Meanwhile, de Gaulle took astute political advantage of the Soviet Union's entry into the war by organizing, in September 1941, the French National Committee, a virtual government in exile, with himself as chairman. The general, however, was far from receiving United States recognition and cooperation.

On the contrary, Roosevelt, urged on by Adm. William D. Leahy, his envoy to Vichy, and by Robert W. Murphy, his representative in Algiers, sought an alternative to de Gaulle, someone more complaisant.

The Americans' choice fell on General Giraud, a Pétainist who was taken out of France to North Africa, where he was appointed French commander in chief in late 1942. At about the same time Adm. François Darlan, a Vichy man who thought the time had come to jump on the Allied bandwagon, arrived in Algiers. A deal was concluded whereby Darlan became the chief French authority in North Africa, but his tenure was cut short by his assassination under mysterious circumstances on Christmas Eve. General Giraud was then appointed civil and military commander.

In these murky dealings de Gaulle could not be ignored completely, for he had support in the colonies and in France; and in a complicated series of maneuvers Roosevelt and Churchill brought de Gaulle and General Giraud together at a conference at Anfa, near Casablanca, in late January 1943. A fragile alliance was fabricated, symbolized by a handshake for cameramen. But General Giraud, with his conservative associations and his political ineptitude, was sacked as co-chairman of the Committee of National Liberation within a year.

Even in control of the committee, however, de Gaulle did not have the confidence of the Americans as the man to govern France after the war. W. Averell Harriman, the diplomat, summed up official feeling when he wrote: "Unfortunately de Gaulle is thinking more of how he is going to rule France than of ways of liberating her. That is his great flaw. Also, he is extremely vain and imagines himself a sort of Joan of Arc, and that makes work with him difficult."

The hunt for a more pliable leader led to proposals to keep de Gaulle out of France after the Normandy landings in June 1944. It also accounted in part for the fact that only a token French force went ashore on D-Day. This so irked de Gaulle that 20 years later he refused to attend commemorative rites at the Normandy beaches. "The Anglo-Saxons," he wrote, "never really treated us as real allies."

Circumventing Britain and the United States, the de Gaulle committee declared itself the provisional government of France; and then, on June 13, the general and a tiny group of aides made a quick, almost stealthy, trip to Bayeux, where the general received a hearty welcome and where he appointed a Gaullist governor for Normandy.

De Gaulle did not return to France until Aug. 20, having met meanwhile with Roosevelt in Washington and established a superficially cordial relationship. One result was Washington's recognition of his committee as "qualified to exercise the administration of France." De Gaulle went on to establish his personal authority in fact in a tremendous outburst of emotional frenzy that convulsed Paris when he led a triumphal march from the Arch of Triumph to the Cathedral of Notre Dame on Aug. 26, 1944.

Paris had been liberated the day before by the combined efforts of armed Parisians, Gen. Jacques Leclerc's Second Armored Division and American troops. But de Gaulle, tall, smartly turned out in his military best, was the one person on whom the hero's mantle seemed to fall. If he at this moment was not France, who was?

In the days that followed, de Gaulle created a moderate Government of National Unanimity, which lasted for 14 fitful months. During its tenure, he took pains to cold-shoulder leftist groups in the Resistance and to disarm their paramilitary units. Even so, he did not satisfy President Harry S Truman, who told him bluntly on a trip to Washington in August 1945 not to expect much American financial help unless he threw out the few Communists in his cabinet.

In October 1945, the French, disavowing the Third Republic, elected a Constituent Assembly. With its convocation, which foreshadowed the Fourth Republic, de Gaulle became a parliamentary executive, a role for which he had no liking. So, giving the excuse that the "regime of parties" had again emerged, he resigned in January 1946. His sojourn, though, was brief, for he emerged from "retirement" in April 1947 to call for formation of a Rally of the French People *(Rassemblement du Peuple Français)*—a party against parties. It was a venture that the general's admirers were later to play down.

At first he attracted thousands to the Rally as, in a bid for centrist and rightist backing, he inveighed against the Communists and the trade unions. The Rally had a grand success in the municipal elections of 1947, gathering nearly 40 percent of the votes. But de Gaulle overplayed his hand by issuing a virtual ultimatum to the National Assembly that sought an immediate general election. The demand agitated the assembly and dismayed many in the Rally's rank and file who still thought a bad republic preferable to a good tyranny. Moreover, the paramilitary character of Rally meetings disquieted public opinion, as did de Gaulle's friendly references to Dr. Konrad Adenauer, the West German leader.

The Rally did not obtain significant big-business support and it failed also to attract the United States, which placed its confidence and its Marshall Plan money in such politicians as Robert Schuman and Jules Moch. De Gaulle seemed too unreliable.

By 1954, when his Rally was in disarray, de Gaulle's spirits were so buffeted that he could say, *"J'étais la France"* ("I was France"). And in July 1955 he announced his retirement from public life. "I say farewell to you," he told newsmen. "We shall not meet again until the tempest again looses itself on France." He was nearing his 65th birthday.

From then until the middle of 1958, he lived at Colombey, where he completed *The War Memoirs of Charles de Gaulle.* He also traveled to the French West Indies and the Pacific. More important, he received politicians at Colombey and journeyed to Paris once a week for political chats in his office on Rue Solférino.

The "tempest" that brought de Gaulle openly back to public life, and to power, was the war in Algeria, under way since 1954. The Fourth Republic, already stung by the loss of Indochina and the defeat at Dienbienphu, was bedeviled by the conflict against the Algerian nationalists. By 1958 some 35,000 French troops were in Algeria attempting to contain 15,000 insurgents.

The brutal war was unpopular in France, where its costs were cutting into a spreading prosperity; but no cabinet knew how to liquidate it without risking an army coup. The crisis came in May 1958, when hysterical Europeans in Algeria seized government offices with the aid of army officers. There was talk of a rightist coup in Paris. Almost automatically attention swung to de Gaulle, and he was ready—with a statement that said: "In the past, the country from its very depth entrusted me with the task of leading it to salvation. Today, with new ordeals facing it, let the country know that I am ready to assume the powers of the Republic."

After two weeks of frenetic political dealing he was invested as premier of France on June 1 and given decree powers for six months with the right within that time to submit a new constitution. He was accepted by the army in the belief that a general would surely support the war.

Abandoning demagoguery and proceeding with caution and adroit double-talk, he moved to dismantle the French Algerians' Committees of Public Safety while appearing to place confidence in Gen. Raoul Salan as the government representative in Algiers. With the immediate crisis muffled, a constitution for the Fifth Republic was drafted that placed effective power in a president rather than in Parliament. It was ratified by an 80 percent majority of the voters, and in December de Gaulle was elected president for a seven-year term that began Jan. 8, 1959.

Certain of his position in France, de Gaulle removed General Salan and, over a year, transferred to France 1,500 army officers associated with the French Algerian diehards. Nevertheless, in January 1960, there was an army-led insurrection in Algiers, which was contained with the arrest of the ringleaders and the cashiering of some rightist generals.

In November of that year de Gaulle suggested an independent Algeria, a proposal that was endorsed in a referendum in France and Algeria in January 1961. Orderly progression to independence was thwarted, however, by the rise of the Secret Army Organization and by the obduracy of many French Algerians. Terrorism spread into France, while the unrest and violence in Algeria culminated in rebellion there in April 1961.

De Gaulle acted with firmness and energy. The revolt collapsed, and three of its four leaders went into hiding while the fourth was jailed.

Finally, in September 1962, an independent Algerian regime was established and within a year about 750,000 French Algerians emigrated to metropolitan France. All this was accomplished in the face of Secret Army terrorism that included two attempts to assassinate the president. In the second attempt, in August 1962, a bullet missed his skull by an inch. Turning to his bodyguard, he remarked: "This is getting to be dangerous. Fortunately, those gentlemen are poor shots."

Once the Algerian problem was solved, de Gaulle was able to flex French muscle in Europe and around the world. A mighty ingredient of the "new" France was her development of an atomic bomb, which came about in 1960, when a device was exploded in the Sahara.

De Gaulle's European policy was aimed at restoring France to a position of greatness. This involved, on the one hand, an entente with the Soviet Union and, on the other, an effort to keep Britain and the United States at a distance. The Russian phase of de Gaulle's policy entailed a dramatic trip to the Soviet Union in mid-1966 and visits to other Eastern European nations.

His relations with Britain, never comfortable, seemed to reflect a belief that she was an American satellite. This was said to account for his veto of Britain's bids (the first rebuff was in 1963) to join the Common Market, a six-nation economic group composed of France, West Germany, Italy, Belgium, the Netherlands and Luxembourg.

De Gaulle profoundly disagreed with United States policy in Europe, and he eventually decided to withdraw France from NATO. He barred American nuclear warheads from French territory and denied French rocket sites to the United States. At the same time he sharpened his attitude toward West Germany, calling that country at one point "America's Foreign Legion in Europe." In addition, he established diplomatic relations with Peking and nettled Washington by condemning the Vietnam war.

His policy toward West Germany, however, proved ambiguous. On the one hand, de Gaulle was alert to the potential dangers of militarism across the Rhine. On the other hand, he sought to mute the hatreds generated by World War II. In this spirit, he toured West Germany and invited German officials to Paris. He seemed to realize that European stability could not be achieved unless the government in Bonn played its part in the economic and political life of Western Europe.

He also strove to exert leadership in the nonaligned world by trying to create an alternative to the dual hegemonies of the United States and the Soviet Union. Polarization of the world into two antithetical camps, he believed, tended to increase global tensions. French nuclear development, he felt, helped to overcome an American-Soviet atomic monopoly.

At the same time, he could not resist shocking American opinion. He encouraged French-Canadian separatism. He courted Latin America, a United States preserve. In the Middle East, he leaned to the Arab cause against the Israelis by cutting off the flow of French arms to Israel.

Indeed, de Gaulle generated strong resentments among many Americans, some of whom even refused to visit France or purchase French-made goods while he was in power.

De Gaulle's first term as president of the Fifth Republic expired in January 1966. He was elected to a second term, but only after a runoff in which he received 55 percent of the votes. The principal attack on him came from the left, temporarily united under François Mitterrand, on account of his essentially conservative domestic policies. Inflation and wage restraints bore heavily on the working class.

It was domestic discontent that eventually brought him down. Grandeur—membership in the nuclear "club," foreign aid in Africa (including support of Biafra) and elsewhere, stockpiling of gold reserves, pioneering in supersonic air travel—cost millions of francs. This meant austerity at home at a time when a nation chiefly of small shopkeepers and farmers was struggling to transform itself into a more modern country.

The transition brought with it tensions in virtually every segment of society. There were dislocations in the countryside as corporate farming increased; in the cities supermarkets began to appear, dooming the neighborhood grocery and meat stores. And more and more industrial workers were employed in larger and larger enterprises.

In education, more students than ever before crowded the universities and studied under curriculums and pedagogical practices that were clearly irrelevant to the times. In an effort to accommodate the influx of students, satellites of older universities were set up, as at Nanterre, just outside Paris.

It was at Nanterre that open rebellion against de Gaulle broke out in the spring of 1968. The issue was reform of education. Students at the graceless concrete school occupied a classroom on March 22, and were routed by the police, who used steel rods as spears. The number of militant students—many of them commuters from Paris—grew, and the authorities closed the university in early May. Thereupon a group from Nanterre met with a Sorbonne group to plan a joint protest.

From this mild beginning sprang "the events of May," a month-long clash of social, economic and political forces that generated a near revolution. The Sorbonne students went on strike and were clubbed and buffeted by the police. The turmoil spread to the provinces, and soon the relatively prosperous sons and daughters of bourgeois parents were battling not just oppressive education but government itself.

Meanwhile, the students' spirit of audacity spread to the workers, who had their own discontents, and soon there were factory sit-ins. These grew despite the efforts of union leaders to calm the situation, and all France seemed engaged in crisis, demonstrations and strikes.

At first aloof to the disorders, de Gaulle passed the early days of the turmoil in writing out in longhand the speeches he was going to deliver in Rumania. And, indeed, he visited that country later in the month.

When he returned to Paris he found that the situation was nearly out of hand; and, after a quick conference with army leaders, then in Germany, to obtain assurances of their support, he began to resolve the crisis, first by acting to pacify the 10 million striking workers with pay increases and then by cracking down further on the students.

Finally, on May 30, he dissolved the National Assembly and warned the country in an emotional radio speech (the government-run television system was on strike) that he would restore law and order with all the means at his disposal. There was an implied threat that 30,000 French troops might be on their way back to France from Germany. De Gaulle feared, he said, the possibility of a Communist "dictatorship."

Immediately after he spoke, hundreds of thousands of his adherents thronged the Place de la Concorde in Paris to voice their support. This segment of society, apprehensive over the possibility of a social revolution, proved to be his temporary bulwark. Leftist elements, including the Communists, backed down from the barricades, deciding to take their chances in the National Assembly elections made necessary by de Gaulle's dissolution of that body. The "days of May" were over.

Posing a choice between chaos and himself, de Gaulle won a big victory in the elections. He seemed more in control than ever, and strong enough to bar devaluation of the franc in the fall of 1968, when most signs pointed to the necessity for such action. However, as Georges Pompidou, then the premier, remarked shortly after the student-worker insurgency, "things would never be quite the same again."

What had taken place during May constituted a fatal undermining of the contention that de Gaulle was the incarnation of France. He might win a National Assembly victory, but it was clear that his policies did not correspond to the aspirations of either French college youths or workers.

The proof that de Gaulle had lost the adherence of his people even as he had won their votes in June 1968 came over a relatively minor issue—the future regional structure of France and the role of its Senate. The matter was to be settled in a referendum in April 1969, which at first created only slight interest.

Then de Gaulle injected himself. The result of the voting was to be a test of public confidence. Precisely why he chose to make the referendum a personal matter is conjectural. As an autocrat he may have felt that he required the extra bolstering that victory would bring him. Perhaps he felt, too, that he could again discomfit his domestic enemies on the left. Perhaps also the megalomania that often accompanies old age may have been a factor in his decision.

In any event he gambled on what he was convinced would be an assured success. His tactics of May and June 1958 were used again: the attempt to frighten the electors with the threat of Communism and chaos should the voting be adverse. Where would they be without de Gaulle? he asked.

The general was unprepared for the results. He was persuaded, until the returns were indubitable, that he would triumph. He left office still dazed.

Retiring once more to Colombey with a secretary, a bodyguard, a chauffeur and his $35,000 pension, he set to writing his memoirs, dating from 1958. *The Renewal*, the first of a projected three-volume *Memoirs of Hope*, was published in October 1970. Such was the magic of his name and interest in the events recounted that 250,000 copies were sold in a few days.

At Colombey, though, he vanished into political silence. When he retired in 1969, the long personalist epoch of Charles de Gaulle was over.

With the words "General de Gaulle is dead. France is a widow," delivered in a trembling voice, President Pompidou announced on radio and television on Nov. 10, 1970, that Charles de Gaulle had died the night before at his country retreat in Colombey-les-Deux-Églises. His 80th birthday would have been Nov. 22nd.

Death came to the wartime leader and peacetime premier and president while he was playing a game of solitaire on a little card table in the quiet of his living room. Stricken with a heart attack, he collapsed at 7:30 P.M. and is believed to have died of a ruptured aorta soon afterward.

According to the general's wishes, no state funeral was held. General de Gaulle was buried Thursday morning in the churchyard of Colombey-les-Deux-Églises in an "extremely simple" ceremony.

A memorial service was held at the same hour—11 A.M.—in Notre Dame Cathedral, and it is there that President Pompidou and other French leaders joined with some 80 chiefs of foreign states or heads of government—among them President Nixon, Premier Aleksei N. Kosygin of the Soviet Union, Prime Minister Heath of Britain—for last homage to the soldier-statesman.

ON THE OLD AND NEW LEADERSHIP

JAMES RESTON

THE DEATH of Charles de Gaulle reminds one of the lovely verse by Stephen Phillips, the English poet:

O for a living man to lead!
That will not babble when we bleed;
O for the silent doer of the deed!
One that is happy in his height,
And one that in a nation's night
Hath solitary certitude of light.

All this he had and it partly explains the genuine sense of loss at his passing, even here on the Potomac, but it is not the full explanation. His "certitude" often infuriated Washington and all but broke America's faith in the common defense of Western civilization, but he had other qualities now uncommon in a world of political technicians.

He knew what he wanted, which is a rare quality in this ambiguous time. He knew the power of the word *no;* he knew when to be silent and when to speak, and he had the gifts of precision, poetry and prophecy.

I once asked him if he really wanted to unite Europe. France will not unite Europe, he replied, and neither will Britain, nor the United States, but China will. There is the force that will bring Russia and Europe back together again.

The Cold War, he said, is a passing phase. America has won it in Europe and doesn't know it, but other great divisions will arise. At the end of the century the critical tension in the world may not be ideological but racial.

If this were true, I asked, was there any other force in the world that could stand out against the pressure of China—could India do it? "India?" he asked. "India is a dust of peoples, living in misery and meditation. . . . Never! Impossible!"

Here again the "certitude" that made him a great Frenchman, and the ranging mind thinking in generations and epochs, but was he a great statesman of the world? The historians of France may have a loftier view of this than the historians of the rest of the Western world.

Even when de Gaulle's nationalistic views were getting the American forces out of France and blocking the integration of Europe, that other great Frenchman (and great world statesman as well), Jean Monnet, used to urge compassion for de Gaulle's views.

"You must always remember," Monnet said, "it is the living de Gaulle who speaks, but it is the dead de Gaulle who acts. You must wait and look back on it all later."

Well, that is what the world is doing now—perhaps far too soon, and in French terms it may be that Monnet was right. In his brave and dangerous liberation of Algeria, de Gaulle undoubtedly allied himself with the historic liberation of the overseas territories.

He may very well have been right in his assumption that the United States would never risk atomic destruction in the defense of France, and therefore France must keep an independent atomic force of its own. But while he knew what he wanted, he wanted too many contradictory things: glory without power; strength without allied unity; equality without size; "a nation of heroes and saints" in a world of scoundrels.

It was easy to understand many of his longings. He hated this big, clattering, homogenized world. His writings were full of the old noble words—*honor, dignity, sacrifice, independence, courage* and *grandeur*—and naturally enough, he resented the fact that Europe, the common home of Dante and Goethe, the center of the political and cultural world for a thousand years, should be dominated by those two clumsy giants, the United States and the Soviet Union.

DE GAULLE'S WORDS: DEFIANT, PROUD, ELOQUENT

From Speeches

Has the last word been spoken? Must hope disappear? Is the defeat final? No. Believe me—I who speak to you in full awareness and tell you that nothing is lost for France. The same means that have conquered us can bring victory one day. Whatever happens, the flame of French resistance must not go out and shall not go out.

—Speech on British Broadcasting Corporation, June 18, 1940.

It was dark yesterday. But this evening there is light. Frenchwomen, Frenchmen, help me.

—Radio speech on June 27, 1958, on return to power.

Well, my dear old country, here we are together then, once again facing a heavy trial. By virtue of the mandate that the people gave me and of the national legitimacy that I have incarnated for 20 years, I call upon all men and all women to support me, whatever happens.

—Appeal broadcast during military uprising in Algiers on Jan. 29, 1960.

I'll tell you what will happen when de Gaulle is gone. Well, I'll tell you this, which may explain which way we intend to move: what is to be feared, in my way of thinking, after the event about which I'm talking, is not a political vacuum, it is rather an overflow.

—News conference, May 25, 1962.

The new Republic has its President. It's I. Here I am, such as I am. I don't say that I'm perfect and that I'm not as old as I am. I don't at all claim to know everything nor to be capable of everything. I know better than anybody that I must have successors and that the nation must choose them so that they follow the same line. But history has conferred upon me, along with the French people, to succeed in certain undertakings.

—Speech on reelection, Dec. 18, 1965.

I have understood you.

—Speech to mutinous throng in Algiers, June 4, 1958.

For a great people to have the free disposition of itself and the means to struggle to preserve it is an absolute imperative, for alliances have no absolute virtues, whatever may be the sentiments on which they are based.

—News conference, Jan. 14, 1963.

Unless the universe is to head toward catastrophe, only a political accord could reestablish peace. The conditions of such an agreement being clear and well known, it is still time to hope. Just as the one in 1954, the agreement would have as its purpose to reestablish and guarantee the neutrality of the peoples of Indochina and their right to self-determination . . . allowing each of them the entire responsibility of their affairs. The contracting parties would therefore be the real powers that are functioning and among the other states, at least the five world powers. But the possibility and, even more, the opening of such a vast and difficult negotiation would of course depend on the decision and the commitment that America would have previously been willing to take to repatriate her forces in a reasonable and fixed time.

—Speech in Phnom Penh, Cambodia, Sept. 1, 1966.

Vive le Québec libre!

—Cry to crowd in Montreal, July 24, 1967.

From Memoirs

France comes from the depths of the ages. She lives, the centuries call to her. But she remains herself throughout time.

All my life, I have built a certain idea of France. Sentiment as well as reason inspires it. The emotional side of me naturally imagines France as the princess of the fairy tales or the Madonna of the frescoes, as though dedicated to a lofty and exceptional destiny. In short, in my view, France cannot be France without grandeur.

In France, it has always been through war that the Merovingians, the Carolingians, the Capetians, the Bonapartes and the Third Republic received and lost supreme authority. That which, in the depths of disaster, was invested in me was recognized first by those Frenchmen who did not give up fighting; then, as events proceeded, by the whole population; finally, through many clashes and resentments, by all the governments of the world. Thanks to which, I was able to lead the country to its salvation.

From 1952 to 1958, I was to take six years to write my war memoirs without intervening in public affairs but without doubting that the infirmity of the system would result, sooner or later, in a grave national crisis.

The one that broke out May 13 in Algiers did not therefore surprise me at all. However, I was not involved in any way in the local agitation, nor in the military movement nor in the political schemes that provoked it and I had no liaison with any element in the area nor with any minister in Paris.

The French people have no mental reservations about accepting the Fifth Republic. For the masses, the question is one of our freedoms, is capable of action and reinstituting a regime which, while respecting sponsibility. The question is one of having a government that wants and is able to solve the problems we face. It is a question of answering "Yes" to de Gaulle to whom confidence is accorded because France is at stake.

If there is one voice that can be heard, one activity than can be effective as to the kind of order to establish in place of the cold war, they are par excellence the voice and the activity of France. But on the condition that they be her own and that the hand she holds out be free.

The end of colonization is a page of our history. By turning it France felt both regret for the past and hope for what was to come. But the one who wrote it for her, was he to survive? It was for destiny to decide. It did on Aug. 22, 1962. That day, in Le Petit-Clamart, the car taking me to a plane . . . is suddenly caught in a carefully organized ambush: machine-gunning at point blank range by several automatic arms, then a pursuit undertaken by armed men in a car. Of the some 150 rounds fired at us, 14 touch our car. Yet—incredible luck—none of us is hit. Let de Gaulle thus continue to follow his path and his vocation!

It is true that though France has lost her special vocation of being constantly in danger, the whole world finds itself subjected to the permanent obsession of a generalized conflict. Two empires, American and Soviet, that have become colossal in relation to the former great powers, confront each other with their forces, their hegemonies and their ideologies. Both dispose of nuclear armament that can at any moment overturn the universe and that make of each, in its own camp, an irresistible protector. A dangerous equilibrium that threatens to end some day in an out-sized war if it does not evolve toward a general easing of tensions!

On assuming the leadership of France, I was determined to free her from the subjections, henceforth without reward, that her empire imposed upon her. One can imagine that I would not do it, as one says, with a light heart. For a man of my age and upbringing, it was really cruel to become, on one's own, the mastermind of such a change.

Still, somehow, romance and reality never quite came together in his policies, and even the other Western allies were never willing to exchange American influence and power, which irritated but protected them, for French poetry and politics, which also irritated but did not protect them.

What he did, above all question, was to restore the pride of a defeated nation, and to bring the voice of France back into the highest councils of the world. He made the masses of his fellow countrymen believe in him, though he believed more in authority than democracy and didn't quite believe in them.

Nobody is really going to weep for the bad old days of the two world wars. They produced unspeakable horrors, which make our present struggles seem almost bearable, but they did produce some spectacular men, and de Gaulle was the last of them in the West.

WALT DISNEY

1901–1966

By Murray Schumach

Walt Disney, who built his whimsical cartoon world on Mickey Mouse, Donald Duck, and Snow White and the Seven Dwarfs into a $100-million-a-year entertainment empire, died in St. Joseph's Hospital in Los Angeles on Dec. 15, 1966. He was 65 years old.

His death, at 9:35 A.M., was attributed to acute circulatory collapse. He had undergone surgery at the hospital a month ago for the removal of a lung tumor that was discovered after he entered the hospital for treatment of an old neck injury received in a polo match. On Nov. 30 he reentered the hospital for a "postoperative checkup."

Just before his last illness, Mr. Disney was supervising the construction of a new Disneyland in Florida, a ski resort in Sequoia National Forest and the renovation of the 10-year-old Disneyland at Anaheim. His motion-picture studio was turning out six new productions and several television shows and he was spearheading the development of the vast University of the Arts, called Cal Art, now under construction here.

Although Mr. Disney held no formal title at Walt Disney Productions, he was in direct charge of the company and was deeply involved in all its operations. Indeed, with the recent decision of Jack L. Warner to sell his interest in the Warner Brothers studio, Mr. Disney was the last of Hollywood's veteran moviemakers who remained in personal control of a major studio.

Roy Disney, Walt Disney's 74-year-old brother, who is president and chairman of Walt Disney Productions and who directs its financial operations, said, "We will continue to operate Walt's company in the way that he had established and guided it. All of the plans for the future that Walt had begun will continue to move ahead."

Besides his brother, Mr. Disney is survived by his widow, Lillian, and two daughters, Mrs. Ron Miller and Mrs. Robert Brown.

From his fertile imagination and industrious factory of drawing boards, Walt Elias Disney fashioned the most popular movie stars ever to come from Hollywood and created one of the most fantastic entertainment empires in history.

In return for the happiness he supplied, the world lavished wealth and tributes upon him. He was probably the only man in Hollywood to have been praised by both the American Legion and the Soviet Union.

Where any other Hollywood producer would have been happy to get one Academy Award—the highest honor in American movies—Mr. Disney smashed all records by accumulating 29 Oscars.

"We're selling corn," Mr. Disney once told a reporter, "and I like corn."

David Low, the late British political cartoonist, called him "the most significant figure in graphic arts since Leonardo."

New York Times Photo

Mr. Disney went from seven-minute animated cartoons to become the first man to mix animation with live action, and he pioneered in making feature-length cartoons. His nature films were almost as popular as his cartoons, and eventually he expanded into feature-length movies using only live actors.

The most successful of his nonanimated productions, *Mary Poppins,* released in 1964, has already grossed close to $50 million. It also won an Oscar for Julie Andrews in the title role.

From a small garage-studio, the Disney enterprise grew into one of the most modern movie studios in the world, with four sound stages on 51 acres. Mr. Disney acquired a 420-acre ranch that was used for shooting exterior shots for his movies and television productions. Among the lucrative by-products of his output were many comic scripts and enormous royalties paid to him by toymakers who used his characters.

Mr. Disney's restless mind created one of the nation's greatest tourist attractions, Disneyland, a 300-acre tract of amusement rides, fantasy spectacles and re-created Americana that cost $50.1 million.

When Disneyland observed its 10th birthday in 1965, it had been visited by some 50 million people. Its international fame was emphasized in 1959 by the then premier of the Soviet Union, Nikita S. Khrushchev, who protested, when visiting Hollywood, that he had been unable to see Disneyland. Security arrangements could not be made in time for Mr. Khrushchev's visit.

Even after Disneyland had proven itself, Mr. Disney declined to consider suggestions that he had better leave well enough alone: "Disneyland will never be completed as long as there is imagination left in the world."

Repeatedly, as Mr. Disney came up with new ideas he encountered considerable skepticism. For Mickey Mouse, the foundation of his realm, Mr. Disney had to pawn and sell almost everything because most exhibitors looked upon it as just another cartoon. But when the public had a chance to speak, the noble-hearted mouse with the high-pitched voice, red pants, yellow shoes and white gloves became the most beloved of Hollywood stars.

When Mr. Disney decided to make the first feature-length cartoon—*Snow White and the Seven Dwarfs*—many Hollywood experts scoffed that no audience would sit through such a long animation. It became one of the biggest money-makers in movie history.

Mr. Disney was thought a fool when he became the first important movie producer to make films for television. His detractors once again were proven wrong.

Mr. Disney's television fame was built on such shows as "Disneyland," "The Mickey Mouse Club," "Zorro," "Davy Crockett" and "Walt Disney's Wonderful World of Color."

He was, however, the only major movie producer who refused to release his movies to television. He contended, with a good deal of profitable evidence, that each seven years there would be another generation that would flock to the movie theaters to see his old films.

Mickey Mouse would have been fame enough for most men. In France he was known as Michel Souris; in Italy, Topolino; in Japan, Miki Kuchi; in Spain, Miguel Ratoncito; in Latin America, El Raton Miguelito; in Sweden, Muse Pigg, and in Russia, Mikki Maus. On D-Day during World War II, Mickey Mouse was the password of Allied Supreme Headquarters in Europe.

But Mickey Mouse was not enough for Mr. Disney. He created Donald Duck, Pluto and Goofy. He dug into books for Dumbo, Bambi, Peter Pan, the Three Little Pigs, Ferdinand the Bull, Cinderella, the Sleeping Beauty, Brer Rabbit, Pinocchio. In *Fantasia,* he blended cartoon stories with classical music.

Though Mr. Disney's cartoon characters differed markedly, they were all alike in two respects: they were lovable and unsophisticated. Most popular were big-eared Mickey of the piping voice; choleric Donald Duck of the unintelligible quacking; Pluto, that most amiable of clumsy dogs, and the seven dwarfs who stole the show from Snow White: Dopey, Grumpy, Bashful, Sneezy, Happy, Sleepy and Doc.

His cartoon creatures were often surrounded with lovely songs. Thus, Snow White had "Some Day My Prince Will Come" and the dwarfs had "Whistle While You Work." From his version of "The Three Little Pigs," his most successful cartoon short, came another international hit, "Who's Afraid of the Big Bad Wolf?" Cliff Edwards as Jiminy Cricket sang "When You Wish Upon a Star" for *Pinocchio.* More recently, *Mary Poppins* introduced "Supercalifragilisticexpialidocious."

Mr. Disney seemed to have had an almost superstitious fear of considering his movies as art, though an exhibition of some of his leading cartoon characters was once held in the Metropolitan Museum of Art in New York. "I've never called this art," he said. "It's show business."

One day, when Mr. Disney was approaching 60 and his black hair and neatly trimmed mustache were gray, he was asked to reduce his success to a formula. His brown eyes became alternately intense and dreamy. He fingered an ashtray as he gazed around an office so cluttered with trophies that it looked like a pawnshop.

"I don't really know," he said. "I guess I'm an optimist. I'm not in business to make unhappy pictures. I love comedy too much. I've always loved comedy. Another thing. Maybe it's because I can still be amazed at the wonders of the world.

"Sometimes I've tried to figure out why Mickey appealed to the whole world. Everybody's tried to figure it out. So far as I know, nobody has. He's a pretty nice fellow who never does anybody any harm, who gets into scrapes through no fault of his own, but always manages to come up grinning. Why, Mickey's even been faithful to one girl, Minnie, all his life. Mickey is so simple and uncomplicated, so easy to understand that you can't help liking him."

But when Dwight D. Eisenhower was president, he found words for Mr. Disney. He called him a "genius as a creator of folklore" and said his "sympathetic attitude toward life has helped our children develop a clean and cheerful view of humanity, with all its frailties and possibilities for good."

When France gave to Mr. Disney its highest artistic decoration as Officier d'Académie, he was cited for his "contribution to education and knowledge" with such nature-study films as *Seal Island, Beaver Valley, Nature's Half Acre* and *The Living Desert.*

This stocky, industrious man who had never graduated from high school received honorary degrees from Harvard and Yale. He was honored by Yale the same day as it honored Thomas Mann, the Nobel Prize–winning novelist. Prof. William Lyon Phelps of Yale said of Mr. Disney: "He has accomplished something that has defied all the efforts and experiments of the laboratories in zoology and biology. He has given animals souls."

By the end of his career, the list of 700 awards and honors that Mr. Disney received from many nations filled 29 typewritten pages and included 29 Oscars, four Emmys and the Presidential Freedom Medal.

There were tributes of a different nature. Toys in the shape of Disney characters sold by the many millions. Paris couturiers and expensive jewelers both used Disney patterns. One of the most astounding exhibitions of popular devotion came in the wake of Mr. Disney's films about Davy Crockett. In a matter of months, youngsters all over the country who would balk at wearing a hat in winter were adorned in coonskin caps in midsummer.

In some ways Mr. Disney resembled the movie pioneers of a generation before him. He was not afraid of risk. One day, when all the world thought of him as a fabulous success, he told an acquaintance, "I'm in great shape, I now owe the bank only eight million."

A friend of 20 years recalled that he once said, "A buck is something to be spent creating." Early in 1960 he declared, "It's not what you have, but how much you can borrow that's important in business."

Mr. Disney had no trouble borrowing money in his later years. Bankers, in fact, sought him out. Last year Walt Disney Productions grossed $110 million. His family owns 38 percent of this publicly held corporation, and all of Retlaw, a company that controls the use of Mr. Disney's name.

Mr. Disney's contract with Walt Disney Productions gave him a basic salary of $182,000 a year and a deferred salary of $2,500 a week, with options to buy up to a 25 percent interest in each of his live-action features. It is understood that he began exercising these options in 1961, but only up to 10 percent. These interests alone would have made him a multimillionaire.

Mr. Disney, like earlier movie executives, insisted on absolute authority. He was savage in rebuking a subordinate. An associate of many years said the boss "could make you feel one inch tall, but he wouldn't let anybody else do it. That was his privilege."

Once in a bargaining dispute with a union of artists, a strike at the Disney studios went on for two months and was settled only after government mediation.

This attitude by Mr. Disney was one of the reasons some artists disparaged him. Another was that he did none of the drawings of his most famous cartoons. Mickey Mouse, for instance, was drawn by Ubbe Iwerks, who was with Mr. Disney almost from the beginning.

However, Mr. Iwerks insisted that Disney could have done the drawings, but was too busy. Mr. Disney did, however, furnish Mickey's voice for all cartoons. He also sat in on all story conferences.

Although Mr. Disney's power and wealth multiplied with his achievements, his manner remained that of some prosperous midwestern storekeeper. Except when imbued with some new Disneyland project or movie idea, he was inclined to be phlegmatic. His nasal speech, delivered slowly, was rarely accompanied by gestures. His phlegmatic manner often masked his independence and tenacity.

Walt Disney was born in Chicago on Dec. 5, 1901. His family moved to Marceline, Mo., when he was a child, and he spent most of his boyhood on a farm.

He recalled that he enjoyed sketching animals on the farm. Later, when his family moved back to Chicago, he went to high school and studied cartoon drawing at night at the Academy of Fine Arts. He did illustrations for the school paper.

When the United States entered World War I he was turned down by the army and navy because he was too young. So he went to France as an ambulance driver for the Red Cross. He decorated the sides of his ambulance with cartoons and had his work published in *Stars and Stripes.*

After the war the young man worked as a cartoonist for advertising agencies. But he was always looking for something better.

When Mr. Disney got a job doing cartoons for advertisements that were shown in theaters between movies, he was determined that that was to be his future. He would say to friends, "This is the most marvelous thing that has ever happened."

In 1920 he organized his own company to make cartoons about fairy tales. He made about a dozen but could not sell them. He was so determined to continue in this field that at times he had no money for food and lived with Mr. Iwerks.

In 1923 Mr. Disney decided to leave Kansas City. He went to Hollywood, where he formed a small company and did a series of film cartoons called "Alice in Cartoonland."

After two years of "Alice in Cartoonland," Mr. Disney dropped it in favor of a series about "Oswald the Rabbit." In 1928 most of his artists decided to break with him and do their own Oswald. Mr. Disney went to New York to try to keep the series but failed. When he returned, he, his wife, his brother Roy and Mr. Iwerks tried to think of a character for a new series. They decided on a mouse. Mrs. Disney named it Mickey.

The first Mickey Mouse cartoon, "Plane Crazy," was taken to New York by Mr. Disney. But the distributors were apathetic. "Felix the Cat" was ruler of the cartoon field, and they saw nothing unusual in a mouse.

When Mr. Disney returned from New York he decided that sound had a future in movies. He made a second Mickey Mouse cartoon, this one with sound, called "Steamboat Bill." In October 1928, the cartoon opened at the Colony Theater in New York. Success was immediate and the Disney empire began.

THE DREAM MERCHANT

BOSLEY CROWTHER

THE POPULAR image of Walt Disney as a shy and benign miracle man who performed varied feats of movie magic to entertain young and old does not do justice nor honor to this remarkable cinema artist and tycoon who rightly achieved an eminence as great as that of any star in Hollywood. Shy and benign he was, at one phase of his extraordinary career. That was when he was beginning as a maker of animated cartoons. That was when he was conceiving and giving birth to Mickey Mouse, his miraculous cartoon character, which took the world by storm. And that was even into the bright years of the creation of Pluto and Donald Duck and all that swarm of zoological creatures that were so greatly enjoyed and loved.

As a weaver of juvenile fancies with his anthropomorphic cartoons, which turned out to be as delightful to grown-ups as they were to the young, Mr. Disney was toiling in the medium that gave him the greatest joy and stimulated his inventiveness and skill to their finest works. There isn't much question among artists that his most original and tasteful films were his animated shorts made in the 1930s, when he was still fairly diffident and benign.

It is not to Mr. Disney's discredit that, when success and fame rightly came to him, he began to expand as a person and as an ambitious businessman. It was natural that he should have flourished under the warm and tinkling rain of public praise, that he should have managed to throw off his shyness, that he should have found it quite pleasant to take bows. Mr. Disney himself often noticed that there was "a lot of the Mouse in me." He was indigenously an actor. He loved to act the father of his brood.

Furthermore, he loved success and what went with it. And, as he and his brother Roy took stock, they agreed that the future of their business and of Walt's creative energies lay in the direction of the then undreamed-of feature-length story cartoon. That was a terra incognita that Mr. Disney approached with the delight of a pioneer. For his first venture in this area he chose the familiar fairy tale, *Snow White and the Seven Dwarfs.*

The enterprise was successful. But it marked a major departure in Mr. Disney's work. It was not an original Disney story, worked out by him and his genii on their storyboard, and it called for animation of human figures as the principal characters.

This, as we now look back upon it, was the Continental Divide in Mr. Disney's creative career. It marked his fateful migration into a new and less personal fantasy realm. He began working with the stories of other people—old, familiar ones mostly—and he took to a kind of representational animation that was not aesthetically felicitous. Not to him.

He was now moving in the area of the big producer, the Hollywood tycoon, and this was a role that he managed with more pretension than comfort and ease. More work was delegated to others. His associates, whom he credited, did the things that he himself formerly executed. The Disney plant was a factory.

In this situation, which was inevitable, you might say, and pressed by economic circumstances that were discouraging to the making of cartoons, it might well have been that Mr. Disney would have quietly withdrawn into a shell, committed his business to his brother, and lived happily ever after on television residuals. And, indeed, I recall an occasion, a visit to him at his studio back in the early 1950s, when I got the distinct impression that something of this sort was going on.

He seemed totally uninterested in movies and wholly, almost weirdly, concerned with the building of a miniature railroad engine and a string of cars in the workshops of the studio. All of his zest for invention, for creating fantasies, seemed to be going into this plaything. I came away feeling sad.

I needn't have been. Mr. Disney, the cinema artist and tycoon, was even then joyously gestating another Mouse. It was born as Disneyland. This great amusement park may be a symbol of mass commercialism in our day. It may be an entertainment supermarket. It may be many things that highbrow citizens frown on. But it is tasteful, wholesome and clean. It is a place of delight for millions, who escape into its massive fantasies.

It and *Mary Poppins,* which he produced and in which he took a hand, were the final achievements of Mr. Disney, the most persistent and successful fantasist of our age. He managed to come out very nicely for an artist in Hollywood.

DWIGHT DAVID EISENHOWER

1890–1969

Military leadership of the victorious Allied forces in Western Europe during World War II invested Dwight David Eisenhower with an immense popularity, almost amounting to devotion, that twice elected him president of the United States. His enormous political success was largely personal, for he was not basically a politician dealing in partisan issues and party maneuvers. What he possessed was a superb talent for gaining the respect and affection of the voters as the man suited to guide the nation through Cold War confrontations with Soviet power around the world and to lead the country to domestic prosperity.

Eisenhower's gift for inspiring confidence in himself perplexed some analysts because he was not a dashing battlefield general nor a masterly military tactician. Apparently what counted most in his generalship also impressed the voters most: an ability to harmonize diverse groups and disparate personalities into a smoothly functioning coalition.

Thus Eisenhower's two terms in the White House were a personal triumph in which he transcended the persons and forces around him. About his bewitching, benign and smiling figure there grew an aura of certain success that weathered shifts in his personal popularity and began to wane only in the years after he left the presidency.

Of all his unquestioned great moments, two stand out as landmarks. One is May 7, 1945, when Gen. Alfred Jodl, chief of the German Armed Forces Operations Staff, surrendered unconditionally to the Allies at a schoolhouse in Rheims, France, culminating the European phase of a terrible conflict that had nearly consumed the world.

The other is Nov. 6, 1956, when Eisenhower was elected to a second term as president by one of the largest votes ever rolled up by a candidate of any party. His vote of 35.5 million has since been eclipsed, but it was a stunning performance at the time.

In the years that followed his military and presidential victories, he retired to the role of elder statesman, counseling his successors in the White House when they sought his advice and working to help unify (but never to lead) the Republican party along moderate lines. In the campaign of 1964, however, he declined to use his prestige to block the nomination of Sen. Barry Goldwater of Arizona. Moderates backing Gov. William W. Scranton of Pennsylvania were disturbed and disheartened.

The sources of Eisenhower's qualities of leadership were far different from those of other contemporary statesmen. Franklin D. Roosevelt was a patrician with a master's manner in handling men; Sir Winston Churchill was an aristocrat born to command; Josef Stalin was a tyrant who ruled by ruthless craft; Nikita S. Khrushchev was a peasant's son given to hearty bluster; Harry S Truman

New York Times Photo

New York Times Photo

was a commoner who led because he was stubborn.

Eisenhower's political appeal, apart from the glory conferred by his military accomplishments, lay in his background and his expression of it. He was a product of Abilene, Kans., a small Middle Western town that did not have a paved street until 1910—the year after his graduation from high school. He was also the product of a close-knit Mennonite German family that passed on to him the simple pieties of 19th-century agricultural America.

Insulated all of his adult life from the rise of industrialism and the anxieties of the job world by the institutional security of army life, Eisenhower preserved these homilies virtually intact: God helps those who help themselves; the devil finds mischief for idle hands; do justice and you will receive justice; prosperity is a sign of divine blessing; a change of heart expiates sin.

The heartwarming sincerity with which he uttered these beliefs and their obvious role in fashioning his life created around him an atmosphere of uncomplicated goodness and uprightness. It disarmed his critics and confounded his enemies.

Eisenhower's scrubbed face, his dimpled, infectious grin, his exuberance, his quick Jovian anger (and his equally swift return to calm), his paternal manner, all fused into a personality that the American public responded to and heeded. Cloaked with the power to command, he preferred to persuade and conciliate; he seemed to radiate goodwill and diplomacy. He was, in short, a man to be trusted, a man to make the complex simple, to do the job.

For these characteristics much was overlooked—his vacations from the White House, his endless golf, his frequent bridge games, his fondness for cowboy stories, his bumbling syntax—for he exemplified the homespun, folksy virtues that many Americans liked to think they themselves possessed, or should ideally possess.

Eisenhower's entrance into politics was reluctant. Before the end of World War II Dr. Douglas Southall Freeman, the historian, suggested that he consider public office, and his reply was, "God forbid!"

In the glow of the war's end, President Harry S Truman offered to assist the general if he wanted to seek the presidency in 1948. "Mr. President," he said, "I don't know who will be your opponent for the presidency, but it will not be I."

Pressure built up to draft Eisenhower for the race in 1948. Both Democrats and Republicans had hopes of snaring him because there was nothing in the public record to indicate which party, if either, held his favor.

The general squelched talk of a draft for the nomination. "I am not available for and could not accept nomination for high public office," he wrote in a letter. At the time he was on leave from the presidency of Columbia University to serve as commander of the North Atlantic Treaty Organization forces in Europe.

Despite Eisenhower's disclaimer, leading Republicans in the East kept their eye on him. In 1950, when the party seemed resurgent in Congress, Thomas E. Dewey of New York, the titular leader, proposed Eisenhower as the nominee for 1952. Soon there was a well-beaten path to Rocquencourt, outside Paris, where the general made his headquarters; it was trod by politicians and businessmen, many of whom assured him, with adroit flattery, of the public clamor for him back home and of the ease with which he could get the nomination.

Having indicated that he would accept the party's designation, however, Eisenhower soon discovered that it was not quite his for the asking. Pitted against him was Sen. Robert A. Taft of Ohio, the "Mr. Republican" of the party's conservative wing. The decisive issue between them, as the general saw it, was isolationism. Indeed, Eisenhower agreed to run after he was convinced that Taft would not commit himself to the principles of NATO.

The struggle was close, and the general was obliged to do some campaigning. Up to the time of the Republican convention in July 1952, the outcome was unresolved. With the party machinery in Ohio senator Robert Taft's hands, the issue hinged on how delegate contests in Texas, Louisiana and

Georgia would be decided. In a maneuver that outwitted and discomfited the opposition, the Eisenhower forces, masterminded by Dewey, put across a "fair play" amendment to the rules that restricted voting by contested delegations already seated. It swung control of the convention away from Taft and led to Eisenhower's nomination.

The victory came after the regular order of the first roll call, when Minnesota switched 19 votes and gave the general the 604 votes he required for nomination. Other shifts eventually brought his total to 845 votes, while Taft slipped from a high of 500 to 280.

As a vice presidential candidate the convention chose Sen. Richard M. Nixon of California, a man known then for his conservative views.

Eisenhower quickly moved to attain party unity by calling on Taft at his convention offices. Later the two had a dramatic breakfast meeting at Columbia University that brought Taft followers into line, for both agreed, in a communiqué, that they sought similar foreign and domestic objectives.

In the broadest terms, Eisenhower campaigned against his Democratic opponent, Gov. Adlai E. Stevenson of Illinois, on a pledge to clean up "the mess in Washington" and to balance the budget. Shortly before the election he promised he would personally go to Korea and try to end the war there. In its day-to-day unfolding, however, the campaign was much akin to a popularity contest. The country was covered with "I Like Ike" buttons, placards and posters; "All the Way With Adlai" was a fervent, but forlorn, cry.

Eisenhower's concepts of loyalty and integrity were tested twice in the campaign, once with his vice presidential running mate, Senator Nixon, and once with Sen. Joseph R. McCarthy, Republican of Wisconsin.

The Nixon case began with the disclosure that a group of California supporters had placed an $18,000 fund at his disposal while he was in the Senate. In a dramatic television appeal to the nation, Nixon made a sweeping denial of wrongdoing, satisfying Eisenhower's insistence that his running mate be "clean as a hound's tooth." Accepting Nixon's version of the fund, Eisenhower exclaimed: "That's my boy."

In the McCarthy episode, the general was persuaded to delete from a campaign speech a defense of General of the Army George C. Marshall, his army mentor, whom Senator McCarthy had impugned as a traitor. Political advisers had told Eisenhower that he needed McCarthy's support to win the election.

These incidents seem not to have aroused adverse voter reaction, for Eisenhower polled 33,936,252 popular votes and 442 votes in the Electoral College; Stevenson received 27,314,992 popular votes and 89 electoral votes.

Significantly, Eisenhower's "crusade" (as he called it) carried four states of the Old Confederacy, a Democratic stronghold for generations. But the vote there, as elsewhere, was a personal tribute. The Republican edge in Congress was slight, and it vanished altogether in 1954 and 1956, indicating how far, in the voters' minds, the general stood above party.

Eisenhower began his first term in January 1953 as a symbol of international goodwill as well as of national high purpose. He had traveled to Korea, where a truce was soon effected, bringing back thousands of servicemen. At home the government climate was benign and the press was friendly, even protective, as a seeming new era opened.

Even the political opposition struck at the men around the president rather than at Eisenhower himself. John Foster Dulles in the State Department and Ezra Taft Benson in Agriculture were popular targets between 1953 and 1957.

Oddly, Old Guard Republicans, long entrenched in Congress, were among Eisenhower's most vocal critics, because the first Republican administration in 20 years did not make a clean break with the New Deal and Fair Deal. The Old Guard objected when the administration eased credit, abandoned efforts to balance the budget and, in addition to letting $5 billion in Korean War taxes lapse, sanctioned a further tax reduction of $2.4 billion. On top of this, the administration put through an extension of insurance coverage under Social Security and accepted a minimum wage of $1 an hour, up from 75 cents.

It was the Democrats who gave Eisenhower the votes he required to pass key legislation.

In his conduct of the White House the new president introduced the staff concept, under which the workload was distributed among associates. Sherman Adams, a former New Hampshire governor, headed the staff with the title "The Assistant to the President." Despite some initial creaking, the system worked smoothly, especially late in the first term, when the president was twice stricken with serious illness.

Eisenhower attached great importance to business success, a fact evident from the many representatives of big business named to his cabinet and other key posts. It was a standing joke that his first cabinet was composed of "eight millionaires and a plumber." Perhaps significantly, the first to depart was the plumber, Martin P. Durkin, who resigned within a year as Secretary of Labor. He said the president had reneged on a promise to press for revision of the Taft-Hartley Act, which restricted the union shop.

At least three businessmen named to Cabinet-level posts—Charles E. Wilson, George M. Humphrey and Harold E. Talbott—were subjected to senatorial questioning on their investments and on possible conflicts of interest between their official and business lives. Talbott, Secretary of the Air Force, later resigned over such charges.

Throughout, the president was irritated by suggestions that his policies favored business at the expense of other segments of the population. He firmly believed that what was good for business was good for the nation.

His contention seemed borne out by the economic boom that began in mid-1954 and continued through the rest of the first term. Because prosperous times followed a mild recession in 1953, tax concessions to business seemed all the more vindicated.

Under Eisenhower, the nation maintained its international leadership even if, at times, its course seemed uncertain and erratic. The administration had high hopes that, with the Korean truce, psychological warfare would give the West an ascendancy in the battle of ideologies. But when Stalin died in 1953, and again when revolt flared three years later in Hungary and elsewhere behind the Iron Curtain, there was no master plan ready to capitalize on developments.

Yet Eisenhower's atoms-for-peace proposal, made before the United Nations in 1953, and his open-skies inspection plan, presented at the summit conference in Geneva in 1955, contributed markedly toward relaxation of world tensions and a more hopeful outlook.

Although the promise of the Geneva conference, attended by Eisenhower, Soviet Premier Nikolai A. Bulganin, French Premier Edgar Fauré and British Prime Minister Anthony Eden, never fully materialized, the meeting did produce a tacit understanding that nuclear war would be avoided.

The neutral and nonaligned powers, notably India, liked Eisenhower's thinking in these areas. This was significant because other U.S. policies perturbed the neutrals. They did not agree that the cause of peace was being served by the ring of defensive alliances drawn around the Soviet bloc on the United States's initiative. Among these was the Southeast Asia Treaty Organization, an alliance set up late in 1954 upon French withdrawal from Indochina.

At that time Eisenhower also wrote a letter to the Diem government of South Vietnam, vaguely pledging United States economic and arms assistance. That letter, scarcely noticed at the time, was later used to justify massive American military involvement in Vietnam.

Although an uneasy détente existed in Europe, tension prevailed in the Orient, especially between the People's Republic of China and the Nationalist regime on Taiwan. This reached a high point in 1955, when the Communists seemed ready to strike at the offshore island. In a dramatic step, Eisenhower asked Congress to underwrite his authority to use American armed forces "if necessary to assure the security" of Taiwan.

Many believed that the resolution, overwhelmingly approved, kept Communist China from moving against Quemoy and Matsu, Nationalist-held islands off China, because of uncertainty as to how the United States would react.

In some areas the United States found itself in trade-and-aid competition with the Soviet Union. Middle East developments in 1955 pointed up the extent of this rivalry. The West, jolted by an Egyptian arms purchase from the Soviet bloc, was drawn into the bidding to finance the Aswan High Dam that the United Arab Republic wanted to build on the Nile. Midway in 1956 the West pulled out of the bidding and in a matter of days the U.A.R. seized the Suez Canal.

Tensions mounted as negotiations failed to produce a formula for operation of the waterway, and by fall events were moving swiftly. After Israeli forces entered Egypt, Britain and France threatened on Oct. 30, 1956, to intervene if the fighting was not halted promptly. With world attention divided between the Mideast and Hungary, in the throes of upheaval, the U.A.R. balked, and Anglo-French forces took action. The conflict was speedily taken to the United Nations, where, in the voting for a cease-fire, the United States sided with the Soviet Union against France and Britain.

The U.A.R. came out of the struggle triumphant. Invasion forces were obliged to withdraw under United Nations pressure; the U.A.R. retained the Suez Canal and financing for the Aswan Dam was arranged with the Soviet Union.

To many Americans, however, events abroad seemed remote in those years. Anxieties centered rather on the president, who suffered two major illnesses toward the end of his first term.

The first, on Sept. 24, 1955, was diagnosed as a coronary thrombosis, a clot in the artery of the heart. It sent the president to the hospital for seven weeks. The second illness occurred eight and a half months later, on June 8, 1956, and was diagnosed as ileitis, an inflammation of the lower part of the small intestine. Eisenhower underwent a successful operation the next day to bypass the ileum, which was obstructing the intestinal tract.

The president was on vacation in Denver when his heart attack occurred. He had just returned to the home of his mother-in-law, Mrs. John S. Doud, from a four-day fishing trip in the Rockies. After complaining of indigestion and intense chest pain, he was taken to the Fitzsimmons Army Hospital in Denver. Heart specialists were called in, including Dr. Paul Dudley White of Boston, who described the attack as "moderate." The patient was cleared to leave the hospital Nov. 10, and he flew to Washington the following day, "happy that the doctors have given me a parole if not a pardon."

Throughout the illness the public was kept minutely informed of the president's progress and of the fact that, with his staff, he continued to direct affairs of state. In these tasks he was aided by Vice President Nixon as well as by Sherman Adams. Despite the smoothness with which the president made decisions and despite the general uneventfulness of his recovery, speculation arose on his availability for a second term.

After being pronounced medically fit by Dr. White, the president consulted earnestly with his closest advisers. They unanimously favored a second term, telling him it was his duty to continue working for peace if his health permitted. This advice led to Eisenhower's announcement on Feb. 29, 1956, that he would run again.

The ileitis attack, coming in June, cast momentary doubt on Eisenhower's candidacy, but a routine recovery from three-hour surgery at the Walter Reed Army Medical Center in Washington relieved public apprehensions. The Republicans renominated him along with Nixon as his running mate.

Eisenhower, at the peak of his popularity, conducted a restricted campaign for a second term in which he stood on his record of peace and prosperity. He made a limited number of radio and television speeches and undertook only two campaign swings that kept him away from the capital overnight.

Stevenson, again the Democratic choice, hammered away at the "breakdown of leadership," at domestic and foreign policies that were "stalled on dead center" and at a "part-time president." He inveighed against a cabinet representative of "the larger interests" and, with references to "the heir apparent," sought to increase the misgivings of some about Nixon.

"Why this anguished cry of some politicians that we have no peace?" Eisenhower asked in the face of attacks on his foreign policy. Countering the charge of undue big-business influence, he demanded to know whether government affairs should be entrusted to "some failure . . . or a successful businessman." He insisted that his administration had brought "sense and order" to Washington.

Developments in the Middle East in October, touched off by the Israeli march into Egypt and the Anglo-French thrust at Suez, unquestionably helped Eisenhower with the voters, for his quick response to those events put the United States on the side of peace.

The election results gave him 35,582,236 votes, a record up to that time, and 457 electoral votes, including those of five southern states. Stevenson's popular vote was 26,031,322, his electoral total 73.

Difficult and fateful problems at home, abroad and in space confronted Eisenhower in his second term.

There was mob violence over school integration in the South, and in September 1957 the president was obliged to send troops to Little Rock, Ark., to enforce court-ordered school desegregation.

Business slumped sharply in the winter of 1957–58 and only slowly recovered. By July 1959, when a steel strike dealt the economy another stinging blow, employment still had not recovered. The national debt climbed higher than ever.

The Soviet Union achieved a stunning scientific success, with strong military implications, when it orbited the first man-made earth satellite in October 1957.

With the collapse of the second summit conference, in May 1960, the perilous stalemate between the Soviet Union and the West over Berlin continued.

Tensions in the Far East reached a peak a month later when the president, in the middle of a trip through the area, was forced to cancel a visit to Japan because of anti-American rioting there.

The widening rift between Cuba and the United States brought economic reprisals on both sides and a threat of Soviet intervention that led Eisenhower to declare that he would never "permit the establishment of a regime dominated by international Communism in the Western Hemisphere."

And in the Middle East a policy designed to promote stability did not prevent the decline of Western influence through civil war in Lebanon and revolution in Iraq.

The demands of the times would have taxed the energy of the healthiest of men, and they were especially heavy for Eisenhower on account of his heart attack and his bout of ileitis. His health was further compromised Nov. 25, 1957, when he suffered an occlusion of a small branch of the middle cerebral artery on the left side. He was left with a mild aphasia (difficulty in speaking) and he was not pronounced recovered from the stroke until March 1, 1958.

Eisenhower sought to preserve his strength and health by daily rests, weekends at his farm at Gettysburg, Pa., and periodic golfing holidays. Although public concern over his physical condition was intense, the president's popularity, as measured by public-opinion polls, began a perceptible decline soon after he took his second oath of office in January 1957.

Large sections of the Republican party's conservative wing were alienated early in 1957 when Eisenhower submitted a $71.8-billion budget, the largest in peacetime history. One of the first to protest was George M. Humphrey, the industrialist who was Secretary of the Treasury. He retired six months later and was succeeded by Robert B. Anderson, a former deputy secretary of defense.

Congress, under Democratic leadership in both houses despite Eisenhower's sweep, did not hesitate to revise the president's legislative program, although it avoided, as had other Congresses, narrow partisanship.

It agreed with Eisenhower on the essentials of foreign aid and extension of the reciprocal trade program; it differed on Defense Department reorganization, and it took the initiative in measures to meet the recession of 1957–58 and the Soviet space challenge.

After Russia orbited its first satellite, a Senate committee under Lyndon B. Johnson of Texas, the Democratic leader, called for a speed-up of United States space programs; but it was not until Feb. 1, 1958, that the president was able to announce the launching of an American satellite, a puny device compared to the Russians' *Sputnik.* In the years that followed, with the illusion of American technological superiority shattered, there was growing criticism of the United States space program.

On the domestic scene the president faced a direct challenge to federal authority that grew out of resistance to the Supreme Court's ruling, in 1954, that racial segregation in the public schools was unconstitutional.

Gov. Orval E. Faubus of Arkansas called out the Arkansas National Guard in September 1957 to prevent Negro students from entering the Little Rock Central High School. When a Federal District Court injunction forced him to withdraw the Guard, rioting broke out and the Negroes had to leave school.

Eisenhower ordered federal troops to Little Rock, where they restored order. In this crisis Eisenhower spoke up for obedience to federal law and the courts, but he avoided a direct commitment to the morality of integration.

During 1957, however, he signed the first major bill since Reconstruction to protect the constitutional rights of minorities. The bill created a Civil Rights Commission to investigate denials of minority rights.

Although the president's handling of the explosive Little Rock situation was applauded in the North and West, his prestige generally dropped with the downturn in the national economy. Starting late in 1957 and accelerating in 1958, the slump brought to an end the period of high employment and prosperity that marked Eisenhower's first term.

Some observers attributed the decline of Eisenhower's influence to his being the first president whose tenure was limited to two terms by the 22nd Amendment. Others felt that the president was delegating too many of his functions to subordinates.

This view appeared to be reinforced in the summer of 1958, when Adams, the stern assistant to the president, who presided over the White House offices, came under investigation for alleged intervention with federal agencies in behalf of his friends.

Much of the disenchantment that had been building up against the administration seemed to culminate in criticism of Adams, one of Eisenhower's closest friends and associates. The president tried to ignore the criticism, insisting that Adams would remain on his staff because "I need him." But Adams resigned anyway, on Sept. 22, 1958.

In the elections that November the Republicans lost 47 House seats and 13 of 21 contested Senate seats. The Democrats controlled Congress by the widest margins since the Roosevelt landslide of 1936.

Few realized it until well afterward, but the elections were the nadir of Eisenhower's political fortunes. The turning point had been the resignation of Adams, for thereafter the president began to take an ever-increasing role in national affairs. By the spring of 1959 some observers were talking about "the new Ike," while others insisted that it was only the reemergence of the old Ike who had so fired the country's imagination in 1952.

One evidence of this change was a firmer attitude toward Congress. In September 1959, Eisenhower vetoed a $1.2-billion public works bill, citing a need for federal economy. The veto was overridden, as was his veto of a bill to raise federal employees' pay in the summer of 1960. The issue here was also economy. The essence of "the new Ike" was that he took a position and defended it with some vigor.

A second evidence of change was in the field of personal diplomacy and involved a visit to the United States by Premier Nikita S. Khrushchev of the Soviet Union in September 1959. Although in later years Eisenhower disclosed that the Khrushchev visit had been authorized through a misunderstanding of his instructions by the State Department, he made the most of it at the time by inviting the Russian leader to the White House and to Camp David, the president's weekend retreat in Maryland. These informal talks resulted in what was termed "the spirit of Camp David," a thaw in the Cold War between the United States and Russia: peaceful coexistence was to replace bellicosity.

The Camp David spirit persisted until May 1960, when a summit meeting in Paris was blasted by the disclosure that the United States was using a U-2 photo-reconnaissance plane over the Soviet Union.

Ten days before the summit meeting was to convene on May 5, Khrushchev announced that an American plane had been shot down over the Soviet Union. He withheld details. That night, in Washington, the National Aeronautics and Space Administration said that the pilot of a weather plane missing since May 1 had reported oxygen difficulties about an hour after takeoff. This, according to the agency, might have caused the Pakistan-based plane to stray over the Russian border.

The following day the Soviet Union said that the U-2 had been shot down by "a remarkable rocket." Meanwhile, the State Department unequivocally denied any "deliberate attempt to violate Soviet air space."

This denial had scarcely been made when the Russians produced Francis Gary Powers, the U-2 pilot, and the confession that he had been on a spying mission across Russian territory from Pakistan to Norway.

Moscow's revelations forced Washington to admit that it had engaged in U-2 espionage for the last four years. For this Eisenhower took full responsibility.

The upshot of the episode was to reflect on the president and his sincerity as a partner in the Camp David spirit. Thus, when he reached Paris May 15, he was on the defensive, but sought to make the most of it. "Far too much is at stake," he said, "to indulge the passions of the moment or to engage in profitless bickering."

His appeal was in vain, for Khrushchev demanded that the United States end its U-2 project, ban future flights and punish those "directly guilty." Angered by the Soviet leader's heavy-handedness, Eisenhower made only one concession, saying the espionage flights had been suspended and "are not to be resumed."

The summit meeting died the next day, as Khrushchev continued his attacks on the United States and refused to take part in a meeting with Eisenhower. His unrelenting recalcitrance tended, however, to shift sympathy to Eisenhower.

It was clear, nevertheless, that the last chance had gone for the president, in the final months of his term, to strengthen hopes for peace in line with the spirit of the first summit meeting at Geneva in 1955 and the Khrushchev visit to America in 1959.

Although Eisenhower regained a measure of popularity in the campaign of 1960 and spoke for the candidacy of Nixon, his vice president, it was not enough to carry the country. The Eisenhower "magic" was his alone, and Sen. John F. Kennedy of Massachusetts ended the eight-year Republican rule of the White House. Eisenhower stepped down Jan. 20, 1961.

Three days earlier, Eisenhower delivered a televised farewell address to the American people that contained a warning that has echoed down through the years.

Noting that a vast military establishment and a huge arms industry had developed in the United States, Eisenhower said: "In the councils of government, we must guard against the acquisition of unwarranted influence, whether sought or unsought, by the military-industrial complex. The potential for the disastrous rise of misplaced power exists and will persist."

A FARM BOY BECOMES A GENERAL

DWIGHT D. EISENHOWER was born in Denison, Tex., on Oct. 14, 1890. He was of German descent. His ancestors belonged to evangelical groups from which evolved the Mennonite sect. Subjected to religious persecution, some of the family had emigrated from Bavaria to Switzerland in the 17th century.

The first Eisenhowers came to America from Switzerland in 1732. They settled in Pennsylvania, first at York and later at Elizabethville, near Harrisburg. They helped establish a Mennonite branch called Brethren of Christ. It also was known as the River Brethren because its members lived near the Susquehanna.

As Mennonites, the Eisenhowers believed in plainness of dress, nonresistance and nonjuring. However, they put on the uniform of the Continental Army in the Revolutionary War and the Union Army in the Civil War.

In 1878 the Rev. Jacob Eisenhower, farmer and merchant, with other River Brethren, followed the covered-wagon trail west to Kansas. He settled on a 160-acre farm near Abilene. His son David, who was born in Elizabethville, Pa., was married in 1885 to Ida Elizabeth Stover of Mount Sydney, Va., in the United Brethren Church at Lecompton, Kans. In later life she joined the Jehovah's Witnesses.

David Eisenhower failed in grocery and banking ventures in Kansas. He then moved to Texas, where he got a job as mechanic in the Cotton Belt Railroad shops at Denison. With him went his wife and the first two of their seven sons.

The future president, their third son, was born in a house near the railroad yards. He was christened David Dwight Eisenhower and is so listed in the family Bible. His mother, however, reversed the order and called him Dwight David. This was partly to distinguish him from David his father and partly to avoid the nickname "Dave."

In 1892, when Dwight was 2 years old, the family returned to Abilene. The father got a job in a creamery and moved his family into a small house on East Fourth Street with an adjoining 2½-acre farm.

One of Dwight's brothers died in infancy. The six remaining boys took turns getting up at dawn to build the kitchen fire and get breakfast started. They took care of the chickens and the garden. They milked the cow and sold farm products from door to door. They did odd jobs and sometimes worked at the creamery with their father.

Even in grade school, Dwight's teachers were impressed with the engaging grin that became his political trademark. At high school, from which he was graduated in 1909, he showed a liking for history, military history and biography, mathematics and athletics.

After high school he at first had no definite idea of what he wanted to do. He worked in the creamery and at other jobs. These included hauling ice and loading wagons. He played semiprofessional baseball, too.

His father could not afford to send him to college. The youth, however, took competitive examinations for both the United States Military Academy at West Point and the Naval Academy at Annapolis.

He finished first in the Annapolis and second in the West Point examinations. He received an appointment to Annapolis only to discover that he would be several months past the age limit of 20 when the next academy year started. But the high man on the West Point list was unable to accept his appointment and it went to Dwight. He entered the Military Academy on July 1, 1911.

At West Point, Cadet Eisenhower won his army "A" in baseball and football. He was regarded as one of the most promising backs in the East until his playing career was halted after he wrenched his knee badly in a game with Tufts College and then, soon afterward, twisted it again riding horseback.

He was graduated with a standing of 61st in a class of 164. Neither his scholastic record nor his deportment was of the best, though he was in the upper half of the class scholastically. A steady shower of demerits had rained down on him throughout his entire four years at the Point.

He was graduated with a "clean sleeve," being neither a cadet officer nor a noncommissioned officer.

His first assignment, as a second lieutenant, was with the 19th Infantry at Fort Sam Houston, San Antonio, Tex. At a dinner-dance there in October 1915 he met Mamie Geneva Doud, daughter of Mr. and Mrs. John Doud of Denver, who was visiting friends.

Lieutenant Eisenhower asked for a date and was told to call back in a month. Instead, he began calling the next day, every 15 minutes. He got a date that evening and appeared four hours early. By December they were engaged. The couple were married in Denver July 1, 1916.

The Eisenhowers had two sons, the first dying in infancy. The second son, John Sheldon Doud Eisenhower, was born in 1922. He went to West Point and became an army officer. He saw service in Europe in World War II and later in Korea. He married Barbara Jean Thompson. They gave the Eisenhowers four grandchildren—Dwight David 2d, born in 1948; Barbara Anne, 1949; Susan Elaine, 1951; and Mary Jean, 1955.

The future president served at Fort Sam Houston from Sept. 13, 1915, until May 28, 1917.

He did not get overseas in World War I. From Fort Sam Houston he went to the 57th Infantry at Leon Springs, Tex., as regimental supply officer. He served there until Sept. 18, 1917.

He was promoted to captain May 15, 1917; to the temporary rank of major June 17, 1918, and to the temporary rank of lieutenant colonel Oct. 14, 1918.

After leaving the 57th Infantry he served as an instructor at the Officers Training Camp at Fort Oglethorpe, Ga., to Dec. 12, 1917, and as instructor at the Army Service Schools, Fort Leavenworth, Kans., to Feb. 28, 1918.

He organized the 65th Battalion Engineers at Camp Meade, Md., and remained there until March 24, 1918; commanded the Camp Colt tank training center at Gettysburg, Pa., until Nov. 18, 1918; commanded Tank Corps troops at Camp Dix, N.J., to Dec. 22, 1918, and at Fort Benning, Ga., to March 15, 1919.

For his World War I services he received the Distinguished Service Medal.

After the war he was reduced to the permanent rank of captain on June 30, 1920, but was promoted to the permanent rank of major July 2.

From Fort Benning he was ordered to Fort Meade, Md. There he was graduated from Infantry Tank School.

He then sailed for the Panama Canal Zone. There he served as executive officer at Camp Gaillard to Sept. 19, 1924.

He was recruiting officer at Fort Logan, Col., until Aug. 19, 1925. Then came an opportunity that helped transform an ordinary military career into a distinguished one. He was sent to the army's Command and General Staff School at Fort Leavenworth. He completed the course with honors in June 1926, standing first among 275 selected army officers.

Next he joined the 24th Infantry at Fort Benning Aug. 15, 1926. He was transferred to Washington Jan. 15, 1927, for service with the American Battle Monuments Commission until Aug. 15, 1927.

He was graduated from the Army War College in Washington June 30, 1928, and returned to duty with the American Battle Monuments Commission.

From Nov. 8, 1929, to Feb. 20, 1933, he was assistant executive officer of the assistant secretary of war in Washington. In that period he was graduated from the Army Industrial College.

In 1930 an official paper he wrote attracted the attention of Gen. Douglas MacArthur, then the Army's chief of staff.

The future president served in the chief of staff's office in Washington until Sept. 24, 1935, and then sailed to Manila as a member of the American Military Mission and assistant to General MacArthur as military adviser of the Commonwealth government of the Philippine Islands.

On July 1, 1936, Major Eisenhower was promoted to the permanent rank of lieutenant colonel. He returned to the United States in 1939, after the outbreak of World War II in Europe.

He joined the 15th Infantry at Fort Ord, Calif., in February 1940, and a few weeks later accompanied his regiment to Fort Lewis, Wash.

On March 11, 1941, he was promoted to the temporary rank of colonel. He was assigned as chief of staff to the Third Army, San Antonio, Tex., on June 24, 1941. He was promoted to the temporary rank of brigadier general on Sept. 29, 1941.

On Dec. 14, 1941, seven days after the Japanese attacked Pearl Harbor, Gen. George C. Marshall, then the Army's chief of staff, called Eisenhower to Washington.

Although he had never commanded troops in battle, he was recognized as a specialist in operations planning and organization. He also had made a reputation as a tactician in the large-scale Louisiana maneuvers of 1941. In this capacity, as well as in others, he impressed General Marshall, who sponsored his army advancements.

Eisenhower was named chief of the War Plans Division, General Staff, Feb. 16, 1942. When the division was reorganized and renamed he became chief of operations for the Army. He was promoted to the temporary rank of major general on March 27, 1942.

In the spring of 1942 he was sent to London to make a survey and recommendations on organization and development of United States forces in the European Theater of Operations. On returning to Washington, he submitted a draft directive for the Commanding General, E.T.O., and recommended another general to carry it out.

General Marshall approved the directive but named Eisenhower to the E.T.O. command to put his own plan into effect. On June 25, 1942, Eisenhower was designated Commanding General, E.T.O., with headquarters in London.

He flew to London, set up headquarters at Norfolk House and in July began planning the invasion of French North Africa. He was promoted to the temporary rank of lieutenant general July 7, 1942.

One of his chief objectives was to encourage harmony among British, French and United States officers at headquarters. Relations with the British and French had to be handled delicately. A story widely circulated at the time emphasized his determination to achieve this aim.

A United States colonel became involved in a quarrel with a British general. The colonel was called on the carpet before Eisenhower, who told him: "I think you have the right of the argument. You called the general a so-and-so and I can understand that, too. But unfortunately you called him a British so-and-so, and for that I am sending you home."

On the eve of the North African invasion Eisenhower flew to Gibraltar, a central command post, to direct the troop landings at Casablanca, Oran and Algiers on Nov. 7. The following day he was named Allied Commander in Chief, North Africa, commanding British, French and United States forces. On Nov. 22 he transferred his headquarters to Algiers.

There he found that Gen. Henri-Honoré Giraud, tentative choice to command the French forces, was being ignored by French military commanders and colonial administrators. They were maintaining loyalty to Adm. Jean François Darlan.

Admiral Darlan had been in command of all French naval forces at the start of the war. After the collapse of French military resistance, he became vice premier of the Vichy regime that ruled France as a puppet of Nazi Germany.

Vichy named him commander in chief of all French forces, and he was in North Africa at the time of the invasion. Captured in Algiers, he ordered French forces in Algeria and Morocco to cease resistance. He was then recognized by the Allies as High Commissioner of French North Africa.

This arrangement brought criticism upon Eisenhower. He took full responsibility for it and defended it as a military necessity. He emphasized that it avoided fighting between Anglo-American and French forces, spared thousands of lives and ensured the success of the landings.

President Franklin D. Roosevelt and Prime Minister Winston Churchill upheld Eisenhower. The incident, however, provoked a worldwide controversy. In the midst of it Admiral Darlan was assassinated by a French youth in Algiers on Christmas Eve 1942.

The fighting in North Africa at first went badly for the Allies. Field Marshal Bernard Law Montgomery was backing the German general, Erwin Rommel, and his dreaded Afrika Korps across Libya into Tunisia, but Allied plans for a quick victory by attacking the rear of the retreating foes were faulty. United States troops were green and their commanders untried.

After the Allied defeat at Kasserine Pass, Eisenhower relieved Maj. Gen. Lloyd R. Fredenall, ranking United States commander in the field.

Eisenhower was promoted to the temporary rank of full general on Feb. 11, 1943. But until the end of the campaign he was uncertain whether he himself might not be replaced. In his book, *Crusade in Europe*, after relating the removal of General Fredenall in July, he added: "Several others, myself included, shared responsibility for our week of reverses."

But the tide turned. In May 1943 the mass surrender of German and Italian forces in Tunisia brought Eisenhower's first military campaign to a successful end. The Afrika Korps was routed and North Africa was liberated.

Eisenhower then directed the invasions of Sicily and Italy. Though the invasion of Italy did not force the Germans out of Italy, it did force the Italians out of the war. Eisenhower was promoted to the permanent rank of brigadier general and major general both on the same day, Aug. 30, 1943. He received the Oak Leaf Cluster to be added to the Distinguished Service Medal he had won in World War I.

In a sustained campaign of 38 days, Eisenhower directed the combined operations leading to the conquest of Sicily and reduced Italy to a state of military impotence.

President Roosevelt personally decorated him with the medal of the Legion of Merit. Announcing Eisenhower's selection in December 1943, as Supreme Allied Commander for the invasion of Western Europe, President Roosevelt said, "The performances in Africa, Sicily and Italy have been brilliant. He knows by practical and successful experience the way to coordinate air, sea and land power."

On Dec. 10, 1943, Eisenhower first learned that he was to be chosen to command the invasion of Western Europe. On June 6, 1944, he directed the landings on the Normandy beaches in France. In between, he had devoted every waking moment to planning the long-awaited second front.

In his planning he had to make two vital decisions. The first dealt with an airborne operation to precede the landings. He planned to drop two United States divisions in a massed paratroop and glider assault onto the Cherbourg Peninsula in the early morning of D-Day.

Their task was to support the assault forces who were to cross the English Channel by boat and land on the Normandy beaches.

Two days before D-Day, at Eisenhower's advance command post near Portsmouth, the great British naval base by the English Channel, his air adviser, Air Chief Marshal Sir Trafford Leigh-Mallory, strongly urged against the airborne operation. He held that it could not succeed and might invite a massacre.

Eisenhower, in *Crusade in Europe*, related what an ordeal it was to have to make this decision: "It would be difficult to conceive of a more soul-racking problem," he wrote. "If my technical expert was correct, then the planned operation was worse than stubborn folly, because even at the enormous cost predicted we could not gain the principal object. . . . I took the problem to no one else. Professional advice and counsel could do no more. I went to my tent alone and sat down to think."

His decision was to take the calculated risk. Although the two divisions were badly mauled, and many of the troops were dropped by mistake into a marsh, the operation was credited with creating confusion behind German lines at the time the invasion forces were landing.

After the war, Eisenhower was asked what he considered the greatest moment of his military career. He replied, "When I got word that the 82d and 101st Airborne Divisions had landed on the Cherbourg Peninsula."

The second great decision that Eisenhower alone had to make was whether to postpone the invasion because of bad weather. It already had been postponed once.

First scheduled for June 5, it was delayed for 24 hours because of a weather forecast of an approaching storm. The weather prediction still looked bad for June 6, and some of Eisenhower's advisers recommended another postponement until the weather was favorable.

But Eisenhower had studied meteorology to learn how to interpret weather reports himself. He decided to go ahead. The silent travail he underwent in making this decision has been described by Lieut. Gen. Walter Bedell Smith, then his chief of staff. Writing in the *Saturday Evening Post* after the war, General Smith related:

"The silence lasted for five full minutes while General Eisenhower sat on a sofa before a bookcase that filled the end of the room. I never realized before the loneliness and isolation of a commander at a time when a momentous decision has to be taken, with full knowledge that the failure or success rests on his judgment alone. He sat there quietly, not getting up to pace with quick strides as he often does. He was tense, weighing every consideration. . . . Finally he looked up and tension was gone from his face. He said briskly, 'Well, we'll go.' "

It turned out that Eisenhower had selected the right day and hour for the invasion from a weather standpoint. Weather conditions still were far from favorable as the assault craft shoved off. Heavy swells on the channel beset the troops with seasickness. Yet they were able to complete the landings.

On the night before the invasion, Eisenhower spent much of his time with the troops. He walked among them from group to group, talking with them and patting them on the back.

Eisenhower rapidly built up reserves of troops, ammunition, armor and supplies in France. On July 25, the United States First Army under Lieut. Gen. Omar N. Bradley achieved the St.-Lô breakthrough from the beachheads.

This success allowed Lieut. Gen. George S. Patton's Third Army to get loose for its spectacular drive inland. Between them, the First and Third armies destroyed a major part of Field Marshal Guenther von Kluge's Seventh Army. This was ground to pieces in the Falaise pocket.

As the Allied forces swept the Germans out of France, Paris was liberated. On Aug. 27 Eisenhower flew there behind the liberating forces of the French general Jacques Le Clerc. He then moved his own headquarters from London to Versailles, near Paris.

Meanwhile, Eisenhower also planned and directed the invasion of Southern France, beginning two months after D-Day in Normandy.

By September the Allied invasion from the West had reached German soil and was battering against the strongly fortified Siegfried Line.

Eisenhower was elevated by President Roosevelt to the temporary rank of General of the Army on Dec. 20, 1944. This five-star rank was established by Congress in World War II.

About this time the Allied campaign met a serious but temporary reverse. Just before Christmas 1944 Field Marshal Karl von Rundstedt opened a surprise counteroffensive into Belgium and Luxembourg. In their last desperate drive, the German troops broke through a weak point in the United States lines and plunged deep into the Ardennes Forest. This event became known as the Battle of the Bulge.

Eisenhower then was faced with a difficult decision comparable to those of D-Day. Field Marshal Montgomery, commanding the British forces north of the Bulge, was separated by it from General Bradley, commanding United States forces to the south.

Though Eisenhower knew his decision would be unpopular with his American subordinates, he unhesitatingly placed Field Marshal Montgomery in temporary command of all troops in the northern part of the Bulge, including American forces that had been under Bradley's command.

The Nazis then were gradually beaten back and the Bulge was wiped out.

The end followed quickly on the German defeat in the Bulge. Eisenhower rallied his armies and sent them crashing across the Rhine for the final campaign. In the spring of 1945 his troops took 317,000 prisoners and broke the back of German resistance in the Ruhr.

March 7, 1945, was a day always remembered by Eisenhower as "one of the happiest of my life." On that day General Bradley telephoned him that German bungling, the failure to blow up the Ludendorf Bridge over the Rhine at Remagen (in the United States sector of the front) had resulted in the capture of the bridge intact.

The capture of the bridge was one of the turning points in the latter phase of the war. To exploit it Eisenhower quickly changed his plans. He decided to make his first thrust across the Rhine there instead of in the British sector. He ordered General Bradley to rush every available man and gun across the bridge before the Germans could destroy it.

On April 23, United States troops met the Russians in the Torgau area on the Elbe River. The Allies smashing from the west and the Russians from the east had crushed Hitler's once-mighty legions.

They also had reduced German cities to rubble by air and artillery bombardment.

The unconditional surrender of Germany was accepted by Eisenhower on May 7, 1945. When Gen. Alfred Jodl of the German army arrived at Allied advance headquarters in a schoolhouse at Rheims, France, Eisenhower put General Smith in charge of the ceremonies and absented himself from the room.

Jodl signed the surrender document before General Smith and other Allied officers. He then was led down the hall to Eisenhower's office.

The German entered the room, clicked his heels and raised his field marshal's baton in salute. In *Crusade in Europe*, Eisenhower wrote of this scene:

"I asked him through the interpreter if he thoroughly understood all provisions of the document he had signed.

"He answered, *'Ja.'*

"I said, 'You will, officially and personally, be held responsible if the terms of this surrender are violated, including its provisions for German commanders to appear in Berlin at the moment set by the Russian High Command to accomplish formal surrender to that Government. That is all.'

"He saluted and left."

An Associated Press correspondent described the scene as follows:

"General Eisenhower's famous smile was absent. There was a moment of heavy silence. Then General Eisenhower spoke.

"He was brief and terse as always. His voice was cold and hard. In a few clipped sentences he made it plain that Germany was a defeated nation and that henceforth all orders to the German people would come from the Allies. He said they would be obeyed.

"Then the Germans filed out. It was over. Nazi Germany had ceased to exist. The war had ended."

Within a few weeks of the German surrender, Eisenhower was invited to Moscow by Premier Josef Stalin and he reviewed a victory parade from the top of Lenin's tomb.

He received Russia's highest award, the jeweled Order of Victory. This had never before been presented to a non-Russian. Only seven Russians had ever received it. Eisenhower also was the first foreign general to receive Russia's highest military decoration, the Order of Suvarov.

The other Allied nations also heaped honors upon him. In London, at Buckingham Palace, King George VI invested him with the Order of Merit. He was the first United States soldier ever to receive this decoration.

In Paris more than one million persons thronged

the streets through which he rode in a triumphal procession. In a ceremony before the Tomb of the Unknown Soldier, Gen. Charles de Gaulle, leader of the French Resistance against the Nazis, conferred upon him the title Fellow of the Liberation.

The general received a series of enthusiastic welcomes in the United States. At Washington on June 18 more than one million persons turned out in the streets for him. Congress praised him in joint session.

The next day New York gave him a roaring welcome, with a ticker tape parade, a reception at City Hall and a dinner at the Waldorf-Astoria Hotel. The police estimated that four million persons had lined the streets to see him.

At West Point there was another hearty welcome for the general. The celebrations ended with ceremonies in Abilene, Kans., where he had spent his boyhood.

Eisenhower then returned to Europe for a short tour of duty as commander of the United States occupation forces and military governor of the United States–occupied zone in Germany, with headquarters at Frankfurt. He was recalled to the United States to succeed Gen. George C. Marshall on Nov. 20, 1945, as the army's chief of staff.

On April 11, 1946, Eisenhower was promoted to the permanent five-star rank of General of the Army. He served as chief of staff until Feb. 7, 1948. He retired from the army on May 2 of that year, taking what he believed to be his farewell salute.

On June 7, 1948, he became president of Columbia University. While there, however, he was called back into uniform on several occasions. The general served as temporary chairman of the Joint Chiefs of Staff under the armed forces unification program.

Eisenhower's final leave of absence from Columbia came in 1950. By that time the threat of aggression from the Soviet Union had become so obvious that nations of the North Atlantic area had formed the North Atlantic Treaty Organization to prepare defense armaments.

On Dec. 19, 1950, the 12 nations that had formed NATO unanimously asked President Truman to let Eisenhower command its military forces. The president consented.

Eisenhower once more put on his military uniform, for the second time as Supreme Commander, Allied Powers, Europe. His mission was to keep the peace in Europe.

The commander established headquarters first at the Hotel Astoria, Paris, and later at Rocquencourt, near Paris. He remained there until the spring of 1952. After a farewell tour of NATO countries, he resigned his command post. On May 30 he turned it over to Gen. Matthew B. Ridgway. At the same time he resigned from the army.

This resignation was withdrawn in 1961 after his retirement from the presidency. At Eisenhower's own request, his successor, President John F. Kennedy, asked Congress that his rank as General of the Army be restored. This was done, and on March 22, 1961, Eisenhower again became a general of the line.

THE MAN AS GENERAL: A Military Appraisal

HANSON W. BALDWIN

DWIGHT D. EISENHOWER was born in an age when personal generalship at high command was a thing of the past. He could not command from horseback, as Napoleon did, nor could he plan in a tent, like Ulysses S. Grant and Robert E. Lee.

General Eisenhower's career spanned an age when the big battalions had been dethroned by the big factories as the arbiters of battle. And he was to live to see the "big bang" replace industrial output as the primary factor of a nation's military strength.

The development of nuclear weapons, with their awful power to devastate great areas, turned the military clock back during President Eisenhower's lifetime, not to superior numbers, not to superior mobilization potential, but to instantly ready professional forces capable of manning the ramparts of the sky. These were forces far different, indeed, from the traditional cavalry and infantry of General Eisenhower's youth.

General Eisenhower, therefore, was born into the age of technological revolution in war—an age when general management, rather than personal generalship, and an ability to capitalize on new technical developments were the hallmarks of military success. He also rose to power in a coalition war, with the need for the qualities of conciliation and patience in a supreme commander.

As an officer General Eisenhower had these qualities in abundance. His great achievement in World War II was as mediator, adjudicator and manager. He fashioned the often discordant elements of many nations into a fighting team that was, perhaps, the most successful combat coalition in history.

Personal generalship, in the old sense, had little to do with this success. But personal leadership did. His straightforward good humor, charm, reasonableness and ability to make friends had a great deal to do with his military success. He was able to win over even some of his most difficult subordinates. This was not always done without strain on General Eisenhower. He might blow his top privately, but rarely publicly. In March 1943 he told this writer in North Africa: "Damn it, I can get along with anybody but Monty!"

He was referring to Field Marshal Montgomery, then commanding the British Eighth Army.

But General Eisenhower, mainly because of his warm and friendly personality, did get along with Field Marshal Montgomery. Despite many differences, the Briton became one of General Eisenhower's warmest admirers.

General Eisenhower had two other great qualities as a leader. He was able to pick good assistants and he had the knack of getting to the heart of a problem quickly, even though the subject matter might be unfamiliar to him. And when the chips were down, he did not lack decisiveness.

His decision to go ahead with the Normandy invasion in June 1944 despite dubious weather prospects has perhaps been both overpublicized and overpraised. It was the correct decision but it was also the easiest and most logical one at that stage of preparations.

Less known, but requiring greater resolution at that early period of the war when his fame was not so firmly established, was General Eisenhower's decision to assault the Italian-held island of Pantelleria in the Mediterranean. This was a prelude to the invasion of Sicily.

The assault plan was so strongly opposed by one of his British subordinates that the differences were carried to Winston Churchill. The British officer held that the island was so heavily fortified that an assault would risk great loss and repulse. General Eisenhower maintained his stand despite great pressure. After heavy preliminary bombing and bombardment Pantelleria surrendered before the first assault wave had reached its shores.

General Eisenhower also demonstrated moral courage and independence of mind. When he was under heavy criticism because of early military setbacks at Kasserine Pass and elsewhere in North Africa and because of some Allied political dealings with Frenchmen described as "Vichyites," he is said to have sent a humorous but frank message to President Roosevelt.

"Tell him," he said, "that I am the best damn lieutenant colonel in the U.S. Army."

His permanent army rank at the time was lieutenant colonel. He held the temporary rank of general. The message implied that if the president did not like his leadership General Eisenhower would be glad to assume the rank and duties of lieutenant colonel.

General Eisenhower was in no way an intellectual

soldier, but he had a native shrewdness and common sense. When he was assigned to high command in North Africa, these traits and his ability to pick good subordinates and get along with people helped him to compensate for his somewhat narrow general knowledge and his limited experience.

In some ways he was at that time still the midwestern farm boy; in a conversation with this writer in Algiers he mispronounced the title Viscount as "Vizcount."

But he learned quickly, and he was never abashed in the company of the great and the near great.

General Eisenhower's commanding roles in World War II did not test him as a tactician; tactics were essentially the province of his division and corps commanders. But he contributed to new tactical thought. The weight of his authority added to the emphasis on air power and its proper utilization on the battlefield, and he became an exponent of the armored personnel carrier to increase the mobility of the infantry man.

As a strategist, history will probably judge General Eisenhower charitably but not as a planner of brilliance.

He had, as a matter of fact, little opportunity to display strategic talents. The strategy of World War II was not born from any one brain; it was a composite of plans developed by many men and approved in the final analysis by the Joint and Combined Chiefs of Staff, Winston Churchill and President Roosevelt. General Eisenhower in World War II was really more the executor of strategy than the maker of it.

But his ideas influenced the composite result—and this influence was generally in favor of the so-called blow to the heart—the most direct attack possible against Germany and the quickest possible end of the fighting.

He was opposed by Winston Churchill, who wished to cancel the invasion of Southern France in the summer of 1944 and possibly substitute a Balkan drive. (General Eisenhower told this writer after the war that his opposition to Churchill's proposed Balkan offensive had been wrong, politically.)

General Eisenhower compromised on the single-thrust versus broad-front approach to Germany. He gave Field Marshal Montgomery heavy backing for his crossing of the Rhine in the north but also continued the attack with American armies in the south.

General Eisenhower was much criticized for not concentrating forces for a smashing blow into the heart of Germany. Yet the broad-front strategy was militarily successful; Germany and Italy were defeated, probably as quickly as possible.

In one major respect, however, the verdict of history will cast a shadow across General Eisenhower's final World War II victories. The halt at the Elbe River, the failure to drive for Berlin and the orders to Gen. George Patton to halt short of Prague are now generally viewed as mistakes—political rather than military.

United States or British capture of Berlin and Prague before the Russians reached those cities might have changed to some extent the postwar political complexion of Europe and would have strengthened the West's hand in its postwar conflict with Communism.

The capture of Berlin prior to Russian conquest was perhaps possible, but not certain. General Eisenhower was undoubtedly persuaded not to attempt it by two factors: the then current but fallacious belief that the Nazis would attempt to continue indefinite resistance from a "national redoubt" in the Alps, and the estimate of Gen. Omar Bradley, commander of the 12th Army Group, that the capture of Berlin might cost 100,000 casualties. Prague could admittedly have been taken without much difficulty well before the advancing Soviet armies reached it.

These "might-have-beens" of history troubled General Eisenhower later. But his defense of his actions was based on the premise that Berlin and Prague were not military objectives and that his concern was to wipe out as quickly as possible organized German resistance.

He, like Gen. George C. Marshall, army chief of staff, then had a kind of political astigmatism, and the unconditional-surrender concept had in it no place for military operations that had essentially political goals.

A RETURN, OFF DUTY, TO SIMPLICITY

UPON LEAVING the White House, Dwight D. Eisenhower went to live on his farm at Gettysburg, Pa., the first real home he had had since entering the army in 1915. He had bought the farm in 1950 for $23,000. He liked the quiet, rolling Pennsylvania countryside and the opportunities that his new leisure afforded him to golf at the nearby Gettysburg Country Club and to paint in oils.

He maintained a small office on the second floor of the former residence of the president of Gettysburg College. There he wrote and painstakingly revised his two-volume memoir, *The White House Years*, and 1967's *At Ease: Stories I Tell My Friends.* There he also saw many visitors and answered letters. The office was sparsely furnished—a desk, an American flag behind it, a bookcase, some Steuben glass, four chairs and a pinkish rug.

Although Eisenhower lived on a farm, he was so far from being a farmer that he once grabbed a bull's tail to move the bull for a visitor. He often complained that he was supporting the farm, rather than the farm supporting him, because his cattle business was not profitable. Actually, of course, he and his wife did not spend all their time in Gettysburg; they wintered at Palm Desert, Calif., and frequently vacationed in Georgia, where the former president golfed at the Augusta National Golf Club.

In retirement, Eisenhower had to do a number of things that had always been done for him. He thought, for example, that he ought to learn to drive an automobile, but a couple of times behind the wheel convinced him he was better off chauffeured, and a sergeant drove him around most of the time. He also discovered that he sometimes had to buy train tickets for himself or dial telephone calls. These were irksome chores for a man who had been waited on most of his mature life.

He felt keenly that he was busier in retirement than he had been as president, yet he also felt a strong responsibility to history to be a model public figure. For this reason he lent his name to such worthy causes as the English-Speaking Union, made speeches to Republican party gatherings, wrote his memoirs and responded to calls for advice from President Kennedy and President Johnson.

He was careful, however, to avoid public roles that might embarrass his successors in the White House. In line with this, he declined an invitation to visit the Soviet Union as a guest of the Kremlin. He did not feel the same hesitation, however, in visiting Western Europe. In July and August of 1962 he and his wife and several of their grandchildren toured Paris, Copenhagen, Stockholm, Cologne and London. He met with Chancellor Konrad Adenauer of West Germany and Sir Winston Churchill.

He revisited Europe the following year, when he appeared in a television film on the Normandy invasion.

Later that year, *Mandate for Change*, the first volume of his presidential memoirs, was published. Prepared with the help of his son, John, Eisenhower's book recounted the events of his first term. The second volume, *Waging Peace, 1956–1960*, was published in 1965 and covered his second term.

It was after his first retirement from the army that Eisenhower wrote *Crusade in Europe*, the story of his career as Allied commander. For the book he was paid $636,000, with a net return of $476,250 after taxes.

In the give-and-take of conversation, Eisenhower

was never a syntactical talker. He was sensitive about this both in the White House and in retirement. He brought the matter up in an informal interview late in 1965, and explained to a reporter that he was "a man of ideas," not of talk, and that when he saw that his listeners understood what he was in the midst of saying he switched to the next point.

Eisenhower conversed with animation. Sometimes he would pace the floor as he talked; he would pound his desk for emphasis, or fling out both arms to suggest the magnitude of some problem. As an aftereffect of his stroke, he had difficulty pronouncing some words, but this impediment was not obtrusive.

A certain mellowness was evident in Eisenhower's conduct after he left the White House, but this involved conscious effort. He realized toward the end of his second administration that he could not afford to let himself become angry, and he rather docilely yielded to intimates who sought to calm him down.

Once he topped a tee shot at Augusta and flared up in such anger that Richard Flohr, his Secret Service guard, grew alarmed. Mr. Flohr ran to the general and, in the manner of a top sergeant talking to a buck private, shouted: "Now you just cut that out right now, Mr. President. And I mean cut it out, or I'm going to put you in that cart and take you right back to the cottage and lock you in." Eisenhower was abashed and quieted down.

Always considerate of his wife, Mamie, Eisenhower traveled much by train in retirement because Mrs. Eisenhower was uncomfortable on airplanes. On many occasions he went out of his way to demonstrate his affection.

Not long before his 75th birthday he was presented with a large bouquet of white carnations at a public ceremony. He put one in his lapel and remarked, "The rest of these are for my sweetheart." To interviewers in his final years he liked to say that "the luckiest thing that ever happened to me was the girl I married."

All his life Eisenhower was influenced by the moralism of his Mennonite forebears, and it seemed only natural to him to consider social, economic and political questions in a moral environment. The Bible was the ultimate source of inspiration and consolation for his parents, and Eisenhower turned to it more and more after he left the presidency.

In the living room of his Gettysburg farm was a well-thumbed Bible bound in soft black morocco. An interviewer asked him about it, and he replied: "I wouldn't want to be portrayed as anything like a student of the Bible, let alone a biblical scholar. But since leaving the White House I have found myself turning to it more and more. I suppose it's just that I have more time for reading what I please than was possible in White House years.

"My favorite passages? Well, that's not easy to answer. But mostly I like to read from the Prophets. In the midst of wars and rumors of wars I don't know anything more helpful to straighten out your thinking. They had a way of putting first things first and it has seemed to me that some of this quality must rub off on a man who reads them with a purpose.

"Then, too, they had a certain dignity of expression—an ennobling quality, if you will—that I have always liked. To me a reading from the Prophets is a reminder of the dignity of man and the essential worthwhileness of the individual."

As an elder statesman after he left the White House, Eisenhower was frequently consulted on national affairs by President Johnson. His advice was sought in particular on American military involvement in Vietnam, which he firmly supported. He suggested that patriotism required united public backing for a victory policy lest United States resolution in Southeast Asia be found wanting by the Communists.

As a revered figure in his party, the general was courted by Republican politicians eager for his endorsement. He professed greater concern, however, for party unity than for personalities; but he broke his rule in 1968 to endorse Richard M. Nixon for the Republican presidential nomination. He cited Nixon's devotion to the party and his experience in government.

In the 1962 midterm election, he campaigned for a party united on moderate stands. Despite pressure from moderates at the 1964 Republican National Convention, he declined to endorse Gov. William W. Scranton of Pennsylvania or oppose Sen. Barry Goldwater of Arizona, fearing a party rift.

"We must learn," he said, "that when a Republican concerns himself too much in condemning this or that faction of decent people in the party, he is hurting himself and the party."

Four years later, in a valedictory address to the party convention, he again stressed party solidarity, but devoted most of his talk to rallying the delegates to meet foreign and domestic challenges to the nation. Warning of Communist peril, he said: "At every level of government we must . . . seek out candid and capable leaders. We need people who can point the way to sound progress, serenity and confidence at home, and respect for America throughout the world."

General Eisenhower had endorsed Nixon on July 18, lauding his "experience, decisiveness and intelligence." At the Walter Reed Army Medical Center in Washington, recuperating from his heart attacks, he received Nixon and other candidates before the November election.

Late in October, he wrote Nixon a "Dear Dick" letter, calling him better equipped for the presidency "than any other political figure I have seen or heard."

Eisenhower's final years were beset by illness. He suffered two mild heart attacks in late 1965; he was operated on for a gall bladder condition in 1966 and was hospitalized three times the following year, twice for stomach ailments and once for an enlarged prostate gland. He suffered another heart attack in April, a fifth one in June and a sixth on Aug. 6, a few hours after addressing the party convention from his hospital room. His seventh heart attack occurred last Aug. 16.

Toward the close of his life Eisenhower was asked to tick off what he considered his greatest achievements and disappointments during his presidency.

Referring to achievements, he told Walter Cronkite of the Columbia Broadcasting System: "When I came to the presidency, the country was rather in an unhappy state. There was bitterness and there was quarreling and so on. I tried to create an atmosphere of greater serenity and mutual confidence, and I think that it was noticeable over those eight years that that was brought about."

In *Waging Peace* he said that the defeat of Richard Nixon in 1960 was "my principal political disappointment." "I cannot ascribe any rational cause for the outcome," he wrote, "for I still believe, as I did then, that any objective comparisons of the relative capacities and qualifications of the two candidates would have resulted in an overwhelming judgment in Nixon's favor."

Eisenhower's major regret was "that as we left the White House I had to admit to little success in making progress in global disarmament or in reducing the bitterness of the East-West struggle." The "bleak record," he said in his book, was not owing to "any lack of striving on our part." "The difficulty was the frozen position of hostility with which the Communists greeted every Western proposal for enforceable, mutual disarmament or for any removal of the causes of tensions that so plague the world."

Eisenhower died in Washington, D.C., on March 28, 1969, after a long fight against heart disease. President Nixon said of him: "He spoke with a moral authority seldom equated in American public life. He was devoted to the common cause of humanity, to his beloved country, and to his family and friends. He was both a great man and a good man. To millions the world over he was a symbol of decency and hope."

HOW THE WORLD'S LEADERS DESCRIBED EISENHOWER

HIS CAREER, military and political, brought General Eisenhower into frequent touch with famous men of state and men of war. Many of them have told of the impression he made upon them in their memoirs, from which the following assessments have been excerpted.

Winston Churchill

Winston Churchill wrote of General Eisenhower in a letter to President Truman just after the German surrender in May 1945:

"Let me tell you what General Eisenhower has meant to us. In him we have had a man who set the unity of the Allied armies above all nationalistic thoughts. In his headquarters unity and strategy were the only reigning spirits. The unity reached such a point that British and American troops could be mixed in the line of battle and large masses could be easily transferred from one command to the other without the slightest difficulty.

"At no time has the principle of alliance between noble races been carried and maintained at so high a pitch. In the name of the British Empire and Commonwealth I express to you our admiration of the firm, farsighted and illuminating character and qualities of General of the Army Eisenhower."

In *The Hinge of Fate*, the fourth volume of his six-volume history, *The Second World War*, Sir Winston described his relationship with General Eisenhower and General Mark Clark as "close and agreeable."

"From the moment they arrived in June," he wrote, "I had arranged a weekly luncheon at Number 10 on Tuesdays. These meetings seemed to be a success. I was nearly always alone with them, and we talked all our affairs over, back and forth as if we were all of one country. I set great value on these personal contacts. Irish stew turned out to be very popular with my American guests, especially with General Eisenhower. My wife was nearly always able to get this. I soon began to call him 'Ike.' "

Harry S Truman

On Aug. 13, 1952, President Truman invited General Eisenhower, the Republican presidential nominee, to a cabinet luncheon and a briefing. The general declined by telegram.

"Eisenhower's telegram angered me," Mr. Truman later wrote. "It was apparent that the politicians had already begun to mishandle him. On Aug. 16 I wrote in longhand this personal letter to Eisenhower:

> Dear Ike:
> I am sorry if I caused you any embarrassment.
>
> What I've always had in mind was and is a continuing foreign policy. You know that is a fact because you had a part in outlining it.
>
> Partisan politics should stop at the boundaries of the United States. I am extremely sorry that you have allowed a bunch of screwballs to come between us.
>
> You have made a bad mistake, and I'm hoping that it won't injure this great Republic.

The last line of the seven-paragraph letter said, 'From a man who has always been your friend and who always intended to be.' " His relationship with General Eisenhower after he became the Republican nominee perplexed and somewhat troubled Mr. Truman, who found the general cold and distant.

Meeting After Election

In volume 2 of his memoirs, *Years of Trial and Hope*, Mr. Truman tells of his meeting with President-elect Eisenhower on Nov. 18, 1952.

"When the general and his aides left, I was troubled," Mr. Truman wrote in the last paragraph of the book. "I had the feeling that, up to this meeting in the White House, General Eisenhower had not grasped the immense job ahead of him. There was something about his attitude during the meeting that I did not understand. It may have been that this meeting made him realize for the first time what the Presidency and the responsibilities of the President were. He may have been awestruck by the long array of problems and decisions the President had to face. If that is so, then I can almost understand his frozen grimness throughout the meeting. But it may have been something else. He may have failed to grasp the true picture of what the Administration had been doing because in the heat of partisan politics he had gotten a badly distorted version of the true facts. Whatever it was, I kept thinking about it."

Charles de Gaulle

General de Gaulle wrote in *Unity, 1942–1944: The War Memoirs of Charles de Gaulle* that on June 16, 1943, when he was head of the Free French, he was invited to a conference with General Eisenhower.

"I purposely arrived last and spoke first," General de Gaulle wrote. " 'I am here,' I told Eisenhower, 'in my capacity as President of the French Government. For it is customary that during operations the chiefs of state and of the government should come in person to the headquarters of the officers in command of the armies they have entrusted to him.' "

General de Gaulle thus sought to put General Eisenhower in a position of subordination to him. General de Gaulle continues: "The inter-Allied commander in chief, making an effort to be pleasant, then declared, in substance, 'I'm preparing, as you know, a very important operation which will soon be launched against Italy and which directly concerns the liberation of Europe and of France.' " General Eisenhower told General de Gaulle that Gen. Henri Giraud must remain at the head of the French command in North Africa.

" 'You are asking a promise of me which I will not give you, for the organization of the French command is the province of the French government, not yours,' " General de Gaulle quotes himself as replying.

"I continued, 'You who are a soldier, do you think that a leader's authority can subsist if it rests on the favor of a foreign power?'

"After a new and heavy silence, the American commander in chief said, 'I quite understand, general, that you have long-standing preoccupations as to the fate of your nation. Please understand that I for my part have immediate military preoccupations.' "

General de Gaulle broke off the interview. The next day the Allied headquarters sent him a note specifying Allied requirements. It ended: "The Allied commander in chief wishes to emphasize the assurances given by the British and American Governments guaranteeing that French sovereignty will be respected in North and West Africa."

"Although this last touch, serving as an ironic conclusion to the demands that contradicted it, was signed by the Allied commander in chief, I recognized in it the procedure frequently employed by Washington and London—paying lip service to rights even while infringing them," General de Gaulle wrote.

"But I knew that such a course of action, if it corresponded to the policies pursued in regard to France by the British and American Governments proceeded from neither the initiative nor the character of General Eisenhower.

"He was a soldier. To him, by nature and by profession, action seemed natural, immediate and simple. To put into play, according to time-honored rules, specific means of a familiar nature—this was how he envisaged warfare and consequently his task. Eisenhower approached the test trained for 35 years by a technique and a philosophy beyond which he was in no way inclined to go.

"Yet now he found himself abruptly invested with an extraordinarily complex role. Removed from the hitherto rigid framework of the American Army, he had become commander in chief of a colossal coalition.

"It was a piece of luck for the Allies that Dwight Eisenhower discovered within himself not only the necessary prudence to deal with these thorny problems, but also an attraction toward the wider horizons that history opened before his career. He knew how to be adroit and flexible. But if he used skill, he was also capable of audacity.

"Yet it was chiefly by method and perseverance that he dominated the situation. By choosing reasonable plans, by sticking firmly to them, by respecting logistics, General Eisenhower led to victory the complicated and prejudicial machinery of the armies of the free world."

General de Gaulle wrote that General Eisenhower could have done more for France and for the French forces than he actually did.

"In my own relations with him, I often had the feeling that this generous-hearted man inclined toward these points of view. But I was soon to see him turn away from them, as if regretfully. Actually, politics dictated his behavior from Washington and necessitated his reserve. He complied, yielding to Roosevelt's authority.

"Nevertheless, if occasionally he went so far as to support the pretexts which tended to keep us in obscurity, I can affirm that he did so without conviction. I even saw him submit to my intervention in his own strategy whenever national interest led me to do so. At heart this great soldier felt, in his turn, that mysterious sympathy which for almost two centuries has brought his country and mine together in the world's great dramas."

General de Gaulle wrote that President Roosevelt's efforts to honor some other authority than his own over France "seemed to me on the same order as Alice's Adventures in Wonderland. The Allies would encounter no other ministers and officials in France than those I had established there. They would find no other French troops than those of which I was the leader. Without any presumptuousness, I could defy General Eisenhower to deal lawfully with anyone I had not designated.

"He himself, moreover, did not dream of doing so. 'You were originally described to me,' he said, 'in an unfavorable sense. Today, I realize that that judgment was in error. For the coming battle, I shall need not the only the cooperation of your forces, but still more the assistance of your officials and the moral support of the French people. I must have your assistance, and I have come to ask you for it.'

" 'Splendid!' I replied. 'You are a man! For you know how to say, "I was wrong." ' "

Bernard Law Montgomery

"It was always very clear to me that Ike and I were poles apart when it came to the conduct of the war," Viscount Montgomery wrote in his memoirs, published in 1958, and he provided extensive detail on the nature and extent of those tactical disagreements.

Toward General Eisenhower the military commander, Viscount Montgomery was frankly and sometimes impatiently critical, but toward General Eisenhower the man, the Viscount was most warmly inclined. "My military doctrine was based on unbalancing the enemy while keeping well-balanced myself. I planned always to make the enemy commit his reserves on a wide front in order to plug holes in his defences; having forced him to do this, I then committed my own reserves on a narrow front in a hard blow. I know from experience how it helped to save men's lives.

"Eisenhower's creed appeared to me to be that there must be aggressive action on the part of everyone at all times. Everybody must attack all the time. I remember Bedell Smith once likened Eisenhower to a football coach; he was up and down the line all the time, encouraging everyone to get on with the game. This philosophy was expensive in life."

The trouble that arose out of various differences in military outlook, Viscount Montgomery wrote, was to "grow and develop into storms which at times threatened to wreck the Allied ship."

But on the last five pages of his memoirs, he describes General Eisenhower as "a remarkable and most lovable man." He said he was "greatly impressed by his quick grasp of a problem and by the way he radiated confidence and kindness."

Viscount Montgomery was a nondrinker and nonsmoker who detested cigarette smoke. General Eisenhower "was a very heavy smoker in those days and at breakfast in our mess tent he lit a cigarette before I had begun the meal." He went on: "We were sitting together and I at once moved my seat to the other side of the table. He quickly sensed that I did not like smoke circulating around me at meal times and apologized, throwing away his cigarette!

"I would not class Ike as a great soldier in the true sense of the word," he wrote. "He might have become one if he had ever had the experience of exercising direct command of a division, corps, an army which, unfortunately for him, did not come his way. But he was a great Supreme Commander—a military statesman. I know of no other person who could have welded the Allied forces into such a fine fighting machine in the way he did, and kept a balance among the many conflicting and disrupting elements which threatened at times to wreck the ship.

"He has the power of drawing the hearts of men towards him as a magnet attracts the bits of metal. He has only to smile at you, and you trust him at once. He is the very incarnation of sincerity. He has great common sense."

Dean Acheson

Mr. Acheson was secretary of state in the Truman administration. In his book, *Sketches from Life: Of Men I Have Known*, published in 1959, Mr. Acheson wrote of a North Atlantic Alliance meeting at Rome in 1951. He said:

"The Supreme Commander, Eisenhower, spoke to us. I had never heard him in a large meeting before and found myself bewildered between the tone and the content of the speech. The tone was inspirational and vigorous; the content was the meagerest intellectual fare. To test the opinion of others, in the recess after the speech, I sought out my wise, shrewd, and humorous friend Mr. Joseph Bech, and asked him how he liked the speech.

" 'Ah,' he said, 'I think before long we shall lose our Supreme Commander.' I was puzzled and doubtless showed it. 'Yes,' he went on, 'the signs are unmistakable. Our commander will soon leave us to run for President of your country.' And so he did, less than four months later."

THE EISENHOWER ERA

MAX FRANKEL

THERE WAS not much shock or weeping in Washington, D. C., when Dwight D. Eisenhower died, because the memories of him remain so plainly cheerful, fond and benign. He left the White House with affection, lived a long and full life, and died a natural death, the way it ought to be for presidents but has not been since Ike. Two somewhat contradictory impressions dominated the talk of him around Washington in the days following his death. People were amazed at how vividly they still remembered the great grin and the true trust that it inspired. Yet they were surprised at how remote they felt from the Eisenhower years.

There has been so much tumult since 1961 that the capital has barely had time to reflect upon General Eisenhower's final struggle out at Walter Reed Hospital.

And few of this city's crisis-hopping residents, except perhaps President Nixon, have had occasion to think back to the days when political assassination meant only verbal assault on character and when urban unrest meant only trouble in remote Little Rock, Ark.

President Eisenhower was shoved into history here by the impatient men of the New Frontier and the Great Society and it is only now that people are taking a second look back to the fifties.

As they do, the general still does not stand out as

a forceful agent of change, but he is seen now to have presided, perhaps more knowingly than many realized, over some great transformations at home and abroad.

It was in the Eisenhower years, during his two terms in office after his election in 1952, that the nation settled down to live uneasily with its concerns about Soviet power and Communist expansion. The talk of preemptive nuclear war and the suspicions of treason in high places were gradually overcome.

The Eisenhower administration wrote a long list of new military commitments around the world, one of which led eventually to war in Vietnam. But the general himself refused to authorize military intervention in Southeast Asia or even to contemplate it against the Soviet invasion of Hungary.

Instead, over time, he engaged the Russians in the first attempts at Soviet-American negotiation. He brought Nikita S. Khrushchev to Camp David in the Catoctins and almost made it to Moscow. The balance of terror, though unstable and still unsettling, gradually became an acceptable fact.

And it was in the Eisenhower years that conservative Americans became grudgingly reconciled to constantly expanding and frequently unbalanced federal budgets. Quietly, if not enthusiastically, they accepted government responsibility for programs of social and economic welfare.

The Eisenhower administration lived in serene ignorance of the ominous Negro migration from the rural South to the urban North. Its great legislative monument is the river of highway concrete that flows round and through the cities, but the rapid deterioration of the quality of life in those cities went unnoticed and untended.

That is why the young Kennedy men chased the Republicans with the promise to "get the country moving again," but it had moved imperceptibly under Eisenhower, too.

The general moved the Republican party firmly away from its last flirtation with isolationism. And though he had little taste for partisan politics and paid scant attention to partisan organization, he was the first Republican in this century to win two consecutive terms in the White House, and moved his party from despair back into significant contention throughout the country. In this, he felt he had "saved" the two-party system itself after 20 years of uninterrupted Democratic rule.

Moreover, it was General Eisenhower's conduct in office that restored to the presidency an element of nonpartisanship and let the nation think that one man, at least from time to time, stood above political interest. By his conduct, also, the general stilled the fear of military domination of government; mostly he was criticized for governing too little instead of too much.

He held down military spending and in his final speech as president sounded the now famous alarm against "unwarranted influence, whether sought or unsought, by the military-industrial complex."

There are those who lived through the Eisenhower years who have never forgiven him his reluctance to condemn the demagoguery of Sen. Joseph R. McCarthy. And there are those who will never forgive him the appointment of Earl Warren as Chief Justice of the United States.

But the rush of history here has also left many who clamor today against the "military-industrial complex" wholly ignorant of the man and the faith that gave them their slogan. It was a simple faith in his country and in the idea of progress, and in its time it was powerful indeed.

T. S. ELIOT

1888–1965

London, Jan. 4—T. S. Eliot, the quiet, gray figure who gave new meaning to English-language poetry, died Jan. 4, 1965, at his home in London. He was 76 years old.

Eliot was an American, born in St. Louis. He moved to England at the beginning of World War I and became wholly identified with Britain, even becoming naturalized in 1927.

Nevertheless, when President Johnson recently awarded the Medal of Freedom to leaders in American literature and public life, Eliot was among those honored. He did not make the trip to the United States, however, to receive the award.

The influence of Eliot began with the publication in 1917 of his poem "The Love Song of J. Alfred Prufrock." Perhaps his most significant contribution came five years later in the lengthy poem *The Waste Land.*

From time to time Eliot would give readings of his poetry in public. He read softly, but when he ended *The Waste Land* in a quick rush of words audiences were always moved.

Eliot was a convert to Anglo-Catholicism, and his religious belief showed up strongly in his later works.

Eliot won the Nobel Prize for Literature in 1948 and was awarded the Order of Merit by Britain in the same year.

This is the way the world ends
This is the way the world ends
This is the way the world ends
Not with a bang but a whimper.

These four lines by Thomas Stearns Eliot, written as the conclusion to "The Hollow Men" in 1925, are probably the most quoted lines of any 20th-century poet writing in English. They are also the essence of Eliot as he established his reputation as a poet of post-World War I disillusion and despair.

They were written by an expatriate from St. Louis, a graduate of Harvard College, who had chosen to live in London and who was working as a bank clerk.

The "bang and the whimper," together with *The Waste Land,* which was published three years earlier, established Eliot as a major poet. From there he went on to mellowness, fame, financial independence and a Nobel Prize, but he always remained, in the layman's view, the poet of gray melancholy.

This view persisted despite Eliot's notable literary criticism that established new pathways in the field and despite his two plays of considerable merit, *The Cocktail Party* and *Murder in the Cathedral.* These, while not of flaming hue, were not yet gray.

Cursed though he might be with that reputation, Eliot's early poems did not represent the more ma-

Bassano/Camera Press

© Rollie McKenna

ture conclusions of his later years about the state of mankind and the world as stated in *Four Quartets* or his delicious sense of humor, which included himself.

One example of his ability to see himself as something less than magisterial was expressed in this poem about himself:

How unpleasant to meet Mr. Eliot!
With his features of clerical cut,
And his brow so grim
And his mouth so prim
And his conversation, so nicely
Restricted to What Precisely
And If and Perhaps and
But . . .

Whereas Eliot began his seminal *The Waste Land* with the line "April is the cruellest month" and ended it 434 lines later with "Shantih shantih shantih," his more seasoned reflections included these lines from *Four Quartets:*

. . . And right action is freedom
From past and future also.
For most of us, this is the aim
Never here to be realized;
Who are only undefeated
Because we have gone on trying;
We, content at last
If our temporal reversion nourish
(Not too far from the yew-tree)
The life of significant soil.

Not only did Eliot shift his philosophic outlook, but his poetic accents also became almost conversational, verging on the informal.

In his later years he had an office in London in the publishing house of Faber & Faber, of which he was a director. There he carried on his business, writing letters and articles, somewhat like the clerkish type he resembled.

In appearance he was then, as he was in early life, a most unlikely figure for a poet. He lacked flamboyance or oddity in dress or manner, and there was nothing of the romantic about him. He carried no auras, cast no arresting eye and wore his heart, as nearly as could be observed, in its proper anatomical place.

His habits of work were equally "unpoetic," for he eschewed bars and cafés for the pleasant and bourgeois comforts of an office with padded chairs and a well-lighted desk.

Talking of his work habits, he once said: "A great deal of my new play, *The Elder Statesman*, was produced in pencil and paper, very roughly. Then I typed it myself first before my wife got to work on it. In typing myself I make alterations, very considerable ones. But whether I write or type, composition of any length, a play for example, means for me regular hours, say 10 to 1. I found that three hours a day is about all I can do of actual composing. I could do the polish perhaps later."

Eliot's dress was a model of the London man of business. He wore a bowler and often carried a tightly rolled umbrella. His accent, which started out as pure American Middle West, did undergo changes, becoming over the years quite British U.

The U was complete and unfeigned, "I am," he said stoutly, "an Anglo-Catholic in religion, a classicist in literature and a royalist in politics."

Even so, his ascetic austerity drew the line at gin rummy, which he delighted to play of an evening. He also kept a signed photograph of Groucho Marx, cigar protuberant, in his study at home.

These touches lend credence to Eliot's attempts in later years to soften some aspects of his credo. His religious beliefs, he asserted, remained unchanged, and he was still in favor of monarchy in all countries having a monarch, but the term *classicism* was no longer so important to him.

The poet was born on Sept. 26, 1888, into a family of some privilege that had a good background in the intellectual, religious and business life of New England. After a year at Milton (Mass.) Academy, he entered Harvard in 1906 in the class that included Walter Lippmann, Heywood Broun, John Reed and Stuart Chase. He completed his undergraduate work in three years and took a Master of Arts degree in his fourth.

Although he never took his doctorate, he completed the dissertation in 1916. It was titled "Experience and Objects of Knowledge in the Philosophy of F. H. Bradley." This thinker's monist view of personality greatly influenced Eliot's poetic sensibility, reinforcing his themes of human isolation in guilt.

His Harvard classmates recall that he dressed with the studied carelessness of a British gentleman, smoked a pipe and liked to be left alone.

This aspect of Eliot was hardly altered when he returned to Harvard in the 1930s for a half year as a sort of poet in residence.

In that sojourn he lived in an undergraduate house near the Charles River and entertained students at least once a week at teas. The tea was always brewed and he poured with great delicacy, his long and tabescent fingers clasping the handle of the silver teapot. The quality of his tea, the excellence of the college-provided petit fours and the rippling flow of his conversation drew overflow crowds of students, who sat on chairs, on the floor and on windowsills.

At these functions, Eliot was shy and patient with the halting undergraduates, and he must have suffered many fools, but such was his courtesy that he never showed impatience openly. He just sat and talked, reclining in a high-backed cloth chair, puffing and relighting his pipe, crossing and uncrossing his tweed-covered legs.

Eliot was an omnivorous and retentive reader. He consumed philosophy, languages and letters and this lent his poetry an erudition and scholarship unmatched in this century. Indeed, he carried scholarship so far as to footnote *The Waste Land* as though it were a thesis for a doctorate.

He was also able, because of his extensive reading, to converse (and hold reasoned views) on a range of subjects from Shakespeare to Karl Marx.

His views and his expression of them were usually pungent.

"No one can go very far in the discerning enjoyment of poetry," he once remarked, "who is incapable of enjoying any poetry other than that of his own time and place. It is in fact a part of the function of education to help us to escape—not from our own time, for we are bound by that—but from the intellectual and emotional limitations of our own time."

He had a strong dislike for most teaching of poetry, and he once recalled that he had been turned against Shakespeare in his youth by didactical instructors.

"I took a dislike to *Julius Caesar* which lasted, I am sorry to say, until I saw the film of Marlon Brando and John Gielgud, and a dislike to *The Merchant of Venice* which persists to this day.

"It may be that a few plays and poems must be sacrificed [in school] in order that we learn that English literature exists and that an ordinary acquaintance with it is desirable."

Eliot believed, moreover, that "unless a teacher is a person who reads poetry for enjoyment he or she cannot stimulate pupils to enjoy it."

Pursuing this theme, he once described how teachers of literature should go about teaching: "My Ideal Teacher will teach the prescribed classics of literature as history, as part of history which every educated person should know something about, whether he likes it or not; and then should lead some of the pupils to enjoyment, and the rest at least to the point of recognizing that there are other persons who do enjoy it. And he will introduce the pupils to contemporary poetry by exciting enjoyment; enjoyment first and understanding second."

Eliot, however, was not one to minimize the difficulties of understanding poetic complexities or of achieving empathy with a poem's mood and feeling. "The reader of a poem," he admonished, "should take at least as much trouble as a barrister reading a decision on a complicated case."

In 1915 Eliot became a teacher in the Highgate School in London, and the next year went to work in Lloyds Bank, Ltd. Hints of this commercial experience, of which he rarely complained, although the work must have been tedious, peep unexpectedly out of his poetry. For instance, "A Cooking Egg" contains these lines:

. . . We two shall lie together, lapt
In five per cent Exchequer Bond

The first poem that started Eliot's reputation was "The Love Song of J. Alfred Prufrock" in 1917. In it he assumed the pose of a fastidious, world-weary, young-old man, aging into ironic wit. The poem is full of exquisitely precise surrealist images and rhythms, but it also has some everyday metaphors. Part of it goes:

I grow old . . . I grow old . . .
I shall wear the bottoms of my trousers rolled.
Shall I part my hair behind?
Do I dare to eat a peach?
Shall I wear white flannel trousers and walk upon the beach . . .

Eliot's strictures on applying concentrated efforts to the understanding of poetry could well apply to his next major poem, *The Waste Land.* Heavily influenced by Ezra Pound (it was, in fact, dedicated to that other poet of obscurity), *The Waste Land* was an expression of gigantic frustration and despair. But it made his reputation, although its author conceded in later years that he wrote it "simply to relieve my own feelings."

The poem, a series of somewhat blurred visions, centers on an imaginary waste region, the home of the Fisher King, a little-known figure in mythology, who is sexually impotent.

Writing on *The Waste Land*, Helen Gardner, an authority on Eliot's writings, noted: "The sense of boredom and horror behind both the beauty and ugliness is expressed by juxtaposition of the beautiful and the ugly." In another reference, Miss Gardner wrote of Eliot's "union of the common and the formal, the colloquial and the remote, the precise and the suggestive."

After *The Waste Land*, Eliot's development was tortured and hesitant, but was clearly marked. His interest in the spiritual development of man rather than in his spiritual inadequacies grew after his early period, when he poked more or less good-natured fun at the Church in such works as "The Hippopotamus." He sees the haloed hippo ascending into heaven:

Blood of the Lamb shall wash him clean
And him shall heavenly arms enfold,
Among the saints he shall be seen
Performing on a harp of gold.
He shall be washed as white as snow,
By all the martyr'd virgins kist,
While the True Church remains below
Wrapt in the old miasmal mist.

In one of his poetry readings at Columbia University, Eliot recited "The Hippopotamus," which had been published in 1914. He said, "It doesn't seem shocking to anybody now, I think, as it did all those years ago." He discussed his comparison between the hippopotamus and the Church:

The True Church need never stir
To gather in its dividends.

He recalled: "A good many years after I had written those lines I became a church warden and we were wondering how to keep the church going on the collections. So one lives and learns."

Eliot was regarded as an important literary critic as well as a poet. Much of his criticism was published in literary reviews or delivered from the lecture platform, without subsequently appearing in book form. His first book of literary criticism, *The Sacred Wood*, was published in 1920.

This book and much of Eliot's subsequent criticism introduced certain types of writing to the intelligent reading public with accompanying evaluation that heightened interest in important writers who were not so well known.

It is possible that Eliot is most widely known through his drama *Murder in the Cathedral*, which was often produced in this country and which was made into a motion picture. It is a grim, sardonic account of the murder of Thomas à Becket, Archbishop of Canterbury, in 1170.

An opera, *Assassinio Nella Cattedrale*, written by Ildebrando Pizzetti, was based on the Eliot drama and was a critical success.

Two of Eliot's plays enjoyed critical success in London and New York. *The Cocktail Party*, published in 1954, was a story of deeply religious experience told against a background of highly literate and amusing British people. *The Confidential Clerk* told of bastardy and general unhappiness.

In his lighter moments (and there were many) Eliot was an unabashed ailurophile. He kept cats at home, bestowing upon them such names as Man in White Spats; he also wrote a book of poems called *Old Possum's Book of Practical Cats*;* and in his dry, cadenced voice he read the verses on the platform and for recordings.

These lines from "The Naming of Cats" illustrate Eliot's profound insight into the narcissistic world of the feline:

But I tell you, a cat needs a name that's
particular,
A name that's peculiar, and more dignified,
Else how can he keep up his tail
perpendicular,
Or spread out his whiskers, or cherish his
pride?
Of names of this kind, I can give you a
quorum,
Such as Munkustrap, Quaxo, or Coricopat,
Such as Bombalurina, or else Jellylorum—
Names that never belong to more than one
cat.
But above and beyond there's still one name
left over,
And that is the name you never will guess;
The name that no human research can
discover—
But THE CAT HIMSELF KNOWS, *and will*
never confess.
When you notice a cat in profound
meditation,
The reason, I tell you, is always the same:
His mind is engaged in a rapt contemplation
Of the thought, of the thought, of the
thought of his name:
His ineffable effable
Effanineffable
Deep and inscrutable singular Name.

Those critical of Eliot's writing accused him of obscurity for its own sake. They found his verses full of coy and precious little mannerisms. They accused him of loading down his writing with obscure code references that could not possibly be known except to a few intimate friends such as Pound. Unless you knew that Eliot called Pound "Mop" and that Pound called Eliot "Possum" you couldn't possibly know what they were getting at, these critics asserted.

In politics, Eliot liked to say that he was a "monarchist," although most of his friends suspected that he saw the monarchial principle as a symbol rather than as a political instrument. The doctrines of Anglo-Catholicism were probably the greatest influence in his later life and writings. He was a vestryman at a fashionable London church.

In 1927, Eliot became the first important American man of letters since Henry James to become a British subject. He said at the time: "Here I am, making a living, enjoying my friends here. I don't want to feel like being a squatter. I might as well take full responsibility."

In 1949, King George VI conferred the Order of Merit on the poet. This is one of Britain's highest awards. No more than 24 persons may hold it at one time.

Eliot returned to his native country many times and in 1948 resided in Princeton, where he worked at the Institute for Advanced Study. In 1950, he gave the first Theodore Spencer Memorial Lecture

* *Old Possum's Book of Practical Cats*, reworked as the musical *Cats*, in 1982 served to give Eliot a posthumous success on Broadway and in the West End.

at Harvard on "Poetry and Drama." He lectured frequently and gave readings of his poems in New York and throughout the country.

Eliot was a rather stooped man of a little over 6 feet who had a somewhat prim appearance that mingled with the slight air of anxiety common to persons who are shy.

In London, Eliot lived in a comfortable, modern apartment in Chelsea, overlooking the Thames. In 1915, he married Miss Vivienne Haigh-Wood, who died in 1947. They had no children.

In January 1957, Eliot married Miss Valerie Fletcher, his private secretary. He was then 68 years old and his bride about 30.

A new play by Eliot, *The Elder Statesman*, was first performed at the Edinburgh Festival in 1958 and ran briefly in London, where it was not received with any particular enthusiasm. It was in the spirit of his previous plays, *The Cocktail Party* and *The Confidential Clerk*, and dealt with the tragic lack of communication between a British father and his son.

In that year Eliot was 70 and in an interview said: "I am just beginning to grow up, to get maturity. In the last few years everything I'd done up to 60 or so has seemed very childish."

In connection with Eliot's 70th birthday, a book entitled *T. S. Eliot: A Symposium for His 70th Birthday* was published. It contained anecdotes about the poet, comment on his writings and other matter concerning Eliot written by 50 persons, most of whom knew him.

Eliot's writings included the following:

Essays—*The Sacred Wood*, 1920; *Andrew Marvell*, 1922; *For Lancelot Andrewes*, 1928; *Dante*, 1929; *Tradition and Experiment in Present-Day Literature*, 1929; *Thoughts After Lambeth*, 1931; *Selected Essays, 1917–1932*, 1932; *John Dryden*, 1932; *The Use of Poetry and the Use of Criticism*, 1933; *After Strange Gods*, 1933; *Essays on Elizabethan Drama*, 1934; *Essays Ancient and Modern*, 1936; and *The Idea of a Christian Society*, 1940.

Plays—*Sweeney Agonistes*, 1932; *The Rock*, 1934; *Murder in the Cathedral*, 1935; and *Family Reunions*, 1939.

Books of Poetry—*Prufrock and Other Observations*, 1917; *Poems*, 1919; *The Waste Land*, 1922; *Poems, 1909–1935*, 1925; *Ash Wednesday*, 1930; *Collected Poems 1909–1935*, 1936; *East Coker*, 1940; *Burnt Norton*, 1941; and *The Dry Salvages*, 1941.

Other essays included *Notes Toward the Definition of Culture*, 1949; *Selected Essays* (new edition), 1950; *Poetry and Drama*, 1951; *The Three Voices of Poetry*, 1954; *Religious Drama: Medieval and Modern*, 1954.

Also *The Literary Essays of Ezra Pound*, 1954; *The Cultivation of Christmas Trees*, 1956; and *On Poetry and Poets*, 1945.

Other published works are the play *The Cocktail Party*, 1950; the film version of *Murder in the Cathedral* (with C. Hoellering), 1951; *The Confidential Clerk*, 1954, *Latin Poems, 1925–1935*, 1954; and *The Elder Statesman*, a play, 1958.

Four Quartets, consisting of four previously published poems as revised, was published in 1943.

The *Complete Poems and Plays* was published in 1952.

ELIOT'S VERSE AND POSTWAR SPIRITUAL DESPAIR

THOMAS LASK

IT IS very likely that when the literary history of our time comes to be written, it will be characterized as the Age of Eliot, just as we speak now of the Age of Pope or Tennyson.

For no man in the period between the two world wars so dominated his time as critic and creator as did T. S. Eliot. And no man did more to help shape the standards by which he was judged. For this ex-

WRITING OF ELIOT

Let us go then, you and I,
When the evening is spread out against the sky
Like a patient etherised upon a table;
Let us go, through certain half-deserted streets,
The muttering retreats
Of restless nights in one-night cheap hotels
And sawdust restaurants with oyster-shells:
Streets that follow like a tedious argument
Of insidious intent
To lead you to an overwhelming question . . .
Oh, do not ask, 'What is it?'
Let us go and make our visit.
. . . .
I grow old . . . I grow old . . .
I shall wear the bottoms of my trousers rolled.

Shall I part my hair behind? Do I dare to eat a peach?
I shall wear white flannel trousers, and walk upon the beach.
I have heard the mermaids singing, each to each.

I do not think they will sing to me.

I have seen them riding seaward on the waves
Combing the white hair of the waves blown back
When the wind blows the water white and black.

We have lingered in the chambers of the sea
By sea-girls wreathed with seaweed red and brown
Till human voices wake us, and we drown.
—*The Love Song of J. Alfred Prufrock* (1917)

April is the cruellest month, breeding
Lilacs out of the dead land, mixing
Memory and desire, stirring
Dull roots with spring rain.
Winter kept us warm, covering
Earth in forgetful snow, feeding
A little life with dried tubers.
Summer surprised us, coming over the Starnbergersee
With a shower of rain; we stopped in the colonnade,
And went on in sunlight, into the Hofgarten,
And drank coffee, and talked for an hour.
Bin gar keine Russin, stamm' aus Litauen, echt deutsch.
And when we were children, staying at the arch-duke's,
My cousin's, he took me out on a sled,
And I was frightened. He said, Marie,
Marie, hold on tight. And down we went.
In the mountains, there you feel free.
I read, much of the night, and go south in the winter.
. . . .
Phlebas the Phoenician, a fortnight dead,
Forgot the cry of gulls, and the deep sea swell
And the profit and loss.
A current under sea
Picked his bones in whispers. As he rose and fell
He passed the stages of his age and youth
Entering the whirlpool.
Gentile or Jew
O you who turn the wheel and look to windward,
Consider Phlebas, who was once handsome and tall as you.
—*The Waste Land* (1922)

CELIA: . . . Can we only love
Something created by our own imagination?
Are we all in fact unloving and unlovable?
Then one *is* alone, and if one is alone
Then lover and belovèd are equally unreal
And the dreamer is no more real than his dreams.
—*The Cocktail Party* (1950)

patriate American caught and expressed in his verse the sense of a doomed world, of fragmentation, of a wasteland of the spirit that moved the generation after the war.

It was a generation that felt tricked by the politicians, felt that the enormous bloodletting of World War I had been a fraud and saw in the disintegrating Europe of their time the symbol of their own lives. Their mood of spiritual despair was exquisitely rendered in Eliot's poetry.

It is said that he resented being spoken of as the poet of a wasteland, and yet the dry tone, the arid physical and spiritual landscape of his early poetry, the bleakness that stared out of his verse, whether he wished it or not, summed up for a generation their own sense of defeat, their sense of barrenness. They echoed his words: "I have seen the moment of my greatness flicker."

By transplanting himself from the America where he was born and nurtured to England, he gave physical proof of the alienation and exile that were hallmarks of the sensibilities of the 1920s.

The tone of fastidious weariness that characterized "Prufrock" was welcomed eagerly by the young on both sides of the Atlantic. In this poem, where high purpose has been dissolved into the niceties of social behavior, they found an excuse for if not an answer to their lack of purpose and direction. In the character of Sweeney who inhabits his poems, Eliot expressed the contrast between the mindless and brutalizing force of the world and the permanent values that are destroyed by it.

But it was *The Waste Land*, whose very form seemed to reflect the title, that gave a heading to the time. The poem, too, by its borrowings from different literatures and cultures, by offering complexities and helping with solutions, also gave a further turn to the critical taste that delighted in explication and esoteric burrowings, which felt that explanation almost came before enjoyment.

With "Ash Wednesday," Eliot turned to the support and succor of faith, and in *Four Quartets* he worked out with a calm music a statement of the strength of abiding belief. There was, too, a mordant and satiric side to the poet, as in "Conversation Galante" and "Cousin Nancy," and a playful one, best found in *Old Possum's Book of Practical Cats.*

In his critical essays Eliot wrote with a transparency of style and certainty of tone that were enormously persuasive. By his disapproval of the overweighted character of Milton's lines, he turned a generation of scholars to the complexities and involved conceits of the Metaphysicals and those who derived from them.

Though perhaps not a formal member of the New Critics, he gave them encouragement and support by his own poetic practice and by the choice of subjects and their treatment in his own work. By borrowings and paraphrases he made new readers aware of the writings of the French symbolist poets.

More than all this, however, by asserting that "poetry is not a turning loose of emotion, but an escape from emotion; it is not the expression of personality, but an escape from personality" and by demanding that the poet must search for the object, situation or event that objectively expresses the emotion, Eliot supplied critical tools to both maker and critic alike.

In his verse plays, Eliot hoped to restore poetic drama to a place it once occupied, though whether there is enough life in his characters and whether their moral dilemmas will carry over to another age must needs be left to time. Only *Murder in the Cathedral* seems to have the necessary staying power, at least in book form, if not on the stage.

Although Eliot's influence began to wane in the last decade of his life, we are still too close to the light he shed to take his measure accurately. That his poems will have a permanent place in the tradition he so cherished is certain. And whatever judgment is made of his criticism, no consideration of 20th-century literature in English will be able to bypass him. If we judge a man by the vacancy that his absence from his time would have caused, T. S. Eliot was a giant.

AN ARTISTIC TRIBUTE TO ELIOT

ANTHONY LEWIS

IGOR STRAVINSKY contributed a new choral work and Henry Moore a huge sculpture. Andrei Vosnesensky recited in Russian, Peter O'Toole and Sir Laurence Olivier and Paul Scofield in English. Groucho Marx was himself.

"Homage to T. S. Eliot" brought these disparate talents together on June 13, 1965. More than 1,200 persons filled the Globe Theater in London for a compelling artistic and theatrical tribute to the American-born poet.

The smash hit of the evening was Eliot's own *Sweeney Agonistes*, which he subtitled *Fragments of an Aristophanic Melodrama.* It was turned into a brief and hysterical musical, faintly reminiscent at times of Kurt Weill's *Three-Penny Opera.*

The music was performed by a jazz combo and sounded something like swing of the 1930s. It was composed for the occasion by John Dankworth, who is a top British jazz performer and composer.

The audience, so familiar with the poetry, roared as Sweeney sang the refrain, "Birth, Copulation and Death." Then there came, along with a soft-shoe routine, "Under the Bam, Under the Boo, Under the Bamboo Tree."

This portion of the program illustrated W. H. Auden's comment that Eliot had in him a lot of the "conscientious churchwarden," but also "a 12-year-old boy who liked to surprise over-solemn wigs by offering them explosive cigars."

The evening began with the new Stravinsky piece, entitled *Introitus* and written in Eliot's memory. It was a spare, ethereal work for six male voices, harp, piano, double bass, viola, four tympani and two gongs.

Then the curtains opened to show the large Moore sculpture revolving slowly on the stage. Of white plaster, it was called *The Archer* and made some think of an inner ear.

There followed the Stravinsky setting of words from Eliot's "Little Gidding," one of the *Four Quartets.* The anthem was sung by the choirboys of Westminster.

Peter O'Toole read "The Love Song of J. Alfred Prufrock." He made the familiar lines—for example, "In the room the women come and go, talking of Michelangelo"—seem more histrionic than they had.

Other actors read other poems, selected by Auden and with brief narration written by the American cultural attaché here, Cleanth Brooks.

Then came Groucho. He began with this sentence: "I never knew what an anachronism was until they invited me to appear here tonight."

Mrs. Eliot, sitting in a box, joined in the laughter as Groucho punctured what had become a somewhat pious atmosphere. He described how Eliot had written him two years ago and asked for his picture.

"Apparently he was a great admirer of mine," Groucho said, "and I don't blame him."

Groucho sent the picture, but Eliot sent it back, saying he wanted one with a cigar. Groucho sent one with a cigar, but Eliot returned it, saying the cigar was at the wrong angle. Finally, the right picture was supplied and installed in Eliot's office along with those of James Joyce and John Millington Synge.

In fact, though Groucho did not mention it on stage tonight, he visited Eliot at home. They talked about baseball, among other things.

Between his own observations, Groucho read tonight from the best-known Eliot whimsy, *Old Possum's Book of Practical Cats.*

Near the end of the program came Mr. Vosnesensky, the Soviet poet. A dark young man with sharp Russian features, he read two of his poems with deep emotion. In accented English he expressed his respect for Eliot.

The evening ended with portions of "Little Gidding" read by Sir Laurence Olivier and then, in a recording, by Eliot himself. His rather plain, undramatic voice made an affecting contrast as he read, "The End Is the Beginning."

'OUR MR. ELIOT' GROWS YOUNGER [1958]

V. S. PRITCHETT

T. S. ELIOT will be 70 on Friday. An American, born in St. Louis, and, like Henry James before him, long a British citizen, Eliot is the greatest living poet writing in English. He is probably the most widely known poet in the world—despite the fact that he is the founding father of difficult, intellectual poetry and has written, along with the poetry, a large body of criticism that drastically revised the long overshadowing opinions of the 19th century. Furthermore, he has revived the poetic drama and has become a fashionable playwright, with works like *Murder in the Cathedral*, *The Cocktail Party* and (this summer at the Edinburgh Festival) *The Elder Statesman.*

When he published "The Love Song of J. Alfred Prufrock" in 1917, *The Waste Land* in 1922, "The Hollow Men" in 1925, Eliot was a revolutionary experimentalist, a man of the generation of Ezra Pound and James Joyce. With the poems "Ash Wednesday" and his 1943 masterwork, *Four Quartets*, he appeared as a metaphysical poet writing on the religious experience. Now Eliot the iconoclast—always iconoclastic on *behalf* of tradition and orthodoxy, which were not highly thought of when he began to write—has become, like the chief character in his latest play, an Elder Statesman. Ten years ago he was awarded the Nobel Prize; he wears the most rarely given British Order of Merit. He is an earnest member of the Anglican Church who has dealt severely with Bertrand Russell, Aldous Huxley and Harold Laski.

Eliot is a member of three famous London clubs that indicate three aspects of his complex personality: the Athenaeum, much frequented by bishops and statesmen; the Garrick, affected by judges, queen's counsels, publishers and the stage; and the Oxford and Cambridge, notable for its university eminences. Few Englishmen have such an officially English persona.

The special quality of Eliot's contribution to English literature springs from his inherited though attenuated New England Puritanism. He is, above all, a man of thought rather than of feeling, a true intellectual. He has sought to revive the mystical and metaphysical traditions of the 17th century—the era of the religious wars. In this he has carried two generations with him in England and America.

His subject is the mind and the soul seeking to rid themselves of the corrosions of the flesh in order to toil in loneliness toward the presence of God. Yet his religious poetry is not didactic; it does not urge but, in the manner of the mystics, it crystallizes the pains, the ecstasies, the forebodings and the vicissitudes of this difficult experience.

Such a poetry, and the criticism that goes with it, is clearly against the obvious drift of modern life. How then do we explain his enormous influence in an age used to irreligion, rationalism, science, Socialism, mass culture, material progress, the cult of happiness and health in everyone in this life?

Eliot's influence may owe something to our mistrust of a civilization that has made two attempts to destroy itself and is undisguisedly preparing a third. From this, Eliot may be said to provide an "escape" or an abstention. But I do not think this really explains his great influence. We come nearer to an explanation when we say that Eliot attempts to restore dignity and integrity to an inner life.

In his critical writing he attacked the rhetoric of Milton and held that Milton was a disastrous influence, at a time when Milton was thought sacred. He attacked Tennyson. He swept the Georgian poets scornfully away—A. E. Housman, for example. He was stern with Matthew Arnold's wit and Arnold's theory that poetry is a criticism of life. He suspected those who spoke of the music of words.

The fact is, the younger Eliot was drastically clearing the ground for his own poetry. And if he has been found pedantic or arid, it is because he brought the Puritan gift for thought and the Puritan suspicion of feeling to his subject.

"When I look back upon my criticism," he says now, "I am astonished to see how dogmatic I have been. I didn't realize it."

On the eve of his 70th birthday, Eliot—or, rather, Mr. Eliot—has consented to an interview. He may be Tom Eliot to his affectionate friends, but he is Mr. Eliot to us, the countless numbers who, for two generations, have been disentangling his images and meanings in most of the universities of the world. It is a safe guess that Mr. Eliot is sometimes Mr. Eliot to himself and that, years ago, when he worked in a London bank dealing with documentary bills and acceptances, he was "our Mr. Eliot," impersonal, prudent and exemplary in bowler hat and umbrella until he went home to fog-smeared Bloomsbury in the evenings and changed the face of English poetry.

They said, when I set out to see him in Russell Square the other day, that his second marriage (his first wife died in 1947) last year to the young woman who had worked with him for 10 years in the publishing house of Faber & Faber (where he conscientiously goes three times a week) had mellowed and softened him. Even so, the admirer of comedian George Robey and the English music hall, the singer of "The One-Eyed Riley," could hardly have been impregnable to geniality.

When one goes up to his little office at the top of Faber's Georgian house in Russell Square, a half-laughing figure with powerful shoulders and active hands comes forward with amused alacrity. He is kind, and fusses courteously and gently about his guest.

He is sardonic, with masculine good nature. His once-black hair is now graying, but his deep-eyed eagle face is still handsome, with that American, leathered sallowness of skin so outstanding in a roomful of Britishers. The eagle's cage is cozy; Mr. Eliot's fine dark eyes gaze, his head is alert, his very ears seem to twinkle. He looks the most spiritually and sartorially assured man on earth. ("Tom is coming to luncheon," Virginia Woolf once wrote to Clive Bell, "and what is more, in a four-piece suit.")

The man leans forward as attentively as an old city merchant or the most disarming of bishops. His voice is slow, lazy and soft; he searches like another Henry James for his word—though for the exact, not the dramatic one. But under the easy, skeptical, stooping, idle manner, there is power—one always finds that in a genius. Mr. Eliot puts up with being interviewed. "It's the penalty of being 70."

He is jealous of revealing where he lives; he astutely dodges most personal questions about his habits. He's the most firmly private of old birds. The trick is in speaking slowly, hesitating, preparing the ground, insuring here and there, so that the interviewer is left with nothing but an engaging collection of subclauses.

About "being 70," he is genuinely astonished. He is astonished at not feeling older and not feeling wise. "But I have never been wise. And I feel younger. I don't believe one grows older," he says, "I think that what happens early on in life is that at a certain age one stands still and stagnates?" The words are put politely, as a question.

I look at the drawings and photographs on the chimney piece of the little room—Virginia Woolf's is among them—at the little china cat, a ginger one, and at a pair of carved wooden animals that look African; at the old-fashioned desk covered with papers, the four tiers of the wire paper tray, the books. It is a domestic little office, furnished in red. The large head and shoulders are massively darkened as he sits against the light and looks smiling down. It is the sort of smile that seems to have chamois gloves on.

"I don't know why people ask my philosophy of life. When you are 70 why is it people seem to think you must have one? Up your sleeve or somewhere. I am sure there are professors who have got one ready the moment they are asked. All thought out. What does it mean—philosophy? of? life?" The voice strays between the words.

"I am astonished," he says, "when I read my work to see the things I thought years ago, the opinions, the moods. They change."

"But you have your beliefs?"

"Ah!" He smiles knowingly. "Ah." And he nods and one nods back. Mr. Eliot undoubtedly has his beliefs. Has he modified his much-disputed opinions on mass education? He evades; he would have to read them again to see. Pressed, he says that others have shared his alarm over mass education—Ortega y Gasset, for example. One can only say the future depends on the appearance of men of genius. We do not see them yet.

What about writers like Sartre who say that some way must be found of reaching the new large audience? "It is inhibiting to speculate on the kind of audience you write for. There is the danger of an audience blunting the edge of a writer. In the end, a work of art makes its own audience. I speak particularly of lyrical poetry—the drama is different. There a third person intervenes, the performer, who transforms the work into something else."

Did he ever wish to lead a political or religious cause or crusade? "No," he laughs with horror, "under no circumstances."

"Under no circumstances whatever?"

Long hesitation. "I would not say under absolutely no circumstances," he grants. "If there were another Dreyfus case—well, perhaps. I have written propaganda, you know, once. *Murder in the Cathedral* was conscious anti-Nazi propaganda." (This rather defiantly. After all, the poets of the 1930s had attacked his conservatism.)

About contemporary writers he thinks he ought not to speak. About the classics: "I find it impossible to reread so many great books. *Crime and Punishment*—not again. Books like that, they have done their work for me. But I've read Browning's *The Ring and the Book* three times."

The soft London English voice goes on, more deliberate and ceremonious in manner than most Englishmen's voices. He is a little amused by his own decorum. One sees that he is a company of actors inside one suit, each twitting the other. This self-irony comes from the American Puritan inheritance. His grandfather, he says, was a powerful Unitarian who ruled his son and his son's sons from the grave, urging them on relentlessly to public duty, charity and good works. "You know—buy yourself some sweets to give to the poor children who haven't got sweets." That creates the comic temperament and the comic verses.

"Are you a townsman or countryman by nature?"

"A townsman," he says. "Many American boys spend nine months in the city and then three by the sea. I'm told I don't write well about the country, but I do write well about the sea, don't you think? I used to do a little bird-watching in the summer." Then, with a characteristic piece of precision and sadness: "The summer—I missed the nesting season, you see. I never saw it."

It puzzles him now to decide how English or how American he is.

"But my poetry is American," he says firmly. "Purely American. I hope my poetry will last. I don't think my criticism will." And when I say that it is held that his poetry and criticism are inseparable, he smiles with an irony that makes me wonder how much he is drawing me out. His criticism was not well written, he says. He speaks of his work as a matter of phases in his life, each one brought to an end, and the end—in his familiar words—a new beginning.

One goes away with his lazy laugh in one's head. He is not to be intruded on. One sits on a bench in Russell Square, in the midst of *The Waste Land.* Mr. Eliot is what is called a culture hero. He has the fear that success is bad for poetry. He fears that very much.

What do the young think of him? For them, he remains the great master as a poet, the great renewer. If the young contend with him, it is not over his poetry or the criticism that encases it, but with his religious and social views. Puritan in love of truth, in self-denial, in self-protection, Mr. Eliot has coldly repelled the natural man.

But a belief in human love as a spiritual power, so lacking in Eliot's writing, appears at last in *The Elder Statesman*, the play written since his marriage. And whether this is a good play or not, it is the expression of a new incarnation. Mr. Eliot, aged 70, is like an explorer. He has rejoined the human race, after long and bitter voyages into regions few minds have the severity and special genius to travel in.

DUKE ELLINGTON

1899–1974

By John S. Wilson

Duke Ellington, who expanded the literature of American music with compositions and performances that drew international critical praise and brought listening and dancing pleasure to two generations, died in New York City on May 24, 1974.

At his death, the phrase "beyond category," which Edward Kennedy Ellington had used as his highest form of praise for others, could quite literally be applied to the Duke himself, whose works were played and praised in settings as diverse as the old Cotton Club, Carnegie Hall and Westminster Abbey.

The noted jazz critic and historian Ralph J. Gleason has called Mr. Ellington "America's most important composer . . . the greatest composer this American society has produced," and summed him up as a "master musician, master psychologist, master choreographer."

"Ellington has created his own musical world which has transcended every attempt to impose category upon it and has emerged as a solid body of work unequalled in American music," Mr. Gleason wrote.

"His songs have become a standard part of the cultural heritage, his longer compositions a part of the finest art of our time and his concerts and personal appearances among the most satisfying for an audience of those of any artist. Every music honor this country can bestow is little enough for such a musical giant as this man. In reality, he has already won them and more by his imprint on the minds of all who have heard him."

Mr. Ellington, whose innate elegance of manner won him his nickname of Duke while he was still a schoolboy in Washington, was a tall, debonair, urbane man with a vitalizing sense of the dramatic and an ironic wit that often served as a protective shield.

Amid the protests voiced in 1965, when a unanimous recommendation by the Pulitzer Prize music jury that Mr. Ellington be given a special citation was rejected by the Pulitzer advisory board, the only comment by the composer, pianist and orchestra leader was, "Fate is being kind to me. Fate doesn't want me to be famous too young." He was then 66 years old.

But beneath a suave, unruffled exterior, Mr. Ellington had a fiery appreciation of his worth and his style. When he was conducting a public rehearsal of his orchestra at the University of Wisconsin in 1972, he took his musicians through a first attempt at his latest composition.

"Letter E," he said to indicate where they were to start playing. But when only half the band began at the proper place, he shouted, "No! E! E as in Ellington! E! E as in Edward! E! E as in Ellington! E as in excellence! E as in elegance! E as in Edward

CBS Records

and Ellington! E! E! E as in all good things! Edward . . . Ellington . . . excellence . . . elegance! E!"

Mr. Ellington combined his musical talents, his excellence and his elegance in a manner that transcended the usual connotations of *jazz,* a word that he consistently rejected in relation to his work.

"In the 1920s I used to try to convince Fletcher Henderson that we ought to call what we're doing 'Negro music,' " Mr. Ellington said in 1965. "But it's too late for that now. The music has become so integrated that you can't tell one part from the other so far as color is concerned. Well, I don't have time to worry about it. I've got too much music on my mind."

As a composer and arranger, Mr. Ellington created an unusual and (as many other orchestra leaders found) inimitable style by building his works on the individualistic sounds of the brilliant instrumentalists he gathered around him—the growling trumpets of Bubber Miley, Cootie Williams and Ray Nance; the virtuoso plunger mute effects of the trombonist Tricky Sam Nanton; the rich, mellow clarinet of Barney Bigard; the exquisite alto saxophone of Johnny Hodges; the huge, sturdy drive of Harry Carney's baritone saxophone. Billy Strayhorn, who was Mr. Ellington's musical right arm, his co-composer and co-arranger from 1939 until his death in 1967, explained that "Ellington plays the piano but his real instrument is his band."

The basis of the Ellington sound eluded other musicians. In the late 1920s, when Mr. Ellington's star was just beginning to rise and Paul Whiteman was the "King of Jazz," Mr. Whiteman and his arranger, Ferde Grofé, spent nights on end at the Cotton Club listening to the Ellington orchestra but, so legend has it, eventually abandoned their efforts to try to notate what the Duke's musicians were playing.

More recently André Previn, who is as familiar with the classical side of music as he is with jazz, shook his head in amazement as he noted that "Stan Kenton can stand in front of a thousand fiddles and a thousand brass and make a dramatic gesture and every studio arranger can nod his head and say, 'Oh, yes, that's done like this.' But Duke merely lifts his finger, three horns make a sound and I don't know what it is."

Although Mr. Ellington's basic working materials were almost invariably the blues and the voice-like manner in which a jazz musician plays his instrument, classically oriented musicians often found a relationship to Debussy, Delius and Ravel in his work. Constant Lambert wrote in 1934 that there is "nothing in Ravel so dexterous in treatment as the varied solos in the middle of the ebullient 'Hot and Bothered' [an Ellington variation on 'Tiger Rag'] and nothing in Stravinsky more dynamic than the final section."

Mr. Ellington was a pioneer in extending jazz composition beyond the customary chorus of 12 or 32 bars. His "Reminiscing in Tempo," written in 1934, was a 12-minute work. Four years later, Paul Whiteman commissioned him to write a concert piece, "Blue Belles of Harlem," for the Whiteman orchestra. Mr. Ellington's first major effort at an extended composition came in 1943, when he wrote "Black, Brown and Beige," which ran for 50 minutes when it was introduced at an Ellington concert in Carnegie Hall.

This was the first of what became an annual series of concerts in the 1940s at Carnegie Hall, for each of which Mr. Ellington prepared such works as "New World A-Comin'," "The Deep South Suite" and "The Perfume Suite." Later, on commission from the Liberian government, he wrote "The Liberian Suite" and, more recently, for Togo, "Togo Brava."

His extended compositions also included "Harlem"; "Night Creatures," introduced by the Ellington band and the Symphony of the Air at Carnegie Hall in 1955; "Suite Thursday," inspired by John Steinbeck's book *Sweet Thursday* and commissioned by the Monterey Jazz Festival in 1960; and a Shakespeare suite, "Such Sweet Thunder," inspired by a Shakespeare Festival in Stratford, Ontario, in 1957.

In 1965, Mr. Ellington moved into a new musical

field, presenting the Concert of Sacred Music of his own composition in Grace Cathedral in San Francisco. The performance, starting with the biblical paraphrase "In the beginning, God . . . ," was developed in typical Ellingtonian style with a company that included his full orchestra, three choirs, a dancer and several guest vocalists.

Mr. Ellington considered the concert "the most important thing I've ever done." It was repeated twice in New York at the Fifth Avenue Presbyterian Church in the same year. Three years later he introduced a Second Sacred Concert in New York at the Cathedral Church of St. John the Divine and, in 1973, a Third Sacred Concert was performed for the first time in London at Westminster Abbey.

But before Mr. Ellington became involved in extended composition, his songs, which included "Solitude," "Sophisticated Lady," "In a Sentimental Mood," "I Let a Song Go Out of My Heart" and "I Got It Bad," had become standards in the popular repertory. In addition, his short instrumental pieces—such as "Black and Tan Fantasy," "The Mooche," "Creole Love Call" and "Mood Indigo"—were established as part of the jazz repertory.

Despite Mr. Ellington's prolific output as a composer—he wrote more than 6,000 pieces of varying length—one of the tunes most closely associated with him, "Take the 'A' Train," which he used as a signature theme for many years, was not written by him. It was composed by his close associate, Mr. Strayhorn.

Other theme tunes used by his band at various times included "East St. Louis Toodle-Oo" and "I Let a Song Go Out of My Heart," both composed by Mr. Ellington, and "Things Ain't What They Used to Be," composed by his son, Mercer.

Mr. Ellington was born in Washington on April 29, 1899, the son of James Edward Ellington and the former Daisy Kennedy. His father was a blueprint maker for the Navy Department, who also worked occasionally as a butler, sometimes at the White House.

In high school, the Duke, whose nickname was given to him by an admiring neighborhood friend when he was 8 years old, was torn between his interests in painting and in music. He won a poster contest sponsored by the National Association for the Advancement of Colored People and in 1917 was offered a scholarship by the Pratt Institute of Applied Art. He turned it down, however, to devote himself to music.

He wrote his first composition, "Soda Fountain Rag," while he was working after school as a soda jerk at the Poodle Dog Café. Some piano lessons he had received at the age of 7 comprised the only formal musical education he had. He learned by listening to the "two-fisted piano players" of the period, paying particular attention to Sticky Mack, Doc Perry, James P. Johnson and Willie (The Lion) Smith.

By the time he was 20 he was making $150 a week playing with his small band at parties and dances. In this year, 1919, Sonny Greer became Mr. Ellington's drummer (he remained with him until 1950, setting a pattern of longevity that was to be followed by many Ellington sidemen).

In 1922 Wilbur Sweatman, then a successful bandleader, asked Mr. Greer to join his band in New York. Mr. Ellington and three other members of the group went along, too, but jobs in New York were so scarce that soon they were all back in Washington. However, the visit gave Mr. Ellington an opportunity to hear the Harlem pianists who became a prime influence on his own playing—Willie (The Lion) Smith, James P. Johnson and Johnson's protégé, Fats Waller.

At Mr. Waller's urging, Duke Ellington and his men returned to New York in 1923. This time they got a job playing at Barron's in Harlem with Elmer Snowden, the group's banjoist, as nominal leader. When they moved downtown to the Hollywood Club (later known as the Kentucky Club) at Broadway and 49th Street, Mr. Snowden left the group and Mr. Ellington assumed the leadership.

During the four and a half years that Ellington's

Washingtonians remained at the Kentucky Club, the group made its first records and did its first radio broadcasts. Late in 1927, when the band had expanded to 10 men, the Cotton Club, a Harlem showplace, found itself in sudden need of an orchestra when King Oliver, whose band was scheduled to open there, decided he had not been offered enough money.

Mr. Ellington got the booking, but first he had to be released from a theater engagement in Philadelphia. This was arranged when the operators of the Cotton Club asked some associates in Philadelphia to call on the theater manager with a proposition: "Be big or you'll be dead." He was big, and Duke Ellington began a five-year association with the Cotton Club.

A crucial factor in spreading the fame of the Ellington band was a nightly radio broadcast from the Cotton Club that was heard across the country, introduced by the Ellington signature theme "East St. Louis Toodle-Oo," with Bubber Miley's growling trumpet setting the mood for the stomping and often exotic music that followed. Mr. Ellington's unique use of growling brass (identified as his "jungle" style) and the rich variety of tonal colors that he drew from his band brought musicians of all schools to the Cotton Club.

In 1930 the Ellington band appeared in its first feature-length movie, *Check and Double Check*, and in 1933 it went overseas for the first time, to Britain and Europe. During the 1930s, the band appeared in several more films—*Murder at the Vanities*, *Belle of the Nineties* and *The Hit Parade*—and made a second European tour in 1939.

When the popularity of swing bands rose in the late 1930s, the Ellington band was overshadowed by the glare of publicity that fell on the bands of Benny Goodman, Artie Shaw and Glenn Miller. But as the swing era faded, the Ellington band hit one of its peaks in 1941 and 1942, years when all the greatest of Mr. Ellington's star sidemen (except Bubber Miley) were together in the band and when Mr. Ellington himself was in an extraordinarily creative period as a composer.

By 1943, however, he was leaving the early phases of his career behind him and turning to the extended compositions and concert presentations that would be an increasingly important part of his work.

In the 1950s, when interest in big bands dropped so low that all but a handful gave up completely or worked on a part-time basis, Mr. Ellington kept his band together even when the economic basis became very shaky.

"It's a matter of whether you want to play music or make money," he said. "I like to keep a band so I can write and hear the music next day. The only way you can do that is to pay the band and keep it on tap 52 weeks a year. If you want to make a real profit, you go out for four months, lay off for four and come back for another four. Of course, you can't hold a band together that way and I like the cats we've got. So, by various little twists and turns, we manage to stay in business and make a musical profit. And a musical profit can put you way ahead of a financial loss."

The fortunes of the Ellington band started to rise again in 1956 when, at the Newport Jazz Festival, a performance of a composition Mr. Ellington had written 20 years before, "Diminuendo and Crescendo in Blue," propelled by a 27-chorus solo by the tenor saxophonist Paul Gonsalves, set off dancing in the aisles that reminded observers of the joyous excitement that Benny Goodman had generated at New York's Paramount Theater in the 1930s.

During the next 15 years, Mr. Ellington's orchestra was heard in all areas of the world, touring the Middle East, the Far East and the Soviet Union under the auspices of the State Department, playing in Africa, South America and Europe. Mr. Ellington wrote scores for five films—*Paris Blues*, *Anatomy of a Murder*, *Assault on a Queen*, *Change of Mind* and a German picture, *Janus.*

He composed a ballet, *The River*, in 1970 for Alvin Ailey and the American Ballet Theater. In

1963 he wrote a pageant of black history, *My People*, which was presented in Chicago. He had also written for the theater earlier in his career—a musical, *Jump for Joy*, produced in Los Angeles in 1941, and a score with lyrics by John Latouche for *Beggar's Holiday*, an adaptation of John Gay's *Beggar's Opera* on Broadway in 1947.

Honors were heaped on him. In 1969, at a celebration of his 70th birthday at the White House, President Nixon awarded him the Presidential Medal of Freedom. President Georges Pompidou of France in 1973 gave him the Legion of Honor. The Royal Swedish Academy of Music elected him a member in 1971. Two African countries, Chad and Togo, issued postage stamps bearing his picture. In 1972, Yale University established the Duke Ellington Fellowship Fund "to preserve and perpetuate the Afro-American musical tradition."

Through all this, Mr. Ellington kept up the steady pace of composing and performing and traveling that he had maintained since the late 1920s. Everywhere he went, his electric piano went with him, for there was scarcely a day in his life when he did not compose something.

"You know how it is," he said. "You go home expecting to go right to bed. But then, on the way, you go past the piano and there's a flirtation. It flirts with you. So, you sit down and try out a couple of chords and when you look up, it's 7 A.M."

Quite logically, Mr. Ellington called his autobiography, published in 1973, *Music Is My Mistress.*

"Music is my mistress," he wrote, "and she plays second fiddle to no one."

Mr. Ellington married Edna Thompson in 1918. Their son, Mercer, was born the following year. The couple were divorced in 1930 and Mr. Ellington's second marriage, to Mildred Dixon, a dancer at the Cotton Club, also ended in divorce.

Mr. Ellington entered Columbia Presybterian Medical Center in New York City at the end of March 1974 for treatment of cancer of both lungs. His condition was complicated when he developed pneumonia in late May. When he died on May 24, he was 75 years old.

FAREWELL TO THE DUKE

TOM BUCKLEY

THE CITY whose hectic rhythms and melancholy sophistication he caught in scores of compositions said farewell to Duke Ellington on May 27, 1974.

An estimated 10,000 persons filled every pew and crowded the aisles of the Episcopal Cathedral Church of St. John the Divine for the funeral service. And 2,500 followed the service by loudspeaker in front of the Amsterdam Avenue entrance of the cathedral.

Earl (Fatha) Hines, Ella Fitzgerald, Mary Lou Williams, Ray Nance, Lou Rawls, McHenry Boatright and Joe Williams, who was accompanied by Hank Jones, Jo Jones and Lyle Atkinson, paid tribute to Mr. Ellington with musical selections that were interpolated into the funeral service.

Aside from Benny Goodman and the Duke's friendly rival of 40 years' standing, William (Count) Basie, who sat in a front pew with his wife, Catherine, there were comparatively few well-known show business and music-world figures among the mourners.

Overwhelmingly, they were plain people, black and white, who arrived by bus and subway or trudged up Morningside Heights from Harlem. It was there, at the old Cotton Club, that Duke Ellington became an international celebrity in the period from 1927 to 1931.

"Duke, he went all over the world after that, but nobody ever loved him better than we did," said an old-time tap dancer who goes by the name of Kid Chocolate.

Representing President Nixon, who presented

the Medal of Freedom, the nation's highest civilian award, to Mr. Ellington at a White House gala on his 70th birthday in 1969, were Pearl Bailey and Stanley Scott, a White House assistant for minority affairs.

With Miss Bailey was her husband, Louis Bellson, who played the drums in the Ellington orchestra in the 1950s.

"The Duke once gave me his definition of music, and I agree with it," he said. "Mass unity sounding in concert—M-U-S-I-C."

Percy E. Sutton, the borough president of Manhattan and an old friend of the Duke, said, "It's the end of an era for Harlem, for New York and for the world."

The Right Rev. Harold Louis Wright, Suffragan Bishop of the New York Diocese and himself a black man, carrying the crozier of his office, presided at the service and pronounced the benediction. He was assisted by the cathedral chapter, who wore stoles of green edged with gold over black robes.

Among the other clergymen who took part in the service were the Rev. John Gensel, pastor of St. Peter's Lutheran Church in Manhattan, and the Rev. Norman O'Connor of the Paulist Fathers, both of whom are jazz experts and were friends of long standing of Mr. Ellington.

Father O'Connor, who wore the white cassock of his order, said, "Duke, we thank you. You loved us madly. We will love you madly, today, tomorrow and forever."

"We love you madly" had been Mr. Ellington's sign-off at his performances for many years.

Father Gensel recalled that Mr. Ellington's interest in religion had deepened in his later years. "He called himself 'God's messenger boy,' " Father Gensel said. "He called himself 'beyond categories' because he knew he was in God's structure."

Stanley Dance, the author of *The World of Duke Ellington*, eulogized him as a rare genius who combined sophistication, primitiveness, irony and childlike innocence. "He was a great innovator and paradoxically a conservative," Mr. Dance said.

The thronged, granite cathedral, by some measurements the largest in the world, fell silent when Miss Fitzgerald, a stout woman wearing a black silk suit and hobbled a bit by arthritis, stood to sing the great Ellington standard, "Solitude," and the stirring old New Orleans funeral hymn, "Just a Closer Walk With Thee."

Seated in the choir and in the nave were many present and former members of the Ellington orchestra, proud in their recollection that for many years the group was indisputably in a class by itself in the world of jazz.

Sonny Greer, the Duke's drummer from the time he came to New York until the illness of his wife forced him to retire in the early 1950s, said, "There was some sort of magnetism in him that you couldn't understand."

There was Cootie Williams, the trumpet star of the great days of the Ellington band from 1927 to 1940 who rejoined it in 1962; Russell Procope, the saxophonist and clarinetist, a "new boy" he said, with only 22 years with the Duke; and Harry Carney, the baritone saxophonist who played with Mr. Ellington without interruption from 1927 until the last date, at Kalamazoo, Mich., in March.

Mr. Procope said the leader had kept from the band the seriousness of his illness during his final days. Many friends and acquaintances became aware that the end might be near for one of the nation's protean creators when they received greeting cards from him a week or so before his death. The cover bore the inscription on a field of blue:

L
G O D
V
E

As the two-hour service ended and Bishop Wright commended the soul of Edward Kennedy Ellington to God, and the pallbearers slid the silver-colored metal coffin onto rollers, Count Basie covered his face with his handkerchief and wept.

The recessional was a recording of the Second Sacred Concert that Mr. Ellington gave at St. John the Divine in 1968. The soaring alto saxophone of Jimmy Hodges, one of the greatest of all Ellingtonians, who died in 1971, filled the gloomy interior with light.

Mr. Ellington was buried at Woodlawn Cemetery in the Bronx, next to the graves of his parents.

THE DUKE: His Creativity—and All That Jazz—Throbs On [1972]

TOM BUCKLEY

DUKE ELLINGTON sat cater-cornered on a folded plaid blanket on the piano bench. "Lemme hear it now," he said. With his left hand he cued the brass section for the biting attack he wanted on the riff theme of "New York, New York."

It is the newest of the countless hundreds of compositions he has written since he began his career with "Soda Fountain Rag" in 1915, and he and his band will probably play it during their concert appearance at the Newport Jazz Festival here this week.

After a few measures the Duke signaled a halt. "Ooh, no, no, no," he said.

"You want the same B-flat as in the first bar?" asked Tyree Glenn, the lead trombonist. "Bah, bah, *beyow*?"

The Duke shook his head.

"What *do* you want?" asked the trombonist, a large, dark pudding of a man with a graying goatee.

"I want it together, mainly," the Duke replied with a laugh. "Play it . . . play it with a drawl and an accent."

He illustrated his conception by bending the word *drawl* with a full southern intonation and tightening his mouth around *accent* so that it came out as pure Mayfair.

"Tyree, keep it that way," he said, after the band had played the figure again.

"I don't know what I did," the trombonist replied, and the 15 musicians in the recording studio in Toronto last week laughed appreciatively.

"C'mon, let's roll it," the Duke said. Behind the glass partition the sound engineer adjusted his dials and switches and started the tape spinning.

Heard all the way through, "New York, New York," was what has come to be thought of as typical Ellington: an easy, rocking tune, built on dark, pulsing chords, featuring a couple of solo choruses by Paul Gonsalves, the lead tenor saxophonist.

Behind, around, underneath and over the wind instruments was the famous Ellington piano. Almost offhandedly, he spun single-note runs and figures, some smooth and glistening as beads of dew on a spider's web, others brittle, shiny and sharply cut as a necklace of jet.

As one long instrumental passage built and swelled, he left the piano and danced a few steps in front of the band. His feet scarcely moved but his hips and shoulders expressed the rhythm.

At the age of 73, Mr. Ellington is getting a bit stiff-legged. His body bends forward from the hips when he walks, and around his right wrist he wears one of those copper bracelets that are supposed to ward off arthritis. A lifelong dedicated hypochondriac, the Duke has found some of his ailments inevitably becoming real with the passage of time.

Even so, his enthusiasm for the endless grind of travel, performance, composition, rehearsal, is undiminished. It may even have increased in recent years and become something of a compulsion with the growing realization that even the longest journey must finally come to an end.

He had been on the road almost continuously since the first of the year. It was a trip that took him and his band to Tokyo, Bangkok, Indonesia and Jakarta, then from Tacoma, Wash., San Francisco and Los Angeles back across the country, playing concerts and dances. Now, on a rare night without a performance or the need to travel, he was making records.

The same sense of a need for haste has also led him to simplify his life. Once a fashion plate, the Duke now seldom dresses up except when he is performing. On this night he wore a loose, long-sleeved woolen polo shirt, a pair of bright blue narrow-legged trousers, long out of fashion, that sagged below a noticeable paunch, and unpolished loafers. On the massive Ellington head was perched, incongruously, a fuzzy, narrow-brimmed blue fedora, punched out into derby shape.

His diet has been simplified, too. No longer a great gourmand, he seldom eats much besides steak and grapefruit. He gave up alcohol years ago, but as a great believer in the need for sugar to fuel his creative processes, he drinks many bottles of Coca-Cola each day and nibbles at peanut brittle, gumdrops and cookies that he buys at roadside stands.

At 11:30 P.M., the Duke left the recording studio. From there he went to a nightclub to hear a singer he was thinking of engaging for a one-week date he was booked to play at the Playboy Club Hotel in Great Gorge, N.J., that began Friday night.

He was greeted at the nightclub by the singer, Aura Rully, who came to Canada from her native Rumania three years ago. She is a striking young woman, with long, dark hair and small, feline features.

The Duke ceremoniously greeted her with four kisses, two on each cheek, took his place at a ringside table and ate a steak and drank tea while listening to her perform. He decided that she would do, and they discussed terms and conditions in whispers when she had finished her set.

At 2 A.M. the Duke was back in his hotel room, talking with Ron Collier, who would do the arrangements that Miss Rully required. From his flight bag the Duke produced a couple of the miniature bottles of Scotch that he picks up on his air travels for visitors and rang for ice and soda.

"This is first-class Scotch," he said, and laughed at the play on words.

"It's not a big sound," said the arranger, speaking of Miss Rully, "but a fantastic range. But I don't know about her reading."

"Well, if she isn't a good reader, she has to have a quick ear to do all those Ella Fitzgerald things," said the Duke. "It works out about the same."

He played cassette tapes of several old Ellington recordings that he wanted the arranger to revise. "She needs something to open with," he said, "something like Joya Sherrill did on 'Mood Indigo.' "

"What about those things you did with Kay Davis?" asked the arranger. He whistled a tune. "What's that one called?"

"You mean 'Transbluency'?" asked the Duke.

"That's it," Mr. Collier replied. "Have you got a chart?"

"No," said the Duke. "It's stuck away somewhere at Tom Whaley's." (Mr. Whaley is the band's copyist.) "It's a good thought for later on."

"How about 'C-Jam Blues'?" The arranger sang, " 'Let's all go / Down to Duke's place.' "

"There's no chart for 'C-Jam,' " the Duke said. "The chart they're *faking* goes back to 1941 or 1942."

Finally, at 3:30 A.M., the arranger, pleading exhaustion and an early deadline, departed. "Now I can get down to work," Mr. Ellington said, laughing, as he closed the door.

At 5 o'clock the next afternoon, which was Wednesday, the Duke, naked except for a chartreuse chiffon scarf wound around his head to protect it from air-conditioning drafts, got out of bed in his hotel suite. He would be leaving in another hour to play a dance date in West Lorne, Ontario, 150 miles to the west.

"I was up till 7 o'clock this morning writing," he said, rolling himself under the covers again. Next to the bed stood a small electric piano that follows him on his travels.

Did his world-ranging trips still provide him with musical inspiration, or was it a case of having been too many places too many times?

"I compose *as* I travel," he said. "Sometimes it doesn't come out until much later. A couple of days ago I was thinking about Russia, where we went last year, and I began writing. It just came out so so naturally. I think I'm going to call it 'European Sunrise Land.' That's a good title." He rolled over in bed and closed his eyes, letting a stream of words pass across the inside of his lids.

"No," he said, after a moment. " 'Continental Sunrise Land.' From the continent you look east and there are all those countries out there in that minor key."

But like many, perhaps most, artists, Mr. Ellington does not really like talking about how his creative processes work, especially when he has just awakened.

"I don't understand this craze to know how everything works," he said grumpily. "People want to know how I do it, or they say they want to get behind the scenes. Why should the audience *ever* be behind the scenes? All it does is pull the petals off the creative flower.

"Magicians, they're the smartest artists in the world," he went on. "They don't tell everybody how it's done. They're not expected to.

"That's going into the stockpile," he said. "For an artist, that's Fort Whatsit, where they keep the gold. It's the secret of the nuclear bomb. I don't think that everybody has got the right to know where the nuclear bombs are kept and how they are turned on and off."

The power of the Ellington creative impulse has, by general agreement, diminished with the passage of the years. The longer compositions that he mainly addresses himself to these days lack the compressed vitality of "Sophisticated Lady," "Mood Indigo," "Warm Valley," "Don't Get Around Much Anymore," "I Got It Bad," to mention a few of the dozens of evergreens he has written.

Once in the musical vanguard, he has continued in his own path while jazz has developed in many other streams. What was once daring and disturbing in his work has come to be seen as conservative. He has been loaded with establishment honors, including the Medal of Freedom, which was presented to him by President Nixon on his 70th birthday.

Although his place at a pinnacle of American musical history is secure, the Duke is still impelled by fierce pride and the desire to go on working.

"There are only a few of us who love what we do enough to stay with it 52 weeks, 365 days a year," he said. "You have to love something to do it like that, win, lose or draw, whether you make a profit or not. I want to keep my band together. I want to hear my music. And I'm going to keep right on doing it."

The telephone rang. It was Harry Carney, the band's baritone saxophonist, an Ellingtonian since 1927. The Duke rides in Mr. Carney's car, rather than in the band's chartered bus, on their trips in the East.

"Got to get going," said the Duke, rolling out of bed and quickly getting into the same clothes he had worn the night before. Downstairs, Mr. Carney was waiting by his battered white Imperial, parked in front of the hotel.

"That Collier is all right," he said. "You know those arrangements we were playing last night. On my part, he wrote 'Harry-tone' instead of baritone. No one ever came up with that one before."

He lighted a cigarette. "This band is different," he said. "Monotony never enters the picture. We play concerts, dances, we play sacred music, we play long compositions. There are so many small places that we visit, and in every one of them there are people who have been listening to Duke and the band on records for years."

The Duke appeared at last, tipped the bellboys royally, and he and Mr. Carney pulled away. They disagreed amiably about directions, stopped for gasoline and a Coke, and got back on the divided highway.

FELIX FRANKFURTER

1882–1965

By Albin Krebs and Anthony Lewis

As lawyer, teacher, judge and goad to society, Felix Frankfurter was a significant influence in American life for more than half a century.

His public career spanned the years from Theodore Roosevelt's presidency to John F. Kennedy's. When he became a Supreme Court Justice, in 1939, he had already won a place in history as an adviser to presidents, the holder of a variety of government jobs and a leader in the fight for dozens of social causes.

As important as his public life was his extraordinary private influence. His friends included many of the great in the worlds of law, journalism, government and scholarship, and he left his imprint on hundreds of students and law clerks who remembered him as they made their way in the world.

The Frankfurter impact on those who knew him—or were meeting him for the first time—was one of personality rather than of any particular philosophy.

He was the most vivacious, the most ebullient of men, bursting with joy and wit and sarcasm, eager to exchange gossip or debate eternal verities—but at any rate, to talk. He was by all odds the greatest talker of his time.

Matthew Josephson wrote in 1940: "Wherever Frankfurter is, there is no boredom. As soon as he bounces in—he never walks, he bounces—the talk and laughter begin, and they never let up."

Few who were ever exposed to it could resist his captivating personality. This was by way of contrast with his judicial philosophy, which was a subject of the greatest controversy, bringing denunciations from some who had been his admirers and praise from former enemies.

What disappointed the admirers was that as a Supreme Court justice he did not always vote on the side of the interests he had championed as a private citizen.

He had been a strong supporter of labor unions, for example. But he upheld the constitutional power of the states to restrict what they—not necessarily he—deemed socially undesirable practices.

In 1940, in *Thornhill* v. *Alabama*, he joined Justice Frank Murphy's broadly written opinion of the court, holding that picketing was a form of expression and that state prohibitions on peaceful picketing violate the Constitution's guarantee of free speech. But in 1941 Justice Frankfurter wrote for the court in the *Meadowmoor Dairies* case, holding that a state could enjoin even peaceful picketing if it became enmeshed in contemporaneous violence.

"It must never be forgotten that the Bill of Rights was the child of the Enlightenment," he wrote. "Back of the guarantee of free speech lay faith in the power of an appeal to reason by all the peaceful means of gaining access to the mind."

New York Times Photo

Another crucial area in the separation of the judge from the man was the right of persons with radical views to speak freely, or remain silent. He had spoken out against Attorney General A. Mitchell Palmer's "Red raids" after World War I. He was one of a handful of lawyers who, along with Charles Evans Hughes, protested them as a violation of civil liberties.

But as a justice he voted repeatedly to sustain governmental action against the Communist party, its leaders and those accused of association with it. He simply did not find in the Constitution grounds to upset legislative action based on detailed congressional findings as to the dangers of the Communist party—however much he personally disagreed with the action.

He was charged with having departed from the ideals of his great heroes, Justices Holmes and Brandeis, who so often dissented against the repression of radical speech. His answer—had he felt free to give one—might have been that Communism was not a world power in their day, and hence not a real threat to this country, but that in any event he was not prepared to upset these congressional determinations no matter what Holmes and Brandeis might have done.

The landmark decision in the Communist area was the case of Eugene Dennis and 10 other party leaders, decided in 1951. The Supreme Court, including Justice Frankfurter, affirmed their conviction under the Smith Act for conspiring to teach and advocate the violent overthrow of the government.

Ten years later, in an opinion by Justice Frankfurter, the Court upheld the requirement of the Internal Security Act of 1950 that the party register with the government as a foreign-controlled Communist organization. The court did not then pass on the 1950 act's penalties for registered groups, including a provision that no member could have a passport.

There was also the long series of cases arising from the refusal of witnesses to testify in congressional investigations of Communism.

The first of these was that of John T. Watkins. The court reversed his contempt conviction in 1957 in a broadly written opinion by Chief Justice Earl Warren that seemed to throw doubt on the validity of all inquiries by the House Committee on Un-American Activities.

In a brief concurring opinion Justice Frankfurter said he understood the Court to decide only a relatively narrow procedural point—that a committee must explain the relevance of its questions to a witness before requiring him to answer.

This turned out to be just about all the Watkins case did mean in the long run. In a number of subsequent cases—most of them decided by 5–4 votes, with Justice Frankfurter in the majority—the court affirmed convictions of men who had refused to tell congressional committees about alleged Communist connections.

Some of the liberal-minded citizens who deplored these and similar decisions understood, and disagreed with, the judicial philosophy underlying Justice Frankfurter's votes. But many others did not understand why he was often unwilling to invoke the judicial power in support of civil liberties.

One factor in the Frankfurter philosophy was the belief that it was undemocratic and dangerous for nine lifetime appointees to veto what legislators had done except in the clearest and most urgent cases. This belief was born of the 1920s and 1930s, when he saw a slim majority on the Supreme Court overturn urgent economic measures undertaken by state and nation.

A corollary view was that for the Court to attempt too much, to press its ideas of wise policy, would be to invite its own destruction. This was another lesson of the 1930s, when a self-willed Court brought itself to the brink of drastic reform.

Last, and not least important, was the thesis that reliance on the courts to preserve our liberties drained responsibility from those who should exercise it—legislatures and the people. He wrote: "Where all the effective means of inducing political changes are left free from interference, education in the abandonment of foolish legislation is itself a training in liberty. To fight out the wise use of legislative authority in the forum of public opinion and before legislative assemblies rather than to transfer such a contest to the judicial arena serves to vindicate the self-confidence of a free people."

Those words are from an opinion that came as a particular shock to Justice Frankfurter's liberal friends—the 1943 opinion holding that a state could require children to salute the flag although their religion forbade the exercise.

Three years later the Court overruled that decision. Justice Frankfurter, this time in dissent, wrote this most passionate defense of his judicial philosophy: "One who belongs to the most vilified and persecuted minority in history is not likely to be insensible to the freedoms guaranteed by our Constitution. Were my purely personal attitude relevant I should wholeheartedly associate myself with the general libertarian views in the court's opinion, representing as they do the thought and action of a lifetime.

"But as judges we are neither Jew nor gentile, neither Catholic nor agnostic . . . As a member of this court I am not justified in writing my private notions of policy into the Constitution, no matter how deeply I may cherish them or how mischievous I may deem their disregard."

Another important statement of his philosophy came in his dissent to the Court's 1962 decision that the apportionment of seats in state legislatures was subject to the constitutional scrutiny of the federal courts. The decision upset one of Justice Frankfurter's most deeply held beliefs, that the courts must stay out of what he termed the "political thicket" of districting problems.

"There is not under our Constitution a judicial remedy for every political mischief," the justice wrote. "In a democratic society like ours, relief must come through an aroused popular conscience that sears the conscience of the people's representatives."

A consistent theme during Justice Frankfurter's years on the Supreme Court was his insistence on fair procedure in the investigation of crime and the treatment of suspects. One of his best-known statements was that "the history of liberty has largely been the history of the observance of procedural safeguards."

Of all the members of the Court during his tenure he took probably the most stringent view of wiretapping. He voted more than once to hold tapping a violation of the Constitution, but there was never a majority with him.

His same feeling for the inviolable character of the citizen's privacy made him give special importance to the Fourth Amendment's prohibition of unreasonable searches and seizures. He often dissented on the ground that the Court was giving federal agents too much leeway to search suspects. He was the author of the significant doctrine that confessions obtained from federal prisoners during unnecessary delays in their arraignment were inadmissible at trial.

The justice's insistence on the niceties of fair criminal procedure sometimes gave way to another strongly held view—his respect for the independence of the states in our federal system. He was not prepared to apply the same rigid standards to the states that he did to the federal government.

Thus he felt that state courts should be free to admit illegally seized evidence, although federal courts might not. He lost this battle in 1961, when the Supreme Court overruled an earlier case and barred illegal evidence from state trials.

A majority of the Court was with him for the proposition that successive federal and state trials of the same man for the same criminal act do not constitute double jeopardy, barred by the Constitution. Justice Frankfurter wrote that Washington and the states constitute separate sovereignties that cannot foreclose each other from acting.

One of his great battles on the Court was against the argument that the first eight amendments to the Constitution—which have been held to bind only the federal government—should be held applicable to the states through the clause of the Fourteenth Amendment assuring due process of law.

The issue arose notably on the question of self-incrimination. A 5–4 majority, including Justice Frankfurter, held that the states need not apply the precise protection against compulsory self-incrimination afforded by the Fifth Amendment in federal cases.

In this, as in so many other closely divided cases, the principal voice on the other side of the argument was that of Justice Hugo L. Black. For years he and Justice Frankfurter were the senior members of the court. They respected and even, in a strange way, liked each other. But they were in fundamental philosophical conflict.

Justice Black believed, as he said, that there were absolutes in the Constitution. It prohibited any governmental restraints on free speech, for example. It applied to the states in exactly the same terms as to the federal government.

To Justice Frankfurter absolutes were anathema. He thought that in every case the relative needs of liberty had to be weighed against the demands of authority. He thought the United States had grown on a process of cautious pragmatism, by trial and error, and he hesitated to impose rigid constitutional formulas on it.

A case that tested the issue nicely was one from Los Angeles in 1952. The police had pumped the stomach of a suspect named Antonio Rochin, against his will, and recovered morphine capsules. Was this an illegal search? A compulsory self-incrimination? If either, were they prohibited in state proceedings?

Justice Frankfurter avoided those pigeonholes. He said Rochin had been denied due process of law in his conviction because the recovery of evidence by stomach-pumping was "conduct that shocks the conscience." Constitutional law professors spoke jokingly thereafter of a stomach test of constitutionality: If it makes you sick, it's not due process.

When in any event the Court's resolution of a problem was subject to correction by Congress, Justice Frankfurter felt freer in devising the solution to a problem.

In the field of interstate commerce, for example, he did not hesitate to strike down state taxes or regulations as infringements on the freedom of commerce. Congress could always pass a statute permitting the disputed state action. In the same way the justice would sometimes strain his interpretation of a congressional statute to avoid a constitutional problem, reasoning that Congress could correct the construction if it was too far-fetched.

But when the Supreme Court was speaking as the ultimate voice in American government—making the final decision on whether the Constitution authorized legislators to act as they did—he was very cautious in interposing his views against those of the legislature. His caution stemmed from his view of the limited function of a judge in a democratic society, a function not including the making of policy.

"If judges want to be preachers," he said in 1955 at a Harvard Law School ceremony in honor of John Marshall, "they should dedicate themselves to the pulpit; if judges want to be primary shapers of policy, the legislature is their place. Self-willed judges are the least defensible offenders against government under law."

The informed critics of Frankfurter the judge felt that he missed greatness by taking too narrow, too timid a view of the judicial function. They argued that he carried judicial self-restraint and deference to the legislature so far as to miss the opportunity for creative inspiration of idealism in government and society. In short, they urged, there are times when legislatures need to be hauled up short and may even privately admit they had strayed from permissible paths.

Perhaps the strongest criticism here is that Justice Frankfurter in his view of the Constitution failed to place liberties of the mind—notably speech and expression—on a higher plane than other rights. Such a hierarchy of values was demanded by, among others, Justice Black.

Before he went on the Court, Justice Frankfurter

made the distinction himself. In a 1938 lecture on Justice Holmes, he said Holmes had "attributed very different legal significance to those liberties of the individual which history has attested as the indispensable conditions of a free society from that which he attached to liberties which derived merely from shifting economic arrangements."

No rational critic would suggest that Justice Frankfurter was insensitive to the individual liberties enshrined in the Constitution. His opinions rejecting any hint of an establishment of religion and any encroachment on academic freedom, among many others, make such a view impossible.

Perhaps most significant is an aspect of his judicial career that is yet shrouded. That is the part that he played in the 1954 decision declaring racial segregation in the public schools unconstitutional.

There is reason to believe that the Court could not have reached that decision unanimously—and perhaps not at all—if the justices had thought the result had to be immediate, total desegregation. The decisive formula was the one permitting implementation of the decision "with all deliberate speed," and in that formula the hand of Justice Frankfurter was evident. The very phrase was his—used in at least five opinions before the school case.

All the arguments about whether he was a "liberal" or "conservative" on the Court made no sense to Justice Frankfurter himself. He rejected the idea that a judicial decision had anything to do with "liberalism" or "conservatism."

Prof. Louis L. Jaffe, in a study of Justice Frankfurter's opinions, wrote: "It is of the very essence of his judicial philosophy that his role as a judge precluded him from having a program couched in these terms of choice."

For every critic of the Frankfurter judicial outlook there was someone to argue that only his scholarship and his sense of history had saved the Supreme Court from many self-destructive errors. In any event, all agreed that the Court had been deeply influenced by his unusual background in the world of law and the world of affairs.

The great judge Learned Hand wrote in 1957 that he considered Justice Frankfurter, because of his views of a judge's role, "the most important figure in our whole judicial system."

"It would be impossible for me to think of any other judge whose continuance in his duties I welcome more unreservedly," Judge Hand said.

President Kennedy used humor to point up Justice Frankfurter's position in a letter to the justice on his 80th birthday, in 1962, shortly after his retirement.

"You seem to be the same age as Eamon de Valera, to whom I was writing only the other day," the President said. "He was born in New York and conquered Ireland, while you seem to have reversed the process by starting in Vienna and taking charge of the constitutional traditions of the United States."

Felix Frankfurter's imprint on American life was the more remarkable because he was an immigrant and a Jew who rose to eminence in a day when neither anti-Semitism nor suspicion of the foreign-born was a rarity.

He was born on Nov. 15, 1882, in Vienna. His father, Leopold, was a poor merchant descended from six generations of rabbis and scholars. When Felix was 12, he and his five brothers and sisters followed their father to New York.

He attended public school, was graduated from City College at 19 and then saved $1,200 during a year as clerk for the New York City Tenement House Commission. He used the money to enter the Harvard Law School.

Between the law school and young Frankfurter it was love at first sight—a love that lasted the rest of his life. He was graduated in 1906 as an honor student, law review editor and friend of the school's great dean, James Barr Ames.

A few months later Theodore Roosevelt's United States Attorney in New York, Henry L. Stimson, asked Dean Ames to recommend a young assistant. Frankfurter was the choice.

Mr. Stimson was another of the heroes who shaped Frankfurter's life. Justice Frankfurter spoke of him often, and in reverential tones, as the man who taught him the meaning of total honor and rectitude.

For four years the young assistant helped Mr. Stimson bust trusts, receiving a personal commendation from President Roosevelt at the White House for his work. In 1911 Mr. Stimson became secretary of war and took young Frankfurter to Washington with him.

In 1914, at the insistence of Louis D. Brandeis of the Boston bar, he was appointed to the Harvard law faculty. He had hardly arrived when he began his extracurricular activity, helping Brandeis to brief and argue the constitutionality of maximum-hours laws before the Supreme Court and handling the issue himself when Brandeis became a justice.

As Archibald MacLeish once put it: "In 1917 he left Cambridge for a Washington weekend with Secretary of War Newton D. Baker, which lasted for two years." He was assistant to the secretaries of war and labor and, finally, chairman of the War Labor Policies Board, handling the wartime labor problems of the country. He came to know Justice Holmes, who called the home Frankfurter shared with other bright young men "the house of truth" because of their philosophical discussions.

During those same years Justice Frankfurter investigated for President Wilson the brutal repression of an Arizona mine strike and the conviction and life sentence of Tom Mooney for an alleged "radical" bombing in San Francisco. He reported that Mooney had been framed—a finding roundly condemned by, among others, Theodore Roosevelt. Twenty years later Mooney was pardoned.

In 1919 Justice Frankfurter went to the Versailles Peace Conference, where he helped to represent the cause of Zionism. (Like Justice Brandeis, he aided Jewish and Zionist causes although he was not a religious Jew.)

He returned to Harvard in 1919. There he remained for the next 20 years, teaching bright students about the world of ideas and teaching them how to think. So analytical was one course, and so oblivious to the usual goal of progressing through a fixed amount of material, that it became known as the "Case-of-the-Month Club." He became a major student and critic of the Supreme Court.

While he taught, he carried on outside activities at a furious pace. He wrote for the *New Republic*—he was an original stockholder. He was a founding member of the American Civil Liberties Union and worked hard for it. He was involved with the National Association for the Advancement of Colored People.

But his most famous activity was in behalf of Nicola Sacco and Bartolomeo Vanzetti, anarchists condemned to death for a holdup murder in Massachusetts. A Frankfurter article in the *Atlantic Monthly* analyzing the evidence and scoring the trial as a miscarriage of justice brought the case to national and world attention. Despite the horrified reproaches of the Boston bar and society, Professor Frankfurter fought for Sacco and Vanzetti until the sentence, now generally regarded as unjust, was executed.

Then came Franklin D. Roosevelt and the New Deal. President Roosevelt was an old friend, and Professor Frankfurter quickly took on an advisory role probably unequaled by any unofficial person outside Washington before or since.

Those who were suspicious of him doubtless tended to exaggerate his influence, but it seems clear that the influence was at least substantial. He helped to draft legislation. He saw the president privately and often—weekly, even daily. Most important, he filled the new administration with eager and able young lawyers who proceeded to remake the government.

"I don't see why I am here as Postmaster General," James A. Farley was quoted as complaining, "since Frankfurter seems to hand out all the patronage."

The professor never saw it as patronage. He was simply helping to find able men for important jobs in a government up against the crisis of the Depression. And he was encouraging his students and former students to undertake what he considered the high duty of public service. In fact, he had sent his students to Washington all through the Republican years.

President Roosevelt asked Professor Frankfurter to be Solicitor General, but he declined. He also turned down, in 1932, nomination to the Supreme Judicial Court of Massachusetts.

By all indications he was to be a professor for life.

On the evening of Jan. 4, 1939, he was in his Cambridge home dressing for dinner when the telephone rang and "there was the ebullient, the exuberant, warmth-enveloping voice of the President of the United States."

For minutes Mr. Roosevelt explained why he could not appoint Professor Frankfurter to the Supreme Court vacancy created by the death of Justice Benjamin N. Cardozo.

"I was getting bored really," Justice Frankfurter wrote, "when he whipped around on the telephone and said, 'But unless you give me an insurmountable objection I'm going to send your name in for the court tomorrow at 12 o'clock.'

"I remember saying, and it is very natural to remember this very vividly, 'All I can say is that I wish my mother were alive.' "

His nomination was violently attacked by the far right, and witnesses appeared at a Senate hearing to denounce his ethnicity, his birth and his politics. Senator Pat McCarran, Democrat of Nevada, asked the nominee whether he believed in "the doctrines of Karl Marx."

"Senator," he replied, "I do not believe you have ever taken an oath to support the Constitution of the United States with fewer reservations than I have or would now, nor do I believe you are more attached to the theories and practices of Americanism than I am."

He was confirmed by voice vote of the Senate, without objection.

Over the years political conservatives, in tones that suggested they were rubbing their eyes in disbelief, came to acknowledge that Felix Frankfurter had been no radical on the Supreme Court but a force for stability and moderation. A particularly genuine tribute came in 1958 from Sen. John W. Bricker, Ohio Republican, who said their differences in political outlook made him the more respect the justice's performance on the bench.

What made Justice Frankfurter's restraint as a judge so remarkable was that, underneath the robe, he remained the man he always had been—a man of the most intense passion. He was small, just a few inches over 5 feet, and emotion filled his slight frame to overflowing.

He loved to argue, his head darting here and there, his hand suddenly gripping the listener's elbow as he made a point. On the bench he would pepper lawyers with questions that approached, and sometimes reached, the heckling level.

The emotional inner man was given away once when a Washington radio station played his favorite music. He requested, among other works, Debussy's *La Mer* and De Falla's *El Amor Brujo*—the lushest and most passionate romantic pieces.

Sometimes his emotions would carry him away in court, and there would be a tense episode with a colleague. The best-known incident came when Chief Justice Earl Warren was so stung by a Frankfurter dissent that he extemporized a rebuttal, charging the justice with "degrading the Court." A few minutes later they were chatting away amiably.

Despite all the disagreement on the Court, Justice Frankfurter's colleagues had the deepest feelings for him. When he returned after retirement, their affection was tangible.

His love and his concern for other human beings—for their own sake, not for their station—had to be observed to be believed.

Childless himself, he had a special love for children, and they for him. He would telephone a friend to rib him for some failing and then spend his time talking with the 5-year-old who answered the phone. Extraordinary affection bound him to his law clerks, who returned from all over the country each year for a dinner.

And there were his friends among the great. He was a friend of Albert Einstein, Thomas Mann, John Dewey, Alfred E. Smith, Alexander Woollcott, Chaim Weizmann, Alfred North Whitehead—of prime ministers and judges and actors and poets too numerous to begin listing.

He read everything—complete reports of the courts of all the English-speaking world, philosophy, science, the most obscure newspaper stories. Newspapers not least. He was a critic of the press, ever ready to tax its shortcomings. But the truth was that he was a frustrated journalist himself. He remarked that the letters to the editor he had drafted in his mind and never sent would fill a volume.

In 1954 a 12-year-old boy he did not know wrote and asked how he should prepare himself to become a lawyer. The justice answered that he should learn of literature, painting and music.

The letter ended: "Stock your mind with the deposit of much good reading, and widen and deepen your feelings by experiencing vicariously as much as possible the wonderful mysteries of the universe, and forget all about your future career."

Justice Frankfurter died at George Washington University Hospital on February 22, 1965, after suffering a heart attack at his home in Washington the day before. He was 82.

A PASSIONATE CONCERN

ANTHONY LEWIS

IN 1945, Sir William Haley, then director of the British Broadcasting Corporation, was surprised to get a letter from an American Supreme Court Justice, Felix Frankfurter. It complimented him on an article Sir William had written about the limits on freedom of speech and informed him that the justice had cited it in an opinion. That was the beginning of a correspondence and a friendship that lasted until Justice Frankfurter's death. In 1952 Sir William became editor of the *Times* of London, of which the justice was a regular and sharp-eyed reader, and the *Times* usually provoked the letters.

Justice Frankfurter would write about a book that Sir William had reviewed—some esoteric work on 18th-century literature, perhaps, that the justice had obtained through the Library of Congress. Or he might comment on a parliamentary jest buried in the lengthy, near-verbatim reports of the sessions of Parliament carried by the *Times*. Law was only an occasional topic.

It was all so characteristic of Felix Frankfurter—the breadth of interest, the fierce inquisitiveness, the love of correspondence as of talk, and not last his fascination for things English.

He read not only the *Times* every day but also the British weeklies.

When the *Economist* carried an article from Washington critical of an opinion of his and labeled only "By a Special Correspondent," he sent a note down from the bench on the Monday morning the issue arrived, asking a friend in the courtroom who the "special correspondent" was, as if he didn't know already.

He was visiting professor at Oxford in 1933–34, and said afterward that it was "the fullest year my wife and I spent—the amplest and most civilized." One thing that impressed him was that people respected his privacy by sending notes instead of telephoning.

One of the many paradoxes about Justice Frankfurter was that he was a great believer in privacy and yet loved to know all about everyone and everything.

Long before he was a judge he valued "the right to be let alone," as his great hero Brandeis called it. He tried while on the Court—unsuccessfully—to write into law Brandeis's dissent from the decision establishing the constitutionality of police wiretapping.

But try to keep a secret from him. He loved to know why the great did what they did and to speculate on the mechanisms that moved them. His conversation roamed over the ideas and the motivations of presidents and premiers as well as judges.

But the important thing was that he was not concerned only about the great. He would somehow hear about a child being born to a friend and send a congratulatory note. He was genuinely concerned about other people's difficulties or illnesses.

Compliments were customarily mixed with chivvying of friends to make sure their heads did not swell. When one acquaintance left Washington, the justice wrote to say that the move was "foolish"—and enclosed a copy of a warm letter on his behalf to an influential person in the city where he was moving.

While in England years ago, he testified before a royal commission on the subject of capital punishment. He was deeply opposed to the death penalty and doubtless took comfort in his last days from the fact that Britain was finally moving to outlaw it.

As a judge he often joined in affirming criminal convictions where the death penalty was involved. This bothered some who found him too "conservative" a judge, as did his consistent judicial sustaining of anti-Communist measures that he personally did not like.

The point, of course, was that he considered his personal views irrelevant to his judicial duty. At least he said so. But like all other statements about this complicated man, it was too simple.

Much as he strived for disinterest, Felix Frankfurter remained a passionate man. What took place in his judicial career was really a struggle to control the passions—an effort wiser and more successful in some directions than in others.

At bottom, there may have been a skepticism about the perfectibility of human beings, including—perhaps especially—judges. He was unwilling to gamble too much on the all-seeing wisdom of any one man or small group, however right their ideas seemed at the moment.

There was an occasion when more than half his Supreme Court colleagues were going to a bar association meeting. Justice Frankfurter, who would never dream of engaging in what he considered a public relations enterprise, commented tartly: "They think they'll win friends because their faces are so beautiful!"

Those who knew him will remember the passion more than the effort at restraint. No one who experienced it could forget the fierce questions, the grip on one's elbow, the sudden turn from banter to challenges of one's deepest assumptions. That was Felix Frankfurter.

THE BRANDEIS-FRANKFURTER LETTERS

DAVID M. MARGOLICK

LOUIS D. BRANDEIS, in his 23 years on the United States Supreme Court, paid Felix Frankfurter, who was then a Harvard law professor, more than $50,000 to further the justice's goals on public policy, according to previously unpublished letters.

A new study that relies in large part on the letters exchanged by two of 20th-century America's most prominent lawyers and jurists discloses that Brandeis, feeling ethically constrained from engaging directly in extrajudicial activities but possessing strong opinions about the political issues of the day, paid Frankfurter an annual retainer for his efforts.

The letters show that each year from 1916 through 1938 Brandeis deposited as much as $3,500 in a special "joint endeavors for the public good" fund he set up for Frankfurter.

"I ought to feel free to make suggestions to you, although they involve some incidental expense," Brandeis wrote in 1916 to Frankfurter, "and you should feel free to incur expense in the public interest."

The financial relationship between the two men ended only when Brandeis retired from the Supreme Court in 1939. Frankfurter, 26 years younger, was named the same year to a different seat on the Court by President Roosevelt.

The retainer arrangement was discovered by Bruce A. Murphy, an assistant professor of political science at Pennsylvania State University, who obtained from the Library of Congress 300 letters between Brandeis and Frankfurter, most of them previously unpublished.

Professor Murphy described his findings in a book titled *The Brandeis/Frankfurter Connection: The Secret Political Activities of Two Supreme Court Justices*, which was published in 1982 by Oxford University Press.

"The fund was designed to free Brandeis from the shackles of remaining nonpolitical on the bench and to permit him to engage freely in political affairs," Professor Murphy wrote. "Frankfurter provided Brandeis the conduit through which he might both inquire freely in the political realm and influence the course of political decisions."

Such a relationship, Professor Murphy wrote, was "unprecedented in Supreme Court history."

The newly detailed activities of the two men raise anew the problem of defining the proper scope of extrajudicial activity by Supreme Court justices, particularly for individuals with strong personalities and political views like Brandeis and Frankfurter.

They also help place in some perspective the recent allegation by John D. Ehrlichman that Chief Justice Warren E. Burger spoke of matters pending before the Court with President Nixon.

"Chief Justice Burger is being held to a standard that does not and has never existed," Professor Murphy said in an interview. "The truth is that justices throughout history have been involved in politics, and Justices Brandeis and Frankfurter were as politically active as any of them."

Professor Murphy's findings also include these points:

Brandeis, steeped in a tradition of individualism and fearing concentration of power in Washington, warned officials in the Roosevelt Administration that he might seek to have two key New Deal measures, the Agricultural Adjustment Act and the National Recovery Act, declared unconstitutional should the laws come before the Court, unless the Roosevelt administration abandoned its collectivist philosophy.

With Frankfurter's assistance, Brandeis's views on contemporary legal and social issues were represented for many years in the *Harvard Law Review* and quoted, often verbatim but without attribution, in unsigned editorials in the *New Republic* magazine.

Evidence from the Brandeis-Frankfurter correspondence, as well as from recently discovered transcripts of a wiretap placed by the Massachusetts state police on Frankfurter's telephone in 1927, suggests additional reasons for Brandeis's decision to disqualify himself from hearing the Sacco-Vanzetti case.

After his own appointment to the bench, Frankfurter broke with Supreme Court tradition and gave an advisory opinion on the constitutionality of the 1940 "destroyers for bases" agreement with Britain. Moreover, he personally reviewed more than 30 drafts of the Lend-Lease bill, which provided military credits to Britain.

Frankfurter campaigned for 56 months to have Henry J. Friendly named to the United States Court of Appeals for the Second Circuit, while seeking to deny Judges Irving R. Kaufman and Harold R. Medina similar appointments.

According to the book, Felix Frankfurter's first encounter with Louis D. Brandeis occurred in 1905, when, as a 22-year-old student at Harvard Law School, he heard Brandeis speak. They began corresponding in 1911, and the young Frankfurter, like many before and after him, became enthralled with the charismatic "people's attorney."

Brandeis recommended Frankfurter for a faculty position at Harvard Law School and appointed him an adviser to the American Zionist movement, which Brandeis headed before his appointment to the Supreme Court in 1916. A few years later, Brandeis referred to Frankfurter in a letter as "half brother-half son."

"Brandeis changed the norms of extrajudicial conduct," Professor Murphy wrote, adding, "His incredibly open and extensive political behavior made it possible for members of the Court to establish intimate advisory relationships with later administrations."

When the Republicans occupied the White House in the 1920s and early 1930s, Brandeis had to be content more with disseminating his ideas than directly affecting public policy. It was a task for which Frankfurter, with his numerous literary contacts and legions of bright, faithful students, was perfectly equipped.

Professor Murphy showed that Frankfurter undertook many chores for his political patron. In some instances, Brandeis asked Frankfurter either to draft legislation designed to remedy what he considered incorrect rulings by his Supreme Court colleagues or to criticize the ruling in the pages of the *Harvard Law Review.* On another occasion, he asked Frankfurter to research a constitutional question being considered by the Court.

Frankfurter, a trustee and contributing editor of the *New Republic*, also saw to it that excerpts from Brandeis's letters—on such topics as the character of Charles A. Lindbergh, President Coolidge's silence on the Teapot Dome scandal and the danger of "big money" in election campaigns—were printed, sometimes verbatim, a few weeks later as unsigned editorials in the magazine.

The financial ties between Frankfurter and Brandeis were to have more immediate ramifications after the 1921 trial of Nicola Sacco and Bartolomeo Vanzetti. In one of the most celebrated legal cases in American history, Sacco and Vanzetti were convicted and sentenced to death for the murder of a paymaster and his guard in Massachusetts. Justice Brandeis declined to participate in the appeals process and refused to hear a request by the convicted men for a stay of execution, citing his family's close ties to a woman active in the pair's defense.

The Brandeis-Frankfurter correspondence discloses, however, that Brandeis encouraged Frankfurter to defend Sacco and Vanzetti in print shortly before they were executed in 1927. Moreover, concerned over expenses incurred by his colleague in this effort, the justice inquired, in a letter dated June 2, 1927, whether "an additional sum might not be appropriate." That August, he deposited an additional $500 in the "public good" account.

The payments, Professor Murphy suggests, put Brandeis in a "compromising position" and may have helped "deprive convicted men of a right to a fair hearing by the Court's most liberal member."

Transcripts from a recently discovered wiretap placed by the Massachusetts state police on Frankfurter's phone at the time of the case indicate that the arrangement might have had an inhibiting effect on Frankfurter as well.

Letters in the Brandeis-Frankfurter correspondence show, moreover, how the two collaborated with Benjamin V. Cohen and Thomas G. Corcoran to draft such key legislation as the Securities Act of 1933. Mr. Cohen and Mr. Corcoran were young Frankfurter protégés who had key positions in the Roosevelt administration.

According to Professor Murphy, Mr. Cohen and Mr. Corcoran visited Brandeis—whom they called "Isaiah," after the biblical prophet—as often as twice monthly. Afterward, Brandeis would forward specific legislative proposals on the matters they had discussed to Frankfurter, who would gather support materials and forward them to Roosevelt. The information would then be returned to Mr. Corcoran and Mr. Cohen, who would draft the legislation and shepherd it through Congress.

Professor Murphy argues that despite similarities in their backgrounds and their long association,

Brandeis and Frankfurter had vastly different approaches to extrajudicial activity.

Brandeis, Professor Murphy says, was content both morally and tactically to stay above the fray and use intermediaries to achieve his political ends. Frankfurter professed to be aloof, writing in his diary in 1943, "I have an austere and even sacerdotal view of the position of a judge on this Court, and that means I have nothing to say on matters that come within a thousand miles of what may fairly be called politics." In reality, Professor Murphy wrote, Frankfurter was an "incessant meddler," more immersed in politics as a Supreme Court justice than he ever was as a Harvard professor.

"One saw President Wilson having to travel to Brandeis's apartment or send an emissary to obtain counsel," the author explains, "whereas not even barring the doors and windows would have kept Frankfurter out of the Roosevelt White House."

Like many of his predecessors on the Court, Frankfurter abandoned judicial restraint to aid his government in wartime. In 1940, for example, he gave Secretary of War Henry L. Stimson an advisory opinion—a practice long frowned upon by the Court—on the constitutionality of Roosevelt's "destroyers-for-bases" agreement with the British.

Further, the book discloses, Frankfurter personally reviewed more than 30 drafts of the Lend-Lease bill in 1941—going so far as to suggest that it be labeled "House Resolution No. 1776" to counteract isolationist opposition—and helped draft the first War Powers Act.

Frankfurter also became involved in partisan politics, according to the book. He took an active role in Roosevelt's campaign for a third term and had some of his young associates write speeches and perform other tasks on Roosevelt's behalf.

One such associate, Joseph L. Rauh, Jr., defended Frankfurter's partisan activities. "If Felix were alive today he'd say that the reelection of F.D.R. was the only way to stop Hitler," said Mr. Rauh, now a Washington lawyer.

While Frankfurter's political influence waned with Roosevelt's death in 1945, the Murphy study discloses one front on which he continued to remain active until the end of his career: appointments to the federal judiciary.

Letters written by the justice to federal appeals court judge Learned Hand and a prominent New York attorney, Charles C. Burlingham, detail Frankfurter's 56-month campaign, beginning in 1954, to place Henry J. Friendly on the Court of Appeals for the Second Circuit. At the same time, the letters show that Frankfurter was equally determined to keep off that court two other judges who had presided over politically sensitive cases in the Truman years, Irving R. Kaufman and Harold R. Medina.

Frankfurter characterized Judge Medina, who heard the prosecution of several Communist party leaders in 1949, as a "Messianic character" and a "superegotist." Of Judge Kaufman, who sentenced Ethel and Julius Rosenberg to death for their role in passing atomic secrets to the Soviet Union, he told Learned Hand, "I despise a judge who feels God told him to impose a death sentence," and added, "I am mean enough to try to stay here long enough so that K. will be too old to succeed me."

Summing up his study, Professor Murphy said in an interview that Brandeis and Frankfurter were "patriotic men who were doing things they believed would advance the cause of the American people and improve our society."

"The real problem," he continued, "is whether you can have one set of rules for well-intentioned actors like Brandeis and Frankfurter, and another for those not so well intentioned."

FRANKFURTER AND THE *BROWN* v. *BOARD OF EDUCATION* DECISION

STUART TAYLOR, JR.

IN EARLY 1987 a recently published oral history shed important new light on the behind-the-scenes drama, including private discussions between Justice Felix Frankfurter and a key Justice Department lawyer, that led up to the Supreme Court's historic 1954 decision striking down school segregation.

The lawyer, Philip Elman, said in the tape-recorded history that Frankfurter gave him confidential information about his and his colleagues' views on the case, *Brown* v. *Board of Education*, information that inspired Mr. Elman to write a crucial argument into the Justice Department's brief.

Mr. Elman's account for the Columbia Oral History Project, as published in the February issue of the *Harvard Law Review*, has provoked great interest and some controversy in legal circles, including strong criticism over the propriety of the Frankfurter-Elman discussions.

Private discussions about a pending case between a judge and one of the lawyers would clearly violate current ethical rules, which are not directly binding on justices of the Supreme Court and had not been codified in detail in the 1950s.

Mr. Elman, a former law clerk for Frankfurter who remained his confidant, said in telephone interviews that their talks may have changed the course of history for the better, although some lawyers said he might be overstating their importance.

Mr. Elman was the principal author of the three briefs the Justice Department filed in the Brown case, widely regarded as the most important Supreme Court decision of the past century.

The department's role in siding, as a friend of the court, with the black plaintiffs who brought the Brown case is widely thought to have been a major factor in winning a 9–0 ruling and the moral authority that went with unanimity. Mr. Elman said the unorthodox legal argument that grew out of his discussions with Frankfurter was a key element in bringing together the fractious Court.

"He told me what he thought, what the other justices were telling him they thought," recalled Mr. Elman.

"*Brown* v. *Board of Education*, which we fully discussed, was an extraordinary case, and the ordinary rules didn't apply," Mr. Elman said. "In that case, I knew everything, or at least he gave me the impression that I knew everything, that was going on at the Court. He told me about what was said in conference and who said it."

Members of the Court ordinarily regard their private conferences as highly confidential and jealously guard their secrecy.

Mr. Elman, who was Justice Frankfurter's clerk from 1941 to 1943 and remained a close confidant until the justice died in 1965, served for many years as the senior career civil rights expert in the Solicitor General's office.

He said the information he had from Frankfurter about the misgivings of some justices, who feared that ordering immediate desegregation would spawn turmoil in the South, inspired him to write into the government's December 1952 brief a proposal that otherwise would not have been made.

This was the argument—viewed by Mr. Elman at the time as legally incorrect and unprincipled but critical to winning a strong majority—that the Court could hold that school segregation violated the rights of millions of black children without ordering an immediate end to these violations.

Rather, desegregation could be phased in gradually—"with all deliberate speed," in the famous phrase used by Chief Justice Earl Warren, at Justice Frankfurter's suggestion, in the Court's 1955 decision on enforcement of the 1954 desegregation ruling.

Mr. Elman said that at the same time he was disclosing some internal Justice Department deliberations to Justice Frankfurter, who was "the grand strategist in all this inside the Court," and was eager for the government to support desegregation.

"I never mentioned my conversations with Frankfurter to anyone," Mr. Elman said. "He didn't regard me as a lawyer for a party; I was still his law clerk. He needed help, lots of help, and there were things I could do in the Department of Justice that he couldn't do, like getting the support of both administrations, Democratic and Republican, for the position he wanted the Court to come out with, so that it would not become a hot political issue."

The oral history also includes such details as the sometimes contemptuous "code names" Frankfurter used for other justices: "Stanley Reed was 'the Chamber,' which means fool, or dolt, or mule in Hebrew; now that might have been difficult for somebody to decipher. The others wouldn't have been. Murphy was 'the Saint.' Roberts was 'the Squire'—he was the country squire."

The rich historical literature on the Brown case and its precursors includes fragmentary references to conversations between Mr. Elman and Justice Frankfurter and to insights Mr. Elman derived from Frankfurter about the Court's leanings in *Brown.* But the *Harvard Law Review* article is the first published account detailing the substance of the Frankfurter-Elman conversations and asserting that they had a key role in the outcome of the case.

The article is excerpted from the transcript of Mr. Elman's reminiscences in interviews conducted in 1983 by Norman Silber, a legal history scholar, for the Columbia Oral History Project.

In interviews this week, Mr. Elman said that contrary to the possible implication in the oral history, his most important discussions with Frankfurter about the Brown case took place before he became directly involved in the case with the filing of the government's first legal brief in December 1952.

Several prominent experts on legal ethics and the Supreme Court said in separate interviews, based on the account in the *Law Review*, that it had clearly been improper for a justice and a lawyer to engage in private discussions about a pending case in which the lawyer was involved.

These experts included Professor Geoffrey Hazard, Jr., of Yale Law School, the principal draftsman of the American Bar Association's Model Rules of Professional Conduct and Code of Judicial Conduct; Solicitor General Charles Fried; and former Solicitors General Erwin N. Griswold and Rex E. Lee.

Mr. Griswold, who knew Justice Frankfurter, worked in the Solicitor General's office from 1929 to 1934 and headed it from 1967 to 1973. He said he was "startled" by Mr. Elman's disclosures.

It was clearly regarded as improper at the time and would clearly be improper now, Mr. Griswold said, for a judge to discuss privately with a lawyer, or a lawyer with a judge, a pending case in which the lawyer was involved.

Mr. Hazard said that while "ethics was more of a tradition and assumed shared understanding as distinct from a body of definite rules" in the 1950s, lawyers for the southern states in the Brown case "could have brought Frankfurter under bitter criticism" if they had known that he was talking privately with one of their adversaries.

But Mr. Elman said in an interview that he had done the right thing under the unique circumstances of the case. "I wasn't an advocate representing a client," he said, "I was on the same side with Frankfurter. We were both representing the same boss. We were both trying to do what was right." He added, "I was almost like a son to him."

Mr. Elman said that Justice Frankfurter, who was appointed by President Roosevelt in 1939 and continued as a close adviser to the president thereafter, would "call me almost every Sunday night at home" from 1941 until his death in 1965.

"Proper or improper, history might have been different, and *Brown* v. *Board of Education* might have come out differently, if I had not known from Frankfurter how he and the other justices felt about the problem," Mr. Elman said.

"You put down a little impropriety on the one side, if that's what it is, and you put down on the other side that without that little impropriety you would not have had this enormous contribution to American constitutional law of the 20th century, which was at long last to bring about the integration of black people to American society," he added.

"I'd rather have that on my tombstone than that I spent 10 years at the Federal Trade Commission fighting mergers."

Mr. Elman, who joined the Solicitor General's Office in 1944, handled all major civil rights cases for the government in the Supreme Court until his appointment to the Federal Trade Commission in 1961.

Aside from calling the Frankfurter-Elman discussions improper, Mr. Griswold and some other lawyers said they thought Mr. Elman had overstated the importance of those discussions and of his own role in the outcome of the Brown case.

These lawyers included William T. Coleman, Jr., chairman of the NAACP Legal Defense and Educational Fund, who also accused Mr. Elman of unfairly depreciating that group's strategy as counsel for the black students who sued in *Brown* and related cases.

Mr. Coleman, who had also been a Frankfurter clerk, said that Mr. Elman's account of his discussions with the justice was "shocking" and could not be true. Frankfurter "would have recognized it was improper and would not have done it," he asserted.

But Joseph L. Rauh, Jr., a prominent civil rights lawyer who was Justice Frankfurter's first law clerk in 1939, supported Mr. Elman's view.

"Whether this was right or wrong, there was nothing venal about it," Mr. Rauh said. "It was as natural as it could be for him to talk to Phil Elman about anything, including pending cases."

He said Justice Frankfurter regarded his first few clerks, who had also been his students at Harvard Law School, as members of his family and "law clerks for life."

While others disputed the importance of the Frankfurter-Elman discussions in shaping the outcome of *Brown*, Mr. Elman said in an interview this week: "I lived through it, and I can tell you it made all the difference in the world."

He said in the oral history that as late as 1952, when the *Brown* case came to the Court, "Frankfurter could not count five sure, or even probable, votes" to overrule *Plessy* v. *Ferguson*, the 1896 decision approving "separate but equal" facilities for blacks.

It took some persuasion to win the vote of Justice Frankfurter himself, who opposed segregation but was wary of overextending the Court's powers by undertaking the enormous task of integrating the school systems in almost half the states, Mr. Elman said.

He said he knew from Justice Frankfurter that Chief Justice Fred M. Vinson was against broadly striking down segregation, that others were leaning the same way and that even opponents of segregation, like Justice Robert H. Jackson, feared immediate desegregation would overextend the Court's powers and unleash turmoil in the South.

The argument for gradual desegregation that Mr. Elman's discussions with Justice Frankfurter inspired, Mr. Elman said, "broke the logjam."

He noted that in arguing that victims of constitutional violations were not entitled to immediate relief "I was on very shaky ground," and that private civil rights advocates had assailed him for failing to urge immediate desegregation.

However, he added, "unlike Frankfurter and me, they couldn't or didn't count the votes on the Court."

The Brown case was still pending at the Court when President Truman was succeeded in early 1953 by President Eisenhower, who was more sympathetic to southern whites. His subordinates at the Justice Department were reluctant to take a position in the case. Mr. Elman said he told Justice Frankfurter this.

The Court, still divided, ordered in the summer of 1953 that *Brown* and related cases be reargued. At Justice Frankfurter's instigation, Mr. Elman said, the Court also invited the government to file another brief.

Mr. Elman said he told the new attorney general, Herbert Brownell, Jr., and other Eisenhower appointees that this invitation was "the equivalent of a royal command," and the government did file another brief criticizing segregation.

He said his argument for gradual desegregation combined with several accidents of history to bring about the right result in the Brown case. One was Chief Justice Vinson's unexpected death in September 1953. Returning for the funeral, Justice Frankfurter was "in high spirits" when Mr. Elman met him at the train station, the lawyer said.

"With that viselike grip of his, he grabbed me by the arm and looking me straight in the eye said, 'Phil, this is the first solid piece of evidence I've ever had that there really is a God,' " Mr. Elman recalled.

The Court unanimously found school segregation unconstitutional on May 17, 1954, in an opinion by the new Chief Justice, Earl Warren.

"The winning formula," Mr. Elman said, "was God plus 'all deliberate speed.' "

BENNY GOODMAN

1909–1986

By John S. Wilson

Benny Goodman became the King of Swing the night of Aug. 21, 1935, at the Palomar Ballroom in Hollywood and led a generation of fans into the Big Band Era in the 1930s. In the following years, he drew throngs to nightclubs and theaters and introduced jazz to Carnegie Hall, toured the world as a representative of a distinctive American culture, was instrumental in breaking the barrier that had kept white and black musical groups separate and developed a band that was a training ground for many other bandleaders, including Harry James, Gene Krupa, Lionel Hampton and Teddy Wilson.

Lionel Hampton, the vibraphonist, recalled that Mr. Goodman was the first major music figure to put black and white musicians together on stage in the 1930s.

"The most important thing that Benny Goodman did," he said, "was to put Teddy Wilson and me in the quartet. It was instant integration. Black people didn't mix with whites then. Benny introduced us as Mr. Lionel Hampton and Mr. Teddy Wilson. He opened the door for Jackie Robinson. He gave music character and style."

In May 1986, Mr. Goodman was awarded an honorary Doctor of Music degree at Columbia University's commencement ceremonies, the latest in a long list of honors that included lifetime achievement awards at the Grammy show in February and from the Kennedy Center in Washington in 1982.

But when he arrived at the Palomar in the summer of 1935 with a 14-piece band that he had formed a year before, there was no aura of success around Mr. Goodman. He was, in fact, so discouraged that he was prepared to give up his band and return to free-lancing. His career as a bandleader had been discouraging. His orchestra had been dismissed from the only two engagements it had had in New York and, after completing a 26-week contract on a network radio program, it had set out on a cross-country trek from New York to California. The reaction to Mr. Goodman's repertory of jazz-based arrangements ranged from bewilderment to antipathy.

"I thought we'd finish the engagement in California and take the train back to New York and that would be it," he recalled many years later. "I'd just be a clarinetist again."

He had tried to adapt to what he had been told the audiences wanted—pop tunes and waltzes. But on this night at the Palomar, starting what he thought would be the band's last engagement, Mr. Goodman decided that if he were going to fail, he would fail on his own terms. He brought out some of his favorite arrangements by Fletcher Henderson—of "Sugar Foot Stomp," "Blue Skies," "Sometimes I'm Happy" and "King Porter Stomp" —which had been his reason for recruiting a band

Retna/David Redfern

that included such jazz specialists as the trumpeter Bunny Berrigan, the pianist Jess Stacy and the drummer Gene Krupa.

As he beat out the tempo for "Sugar Foot Stomp," the band dug into the Henderson arrangement. Then Mr. Berrigan rose up in the trumpet section, playing a crackling solo. As the sound of his horn exploded across the ballroom, a responsive roar went up from the listeners and they surged around the bandstand, cheering.

Mr. Goodman looked around in amazement. He was stunned by the sudden change but, he said later, that roar "was one of the sweetest sounds I ever heard in my life."

This stunning reversal in audience acceptance in Hollywood has been attributed to two factors. Although the "Let's Dance" program was on the air for only three hours, the bands actually played for five hours because, in those pretape days, the program had to be played a second time for the West Coast. By the time young listeners in California heard the Goodman band, it was warmed up and bringing out its best arrangements.

California was also developing a new type of radio entertainer, the disk jockey. The first celebrity disk jockey was Al Jarvis in Los Angeles, who had a program of recordings called "The Make Believe Ballroom" (a title later used in New York by Martin Block). Mr. Jarvis had been plugging the Goodman band's records and, when the band reached the Palomar, the audience, thanks to Mr. Jarvis, knew and was anxious to hear his choice Henderson arrangements.

The crowd's roar would follow him for years at precedent-setting events not only during the swing era, which lasted into the mid-1940s, but also decades later when, in the 1960s, he toured the Soviet Union with his band. He heard that same sound at the "Paramount riot," in March 1937, when he played at the Paramount Theater in New York for the first time.

Teenagers, who had followed the band on radio and had bought its records but could not afford the prices of such places as the Manhattan Room of the Hotel Pennsylvania, where the band usually played, were lined up around the theater at 6 A.M. to get into the morning show for 35 cents. During that day, more than 21,000 people jammed into the theater to bounce deliriously in the seats or shag in the aisles and battle ushers as they made desperate lunges toward the stage.

Mr. Goodman heard the roar again in January 1938, when, looking stiff and uncomfortable in white tie and tails, he led his orchestra in the first jazz concert ever given in Carnegie Hall, for an audience that showed its enthusiasm by beating out the band's rhythm with pounding feet that rocked the old hall's balconies.

There had been big bands that played swinging dance music before Mr. Goodman organized his orchestra. Fletcher Henderson led a groundbreaking black jazz band in the mid-1920s, and in his wake came Duke Ellington, Earl Hines and Jimmie Lunceford, all black. There had also been big, jazz-oriented white bands—Jean Goldkette's Orchestra, the Casa Loma Orchestra and the band in which Mr. Goodman began playing when he was 16 years old, Ben Pollack's Orchestra.

But Mr. Goodman's band arrived at a moment when the public's ear had been attuned by these earlier bands. Mr. Goodman provided a blend of jazz and contemporary popular music that filled this demand so successfully that, for a brief period, jazz and popular music were one and the same. His band also represented a blend of the freedom of jazz improvisation and the discipline that Mr. Goodman demanded from his musicians and, even more, from himself. He practiced his clarinet, his trumpeter Harry James once said, "15 times more than the whole band combined."

"All the time I was with Goodman, he was never satisfied," Jess Stacy, the pianist, once said. "With him, perfection was just around the corner. I figure Benny will die in bed with that damn clarinet."

In rehearsal or performance, Mr. Goodman's musicians dreaded "the ray"—a long, accusatory, poker-faced glare over the top of his glasses at anyone who had committed a false musical move. "If you're interested in music," Mr. Goodman once said, "you can't slop around. I expected things and they had to be done."

This discipline and his feeling for tempo produced performances that audiences that had not been exposed to much jazz found more exciting than the looser, more deeply jazz flavored playing of Mr. Henderson's band, in which many of Mr. Goodman's most popular arrangements originated.

"Benny was very conscious of tempos," Willard Alexander, a booking agent who was one of the band's earliest supporters, once said. "His music had a kind of lilt, a feel. I remember one time we dropped into the Roosevelt Grill when Guy Lombardo was playing there. Benny said to me, 'You know, this Lombardo's got something.' I thought he was putting me on. But he wasn't. 'You know his secret,' Benny said. 'He never plays a song in the wrong tempo.' "

"Benny was a phenomenon," Mr. Alexander went on. "He was not really the biggest band of the Swing Era. Glenn Miller's was. But Benny was the biggest *new* thing in this type of presentation. He was even different physically, contrary to what everybody expected in a band leader. No glamour. No sex appeal. But a well-grounded musician. Once he hit, in came the others in the same pattern. Tommy Dorsey, Glenn Miller. Like Goodman, they were not the typical Hollywood glamour boys. They wore glasses. They had musical experience. They were not young or green. And they had a lot of background."

Mr. Goodman's background went back to Chicago, where he was born on May 30, 1909, the eighth of 12 children in the family of an immigrant tailor who rarely earned more than $20 a week. He was 10 when he got a clarinet on loan from a local synagogue that also provided music lessons. His brother, Harry, the biggest of the Goodman boys, was given a tuba. Freddy, the next largest, received a trumpet. In later years, Benny Goodman wondered what kind of career he might have had "if I had been 20 pounds heavier and two inches taller."

When he was 12, the youth won $5 at a Chicago theater doing an imitation of Ted Lewis, and by the time he was 14 he was making $48 a week playing four nights in the neighborhood band. He also played in the band at Hull House, the celebrated Chicago settlement house, and studied for two years with Franz Shoepp, a clarinetist in the Chicago Symphony, a strict disciplinarian who, Mr. Goodman said, "did more for me musically than anyone I ever knew."

Still wearing short pants, he became part of a clique of teenage jazz musicians that included the cornetist Jimmy McPartland, the saxophonist Bud Freedman and the drummer Dave Tough, who were fascinated by the jazz sounds that flowed through Chicago in the 1920s. He absorbed in his own playing the beautiful tone and sparkling flow of Jimmie Noone, the clarinetist.

Leon Rappolo, clarinetist in the New Orleans Rhythm Kings, who leaned so far back in his chair when he played that he seemed to be lying down, influenced both Mr. Goodman's style and his posture. When Ben Pollack, the drummer in the Rhythm Kings, formed a band in California, he sent back to Chicago for "the kid in the short pants, the kid who played lying down, like Rappolo."

Mr. Goodman was 16 when he joined the Pollack band in Venice, Calif., in 1926. He remained in the band for four years, when Glenn Miller, Jack Teagarden, Bud Freeman, Jimmy McPartland and Mr. Goodman's brother, Harry, were in the band. For the last two years, the Pollack band was based in New York, playing at the Little Club and at the Park Central Hotel (now the Omni Park Hotel) and doubling in the pit of a musical, *Hello, Daddy*.

In the fall of 1929, after some disagreements with Mr. Pollack, Mr. Goodman left the band and began to free-lance on radio and records, making as much as $350 to $400 a week in the early days of the Depression. In 1933, he met a young jazz fan and jazz activist, John Hammond, whose enthusiasm, insight and energy were to have a profound effect on the careers of Mr. Goodman, Billie Holiday, Count Basie and Charlie Christian, the short-lived, precedent-setting electric guitarist who played in Mr. Goodman's band for two years before his death in 1941.

Mr. Hammond, who had a commission to make some jazz records for release in England, asked Mr. Goodman to lead a band for this purpose. Mr. Goodman chose some of his free-lance friends, a group that Mr. Hammond augmented by borrowing Gene Krupa and Jack Teagarden from Mal Hallett's orchestra in Boston.

These records, released as by "Benny Goodman and His Orchestra," planted a seed that took root in 1934, when, with his free-lance income reduced to $40 a week, Mr. Goodman heard that Billy Rose was auditioning bands for a new club called the Music Hall. With the help of Mr. Hammond, he started putting a band together.

"There were practically no hot bands using white musicians at the time," Mr. Goodman later recalled, "and there was a lot of talent around town, both in jobs and laying off, that hadn't gotten the breaks."

His concept was a jazz band made up of young musicians who read well and played in tune, a group with a tight, small-band quality in which every man could be a soloist. The band he and Mr. Hammond assembled included Claude Thornhill, the pianist, who soon returned to studio work, and three musicians who remained with Mr. Goodman through the band's early days of glory—Red Ballard, trombonist; Arthur Rollini (brother of Adrian), saxophonist; and Hymie Schertzer. Mr. Schertzer's alto saxophone later gave the Goodman saxophone section its sheen, but he was hired because Mr. Goodman had heard he would need a violin in his band to accompany the shows at the Music Hall and Mr. Schertzer could play violin as well as saxophone.

Ironically, Mr. Goodman's band was not able to play the routine accompanying music for the Music Hall's vaudeville acts—tumblers, a fire eater, a dog act—to Billy Rose's satisfaction. They were on the verge of being released when a compromise was reached—a second band would play for the shows and Mr. Goodman's band would play for dancing.

Three months later, when the Music Hall's management changed, the band was let go. But before that happened, the band auditioned for a prospective three-hour weekly radio program to be divided among Latin music, "sweet" music and "hot" music. Xavier Cugat had already been signed as the Latin band. Murray Kellner (as Kel Murray) led the "sweet" band. The sponsor, the National Biscuit Company, lined up several "hot" bands and had some of its employees vote on them. Benny Goodman won by one vote.

During the 26 weeks that Mr. Goodman played on this "Let's Dance" program, he had a budget with which to buy eight arrangements a week at $37.50 each. Edgar Sampson's $37.50 arrangement of "Stompin' at the Savoy," played on the first "Let's Dance" broadcast, became one of Mr. Goodman's classics.

Another arranger, Gordon Jenkins, wrote "Goodbye," which became Mr. Goodman's closing theme. He also got his opening signature, "Let's Dance," from the show—a "hot" arrangement of Carl Maria von Weber's "Invitation to the Dance" written by George Bassman, who also provided a Latin version for Mr. Cugat and a "sweet" version for Mr. Kellner.

But the most important collection of arrangements that Mr. Goodman got for his $37.50 came from Fletcher Henderson, who, in 1934, had given up the big band he had led for 11 years. Some of these arrangements had originally been played by the Henderson band. "King Porter Stomp" and "Big John Special" were the first two, providing Mr. Goodman with the basis for the library of what became known as "killer-dillers." But, at Mr. Goodman's urging, Mr. Henderson also wrote arrangements of popular songs that established the melodic and swinging style of the Goodman band.

"Fletcher's ideas were far ahead of anybody else's at the time," Mr. Goodman said. "Without Fletcher, I probably would have had a pretty good band, but it would have been something quite different from what it eventually turned out to be."

Mr. Henderson's insistently swinging scores typify the Goodman band's style. George Simon, in his book *The Big Bands*, described them as "simple, swinging arrangements in which complete sections played with the feeling of a single jazz soloist."

"In addition," Mr. Simon wrote, "Henderson would set off one section against another, rolling saxes versus crisp brass, an approach quite different from the less rhythmic, more lethargic-sounding ensembles of most dance bands."

After the "Let's Dance" program went off the air, Mr. Goodman's band was, inexplicably, booked into the Roosevelt Grill as a summer replacement for Guy Lombardo's "Sweetest Music This Side of Heaven." Mr. Goodman's musicians had scarcely let out their first "hot" blast on opening night at the Roosevelt when they were given their two weeks' notice. The trail of discouragement continued as the band headed west toward California and the sudden turnaround at the Palomar Ballroom.

So, instead of taking the train back to New York, Mr. Goodman stayed at the Palomar for two months. Then the band went to Chicago, where, booked into the Joseph Urban Room of the Congress Hotel, it stayed for six months. In Chicago it was billed for the first time as a "swing" band, with the word in quotes—"as if," Mr. Goodman remarked, "it was something in a foreign language."

The word had been used for years by musicians—Duke Ellington wrote "It Don't Mean a Thing if It Ain't Got That Swing" in 1932. But the general public seized on *swing* as a trendy catchword. However, references to Mr. Goodman as the "King of Swing" made him nervous.

"I didn't know how long it was going to last," he explained, "and I didn't want to be tied down to something people might say was old-fashioned just because they tired of the name in a year or so."

But swing fever was on the rise, and in December 1935 some of Mr. Goodman's fans organized what may have been the first jazz concert. It was advertised as a "Tea Dance" and it was held in the Joseph Urban Room. But it was a sit-down-and-listen affair, and a few people who instinctively tried to dance were booed off the floor. The response was so enthusiastic that another concert was organized for Easter Sunday in 1936. This time Mr. Goodman flew Teddy Wilson, the pianist, out to Chicago from New York.

Less than a year before, Mr. Goodman had jammed with Mr. Wilson at the home of Mildred Bailey, the singer, accompanied on drums by Miss Bailey's cousin, Carl Bellinger. This led to some recordings by a trio made up of Mr. Goodman, Mr. Wilson and Gene Krupa, the Goodman band's drummer, made just before Mr. Goodman's fateful trip to the West Coast. This Chicago concert was the first time the trio performed in public. The performance was so successful that Mr. Goodman decided to keep Mr. Wilson and the trio as a regular part of his troupe.

This created a precedent, quickly copied by other swing bands, of having a small group within the big band. And by making Mr. Wilson, a black, a part of his entourage, Mr. Goodman broke through the color barrier that, until then, had kept white bands white and black bands black. A few months later, while the band was in Hollywood making its first movie, *The Big Broadcast of 1937*, Mr. Goodman heard Lionel Hampton leading a band at the Paradise Café and, after enjoying an after-hours jam session with him, persuaded Mr. Hampton to add his vibraphone to the trio, making it a quartet that was 50 percent black.

For the next four years the Goodman band rode on the crest of Swing Era popularity, despite a brief challenge from another clarinet-playing leader, Artie Shaw. The cheers and shouts of approval were seemingly endless. In 1938, when the band's second film, *Hollywood Hotel*, opened in New York, the *New York Times* film critic, Frank Nugent, reported: "You couldn't hear anything but the audience except when the picture worked its volume to a storm-warning level. It would have taken more than that, though, to override their howling when Mr. Goodman's clarinet came into camera range."

Not long after appearing in the film, Mr. Goodman performed with other jazz musicians in the Broadway musical *Swingin' the Dream*, which opened in 1939.

The eye of the Goodman whirlwind was the Hotel Pennsylvania in New York, where the band spent several months each year. When Mr. Goodman's mother came to hear his band for the first time, she looked around in amazement.

"This is the way he makes a living?" she asked.

In the summer of 1940, despite a steady load of engagements, Mr. Goodman broke up his band to take three months off to undergo surgery for a painful case of sciatica. When he reorganized his band in October of that year, the bulk of the arranging was taken over by Eddie Sauter, a trumpet player who had played and arranged for Red Norvo and who, in the 1950s, would be co-leader of an adventurous band with Bill Finegan. Mr. Finegan was making his reputation as an arranger with Glenn Miller at the very time that Mr. Sauter began arranging for the new Goodman band.

For this 1940s band, Mr. Goodman lured away Duke Ellington's trumpet star, Cootie Williams. He had a brilliant 18-year-old pianist, Mel Powell, and such veterans as Charlie Christian, Dave Tough, Billy Butterfield, Lou McGarity and Georgie Auld. In the opinion of many Goodman fanciers, this band of the early 1940s, less publicized than his band of the 1930s but with Mr. Sauter's provocative arrangements, was the finest of the Benny Goodman bands.

It was during the 1940s also that Mr. Goodman appeared in another Broadway musical, this time with a small group. The show was *Seven Lively Arts*, which opened in December 1944.

Mr. Goodman continued to lead a big band until 1950. After World War II, he tried, briefly, to adapt to the new jazz style—bebop—but soon gave it up, to the relief of proponents of both bebop and swing.

Meanwhile, Mr. Goodman carried on a dalliance with classical music. In 1935 John Hammond, who, despite his devotion to jazz, expressed himself musically by playing viola in classical string quartets, enticed Mr. Goodman to join his quartet in playing the Mozart Clarinet Quintet. It was an intoxicating whiff for the clarinetist.

He subsequently played, and recorded, with the Budapest Quartet, with Joseph Szigeti and with symphony orchestras. He commissioned works by Béla Bartók, Aaron Copland and Paul Hindemith. During the 1940s, he studied with Reginald Kell, a renowned classical clarinetist, learning a new embouchure that required the use of a new set of facial muscles and a change in fingering for which he had his finger calluses surgically removed.

In 1955, *The Benny Goodman Story*, a biographical film, was made; in it Steve Allen played Mr. Goodman, and the producer assembled a band studded with former Goodman sidemen to play the sound track. Through the 1950s, 1960s and 1970s, Goodman formed small groups and big bands sporadically for concerts and tours, concentrating on the hits he had established in the Swing Era.

Mr. Goodman took his music around the world, playing duets with the King of Thailand, a fellow clarinetist. At the 1958 World's Fair in Brussels, his band was regarded as one of the best American exhibits. He took a band to the Soviet Union in 1962 as part of a cultural exchange arrangement, producing a mixture of adulation and controversy, including an impromptu debate on jazz with Premier Nikita S. Khrushchev.

In 1941, Mr. Goodman married Alice Duckworth, the sister of his friend John Hammond. She died in 1979. Mr. Goodman died in his Manhattan apartment of a heart attack on June 12, 1986. He was 77 years old.

HAILE SELASSIE

1892–1975

By Alden Whitman

As a symbol of regal power, His Imperial Majesty the Conquering Lion of the Tribe of Judah, Haile Selassie I, Elect of God, Emperor of Ethiopia, ruled his ancient realm like a medieval autocrat.

Seized in a military coup in March 1975, after almost a year of festering discontent with his regime, Haile Selassie, who was accustomed to Rolls-Royces, was hustled from his spacious palace to an army officer's bungalow in the back seat of a blue Volkswagen. The final confrontation between the aged and frail emperor and the young and robust army men was like a scene from a Verdi opera. Haile Selassie scolded and insulted the officers as insolent, and they, with mounting ire, decided on the spot to take him to a military camp rather than to another palace. And on the way, he was jeered by crowds yelling "Thief! Thief!"

Haile Selassie's troubles began in 1973 with disquiet in the countryside and in the peasant-based army over government attempts to hush up a drought that eventually took 100,000 lives in two northern provinces. The unrest was compounded in February 1974, when mutinies broke out in the military over low pay; and a secessionist guerrilla war in Eritrea complicated the emperor's problems. In the spring and summer, after riots in Addis Ababa, the capital, his absolute power was gradually circumscribed.

Ironically, Haile Selassie initiated the changes that led to his downfall—the military training program that exposed Ethiopian officers to representative institutions in the United States, and Haile Selassie I University, where students learned to think about political economy. The emperor, however, could not seem to adapt to new concepts, and he lost touch with his subjects in recent years, showing more affection for his pet cheetahs and dogs, diplomats said, than for his human entourage.

In the working out of Haile Selassie's cautious reforms, a thin layer of technocrats and intellectuals was created, a group that perceived the country far differently than the tradition-bound emperor did. The reform process, moreover, created a dependency on the United States, which equipped the army and which drew Ethiopia into the periphery of superpower politics.

This came about because of the country's strategic position on the Red Sea. The Soviet Union, likewise alert to geopolitics, equipped the military forces of Somalia, which also lies on the Red Sea and abuts Ethiopia on the southeast. For years the two countries quarreled over their border, adding to tensions inside both nations.

The combination of circumstances that led to Haile Selassie's downfall tended to obscure his accomplishments in leading a largely illiterate, rural and feudal country with 2,000 languages and dia-

AP/WIDE WORLD

The Emperor in dress uniform in 1935

lects into the 19th, if not the 20th, century. And it also shadowed his contributions to African unity. An African who met the emperor at the United Nations Security Council session in Addis Ababa in 1972 summed up a widespread feeling when he said: "Haile Selassie is one of the world's great men. He did a lot for his country and early became a respected voice for Africa and for the third world."

If the pace of change was snailish under the emperor, it was deliberately so. "We must make progress slowly so as to preserve the progress we have already made," he said frequently of his reign, in which slavery was legally abolished and limited democratic structures instituted.

But he was also regarded as one who ruled too strictly by prerogative for the benefit of his family and friends. And at his ouster he was popularly accused as an exploiter who had secretly sent billions of dollars to private bank accounts abroad.

The drama of his departure from power and the intrigues that preceded it were kin to the events of his long life.

Coming to power in a palace coup and, later, discomfiting his enemies in battle, Haile Selassie was driven into exile by the troops of Fascist Italy after the civilized world had spurned his eloquent and poignant appeals for help.

Restored to his capital in World War II, he obtained for Ethiopia a coastline on the Red Sea, skillfully courted foreign economic aid, strove to improve education, quashed an attempted coup and, despite the anachronisms of his person and the archaisms of his country, emerged as an elder statesman of African anticolonialism.

The prestige and power of Haile Selassie, waxing over more than a half century, made him larger than life. With a splendid sense of theater, he lived up to, and even surpassed, the role in which he was cast.

Once the emperor was distributing gifts to men who served the Ethiopian cause in World War II. After he had finished, one man approached him and complained that he had been overlooked.

"You lie," Haile Selassie replied, calling the petitioner by name and citing the exact place, day and hour at which he had been rewarded for obtaining a string of mules for the army.

The man flushed and trembled, for he had never suspected that the emperor would remember, since scores of others had been honored at the same time. He started to inch away, but the emperor summoned him back and tossed him a bundle of bank notes anyway.

Such magnificent and munificent gestures tended to obscure the fact that the emperor looked emaciated and was only 5 feet 4 inches tall. But he managed to convey an imposing presence and an air of cold command whether he was seated at his desk in military uniform with a blazing array of decorations across his chest; or whether he was standing, caped, on the rostrum of the League of Nations; or whether, seated bolt unright in his green or maroon Rolls-Royce, he was motoring through the dusty streets of Addis Ababa as his subjects lay prostrate while he passed.

What helped to make Haile Selassie so physically imposing was his bearded and dark-complexioned face, his aquiline nose over full lips and his steady, penetrating black eyes. It was a mien both melancholy and fearsome, the visage of one who ruled by the precepts of John Stuart Mill as well as by those of Niccolo Machiavelli, by compassion as well as cruelty, for he could be generous to loyal subordinates, or he could hang the rebellious, or he could keep a rival imprisoned in golden chains.

The limit of his emotional expression was a sad smile, so enigmatic that his true feelings seemed deeply mysterious.

To many in the West, especially in the United States, Haile Selassie was a storied figure. He was the 225th emperor of Ethiopia in a line that he traced to Menelik I, who was credited with being the child of King Solomon and the Queen of Sheba, identified in Ethiopia as Queen Makeda. (The constitution of 1955 specified Haile Selassie's direct descent from Menelik I.)

Unbending on protocol and punctilio, the emperor, in his public appearances, recalled the splendor and opulence of Suleiman the Magnificent or Louis XIV, with the difference that he lived and worked in a modern atmosphere and journeyed abroad in a commandeered Ethiopian Airlines plane. He once had three palaces; but after he transformed the Gueneteleul Palace into the Haile Selassie I University in 1960, he was reduced to a palace to live in—the Jubilee—and one to work in—the Ghibi.

Around the clock, he was guarded by lions and cheetahs, protected by imperial bodyguards, trailed by his pet papillon dogs, flanked by a multitude of chamberlains and flunkies and sustained by a tradition of reverence for his person. He took seriously the doctrine of the divine right of kings, and he never allowed his subjects to forget that he considered himself the Elect of God. Indeed, he combined in his person the temporal sovereignty of the state and the leadership of the Ethiopian Orthodox Church, the country's established church.

In moments of relaxation—and these were few, for he was an extraordinarily hardworking monarch—Haile Selassie displayed considerable charm. He spoke softly (in halting English if necessary), and he had a mind well furnished with small talk derived from his daily scrutiny of the world press and from viewing films and newsreels. He absorbed information from his extensive travels about the world. His talk, though light, was not likely to be gay or mirth-provoking or quotable. He referred to himself always with the imperial "we."

In his latter years he was a lonely man beneath the panoply of office. He had outlived his wife of 50 years, who died in 1962, and four of his six children. He had, though, more than a dozen grandchildren and some great-grandchildren, with whom he liked to surround himself at dinner.

In African affairs, Haile Selassie's courage and his tenacity as a nationalist gave him a position of leadership among such anticolonialist statesmen as Jomo Kenyatta of Kenya, Sekou Touré of Guinea and Kenneth Kaunda of Zambia. Despite his autocratic rule, the emperor represented independence from overt foreign domination as well as the artful acquisition of foreign economic aid. It was Haile Selassie who convoked the first meeting of the Organization of African Unity in 1963 and devised the charter for the 38-nation bloc. Its headquarters are in Addis Ababa.

Moreover, at Haile Selassie's suggestion a United Nations Economic Commission for Africa was set up. Its secretariat is also in Addis Ababa, in a lavish $1.75-million building erected at the emperor's bidding.

In Ethiopia, he was an object of veneration to the masses of people until his overthrow, but to the new urban elite the centralization of authority in his person and the tepidity of reform had been unpalatable for some time. The two constitutions the emperor granted, one in 1931 and the other in 1955, were both criticized because the cabinet was responsible to Haile Selassie and because there was no provision for political parties.

Economic reform, especially changes in the age-old system of land tenure, was far too slow, critics said, with the result that the country's agriculture and animal husbandry—the mainstays of its economy—were operated on a primitive level. Coffee, cereals and beans were the main cash crops; meat and animal products also contributed heavily to the gross national product. Manufacturing and power, on the other hand, accounted for only 3 percent of the GNP.

Haile Selassie's kingdom was a wild and sprawling country of 455,000 square miles (about the size of Texas, Louisiana, Arkansas and Oklahoma combined) and 26 million people (an accepted guess in the absence of any census). There were a score of tribes, at least one so primitive that its men castrated their enemies to win favor with an intended bride. There were many languages, but Amharic, the official tongue, was spoken in some degree by only 50 percent of the people.

Although the state religion was a Monophysite Christianity, a substantial portion of the population, perhaps 40 percent, was Moslem. In addition, there were Animists and Jews. The multiplicity of religions and customs accented Ethiopia's lack of homogeneity and its general backwardness, for it was a country without a developed highway or rail system and without organized health and social services. The bulk of the people lived in mud and straw huts, even in Addis Ababa.

In the capital, the contrast between the old and the new was especially striking, for its few modern buildings cast their shadow on the far more numerous ancient structures that included, until a few years ago, the Imperial Brothel and the square in which public hangings were carried out.

Of the dominant Amhara tribe, Haile Selassie was born in Ejarsa Gora, in a mud and wattle house, on July 23, 1892. He was named Lij Tafari Makonnen and he was the only legitimate son of Ras Makonnen, governor of Harar, to survive infancy.

The boy's father was a cousin and close ally of Emperor Menelik II, who was without a legitimate direct male heir. When Ras Makonnen died in 1906, his son, who already had a rudimentary education and spoke French, was summoned to the court at Addis Ababa, where he was further schooled both in book learning and in the devious intrigues of Menelik's household.

Tafari was passed over on the death of Menelik II in 1913 in favor of the emperor's grandson Lij Yasu, a handsome, dissolute and athletic young man. Tafari, meantime, had married Lij Yasu's niece, Waizero Menen, after her divorce, and had attained practical experience in government as governor of a province.

Lij Yasu, who was never formally crowned, was converted to Islam and excommunicated by the Ethiopian church. And in the palace coup that followed, Tafari made himself the heir presumptive to the throne and regent for Zauditu, a daughter of Menelik, who was proclaimed empress.

Emerging as the strongman, Tafari got rid of the husband of the empress, putting her under his control, and, capturing Lij Yasu, imprisoned him for the rest of his life. The golden chains in which he was held were not so confining, however, as to prevent him from enjoying the variety of women with whom Tafari plied him.

With his other warlord enemies among the nobles Tafari was less indulgent. "He creeps like a mouse, but he has the jaws of a lion," one of them said. By force of arms and executions he brought an end to the chaos that threatened to envelop Ethiopia and turned his country's eyes ever so slightly toward the outside world.

In 1923 Tafari had the kingdom accepted as a member of the League of Nations. He acted in the hope that league membership would exempt Ethiopia from the colonial ambitions of other countries.

In the following year Tafari, having bulwarked his power at home, undertook an extensive foreign tour. "We need European progress," he explained, "only because we are surrounded by it."

Everywhere he went in Europe, Tafari, with his six lions and four zebras and 30 attendants, created a lasting impression. His modern outlook won him friends; so did his assertions that Ethiopia required innovation and development.

One fruit of his trip was the Tafari Makonnen School, which he founded and staffed with European teachers. (Education was one of the chief interests of Tafari when he became emperor, and he established primary and secondary schools throughout the country as well as the Haile Selassie I University. Even so, at the end of his reign, only 500,000 school-age children of a potential 3.2 million were enrolled.)

Friction between the empress and her regent grew in the late 1920s. Believing in 1928 that she had the upper hand, the empress attempted a coup, but she was thwarted by the cunning and alertness of Tafari, who forced her to crown him King of Ethiopia. Two years later, after her mysterious death, Tafari was crowned emperor and took the name of Haile Selassie, which means "Power of the Holy Trinity."

The coronation, on Nov. 2, 1930, was an event of

unparalleled sumptuousness in a city that, one observer said, "resembled a shantytown with wedding-cake trimmings." There were only one or two buildings of more than one story, the rest being a tumbled mass of mud huts. Distinguished foreign delegations mingled with the city's 20,000 prostitutes.

Describing the coronation, Leonard Mosley wrote in his book, *Haile Selassie: The Conquering Lion*: "Shortly before dawn on the morning of Nov. 2, before the world press, the foreign guests and a great concourse of rases [nobles] in their lion's manes and most resplendent robes, Abuna Kyril [the archbishop] anointed the head of Haile Selassie and placed on it the triple crown of Ethiopia.

"Simultaneously, the rases put on their coronets, then made their obeisances to him, after which the celebratory shooting, shouting, loolooing, feasting, dancing and drinking broke out all over the city."

The emperor's initial ventures into reform, in which he changed the status of his people from chattels of the nobles into subjects of the state, culminated in a constitution in 1931. Although its limits on the royal prerogative were negligible, it was a step away from feudalism.

At the same time, administrative changes improved the civil service, and a tax system was introduced. Road building and other public works were undertaken. Moreover, several edicts against slavery were promulgated, if not enforced. Virtually total abolition was not accomplished until 1964.

In 1934 Benito Mussolini, the dictator of Fascist Italy, moved against Ethiopia in a border incident. His pretense, that of bringing civilization to a backward country, concealed Italian imperial ambitions for an African colony to supplement Italian Somaliland and Eritrea. In the diplomatic footwork that followed the border clash, the emperor referred the dispute to the League of Nations for mediation; but Britain and France gave Mussolini to understand that he could expect a free hand in Ethiopia.

"Could we not have called Musso's bluff and at least postponed this war?" Winston Churchill asked later. "The answer I'm sure is yes. We built Musso into a great power."

Deserted by Britain and France, Ethiopia fell to Italian arms shortly after the Fascist invasion began on Oct. 2, 1935. By April 1936 the conflict ("This isn't a war, it isn't even a slaughter," a British eyewitness said. "It's the torture of tens of thousands of men, women and children with bombs and poison gas") was over. On May 2 Haile Selassie went into exile.

The emperor went first to Jerusalem to pray, and then to Britain as a private guest. Still convinced that the League could be rallied to his cause, he appealed to it and its members not to recognize the Italian conquest. Shamed, the League permitted him to state his case, and his appearance before the delegates assembled in Geneva on June 30, 1936, was a moment in history that few who witnessed it ever forgot.

Aloof, dignified, gazing in contempt at the Fascist journalists who shouted at him, and looking directly at the uneasy, shuffling delegates, he began his speech in Amharic by saying: "I, Haile Selassie I, Emperor of Ethiopia, am here today to claim that justice that is due to my people and the assistance promised to it eight months ago by 52 nations who asserted that an act of aggression had been committed in violation of international treaties."

After reciting the principal events of the war and his betrayal by the big powers, he continued: "I assert that the issue before the Assembly today is not merely a question of the settlement in the matter of Italian aggression. It is a question of collective security; of the very existence of the League; of the trust placed by states in international treaties; of the value of promises made to small states that their integrity and independence shall be respected and assured. . . .

"In a word, it is international morality that is at stake. . . .

"Outside of the Kingdom of God, there is not on this earth any nation that is higher than any other. If a strong government finds that it can, with impunity, destroy a weak people, then the hour has struck for that weak people to appeal to the League of Nations to give its judgment in all freedom. God and history will remember your judgment.

"Placed by the aggressor face to face with the accomplished fact, are states going to set up the terrible precedent of bowing before force?

"I ask the great powers, who have promised the guarantee of collective security to small states—those small states over whom hangs the threat that they may one day suffer the fate of Ethiopia: What measures do they intend to take? . . . What answer am I to take back to my people?"

As Haile Selassie concluded what was certainly his saddest (and greatest) hour and moved from the tribunal to a scatter of embarrassed applause, he murmured: "It is us today. It will be you tomorrow."

In practical terms the emperor's speech was a magnificent but futile gesture, for one by one the powers recognized the Italian regime in East Africa. Haile Selassie, meantime, went to live as an unwanted guest in Bath, England; he was so broke that the local bookshop stopped his credit.

The emperor was rescued from this seedy oblivion on May 10, 1940, when Italy entered World War II as an enemy of Britain. Churchill, long a friend, had him flown incognito, as Mr. Strong, to Africa. Landing at Alexandria, he spent the night in the men's room of the Italian Yacht Club before going on to Khartoum in the Sudan. There he helped to organize an army of liberation with the aid of Orde Wingate, one of the most picturesque British officers in the war.

The result of these exertions was that Haile Selassie returned to his country on Jan. 20, 1941, and made his state entry into Addis Ababa on May 5 in the back of an Alfa Romeo motorcar. It was five years to the day since the Italians had entered the city. The country remained under British administration, however, until Jan. 31, 1942, when London recognized Ethiopia as a sovereign state.

In the years that followed the restoration, Haile Selassie enhanced his personal power while acting slowly to solve the country's grave economic and social problems. Some advance in education was also made, for 200 school buildings were put up between 1942 and 1952. In this period, too, a new force was reaching manhood in the kingdom—the educated elite whose travels and schooling abroad made them restive over their nation's introversions.

Partly as the result of pressure from this group and partly because of the rising tide of anticolonialism in Africa, Haile Selassie granted a new constitution in 1955. It promised his subjects equal rights under the law, plus a vote; but it also retained his traditional prerogatives. One clause read: "By virtue of His Imperial Blood as well as by the anointing which He has received, the person of the Emperor is sacred. His dignity is inviolable and His Power indisputable. He is, consequently, entitled to all the honors due Him in accordance with tradition and the present Constitution. Anyone so bold as to seek to injure the Emperor will be punished."

The surface placidity of Ethiopia was shattered in 1960, when Haile Selassie was absent on a state trip to Brazil. The imperial bodyguard mutinied and some members of the royal family, including Crown Prince Asfa Wossen, joined an attempt to dethrone the emperor and promote faster social and economic progress. The emperor returned to Addis Ababa, crushed the revolt and had the commander of the bodyguard publicly hanged for treason. The crown prince was put out of favor, from which he finally emerged, but slowly.

The attempted coup led the emperor to try to communicate more directly with his subjects in radio talks and to indicate what he was doing for them in his paternal fashion.

One such advance was foreign aid. In the final years of his reign he contrived to obtain help from diverse sources without creating crosscurrents among the donors. Italy and Yugoslavia built dams for him; the Addis Ababa airport was constructed by the United States; the Soviet Union put up a polytechnic institute on the shores of Lake Tana, source of the Blue Nile.

The emperor much enjoyed state visits—to Marshal Tito of Yugoslavia, to Queen Elizabeth II of Britain, to the United States, where he was the guest of Presidents Truman, Eisenhower, Kennedy, Johnson and Nixon. In all, he traveled to more than 60 countries, including China, where he was received in 1971 by Mao Zedong.

HO CHI MINH

1890–1969

By Alden Whitman

Among 20th-century statesmen, Ho Chi Minh was remarkable both for the tenacity and patience with which he pursued his goal of Vietnamese independence and for his success in blending Communism with nationalism.

From his youth Ho espoused freedom for the French colony of Vietnam. He persevered through years when his chances of attaining his objective were so minuscule as to seem ridiculous. Ultimately, he organized the defeat of the French in 1954 in the historic battle of Dienbienphu. This battle, a triumph of guerrilla strategy, came nine years after he was named president of the Democratic Republic of Vietnam.

After the supposed temporary division of Vietnam at the 17th parallel by the Geneva Agreement of 1954 and after that division became hardened by United States support of Ngo Dinh Diem in the South, Ho led his countrymen in the North against the onslaughts of American military might. In the war, Ho's capital of Hanoi, among other cities, was repeatedly bombed by American planes.

At the same time Ho was an inspiration for the National Liberation Front, or Vietcong, which operated in South Vietnam in the long, bloody and costly conflict against the Saigon regime and its American allies.

In the war, in which the United States became increasingly involved, especially after 1964, Ho maintained an exquisite balance in his relations with the Soviet Union and the People's Republic of China. These Communist countries, at ideological sword's points, were Ho's principal suppliers of food and war goods. It was a measure of his diplomacy that he kept on friendly terms with each.*

To the 19 million people north of the 17th parallel and to other millions below it, the small, frail, ivorylike figure of Ho, with its long ascetic face, straggly goatee, sunken cheeks and luminous eyes, was that of a patriarch, the George Washington of his nation. Although his name was not attached to public squares, buildings, factories, airports or monuments, his magnetism was undoubted, as was the affection that the average citizen had for him.

He was universally called "Uncle Ho," a sobriquet also used in the North Vietnamese press. Before the exigencies of war confined him to official duties, Ho regularly visited villages and towns. Simply clad, he was especially fond of dropping into schools and chatting with the children. Westerners who knew him were convinced that, whatever his guile in larger political matters, there was no pose in his expressions of feeling for the common people.

---

* In 1979 relations between China and Vietnam became so strained that they exploded into vicious fighting along the 490-mile China-Vietnam border. Relations still remain poor.

Camera Press

Ho Chi Minh greeting children in Tam Son in 1960

Indeed, Ho's personal popularity was such that it was generally conceded, even by many of his political foes, that Vietnam would have been unified under his leadership had the countrywide elections pledged at Geneva taken place. As it was, major segments of South Vietnam were effectively controlled by the National Liberation Front despite the presence of hundreds of thousands of American troops.

Intelligent, resourceful and dedicated, though ruthless, Ho created a favorable impression on many of those who dealt with him. One such was Harry Ashmore of the Center for the Study of Democratic Institutions and former editor of the *Arkansas Gazette*.

Mr. Ashmore and the late William C. Baggs, editor of the *Miami News*, were among the last Americans to talk with Ho at length when they visited Hanoi in early 1967.

"Ho was a courtly, urbane, highly sophisticated man with a gentle manner and without personal venom," Mr. Ashmore recalled in an interview. At the meeting Ho was dressed in his characteristic high-necked white pajamalike garment, called a *cunao*, and he wore open-toed rubber sandals. He chain-smoked cigarettes, American-made Salems.

Their hour-long conversation started out in Vietnamese with an interpreter, Mr. Ashmore said, but soon shifted to English. Ho astonished Mr. Ashmore by his adeptness in English, which was one of several languages—the principal others were Chinese, French, German and Russian—in which he was fluent.

At one point Ho reminded Mr. Ashmore and Mr. Baggs that he had once been in the United States. "I think I know the American people," Ho said, "and I don't understand how they can support their involvement in this war. Is the Statue of Liberty standing on her head?"

This was a rhetorical question that Ho also posed to other Americans in an effort to point up what to his mind was an inconsistency: a colonial people who had gained independence in a revolution were fighting to suppress the independence of another colonial people.

Ho's knowledge of American history was keen, and he put it to advantage in the summer of 1945, when he was writing the Declaration of Independence of the Democratic Republic of Vietnam. He remembered the contents of the American Declaration of Independence, but not its precise wording. From an American military mission then working with him he tried in vain to obtain a copy of the document, and when none could supply it Ho paraphrased it out of his recollections.

Thus his declaration begins, "All men are created equal; they are endowed by their Creator with certain inalienable Rights; among these are Life, Liberty, and the pursuit of Happiness." After explaining that this meant that "all the peoples on the earth are equal from birth, all the peoples have a right to live, to be happy and free," Ho went on to enumerate, in the manner of the American declaration, the grievances of his people and to proclaim their independence.

Apart from Americans, Ho struck a spark with many others who came in contact with him over the years. "Extraordinarily likable and friendly" was the description of Jawaharlal Nehru, the Indian leader. Paul Mus, the French Orientalist who conducted delicate talks with Ho in 1946 and 1947, found him an "intransigent and incorruptible revolutionary, à la Saint Just."

A French naval commander who observed the slender Vietnamese for the three weeks he was a ship's passenger concluded that Ho was an "intelligent and charming man who is also a passionate idealist entirely devoted to the cause he has espoused" and a person with "naive faith in the politico-social slogans of our times and, generally, in everything that is printed."

Ho was an enormously pragmatic Communist, a doer rather than a theoretician. His speeches and articles were brought together in a four-volume *Selected Works of Ho Chi Minh*, issued in Hanoi between 1960 and 1962. Bernard B. Fall, an American authority on Vietnam, published a collection of these in English in 1967 under the title *Ho Chi Minh on Revolution*. They are simply and clearly worded documents, most of them agitational or polemical in nature and hardly likely to add to the body of Marxist doctrine.

Like Mao Zedong, Ho composed poetry, some of it considered quite affecting. One of his poems, written when he was a prisoner of the Chinese Nationalists in 1942–43, is called "Autumn Night" and reads (in translation by Aileen Palmer):

In front of the gate, the guard stands with his rifle.
Above, untidy clouds are carrying away the moon.
The bedbugs are swarming around like army tanks on maneuvers,
While the mosquitoes form squadrons, attacking like fighter planes.
My heart travels a thousand li *toward my native land.*
My dream intertwines with sadness like a skein of a thousand threads.
Innocent, I have now endured a whole year in prison.
Using my tears for ink, I turn my thoughts into verses.

Ho's rise to power and world eminence was not a fully documented story. On the contrary, its details at some crucial points are imprecise. This led at one time to the suspicion that there were two Hos, a notion that was discounted by the French Sûreté when it compared photographs of the early and the late Ho.

One explanation for the confusion is that Ho used about a dozen aliases, of which Ho Chi Minh (which can be translated as Ho, the Shedder of Light) was but one. Another was Ho's own reluctance to disclose biographical information. "You know, I am an old man, and an old man likes to hold on to his little mysteries," he told Mr. Fall. With a twinkle, he continued, "Wait until I'm dead. Then you can write about me all you want."

Nonetheless, Mr. Fall reported, before he left Hanoi he received a brief, unsigned summary of Ho's life "obviously delivered on the old man's instructions."

Despite Ho's apparent self-effacement, he did have a touch of personal vanity. Mr. Fall recalled having shown the Vietnamese leader a sketch of him by Mrs. Fall. "Yes, that is very good. That looks very much like me," Ho exclaimed. He took a bouquet of flowers from a nearby table and, handing it to Mr. Fall, said: "Tell her for me that the drawing is very good and give her the bouquet and kiss her on both cheeks for me."

Although there is some uncertainty over Ho's birthdate, the most reliable evidence indicates he was born May 19, 1890, in Kimlien, a village in Nghe-An Province in central Vietnam. Many sources give his true name as Nguyen Ai Quoc, or Nguyen the Patriot. However, Wilfred Burchett, an Australian-born correspondent who knew Ho well, believes (and it is now generally accepted) that Ho's birth name was Nguyen Tat Thanh.

He was said to be the youngest of three children. His father was only slightly better off than the rice peasants of the area, but he was apparently a man of some determination, for by rote learning he passed examinations that gave him a job in the imperial administration just when French rule was beginning.

An ardent nationalist, Ho's father refused to learn French, the language of the conquerors of his country, and joined anti-French secret societies. Young Ho got his first underground experience as his father's messenger in the anti-French network. Shortly, the father lost his government job and became a healer, dispensing traditional Oriental potions.

Ho's mother was believed to have been of peasant origin, but he never spoke of her.

Ho received his basic education from his father and from the village school, going on to a few years of high school at the Lycée Quoc-Hoc in the old imperial capital of Hue. This institution, founded by the father of Ngo Dinh Diem, was designed to perpetuate Vietnamese national traditions. It had a distinguished roster of graduates that included Vo Nguyen Giap, the guerrilla general, and Pham Van Dong, former premier of North Vietnam.

Ho left the school in 1910 without a diploma and taught briefly at a private institution in a South Annam fishing town. It was while he was there, according to now accepted sources, that he decided to go to Europe. As a step toward that goal, he went to a trade school in Saigon in the summer of 1911 where he learned the duties of a kitchen boy and pastry cook's helper, skills in demand by Europeans of that day.

His training enabled him to sign aboard the *Latouche-Treville* as a kitchen boy, a job so menial that he worked under the alias Ba. In his travels, he visited Marseilles and ports in Africa and North America.

Explaining the crucial significance of these voyages for Ho's education as a revolutionary, Mr. Fall wrote in *The Two Vietnams*: "His contacts with the white colonizers on their home grounds shattered any of his illusions as to their 'superiority,' and his association with sailors from Brittany, Cornwall and the Frisian Islands—as illiterate and superstitious as the most backward Vietnamese rice farmer—did the rest.

"Ho still likes to tell the story of the arrival of his ship at an African port where, he claims, natives were compelled to jump into the shark-infested waters to secure the moorings of the vessel and were killed by the sharks under the indifferent eyes of passengers and crew.

"But his contacts with Europe also brought him the revelation of his own personal worth and dignity; when he went ashore in Europe in a Western suit, whites, for the first time in his life, addressed him as 'monsieur,' instead of using the deprecating 'tu,' reserved in France for children but used in Indochina by Frenchmen when addressing natives, no matter how educated."

In his years at sea, Ho read widely—Shakespeare, Tolstoy, Marx, Zola. He was even then, according to later accounts, an ascetic and something of a puritan, who was offended when prostitutes clambered aboard his ship in Marseilles. "Why don't the French civilize their own people before they pretend to civilize us?" he is said to have remarked.

(Ho, incidentally, is believed to have been a bachelor, although the record on this point is far from clear.)

With the advent of World War I, Ho went to live in London, where he worked as a snow shoveler and as a cook's helper under Escoffier, the master chef, at the Carlton Hotel. Escoffier, it is said, promoted Ho to a job in the pastry kitchen and wanted to teach him the art of cuisine. However that may be, the 24-year-old Vietnamese was more interested in politics. He joined the Overseas Workers Association, composed mostly of Asians, and agitated for, among other things, Irish independence.

Sometime during the war, Ho gave up the Carlton's kitchen for the sea and journeyed to the United States. He is believed to have lived in Harlem for a while. Ho himself often referred to his American visit, although he was hazy about the details. According to his close associate, Pham Van Dong, what impressed Ho in the United States were "the barbarities and ugliness of American capitalism, the Ku Klux Klan mobs, the lynching of Negroes."

Out of Ho's American experiences came a pamphlet, issued in Moscow in 1924, called *"La Race Noire"* ("The Black Race"), which assailed racial practices in America and Europe.

About 1918 Ho returned to France and lived in a tiny flat in the Montmartre section of Paris, eking out a living by retouching photos under the name of Nguyen Ai Quoc.

At the Versailles Peace Conference of 1919 Ho emerged as a self-appointed spokesman for his native land. Seeing in Woodrow Wilson's proposal for self-determination of peoples the possibility of Vietnam's independence, Ho, dressed in a hired black suit and bowler hat, traveled to the Palace of Versailles to present his case. He was, of course, not received, although he offered a program for Vietnam. Its proposals did not include independence, but basic freedoms and equality between the French rulers and the native population.

Whatever hopes Ho may have held for French liberation of Vietnam were destroyed in his mind by the failure of the Versailles Conference to settle colonial issues. His faith was now transferred to Socialist action. Indeed, his first recorded speech was at a congress of the French Socialist party in 1920, and it was a plea not for world revolution but "against the imperialists who have committed abhorrent crimes on my native land." He bid the party "act practically to support the oppressed natives."

Immediately afterward Ho became, fatefully, a founding member of the French Communist party because he considered that the Socialists were equivocating on the colonial issue whereas the Communists were willing to promote national liberation.

"I don't understand a thing about strategy, tactics and all the other big words you use," he told the delegates, "but I understand well one single thing: The Third International concerns itself a great deal with the colonial question. Its delegates promise to help the oppressed colonial peoples to regain their liberty and independence. The adherents of the Second International have not said a word about the fate of the colonial areas."

With his decision to join the Communists, Ho's career took a marked turn. For one thing, he became the French party's resident expert on colonial affairs and edited *Le Paria* (*The Outcast*), the weekly paper of the Intercolonial Union, which he was instrumental in founding in 1921.

For another thing, the fragile-looking Ho became an orator of sorts, traveling around France to speak to throngs of Vietnamese soldiers and war workers who were awaiting repatriation.

In addition, Ho gravitated to Moscow, the nerve center of world Communism. He went there first in 1922 for the Fourth Comintern Congress, where he met Lenin and became a member of the Comintern's Southeast Asia Bureau. By all accounts, Ho was vocal and energetic, meeting all the reigning Communists and helping to organize the Krestintern, or Peasant International, for revolutionary work among colonial peoples.

After a brief sojourn in France, Ho was back in Moscow, his base for many years thereafter. He attended the University of the Toilers of the East, receiving formal training in Marxism and the techniques of agitation and propaganda.

Following his studies in Moscow, Ho was dispatched to Canton, China, in 1925 as an interpreter for Michael Borodin, one of the leaders of the Soviet mission to help Chiang Kai-shek, then in Communist favor as an heir of Sun Yat-sen. Once in Canton, Ho set about to spread the spirit of revolution in the Far East. He organized Vietnamese refugees into the Vietnam Revolutionary Youth Association and set up the League of Oppressed Peoples of Asia, which soon became the South Seas Communist party, the forerunner of various national Communist groups, including Ho's own Indochinese Communist party of 1930.

For two years, until July 1927, when Chiang turned on his Communist allies, Ho sent apt Vietnamese to Chiang's military school at Huangpu while conducting a crash training course in political agitation for his compatriots.

After the Chiang-Communist break, Ho fled to Moscow by way of the Gobi. His life immediately thereafter is not clear, but it is believed that he lived in Berlin for a time and traveled in Belgium, Switzerland and Italy, using a variety of aliases and passports.

After 1928 Ho turned up in eastern Thailand, disguised as a shaven-headed Buddhist monk. He traveled among Vietnamese exiles and organized political groups; he published newspapers that were smuggled over the border into Vietnam.

In that same year a peasant rebellion erupted in Vietnam, which the Communists backed. On its suppression by the French, Ho was sentenced to death in absentia. At the time he was in a British jail in Hong Kong, having been arrested there in 1931 for subversive activities.

The French sought his extradition, but Ho argued that he was a political refugee and not subject to extradition. The case, which was handled in London by Sir Stafford Cripps in a plea to the Privy Council, was decided for Ho. He was released, and fled Hong Kong in disguise (this time as a Chinese merchant) and made his way back to Moscow.

There he attended Communist schools—the Institute for National and Colonial Questions and the celebrated Lenin School. He was, however, back in China in 1938, now as a communications operator with Mao's renowned Eighth Route Army. Subsequently, he found his way south and entered Vietnam in 1940 for the first time in 30 years.

The timing was a masterstroke, for the Japanese, virtually unopposed, had taken effective control of the Indochinese Peninsula and the French administrators, most of them Vichy adherents, agreed to cooperate with the Japanese. With great daring and imagination, Ho took advantage of World War II to piece together a coalition of Vietnamese nationalists and Communists into what was called the Vietminh, or Independence Front.

The Vietminh created a 10,000-man guerrilla force, "Men in Black," that battled the Japanese in the jungles with notable success.

Ho's actions projected him onto the world scene as the leading Vietnamese nationalist and as an ally of the United States against the Japanese. "I was a Communist," he said then, "but I am no longer one. I am a member of the Vietnamese family, nothing else."

In 1942 Ho was sent to Kunming, reportedly at the request of his American military aides. He was arrested there by Chiang Kai-shek's men and jailed until September 1943, when he was released, it has been said, by American request.

On his release, according to Mr. Fall, Ho cooperated with a Chinese Nationalist general in forming a wide Vietnamese freedom group. One result of this was that in 1944 Ho accepted a portfolio in the provisional republican government of Vietnam. That government was largely a paper affair, but it permitted Ho to court vigorously the American Office of Strategic Services. Thus when Ho's Vietminh took over Hanoi in 1945, senior American military officials were in his entourage. It was in this period that he took the name Ho Chi Minh.

With the end of World War II, Ho proclaimed the independence of Vietnam, but it took nine years for his declaration to become an effective fact. First, under the Big Three Agreement at Potsdam, the Chinese Nationalists occupied Hanoi and the northern sector of Vietnam. Second, the French (in British ships) arrived to reclaim Saigon and the southern segment of the country. And third, Ho's nationalist coalition was strained under pressure of these events.

Forming a new guerrilla force around the Vietminh, Ho and his colleagues, according to most accounts, dealt summarily with dissidents unwilling to fight in Ho's fashion for independence. Assassinations were frequently reported. Meantime, as the Chinese withdrew from the north and the French advanced from the south, Ho negotiated with the French to save his nationalist regime.

In a compromise that Ho worked out in Paris in 1946, he agreed to let the Democratic Republic of Vietnam become a part of the French Union as a free state within the Indochina federation. The French recognized Ho as chief of state and promised a plebiscite in the south on the question of a unified Vietnam under Ho.

By the start of 1947, the agreement had broken down, and Ho's men were fighting the French army. The Vietminh guerrillas held the jungles and the villages, the French the cities. For seven years the war raged as Ho's forces gathered strength, squeezing the French more and more. For most of this time, Ho was diplomatically isolated, for he was not recognized by Communist China or the Soviet

Union until his victory over the French was virtually assured.

In an effort to shore up their political forces, the French resurrected Bao Dai, the puppet of the Japanese who held the title of emperor. Corrupt and pleasure-loving, he soon moved with his mistresses to France, leaving a weak and splintered regime in Saigon.

This, of course, proved no support for the French army, which was also sapped by General Giap's guerrilla tactics. Finally, on May 8, 1954, the French forces were decisively defeated at Dienbienphu. The Indochina war ended officially in July at a cost to the French of 172,000 casualties and to the Vietminh of perhaps three times that many.

The cease-fire accord was signed in Geneva July 21, 1954, and it represented far less than Ho's hopes. But by that time the United States was involved in Vietnam on the French side through $800 million a year in economic aid. Fear of Communist expansion in Asia dominated Washington, with Vice President Richard M. Nixon saying, "If, to avoid further Communist expansion in Asia, we must take the risk of putting our boys in, I think the executive branch has to do it."

The Geneva Accord, however, divided Vietnam at the 17th parallel, creating a North and a South Vietnam. It removed the French administration from the peninsula and provided for Vietnam-wide elections in 1956 as a means of unifying the country.

Although a party to the Geneva Accord, the United States declined to sign it. South Vietnam, also a nonsignatory, refused to hold the elections. Meantime, the United States built up its military mission in Saigon and its support of the regime of President Ngo Dinh Diem as a counter to continued guerrilla activity of the National Liberation Front, which became pronounced after 1956.

The Front, technically independent of Ho Chi Minh in the North, increased its sway into the 1960s. It supplied itself from captured American arms and from matériel that came through from the North. Beginning in 1964, thousands of American troops were poured into South Vietnam to battle the Vietcong and then to bomb North Vietnam.

The halt of American bombing in 1968 finally led to the peace negotiations in Paris, but in the meantime the fighting in South Vietnam continued.

Throughout, Ho was confident of victory. In 1962, when the war was still a localized conflict between the South Vietnamese forces and 11,000 American advisers on the one hand and a smaller guerrilla force on the other, he told a French visitor: "It took us eight years of bitter fighting to defeat you French, and you knew the country and had some old friendships here. Now the South Vietnamese regime is well-armed and helped by the Americans.

"The Americans are much stronger than the French, though they know us less well. So it perhaps may take 10 years to do it, but our heroic compatriots in the South will defeat them in the end."

Ho was still confident in early 1967, when he talked with Mr. Ashmore and Mr. Baggs. "We have been fighting for our independence for more than 25 years," he told them, "and of course we cherish peace, but we will never surrender our independence to purchase a peace with the United States or any party."

At the close of his conversation, he clenched his right fist and said emotionally, "You must know of our resolution. Not even your nuclear weapons would force us to surrender after so long and violent a struggle for the independence of our country."

About his own death he appeared unemotional. He had been urged to give up cigarettes, but he persisted in smoking. "When you are as old as I am," he remarked, "you do not worry about the harm of cigarettes."

HO'S DEATH IN HANOI

TILLMAN DURDIN

HONG KONG, Thursday, Sept. 4, 1969—President Ho Chi Minh of North Vietnam died yesterday morning in Hanoi at the age of 79.

A Hanoi radio report at 7 A.M. this morning announced that he succumbed at 9:47 A.M. Hanoi time yesterday "after a very sudden, serious heart attack."

The radio disclosed only at 4 A.M. yesterday that President Ho had been gravely ill for several weeks and was under emergency treatment day and night by "a collective of professors and medical doctors."

There was no explanation for the delay of almost 24 hours in announcing the president's death.

Under the North Vietnamese Constitution, the vice president takes over if the president dies or is incapacitated, pending a new election. The vice president is an obscure figure, Ton Duc Thang, 81.

[In San Clemente, Calif., the Western White House said that President Nixon would have no comment on Mr. Ho's death.]

The Hanoi government announcement, in the form of a government communiqué issued in the name of the Central Committee of the Vietnam Workers (Communist) party, the Standing Committee of the National Assembly and the Council of Ministers, said: "We feel boundless grief in informing the entire party and the entire Vietnamese people that Comrade Ho Chi Minh, President of the Central Committee of the Vietnam Workers party and President of the Democratic Republic of Vietnam, passed away at 9:47, Sept. 3, 1969, after a very sudden, serious heart attack at the age of 79. Everybody has done his best, determined to cure the President at all costs. But due to his advanced age President Ho Chi Minh has departed from us."

After the first announcement of Mr. Ho's death, the Hanoi radio was being organized "with the most solemn rites of our country" and a period of mourning from today until next Wednesday has been fixed.

A further special communiqué recapitulated the account of the death and described Mr. Ho as "the great, beloved leader of our Vietnamese working class and nation who all his life devotedly served the revolution, the people and the fatherland."

J. EDGAR HOOVER

1895–1972

By Christopher Lydon

When J. Edgar Hoover ambled through the Mayflower Hotel in Washington after one of his ritual fruit-salad-and-coffee lunches a year before he died, he passed almost unnoticed.

The once ruddy face was puffy and pale. The brushed-back, gray-brown hair was straight and thin—not the wiry, dark curls of a few years ago. He walked stiffly, although his figure was trim and erect. Behind his glasses, his dark brown eyes looked fixed, and he seemed to be daydreaming.

At the age of 77, the legendary G-man—in his 48th year as director of the Federal Bureau of Investigation—the most enduring and perhaps, if there is such a thing as a cumulative total, the most powerful official in the long span of the American government—looked deceptively like any other old gentleman in the hotel lobby.

In one of his rare reflections on mortality a few years ago, Mr. Hoover told a reporter, "The greatest enemy is time." Time's advances against this seemingly indestructible official had become obvious. But then, Mr. Hoover was always more human than he or the myth admitted.

Mr. Hoover's power was a compound of performance and politics, publicity and personality. At the base of it all, however, was an extraordinary record of innovation and modernization in law enforcement—most of it in the first decade or so of his tenure.

The centralized fingerprint file (the print total passed the 200 million mark in 1972) at the Identification Division (1925) and the crime laboratory (1932) are landmarks in the gradual application of science to police work. The National Police Academy (1935) has trained the leadership elite of local forces throughout the country. Mr. Hoover's recruitment of lawyers and accountants, although they now make up only 32 percent of the special agent corps, set a world standard of professionalism.

The National Crime Information Center enables 4,000 local law enforcement agencies to enter records and get questions answered on a network of 35 computer systems, with its headquarters at the F.B.I. office here.

From the start, Mr. Hoover got results. His bureau rounded up the gangsters in the 1930s. It made the once epidemic crime of kidnapping a rarity ("virtually extinct," as the director's friends like to say). It arrested German saboteurs within days after their submarines landed them on the Atlantic Coast. And, in one of its most sensational coups, the F.B.I. seized the slayers of Mrs. Viola Gregg Liuzzo only hours after the civil rights worker's shotgun death in Alabama in 1965.

The F.B.I. does not catch everybody, and it is sometimes many months before any of its "most wanted" suspects are arrested. But Mr. Hoover ex-

New York Times Photo

AP/WIDE WORLD

ecuted enough seemingly miraculous swoops to make any specific criticism perilous.

Mr. Hoover always understood the subtle currents of power among officials in Washington better than anyone around him. Not a New Dealer at heart, he had nonetheless dazzled President Franklin D. Roosevelt with his celebrated success against kidnappers.

Roosevelt liked him; he slapped the F.B.I. director's back and laughed when Mr. Hoover confessed that an agent had been caught in the act of illegal wiretapping, and he was amused at the bureau's temerity in putting a spy on Harry Hopkins, Roosevelt's counselor, in London. Roosevelt's assignment of counterespionage duties to the F.B.I. as war loomed in 1936 expanded the bureau's size and heightened Mr. Hoover's prestige.

But, when the Republicans won the White House again in 1952, Mr. Hoover's loyalty swung immediately to the new team.

The more awesome Mr. Hoover's power grew, the more plainly he would state, for the record, that there was nothing "political" about the bureau, that the F.B.I. was simply a "fact-finding agency" that "never makes recommendations or draws conclusions." The most pointed such declaration, coming in the furor about Harry Dexter White in 1953, was, paradoxically, one of Mr. Hoover's most political acts.

In a speech in Chicago, Herbert Brownell, President Eisenhower's attorney general, said that Mr. White, who had served as Assistant Secretary of the Treasury under Roosevelt, was named in 1946 as the United States executive director of the International Monetary Fund even though President Truman had been told that Mr. White was a Soviet spy. Mr. Truman, in retirement, replied that the F.B.I. had contributed to the judgment that it would be safer to keep Mr. White in office, under observation, than to dismiss him.

Rushing before Senate investigators, Mr. Hoover did not question the "conclusion" that Mr. White was a spy—although the F.B.I.'s evidence had not been enough to persuade a grand jury to indict Mr. White before he died in 1948. As for Mr. White's promotion to the International Monetary Fund, Mr. Hoover stated emphatically that, while he knew of Mr. Truman's reasoning, he had not been in on the decision nor had he approved it.

At a time when the Republican party chairman was promising to make Communism in government the central issue of the 1954 congressional campaign, Mr. Hoover's eager testimony was taken by some to be a boldly partisan move.

House Speaker Sam Rayburn was one of many Democrats who never forgave Mr. Hoover and encouraged speculation that a Democratic president would find a new F.B.I. director.

But Mr. Hoover's reappointment was virtually the first decision John F. Kennedy announced on the day after his election to the presidency in 1960.

Despite its acrimonious ending, the Hoover-Kennedy relationship started out cordially, based apparently on Mr. Hoover's long acquaintance with the president's father, the late Joseph P. Kennedy.

Robert Kennedy had urged the president-elect to retain Mr. Hoover; and when John Kennedy weighed assignments for his brother, Mr. Hoover urged him to follow his instinct and make Robert the attorney general.

Later, Robert Kennedy and Mr. Hoover fought a long tug-of-war over the assignment of agents to civil rights and organized crime cases. Mr. Hoover was not used to having an immediate boss who could block his access to the White House. He was annoyed when the attorney general installed a "hot line" between their Justice Department offices, and was even more annoyed when Robert Kennedy had the F.B.I. phone moved from the desk of Helen Gandy, Mr. Hoover's long-time secretary, to the director's desk.

Robert Kennedy never forgave Mr. Hoover for the cold telephone call that brought the first word of his brother's assassination. Mr. Hoover's voice, Robert Kennedy told William Manchester, the author, was "not quite as excited as if he were reporting the fact that he had found a Communist on the faculty of Howard University."

Later, according to William W. Turner, a former agent who wrote an unflattering book titled *Hoover's F.B.I.*, Robert Kennedy called back on the hot line. "Hoover was in his office with several aides," Mr. Turner wrote, "when it rang . . . and rang . . . and rang. When it stopped ringing, the director snapped to an aide, 'Now get that phone back on Miss Gandy's desk.' "

Although Robert Kennedy remained attorney general until the summer of 1964, he and Mr. Hoover never spoke again after the president's assassination.

Until Representative Hale Boggs of Louisiana, the House Majority Leader, criticized Mr. Hoover in the House in 1972 as a "feudal baron" and a wiretapper, the F.B.I. director had been sacrosanct in Congress's deference. The case of former Sen. Edward V. Long, a Missouri Democrat who denounced government wiretapping and was quickly undone by *Life* magazine's disclosure, leaked from the F.B.I., that he was splitting legal fees with a teamster lawyer in St. Louis, is often cited as an example of the director's tactics.

Mr. Hoover insisted that he did not tap the phones or "bug" the offices of Congressmen, and Mr. Boggs failed notably to prove the contrary. But Mr. Hoover always had other ways to keep critics in line anyway.

The late Sen. Kenneth D. McKellar, a Tennessee Democrat and chairman of the Senate Appropriations Committee, harassed Mr. Hoover from time to time in the 1930s, and in the spring of 1936 drew the blushing testimony that the director of the F.B.I. had never made an arrest.

Less than a month later, as if by magic, Mr. Hoover led a raid in New Orleans that captured Alvin (Kreepy) Karpis, a star of the Ma Barker mob.

By his own account, Mr. Hoover rushed up to the unsuspecting Karpis as he sat in a car, threatened him with a gun, then snapped out the order to other agents: "Put the cuffs on him, boys." In his recently published memoirs, Karpis contends that Mr. Hoover "hid until I was safely covered by many guns. He waited until he was told the coast was clear. Then he came out to reap the glory."

Karpis's account is obviously suspect, and about 35 years too late to undo Senator McKellar's embarrassment. When Senator McKellar tried to cut $225,000 out of the F.B.I. budget that year, Sen. Arthur H. Vandenberg of Michigan denounced him, according to one report of the Senate debate, "as a miser whose parsimony would cause the threat of kidnapping to hang once more over every cradle in America." Mr. Hoover's full budget request was then passed by a resounding voice vote. Since that time, the Senate has never questioned the F.B.I. budget as reported by the House.

As some of the men closest to him volunteer, Mr. Hoover's primary genius might well have been publicity. However, the real foundations of his legend are built on more solid stuff than press relations; certainly his image was never dependent on the goodwill of newspapermen, to whom Mr. Hoover was normally inaccessible.

Mr. Hoover never held a news conference. The closest thing he had to a mouthpiece in the press was not a political pundit or a crime reporter but the late Walter Winchell, the Broadway gossip columnist, who traveled with an F.B.I. escort and carried an item about "G-man Hoover" almost every day.

The making of the Hoover folk hero, in which Mr. Winchell played a large part, was undertaken purposefully in the early 1930s—long after the director's quiet administrative mastery had established him securely.

Speakeasies were the fashion. Gangsterism ravaged the land, capturing headlines and, in a sense, the public fancy. For Mr. Hoover, the last straw was the Kansas City massacre of June 17, 1933, in which Charles (Pretty Boy) Floyd and his gang killed five men, including an F.B.I. agent and three local policemen. "If there is going to be publicity," the director raged, "let it be on the side of law and order."

Looking around for a symbol, Mr. Hoover found

himself, and proceeded to orchestrate a dazzling range of movies, books, radio dramas and comic strips.

Mr. Hoover understood pop culture and its evolution. He promoted "junior G-man" clubs for boys, and sold two and a half million copies of *Masters of Deceit*, a book on Communism. His "10 most wanted" list made a lot of seedy drifters into headline material. In the age of television, he shrewdly reserved the right to select the actor (Efrem Zimbalist, Jr.) who would represent the F.B.I. in millions of living rooms in a popular television series.

The late Sen. George Norris of Nebraska called Mr. Hoover "the greatest hound for publicity on the American continent." Even Chief Justice Harlan Fiske Stone, who had appointed the F.B.I. director in 1924, observed critically that "one of the great secrets of Scotland Yard has been that its movements are never advertised."

But Mr. Hoover, once committed to a public fight on crime, played the role with all his fierce energy. He unquestionably made a brilliant success of it. Even after political pot shots at the director became fashionable in recent years, a Gallup poll for *Newsweek* magazine in the spring of 1971 showed that 80 percent of those who had any opinion about Mr. Hoover rated his performance "good" or "excellent."

Any general accounting of the F.B.I. director's power must also take note of the fact that his personality, as well as his office, has always inspired fear. Francis Biddle, President Roosevelt's attorney general in the early 1940s, sensed that behind Mr. Hoover's "absolute self-control" was "a temper that might show great violence if he did not hold it on leash, subject to the domination of a will that is the master of his temperament."

There were hints of that temper in his passionate criticisms—favorite phrases such as "mental halitosis," and the "jellyfish" tag he put on former attorney general Ramsey Clark. And Mr. Hoover had a hair-trigger sensitivity to criticism.

When the Warren Commission was investigating President Kennedy's assassination and said that the F.B.I. had not shared its intelligence fully with the Secret Service, Mr. Hoover lashed out at what he called "a classic example of Monday morning quarterbacking," a charge that gravely displeased President Johnson.

And when the Rev. Dr. Martin Luther King, Jr., said that southern blacks could not turn to their local F.B.I. offices with any assurance of sympathy or zeal for civil rights, Mr. Hoover called Dr. King "the most notorious liar in the country." Later, Mr. Hoover had his staff invite newsmen to hear the taped record of F.B.I. bugs in Dr. King's hotel rooms as evidence that "moral degenerates," as Mr. Hoover put it, were leading the civil rights movement. This was a rare extension of Mr. Hoover's lifelong practice of entertaining attorneys general and presidents with spicy details about the secret lives of famous people.

Critics within the F.B.I. were crushed summarily, and men who were thought to have been good friends of the director revealed deeper levels of hostility in casual conversations. "I'm afraid of him," said a former aide who would seem to have been secure in a new and completely different public career. "I can't imagine what he'd do to me, but I'd rather not mess with him."

John Edgar Hoover was born in Washington on New Year's Day in 1895, the youngest of three children of Dickerson N. Hoover, an easygoing federal official, and the former Annie M. Scheitlin, the granddaughter of Switzerland's first consul general in America.

The Hoovers' stucco house on Seward Square was later torn down, but Mr. Hoover's birthplace is memorialized in a stained-glass window of the Presbyterian church that stands on the site of the house.

Mrs. Hoover, who has been described as "old-world strict," instilled in her son an intense discipline and stern sensitivity to moral issues. By all accounts, she was the dominant influence on his character.

As a boy, he was known as "Speed"—a reference, apparently, to his agile mind, rattling speech and efficiency as a grocery delivery boy in the Capitol Hill section of Washington.

Admirers have compared his physique to Babe Ruth's—heavy torso, spindly legs—and, indeed, his flattened nose was the result of a hard-hit baseball. But Mr. Hoover was never an athlete. Remembering the day in 1909 when the football coach at Central High School rejected the puny volunteer brought twinges ever after.

In his disappointment, young Hoover turned all the more intensely to the school's military drill team, of which he became captain, and to public speaking. According to one biographer, he never had a regular girlfriend in high school; friends teased him, wrote Mildred H. Comfort, "and accused him of being in love with Company A," an institutional attachment foreshadowing his marriage to the F.B.I.

As a debater, young Hoover argued "The Fallacies of Women Suffrage" with gusto and competitive success. He was valedictorian of his class and was described in the school yearbook as "a gentleman of dauntless courage and stainless honor." In his high school days, he also was a choirboy and Sunday school instructor.

Although the University of Virginia offered him a liberal arts scholarship, Mr. Hoover feared that his living expenses would be a burden on his father. Instead, he took a $30-a-month clerk's job at the Library of Congress (he would apply indexing lessons to law enforcement later), and enrolled at George Washington University, where he was able to win his law degree in three years.

With a master's degree in 1917, Mr. Hoover passed the bar and moved into a $1,200-a-year job at the Department of Justice—his only employer over a stretch that exceeded 55 years.

From the start, according to Jack Alexander's 1937 profile of Mr. Hoover in *The New Yorker*, he stood out from the other young lawyers around him.

"He dressed better than most, a bit on the dandyish side," Mr. Alexander wrote. "He had an exceptional capacity for detail work, and he handled small chores with enthusiasm and thoroughness. He constantly sought new responsibilities to shoulder, and welcomed chances to work overtime. When he was in conference with an official of his department, his manner was that of a young man who confidently expected to rise."

Mr. Hoover's first assignment in "counter-radical activities" left a profound mark. This was at the end of President Wilson's second term, the era of the "Red raids" under Attorney General A. Mitchell Palmer. Evidently caught up in the official agitation about bombs and Bolshevism, Mr. Hoover took charge of assembling a card file on 450,000 "radicals," and built his first informer network—a controversial tool of police work that he used with dramatic results later against the Communist party and the Ku Klux Klan.

Many years later, Mr. Hoover said he had always "deplored" the hysterical dragnet arrests of thousands of innocent aliens in 1919 and 1920, but the record is also clear that, as the head of the new General Intelligence Division at the Justice Department, he was responsible for planning the raids, if not their execution.

A still darker era followed under President Harding. Within the Justice Department, according to Alpheus T. Mason, the historian, the Bureau of Investigation "had become a private secret service for corrupt forces within the government." Mr. Hoover nearly quit in disgust.

When Harlan Fiske Stone became attorney general under President Coolidge in 1924, he determined to rebuild the bureau after the image of Scotland Yard and sought, as his director, a man experienced in police work but free of the "more usual police tradition that it takes a crook to catch a crook and that lawlessness and brutality are more to be relied upon than skill and special training."

Secretary of Commerce Herbert Hoover, an untainted holdover from the Harding administration, recommended J. Edgar (no relation) as "a lawyer of uncommon ability and character."

Attorney General Stone, who held the appointive power, offered him the job. But Mr. Hoover, who was then only 29 years old, did not leap at what was unmistakably the chance of a lifetime.

With confidence and cunning that were very much in character, he said he would accept the assignment only if appointments to the bureau were divorced entirely from outside politics and if he would have sole control over merit promotions. Mr. Stone replied that he would not allow Mr. Hoover to take the job under any other conditions. And thus in 1924 the modern bureau—renamed the Federal Bureau of Investigation in 1935—was born.

From the start, Mr. Hoover's personal grip on all the important strings was the organizing principle at the bureau. It had everything to do with discipline and morale; Mr. Hoover made Siberia assignments and the compassionate transfers. It had a lot to do with the agency's efficiency and its incomparable record of probity. Under the Hoover inspection system, there were no secrets and no independent power centers in the F.B.I. In recent years, the system also seemed to have inhibited the bureau from taking worthwhile risks. "The first rule," according to one former agent, was "Do not embarrass the director."

The insulation from outside politics meant free play for Hoover politics. The 15,000 F.B.I. employees had neither the Civil Service nor a union to inhibit the director's whims. He shaped the bureau in his own Victorian image, and changed in the process himself.

Personal affairs were strictly regulated at the bureau. Women were not allowed to smoke on the job. No one got a coffee break. A clerk was once dismissed for playing with a yo-yo in the halls. In a case that went to court in 1967, a 26-year-old clerk was dismissed for keeping a girlfriend in his apartment overnight. Agents have been reprimanded for reading *Playboy* magazine and transferred for being overweight.

Mr. Hoover wore custom-made Brooks Brothers shirts and suits, and he ordered his agents to dress carefully, like young businessmen. The unofficial uniform for an agent included a white shirt, dark suit, snap-brim hat and a handkerchief in the jacket pocket.

One-man rule also bred sycophancy. Flattery worked wonders around Mr. Hoover, according to an inside student of the director's office. "Let's say you're an agent," he said. "Go in there and tell him he looks better than ever, that you are inspired by his leadership, that he's saving America and you hope he lives forever. As soon as you leave there will be a memo from the director saying, 'This man has executive ability.' A lot of agents have caught on."

Agents admittedly quaked at the thought of the director's disapproval, expressed typically in the bright blue ink of Mr. Hoover's stub pen in the margins of their memorandums. His language was vehement ("This is asinine!"); the filling of all four borders around a typewritten sheet was known as a "four-bagger." Once, it is said, when an assistant's memorandum so filled the page that Mr. Hoover barely had room for a comment, he wrote, "Watch the borders," and his puzzled but obedient aides dispatched agents to patrol the Canadian and Mexican borders for a week.

Friends and detractors all agreed that the system mirrored and fed a colossal ego. In the office, for instance, Mr. Hoover never circulated; people came to him. He sat amid flags behind a raised, polished mahogany desk at the end of a 35-foot office. Visitors, if they sat, sank into deep leather chairs and inevitably looked up to the throned director.

A day in the life of J. Edgar Hoover testified to his unflagging energy and to the power of habit. The few changes in his routine were forced on him: His friend Clyde Tolson, the F.B.I.'s associate director, was not well enough to walk the last few blocks to the office in recent days, so their morning strolls along Constitution Avenue were abandoned. The old Harvey's Restaurant was razed, so Mr. Hoover and Mr. Tolson had lunch instead at the Mayflower Hotel next door on Connecticut Avenue.

Old patterns persisted. The chauffeur picked up Mr. Hoover and then Mr. Tolson, about 9 o'clock every morning, and delivered them to the office about 9:30.

At the end the director was still the complete master of the bureau's huge flow of paperwork. He did little sleuthing himself, but he kept abreast of the F.B.I.'s major cases. Certain categories of business were handled by Mr. Hoover alone, including high-level personnel decisions, liaison in other than routine matters with Congress, the attorney general and the White House, and anything that brought unfavorable publicity on the bureau.

He left for lunch at 11:30 A.M., returned by 12:45 P.M. and usually took work home with him when he left for the day at 4:30.

There were things he did not do anymore. He outlived the Stork Club in New York, where he long enjoyed café society's attention and the friendship of Sherman Billingsley, the owner. He no longer tended the azaleas around his house. He had to give up his favorite angel food cake and chocolate cream pie to keep his weight down. Once an avid walker, he said that "conditions in this city," presumably a reference to the crime rate, kept him out of Rock Creek Park, formerly a favorite stamping ground near his house.

Still, the continuities in his life were as noticeable as the changes: the Jack Daniel's whiskey before dinner; the Miami vacation during the last two weeks of December and the July break and physical checkup in La Jolla, Calif.; the passion for horse racing; and above all, the friendship with Mr. Tolson, a fellow bachelor with whom Mr. Hoover had lunch and dinner six days a week since the late 1920s.

Mr. Tolson, who always stayed a respectful step behind Mr. Hoover in their famous walks together, lagged severely after two strokes and open-heart surgery. But the friendship was as fast as ever, and, through a special personnel device that Mr. Hoover engineered to get around Mr. Tolson's physical disability, Mr. Tolson remained the bureau's second-ranking officer.

Together they frequented the racetracks around Washington, as well as Gulfstream in Miami and Delmar in La Jolla. Mr. Hoover, who applied the same analytical imagination to the racing charts that he once used on kidnapping rings, was still bothered by touts who recognized him and wanted to tip him on a sure thing. But he bet only $2 on each race and would leave in disgust if his losses went over $10. Friends say it was Mr. Tolson, not Mr. Hoover, who sent junior F.B.I. agents around to the $50 and $100 windows with heavy side bets.

Mr. Hoover's humor usually ran to heavy-handed practical jokes. The late Julius Lulley, the restaurateur who always kept a special table set for Mr. Hoover and Mr. Tolson at Harvey's, once found his Maryland farm dotted with F.B.I. "wanted" posters bearing Mr. Lulley's picture.

Years ago, when Guy Hottel, a Hoover bodyguard and friend, got married, the F.B.I. director found out where Mr. Hottel was going on his honeymoon and conspired with the Virginia state police to have the newlyweds picked up and held overnight on a fake charge.

Mr. Hoover was not always quick to appreciate other people's jokes. In his saloon-going days in New York, it was said that he avoided Toots Shor's restaurant because of the insults that were Mr. Shor's trademark.

However, there always was a droll undercurrent in many of Mr. Hoover's utterances—as in his W. C. Fields-like defense of racetracks as an outlet for people's emotions, "which, if they weren't at the track, they might use for less laudable escapades."

And Mr. Hoover recently took to public kidding about himself—the clearest sign of his rejuvenation under President Nixon and Attorney General John N. Mitchell.

Perhaps the most widely asked question about Mr. Hoover was why he stayed on the job, but that, too, had been around a while. Even in the 1930s his long tenure was considered remarkable. During the 1940s, a former aide recalls, "every year he'd ask for a computation of his retirement and there'd be a rumor that the old boy was stepping down." The inside gossip in the 1950s was that Mr. Hoover had approved plans for the construction of his retirement villa at La Jolla.

After John Kennedy reappointed Mr. Hoover in 1960, it was thought he would bow out around the mandatory retirement age of 70, which would have come on New Year's Day 1965. But as early as May 1964, President Johnson waived the retirement law. The next obvious milestone was his 75th birthday in January 1970, but that passed without incident, like all the rest.

Some people said that Mr. Hoover wanted to see the completion of the new $102-million F.B.I. Building on Pennsylvania Avenue. He said he would stay on the job as long as his physical condition permitted. But why? "I've always been against retiring a man by age," he said. "The longer a man is with us, the more valuable he becomes."

The men around Mr. Hoover pointed to his egotism—a sense of his own indispensability—and to the lack of family and interests that consoled other men in retirement. "For him the bureau is everything," said a friend.

Mr. Hoover died at his home in Washington, D.C., during the night of May 2, 1972, from the effects of hypertensive cardio-vascular disease. He was 77.

A MAN WHOSE LIKE WILL NOT BE SEEN AGAIN

TOM WICKER

THE DEATH of J. Edgar Hoover brought an end to an era. That has been said of many men, but in the case of Mr. Hoover—who, at 77, had been director of the Federal Bureau of Investigation for 48 years—it was really true. The Hoover era almost exactly spanned the years since the United States emerged from World War I to find itself a world power; and in the half century that followed, he became one of the few constants in a rapidly changing nation, an endlessly evolving society.

The director's views and values never ceased to reflect the vanished America that had shaped him; but his remarkable combination of bureaucratic and political skills, public relations genius, dictatorial methods and law enforcement professionalism enabled him to retain unmatched power and status in Washington through Prohibition, the Depression, the gangster days of the 1930s, World War II, the Cold War, Korea, Vietnam and the radical political activism of the 1960s.

Eight presidents depended on or tolerated him; Congress feared and favored him, from the "Red scares" of the early 1920s to the trial of Philip Berrigan; and he became the only high public official for whom the federal retirement rules were specifically set aside so that he could serve on, as it seemed, forever. When his housekeeper found him one morning, slumped by his bed, dead of natural causes, even J. Edgar Hoover's enemies—by whom the truculent old man liked to say he had been "distinguished"—conceded that his like would not be seen again.

For many Americans, that was a relief; but for others, Mr. Hoover's death symbolized the passing of much that they had valued—old-fashioned patriotism; rigid "moral" values; a stern code of authority; a political and social attitude uncomfortable with the strident demands of minorities, young people, liberated women, gays; and a view of "law and order" as the first priority of government. Both for them, and for those others who believed Mr. Hoover had outlasted his time, the question of his successor was a matter of vital importance.

The director, after all, had presided over one of the major agencies of the federal government; he had almost unlimited powers over its thousands of agents and its substantial budget; he had custody of its massive accumulation of reports, files, fingerprints, dossiers; he had, by custom and necessity, direct links to any man who might sit in the White House; and thus he had the potential for extending a vast and effective secret police system into the life of virtually every American. J. Edgar Hoover had personally had that potential; the question whether his successor also should have it could hardly be answered without searching study of the way Mr. Hoover had handled it.

The historical record is likely to accord him both good and bad marks. Up to the end of World War II, few officials had earned such esteem, in making an honest, efficient and feared federal force of what had been a corrupt and sleazy agency; in developing scientific investigative techniques; in the F.B.I.'s effective wars on bank robbery and kidnapping and the gangsterism of Depression days; in its successful counterespionage activities during World War II. In these achievements and more, J. Edgar Hoover compiled a remarkable personal record.

With his flair for publicity—he invented the "10 most wanted" list and shrewdly cooperated in "G-man" movies and radio programs—he made himself a legend in the nation; and with his masterly bureaucracy, he made himself a fixture in Washington.

But the postwar era brought new problems. Hot war became the Cold War; in its late Stalinist phase, Communism became the new international threat. Seen as a revolutionary and aggressive ideology, its intrusion from abroad into American life seemed a more formidable "fifth column" than the spies and saboteurs of World War II ever had; and since it was J. Edgar Hoover's F.B.I. that had taken care of the latter, it became the new mission of the G-men to take on the Communists. But the task was subtly, perhaps fatally different; the Communist threat, if it had any substance at all, was far more a matter of domestic subversion than of foreign agents. Thus it was that the F.B.I. moved into what a group of academic and other specialists on the agency, meeting in 1971 at Princeton, concluded was now its principal concern—domestic political surveillance.

Moreover, Mr. Hoover's public relations techniques, glorifying his agency's mortal combat with the "masters of deceit" in the Communist "movement," probably contributed as much as any other single factor to the virulent anti-Communism of the public and its politicians in the 1950s and early 1960s; and that public attitude had its effect on government policies, from the nonrecognition of Communist China to the fiasco at the Bay of Pigs. Concurrently to those Americans less fearful of the Reds than for their own political institutions, the F.B.I.'s political surveillance came to seem an alarming secret police threat; in some ways, that fear may have been little more justified than the fear of Communists but it nevertheless began to undermine confidence in the F.B.I. and in J. Edgar Hoover personally.

Despite the bureau's front-page warfare on Communism, it also began to be apparent in the late 1950s and early 1960s that the bureau had been considerably less than alert, eager and effective in protecting the civil rights of blacks, and of whites who tried to help them in the years of upheaval that followed the Supreme Court's order for the desegregation of schools.

President Kennedy had made the reappointment of Mr. Hoover the first order of business after his election in 1960, but Robert Kennedy, arriving at the Justice Department intent on wiping out organized crime, found that the F.B.I. scarcely admitted the existence of organized crime. Students of the agency contend that these deficiencies, too, were to some extent the result of F.B.I. concentration on Communism—which the director considered more of a threat than segregation and more rewarding in publicity and bigger budgets than organized crime.

During the Kennedy and Johnson administrations, these defects were to some extent rectified; but as black and antiwar militance became powerful in the 1960s, the domestic surveillance of the F.B.I. became more and more extensive.

In recent years, therefore, the director and the F.B.I. he created had become engulfed in controversy, primarily over the agency's surveillance and Mr. Hoover's personal activities—such as his feud with the Rev. Dr. Martin Luther King and his powerful political opposition to a consular treaty with the Soviet Union.

The director was charged also with letting his agency's general effectiveness slip. Critics thought both were outdated—that the F.B.I. National Academy, for instance, reflecting Mr. Hoover's views, taught little that was relevant to the modern problems of police in central cities. They said F.B.I. agents were overwhelmed by Mr. Hoover's bureaucratic demands and intimidated by his dictatorial discipline.

But J. Edgar Hoover was never charged with being too weak to resist improper political demands; over the long pull, his stewardship of the F.B.I. files was reasonably good—but just flawed enough to suggest the damage that could be done by a weaker or less scrupulous successor. His long career suggested, therefore, the need for a replacement with a reassuring public reputation for strength and integrity, as well as one more in tune with the last third of the 20th century than the first third. Law enforcement experience seems equally necessary, as well as freedom from entangling political commitments.

EDWARD HOPPER

1882–1967

Edward Hopper attained a reputation as one of America's most distinguished and most individualistic painters. He remained resolutely determined to paint everyday subjects realistically throughout a long career that spanned numerous changes in contemporary art.

"My aim in painting," Mr. Hopper once observed, "has always been the most exact transcription possible of my most intimate impressions of nature."

"In general," he added, "it can be said that a nation's art is greatest when it most reflects the character of its people."

His city people sitting at the all-night lunch stand, his apartment dwellers reading newspapers in barren rooms, his plain-bodied girls dressing in the morning light, his usherettes trapped in the cheap and plushy gloom of the movie palace were painted by Mr. Hopper with a respect for their right to inner privacy in the face of mass living.

Mr. Hopper, who would study a subject for months and then paint it from memory in a spurt of energy, maintained a limited output of only a few paintings a year. He said he never wanted to repeat himself.

Living simply in his quarters on Manhattan's Washington Square, which contained two studios, a bedroom and a kitchen, Mr. Hopper was brooding and secretive about his work. He painted in solitude in his bare, white-walled studio. Asked what he was painting, he would reply: "Go to my dealer."

He hated ostentation, dressed simply in tweeds and ate frugally, sometimes eating with his wife in local restaurants and sometimes from cans in his spare apartment. The artist enjoyed driving, felt good behind the wheel of a car and made several trips through the country.

While contemporaries like Rockwell Kent and George Bellows gained swift fame when American art began to veer away from conservatism early in the 20th century, Mr. Hopper declined to follow the trends and labored for years in obscurity. He was 43 years old before recognition came to him.

The loneliness he probably felt as he worked aloof from dominant trends and influences pervades all of his work, and has become his hallmark. His carefully detailed Victorian houses, city streets, roadside lunch counters, theater interiors and New England cottages are typical parts of the American scene. They are utterly devoid of any American hustle-bustle, however. The calm that precedes a storm, or follows desertion, or appears through a window to the fleeting glimpse of a passerby, prevails.

His reflective and personal style was modern in spirit without being quite attachable to any modern school; he began, and to the end continued, as an artist who put his faith neither in tradition nor in innovation, but completely in his own vision.

Peter A. Juley & Son Collection
National Museum of American Art
Smithsonian Institution

Whitney Museum of American Art, Josephine N. Hopper Bequest
Photograph by Geoffrey Clements

Writing at the time of the retrospective exhibition of Mr. Hopper's work at the Whitney Museum of American Art in 1964, John Canaday, art critic of *The New York Times*, characterized the artist as "a rangy, big-boned man whose appearance suggests that he might have been a member of his college crew around the year 1900."

"Nothing suggests the wiry compactness of the long-distance runner," the critic continued, "but a long-distance runner is what Edward Hopper has always been. His steady pace does not decrease from year to year, although today he is so far ahead of the field that you would think he might slow down a little.

"The best of his American competitors have hardly got their second wind and are not yet in sight behind him, and his only international competitor is Pablo Picasso."

Edward Hopper was born in Nyack, N.Y., July 22, 1882. He came to New York to study art in 1900, and continued to live and work here the rest of his life, except for summers in New England and short periods abroad.

Mr. Hopper's ancestry was English, Welsh, Dutch and Danish. His parents, Garrett Henry Hopper and the former Elizabeth Griffiths Smith, sent him to a private day school in Nyack, and he graduated from the local high school.

During the winter of 1899–1900, he studied commercial illustration in New York. Shortly afterward he enrolled at the New York School of Art, where his fellow students included George Bellows, Guy Pène du Bois, Eugene Speicher and Mr. Kent. For five years he worked under Kenneth Hayes Miller and Robert Henri, the latter a leading pioneer in the movement from idyllic to realistic painting scornfully dubbed the "Ash Can" school.

During the next four years Mr. Hopper painted in Europe for periods of several months, chiefly in France and Spain. He was known to the modernists then painting abroad, but was not a part of their circle, and was little influenced by them.

In 1913 the artist exhibited with other nonacademic painters at the revolutionary Armory Show, and achieved his first sale—a canvas titled *The Sailboat*.

He continued painting in Maine during the next two summers, but in 1915 gave it up and turned to etching. His etchings were hailed as genuine, lasting contributions to American art, and brought him awards in Los Angeles and Chicago.

Heartened by an exhibition of his watercolors at the Rehn Galleries here in 1924, Mr. Hopper resumed painting in oils. Critical interest and admiration for his work began to grow, and in 1933 he achieved major recognition—a one-man retrospective exhibition at the Museum of Modern Art.

At that time, Mr. Hopper had sold only two canvases. One of these had been bought in 1931 by the Metropolitan Museum of Art, which had previously been indifferent, if not hostile, to "modern" painters. It was *Tables for Ladies*.

The artist had also received the honor of being one of 19 living American artists chosen by the new Museum of Modern Art for its second exhibition, in 1929. The museum had just opened, a month previously, with an exhibition of works by Cézanne, Van Gogh, Seurat and Gauguin that had attracted 47,000 visitors.

In 1937, the Metropolitan bought a second painting, *From Williamsburg Bridge*, from Mr. Hopper.

A wave of modernism had engulfed American realism early in the 1920s, but Mr. Hopper had persisted in painting starkly realistic though brightly colored aspects of contemporary life.

The Depression brought the attention of the abstractionists back to the American scene. They began to paint it realistically again, many in anger because of the poverty and suffering they saw.

The revival of realism brought fresh admiration to Mr. Hopper, who had been painting it all along, with steadily improving technique, deepening perception and a poet's sense of mood. He was cited as the esthetic heir of Winslow Homer and as one of the two 20th-century American artists—the other was Charles Burchfield—who had achieved the most complete and most individual expression of romantic realism.

A 6-foot-5-inch, lumbering man with a frank and quietly brooding face, Mr. Hopper accepted his belated success calmly. He continued to live and work in his top-floor apartment studio in Washington Square North or at his summer home in Truro, Mass. Occasionally he and his wife, who also painted, would take long automobile trips around the country, during which he would make sketches for future oils and watercolors.

In December 1944, Mr. Hopper was elected to life membership in the National Institute of Arts and Letters. In 1932 he had rejected "without explanation" an invitation to membership in the conservative National Academy of Design.

Another retrospective exhibition devoted to Mr. Hopper was held in 1950 at the Whitney Museum in New York. "In the main his view of life is searching, compassionate and profound," the critic Robert M. Coates commented.

"At his best he can invest the simplest subjects with a magic and mystery it would be hard to duplicate," Mr. Coates added.

In 1953 Mr. Hopper received an honorary degree from Rutgers University. Two years later he was presented with the gold medal of the National Institute of Arts and Letters. He is represented in major museums of the United States and England.

The artist received many important art awards. His first "art" prize was $300 in 1918 for a war poster titled "Smash the Hun." It portrayed a muscular-looking shipbuilder brandishing a hammer at three blood-covered German bayonets projecting from the lower corner of the canvas.

In 1957 he received the $2,000 first prize in the fourth International Hallmark Award competition, and he also was awarded a silver medallion by the New York Board of Trade.

Three years later Mr. Hopper won the Art in America annual award for outstanding contribution to American art. The $1,000 cash prize and medal are sponsored by the magazine *Art in America*, and the winner is chosen in a poll of artists, critics, teachers, museum directors and others involved in the arts.

In 1961 Mr. Hopper's painting *House of Squam Light, Cape Ann* was selected by Mrs. John F. Kennedy with 10 other oils and watercolors from the Boston Museum of Fine Arts to be displayed at the White House to help broaden knowledge and appreciation of American artists and craftsmen.

The retrospective exhibition of Mr. Hopper's work that was held at the Whitney Museum in 1964 covered 55 years of his painting.

"Hopper has always been a master in the painting of light, not the broken, sparkling light of impressionism, but the steady light of the sun on flat surfaces," Mr. Canaday wrote. "When his paintings include figures, they are usually isolated not only within the picture, but also within themselves."

"In the face of nature, or what is left of it," Mr. Canaday observed later, "Hopper always checks himself well this side of lyricism and reminds us—for instance, by showing us the roadside gasoline pump in front of a pine forest—that nature in an urbanized century is only a relative concept.

"He can paint, as few painters can, the purity of the sky, the freshness of morning near the sea, the soft clarity of the light that strikes across dunes or grass and onto white clapboards.

"But nature is never an ineffable mystery for Hopper; he has no interest in the ineffable—or at least, by the evidence, he does not regard painting as a medium for expression of the ineffable.

"Nature for him is reduced in scale by the presence of men, by their cottages and lighthouses. The people who sit on porches or by open windows are warmed by the sun and refreshed by the air, but are inspired to no philosophical ponderings.

"By giving us a picture, Hopper supplies us with his selection of raw material for such ponderings if we want to make them for ourselves, but he does not dictate their direction."

In August 1966 the directors of the MacDowell

Colony awarded the Edward MacDowell medal for outstanding contributions to the arts to Mr. Hopper.

Mr. Hopper was selected as the tone-setting "elder statesman" of the United States exhibit at Brazil's São Paulo Biennial in 1967.

The exhibition was assembled by William C. Seitz, director of Brandeis University's Rose Art Museum. Mr. Seitz said: "At this time, in my opinion, there is no other master—surely no one who has not already been widely seen abroad—who can better represent both what is finest and most characteristic in the art of the United States.

"A pioneer in representing 'unpaintable' American subjects, he provides a bridge from the beginning of the century and the Ash Can school to the decade of pop art."

Mr. Hopper died in his studio in New York on May 15, 1967. He was 84 years old.

AN INTEGRITY IN REALISM

HILTON KRAMER

THE WORK of Edward Hopper occupies a special and somewhat paradoxical place in the history of modern painting in America. For decades he was our foremost realist—a painter whose homely and often desolate scenes of American life and the American landscape had come to exert an enormously wide appeal. Yet the popular side of Hopper's art, with its rich vein of pictorial anecdote and its evocation of familiar emotions, was not the real basis of the critical fame he enjoyed in the later years of his career. It was, above all, the esthetic integrity of Hopper's work—the extraordinary degree to which he was able to endow a very personal vision of American life with a stark and original pictorial form—that won him the admiration not only of like-minded fellow realists but of many members of the avant-garde as well.

Hopper was an artist intensely preoccupied with images of isolation, loneliness and silence. Some of these images are nocturnal and eerie; many are sun-drenched and, if anything, even more eerie. Indeed, he conferred on the most commonplace sort of daylight scene—women standing in doorways or windows of old Cape Cod houses, figures sitting in city hotel rooms, offices and cafeterias—an almost novelistic anxiety and tension. There is always an atmosphere of ennui and vague menace.

The scene is always very precisely observed, moreover. Hopper had a wonderful eye for detail. One could almost write a history of native American architecture and interior decor based on the visual evidence of his pictures. Yet he absorbed this painstaking observation into a vision entirely his own. The architectural structures and spaces in Hopper's paintings are scenes in a private scenario that the artist developed from picture to picture—a scenario of macabre presences and haunted feelings.

His success in realizing and sustaining this severe vision undoubtedly owed much to his early experience as an illustrator. Yet the paintings of Hopper's maturity transcend the limitations of illustration, for their strength derives as much from their purity of form as from the vision this form was designed to serve.

The crux of Hopper's pictorial esthetic is to be found in the very strict, economical geometry that governs every detail of his painting. In Hopper's best work, the anecdote is located in a rigorously designed pattern of light-filled space. Every observable element in the picture is a coefficient of this geometry of light.

There is thus something forbidding and puritanical in both the form and the content of Hopper's art—something hard and unyielding that his more sentimental admirers have tended to overlook in their haste to enjoy the superficial pleasures of his work. But it is this hardness that gives his work its great unity and strength. In years to come, Hopper's reputation will undergo, I believe, a change similar to the one that overtook Robert Frost's. The folksy side of his art will yield to a greater sense of its dark message.

THE WORLD OF EDWARD HOPPER [1971]

JAMES R. MELLOW

EDWARD HOPPER was a man of stubborn loyalties. During a career that stretched back for nearly seven decades as a painter—from 1900, when he began studying with Robert Henri, leader of the Ash Can school, until his death in 1967 at the age of 84—Hopper remained dedicated to one wife (Josephine Nivison, a Henri student as well, whom he had married in 1924), one dealer (Frank Rehn, who had given him his first one-man gallery exhibition the same year), a style of painting that remained uncompromisingly realistic through every major movement and minor fad that shook the art world. (Hopper had lived past a good many of them: from Fauvism and Cubism, early in the century, to the American styles—Abstract Expressionism, Hard-Edge, Pop Art—that dominated the international scene in his old age, when he was regarded as the country's foremost realist.)

Through those years, Hopper cultivated the same essential themes—the tawdry architecture of the city with its all-night luncheonettes, corner drugstores, second-floor chop suey restaurants; the isolation of lonely individuals and bored couples in rented rooms; the decline of small-town America, bleaching in the sun—themes that became so doggedly personal, in time, and in which he discovered such unexpected beauty, that they seemed uniquely his own. Toward the end of his life, in a rare moment of self-assertion, Hopper could claim: "The only real influence I've ever had was myself."

Hopper was, undoubtedly, America's most tight-lipped contemporary master. Attempts to draw him out inevitably met with a prolonged, uncomfortable silence. Behind the silence, Hopper would formulate, then deliver one or two impregnable sentences that, like his art, revealed only so much of himself as he wanted revealed and never a bit more. Lloyd Goodrich, former director of the Whitney Museum and a friend of Hopper's for 40 years—Goodrich's lavishly illustrated monograph on the artist was published by Abrams in 1971—recalls that in order to get Hopper to discuss his work at all, he would have to stand the painter directly in front of one of his pictures and proceed to question him about it. Slowly, each word carefully considered, Hopper would explain some technical challenge the picture had involved, persistently avoiding all attempts to analyze its subject. Inevitably, Mrs. Hopper—who took a proprietary air toward her husband and his work that others found irritating—would interrupt the conversation, allowing Hopper to retreat into his usual silence.

Hopper's reticence was legendary: he seems never to have wanted the meaning of a work crystallized verbally, preferring to keep it, always, in solution in the picture. When the Whitney acquired his 1960 painting *Second Story Sunlight*, depicting a voluptuous young woman and an old one sitting on the second-floor porch of a white frame house, Hopper's response to a Whitney questionnaire was adamantly plain: "This picture is an attempt to paint sunlight as white, with almost or no yellow pigment in the white. Any psychologic idea will have to be supplied by the viewer." (Having once formulated an idea, Hopper apparently stuck with it: he used the same words—verbatim—in a 1961 interview with art writer Katharine Kuh.)

"A Great Stone Face" was how critic Brian O'Doherty described Hopper—or, at least, the legendary Hopper, the quiet man of American painting. In the course of four years of occasional visits and conversations, O'Doherty discovered, he said, "a good deal of life" behind the stone facade. He managed to draw the artist out sufficiently to produce the incisive profile that appeared in *Art in America* on the occasion of Hopper's impressive 1964 retrospective at the Whitney. It presents Hopper in some unusually expansive moments, discussing certain features of his work, even confessing that one of his recent paintings—the 1963 *Intermission*, showing a woman, alone, in a row of empty theater seats—was "pretty good," but then immediately qualifying his statement with, "Maybe it's too complete, not suggestive enough." (Even at the height of his fame, Hopper was to remain persistently uncertain about the success of his work.)

Hopper disagreed, too, with those critics—the vast majority—who saw his work as a commentary on the alienation of American life. "The loneliness thing is overdone," he said. "It formulates something you don't want formulated." But several months later, back to the same question because of O'Doherty's insistence, he was willing to concede, "Maybe they're right," then clammed up tight on the subject.

The important Hopper exhibition that opens this Friday at the Whitney Museum—157 paintings, watercolors, drawings and prints, covering several unknown aspects of the artist's career—is a prime case of Hopper's mystifying reticence. The works are all drawn from the staggering Hopper bequest—more than 1,000 items, the entire contents of his studio at the time of his death on May 15, 1967—that Hopper willed to the Whitney. The museum learned of this windfall—probably the largest donation an American artist has ever made to a single American institution—only after the death of Mrs. Hopper in March 1968. Hopper had never mentioned his intention to his friend Goodrich; he left the work to his wife, with the provision that it be given to the Whitney when she died. Considering his lengthy friendship with Goodrich, who had consistently championed his work, producing an earlier monograph on the artist and organizing two retrospectives at the Whitney (in 1950 and 1964), as well as Hopper's long association with the Whitney, dating back to the 1920s, when it was the Whitney Studio Club on West Fourth Street, Hopper's choice of institution was hardly surprising—it was simply another example of his staunch loyalty.

What was totally unexpected, however, was the amount of work remaining in the estate. Hopper had told Goodrich, years before, that he had destroyed much of his early work. In the mid-1940s, too, when Goodrich began making a comprehensive catalog of Hopper's *oeuvre,* the Hoppers had supplied him with a series of ordinary office ledgers in which, supposedly, every one of Hopper's works was registered. The ledgers—bequeathed to Goodrich personally—are a fund of valuable information. They detail the dates when pictures were completed, record the prices when sold, indicate where the pictures were first exhibited. They chronicle, too, the rising prices of Hopper's works, from the meager $10 or $15 his etchings brought in the early 1920s to the $20,000 his oils commanded in the late years. More valuable, they contain Hopper's own sketches of the major oils. Among their incidental benefits are Mrs. Hopper's chatty notations, written in a small, crabbed hand, supplying tidbits of personal information. The notes for the 1940 painting *Gas*, for example, indicate that the picture was brought back to New York from Cape Cod early in October "on hasty trip home to register for Willkie."

The ledgers would ordinarily have been a cataloger's dream, but when Goodrich and his research assistant, Mrs. Elizabeth Streibert, began sorting through the cartons of Hopper's works that had been deposited in a New York warehouse pending settlement of the estate, they discovered a treasure trove of unrecorded Hoppers: early student paintings reflecting Robert Henri's bravura technique—an influence that Hopper, who had a marked preference for clean, decisive forms, admitted it had taken him 10 years to get over; Parisian cityscapes—the results of three lengthy stays in Europe in 1906, 1909 and 1910; an unusual series of early nudes, sketched at the model sessions at the old Whitney

Studio Club; watercolors and oils of stolid New England frame houses, isolated farm buildings, lighthouses, painted "from the fact," as Hopper termed it, during the summers he and his wife spent at Gloucester, Mass., and in Maine during the 1920s. There were, as well, a number of handsome oils—like the 1929 *Railroad Sunset*, an observation tower silhouetted against a broad expanse of sky, a picture that looks forward to the spare structural simplicity of Hopper's late works.

It was clear that the Hoppers had recorded in the ledgers only works that had been exhibited or sold or turned over to Hopper's gallery. "They let me go on compiling the catalog on the basis of the ledgers," Goodrich says, shaking his head. "Neither one of them said a word to me."

If there was a single dramatic year in Hopper's otherwise plodding career, it was 1924. It was in that year that he walked into the Frank Rehn Gallery one day at lunchtime with a bundle of watercolors under his arm. Rehn and his assistant, John Clancy (now director of the gallery), both liked the work so well that Rehn decided to give him a show. The exhibition, held in November, consisted of 11 watercolors, mostly Gloucester scenes and houses. It was a sellout; Hopper, in fact, brought in five more pictures, which sold as well. It was also in that year that he married Josephine and gave up working as a commercial illustrator.

Before that, Hopper's career had given no particular evidence of success. Born in Nyack, N.Y., in 1882—his father had a dry goods business—he encountered no parental objections when he decided to make art his profession. His parents, however, did suggest that he take up commercial art as a more practical career, and he enrolled in a commercial art school in New York in 1899. For more than two decades, he earned his living as a commercial artist, disliking the work intensely, but saving his money in order to afford summer painting trips in New England and lengthier visits abroad.

In Paris, where young American painters like Patrick Henry Bruce, whom he knew from Henri's classes, were joining the vanguard struggles of Fauvism and Cubism, Hopper remained aloof, living quietly with a French family on the Rue deLille, visiting the Louvre, teaching himself French. His one success in the early years was freakish: he entered a single painting, *Sailing*, in the historic 1913 Armory Show in New York and it was sold for $250. It was 10 years, however, before he made another sale.

Hopper's first successes in a variety of media (he had taken up etching in 1915, watercolor in 1923) came in the 1920s and 1930s, but they proved irksome on one count. Inevitably, he was classified with the popular American Scene painters—regional artists like Thomas Hart Benton, John Stuart Curry and Grant Wood—who were mythicizing grassroots America. The identification, which stuck with him for years, rankled Hopper. It could bring a perceptible rise to his usually laconic voice. "I hate the word American Scene. I hate the term," he said. "It has been applied to American painters who definitely tried very hard to be American and I never did. I just tried to be myself."

In the 1940s and 1950s, when abstraction moved into the foreground of American art, Hopper held his ground as the dean of American realists; the public liked the haunting familiarity of his scenes; the critics admired his rigorous sense of form. Never exactly a prolific artist, in his late years he produced only two or three oils a year, the subjects carefully considered and planned beforehand. Goodrich, for example, visited the Hoppers in South Truro, Mass., in the late summer of 1958—they had built a modest shingle house overlooking the sea there in 1930—and discovered only the wooden stretchers for a painting, without canvas, resting on his easel. "He's been looking at that all summer," Mrs. Hopper told him. The painting that eventually resulted, *Sunlight in a Cafeteria*, was a far cry from the windswept landscape in which it had been pondered—two idle patrons in a bland, sun-drenched city interior.

Hopper's late works, like *Sunlight in a Cafeteria*, and even more, his 1963 *Sun in an Empty Room* (rooms devoid of the human presence held a certain fascination for him), were increasingly purged of unnecessary detail, the compositions more elemental in design. But attempts to relate these works to a trend toward abstractionism met with Hopper's frank disapproval. Once, when Goodrich informed him that in a recent slide lecture he had made a successful comparison between a Mondrian and one of Hopper's pictures—*High Noon*, a severely angular frame house with a woman standing in the doorway—Hopper's only comment was, "You kill me."

In 1955, Hopper was awarded one of the top cultural awards in the country, the Gold Medal of the National Institute of Arts and Letters, but did not even attend the ceremonies—he and Jo were traveling in Mexico. (The painter Henry Varnum Poor, making the presentation, announced: "From the safe distance of Monterrey, Mexico, Edward Hopper has sent his acceptance speech. . . . It is two paragraphs long. If he were here to make it by spoken word it would have been 'Thanks,' or, if he felt really expansive, 'Thanks a lot.' ") The last honor he received was the selection of 40 of his oils for the American representation at the São Paulo Biennial of 1967, usually a vanguard affair. It may have been a mixed blessing, however, since Hopper's work provided the focal point for an exhibition of latter-day American Scenists, among them a large contingent of Pop artists.

The perfect Hopper retrospective—that is, the most revealing—would concentrate, I believe, not simply on the chronology of his work, but on the chronology of its persistent themes. Light, for instance, is the motivating force in nearly all of Hopper's paintings. The titles of any handful of his works—*House at Dusk*, *Early Sunday Morning*, *Cape Cod Evening*, *Office at Night*—indicate its importance. The drama of light in Hopper is explored in all its variations: the relentless early light toward which a woman turns her face in *Cape Cod Morning*; the lingering russet light that bathes the gas station on the deserted country road in *Gas*; the hard electric glare of the corner luncheonette, cutting into the darkened streets of *Nighthawks*.

Hopper's most celebrated subject, New York—"The American city that I know best and like most," he said—was treated from his own personal angle. Hopper never seems to have been interested in skyscrapers or the dramatic New York skyline. Instead, he fixed upon the remnants of its 19th-century architecture: a stretch of small street-level stores in a row of brownstones; the strange rooftop vistas of chimneys and vents on four- and five-story buildings. When he turned to decaying small-town America, it was the architectural relics of another era that interested him: modest frame houses with their ornate trim; pretentious Victorian mansions that had become victims of industrial realities, railroad tracks cutting across their diminished front yards.

In many of his pictures, Hopper seems to have kept nature at a distance. Judging from a remark he made to O'Doherty, he viewed it as somewhat suspect. "Do you notice how artificial trees look at night? Trees look like theater at night," he told the critic. On occasion, he could endow nature with a feeling of ominousness: The grove of locust trees in *Cape Cod Evening*, for example, looks like an invading army advancing toward a stalwart white house.

When he painted houses, Hopper usually preferred those that stood on isolated ground, bereft of any softening vegetation. In this respect, photographer Arnold Newman's 1960 portrait reveals the artist's tastes. In the foreground Hopper sits on a painted bench, his stern features etched by hard light, his tall frame hunched over. Behind him, rising on a hillock of low-growing weeds and field flowers, the Truro house stands foursquare on its foundation, unrelieved by shrubbery or the mitigating shade of trees.

The theater—not just the homely dramas glimpsed through the proscenium windows of New York brownstones, but the theater itself—was a major theme in Hopper's paintings: the lonely woman in *Intermission*; the couple taking their seats in *Two on the Aisle*; the brassy stripper parading across the stage in *Girlie Show*. (The latter painting reminds one, too, of the undercurrent of sensuality that runs through Hopper's art: the women undressing for bed or standing nude in their bleak rooms.)

One of Hopper's most important paintings on a theatrical subject is the 1939 *New York Movie*, now in the collection of the Museum of Modern Art. The Whitney Museum, as a result of the Hopper bequest, has acquired some 50 preparatory drawings for the picture—certainly an index of the painting's significance for the artist. The detailed sketches of gilded pillars, curtained exitways, wall sconces, ceiling fixtures, were taken from New York theaters—the Globe, the Strand, the Palace. Jo Hopper, standing in the hall landing of their Washington Square apartment, posed for the bored usherette, leaning against the wall. Hopper's method, in his later oils, was like Balzac's: steeping himself in a milieu, fastening upon vivid details until he could produce the perfect composite image, bristling with life. *New York Movie* is at once every 1930s movie you've ever seen and none of them. The patrons—an isolated man and a woman—sit in their plush seats, immobilized in front of the latest product of the dream factory, a not-quite-identifiable landscape, shimmering on the screen.

Hopper's world, it should be noted, is a world of adults only; children never intrude upon the scene. He uses his figures sparingly: solitary men or women, manageable groups of three or four—never crowds. And there is, throughout his work, an ever-recurring couple—the bored young marrieds of *Room in New York*, the boss and his secretary in *Office at Night*, the seedy, aging couple in *Hotel by a Railroad*—actors in a continuous private scenario that is drawn, one suspects, from Hopper's own cloistral married life.

During the 43 years of their marriage, Hopper and his wife were inseparable. Childless, they lived together and worked together daily, wintering in New York, summering at the Cape, except for occasional trips elsewhere. Once, when Hopper had been invited to judge an exhibition at a Virginia museum, the officials extended an invitation to him to stay at a local home. The invitation was sent through the Rehn Gallery—Hopper and Jo were traveling at the time—and Frank Rehn hastily called the museum. "For heaven's sake," he told them, "invite Mrs. Hopper. If she doesn't go, he doesn't go." Mrs. Hopper posed for virtually all the nudes and female figures that were required in Hopper's paintings.

Until the end of their lives, the Hoppers lived with an almost comic frugality. Even when Hopper's oils were bringing $15,000 and $20,000, the pair continued to eat in the same inexpensive Village restaurants they had frequented for years. John Clancy recalls that he was one of the few people ever invited to lunch at the Hoppers' New York studio—and then only because he was there on business at the time. It was a modest lunch: canned soup, cake and coffee.

Once, in a moment of extravagance, Hopper bought his wife a fur coat, and Jo was angry with him for six months. The only luxuries they permitted themselves were traveling—trips to Mexico, New Mexico, the West Coast—and the clothes bought at Abercrombie & Fitch for serviceability and wear. They were, it seems, two dropouts from the great American dream of conspicuous consumption.

By all accounts, Jo Hopper was a vivacious, high-spirited and difficult woman. A painter herself, she was convinced of the value of her work and willed it to the Whitney, along with her husband's. (The bequest consists of generally pleasant, lightweight works: flowers, sweet-faced children, gaily colored scenic views.) With visitors and friends, Jo Hopper would set up a barrage of conversation around her usually resigned husband—an indefatigable tug piping around a somnolent gray cruiser—effectively blocking discussions, sidetracking the subject when it veered off in directions where she didn't wish to go.

O'Doherty recalls a visit in which Hopper spoke to him about a self-portrait, done many years before. When he expressed a real interest in seeing it, Mrs.

Hopper put a stop to the discussion, declaring she had destroyed the picture. (The painting—a rare item in Hopper's *oeuvre*—turned up in the bequest. It was matched by Mrs. Hopper's own oil portrait of her husband, a gray, fussed-over work with a strange, probably inadvertent, halo effect showing behind his head.) Hopper did a striking portrait of his wife as well, *Jo Painting*; the look of determination he captured in her profile makes it clear that Jo Hopper was a formidable woman.

"They could be appallingly frank with each other," Goodrich remembers, but despite the bickering, he felt, "there was no mistaking their deep mutual attachment and dependence." The difficulties were not all one-sided. Mrs. Hopper complained: "Sometimes talking with Eddie is just like dropping a stone in a well, except that it doesn't thump when it hits bottom." Hopper's relationship to his wife, it appears, was much like his relationship to his art: silent, patient, totally committed to the nagging problems involved.

The brownstone at No. 3 Washington Square North where the Hoppers lived—Hopper had first moved there in 1913—is leased by New York University and now houses offices of its School of Social Work. In the entryway, Hopper's soiled name card is still in place by the bell, and the bright yellow stripes he painted on the edges of the stairs so that Mrs. Hopper could see them on her way down in the dim light are still visible on the four steep flights that lead up to the apartment. Joseph Roberto, the university's architect, who is in the process of restoring the Hoppers' studio (it will serve both as a memorial and a faculty lounge) explains that the rooms have been used for storage since the Hoppers' deaths.

On the fifth floor, we are met by Ed Brady, a graying, bouncy man, carrying a large old-fashioned briefcase. Brady has been the handyman for the block of buildings, including No. 3, since the early 1940s and he knew the Hoppers well. In their last years, they depended upon him a good deal; he did errands for them and looked in on them regularly. When Hopper was no longer able to drive, Brady would drive them up to Truro for the summer—in the Hoppers' old 1956 Buick—returning himself by bus. He pulls out of his briefcase several well-thumbed back issues of *Life* and *Time*, containing features on Hopper and his work, obviously proud of his association with the artist. Brady is one of the beneficiaries of Mrs. Hopper's will.

Hopper's studio in the south end of the building was not damaged in the disastrous fire, earlier in 1971, that gutted the north end of the building, which faces on Washington Mews. But the studio has recently been rewired and a layer of fine plaster dust covers the stored equipment and odds and ends of furniture, little of which belonged to the Hoppers. The room is flooded with a pleasant soft light, sifting down from a skylight on its northern end.

Hopper was photographed several times against the white studio wall with its white marble fireplace—the wall one first sees on entering the room. He kept his studio ascetically bare, not even hanging his own pictures. One gets the impression, from the slow, painstaking way in which he worked, that once he had finished a picture, he had it so firmly in mind that it was no longer necessary for him to look at it—or, perhaps, that the effort of concentration he bent upon each picture was so intense that it allowed for no distractions, not even the distraction of his own paintings hanging on the wall.

Roberto has managed to rescue a few personal items belonging to the Hoppers: a plain, glassed-in bookcase, of the kind one finds in Salvation Army stores nowadays; a badly stained canvas rain hat; and the old brown felt hat, belonging to Hopper, that had hung on the arm of his etching press for 20 or more years after he had given up pulling his own prints. He has also persuaded the Bank of New York, which administered the Hopper estate, to donate the etching press—now standing, with its antiquated fixtures and ancient cream-colored paint, in the corner, covered by a light film of dust—to the memorial, along with Hopper's old-fashioned, handmade easel, which has been dismantled and stored until the restoration is completed.

Mrs. Hopper's studio, in back of her husband's, is flooded with the same impassive light. A cheap wooden dresser, painted a shade of dusky rose that was popular in the 1940s, stands forlornly near the center of the room, its drawers pulled open and empty. It is one of the sturdy, inexpensive items of furniture with which the Hoppers furnished their apartment. Between the two connecting studios is a tiny kitchenette, no wider than the 1930s-vintage upright gas range on which the Hoppers cooked their meals. Their small hall bedroom is now occupied as a faculty office. The hall bathroom, with its antiquated fixtures and ancient cream-colored paint, is just as the Hoppers left it—even, one suspects, to the leaky faucet, patiently dripping into the sink.

Hopper spent the last months of his life in the studio, confined to a wheelchair, suffering from a prostate ailment for which he had had several operations. Unable to paint, he was reduced to simply waiting out the days while the light bloomed and faded in his white room—that condition of waiting in small, confined spaces that he had pictured often in his paintings. Ed Brady would wheel him to the hall john and help him into bed in the evenings—a proud man, serving out the last indignities of the flesh.

Jo Hopper lived on in the studio after her husband's death. She was 84, the only tenant in the south section of the building, the university having taken over the lower floors. When university officials tried to persuade her to move to one of their other properties where she would have the advantage of an elevator, she refused. Brady would come by at noontime, bringing his lunch ("She'd talk my ear off," he says). He regularly did her shopping for her ("If I spent 69 cents for a cake, she'd complain"—this said more in simple amazement than disapproval). In the evenings, he brought over a hot meal from a nearby restaurant ("Tuesday nights was chicken à la king").

One day, Mrs. Hopper brought out a stack of 20 or more of her husband's pictures and told Brady to burn them. They were Edward's early work, she said, and not good. "So help me God, I don't know anything about art," Brady says, "but some of them were the most beautiful nudes you've ever seen, painted on wooden panels. But as my wife says, 'At least you kept faith with her.' " Mrs. Hopper had carefully torn up beforehand the watercolors that were in the batch.

Several months after she had been living alone, Mrs. Hopper fell and broke her hip. She managed to drag herself to the phone and summon help. Brady had to climb in through the front window in order to get to her. Released from the hospital, she returned to the apartment, still determined to live alone. One Monday morning, a secretary, coming to work on the floor below, heard her moaning and calling for help. She was taken to St. Vincent's Hospital, where she died of lung cancer. The Hopper estate, which is said to be near final settlement, is valued at slightly less than a million dollars.

Hopper's final observations on his art and his life were left, characteristically, in the form of a painting—his last painting, in fact, completed at South Truro in the fall of 1965. *Two Comedians* is probably Hopper's most mordant commentary on a number of his chosen themes—the remorseless human comedy, the theater as an abiding image of life, the artificiality of nature, his own long marital life. It depicts a man and a woman in clown costumes bowing out before the last curtain. Behind them is a darkened stage; to their side, flats of painted scenery, representing luxuriant foliage.

Before her death, Jo Hopper confirmed to Goodrich that the couple represented her and her husband.

LYNDON BAINES JOHNSON

1908–1973

By Albin Krebs

"I shall not seek, and I will not accept, the nomination of my party for another term as your president," Lyndon Baines Johnson told a startled nationwide television audience the night of March 31, 1968.

Despite the fact that the nation was frustrated and angry about the war in Vietnam, troubled by racial strife and caught up in inflation, most Americans had more or less assumed that Mr. Johnson, the highly political and mightily proud 36th President of the United States, would run for reelection in 1968.

But in his televised speech, Mr. Johnson first gave the long-awaited word that he had ordered a major reduction in the bombing of Communist North Vietnam and called for peace talks.

Then, after acknowledging that there was "division in the American house," Mr. Johnson added his withdrawal statement, which had not been in his prepared text:

"What we won when all of our people were united must not now be lost in suspicion, distrust, selfishness and politics among our people," he said. "Believing this as I do, I have concluded that I should not permit the presidency to become involved in the partisan divisions that are developing in this political year."

Then he said he would not be a candidate for another term.

With those electrifying words, Mr. Johnson in effect admitted the shattering of a dream he had cherished since Nov. 22, 1963, when a madman's bullet killed his predecessor and made him president, that he would restore peace and serenity to the American people.

He set forth those goals in a ringing speech before a joint session of Congress on March 15, 1965. "This is the richest and most powerful country which ever occupied this globe," he said. "The might of past empires is little compared to ours. But I do not want to be the president who built empires, or sought grandeur, or extended dominion.

"I want to be the president who educated young children to the wonders of their world.

"I want to be the president who helped to feed the hungry and to prepare them to be taxpayers instead of tax-eaters.

"I want to be the president who helped the poor to find their own way and who protected the right of every citizen to vote in every election.

"I want to be the president who helped to end hatred among his fellow men and who promoted love among the people of all races, all regions and all parties.

"I want to be the president who helped to end war among the brothers of this earth."

These were Lyndon Johnson's aims, but few of them were to be achieved. Less than two years after

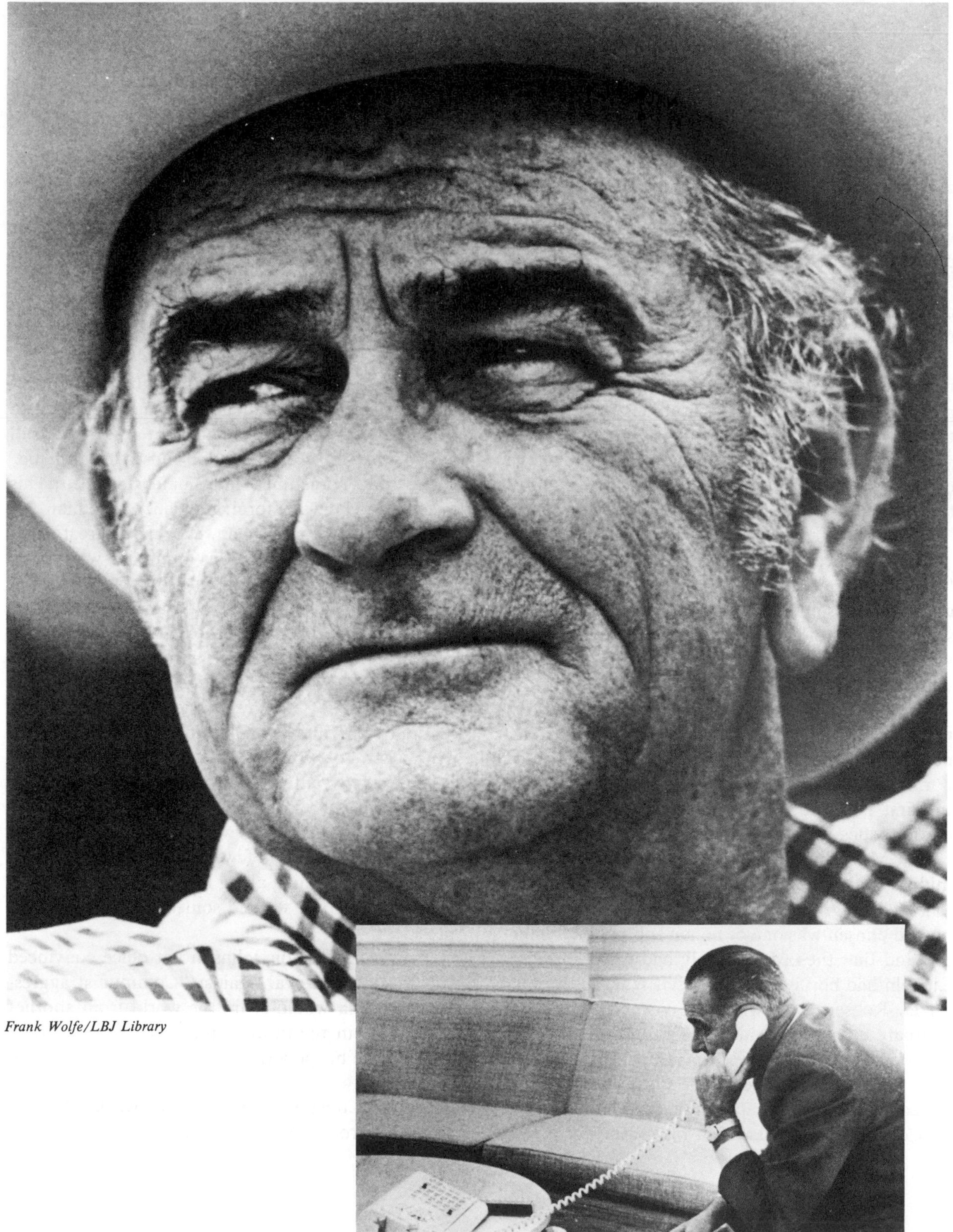

Frank Wolfe/LBJ Library

UPI/Bettmann Newsphotos

that fateful day in Dallas when John F. Kennedy was shot, and less than a year after he had been chosen president in his own right, Mr. Johnson found himself trapped in a remote, bloody and incredibly costly war that, it seemed, would never end.

Progressively the budgets of his administration were mortgaged to that war, and its unpopularity drained his political strength.

Moreover, the cities of America were ravaged by decay and racial dissension, and the white majority responded with anger, fear and vindictiveness.

By the time he left office on Jan. 20, 1969, his nation's reputation for violence, far from having diminished, had grown abroad to monstrous proportions.

The name of Lyndon Johnson, like that of the other three Democratic presidents who served full terms in this century, had become inextricably linked with war and its consequences.

By all indications, the war in Vietnam was the least popular of the nation's wars in this century, and Mr. Johnson became by far the most controversial wartime leader. Bitter controversy born of the war swirled around the president and drowned the memory of his good legislative works.

Historians will long debate how and why he took the nation into the Vietnam quagmire. His contemporaries, unwilling to await that judgment, berated him from all sides, not only for getting involved in the first place but also for his military and diplomatic tactics throughout.

But Mr. Johnson tried always to steer deftly to a middle course between the extremes of public opinion. He held grimly to the conviction that the course he had chosen was one of honor and national interest, and that the ordeal simply had to be borne, as Lincoln had borne his in the Civil War, and Franklin D. Roosevelt, to whom he wanted most to be compared, had borne his in this century.

In doing so, he knew that he had sacrificed not only popularity and the people's love, for which he lusted, but also the great domestic accomplishments that once had seemed within his grasp. For a man with a gargantuan appetite for achievement, this was a bitter pill to swallow.

Convinced as he was that he had pursued the right, even the just, course, by mid-1968 Lyndon Johnson made it plain that he was a deeply disillusioned and frustrated man, ready to shake off the shackles the presidency by then represented.

Those who knew him knew this, but they would also remember that the essential Lyndon Johnson, forged in the political fires over a period of some 40 years, was an intense dynamo of a man, a mover, a shaker, a doer.

He was a zestful man who brought to the presidency a genuine love of politics, of the infighting and conniving and the sense of public interest that are all part of that most exacting and most vexing game.

He was sometimes inordinately loyal to his friends, and he was a forgiving man, a kind man. He was also often a cruel man, capable of great rages and monumental castigations of anyone who dared cross him. His vanity was legend, his compassion for a friend in trouble limitless. He was incredibly thin-skinned when criticized by the press, yet he held few grudges long. And he could shrug off attacks with the homily, "My Daddy told me that if you don't want to get shot at, stay off the firing line."

But by the time he had decided to leave the presidency, Mr. Johnson had apparently concluded that he no longer wanted to be on the firing line.

The man who had been fond of saying, "Let us reason together," and "I want to be president of all the people," had found fewer and fewer of his fellow Americans reasoning along his lines, and vast numbers of the people wanted someone else to be their president.

However, Lyndon Johnson left office convinced still that a small war against "Communist aggression" in Asia would spare the world from another global war in the future, and he seemed confident that in time his policies would be vindicated by history.

He was a man who slept little and worked himself and those around him like Texas field hands. He was constantly on the telephone, ordering, wheedling, threatening, wheeling and dealing, striving always to keep abreast of every matter that affected the interests of the United States—and Lyndon Johnson.

Although it was often said that Lyndon Baines Johnson was born for the presidency, it seemed quite unlikely that he would ever attain it.

For one thing, Mr. Johnson was not a revered theorist of government or the proponent of great change and innovation. Nor was he a polished orator, a magnetic personality, a powerful factional leader.

His personal and political career had been clouded by charges of vulgarism and provincialism, of opportunism and "wheeling and dealing," by his disputed election to the Senate in 1948, his ownership of lucrative, government-regulated television broadcasting rights, and by the tangled affairs of his protégé, Robert G. Baker, who was secretary to the Democratic majority in the Senate during Mr. Johnson's most influential years there.

Moreover, Mr. Johnson was a southerner, and there had been no southerner in the White House since Woodrow Wilson, a Virginian, had left it in 1921.

All these factors contributed to the unlikelihood that Mr. Johnson would ever become president, short of the sort of accident that indeed gave him that high office. But the fact that he would go into politics seemed certain from the start.

Mr. Johnson's father, his father's father and his mother's father all served in the Texas legislature. He was, as he put it, "born into politics."

It was said that on Aug. 27, 1908, Mr. Johnson's rancher grandfather, Sam Johnson, Sr., rode on horseback around Johnson City, Tex., proclaiming that "a United States senator was born this morning—my grandson."

Lyndon Johnson was born in the three-room Johnson home at Hye, near the small villages of Stonewall and Johnson City, in the sere hills of southwest Texas. He was the eldest of five children, the others being Rebekah, Josefa, Sam Houston and Lucia.

The Johnson family was extremely poor. Money was scarce in the back-country hills, cattle raising was risky at best and the oil boom had not yet come to Texas. Water was a problem, and since the land was mesquite-choked, arid and sulphurous, farming was not, as the future president was to put it, "worth a cotton-pickin' damn."

Growing up in the "jackrabbit country" along the Pedernales River, Mr. Johnson was extremely close to his parents. He recalled in later years that his father, Samuel Ealy Johnson, Jr., having high hopes for his firstborn, would shake the boy awake mornings with the cry "Son, get up! Every boy in town has a two-hour start on you." (In his Senate office years later, an adage of his father's hung on Mr. Johnson's wall: "When you're talkin', you ain't learnin' nothin'.")

From his mother, Rebekah Baines Johnson, Lyndon gained a lifetime respect for the value of an education, although at first he balked at going to college. Mrs. Johnson had worked her own way through college and had taught "expression" in rural schools, and she taught her son the alphabet with A-B-C blocks.

Mrs. Johnson also taught Lyndon how to read, first with Mother Goose rhymes, then with lines from Longfellow and Tennyson, which the child did not enjoy. Then, and for the rest of his life, Mr. Johnson abhorred fiction. When his mother read to him, he would ask insistently, "But, Ma, is it real? Did it really happen?"

Lyndon could read by the time he was 4 and he was in school at the age of 5. He rode to classes on a donkey and was thus the butt of many jokes. Fistfights with schoolmates were not uncommon, but the youth managed to be popular. Although he was not bookish and his grades were mediocre, he was president of his high school graduating class of seven students as well as of the debate team.

The team made it to the state debate finals.

When Lyndon lost his match, he recalled later, "I went to the bathroom and was sick." Then, as in later years, Lyndon Johnson hated to lose—and even to associate with losers, or what he called "cain't-doers."

Out of school at 15, Lyndon resisted parental suggestions that he go to college; instead he hitchhiked to California with five other boys. They split up there and, according to Mr. Johnson, "Up and down the Pacific Coast I tramped, washing dishes, waiting on tables, doing farm work and growing thinner and more homesick."

He returned to Texas, but college still struck him as a loathsome prospect, and for a time he worked on a road gang. Finally, he told his parents he was "sick of working with my hands," and with $75 borrowed on his own signature, in February 1927 he entered Southwest Texas State Teachers College at San Marcos.

There he worked as a janitor, housepainter and secretary to the college president. He was a star debater and editor of the school paper. Already a reservoir of cyclonic energy, not to mention supreme self-confidence, Lyndon had no intention of "wasting" four years getting a degree. And even though he had to complete three months of precollege work plus the regular course, he was graduated in three years at the age of 22.

His first full-time job was teaching public speaking and English at Sam Houston High School in Houston. Many Mexican-Americans attended the school, and there was discrimination against them there and in the community. Mr. Johnson encouraged the children to learn English so they could get along better in society.

Mr. Johnson obviously liked the Mexican-Americans. He learned to speak with them in a relaxed pidgin Spanish and, in the years to come, in their company he could unashamedly return affectionate *abrazo* for *abrazo*. In Houston he laid the groundwork for what was to become, in Texas politics, a reputation as the special friend and champion of the state's Mexican-American minority. As that minority grew in influence and affluence, Lyndon Johnson reaped considerable political benefits.

While still teaching in Houston, Mr. Johnson went to work as a volunteer in the 1931 congressional campaign of Richard M. Kleberg, Sr., one of the owners of the mammoth King Ranch and a friend of his father. Mr. Kleberg won the special election for a House seat. The tall, gangling Mr. Johnson went to Washington with him as his legislative assistant.

Lyndon Johnson hit Capitol Hill in those Depression days like a Texas tornado. He called persistently on federal bureaus, seeking drought relief, unemployment relief, civil service jobs, anything that was available for the folks back home. In those early days in Washington, Mr. Johnson had the not inconsiderable help of Sam Rayburn, soon to become the powerful Speaker of the House. Mr. Rayburn had been an old friend of Lyndon's father, with whom he had served in the Texas House of Representatives.

By 1934, young Mr. Johnson was a man-about-Washington, with friends in nearly every office in the capital.

He shuttled between Washington and Texas, tending Mr. Kleberg's political fences. It was on such a flying trip to Austin, in September 1934, that he met Claudia Alta Taylor, who had been nicknamed Lady Bird by a nurse when she was a child. Their whirlwind courtship began three minutes after they met, when Mr. Johnson asked Lady Bird for a date. She declined. But Miss Taylor—the daughter of a well-to-do East Texan and fresh out of the University of Texas—was barraged by telegrams and telephone calls from Washington, all from a very determined young man who was intent on having his way. He did, and they were married on Nov. 17, 1934.

Back in Washington, Mr. Johnson attended law school at George Washington University, but in 1935, not yet 27 years old and still short of his law degree, he was—at Sam Rayburn's behest—appointed Texas state director of the National Youth Administration.

The job gave Mr. Johnson a splendid opportunity. By then he had firmly decided to get into the political big leagues, and so his new post was superbly designed to give him grass-roots links with young Texans just coming of voting age. He whirled around the state, making friends, passing out favors and getting his name into the newspapers.

His chance to run for office came in 1937. The United States Representative from his district, James P. Buchanan, died, and a special election to fill out the term was called. Mr. Johnson was one of 10 candidates in a no-primary, no-runoff, winner-take-all race.

In that election, Mr. Johnson showed the acute political sense that was to become his trademark. He needed a gimmick to distinguish his candidacy from those of his rivals, and he found it in support of the New Deal, which had fallen into disfavor with conservatives and businessmen in Texas. President Roosevelt's plan to "pack" the Supreme Court served to harden their resistance.

It happened that Mr. Johnson was an admirer of Mr. Roosevelt, and that he approved of the New Deal without reservation. He took a firm stand in support of the president, particularly his proposal to increase the membership of the Supreme Court. The tactic served to force his rivals to gang up on him—and put him into the limelight. He was no longer an unknown.

The result was that when the ballots were counted, Lyndon Johnson had piled up twice as many votes as his nearest opponent. He had won the first of his six House terms handily, along with the delight and gratitude of Franklin Delano Roosevelt. The president, who chanced to be cruising in the Gulf of Mexico off Galveston on Election Day, invited young Mr. Johnson aboard ship, and a mutually beneficial friendship blossomed. (When Mr. Roosevelt died, Mr. Johnson said mournfully: "He was like a Daddy to me.")

Mr. Johnson was sworn in as a member of Congress on May 14, 1937. The president, convinced that he was a "comer," wangled him, with the cooperation of Mr. Rayburn, a coveted assignment to the Naval Affairs Committee, an unusual piece of luck for a junior congressman, who would normally have to be content with a lackluster position on a minor committee.

The late 1930s was the high-water mark of the "Texas era" in Washington, with such natives as Mr. Rayburn, John Nance Garner (Mr. Roosevelt's first vice president), Tom Connally and Jesse Jones riding high. Mr. Johnson fitted well into that galaxy, benefited from its favors and in time shone with a light all his own.

He won reelection easily in 1938, and in 1940 he breezed through to a second full term without formal opposition. The same year his House Democratic colleagues recognized his political talents by electing him chairman of their campaign committee.

Meanwhile, Mr. Johnson kept his political fences in Texas in good repair by obtaining more than his share of conservation and public works projects for his district. Among these was a flood-control and electricity-generating dam-and-spillway system for the Pedernales River, which runs through what is now the LBJ Ranch at Johnson City.

In 1941 Mr. Johnson had to take a step back on the political ladder he was fast climbing. After the death of Senator Morris Sheppard, he called on his friend, Mr. Roosevelt, and then announced, on the steps of the White House, that he planned to run, with the president's support, for the vacant Senate seat.

But this was a different year and a different kind of race from his first one. Mr. Roosevelt was in supreme disfavor in Texas by then, and so it was probably a mistake for Mr. Johnson to have the president openly "telling Texas how to vote," as the cry across the state had it. Mr. Johnson lost the race, by 1,311 votes, to the colorful former governor W. Lee (Pappy) O'Daniel, a reactionary self-styled hillbilly. It was the only defeat he ever suffered at the hands of the electorate.

Fortunately for Mr. Johnson, he did not have to relinquish his House seat to participate in the special election, and he returned to his duties in Washington. One of these duties was to vote, in December 1941, for a declaration of war against Japan. Three days after Pearl Harbor was attacked by the Japanese, he was commissioned a lieutenant commander in the navy and dispatched to the Pacific on a three-man team to make a personal survey of battle conditions for the president.

It was a noncombat assignment, but Mr. Johnson did fly on some missions as an observer, surviving crash landings on two occasions. General Douglas MacArthur awarded him the Silver Star for gallantry in action. Seven months after he went into uniform, Mr. Johnson's naval career ended, when President Roosevelt ordered all members of Congress in military service to return to their duties on Capitol Hill.

During his absence, Mr. Johnson's congressional office was maintained by his wife. Upon his return to Washington in July 1942, he found his political affairs in excellent shape.

At this time the Johnsons made a private decision that was to have an important bearing on the future. A virtually bankrupt radio station in Austin, one that blanketed all seven counties of Mr. Johnson's 10th District and some others besides, came up for sale. It was an unpromising investment, since in 1942 it had lost $7,000 on revenues of more than $26,000, but the Johnsons looked upon the station as a useful tool for his political career.

Mrs. Johnson had recently inherited about $65,000 from her grandmother. After much deliberation, she and her husband decided to risk a bid on the broadcasting property. They did, at $17,500, and the station, debts and all, became theirs.

The station, KTBC, and later KTBC-TV, became Mrs. Johnson's particular preoccupation while her husband carried on in the realm of politics. Its fortunes spiraled upward under her canny management, and by 1964 the station's assets were listed at $3.2 million. At that time the Johnsons put their holdings in a family trust, in which they remained until Mr. Johnson left the White House in 1969.

In the late 1940s, Mr. Johnson's liberal New Deal voting record began showing lapses. The man who had voted enthusiastically for the Wagner Act of 1935—"labor's Magna Carta," as it was called—in 1946 voted also for the Taft-Hartley Act, denounced by some of his colleagues as "a slave labor bill." (Mr. Johnson, as a senator, also was lukewarm, at best, on civil rights proposals urged upon the Republican-controlled 80th Congress by President Harry S Truman.)

By 1948, Mr. Johnson was ready for another try at the Senate. Mr. O'Daniel, who had defeated him in 1941, had decided not to run again, but Mr. Johnson faced a formidable opponent in former governor Coke Stevenson, who was widely popular and soundly conservative. In the Democratic primary—in which there were a total of 11 candidates—Mr. Stevenson outpolled Mr. Johnson, 477,077 to 405,617, but neither had a clear majority and there had to be a runoff.

Mr. Johnson campaigned in a helicopter and by plane, something new and exciting in those days, and concentrated on the metropolitan areas where Mr. Stevenson had shown the most strength. There was a runoff, and Mr. Johnson squeaked to victory by a margin of only 87 votes of 988,295 cast.

There were accusations of ballot-box irregularities—particularly in south Texas, Mr. Johnson's Mexican-American stronghold. Mr. Stevenson filed suits in county, state and federal courts; but Mr. Johnson, blithely filing countersuits, won all down the line. The state Democratic Executive Committee finally certified his primary election, and in the general election he defeated his Republican opponent by a 2-to-1 margin.

But for years afterward, Mr. Johnson was derisively called "Landslide Lyndon" and there were persistent charges that the election had been "fixed." During the 1964 presidential race, extreme right-wingers, who loathed Mr. Johnson monumentally, charged that the 1948 election was the platform for his alleged "tower of illegitimate power."

Mr. Johnson's career in the Senate matched in vigor and ambition his career in the House, but it was marked also by maturity and a growing sophistication.

While observing the unwritten rule that freshman senators should be seen and not heard, Mr. Johnson cultivated the veteran Sen. Richard Russell of Georgia, a member of the Senate's "inner club" and chairman of the powerful Armed Services Committee. After the outbreak of the Korean War, he won a seat on that committee. And after he charged that the country had demobilized too swiftly after World War II and embarked on a "delay-defeat-retreat" policy, he found himself appointed chairman of a new Senate Armed Forces preparedness subcommittee.

Despite his criticism of the nation's defense policies, Mr. Johnson stood firmly with President Truman on Korean policy. When the Republicans and many Democrats blamed the war on Mr. Truman, he said with characteristic bluntness and simplicity: "The Communists, not President Truman, were responsible for the invasion of South Korea. The quicker we direct our hostility to the enemy instead of to our leaders the quicker we will get the job done."

In 1951 Mr. Johnson was elected Majority Whip, a testament to his growing capacity to make friends and wield influence. His choice for the 1952 Democratic nomination for president was his friend Mr. Russell, but he gave his full support to Adlai E. Stevenson when the Illinois governor captured the nomination.

The Democrats lost majority control in the Senate in the 1952 election, which brought Dwight D. Eisenhower into the White House. Mr. Johnson became Democratic Minority Leader. At 44, he was the youngest man ever to hold that position.

The Republicans lost control of both houses of Congress in 1954 and Mr. Johnson became majority leader in the Senate. Again, he was the youngest ever to hold such a position.

In the years that followed, Mr. Johnson was to gain the gratitude of Mr. Eisenhower for his active cooperation with the Republican branch on legislative matters. He also incurred the scarcely disguised dislike and distrust of many liberals in his own party, who believed he was too conservative and was carrying bipartisanship too far.

His achievements as Senate Majority Leader became something of a legend in Washington. He was said by many to have been the most proficient of any who ever held the post, for, without resorting to bombast or open exhibitions of punishment or reward, he adroitly got temperamental and independent-minded senators to see things his way.

Mr. Johnson exhibited an uncanny ability to count noses, to know precisely, long before a vote was taken, what chances a given bill had for passage. He gave patronage favors in return for voting favors, and, according to one admiring colleague, "Lyndon had a mind like a ledger—accounts payable, accounts receivable—and every transaction he ever made with any of us was recorded in it."

During those years Mr. Johnson, always a powerhouse, moved so fast and so furiously and with such blinding effect that, it was said, when someone once asked a page boy if he had seen Senator Johnson, the youth replied, "I haven't seen anything but a burning bush."

Hardworking Lyndon Johnson very nearly burned himself out. In July 1955 he suffered a massive heart attack—"about as bad as a man can have and still live," as he described it—that put him on the sidelines for six months. As a friend put it, "he organized his recovery like one of his political campaigns." He gave up the chili dishes he favored and also his three-pack-a-day cigarette habit, trimmed down from 220 to 180 pounds and cut his normal working day from 18 to 14 hours.

In January 1956 Mr. Johnson returned to his Senate post and within weeks his colleagues were worriedly complaining that, again, his tremendous energy might be endangering his health. But he seemed to thrive on hard work.

The heart attack put a temporary damper on speculation that Mr. Johnson was a leading contender for his party's presidential nomination. The speculation had arisen as Mr. Johnson seemed to be trying to divest himself of the image that he was a straight-down-the-line "southern senator," meaning a segregationist.

As early as 1954, Mr. Johnson had acted independently of his fellow southerners when he refused to sign the "Southern Manifesto" that all other senators from the South did sign, denouncing the Supreme Court decision on desegregation of public schools. He was openly proud of having piloted through the Senate, in 1957, the first civil rights bill since Reconstruction, and in 1960 he helped beat back a filibuster aimed at blocking an expanded civil rights measure.

Mr. Johnson's decision to seek the presidential nomination in 1960 was handled as cagily as he handled most political decisions in his life. He allowed friends to mount an unofficial campaign for him as early as December 1959, but withheld his own announcement until the following July, shortly before the opening of the 1960 convention.

Many observers contended that he never seriously believed he could take the prize away from Sen. John F. Kennedy, starting as late as he did to win delegates. Mr. Kennedy went into the convention at Los Angeles with impressive primary victories, plus the solid results of hard work and sharp dealing with state conventions by his staff and most notably by his younger brother Robert.

Mr. Kennedy had the nomination clinched before the completion of the first roll call. His selection of Mr. Johnson as his vice presidential running mate came as a distinct surprise. So did Mr. Johnson's acceptance. His old friend, Mr. Rayburn, who had placed his name in nomination to lead the ticket, tearfully pleaded with him not to be "fool enough" to surrender his powerful Senate leadership in favor of the largely ceremonial position of vice president.

But having accepted the Kennedy offer willingly, even eagerly, Mr. Johnson said shortly after the convention: "I recognized that there were only two offices in the land in which all the people had a choice. And I felt it offered a good opportunity, that it would be quite a challenge, and that it would be good for the party and the country."

It was common knowledge at the time that there was no love lost between Mr. Kennedy and Mr. Johnson, but Mr. Kennedy could obviously benefit from Mr. Johnson's considerable presence on his ticket. As a Roman Catholic easterner, Mr. Kennedy's position in the southern Bible Belt, traditionally regarded as a bastion of anti-Catholicism, was not strong. He was also on shaky ground in the West. The Johnson image of a Texan, a westerner, and a bit of a conservative would be helpful.

Mr. Johnson's campaign train, from which emanated almost constantly the strains of his favorite song, "Yellow Rose of Texas," took the Johnsons across the heart, width and breadth of the Old Confederacy, making whistle-stops from Washington to New Orleans and on up to Memphis.

Besides making speeches, the candidate talked in private with hundreds of local, district and state politicians. A close associate said he reminded his listeners in these talks that, as Senate Majority Leader, he had done more for the modern South and its politicians than any other man. And indeed he had done much for them, in obtaining dams, rural electrification, defense installations, government contracts and other so-called pork-barrel favors.

Mr. Kennedy was, like Mr. Johnson, a formidable campaigner, yet the Democratic ticket finally triumphed over the Republican team of Richard M. Nixon and Henry Cabot Lodge by the smallest vote margin in this century. Of the 69 million votes cast, the Democrats won by approximately 113,000 votes. The electoral vote was 303 to 219.

Mr. Kennedy credited Mr. Johnson with cutting down the anticipated Nixon-Lodge vote in the South and West. In Texas, vote analysts agreed that Mr. Johnson's Mexican-American constituency was responsible for swinging the state into the Democratic column.

Early in his vice presidency, Mr. Johnson found it difficult to accustom himself to living in the shade traditionally reserved for holders of his office. Before long, however, Mr. Kennedy, who was said to have developed a warm personal regard for Mr. Johnson during and immediately following the campaign, took steps to make Mr. Johnson the most active vice president in history.

The president sent him on missions to 33 countries. Many of the missions were ceremonial, but not all. Mr. Johnson could indeed reap snickers by befriending a camel driver in Karachi, Pakistan, and entertaining him in the United States. But he also flew to beleaguered West Berlin in August 1961, and said, "This city can never be bullied into the surrender of its freedom."

Mr. Johnson was brought into some of the inner circles of the Kennedy administration. He sat in on National Security Council meetings, was placed in charge of the president's program to eliminate job discrimination at plants doing business with the government and assigned the responsibility of keeping the administration's eye on the nation's space program—which, as a senator, he had been instrumental in getting off the ground.

Still, there were persistent rumors in 1963 that Mr. Kennedy was going to "dump" Mr. Johnson from his ticket in 1964. At his last news conference, held less than a month before the Dallas tragedy, the president emphatically stated that Mr. Johnson would be his running mate in 1964.

Mr. Kennedy also acceded to Mr. Johnson's request that he accompany him to Texas on a political fence-mending trip. In Texas, pro- and anti-Johnson, liberal and conservative, Democratic factions had been feuding for years. The President of the United States might be just the man to patch up the feud, to give the party a united cast as it headed for the next year's elections.

And so John F. Kennedy went with Lyndon Johnson to Texas on Nov. 21, 1963. The following day, Mr. Johnson and his wife rode in a motorcade through the sunlit streets of Dallas, behind an open limousine bearing John and Jacqueline Kennedy and Gov. John Connally of Texas.

Lee Harvey Oswald fired three shots from a window of the Texas Book Depository, and a president was dead.

Lyndon Johnson, a Texas ranch boy who had fought his way up the political ladder to become vice president of his country, became the 36th President of the United States at the age of 55.

Millions of Americans, stunned and frightened by the violence at Dallas, found consolation in the fact that, whether they liked him or not, Lyndon Johnson, propelled by chance into the presidency, was as well equipped by experience for his task as any man in history.

AFTER A TIME OF TRAGEDY, A BEGINNING TOWARD THE "GREAT SOCIETY"

VICE PRESIDENT JOHNSON and his wife had planned to entertain President and Mrs. Kennedy at their ranch in Johnson City, Tex., the night of Nov. 22, 1963.

But that afternoon, while he rode in a motorcade through the streets of Dallas, President Kennedy was killed by a sniper.

The Johnsons were riding in the third car of the motorcade. A Secret Service agent heard the assassin's shots and, as Mr. Johnson later recalled it, the agent "vaulted across the front seat . . . pushed me to the floor and shielded my body with his own body, ready to sacrifice his life for mine."

At Parkland Memorial Hospital, while President Kennedy lay dying, the frightened man who was to succeed him in only a few minutes stood in a hallway, muttering over and over, "The international Communists did it . . . The international Communists did it."

At 1:13 P.M., 43 minutes after he had been shot,

John Fitzgerald Kennedy, the young and dashing 35th President of the United States, was pronounced dead.

Thirteen minutes later, Mr. Johnson was hustled into an unmarked police car to be driven at breakneck speed to Love Field, where Air Force One, the presidential jet, was waiting. Fearing possible conspirators of the assassin, Mr. Johnson made the trip crouched on the floor of the police car.

The somber-faced Texan took the oath of office as President of the United States in the cramped executive suite of Air Force One. At his right stood his wife, Lady Bird, to his left the numbed and grief-stricken Jacqueline Kennedy, who still wore a pink wool suit spattered with her husband's blood. Instead of a Bible, Federal District Judge Sarah T. Hughes used a Roman Catholic missal to administer the oath to Mr. Johnson.

Air Force One, carrying the new president and his predecessor's body, took off immediately for Washington.

Dusk had fallen over Andrews Air Force Base, near Washington, when the jet rolled to a halt. A nationwide television audience watched, stunned, as Mr. Kennedy's casket was taken off the plane.

Then, under the harsh glare of the arc lights that flooded the plane, Mr. Johnson stepped forward and read the nation 57 words of reassurance from a white card: "This is a sad time for all people. We have suffered a loss that cannot be weighed. For me, it is a deep personal tragedy. I know the world shares the sorrow that Mrs. Kennedy and her family bear. I will do my best. That is all I can do. I ask for your help—and God's."

Under the gravest of circumstances, the torch of leadership had been passed on. The new chief executive did not publicly take it up until five days after the assassination, when he stood before a joint session of Congress and said, "Let us continue."

Then he quickly made it apparent that what he meant was passage of Mr. Kennedy's entire legislative program, including civil rights laws and an unorthodox tax reduction to stimulate the economy.

In his rich southern drawl, Mr. Johnson told Congress: "We have talked long enough in this country about equal rights. We have talked for 100 years or more. It is time now to write it in the books of law."

He made it clear that he intended to keep the Kennedy vision for the world and pronounced it with unexpected force and eloquence: "We will be unceasing in our search for peace, resourceful in our pursuit of areas of agreement even with those with whom we differ, and generous and loyal to those who join us in common cause."

For a few months, Mr. Johnson kept the staff of President Kennedy beside his own in the White House, as for years he was to retain the services of many of the key members of the Kennedy cabinet, notably Secretary of State Dean Rusk and Secretary of Defense Robert McNamara. He even kept on, for more than a year, Attorney General Robert F. Kennedy, the late president's brother, despite the fact that he loathed him and the feeling was mutual.

It was in his first 15 months in office that Mr. Johnson best demonstrated the qualities for which he hoped to be remembered—by masterly managing the transition of power from the slain president to himself, by breaking legislative logjams of decades' duration, by restoring faith in the viability of the American system of divided legislative and executive powers, by proving the nation's capacity to withstand the horror of assassination and by persuading the world of the strength and continuity of American institutions.

In putting his own brand on the presidency, he brought to the office a profound respect for the balancing force of Congress. He restored communications between the executive and legislative branches of government to such an extent that the 1964 congressional record was described as the most fruitful in a decade.

Shrewd management of his relations with Congress brought about quick action on a tax-cut bill only weeks after Mr. Johnson became president. He paved the way for the $11 billion cut by slashing the budget by $900 million, which apparently impressed the economy blocs.

In July 1964 Mr. Johnson proudly signed into law the most sweeping civil rights bill since Reconstruction days. The measure had been submitted to Congress in June 1963 by Mr. Kennedy, and Mr. Johnson had pushed hard for its enactment from the time he became president.

The bill passed the Senate after a 15-week southern filibuster. It outlawed discrimination in places of public accommodation, publicly owned facilities, employment and union membership, as well as in federally aided programs. A major feature of the legislation was the new power it gave the attorney general to speed school desegregation and to enforce the Negro's right to vote.

To get the legislation he wanted, the president used with great success what came to be known in Washington as "the Johnson treatment."

The treatment consisted of a combination of cajolery, flattery, concession, arm-twisting threats and outright wooing, all applied by Mr. Johnson with an endless succession of telephone calls, bourbon-and-Scotch lunches, barnyard jokes, the squeezing of elbows, the friendly arm around the shoulder, the cold stare when crossed. The technique was aimed at finding and touching the most sensitive nerve in Mr. Johnson's target—and, he said, "most often, that was the target's self-interest."

He used variations of the treatment to win a victory that had eluded the administrations of both Dwight D. Eisenhower and John F. Kennedy over a period of more than five years. That was the settlement of the so-called featherbedding dispute over work-rule changes between the nation's railroads and the railroad unions.

When a nationwide rail strike was called by the unions for April 10, 1964, Mr. Johnson invited railroad and union leaders to the White House on April 9. The two sides agreed there would be no strike before April 25 and promised they would once more try to reach a settlement.

On April 21, labor fell in line for a settlement and the president turned the treatment on the nine management representatives. He popped in and out of their meetings, sent special emissaries to persuade them that they must agree to settle, and ate and drank with them. Finally, when he sensed it was a do-or-die proposition, he sat down with the management men, thinking, he confided to an aide, they were probably 7-to-2 against him.

When one management representative began the meeting with "I'm just an old country boy . . . ," old country boy Lyndon Johnson imperiously shushed him.

"Hold it," he snapped, "stop right there. When I hear that around this town, I put my hand on my billfold. Don't start that with me."

The astonished butt of the presidential dressing-down joined the laughter and said, "By God, I was just going to say that I'm ready to sign up." Mr. Johnson said later that he believed "that broke the deadlock, but of course I'll never know what he was going to say when I broke in."

The business community's initial reaction to Mr. Johnson was most favorable, in contrast to its attitude toward Mr. Kennedy, who was looked upon with suspicion by business after his crackdown on the steel industry over a price increase early in his administration.

Mr. Johnson courted business in an hour-long, off-the-cuff speech before the United States Chamber of Commerce in 1964. Combining Texas blarney, homespun wit and candor ("Jettison your martyr complex . . . Stop obstructing the government . . . Join with labor to help us hold down inflation . . ."), he won a standing ovation.

Henry Ford 2d, who admitted he had never voted for a Democrat for president, pronounced Mr. Johnson "terrific" and said he intended to vote for him in 1964.

There were occasions, of course, when business was less than enchanted with Mr. Johnson. In the latter part of 1965, for example, when the aluminum and copper industries announced price rises that the administration felt were inflationary, the government threatened to release some of its stockpiles of the metals to keep prices down.

Early in his administration, the president declared what he called a "war on poverty." With Mrs. Johnson he made two trips to the distressed Appalachia area to dramatize the need for an antipoverty drive for which he asked Congress to appropriate $1 billion.

He first spoke of the Great Society, the catchphrase with which he sought to identify his administration—as the New Deal was identified with Franklin D. Roosevelt's and the New Frontier with Mr. Kennedy's—in a commencement address at the University of Michigan on May 22, 1964. He repeated the call six days later in New York.

"I ask you to march with me along the road to the future," he said, "the road that leads to the Great Society, where no child will go unfed and no youngster will go unschooled . . . where every human being has dignity and every worker has a job; where education is blind to color and employment is unaware of race; where decency prevails and courage abounds . . ."

The Great Society became the slogan of Mr. Johnson's 1964 campaign to win a full four-year term in office, and well into that term he often promised that America could indeed become the Great Society. But he used the tag less and less as the nation became embroiled in racial strife, civil disorders and the ruinous war in Vietnam.

As the 1964 Democratic convention drew near, however, Mr. Johnson seemed to enjoy great popularity, and there was general approval of his handling of domestic problems and programs. He was also praised, during that period, for his cautious approach to foreign crises.

After rioting broke out in the Panama Canal Zone on Jan. 9, 1964, as an outgrowth of a schoolboy dispute over the flying of United States and Panamanian flags in the Zone, Panama suspended diplomatic relations with the United States and demanded revision of the 1903 Canal Zone treaty.

Working through the Organization of American States, Mr. Johnson finally persuaded the Panamanians to resume relations with this country, and eventually the United States granted Panama concessions in the Zone. Throughout, Mr. Johnson appeared to proceed with a steady hand.

He was equally unruffled in February 1964, when Premier Fidel Castro cut off the water supply for the United States Navy base at Guantánamo Bay, Cuba. He ordered water shipped to the base in tankers, and set in motion a crash program to build a desalinization plant at Guantánamo, making the base no longer dependent on the Castro regime for its water.

Mr. Johnson's record in the months after Mr. Kennedy's assassination, in addition to his previously unconcealed presidential ambitions, left no doubts in the minds of Democrats and Republicans alike that he would be his party's nominee in the 1964 election. The only real question was who would be his running mate.

Robert F. Kennedy, still attorney general, was believed to want the nomination, but Mr. Johnson quickly ruled him out by laying down the rule that no member of his cabinet would be his candidate. He then began to leak the names of several other possible candidates, including Sen. Eugene J. McCarthy, who four years later was to become one of the president's most severe Vietnam war critics.

Finally, after what some called his phony manipulations had achieved the desired effect —suspense and titillation—Mr. Johnson broke precedent and flew up to Atlantic City to personally tell the delegates to the Democratic convention that he had chosen Sen. Hubert H. Humphrey of Minnesota.

An incident connected with that flight illustrates how Mr. Johnson sometimes treated the men who worked for him. To his subordinates at the White House, he was a driving taskmaster who could blaze with anger at incompetence and negligence. He respected and even liked his aides, but on occasion, such as the one involving the flight to Atlantic City, he was entirely capable of insulting them publicly.

The idea to fly to Atlantic City had been supplied

by Pierre Salinger, Mr. Kennedy's press secretary, who had stayed on in the same capacity for Mr. Johnson before resigning to run unsuccessfully for the Senate in California. Mr. Johnson so liked the idea that he couldn't resist the temptation to turn to George Reedy, his new press secretary, and tell him scornfully, in the presence of newsmen, "Why don't you ever have good ideas like Pierre?" A shaken Mr. Reedy wrote out his resignation, but later tore it up after Mr. Johnson apologized, in private, for his offhand cruelty.

In the campaign Mr. Johnson advocated big government programs that he called vital to the nation's welfare. His Republican opponent, Barry Goldwater, the conservative senator from Arizona, called for cuts in government spending and less "Washington control" of the affairs of individuals and business.

Much campaign oratory was given over to arguments as to whether Mr. Goldwater had an "itchy finger" that might, if he became president, press the button that could plunge the nation into atomic holocaust. The Democrats charged that a President Goldwater might feel constrained to escalate the United States participation in the fighting in Vietnam, while Mr. Johnson would do no such thing and indeed would seek peace in Southeast Asia.

Senator Goldwater's campaign was in marked contrast to Mr. Johnson's. The senator held himself aloof and seldom mingled with the crowds, while Mr. Johnson kept his Secret Service guards constantly in jitters by breaking away and joining the throngs, shaking dozens of outstretched hands.

"Come on down to the speakin'," he would call through a bullhorn as his custom-built, bubble-top, armor-plated limousine cruised into a town. "Y'all don't need to dress up. It's not formal. Bring the kids and the dogs and come on down to the speakin'."

On both sides, the campaign was a relatively clean one. Mr. Johnson's supporters had a few episodes verging on the scandalous that had to be explained to the voters.

One involved Robert G. Baker, a good and loyal friend of Mr. Johnson, who had served as secretary to the Senate Democratic majority at the time Mr. Johnson was majority leader. Just before the assassination of Mr. Kennedy, it was disclosed that Bobby Baker had used official influence to amass for himself a sizable fortune.

A Senate subcommittee investigation disclosed that Mr. Baker had arranged a deal between an insurance man and the LBJ Company, the Johnson family communications concern in Austin, collecting a considerable fee on it. Mr. Baker, it was testified, showed his gratitude to the then vice president by giving him an $800 stereophonic system.

The Baker investigation never officially linked Mr. Johnson to Mr. Baker's alleged unethical practices, but the whole affair remained a source of embarrassment for the president. (In 1967, Mr. Baker was convicted of income tax evasion, theft and conspiracy to defraud the government, but Mr. Johnson was not involved in the case.)

During the campaign, the Johnson family fortune, which included the LBJ Company and its television and radio stations, plus real estate in Texas, Missouri, Alabama and Louisiana, became a political issue that led to release of a reputable accounting firm's audit of the family interests. The official worth was put at $3.2 million, but this was the value of the properties and assets at cost. Actually, the selling value of the Johnson assets was estimated at about $15 million.

In revealing his financial statement, Mr. Johnson pointed out that exactly a week after he became president, the family stock and property had been put into the hands of trustees who had the power to sell and reinvest and were under instructions to furnish the Johnsons only with information needed to complete their tax returns. The properties did, of course, revert to the Johnsons when Mr. Johnson left the White House in 1969.

On Election Day 1964, the Johnsons were at their ranch house in Johnson City, the unofficial White House during the Johnson administration. The house was the old family homestead, much added to, replete with piped-in Muzak tunes in every room and a heated swimming pool. The president voted, then spent the day riding around his lavish spread, dotted with herds of Herefords and purebred Angus cattle nibbling at sweeping expanses of grass.

That night, as the votes were counted across the nation, it became quickly apparent that tens of thousands of Republicans had deserted their party to vote for Mr. Johnson. The people rewarded him with a record-breaking majority of 61 percent of the popular vote.

Mr. Johnson called the result a "mandate for unity."

UNDER THE SHADOW OF VIETNAM

MRS. LYNDON B. JOHNSON held the Bible on which her husband's left hand rested as Chief Justice Earl Warren administered the oath of office to Mr. Johnson at his inauguration to his full term in the presidency on Jan. 20, 1965.

Mr. Johnson wore an ordinary business suit, in contrast to the formal clothes worn by most of his predecessors at their inaugurations. His 1,500-word inaugural address was one of the shortest in history. In it he said: "In a land of great wealth, families must not live in hopeless poverty. In a land rich in harvest, children must not go hungry. In a land of healing miracles, neighbors must not suffer and die untended. In a land of great learning and scholars, young people must be taught to read and write."

To the world Mr. Johnson said: "We aspire to nothing that belongs to others. We seek no dominion over our fellow man, but man's dominion over tyranny and misery."

The president had good reason to believe that many of his dreams for a better America could become reality, for the voters, while putting him into office in a landslide, had given him a Congress dominated by 295 Democrats against 140 Republicans in the House of Representatives and 68 Democrats against 32 Republicans in the Senate.

What the president called "the fabulous 89th" Congress soon began to enact far-reaching programs that had been bogged down in the legislative body for up to 30 years. Suddenly, they began to breeze through for signature by an exultant chief executive. The Congress passed 86 administration measures, despite the fact that the Republicans called much of the legislation unwise and charged that it was rammed through by the Johnson administration by means of sheer political power and with insufficient debate.

Among the measures that would have the most far-reaching effect on the quality of American life in the future was the bill to provide virtually free medical and hospital care for the aged under Social Security.

The measure, popularly known as the Medicare bill, was signed into law by the president on July 30, 1965, in the presence of former President Harry S Truman. Mr. Johnson chose the Truman Library in Independence, Mo., as the site of the signing of the bill in tribute to Mr. Truman, who had unsuccessfully sought Medicare legislation during his own administration.

Among Mr. Johnson's other notable successes during those first euphoric months of his full term in office were a massive program of federal aid to elementary and secondary schools as well as greatly expanded help to colleges and college students; new safeguards for Negro voting rights; reform of the immigration laws; grants for the "model cities" development program and a program of rent subsidies for poor tenants; a higher minimum wage; increased funds for the antipoverty program; a series of measures to protect the consumer from fraudulent packaging and advertising; and a substantial start on efforts to rid the air and streams of pollution.

All these and tax cuts, too, were realized by the

president, with the help of the 89th Congress, as were new health programs, greater support for the arts and humanities, a constitutional amendment to clarify the chain of executive command in case of presidential disability, and two more cabinet offices, Secretary of Transportation and Secretary of Housing and Urban Development.

To the latter post he named Robert C. Weaver, the first Negro to hold cabinet rank. The president also appointed the first Negro ever to sit on the Supreme Court, Thurgood Marshall, who had won fame as a brilliant trial lawyer for Negro rights before Mr. Johnson appointed him Solicitor General of the United States.

He appointed other Negroes to high office and championed their cause, so that, he said, "now, maybe, every Negro kid in the United States could think, 'Goddamn it, maybe I can be a judge some day—or president.' I never thought I could be president. I want to put some incentive in them."

On many occasions, Mr. Johnson lent his prestigious southern accent to the cry of nonviolent Negro demonstrations that "we shall overcome," and on one such occasion he used that phrase—the anthem of the civil rights movement—in urging Congress to enact strong voting rights legislation.

On March 16, 1965, he told Congress: "It is not just Negroes but really it is all of us who must overcome the crippling legacy of bigotry and injustice. And we shall overcome."

By habit and training, Mr. Johnson was a child of Congress, and the passing of legislation and the shaping of federal programs were to him the essence of government. It appeared that, ideally, he would have liked to cut off the world at both oceans to let America put her own house in order and to help all Americans arrange for their welfare through normal political processes.

But events were not to allow him to take that course.

Since he had, over the years, been acknowledged as something of a master at handling domestic problems that lent themselves to the legislative process, perhaps Mr. Johnson could have smoothly handled the purely domestic perplexities that were soon to besiege him—had he not become embroiled in seemingly insoluble, highly explosive situations abroad.

As early as April 1965, Mr. Johnson was severely criticized for his handling of a political crisis in the Dominican Republic. He rushed two divisions of American troops there—too swiftly and without proper notification to the Organization of American States, his critics charged—on the suspicion that Communists and Castroites were about to seize power there.

The troops helped put down the leftist forces in the Dominican Republic, amid many cries throughout the Western Hemisphere that Uncle Sam had abandoned his so-called good-neighbor policy and was once more wielding the big stick.

Having foiled the leftists in Santo Domingo, the president, using typical Johnson wheeler-dealer tactics, it was charged, applied his political and economic influence to bar the extreme right, as well as the left, from power, and to arrange an election that gave control to moderate rightists.

Two years later, Mr. Johnson was able to bind up some of the wounds inflicted in the hemisphere by his management of the Dominican crisis when he summoned a meeting of all the Latin American heads of state. The conference, at Punta del Este, Uruguay, was called to demonstrate his more positive interests in the hemisphere's economic development.

However, throughout his administration, a great shadow was cast over all his efforts abroad. It was the shadow of war, of the tragic, ugly, bloody, seemingly endless war in Vietnam.

Even Mr. Johnson's most severe critics would agree that in substantial measure the president inherited the problem of Vietnam.

South Vietnam, carved out of what had been French Indochina after France lost that colony with the fall of Dienbienphu in 1954, had plagued both President Dwight D. Eisenhower and President John F. Kennedy. They sent military advisers to help organize the South Vietnamese army to combat the guerrilla tactics of the Communist rebels, the Vietcong, who were aided and armed by Communist North Vietnam. But it was President Johnson's fate to commit American troops to a long and costly land war in South Vietnam.

The stage for his escalation of the war was actually set in August 1964, after Communist PT boats had attacked United States destroyers in the Gulf of Tonkin. Mr. Johnson obtained congressional approval of a resolution granting him full support for "all necessary action to protect our armed forces." (It was not until many months later, in bitter wrangling before the Senate Foreign Relations Committee, that doubt was cast on the intelligence information concerning the Tonkin incident that impelled Congress to give Mr. Johnson "a blank check to escalate the war," as some critics charged.)

In February 1965 there were about 20,000 American servicemen in South Vietnam, functioning in the limited capacity of advising and giving logistic support to the weakening native forces.

At that time, there came to Mr. Johnson the grim news that the Saigon government, which the United States had repeatedly promised to defend, stood in imminent danger of collapse, that the Vietcong insurgents were on the march, and that together with North Vietnamese army units smuggled into the South they had begun a final and feasible drive for victory.

The choice to the president seemed to be either a great infusion of American military power or defeat and withdrawal as the Vietcong and Communists gradually took over. Feeling committed to the defense of South Vietnam by his predecessors; resolved, perhaps, not to start his full term of office with an international defeat; and led by his military and diplomatic advisers to believe that only a few months of direct military action would settle the matter, Mr. Johnson plunged ahead.

He authorized what soon became the daily, although selective, air bombardment of North Vietnam, which he blamed for planning and supplying the campaign of the Vietcong in South Vietnam. By July 1965 Mr. Johnson had sent 75,000 American troops into the war zone and was planning an increase to 125,000. By November there were 160,000 American troops there.

Every few months, the president's advisers calculated that just a bit more strength would tip the scales and turn Vietnam into a victory. But three years after the escalation had begun, and as Mr. Johnson approached the end of his White House tenure, the number of troops in Vietnam soared past a half million, and there was still no end in sight. The severity of the internal debates and doubts over escalation of the war was disclosed in the Pentagon Papers, published in late 1971.

What was more tragic, more and more lives were being sacrificed to the Vietnam quagmire. By the end of January 1969, some two weeks after Mr. Johnson left office, more than 31,000 Americans had been killed in Vietnam and nearly 435,000 had been hospitalized with wounds.

In financial terms, the cost of the war became staggering. It went from $103 million in 1965, the year Mr. Johnson began the escalation, to $5.8 billion in 1966, to more than $20 billion the following year, to $26.5 billion in 1968, and finally, for the 1969 fiscal year, an estimated $28.8 billion.

Despite the expenditure of lives and dollars, however, most of the increased American effort was offset by more men and supplies from North Vietnam.

Too, Communist China and the Soviet Union, themselves competing for authority in the Communist world, supplied the North Vietnamese and effectively protected them from total devastation or invasion with the implied threat to the United States of their own direct involvement in the war.

Often, as criticism of his war policies grew both at home and abroad, the president pleaded for understanding. "We will never be second in the search for . . . a peaceful settlement in Vietnam," he said. "We remain ready for unconditional discussions."

From time to time, he stopped or reduced the bombing of North Vietnam to reinforce his calls for negotiation. Late in 1965, for example, during a truce, he set in motion a massive "peace offensive" in which Ambassador at Large W. Averell Harriman, Vice President Hubert H. Humphrey and many other officials flew to capitals on both sides of the Iron Curtain to enlist support for a Johnson peace plan.

Hanoi, Beijing and Moscow denounced the peace offensive as a fraud designed as a smoke screen for further escalation of the war.

Despite such disappointments, the president continued to hammer home what he conceived as the central issue of the war, which was, simply, who was to control Vietnam.

The Vietcong, and their political arm, the Communist-backed National Liberation Front, claimed to be the only legitimate governing force in South Vietnam. So did the United States–backed Saigon government, controlled largely by leaders of the South Vietnam armed forces.

Mr. Johnson steadfastly refused to pursue a settlement that would give the Liberation Front too great a share of political power in Saigon, fearing that total power was the Front's long-range aim. The other side refused to settle for anything less.

But, as the president said in his State of the Union Address on Jan. 12, 1966, "There are no arbitrary limits to our search for peace. . . . We will meet at any conference table; we will discuss any proposals—4 points or 14 or 40—and we will work . . . for a cease-fire now or once discussions have begun. We'll respond if others reduce their use of force. . . ."

On all except the central issue of the Front's power in Saigon, Mr. Johnson tried to be conciliatory, even generous. He refused to whip up hate for the enemy and he offered to spend, after the war, billions to help rebuild Vietnam and to help develop the economies of both the North and South.

But beyond charity, Mr. Johnson believed, the dominant issue was whether the United States would keep its word and prevent the forcible overthrow or conquest of a country it had promised to defend. The violation of such a promise, he insisted, would imperil dozens of other nations—especially those on the periphery of Communist China—and hence the peace of the world.

Many Americans agreed, and they also went along with Mr. Johnson's contention that promises and commitments, once made, could be violated only at the nation's peril. His stance won the approval of such diverse Republicans as General Eisenhower, Richard M. Nixon and Barry Goldwater.

However, a large and highly vocal minority of Americans disagreed, sometimes violently, with Mr. Johnson's pursuit of the war in Vietnam. Some came to hate him and the war so passionately that they doubted he had any purpose in continuing the conflict except what they saw as a jingoist refusal to accept defeat or to admit mistakes.

Americans gradually divided themselves into hawks and doves—those who would take even more vigorous military action than Mr. Johnson did to end the fighting, and those who would fight less and negotiate some face-saving end to the ordeal.

Partly because of displeasure with the war, a critical Congress, and especially its Senate Foreign Relations Committee, tore to shreds even Mr. Johnson's modest foreign aid programs for the hemisphere and other regions. And in a series of damaging public hearings in 1966, conducted by Mr. Johnson's fellow Democrat, Sen. J. William Fulbright, the Foreign Relations Committee challenged all the assumptions of the president's policies in Vietnam, toward Communist China and even Western Europe.

More carefully than many of his critics, however, Mr. Johnson sought to compartmentalize his foreign policies against the effects of Vietnam.

He constantly prodded the Soviet Union for a wider measure of agreement, and although Moscow refused while the war lasted to be conspicuously friendly, it did negotiate on some issues. Notably, it came to terms with Washington on treaties to limit the spread of nuclear weapons and to limit the use of such weapons in outer space.

The arms race continued, however, and the Russians nearly caught up to the United States in the number of land-based long-range missiles. Both sides began work on antimissile missile defenses. Their arms sales, linked with political deals with their friends, stimulated conflict in several regions, particularly the Middle East.

One such conflict erupted into a brief but dangerous war in which Israel was pitted against her Arab neighbors in June 1967. Mr. Johnson dexterously maneuvered the Russians into agreeing that both Moscow and Washington would stay out of the conflict, which both knew to mean a deal to assure victory to the Israelis.

The war in the Mideast resulted in an emergency session of the United Nations, which brought Soviet Premier Aleksei N. Kosygin to New York to explain the Russian view of the crisis. After much delicate diplomacy, it was decided that the premier and the president would hold a summit meeting in the small college town of Glassboro, N.J.

Nothing really concrete came out of the Glassboro talks, but they produced what came to be known as "the spirit of Glassboro," a subtle easing of tensions between the two great superpowers of the Soviet Union and the United States that Mr. Johnson said made the world "a little less dangerous."

The East-West confrontation across the heart of Europe remained quiet throughout the Johnson years, although the political sands continued to shift on both sides of the line. The European Common Market flourished, but at the price of accepting French president Charles de Gaulle's exclusion of Britain from the market and his imperious strictures against American influence. Thus the North Atlantic Treaty Organization foundered, becoming only a formal excuse for the retention of six American divisions in West Germany.

In Communist Europe, there was rebellion against Soviet dominance, particularly in Czechoslovakia, where liberalization of the Communist regime was crushed by Soviet and Soviet-bloc troops. There was also a gradual movement in the Communist sphere toward political arrangements that would promote economic development through cooperation with the West. Mr. Johnson had hoped to influence this trend through a major campaign for trade with the European Communist bloc of nations, but Congress, while criticizing his Vietnam war policies on the one hand, refused to cooperate with him on the other by "rewarding" North Vietnam's friends and allies with trade concessions.

Everywhere he turned, at home and abroad, it seemed, Lyndon Johnson ran headlong into the limitations set for him by the war, which sapped not only money but also governmental energy and priority. And, sadly, the war distracted the nation and its leader from what under any circumstances would have been a monumental problem, the decay of the cities and the revolt of the Negroes in the ghettos.

Only a week after Mr. Johnson had triumphantly signed the Voting Rights Act of 1965, the nation was vividly reminded that the race problem was far from reconciled. Wild rioting engulfed the Watts Negro ghetto of Los Angeles.

In succeeding summers, the looting and arson and shooting spread from city to city, ghetto to ghetto. Newark, Detroit and other cities were in open rebellion for several days in 1967, and after the assassination in April 1968 of the Rev. Dr. Martin Luther King, Jr., the moderate, nonviolent civil rights leader, dozens of cities across the nation were the scenes of frightening rioting.

Much of this occurred even while new civil rights laws, tardy relief programs and antisegregation orders were being put into effect, but the Negro, weary of having waited for generations for equality of opportunity and the end of racism in America, continued to press his revolt.

Mr. Johnson did what he could with limited resources for more education and job training and job opportunity, but he had to contend with a fearful and often angry white community that demanded repression of the rioters and rebelled against still more federal spending to "reward" them.

Behind the riots lay the decay of the cores of the nation's major cities and the pervasive patterns of discrimination that kept poor Negroes imprisoned there. And behind the angry white response lay the deterioration of much of the quality of life in middle-class America, despite a booming economy and, for most of the people, an unparalleled prosperity.

Transportation systems were clogged, the air and water were polluted, public services were strained. Crime rates soared. To their elders, the young seemed embarked on a permissive new pursuit of an irresponsible life-style based on drugs, sex and rebellion against authority.

Mr. Johnson kept urging the nation to think positively, to remember what was "right with America." He regarded its problems as challenges, not defeats, and he tried to devise programs to deal with them.

During his five years in office, he doubled the size of the federal budget, to nearly $200 billion, and tripled the amounts spent for education and health. His budgets tripled the amount of money spent on aid to the poor. He designed significant programs to attack urban blight, crime and pollution.

Yet Congress, no doubt reflecting the mood of the nation, long resisted his proposals to raise taxes even modestly to prevent the war in Vietnam from gutting all domestic programs. And, despite prosperity, the nation's military commitments abroad produced a net outflow of dollars and hence a constant drain on American gold reserves.

Thus Mr. Johnson was forced to devote much of his time to managing and manipulating the economy, to reducing the deficit in international payments, to holding federal spending to the barest minimum and to keeping down wages and prices.

As commander in chief, Mr. Johnson exhibited a complex mixture of admiration for his generals and admirals with suspicion and fear of the advice they gave him. He eventually became a virtual prisoner of the military logic that plotted strategy in Vietnam, but he never ceased to question the professional military men to a degree that some of them resented.

Although nominally head of his party, Mr. Johnson never worked easily with the Democratic National Committee or its affiliates. He did try, desultorily, in 1966 to help party candidates win reelection to Congress but, sensing a doomed cause, backed away. The Democrats lost eight state houses, three Senate seats and 47 House seats.

Political friendship caused the President to appoint Abe Fortas a Supreme Court justice—much to Mr. Johnson's ultimate sorrow. In 1969 Mr. Fortas had to resign amid criticism of his financial dealings.

At the outset of his presidency, Mr. Johnson was admired by many, if not precisely loved. He showed what many considered likable traits of rustic humor, earthiness, folksiness, sentimentality and old-fashioned patriotism. Later, however, many, who had supported him came to loathe him because of his war policies, and they came to consider him vulgar, tasteless and insular.

Mr. Johnson brought to the White House the manners of the raucous West, more forcibly than any president since Andrew Jackson. White House visitors were taken by him on exhaustive tours of what Mr. Johnson liked to call "your house," and specially favored guests were given a glimpse of his bedroom and bathroom as well.

With his lust for life and action, Mr. Johnson was perhaps naturally undisciplined in some of his personal habits. He ate hugely and had to suffer through periodic diets to take off the 20 or 30 additional pounds that would easily creep up on his 200-pound frame.

Mr. Johnson's language around men could be excessively profane, but in the presence of women he had an exaggerated sense of courtly decorum. He usually addressed them as "Ma'am."

The tall Texan liked expensive, elaborately tailored clothes, suits with narrow lapels and outsized shirt collars, all to give a streamlined appearance to his somewhat ungainly form. He placed a cowboy's high premium on highly polished shoes or leather of any kind.

On his frequent retreats to the LBJ Ranch, Mr. Johnson was a colorful and solicitous host. He once held a news conference on the banks of the Pedernales River, with a bale of hay for a rostrum, and ended it by riding off on a Tennessee walking horse. Dignified diplomats were entertained at barbecues.

While touring the ranch, Mr. Johnson once took

a Secret Service agent's pistol and blazed away at an armadillo. On another occasion the president drove a group of reporters on a wild, 90-mile-an-hour ride on a highway near the ranch, a bottle of beer on his dashboard. He was widely criticized for that beer-drinking ride.

On another occasion, the nation's dog lovers set up a considerable howl after they saw news photographs of the president holding up his beagles, Him and Her, by their ears "to make them bark—it's good for them," as he put it.

Another round of criticism was stirred by his public display of an operation scar. While recuperating in October 1965 from an operation to remove a benign polyp from his abdomen, the president impulsively pulled up his shirttail to let newsmen see his incision. The photographs that resulted were splashed across hundreds of front pages, and the White House received hundreds of letters expressing shock and disgust that a president could be, as some said, "so coarse."

Mr. Johnson was never at ease in press conferences, especially large televised ones, for he knew he did not come off well on television. Newsmen were invited to his office at a moment's notice for informal conferences. He held one while strolling on the White House grounds, and to another he invited the newsmen's wives and children and served them cookies and punch.

The president seemed genuinely to want to be liked, even loved. Yet, as the nation sank deeper and deeper into the horror of Vietnam, his popularity continued to wane. The intellectual community, which in general had supported his election, found him vulgar and tiresome and untrustworthy. Much of the press treated him as crude and temperamental.

The impression spread that Mr. Johnson suffered from what was euphemistically called a "credibility gap"—a tendency to misstate and misrepresent issues and facts to the country.

In many respects, this was merely a new phrase for an old complaint about the self-serving nature of official propaganda; "managing the news" was an earlier one. But here again, many of the worst suspicions about Mr. Johnson were traceable to the war. The president had appeared to promise to avoid such a war in the 1964 campaign, and on many occasions thereafter he mistakenly represented it as going well.

As the time grew near for him to decide whether he would run for reelection in 1968, Mr. Johnson found himself being berated by hawks and doves alike on the war, by both whites and blacks on race relations.

The opposition to him became so great, so bitter, and so often unfair, that he had reason to fear moving among the people, something that in happier days he enjoyed and did effectively and well.

In his own party, opponents of the Vietnam war and critics of his domestic failures were getting more and more attention. Two Democratic senators, Eugene J. McCarthy of Minnesota and Robert F. Kennedy of New York (who was assassinated in June 1968), had gone to the electorate in state primaries to challenge his right to renomination.

The national opinion polls showed that the public's confidence in the president's handling of his office had plunged so low that there was serious doubt he could win the November election against the Republican front-runner, Richard M. Nixon, even should he receive the Democratic nomination.

When, on March 31, 1968, he announced he would not run for reelection, Mr. Johnson said he was withdrawing from politics in the name of national unity and for the "ultimate strength of our country." He did not sound bitter; rather, there was a note of relief in his voice.

Mr. Johnson coupled his declaration with an announcement that he had ordered the bombing of North Vietnam restricted to the area below the 19th parallel, and he called for peace talks. Three days later the North Vietnamese agreed to preliminary discussions, and by mid-May, negotiations had begun.

On Dec. 22, 1968, a month before he left office, Mr. Johnson could note with pride that North Korea had released 82 crew members of the United

States intelligence ship *Pueblo* who had been imprisoned since Jan. 23, 1968, when their ship was captured by the Communists. At the time he had resisted congressional and popular demands that force be used to effect the return of the ship.

On Jan. 20, 1969, Mr. Johnson turned over the presidency to Mr. Nixon, the Republican who defeated Vice President Hubert H. Humphrey in the 1968 election. He left Washington the same day, going home to Texas to write his memoirs for the record price of $1.5 million.

Back home, he seemed relaxed and happy, surprising many who believed he could derive little pleasure from life out of the limelight and unnourished by politics. For the first time in years, no demanding schedule determined the course of his days. He had no set time to rise or sleep. He enjoyed his family and his ranch; he went to football games, attended to his correspondence, saw old friends and worked on his book.

In May 1971 the $18.6-million Lyndon Baines Johnson Library complex in Austin on the University of Texas campus was dedicated in nationally televised ceremonies that drew 3,000 guests, including President Nixon. The library was designed to house 31 million pages of documents, 500,000 photographs and memorabilia.

Mr. Johnson's memoirs, *The Vantage Point: Perspectives of the Presidency, 1963-1969*, were published Nov. 1, 1971, by Holt, Rinehart & Winston.

In the *New York Times Book Review*, David Halberstam said: "The real story of the Johnsonian presidency is not to be found in this book. It is his story as he would have it, his view of how he would like things to be."

Lyndon Johnson had sought greatness, but at the time he gave up the Presidency many Americans would not say he had achieved it. Many more had chosen to forget the good he had done because they so despised his handling of the war in Vietnam.

One of the first judgments of him by a historian came from Dr. Eric F. Goldman, a Princeton University professor who had served Mr. Johnson as a special consultant in the White House. Dr. Goldman's relationship with Mr. Johnson had been stormy, but, looking back, the historian took a compassionate view of the president.

In his book *The Tragedy of Lyndon Johnson*, Dr. Goldman wrote: "Lyndon Johnson could win votes, enact laws, maneuver mountains. He could not acquire that something beyond, which cannot be won, enacted or maneuvered but must be freely given . . . that respect, affection and rapport which alone permit an American President genuinely to lead. In his periods of triumph and of downsweep, in peace as in war, he stood the tragic figure of an extraordinarily gifted President who was the wrong man from the wrong place at the wrong time under the wrong circumstances."

Mr. Johnson's view of what he achieved might be summed up in a homily he once delivered to a group of young people.

"To hunger for use and to go unused is the worst hunger of all," he said. "Few men have the power by a single act or by a single lifetime to shape history for themselves. Presidents, for example, quickly realize that while a single act might destroy the world they live in, no one single decision can make life suddenly better or can turn history around for the good."

A PERSONAL POLITICIAN

MAX FRANKEL

HE WAS larger than life, almost a caricature of the Texas caricature that he could never shake, but he never lost his humanity, because with Lyndon Johnson everything was really personal.

The war that overwhelmed his years in the White House was personal—a test of endurance against Ho Chi Minh, which he acknowledged having lost in the end, no matter who actually won the spoils of battle.

The Great Society was personal, because a lackluster education in his own life had saved him from shiftlessness and he deemed learning of any kind to be forevermore the way to get ahead in this world.

The civil rights laws that he wanted as his monument were, in the end, highly personal, because they were drawn on the testimony of his Negro cook about her humiliations whenever she traveled without reliable food or lodging between Washington and the Texas ranch.

And even politics, the business in which he excelled and in which he took such great pride, was to him only a personal, face-to-face thing. If he had talked George Meany into acquiescence on a point, he thought he had won over all of American labor. If he had conquered influential Sen. Richard Russell of Georgia on a budget matter, he thought he had won over the Southland.

In this fashion, he had been able to encompass every issue and every center of power in his years as majority leader of the Senate. But from the White House, even his huge reach fell short and his incredibly hard work and keen mind felt often overwhelmed.

Insecure despite his size and force, L.B.J. felt from the moment of John Kennedy's death in Dallas that the nation would never accept his southern speech and rural manners as a replacement for the slain prince.

So he clung to the Kennedy men and boasted of their Ph.D. degrees and he was afraid, even after his landslide election in 1964, to bring his own men to the capital.

And he could not comprehend, to the moment of death, how so many Kennedy partisans around the country could turn against him because of a war in which he felt he had taken the counsel of his predecessor's cabinet and aides.

So he took it personally. He thought he saw a plot to promote yet another Kennedy and he thought he saw his fate as being merely the caretaker between two Kennedy administrations and he hated the thought and all who made it seem so real.

In his own mind, he felt certain that history would bring vindication:

A southerner who brought blacks to the ultimate legal equality, with their own seat on the Supreme Court and a Court that ruled in their cause.

A conservative kept alive in politics by conservative votes for Texas interests, who made war on poverty a principal concern of the federal government.

A wartime leader who was governed to the end by respect and occasionally even compassion for his "enemy," who really wanted to extend the Great Society to the Mekong River and who systematically refused to whip the nation into an anti-Communist frenzy.

A backwoods boy of modest learning who gave what seemed to him the disrespectful establishment figures of the East the scope and mandate for great social works.

That is how he saw himself and how he expected to be seen in history. He confronted antagonists to the end, always hoping that reason and short ideals and long conversations—really monologues—could find a compromise for every conflict.

Although overcome by a bitter war and the hatreds that it spawned throughout the country, Lyndon Johnson remained a man who hated conflict and who feared confrontation for himself and his country.

He made the Joint Chiefs of Staff testify in writing that he should really stand at the siege of Khe San.

He made all his diplomatic advisers commit themselves in writing to the advice that he really go to meet Soviet premier Kosygin at Glassboro, N.J.

He won from his wife, Lady Bird, a written recommendation that he ride into battle against Barry Goldwater in 1964 and that he should buck the battle for reelection in 1968. He never did want to stand alone.

"Well, Max," he asked an acquaintance on the morning after the surprise announcement of his intended retirement in 1968, "do you still believe in the First Amendment?" He thought free speech and free assembly had destroyed him, but he went on to confess that he believed in the First Amendment.

He wanted everyone with him all the time and when they weren't, it broke his heart.

ACROSS THE PEDERNALES [1973]

BILL MOYERS

I WAS in Minneapolis, filming a public television show with Chippewa Indians, when the radio flashed the news of President Johnson's death.

As I walked into the tribal hall, one Indian, who knew that I had worked for Mr. Johnson, pulled me aside and said, "A mighty wind has been stilled. I'm sorry."

Lyndon Johnson struck people that way. Friends, enemies and strangers alike felt the force of his enormous, restless energy. Like the Chippewa's "mighty wind" he could be awesome, capricious and inexplicable—his presence, as Washington learned after 1968, felt even by his absence.

I was drawn to him early. To a generation of ambitious Texans, Lyndon Johnson was as big as the state itself and just as promising. To a small-town kid with an overwrought Baptist conscience he showed how to get things done in a hurry. We were short on philosophy in Texas, short on history and philosophy, too. On the frontier, which Texas remained until late, life was its own reason for living, action its own justification. And you didn't read a textbook on how to climb the greasy pole; you just started climbing. How often I would hear him say: "Don't just stand there, son, get busy."

But power had a purpose for L.B.J. It was the way to deliver the goods. If you shared in the rewards (his mother, he told me, insisted that "If you do good, you'll make good"), so be it; the "folks" were always the real winners. The greatest good for the greatest number, he preached, and the largesse was pouring in: rural electricity, dams, highways, defense contracts, space projects, aerospace plants. "This is what your government did," he told his hill-country friends as he patted a new R.E.A. building as if it were a newborn calf.

His critics smirked when he said that what most people want "is a rug on the floor, a picture on the wall and music in the house." Their criticism bothered him least of all. "Those S.O.B.s got it all," he said. "The folks I'm talking about don't even have the simple decencies, and they outnumber that slicked-down crowd"—here he would wrinkle his nose as if squinting through pince-nez—"ten million to one."

So I wrote him for a summer job. Later he told me the letter was impertinent, my suggesting that he was out of touch with young Texas voters and offering to help him reach them; but, maybe because he had also been brash and not a little cocky when he was 18, he told me to come to Washington, sight unseen.

I flew there aboard an old two-engine Convair, my first trip east of the Red River, and landed expecting to counsel the mighty. Instead I wound up in a tiny airless room so deep in the basement labyrinth of the Capitol that one old senator who had stashed his mistress in a nearby hideaway got lost coming back from a quorum call and couldn't find her for hours.

I spent my first night in Washington—from 5 P.M. to the following noon—completing my first assignment for Lyndon B. Johnson: addressing 100,000 letters to Texas voters one at a time on an ancient machine operated by pumping the right foot up and down, like a sewing machine. I stopped only to go to the bathroom and to assure Senator —'s girlfriend, who kept poking her tearful face in the door to inquire how long quorum calls lasted (I didn't know), that he was certain to return (I didn't know that, either).

I emerged the next day squinting in the light,

hobbling on my now-stunted right foot, and wondering how L.B.J. would reward me. I soon found out. "I'm going to promote you to an upstairs room," he announced. I reported there immediately—and got to put stamps on all those letters I had just addressed. Some reward.

Years later I told him how my illusions had suffered those first two days in Washington. "Politics is stamps, spit and shakin' hands," he said. Then he smiled: "Besides, whom the Lord liketh, He chasteneth." Not quite a literal translation, but I got the point.

Throughout his career Lyndon Johnson carried on that kind of love affair with the country, a onetime schoolteacher from Cotulla, Texas, forever trying to instruct his charges.

He taught us that the country is "peepul," with names, faces and dreams. He came to despise the bureaucracy his own programs created because they started dealing in "categories" and assigning numbers to human beings whose names were Hathie, Joe Henry, Fritz or Betty Lou—people who lived down the road, across the Pedernales. Once he cut an H.E.W. official off in mid-sentence with the outburst: "Goddamit, you make those folks sound like subjects instead of citizens."

Another time he ripped into a group of government lawyers who had drafted an Appalachian assistance bill. "Who the hell can read this gobbledy-gook?" he thundered. "But that's a technical document, sir," one of the men replied. The president gave him a long, merciless stare, then with his own black felt pen he rewrote the establishing clause. "There!" he said, holding the document out before him with a flourish. "Now they'll know down in Morgantown what we're talking about."

As the Manila Conference droned to a close in 1966 the president was handed a draft of the final memorandum of agreement. He was aghast at its flat, sterile, polysyllabic prose: "Come on," he whispered, pulling at my sleeve, and we left without so much as an "excuse me" to the dignitaries around the table. At the door he stopped long enough to whisper to the Secret Service agent: "Don't let one of 'em out until I get back."

In the next room he handed me a pad and his own pen. "Now I want to rewrite that preamble so it can be read in the public square at Johnson City," he said. We labored for an hour while Marshal Ky, President Thieu, Dean Rusk and other assorted, perplexed personages waited in the next room. The president dictated, edited, looked over my shoulder as I added what I could, finally picked up the pad, read silently, nodded, and stalked back toward the conference room. He stopped at the door and, winking at me, said, "I want you to leak this to Smitty (Merriam Smith of UPI) first. It gets home first that way, and when ol' Judge Moursund reads this he'll know what we're trying to do out here with his money."

He taught us there's no progress without some giving up, that a nation of 200 million will stagnate without compromise. Some people scoffed as he reached for consensus, charging him with trying to please all the people all the time. But to him politics meant inclusion—"Noah wanted some of all the animals on board," he said, "not just critters with four legs." If consent of the governed is essential to democracy, to L.B.J. compromise was its lubricant.

On the day I resigned, we rode around his ranch for hours. "You were born over there with those Choctaw Indians," he said. "Bet you don't know where the word *okay* came from."

I didn't.

"Right from the Choctaws themselves," he said. "It meant 'we can agree now, if you aren't so all-fired set on perfection.' " If he had been born in another time, I thought, he would have made his living as a horse trader. Instead, he bent this remarkable talent for getting agreement from disparate men to making things happen. He taught us, after years of stalemate, that the legislative process can function.

Why, then, wasn't he willing to compromise in Vietnam? The irony is, he thought he was. "Well, boys, I've gone the second, third and fourth mile tonight," he said after his Johns Hopkins speech in 1965. He had proposed a multibillion-dollar rehabilitation program for Indochina, including North Vietnam, and he was convinced that it was a bargain Ho Chi Minh couldn't turn down. Another time he made another offer, in secrecy, and Ho again said no. "I don't understand it," he said, with a note of sadness in his voice. "George Meany would've grabbed at a deal like that."

Therein may be the biggest lesson Lyndon Johnson may inadvertently have taught us. We think of ourselves as a broad-minded, good-intentioned, generous people, pursuing worthy goals in a world we assume is aching to copy us. "Surely," the logic goes, "all we have to do is offer them what we would want if we were in their place."

This is not a lesson in the limits of power. Lyndon Johnson knew better than most the fragile nature of power, its shortcomings, the countertides it inevitably provokes. "Hurry, boys, hurry," he would implore his staff after his great electoral triumph of '64. "Get that legislation up to the Hill and out. Eighteen months from now ol' Landslide Lyndon will be Lame-Duck Lyndon."

He knew the limits of power. What he had to learn the hard way, and teach us as he went along, was something about the limits of perception. What made Lyndon Johnson such a unique and authentic figure—half Texas hill country, half Washington—may have also been his undoing. He was so much a creature of those places that he may have shaped the world in their image. And this image would hem him in, causing him to see others as he saw himself. It was this that made him such an American man when the world was in reality reaching for other models.

I don't know; this is conjecture. What I do know is that Lyndon Johnson was cut ten sizes larger than any of us. This made him coarser, more intemperate, more ambitious, cunning and devious. But it also made him more generous, intelligent, progressive and hopeful for the country. He was, inside, a soft man—I saw him weep as he watched television reports from Selma, Ala.: "My God," he said, "those are people they're beating. Those are Americans." Inside, I don't think he had what it took to prosecute a war wholeheartedly, and in the end he may yet teach us that democracy just doesn't have the heart for those dirty little wars.

He's gone now, and history will take a fuller measure of the man than those of us who served him. I suspect he would have enjoyed what his fellow politicians are saying about him today. I know he would believe them.

Our own relationship was strained toward the close and he died before the prodigal got home. But he did more for me than any man and I loved him.

"AND . . . WE . . . SHALL . . . OVERCOME" [1978]

DORIS KEARNS

ON MARCH 15, 1965, President Lyndon B. Johnson gave what was probably the most important speech of the decade. Before a joint session of the Congress, Mr. Johnson responded to the violent attacks on civil rights demonstrations in Selma, Ala., with a demand for immediate passage of a bill guaranteeing black Americans the right to vote. The speech was Mr. Johnson at his best—homely, compassionate, audacious and noble—a hard, practical appeal embedded in a strong moral statement.

"I speak tonight," the president began, "for the dignity of man and the destiny of democracy. . . . There is no constitutional issue here. The command of the Constitution is plain. There is no moral issue. It is wrong . . . to deny any of your fellow Americans the right to vote. What happened in Selma is part of a far larger movement which reaches into every section and state of America. It is the effort of American Negroes to secure for themselves the full blessings of American life. Their cause must be our cause too. Because it is not just Negroes, but really it is all of us who must overcome the crippling legacy of bigotry and injustice."

Here Mr. Johnson stopped. He raised his arms and repeated four words from an old Baptist hymn that had become the marching song of the civil rights movement: "And . . . we . . . shall . . . overcome."

At this moment, as an observer described it: "The whole chamber was on its feet. . . . In the galleries Negroes and whites, some in the rumpled sports shirts of bus rides from the demonstrations, others in trim professional suits, wept unabashedly."

Four months later, Mr. Johnson's expectations were incorporated into law. And it was a law that worked. In the decade following its passage, the 1965 Voting Rights Act has had a remarkable effect upon political life in the South. Since 1965 black registration has increased by over one million, and the number of black elected officials has increased by more than 2,000 percent. In 1965 approximately 70 black southerners held elective office. Today blacks hold nearly 1,500 elective positions in city government, law enforcement and state legislatures in the eleven southern states. And most important, the presence of blacks as an actual and potential political force has moderated the climate of political opinion in the South and affected the behavior of officials at all levels, from governor to sheriff to police commissioner to school committeeman.

But progress in the South, as all of us in Massachusetts are painfully aware, has not been matched by progress in the North—a contrast dramatically foreshadowed in 1965 when, six days after the signing of the Voting Rights Act, large-scale riots broke out in the Watts district of Los Angeles, to be followed by more than 100 similar outbursts, stretching through three long summers, leaving hundreds of people dead, thousands wounded and billions of dollars in property damage. Lyndon Johnson's reaction to the riots—disbelief, shock, hurt and, finally, anger—mirrored that of many Americans who simply could not understand how the blacks could be so ungrateful for all their white benefactors thought they were doing.

"How is it possible," Mr. Johnson later asked, "that all these people could be so ungrateful to me after I had given them so much? Take the Negroes. I fought for them from the first day I came into office. I tried to make it possible for every child of every color to grow up in a nice house, to eat a solid breakfast, to attend a decent school, and to get a good and lasting job. I asked so little in return. Just a little thanks. Just a little appreciation. That's all. But look at what I got instead. Riots in 175 cities. Looting. Burning. Shooting. It ruined everything . . . and the poor, they, too, turned against me. When Congress cut the funds for the Great Society, they made me Mr. Villain. I remember once going to visit a poor family in Appalachia. They had seven children, all skinny and sick. I promised the mother and father I would make things better for them. I told them all my hopes for their future. They seemed real happy to talk with me, and I felt good about that. But then as I walked toward the door, I noticed two pictures on the shabby wall. One was Jesus Christ on the cross; the other was John Kennedy. I felt as if I'd been slapped in the face."

Still, at more reflective moments, Mr. Johnson showed that he understood the answers to his own questions. "God knows how little we've really moved on this issue, despite all the fanfare," he explained, long after he had left the White House. "As I see it, I've moved the Negro from D+ to C−. He's still nowhere. He knows it. And that's why he's out in the streets. Hell, I'd be there too. It was bad enough in the South—especially from the standpoint of education—but at least there the Negro knew he was really loved and cared for, which he never was in the North, where children live with rats and have no place to sleep and come from broken homes and get rejected from the army.

"We'll never know how high a price we paid for the unkindness and injustice we've inflicted on people—the Negroes, Mexicans and Jews—and everyone who really believes he has been discriminated against in any way is part of that great human price. No matter how well you may think you know a Negro, if you really know one, there'll come the time when you look at him and see how deep his bitterness is.

"Prejudice—you know my feeling all along has been that prejudice about color is not the big factor. Maybe the Poles do hate the Negroes, but I think fear is the cause of their hatred, not prejudice—anyone who's afraid of losing his job to another man will soon turn to hate that other man. Now I thought when we got unemployment down, we'd eliminated that fear. When I got the tax bill passed in '64 . . . and when I got the stock market up and everyone was making money, with wages going up even higher than prices, I figured if there was a time when jealousy wouldn't assert itself, it would be this one."

But the healthy economy that Johnson recognized as essential to the continuing progress of black Americans fell victim to the war in Vietnam and to the spirals of inflation and recession that followed through succeeding presidencies. And as the general unemployment rate has risen, and as conditions on city streets and in city schools have worsened, the progress made by blacks in the 1960s has eroded. Even worse, in the absence of courageous national political leadership, the political dialogue has degenerated from hope to bitterness, turning a legitimate concern for miserable conditions in city schools into the issue of busing, tragically obscuring the vision and misdirecting the energies of all those who genuinely care about improvement.

The presidential primaries to date offer little hope for that moral leadership at the highest level that Lyndon Johnson understood as essential to any forward movement on race: "Now I knew that as President I couldn't make people want to integrate their schools or open their doors to blacks, but I could make them feel guilty for not doing it and I believed it was my moral responsibility to do precisely that—to use the moral suasion of my office to make people feel that segregation was a curse they'd carry with them to their graves."

Listening to those words makes one almost wish to see again that large, formidable, sometimes frightening man whose instinctive comprehension of his fellow Americans—bred of his own experience on the Pedernales banks—earned him a lasting place in the annals of history through his contributions to civil rights.

HELEN KELLER

1880–1968

By Alden Whitman

For the first 18 months of her life Helen Keller was a normal infant who cooed and cried, learned to recognize the voices of her father and mother and took joy in looking at their faces and at objects about her home. "Then," as she recalled later, "came the illness which closed my eyes and ears and plunged me into the unconsciousness of a newborn baby."

The illness, perhaps scarlet fever, vanished as quickly as it struck, but it erased not only the child's vision and hearing but also, as a result, her powers of articulate speech.

Her life thereafter, as a girl and as a woman, became a triumph over crushing adversity and shattering affliction. In time, Miss Keller learned to circumvent her blindness, deafness and muteness; she could "see" and "hear" with exceptional acuity; she even learned to talk passably and to dance in time to a fox-trot or a waltz. Her remarkable mind unfolded, and she was in and of the world, a full and happy participant in life.

What set Miss Keller apart was that no similarly afflicted person before had done more than acquire the simplest skills.

But she was graduated from Radcliffe; she became an artful and subtle writer; she led a vigorous life; she developed into a crusading humanitarian who espoused Socialism; and she energized movements that revolutionized help for the blind and the deaf.

Her tremendous accomplishments and the force of assertive personality that underlay them were released through the devotion and skill of Anne Sullivan Macy, her teacher, through whom in large degree she expressed herself. Mrs. Macy was succeeded, at her death in 1936, by Polly Thomson, who died in 1960. Since then Miss Keller's companion had been Mrs. Winifred Corbally.

Miss Keller's life was so long and so crowded with improbable feats—from riding horseback to learning Greek—and she was so serene yet so determined in her advocacy of beneficent causes that she became a great legend. She always seemed to be standing before the world as an example of unquenchable will.

Many who observed her—and to some she was a curiosity and a publicity seeker—found it difficult to believe that a person so handicapped could acquire the profound knowledge and the sensitive perception and writing talent that she exhibited when she was mature. Yet no substantial proof was ever adduced that Miss Keller was anything less than she appeared—a person whose character impelled her to perform the seemingly impossible. With the years, the skepticism, once overt, dwindled as her stature as a heroic woman increased.

American Foundation for the Blind

Helen Keller, left, and Anne Sullivan Macy

New York Times Photo

Miss Keller always insisted that there was nothing mysterious or miraculous about her achievements. All that she was and did, she said, could be explained directly and without reference to a "sixth sense." Her dark and silent world was held in her hand and shaped with her mind. Concededly, her sense of smell was exceedingly keen, and she could orient herself by the aroma from many objects. On the other hand, her sense of touch was less finely developed than in many other blind people.

Tall, handsome, gracious, poised, Miss Keller had a sparkling humor and a warm handclasp that won her friends easily. She exuded vitality and optimism. "My life has been happy because I have had wonderful friends and plenty of interesting work to do," she once remarked, adding: "I seldom think about my limitations, and they never make me sad. Perhaps there is just a touch of yearning at times, but it is vague, like a breeze among flowers. The wind passes, and the flowers are content."

This equanimity was scarcely foreshadowed in her early years. Helen Adams Keller was born on June 27, 1880, on a farm near Tuscumbia, Ala. Her father was Arthur Keller, an intermittently prosperous country gentleman who had served in the Confederate Army. Her mother was the former Kate Adams.

After Helen's illness, her infancy and early childhood were a succession of days of frustration, manifest by outbursts of anger and fractious behavior. "A wild, unruly child" who kicked, scratched and screamed was how she afterward described herself.

Her distracted parents were without hope until Mrs. Keller came across a passage in Charles Dickens's *American Notes* describing the training of the blind Laura Bridgman, who had been taught to be a sewing teacher by Dr. Samuel Gridley Howe of the Perkins Institution in Boston. Dr. Howe, husband of the author of "The Battle Hymn of the Republic," was a pioneer teacher of the blind and the mute.

Shortly thereafter the Kellers heard of a Baltimore eye physician who was interested in the blind, and they took their daughter to him. He said that Helen could be educated and put her parents in touch with Alexander Graham Bell, the inventor of the telephone and an authority on teaching speech to the deaf. After examining the child, Bell advised the Kellers to ask his son-in-law, Michael Anagnos, director of the Perkins Institution, about obtaining a teacher for Helen.

The teacher Mr. Anagnos selected was 20-year-old Anne Mansfield Sullivan, who was called Annie. Partly blind, Miss Sullivan had learned at Perkins how to communicate with the deaf and blind through a hand alphabet signaled by touch into the patient's palm.

"The most important day I remember in all my life is the one on which my teacher came to me," Miss Keller wrote later. "It was the third of March, 1887, three months before I was 7 years old.

"I stood on the porch, dumb, expectant. I guessed vaguely from my mother's signs and from the hurrying to and fro in the house that something unusual was about to happen, so I went to the door and waited on the steps."

Helen, her brown hair tumbled, her pinafore soiled, her black shoes tied with white string, jerked Miss Sullivan's bag away from her, rummaged in it for candy and, finding none, flew into a rage.

Of her savage pupil, Miss Sullivan wrote: "She has a fine head, and it is set on her shoulders just right. Her face is hard to describe. It is intelligent, but it lacks mobility, or soul, or something. Her mouth is large and finely shaped. You can see at a glance that she is blind. One eye is larger than the other and protrudes noticeably. She rarely smiles."

It was days before Miss Sullivan, whom Miss Keller throughout her life called "Teacher," could calm the rages and fears of the child and begin to spell words into her hand. The problem was of associating words and objects or actions: What was a doll, what was water? Miss Sullivan's solution was a stroke of genius. Recounting it, Miss Keller wrote: "We walked down the path to the well-house, attracted by the fragrance of the honey-suckle with which it was covered. Someone was drawing water and my teacher placed my hand under the spout.

"As the cool stream gushed over one hand she spelled into the other the word water, first slowly, then rapidly. I stood still, my whole attention fixed upon the motions of her fingers. Suddenly I felt a misty consciousness as of something forgotten—a thrill of returning thought; and somehow the mystery of language was revealed to me.

"I knew then that 'w-a-t-e-r' meant the wonderful cool something that was flowing over my hand. That living word awakened my soul, gave it light, hope, joy, set it free. There were barriers still, it is true, but barriers that in time could be swept away."

Miss Sullivan had been told at Perkins that if she wished to teach Helen she must not spoil her. As a result, she was soon locked in physical combat with her pupil. This struggle was to thrill theater and film audiences later when it was portrayed in *The Miracle Worker* by Anne Bancroft as Annie Sullivan and Patty Duke as Helen.

The play was by William Gibson, who based it on *Anne Sullivan Macy: The Story Behind Helen Keller* by Nella Braddy, a friend of Miss Keller. Opening in New York in October 1959, it ran 702 performances.

Typical of the battles between child and teacher was a dinner table struggle in which Helen, uttering eerie screams, tried to jerk Miss Sullivan's chair from under her.

"She pinched me and I slapped her face every time she did," Miss Sullivan wrote. "I gave her a spoon which she threw on the floor. I forced her out of the chair and made her pick it up. Then we had another tussle over folding her napkin. It was another hour before I succeeded in getting her napkin folded. Then I let her out into the warm sunshine and went to my room and threw myself on the bed, exhausted."

Once Helen became more socialized and once she began to learn, her hunger for knowledge was insatiable. In a few hours one April day she added 30 words to her vocabulary. Abstractions—the meaning of the word *love,* for example—proved difficult, but her teacher's patience and ingenuity prevailed.

Helen's next opening into the world was learning to read. "As soon as I could spell a few words my teacher gave me slips of cardboard on which were printed words in raised letters," she recalled. "I quickly learned that each printed word stood for an object, an act or a quality.

"I had a frame in which I could arrange the words in little sentences; but before I ever put sentences in the frame I used to make them in objects. I found the slips of paper which represented, for example, 'doll,' 'is,' 'on,' 'bed' and placed each name on its object; then I put my doll on the bed with the words *is, on, bed* arranged beside the doll, thus making a sentence of the words, and at the same time carrying out the idea of the sentence with the things themselves."

Helen read her first connected story in May 1887, and from that time "devoured everything in the shape of a printed page that has come within the reach of my hungry fingertips."

After three months with her pupil, Miss Sullivan wrote to Mr. Anagnos: "Something tells me that I am going to succeed beyond all my dreams."

Helen's progress was so rapid that in May 1888 she made her first trip to the Perkins Institution in Boston, where she learned to read Braille and to mix with other afflicted children. For several years she spent the winters in the North and the summers with her family. It was in the spring of 1890 that Helen was taught to speak by Sarah Fuller of the Horace Mann School.

"Miss Fuller's method was this," Miss Keller recalled. "She passed my hand lightly over her face, and let me feel the position of her tongue and lips when she made a sound. I was eager to imitate every motion and in an hour had learned six elements of speech: M, P, A, S, T, I. I shall never forget the surprise and delight I felt when I uttered my first connected sentence: 'It is warm.' "

Even so, it took a long time for the child to put her rushing thoughts into words. Most often Miss Sullivan or Miss Thomson was obliged to translate the sounds, for it took a trained ear to distinguish them accurately. When Miss Keller spoke very slowly and employed monosyllabic words, she was fairly readily understandable.

At the same time the child learned to lip-read by placing her fingers on the lips and throat of those who talked with her. But one had to talk slowly with her, articulating each word carefully. Nonetheless, her crude speech and her lip-reading facility further opened her mind and enlarged her experience.

Each of the young girl's advances brought pressure on her from her elders for new wonders, and this inevitably fed public skepticism. This was intensified when, in 1892, a story appeared under her name that was easily identified as similar in thought and language to an already published fable. Although she denied the charge of plagiarism, the episode hurt Miss Keller for many years.

In that period, she was also exploited through such incidents as publicized trips to Niagara Falls and visits to the World's Fair of 1893 in the company of Bell.

When she was 14, in 1894, Miss Keller undertook formal schooling, first at the Wright-Humason School for the Deaf in New York and then at the Cambridge (Mass.) School for Young Ladies. With Miss Sullivan at her side and spelling into her hand, Miss Keller prepared herself for admission to Radcliffe, which she entered in the fall of 1900. It was indeed an amazing feat, for the examinations she took were those given to unhandicapped applicants, but no more astonishing than her graduation cum laude in 1904, with honors in German and English. Miss Sullivan was with her when she received her diploma, which she obtained by sheer stubbornness and determination.

"I slip back many times," she wrote of her college years. "I fall, I stand still. I run against the edge of hidden obstacles. I lose my temper and find it again, and keep it better. I trudge on, I gain a little. I feel encouraged. I get more eager and climb higher and begin to see widening horizons."

While still in Radcliffe, Miss Keller wrote, on her Hammond typewriter, her first autobiography. *The Story of My Life* was published serially in the *Ladies' Home Journal* and, in 1902, as a book. It consisted largely of themes written for an English composition course conducted by Prof. Charles Townsend Copeland, Harvard's celebrated "Copey."

Most reviewers found the book well written, but some critics, including that of *the Nation,* scoffed. "All of her knowledge is hearsay knowledge," *the Nation* said, "her very sensations are for the most part vicarious and she writes of things beyond her power of perception and with the assurance of one who had verified every word."

Miss Keller's defenders replied that she had ways of knowing things not reckoned by others. When she wrote of the New York subway that it "opened its jaws like a great beast," it was pointed out that she had stroked a lion's mouth and knew whereof she spoke. At a circus zoo she had also shaken hands with a bear, patted a leopard and let a snake curl itself around her.

"I have always felt I was using the five senses within me, that is why my life has been so full and complete," Miss Keller said at the time. She added that it was quite natural for her to use the words *look, see* and *hear* as if she were seeing and hearing in the full physical sense.

After college Miss Keller continued to write, publishing *The World I Live In* in 1908, *The Song of the Stone Wall* in 1910 and *Out of the Dark* in 1913. Her writings, mostly inspirational articles, also appeared in national magazines of the time. And with Miss Sullivan at her side she took to the lecture platform.

After her formal talks—these were interpreted sentence by sentence by Miss Sullivan—Miss Keller answered questions, such as "Do you close your eyes when you go to sleep?" Her stock response was, "I never stayed awake to see."

Meantime, Miss Keller was developing a largeness of spirit on social issues, partly as a result of walks through industrial slums, partly because of her special interest in the high incidence of blindness among the poor and partly because of her conversations with John Macy, Miss Sullivan's husband, a social critic. She was further impelled toward Socialism in 1908 when she read H. G. Wells's *New Worlds for Old.*

These influences, in turn, led her to read Marx and Engels in German Braille, and in 1909 she joined the Socialist party in Massachusetts. For many years she was an active member, writing incisive articles in defense of Socialism, lecturing for the party, supporting trade unions and strikes and opposing American entry into World War I. She was among those Socialists who welcomed the Bolshevik Revolution in Russia in 1917.

Although Miss Keller's Socialist activities diminished after 1921, when she decided that her chief life work was to raise funds for the American Foundation for the Blind, she was always responsive to Socialist and Communist appeals for help in causes involving oppression or exploitation of labor. As late as 1957 she sent a warm greeting to Elizabeth Gurley Flynn, the Communist leader, then in jail on charges of violating the Smith Act.

When literary tastes changed after World War I, Miss Keller's income from her writings dwindled, and, to make money, she ventured into vaudeville. She, with Miss Sullivan, was astonishingly successful; no Radcliffe graduate ever did better in variety than she. Harry and Herman Weber, the variety entrepreneurs, presented her in a 20-minute act that toured the country between 1920 and 1924. (Although some of her friends were scandalized, Miss Keller enjoyed herself enormously and argued that her appearances helped the cause of the blind.)

In the Keller-Sullivan act, the rising curtain showed a drawing room with a garden seen through French windows. Miss Sullivan came on stage to the strains of Mendelssohn's "Spring Song" and told a little about Miss Keller's life. Then the star parted a curtain, entered and spoke for a few minutes. The *Times* review of her debut at the Palace said: "Helen Keller has conquered again, and the Monday afternoon audience at the Palace, one of the most critical and cynical in the world, was hers."

On the vaudeville tour, Miss Keller, who had already met scores of famous people, formed friendships with such celebrities as Sophie Tucker, Charlie Chaplin, Enrico Caruso, Jascha Heifetz and Harpo Marx.

In the 1920s, Miss Keller, Miss Sullivan and her husband, and Miss Thomson (who had joined the household in 1914) moved from Wrentham, Mass., to Forest Hills, Queens, in New York. Miss Keller used this home as a base for her extensive fundraising tours for the American Foundation for the Blind, of which she was counselor until her death. In this effort she talked in churches, synagogues and town halls. She not only collected money, but also sought to alleviate the living and working conditions of the blind. In those years the blind were frequently ill-educated and maintained in asylums; her endeavors were a major factor in changing these conditions.

A tireless traveler, Miss Keller toured the world with Miss Sullivan and Miss Thomson in the years before World War II. Everywhere she went she lectured in behalf of the blind and the deaf; and, inevitably, she met everyone of consequence. She also found time for writing: *My Religion* in 1927; *Midstream—My Later Life* in 1930; *Peace at Eventide* in 1932; *Helen Keller's Journal* in 1938 and *Teacher* in 1955.

The *Journal,* one of her most luminous books, discloses the acuity and range of Miss Keller's mind in the 1930s. In her comments on political, social and literary matters, she condemned Hitlerism, cheered the sitdown strikes of John L. Lewis's Committee for Industrial Organization and criticized Margaret Mitchell's *Gone With the Wind* as overlooking the brutalities of southern slavery.

Although she did not refer to it conspicuously, Miss Keller was religious, but not a churchgoer. While quite young she was converted to the mystic New Church doctrines of Emanuel Swedenborg. The object of his doctrine was to make Christianity a living reality on earth through divinc lovc, a theology that fitted Miss Keller's sense of social mission.

Although Miss Keller's serenity was buttressed by her religious faith, she was subjected in adulthood to criticisms and crises that sometimes unsettled her. Other people, she discovered, were attempting to run her life, and she was helpless to counter them. The most frustrating such episode occurred in 1916 during an illness of Miss Sullivan.

Miss Keller, then 36, fell in love with Peter Fagan, a 29-year-old Socialist and newspaperman who was her temporary secretary. The couple took out a marriage license, intending a secret wedding. But a Boston reporter found out about the license, and his witless article on the romance horrified the stern Mrs. Keller, who ordered Mr. Fagan out of the house and broke up the love affair.

"The love which had come, unseen and unexpected, departed with tempest on his wings," Miss Keller wrote in sadness, adding that the love remained with her as "a little island of joy surrounded by dark waters."

For years her spinsterhood was a chief disappointment. "If I could see," she said bitterly, "I would marry first of all."

With Miss Sullivan's death in 1936, Miss Keller and Miss Thomson moved from New York to Westport, Conn., Miss Keller's home for the rest of her life. At Westport she made friends with its artists (Jo Davidson executed a sculpture of her) and its writers (Van Wyck Brooks wrote a biographical sketch).

With Mr. and Mrs. Davidson, Miss Keller and Miss Thomson toured France and Italy in 1950, where Miss Keller saw great sculptures with her fingers under Mr. Davidson's tutelage. "What a privilege it has been," Mrs. Davidson remarked to a friend, "to live with Helen and Polly. Every day Helen delights us more and more—her noble simplicity, her ability to drink in the feel of things, and that spring of joyousness that bubbles up to the surface at the slightest pressure."

In her middle and late years Miss Keller's income was derived from her book royalties and a stipend from the Foundation for the Blind. After Miss Thomson's death in 1960, a trustee conducted most of her affairs.

For her work in behalf of the blind and the deaf, in which she was actively engaged up to 1962, Miss Keller was honored by universities and institutions throughout the world—the universities of Harvard, Glasgow, Berlin and Delhi among them. She was received in the White House by every president from Grover Cleveland to John F. Kennedy.

In 1964 she was one of 30 Americans on whom President Johnson conferred the nation's highest civilian recognition, the Presidential Medal of Freedom.

Despite the celebrity that accrued to her and the air of awesomeness with which she was surrounded in her later years, Miss Keller retained an unaffected personality and a certainty that her optimistic attitude toward life was justified.

"I believe that all through these dark and silent years God has been using my life for a purpose I do not know," she said recently, adding: "But one day I shall understand and then I will be satisfied."

Miss Keller died in her sleep at her home in Westport, Conn., on June 1, 1968. She was 87.

THE DAY HELEN KELLER CAME BACKSTAGE

RUTH GORDON

WHEN I was a little girl I lived in Wollaston, Mass., and one day riding into Boston on the train, a short distance before we got to Boston's South Station, my mother pointed out, on the right, an old brick building. "That's the Perkins Institute," she said, "where blind people are taught to read and write. That's where Mrs. Keller brought her little girl Helen."

I met her in 1941, New York City. Alexander Woollcott rang me up. "What are you doing this afternoon and whatever it is get out of it. Come up here at four. Something *great!*"

"What are we going to do, read Braille?" I asked. And astonished myself. What did *that* mean?

Silence at the other end of the phone.

"Alec?" I asked. "Alec, are you there?"

"Why'd you say that?"

"I don't know. Did *you* ever say anything silly?"

"Rarely. Why *did* you? You must've had *some* idea."

"No, I didn't," I said. "What's going to be so great at four?"

There was a pause. Then he said, "Helen Keller's coming to tea."

When I said, "What are we going to do, read Braille?" it startled Woollcott. And when he said, "Helen Keller's coming to tea," that startled *me.*

I still don't know why I said it.

A little before four, I got to the Hotel Gotham. A little before: Woollcott could turn on you if you were not on time. And even more important, I did not want to miss one moment of Helen Keller.

"How could you know Helen Keller," I asked, "and not talk about it?"

"Known her for years," he said and there was a knock at the door. Two ladies arm in arm. He certainly *had* known her for years, he planted a big kiss on Helen Keller's cheek. Then one on Polly Thomson's. And sometime after that, he remembered me. "Helen, this is Ruth Gordon. Polly, Ruth."

Do we know when a great moment is going on? I think so. I think a great moment makes itself felt. And this winter afternoon at the Hotel Gotham I knew was a great moment. And part of this great moment was, it was a total surprise. Sitting on that Gotham Hotel sofa was a legend in a terribly pretty dress. An immortal with lipstick and powder and just a touch of eye shade. She and her companion, Polly Thomson, could have been two charming anybodies, except for their terrific gaiety. And except for Helen's clouded speech, which Polly made clear to us. And when we talked, she tapped out on Helen's hand what *we* said. Except for that, they were two adorable ladies hell-bent on having a good time.

"Tea?" asked Woollcott.

Polly tapped. Helen didn't look very interested.

"Something stronger?"

Polly tapped. Helen brightened up.

"Old-fashioned?"

Polly tapped. Helen made enthusiastic sounds.

That afternoon in 1941 we all had a good time. We all laughed a lot. And Helen laughed hardest when the joke was on her. To remember Alec's face, she patted it all over. Then she patted his mustache. Then she patted it again and made sounds. "Helen says she thinks your mustache has gotten smaller, Alec."

Woollcott leaned over and patted Helen's face. "Tell her hers hasn't." Polly tapped; Helen laughed more than anybody.

The next time I saw her was also due to Woollcott. He died. It was 1943. His last will and testament said, "No memorial service," but once he was no longer with us, his friends got out of line. They arranged a memorial service to be held at McMillin Auditorium, Columbia University, on a January morning at 10 A.M.

Ten A.M.! Most of Woollcott's friends were late sleepers, but 10 A.M. was when McMillin Auditorium was available, so that January morning a lot of new alarm clocks went off in a lot of unaccustomed ears. And what *else* was unaccustomed, New York chose that morning to have a blizzard. Snow came pelting down as if the property man had gone raving mad. The mayor looked out the window and ordered all private cars off the streets. A hush fell on New York City except up at McMillin where Woollcott's sleepy, exasperated friends filled every seat in the big auditorium.

Only Guthrie McClintic—great director that he was—was wide awake enough to direct his yellow taxi to wait. And after the ceremony and after we had buckled on our galoshes, after we had pulled on our warm coats and mufflers and mittens, Guthrie directed his wife, Katharine Cornell, and Helen Keller and Polly Thomson into his yellow taxi. *I* was only included because I was playing in his production of *The Three Sisters* and he didn't want me to get lost in a snowdrift and have the understudy go on. Well, that's show business. Sometimes it's rough and sometimes you get the breaks and that morning I got the break of being squeezed into Guthrie's yellow taxi along with Helen and Kit and Polly and off we skidded down Morningside Heights.

As we lurched around icy curves, feelings got a lot less serious; things became more informal when we kept falling all over each other. Once we all landed on the taxi floor in a woolly heap and as Helen untangled herself she spoke. "Wouldn't Alec be delighted," repeated Polly, "at how much trouble he is causing his friends."

The next time I saw Helen Keller, she was my guest at *The Matchmaker.* I remembered she always came to the plays Kit Cornell was in and I invited her to the Royale Theater on West 45th Street.

Polly wrote that Helen would be delighted. A Wednesday matinee would be best. And might they have five tickets and a script of the play for them to read in advance? The script and the five tickets were sent to Helen's house, Arcan Ridge, in Westport, Conn. Back came a check. Well, that wasn't the idea. Back went the check to Arcan Ridge and a few days later there arrived a big luxurious bottle of Gardenia Bath Oil from Henri Bendel's elegant store with a message from Helen that she was looking forward to Wednesday. One knows great moments. What about bathing in gardenia-scented bath oil, the gift of Helen Keller!

That Wednesday matinee was the best performance we ever did. *The Matchmaker* had played in London, Berlin, Edinburgh, but we never played it as well as that Wednesday. When the curtain fell, the stage manager went out into the theater to bring our great lady and her friends backstage. Nobody had arranged it, but the whole *Matchmaker* company stood discreetly at the side of the stage to see her pass. Distinguished people had come backstage in the course of the run, but only for Helen Keller did the *Matchmaker* company stand and wait.

And then she was in the dressing room. With Polly Thomson. With her three lady friends from the Lighthouse, the great charitable organization for the blind—and again *such* a sense of somebody having a good time, *again* her radiant smile. And her lovely clothes. That spring afternoon an Alice blue suit, a spring hat with flowers and a ribbon. Such a surprise for an immortal to look chic! "Helen," I said, "you are in my dressing room, but if anyone walked in here, they would take *you* for the actress."

To remember just what I looked like, she reached over and patted my face, my red wig that I wore as Mrs. Dolly Gallagher Levi, my period costume, the bodice, the sleeves, the 1880 taffeta bustle. Then her hand stopped and suddenly she looked moved. She spoke and Polly looked moved. "Helen says she hasn't thought of a bustle since she was a little girl. Her mother wore one."

The Boston train. The old brick building. "That's where Mrs. Keller brought *her* little girl Helen."

I asked if she followed the play. Polly tapped. Helen nodded enthusiastically. Polly said, "When you got to the monologue in the last act, which Helen had so admired when we read the manuscript, she pushed my hand away. She didn't want me to tap it out for her. She wanted to 'hear' it for herself. She knew every word, as you came to it. Laughed when the audience did. Was moved when they were."

The great moment was over. We spoke briefly of Alec Woollcott and I held out to her a picture I kept of him in a jinrickshaw from the Chicago World's Fair. When she left, Arthur Hill was waiting to show her to her car. "Oh, we don't have a car," said Polly. "Every taxi driver knows Helen and stops."

Outside on 45th Street, the whole matinee audience waited to see her come out. Arthur Hill, not as confident of New York taxi drivers as Polly, rushed ahead. He beckoned to a taxi. It dove out of sight into the after-matinee crush. Then Helen came through the matinee ladies, stood at the curb in her lovely Alice blue suit, smiling her radiant confident smile and a screech of brakes let Arthur Hill know that life *can* be beautiful. *Two* taxis pulled up to the curb.

A few days later a letter arrived. "Dear Ruth Gordon, While the memory of Wednesday's matinee sparkles in my mind, I want to write you grateful thanks. Whenever Polly and I recall *The Matchmaker,* the imps of laughter dance in our hearts. Also, you were a darling to let us see you after the play when you must have felt tired. . . . It was good to see Alec's picture. Devotedly your friend, Helen Keller."

It was typed—beautifully typed—by her. And soon after, a package was delivered. Her Book. *Teacher.* Here is what she wrote in her own hand. With a lead pencil. Each word perfectly spaced.

> *To Ruth Gordon*
> *who is loved not*
> *only for her dramatic art*
> *but also for her sunny*
> *sweetness and her heart of*
> *gold.*
>
> *Affectionately*
> Helen Keller
> *February 17, 1956*

I set this down in all humility. Whether it is so or not, that is what Helen Keller—with her love of people, her confidence in the human race—that is what Helen Keller thought of me.

THE TIME HELEN KELLER PLAYED THE PALACE [JUNE 1962]

HELEN KELLER, who will be 82 this month, may sometimes recall a little-known phase of her long life. For nearly two years back in the frenzied Twenties she was in vaudeville, and a very good trouper she was, too. She was in her late thirties then and was already part of the American legend for her fight to break through the wall of deafness and blindness that enclosed her. She opened at the Palace on Monday, Feb. 23, 1920, on a bill that included Bessie Clayton, the dancer, who had the top billing. Miss Keller's act was designed to give the public a chance to see a woman whose courage and brilliance of mind were by way of making her a world figure. The only other similarly handicapped woman who had been capable of receiving instruction had become a sewing teacher. Helen Keller had been graduated *cum laude* from Radcliffe College.

Her act lasted about 20 minutes. The rising curtain showed a drawing room with a fire in the fireplace, a garden seen through French windows. There was a grand piano upon which stood a large vase of flowers. Mrs. Anne Sullivan Macy, Miss Keller's teacher since Helen was 6, entered as the orchestra played Mendelssohn's "Spring Song." She told who Helen Keller was and a little of her story. Miss Keller parted a curtain and came to the stage as Annie Sullivan left. Helen Keller stood for a moment alone, her beautiful but sightless blue eyes directed toward the gallery. Then her teacher returned to her side and Helen Keller spoke for a few minutes in the strange but fascinating voice she had learned to use. As the piano was played she showed how she could beat time to the music. The audience was invited to ask questions. These questions were conveyed to Miss Keller by Annie Sullivan by finger taps in Miss Keller's hand, the usual method of communication between the teacher and the pupil. There was more soft music. Then came Miss Keller's bow and the invariably enthusiastic applause.

Miss Keller's act was reviewed extensively and

favorably the following morning. *The New York Times* said: "The widespread interest in the achievements of Helen Keller was indicated anew in the enthusiastic reception accorded Miss Keller at the Palace Theatre yesterday, upon the occasion of her first appearance on the vaudeville stage—the first, that is, if a preliminary week in the outlying regions is disregarded [she had opened prudently in White Plains]. . . . Her replies [to the questions] could be heard with distinctness in all but the farthest corners of the auditorium." "Before she had been on the stage two minutes," another paper wrote, "Helen Keller had conquered again, and the Monday afternoon audience at the Palace, one of the most critical and cynical in the world, was hers." The talented Bessie Clayton, who danced her way into the hearts of thousands in the Weber & Fields days, was not mentioned. Miss Keller was held over for a second week, always a sign of success at the Palace.

While there were no complaints against the act itself, a few people believed that it was undignified for Helen Keller to appear on the same bill with Broadway patter acts, bounding Algerians, trained seals and acrobats. She had already been on the lecture platform and had appeared in private homes and before university groups, but her *entrepreneur,* Harry Weber, frankly noted the plain fact that the lecture platform did not pay nearly so much as vaudeville. In her book on Anne Sullivan Macy, Nella Braddy Henney said that Helen Keller and Annie Sullivan, as everybody called her, were popular with other vaudeville actors billed with them during their tours about the country. One of these lasted 40 weeks. Polly Thomson, who was then Miss Keller's secretary, accompanied the pair on the tours. She said that she had been taught makeup by none other than the great Sophie Tucker.

MARTIN LUTHER KING, JR.

1929–1968

By Murray Schumach

To many millions of American Negroes, the Rev. Dr. Martin Luther King, Jr., was the prophet of their crusade for racial equality. He was their voice of anguish, their eloquence in humiliation, their battle cry for human dignity. He forged for them the weapons of nonviolence that withstood and blunted the ferocity of segregation.

And to many millions of American whites, he was one of a group of Negroes who preserved the bridge of communication between races when racial warfare threatened the United States in the 1960s, as Negroes sought the full emancipation pledged to them a century before by Abraham Lincoln.

To the world Dr. King had the stature that accrued to a winner of the Nobel Peace Prize; a man with access to the White House and the Vatican; a veritable hero in the African states that were just emerging from colonialism.

In his dedication to nonviolence, Dr. King was caught between white and Negro extremists as racial tensions erupted into arson, gunfire and looting in many of the nation's cities during the summer of 1967.

Militant Negroes, with the cry of "Burn, baby, burn," argued that only by violence and segregation could the Negro attain self-respect, dignity and real equality in the United States.

Floyd B. McKissick, when director of the Congress of Racial Equality, declared in August of that year that it was a "foolish assumption to try to sell nonviolence to the ghettos."

And white extremists, not bothering to make distinctions between degrees of Negro militancy, looked upon Dr. King as one of their chief enemies.

In the months shortly before he died, efforts by Dr. King to utilize nonviolent methods exploded into violence.

In the last week in March of 1968, when he led a protest march through downtown Memphis, Tenn., in support of the city's striking sanitation workers, a group of Negro youths suddenly began breaking store windows and looting, and one Negro was shot to death.

Two days later, however, Dr. King said he would stage another demonstration and attributed the violence to his own "miscalculation."

At the time he was assassinated in Memphis, Dr. King was involved in one of his greatest plans to dramatize the plight of the poor and stir Congress to help Negroes.

He called this venture the "Poor People's Campaign." It was to be a huge "camp-in" either in Washington or in Chicago during the Democratic National Convention.

In one of his last public pronouncements before the shooting, Dr. King told an audience in a Harlem church on March 26, 1968: "We need an alternative

AP/WIDE WORLD

to riots and to timid supplication. Nonviolence is our most potent weapon."

His strong beliefs in civil rights and nonviolence made him one of the leading opponents of American participation in the war in Vietnam. To him the war was unjust, diverting vast sums from programs to alleviate the condition of the Negro poor in this country. He called the conflict "one of history's most cruel and senseless wars."

In January 1968, he said: "We need to make clear in this political year, to Congressmen on both sides of the aisle and to the President of the United States that we will no longer vote for men who continue to see the killing of Vietnamese and Americans as the best way of advancing the goals of freedom and self-determination in Southeast Asia."

Inevitably, as a symbol of integration, he became the object of unrelenting attacks and vilification. His home was bombed. He was spat upon and mocked. He was struck and kicked. He was stabbed, almost fatally, by a deranged Negro woman. He was frequently thrown into jail. Threats became so commonplace that his wife could ignore burning crosses on the lawn and ominous phone calls. Through it all he adhered to the creed of passive disobedience that infuriated segregationists.

The adulation that was heaped upon him eventually irritated even some Negroes in the civil rights movement who worked hard, but in relative obscurity. They pointed out—and Dr. King admitted—that he was a poor administrator. Sometimes, with sarcasm, they referred to him, privately, as "De Lawd." They noted that Dr. King's successes were built on the labors of many who had gone before him, the noncoms and privates of the civil rights army who fought without benefit of headlines and television cameras.

The Negro extremists he criticized were contemptuous of Dr. King. They dismissed his passion for nonviolence as another form of servility to white people. They called him an "Uncle Tom" and charged that he was hindering the Negro struggle for equality.

Dr. King's belief in nonviolence was subjected to intense pressure in 1966, when some Negro groups adopted the slogan "black power" in the aftermath of civil rights marches into Mississippi and race riots in northern cities. He rejected the idea, saying: "The Negro needs the white man to free him from his fears. The white man needs the Negro to free him from his guilt. A doctrine of black supremacy is as evil as a doctrine of white supremacy."

The doctrine of "black power" threatened to split the Negro civil rights movement and antagonize white liberals who had been supporting Negro causes, and Dr. King suggested "militant nonviolence" as a formula for progress with peace.

At the root of his civil rights convictions was an even more profound faith in the basic goodness of man and the great potential of American democracy. These beliefs gave to his speeches a fervor that could not be stilled by criticism.

Scores of millions of Americans—white as well as Negro—who sat before television sets in the summer of 1963 to watch the awesome march of some 200,000 blacks and whites on Washington were deeply stirred when Dr. King, in the shadow of the Lincoln Memorial, said: "Even though we face the difficulties of today and tomorrow, I still have a dream. I have a dream that one day this nation will rise up and live out the true meaning of its creed: 'We hold these truths to be self-evident, that all men are created equal.' "

And all over the world, men were moved as they read his words of Dec. 10, 1964, when he became the third member of his race to receive the Nobel Peace Prize.

"I refuse to accept the idea that man is mere flotsam and jetsam in the river of life which surrounds him," he said. "I refuse to accept the view that mankind is so tragically bound to the starless midnight of racism and war that the bright daybreak of peace and brotherhood can never become a reality.

"I refuse to accept the cynical notion that nation after nation must spiral down a militaristic stairway into the hell of thermonuclear destruction. I believe that unarmed truth and unconditional love will have the final word in reality. This is why right, temporarily defeated, is stronger than evil triumphant."

For the poor and unlettered of his own race, Dr. King embraced the rhythm and passion of the revivalist and evangelist. Dr. King had the touch, as he illustrated in a church in Albany, Ga., in 1962: "So listen to me, children: Put on your marching shoes; don'cha get weary; though the path ahead may be dark and dreary, we're walking for freedom, children."

Or there was the meeting in Gadsden, Ala., late in 1963, when he displayed another side of his ability before an audience of poor Negroes. It went as follows:

> KING: I hear they are beating you.
> AUDIENCE: Yes, yes.
> KING: I hear they are cursing you.
> AUDIENCE: Yes, yes.
> KING: I hear they are going into your homes and doing nasty things and beating you.
> AUDIENCE: Yes, yes.
> KING: Some of you have knives, and I ask you to put them up. Some of you have arms, and I ask you to put them up; get the weapon of nonviolence, the breastplate of righteousness, the armor of truth, and just keep marching.

It was said that so devoted was his vast following that even among illiterates he could, by calm discussion of Platonic dogma, evoke deep cries of "Amen."

Dr. King also had a way of reducing complex issues to terms that anyone could understand. Thus, in the summer of 1965, when there was widespread discontent among Negroes about their struggle for equality of employment, he declared: "What good does it do to be able to eat at a lunch counter if you can't buy a hamburger?"

The enormous impact of Dr. King's words was one of the reasons he was in the President's Room in the Capitol on Aug. 6, 1965, when President Johnson signed the Voting Rights Act that struck down literacy tests, provided federal registrars to assure the ballot to unregistered Negroes and marked the growth of the Negro as a political force in the South.

Dr. King's effectiveness was enhanced and given continuity by the fact that he had an organization behind him. Formed in 1960, with headquarters in Atlanta, it was called the Southern Christian Leadership Conference, familiarly known as SLICK. Allied with it was another organization formed under Dr. King's sponsorship, the Student Nonviolent Coordinating Committee, often referred to as SNICK.

These two organizations reached the country, though their basic strength was in the South. They brought together Negro clergymen, businessmen, professional men and students. They raised the money and planned the sit-ins, the campaigns for Negro vote registration, the demonstrations by which Negroes hacked away at segregationist resistance, lowering the barriers against Negroes in the political, economic and social life of the nation.

This minister, who became the most famous spokesman for Negro rights since Booker T. Washington, was not particularly impressive in appearance. About 5 feet 8 inches tall, he had an oval face with almond-shaped eyes that looked almost dreamy when he was off the platform. His neck and shoulders were heavily muscled but his hands were almost delicate.

There was little of the rabble-rouser in his oratory. He was not prone to extravagant gestures or loud peroration. Occasionally, after a particularly telling sentence, he would tilt his head a bit and fall silent as though waiting for the echoes of his thought to spread through the hall, church or street.

In private gatherings, Dr. King lacked the laughing gregariousness that often makes for popularity. Some thought he was without a sense of humor. He was not a gifted raconteur. He did not have the flamboyance of a Representative Adam Clayton Powell, Jr., or the cool strategic brilliance of Roy Wilkins, head of the National Association for the Advancement of Colored People.

What Dr. King did have was an instinct for the

right moment to make his moves. Some critics looked upon this as pure opportunism. Nevertheless, it was this sense of timing that raised him, in 1955, from a newly arrived minister in Montgomery, Ala., with his first church, to a figure of national prominence.

Negroes in that city had begun a boycott of buses to win the right to sit where they pleased instead of being forced to move to the rear of buses, in southern tradition, or to surrender seats to white people when a bus was crowded.

The 381-day boycott by Negroes was already under way when the young pastor was placed in charge of the campaign. It has been said that one of the reasons he got the job was because he was so new in the area he had not antagonized any of the Negro factions. Even while the boycott was under way, a board of directors handled the bulk of the administrative work.

However, it was Dr. King who dramatized the boycott with his decision to make it the testing ground, before the eyes of the nation, of his belief in the civil disobedience teachings of Thoreau and Gandhi. When he was arrested during the Montgomery boycott, he said: "If we are arrested every day, if we are exploited every day, if we are trampled over every day, don't ever let anyone pull you so low as to hate them. We must use the weapon of love. We must have compassion and understanding for those who hate us. We must realize so many people are taught to hate us that they are not totally responsible for their hate. But we stand in life at midnight; we are always on the threshold of a new dawn."

Even more dramatic, in some ways, was his reaction to the bombing of his home during the boycott. He was away at the time and rushed back fearful for his wife and children. They were not injured. But when he reached the modest house, more than a thousand Negroes had already gathered and were in an ugly mood, seeking revenge against the white people. The police were jittery. Quickly, Dr. King pacified the crowd and there was no trouble.

Dr. King was even more impressive during the "big push" in Birmingham, which began in April 1963. With the minister in the limelight, Negroes there began a campaign of sit-ins at lunch counters, of picketing and protest marches. Hundreds of children, used in the campaign, were jailed.

The entire world was stirred when the police turned dogs on the demonstrators. Dr. King was jailed for five days. While he was in prison he issued a 9,000-word letter that created considerable controversy among white people, alienating some sympathizers who thought Dr. King was being too aggressive.

In the letter he wrote: "I have almost reached the regrettable conclusion that the Negro's great stumbling block in the stride toward freedom is not the White Citizens Counciler or the Ku Klux Klanner, but the white moderate who is more devoted to order than to justice; who prefers a negative peace, which is the absence of tension, to a positive peace, which is the presence of justice."

Some critics of Dr. King said that one reason for this letter was to answer Negro intellectuals, such as the writer James Baldwin, who were impatient with Dr. King's belief in brotherhood. Whatever the reasons, the role of Dr. King in Birmingham added to his stature and showed that his enormous following was deeply devoted to him.

He demonstrated this in a threatening situation in Albany, Ga., after four Negro girls were killed in the bombing of a church. Dr. King said at the funeral: "In spite of the darkness of this hour, we must not despair. We must not lose faith in our white brothers."

As Dr. King's words grew more potent and he was invited to the White House by Presidents Kennedy and Johnson, some critics—Negroes as well as whites—noted that sometimes, despite all the publicity he attracted, he left campaigns unfinished or else failed to attain his goals.

Dr. King was aware of this. But he pointed out, in 1964, in St. Augustine, Fla., one of the toughest civil rights battlegrounds, that there were important intangibles.

"Even if we do not get all we should," he said, "movements such as this tend more and more to give a Negro the sense of self-respect that he needs. It tends to generate courage in Negroes outside the movement. It brings intangible results outside the community where it is carried out. There is a hardening of attitudes in situations like this. But other cities see and say: 'We don't want to be another Albany or Birmingham,' and they make changes. Some communities, like this one, had to bear the cross."

It was in this city that Negroes marched into the fists of the mob singing "We love everybody."

There was no false modesty in Dr. King's self-appraisal of his role in the civil rights movement.

"History," he said, "has thrust me into this position. It would be both immoral and a sign of ingratitude if I did not face my moral responsibility to do what I can in this struggle."

Another time he compared himself to Socrates as one of "the creative gadflies of society."

At times he addressed himself deliberately to the white people of the nation. Once, he said: "We will match your capacity to inflict suffering with our capacity to endure suffering. We will meet your physical force with soul force. We will not hate you, but we cannot in all good conscience obey your unjust laws . . . We will soon wear you down by our capacity to suffer. And in winning our freedom we will so appeal to your heart and conscience that we will win you in the process."

The enormous influence of Dr. King's voice in the turbulent racial conflict reached into New York in 1964. In the summer of that year racial rioting exploded in New York and in other northern cities with large Negro populations. There was widespread fear that the disorders, particularly in Harlem, might set off unprecedented racial violence.

At this point Dr. King became one of the major intermediaries in restoring order. He conferred with Mayor Robert F. Wagner and with Negro leaders. A statement was issued, of which he was one of the signers, calling for "a broad curtailment if not total moratorium on mass demonstrations until after the presidential elections."

The following year, Dr. King was once more in the headlines and on television—this time leading a drive for Negro voter registration in Selma, Ala. Negroes were arrested by the hundreds. Dr. King was punched and kicked by a white man when, during this period of protest, he became the first Negro to register at a century-old hotel in Selma.

Martin Luther King, Jr., was born Jan. 15, 1929, in a house on Auburn Avenue in Atlanta. As a child his name was Michael Luther King and so was his father's. His father changed both their names legally to Martin Luther King in honor of the Protestant reformer.

Auburn Avenue is one of the nation's most widely known Negro sections. Many successful Negro business or professional men have lived there. The Rev. Martin Luther King, Sr., was pastor of the Ebenezer Baptist Church at Jackson Street and Auburn Avenue.

Young Martin went to Atlanta's Morehouse College, a Negro institution whose students acquired what was sometimes called the "Morehouse swank." The president of Morehouse, Dr. B. E. Mays, took a special interest in Martin, who had decided, in his junior year, to be a clergyman.

He was ordained a minister in his father's church in 1947. It was in this church he was to say, some years later: "America, you've strayed away. You've trampled over 19 million of your brethren. All men are created equal. Not some men. Not white men. All men. America, rise up and come home."

Before Dr. King had his own church he pursued his studies in the integrated Crozier Theological Seminary in Chester, Pa. He was one of six Negroes in a student body of about a hundred. He became the first Negro class president. He was named the outstanding student and won a fellowship to study for a doctorate at the school of his choice. The young man enrolled at Boston College in 1951.

For his doctoral thesis he sought to resolve the differences between the Harvard theologian Paul Tillich and the neonaturalist philosopher Henry Nelson Wieman. During this period he took courses at Harvard, as well.

While he was working on his doctorate he met Coretta Scott, a graduate of Antioch College, who was doing graduate work in music. He married the singer in 1953. They had four children: Yolanda, Martin Luther King 3d, Dexter Scott and Bernice.

In 1954 Dr. King became pastor of the Dexter Avenue Baptist Church in Montgomery, Ala. At that time few of Montgomery's white residents saw any reason for a major dispute with the city's 50,000 Negroes. They did not seem to realize how deeply the Negroes resented segregated seating on buses, for instance.

On Dec. 1, 1955, they learned, almost by accident. Mrs. Rosa Parks, a Negro seamstress, refused to comply with a bus driver's order to give up her seat to a white passenger. She was tired, she said. Her feet hurt from a day of shopping.

Mrs. Parks had been a local secretary for the National Association for the Advancement of Colored People. She was arrested, convicted of refusing to obey the bus conductor and fined $10 and costs, a total of $14. Almost as spontaneous as Mrs. Parks's act was the rallying of many Negro leaders in the city to help her.

From a protest begun over a Negro woman's tired feet Dr. King began his public career.

In 1959 Dr. King and his family moved back to Atlanta, where he became a co-pastor, with his father, of the Ebenezer Baptist Church.

As his fame increased, public interest in his beliefs led him to write books. It was while he was autographing one of these books, *Stride Toward Freedom,* in a Harlem department store that he was stabbed by a Negro woman.

It was in these books that he summarized, in detail, his beliefs as well as his career. Thus, in *Why We Can't Wait,* he wrote: "The Negro knows he is right. He has not organized for conquest or to gain spoils or to enslave those who have injured him. His goal is not to capture that which belongs to someone else. He merely wants, and will have, what is honorably his."

The possibility that he might someday be assassinated was considered by Dr. King on June 5, 1964, when he reported, in St. Augustine, Fla., that his life had been threatened. He said: "Well, if physical death is the price that I must pay to free my white brothers and sisters from a permanent death of the spirit, then nothing can be more redemptive."

THE ASSASSINATION

EARL CALDWELL

APRIL 5, 1968—The Rev. Dr. Martin Luther King, Jr., who preached nonviolence and racial brotherhood, was fatally shot in Memphis on the evening of April 4, 1968, by a distant gunman who then raced away and escaped.

Four thousand National Guard troops were ordered into Memphis by Gov. Buford Ellington after the 39-year-old Nobel Prize–winning civil rights leader died.

A curfew was imposed on the shocked city of 550,000 inhabitants, 40 percent of whom are Negro.

But the police said the tragedy had been followed by incidents that included sporadic shooting, fires, bricks and bottles thrown at policemen, and looting that started in Negro districts and then spread over the city.

Police Director Frank Holloman said the assassin might have been a white man who was "50 to 100 yards away in a flophouse."

Chief of Detectives W. P. Huston said a late-model white Mustang was believed to have been the killer's getaway car. Its occupant was described as a bareheaded white man in his 30s, wearing a black suit and black tie.

The detective chief said the police had chased two cars near the motel where Dr. King was shot and had halted one that had two out-of-town men as occupants. The men were questioned but seemed to have nothing to do with the killing, he said.

A high-powered 30.06-caliber rifle was found about a block from the scene of the shooting, on South Main Street. "We think it's the gun," Chief Huston said, reporting it would be turned over to the Federal Bureau of Investigation.

Dr. King was shot while he leaned over a second-floor railing outside his room at the Lorraine Motel. He was chatting with two friends just before starting for dinner.

One of the friends was a musician, and Dr. King had just asked him to play a Negro spiritual, "Precious Lord, Take My Hand," at a rally that was to have been held two hours later in support of striking Memphis sanitation men.

Paul Hess, assistant administrator at St. Joseph's Hospital, where Dr. King died despite emergency surgery, said the minister had "received a gunshot wound on the right side of the neck, at the root of the neck, a gaping wound."

"He was pronounced dead at 7:05 P.M. Central Standard Time [8:05 P.M. New York time] by staff doctors," Mr. Hess said. "They did everything humanly possible."

Dr. King's mourning associates sought to calm the people they met by recalling his messages of peace, but there was widespread concern by law enforcement officers here and elsewhere over potential reactions.

In a television broadcast after the curfew was ordered here, Mr. Holloman said that "rioting has broken out in parts of the city" and "looting is rampant."

Dr. King had come back to Memphis Wednesday morning, April 3, to organize support once again for 1,300 sanitation workers who had been striking since Lincoln's Birthday. Just a week earlier he led a march in the strikers' cause that ended in violence. A 16-year-old Negro was killed, 62 persons were injured and 200 were arrested.

On April 4, Dr. King had been in his second-floor room—Number 306—throughout the day. Just about 6 P.M. he emerged, wearing a silkish-looking black suit and white shirt.

Solomon Jones, Jr., his driver, had been waiting to take him by car to the home of the Rev. Samuel Kyles of Memphis for dinner. Mr. Jones said later he had observed, "It's cold outside, put your topcoat on," and Dr. King had replied, "O.K., I will."

Dr. King, an open-faced, genial man, leaned over a green iron railing to chat with an associate, Jesse Jackson, standing just below him in a courtyard parking lot.

"Do you know Ben?" Mr. Jackson asked, introducing Ben Branch of Chicago, a musician who was to play at the night's rally.

"Yes, that's my man!" Dr. King glowed.

The two men recalled Dr. King's asking for the playing of the spiritual. "I really want you to play that tonight," Dr. King said, enthusiastically.

The Rev. Ralph W. Abernathy, perhaps Dr. King's closest friend, was just about to come out of the motel room when the sudden loud noise burst out.

Dr. King toppled to the concrete second-floor walkway. Blood gushed from the right jaw and neck area. His necktie had been ripped off by the blast.

"He had just bent over," Mr. Jackson recalled later. "If he had been standing up, he wouldn't have been hit in the face."

"When I turned around," Mr. Jackson went on, bitterly, "I saw police coming from everywhere. They said, 'Where did it come from?' And I said, 'Behind you.' The police were coming from where the shot came."

Mr. Branch asserted that the shot had come from "the hill on the other side of the street."

"When I looked up, the police and the sheriff's deputies were running all around," Mr. Branch declared.

"We didn't need to call the police," Mr. Jackson said. "They were here all over the place."

Mr. Kyles said Dr. King had stood in the open "about three minutes."

Mr. Jones, the driver, said that a squad car with four policemen in it drove down the street only moments before the gunshot. The police had been circulating throughout the motel area on precautionary patrols.

After the shot, Mr. Jones said, he saw a man "with something white on his face" creep away from a thicket across the street.

Someone rushed up with a towel to stem the flow of Dr. King's blood. Mr. Kyles said he put a blanket over Dr. King, but "I knew he was gone." He ran down the stairs and tried to telephone from the motel office for an ambulance.

Mr. Abernathy hurried up with a second, larger towel.

Policemen were pouring into the motel area, carrying rifles and shotguns and wearing riot helmets.

But the King aides said it seemed to be 10 or 15 minutes before a fire department ambulance arrived.

Dr. King was apparently still living when he reached the St. Joseph's Hospital operating room for emergency surgery. He was borne in on a stretcher, the bloody towel over his head.

It was the same emergency room to which James H. Meredith, the first Negro enrolled at the University of Mississippi, was taken after he was ambushed and shot in June 1965 at Hernando, Miss., a few miles south of Memphis. Mr. Meredith was not seriously hurt.

Outside the emergency room some of Dr. King's aides waited in forlorn hope. One was Chauncey Eskridge, his legal adviser. He broke into sobs when Dr. King's death was announced.

"A man full of life, full of love and he was shot," Mr. Eskridge said. "He had always lived with that expectation—but nobody ever expected it to happen."

But the Rev. Andrew Young, executive director of Dr. King's Southern Christian Leadership Conference, recalled there had been some talk Wednesday night about possible harm to Dr. King in Memphis.

Mr. Young recalled: "He said he had reached the pinnacle of fulfillment with his nonviolent movement, and these reports did not bother him."

Mr. Young believed that the fatal shot might have been fired from a passing car. "It sounded like a firecracker," he said.

In a nearby building, a newsman who had been watching a television program thought, however, that "it was a tremendous blast that sounded like a bomb."

There were perhaps 15 persons in the motel courtyard area when Dr. King was shot, all believed to be Negroes and Dr. King's associates.

Past the courtyard is a small empty swimming pool. Then comes Mulberry Street, a short street only three blocks away from storied Beale Street on the fringe of downtown Memphis.

On the other side of the street is a six-foot brick restraining wall, with bushes and grass atop it and a hillside going on to a patch of trees. Behind the trees is a rusty wire fence enclosing backyards of two-story brick and frame houses.

At the corner at Butler Street is a newish-looking white brick fire station.

Police were reported to have chased a late-model blue or white car through Memphis and north to Millington. A civilian in another car that had a citizens band radio was also reported to have pursued the fleeing car and to have opened fire on it.

The police first cordoned off an area of about five blocks around the Lorraine Motel, chosen by Dr. King for his stay here because it is Negro-owned. The two-story motel is an addition to a small two-story hotel in a largely Negro area.

Mayor Henry Loeb had ordered a curfew here after last week's disorder, and National Guard units had been on duty for five days until they were deactivated Wednesday.

Last night the mayor reinstated the curfew at

6:35 and declared: "After the tragedy which has happened in Memphis tonight, for the protection of all our citizens, we are putting the curfew back in effect. All movement is restricted except for health or emergency reasons."

Governor Ellington, calling out the National Guard and pledging all necessary action by the state to prevent disorder, announced: "For the second time in recent days, I most earnestly ask the people of Memphis and Shelby County to remain calm. I do so again tonight in the face of this most regrettable incident.

"Every possible action is being taken to apprehend the person or persons responsible for committing this act.

"We are also taking precautionary steps to prevent any acts of disorder. I can fully appreciate the feelings and emotions which this crime has aroused, but for the benefit of everyone, all of our citizens must exercise restraint, caution and good judgment."

National Guard planes flew over the state to bring in contingents of riot-trained highway patrolmen. Units of the Arkansas State Patrol were deputized and brought into Memphis.

Sixty arrests were made for looting, burglary and disorderly conduct, Chief Bartholomew said.

In Memphis, Dr. King's chief associates met in his room after he died. They included Mr. Young, Mr. Abernathy, Mr. Jackson, the Rev. James Bevel and Hosea Williams.

They had to step across a drying pool of Dr. King's blood to enter. Someone had thrown a crumpled pack of cigarettes into the blood.

After 15 minutes they emerged. Mr. Jackson looked at the blood. He embraced Mr. Abernathy.

"Stand tall!" somebody exhorted.

"Murder! Murder!" Mr. Bevel groaned. "Doc said that's not the way."

"Doc" was what they often called Dr. King.

Then the murdered leader's aides said they would go on to the hall where tonight's rally was to have been held. They wanted to urge calm upon the mourners.

Some policemen sought to dissuade them.

But eventually the group did start out, with a police escort.

At the Federal Bureau of Investigation office here, Robert Jensen, special agent in charge, said the F.B.I. had entered the murder investigation at the request of Attorney General Ramsey Clark.

Last night Dr. King's body was taken to the Shelby County morgue, according to the police. They said it would be up to Dr. Derry Francisco, county medical examiner, to order further disposition.

THE MEMPHIS MARCH

J. ANTHONY LUKAS

APRIL 8, 1968—Mrs. Martin Luther King, Jr., led a massive, orderly, silent march today through the streets of this city, where her husband was killed by a sniper's bullet four days before.

Then, standing against the white marble facade of the Memphis City Hall on the banks of the Mississippi, she told the huge crowd spread out before her in City Hall Plaza that "we must carry on because this is the way he would have wanted it."

Wearing a simple black dress, and with her face lifted up to the gray skies from which a few drops had begun to fall, she challenged the throng to "go forward from this experience, which to me represents the Crucifixion, on toward the resurrection and redemption of his spirit."

"Somehow," she said, "I hope in this resurrection experience the will will be created within the hearts, and minds, and the souls, and the spirits of those who have the power to make changes come about."

Then, her voice breaking, she said, "How many

men must die before we can really have a free and true and peaceful society? How long will it take?"

The crowd, many of whom had come to Memphis from all over the country, gave Mrs. King's words repeated and prolonged applause that echoed off the deserted office buildings ringing the plaza.

Estimates of the number of marchers varied sharply. Bayard Rustin, one of the march organizers, told the rally that his assistants had counted 42,000 persons. But a police spokesman said the police had counted only slightly more than 19,000.

Whatever the number, the procession represented an impressive rallying of forces to honor Dr. King and to support the cause he had come here to fight for—the demands of the city's predominantly Negro garbagemen for union recognition and a dues check-off.

Among those who marched in the first ranks today were Walter P. Reuther, president of the United Automobile Workers; Dr. Benjamin Spock, the pediatrician, a leader of the peace movement; Rabbi Joachim Prinz, past president of the American Jewish Congress; Mario Procaccino, New York City Controller; Eugene Nickerson, Nassau County Executive; Harry Belafonte, the singer; and Ossie Davis, the actor.

Also in the front ranks, next to Mrs. King—who walked where her husband would have walked—were his colleagues and friends in the Southern Christian Leadership Conference.

The Rev. Ralph D. Abernathy, Dr. King's long-time lieutenant and his successor as head of the leadership conference, strode beside her and held her hand tightly clasped in his.

Mr. Abernathy gave perhaps the most emotional speech at the three-hour City Hall rally. Pounding the wooden lectern repeatedly with his clenched fists, he said: "We are bound for the promised land and we aren't going to let nobody, whether it be Mayor [Henry] Loeb [of Memphis], whether it be the governor of the state of Tennessee, whether it be the National Guard or the police force, whether it be Lyndon Baines Johnson or the Congress of the United States, we aren't going to let nobody turn us around."

The aroused crowd responded repeatedly with "Amen, amen" and "Tell it like it is."

"I have been on top of the mountain," Mr. Abernathy said. "I have talked to God about it, and God told me that Martin did not get there but you have been so close to Martin I am going to help you get there. If God will lead me I am going to lead my people into the promised land."

Despite the emotion generated by the speakers and the march itself, there was no violence anywhere along the route of march.

This was due largely to emphatic insistence on nonviolence by Mr. Rustin and the march's other organizers and to elaborate training sessions for the 500 march marshals, Negro community leaders who kept tight control of the marchers.

It was due also to restraint by the more than 800 Memphis policemen and 5,000 Tennessee National Guardsmen mobilized along the route of march or nearby.

The Guardsmen—the great majority of whom were white—stood at ease, their rifles with fixed bayonets on the ground before them, as the marchers moved by. Behind them in adjoining streets the marchers could see jeeps and trucks filled with other armed troops. But there was not one incident reported between troops or policemen and the marchers.

The police reported a few cases of looting in outlying parts of the city and two shooting incidents, in which nobody was hurt. But they said these had nothing to do with the march.

The peacefulness of today's march was in striking contrast to the first march Dr. King led here, on March 28, which deteriorated into rioting. Dr. King was so disturbed by this marring of his record for nonviolence that he came back here last week to plan the march held today as a demonstration of his capacity to keep his movement nonviolent.

The procession started at the Clayborn Temple

African Methodist Episcopal Church, about 15 blocks south of City Hall, along the Mississippi.

Marchers began gathering at about 9 A.M. in the streets around the church, where they were given printed black-and-white signs reading "Union Justice Now," "Honor King: End Racism!" and "I Am a Man." Some marchers brought their own signs and banners.

The march had been scheduled to begin at 11 A.M., but there was a delay because fog here and in Atlanta held up planes bringing in prominent persons including Mrs. King, Gov. Nelson Rockefeller, and Harry Belafonte.

Finally, at 11:16 A.M., with Mrs. King and other awaited persons still missing, the march moved out from the church along Hernando Street and swung east into Linden Avenue, through a Negro section of town.

The march was led by the Rev. James M. Lawson, chairman of the Committee on the Move for Equality, which has been the spearhead of the Memphis movement; Mr. Reuther; Donald Slaiman, head of the Civil Rights Department of the American Federation of Labor and Congress of Industrial Organizations, and several others.

The procession moved past ramshackle frame houses where Negro men in blue jeans and tattered sweaters leaned against peeling white pillars; past the dusty windows of Alma and Ruth's Beauty Bar and the sagging door of the Outer Limits Cafe.

It swung onto Main Street, the wide thoroughfare that parallels the river. The big department stores and specialty shops along the street were locked tight. A few had put signs in their windows announcing that they were closed "in honor of Dr. King" or "in a spirit of community cooperation," but most had simply stripped their windows bare of any lootable goods.

A few white residents leaned against buildings on Main Street, their faces impassive. Negro spectators, some in bright pullovers and toreador pants, kept pace with the marchers, smiles of excitement and delight on their faces.

At Beale Street, famed as one of the nation's great jazz centers decades ago, the march suddenly halted and word circulated that Mrs. King had landed at the airport and that the march would wait until she arrived.

Twenty minutes later, preceded by police motorcycles, her car pulled up and Mrs. King got out, followed by her three oldest children: Yolanda, 12 years old; Martin Luther 3d, 10; and Dexter, 7.

Mr. Belafonte escorted them into the march, where they were welcomed with warm embraces by Mr. Abernathy and other Negro leaders who had also just arrived.

Then the march moved out again, with Mrs. King and her children at the head. As it approached City Hall Plaza, marshals told the marchers, "Everybody maintain silence" and "No smoking or chewing gum."

On the sidewalk a white girl with a blond beehive hairdo squealed to a companion, "Oh, I'm so excited, I've never seen Harry Belafonte before."

The procession moved with measured pace, sometimes eight, sometimes 10 or 15 abreast, among them representatives of almost every walk of life: white college students in nubby sweaters and white sneakers; Negro garbagemen in denim overalls; young girls in short skirts and high boots; Roman Catholic priests in high white collars; middle-aged white businessmen and professional men and their gray-haired wives; Negro housewives with flowered hats; nuns in flowing robes; labor unionists, professors, ministers, teachers.

Most linked hands or arms, black and white side by side. Observers estimated about 70 percent of the marchers were Negro and 30 percent were white.

At City Hall the marchers moved quietly into rank after rank in front of the wooden stand set up before the huge bronze Memphis seal showing a Mississippi riverboat and a stalk of cotton. Ossie Davis opened the rally, followed by Mr. Belafonte, who paid a glowing tribute to Mrs. King.

He also delivered a bristling denunciation of what he called "the bestiality and the decay of the white world."

"I hope that now the white man will come to his senses," he said. "Perhaps after that we can appeal to his soul, because that's all that is left."

The throng then sang "O Lord, Guard My Feet, While I Run This Race," one of Dr. King's favorite hymns. It was led by the Rev. S. P. Kyle, a Memphis minister who was with Dr. King the night he was shot.

Among those who spoke during the rally was Jerry Wurf, president of the American Federation of State, County and Municipal Employees, the union that organized the Memphis garbage workers.

Mr. Wurf, who had been in negotiations with city officials here until 6 o'clock this morning in a vain effort to settle the garbage strike before today's march, told the crowd: "As long as these 1,300 men have no freedom, no dignity, none of us have dignity."

Mr. Reuther said that "the whitest American can't be free until he gives his hand to the blackest American."

Mr. Reuther announced a United Automobile Workers gift of $50,000 to support the striking garbagemen.

Dr. Spock ended the rally by urging white Americans to go beyond eulogies for Dr. King to some positive action, "because we are the group that have been the oppressors."

THE FUNERAL IN ATLANTA

HOMER BIGART

APRIL 9, 1968—The coffin of the Rev. Dr. Martin Luther King, Jr., was carried through the streets of Atlanta on April 9, 1968, on a crude farm wagon pulled by two Georgia mules. It was followed by tens of thousands of mourners, black and white, the lowly and the powerful, mingling in silent tribute to the slain Negro civil rights leader.

It was one of the strangest corteges ever seen in the land.

The body of Dr. King, the advocate of racial progress through nonviolence, who was shot by a sniper in Memphis, lay in a gleaming African mahogany coffin that rested on the rough planks of the faded green cart. The wagon and the mules were symbols of Dr. King's identification with the poor.

Behind the wagon marched some of the nation's highest figures in finance, politics, religion and government. In sultry 80-degree heat Governor Rockefeller of New York and Sen. Robert F. Kennedy made the three-and-one-half-mile walk from Ebenezer Baptist Church, where a funeral service was held, across the city to an open-air general service at Morehouse College.

The service at the church began at 10:43 A.M., 13 minutes after the scheduled start. By the time the march from the church to the college and the 90-minute memorial service there were over, it was 5:30 P.M. before Dr. King was buried in South View Cemetery.

The Atlanta police declined to estimate the size of the crowd, but unofficial estimates put the number of marchers at about 50,000, with perhaps 100,000 more viewing the procession and the service on the campus.

Observers estimated the proportion of whites in the procession and at the two services at about 10 percent.

Dozens of mourners fainted from the heat and the pressing of the crowds.

All of the avowed candidates for presidential nomination attended the service in Ebenezer Church, where Dr. King was co-pastor with his father.

Besides Senator Kennedy of New York, the mourners included his rival for the Democratic nomination, Sen. Eugene J. McCarthy of Minnesota. Former Vice President Richard M. Nixon, the only announced major candidate for the Republican nomination, was there.

Representing the White House was Vice President Humphrey, who is expected to announce for the Democratic nomination soon.

Although the visiting politicians were received courteously by the largely middle-class Negro crowd and Senator Kennedy was cheered, cries of "politicking" greeted Mr. Nixon as he entered the church.

Some of the younger militants murmured privately about "crocodile tears" and vote-seeking.

In the throng there were, too, a scattering of bishops in ecclesiastical robes, some African envoys, labor potentates and some famous Negro names in the theater, the cinema and sports.

From Washington came 50 members of the House of Representatives and 30 senators. A regiment of mayors appeared, some of them from cities recently torn by riots.

But the figure that evoked the sharpest pang of sentiment was Mrs. John F. Kennedy, widowed—like Coretta King—by an assassin.

Recognized by surging crowds as she was led toward the church, Mrs. Kennedy was suddenly caught up in such a pressure of people that she had to be pulled and pushed through the narrow door. For a moment her face appeared strained and frightened.

Soon after Mrs. Kennedy disappeared through the door, there was another commotion. Stokely Carmichael, the black power apostle, appeared, wearing a light blue turtleneck sweater under a dark coat and accompanied by six bodyguards.

The church was already jammed—Governor Rockefeller, Mayor Lindsay of New York and Gov. George Romney of Michigan had yielded their seats to women and were standing in the aisle. Carmichael had been invited—there was a seat for him—but the doormen were dubious about the bodyguards.

So there was a milling confrontation at the entrance. Some of Carmichael's followers, thinking he himself was being kept out, shouted: "You'd better let him in" and "He's a black man." Finally the whole group was allowed to enter.

At times the clamor for admission was loud enough to disturb the service, which had started late because the principal mourners, including the immediate family, were unable to get into the church.

Dr. King's brother, the Rev. A. D. King, emerged to appeal for order. Stepping onto the back of a black hearse that was to be used to carry flowers, he pleaded: "At this hour our hearts are very heavy. Please let the family through. You would want Dr. King's wife, children, mother and father to have an opportunity of seeing this service. Please don't make Mrs. King have to fight her way in."

No one budged. Dr. King's brother said: "If we can't receive your cooperation, we have but one choice—to remove the body and bury it privately."

Then there was less tumult and jostling. Inside the church, Governors Rockefeller and Romney and Mayor Lindsay were led to seats at the center of the church. Mrs. Kennedy sat next to Sen. Edward M. Kennedy of Massachusetts, near the front. Vice President Humphrey, who entered through a side door just before the service started, walked up close to the coffin and greeted Dr. King's parents in the front row.

Seated among the New York delegation were the Right Rev. Horace W. B. Donegan, Episcopal bishop of New York; the Most Rev. Terence J. Cooke, the new Roman Catholic archbishop of New York, whose bright purple episcopal robes made him conspicuous among the mourners; Archbishop Iakovos, Greek Orthodox primate of North and South America, and Rabbi Henry Siegman, executive vice president of the Synagogue Council of America.

At the request of Mrs. King, the church service included a taped excerpt from the last sermon Dr. King preached at the church, on Feb. 4.

The congregation was visibly moved, and some wept openly, as the voice of Dr. King said: "If any of you are around when I have to meet my day, I don't want a long funeral. And if you get somebody to deliver the eulogy, tell him not to talk too long. Tell him not to mention that I have a Nobel Peace Prize—that isn't important.

"Tell him not to mention that I have 300 or 400 other awards—that's not important.

"Tell him not to mention where I went to school.

"I'd like somebody to mention that day that Martin Luther King, Jr., tried to give his life serving others.

"I'd like for somebody to say that day that Martin Luther King, Jr., tried to love somebody. . . .

"I want you to be able to say that day that I did try to feed the hungry. I want you to be able to say that day that I did try in my life to clothe the naked. And I want you to say that I tried to love and serve humanity."

The Rev. Ralph D. Abernathy, who succeeds Dr. King as president of the Southern Christian Leadership Conference, opened the church service by calling Dr. King's murder "one of the darkest hours of mankind."

A brief tribute to Dr. King was delivered by Dr. L. Harold DeWolfe, dean of Wesley Theological Seminary, Washington, who had taught Dr. King at Boston University. Dr. DeWolfe, the only white participant in the service, said that "Dr. King sought to relieve the slavery of the oppressors as well as that of the oppressed.

"It is now for us, all the millions of the living who care, to take up his torch of love," he said. "It is for us to finish his work, to end the awful destruction in Vietnam, to root out every trace of race prejudice from our lives, to bring the massive powers of this nation to aid the oppressed and to heal the hate-scarred world."

The service was an hour longer than expected, and it was past noon when the coffin was carried out and placed on the cart.

Many of the dignitaries did not make the march. Others dropped out along the way.

The procession moved down Auburn Street, past a clutter of closed taverns and honky-tonks and into the downtown business district. Here the sidewalk crowds were predominantly white.

Most of the men doffed their hats as the mule wagon passed. A few who did not do so obeyed quickly when marchers politely asked them to.

The line of march led past the domed State Capitol, where the segregationist governor, Lester G. Maddox, was sitting in his office under heavy guard.

Governor Maddox's decision not to participate in the funeral was hailed by Charles Morgan, Jr., one of the three white directors of the Southern Christian Leadership Conference, as "an honest act at a time when very few honest acts are performed."

"Of course," Mr. Morgan added, "the governor's attendance would have been a desecration."

Without bands, the procession seemed strangely silent as it toiled past City Hall, draped in mourning. But as the marchers moved over the long Hunter Street viaduct into the largely Negro West Side, they occasionally broke into the songs that Dr. King loved, "We Shall Overcome" and "This Little Light of Mine."

It was nearly 3 P.M. by the time the memorial service began on the campus of Morehouse College, where Dr. King had been an undergraduate. Again the crush of crowds around Dr. King's family became so great that the service was interrupted for nearly 15 minutes while clergymen pleaded with the people to stand back. Many fainted.

In the eulogy at Morehouse, Dr. Benjamin H. Mays, president emeritus of Morehouse, said: "I make bold to assert that it took more courage for King to practice nonviolence than it took his assassin to fire the fatal shot.

"The assassin is a coward: he committed his foul act and fled. When Martin Luther disobeyed an unjust law, he accepted the consequences of his actions. He never ran away and he never begged for mercy."

Dr. Mays said that although Dr. King was "deeply committed to a program of freedom for Negroes, he had a love and concern for all kinds of people."

South View Cemetery, where Dr. King was buried, was abloom with dogwood and the fresh green boughs of April.

Crowds of Negroes and whites had lined the four-mile route from the campus to the cemetery. The little hillside graveyard was founded in 1866, right after the Civil War, by six Negroes who were tired of taking their dead to the back gates of the municipal cemeteries.

Dr. King's coffin was taken from the college to the cemetery in a hearse.

The interment rites were brief. Mr. Abernathy intoned: "The cemetery is too small for his spirit but we submit his body to the ground. The grave is too narrow for his soul, but we commit his body to the ground. No coffin, no crypt, no stone can hold his greatness. But we submit his body to the ground."

Dr. King was buried beside his grandparents. An epitaph on the tombstone, derived from a Negro spiritual, reads: "Free at last; free at last; thank God Almighty I'm free at last."

THE TIME FOR FREEDOM HAS COME [1961]

MARTIN LUTHER KING, JR.

ON A chill morning in the autumn of 1956, an elderly, toil-worn Negro woman in Montgomery, Ala., began her slow, painful four-mile walk to her job. It was the tenth month of the Montgomery bus boycott, which had begun with a life expectancy of one week. The old woman's difficult progress led a passerby to inquire sympathetically if her feet were tired. Her simple answer became the boycotters' watchword. "Yes, friend, my feet is real tired, but my soul is rested."

Five years passed and once more Montgomery arrested the world's attention. Now the symbolic segregationist is not a stubborn, rude bus driver. He emerges in 1961 as a hoodlum stomping the bleeding face of a Freedom Rider. But neither is the Negro today an elderly woman whose grammar is uncertain; rather, he is college-bred, Ivy League–clad, youthful, articulate and resolute. He has the imagination and drive of the young, tamed by discipline and commitment. The nation and the world have reacted with astonishment at these students cast from a new mold, unaware that a chain reaction was accumulating explosive force behind a strangely different facade.

Generating these changes is a phenomenon Victor Hugo described in these words: "There is no greater power on earth than an idea whose time has come." In the decade of the sixties the time for freedom for the Negro has come. This simple truth illuminates the motivations, the tactics and the objectives of the students' daring and imaginative movement.

The young Negro is not in revolt, as some have suggested, against a single pattern of timid, fumbling, conservative leadership. Nor is his conduct to be explained in terms of youth's excesses. He is carrying forward a revolutionary destiny of a whole people consciously and deliberately. Hence the extraordinary willingness to fill the jails as if they were honors classes and the boldness to absorb brutality, even to the point of death, and remain nonviolent. His inner strength derives from his goal of freedom and the leadership role he has grasped even at a time when some of his white counterparts still grope in philosophical confusion searching for a personal goal with human values, searching for security from economic instability, and seeking relief from the haunting fear of nuclear destruction.

The campuses of Negro colleges are infused with a dynamism of both action and philosophical discussion. The needs of a surging period of change have had an impact on all Negro groups, sweeping away conventional trivialities and escapism.

Even in the Thirties, when the college campus was alive with social thought, only a minority was involved in action. Now, during the sit-in phase, when a few students were suspended or expelled, more than one college saw the total student body involved in a walkout protest. This is a change in student activity of profound significance. Seldom, if ever, in American history has a student movement engulfed the whole student body of a college.

In another dimension an equally striking change is altering the Negro campuses. Not long ago the Negro collegian imitated the white collegian. In attire, in athletics, in social life, imitation was the rule. For the future, he looked to a professional life cast in the image of the middle-class white professional. He imitated with such energy that Gunnar Myrdal described the ambitious Negro as "an exaggerated American."

Today the imitation has ceased. The Negro collegian now initiates. Groping for unique forms of protest, he created the sit-ins and Freedom Rides. Overnight his white fellow students began to imitate him. As the movement took hold, a revival of social awareness spread across campuses from Cambridge to California. It spilled over the boundaries of the single issue of desegregation and encompassed questions of peace, civil liberties, capital punishment and others. It penetrated the ivy-covered walls of the traditional institutions as well as the glass-and-stainless-steel structures of the newly established colleges.

A consciousness of leadership, a sense of destiny have given a maturity and a dedication to this generation of Negro students which have few precedents. As a minister, I am often given promises of dedication. Instinctively I examine the degree of sincerity. The striking quality in Negro students I have met is the intensity and depth of their commitment. I am no longer surprised to meet attractive, stylishly dressed young girls whose charm and personality would grace a junior prom and to hear them declare in unmistakably sincere terms, "Dr. King, I am ready to die if I must."

Many of the students, when pressed to express their inner feelings, identify themselves with students in Africa, Asia and South America. The liberation struggle in Africa has been the greatest single international influence on American Negro students. Frequently I hear them say that if their African brothers can break the bonds of colonialism, surely the American Negro can break Jim Crow.

African leaders such as President Kwame Nkrumah of Ghana, Governor General Nnamdi Azikiwe of Nigeria, Dr. Tom Mboya of Kenya and Dr. Hastings Banda of Nyasaland are popular heroes on most Negro college campuses. Many groups demonstrated or otherwise protested when the Congo leader, Patrice Lumumba, was assassinated. The newspapers were mistaken when they interpreted these outbursts of indignation as "Communist-inspired."

Part of the impatience of Negro youth stems from their observation that change is taking place rapidly in Africa and other parts of the world, but comparatively slowly in the South. When the United States Supreme Court handed down its historic desegregation decision in 1954, many of us, perhaps naively, thought that great and sweeping school integration would ensue. Yet, today, seven years later, only 7 percent of the Negro children of the South have been placed in desegregated schools. At the current rate it will take 93 more years to desegregate the public schools of the South. The collegians say, "We can't wait that long," or simply, "We won't wait!"

Negro students are coming to understand that education and learning have become tools for shaping the future and not devices of privilege for an exclusive few. Behind this spiritual explosion is the shattering of a material atom.

The future of the Negro college student has long been locked within the narrow walls of limited opportunity. Only a few professions could be practiced by Negroes and, but for a few exceptions, behind barriers of segregation in the North as well as the South. Few frustrations can compare with the experience of struggling with complex academic subjects, straining to absorb concepts which may never be used, or only half-utilized under conditions insulting to the trained mind.

A Negro intern blurted out to me shortly after his patient died, "I wish I were not so well trained because then I would never know how many of these people need not die for lack of proper equipment, adequate postoperative care and timely admission. I'm not practicing good medicine. I'm presiding over tragedies which the absence of good medicine creates."

The Negro lawyer knows his practice will bulk large with criminal cases. The law of wills, of corporations, of taxation will only infrequently reach his office because the clientele he serves has had little opportunity to accumulate property. In his courtroom experience in the South, his clients and witnesses will probably be segregated and he, as well as they, will seldom be referred to as "Mister." Even worse, all too often he knows that the verdict was sealed the moment the arrest was made.

These are but a few examples of the real experience of the Negro professional, seen clearly by the student who has been asked to study with serious purpose. Obviously his incentive has been smothered and weakened. But today, more than ever, the Negro realizes that, while studying, he can also act to change the conditions which cripple his future. In the struggle to desegregate society he is altering it directly for himself as well as for future generations.

There is another respect in which the Negro student is benefiting, while simultaneously contributing to society as a whole. He is learning social responsibility; he is learning to earn, through his own direct sacrifice, the result he seeks. There are those who would make him soft, pliable and conformist—a mechanical organization man or an uncreative status seeker. But the experience of Negro youth is as harsh and demanding as that of the pioneer on the untamed frontier. Because his struggle is complex, there is no place in it for the frivolous or rowdy. Knowledge and discipline are as indispensable as courage and self-sacrifice. Hence the forging of priceless qualities of character is taking place daily as a high moral goal is pursued.

Inevitably there will emerge from this caldron a mature man, experienced in life's lessons, socially aware, unafraid of experimentation and, most of all, imbued with the spirit of service and dedication to a great ideal. The movement therefore gives to its participants a double education—academic learning from books and classes, and life's lessons from responsible participation in social action. Indeed, the answer to the quest for a more mature, educated American, to compete successfully with the young people of other lands, may be present in this new movement.

Of course, not every student in our struggle has gained from it. This would be more than any humanly designed plan could realize. For some, the opportunity for personal advantage presented itself and their character was not equal to the challenge. A small percentage of students have found it convenient to escape from their own inadequacies by identifying with the sit-ins and other activities. They are, however, relatively few because this is a form of escape in which the flight from responsibility imposes even greater responsibilities and risks.

It is not a solemn life, for all of its seriousness. During a vigorous debate among a group of students discussing the moral and practical soundness of nonviolence, a majority rejected the employment of force. As the minority dwindled to a single student, he finally declared, "All I know is that, if rabbits could throw rocks, there would be fewer hunters in the forest."

This is more than a witty remark to relieve the tensions of serious and even grim discussion. It expresses some of the pent-up impatience, some of the discontent and some of the despair produced by minute corrections in the face of enormous evil. Students necessarily have conflicting reactions. It is understandable that violence presents itself as a quick, effective answer for a few.

For the large majority, however, nonviolent, direct action has emerged as the better and more successful way out. It does not require that they abandon their discontent. This discontent is a sound, healthy social response to the injustice and brutality they see around them. Nonviolence offers a method by which they can fight the evil with which they cannot live. It offers a unique weapon which, without firing a single bullet, disarms the adversary. It exposes his moral defenses, weakens his morale, and at the same time works on his conscience.

Another weapon Negro students have employed creatively in their nonviolent struggle is satire. It has enabled them to avoid corrosive anger while pressing the cutting edge of ridicule against the opponent. When they have been admonished to "go slow," patiently to wait for gradual change, with a straight face they will assure you that they are diligently searching for the happy medium between the two extremes of moderation and gradualism.

It is perhaps the special quality of nonviolent direct action, which sublimates anger, that explains why so few students are attracted to extreme nationalist sects advocating black supremacy. The students have anger under controlling bonds of discipline. Hence they can answer appeals for cooling-off periods by advocating cooling-off for those who are hot with anger and violence.

Much has been made of the willingness of these devotees of nonviolent social action to break the law. Paradoxically, although they have embraced Thoreau's and Gandhi's civil disobedience on a scale dwarfing any past experience in American history, they do respect law. They feel a moral responsibility to obey just laws. But they recognize that there are also unjust laws.

From a purely moral point of view, an unjust law is one that is out of harmony with the moral law of the universe. More concretely, an unjust law is one in which the minority is compelled to observe a code that is not binding on the majority. An unjust law is one in which people are required to obey a code that they had no part in making because they were denied the right to vote.

In disobeying such unjust laws, the students do so peacefully, openly and nonviolently. Most important, they willingly accept the penalty, whatever it is, for in this way the public comes to reexamine the law in question and will thus decide whether it uplifts or degrades man.

This distinguishes their position on civil disobedience from the "uncivil disobedience" of the segregationist. In the face of laws they consider unjust, the racists seek to defy, evade and circumvent the law, and they are unwilling to accept the penalty. The end result of their defiance is anarchy and disrespect for the law. The students, on the other hand, believe that he who openly disobeys a law, a law conscience tells him is unjust, and then willingly accepts the penalty, gives evidence thereby that he so respects that law that he belongs in jail until it is changed. Their appeal is to the conscience.

Beyond this, the students appear to have perceived what an older generation overlooked in the role of law. The law tends to declare rights—it does not deliver them. A catalyst is needed to breathe life experience into a judicial decision by the persistent exercise of the rights until they become usual and ordinary in human conduct. They have offered their energies, their bodies to effect this result. They see themselves the obstetricians at the birth of a new order. It is in this manner that the students have related themselves to and materialized "the idea whose time has come."

In a sense, the victories of the past two years have been spectacular and considerable. Because of the student sitters, more than 150 cities in the South have integrated their lunch counters. Actually, the current breakthroughs have come about partly as a result of the patient legal, civil and social ground clearing of the previous decades. Then, too, but slowly, the national government is realizing that our so-called domestic race relations are a major force in our foreign relations. Our image abroad reflects our behavior at home.

Many liberals, of the North as well as the South, when they list the unprecedented progress of the past few years, yearn for a "cooling-off" period; not too fast, they say, we may lose all that we have gained if we push faster than the violent ones can be persuaded to yield.

This view, though understandable, is a misreading of the goals of the young Negroes. They are not after "mere tokens" of integration ("tokenism," they call it); rather, theirs is a revolt against the whole system of Jim Crow and they are prepared to sit in, kneel in, wade in and stand in until every waiting room, rest room, theater and other facility throughout the nation that is supposedly open to the public is in fact open to Negroes, Mexicans, Indians, Jews or what have you. Theirs is total commitment to this goal of equality and dignity. And for this achievement they are prepared to pay the costs—whatever they are—in suffering and hardship as long as may be necessary.

Indeed, these students are not struggling for themselves alone. They are seeking to save the soul of America. They are taking our whole nation back to those great wells of democracy which were dug deep by the Founding Fathers in the formulation of the Constitution and the Declaration of Independence. In sitting down at the lunch counters they are in reality standing up for the best in the American dream. They courageously go to the jails of the South in order to get America out of the dilemma in which she finds herself as a result of the continued existence of segregation. One day historians will record this student movement as one of the most significant epics of our heritage.

But should we, as a nation, sit by as spectators when the social unrest seethes? Most of us recognize that the Jim Crow system is doomed. If so, would it not be the wise and human thing to abolish the system surely and swiftly? This would not be difficult, if our national government would exercise its full powers to enforce federal laws and court decisions and do so on a scale commensurate with the problems and with an unmistakable decisiveness. Moreover, we would need our religious, civic and economic leaders to mobilize their forces behind a real honest-to-goodness "End Jim Crow Now" campaign.

This is the challenge of these young people to us and our ideals. It is also an expression of their new-found faith in themselves as well as in their fellow man.

In an effort to understand the students and to help them understand themselves, I asked one student I know to find a quotation expressing his feeling about our struggle. He was an inarticulate young man, athletically expert and far more poetic with a basketball than with words, but few would have found the quotation he typed on a card and left on my desk early one morning:

I sought my soul, but my soul
I could not see,
I sought my God, but he eluded
me,
I sought my brother, and I
found all three.

THE MARCH ON WASHINGTON

E. W. KENWORTHY

MORE THAN 200,000 Americans, most of them black but many of them white, demonstrated in Washington, D.C., on August 28, 1963, for a full and speedy program of civil rights and equal job opportunities.

It was the greatest assembly for a redress of grievances that this capital has ever seen.

One hundred years and 240 days after Abraham Lincoln enjoined the emancipated slaves to "abstain from all violence" and "labor faithfully for reasonable wages," this vast throng proclaimed in march and song and through the speeches of their leaders that they were still waiting for the freedom and the jobs.

There was no violence to mar the demonstration. In fact, at times there was an air of hootenanny about it as groups of schoolchildren clapped hands and swung into the familiar freedom songs.

But if the crowd was good-natured, the underlying tone was one of dead seriousness. The emphasis was on "freedom" and "now." At the same time the leaders emphasized, paradoxically but realistically, that the struggle was just beginning.

On Capitol Hill, opinion was divided about the impact of the demonstration in stimulating congressional action on civil rights legislation. But at the White House, President Kennedy declared that the cause of 20,000,000 Negroes had been advanced by the march.

The march leaders went from the shadows of the Lincoln Memorial to the White House to meet with the president for 75 minutes. Afterward, Mr. Kennedy issued a 400-word statement praising the marchers for the "deep fervor and the quiet dignity" that had characterized the demonstration.

The nation, the president said, "can properly be proud of the demonstration that has occurred here today."

The main target of the demonstration was Congress, where committees are now considering the administration's civil rights bill.

At the Lincoln Memorial this afternoon, some speakers, knowing little of the ways of Congress, assumed that the passage of a strengthened civil rights bill had been assured by the moving events of the day.

But from statements by congressional leaders, after they had met with the march committee this morning, this did not seem certain at all. These statements came before the demonstration.

Senator Mike Mansfield of Montana, the Senate Democratic leader, said he could not say whether the mass protest would speed the legislation, which faces a filibuster by southerners.

Senator Everett McKinley Dirksen of Illinois, the Republican leader, said he thought the demonstration would be neither an advantage nor a disadvantage to the prospects for the civil rights bill.

The human tide that swept over the Mall between the shrines of Washington and Lincoln fell back faster than it came on. As soon as the ceremony broke up this afternoon, the exodus began. With astounding speed, the last buses and trains cleared the city by mid-evening.

At 9 P.M. the city was as calm as the waters of the Reflecting Pool between the two memorials.

At the Lincoln Memorial early in the afternoon, in the midst of a songfest before the addresses, Josephine Baker, the singer, who had flown from her home in Paris, said to the thousands stretching down both sides of the Reflecting Pool: "You are on the eve of a complete victory. You can't go wrong. The world is behind you."

Miss Baker said, as if she saw a dream coming true before her eyes, that "this is the happiest day of my life."

But of all the 10 leaders of the march on Washington who followed her, only the Rev. Dr. Martin Luther King, Jr., president of the Southern Christian Leadership Conference, saw that dream so hopefully.

The other leaders, except for the three clergymen among the 10, concentrated on the struggle ahead and spoke in tough, even harsh, language.

But paradoxically it was Dr. King—who had suffered perhaps most of all—who ignited the crowd with words that might have been written by the sad, brooding man enshrined within.

As he arose, a great roar welled up from the crowd. When he started to speak, a hush fell.

"Even though we face the difficulties of today and tomorrow, I still have a dream," he said.

"It is a dream chiefly rooted in the American dream," he went on.

"I have a dream that one day this nation will rise up and live out the true meaning of its creed: 'We hold these truths to be self-evident, that all men are created equal.'

"I have a dream . . ." The vast throng listening intently to him roared.

". . . that one day on the red hills of Georgia, the sons of former slaves and the sons of former slave owners will be able to sit together at the table of brotherhood.

"I have a dream . . ." The crowd roared.

". . . that one day even the state of Mississippi, a state sweltering with the heat of injustice, sweltering with the heat of oppression, will be transformed into an oasis of freedom and justice.

"I have a dream . . ." The crowd roared.

". . . that my four little children will one day live in a nation where they will not be judged by the color of their skin but by the content of their character.

"I have a dream . . ." The crowd roared.

". . . that one day every valley shall be exalted, every hill and mountain shall be made low, the rough places will be made plain, and the crooked places will be made straight, and the glory of the Lord shall be revealed and all flesh shall see it together."

As Dr. King concluded with a quotation from a Negro hymn—"Free at last, free at last, thank God Almighty"—the crowd, recognizing that he was finishing, roared once again and waved their signs and pennants.

But the civil rights leaders, who knew the strength of the forces arrayed against them from past battles, knew also that a hard struggle lay ahead. The tone of their speeches was frequently militant.

Roy Wilkins, executive secretary of the National Association for the Advancement of Colored People, made plain that he and his colleagues thought the president's civil rights bill did not go nearly far enough. He said: "The president's proposals represent so moderate an approach that if any one is weakened or eliminated, the remainder will be little more than sugar water. Indeed, the package needs strengthening."

Harshest of all the speakers was John Lewis, chairman of the Student Nonviolent Coordinating Committee.

"My friends," he said, "let us not forget that we are involved in a serious social revolution. But by and large American politics is dominated by politicians who build their career on immoral compromising and ally themselves with open forms of political, economic and social exploitation."

He concluded: "They're talking about slowdown and stop. We will not stop.

"If we do not get meaningful legislation out of this Congress, the time will come when we will not confine our marching to Washington. We will march through the South, through the streets of Jackson, through the streets of Danville, through the streets of Cambridge, through the streets of Birmingham.

"But we will march with the spirit of love and the spirit of dignity that we have shown here today."

In the original text of the speech, distributed last night, Mr. Lewis had said: "We will not wait for the president, the Justice Department, nor the Congress, but we will take matters into our own hands and create a source of power, outside of any national structure, that could and would assure us a victory."

He also said in the original text that "we will march through the South, through the heart of Dixie, the way Sherman did."

It was understood that at least the last of these statements was changed as the result of a protest by the Most Rev. Patrick J. O'Boyle, Roman Catholic archbishop of Washington, who refused to give the invocation if the offending words were spoken by Mr. Lewis.

The great day really began the night before. As a half-moon rose over the lagoon by the Jefferson Memorial and the tall, lighted shaft of the Washington Monument gleamed in the Reflecting Pool, a file of Negroes from out of town began climbing the steps of the Lincoln Memorial.

There, while the carpenters nailed the last planks on the television platforms for the next day and the TV technicians called through the loudspeakers, "Final audio, one, two, three, four," a middle-aged Negro couple, the man's arm around the shoulders of his plump wife, stood and read with their lips: "If we shall suppose that American slavery is one of the offenses which in the providence of God must needs come but which having continued through His appointed time, He now wills to remove. . ."

The day dawned clear and cool. At 7 A.M. the town had a Sunday appearance, except for the shuttle buses drawn up in front of Union Station, waiting.

By 10 A.M. there were 40,000 on the slopes around the Washington Monument. An hour later the police estimated the crowd at 90,000. And still they poured in.

Because some things went wrong at the monument, everything was right. Most of the stage-and-screen celebrities from New York and Hollywood who were scheduled to begin entertaining the crowd at 10 did not arrive at the airport until 11:15.

As a result the whole affair at the monument grounds began to take on the spontaneity of a church picnic. Even before the entertainment was to begin, groups of high school students were singing with wonderful improvisations and hand-clapping all over the monument slope.

Civil rights demonstrators who had been released from jail in Danville, Va., were singing:

Move on, move on,
Till all the world is free.

And members of Local 144 of the Hotel and Allied Service Employes Union from New York City, an integrated local since 1950, were stomping:

Oh, freedom, we shall not,
we shall not be moved,
Just like a tree that's
planted by the water.

Then the pros took over, starting with the folk singers. The crowd joined in with them.

Joan Baez started things rolling with "the song"—"We Shall Overcome."

Oh deep in my heart I do believe
We shall overcome someday.

And Peter, Paul and Mary sang "How many times must a man look up before he can see the sky?" And Odetta's great, full-throated voice carried almost to Capitol Hill: "If they ask you who you are, tell them you're a child of God."

Jackie Robinson told the crowd that "we cannot be turned back," and Norman Thomas, the venerable Socialist, said, "I'm glad I lived long enough to see this day."

The march to the Lincoln Memorial was supposed to start at 11:30, behind the leaders. But at 11:20 it set off spontaneously down Constitution Avenue behind the Kenilworth Knights, a local drum-and-bugle corps dazzling in yellow silk blazers, green trousers and green berets.

Apparently forgotten was the intention to make the march to the Lincoln Memorial a solemn tribute to Medgar W. Evers, the N.A.A.C.P. official murdered in Jackson, Miss., on June 12, 1963, and others who had died for the cause of civil rights.

The leaders were lost, and they never did get to the head of the parade.

The leaders included also Walter P. Reuther, head of the United Automobile Workers; A. Philip Randolph, head of the American Negro Labor Council; the Rev. Dr. Eugene Carson Blake, vice chairman of the Commission on Religion and Race of the National Council of Churches; Mathew Ahmann, executive director of the National Catholic Conference for Interracial Justice; Rabbi Joachim Prinz, president of the American Jewish Congress; Whitney M. Young, Jr., executive director of the National Urban League, and James Farmer, president of the Congress of Racial Equality.

All spoke at the memorial except Mr. Farmer, who is in jail in Louisiana following his arrest as a result of a civil rights demonstration. His speech was read by Floyd B. McKissick, CORE national chairman.

At the close of the ceremonies at the Lincoln Memorial, Bayard Rustin, the organizer of the march, asked Mr. Randolph, who conceived it, to lead the vast throng in a pledge.

Repeating after Mr. Randolph, the marchers pledged "complete personal commitment to the struggle for jobs and freedom for Americans" and "to carry the message of the march to my friends and neighbors back home and arouse them to an equal commitment and an equal effort."

"I HAVE A DREAM . . ."

JAMES RESTON

ABRAHAM LINCOLN, who presided in his stone temple on August 28, 1963 above the children of the slaves he emancipated, may have used just the right words to sum up the general reaction to the Negroes' massive march on Washington. "I think," he wrote to Gov. Andrew G. Curtin of Pennsylvania in 1861, "the necessity of being ready increases. Look to it." Washington may not have changed a vote today, but it is a little more conscious tonight of the necessity of being ready for freedom. It may not "look to it" at once, since it is looking to so many things, but it will be a long time before it forgets the melodious and melancholy voice of the Rev. Dr. Martin Luther King, Jr., crying out his dreams to the multitude.

It was Dr. King who, near the end of the day, touched the vast audience. Until then the pilgrimage was merely a great spectacle. Only those marchers from the embattled towns in the Old Confederacy had anything like the old crusading zeal. For many the day seemed an adventure, a long outing in the late summer sun—part liberation from home, part Sunday School picnic, part political convention, and part fish fry.

But Dr. King brought them alive in the late afternoon with a peroration that was an anguished echo from all the old American reformers. Roger Williams calling for religious liberty, Sam Adams calling for political liberty, old man Thoreau denouncing coercion, William Lloyd Garrison demanding emancipation, and Eugene V. Debs crying for economic equality—Dr. King echoed them all.

"I have a dream," he cried again and again. And each time the dream was a promise out of our ancient articles of faith: phrases from the Constitution, lines from the great anthem of the nation, guarantees from the Bill of Rights, all ending with a vision that they might one day all come true.

Dr. King touched all the themes of the day, only better than anybody else. He was full of the symbolism of Lincoln and Gandhi, and the cadences of the Bible. He was both militant and sad, and he sent the crowd away feeling that the long journey had been worthwhile.

This demonstration impressed political Washington because it combined a number of things no politician can ignore. It had the force of numbers. It had the melodies of both the church and the theater. And it was able to invoke the principles of the Founding Fathers to rebuke the inequalities and hypocrisies of modern American life.

There was a paradox in the day's performance. The Negro leaders demanded equality "now," while insisting that this was only the "beginning" of the struggle. Yet it was clear that the "now," which appeared on almost every placard on Constitution Avenue, was merely an opening demand, while the exhortation to increase the struggle was what was really on the leaders' minds.

The question of the day, of course, was raised by Dr. King's theme: Was this all a dream or will it help the dream come true?

No doubt this vast effort helped the Negro drive against discrimination. It was better covered by television and the press than any event here since President Kennedy's inauguration, and, since indifference is almost as great a problem to the Negro as hostility, this was a plus.

None of the dreadful things Washington feared came about. The racial hooligans were scarce. Even the local Nazi, George Lincoln Rockwell, minded

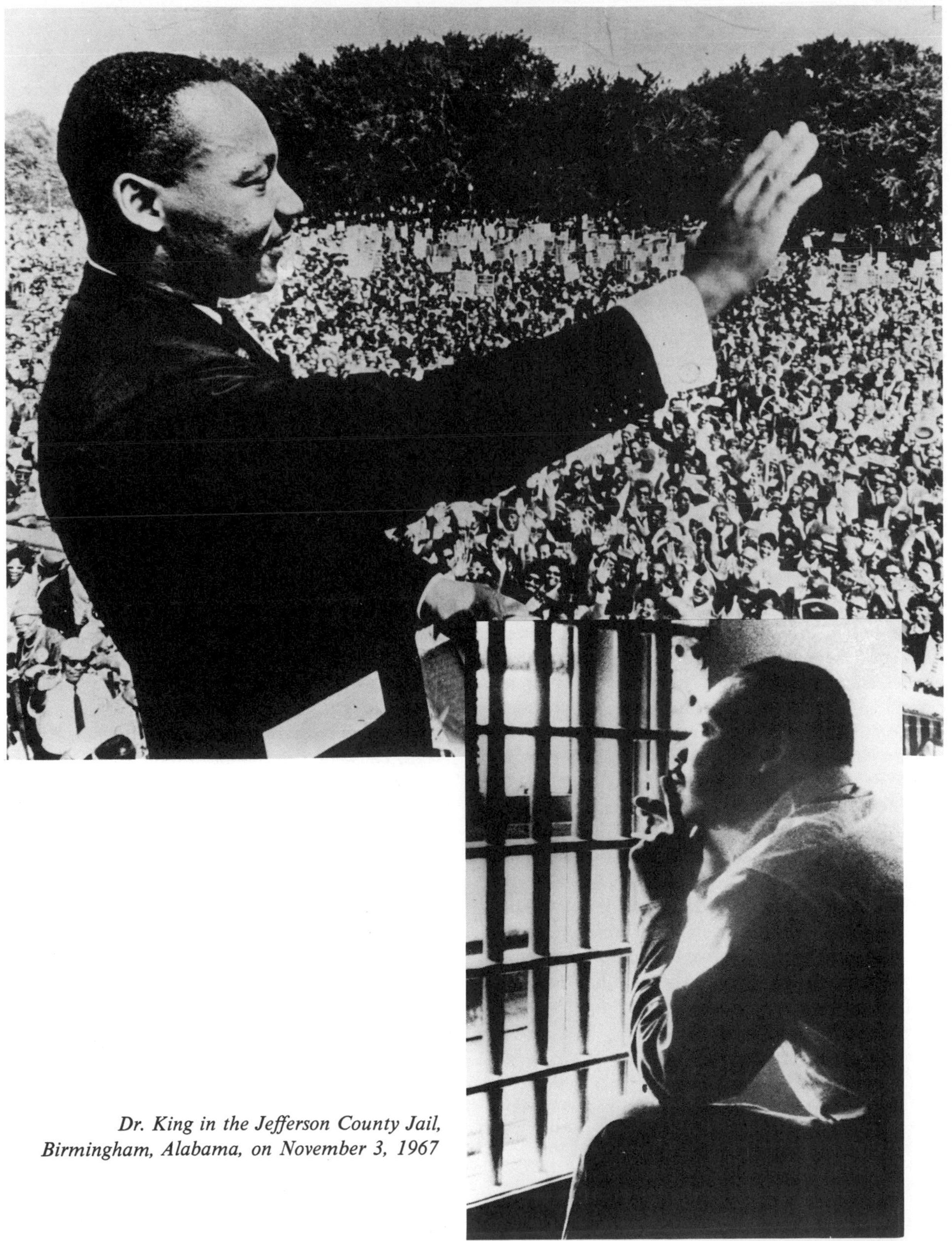

Dr. King in the Jefferson County Jail, Birmingham, Alabama, on November 3, 1967

UPI/Bettmann Newsphotos

his manners, which is an extraordinary innovation for him. And there were fewer arrests than on any normal day in Washington, probably because all the saloons and hootch peddlers were closed.

The crowd obviously impressed the politicians. The presence of nearly a quarter of a million petitioners anywhere always makes a senator think. He seldom ignores that many potential votes, and it did not escape the notice of congressmen that these Negro organizations, some of which had almost as much trouble getting out a crowd as the Washington Senators several years ago, were now capable of organizing the largest demonstrating throng ever gathered at one spot in the District of Columbia.

It is a question whether this rally raised too many hopes among the Negroes or inspired the Negroes here to work harder for equality when they got back home. Most observers here think the latter is true, even though all the talk of "Freedom NOW" and instant integration is bound to lead to some disappointment.

The meetings between the Negro leaders on the one hand and President Kennedy and the congressional leaders on the other also went well and probably helped the Negro cause. The Negro leaders were careful not to seem to be putting improper pressure on Congress. They made no specific requests or threats, but they argued their case in small groups and kept the crowd off Capitol Hill.

Whether this will win any new votes for the civil rights and economic legislation will probably depend on the overall effect of the day's events on the television audience.

This is the major imponderable of the day. The speeches were varied and spotty. Like their white political brethren, the Negroes cannot run a political meeting without letting everybody talk. Also, the platform was a bedlam of moving figures who seemed to be interested in everything except listening to the speaker. This distracted the audience.

Nevertheless, Dr. King and Roy Wilkins, head of the National Association for the Advancement of Colored People, and one or two others got the message across. James Baldwin, the author, summed up the day succinctly. The day was important in itself, he said, and "what we do with this day is even more important."

He was convinced that the country was finally grappling with the Negro problem instead of evading it; that the Negro himself was "for the first time" aware of his value as a human being and was "no longer at the mercy of what the white people imagine the Negro to be."

On the whole, the speeches were not calculated to make Republican politicians very happy with the Negro. This may hurt, for without substantial Republican support, the Kennedy program on civil rights and jobs is not going through.

Apparently this point impressed President Kennedy, who listened to some of the speeches on television. When the Negro leaders came out of the White House, Dr. King emphasized that bipartisan support was essential for passage of the Kennedy civil rights program.

Aside from this, the advantages of the day for the Negro cause outran the disadvantages.

Above all, they got over Lincoln's point that "the necessity of being ready increases." For they left no doubt that this was not the climax of their campaign for equality but merely the beginning, that they were going to stay in the streets until they could get equality in the schools, restaurants, houses and employment agencies of the nation, and that, as they demonstrated here today, they had found an effective way to demonstrate for changes in the laws without breaking the law themselves.

DR. KING IN PHILADELPHIA, MISS. [1964]

JOHN HERBERS

VIRTUALLY EVERYONE in Mississippi knew that the Rev. Dr. Martin Luther King, Jr., was to visit Philadelphia on July 24, 1964.

Among those who did not were the boys in the Negro community center, which sits atop a red gravel hill across the street from the Evers Hotel. They scrambled to the door in amazement when Dr. King in his black Oldsmobile and 14 other cars carrying Federal Bureau of Investigation agents and newsmen rolled up in a cloud of orange dust.

First, Dr. King challenged Robert Hudson, a teenager, to a game of pool while members of his staff rounded up an audience. After losing a game of eight-ball, the integration leader climbed on a bench and told 60 curious Negroes that he was here in the interest of three missing civil rights workers.*

"Three young men came here to help set you free," he said. "They probably lost their lives. I know what you have suffered in this state, the lynching and the murders.

"But things are going to get better. Walk together, children, don't you get weary."

It probably was the first freedom rally held in this town of 5,600 people. An old woman came up to Dr. King and said, "I just want to touch you."

Dr. King is on a five-day tour of the state, raising money and support for the Mississippi Freedom Democratic party. This is a new group that will challenge the regular state Democrats for the state seats at the national convention in Atlantic City Aug. 24.

As Dr. King stepped out of the community center there was a clap of thunder and drops of rain fell on the gravel road. Little boys in ragged clothes looked in astonishment as the entourage of Negro leaders, F.B.I. agents, cameramen and reporters piled into the cars and rolled away.

Groups of whites and Choctaw Indians stood on the sidewalks and stared as the caravan passed the courthouse and headed down Highway 16 for the Mount Zion Methodist Church.

The church, 12 miles east of this city, was to have been used for one of the Freedom Schools in the Mississippi Summer Project. It was burned by night riders shortly after midnight on June 17.

The three missing workers—Michael Schwerner, 24 years old, of Brooklyn; James E. Chaney, 21, of Meridian, Miss.; and Andrew Goodman, 21, of New York—had inspected the ruins of the church on June 21.

They were arrested later that day and held for several hours in the Neshoba County jail. Authorities said they were released about 10:30 P.M. They have not been seen since.

Dr. King stepped through the ashes and stood on the brick foundation.

"As I stand here on the site of this church, I have mixed emotions," he said. "I feel sorry for those who were hurt by this. On the other hand, I rejoice that there are churches relevant enough that people of ill will will be willing to burn them. I think this church was burned because it took a stand."

Dr. King then went to Meridian to address a mass rally. He was accompanied on the trip by members of his staff and by John Lewis, chairman of the Student Nonviolent Coordinating Committee. He is scheduled to return tomorrow to Atlanta where he is president of the Southern Christian Leadership Conference.

On his trip to Mississippi he was accompanied constantly by F.B.I. agents, state and local police. He has attracted large crowds of Negroes but few whites.

---

* On Aug. 4, 1964, the bodies of the three young men were found in an earthen dam on a farm a few miles from the town of Philadelphia, Miss. In December the F.B.I. arrested 21 white Mississippians, including the deputy sheriff who stopped the three men, allegedly for speeding, shortly before they vanished. Charges against the 21 were subsequently dropped in state court; six of them were sent to jail, however, for violating federal civil rights laws.

NONVIOLENCE— Powerful Rights Weapon [1965]

JOHN HERBERS

ON THE morning of Feb. 3, 1965, Malcolm X showed up unexpectedly in Selma, Ala., where the Rev. Dr. Martin Luther King, Jr., was leading a nonviolent movement against the area's restrictions on Negro voting.

Dr. King was, by his own design, in jail. Other civil rights leaders who were not were somewhat disturbed by the appearance of the Black Nationalist leader at the Browns Chapel Methodist Church.

The church was packed with Negroes waiting to march on the Dallas County Courthouse, where Sheriff James G. Clark and his deputies were waiting with guns, nightsticks and cattle prods.

A succession of speakers had brought the audience to a delicately balanced posture of deep resentment against the white man's injustices, yet a determination to refrain from the use of physical force while moving against the white community.

Would Malcolm, an outspoken foe of nonviolence, tip the scales and send the marchers to the courthouse prepared to do battle with the Dallas County sheriff's posse?

The leaders reluctantly decided to let him speak because of their policy of open meetings. For Malcolm, his remarks were restrained. Yet they contained strong undertones of violence, of his belief that even Dr. King would someday abandon the nonviolent technique.

He received polite applause, but by the time the Negroes began their march on the courthouse it was apparent that Malcolm had made no contact with his audience.

The failure of men like Malcolm, or even less militant spokesmen for black supremacy, to establish a rapport with southern Negroes points up how well-established and accepted the nonviolent method, with its goal of assimilation rather than estrangement, has become.

The Muslims and other groups that preach violence and black supremacy have never been able to make significant inroads in the South.

Nonviolence, as defined by Dr. King and other leaders, is a method of peaceful protest by oppressed people. Its use frequently leads to violent disruption and stirs hatred, particularly on the part of the oppressor. But the leaders say this may be necessary in order to cure the ills of the society.

In a classical nonviolent situation, the oppressed engage in mass demonstrations or in one or more forms of civil disobedience so as to cause the oppressor to retaliate. The object is to plague the oppressor by filling up the jails or to cause him to engage in violence on the streets.

Negroes justify the bringing of violence on themselves by saying that they have long been subjected to violence anyway; that the nonviolent movement simply moves it from the jail cells and dark alleys out into the open for all the world to see. Conflicts that have festered beneath the surface are exposed.

It is expected that mass arrests and violence against Negroes will attract attention and stir the conscience of someone in a position to free the oppressed—the national government, the church, the white moderate who has not come face-to-face with the problem in the past.

"Civilization and violence are antithetical concepts," Dr. King said in accepting the 1964 Nobel Peace Prize. "Negroes of the United States, following the people of India, have demonstrated that nonviolence is not sterile passivity, but a powerful moral force which makes for social transformation. Sooner or later, all the people of the world will have to discover a way to live together in peace. . . .

"If this is to be achieved," he said, "man must evolve for all human conflict a method which rejects revenge, aggression and retaliation. The foundation of such a method is love."

Participants in the movement are constantly reminded that they must harbor no hatred for whites while moving for social change. "Hate is too great a burden to bear," Dr. King says in almost every talk.

Nonviolence has not always prevailed in the southern civil rights movement. In Monroe, N.C., Robert Williams, a former leader in the National Association for the Advancement of Colored People, urged Negroes to arm themselves and meet violence with violence. Militants from other cities joined the Monroe movement.

After a riot in the town square, Negroes kidnapped a white couple who happened to be in the area and held them for several hours as hostages. Mr. Williams fled to Cuba, where he found asylum. He left behind a town torn by bitterness and misunderstanding.

This, however, was an aberration. While Negroes in scattered areas across the South—mostly in rural communities or small towns—have armed themselves for defense, the vast majority of those engaged in the civil rights movement have refrained from violence.

Last year, before passage of the 1964 Civil Rights Act, there were indications that southern Negroes were beginning to lose faith in the nonviolent technique. In Atlanta, Nashville and other cities, demonstrators fought the police in disorderly protests against segregated public accommodations.

A mood of despair—caused by the slow progress of desegregation, reports of a white backlash in the North and uncertainty about where the movement was going—was felt in the civil rights organizations.

This was largely dissipated by passage of the Civil Rights Act and by the overwhelming defeat of Barry Goldwater in the presidential election. Most civil rights leaders felt that the nonviolent technique had been vindicated.

The use of nonviolence does not always follow the classical definition, and changing conditions in the South have brought changes in its application. Even among Negro leaders there is a division of opinion about whether certain practices are in the nonviolent tradition.

A few years ago it was a fairly simple matter in most any southern community to arouse the anger of whites and fill up the jails by conducting sit-ins or mass demonstrations. But the Civil Rights Act has narrowed the field of civil disobedience and even in the Deep South law enforcement officers have become sophisticated in dealing with the movement.

Even in towns like Magnolia, Miss., the authorities let Negroes demonstrate around the courthouse rather than arrest them and attract attention to the town.

In Selma, an unsophisticated sheriff accommodated the movement with mass arrests, but even so there is almost a daily contest between Negroes trying to be arrested and law enforcement officers trying not to make arrests.

This led to use of the night march, which the police are more certain to put down and which is more likely to lead to violence on the part of whites.

Selma Negroes know that Sheriff James G. Clark has a low boiling point. One quiet day when the movement was attracting little attention, Sheriff Clark seemed determined to restrain himself during a demonstration. But the Rev. C. T. Vivian, one of Dr. King's assistants, hurled insults at him on the courthouse steps until the sheriff responded with a left jab to the mouth.

When violence by whites is most intense, leaders find it difficult to keep all participants in the movement nonviolent. When state troopers broke up a night demonstration in Marion, Ala., with nightsticks, some Negroes retaliated by throwing bricks and bottles.

Most observers, however, feel that the overall restraint by Negroes has been remarkable. This is believed to be due largely to the religious orientation that the movement in the South has had. It is based on faith, hope and patience.

Civil rights leaders say that although nonviolence is not perfect it is the least destructive and most creative method of protesting Negro grievances. They believe that its use, more than any other factor, is responsible for passage of the civil rights bill and for most of the voluntary gains that have been made in the South in recent years.

This is borne out by the fact that many southern whites have embraced it as the best means of preventing violent disorders. It is of some significance that when Dr. King was honored at a dinner by white Atlanta leaders recently the meeting was concluded by everyone singing "We Shall Overcome," the theme song of the nonviolent movement.

MARCHING OUT OF SELMA [1965]

ROY REED

BACKED BY the armed might of the United States, 3,200 persons marched out of Selma, Ala., on March 21, 1965, on the first leg of a historic venture in nonviolent protest.

The marchers, or at least many of them, are on their way to the State Capitol at Montgomery to submit a petition for Negro rights to Gov. George C. Wallace, a man with little sympathy for their cause.

Today was the third attempt for the Alabama Freedom March. On the first two, the marchers were stopped by state troopers, the first time with tear gas and clubs.

The troopers were on hand today, but they limited themselves to helping federal troops handle traffic on U.S. Highway 80 as the marchers left Selma.

Hundreds of army and federalized National Guard troops stood guard in Selma and lined the highway out of town to protect the marchers. The troops were sent by President Johnson after Governor Wallace said that Alabama could not afford the expense of protecting the march.

The marchers were in festive humor as they started. The tone was set by the Rev. Ralph D. Abernathy, top aide to the Rev. Dr. Martin Luther King, Jr., in the Southern Christian Leadership Conference, as he introduced Dr. King for an address before the march started.

"When we get to Montgomery," Mr. Abernathy said, "we are going to go to Governor Wallace's door and say, 'George, it's all over now. We've got the ballot.' "

The throng laughed and cheered.

The marchers, a large majority of them Negroes, walked a little over seven miles today.

Governor Wallace is not expected to be at the State Capitol when the marchers arrive at the end of their 54-mile journey. An aide has said that he will probably be "in Michigan, or someplace" making a speech Thursday.

Not enough buses could be found to escort 2,900 of the 3,200 marchers back to Selma tonight in line with a federal court order limiting the number to 300 along a two-lane stretch of highway.

The authorities feared for the safety of those returning to Selma. Justice Department officials finally arranged with the Southern Railway for a special train of the Western Railway of Alabama to take them back. The Western is a subsidiary of the Southern.

Highway 80 narrows from a four-lane to a two-lane road about five miles past the point where the marchers stopped tonight. It widens to four lanes again as it approaches Montgomery.

In his talk at the start of the march, Dr. King praised President Johnson, saying of his voting rights message to Congress last Monday: "Never has a president spoken so eloquently or so sincerely on the question of civil rights."

Then he turned to the crowd in front of Browns Chapel Methodist Church, the thousands of whites and Negroes from Alabama and around the country who were congregated for the march, and said: "You will be the people that will light a new chapter in the history books of our nation. Those of us who are Negroes don't have much. We have known the long night of poverty. Because of the system, we don't have much education and some of us don't know how to make our nouns and verbs agree. But thank God we have our bodies, our feet and our souls.

"Walk together, children, don't you get weary, and it will lead us to the promised land. And Alabama will be a new Alabama, and America will be a new America."

Dr. King's sense of history, if not his optimism, seemed well placed. The Alabama march appears destined for a niche in the annals of the great protest demonstrations.

The march is the culmination of a turbulent nine-week campaign that began as an effort to abolish restrictions on Negro voting in the Alabama Black Belt and widened finally to encompass a general protest against racial injustice in the state.

The drive has left two men dead and scores injured. Some 3,800 persons have been arrested in Selma and neighboring communities.

The march got under way at 12:47 P.M., 2 hours 47 minutes late, after a confused flurry of last-minute planning and organizing.

The marchers reached the first night's campsite, 7.3 miles east of Selma, at 5:30. When they got there they found four big tents pitched in a Negro farmer's field.

Leading the march with Dr. King were Dr. Ralph J. Bunche, United Nations Under Secretary for Special Political Affairs; the Right Rev. Richard Millard, Suffragan Bishop of the Episcopal Diocese of California; and Cager Lee, grandfather of Jimmie Lee Jackson, the young Negro killed by a state trooper last month at Marion, Ala.

Also among the leaders were John Lewis, president of the Student Nonviolent Coordinating Committee; Deaconess Phyllis Edwards of the Episcopal Diocese of California; Rabbi Abraham Heschel, professor of Jewish mysticism and ethics at the Jewish Theological Seminary in New York; Mr. Abernathy; and the Rev. Frederick D. Reese, a Negro minister from Selma, who is president of the Dallas County Voters League.

About 2,000 white and Negro spectators watched the procession leave town. That was 4,000 fewer than army intelligence had predicted.

About 150 whites watched in silence as the march turned from Alabama Avenue and headed down Broad Street toward Edmund Pettus Bridge. A white man hoisted his young son to his shoulder to give the lad a better view. Several persons snapped pictures.

Brig. Gen. Henry V. Graham, a National Guard officer, commanded all federal troops on the scene, including the regular army military policemen. General Graham, a tall, square-jawed man, stood in the middle of Pettus Bridge wearing a helmet as he directed the operation.

Two state trooper cars led the procession across the bridge. In the lead car was Maj. John Cloud, the man who directed the rout, with tear gas and nightsticks, of 525 Negro marchers near the foot of the same bridge two weeks before.

The marchers passed the site of the bloody incident without signal, except for a reminder from a white heckler.

It was to protest the officers' rout of the first marchers that the Rev. James J. Reeb, a white Unitarian minister from Boston, came to Selma with scores of other clergymen. While he was here, Mr. Reeb was fatally beaten by a band of white men on March 9.

The heckler held up a sign as the procession left Pettus Bridge early this afternoon. It read "Too bad, Reeb."

A few feet away, another white spectator held a sign saying, "I hate niggers."

More whites heckled from a railroad embankment running along the highway. They apparently were upset over the way the marchers were carrying a United States flag. They were carrying it upside down, the position of the distress signal.

On down the road, three cars painted with anti-Negro slogans passed in the south section of the four-lane highway. One car, with a Mississippi license plate, bore the words "Meridian, Miss., hates niggers." A Confederate flag flew from the radio aerial. The lettering on another car said "Go home scum."

Back in town some 20 stragglers ran up Broad Street toward the bridge with knapsacks bouncing on their backs, trying to catch the procession, which had already disappeared over the bridge. The marchers walked on the left side of the highway.

The federal presence was everywhere, even in the air. About a dozen planes and helicopters, many of them manned by military personnel, flew over the procession constantly.

John Doar, head of the civil rights division of the Justice Department, walked to one side at the head of the march, watching.

Maj. Gen. Carl C. Turner, Provost Marshal General of the United States Army, was on the scene as the personal representative of the Army Chief of Staff, Gen. Harold K. Johnson.

By radio, federal agents reported minute by minute to the Justice Department and the Pentagon in Washington.

M.P.s guarded every crossroad, leapfrogging in jeeps to stay ahead of the march.

There was one report of violence. An unidentified white minister riding in an advance car was said to have been attacked by four white men when he got out of the car on the side of the road.

A spokesman for the marchers said the minister had been struck on the face once and knocked to the ground but had not been seriously hurt.

Today's leg of the journey was cut short by four miles by a court injunction obtained by a white landowner who did not want the marchers camping overnight on his land. A Negro tenant had agreed to let them camp there.

The march leaders found a new campsite. The Negro farmer's field where they slept tonight is about a quarter of a mile south of the highway.

The field is about 500 yards from the New Sister Springs Baptist Church. It was at the church that the marchers returning to Selma tonight boarded rented Greyhound buses and numerous automobiles that shuttled them to the railway loading point about a mile from the campsite.

Most of those who left the march this way spent the night, as many had spent previous nights, with Negro families in Selma.

Some will remain in Alabama and rejoin the march Thursday, the final day. Leaders of the march hope to arrive at Montgomery in impressive numbers.

The military authorities are concerned about protection for the marchers at night. Show business personalities such as Harry Belafonte and Lena Horne are scheduled to entertain the group every night. The officials fear that outsiders may come to the camps to see and hear the entertainers and that troublemakers may infiltrate at the same time.

A military spokesman said the troops had no authority to search cars for weapons.

Although the weather was relatively warm for the beginning of the march, the temperature dropped below freezing.

The coming of the troops to Selma produced none of the crushing grimness of the federal presence that characterized the government's intervention at Little Rock, Ark., in 1957 and Oxford, Miss., in 1962.

The main difference is that troops were used in the earlier instances to suppress violence already out of hand, or threatening to get out of hand, while they were brought here to prevent violence.

Most of Selma's whites today went about their Sunday morning business, which is church, and only a few bothered with the commotion on Sylvan Street.

About 30 whites gathered at Broad Street and Alabama Avenue at midmorning to wait for the march to go by. The march was late, as expected, and while they waited half a dozen spectators joshed with the four armed military policemen stationed there.

The state and local authorities have repeatedly urged Alabama whites to stay away from U.S. Highway 80 while the march is in progress.

Early this morning two or three armed M.P.s

were deployed at each intersection on the march route in the city. More were strung out along Highway 80 on the other side of Edmund Pettus Bridge. Several state troopers were scattered along the highway on the outskirts of the city.

At Craig Air Force Base, five miles east on Highway 80, a dozen big army trucks could be seen from the road. They were filled with armed troops.

The temperature was two degrees above freezing when people began gathering in Sylvan Street this morning. The sun came out brilliantly, and by 11 A.M. the temperature was up to 42 degrees.

The marchers were out in everything from shirt sleeves to heavy coats. One elderly Negro wore a dress air force topcoat and a heavy wool headpiece that covered his head, throat and most of his face.

Paul R. Screvane, president of the New York City Council, showed up in a suit and blue overcoat. He and Mrs. Constance Baker Motley, Manhattan's Negro borough president, joined the milling crowd in front of Browns Chapel at midmorning.

Mr. Screvane explained why he was there.

"We came to represent Mayor Wagner and, we hope, the people of New York, in what we consider to be a just cause," he said.

Dozens of union officials and clergymen came in today and joined the hundreds of ministers and students and civil rights workers already here.

A fresh college group arrived, 33 students and three professors from Canisius College, a Roman Catholic institution in Buffalo, N.Y. A sign thrust up from the group said "Civil Man Wants Civil Rights."

Early today, plans for the march were still being hammered out. At 8 A.M., 400 or 500 persons milled in the street.

Milling has become the style of the movement in recent weeks, and the character of the milling has changed as hundreds of whites from the North, East and West have come into town to add their protest to the Negroes'. The outsiders mill with a greater air of purpose.

The marchers who showed up very early today in front of Browns Chapel were from the hard core of the movement. Others did not begin to appear on Sylvan Street until the sun was high.

The Alabama Freedom March has a long history, as the leaders see it. The Rev. Andrew Young, executive assistant to Dr. King in the Southern Christian Leadership Conference, told reporters last night that the whole Alabama project went back to the Birmingham church bombing of 1963 in which five Negro children were killed.

"At that time," he said, "we began to ask ourselves, 'What can we do to change the climate of an entire state?' "

The Black Belt movement began that year. The Student Nonviolent Coordinating Committee moved into Selma, which calls itself queen of the Alabama Black Belt—the swath of rich, dark soil and heavy Negro population across south-central Alabama—and began holding meetings and demonstrations.

Dr. King and the Southern Christian Leadership Conference came here in January 1965 and put the Selma movement on the map.

DR. KING IN MONTGOMERY [1965]

ROY REED

THE REV. DR. MARTIN LUTHER KING, JR., led 25,000 Negroes and whites to the shadow of the State Capitol on March 25, 1965, and challenged Alabama to put an end to racial discrimination.

Gov. George C. Wallace sent word about 2 P.M. that he would receive a delegation from the marchers after the rally, but the delegation met twice with rebuffs when it tried to see him. State policemen stopped the group the first time at the edge of the Capitol grounds and said no one was to be let through.

The delegation was later admitted to the Capitol,

but was told that the governor had closed his office for the day. The group left without giving its petition to anyone.

The Alabama Freedom March from Selma to Montgomery ended shortly after noon at the foot of the Capitol steps, and as people from all over the nation stood facing the white-columned statehouse, Dr. King assured them: "We are not about to turn around. We are on the move now. Yes, we are on the move and no wave of racism can stop us."

The throng let out a mighty cheer, so loud that it was easily audible 75 yards away in the office of Governor Wallace, where the governor was seen several times parting the venetian blinds of a window overlooking the rally.

Even though the 54-mile march from Selma was a dramatization of a grievance, its windup at the steps of the Capitol carried the trappings of triumph.

The march was hailed by several speakers as the greatest demonstration in the history of the civil rights movement. The caravan that followed Dr. King up Dexter Avenue, up the broad slope that once accommodated the inaugural parade of the president of the Confederate States of America, comprised friends of the civil rights movement from all sections of America and some from abroad.

Virtually all of the notables of the movement were there, and the speakers' platform held two Negro winners of the Nobel Peace Prize, Dr. King and Dr. Ralph J. Bunche, United Nations Under Secretary for Special Political Affairs.

Other Negro leaders included Roy Wilkins, executive director of the National Association for the Advancement of Colored People; Whitney M. Young, director of the National Urban League; A. Philip Randolph, president of the Brotherhood of Sleeping Car Porters; Bayard A. Rustin, who with Mr. Randolph was one of the organizers of the March on Washington in 1963; and John Lewis, president of the Student Nonviolent Coordinating Committee.

Other notables included James Baldwin, the author; Harry Belafonte, the singer; Joan Baez, the folk singer; and others.

The march started Sunday at Selma. It reached the outskirts of Montgomery yesterday after four days and nights on the road under the protection of army troops and federalized Alabama National Guardsmen. The troops were sent by President Johnson after Governor Wallace said Alabama could not afford the expense of protecting the marchers.

The little band that made the entire march, much of it through desolate lowlands, was joined by thousands who flocked to Montgomery to walk the last three and one-half miles of the trip to the Capitol.

The marchers carried with them a petition to Governor Wallace saying: "We have come not only five days and 50 miles but we have come from three centuries of suffering and hardship. We have come to you, the governor of Alabama, to declare that we must have our freedom NOW. We must have the right to vote; we must have equal protection of the law and an end to police brutality."

Federal troops who guarded the marchers and brought them safely to Montgomery were out in force at the Capitol today. Eight hundred troops lined Dexter Avenue, one soldier about every 25 feet behind wooden barricades set between the street and the sidewalks.

Troops stood on the roofs of buildings along the march route through downtown Montgomery and on those of the office buildings looking out on the rally at the Capitol steps.

The rally never got onto state property. It was confined to the street in front of the steps.

The throng stretched down eight-laned Dexter Avenue a block and a half. Its cheers could be heard for blocks.

The line of marchers who walked from the City of St. Jude, a Catholic school and hospital where they spent last night, stretched out so long that when Dr. King and the other leaders reached the makeshift speakers' platform at the head of Dexter Avenue, the end of the line did not arrive for nearly an hour and a half.

Tension was high in the city, particularly after the rally, as the thousands of visitors scurried for taxis, buses, trains, cars and airplanes to get out of town before nightfall.

Dr. King, in an interview after the rally, said the civil rights campaign would continue in the Alabama Black Belt.

"We will continue to march people to the courthouses," he said. "If there is resistance, naturally we will have to expose the resistance and the injustice we still face. There could be violence in some areas, but we feel a moral compulsion to go forward, anyway."

He said the Negro movement would turn much of its attention in the weeks ahead to trying to pass President Johnson's voting rights bill in Congress.

"We want immediate passage," he said. "We will lobby for this in many areas of the country."

In his address at the end of the three-and-a-half-hour rally, Dr. King urged his listeners onward in the civil rights struggle.

"Let us march on segregated schools until every vestige of segregation and inferior education becomes a thing of the past and Negroes and whites study side by side in the socially healing context of the classroom," he said.

"Let us march on ballot boxes, march on ballot boxes until race baiters disappear from the political arena."

He referred to the tumultuous events at Selma in the last two months, during which time the voting rights campaign that he began there turned into a general protest against racial injustice, with two men dead and scores injured.

"Yet Selma, Alabama, has become a shining moment in the conscience of man," he said. "If the worst in American life lurked in the dark streets, the best of American instincts arose passionately from across the nation to overcome it.

"The confrontation of good and evil compressed in the tiny community of Selma generated the massive power that turned the whole nation to a new course," he said.

"Alabama has tried to nurture and defend evil, but the evil is choking to death in the dusty roads and streets of this state."

Dr. King spoke with passion, and the thousands sitting in the street beneath him responded with repeated outbursts of approval.

Several times he urged his followers to continue their support of nonviolent demonstrations, with the aim of achieving understanding with the white community.

"Our aim must never be to defeat or humiliate the white man," he said, "but to win his friendship and understanding. We must come to see that the end we seek is a society at peace with itself, a society that can live with its conscience."

He ended his address with a peroration on the theme "How long must justice be crucified and truth buried?" a spirited quotation of a verse of "The Battle Hymn of the Republic" and finally a burst of "Glory, hallelujah!" repeated four times.

The crowd rose to its feet in one great surge, and the applause and cheering reverberated through the Capitol grounds.

Two or three dozen state employees who had watched from the Capitol steps stood impassively.

The committee of 18 Negro and two white Alabamians designated to deliver the Negroes' petition to Governor Wallace walked the one, uphill block from the Dexter Avenue Baptist Church to Bainbridge Street at about 5:40 P.M. (C.S.T.).

State police jurisdiction over the Capitol grounds begins at the curb closest to the Capitol steps, and 70 blue-helmeted state troopers had been deployed at the curb line of Bainbridge Street half an hour before the committee arrived. They were backed by 50 uniformed conservation patrolmen, standing two deep halfway up the Capitol steps.

When at the Capitol steps, the Rev. Joseph E. Lowrey, a Negro from Birmingham, serving as chairman of the delegation, asked Maj. W. L. Allen of the Alabama Highway Patrol to let the committee pass. The officer replied: "I don't know anything about that." He said his orders were to let no one through.

A delegation of Governor Wallace's top aides was already gathering inside the locked front door of the Capitol.

Instructions were then issued to Major Allen from inside the Capitol over an army walkie-talkie. Maj. Gen. Alfred C. Harrison, the Alabama Adjutant General, who was dressed in civilian clothes, gave these instructions. The committee then walked up the Capitol steps.

About 10 feet inside the door, however, Mr. Lowrey came face to face with Cecil C. Jackson, Jr., the governor's executive secretary. Mr. Jackson was crippled by polio as a youth. He stood in Mr. Lowrey's path on aluminum crutches.

"The Capitol is closed today," Mr. Jackson began, in a calm, steady voice. "The governor has designated me to receive your petition."

"We are very sorry that he cannot see us," Mr. Lowrey replied, almost immediately, clasping copies of the petition to his chest. "Please advise the governor that as citizens of this state we have legitimate grievances to present to him. Please advise the governor that we will return at another time."

"That would be appropriate," Mr. Jackson answered. The petitions never left Mr. Lowrey's hands.

EXCERPTS FROM DR. KING'S MONTGOMERY ADDRESS [MARCH 25, 1965]

MY DEAR and abiding friends, Ralph Abernathy, and all the distinguished Americans seated here on the rostrum, my friends and co-workers of the state of Alabama and to all of the freedom-loving people who have assembled here this afternoon, from all over our nation and from all over the world:

Last Sunday more than 8,000 of us started on a mighty walk from Selma, Alabama. We have walked on meandering highways and rested our bodies on rocky byways. Some of our faces are burned from the outpourings of the sweltering sun. Some have literally slept in the mud. We have been drenched by the rains.

Our bodies are tired, and our feet are somewhat sore, but today as I stand before you and think back over that great march, I can say as Sister Pollard said, a 70-year-old Negro woman who lived in this community during the bus boycott and one day she was asked while walking if she didn't want a ride and when she answered "No," the person said, "Well, aren't you tired?" And with her ungrammatical profundity, she said, "My feets is tired, but my soul is rested."

And in a real sense this afternoon, we can say that our feet are tired but our souls are rested.

They told us we wouldn't get here. And there were those who said that we would get here only over their dead bodies, but all the world today knows that we are here and that we are standing before the forces of power in the state of Alabama saying "We ain't goin' let nobody turn us around."

The Civil Rights Act of 1964 gave Negroes some part of their rightful dignity, but without the vote it was dignity without strength.

Once more the method of nonviolent resistance was unsheathed from its scabbard and once again an entire community was mobilized to confront the adversary. And again the brutality of a dying order shrieks across the land. Yet Selma, Alabama, became a shining moment in the conscience of man.

There never was a moment in American history more honorable and more inspiring than the pilgrimage of clergymen and laymen of every race and faith pouring into Selma to face danger at the side of its embattled Negroes.

Confrontation of good and evil compressed in the tiny community of Selma generated the massive power to turn the whole nation to a new course. A president born in the South had the sensitivity to feel the will of the country, and in an address that will live in history as one of the most passionate pleas for human rights ever made by a president of our nation, he pledged the might of the federal government to cast off the centuries-old blight. President Johnson rightly praised the courage of the Negro for awakening the conscience of the nation.

On our part we must pay our profound respects to the white Americans who cherish their democratic traditions over the ugly customs and privileges of generations and come forth boldly to join hands with us. From Montgomery to Birmingham, from Birmingham to Selma, from Selma back to Montgomery, a trail wound in a circle and often bloody, yet it has become a highway up from darkness. Alabama has tried to nurture and defend evil, but the evil is choking to death in the dusty roads and streets of this state.

So I stand before you this afternoon with the conviction that segregation is on its deathbed in Alabama and the only thing uncertain about it is how costly the segregationists and Wallace will make the funeral.

Our whole campaign in Alabama has been centered around the right to vote. In focusing the attention of the nation and the world today on the flagrant denial of the right to vote, we are exposing the very origin, the root cause, of racial segregation in the Southland.

The threat of the free exercise of the ballot by the Negro and the white masses alike resulted in the establishing of a segregated society. They segregated southern money from the poor whites; they segregated southern mores from the rich whites; they segregated southern churches from Christianity; they segregated southern minds from honest thinking; and they segregated the Negro from everything.

We have come a long way since that travesty of justice was perpetrated upon the American mind. Today I want to tell the city of Selma. Today I want to say to the state of Alabama. Today I want to say to the people of America and the nations of the world: We are not about to turn around. We are on the move now. Yes, we are on the move and no wave of racism can stop us.

We are on the move now. The burning of our churches will not deter us. We are on the move now. The bombing of our homes will not dissuade us. We are on the move now. The beating and killing of our clergymen and young people will not divert us. We are on the move now. The arrest and release of known murderers will not discourage us. We are on the move now.

Like an idea whose time has come, not even the marching of mighty armies can halt us. We are moving to the land of freedom.

Let us therefore continue our triumph and march to the realization of the American dream. Let us march on segregated housing, until every ghetto of social and economic depression dissolves and Negroes and whites live side by side in decent, safe and sanitary housing.

Let us march on segregated schools until every vestige of segregated and inferior education becomes a thing of the past and Negroes and whites study side by side in the socially healing context of the classroom.

Let us march on poverty, until no American parent has to skip a meal so that their children may march on poverty, until no starved man walks the streets of our cities and towns in search of jobs that do not exist.

Let us march on ballot boxes, march on ballot boxes until race baiters disappear from the political arena. Let us march on ballot boxes until the Wallaces of our nation tremble away in silence.

Let us march on ballot boxes, until we send to our city councils, state legislatures, and the United States Congress men who will not fear to do justice, love, mercy, and walk humbly with their God. Let us march on ballot boxes until all over Alabama God's children will be able to walk the earth in decency and honor.

For all of us today the battle is in our hands. The road ahead is not altogether a smooth one. There are no broad highways to lead us easily and unevitably to quick solutions. We must keep going.

My people, my people, listen! The battle is in our hands. The battle is in our hands in Mississippi and Alabama, and all over the United States.

So as we go away this afternoon, let us go away more than ever before committed to the struggle and committed to nonviolence. I must admit to you there are still some difficulties ahead. We are still in for a season of suffering in many of the Black Belt counties of Alabama, many areas of Mississippi, many areas of Louisiana.

I must admit to you there are still jail cells waiting for us, dark and difficult moments. We will go on with the faith that nonviolence and its power transformed dark yesterdays into bright tomorrows. We will be able to change all of these conditions.

Our aim must never be to defeat or humiliate the white man but to win his friendship and understanding. We must come to see that the end we seek is a society at peace with itself, a society that can live with its conscience. That will be a day not of the white man, not of the black man. That will be the day of man as man.

I know you are asking today, "How long will it take?" I come to say to you this afternoon however difficult the moment, however frustrating the hour, it will not be long, because truth pressed to earth will rise again.

How long? Not long, because no lie can live forever.

How long? Not long, because you still reap what you sow.

How long? Not long, because the arm of the moral universe is long but it bends toward justice.

How long? Not long, " 'cause mine eyes have seen the glory of the coming of the Lord, trampling out the vintage where the grapes of wrath are stored. He has loosed the fateful lightning of his terrible swift sword. His truth is marching on.

"He has sounded forth the trumpets that shall never call retreat. He is lifting up the hearts of man before His judgment seat. Oh, be swift, my soul, to answer Him. Be jubilant my feet. Our God is marching on."

DR. KING'S STATEMENT IN MEMPHIS
[April 3, 1968]

I LEFT Atlanta this morning, and as we got started on the plane—there were six of us—the pilot said over the public address system: "We're sorry for the delay, but we have Dr. Martin Luther King on the plane. And to be sure of that, all of the bags were checked. And to be sure that nothing would be wrong on the plane, we had to check out everything carefully. And we've had the plane protected and guarded all night."

And then I got into Memphis. And some began to say the threats—or talk about the threats that were out. Or what would happen to me from some of our sick white brothers.

Well, I don't know what will happen now. We've got some difficult days ahead. But it really doesn't matter with me now. Because I've been to the mountaintop. I won't mind.

Like anybody, I would like to live a long life. Longevity has its place. But I'm not concerned about that now. I just want to do God's will.

And He's allowed me to go up to the mountain. And I've looked over, and I've seen the promised land.

I may not get there with you, but I want you to know tonight that we as a people will get to the promised land.

So I'm happy tonight. I'm not worried about anything. I'm not fearing any man. Mine eyes have seen the glory of the coming of the Lord.

"A DRUM MAJOR FOR JUSTICE"

FROM A sermon delivered at Ebenezer Baptist Church in Atlanta by the Rev. Dr. Martin Luther King, Jr., and published by The Times *on April 9, 1968, four days after he was murdered.*

Every now and then I guess we all think realistically about that day when we will be victimized with what is life's final common denominator—that something we call death. We all think about it and every now and then I think about my own death and I think about my own funeral. And I don't think about it in a morbid sense. And every now and then I ask myself what it is that I would want said and I leave the word to you this morning.

If any of you are around when I have to meet my day, I don't want a long funeral.

And if you get somebody to deliver the eulogy tell him not to talk too long.

And every now and then I wonder what I want him to say.

Tell him not to mention that I have a Nobel Peace Prize—that isn't important.

Tell him not to mention that I have 300 or 400 other awards—that's not important. Tell him not to mention where I went to school.

I'd like somebody to mention that day that Martin Luther King, Jr., tried to give his life serving others.

I'd like for somebody to say that day that Martin Luther King, Jr., tried to love somebody.

I want you to say that day that I tried to be right and to walk with them. I want you to be able to say that day that I did try to feed the hungry. I want you to be able to say that day that I did try in my life to clothe the naked. I want you to say on that day that I did try in my life to visit those who were in prison. And I want you to say that I tried to love and serve humanity.

Yes, if you want to, say that I was a drum major. Say that I was a drum major for justice. Say that I was a drum major for peace. I was a drum major for righteousness.

And all of the other shallow things will not matter.

I won't have any money to leave behind. I won't have the fine and luxurious things of life to leave behind. But I just want to leave a committed life behind.

THE F.B.I. AND DR. KING

NICHOLAS M. HORROCK

MARCH 8, 1975—The Federal Bureau of Investigation mailed what some agents considered an "unsavory" tape recording made from an electronic room bug to Coretta King to frighten her husband, the Rev. Dr. Martin Luther King, Jr., into halting his criticism of the bureau, according to a former high official of the agency.

The mailing of the tape recording to Mrs. King was part of nearly a decade of "harassment" of the late civil rights leader by the bureau, several former agents and officials say.

One retired agent, Arthur Murtagh, who was attached to the F.B.I.'s Atlanta field office, said the moves against Dr. King were second in size "only to the way they went after Jimmy Hoffa."

Yet there was never a criminal prosecution of Dr. King and, these former F.B.I. men say, there was a "dubious" national security rationale for what they said were thousands of hours of electronic and physical surveillance. These sources believe that the alleged harassment of Dr. King should be investigated by the congressional committees on intelligence.

Several have written to the Senate Select Committee on Intelligence.

The sending to a private citizen of a tape recording obtained by a national security electronic surveillance is a violation of F.B.I. regulations and was a potential violation of the Federal Communications Act and the Federal Criminal Code.

The surveillance of Dr. King was briefly noted in 1974 in a report by William B. Sambe, then the attorney general, and Clarence M. Kelly, director of the F.B.I., on the bureau's Counterintelligence Program, or Cointelpro. The report said that Cointelpro techniques included "investigating the love life of a group leader for dissemination to the press." Justice Department officials later identified the group leader as Dr. King.

A spokesman for the bureau said it had "no comment" on the alleged harassment of Dr. King.

The former high F.B.I. official who brought the matter to the attention of *The New York Times* asked to remain anonymous in the expectation that he might be called to testify in investigations of the bureau.

He said that in late 1964, after Dr. King criticized the F.B.I. for having assigned agents with southern backgrounds to handle civil rights cases, the late director, J. Edgar Hoover, ordered William C. Sullivan, then in charge of the bureau's counterintelligence operations, to arrange to send a copy of a tape recording secretly to Mrs. King in such a manner that it could not be traced to the F.B.I.

The source said that a copy of a tape recording was made by the bureau's laboratory. It was wrapped in a small, plain, unmarked package with no return address, and delivered to Mr. Sullivan's office, the source said; it had been addressed to Mrs. Coretta King, Atlanta, Ga.

Another source, attached to the bureau at the time, said that he believed the recording was of a party held by Dr. King and officials of the Southern Christian Leadership Conference, which Dr. King headed, in the Willard Hotel in Washington in the fall of 1963. The source said the party had been picked up by an F.B.I. electronic bug in the room and put on tape.

Bureau officials, according to sources at the time, felt that the content of the tape was detrimental to Dr. King and some of his associates because it recounted activities at the party they thought did not conform with the rights leader's position as a religious leader.

The tape and the package had been prepared so they could not be traced, one source said. He said Mr. Hoover wanted the tape mailed from somewhere in Florida and that Mr. Sullivan had ordered a special agent to fly to Tampa and mail the tape to Mrs. King. The source stressed that the agent had no idea of the contents.

The source said that Mr. Hoover believed the sending of the tape to Mrs. King would stop Dr. King's criticism of the bureau and break up his marriage as well.

Mrs. King said in a telephone interview that she recalled receiving a tape recording in January 1965.

"I received a tape that was rather curious—unlabeled," she said. "As a matter of fact, Martin and I listened to the tape and we found much of it unintelligible. We concluded there was nothing in the tape to discredit him."

Mrs. King said that she and her husband immediately realized that the tape had been made covertly and "presumed" it had been made by the F.B.I.

Mr. Murtagh, 53 years old, who now lives in Constable, N.Y., said the "trick" of sending the tape to Mrs. King to discredit her husband was well known "among senior agents in the Atlanta bureau and some of them bragged about it as a smart stunt."

According to two former senior F.B.I. officials, a wiretap on Dr. King later picked up a conversation in which Dr. King told a friend that he was deeply concerned about the pressure being placed upon him.

S.C.L.C. sources from that era say that Dr. King never wavered in his leadership of the movement and that the harassment failed.

The following incidents of harassment were either confirmed in earlier press accounts or uncovered in interviews with high bureau officials:

Mr. Murtagh and a former senior bureau official confirmed the bureau tried to disrupt plans for a banquet in Atlanta in 1964 by business leaders to laud Dr. King's winning of the Nobel Prize. It included covert contacts with community leaders with charges about Dr. King's personal life.

Two former bureau officials said that a "monograph" on Dr. King's personal life was circulated among government officials by the bureau during the Kennedy administration. President Kennedy became aware of what was going on and ordered Mr. Hoover to retrieve every copy of the monograph.

Mr. Murtagh said that efforts at harassment of S.C.L.C. leaders continued after Dr. King's assassination in 1968. He said he was ordered by bureau officials to obtain handwriting samples of Andrew Young, now a Democratic representative from Georgia, later ambassador to the United Nations and mayor of Atlanta; and Hosea Williams, twice a national executive director of the Southern Christian Leadership Conference and a member of the Georgia legislature, to permit bureau experts to forge letters over the Young and Williams signatures that would harm their careers. Mr. Murtagh said he refused the assignment.

Two former senior F.B.I. officials said the bureau "routinely" sought to prevent Dr. King from receiving honorary degrees from colleges and universities by planting stories about his personal life, including charges that he directed S.C.L.C. funds to his own use and to Swiss bank accounts.

Mr. Murtagh and other sources said there was a consistent practice of anonymous telephone calls, sometimes to make false fire alarm reports at locations where Dr. King was to speak and in other instances to friends and associates of Dr. King, trying to sow distrust among them.

In 1961 and 1962, bureau intelligence experts reportedly became convinced that two members of the Communist party had infiltrated the S.C.L.C. The intelligence men urged then Attorney General Robert F. Kennedy to open a national security investigation of Dr. King, and he complied.

Reliable sources said that Dr. King was under electronic surveillance well before Mr. Kennedy had made his decision. On two occasions, members of the Kennedy administration warned the S.C.L.C. leaders to disassociate themselves from the alleged Communists because they were leaving Dr. King open to attacks by southern conservatives in the Senate, but Dr. King refused to do so unless the government produced evidence of Communist affiliation.

In 1963, Mr. Kennedy authorized a national security wiretap—then legal under federal law—on Dr. King. Court testimony and interviews with F.B.I. and Justice Department officials indicate that the electronic surveillance continued for at least two years, from 1963 to 1965, and produced a massive amount of recordings. One estimate held that 5,000 separate conversations went on tape.

Former agents said the room bugs were planted in hotels from coast to coast as Dr. King moved about the country.

Despite this massive surveillance, veteran agents said, there was never a recommendation for prosecution for violation of any federal or state law. Nor, several sources said, were grounds for any national security concern ever established.

In a 1969 federal court case involving the boxer Muhammad Ali, a federal agent testified that he believed the tapes from the King investigation had been destroyed. But other sources among former bureau officials maintain that the tapes or transcripts of the tapes are still in the bureau and may be part of the material disclosed 10 days ago by Attorney General Edward H. Levi.

Mr. Murtagh said the bureau surveillance of the S.C.L.C. failed because it concentrated on gathering information about the mores and personal lives of the rights group's officials.

"This was a little naive because S.C.L.C. officials told me they couldn't care less," Mr. Murtagh said.

Under laws in force when the tape was reportedly

mailed, it was both a potential crime and a violation of bureau regulations to use the tape in this manner.

The Federal Communications Act in force in 1964–1965 prohibited a police or government agency from disclosing the contents of a taped or bugged conversation to a third party. Another section of the federal criminal statutes makes it a crime for federal employees to convert government property and records to other than official use.

DR. KING'S DREAM LIVES ON IN EAST ORANGE [1986]

MICHAEL WINERIP

THE ROGERS twins, Kendall and Kenneth, are only in first grade, in East Orange, N.J., but they know the whole story on Martin Luther King.

"This one time Rosa Parks was sitting in the front of the bus," said Kendall, "and this white lady said, 'Get up,' and that bus driver called the police."

"And," said Kenneth, "Rosa Parks called up Martin Luther King and said, 'Get me out of jail, Martin.' "

The Rogers twins know who killed Dr. King, because their music teacher told them. They know when he died because it was on the bulletin board. They know that he was special because they wore ties to school on his birthday last Wednesday and signed a pledge to live his dream.

Nowadays, Dr. King is a hero in most places, but he is a very big hero to children in East Orange, where the school system is 98 percent black. They can sympathize: as a third grader, Nekiesha Jeter, wrote, "He did not fight and it was hard not to fight and I mean hard."

Indeed, if Dr. King were able to visit East Orange in 1986, he would find all the promise and sadness of urban schools. Keisha Lowen, a seventh grader, put it this way: "He might feel satisfied to see what he tried to do was half-accomplished."

At Scott High, he would find that more than half the seniors go to college, though not one went to an Ivy League school last year. He would find that despite high local taxes for education, East Orange spending per pupil is $2,700, compared with $4,200 in mostly white West Orange.

"He'd be pleased to see how we work together and are not beat down just because we're an urban district," said Reggie Lewis, a senior. "He'd like this school," said a sixth grader, Preston Lyde. "It teaches you it's not easy going in life."

Said Dwayne Otis, a senior, "A lot of students, he'd be disappointed they're just sliding by." He would find a dropout rate of 43 percent.

He would find that Emily McHugh has studied French, Spanish and Latin; that John Eubanks is only a freshman and starts on the tennis team, that Dwayne Otis has already been accepted to Purdue's engineering program.

He would find a district that 30 years ago was upper middle class and now has a median household income of $13,300, far below the state average.

He would find a district that was 75 percent white in 1960, was one-third white in 1970 and is 0.3 percent white today.

"He would have liked it mixed," said Emily McHugh, a senior. "When my oldest brother was here in 1973, it was nicely mixed. I wish it was that way today. It's like isolation. To maneuver in the world, you have to deal with all kinds."

Dr. King would find a place where most black children do not have a white friend. Said Mae Bean, a fifth grader, "I have very, very little white friends."

"I used to have one white friend, Angel, but he moved away," said Kevin Greene, of the seventh grade.

"It's not real segregation here," said Leidene King, a ninth grader. "They can come to East Orange if they're white, we won't hold it against them."

He would find that the children know most whites will not come. Said Khalil Callier, a fifth grader, "The whites don't like the neighborhoods and the people around here."

"It's black," said Tyrick Harris, "because most blacks like a low-rate house."

He would hear cynicism about whites. "They may work with us," said Reggie Lewis, "but they don't live with us or go to school with us."

And he would find that the children of East Orange have not forgotten him. As a second grader, Noel Fernandez, said, "Dr. King would have been delighted to see the children."

In many homes, he is the first historical figure they hear of. "When I was 6," said Preston Lyde, "my mother hung this picture, and I said: 'Who is that? That's my grandfather?' and she said, 'Dr. Martin Luther King, Jr.' "

The parents of Joy Knight, a tenth grader, said when they lived in the South—before Dr. King—they could not sit in restaurants, and had to order takeout food from a side window.

The students have been studying him. "He was a nonviolence man," said a third grader, Ron Sanders.

"He fought the bad laws," said a second grader, Valerie Fitzhugh. When asked why the laws were bad, she said: "The president wouldn't make those bad laws. Maybe white people made them up themselves."

"He didn't slow down," said Tyrick Harris. "He just kept moving."

"Our people would still be on the back of the bus," said Reggie Lewis, "if it wasn't for the 1955 Montgomery bus boycott."

The few nonblacks who move here are surprised to discover how important Dr. King is. Frank Veliz used to go to a mostly Hispanic school in the Bronx. "When I heard about Dr. King here, I kind of liked him, because he wanted peace, and these days it's kind of hard to find people like that."

Students rate him high. Rhashonda James, a third grader, compared him to Stevie Wonder. Chon Houston, a fourth grader, could not think of any whites as important: "I can't remember any white famous people who helped black people."

Preston Lyde, a sixth grader, compared him to Benjamin Banneker, the 18th-century black astronomer.

Tyrick Harris said, "He's higher than a president, yeah."

A tenth grader, Natalie Darden, said Shirley Chisholm was like Dr. King; Derrick Canada, a junior, said Moses; Reggie Lewis, a senior, named Louis Farrakhan.

Dwayne Otis, a senior, said his own father was the same kind of man, because he went back to school nights to get his degree.

This past week they celebrated Dr. King in school according to their age. Fifth graders wrote "I have a dream" essays, and for several the dream was a city with no trash or robbers. They sang the "Happy Birthday" song that Stevie Wonder wrote in honor of Dr. King.

Eighth graders debated violence versus nonviolence, one side for Malcolm X, the other for Dr. King.

Tyrick Harris noted, "When Dr. King's house got bombed, he said, 'Put your swords away.' He said, 'He who lives by the sword will perish by the sword,' but it didn't really go that way. He didn't live by the sword yet he still perished by the sword."

A day off for Dr. King is nothing new here. For years, East Orange schools closed for his birthday. Many felt it was good the country was catching on.

"I say it's about time," Natalie Darden said. Joy Knight said years from now, if children do not know who Dr. King was, his holiday would come up, and they would be curious to learn more about him.

The youngest said they would be thinking of him

tomorrow, during their day off for the holiday. A second grader, James Sharp, said he might go to the library and study more on him with his cousin, Keshia.

Clifton Dunston, a sixth grader, said, "I'll be looking at different TV pictures of him on each and every channel."

At high school, only a few like Reggie Lewis were planning something special. He will give a speech about Dr. King and blackness at a city celebration.

Leidene King said she expected to go shopping for new clothes she needs for a fashion show at her charm school in Newark.

Derrick Canada, a starter on the boys' basketball team, said he will probably be practicing, and so will Cheryline Hewitt, a girls' starter.

Natalie Darden said on Dr. King's day she would be studying for midterms.

JOHN LENNON

1940-1980

By Robert Palmer

The Beatles united a generation of young people with their songs, their attitudes and their sense of style, and John Lennon was the thinking person's Beatle.

Of the four, he was the Beatle who wrote books, the Beatle who embroiled the group in a potentially disastrous controversy by suggesting in an interview that they were more popular than Jesus, the Beatle who embraced the poetic innovations of Bob Dylan in the mid-1960s and shocked Beatles fans by jumping into performance art, happenings and political protests in the late 1960s and early 1970s.

He was the Beatle who announced, in one of his first solo albums after the breakup of the Beatles, that "The Dream Is Over"—the dream of community through peace, love, mysticism and psychedelic drugs that the Beatles had encouraged and advertised.

And yet, paradoxically, Mr. Lennon never lost sight of that dream. "The media are saying that the sixties were stupid and naive," he remarked in an interview a month before he died. "But look at how much of what was sniggered about in the sixties has become mainstream—health food, therapies and all the rest. And love and peace weren't invented in the sixties. What about Gandhi? What about Christ? The naïveté is to buy the idea that the sixties were naive."

To protest Britain's involvement in the Nigerian civil war and British support of the United States' role in Vietnam, Mr. Lennon, named a Member of the Order of the British Empire by Queen Elizabeth in 1965, returned his award. The award, the lowest of five divisions of the order, was presented to the four Beatles for service to their country.

John Lennon was born Oct. 9, 1940, in Liverpool, England. In his early teens he felt the full force of Elvis Presley, Little Richard and Jerry Lee Lewis—the earliest American rock and roll. When he was 15, he organized his first rock and roll group, the Quarrymen, continuing it after he entered art school, enlisting the services of Paul McCartney and George Harrison, and later Ringo Starr.

From 1958 to 1962 the group (renamed the Silver Beatles and later the Beatles) worked steadily in the port cities of Liverpool and Hamburg, West Germany. In 1961 they came to the attention of Brian Epstein, who secured a recording contract for them, plotted and executed their conquest of Europe, and arranged their first tour of the United States early in 1964.

Mr. Lennon and Paul McCartney were the group's lead vocalists and songwriters, and as the Beatles grew more and more popular worldwide, their songs grew more complex. By the mid-1960s the Beatles were leaders of a worldwide rock movement that believed music with a beat could and should be intelligent and innovative as well.

The Beatles were the first popular rock and roll band to write their own material, to address a range

Photo Trends

Bob Gruen/Star File

of serious subjects and to embrace influences that ranged from Mr. Dylan's folk poetry to Indian classical music to Karlheinz Stockhausen's electronic sound collages. They changed the face of popular music, and popular culture, radically and irrevocably.

Beginning with the mid-1960s album *Rubber Soul,* the Lennon-McCartney songwriting partnership began to unravel. Mr. McCartney began concentrating on pure pop, contributing ballads like "Michelle" and "Eleanor Rigby." Mr. Lennon wrote more complex songs, embodying the conflicts he was feeling acutely as a Beatle: between his private life as an intellectual and an artist and his public persona; between his role as a pop musician and a generational spokesman, and the unresolved personal problems of his childhood.

Out of this turmoil came exquisite songs of euphoria and confusion ("Strawberry Fields Forever" and "Lucy in the Sky with Diamonds"), some of the first and best examples of pop surrealism ("I Am the Walrus" and "Happiness Is a Warm Gun"), and electronic experiments that prefigured Mr. Lennon's later collaborations with the conceptual artist Yoko Ono.

Mr. Lennon met Miss Ono in 1966, and by 1969, when they married, their romance was being blamed for the disintegration of the Beatles, who officially disbanded in 1970. The couple's demystification of the Beatles began with their *Two Virgins* album, with its celebrated cover showing them nude, and continued with a series of albums that grafted Miss Ono's experimental and sometimes intensely grating vocal techniques onto Mr. Lennon's sensibility.

The music was dismissed by most critics and fans at the time, but it has been an important influence on some of the brightest talents in the most recent wave of rock performers.

Mr. Lennon's post-Beatles albums continued to mirror his internal struggles, particularly *John Lennon/Plastic Ono Band* (1970), which followed several months of "primal scream" therapy with Arthur Janov and included songs that attempted to exorcise childhood traumas. But Mr. Lennon was also, and perhaps first of all, one of the most talented pop tunesmiths of modern times, as he proved with the subsequent albums *Imagine* (1971) and *Mind Games* (1973).

In 1975, after recording an album of rock and roll oldies that he recently expressed some dissatisfaction with, Mr. Lennon stopped making records to concentrate on rearing his and Yoko's son, Sean, who is now 5 years old. (Mr. Lennon also has a son, Julian, by his first wife, Cynthia).

In his own words, he was a "househusband," tending to domestic duties while Miss Ono supervised the couple's investments and other business matters.

Finally, in August, the Lennons began making a new album, *Double Fantasy,* which was released by Geffen Records a month before he was murdered in 1980 and is now in the national top 20. Mr. Lennon's first new single in five years, in the top 10, is optimistically titled "Starting Over."

The album was conceived as a "dialogue on love," with songs by Mr. Lennon alternating with songs by Miss Ono.

THE MURDER OF JOHN LENNON

LES LEDBETTER

JOHN LENNON, one of the four Beatles, was shot and killed Dec. 8, 1980, while entering the apartment building where he lived, the Dakota, on Manhattan's Upper West Side. A suspect was seized at the scene.

The 40-year-old Mr. Lennon was shot in the back twice after getting out of a limousine and walking into an entranceway of the Dakota at 1 West 72d Street, Sgt. Robert Barnes of the 20th Precinct said.

"Obviously the man was waiting for him," Sergeant Barnes said of the assailant. The suspect was identified as Mark David Chapman, 25, of Honolulu, who had been living in New York for about a week, according to James L. Sullivan, chief of detectives in the New York City Police Department. Mr. Chapman was charged with murder and possession of a deadly weapon.

Lieut. John Schick of the 20th Precinct said the gunman let the Lennons pass him and enter the building's passageway before shooting Mr. Lennon. Lieutenant Schick said the man called out "Mr. Lennon" and then stepped from an alcove, pulled a gun from under his coat and fired several shots into Mr. Lennon while standing in a combat position. Mr. Lennon then struggled up six stairs and inside the alcove to a guard area where he said "I'm shot," and collapsed.

Mr. Lennon's wife, Yoko Ono, was with the singer when he was shot. She was not injured.

David Geffen, a recording executive, read this statement from Miss Ono: "John loved and prayed for the human race, please do the same for him."

Witnesses said Mr. Lennon was wearing a white T-shirt and dungaree jacket when he was shot. They said Miss Ono screamed, "Help me. Help me."

They said the suspect paced back and forth in the entranceway to the Dakota after shooting the musician, arguing with the doorman and holding the gun in his hand pointing downward.

An eyewitness, who only gave her first name, Nina, said that she had approached the suspect after the shooting.

"I asked him what had happened and he said, 'I'd go away if I were you,' " she said.

One witness, Ben Eruchson, a cabdriver from Brooklyn, said, "He could have gotten away. He had plenty of time."

Jeff Smith, a neighbor, said that he heard five shots fired shortly before 11 P.M. Other witnesses said they heard four when the shooting occurred at 10:45 P.M.

There were bullet holes in the structure and blood on the bricks of the building.

Immediately after Mr. Lennon was shot, hundreds of people began to gather at West 72d Street and Central Park West. A number of them were crying. By 1 A.M., the crowd had grown to 1,000.

Witnesses said that the shooting took place in the West 72d Street entranceway of the Dakota, just past the lobby attendant's office.

Mr. Lennon was taken into the office after being shot. Shortly after, he was taken to Roosevelt Hospital, where he was pronounced dead in the emergency room, according to a hospital spokesman. A crowd similar to the one gathered outside the Dakota soon assembled outside the hospital, witnesses said.

Police Officer Anthony Palma, who drove Miss Ono to the hospital, described her as "very hysterical" and said she sobbed: "Tell me it isn't true."

Jack Douglas, Mr. Lennon's producer, said he and the Lennons had been at a studio called the Record Plant in midtown earlier in the evening and that Mr. Lennon had left at 10:30 P.M. Mr. Lennon said he was going to get something to eat and then go home, according to Mr. Douglas.

Employees at the Dakota said someone resembling the alleged assailant had obtained an autograph from Mr. Lennon earlier in the day.

Chief Sullivan said the suspect had been seen in the neighborhood of the Dakota for several days.

"Some people said they heard six shots and said John was hit twice," Mr. Strub said. "The police said he was hit in the back."

He said others on the street had told him the assailant had been "crouching in the archway of the Dakota."

He said the suspect was put into another police car.

"He had a smirk on his face" when the police took him away, Mr. Strub said.

The suspect, Mr. Chapman, was described as a stocky man wearing a white shirt and brown pants, wire-rimmed glasses and a coat. Sergeant Barnes said a .38-caliber revolver, believed to be the murder weapon, had been recovered.

Mr. Lennon, who was widely thought to be the

most intellectual and outspoken of the Beatles during their heyday, was responsible for writing many of the songs that launched them in the early 1960s and changed the course of rock music.

The other members of the group were Paul McCartney, George Harrison and Ringo Starr. Mr. McCartney has his own musical group, called Wings. Mr. Harrison and Mr. Starr are still active in the music business.

In an interview earlier this year—his first major interview in five years—Mr. Lennon said he had wanted to leave the Beatles as early as 1966 but did not make the move until four years later because he "just didn't have the guts."

Mr. Lennon attended secondary school in Liverpool and then went on to Liverpool College of Art, where he married a classmate, Cynthia Powell.

They were later divorced. In 1969, Mr. Lennon married Miss Ono, a Japanese-American artist, who was pregnant. He later said, "We went to Paris on our honeymoon, then interrupted our honeymoon to get married on the Rock of Gibraltar."

The Beatles' music was as much a staple of the revolutionary 1960s as the Vietnam War, whose protesters sang Beatles songs in addition to letting their hair grow long in imitation of the musicians.

"I Want to Hold Your Hand," "Love Me Do" and "She Loves You" stayed on the top of the hit parades for months and heralded Beatlemania, the frenzy whipped up among their teenage fans around the world.

After the breakup of the group in 1970, Mr. Lennon and Miss Ono lived in seclusion in New York for several years, but the couple were on the front page again in a messy deportation hearing.

The United States government contended that Mr. Lennon, a British subject, was ineligible for permanent residence because of a 1968 drug conviction in Britain. Mr. Lennon eventually was allowed to stay in the United States.

LEADER OF A ROCK GROUP THAT HELPED DEFINE A GENERATION

BY JOHN ROCKWELL

THE BEATLES were without any question the most popular, most influential of all rock groups, and John Lennon was the most impassioned, and probably the most deeply talented, of all the Beatles.

In 1964, when the Beatles first reached America to appear on the Ed Sullivan television program, bemused adult observers found it difficult to distinguish them. They all seemed similarly gray-suited, mop-topped mannequins; what seized their attention was that their songs—"I Want to Hold Your Hand" was the archetype—celebrated teen love in a way that teenagers hadn't responded to since the days of Elvis Presley and Frank Sinatra.

But soon thereafter, as the Beatles began to define their generation, it became apparent that Mr. Lennon and Paul McCartney were actually the creative forces behind the band. Ringo Starr was cute and cuddly and George Harrison played eloquent lead guitar and helped channel the Beatles' energies into Eastern mysticism. But it was Mr. Lennon and Paul McCartney who counted.

The two composed most of the band's songs and were the lead singers. At first they collaborated closely, sharing lyrics and music. Later they tended to compose separately, but for reasons of legality and personal loyalty the songs were still credited to both jointly.

Mr. Lennon and Mr. McCartney worked together in a classically complementary manner. Mr. McCartney was the sunny, bright one, the purveyor of lilting ballads and cheery love songs. Mr. Lennon was the harder, fiercer man, the true rocker of the foursome. He had the grittiest singing voice, and the deepest, most convoluted sense of rock's anger and potential triumph.

The Beatles' influence expressed itself first of all in the simple sociological dimensions of their success, unmatched in pop music history to this day. But the band also managed almost singlehandedly to transform the innocent entertainment of rock and roll into the artistically self-conscious pretensions of rock. Mr. Lennon, with his eager willingness to explore the ramifications of the psychedelic experience, led that transformation more than any other Beatle.

But ironically, it was that very evolution away from the rude energy of early Beatles rock and roll that crystallized Mr. Lennon's dilemma for the 1970s. He was once quoted as saying that the band had never made better, more intense music than it had in the cellar nightclubs of Hamburg in 1962. In the 1970s, he tried to find a way to recapture the power of his youth and to reconcile it with his adulthood, but he had severe difficulties in doing so.

The dichotomy between Mr. Lennon's drive and Mr. McCartney's softness manifested itself ever more strongly after the band broke up in 1970, and ironically reaffirmed what each man had brought to the other. On his own, Mr. Lennon's solo albums sometimes reached real eloquence (above all, *Imagine*). But too often he degenerated into self-indulgent howling—frequently abetted by his wife, the Japanese-born conceptual artist Yoko Ono. At the same time, Mr. McCartney, shorn of Mr. Lennon's toughening influence, drifted ever more thoughtlessly into frothy pop.

Throughout his life, from even before the Beatles came together, Mr. Lennon seemed a seeker. His first and perhaps ultimate way to salvation was rock music itself, which he mastered and conveyed with a passion and intensity rarely equaled in the genre. And he managed in the 1960s to leaven that passion with a delightful wit.

But as the Beatles grew, seemingly unstoppably, into the phenomenon they became, Mr. Lennon appeared to grow troubled in his search, and to broaden it to include politics, religion and the self. In so doing he lost the focus his music had previously given him, and tended to rant emptily. All of the psychedelic adventures, sleep-in protests, nude album covers and primal screaming in the world could not replace the void that rock had once filled.

In the latter half of the 1970s, Mr. Lennon withdrew almost completely into himself, and into the rearing of his young son, Sean. *Double Fantasy,* the recently released album that he and Miss Ono created, was in reality more of an extension of that domestic introversion than a break from it. Mr. Lennon's songs on the record, even though they have done well commercially, represent a tired recycling of his youthful idioms—a sincere but misguided and slightly desperate fixation on domestic happiness that really doesn't suit rock at all.

As such, even in failure, he remained a spokesman for his generation, as true in personal retreat as he had been in the joyful assertion and tortured protests of his earlier years.

MOURNERS COME AND GO TO SAD TONES OF BEATLES' MUSIC

WILLIAM E. FARRELL

DEC. 10, 1980—The filigreed wrought-iron entry gate to the Dakota apartment house is a wailing wall completely covered with flowers, messages of love and peace, Christmas wreaths and a long tinsel streamer that was crudely framed like a crucifix until the wind got hold of it.

An informal procession of mourners—groups of friends, tearful couples, sad-faced stragglers—walks along 72d Street from bus and subway stops to the open-air wake in front of John Lennon's apartment house, a Victorian landmark as dark and brooding as a tale by Poe.

Many of them carry small bouquets or single flowers that they place in crannies in the gate before the police politely urge them to get behind the barricades running alongside the Dakota. The iron mouth of a roaring lion on the gate is stopped by a sticker the size of an envelope. It says "The Beatles."

The crowd gathered early in the morning when the word got out that John Lennon had been slain in the entranceway to his home. Long before dawn, hundreds had come to recite the Lord's Prayer and to sing Lennon's songs while candles burned in some of the Dakota's huge windows. The mourners ebb and flow. Sometimes there are more than a thousand, sometimes no more than a couple of hundred. They keep coming and going.

The scene in front of the Dakota is a 1980s Bruegel painting in its busyness, its congestion and its color. Morning joggers, in shorts, headbands and knee warmers, break their "me generation" stride to pay homage. Some young men in three-piece business suits stop by. Platoons of men and women, carefully coiffed and wearing a dizzying array of designer jeans, stand behind the barricades with young boys and girls in ratty hairdos and army surplus gear, those nostalgic fixtures of the 1960s.

The crowd is permeated by news representatives—newspaper reporters with pads, television crews, radio reporters sticking microphones in front of people and asking, "What's your reaction?"

"Get the ambience," a vexed reporter says to a camera crew. Spectators eye police press cards fixed to coats—lingering over the television crowd, giving the print reporters a quick bypass. A young girl becomes shrill and hysterical and is held for a long time by a boyfriend while a paparazzi surge of 20 photographers surrounds her. Shutters click mercilessly in hope of the perfect picture of a fan's grief.

"There's a hundred of you filming that poor girl," says a bewildered policeman trying to contain a sudden crowd of voyeurs who think a celebrity has been sighted.

"Where'd he get shot?" a boy asks.

"Right over there, man," another replies and points wrongly to a spot in front of the Dakota.

One man in his 20s has a small audience as he describes what happened in an inaccurate account that nonetheless has the compelling force of myth.

Many of the spectators are equipped with still cameras and movie cameras. A man from Virginia ducks out of his bus tour of New York and, still wearing his tour tag ("Hi, I'm Ashley"), is snapping everything in sight. A young girl makes a movie record of her friend holding a huge white gladiolus before it is placed in the gate.

There are huge portable radios everywhere—cacophonous boxes blaring taped Beatles music transformed into dirges by the occasion. Frequently, different songs merge incoherently in the cold air. Others are tuned into all-news radio stations that tell the spectators where they are and why they are there.

One station has a call-in segment in which people phone the station to react to John Lennon's death while those who have come to his home to express their sorrow listen. Eerily, a group huddles near a radio featuring an excerpt from his last interview.

"You have to give thanks to God or whatever it is up there to the fact that we all survived," he says.

One radio commentator makes much of the fact that John Lennon spent a large part of the 1970s in seclusion, and the thought occurs that so did many of this crowd now once again massed together on a public street in a reprise of the activism of the 1960s.

"My generation doesn't stick together no more," says a distraught woman in her 20s.

"Nobody cares no more," says her companion. Near them a young group sings "Hey Jude" for a television camera that zeroes in on them.

Down the block from the Dakota, heading toward Columbus Avenue, a woman walks alone trying to hide her tears. She is one of the many who has lost a hero and who reached an awful milestone in her life when she woke up and heard about the death of a contemporary. A few feet behind her a man with a portable radio sits on a building stoop listening to the Beatles singing "It's been a hard day's night."

MUST AN ARTIST SELF-DESTRUCT?

[An Interview with John Lennon Recorded in the Fall of 1980]

ROBERT PALMER

"IS IT possible to have a life centered around a family and a child and still be an artist?" asked John Lennon. For Mr. Lennon, widely regarded as the most thoughtful and outspoken of the four Beatles during their heyday in the 1960s, the question is far from rhetorical. Together with his wife, Yoko Ono, and their 5-year-old son, Sean, the 40-year-old Mr. Lennon has been engrossed in a settled family life since dropping out of the music business five years ago. Now, with Miss Ono, he is reentering the pop mainstream with a new album, *Double Fantasy.*

In a series of candid conversations that took place in a recording studio during the making of the album, and at the Lennons' New York apartment after its completion, both artists talked at length about the demands of making music versus the demands of a family. "In a way," Mr. Lennon said, "we're involved in a kind of experiment. Could the family be the inspiration for art, instead of drinking or drugs or whatever? I'm interested in finding that out."

At the door of the family's apartment in the Dakota apartment building, Mr. Lennon greeted me, smiling broadly, one hand on his heart, the other arm outstretched, like a 1930s crooner. "Pardon me," he sang, "if I'm sentimental . . ." The Warner Brothers-distributed Geffen label had just released a single, "Starting Over," backed with Miss Ono's "Kiss Kiss Kiss," from the album.

I'd written the preceding week that while Mr. Lennon's pop craftsmanship was intact, the song's lyrics seemed a bit obvious and sentimental.

We sat down at a plain wooden table in the middle of a spacious kitchen that had a stereo, a large video screen, and a couch and lounging area at one end. There were Italian cookies and pastries on the table, and Mr. Lennon brewed a pot of coffee. "I've heard 'Starting Over' hundreds of times now," Miss Ono said, "but I still get choked up and cry sometimes when I hear it, because . . . well, in the sixties, we went through this thing with everybody feeling that we were going to be free. And it turned into a big orgy; in the end, the women realized that all the sexual liberation was really just for men. And now here's a guy, John, saying to a woman, let's start over again, let's try. These are times when women are still bitter about these things, and I think men have to make that first move." "The sixties," Mr. Lennon said with a smile, sitting down with the coffee. "When I met Yoko, we were two poets in velvet cloaks—almost literally—both full of positive ideas for the world, but for ourselves those ideas didn't count. We were both self-destructive; I'd come up thinking of myself not so much as a *musician,* you know, but as a writer, and the big examples in England were Dylan Thomas and Brendan Behan. I'd just naively accepted the idea that an artist had to self-destruct in order to create. And we both came out of that through the gift of having the baby.

"By 1975 I wasn't really enjoying what I was doing anyway. I was a machine that was supposed to produce so much creative *something* and give it out periodically for approval or to justify my existence on earth. But I don't think I would have been able to just withdraw from the whole music business if it hadn't been for Sean. I gave him five years, taking care of him while Yoko ran our business affairs, but it's going on, and I feel it should go on. When I look at the relative importance of what life is about, I can't quite convince myself that making a record or having a career is more important or even as important as my child, or any child."

Mr. Lennon lit a cigarette and pushed a tempting chocolate cake to the far end of the table. "Another thing those five years did for me," he said, "was to move a lot of intellectual garbage out of the way and allow whatever it is in me that wants to express itself to do it naturally. This is a digression, but going back to the beginnings of rock and roll, Elvis and Jerry Lee Lewis and so on were working-class entertainment; *they* were working class. The Beatles were slightly less working class; for Paul McCartney and me, at least, going to university was a possibility. I had all this artsy stuff in me anyway, so we put a little more intellect into our music, just because of what we were. And gradually, expectations for the Beatles became educated, middle-class expectations. And *I* tended to get too intellectual about pop music. I had this sort of critic John Lennon sitting over me saying, 'You did that already, you can't do it again. You can't say it that simply.' Now the music's coming *through* me again."

The *Double Fantasy* album, subtitled "A Heart Play," isn't going to be accused of being overly intellectual. Mr. Lennon's songs are direct and, in their celebrations of enduring love and the pleasures of home and hearth, they will undoubtedly strike some listeners as simplistic, finely crafted though they are. Miss Ono's songs tend to have more bite, though "I'm Your Angel," a piece of 1930s-style whimsy, wouldn't sound out of place in a Walt Disney movie. "For me," Mr. Lennon said, "a lot of the so-called avant-garde in pop is pseudointellectual—which is something I contributed to. Basically, you just want a good record, right? You can enjoy it no matter what level it's on, whether it makes you want to dance or makes you want to lie down and think about the universe."

"I'm not impressed by pop that plays a lot of intellectual games," Miss Ono added. "The more you intellectualize, the more you get lost."

. . .

At work at a recording console in New York's Hit Factory, bracing himself with a strong cup of coffee, Mr. Lennon looked trimmer than he had in the late 1960s and early 1970s; and in his black jeans, black work shirt and wire-rimmed glasses, he seemed more like John Lennon, pop star, than like a "househusband," as he's taken to calling himself. Miss Ono, a founding member of the 1960s performance art vanguard known as the Fluxus movement (other participants included John Cage, La Monte Young and Nam June Paik)—was sitting at the console, too, and they were both listening to Mr. Lennon's song "Starting Over," which was to be the first selection and the first single from their new album. "I don't think you should put another voice on it, John," she said as she lit a cigarette. The song already boasted a rich mesh of voices, some provided by backup singers and some by Mr. Lennon, whose reedy tenor and personal inflection are still immediately recognizable.

"Mother," he said in measured tones—he often calls Miss Ono "Mother," apparently with a great deal of respect—"I don't want to double the same part, I'm hearing another harmony that I want to try." Mr. Lennon turned to explain. "Back when we were doing Beatles records, I used to want to double-track my voice on everything mostly to make it stronger. Now"—he waved his arm to indicate the expanse of blinking, whirring equipment, some of it computerized—"you don't have to do that." He downed the rest of his coffee and walked out into the studio, glancing on the way at the large color photograph of Sean that hung from a monitor speaker. "I'll bet," he mused aloud, "that I miss him a lot more than he misses me."

Recording studios have changed a great deal since the Beatles recorded *Sgt. Pepper's Lonely Hearts Club Band* on a four-track machine—for that matter, they've changed since 1975. Helping the Lennons explore the possibilities of new technology were Jack Douglas, who had worked for them as an engineer in the early 1970s and now produces popular rock groups like Cheap Trick, and the engineer, Lee DeCarlo, a burly Vietnam veteran with a dreamy, bearish smile. "They've been a big help," Miss Ono said as the two busily adjusted settings and Mr. Lennon cleared his throat into a microphone. "But the two of us are very headstrong. For the final word on my songs I always look to John, and the final word on his comes from me."

Mr. Lennon practiced singing along with the track, which had been recorded in an intensive series of sessions that began on Aug. 8. It was a melodious, loping tune with a 1950s backbeat, and the more he ran over it, the more scraps of Beatles songs he was able to insert, just for fun. "Why don't we do it in the road?" he sang, echoing the title line from one of his songs on the Beatles' *White Album* when he should have been singing "why don't we take off alone?" But soon he turned serious and was able to perfect his harmony part after only a few tries. It made the band sound uncannily like a Beatles record, though the backing band was composed of New York studio professionals.

Miss Ono had been taking care of business details while Mr. Lennon sang. Periodically, a Japanese assistant would bring her hot tea and a pad with telephone messages in Japanese characters—from photographers, journalists asking for interviews, record company representatives (the album, and the Lennons' immediate future as recording artists, hadn't yet been assigned to any company, and the bidding was intense). She'd gone into a room adjoining the studio to return the most important calls. "Well, Mother," Mr. Lennon said, plainly elated that his work was going so well, "I'm done for now. Time to work on one of your songs." He stretched out on a nearby couch and went to sleep.

After hearing Mr. Lennon's melodious pop, Miss Ono's song "Give Me Something" was a little startling. Propelled by a serpentine chromatic guitar figure from the former David Bowie sideman Earl Slick and clocking in at a brisk 1 minute and 38 seconds, it offered a vision that was considerably bleaker than Mr. Lennon's reassuring "Starting Over." There was a screaming solo from Earl Slick and the song abruptly crashed to a halt.

"You know what I listened to for the last five years?" Mr. Lennon asked after his nap. "Muzak! For the kind of chores I was doing around the house, it was perfect. I know people are going to say, 'Oh, that's because he's got to be 40 and got soft.' Well, it might be that; it's irrelevant to me. The attitude is that when you change when you get older, there's something *wrong* with that, but the world is stupid enough as it is; if the young were running it, it would be really dumb. Whatever changes I'm going through because I'm 40 I'm thankful for, because they give me some insight into the madness I've been living in all my life."

THE REAL WAY TO REMEMBER LENNON

ROBERT PALMER

DEC. 9, 1981—"Everybody loves you when you're six foot in the ground," John Lennon sang in 1974 on his album *Walls and Bridges.* As usual, he was being trenchant, and as usual, he was right. He was loved by millions when he was alive, but in the year that has passed since last Dec. 8, when he was shot down outside the Dakota, it seems he has been loved by just about everybody, indiscriminately.

Books about Mr. Lennon were hastily thrown together and rushed into print within a few weeks of his death. They were all "tributes," "remembrances," testimonials to what a wonderful artist and all-round wonderful guy he was. The anniversary of the shooting has brought forth a torrent of radio and television "tributes," many exercises in nostalgia-by-the-book: film clips from *A Hard Day's*

Night, snatches of Beatles songs, glimpses of John F. Kennedy and other early 1960s icons and newsreel voices lamenting the passing of an era.

The Cincinnati Pops Orchestra, the hammy belter David Clayton Thomas and the pop singer Roberta Flack, none of whom have the remotest relationship to rock and roll as Lennon perceived and created it, will take "A Tribute to John Lennon: A Concert in His Memory" into Radio City Music Hall tomorrow night. If Lennon could somehow comment on all these outpourings of love, his response would undoubtedly be unprintable.

"I'm sick and tired of hearing things from uptight short-sighted narrow-minded hypocritics," Lennon practically shrieked on his second post-Beatles album, *Imagine.* Now *that* was Lennon—opinionated, outspoken, engaged and combative. The major fallacy of the majority of "tributes" is that they are tributes to Beatle John.

Lennon was justly proud of his work with the Beatles, but he did his best to torpedo the Beatles myth, beginning with his first post-Beatles album, *John Lennon/Plastic Ono Band,* released in 1970.

"I don't believe in Beatles," he announced on that album in a song called "God." "I just believe in me, in Yoko and me. The dream is over."

In retrospect, it's evident that Lennon was chipping away at the Beatles' four-lovable-moptops image early on. In the mid-1960s, when the Beatles should have been on top of the world, he wrote and sang "Help!"—and he meant it. When Paul McCartney was writing "Yesterday," Lennon was writing "Norwegian Wood," a thinly veiled account of an extramarital affair.

And once he was freed from the constraints he had felt as a member of the Fab Four, he no longer felt the need to thinly veil anything. In 1969, he wrote and recorded "Cold Turkey," a graphic account of his first brush with heroin addiction and the torment of withdrawal. On his *Plastic Ono Band* album, he sang about his mother's death, his early insecurity and his continuing feelings of isolation and paranoia. And on his next album, *Imagine,* he posed some of the most difficult questions and confronted some of the most bitter realizations that a pop singer has ever grappled with.

"How can I give love when I just don't know how to give?" he asked. "How can I give love when love is something I ain't never had?" In order to "be somebody," he counseled, "you got to shove." And he warned that while "you can hide your face behind a smile, one thing you can't hide is when you're crippled inside."

These aren't the Lennon songs one hears on the radio, and they aren't the Lennon songs pop singers work into their "tribute" medleys. But to many of Lennon's longtime admirers, they are *the* Lennon songs, the true measure of the man.

At the same time, they are not the whole story. Lennon somehow managed to be both an acerbic, hardheaded analyst of himself and his times and a cockeyed optimist. And most of the tributes that have been lavished on him since his death have failed to grapple with either of these extremes.

A recent review of "The Playboy Interviews With John Lennon and Yoko Ono" is typical. Lennon's soul-searching candor, it says, is "often rather embarrassing." His optimism is dismissed as "the requisite shoveling of cosmic gumdrops, the gratuitous harping on Peace and Love and Living in the Now."

How Lennon would have hated being patronized in this manner! "As if love and peace were invented in the sixties," he snorted when this writer interviewed him a month before his death. "As if Gandhi didn't exist or Christ didn't exist. Naïveté is something the media attributed to the sixties, by saying:

'We told you they were all stupid, those hippies. They were so naive. The reality is disco and drugs and *A Clockwork Orange,* you see.'

"But the naïveté is to buy the idea that the sixties were naive. The musicians weren't naive; they were playing the music for the sake of the music. And look at the things that have come out of the sixties—health food, therapies, meditation, all these things have become mainstream."

Those who choose to love Lennon by attempting to sanitize his memory can point to the domestic sweetness of *Double Fantasy,* the "comeback" album he made with his wife, Miss Ono, in the months before his death. Lennon finally seemed to be at peace with himself in those final months, and his songs reflected that peace truthfully; the album's tougher, more questioning songs were by Miss Ono.

But *Double Fantasy* was not Lennon's final piece of work. The night of his death he had finished work on Miss Ono's "Walking on Thin Ice," a profoundly disturbing song, shot full of foreboding.

Encouraged by favorable reviews of Miss Ono's contributions to *Double Fantasy,* Lennon pulled out the stops on "Thin Ice." He helped Miss Ono craft an arrangement that was as abrasively up-to-the-minute as any New Wave disk, and he contributed one of the most violent, wrenching guitar solos in the history of rock and roll.

According to Miss Ono and to the Lennons' co-producer, Jack Douglas, Lennon saw "Walking on Thin Ice" as the beginning of a new phase in his music, a phase more in line with the provocative lyrics and astringent musical textures of albums like *Plastic Ono Band* and *Imagine.*

One night shortly before his death, Lennon talked at some length and with considerable pride about the dissonant, howling feedback solos he had contributed to some of Miss Ono's most extreme disks in the early 1970s. He expressed the desire to indulge in such brinksmanship again, and he and Miss Ono said they intended to follow up *Double Fantasy* with records that would grow more and more experimental, more and more challenging.

Lennon enjoyed stirring things up. There was something almost anarchic in his quick, unrestrained laughter, something that wanted to test the limits of the situation behind his most relaxed smile. It's the wildness of the laughter, the challenge behind the smile that I'll remember, and love. Beatle John belongs to an era that is gone now, but honest, ornery John Lennon belongs to the ages.

JOHN L. LEWIS

1880–1969

By Alden Whitman

For 40 years, and especially during the turbulent 1930s, 1940s and early 1950s, John Llewellyn Lewis, a pugnacious man of righteous wrath and rococo rhetoric, was a dominant figure in the American labor movement. He aspired to national political and economic power, but they both eluded his grasp except for fleeting moments. He nudged greatness as a labor leader only to end in isolation from the mainstream of trade unionism.

But in his headline years Mr. Lewis, with his black leonine mane, his snaggly reddish eyebrows and his outthrust-jaw stubbornness, was an idol without peer to millions of workers and the symbol of blackest malevolence to millions in the middle and upper classes.

Gruff and unsmiling in public, his broad-brimmed fedora tilted over his eyes, he reveled in the dramatic tensions he helped to create, and he sparkled whether he was in center stage or whether he was the deep stentorian voice from the wings. As the thunderer for labor he was unexcelled.

Starting in 1935, when coal was the country's kingpin fuel and he was president of the United Mine Workers of America, Mr. Lewis shattered the complacent craft-union American Federation of Labor by setting up the Committee for Industrial Organization to organize workers into single unions for each big industry.

He went on to lead convulsive sitdown strikes, to humble the auto industry and Big Steel, to endorse and then to break bitterly with President Franklin D. Roosevelt, to defy the government in coal mine disputes in World War II, and to battle with President Harry S Truman in two coal strikes in which he was twice held in contempt of federal court and fined.

In the course of tumultuous labor politics, Mr. Lewis's wealthy and influential union left the American Federation of Labor and then rejoined it after leaving the Congress of Industrial Organizations. Finally, Mr. Lewis took his union out of the A.F.L. in the late 1940s and went it alone. Although he wrote history for all labor, and with seldom a dull line, the mine union, which he ruled with a fierce pride, held his steadiest focus.

Addressing the miners, he summed up his efforts in their behalf: "I have never faltered or failed to present the cause or plead the case of the mine workers of this country. I have pleaded your case not in the quavering tones of a mendicant asking alms, but in the thundering voice of the captain of a mighty host, demanding the rights to which free men are entitled."

Soot-smirched miners heeded Mr. Lewis without question. If he called for a shutdown, the pits were deserted. If he wanted the mines run on a three-day week, as he did during contract talks in 1949–50, that was the way they were operated. For their un-

AP/WIDE WORLD

George Tames/The New York Times

swerving loyalty the miners received periodic wage increases, vacation pay, pensions at age 60, pay for underground travel time, improved mine safety and many other benefits.

In the larger context of American life, Mr. Lewis, by force of personality, was able to bend public officials to his will. Perhaps the most notable instance of this occurred during the 1937 C.I.O. sitdown strike in General Motors plants in Flint, Mich. The strikers had ignored an injunction to leave the factories and Gov. Frank Murphy was about to declare a state of insurrection and order the National Guard to evict the workers. The governor took a copy of his order to Mr. Lewis in his Detroit hotel in an 11th-hour effort to get him to end the strike.

After Mr. Lewis had refused, Governor Murphy asked him what he would do if the Guard were called out. Mr. Lewis replied: "You want my answer, sir? I give it to you. Tomorrow morning, I shall personally enter General Motors plant Chevrolet No. 4. I shall order the men to disregard your order. I shall then walk up to the largest window in the plant, open it, divest myself of my outer raiment, remove my shirt and bare my bosom. Then when you order your troops to fire, mine will be the first breast those bullets will strike.

"And as my body falls from that window to the ground, you listen to the voice of your grandfather [he had been hanged in Ireland by the British for rebellion] as he whispers in your ear, 'Frank, are you sure you are doing the right thing?' "

Color draining from his face and his body quivering, the governor left the room. The order was not issued.

Mr. Lewis was also the master of the oblique approach, which he demonstrated in dealings with Myron Taylor, chairman of the United States Steel Corporation, in 1937. He charmed the industrialist by chatting with him in his Fifth Avenue mansion about Gothic tapestries and statuary. He flattered Mrs. Taylor. He also convinced Mr. Taylor, in a series of conversations, that Big Steel would be wise to recognize the Steel Workers Organizing Committee of the C.I.O. Mr. Taylor, in turn, persuaded other steelmen to deal with Mr. Lewis. The result was a stunning victory for the C.I.O.

A superb orator with a bass-baritone that could shake an auditorium without electrical amplification or that could be muted to a whisper audible in the last rows, Mr. Lewis swayed thousands of emotion-hungry audiences.

With mine operators in wage negotiations Mr. Lewis was equally effective. C. L. Sulzberger, in his book *Sit Down with John L. Lewis,* related this episode from contract talks in the early thirties: "Lewis began to walk up and down. Back and forth he went, deftly, stolidly, with a peculiar, light-footed stride, throwing his chest forward. He stuck a cigar in his mouth, folded his nubby hands behind him.

" 'Gentlemen,' he said, speaking in a slow, tricky way. 'Gentlemen, I speak to you for my people. I speak to you for the miners' families in the broad Ohio Valley, the Pennsylvania mountains and the black West Virginia hills.

" 'There, the shanties lean over as if intoxicated by the smoke fumes of the mine dumps. But the more pretentious ones boast a porch, with the banisters broken here and there, presenting the aspect of a snaggly-tooth child. Some of the windows are wide open to flies, which can feast nearby on garbage and answer the family dinner call in double-quick time.

" 'But there is no dinner call. The little children are gathered around a bare table without anything to eat. Their mothers are saying, "We want bread."

" 'They are not asking for more than a little. They are not asking for a $100,000 yacht like yours, Mr. —,' suddenly pointing his threatening cigar, 'or for a Rolls-Royce limousine like yours, Mr. —,' transfixing him with his beetle-browed gaze. 'A slim crust of bread . . .' "

The operators, according to Mr. Sulzberger's book, squirmed, and one of them muttered, "Tell him to stop. Tell him we'll settle."

On other contract occasions he could be more blunt. In 1949 talks, A. H. Raskin of *The Times* reported, Mr. Lewis intransigently told the chief negotiator for the operators: "You need men and I have all the men and they are in the palm of my hand; and now I ask, 'What am I bid?' "

Many thought Mr. Lewis merely theatrical. In a sense he was, for his histrionics were in the grand manner; but when he was speaking from a position of strength there was nothing hollow about his acting. On the other hand, when he lacked public sympathy—as in his court battles in the late 1940s—he tended to bombast.

Those who crossed Mr. Lewis discovered there was sting to his tongue. When, in 1939, John Nance Garner, then the vice president, took exception to some of the labor leader's views, Mr. Lewis called him "a labor-baiting, poker-playing, whisky-drinking, evil old man."

Of William Green, president of the A.F.L., he once said: "I have done a lot of exploring of Bill's mind and I give you my word there is nothing there."

He characterized Walter Reuther, head of the United Automobile Workers Union, as "an earnest Marxist chronically inebriated, I think, by the exuberance of his own verbosity."

George Meany, president of the A.F.L.-C.I.O., was dismissed as "an honest plumber trying to abolish sin in the labor movement."

Mr. Lewis's showmanship sometimes tended to obscure his matchless fund of knowledge about coal production and marketing. In appearances before congressional committees he was the professor lecturing sophomores on fuel economics.

He was also exceedingly well read in the classics of English literature, in the Bible, in Napoleonic lore, in American history and in labor-industry problems. His talk was laced with literary allusions.

Mr. Lewis was often pictured as a radical, especially by those who opposed his type of trade unionism. Basically, however, Mr. Lewis's economic and political views tended to be conservative. A Republican in the 1920s, he was twice considered for appointment as secretary of labor. He supported President Roosevelt in 1936 and was on close personal terms with him until the outbreak of World War II in Europe in 1939, when, fearing American involvement, he switched to Wendell L. Willkie, the Republican leader. He later fell out with President Truman, and, although he never again became an ardent Republican, neither was he a staunch Democrat.

Although much of the public may have equated Mr. Lewis with bellicosity, he was actually an amiable and courtly person, possessed of a nimble wit and a pleasant laugh. In private he was also gracious and conciliatory, and he was hospitable, even to those with whom he disagreed.

"I am not disappointed about anything," he remarked toward the close of his active union leadership, when it was suggested that he had failed to exercise enduring labor and political influence. "When you see those editorials about me being a bitter, disappointed old man, just remember that I do my laughing in private."

Mr. Lewis, whose salary rose over the years to $50,000 a year plus expenses, was not a flashy liver. He had a modest, book-lined house on a quiet street in Alexandria, Va., and shunned most Washington parties.

Fastidious about the trim of his hair and his sartorial appearance, he had a fondness for well-tailored suits and excellent shirts and ties. He liked to travel in high-powered cars and he liked to lunch at the Sheraton-Carlton in Washington. But he passed up gourmet viands for meals of steak or roast beef and potatoes, topped off with banana cream pie, which accounted for his weight of 230 pounds in his earlier years. He occasionally sipped a glass of sherry or a weak highball for sociability's sake. He smoked Havana cigars, or sometimes chewed them unlighted.

John Lewis was born to the coal mines and to unionism. His father was Thomas Lewis, a miner who had emigrated from Wales to Lucas, Iowa. His mother, Louisa Watkins Lewis, was also Welsh and the daughter of a miner. John, their first child—

there were in all six sons and two daughters—was born Feb. 12, 1880, in Lucas.

For his role in a Knights of Labor strike, Thomas Lewis was blacklisted for several years, and talk of militant trade unionism and of the miners' hazardous lot filled John's childhood.

The youngster left school after the seventh grade and was toiling in the mines at 15. In his leisure time he organized both a debating and a baseball team. And he read, at first planlessly and then guided by Myrta Bell, the daughter of a Lucas physician, who became his wife in 1907.

But before that, when John was 21, he left Lucas and wandered the West as a casual laborer for five years. He mined copper in Montana, silver in Utah, coal in Colorado, gold in Arizona.

Returning to Lucas and a mine job, he was elected a delegate to the national convention of the United Mine Workers, which traced its history to 1849. It was his first step to union leadership. The next was to move to Panama, Ill., with his five brothers, and in a year he was president of the local mine union there.

He shortly became Illinois lobbyist for the union and, in 1911, he was named general field agent for the A.F.L. by Samuel Gompers, then its president. This gave him a chance to travel widely and to get to know the ins and outs of labor politics. One result was that Mr. Lewis built a large personal following in the mine union, for which he became chief statistician in 1917 and later that year vice president. In 1920 he became president, an office he did not relinquish for 40 years.

In World War I he sat on the National Defense Council, where he successfully opposed proposals for government operation of the mines. His first major confrontation with the government occurred in 1919 in a strike of 400,000 miners. It was denounced by President Woodrow Wilson, and Mr. Lewis sent his men back to the pits after the government had obtained an injunction.

All through the 1920s Mr. Lewis worked to consolidate his power in the union and to enlarge its membership. He fought the operators on the one hand and the Communists on the other. He earned a reputation as a Red-baiter and for his imagination for "Moscow plots." He purged his union opponents from time to time on, it was said, flimsy charges.

His attitude toward the Communists softened in the 1930s, when party members were among the most active organizers of the C.I.O. Chided, he retorted: "Industry should not complain if we allow Communists in our organization. Industry employs them."

The genesis of the C.I.O. was in the plague years of the Depression when unemployment mounted to 15 million workers. Union working and wage standards were toppled; the A.F.L. lost thousands of members, and with them its effectiveness. The mine union itself dropped to 100,000 members.

At the same time it became evident that organization of workers by skilled crafts, which was the basis of the A.F.L., was unrealistic in most major industries, where unskilled or semiskilled workers constituted the majority of employees. This situation led to the C.I.O.'s efforts to organize the unorganized.

That was made possible in part by Section 7A of the National Industrial Recovery Act, adopted in 1933 as part of President Roosevelt's attempt to reverse the Depression. Section 7A, often called Labor's Magna Carta, gave workers the right to organize and bargain collectively through representatives of their choice. It was Mr. Lewis who was chiefly instrumental in getting the section into the N.I.R.A.

With its adoption he sent scores of organizers into the coal fields with the cry, "The president wants you to join the union," and in two years membership rose to 400,000.

The C.I.O. came into being after the A.F.L. convention of 1935, in which tensions between industrial and craft unions erupted in a fistfight between William Hutcheson of the Carpenters Union and Mr. Lewis. When the convention adjourned, Mr. Lewis met to form the C.I.O. with, among others, Charles P. Howard of the International Typographical Union; David Dubinsky of the International Ladies Garment Workers; Thomas McMahon of the Textile Workers; and Sidney Hillman of the Amalgamated Clothing Workers.

Subsequently these and other unions backing the C.I.O. were expelled from the A.F.L., but it was an empty gesture for, virtually from the outset, workers responded to the C.I.O. campaigns in the basic industries. First autos capitulated, then Big Steel, then others, until four million workers were enrolled in C.I.O. unions. But the steady procession of successes was interrupted in late 1937 by Little Steel, the smaller fabricators, and especially by Tom Girdler of Republic Steel.

The Little Steel strike, an old-fashioned walkout, was marked by violence. In Chicago on Memorial Day the police shot and killed 10 strikers and sympathizers, and there was sporadic shooting elsewhere. In the course of the strike, which was lost, President Roosevelt was asked what he thought of the dispute. "A plague on both your houses," he replied, a remark that enraged Mr. Lewis, whose union had contributed $500,000—$120,000 as an outright gift—to the president's 1936 campaign. His retort was: "It ill behooves one who has supped at labor's table and who has been sheltered in labor's house to curse with equal fervor and fine impartiality both labor and its adversaries when they become locked in deadly embrace."

Mr. Lewis followed this excoriation with others equally acerbic in the campaign of 1940, in which he sought to rally organized labor against the Roosevelt third-term bid. "Sustain me now, or repudiate me," he said in accusing the president of Caesarism. After Mr. Roosevelt won the election Mr. Lewis resigned as head of what was then the Congress of Industrial Organizations, and Philip Murray, a Lewis lieutenant, took over. In 1942, however, Mr. Lewis broke with Mr. Murray, his "former friend," and the mine union left the C.I.O.

Mr. Lewis's period of greatest national influence, waning since 1940, concluded at that point. But from 1935 to 1942, when he symbolized the C.I.O., his name brought millions into the ranks of organized labor. Its magical incantation seemed to these workers to offer the promise of higher wages, better working conditions, union recognition. The name stirred hopes among those who toiled in textile mills, in rubber and tire factories, on the docks, in brass foundries, in shipbuilding, in glass works, in garment and glove shops, and even on the farms.

Mr. Lewis, at that time, was larger than life. But his charisma was diminished after he quit the C.I.O.

Four years later he and his union were back in the A.F.L., but their stay lasted less than two years. Again there was a battle of words, this time over a provision of the Taft-Hartley Act requiring union officials to swear they were not Communists. The A.F.L. was willing to comply with the act; Mr. Lewis was not. To him the law was "damnable, vicious, unwholesome and a slave statute." As for the A.F.L., it had "no head, its neck just growed and haired over." The mine union then went its independent way.

Meantime, Mr. Lewis was tangling with the government. A series of wartime strikes won substantial wage increases, including portal-to-portal pay for the miners. This compensated them for underground travel, from the shaft head to the coal face and return.

Then in the spring of 1946 he called a soft-coal strike in a bid for royalties on each ton of coal mined, the money to go into the union's health and welfare fund. President Truman ordered the mines seized and the strike ended on May 29 with a wage increase and a royalty arrangement. A hard-coal strike followed almost immediately, but it ended quickly on just about the same terms as were obtained in the bituminous fields.

Peace, however, was short-lived. In November Mr. Lewis denounced the contract under which the government had been running the mines. Quickly, on motion of the government, Federal Judge T. Alan Goldsborough issued an order restraining Mr. Lewis from maintaining the contract-termination notice.

President Truman ordered the Justice Department to seek a contempt citation if Mr. Lewis disobeyed the court. And when the union chief made no move to halt the walkout, the judge found him and the union guilty of civil and criminal contempt. A fine of $10,000 was imposed on Mr. Lewis and $3.5 million on the union.

Three days later, Mr. Lewis sent the miners back to work pending appeal of the contempt ruling to the Supreme Court. In a 7–2 decision in March 1947, that tribunal upheld the contempt judgment and the fine against Mr. Lewis. The fine against the union was reduced, however, to $700,000, with $2.8 million more to be assessed if a strike occurred during the government's operation of the mines. Mr. Lewis complied with the court and purged himself and the union of contempt.

In 1948, after the government had returned the mines to the operators, Mr. Lewis was once again in court. The miners were idle in a pension dispute, and Judge Goldsborough ordered Mr. Lewis and the union to end the walkout. Mr. Lewis declined and was fined $20,000 and the union $1.4 million. The fines were eventually paid.

At the mine-union convention in 1948 Mr. Lewis stormed against Mr. Truman for persecuting the union.

"He is a man totally unfitted for the position," Mr. Lewis said of the president. "His principles are elastic. He is careless with the truth. He is a malignant, scheming sort of individual who is dangerous not only to the United Mine Workers but dangerous to the United States of America."

The two men composed their differences before the end of Mr. Truman's tenure, and in 1952 the president reversed a ruling of his Wage Stabilization Board to permit a wage increase that Mr. Lewis had negotiated for the miners.

As a result of the royalty fees that Mr. Lewis won from the mine operators, his union initiated a pension program in 1948.

By his flair for dramatizing the problems of his miners, Mr. Lewis also won a long struggle for federal mine inspection in 1952. When 119 miners perished in a West Frankfort, Ill., mine explosion in 1951, he flew to the scene, inspected the shafts and assailed Congress for failing to enact safety legislation. In dramatic testimony before a Senate subcommittee, he called on Congress to give the federal government power to close unsafe mines.

The Federal Mine Safety Law was enacted. It set up a board of review of which the union's safety director was a member. To insure its passage, Mr. Lewis called a 10-day "memorial" stoppage.

In the 1950s coal lost its dominance as a fuel. Oil and gas became competitive. To meet the crisis Mr. Lewis cooperated with the mine operators in introducing mechanization into coal production. This made it possible in 1952, for example, for 375,000 bituminous miners to produce more coal than double that number could have dug 30 years before.

He also convinced the operators that it was wise to close uneconomic mines and pay high wages in the efficient ones. This was done quietly, in contrast to his former tactics, and by 1955 the miners' daily scale was $20.25—well above the standard in other mass industries. When he stepped down as union chief in 1960, the scale was $24.25 a day. By that time the welfare and pension fund had collected $1.3 billion, had a reserve of $130 million and had aided more than a million persons. Miners were enabled to retire at 60 with a pension of $100 a month. In 1960, a total of 70,000 were receiving these retirement benefits.

In the last years of the 1950s Mr. Lewis clamped down on unauthorized strikes. Laying down the law at the union convention in 1956, he warned fractious miners that "you'll be fully conscious that I'm breathing down your necks" if they struck.

When he announced late in 1959 that he was preparing to retire, the operators expressed regret. They praised him both for his "outstanding ability" and as "an extraordinarily fine person."

In his farewell address to his union he said: "The years have been long and the individual burdens oppressive, yet progress has been great.

"At first, your wages were low, your hours long, your labor perilous, your health disregarded, your children without opportunity, your union weak, your fellow citizens and public representatives indifferent to your wrongs.

"Today, because of your fortitude and your deep loyalty to your union, your wages are the highest in the land, your working hours the lowest, your safety more assured, your health more guarded, your old age protected, your children equal in opportunity with their generation and your union strong with material resources."

He retired on an annual pension of $50,000 and was voted the title of president emeritus.

Mr. Lewis died in Washington on June 11, 1969. He was 89.

CHARLES A. LINDBERGH

1902–1974

By Alden Whitman

In Paris at 10:22 P.M. on May 21, 1927, Charles Augustus Lindbergh, a onetime central Minnesota farm boy, became an international celebrity. A fame enveloped the 25-year-old American that was to last him for the remainder of his life, transforming him in a frenzied instant from an obscure aviator into a historical figure.

The consequences of this fame were to exhilarate him, to involve him in profound grief, to engage him in fierce controversy, to turn him into an embittered fugitive from the public, to accentuate his individualism to the point where he became a loner, to give him a special sense of his own importance, to allow him to play an enormous role in the growth of commercial aviation as well as to be a figure in missile and space technology, to give him influence in military affairs, and to raise a significant voice for conservation, a concern that marked his older years.

All these things were touched off when a former stunt flier and airmail pilot touched down the wheels of his small and delicate monoplane, the *Spirit of St. Louis,* on the tarmac of Le Bourget 33½ hours after having lifted the craft off Roosevelt Field on Long Island. Thousands—no one knows how many—trampled through fences and over guards to surround the silvery plane and to acclaim, in a wild outburst of emotion, the first man to fly the Atlantic solo nonstop from the United States to Europe—a feat that was equivalent in the public mind then to the first human step on the moon 42 years later. Icarus had at last succeeded, a daring man alone had attained the unattainable.

What enhanced the feat for many was that Lindbergh was a tall, handsome bachelor with a becoming smile, an errant lock of blond hair over his forehead and a pleasing outward modesty and guilelessness. He was the flawless El Cid, the gleaming Galahad, Frank Merriwell in the flesh.

The delirium that engulfed Paris swirled out over the civilized world. Banner headlines heralded the event. Medals galore were bestowed on Lindbergh. He was gushed over, adulated, worshiped, feted in France, Belgium and Britain. President Calvin Coolidge sent the cruiser *Memphis,* flagship of the United States European Fleet, to bring him and the *Spirit of St. Louis* back to the United States and later awarded him the Medal of Honor, previously reserved only for military heroes. And already a captain in the United States Officers Reserve Corps, Lindbergh was jumped to a full colonel.

As the cruiser steamed up Chesapeake Bay, she was met by four destroyers, two army blimps and 40 airplanes from the Army, Navy and Marine Corps. Debarking at Washington in a civilian's blue serge suit, Lindbergh was glorified by the president, who said that the transatlantic flight was "the same story of valor and victory by a son of the people that shines through every page of American history."

Missouri Historical Society, St. Louis

The panoplied Washington reception, which was topped by an award—the first in the nation's history—of the Distinguished Flying Cross, was followed by an even noisier outpouring in New York, where four million people spilled into the streets. Ticker tape and confetti rained on the Broadway parade, and the day was climaxed by a banquet for 4,000 guests. "We measure heroes as we do ships, by their displacement," the bewhiskered Charles Evans Hughes told the multitude. "Colonel Lindbergh has displaced everything."

And then there were triumphal parades and receptions, seemingly endless, in other cities. Lindbergh eventually flew the *Spirit of St. Louis* to every state in the Union. Everywhere he went a throng collected. Even a supposedly private visit to Orville Wright, co-inventor of the airplane, was noised about, and crowds appeared.

Lindbergh, at one point, was "so filled up with listening to this hero guff that I was ready to shout murder."

What the parades, the pandemonium, the oratory, the hero worship obscured was that Lindbergh's epic flight was a most minutely planned venture by a professional flier with 2,000 air hours amassed over five years. "Why shouldn't I fly from New York to Paris?" he had asked himself in September 1926. "I have more than four years of aviation behind me. I've barnstormed over half of the 48 states. I've flown my mail through the worst of nights."

There had been two previous Atlantic flights—both in 1919, the first when one of three navy craft flew from Newfoundland to the Azores; and the second when John Alcock and Arthur Brown made it from Newfoundland to Ireland. But no one had made the crossing alone, or from continent to continent.

Once he conceived the notion of the flight, Lindbergh, with characteristic energy, began to elaborate the details. He helped design the plane to his specifications, calculating every ounce that went into it. He laid out his route. Every foreseeable circumstance was checked out.

Two elements could not be figured: the weather and his ability to stay awake. With the weather he took a calculated risk. Fighting off sleep proved a problem, and only his indomitable determination overcame that, although he conceded there were moments of touch-and-go.

One of the attractions for the Paris flight was a $25,000 prize, for which there were several competitors, among them Clarence Chamberlin and Adm. Richard E. Byrd. Lindbergh, though, was confident he could be first and be successful. He was motivated, he told this writer in later years, by a desire to improve his standing as a pilot as well as by an eagerness to win the prize. And although there was great interest in him before takeoff time (his hope and that of his rivals to fly the Atlantic had excited wide newspaper coverage), Lindbergh had not calculated the response to his achievement, the degree to which he would be lionized or the extent to which he would be regarded as public property, especially by reporters and photographers, whom he came quickly to detest.

"The situation I encountered was extraordinary in the extreme, and often fantastic," he recalled, and cited, as an example, a woman who "wanted to rent the hotel room I was leaving so she could take a bath in the same tub."

Overwhelmed, without precedents to guide him, pressed by dizzying demands on his time, Lindbergh was happy to accept an invitation from Harry Guggenheim, a very rich and very conservative financier who was connected with the Daniel Guggenheim Fund for the Promotion of Aeronautics, to escape for a while to his Long Island estate. The invitation was at the suggestion of Dwight Morrow, the Morgan banker, who told Mr. Guggenheim, "Harry, almost everyone in the country is after this young fellow, trying to exploit him. Isn't there something you and the fund can do, to save him from the wolves?"

At Falaise, the Guggenheim castle, which was

perhaps the most opulent private home he had stayed in, the aviator was able to catch his breath for three weeks and rewrite the ghost-written manuscript that became the book *We.* He also retained Henry Breckinridge, a conservative Wall Street lawyer, to help handle his affairs. Many of his new associates held conservative views, which his father, a neo-Populist Republican, spent 20 years fighting.

Lindbergh was not conceived of then as a possible political figure, but rather as a nice young man, perhaps a little unpolished socially, who deserved the best that could be provided. His new friends were considerate of his strong individualism. They did not impose flattery; they were respectful and, above all, helpful. The income from *We* and from his flight articles in *The New York Times* made him a millionaire—a considerable eminence for a man accustomed to thinking hard before he spent $5. His friends helped him invest his fortune.

And after Lindbergh made his goodwill flights around the country and to Latin America in the *Spirit of St. Louis,* his friends saw to it that he got a job in keeping with his interest in aviation and his status. The position was as an adviser in both Pan American World Airways and the predecessor of Trans World Airlines in laying out transatlantic, transcontinental and Caribbean air routes for the commercial aviation that his Paris flight had done so much to popularize.

The conservative views that Lindbergh later articulated, the remarks about Jews that proved so startling when he was opposing American entry into World War II, his adverse opinion of the Soviet Union, his belief in Western civilization—these were all a reflection of a worldview prevalent among his friends, which he absorbed over the years. An engineer and aviator of genius, he was, however, not an intellectual, nor a consistent reader, nor a social analyst.

The assumptions of this elitism accounted for his conviction that "America should lead the world in the development of flight," that "a conflict between English and German groups of nations would [be] a fratricidal war," that race was a valid judgmental concept and that to accomplish an objective one should deal with "the top people." It also accounted for what many people thought was his anti-Semitism.

Lindbergh did not regard himself as an anti-Semite. Indeed, he was shocked a couple of years ago when this writer put the question to him. "Good God, no," he responded, citing his fondness for Jews he had known or dealt with. Nor did he condone the Nazi treatment of German Jews, much less Hitler's genocidal policies. On the other hand, he accepted as fact that American Jewish groups were among those promoting United States involvement in World War II.

He voiced these views in a speech in Des Moines, Iowa, on Sept. 11, 1941. After asserting that those groups responsible for seeking American "entanglement in European affairs" were "the British, the Jewish and the Roosevelt administration," he went on to say: "It is not difficult to understand why Jewish people desire the overthrow of Nazi Germany. The persecution they suffered in Germany would be sufficient to make bitter enemies of any race. No person with a sense of the dignity of mankind can condone the persecution the Jewish race suffered in Germany.

"But no person of honesty and vision can look on their prowar policy here today without seeing the dangers involved in such a policy, both for us and for them.

"Instead of agitating for war, the Jewish groups in this country should be opposing it in every possible way, for they will be among the first to feel its consequences. Tolerance is a virtue that depends upon peace and strength. A few farsighted Jewish people realize this and stand opposed to intervention. But the majority still do not. Their greatest danger to their country lies in their large ownership and influence in our motion pictures, our press, our radio and our government."

The speech evoked a nationwide outcry. Lindbergh, it was said, had not only impugned the patriotism of American Jews, but also had used the word *race,* a word many Jews considered both pejorative and inaccurate. Lindbergh never withdrew his remarks, which he considered statements of "obvious fact." "The violence of the reaction to my naming these groups was significant and extremely interesting," he said 25 years later. "In hindsight, I would not change my action."

Lindbergh's attitude toward the Jews was matched by an adamantine stubbornness on other matters. These together sometimes cast him in an unfavorable public light.

One example of his unwillingness to concede that he might have acted unwisely involved the Service Cross of the German Eagle, a civilian medal that was awarded him in 1938 by Hermann Goering, the Nazi leader, "at the direction" of Hitler. The presentation, a surprise to Lindbergh, was made at a stag dinner in the home of the American ambassador to Berlin and was, he was told, in recognition of his services to aviation, especially his 1927 flight.

The award was reported briefly in the newspapers and stirred little criticism. However, the night of the award Mrs. Lindbergh told her husband that it was "the albatross," and she urged him to return it. Lindbergh took the position then and later that to do so would affront the ambassador, as well as Goering, who was technically his host in Germany.

Although he never wore the medal (he gave it to the Lindbergh collection of the Missouri Historical Society in St. Louis, along with other awards and trophies), it became an issue when he opposed American war involvement. It led, among other things, to his being called a Fascist sympathizer, particularly when he declined a suggestion in 1942 to repudiate it; and the medal plagued his reputation for the rest of his life.

He disdained the criticism, however, saying: "Personally, I am not at all concerned about any damage that may have been done to my reputation by the presentation of the medal.

"I felt the throwing back of the medal was like taking part in a child's spitting contest. If I must fight, I'll fight; but I prefer not to spit at my enemy beforehand. Also, I felt Goering had given me the medal with good intent and in friendship. Regardless of how much I disagreed with him about other things, or later on, I did not want to throw it back in his face."

Nonetheless, Lindbergh, in his later years, was defensive in reciting the medal episode and sensitive in having it known that his wife was among his critics.

Like most people, Lindbergh was a bundle of unresolved contradictions. Stubborn, proud, unable to see how Jews might be offended by "obvious facts," blind to the villainies of Hitlerism, he was, in his relationships with his few close friends, a considerate, delightful, sensitive, helpful, unpretentious person who did not obtrude his social and political views, nor make agreeing with them a condition of steadfast friendship.

Although he was the object of much flattery and one who succumbed to some of it, he did not like a fuss made over him. He sometimes sounded pompous in print, but he was not in person. Indeed, he was a man of genuinely simple tastes who was happier in a sleeping bag than in a luxury hotel, who preferred eating wild boar with his fingers in the jungle to dining in expensive restaurants, who found more inner satisfaction with primitive than with sophisticated people and who was more at ease in knockabout attire than in street dress.

Lindbergh's life, like his personality, was full of shadows and enigmas. Born Feb. 4, 1902, in Detroit, he was the son of C. A. Lindbergh, a prosperous Little Falls, Minn., lawyer and land speculator, and his second wife, Evangeline Lodge Land. The elder Lindbergh's first wife had died, leaving him two daughters. Charles Augustus Lindbergh, Jr., was born in Detroit because his mother's uncle was a physician there. He was returned to Little Falls six weeks later and lived in that small town, the center of a farming and timbering community, with few interruptions until he was 18.

His paternal antecedents were Swedes, who

changed their name from Mansons to Lindbergh when they emigrated from Sweden in 1860. They had a history of independence and vigor. The Lands, of Irish and English background, arrived in the United States shortly after 1812. Lindbergh's maternal grandfather was C. H. Land, a dentist and inventor. Both Dr. Land and C. A. Lindbergh were strong advocates of free inquiry and individual initiative, and both impressed on young Charles the merits of personal independence.

Lindbergh's youth was spent close to nature. His deep feeling for it was encouraged by his father, and these early attitudes surfaced toward the end of his life, when he devoted much of his fantastic energy to the cause of conservation. Also early in life, he showed a marked aptitude for mechanical contrivances. When he was 8 or 9, he worked out an ingenious and complicated system for getting ice from the icehouse into the icebox.

Charles's world was jolted when his father was elected to the House of Representatives, where he served from 1907 to 1917. He went to Washington, his first venture into a metropolis, and disliked it. About that time, his mother and father ceased living together, although for appearance' sake there was no legal separation and both parents took care to give the child a sense of security.

Apart from saying that the separation was "a tragic situation" for his parents, Lindbergh shut his lips about the situation and shied from talking about the psychic hurts that he bore. He was equally taciturn on other personal matters.

The future aviator's interest in flying was sparked in 1908 or 1909, when, one day, he heard a buzzing in the sky and climbed out of a dormer window onto the roof of his home to witness a frail biplane skimming through the clouds.

"Afterward, I remember lying in the grass and looking up at the clouds and thinking how much fun it would be to fly up there among those clouds," he recalled in later years, adding: "I didn't think of the hazards—I was just interested in getting up there in the clouds."

But he was torn for a time by a strong yearning to go to Alaska, a land pictured as a wild frontier and the source of mythic Gold Rush tales. For him Alaska was also the scene of Robert W. Service's verse, some of which he memorized so thoroughly that he could recite it faultlessly in old age.

Although Lindbergh Sr. led an active and exciting political life as a maverick Republican who battled (and helped to overthrow) the entrenched establishment in the House, led an assault on "the money trust" and voted against American entry into World War I, his son was bored by politics and all the speeches. The issues that his father espoused in Congress and later as a Farmer-Laborite supporter of Robert LaFollette failed, so the son said, to make any impressions on him. His mother, too, eschewed political thinking.

In World War I, Lindbergh operated the family farm, leaving it in the fall of 1920 to study engineering at the University of Wisconsin. His grades were poor and he left after a year and a half, but not before learning how to shoot quarters out of the outstretched fingers of his friends at 50 feet with a rifle.

From Wisconsin, he motorcycled to the Nebraska Aircraft Corporation in Lincoln, which was then producing an airplane and giving flying lessons to promote the product. "I can still smell the odor of dope [cellulose acetate or nitrate] that permeated each breath," he said years later in recalling his first close-up view of an aircraft.

Lindbergh took his first flight April 9, 1922. In succeeding months he learned to fly, to wing-walk and to parachute. Of equal importance, he absorbed all there was to know about the planes of that day and the various styles of flying. And he made friends with fliers who passed through Lincoln and with Harlan A. (Bud) Gurney, with whom, among others, he barnstormed over the Midwest. Called Slim by his friends because of his lithe, gangling body and 6-foot-2½-inch height, Lindbergh was billed to the public as "Daredevil Lindbergh" for his stunt feats.

However, he did not solo until April 1923, when

he purchased his first plane, a Jenny, in Georgia. Shortly afterward he began to earn his living as a flier by taking up passengers in various towns at $5 a ride. It was all seat-of-the-pants flying and Lindbergh gloried in it; but he gave it up to enlist in the army in March 1924, so he could attend the army flying school at Brooks Field, San Antonio, Tex. For the first time, he found some joy in textbooks and classes.

Indeed, he was graduated as the top man in his class, and was commissioned a second lieutenant in the Army Air Service Reserve in March 1925. He was by this time an experienced flier. He spent some time as an air circus stunt flier at county fairs and the like before being hired by the Robertson Aircraft Company of St. Louis as the chief pilot on the mail run to Chicago. He made the first run in April 1926. It was the only paycheck job in the normal sense of the word that he ever held.

Meantime, he had made a further commitment to the military by joining the Missouri National Guard, where he taught other pilots and became a first lieutenant.

On one of his flights to Chicago in September 1926, he was musing about the possibilities of long-distance trips, and he "startled" himself by thinking "I could fly nonstop between New York and Paris."

In many ways, Lindbergh's life was a series of responses to imperatives. When he became convinced that he "ought" to do something—he ought to oppose entry into World War II, he ought to speak out for conservation—he reacted with vigor and dispatch. And virtually immediately he began to plan the details of the trip—getting financial backing, getting a specially designed plane, mapping the route, seeking to eliminate any chance of failure.

Ultimately, he persuaded a group of St. Louis businessmen to put up $15,000, which was one reason why the plane was called the *Spirit of St. Louis.* After many racking incidents, the Ryan Company, with Lindbergh's help, designed and built a craft tailored for him, and the Wright Company built an engine of 223 horsepower to accommodate the plane.

For several years after the Paris flight, Lindbergh lived in the glare of publicity and popping camera flashbulbs. The public would not let him alone. "I recall stepping out of a building on Wall Street, and having almost everyone on the street turn and follow me," he said. He was regarded as a sort of oracle, and his opinion was solicited on every conceivable subject.

He was, moreover, linked falsely in the press with a number of women. His interest, however, was in Anne Spencer Morrow, the beautiful blue-eyed daughter of Dwight Morrow, then ambassador to Mexico. The couple met in Mexico City at Christmastime in 1927, when Miss Morrow, then a Smith student, went there for the holidays. They were married in a private ceremony in the Morrow home in New Jersey on May 27, 1929.

The marriage was a union of opposites. Sensitive, retiring, a poet, Mrs. Lindbergh wanted nothing so much as a life of peace and quiet. Seldom coddling her, her husband proved hyperactive, happy to be a nomad who was rarely at home for long periods. Yet despite some moments of tension, the marriage was an enduring and affectionate one.

For a while Mrs. Lindbergh accompanied her husband on many of his trips—to the Caribbean, where he was laying out air routes; to Europe and to Asia. He had taught her to fly, and she learned to navigate and to operate a Morse code radio. *North to the Orient* is her chronicle of one of these flights.

Their first child, Charles Augustus 3d, was born June 24, 1930. Twenty months later, when Mrs. Lindbergh was pregnant with their second child, the baby was kidnapped from his nursery in his parents' home in Hopewell, N.J. The date was March 1, 1932. On May 12 the baby's body was found in a shallow grave not far from the house.

In between, there was a bizarre hunt for the child that included payment of a $50,000 ransom at a cemetery in the Bronx and a cast of characters that ranged from Dr. John F. (Jafsie) Condon, a school principal, to Gaston B. Means, a swindler. There were false leads and sensations galore, through all of which Lindbergh bore himself with great public stoicism.

His private emotions were never disclosed, and about the only references that he made in later years to the kidnapping and murder were fleeting mentions of "that New Jersey business."

If public attention glared on Lindbergh during the hunt for his son, it positively poured down on him with the arrest and trial of Bruno Richard Hauptmann, a Bronx carpenter, in 1934. The trial, which Lindbergh attended daily, was reported with diligence and sensationalism. Lindbergh received up to 100,000 letters a week, and the Hopewell estate, which he had long since left, was overrun with curiosity seekers, one of whom dug up and lugged off the earth where the baby was found buried.

After a six-week trial, in which a web of circumstantial evidence was woven about Hauptmann, he was found guilty and executed. Although there were doubts (Hauptmann, the German-born father of a son about the age of Lindbergh's son, denied he was guilty), Lindbergh was satisfied that "Hauptmann did the thing."

Meantime, there were new threats to kidnap Lindbergh's second son, Jon, and the family was living an abnormal existence. Lindbergh was telling friends that Americans exhibited "a morbid curiosity over crimes and murder trials" and lacked "respect for law, or the rights of others." Against this background, Lindbergh took his family to England to seek a safe, secluded residence away from "the tremendous public hysteria" that surrounded him in the United States.

One result of the case was passage of the so-called Lindbergh law, which made kidnapping a federal crime. Part of the statute was ruled unconstitutional in 1967.

Before departing, Lindbergh completed a scientific project on which he had been working with dedication and enthusiasm since 1930. It was the design and building of a tissue-perfusion apparatus at Rockefeller Institute (now University) in New York. He was introduced to the project by Dr. Alexis Carrel, who had won the Nobel Prize for physiology and medicine in 1912 for development of blood vessel transplant procedures. The French-born Carrel was interested in the 1930s in living organs outside the body, and the problem was to devise an instrument to perfuse these organs and keep them alive.

"For me," Lindbergh recalled, "that began an association with an extraordinarily great man. To me, his true greatness lay in the unlimited penetration, curiosity and scope of his mind, in his fearlessness of opinion, in his deep concerns about the trends of modern civilization and their effect on his fellow man."

In addition to perfecting a pump—an important breakthrough in its time—Lindbergh invented a quick way of separating serum from whole blood by means of a centrifuge. The Lindbergh-Carrel friendship lasted for 14 years, until the scientist's death in 1944.

A brilliant investigator, Carrel tinkered with philosophy and other matters; and his thoughts in these areas were sometimes quirky. He believed, for example, in extrasensory perception. He also spoke against "industrial civilization" and suggested that "we ought to try to produce a certain number of individuals above the mental stature we observe in the best." He said, moreover, that "only the elite make the progress of the masses possible."

Some of these notions rubbed off on Lindbergh and were reflected in his little-known book, *Of Flight and Life,* in which he inveighed against "scientific materialism." In this 1948 book, he said, "I believe the values we are creating and the standards we are now following will lead to the end of our civilization, and that if we do not control our science by a higher moral force, it will destroy us with its materialistic values."

In his plea for the recognition of metaphysical values, Lindbergh wrote: "To progress, even to survive, we must learn to apply the truths of God to the actions and relationships of men, to the direction of our science. We must learn from the sermons of

Christ, the wisdom of Laotzu, the teachings of Buddha."

But Lindbergh, in this book, also espoused a doctrine of American superiority in the world. "For Americans, the doctrine of universal equality is a doctrine of death," he wrote. "If we ever become an equal people among other peoples of the world, our civilization will fall."

When Lindbergh went abroad to live, first in Britain and then in France, he was 33 years old. He was immediately treated with courtesy and respect—and given the privacy he so much desired. His new friends were in the upper reaches of British society and Tory politics.

Moreover, as a distinguished aviator, he was invited to visit airplane factories in France by the French Air Ministry. He was also invited by the German government to inspect the Luftwaffe and warplane factories in the Reich. He received red-carpet treatment, visited many factories and was told repeatedly that the Nazis were eager "to create an air force second to none." He visited Germany several times before 1938 and was increasingly impressed with the quality of the air force.

It seemed to him all the more fearsome by comparison with the air arm in Britain, France and the Soviet Union. By 1939 he had concluded that the power of the Luftwaffe was overwhelming, and that the air forces of other European countries were comparatively insignificant. In off-the-record conversations with the leaders of these countries, the Soviet Union excepted, he sought to warn them of the perils they were facing.

Neither then nor later did Lindbergh, according to his journals, believe that German air power would be the decisive factor in a war so much as it would be an essential element. And he said he sought to impress on France, Britain and the United States the need to bestir themselves.

Lindbergh and his family returned to the United States in 1939 shortly before World War II broke out. He felt he ought to do all he could to prevent American involvement. Not a pacifist or an isolationist, he was a noninterventionist.

"My opposition to World War II resulted from the growing conviction that such a war would probably devastate Europe, kill millions of men and possibly result in the end of Western civilization," he told this writer a few years ago, adding: "Under the circumstances of prewar Europe, I concluded that Germany could not be defeated without the active intervention of the United States. I doubted that Germany could be defeated even with American intervention.

"Obviously this depended a great deal on the relationship between Germany and Russia. But if Germany were defeated, it seemed to me almost certain that Russia would be the real victor and that a Stalin-dominated Europe would be even worse than a Hitler-dominated Europe.

"I felt that the wisest policy for Western powers would be to arm, stay neutral and let Germany and Russia clash—and thereafter to feel their way according to changing circumstances. I still think this would have been the wisest policy."

Lindbergh made his first antiwar speech—a radio talk—on Sept. 17, 1939. It was arranged by Fulton Lewis, a well-known conservative commentator.

In the months that followed, he made other radio speeches and worked actively with other antiwar personalities in public and private life, including Sen. Burton K. Wheeler of Montana; Sen. Harry F. Byrd of Virginia; former President Herbert Hoover; Sen. William Borah of Idaho; Henry Ford; Merwin K. Hart, an avowed right-winger; William Castle, a diplomat; Dean Carl Ackerman of the Columbia Journalism School; Theodore Roosevelt, Jr.; and James E. Van Zandt, head of the American Legion.

Lindbergh spoke and worked under his own auspices until April 1941, when he joined the national board of the America First Committee, the country's principal antiwar group. Although its membership was heterogeneous, its effective leadership rested with Robert E. Wood, board chairman of Sears, Roebuck & Co., and Robert R. McCormick, publisher of the Chicago *Tribune.* Both were arch-conservatives and zealous haters of President Franklin D. Roosevelt.

America First was strongest in the Midwest, the traditional seat of the nation's isolationist attitudes; but it was also a powerful force in New York and Boston. Popular support for its antiwar objectives was widespread, and Lindbergh epitomized that support. He rallied millions to the cause with such effectiveness that Roosevelt considered him a major threat.

The president vented his anger at a news conference in April 1941. Roosevelt was asked why he did not call Lindbergh, an army officer, into uniform. The reason, he replied, was that Lindbergh was a defeatist, and he went on to compare him with Representative Clement L. Vallandigham, a Civil War congressman from Ohio, the chief spokesman of a group called the Copperheads, who said the North could never win. Roosevelt's attack was perhaps set off by a Lindbergh magazine article that declared, "While our leaders have shouted for peace, they have consistently directed us toward war."

Considering his honor impugned, Lindbergh resigned his commission. "If I did not tender my resignation," he said in the published version of his *Wartime Journals,* "I would lose something in my own character that means even more to me than my commission in the Air Corps.

"No one else would know it, but I would. And if I take this insult from Roosevelt, more, and worse, will be probably be forthcoming."

Thirty years later Lindbergh still felt wronged by the president, and professed not to see that he himself had questioned Roosevelt's integrity.

With Pearl Harbor, America First collapsed and Lindbergh sought to join the armed forces. "Now that we are at war I want to contribute as best I can to my country's war effort," he wrote. "It is vital for us to carry on this war as intelligently, as constructively, and as successfully as we can, and I want to do my part."

His bid to soldier was rebuffed, however, an action for which he blamed Roosevelt personally. Lindbergh, then 39, joined the Ford Motor Company as a consultant, working at the Willow Run plant in Michigan, which was producing bombers. Later he was a consultant to the United Aircraft Corporation, attached chiefly to its Vought-Sikorsky Division in Stratford, Conn. Vought was producing the Navy Corsair F4U. As part of his job, Lindbergh traveled to the Pacific war area in 1944 to study the Corsair under service conditions, and, as a civilian, flew 50 missions against the Japanese.

The flier had at least one very close brush with death, in a dogfight near Biak Island. He described this and other combat episodes in the *Wartime Journals,* and they constitute the best writing in the book.

After the war, Lindbergh went to Germany for the Naval Technical Mission in Europe to study developments in Nazi aircraft and missiles. He had been interested in rocketry since 1929, when he sought out Dr. Robert Goddard, then an obscure physics professor at Clark University, in Worcester, Mass. (Goddard, who had been ridiculed for his ideas, has since been recognized as a space flight pioneer.)

Lindbergh was always proud of his association with Goddard and of having raised money to fund his experiments. For 16 years, until his death in 1945, Goddard, also a loner, received Lindbergh's help and encouragement; and Goddard's basic rocketry patents were used in the development of United States missiles after the war. The aviator's crucial assistance to Goddard did not become well known until Goddard's biography was published in 1963, a book for which Lindbergh wrote an introduction.

For more than 15 years after the war Lindbergh virtually disappeared from the news. He was a member of Army Ordnance's CHORE project at the University of Chicago; he was consultant to the Secretary of the Air Force; he took part in the reorganization of the Strategic Air Command; and he was a member of scientific ballistic missile committees of the Air Force and the Defense Department. In 1954, he was commissioned a brigadier general in the Air Force Reserve.

Much of the aviator's work in these years dealt with security-classified projects; but it is believed that he was active in rocketry and space flight programs, where his technical expertise was valuable. He enjoyed top-secret clearance, and spoke of his tasks as having to do with security.

In this period, Lindbergh completed his autobiographical account of his 1927 flight, which had been written in bits and pieces in various parts of the world over 14 years. *The Spirit of St. Louis,* published in 1953, won the Pulitzer Prize for biography in 1954 and was made into a movie three years later, with James Stewart as the lead. The book was intended to supersede *We,* which, written in haste, had never satisfied the aviator as an accurate account of his flight.

Starting sometime after the war, he rejoined Pan American as a consultant for the nominal fee of $600 a month. The job, which eventually led to his working on the design specifications for the Boeing 747, allowed him great freedom to travel and to develop any interest he chose. And travel he did, seemingly having no settled abode.

In Africa, in 1964, he found an interest that was to occupy his last years and to bring him out of his public reticence and reclusiveness. The issue was conservation.

"Lying under an acacia tree with the sounds of the dawn around me," he recalled, "I realized more clearly the facts that man should never overlook: that the construction of an airplane, for instance, is simple when compared to the evolutionary achievement of a bird; that airplanes depend on an advanced civilization, and that where civilization is most advanced few birds exist.

"I realized that if I had to choose, I would rather have birds than airplanes."

He concluded, he said, "that I ought to do something."

That imperative, which unfolded slowly, led him to activity in conservation organizations, to having a large hand in saving the humpback and the blue whales, to concern for endangered species and to public advocacy of steps to save the world's environment.

He made his first public speech in 1968—the first since 1941—to the Alaska legislature. The following year he granted what amounted to his first newspaper interview in 35 years, to *The New York Times.*

Lindbergh said that he had unveiled himself because he thought the cause of conservation so urgent. "I have had enough publicity for 15 lives," he said, "and I seek no more of it, but where I can accomplish a purpose I will do things I otherwise abhor."

There was no doubt that his leadership was effective.

Even though he was talking to a generation born long after his Paris flight, his person and his name evoked a tangible response. He did not pretend to be an expert, but had a singular ability to stir response and activity, to enunciate general principles and to cheer people on.

This was, perhaps, the ultimate enigma of his life; for beneath his outer coating was a man who kept more to himself (and perhaps to his wife) than he ever gave to the public.

Charles A. Lindbergh died Aug. 26, 1974, at his simple seaside home in Kipahulu, Maui, Hawaii. He was 72 years old.

LUCK ISN'T ENOUGH [1927]

CAPTAIN CHARLES A. LINDBERGH

PARIS, MAY 22, 1927—Well, here I am in the hands of American Ambassador Herrick. From what I have seen of it, I am sure I am going to like Paris.

It isn't part of my plans to fly my plane back to the United States, although that doesn't mean I have finished my flying career. If I thought that was going to be the result of my flight across the Atlantic, you may be sure I would never have undertaken it. Indeed, I hope that I will be able to do some flying over here in Europe—that is, if the souvenir hunters left enough of my plane last night.

Incidentally, that reception I got was the most dangerous part of the whole flight. If wind and storm had handled me as vigorously as that Reception Committee of Fifty Thousand I would never have reached Paris and wouldn't be eating a 3-o'-clock-in-the-afternoon breakfast here in Uncle Sam's Embassy.

There's one thing I wish to get straight about this flight. They call me "Lucky," but luck isn't enough. As a matter of fact, I had what I regarded and still regard as the best existing plane to make the flight from New York to Paris. I had what I regard as the best engine, and I was equipped with what were in the circumstances the best possible instruments for making such efforts. I hope I made good use of what I had.

That I landed with considerable gasoline left means that I had recalled the fact that so many flights had failed because of lack of fuel, and that was one mistake I tried to avoid.

All in all, I couldn't complain of the weather. It wasn't what was predicted. It was worse in some places and better in others. In fact, it was so bad once that for a moment there came over me the temptation to turn back. But then I figured it was probably just as bad behind me as in front of me, so I kept on toward Paris.

As you know, We (that's my ship and I) took off rather suddenly. We had a report somewhere around 4 o'clock in the afternoon before that the weather would be fine, so we thought we would try it.

We had been told we might expect good weather mostly during the whole of the way. But we struck fog and rain over the coast not far from the start. Actually, it was comparatively easy to get to Newfoundland, but real bad weather began just about dark, after leaving Newfoundland, and continued until about four hours after daybreak. We hadn't expected that at all, and it sort of took us by surprise, morally and physically. That was when I began to think about turning back.

Then sleet began, and, as all aviators know, in a sleet storm one may be forced down in a very few minutes. It got worse and worse. There, above and below me, and on both sides, was that driving storm. I made several detours trying to get out of it, but in vain. I flew as low as ten feet above the water and then mounted up to ten thousand feet. Along toward morning the storm eased off, and I came down to a comparatively low level.

I had seen one ship just before losing sight of Newfoundland, and I saw the glow of several others afterward through the mist and storm. During the day I saw no ships until near Ireland.

I had, as I said, no trouble before I hit the storm I referred to. We had taken off at 7:55 in the morning. The field was slightly damp and soft, so the take-off was longer than it would have been otherwise. I had no trouble getting over the houses and trees. I kept out of the way of every obstacle and was careful not to take any unnecessary chances. As soon as I cleared everything, the motor was throttled down to three-fourths and kept there during the whole flight, except when I tried to climb over the storm.

Soon after starting I was out of sight of land for 300 miles, from Cape Cod over the sea to Nova Scotia. The motor was acting perfectly and was carrying well the huge load of 451 gallons of gasoline and 20 gallons of oil, which gave my ship the greatest cruising radius of any plane of its type.

I passed over St. John's, N.F., purposely going out of my way a few miles to check up. I went right through the narrow pass, going down so low that it could be definitely established where I was at that hour. That was the last place I saw before taking to the open sea.

I had made preparations before I started for a forced landing if it became necessary, but after I started I never thought much about the possibility of such a landing. I was ready for it, but I saw no use thinking about it, inasmuch as one place would have been about as good or as bad as another.

Despite the talk about my periscope, I had no trouble in regard to visibility. The view I had on both sides was quite good enough for navigating the ocean, and the purpose of the periscope was only to enable me to see any obstacle directly in front of me. The periscope was useful in starting from New York and landing in Paris. Other than that I used it very little. I kept a map in front of me and an instrument showing practically where I was all of the time.

Shortly after leaving Newfoundland I began to see icebergs. There was a low fog and even through it I could make out bergs clearly. It began to get very cold, but I was well prepared for cold. I had on ordinary flying clothing, but I was down in the cockpit, which protected me, and I never suffered from the weather.

Within an hour after leaving the coast it became dark. Then I struck clouds and decided to try to get over them. For a while I succeeded, at a height of 10,000 feet. I flew at this height until early morning. The engine was working beautifully and I was not sleepy at all. I felt just as if I was driving a motorcar over a smooth road, only it was easier.

Then it began to get light and the clouds got higher. I went under some and over others. There was sleet in all of those clouds and the sleet began to cling to the plane. That worried me a great deal and I debated whether I should keep on or go back. I decided I must not think any more about going back. I realized that it was henceforth only a question of getting there. It was too far to turn back.

The engine was working perfectly, and that cheered me. I was going along a hundred miles an hour and I knew that if the motor kept on turning I would get there. After that I thought only about navigating, and then I thought that I wasn't so badly off after all.

It was true that the flight was thirty-four hours long, and that at almost any moment in it a forced landing might be what you might call "rather interesting," but I remembered that the flying boys I knew back home spent some hours almost every week in bad flying when a forced landing would have been just as bad for them as a forced landing would have been for me. Those boys don't get credit for it, that's all, and without doubt in a few years many people will be taking just as many chances as I took.

The only real danger I had was at night. In the daytime I knew where I was going, but in the evening and at night it was largely a matter of guesswork. However, my instruments were so good that I never could get more than 200 miles off my course, and that was easy to correct, and I had enough extra gasoline to take care of a number of such deviations. All in all, the trip over the Atlantic, especially the latter half, was much better than I expected.

Laymen have made a great deal of the fact that I sailed without a navigator and without the ordinary stock of navigation instruments, but my real director was my earth inductor compass. I also had a magnetic compass, but it was the inductor compass which guided me so faithfully that I hit the Irish coast only three miles from the theoretic point that I might have hit if I had had a navigator. I replaced a navigator's weight by the inductor compass. This compass behaved so admirably that I am ashamed to hear anyone talk about my luck. Maybe I am lucky, but all the same I knew at every moment where I was going.

The inductor compass is based on the principle of the relation between the earth's magnetic field and the magnetic field generated in the airplane. When the course has been set so that the needle registered zero on this compass, any deviation, from any cause, would cause the needle to swing away from zero in the direction of the error. By flying the plane with the needle at an equal distance on the other side of zero and for about the same time the error had been committed, the plane would be back on her course again. This inductor compass was so accurate that I really needed no other guide.

Fairly early in the afternoon I saw a fleet of fishing boats. On some of them I could see no one, but on one of them I saw some men and flew down, almost touching the craft, and yelled at them, asking if I was on the right road to Ireland.

They just stared. Maybe they didn't hear me. Or maybe they thought I was just a crazy fool.

An hour later I saw land. I have forgotten just what time it was. It must have been shortly before 4 o'clock. It was rocky land and all my study told me it was Ireland. And it was Ireland!

I slowed down and flew low enough to study the land and be sure of where I was and, believe me, it was a beautiful sight. It was the most wonderful-looking piece of natural scenery I have ever beheld.

After I had made up my mind that it was Ireland, the right place for me to strike rather than Spain or some other country, the rest was child's play. I had my course all marked out carefully from approximately the place where I hit the coast, and you know it is quite easy to fly over strange territory if you have good maps and your course prepared.

I flew quite low enough over Ireland to be seen, but apparently no great attention was paid to me. I also flew low over England, mounted a little over the Channel and then came down close to land when I passed a little west of Cherbourg. From Cherbourg I headed for the Seine and followed it upstream.

I noticed it gets dark much later over here than in New York and I was thankful for that. What especially pleased me was the ease with which I followed my course after hitting the coast of Ireland.

When I was about half an hour away from Paris I began to see rockets and Very lights [pyrotechnic signals using balls of fire] sent up from the airfield, and I knew I was all right.

I saw an immense vertical electric sign, which I made out to be the Eiffel Tower. I circled Paris once and immediately saw Le Bourget [the aviation field], although I didn't know at first what it was. I saw a lot of lights, but in the dark I couldn't make out any hangars. I sent Morse signals as I flew over the field, but no one appears to have seen them. The only mistake in all my calculations was that I thought Le Bourget was northeast rather than east of Paris.

Fearing for a moment that the field I had seen—remember I couldn't see the crowd—was some other airfield than Le Bourget, I flew back over Paris to the northwest, looking for Le Bourget. I was slightly confused by the fact that whereas in America when a ship is to land, beacons are put out when floodlights are turned on, at Le Bourget both beacons and floodlights were going at the same time.

I was anxious to land where I was being awaited. So when I didn't find another airfield, I flew back toward the first lights I had seen, and flying low I saw the lights of numberless automobiles. I decided that was the right place, and I landed.

I appreciated the reception which had been prepared for me, and had intended taxiing up to the front of the hangars, but no sooner had my plane touched ground than a human sea swept toward it. I saw there was danger of killing people with my propeller, and I quickly came to a stop.

That reception was the most dangerous part of the trip. Never in my life have I seen anything like that human sea. It isn't clear to me yet just what happened. Before I knew it I had been hoisted out of the cockpit, and one moment was on the shoulders of some men and the next moment on the ground.

It seemed to be even more dangerous for my plane than for me. I saw one man tear away the switch and another took something out of the cockpit. Then, when they started cutting pieces of cloth from the wings, I struggled to get back to the plane, but it was impossible.

A brave man with good intentions tried to clear a way for me with a club. Swinging the club back, he caught me on the back of the head.

It isn't true that I was exhausted. I was tired, but I wasn't exhausted.

Several French officers asked me to come away with them and I went, casting anxious glances at my ship. I haven't seen it since, but I am afraid it suffered. I would regret that very much because I want to use it again.

But I must remember that crowd did welcome me. Good Lord! There must have been a million of them. Other men will fly the Atlantic as I did, but I think it safe to guess that none of them will get any warmer reception than I got.

Finally I got here to Ambassador Herrick's house and I have certainly been all right since then.

I don't know how long I will stay in Paris. It looks like a good place. I have been asked if I intend to fly back to New York. I don't think I shall try that. But I certainly hope to get to do a little flying over here. Flying is my job and because I did this job successfully it doesn't mean I'm through.

I look forward to the day when transatlantic flying will be a regular thing. It is a question largely of money. If people can be found willing to spend enough to make proper preparations, there is no reason why it can't be made very practical. Of course, there are many things to be studied, one of the important points being whether the single-motor or multi-motor ship is best. I understand there is soon to be a transatlantic flight made with a tri-motor plane. [This is evidently a reference to Commander Byrd's projected flight in the *America*.]

I didn't bring any extra clothes with me. I am wearing a borrowed suit now. It was a case of clothes or gasoline, and I took the gasoline. I have a check on a Paris bank and am going to cash it tomorrow morning, buy shirts, socks, and other things. I expect to have a good time in Paris.

But I do want to do a little flying over here.

LINDBERGH DOES IT!
To Paris in 33½ Hours; Flies 1,000 Miles Through Snow and Sleet; Cheering French Carry Him Off Field

EDWIN L. JAMES

PARIS, MAY 21, 1927—Lindbergh did it. Twenty minutes after 10 o'clock tonight suddenly and softly there slipped out of the darkness a gray-white airplane as 25,000 pairs of eyes strained toward it. At 10:24 the *Spirit of St. Louis* landed and lines of soldiers, ranks of policemen and stout steel fences went down before a mad rush as irresistible as the tides of the ocean.

"Well, I made it," smiled Lindbergh, as the little white monoplane came to a halt in the middle of the field and the first vanguard reached the plane. Lindbergh made a move to jump out. Twenty hands reached for him and lifted him out as if he were a baby. Several thousands were around the plane in a minute. Thousands more broke the barriers of iron rails round the field, cheering wildly.

As he was lifted to the ground Lindbergh was pale, and with his hair unkempt, he looked completely worn out. He had strength enough, however, to smile, and waved his hand to the crowd. Soldiers with fixed bayonets were unable to keep back the crowd.

United States Ambassador Herrick was among the first to welcome and congratulate the hero.

A *New York Times* man was one of the first to reach the machine after its graceful descent to the field. Those first to arrive at the plane had a picture that will live in their minds for the rest of their lives. His cap off, his famous locks falling in disarray around his eyes, "Lucky Lindy" sat peering out over over the rim of the little cockpit of his machine.

It was high drama. Picture the scene. Almost if not quite 100,000 people were massed on the east side of Le Bourget airfield. Some of them had been there six and seven hours.

Off to the left, the giant phare lighthouse of Mount Valerien flashed its guiding light 300 miles into the air. Closer on the left, Le Bourget Lighthouse twinkled, and off to the right another giant revolving phare sent its beams high into the heavens.

Big arc lights on all sides with enormous electric glares were flooding the landing field. From time to time rockets rose and burst in varied lights over the field.

Seven-thirty, the hour announced for the arrival, had come and gone. Then 8 o'clock came, and no Lindbergh; at 9 o'clock the sun had set but then came reports that Lindbergh had been seen over

Cork. Then he had been seen over Valentia in Ireland and then over Plymouth.

Suddenly a message spread like lightning: the aviator had been seen over Cherbourg. However, remembering the messages telling of Captain Nungesser's flight, the crowd was skeptical.

"One chance in a thousand!" "Oh, he cannot do it without navigating instruments!" "It's a pity, because he was a brave boy." Pessimism had spread over the great throng by 10 o'clock.

The stars came out and a chill wind blew.

Suddenly the field lights flooded their glares onto the landing ground and there came the roar of an airplane's motor. The crowd was still, then began a cheer, but two minutes later the landing glares went dark for the searchlight had identified the plane and it was not Captain Lindbergh's.

Stamping their feet in the cold, the crowd waited patiently. It seemed quite apparent that nearly everyone was willing to wait all night, hoping against hope.

Suddenly—it was 10:16 exactly—another motor roared over the heads of the crowd. In the sky one caught a glimpse of a white-gray plane, and for an instant heard the sound of one. Then it dimmed, and the idea spread that it was yet another disappointment.

Again landing lights glared and almost by the time they had flooded the field the gray-white plane had lighted on the far side nearly half a mile from the crowd. It seemed to stop almost as it hit the ground, so gently did it land.

And then occurred a scene that almost passed description. Two companies of soldiers with fixed bayonets and the Le Bourget field police, reinforced by Paris agents, had held the crowd in good order. But as the lights showed the plane landing, [looking] much as if a picture had been thrown [i.e., projected] on a moving picture screen, there was a mad rush.

The movement of humanity swept over soldiers and by policemen and there was the wild sight of thousands of men and women rushing madly across half a mile of the not-too-even ground. Soldiers and police tried for one small moment to stem the tide, then they joined it, rushing as madly as anyone else toward the aviator and his plane.

The first people to reach the plane were two workmen of the aviation field and half a dozen Frenchmen.

"*Cette fois, ça va!*" they cried. ("This time, it's done!")

Captain Lindbergh answered: "Well, I made it."

An instant later he was on the shoulders of half a dozen persons who tried to bear him from the field.

The crowd crushed about the aviator and his progress was halted until a squad of soldiers with fixed bayonets cleared a way for him.

It was two French aviators—Major Pierre Weiss and Sergeant de Troyer—who rescued Captain Lindbergh from the frenzied mob. When it seemed that the excited Frenchmen and -women would overwhelm the frail figure that was being carried on the shoulders of a half dozen men, the two aviators rushed up with a Renault car and, hastily snatching Lindy from the crowd, sped across the field to the commandant's office.

Then followed an almost cruel rush to get near the chairman. Women were thrown down and a number trampled badly. The doors of the small building were closed, but the windows were forced by enthusiasts, who were promptly ejected by soldiers.

Spurred on by reports spread in Paris of the approach of the aviator, other thousands began to arrive from the capital. The police estimate that within half an hour after Captain Lindbergh landed there were probably 100,000 storming the little building to get a sight of the idol of the evening.

Suddenly he appeared at a window, waving his helmet. It was then that, amid cheers for him, came five minutes of cheering for Captain Nungesser.

While the gallant aviator was resting in the Aviators' Club, part of the crowd turned toward his airplane. It had landed in the pink of condition. Before the police could intervene the spectators, turned souvenir-mad, had stripped the plane of everything that could be taken off, and some were even cutting pieces of linen from the wings when a squad of soldiers with fixed bayonets quickly surrounded the *Spirit of St. Louis* and guarded it while mechanics wheeled it into a shed, but only after it had been considerably marred.

While the crowd was waiting, Captain Lindbergh was taken away from the field about midnight, to seek a well-earned repose.

The thing that Captain Lindbergh emphasized more than anything else to the American committee that welcomed him, and later to newspapermen, was that he felt no special strain.

"I could have gone one-half again as much," he said with conviction.

Not since the armistice of 1918 has Paris witnessed a downright demonstration of popular enthusiasm and excitement equal to that displayed by the throngs flocking to the boulevards for news of the American flier, whose personality has captured the hearts of the Parisian multitude.

Thirty thousand people had gathered at the Place de l'Opera and the Square du Havre, near St. Lazare station, where illuminated advertising signs flashed bulletins on the progress of the flier. In front of the office of the Paris *Matin* in the Boulevard Poissonnière the crowds quickly filled the streets, so that extra police details had the greatest difficulty in keeping the traffic moving in two narrow files between the mobs that repeatedly choked the entire street.

From the moment when the last evening editions appeared, at 6:30, until shortly after 9 there was a curious reaction, due to the fact that news seemed to be at a standstill. The throngs waited, hushed and silent, for confirmation.

It was a tense period when the thought in every mind was that they were witnessing a repetition of the deception that two weeks ago turned victory into mourning for the French aviators Nungesser and Coli. Suppose the news flashed from the *Empress of France* that the American flier was seen off the coast of Ireland proved false, as deceiving as the word flashed that Nungesser's *White Bird* had been sighted off Nova Scotia!

During a long, tense period no confirmation came. The people stood quietly, but the strain was becoming almost unbearable, permeating through the crowd. Pessimistic phrases were repeated. "It's too much to think it possible." "They shouldn't have let him go." "All alone, he has no chance if he should be overcome with exhaustion."

To these comments the inevitable reply was, "Don't give up hope. There's still time."

All this showed the French throng was unanimously eager for the American's safety and straining every wish for his ultimate victory.

A Frenchwoman dressed in mourning and sitting in a big limousine was seen wiping her eyes when the bulletins failed to flash confirmation that Lindbergh's plane had been sighted off Ireland. A woman selling papers nearby brushed her own tears aside, exclaiming: "You're right to feel so, madame. In such things there is no nationality—he's some mother's son."

Something of the same despair that the crowds evinced two weeks ago spread as an unconfirmed rumor was circulated that Lindbergh had been forced down. Soon after 9 o'clock this was turned to a cheering, shouting pandemonium when *Le Matin* posted a bulletin announcing that the Lindbergh plane had been sighted over Cherbourg.

The crowd applauded and surged into the street, halting traffic in a series of delirious manifestations that lasted for 10 minutes with cries of "*Vive Lindbergh,*" "*Vive l'Americain.*" The news was followed by a general rush for taxicabs and subway stations, thousands being seized simultaneously with the idea of going to Le Bourget to witness the arrival of the victorious airman.

All roads leading toward the airfield were jammed with traffic, though thousands still clung to their places before the boulevard bulletin boards. Other throngs moved toward the Etoile, lining ways of access to the hotel where it had been announced the American's rooms were reserved, in the hope of catching a glimpse of the international hero as he passed in triumph from the airdrome.

Ovation after ovation followed the news of Lindbergh's startling progress through France, the crowds steadily augmenting until they filled the entire block. The throng was estimated at 15,000 people. After Cherbourg word was flashed that the plane had traversed Louvirs, then the outskirts of Paris.

In a perfect frenzy the huge crowd hailed the announcement that Lindbergh had landed at Le Bourget. Straw hats sailed in the air, handkerchiefs fluttered and a roar of cheers and clapping spread through the throng and was carried along down the boulevards, where the crowds seated in the café terraces rushed into the streets and joined in the demonstration.

From the tops of motorbuses, stopped in traffic, joyful figures demonstrated their glee, the police abandoning their efforts to restrain the throng and joining in the general elation.

From the first recheering of *"Vive l'Americain"* rolled up a mighty shout, "The flags," the same cry that two weeks ago gave rise to the false rumor of an anti-American demonstration, when it was falsely reported that a mob demanded the removal of the American flag from the *Matin* office.

For several minutes this cry was renewed until the proprietor of a motion picture house unfurled a little American flag, which was greeted with cheer upon cheer and which became the mightiest pro-American demonstration seen in France since the days of the war, when, as the Yankee troops landed, three large American flags beside the French tricolor hung from *Le Matin*'s window in the glare of searchlights.

There could be no mistaking the sincerity of these cheers, which were prolonged as a Frenchman in the crowd rushed up to the American demonstrators, wringing their hands in congratulations.

Extra papers telling the tale of the American's triumph in bulletin form sold as fast as the newsmen could distribute them.

The throng slowly dispersed in a general procession toward Montmartre, where many hundreds were to spend the remainder of the night in a celebration.

What appealed to the French aviators as the uncanny part of Captain Lindbergh's performance was his lack of navigating instruments. Old and experienced airmen, in conversations during their wait for him, said he had one chance in a thousand because, while he might head in a given compass direction in leaving America, the winds might put him many hundreds of miles out of his path.

Guesses were made that he might land in Spain, in Portugal, in Northern Africa or in Ireland or even Norway. But the flier landed at Le Bourget as simply as you please and as accurately as if he had half a dozen navigators aboard.

When the news of Captain Lindbergh's arrival reached Paris tens of thousands of people started for Le Bourget Field. They met the crowds starting to come home and there ensued the worst traffic tangle the French capital has had. The police estimate that 12,000 automobiles became involved in the tangle and many of the cars did not get back to the city until after 3 o'clock this morning.

For two hours there was a hopeless mixup with no movement in any direction. The emergency traffic police brought from Paris worked nearly all night in straightening out the mess.

French papers estimated that at midnight 150,000 people were trying to get to or from Le Bourget, and there were frequent exhibitions of temper that acted as a great contrast to the enthusiastic joy that greeted the arrival of the American hero.

Soon after Lindbergh landed an employee of the Bourse telegraph office arrived with more than 700 cablegrams for him, but the employee was unable to get within half a mile of the addressee.

HE COULD HAVE GONE 500 MILES FARTHER

CARLYLE MACDONALD

PARIS, SUNDAY, May 22—Captain Lindbergh was discovered at the American Embassy at 2:30 this morning. Attired in a pair of Ambassador Herrick's pajamas, he sat on the edge of a bed and talked of his flight. At the last moment Ambassador Herrick had canceled the plans of the reception committee and, by unanimous consent, took the flier to the embassy in the Place d'Iéna.

A staff of American doctors who had arrived at Le Bourget Field early to minister to an "exhausted" aviator found instead a bright-eyed, smiling youth who refused to be examined.

"Oh, don't bother; I am all right," he said.

"I'd like to have a bath and a glass of milk. I would feel better," Lindbergh replied when the ambassador asked him what he would like to have.

A bath was drawn immediately and in less than five minutes the youth had disrobed in one of the embassy guest rooms, taken his bath and was out again drinking a bottle of milk and eating a roll.

"There is no use worrying about me, Mr. Ambassador," Lindbergh insisted when Mr. Herrick and members of the embassy staff wanted him to be examined by doctors and then go to bed immediately.

It was apparent that the young man was too full of his experiences to want sleep, and he sat on the bed and chatted with the ambassador, his son and daughter-in-law.

By this time a corps of frantic newspapermen who had been madly chasing the airman, following one false scent after another, had finally tracked him to the embassy. In a body they descended upon the ambassador, who received them in the salon and informed them that he had just left Lindbergh with strict instructions to go to sleep.

As Mr. Herrick was talking with the reporters his son-in-law came downstairs and said that Lindbergh had rung and announced that he did not care to go to sleep just yet and that he would be glad to see the newspapermen for a few minutes. A cheer went up from the group, who dashed by Mr. Herrick and rushed upstairs.

In the blue-and-gold room, with a soft light glowing, sat the conqueror of the Atlantic. He immediately stood up and held out his hands to greet his callers, the *New York Times* correspondent being first to greet him.

"Sit down, please," urged everyone with one voice, but Lindbergh only smiled again his famous boyish smile and said, "It's almost as easy to stand up as it is to sit down."

Questions were fired at him from all sides about his trip across the ocean, but Lindbergh seemed to dismiss them all with brief, nonchalant answers.

"I expected trouble over Newfoundland because I had been warned that the situation there was unfavorable. But I got over that hazard with no trouble whatsoever.

"However, it wasn't easy going. I had sleet and snow for over 1,000 miles. Sometimes it was too high to fly over and sometimes too low to fly under, so I just had to go through it as best I could.

"I flew as low as 10 feet in some places and as high as 10,000 in others. I passed no ships in the daytime, but at night I saw the lights of several ships, the night being bright and clear."

Everyone then wanted to know if the flier had been sleepy on the voyage.

"I didn't really get what you might call downright sleepy," he said, "but I think I sort of nodded several times. In fact, I could have flown half that distance again. I had enough fuel left to go 1,000 miles, I think—certainly 500—although I had no time to examine my fuel tanks, the crowds were so terrific.

"If it wasn't for the soldiers and two French aviators I think I might have been injured by wild enthusiasts in the throng. Anyway, I paid no attention to economy of fuel during the voyage."

Ambassador Herrick then asked the young aviator if he had any difficulty finding his way once he reached Europe.

"Well, you know this is my first trip to Europe, and I just had to take a chance," was his reply.

He added, with another of his smiles, that he liked what he had seen of Paris and he wanted to stay as long as he could.

The American youth said that never once during the trip had he doubted his eventual success, and when he was over Cherbourg, or what he thought was Cherbourg, he knew he would make it.

"About 40 miles away from Paris," he continued, "I began to see the old trench flares they were sending up at Le Bourget. I knew then I had made it, and as I approached the field with all its lights it was a simple matter to circle once and then pick a spot sufficiently far away from the crowd to land O.K.

"I landed perfectly. Then the crowd descended on me, and it was all over but the handshaking."

Lindbergh refused to take seriously the problem of flying the Atlantic, when he was asked how he had performed the almost unbelievable feat.

"You know, flying a good airplane doesn't require near as much attention as a motorcar," he explained.

"I had four sandwiches when I left New York," he said. "I only ate one and a half during the whole trip and drank a little water. I don't suppose I had time to eat any more, because you know it surprised me how short a distance it is to Europe."

By this time the interview had lasted for seven or eight minutes and Mr. Herrick insisted that it would involve too much strain on the flier to submit him to further questioning. Everyone then withdrew, and with a cheery "good-night" and a final handshake with the ambassador, Lindbergh hopped into bed like a schoolboy after a hard day's play, and before this correspondent left the embassy word came downstairs that Lindbergh was sound asleep.

Immediately after this Mr. Herrick sent the following cable to Lindbergh's mother in Detroit:

"Warmest congratulations. Your incomparable son has honored me by becoming my guest. He is in fine condition and sleeping sweetly under Uncle Sam's roof. MYRON HERRICK."

Lindbergh brought no baggage, so a hasty wardrobe was assembled for him at the embassy from the personal effects of Ambassador Herrick and his son, Parmely.

The young flier, however, did bring three letters, the only excess baggage he carried. Two were from Theodore Roosevelt for Ambassador Herrick and his son, and the third was addressed to the ambassador and was from Charles Lawrence of the Wright firm that built the motor for the *Spirit of St. Louis.*

JOE LOUIS

1914–1981

By Deane McGowen

Slow of foot but redeemingly fast of hands, Joe Louis dominated heavyweight boxing in a long reign. As world champion, he defended his title 25 times, facing all challengers and fighting the best that the world could offer. In the opinion of many experts, the plain, simple, unobtrusive Brown Bomber—as he was known—with his crushing left jab and hook, was probably the best heavyweight fighter of all time.

The 6-foot-1½-inch, 197-pound Louis won his title June 22, 1937, in Chicago by knocking out James J. Braddock in eight rounds, thus becoming the first black heavyweight champion since Jack Johnson, who had reigned earlier in the century. Before Louis retired undefeated as champion on March 1, 1949, his last title defense was against Jersey Joe Walcott. Louis knocked him out in New York on June 25, 1948.

As the titleholder, his fights had grossed more than $4.6 million, of which he received about $800,000.

Because he wasted little time in dispatching his opponents, Louis's earnings per round were extraordinarily high. Of the 25 defenses, only three went the full 15 rounds. Tony Galento, for example, survived four rounds in 1939, and Buddy Baer managed one round in 1942.

Excluding exhibitions, Louis won 68 professional fights and lost only three. He scored 54 knockouts, including five in the first round. After retiring, he continued to appear in exhibitions and in 1950 he decided to make a comeback, but was beaten by Ezzard Charles in 15 rounds. His final professional bout took place on Oct. 26, 1951, when he lost to Rocky Marciano in New York.

The most spectacular victim of Louis's robust punches was Max Schmeling, the German fighter who was personally hailed by Adolf Hitler as a paragon of Teutonic manhood. Schmeling, who had knocked out Louis in 12 rounds in 1936, was given a return bout on June 22, 1938, in Yankee Stadium. He was knocked out in 2 minutes 4 seconds of the first round.

Describing the bout in *The New York Times,* John Kieran wrote: "Well, of all things! It's on and it's over. Just as Joe promised. He stepped in and started a lightning attack. Lefts and rights—Bang! Bang! Bang! Schmeling reeled into the ropes on the first-base side of the ring and clung like a shipwrecked soldier to a lifeline.

"Swaying on the ropes, Max peered out in a bewildered manner. He pushed himself off and Louis struck like dark lightning again. A ripping left and a smashing right. The right was the crusher. Schmeling went down. He was up again and then, under another fusillade, down again. Once more, and barely able to stand, and then down for the third and final time."

New York Times Photo

Joe Louis throwing a right against Billy Conn in the 1941 match

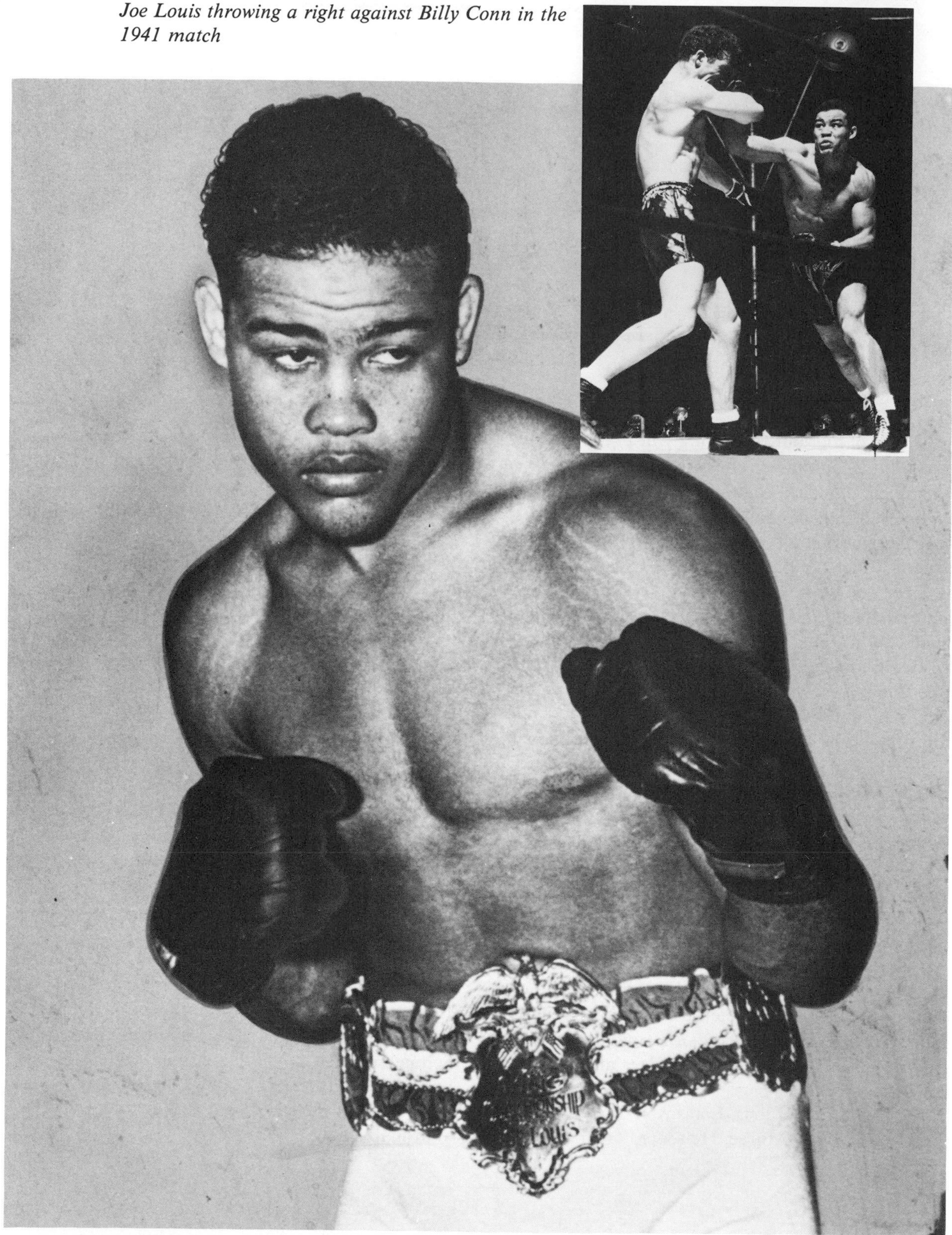

AP/WIDE WORLD

Not all of Louis's fights were so savage. Many of his adversaries entered the ring already quaking and his task of finishing them off was thus a matter of a half dozen solid punches at the proper moment.

There was no Joe Louis behind any facade. He was the same slow-spoken, considerate person in a close social group as he was to the vast crowds that surged in on him to hang on his every word when he was at the apogee of the boxing world.

A simple dignity was characteristic of Louis, who never pretended that his sharecropper origins in Alabama were more than humble.

Louis was born Joseph Louis Barrow on May 13, 1914, in the cotton field country near Lafayette, Ala., the eighth child of Munn and Lilly Barrow. His boyhood was one of want and little schooling.

In his teens, he did odd jobs to help his family until they moved to Detroit. He worked as a laborer there in the River Rouge plant of the Ford Company.

The future champion attended Bronson Vocational School for a time to learn cabinetmaking, before turning to amateur boxing at the request of a schoolmate. He made his boxing debut in an amateur tournament in Detroit, as a light-heavyweight.

He lost the decision, getting knocked down three times by Johnny Miller in a three-rounder. However, he persevered and, in 1934, won the national Amateur Athletic Union light-heavyweight title. That ended his career as an amateur. His record included 43 knockout victories in 54 bouts.

On July 4, 1934, Louis appeared as a professional fighter for the first time and knocked out Jack Kracken in one round in Chicago.

Much of Louis's success was due to the capable manner in which he was handled as a professional. His amateur record brought him to the attention of Julian Black and John Roxborough, who engaged the late Jack Blackburn, one of the ring's great competitors, to polish the rough spots in the young fighter's style and to get the maximum results out of his tremendous strength and punching power.

Louis had 11 more fights in 1934 and 14 in 1935. By then his prowess had attracted the attention of Mike Jacobs in New York.

Mr. Jacobs was competing against Madison Square Garden for the right to promote boxing. He went to Detroit to see Louis fight Natie Brown in March 1935.

After outpointing Brown, Louis soon joined the New York promoter.

On June 25, 1935, Louis appeared for the first time before New York fans and was an immediate success, knocking out Primo Carnera in six rounds. He was so impressive that fans clamored for a match between him and Max Baer. Baer had lost the heavyweight championship to Braddock only two weeks before Louis stopped Carnera.

Louis and Baer met on Sept. 24 of that year, and the young fighter, already recognized as a punching machine, pounded Baer into helplessness in four rounds.

Altogether Louis had 14 bouts in 1935 and earned a total of $368,037, an almost incredible sum then for a fighter in his second year as a professional.

On June 19, 1936, Louis had his first meeting with Schmeling in New York and suffered his first professional defeat, a 12th-round knockout.

Schmeling told reporters before the bout that he had seen faults in Louis's style. After the bout, Schmeling disclosed that Louis had a habit of lowering his left shoulder and arm, leaving his chin open for a right-hand counterpunch.

Schmeling floored Louis with that weapon in the fourth round, and finally knocked him out with more of the right-hand blows in the 12th.

Schmeling was promised a title bout against Braddock after he stopped Louis, but Mr. Jacobs wanted Louis to get the chance. After stalling Schmeling, Braddock agreed to meet Louis.

They fought in Chicago and Louis knocked out Braddock in the eighth round to win the heavyweight title.

In 1938 the new champion had only three bouts, but one of those was his second against Schmeling.

Germany was then expounding its superman

propaganda to the world, and Hitler had made it known that Schmeling was one of those supermen.

Schmeling made the mistake of believing Hitler and made some disparaging remarks about Americans in general and blacks in particular.

When Louis and the challenger met on June 22, 1938, in New York, the champion was in a rage. Louis cut his opponent down with terrific head and body punches. Schmeling went to a local hospital to recuperate before he returned to Germany.

The 2-minute-4-second time span was a record for turning back a challenger in a heavyweight title bout. The bout was the first million-dollar gate Louis attracted during his career.

After that Louis had things pretty much his own way in the ring. Tony Galento had him on the canvas briefly in 1939, Arturo Godoy's crouching nose-to-the-floor tactics puzzled Louis the full 15 rounds in 1940, and Buddy Baer, brother of Max, knocked Louis out of the ring for a nine-count in 1941 before losing.

That last event came during Louis's so-called bum-of-the-month campaign. During it, beginning in December 1940, he met challengers at the rate of one a month, a performance that no other heavyweight champion ever attempted.

Louis came close to losing his crown in the first fight with Billy Conn of Pittsburgh on June 18, 1941, at the Polo Grounds. Conn, the light-heavyweight king, relinquished his title to meet Louis.

Before that fight many boxing writers had said that Conn would be too speedy and would outbox Louis. The champion had the perfect answer when he said, "He can run but he can't hide."

For 12 rounds Louis received a lesson in boxing from the stylish challenger. However, in the 13th, Conn dropped his successful tactics and attempted to slug it out with Louis. The move cost him the championship. Louis knocked him out with two seconds left in the round.

Three months later Louis stopped Lou Nova, and in January 1942 he defeated Buddy Baer again, in 2:56 of the first round. That bout, in Madison Square Garden, was for the Navy Relief Society, which received $47,000.

Two months later Louis knocked out Abe Simon in the sixth round of a fight in New York. The Army Relief Society gained by $36,146. Louis then went into the army as a private.

As a soldier, Louis traveled more than 21,000 miles and staged 96 boxing exhibitions before two million soldiers.

Louis came out of the army on Oct. 1, 1945, and shortly after signed to defend his title against Conn. The bout was the second million-dollar gate Louis drew and earned him the largest purse of his career, $625,916.44. The champion stopped Conn in the eighth round at Yankee Stadium on June 19, 1946.

The champion defended his title three more times after the Conn fight, knocking out Tami Mauriello and Jersey Joe Walcott twice. After the second Walcott bout on June 25, 1948, Louis retired—officially on March 1, 1949.

He later tried a comeback but failed to regain his championship form. Ezzard Charles outpointed him in 15 rounds at Yankee Stadium on Sept. 27, 1950. A year later Louis's ring career came to an end when Rocky Marciano knocked him out in the eighth round of their bout at Madison Square Garden on Oct. 26, 1951.

Although he made a lot of money, it passed through his fingers quickly—and without the sort of accounting that the Internal Revenue Service expects. As a result, the government calculated that his delinquent taxes—after penalties and interest—amounted to $1.25 million, a sum that Louis found staggering. "I liked the good life," Louis said. "I just don't know where the money went. I wish I did. I got 50 percent of each purse and all kinds of expenses came out of my cut." In the mid-1960s, an accommodation was reached with the government and the boxer was able to pay off his obligations.

In 1965, Dana Latham, the commissioner of the Internal Revenue Service, informed Congress: "We have gotten all we could possibly get from Mr.

Louis, leaving him with some hope that he can live. His earning days are over."

Louis was not officially forgiven by the tax collectors, but attempts at getting the money he owed ceased, according to a close friend of the boxer.

Out of the ring for good, Louis tried to establish himself in a variety of careers. He wrestled briefly and engaged in various sports and commercial promotions. In 1969, he and Billy Conn, who had lost twice to Louis in title fights, set up the Joe Louis Food Franchise Corporation in the hope of operating an interracial chain of food shops.

In 1969, he collapsed on a lower Manhattan street, and was rushed to Beekman Downtown Hospital for treatment of what was then described as "a physical breakdown."

And in 1970, he spent five months at the Colorado Psychiatric Hospital and the Veterans Administration Hospital in Denver. He was hospitalized by his wife, Martha, and his son, Joe Louis Barrow, Jr., suffering from paranoia. Because of his confinement he was unable to attend a tribute to him in Detroit that was attended by more than 8,000 people.

Louis disclosed the truth about some of his problems in 1971 in a book, *Brown Bomber: The Pilgrimage of Joe Louis,* by Barney Nagler. He said that his collapse in 1969 had been caused by cocaine. And he admitted that his hospitalization had been prompted by his fear of a plot to destroy him.

Louis's son once said of his father: "I couldn't help thinking of Arthur Miller's play *Death of a Salesman.* In the play, the man's name was Willy Loman, wasn't it? Well, there's a correlation between them. Wasn't Willy a grand guy, just like my father, and then he started growing old and losing his customers? He was never really aware that he had lost his territory. That's the tragedy of it, just like my father's."

Louis's third wife, Martha, said, during her husband's troubles, "Joe's not broke. He's rich-rich with friends. If he said he needed a dollar, a million people would send him a dollar and he'd be a millionaire."

Joe Louis was more than just a boxing champion. He also had a role in the social history of the United States. In a 1970 article about Louis in *Ebony* magazine, Chester Higgins wrote: "He gave inspiration to downtrodden and despised people. When Joe Louis fought, blacks in ghettos across the land were indoors glued to their radios, and when Louis won, as he nearly always did, they hit the streets whooping and hollering in celebration. For Joe's victory was their victory, a means of striking back at an oppressive and hateful environment. Louis was the black Atlas on whose broad shoulders blacks were lifted, for in those days, there were few authentic black heroes."

In 1974 he took time off from his job as a "greeter" at Caesar's Palace in Las Vegas, Nev., to referee the heavyweight fight between Joe Frazier and Jerry Quarry, proclaiming Frazier the winner after the fifth round because of heavy cuts on Quarry's face.

Mr. Louis and Marva Trotter, a 19-year-old Chicago secretary, were married on Sept. 24, 1935. The marriage took place in a Harlem apartment just a few hours before Louis stepped into the ring and knocked out Max Baer.

The couple were divorced in March 1945, but remarried a year later. They were divorced a second time in February 1949. A daughter, Jacqueline, was born to the couple on Feb. 8, 1943, and a son, Joe Jr., on May 28, 1947.

Mr. Louis's third marriage was to Rose Morgan, a New York cosmetics manufacturer, on Christmas Day 1955.

His fourth marriage was to Mrs. Martha Jackson, a Los Angeles lawyer. It took place March 17, 1959, after his union with Rose Morgan Louis was terminated by annulment.

Since 1977, Mr. Louis had been confined to a wheelchair following surgery to correct an aortic aneurysm. His health over the last decade had been poor, beset with heart problems, emotional disorders and strokes. An electronic pacemaker was implanted near his heart last Dec. 23 in Houston.

Mr. Louis died of cardiac arrest in Las Vegas, Nev., on April 12, 1981. He was 66 years old.

Mr. Louis's death came only a few hours after he had attended the heavyweight championship fight on Saturday night between Larry Holmes and Trevor Berbick at Caesar's Palace.

A SENSE OF DIGNITY

RED SMITH

WHEN JOE LOUIS'S tax troubles were still making headlines, a man told him: "You were 15 years ahead of your time. You should have been around today to cut in on these multimillion-dollar closed-circuit shows."

"No," Joe said, "when I was boxing I made $5 million and wound up broke, owing the government a million. If I was boxing today I'd make $10 million and wind up broke, owing the government two million."

Joe Louis Barrow lived a month less than 67 years. He was heavyweight champion of the world in an era when the heavyweight champion was, in the view of many, the greatest man in the world. He held the title for 12 years, defended it 25 times and retired undefeated as a champion.

Not once in 66 years was he known to utter a word of complaint or bitterness or offer an excuse for anything. To be sure, he had nothing to make excuses about. In 71 recorded fights he lost three times, on a knockout by Max Schmeling before he won the championship, on a decision to Ezzard Charles when he tried to regain the title, and finally on a knockout by Rocky Marciano when that young man was on his way to the top.

Joe had just celebrated his 21st birthday when he came to New York the first time. This was 1935, not a long time ago, yet some people still saw any black man as the stereotyped darky, who loved dancing and watermelon. Some news photographers bought a watermelon and asked Joe to pose eating a slice. He refused, saying he didn't like watermelon.

"And the funny thing is," said Harry Markson, telling the story, "Joe loves watermelon."

At 21, this unlettered son of Alabama sharecroppers had the perception to realize what the pictures would imply and the quiet dignity to have no part of the charade. Dignity was always a word that applied to him. Dignity and candor.

Early in Muhammad Ali's splendacious reign as heavyweight champion, he hired Joe as an "adviser" and they appeared on television together.

"Joe, you really think you coulda whupped me?" Ali said.

"When I had the title," Joe said, "I went on what they called a bum-of-the-month tour."

Ali's voice rose three octaves. "You mean I'm a bum?"

"You woulda been on the tour," Joe told his new employer.

During World War II, Joe defended his championship against Buddy Baer for the benefit of the Naval Relief Fund. Wendell Willkie, defeated candidate for president of the United States, made a resounding speech in the ring. "And you, Max Baer," he said, "and you, Joe Louee . . ." Earlier that day Harry Markson, then doing publicity on Mike Jacob's promotions in Madison Square Garden, offered to write a few words for Joe in case he was called on to speak. Joe said no, thanks, he wouldn't be invited.

To his surprise, he was asked to address the crowd. Unprepared though he was, he said a few altogether appropriate words, assuring listeners that we would win the war "because we're on God's side." Dignity. If memory serves, Buddy Baer wasn't called on. Before the first round ended, he couldn't speak, being unconscious.

This story has been told here before but perhaps it will bear repeating. Before Floyd Patterson's second match with Sonny Liston, the one in Las Vegas, a visitor remarked to Joe that every time Floyd talked with the press he spoke of losing. "If I lose, if I lose bad, if I'm humiliated," he would start over again at the bottom and work his way back to main events.

"A fighter can't think that way," Joe said, "and he can't talk that way."

"It seems to me," his companion said, "that any time a man of intelligence goes into an athletic contest, he realizes that he stands a chance of losing."

"Oh, I think I reckanized it," Joe said. "Especially when I was just starting out and scared. After I won the title I didn't think about it no more. Oh, I knew that if I kept on fighting, some guy would come along and take the title away from me, but not this guy, never tonight."

Joe Louis may very well have been the greatest fighter who ever lived. Comparisons with Jack Dempsey and Gene Tunney and others are foolish, and there is no shadow of doubt here that he would have caught and destroyed Muhammad Ali as he caught Billy Conn and other skillful boxers.

At the top of his game he would have outboxed Rocky Marciano and perhaps have taken him out, though after 49 fights without a defeat or draw, Rocky said he had never been dazed by a punch, even the punches that floored him. Joe's aging legs betrayed him when he finally fought Marciano.

That was his last competitive match, though he boxed a few exhibitions afterward. Marciano knocked him out of the ring in the eighth round, and afterward Joe lay on his stomach on a rubbing table with his right ear pillowed on a towel. He wore his faded dressing gown of blue and red, with a raincoat spread over it. His left hand was in a bucket of ice on the floor and a handler massaged his left ear with ice. With his face squashed against the padding of the table, newspapermen had to kneel with their heads close to his lips to hear his words.

He said the best man had won. Asked whether Marciano could hit harder than Schmeling, who had knocked him out 15 years earlier, Joe said: "This kid knocked me out with what? Two punches. Schmeling knocked me out with—musta been a hundred punches. But I was 22 years old then. You can take more then than later on."

"Did age count tonight, Joe?"

"Ugh," Joe said, and bobbed his head.

LOUIS DEFEATS SCHMELING BY A KNOCKOUT IN FIRST [1938]

JAMES P. DAWSON

THE EXPLODING fists of Joe Louis crushed Max Schmeling on June 22, 1938, in the ring at the Yankee Stadium and kept sacred that time-worn legend of boxing that no former heavyweight champion has ever regained the title.

The Brown Bomber from Detroit, with the most furious early assault he has ever exhibited here, knocked out Schmeling in the first round of what was to have been a 15-round battle to retain the title he won last year from James J. Braddock. He has now defended it successfully four times.

In exactly 2 minutes and 4 seconds of fighting Louis polished off the Black Uhlan from the Rhine, but, though the battle was short, it was furious and savage while it lasted, packed with thrills that held three knockdowns of the ambitious ex-champion, every moment tense for a crowd of about 80,000.

This gathering, truly representative and comparing favorably with the largest crowds in boxing's history, paid receipts estimated at between $900,000 and $1,000,000 to see whether Schmeling could repeat the knockout he administered to Louis just two years ago here and be the first ex-heavyweight champion to come back into the title, or whether the Bomber could avenge his defeat as he promised.

As far as the length of the battle was concerned, the investment in seats, which ran to $30 each, was a poor one. But for excitement, for drama, for pulse-throbs, those who came from near and far felt themselves well repaid because they saw a fight that, though it was one of the shortest heavyweight championships on record, was surpassed by few for thrills.

With the right hand that Schmeling held in contempt Louis knocked out his foe. Three times under its impact the German fighter hit the ring floor. The first time Schmeling regained his feet laboriously at the count of three. From the second knockdown Schmeling, dazed but game, bounced up instinctively before the count had gone beyond one.

On the third knockdown Schmeling's trainer and closest friend, Max Machon, hurled a towel into the ring, European fashion, admitting defeat for his man. The towel sailed through the air when the count on the prostrate Max had reached three.

The signal is ignored in American boxing, has been for years, and Referee Arthur Donovan, before he had a chance to pick up the count in unison with knockdown timekeeper Eddie Josephs, who was outside the ring, gathered the white emblem in a ball and hurled it through the ropes.

Returning to Schmeling's crumpled figure, Donovan took one look and signaled an end of the battle. The count at that time was five on the third knockdown. Further counting was useless. Donovan could have counted off a century and Max could not have regained his feet. The German was thoroughly "out."

It was as if he had been pole-axed. His brain was awhirl, his body, his head, his jaws ached and pained, his senses were numbed from that furious, paralyzing punching he had taken even in the short space of time the battle consumed.

Following the bout, Schmeling claimed he was fouled. He said that he was hit a kidney punch, a devastating right, which so shocked his nervous system that he was dazed and his vision was blurred. To observers at the ringside, however, with all due respect to Schmeling's thoughts on the subject, the punches that dazed him were thundering blows to the head, jaw and body in bewildering succession, blows of the old Alabama Assassin reincarnated last night for a special occasion.

Louis wanted to erase the memory of that 1936 knockout he suffered in 12 rounds. It was the one blot on his brilliant record. He aimed to square the account and he did.

Because of the excitement attending the finish, Louis, in the records, will be deprived of a clean-cut knockout. It will appear as a technical knockout because Referee Donovan didn't complete the full 10-second count over Schmeling. But this is merely a technicality. No fighter ever was more thoroughly knocked out than was Max last night.

Thrilling to the spectacle of this short, savage victory that held so much significance was a gathering that included a member of President Roosevelt's cabinet, Postmaster General James A. Farley; governors of several states; mayors of cities in the East, South and Middle West; representatives and senators; judges and lawyers; politicians; doctors; figures of prominence in the professional world; leaders of banking, industry and commerce; stars of the stage and screen; ring champions of the past and present; leaders in other sports and other fields—all assembled eagerly awaiting the struggle whose appeal drew them from distant parts of the country and from Europe.

In addition to those looking on at the spectacle, there were millions listening in virtually all over the world, for this battle was broadcast in four languages, English, German, Spanish and Portuguese, so intense was the interest in its outcome.

Louis, hero of one of the greatest stories ever written in the ring, owner of a record of 38 victories in 39 bouts spread over four years, entered the ring the favorite to win at odds of 1 to 2. He won like a 1-to-10 shot. The knockout betting was at even money, take your pick. It could have been on Louis at 1 to 10, for Schmeling never had a chance. His number was up from the clang of the opening gong.

Schmeling, 32-year-old campaigner over a period of 14 years, aspired to the unparalleled distinction of being the first man to regain the heavyweight crown. He suffered, instead, the fate that overtook Jim Corbett, Bob Fitzsimmons, Jim Jeffries and Jack Dempsey, ring immortals all, who tried and failed.

The fury of Louis's attack explains the result in a nutshell. The defending champion came into the ring geared on high. He never stopped punching until his rival was a crumpled, inert, helpless figure, diving headlong into the resined canvas, rolling over there spasmodically, instinctively trying to come erect, his spirit willing to return to the attack, his flesh weak, for mind and muscle could not be expected to function harmoniously under the terrific battering Schmeling absorbed in those fleeting two minutes.

Emphasizing the savagery with which Louis went after this victory was Schmeling's feeble effort at retaliation. The German ex-champion threw exactly two punches. That is how completely the Bomber established his mastery in this second struggle with the Black Uhlan.

With the opening gong, Louis crept softly out of his corner, pantherlike, eyes alert, arms poised, fists cocked to strike from any angle as he met Schmeling short of the ring's center. Max backed carefully toward his own corner, watching Louis intently, his right, the right that thudded so punishingly against Joe's jaw and temple two years ago, ready to strike over or under a left guard. At least, that was Schmeling's prearranged plan.

But Louis wasted only a few seconds in studying his foe, menacing Max meanwhile with a spearing left, before quickly going to work.

Like flashes from the blue, the Bomber's sharp, powerful left started suddenly pumping into Schmeling's face. The blows tilted Max's head back, made his eyes blink, unquestionably stung him. The German's head was going backward as if on hinges.

Max's face was exposed to a left hook attack, and Louis interspersed his onslaught with a few of these blows, gradually forcing Schmeling back to the ropes and preventing the German from making an offensive or countermove, so fast and sharp and true was the opening fire of the defending champion.

Schmeling suddenly shot a right over Louis's left for the jaw, but the blow was short and they went close. At long range again, Joe stuck and stabbed with his left to the face and head, trying to open a lane through Schmeling's protecting arms and gloves for a more forceful shot from the right.

But the opening didn't come immediately. Instead, Schmeling again lunged forward, his right arching as it drove for Louis's jaw, and it landed on the champion's head as the Schmeling admirers in the tremendous crowd roared encouragement.

Louis, however, only scowled and stepped forward, this time with a terrific right to Schmeling's jaw that banged Max against the ropes, his body partly turned toward the right from Louis.

Schmeling shook to his heels under the impact of that blow, but he gave no sign of toppling. And Joe, like a tiger, leaped upon him, driving a right to the ribs as Schmeling half turned—apparently the blow Schmeling later claimed was foul—swinging with might and main, lefts and rights that thudded against Schmeling's bobbing head, grazed or cracked on Max's jaw, and swishing murderous-looking left hooks into Schmeling's stomach as the crumpling ex-champion grimaced in pain, his face wearing the expression of a fighter protesting "foul."

Shaken when he first landed against the ropes, Schmeling was rendered groggy under the furious assault to which Louis subjected him while he stood there trying unsuccessfully to avoid the blows or grasp a chance to clinch.

Suddenly the Bomber's right, sharp and true with the weight of his 198¾ pounds back of it as well as his knack of driving it home, landed cleanly on Schmeling's jaw. Max toppled forward and down. He was hurt and stunned, but gamely the German came erect at the count of three.

Louis was on him in a jiffy, with the fury of a

jungle beast. After propping the tottering Schmeling with a jolting left to the face, the Bomber's deadly right fist again exploded in Max's face, and under another crack on the jaw Schmeling went down. This time, however, the German regained his feet before the count progressed beyond one.

But Schmeling was helpless. He staggered drunkenly for a few backward steps, the crowd in an uproar as Louis stealthily followed and measured his man. Max was an open target. His jaw was unprotected and inviting. His midsection was a mark for punches. The kill was within Louis's grasp. He lost no time in ceremony.

Spearing Schmeling with blinding straight lefts, numbing Max with powerful left hooks that were sharp, true and destructive, Louis set the stage for one finishing right to the jaw, released the blow and landed in a flash, and the German toppled over in a headlong dive, completely unconscious.

The din of the crowd echoed over the arena, cheers for the conquering Louis, shrieks of entreaty and shouts of advice for Schmeling. But this thunderous roar was unheard by the befogged Schmeling and was ignored by the Bomber, intent only on the destruction of his foe.

In routine fashion, Eddie Josephs, a licensed referee converted into a knockdown timekeeper, started the count over the stricken Schmeling. He counted one, then two, as Referee Donovan went about the duty of signaling Louis to the farthest neutral corner.

At "three" a white towel sailed aloft from Schmeling's corner, hurled by the ever-faithful Machon, who realized, as did everyone else in the vast gathering, that Schmeling was knocked out, if he was not, indeed, badly hurt.

The towel fell in the ring a few feet from Schmeling. It is the custom in European rings to recognize this gesture as a concession of defeat. It used to be recognized here. But for many years now it has been banned, and Referee Donovan, disregarding the emblem of surrender, tossed it through the ropes and out of the ring.

When he returned to the prostrate figure of Schmeling, moving convulsively on the ring floor doubtless with that instinctive impulse to arise, the count had reached "five." One look was enough for Donovan. Instantly he spread his arms in a signal that meant the end of the bout, although timekeeper Josephs, as he is duty bound to do, continued counting outside the ring.

This led to confusion at the finish. Some thought the third knockdown count was eight. Actually, the bout was ended at the count of five, the three seconds beyond that time being a gesture against emergency that was superfluous. Schmeling could not have arisen inside the legal 10-second stretch. His hopes were blasted. He was a thoroughly beaten man.

In a few moments, however, as police swarmed into the ring and his handlers worked over him in the corner to which he was assisted, Schmeling returned to consciousness. He was able to smile bravely as he walked across the ring to shake the hand of the conquering Louis, a gesture that carried the impression, somehow, that Max realized at long last that Louis is his master now and for all time.

"Now I feel like the champion."

These were Joe Louis's first words on his arrival in his dressing room.

"I've been waiting a long time for this night," he added, "and I sure do feel pretty glad about everything. I was a little bit sore at some of the things Max said. Maybe he didn't say them, maybe they put those words in his mouth, but he didn't deny them, and that's what made me mad."

What Louis referred to, probably, was the statement attributed to Schmeling a month ago, to the effect that the Negro would always be afraid of him. Something must have rankled Joe, for the savagery with which he battered down the German was never displayed in his other bouts here.

Most of Louis's remarks were addressed to Gov. Frank Murphy of Michigan, one of the first admitted to the champion's dressing room.

The governor admittedly was "full of hero-worship" as he shook hands with the Detroit boxer who, on his own account, was immeasurably pleased with Murphy's visit.

"You'll never know how my heart thumped during that round, Joe," said the governor.

"I'm glad I made it short for you, sir," responded the champion, who looked exactly like a wool-gathering youngster standing in awe of royalty, instead of a young man who had just earned about $400,000 in 124 seconds.

Louis's managers, Julian Black and John Roxborough, were incensed at Schmeling's claim of foul at first, then laughed it off, saying, "That's for German consumption."

Asked if Schmeling would be considered for a return fight, Black replied, "Certainly not. We've demonstrated tonight that Joe is just too good for Schmeling. We've had enough of him, and he certainly has had enough of us!"

The champion's immediate plans are indefinite. He'll stay around to collect his check today, and probably take in the ball game at the Polo Grounds.

Idol's Downfall Saddens Germans

All Germany, clustered about its short-wave radio sets in the early morning hours, was thunderstruck and almost unbelieving at the unexpected news that "Unser Maxe" Schmeling had failed in his heavyweight comeback try, and failed by the knockout route. Their high hopes of hearing that black-browed Schmeling had fought his way back to the heavyweight championship were dashed so suddenly that the ardor of radio parties and café gatherings was quickly dampened.

Heavy-lidded Germans, who had stayed up till 3 A.M. for the short-wave broadcast only to hear a 2:04-minute fight end with dramatic dispatch, climbed into bed a saddened lot at Joe Louis's victory.

All over the Reich they had clustered in homes, restaurants and cafés to hear the fight they hoped would bring the world's championship to Germany.

It was said Adolf Hitler at his Bavarian mountain retreat was among those who heard the disheartening news.

The maid at Schmeling's Berlin home was so disappointed by the knockout she said she would not awaken Maxie's movie actress wife, Anny Ondra, who left instructions not to be aroused until after the fight.

"I think morning will be time enough to tell her," said the maid, who had stayed up in hope of being able to bear her good news.

The Sportsbar, where Schmeling and his cronies have a regularly reserved table, was "like a tomb," a waiter lamented after the radio told the sad story to patrons looking glumly into their beer steins.

Schmeling's German pals said their only comment was an echo of what the German announcer said at the close of his broadcast from the Yankee Stadium ringside: "We sympathize with you, Max, although you lost as a fair sportsman.

"We will show you on your return that reports in foreign newspapers that you would be thrown into jail are untrue."

K. Metzner, head of the German Boxing Federation, who listened to the broadcast with members of the International European Boxing Federation (FIFA), believed the fight, because of its sudden end, did not give a clear picture of whether Louis or Schmeling was the better fighter.

He said Louis undoubtedly was in excellent form. Schmeling, he thought, watched Louis's left hand too closely, whereas since their last meeting two years ago Louis had developed a powerful right.

He said it was hard to judge whether trainer Machon's action in throwing in the towel was the proper move, thus making the fight end as a technical knockout.

He added Schmeling could be sure of as hearty a reception at home as ever.

MAO ZEDONG

1893–1976

By Fox Butterfield

Mao Zedong, who began as an obscure peasant, died in Beijing on Sept. 9, 1976, as one of history's great revolutionary figures. He was 82 years old.

Born at a time when China was wracked by civil strife, beset with terrible poverty and encroached on by more advanced foreign powers, Mao lived to fulfill his boyhood dream of restoring it to its traditional place as a great nation. In Chinese terms, he ranked with Qin Shihuang, the first emperor, who unified China in 221 B.C., and was the man Chairman Mao most liked to compare himself to.

With incredible perseverance and consummately conceived strategy, he harnessed the forces of agrarian discontent and nationalism to turn a tiny band of peasants into an army of millions, which he led to victory throughout China in 1949 after 20 years of fighting. Along the way the army fought battles as big as Stalingrad and suffered through a heroic march as long as Alexander's.

Then, after establishing the Chinese People's Republic, Mao launched a series of sweeping, sometimes convulsive campaigns to transform a semifeudal, largely illiterate and predominantly agricultural country encompassing almost four million square miles and a fifth of the world's population into a modern, industrialized socialist state. By the time of his death China had manufactured its own nuclear bombs and guided missiles and had become a major oil producer.

With China's resurgence, Mao also charted a new course in foreign affairs, putting an end to a century of humiliation under the "unequal treaties" imposed by the West and winning new recognition and respect. Finally, in 1972, even the United States abandoned its 20 years of implacable hostility when President Richard M. Nixon journeyed to Beijing, where he was received by a smiling Mao.

At the same time Mao brooked no opposition to his control. To consolidate his new regime in the early 1950s he launched a campaign in which hundreds of thousands were executed. In the late 1950s, despite criticism from other party leaders, he ordered the Great Leap Forward, ultimately causing widespread disruption and food shortages. Throughout his years in power he toppled one of his rivals after another in the party. In the Cultural Revolution he risked throwing the country into chaos.

While China achieved enormous economic progress under Mao, some critics felt his constant political campaigns and his emphasis on conformity finally reduced many Chinese to a dispirited, anxious mass ready to go along with the latest shift in the political wind.

One of the most remarkable personalities of the 20th century, Mao was an infinitely complex man—by turns shrewd and realistic, then impatient and a romantic dreamer, an individualist but also a strict disciplinarian. His motives seemed a mixture of the

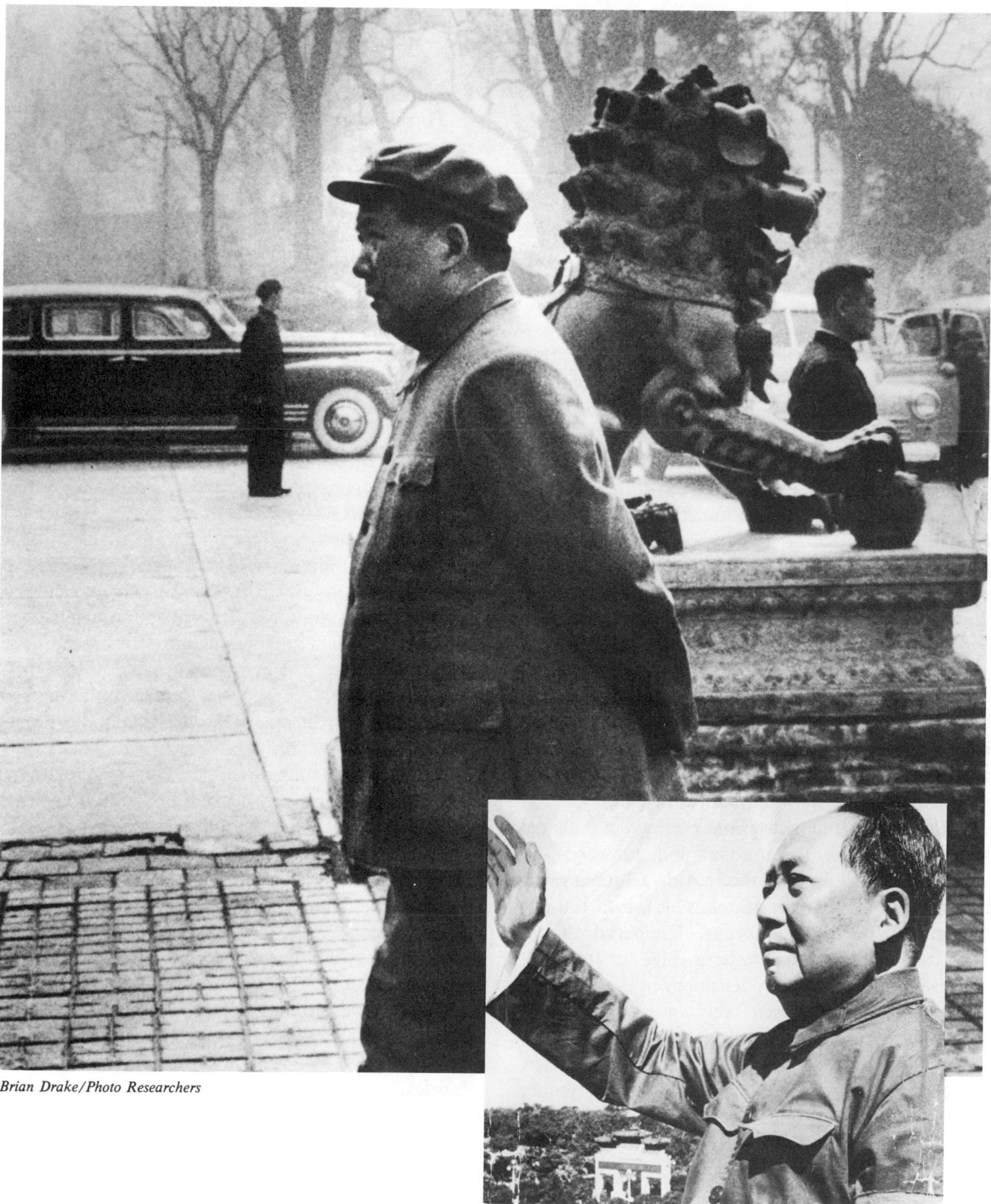

Brian Drake/Photo Researchers

UPI/Bettmann Newsphotos

humanitarian and the totalitarian. He himself once commented that he was "part monkey, part tiger," and perhaps after all he was driven by the same contradictions he was fond of analyzing in the world around him.

Like many Chinese of the past 100 years, angered by the insults of imperialism, he wanted to tear China down to make it stronger. He envisioned creating in China an egalitarian, revolutionary utopia in which mass enthusiasm provided the motive force.

"I have witnessed the tremendous energy of the masses," Mao wrote in 1958 in the midst of the Great Leap Forward, one of his biggest but ultimately most disruptive campaigns. "On this foundation it is possible to accomplish any task whatsoever." The two sentences are a striking summary of his thought.

Unlike many great leaders, Mao never exercised, or sought, absolute control over day-to-day affairs. But the man who rose from humble beginnings in a Hunan village became a virtual sovereign, if not a living god, to the 800 million Chinese. His very words were the doctrine of the state. Printed in millions of little red plastic-bound books as *Quotations from Chairman Mao Zedong*, they were taken to possess invincible magic properties.

Although Mao was a devoted Leninist who, like his Russian predecessor, stressed the need for a tightly organized and disciplined party, he came to cast himself above his party and sought to replace it with a personal cult when it thwarted him.

Despite awesome power and prestige, in the later years of his life—from about 1960 onward—he seemed obsessed by anxieties that the Chinese revolution was in danger of slipping back into the old elitism and bureaucratic ways of imperial China. This danger appeared all the greater, in his eyes, because of the concurrent development in the Soviet Union of what he termed "revisionism." In Mao's view, Nikita S. Khrushchev's emphasis on material incentives to increase consumer-oriented production and the clear emergence of a privileged party elite were anathema. Looking at problems in China, Mao complained in 1964, with perhaps characteristic exaggeration, "You can buy a branch secretary for a few packs of cigarettes, not to mention marrying a daughter to him."

To revitalize China, to cleanse the party and to insure that the revolution survived him, Mao launched the Great Proletarian Cultural Revolution in 1966. As he conceded later, it had consequences even he did not foresee.

Hundreds of thousands of youngsters were mobilized as Red Guards. Often unruly, given to fighting among themselves, they roamed the country and humiliated and chastised Mao's opponents in the party after his call to "bombard the headquarters." After two years of turmoil, economic disruption and even bloodshed, order was finally restored, with help from the increasingly powerful army under Lin Biao, then minister of defense, and some surviving party leaders of a less radical bent such as Prime Minister Zhou Enlai.

But Mao had severely undermined the critical and long-standing unity of the party, forged in the 1930s during the epochal Long March—an anabasis of 6,000 miles that took the fledgling army over mountains, rivers and wastelands from Jiangxi, in South China, to Shaanxi, in the northwest. Foremost among those purged in the Cultural Revolution were Liu Shaoqi, head of state, and Deng Xiaoping, the secretary general of the party, who were labeled "capitalist roaders." Mr. Liu, for years one of Mao's closest associates, had served as head of state since 1959, when Mao relinquished the post in order to give his potential successors more experience. Mao's only official post after that was chairman of the Chinese Communist party's Central Committee.

Marshal Lin, for his role in keeping the army behind Mao and his constant and fulsome praise, was termed "Comrade Mao Zedong's close comrade in arms and successor" and his inheritance was engraved in the 1969 party constitution. But Marshal Lin lasted only two years; according to the official version, he died in a plane crash in Mongolia in 1971 after trying to escape to the Soviet Union when his plot to kill Mao was discovered. Even more bizarre, Mao insisted in letters and speeches that have since reached the outside world that he had been suspicious of Marshal Lin as early as 1966 and had used him only to help get rid of Mr. Liu.

For several years after Marshal Lin's death, the redoubtable Mr. Zhou, a master administrator and conciliator, helped the visibly aging Mao lead the country and embark on what seemed a sustained period of economic growth. But Mr. Zhou's death from cancer in January 1976 left the daily leadership in the hands of Mr. Deng, the former party secretary general, whom Mr. Zhou resurrected in 1973, evidently with Mao's approval, and installed as senior deputy prime minister and likely successor.

Mr. Deng then fell victim to Mao's suspicions even more quickly than had Mr. Liu and Marshal Lin. Only three months after Mr. Zhou's demise, Mr. Deng was stripped of his posts, castigated once again as a "capitalist roader within the party" and accused by Mao of misinterpreting his personal directives by overstressing economic development.

In these later years there were some who thought that Mao appeared as an aging autocrat, given more and more to whim. His invitation last winter to Mr. Nixon to revisit Beijing, the scene of Mr. Nixon's greatest triumph as president, was viewed as a possible sign of a man becoming divorced from reality, though it was understandable in Chinese terms as a kind gesture to a good friend.

Mao made his last public appearance in 1971; in published photographs since then he often looked like a sick man. His apparent difficulty in controlling the movement of his hands and face and his slurred speech stirred speculation that he had suffered a stroke or had Parkinson's disease.

Yet he continued to receive a succession of foreign visitors in his book-lined study, sitting slouched down in a tartan-covered chair, and he apparently remained active in the political conflict that divided Beijing. One of his last acts, it was said, was to select a final successor, Hua Guofeng, a relative unknown who had spent his early party career in Mao's home district, Xiangtan, in Hunan. Whether the two men had a close personal relationship was not clear.

In recent years Mao had also been preoccupied with China's monumental quarrel with the Soviet Union, one of the pivotal developments of the postwar world. From the Chinese side the conflict was partly doctrinal, over Mao's concern that Soviet revisionism was a dangerous heresy that threatened to subvert the Chinese revolution. It was partly political and military, concerned with Mao's effort first to resist Moscow's domination of the Chinese party and later to defend against Soviet troops on China's border. It was partly territorial, over Beijing's contention that Czarist Russia had annexed Chinese territory.

Although few outsiders perceived it until the quarrel surfaced in the early 1960s, it is clear now that the trouble had its origin in the earliest contact between the Chinese Communists and the Russians in the 1920s. It was a period when Mao and others in the newly organized Chinese party were groping for a way to power, and Stalin, from the distance of Moscow, gave them orders that repeatedly led them into disaster.

Stalin and his representatives from the Communist International who served as advisers in China—Mao dubbed them "imperial envoys"—first directed the Communists to ally with Chiang Kai-shek's Nationalists. Then, after Generalissimo Chiang turned on the Communists in 1927, massacring thousands, Stalin ordered the party to anticipate a "revolutionary upsurge" in the cities by the (largely nonexistent) proletariat.

Mao was shorn of his posts and power in the early 1930s as a result of direct Soviet interference. It was only after the Communists were forced to begin the Long March in 1934, after more errors in strategy, that Mao won command because of his genius for organizing and leading peasant guerrillas in a revolution in the countryside.

When Mao traveled triumphantly to Moscow—it

was his first journey abroad—at the end of 1949, soon after setting up his government, he immediately ran into the first foreign policy crisis of the People's Republic of China in the form of a two-month argument with Stalin over terms of an aid agreement and Soviet concessions. Although Mao was to try the Soviet model of economic development, with its emphasis on heavy industry, for a few years, by the mid-1950s he came to have doubts about it, both for its utility in a basically agricultural country such as China and because of the bureaucratic, elitist and capitalistic tendencies—material incentives—it brought with it.

A series of events in the mid- and late 1950s turned this history of uneasy relations into bitter wrangling and eventually open armed clashes. First among these was Nikita S. Khrushchev's speech in 1956 denouncing Stalin for his brutality and personality cult. Mao, who by then envisioned himself as the world's major Marxist-Leninist thinker and revolutionary, was caught by surprise. He resented not being consulted, and he was put in an awkward position by revelations by Mr. Khrushchev, then the party leader.

There followed in rapid succession the evident Soviet complicity in the affair of Peng Dehuai, the Chinese defense minister who was purged in 1959 after criticizing Mao for the chaos of the Great Leap Forward, Moscow's failure to support Beijing in a border clash with India, the offshore islands crisis with Taiwan and Washington, and finally the abrupt withdrawal of all Soviet technicians in July 1960, canceling hundreds of agreements to build factories and other installations.

At the same time Mr. Khrushchev labeled the Chinese leaders as madmen in a speech to the Rumanian party congress, and Mao was soon to tell his colleagues that "the party and state leadership of the Soviet Union have been usurped by revisionists."

The conflict reached its climax in the winter of 1969, when Soviet and Chinese patrols clashed along the frozen banks of the Ussuri River. Thereafter the Russians continued to build up their army, navy and air force along the Chinese frontier until a fourth of their troops were stationed in the area.

Mao spent hours lecturing every visiting head of state on the danger of Soviet expansionism—hegemonism, as he termed it. His belief that Soviet "social-imperialism" was the greatest threat to peace enabled him to take a more sanguine view of the United States and helped bring about the gradual improvement in relations after 1972.

Although Mao commanded enormous authority—in 1955, in a casual talk with local officials, he overturned the provisions of the five-year plan fixed only a day before by the National People's Congress—he shunned the trappings of might. He seldom appeared in public, perhaps to preserve a sense of awe and mystery, and he eschewed fancy dress or medals, in conformity with the simple standard he himself had set during his guerrilla days. Whatever the occasion, he wore only a plain gray tunic buttoned to the neck, and trousers to match, that came to be called a Mao suit in the West and for a period in the 1970s became a fashion craze.

Edgar Snow, the American journalist who in 1936 became the first Westerner to meet Mao, felt that his style owed much to the simplicity, if not roughness and crudeness, of his peasant upbringing. He had the "personal habits of a peasant, plain speaking and plain living," Mr. Snow reported after a visit to the Communists' guerrilla headquarters in Shaanxi, near Yanan. Mao was completely indifferent to personal appearance; he lived in a two-room cave like other peasants "with bare, poor, map-covered walls." His chief luxury was a mosquito net, Mr. Snow found, and he owned only his blankets and two cotton uniforms.

"Mao's food was the same as everybody's, but being a Hunanese he had the southerner's *ai-la*, or love of pepper." Mr. Snow wrote. "He even had pepper cooked into his bread. Except for this passion, he scarcely seemed to notice what he ate."

In the classic *Red Star Over China*, the first public account of Mao, Mr. Snow wrote that he found Mao "a gaunt, rather Lincolnesque figure, above average height for a Chinese, somewhat stooped, with a head of thick black hair grown very long, and with large searching eyes, a high-bridged nose and prominent cheekbones." The account continued: "My fleeting impression was of an intellectual face of great shrewdness.

"He appears to be quite free from symptoms of megalomania," Mr. Snow said—the cult of Mao would not begin until the first "rectification" campaign in 1942. But, Mr. Snow added, "he has a deep sense of personal dignity, and something about him suggests a power of ruthless decision."

Agnes Smedley, another journalist who encountered Mao in Yanan at that time, felt that though he could communicate intensely with a few intimate friends, he remained on the whole reserved and aloof. "The sinister quality I had at first felt so strongly in him proved to be a spiritual isolation," she related. "As Zhu De [the military commander] of the Red Army was loved, Mao Zedong was respected. The few who came to know him best had affection for him, but his spirit dwelt within himself, isolating him."

Other American visitors—diplomats, army officers and journalists—who trooped to Yanan in the 1940s during an optimistic interlude when Washington hoped to bring Mao and Chiang together to fight the Japanese, inevitably were impressed by Mao's obvious earnestness and by his willingness to sacrifice personal comfort for the pursuit of an ideal. In these he contrasted all too clearly with the corruption and indifference of most Nationalist leaders.

Some of Mao's dedication, toughness and reserve may also have been the product of his bitter personal experiences along the road to power. His sister and his second wife, Yang Kaihui, were executed in 1930 by General Chiang, a younger brother was killed fighting a rear-guard action during the Long March, another younger brother was executed in 1943 in Xinjiang and Mao's eldest son was killed in the Korean War. Another son, according to Red Guard sources during the Cultural Revolution, was said to have gone mad because of the way he was brought up by a "bourgeois" family after his mother was executed. (Other accounts say the son was mentally retarded. Still others have him giving speeches in praise of his father.)

Mao also had several close brushes with death. In 1927, when he was organizing peasants and workers in Hunan, he was captured by local pro-Kuomintang—that is, pro-Nationalist—militiamen, who marched him back to their headquarters to be shot. Just in sight of their office, Mao broke loose and fled into a nearby field, where he hid in tall grass until sunset.

"The soldiers pursued me, and forced some peasants to help them search for me," he related to Mr. Snow. "Many times they came very near, once or twice so close that I could almost have touched them, but somehow I escaped discovery. At last when it was dusk they abandoned the search."

He was certainly mindful of the cost of the revolution to his family and friends. In a talk in 1964 with Mao Yuanxin, the son of his executed brother, Mao recalled: "Very many members of our family have given their lives, killed by the Kuomintang and the American imperialists. You grew up eating honey, and thus far you have never known suffering. In the future, if you do not become a rightist, but rather a centrist, I shall be satisfied. You have never suffered—how can you be a leftist?"

Perhaps his losses contributed to Mao's attitude toward his enemies. Unlike Stalin, Mao never sought to put vast numbers of his opponents in the party to death. Instead, in a very Chinese, even Confucian, way, he believed in the power of education to reform them and sent them off to labor camps or the countryside for reindoctrination and redemption.

However, he did not cavil at killing those whom he considered true counterrevolutionaries. One of the first instances of this occurred in late 1930 in the small town of Futian, in the Communists' base area, which Mao had built up since 1927. In putting down a revolt by soldiers who challenged his rule, Mao had 2,000 to 3,000 officers and men executed. In the early 1950s, to consolidate the Communists' power, Mao launched a violent campaign against counterrevolutionaries. According to an estimate accepted by Stuart Schram, Mao's most careful and sensitive biographer, from a million to three million people, including landlords, nationalist agents and others suspected of being "class enemies," were executed.

"There is no evidence whatever," wrote Stuart Schram, that Mao "took pleasure in killing or torturing. But he has never hesitated to employ violence whenever he believed it necessary. No doubt, Mao regarded it all as a natural part of revolutionary struggle. He gave no quarter, and he asked for none."

As Mao himself put it, in one of the most celebrated passages in his writing, his 1927 "report of an investigation into the peasant movement": "A revolution is not the same as inviting people to dinner or writing an essay or painting a picture or embroidering a flower; it cannot be anything so refined, so calm and gentle, or so 'mild, kind, courteous, restrained and magnanimous' [the virtues of Confucius as described by a disciple]. A revolution is an uprising, an act of violence whereby one class overthrows the authority of another. To put it bluntly, it was necessary to bring about a brief reign of terror in every rural area."

Little is known about Mao's personal life or habits, which he kept sheltered from the glare of publicity. He was an inordinate cigarette smoker, and during the Long March, when cut off from regular sources of supply, is said to have experimented by smoking various leaves. Perhaps because of his habit, his voice was husky and he coughed a good deal in later life.

He apparently liked to work 13 or 14 hours a day, and Mr. Snow found that he frequently stayed up until 2 or 3 in the morning reading and going over reports. Despite infirmity in his last years, Mao had an iron constitution that he consciously developed as a student in Changsha, the provincial capital of Hunan.

In this process Mao and his student friends—"a serious-minded little group" that "had no time for love or romance," Mao recalled—were trying to overcome the traditional Chinese prejudice that any physical labor or exercise was lower class. Mao himself was so much a product of this tradition that when the Chinese revolution of 1911 broke out and he joined the army for a few months in a burst of enthusiasm, he spent much of his salary of $7 a month to pay carriers to fetch his water since intellectuals did not do that kind of work.

Physical strength, courage and military prowess remained a basic theme of Mao's life. Even his first published writing, an essay written in 1917, was a plea that Chinese people exercise more. "Our nation is wanting in strength," it began. "The military spirit has not been encouraged."

Whether, in another period—July 1966—Mao actually took his widely publicized swim in the Yangtze for 65 minutes is perhaps more a matter of legend than of fact. But his approach to swimming typified his dogged pursuit of an objective.

"I say that if you are resolved to do it, you can certainly learn, whether you are young or old," Mao once advised his principal military officers in discussing the need to improve themselves. "I will give you an example. I really learned to swim well only in 1954; previously I had not mastered it. In 1954, there was an indoor pool at Qinghua University [in Beijing]. I went there every day with my bag, changed my clothes, and for three months without interruption I studied the nature of water. Water doesn't drown people. Water is afraid of people."

A voracious reader, Mao enjoyed both the Chinese classics and novels he had devoured as a boy, and Western history, literature and philosophy, which he read in translation. He often impressed his visitors with an apt allusion to literature or a salty proverb, but he could be remarkably offhand and whimsical for the leader of a country. In the 1950s, when he was still head of state, he once greeted a particularly tall Western diplomat with the exclamation "My God! As tall as that!"

Mao's informal style, his pithy and frequent use

of Chinese metaphors and his transcendent charisma made him a natural leader for the masses of peasants. A Chinese writer observed that "Mao Zedong is fundamentally a character from a Chinese novel or opera."

In his later years Mao spent most of his time in his simple, yellowish residence inside Beijing's Forbidden City, cut off from all but a small group of people. Some of these were female nurses who helped him walk; others were the three women interpreters who usually translated for him when there were foreign visitors. Given his difficult Hunan accent and speech problem, one of the women had to translate his words into comprehensible Mandarin Chinese.

Assigned to do that was Wang Hairong, whom some believed was his niece but others thought was the daughter of one of his favorite teachers. In any event, in the spring of 1976, after the downfall of Deng Xiaoping, Miss Wang and the two others were suddenly replaced without an announcement, stirring speculation that someone else in the entourage was jealous of their position.

For all the overwhelming changes Mao brought to China, the drama of how he and others at the top of the Communist hierarchy reached decisions seemed a tale from the Ming Dynasty court.

Who Mao's aides were, for example, who arranged his appointments, prepared documents for him to read and sign in his study behind the red velvet drapes or carried his orders to the Central Committee—all this is not known outside China. One key figure in the mystery was certainly Jiang Qing, his fourth wife, an outspoken, sometimes vitriolic woman who claimed the mantle of his most faithful disciple.

Mao considered that he had been married only three times—his first wife was a peasant girl to whom his parents married him when he was only 14 and she was 20. He never lived with her, and as he told Mr. Snow, "I did not consider her my wife and at this time gave little thought to her."

His second wife, Yang Kaihui, the woman executed in 1930, was the daughter of one of Mao's most influential teachers in Changsha, Yang Zhangqi, a professor of ethics. Professor Yang was to introduce the young Mao to Li Dazhao, a brilliant nationalistic intellectual and writer in Beijing who was one of the founders of the Communist movement in China.

Although Mao has sometimes been adjudged an ascetic man, bent only on the pursuit of revolution and power, he evidently could also be sentimental and romantic. In 1937, in reply to a commemorative poem written by a woman whose husband was a Communist leader killed in battle, Mao composed the following verse:

I lost my proud poplar, and you your willow,
Poplar and willow soar lightly to the heaven of heavens.
Wu Kang, asked what he has to offer,
Presents them respectfully with cassia wine.
The lonely goddess in the moon spreads her ample sleeves
To dance for these faithful souls in the endless sky.
Of a sudden comes word of the tiger's defeat on earth,
And they break into tears of torrential rain.

The official interpretation accompanying a later collection of Mao's poems points out that his second wife's surname means "poplar" while the name of the man killed in battle means "willow."

According to an ancient legend, Wu Kang, mentioned in the third line, had committed certain crimes in his search for immortality and was condemned to cut down a cassia tree on the moon. Each time he raises his ax the tree becomes whole again, and thus he must go on felling it for eternity. The tiger in the seventh line refers to the Kuomintang regime Mao was fighting, and, hence, the last couplet describes the emotion of Mao's lost companion at the final triumph of the revolution. The official interpretation found that the poem contained a "large element of revolutionary romanticism."

In 1928, while Mao's second wife was still alive and he was 35, he began living with an 18-year-old, He Zizhen. By some accounts she was a forceful character and a commander of a women's regiment; she was also said to have been the daughter of a landlord. In any case she married Mao in 1930, after Miss Yang was executed, and later accompanied him on the perilous and exhausting Long March, one of the few women to take part. One of the five children she bore Mao was born on the march.

The rigors evidently broke her health, and not long after reaching the Communists' new base area in Yanan, in the northwest, she was sent to the Soviet Union for medical treatment. While she was away, there arrived in Yanan a minor movie actress from Shanghai, Lan Ping, who, in contrast to the plain-living and isolated Communists, must have seemed glamorous and attractive. According to one version, she came to Mao's notice after ostentatiously sitting in the front row at one of his lectures and clapping loudly. It was apparently love at first sight for Mao, and Miss Lan—with her name changed to Jiang Qing—was soon living in Mao's cave house.

Their affair reportedly angered some of Mao's colleagues, who felt that he had betrayed his faithful companion of the Long March, Miss He, a genuine Communist, for the seductive Miss Jiang. To win approval for their marriage Mao is said to have pledged that Miss Jiang would stay out of politics. This may have been the origin of the widespread suspicion of and distaste for her among party leaders that have dogged her since.

Miss Jiang did keep a low profile for much of the next three decades, but in 1964, when Mao grew dissatisfied with the party and prepared to launch the Cultural Revolution, he turned to her as one of the few people he could trust.

She undertook a vigorous reform of the popular traditional opera and the movies, demanding that they inject heavy doses of "class struggle" into every performance and paint all heroes in the whitest whites and villains in the blackest blacks. She also lined up a leftist literary critic in Shanghai, Yao Wenyuan, who was willing to write a scathing attack on a play, *Hai Rui Dismissed from Office*, that was an allegorical criticism of Mao. The publication of the article in November 1965 in Shanghai—Mao could not get it printed in Beijing, where his opponents were in control—signaled the start of the Cultural Revolution.

Miss Jiang was soon promoted to a commanding position in the group Mao established to direct the Cultural Revolution, and she vastly increased her unpopularity by making stinging personal attacks on many leading officials.

When the Cultural Revolution subsided, Miss Jiang's authority was reduced, but in the following years she continued to try to exert her influence. She may have been instrumental in the downfall of Mr. Deng early in 1976. He was accused of, among other crimes, failing to attend any of her model operas and trying to cut off a state subsidy to her pet production brigade near Tianjin.

How Mao regarded his controversial wife is difficult to say. She once indicated to an American scholar, Roxane Witke, that she and Mao were not always close personally. In 1957, when Mao made his second trip to Moscow, she happened to be there in the hospital but he neither stopped in to see her nor phoned, she related. Later, at the start of the Cultural Revolution, Mao wrote her a letter that is often cited by her detractors in the party.

"I think you also ought to pay attention to this problem," he wrote. "Don't be obsessed by victory. It is necessary to constantly remind ourselves of our own weaknesses, deficiencies and mistakes. I have on countless occasions reminded you of this. The last time was in April in Shanghai."

Although Miss Jiang had a reputation among Chinese for being rancorous and spiteful, Americans who met her during the visits to Beijing by Presidents Nixon and Ford found her gay and vivacious. Miss Witke was impressed with her evident devotion to Mao's cause and felt she had suffered from being a woman in a world where men predominated.

Mao's apparent fondness for women and the checkered pattern of his married life contrasted sharply with the monotonous austerity and Puritanism he enforced since 1949. Romance is now frowned on as a decadent bourgeois idea, and the age when women may marry has been pushed back to 25 and for men to 28.

Marriage was not the only instance of a certain willingness on Mao's part to bend the rules for himself. Though he insisted that all plays, novels, poems and paintings follow the often-stultifying code of socialist realism—"So far as we are concerned, art and literature are intended for the people," he said in talks at Yanan in 1942 that became the basis of a rigid artistic canon—he continued to write poetry as he chose, much of it in difficult classical forms with obscure allusions to the now-discredited Chinese classics. This contradiction, Mr. Schram, his biographer, noted, "seems to fill him with a mixture of embarrassment and pride."

Looking into Mao's endlessly complex character, Mr. Schram concluded that he was fundamentally a Chinese patriot. Mao dated his attainment of "a certain amount of political consciousness" from the reading of a pamphlet in 1909, when he was 16, that deplored China's "loss" of Korea, Taiwan, Indochina, Burma and other tributary states. In 1936, speaking with Mr. Snow, Mao still recalled the opening sentence of the pamphlet: "Alas, China will be subjugated."

In Mao's case his native xenophobia was to be reinforced by his discovery of Leninism, in which imperialism was blamed for the backwardness of countries like China. But, Mr. Schram wrote, while Mao became "a deeply convinced Leninist revolutionary, and while the categories in which he reasons are Marxist categories, the deepest springs of his personality are, to a large extent, to be found in the Chinese tradition, and China's glory is at least as important to him as is world revolution."

Mr. Schram noted that in the closing years of Mao's life, he went so far as to subtly play down the importance of Marxism-Leninism in the Chinese revolution, envisioning it only as a storehouse of political techniques. This was in some ways a throwback to the views of 19th-century conservative Chinese imperial officials who wanted to strengthen China against the West but insisted that it borrow only Western "techniques" like gunboats and parliaments without bringing in "Western learning," which might subvert the Chinese essence. As Mao put it in 1965, consciously referring to the 19th-century formulation: "We cannot adopt Western learning as the substance. We can only use Western technology."

Mao's contribution to Marxism-Leninism lay not in his theoretical writings, which were often plodding and in which he showed little interest himself, but in his Sinification of Marxism. When the Chinese Communists were floundering and faced extinction because of their orthodox concentration on the cities and the proletariat, Mao discovered the peasantry. He succeeded in imposing a party organized along tight Leninist lines and, animated by certain basic Marxist tenets, on a largely peasant base.

With suitable indoctrination, as Mao saw it, both the Chinese peasantry and Chinese intellectuals, who made up much of the party's leadership, could develop a "proletarian" consciousness. As Prof. Benjamin I. Schwartz of Harvard wrote in his pioneering study, *Chinese Communism and the Rise of Mao*, it was "a heresy in act never made explicit in theory."

The other basic element in Mao's approach to revolution was his inordinate belief in the power of the human will to overcome material obstacles and his conception that the necessary energy to propel the revolution lay stored among the masses. The potential energy of the peasantry was borne home to him with sudden force in 1927, when he embarked on the investigation of the peasant movement in his home province that formed the basis of his famous report. The liberation Mao found at work in village after village, with peasants overthrowing their landlords, had an enormous impact on him.

Beginning with these two basic insights—the importance of the peasantry to revolution in China and the power of the human will—Mao went on to elaborate the strategy and tactics for the entire revolution. First, he recognized the importance of winning the support of the people, who were, as he put it in his widely quoted formulation, like the ocean in which the guerrillas must swim like fish. Talking with André Malraux in 1964, Mao related: "You must realize that before us, among the masses, no one had addressed themselves to women or to the young. Nor, of course, to the peasants. For the first time in their lives, every one of them felt involved."

Similarly, to keep the allegiance of his guerrilla fighters, who received no pay and often inadequate food and weapons, Mao developed careful rules of behavior.

"The reason why the Red Army has been able to carry on in spite of such poor material conditions and such frequent engagements," he wrote, "is its practice of democracy. The officers do not beat the men; officers and men receive equal treatment; soldiers are free to hold meetings and to speak out; trivial formalities have been done away with; and the accounts are open for all to inspect. The soldiers handle the mess arrangements. All this gives great satisfaction to the soldiers."

For military tactics Mao drew on his boyhood reading of China's classic swashbuckling novels such as *The Romance of the Three Kingdoms* and *The Water Margin*, which describe in vivid detail the exploits and stratagems of ancient warriors and bandits. Not surprisingly, Mao's military tactics—which were to play an important role in Vietnam—bore a close resemblance to those of Sun Tzu, the military writer of the 5th century B.C.

The basic problem was to find a way for a guerrilla force to overcome General Chiang's much larger and better equipped army. To this end Mao applied two principles—concentration of force so that he attacked only when he had a numerical advantage, and surprise.

"We use the few to defeat the many. That is no longer a secret, and in general the enemy is now well acquainted with our method. But he can neither prevent our victories nor avoid his own losses, because he does not know when and where we shall act. This we keep secret. The Red Army generally operates by surprise attacks."

Mao's military precepts were summed up in a four-line slogan his troops memorized:

The enemy advances: we retreat.
The enemy camps; we harass.
The enemy tires; we attack.
The enemy retreats; we pursue.

To these Mao was to add the concept of a base area where his guerrillas could rest and replenish their supplies, and from which, over time, they could expand. In the end, this strategy led to victory.

The supreme moment came on Oct. 1, 1949, when Mao, at age 54, stood on the high balcony of Tian An Men, the Gate of Heavenly Peace in Beijing through which tribute bearers had once come to prostrate themselves before the emperors, and proclaimed the People's Republic of China.

Processions had filled the square in front of the scarlet, brass-studded gate. The air was chilly with the wind from the Gobi. Mao, wearing a drab cloth cap and a worn tunic and trousers, had Mr. Zhou and Marshal Zhu with him. Below them the immense throng shouted: "May Mao Zedong live 10,000 years!"

Suddenly there came a hush. Sliding up the immense white staff in the square was a small bundle that cracked open as it neared the top to reveal a flag 30 feet broad, bloodred, with five yellow stars in the upper left quadrant. Guns roared in salute. On cue the crowd broke out in the new national anthem, and Mao stepped to the microphone amid more cheers.

"The Central Governing Council of the People's Republic of China today assumes power in Beijing," he announced. A week before, speaking to the Chinese People's Political Consultative Conference, he said: "Our nation will never again be an insulted nation. We have stood up. Let the domestic and foreign reactionaries tremble before us."

His words came 28 years after he and 11 others founded the Chinese Communist party in Shanghai. Its membership then was 52. "A small spark can start a prairie fire," Mao once said. It had.

Mao was born in a tile-roofed house surrounded by rice fields and low hills in Shaoshan, a village in Hunan Province, in central China, on Dec. 26, 1893. His father, Mao Rensheng, was a tall, sturdily built peasant, industrious and thrifty, despotic and high-handed. Through hard work, saving and some small trading he raised himself from being a landless former soldier to what his son later described as the status of a "rich peasant," though in the China of those days that hardly meant being wealthy.

Mao's mother, Wen Jimei, was a hardy woman who worked in the house and fields. A Buddhist, she exhibited a warmhearted kindness toward her children much in contrast to her husband's patriarchal sternness. During famines, when her husband—he disapproved of charity—was not watching, she would give food to the poor who came begging.

The China into which Mao was born was a restive empire on the point of its final breakup, which came in 1911. Since the middle of the 19th century the ruling Qing Dynasty had been beset by rural uprisings, most notably the Taiping revolt in the 1860s, and by the encroachments of foreign powers that challenged China's traditional belief in its superiority.

The mandarins who governed on behalf of the emperor in Beijing seemed helpless to stop either the internal decay or the foreign incursions. Corrupt, smug, the product of a rarefied examination system based on the Confucian classics, they procrastinated. China had no industry, and its peasants, 85 percent of the population, were mired in poverty and ignorance, subject to the constant threat of starvation and extortionate demands by landlords.

When Mao was 6, his father set him to work in the rice fields. But, wanting the youngster to learn enough characters to keep the family's accounts, Mao's father also sent him to the village primary school. The curriculum was the Confucian Analects, learned by rote in the old style. Mao preferred Chinese novels, "especially stories of rebellions," he later recalled, which he used to read in school, "covering them up with a classic when the teacher walked past."

At 13 Mao left the school, working long hours on the farm during the day and keeping the accounts at night. His father frequently beat Mao and his two younger brothers and gave them only the most meager food, never meat or eggs.

At this point there occurred an incident that Western writers have seized on as a seminal clue to Mao's later life. During a reception, Mao's father began to berate him for being lazy and useless. Infuriated, Mao fled to a nearby pond, threatening to jump in. Eventually the quarrel was resolved by compromise when Mao agreed to kowtow—on one knee only—in exchange for his father's promise to stop the beatings. "Thus the war ended," Mao recalled, "and from it I learned that when I defended my rights by open rebellion my father relented, but when I remained meek and submissive he only cursed and beat me the more."

Some scholars have also noted the possible influence on Mao of growing up in Hunan, a subtropical region whose many rivers and mountains made it a favorite haunt for bandits and secret societies. Hunanese are also famed for their vigorous personalities and their political talents as well as their love of red pepper, and they have produced a disproportionate number of leaders in the 19th and 20th centuries.

Although out of school, Mao retained his passion for reading in his spare time, and at 16, over his father's opposition, enrolled in a modern higher primary school nearby. It was at this school, in a busy market town, that Mao's real intellectual and political development began. In newspapers a cousin sent him he learned of the nationalistic late 19th-century reformers, and in a book, *Great Heroes of the World*, he read about Washington and Napoleon (from his earliest days Mao was fascinated by martial exploits).

Most of his fellow students were sons of landlords, expensively dressed and genteel in manner. Mao had only one decent suit and generally went about in an old, frayed coat and trousers. Moreover, because he had been forced to interrupt his education for several years, he was much older than the others and towered above them. As a result this tall, ragged, uncouth "new boy" met with a mixture of ridicule and hostility. The experience may also have left its mark in his attitude toward the landlord class.

After a year wanderlust took Mao off to the provincial capital, Changsha, where he entered a junior high school. The year was 1911, the time of the overthrow of the Manchu Dynasty, and Mao was caught up in the political turmoil that swept the country. He cut off his pigtail, a rebellious act, and it was then that he joined a local army unit. After several more months of drifting and scanning classified ads in the press for opportunities, he spent half a year in the provincial library, where he read translations of Adam Smith's *Wealth of Nations*, Darwin's *On the Origin of Species* and Rousseau's *Social Contract*. He also saw a map of the world for the first time.

In 1913 Mao enrolled in the provincial normal school in Changsha, where he received his last five years of formal education. Although it was really only a high school, its standards were high, and Mao was particularly influenced by his ethics teacher, Prof. Yang Zhangqi, whose daughter he was later to marry. Professor Yang, who had studied in Japan and Europe, advocated combining Western and Chinese ideas to prod China back to life. Through him Mao soon found himself in touch with the mainstream of intellectual life, which was then caught up in what was called the May 4th Movement, an explosive nationalistic effort to modernize Chinese culture.

It was at this time that Mao published his first writing, an article for the popular Beijing magazine *New Youth*, on the need for physical fitness to build military strength. He also began to display his genius for leadership, setting up a radical student group.

Having graduated from the normal school in 1918, Mao set off that fall for Beijing. The timing was critical. It was a period when intellectuals were turning from one Western "ism" to another in search of the latest and most potent elixir to revive their nation. In Mao's case, as he later wrote, he arrived just when "the salvos of the October Revolution" in Russia were bringing Marxism to China.

Mao secured a menial job as a library assistant at Beijing University under Li Dazhao, who had published an influential article, "The Victory of Bolshevism," and who had just founded the first Marxist study society in China. Mao was still somewhat "confused, looking for a road," but he was becoming "more and more radical."

Early the next spring he left Beijing for Shanghai, where he saw off some friends on their way to study in France; he was reluctant to go because of his lack of ability in foreign languages. Over the next two years he moved between Shanghai, Beijing and Changsha, teaching part of the time and throwing himself into organizing radical student groups and editing two popular journals that were suppressed by the local warlord government.

One article he published at the time, "The Great Union of the Popular Masses," which held that the vast majority of Chinese were progressive and constituted a mighty force for change, reflected what Mr. Schram has called Mao's populist tendency. In the biographer's opinion, "this idea can be regarded as the bridge which led him from the relatively conservative and traditionalist nationalism of 1917 to a genuinely Marxist viewpoint."

In the fall of 1920 Mao copied the example of his former boss in Beijing, Mr. Li, who had just established a small Communist group there, and formed one in Changsha. The following July, Mao and the

11 other delegates met in Shanghai to form the Chinese party.

The first congress was forced by a police raid to flee from its original meeting place in a girls' school to a holiday boat on a nearby lake. Filled with a new sense of zeal, Mao returned to Hunan, where, in orthodox Marxist fashion, he set about organizing labor unions and strikes. He had found his true vocation as a revolutionary.

The embryonic party fell heavily under the influence of the Russians, who helped engineer an alliance between the Chinese Communists and the much stronger Nationalists of Sun Yat-sen. Stalin's goals in this, as in all his later moves in China, did not necessarily coincide with those of the Chinese Communists, and therein lay the source of much of the later friction.

Stalin wanted first to secure a friendly buffer on his eastern flank, so had to avoid any upheaval that would invite Western intervention. Second, he sought control over the Chinese party. His policy of alliance with the Nationalists worked well enough for the first few years, giving the Communists a chance to expand, but in 1927 it suddenly became a disaster when General Chiang, who had succeeded to leadership of the Nationalists in 1925, turned on the Communists and carried out his massacre.

Perhaps because of Mao's populism and his highly nationalistic feelings, he was one of the most enthusiastic supporters of the alliance. His patriotism was always near the surface.

Criticism of his dual role had a fortuitous result, eventually making him uncomfortable enough so that in 1925 he returned to his native village for a rest and, in the process, encountered a wave of peasant unrest. "Formerly I had not fully realized the degree of class among the peasantry," he told Edgar Snow. From this time on Mao was to take a major interest in the peasantry—first lecturing at the Kuomintang's Peasant Movement Training Institute in Canton in 1926, then in early 1927 making his renowned inspection of the Hunanese countryside, and finally, in the fall of 1927, after the Communists split with General Chiang, he led his small band of surviving supporters up into the Qinggang Mountains to start the search for power all over again—on his terms.

The period from 1927 to 1935, when Mao finally won command of the party, was filled with complex wrangling over leadership and policy. The principal figures in the party (who remained in the security of the international settlement in Shanghai) and Stalin kept looking for a "revolutionary upsurge," and in accordance with conventional Marxist dogma planned attacks on cities. Mao, cut off in the countryside, was condemned for his peasant "deviation," though he was not often informed of the latest shifts in line or of his demotions until much later. Twice, in 1927 and 1930, he was directed to lead attacks on cities, both ending in catastrophic defeats. Mao was to recall: "Long ago the Chinese Communists had firsthand experience of some of Stalin's mistakes."

The Qinggangshan area where Mao gradually worked out his own strategy was a storybook setting: A range of precipitous mountains on the border between Jiangxi and Hunan, it was an almost impregnable vastness populated only by a few simple villages and by groups of bandits. By allying with these bandits and drawing on the peasants, whom he rewarded by reducing rents, Mao built his band of 1,000 soldiers into 100,000 by 1934. A capital was declared at Ruijin, in southern Jiangxi.

Mao's very success proved his undoing. In 1931 the party Central Committee moved up to Jiangxi from Shanghai and proceeded to strip him of his posts in the party and army, with Mr. Zhou replacing him as chief commissar in 1933. One of Mao's few steadfast supporters at this time was Mr. Deng, whom Mao was to oust from high position in 1976.

The loss of control was doubly grave because it coincided with the fifth of General Chiang's encirclement campaigns to wipe out the Communists. The previous efforts had failed in the face of Mao's tactics, withdrawing when outnumbered and then launching surprise attacks in overwhelming force on isolated units. Now the other Communist leaders tried the Nationalists head-on, but General Chiang had 700,000 men—a 7-to-1 advantage—and on the advice of a Nazi general, Hans von Steeckt, slowly strangled the Communists with a ring of barbed wire and machine-gun emplacements.

The only answer was flight. On Oct. 15, 1934, the main body of the Communist army broke through the Nationalist lines and headed southwest, beginning the Long March. Neither their destination nor their purpose was clear. Some thought of finding a new base area; others, including Mao, spoke of going north to fight the Japanese, who had been expanding farther and farther into China since 1931.

Of the 90,000 Communists who broke out, only 20,000 would eventually reach the new base area in Shaanxi, in the northwest, over a year and 6,000 miles later. For all its hardships, the Long March both saved and strengthened the Communists, giving them a legend of invincibility, a guerrilla ethic, a firm discipline and unity, and a new leader—Mao. He was finally given command, after several more blunders along the march, when the army stopped at the remote town of Zunyi, in Guizhou Province, in January 1935. Zunyi had been captured without firing a shot by using a ruse straight out of the *Romance of the Three Kingdoms*, involving captured Kuomintang uniforms and banners.

In Yanan, just below the Great Wall, the area where Chinese civilization originally developed over 3,000 years before, Mao proceeded to build a new party and state fully in his own image. This was a critical period, for the ideas he worked out in Yanan he would turn back to nostalgically in the late 1950s and 1960s, when he launched the Great Leap Forward and the Cultural Revolution. Among them were the sending of party cadres down to the countryside for ideological remolding, and the stress on self-reliance, mutual aid teams on farms and popularized education.

Mao's mood at this time was perhaps best suggested by his poem "Snow," written in February 1936, shortly after his arrival in the northwest. A ringing affirmation of his links with China's glorious past and his love for the land, it reads:

This is the scene in that northern land;
A hundred leagues are sealed with ice,
A thousand leagues of whirling snow.
On either side of the Great Wall
One vastness is all you see.
From end to end of the great river
The rushing torrent is frozen and lost.
The mountains dance like silver snakes.
The highlands roll like waxen elephants,
As if they sought to vie in height with the
Lord of heaven,
And on a sunny day
See how the white-robed beauty is adorned
with rouge, enchantment beyond compare.
Lured by such great beauty in our landscape
Innumerable heroes have rivaled one another
to bow in homage.
But alas, Qin Shihuang and Han Wudi were
rather lacking in culture,
Tang Taizong and Song Taizu had little
taste for poetry,
And Genghis Khan, the favorite son of
heaven for a day,
knew only how to bend his bow to shoot
great vultures.
Now they are all past and gone.
To find heroes in the grand manner,
We must look rather in the present.

The most decisive stroke by Mao at this time was his genius in making the Communists the incarnation of Chinese resistance to the Japanese. The Japanese invasion, which began in 1931 in Manchuria and culminated in full-scale war in 1937, had provoked an enormous wave of popular resentment.

In the face of this, General Chiang continued to insist that his army would fight the Communists first and deal with the Japanese later. This strategy backfired in December 1936, when pro-Nationalist troops under Zhang Xueliang, the young warlord whom the Japanese had driven from Manchuria, kidnapped General Chiang at Xian, near the Communists' base area. Chiang was released only after agreeing to a second united front with the Communists to fight the Japanese.

Although frictions were obvious from the start, the agreement gave Mao a badly needed breathing spell and the chance to expand Communist areas across the whole of North China under the guise of fighting the Japanese. For this the Communists were well prepared by their guerrilla training. By the end of the war in 1945, Communist troops, renamed the Eighth Route Army, had increased to a formidable force of a million men covering an area inhabited by 100 million people.

By an accident of history the Japanese invasion was to prove "perhaps the most important single factor in Mao's rise to power," Mr. Schram concluded in his biography.

Using this time of relative stability to read and write broadly, Mao systematized his thought. Several of his most important books and speeches were produced in the Yanan period, including *On Protracted War*, *The Chinese Revolution and the Chinese Communist Party*, *On New Democracy*, and *On Practice* and *On Contradiction*.

One of his most quoted speeches came in 1938: "Every Communist must grasp the truth: 'Political power grows out of the barrel of a gun.' Our principle is that the party commands the gun, and the gun will never be allowed to command the party. But it is also true that with guns at our disposal we can really build up the party organization."

In 1942, to discipline the thousands of new officials the party was enrolling and to insure their fidelity to his thought, Mao launched the first rectification campaign. It was the beginning of thought reform, and it was also the start of the cult of Mao. He lent the cult a hand by ordering the study of his works. (In the Cultural Revolution he would promote an article praising his thought that he had helped compose.)

The rectification campaign had another purpose—to end what Mao saw as overreliance on Soviet guidance: "There is no such thing as abstract Marxism, but only concrete Marxism. What we call concrete Marxism is Marxism that has taken on a national form. Consequently the Sinification of Marxism—that is to say, making certain that in all of its manifestations it is imbued with Chinese peculiarities—becomes a problem that must be understood and solved by the whole party." This was a call for independence from Moscow.

For a brief time in 1944–45 Mao and the Americans had a short-lived courtship. American diplomats and journalists who were allowed into Yanan at this time, when Washington hoped to bring the Communists and Nationalists together against the Japanese, were invariably impressed by Mao and his army's accomplishments. Mao, for his part, looked to the possibility of winning some of the United States aid that was flowing to General Chiang for use against Tokyo.

"The work which we Communists are carrying on today is the very same work which was carried on earlier in America by Washington, Jefferson and Lincoln," said an encouraging editorial in the official party newspaper on July 4, 1944. But General Chiang's intransigence blocked all efforts in this direction.

When the war ended in 1945, Washington endeavored to play a dual role. On the one hand it helped General Chiang by continuing aid to him and airlifting thousands of his troops to occupy Japanese positions in Manchuria ahead of the advancing Communists. On the other hand it sponsored negotiations for a coalition government. At the urging of the Americans Mao flew to Chongqing—his first airplane flight—where he held 43 days of ultimately futile talks with General Chiang. In November 1945 President Harry S Truman dispatched Gen. George C. Marshall to China as his special envoy; he would continue trying to arrange a cease-fire and coalition government until January 1947, but full-scale civil war had broken out early in 1946.

General Chiang was vastly overconfident. He had American backing, apparent neutrality on the part of Stalin, who was not eager to see Mao win, and a 4-to-1 numerical advantage. But his army was racked by corruption, punishing inflation and an incompetent officer corps in which promotion was based entirely on loyalty. The general war-weariness and hostility of the populace to the Nationalists also played a role.

By the middle of 1947 the Nationalists' advantage had been reduced to 2 to 1, and by mid-1948 the two sides were almost even. Nationalist generals began surrendering in packs, and within a year it was all over.

Over the next five years much of China's development followed the orthodox Soviet model. Mao had proclaimed in 1949 that henceforth China would "lean to one side" in cooperation with the Soviet Union, and so it seemed. The first five-year plan (1953–57) placed emphasis on heavy industry, centralized planning, technical expertise and a large defense buildup in the Soviet pattern.

Part of this may have been the result of what Mao later maintained was his decision in 1949 to retreat to a "second line" and leave "day-to-day work" to others. He did this, he said, "out of concern for state security and in view of the lessons of Stalin in the Soviet Union." "Many things are left to other people, so that other people's prestige is built up, and when I go to see God there won't be such a big upheaval in the state," he wrote. "It seems there are some things which the comrades in the first line have not managed too well."

Whatever the case, China was disrupted in 1950 by the Korean War. Although its exact origins are still obscure and controversial, the weight of evidence seems to indicate that the war was basically a Soviet initiative and that Mao was not consulted. The war had terrible consequences for the new state. It prompted President Truman to order the defense of Taiwan, which General Chiang had retreated to in 1949; it froze Mao's relations with Washington for two decades; it cost tens of thousands of Chinese lives and funds urgently needed for reconstruction.

The war over, Mao began to grow impatient with the speed of China's development and the way Socialism was being introduced. In 1955 he ordered an acceleration in the tempo of collectivization in the countryside.

If over the succeeding years China often appeared to follow a zigzag course, it must have been largely a result of shifting of gears as Mao alternated between his warlike, utopian outlook and his more prudent realism in the face of obvious economic difficulties.

In 1956, following Mr. Khrushchev's revelations of Stalin's excesses, the riots in Poland and the uprising in Hungary, Mao took a new tack and proclaimed the policy of "let a hundred flowers bloom." He hoped that some relaxation of tight controls would bring forth useful but limited criticism of the party to avert similar problems in China and at the same time encourage Chinese intellectuals to become good Communists. But he did not intend full-scale liberalization.

In a speech, "On the Correct Handling of Contradictions Among the People," in February 1957, Mao outlined his own typically two-sided or contradictory rationale for this. China should have both more freedom and more discipline, an impossibility in Western eyes but not to Mao, who saw similar contradictions or dichotomies everywhere. He said, "If there were no contradictions and no struggle, there would be no world, no progress, no life, and there would be nothing at all."

The trick lay in analyzing contradictions correctly. As Mao put it in 1957: "Within the ranks of our people democracy stands in relation to centralism and freedom to discipline. They are two conflicting aspects of a single entity, contradictory as well as united, and we should not one-sidedly emphasize one to the detriment of the other."

Mao's tendency to reason in this fashion owed much to the dialectics of Marxism, but it may also have had its origin in the Chinese theory of yin and yang, the two great alternating forces, which Mao absorbed as a boy.

When, contrary to Mao's expectation, the hundred-flowers policy led to a vast outpouring of criticism that called the Communist party itself into question, he quickly switched to the other side of his formula—discipline—and instituted a tough rectification campaign.

It was at this time that he made his second trip to Moscow, in November 1957, and created a sensation by declaring that there was no need to fear nuclear war. "I said that if the worse came to the worst and half of mankind died, the other half would remain, while imperialism would be razed to the ground, and the whole world would become Socialist: in a number of years there would be 2.7 billion people again and definitely more."

This remark accorded with Mao's deeply held belief that men, not machines or weapons, were the decisive factor. In 1947, in an interview, he had declared: "The atom bomb is a paper tiger used by the U.S. reactionaries to scare people. It looks terrible, but in fact it isn't. Of course, the atom bomb is a weapon of mass slaughter, but the outcome of a war is decided by people, not by one or two new types of weapon." It was a guerrilla's view.

In Mao's recollection, this period, the winter of 1957–58, marked a great watershed in China. His misgivings about the Soviet Union had reached the breaking point, and he resolved to put an end to copying the Russians. He reached back to the wellsprings of his experience in Jiangxi and Yanan, reemphasizing the countryside and the potential energy of the peasantry in overcoming material obstacles. China was to make "a great leap forward." By reorganizing the peasants into communes, Mao would release their energy, vastly increase agricultural production and catch up with the West overnight. It was a vision, not a plan.

As Mao described it: "China's 600 million people have two remarkable peculiarities; they are, first of all, poor, and secondly blank. That may seem like a bad thing, but it is really a good thing. Poor people want change, want to do things, want revolution. A clean sheet of paper has no blotches, and so the newest and most beautiful words can be written on it."

All China went to work at a fever pitch. Peasants set up backyard blast furnaces to make their own steel, the symbol of industrialization. Cadres became dizzy with success and reported a 100 percent jump in agricultural production in a single year. A jingle by peasants in Hunan caught the mood: "Setting up a people's commune is like going to heaven. The achievements of a single night surpass those of several millennia."

It was not so easy. Terrible dislocations ensued, food grew scarce and there was even some starvation. It took three years to restore the economy.

These steps led to the first serious challenge to Mao's leadership since the early 1930s. At a Central Committee meeting in the summer of 1959 at the mountain resort of Lushan, he was boldly criticized by Peng Dehuai, then minister of defense. Under the impact of Mr. Peng's attacks, Mao became tense and irritable. "Now that you have said so much, let me say something, will you," he finally told the group. "I have taken sleeping pills three times, but I cannot go to sleep."

Candidly accepting some of the onus for the disaster, he declared: "The chaos was in a grand scale, and I take responsibility. I am a complete outsider when it comes to economic construction, and I understand nothing about industrial planning."

But with devastating tactical skill Mao also counterattacked and ousted Mr. Peng from his post. This done, Mao was satisfied to leave the running of China to others, and over the next few years concentrated on foreign affairs, particularly the growing quarrel with Moscow.

Foreign policy often seemed to swing almost as wildly as domestic political campaigns; from intervention in Korea to the Bandung (Indonesia) conference and the five principles of peaceful coexistence, from calls for world revolution to President Nixon's trip and the Shanghai communiqué. Behind these shifts, scholars agree, it was Mao himself who made all the fundamental decisions, even if Mr. Zhou was often China's ambassador to the world.

Moreover, underneath these swings Mao adhered to several deeply held ideas.

First, China would pursue a strictly defensive policy; it would not, for example, intervene in Vietnam. "Others may come and attack us, but we shall not fight outside our borders," Mao told the Central Committee. "I say we will not be provoked."

Second, he was committed to supporting revolutionary movements in the third world. But with his penchant for reasoning in contradictions, he worked out a way of conducting correct diplomatic relations with a government at the same time as he aided Communist guerrillas dedicated to overthrowing it.

Third, Mao was dedicated to making China a great power again, and he recognized early that only by building it up economically and militarily would the imperialists, led by the United States, come to accept it. Time proved him right. In the mid-1970s, after the thaw in relations with the United States, China's formerly hostile neighbors in Southeast Asia followed suit.

At the same time Mao became increasingly obsessed with the Soviet Union, both as an external threat and as a heretical internal system that might subvert the Chinese revolution. After the 1959 encounter with Mr. Peng, Mao may have already felt that the party had betrayed him and was in the hands of the bureaucrats who wanted to follow the Soviet example of gradual growth based on a party elite, material incentives and heavy industry. In addition, Mao came to have doubts about China's youth; as he told Mr. Malraux in August 1965, "This youth is showing dangerous tendencies.

"Humanity left to its own does not necessarily reestablish capitalism, but it does reestablish inequality," he said. "The forces tending toward the creation of new classes are powerful."

"Revolutions and children have to be trained if they are to be properly brought up," he added. "Youth must be put to the test."

The test, which Mao launched that fall, was the Cultural Revolution. In many ways it was the longest culmination of his life, bringing together his favorite themes. "Once class struggle is grasped, miracles are possible," he remarked not long before the start of the Cultural Revolution in what might have been his motto. The movement was also his ultimate revolt against the influence of the Soviet Union, its elitism and bureaucracy.

Mao remained uncertain of what would follow him. As he told Edgar Snow in 1965, in 1,000 years even Marx and Lenin might "appear rather ridiculous."

Last year, in a poem addressed to the dying Zhou Enlai, he put it more poignantly:

Loyal parents who sacrificed so much for the nation
Never feared the ultimate fate.
Now that the country has become red, who will be its guardian?
Our mission, unfinished, may take a thousand years.
The struggle tires us, and our hair is gray.

The poem concludes: "You and I, old friends, can we just watch our efforts be washed away?"

BEIJING'S ASSESSMENT OF MAO [1981]

JAMES P. STERBA

JUNE 30, 1981—The Chinese Communist Party said today that Mao Zedong, the man who led it to power and ruled China for 27 years, had been a brilliant revolutionary who turned into a blundering national leader.

The party said that his contributions "far outweigh" his mistakes, but that both were monumental.

Mao, who was long regarded as a godlike figure beyond criticism, came under attack in a 35,000-word statement for his role in starting the Cultural Revolution, a 10-year period of social turmoil that ended with his death in 1976.

But the party's assessment of its rule since it seized power in China in 1949 also praised Mao as a "respected and beloved great leader and teacher."

The assessment was an effort by the present leaders, many of whom were purged and imprisoned during the Cultural Revolution, to sum up the Maoist era. It was issued on the eve of the 60th anniversary of the party's founding.

It also came one day after Hua Guofeng, a man associated with Maoist policies, was replaced as party chairman by Hu Yaobang, an associate of China's principal ruler, Deng Xiaoping, who is the party's senior deputy chairman.

The document, approved by the Central Committee after more than a year of drafting and debate, says that Mao betrayed his own philosophy starting in the late 1950s by steering China into radical political and economic campaigns that did not work because they emphasized class struggle and quick results instead of slow step-by-step modernization and party building.

It says that China has now returned to the "scientific principles of Mao Zedong's thought" for a "period of peaceful development."

The nation's problem is not political but economic, the document says, adding that "all our party work must be subordinated to and serve this central task—economic construction."

The party began to move in that direction in 1978 under Mr. Deng, the document says. Although Mr. Deng shares blame in the report for some past mistakes, he is not criticized personally. His ideas and policies are said to have been correct all along.

Here, for example, is how the document portrays the period in which Mr. Deng was first brought back into the government in January 1975 as the senior deputy prime minister after having been purged in the Cultural Revolution.

According to the report, when Prime Minister Zhou Enlai was seriously ill in 1975, Mr. Deng took charge with Mao's support and tried to undo some of the chaos caused by the Cultural Revolution and the so-called Gang of Four, the name given to Mao's radical associates, including his wife, Jiang Qing, who have since been purged.

Mr. Deng presided over various meetings and "the situation took an obvious turn for the better," the report states.

"However," it goes on, "Comrade Mao Zedong could not bear to accept systematic correction of the errors of the Cultural Revolution by Comrade Deng Xiaoping."

Mao was said to have attacked Mr. Deng as a "right deviationist" and once again plunged the nation into turmoil. The report says Mao purged Mr. Deng a second time in 1976 after the Tian An Men incident in which thousands of supporters of Zhou, who had died in January 1976, turned out in defiance of orders at a wreath-laying and memorial demonstration. The report says Mao did not recognize that this was a demonstration against the Gang of Four.

"In essence, the movement was a demonstration of support for the party's correct leadership as represented by Deng Xiaoping," the report says. "It laid the ground for massive popular support for the subsequent overthrow of the counterrevolutionary Jiang Qing clique."

It was only after Mao's death and the purge of the Gang of Four that Mr. Deng was again returned to leadership in the summer of 1977.

In discussing an earlier stormy period known as the Great Leap Forward, the report says that Mao and others became "smug" in 1958 over their economic successes and launched the Great Leap and other economic policies that "overlooked objective economic laws."

The Great Leap, a crash program of economic development in 1958–59 leading to the withdrawal of Soviet economic aid, caused "serious losses to our country and people," the report says.

Although the collective leadership must take some blame for the troubles of that period, it adds, Mao "must be held chiefly responsible."

"During this period, his theoretical and practical mistakes concerning class struggle in a socialist society became increasingly serious, his personal arbitrariness gradually undermined democratic centralism in party life, and the personality cult grew graver and graver," the assessment says.

Although the report mentions "suffering" and "serious losses" caused by the mistakes of Mao and others, there is no mention of the number of deaths, imprisonments or labor camp sentences handed out during these periods.

The Cultural Revolution, "a grave blunder," was declared to be Mao's worst mistake. The report says: "The Cultural Revolution, which lasted from May 1966 to October 1976, was responsible for the most severe setback and heaviest losses suffered by the party, the state and the people since the founding of the People's Republic. It was initiated and led by Comrade Mao Zedong."

For several years after Mao's death, the Cultural Revolution was labeled the work of the Gang of Four because Mao was not yet open to attack.

According to the party document, Mao believed erroneously that the party had been infiltrated by "bourgeoisie, counterrevolutionaries and capitalist roaders" and that to root them out he would have to wage continuing revolution. Mr. Deng was among those denounced and purged as a capitalist roader during that period.

"Many things denounced as revisionist or capitalist during the Cultural Revolution were actually Marxist and socialist principles, many of which had been set forth or supported by Comrade Mao Zedong himself," the report says.

It says that Mao "confused right and wrong and the people with the enemy."

"While making serious mistakes," the report goes on, "he repeatedly urged the whole party to study the works of Marx, Engels and Lenin conscientiously and imagined that his theory and practice were Marxist and that they were essential for the consolidation of the dictatorship of the proletariat. Herein lies his tragedy."

That tragedy, the report says, is that Mao did many good things during the Cultural Revolution at the same time he was promoting disasters.

The party report says: "It would be entirely wrong to try to negate the scientific value of Mao Zedong's thought and to deny its guiding role in our revolution and construction just because Comrade Mao Zedong made mistakes in his later years."

But, it adds, it would be equally wrong "to regard whatever he said as the unalterable truth which must be mechanically applied everywhere."

MAO'S WIDOW MAKES DOLLS WITH A VENGEANCE [1983]

CHRISTOPHER S. WREN

IN JANUARY 1981 the radicals known as the Gang of Four were found guilty of almost all the evils that racked China during the bitter decade of the Cultural Revolution.

At the time of their conviction, the two ringleaders—Jiang Qing, the widow of Chairman Mao Zedong, and Zhang Chunqiao, a former mayor of Shanghai—were given suspended death sentences that could be changed to life imprisonment in two years if they repented suitably.

Wang Hongwen, once a deputy chairman of the Communist party, got a life sentence, and Yao Wenyuan, a propagandist, was given 20 years in prison.

During the long show trial, Miss Jiang taunted the court to execute her, shouting that "it is more glorious to have my head chopped off." There is no sign that Mao's widow, having been blamed for everything that went awry in the chairman's last years, has shown the slightest remorse.

But no one expects her or Mr. Zhang to be executed, if only because it might inflame dormant Maoist passions. Last August the party chief, Hu Yaobang, told some French reporters that "Jiang Qing lives well in prison, but she persists in behaving as a political and ideological enemy of our people."

Mr. Hu ventured that a court reviewing her case

QUOTATIONS FROM CHAIRMAN MAO

A man's head is not like a scallion, which will grow again if you cut it off; if you cut it off wrongly, then even if you want to correct your error, there is no way of doing it. (1956)

Our nation will never again be an insulted nation. We have stood up. (1949)

The Red Army is like a furnace in which all captured soldiers are melted down and transformed the moment they come over. In China not only the masses of workers and peasants need democracy, but the army needs it even more urgently. (1928)

The popular masses are like water, and the army is like a fish. How then can it be said that when there is water, a fish will have difficulty in preserving its existence? An army which fails to maintain good discipline gets into opposition with the popular masses, and thus by its own action dries up the water. (1938)

Every Communist must understand this truth: Political power grows out of the barrel of a gun. Our principle is that the party commands the gun; the gun shall never be allowed to command the party. (1938)

Within the ranks of our people, democracy stands in relation to centralism, and freedom to discipline. They are two conflicting aspects of a single entity, contradictory as well as united, and we should not one-sidedly emphasize one to the detriment of the other. Within the ranks of the people, we cannot do without freedom, nor can we do without discipline. All this is well understood by the masses of the people. (1937)

In a big country such as ours, it is nothing to get alarmed about if small numbers of people create disturbances; rather we should turn such things to advantage to help us get rid of bureaucratism. (1957)

We are not only good at destroying the old world, we are also good at building the new. (1949)

"will take account of the circumstances and reduce her sentence." When Peng Zhen, another member of the ruling Politburo, visited Yugoslavia last summer, he too said that Miss Jiang would not be executed. "Jiang Qing will remain alive and we shall continue to feed her," Mr. Peng told a Belgrade newspaper. "She has only one mouth."

The leadership must figure out how to justify the reprieve of Miss Jiang, whom most ordinary Chinese still detest because of her role in the repressive years of the Cultural Revolution, because she has shown none of the contrition demanded by law. The weekly *Literary Digest* hinted last month at a face-saving solution. It quoted a university student in Beijing as saying: "Jiang Qing's crime did not consist of directly killing anyone. If she is spared, she will act as a teacher of a negative lesson."

It is rumored that Jiang Qing, now 69 years old, is confined to Qincheng Prison in suburban Beijing, where she has been put to work making dolls. Prisoners in China must do something useful. But according to one version, she has embroidered her name on each doll so they cannot be sold and are now piling up in a warehouse.

As for the three other members of the Gang of Four, Zhang Chunqiao, now 65, is said to be dying of throat cancer. Wang Hongwen, 47, who turned state's evidence at the trial, has become a model convict at a labor camp in Shaanxi Province, where he impresses warders and prisoners alike with his positive attitude. Yao Wenyuan, 51, is working as a prison librarian and has fleshed out to nearly 230 pounds.

GROUCHO MARX

1890–1977

By Albin Krebs

Effrontery, of the most lunatic, unsquelchable sort, was the chief stock in trade of Groucho Marx. As the key man in the most celebrated brother act in motion pictures, he developed the insult into an art form. And he used the insult, delivered with maniacal glee, to shatter the egos of the pompous—and to plunge his audiences into helpless laughter.

The comedy world of Groucho Marx and his brothers Harpo and Chico was wildly chaotic, grounded in slapstick farce, lowbrow vaudeville corn, free-spirited anarchy and zany assaults on the myths and virtues of middle-class America.

The private world of Groucho Marx was not far removed from his public image. He was the kind of man who could, during his wedding ceremony, fling insults at the minister and, 21 years later, when his wife was leaving him for good, shake hands with her and say, "Well it's been nice knowing you; if you're ever in the neighborhood again, drop in."

Groucho was larger and more antic than life. He was the gruesomely stooped man in the swallowtail coat who took great loping steps across the stage or screen, holding a long, plump cigar behind him. His seemingly depraved eyes rolled and leered from behind steel-rimmed glasses. Below his large nose a smudge of black greasepaint passed for a mustache.

His humor was based on the improbable, the unexpected, the outrageous. In a Marx Brothers play he would interrupt a scene by stepping to the footlights to inquire urgently, "Is there a doctor in the house?" When an unsuspecting physician rose, he would demand to know: "If you're a doctor, why aren't you at the hospital making your patients miserable, instead of wasting your time here with that blonde?" And during one of his television quiz shows, which were immensely popular in the 1950s, when a contestant was asked her age and said she was "approaching 40," he replied, "From which direction?"

But Groucho's expertly delivered, rapid-fire insults were more mad than maddening; they really weren't unkind, for they evolved from his interest in humor that deflated rather than annihilated. This quality was, in fact, the distinguishing mark of the comedy so richly dispensed by Groucho Marx, his brothers and their great contemporaries, such as Charles Chaplin, W. C. Fields and Buster Keaton.

"It was the type of humor that made people laugh at themselves," Groucho said in 1968, "rather than the sort that prevails today—the sick, black, merely smart-aleck stuff designed to evoke malicious laughter at the other fellow."

Throughout his hectic life the comedian remained able to laugh at himself. He even appeared not to take seriously the fact that his early years were passed in extreme poverty. For example, when it was suggested that his rags-to-riches rise bore Lin-

colnesque overtones, he said, "There weren't any rails to split in the neighborhood around 93d Street and Third Avenue. Just the third rail on the El, and there wasn't much of a future in fooling around with that."

Julius Henry Marx was born Oct. 2, 1890, in a tenement on East 93d Street. His Alsatian-born father, Samuel Marx, was an unsuccessful tailor; his mother, the former Minnie Schoenberg, was the stagestruck sister of Al Shean, of the comedy team of Gallagher and Shean.

Mrs. Marx pushed all five of her sons into show business, partly because she was the embodiment of the "stage mother," but also because every member of the family had to be a breadwinner. At 10, Groucho was singing soprano with the Gus Edwards vaudeville troupe, and at 14 he completed his formal education by quitting P.S. 86. "If I intended to eat, I would have to scratch for it," he wrote years later.

Still in his teens, Groucho got a $4-a-week job with the Le May Trio, an act that broke up in Denver, leaving him penniless. He worked in a grocery store long enough to earn train fare back to New York, where his mother was putting together an act called the Six Musical Mascots.

It consisted of Groucho and two of his brothers, Adolph (later Harpo) and Milton (Gummo), an attractive soprano named Janie O'Riley, Mrs. Marx and her sister Hannah. Mrs. Marx soon realized that she and her sister were so bad that the act was doomed unless they left it. They retired from show business.

What was left was the Four Nightingales, an act that, in the course of its travels through whistle-stop towns in the South and Midwest, changed its name to the Marx Brothers and Co. Harmony singing, popular on the vaudeville circuit at the time, was the basis of the act before the brothers fairly stumbled onto the format that was to make them famous.

They did so when they played a seedy little theater in Nacogdoches, Tex., in 1914.

"Our act was so lousy," Groucho said, "that when word passed through the audience of numbskull Texans that a mule had run away, they got up en masse to go out and see something livelier. We were accustomed to heckling and insults, but that made us furious, so when those guys wearing 10-gallon hats over pint-size brains came back, we let them have it. It wasn't the best line I ever ad-libbed, but I recall I told them 'Nacogdoches—is full of roaches.' And—ultimate insult—I called those Texans 'damn Yankees.' "

The audience loved the insults and the ad-libs, and from that point on, the Marxes sang less and worked in more jokes, puns and one-liners. They used carefully plotted sketches, but never hesitated to throw in topical ad-libs.

The Marx Brothers perfected their style and characterizations over several years of one-night stands. They got their nutty names from Art Fisher, a monologuist whose hobby was making up nicknames. Harpo's name came from the instrument he played, Gummo's from his gumshoes, Chico's from his reputation as a lady-killer, and Zeppo's from Zippo, star of a chimpanzee act. Because of his saturnine disposition, Groucho's name was a natural.

Groucho first wore his famous frock coat in a sketch called "Fun in Hi Skule," in which he played the professor. He adopted the omnipresent cigar because he liked to smoke cigars in the first place, and they served as useful props. "If you forget a line," he said, "all you have to do is stick the cigar in your mouth and puff on it until you think of what you've forgotten."

The painted-on mustache, which was Groucho's chief trademark for 30 years, until he grew a real one, resulted from a dispute with the manager of the Fifth Avenue Theater. One night Groucho arrived too late to put on his paste-on mustache. Instead he drew one on with greasepaint. After the show the manager demanded "the same mustache you gave 'em at the Palace," so Groucho handed him the fake mustache. The greasepaint smear was thenceforward substituted.

The Marxes' first Broadway hit was *I'll Say She Is,* in 1924. It was a success largely on the strength of a rhapsodic review in *The New Yorker* by Alexander Woollcott, who spent the rest of his life pouring praise upon the brothers, Groucho in particular.

In 1929 Groucho very nearly suffered a nervous breakdown. He and his brothers filmed *The Cocoanuts,* which had been their second Broadway hit, on Long Island during the day, and appeared nightly in the stage version of *Animal Crackers* (which was committed to film in 1930). He had invested all his savings, $240,000, in the stock market, and lost it all in the crash. Under the strain of too much work and worry over finances, he developed insomnia, which plagued him the rest of his life.

Animal Crackers gave Groucho his most celebrated character, Capt. Jeffrey T. Spaulding, the bumbling African explorer, as well as a monologue that Groucho aficionados have loved over the years. The monologue depended heavily for its humor on Groucho's wildly comic delivery, but even in print it suggests the outrageousness of the Marx manner.

The monologue is a lampoon of the African adventure saga, delivered by Groucho (Spaulding) before guests at a rich woman's soiree. "Africa is God's country, and He can have it," Groucho begins. "Well, sir, we left New York drunk and early on the morning of Feb. 2. After 15 days on the water and six on the boat, we finally arrived on the shores of Africa. . . . One morning I shot an elephant in my pajamas. How he got in my pajamas, I don't know. . . . But that's entirely irrelephant. . . ." And so on.

Groucho, the master of the ad-lib, refused to follow the scripts of his plays and movies, although some of them were turned out by such masters of comedy writing as George S. Kaufman, Morrie Ryskind and S. J. Perelman. Some of his ad-libs worked so well that they were incorporated into the script. For example, in *Horse Feathers* (1932), an actor said to Groucho, "Jennings has been waiting for an hour and he is waxing wroth," to which Groucho replied, "Tell Roth to wax Jennings for a change." The line went into the script.

In *Animal Crackers,* as well as eight other Marx Brothers pictures, Groucho's long-suffering comic foil was Margaret Dumont, whose haughty demeanor suggested the epitome of the grande dame. In their scenes, Groucho was invariably the mangy lover intent on fleecing the rich society matron of her last cent, while at the same time hurling at her the most ungentlemanly insults.

"You're the most beautiful woman I've ever seen, which doesn't say much for you," he ardently told Miss Dumont in *Animal Crackers.* In *Duck Soup* (1933), as he, Chico and Harpo fended off Miss Dumont's enemies, he said of her, "Remember, we're fighting for her honor—which is probably more than she ever did."

The most popular of the Marx Brothers movies was *A Night at the Opera* (1935), produced for Metro-Goldwyn-Mayer by Irving Thalberg, who quickly learned he was dealing with zanies. After he kept the Marxes waiting in his office for more than two hours, Groucho instructed his brothers to disrobe. When Mr. Thalberg finally came out to greet them, he found Groucho, Chico and Harpo before the fireplace, roasting marshmallows in the nude.

Groucho was the quack Dr. Hackenbush in *A Day at the Races* (1937). It was his favorite role because, he said, "It tickled up the medical profession, and I think it can stand a bit of lampooning now and then."

By 1939, with the release of *The Marx Brothers at the Circus,* he and his brothers were tiring of making movies. "I continued to appear in them," he said, "but the fun had gone out of picture-making. I was like an old pug, still going through the motions, but now doing it solely for the money."

The Marx Brothers wound up their MGM contract with *Go West* (1940) and *The Big Store* (1941). They were idle until 1946, when they made *A Night in Casablanca,* and broke up the brother act for good in 1949 with *Love Happy.*

(Gummo had left the act many years previously, even before the brothers made their Broadway debut, to become a theatrical agent. Zeppo quit the act after *Duck Soup* in 1933, also to become an agent. Chico died in 1961, Harpo three years later.)

With "You Bet Your Life," a radio-television quiz show that began in 1947 and lasted a decade, Groucho forged a new career for himself as a single. The program, at one time the highest-rated TV show in the country and the winner of several broadcasting awards, featured the quizmaster's irreverent insult humor rather than jackpot cash awards.

On one program, when a contestant developed mike-fright and was unable to utter a word, Groucho said, "Either this man is dead, or my watch is stopped." Interviewing a tree surgeon, he asked, "Have you ever fallen out of any of your patients?"

Groucho's eccentric antics carried over into his private life. He kept an air rifle beside his bed, and when he heard a howling dog, he would bound to the window to shoot at it. He drove his family to distraction, according to his son, Arthur, by practicing on the guitar for stretches of six hours, or playing Gilbert and Sullivan recordings into the wee hours.

He tried to master golf, with results so unsatisfactory that on one occasion, while playing on a course overlooking the Pacific, he walked to a cliff, dropped his golf balls one by one into the sea and then tossed his bagful of clubs after them. "He turned away with a benignly happy look on his face," a fellow player reported.

The comedian married his first wife, the former Ruth Johnson, in 1920, not long after he and his brothers opened in an act called "Home Again" at the Palace Theater and landed at last in the big time. The wedding ceremony was as chaotic as any Marx Brothers routine. While Chico and Harpo skittered about the room carrying potted palms, Groucho harangued the minister with remarks such as "Why are you going so fast? This is a five-buck ceremony. Aren't we entitled to at least five minutes of your time?" The marriage, which produced two children, Miriam and Arthur, lasted until 1942.

In 1945 he married the former Catherine Gorcey, and they had a daughter, Melinda, of whom he was inordinately proud. When Melinda was prevented from swimming with friends in a pool at a country club that excluded Jews, her father wrote the club president an indignant, highly publicized letter in which he said, "Since my little daughter is only half-Jewish, would it be all right if she went in the pool only up to her waist?"

His second marriage ended in divorce in 1950. He married a former model, Eden Hartford, in 1953, when he was past 60 and she was 24.

That marriage broke up in 1969, and Groucho did not marry again. Still, for a number of years, he sought to maintain his image as a leering satyr and seldom let himself be seen in public without the company of a young and beautiful woman. In 1972, when he returned to the New York stage for the first time in 43 years to give a one-man, one-performance show at Carnegie Hall, he was accompanied by Erin Fleming. Miss Fleming had been his "secretary-companion," as she was described then, since his third divorce.

By the time of the Carnegie concert, Groucho, who had shaved four years off his actual age for decades, was no longer lying about the fact that he was past 80. He looked it, too. His voice was feeble and he could hardly hear, even with his hearing aid, but his eyes were still merrily bright.

In November 1976 he was to have been lionized in Washington, where he intended to present Marxian memorabilia, including the pith helmet he wore as Captain Spaulding in *Animal Crackers,* to the Smithsonian Institution. But the trip was canceled at the last minute, ostensibly because Miss Fleming had the flu and he would not go anywhere without her.

Groucho went to the hospital for an operation on his hip last March. As he was recuperating, confined to his Beverly Hills home, an unpleasant court battle went on over the management of his estate, which was estimated at $2.5 million at the time he divorced his third wife.

Three years ago, Miss Fleming was appointed his guardian. She also was temporary conservator for the estate, and Groucho's son, Arthur Marx, sought to replace her in that position. According to the testimony, Miss Fleming, now 37, had exerted a baneful influence over Groucho, even threatening his well-being, though others declared that she was the only reason he was clinging to life then.

The court compromised by appointing Groucho's friend of 45 years, Nat Perrin, the screenwriter, as temporary conservator. A grandson, Andrew, 27, was later named permanent conservator.

Early in 1973, Arthur published *Son of Groucho*, a memoir. In it, he recalled his father as a singularly penurious man who, when going out to dine in an expensive Hollywood restaurant, would park blocks away to save a parking fee.

His stinginess notwithstanding, and despite the pains he took to make himself financially secure, Groucho, his son reported, was not terribly well off in his old age, chiefly because of the expensive alimony and property settlements resulting from his three divorces.

Groucho's irresponsibility in his personal dealings was legendary. It was not unusual for him to call a friend in the middle of the night—this was one of his ways of taking the boredom out of his insomnia—and launch into a barrage of abuse: "This is Professor Waldemar Strumbelknauff. Aren't you ashamed of yourself, beating your children that way? If you were a man you'd come over here and knock my teeth out. If you were half a man you'd knock half my teeth out. . . . This is Groucho. How are you? As if I really care." And then he'd hang up.

He grew to hate New York, because he was expected to wear a tie when he went out. He was so addicted to informal wear that he shunned parties, developing, immediately upon being told he was expected to go to one, "a grippe-y feeling." When he himself entertained, he often took leave of his guests at an early hour, telling them to "go ahead and get drunk on my booze and make fools of yourselves—I don't care because I'm going to bed."

The comedian, who supplemented his meager formal education by reading omnivorously, greatly admired writers. He considered George Bernard Shaw's observation that "Groucho Marx is the world's greatest living actor" as the compliment of his lifetime. For some years he carried on a correspondence with T. S. Eliot, and in 1965 was invited to speak at a memorial service for the poet. Typically, he used the occasion to say something outrageous: "Apparently Mr. Eliot was a great admirer of mine—and I don't blame him."

Groucho Marx was actually a moody man, those who knew him best said. They insisted that beneath his brash, fast-talking exterior, he was thoughtful, shy and kindhearted. His longtime friend, the songwriter Harry Ruby, said, "The guy doesn't mean to be insulting; it's an involuntary notion with him, like a compulsion neurosis." And to his son, Arthur, Groucho was "a sentimentalist, but he'd rather be found dead than have you know it."

Groucho himself admitted that "my trouble is that I don't like to let just everybody get in a word edgewise, and can't stand anyone else having the last word." To make sure this wouldn't happen to him ultimately, he took the precaution of writing his epitaph in advance: "I hope they buried me near a straight man."

Groucho Marx died from pneumonia on Aug. 19, 1977, in Los Angeles. He was 87 years old.

GROUCHO WAS HILARIOUS, BUT ALSO A LITTLE SCARY

VINCENT CANBY

THE RECENT death of the incomparable Groucho Marx, frail and ailing at the age of 87 and the center of the sort of custody battle that is most often fought over children, evokes all sorts of associations and memories, none of them sentimental. I think of Groucho lolling in a canoe that is being paddled by

Thelma Todd in *Horsefeathers* (1932), and enthusiastically greeting each new arrival in that stuffed stateroom in *A Night at the Opera* (1935), with a special leer for the manicurist. I see him instructing the contestants on "You Bet Your Life" about the magic word—*sausages,* it says at the bottom (or is it top?) of my TV screen—and surviving, unscathed, the witlessness of a single act in *Double Dynamite* (1951), whose title referred to Groucho's co-star, Jane Russell. I recall also one of Groucho's funnier improvised performances 10 years ago at lunch in the King Cole Bar of the St. Regis. An especially firm, unsmiling maitre d' stood by as Groucho studied the menu.

GROUCHO: "I'll have . . ."
MAITRE D' (cutting in): "The chicken pot pie is very good."
GROUCHO (suspiciously): "So you're pushing chicken pot pie?"
MAITRE D': "It's very good."
GROUCHO: "I'll have . . ."
MAITRE D': "If it's not a 'Chef's Recommendation' it will take at least 20 minutes."
GROUCHO: "Well, *he's* an independent sort!"
MAITRE D': "Chicken pot pie?"

Groucho hadn't spent all that time in vaudeville for nothing. He knew how the real-life sketch had to end—with his being intimidated into ordering the chicken pot pie and then finding it barely edible even if it were not bad. By that time Groucho had become the first and the truest of what might be called the all-media comedians, having made his way from vaudeville to musical comedy, motion pictures, radio and television and, finally, the world, when his public and private personalities had become so effectively fused by being confused.

It's a bit of a shock to realize that Groucho was only one year younger than Charlie Chaplin and five years *older* than Buster Keaton, both of whom are almost completely identified with the great days of the silent cinema, while Groucho, who shared their generation, owes his fame exclusively to sound and electronics.

It also makes me wonder about any critic's ability to respond fully to the popular comedy of his own time.

Silent comedy—the comedy of Keaton and Chaplin—is now sanctified to such a degree that a lot of critics still wonder whether there is really any such thing as sound-movie comedy. When sound came in, comedy became as noisy, arrogant and anarchic as it was on the stage; the pathetic gesture that had given silent comedy its classic sweetness now became something to ridicule. It's not, I think, that the moviegoing public somehow grew up, became more sophisticated overnight when sound came in, making impossible the kind of comedy that Chaplin and Keaton were best at, but that sound forced movie comedy to adopt new attitudes that recognized and understood the extra dimension of sound films.

Silent films, even when they have music scores and sound effects, are reveries, slightly removed, even fantastic, compared to sound movies that demand the attention of both ear and eye. It may not be too much to suggest that silent films remain private experiences while sound movies are public happenings.

Which may explain why the media comedians—led by Groucho and including Jack Benny, Bob Hope, Fred Allen and George Burns—all developed public personalities closely though not exclusively associated with the private person. Jack Benny may not have been the stingy fellow he took such delight in portraying, and though he always said he couldn't be funny without a team of writers, he was in truth extremely witty, his irony and sarcasm as perfectly timed in private conversation as in any public performance.

Nobody ever confused Chaplin with the Little Tramp—they knew too much about his wives, his divorces and his million-dollar contracts—but when people approached Groucho apprehensively or belligerently, expecting something epically rude and unexpected, they often got it. Groucho—I think it's a matter of public record—was not the easiest fellow

A GROUCHO MARX SAMPLER

GROUCHO: Oscar [Levant], you look tired. Why don't you come to my house for dinner? I've got the most wonderful cook in town, I've saved a steak four inches thick and we'll have a dessert that's out of this world.
LEVANT: What's your address?
GROUCHO: Wouldn't you like to know!

To a dinner of screenwriters:

"We in the industry know that behind every successful screenwriter stands a woman. And behind her stands his wife.

"Edgar Allan Poe created deathless prose in a drafty garret. Shakespeare wrote *Hamlet* on a crust of bread—didn't even have paper. And Balzac, the greatest French novelist of all time, forced himself to write all night by chaining himself to his bedpost. But he got the maid in trouble anyway. And so I say to you writers, keep your imagination in the stars, your prose in the heavens and your price in the gutter. I thank you—Balzac thanks you—and the maid thanks Balzac."

Overseas entertaining troops for the U.S.O., Groucho finds himself in a general's headquarters. A Signal Corps phone rings and Groucho grabs it: "World War Two-oo."

STRAIGHT MAN: Stop at a Western Union office. I want to wire my father.
GROUCHO: What's the matter? Can't he stand up by himself?

From *Monkey Business:*

"Afraid? Me? A man who's licked his weight in wild caterpillars? Afraid? You bet I'm afraid."

ZEPPO: The garbage man is here.
GROUCHO: Tell him we don't want any.

CHICO: I would like to say good-bye to your wife.
GROUCHO: Who wouldn't?

From an interview:

"I always wanted to be rich. I still want to be rich. Why, years ago I came to Los Angeles without a nickel in my pocket. Now I have a nickel in my pocket. Unfortunately, the nickel today isn't worth what it used to be. Do you know what this country needs? A seven-cent nickel. We've been using the five-cent nickel since 1492. So why not give the seven-cent nickel a chance? If that works out, next year we could have an eight-cent nickel. And so on."

"I wouldn't belong to any club that would have me for a member."

GROUCHO: Have you got any stewed prunes?
WAITRESS: Yes.
GROUCHO: Well, give 'em some black coffee. That'll sober 'em up.

"I have no advice to give young actors. To young, struggling actresses, my advice is to keep struggling. If you struggle long enough, you will never get in trouble, and if you never get in trouble you will never be much of an actress."

From *Horsefeathers*:

"I'd horsewhip you if I had a horse."

A MAN [who has just introduced his wife to Groucho]: Matilda's just dying for you to say something insulting to her.
GROUCHO: You ought to be ashamed of yourself. With a wife like that, it should be easy to think of your own insults.

WOMAN: I'm from South Wales.
GROUCHO: Did you ever meet a fellow named Jonah? He lived in whales for a while.

FRANKIE AVALON: I'm a singer.
GROUCHO: You mean you're a sewing machine?

INTERVIEWER: Will there always be a Groucho?
GROUCHO: There'll always be a Groucho, just as there will always be an England—although lately, England hasn't been doing so well.

to get along with. Did the private personality shape the public one? Much more so, I suspect, with Groucho and another great old-timer, W. C. Fields, than with either Chaplin or Keaton.

Critics, who by definition like to worry, have been inclined to fret over the obvious stage origins of the great early Marx Brothers comedies, including *Animal Crackers* (1930), the one that takes place at the Long Island estate of Mrs. Rittenhouse (Margaret Dumont), in which Groucho says, "Mrs. Rittenhouse, ever since I saw you I've swept you off my feet," and *Horsefeathers,* in which Groucho, by some awful fluke, becomes the president of Huxley College.

The fret, I find, is usually of more theoretical interest than practical. If one laughs or is moved, the comedy works. If not, it's dead no matter what devices or styles are employed. Does it really matter that *Animal Crackers* was a hugely successful stage vehicle before being a sidesplitting movie? I think not, since it showed how films could accommodate outsiders and exploit their particular talents.

Jacques Tati, I suppose, has come as close as anyone to finding an essential sound-movie form in such classics as *Traffic* and *Playtime,* but that doesn't mean we have to downgrade the brilliance of Woody Allen's *Take the Money and Run* and *Bananas* because they are virtually translations of his freely associating nightclub monologues.

Woody has gone on to make more and more "cinematic" movies—at the same time gradually transforming the early schlemiel of those first films into the hugely funny, moving and self-aware hero of *Annie Hall.* This is extraordinarily exciting to watch, but it doesn't diminish the accomplishments of those two early comedies.

That was not Groucho's direction. With his brothers he sort of passed through motion pictures to his even greater reward in television, for it was the close-up exposures on "You Bet Your Life" in which we could see the quintessential Groucho character that he merely suggested when he was playing Wolf J. Flywheel or Rufus T. Firefly or Capt. Jeffrey Spaulding. And, paradoxically, it was when his quick, snappy retorts were not especially funny, or when they were a predictable twist on what had been said earlier, that we'd get a glimpse of what dealing with Groucho meant and what he represented.

Behind his wisecracks lay a kind of Beckett landscape, hard, bleak, cosmically disinterested. Groucho, in top form, was unbeatable, hilarious; one marveled at the speed with which the brain operated. But he was also a little scary. One suspected something merciless there, and it's that something that lights up the Marx Brothers movies, gives them their dimension and is why we continue to go back to see them again and again, even when we're told they aren't truly—or originally—cinematic.

GOLDA MEIR

1898–1978

By Israel Shenker

For five years Golda Meir was prime minister of Israel. Her often-stated ambition was to see Israel accepted by its Arab neighbors and living in peace. With firmness and determination, she sought but failed to achieve those aims. "We say 'peace' and the echo comes back from the other side, 'war,' " she once lamented. "We don't want wars even when we win."

It was her fate to lead the Israeli government when the forces of Egypt and Syria attacked in October 1973 in a costly war that Israel almost lost before it could mobilize and fight to an inconclusive end, in which both sides would claim tenuous victories.

"We do not rejoice in victories," she said. "We rejoice when a new kind of cotton is grown and when strawberries bloom in Israel."

Mrs. Meir left office in 1974. When President Anwar el-Sadat of Egypt made the dramatic announcement of his decision to visit Jerusalem in November 1977, Mrs. Meir—who was in New York for the opening of the Broadway show *Golda,* an account of her life starring Anne Bancroft—hailed it as a brilliant move but advised a wait-and-see attitude pending more concrete results.

When President Sadat arrived in Israel, he seemed more at ease with her than with any of the other prominent Israelis he saw, and she gave him a gift for a newly born grandchild. He later confided to interviewers that he would have preferred to negotiate with her because he regarded her as "a tough old lady" who had the will to persevere on the road to peace.

Her toughness was legendary while she ran the Israeli cabinet. After she left, the Labor party, which she had led, became more fractious than ever and, beset by charges of corruption, went down to a stunning defeat in the spring of 1977 at the hands of a right-wing coalition led by Menachem Begin, who became prime minister. After that, the Labor party experienced a bewildering slide into something close to irrelevance in the political arena.

Mrs. Meir had a gift for making complex issues appear simple and expressing her views in plain but emotional terms: "Our generation reclaimed the land, our children fought the war and our grandchildren should enjoy the peace." Even when she spoke to an audience of thousands, it could sound as though she was speaking in her living room.

At a small gathering in New York some years ago, Mrs. Meir heard an overdramatized version of an appeal she had made to President John F. Kennedy for arms. "If I had spoken to Kennedy so beautifully," she commented, "I would have gotten more arms." Once when an aide suggested a statement to make to waiting reporters, she rejoined, "You can't improve on saying nothing." Her mother used to advise: "When you say no, you never regret it."

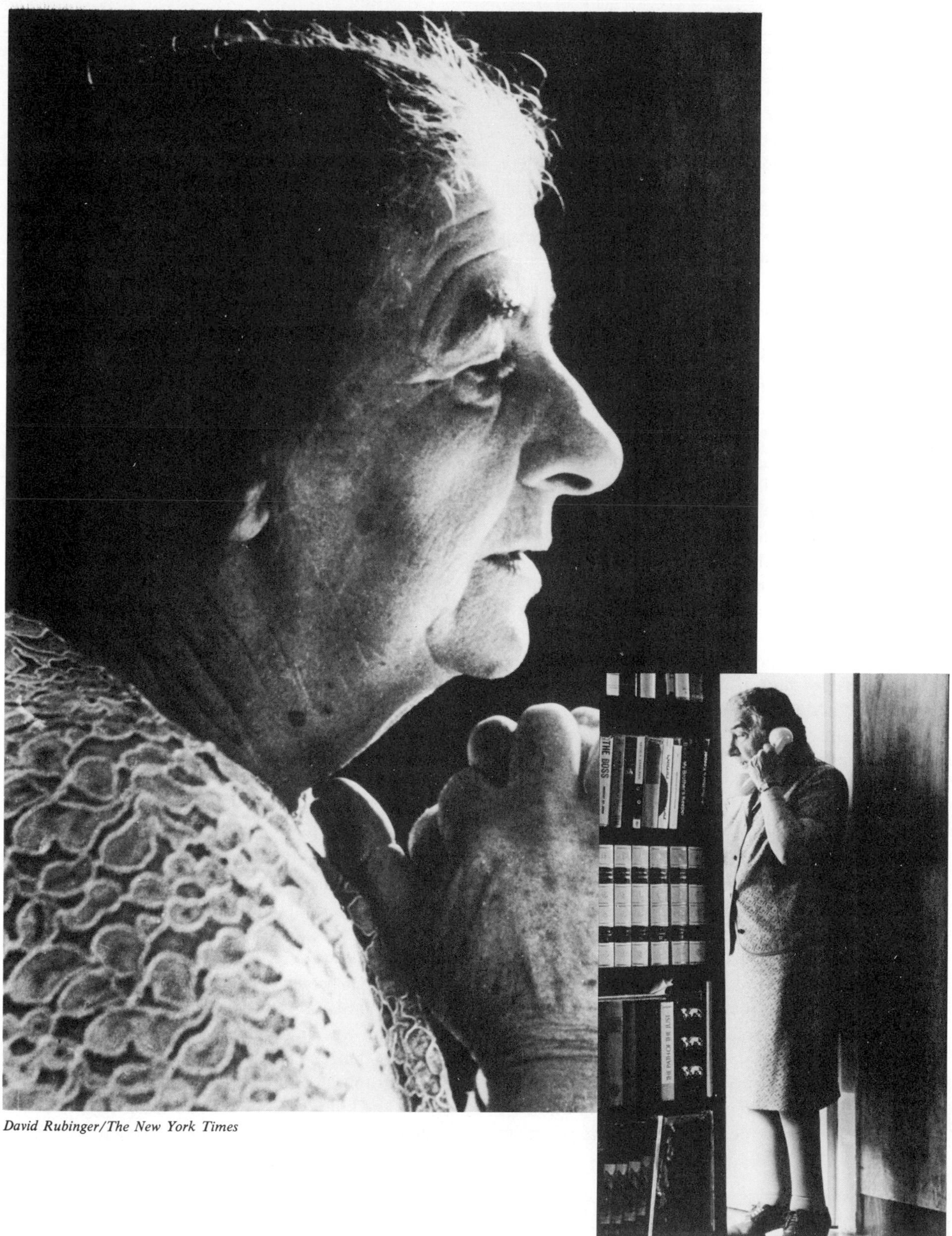

David Rubinger/The New York Times

UPI/Bettmann Newsphotos

Golda Mabovitch was born on May 3, 1898, in Kiev, in the Russian Empire. Her first memory was of her father nailing boards over the front door during rumors that a pogrom was imminent. "If there is any explanation necessary for the direction which my life has taken," she said years later, "perhaps it is the desire and the determination to save Jewish children from a similar scene and from a similar experience.

"I have a pogrom complex—I have, I plead guilty," she went on. Alluding to the six million Jews killed by the Nazis, she added: "There are many Jews who don't have complexes anymore. But we who lived through it have a complex of gas chambers."

In Russia life was not far from death. "I was always a little too cold outside and a little too empty inside," she recalled. Her food was sometimes given to her younger sister, Zipke; their older sister, Sheyna, often fainted from hunger.

In 1906 the family emigrated to the United States, where Golda's father had spent three years in Milwaukee saving to prepare the way. When he could find employment he worked as a carpenter, and his wife set herself up in a small grocery, the bane of Golda's existence. Beginning at age 8, Golda had to run the store each morning while her mother was at the market buying supplies. The child arrived late for school every day, having cried all the way from home.

At age 11 she organized her first public meeting and gave her first public speech, to raise money for school textbooks. Not many years later her mother pressed her to give up the idea of high school, spend her days working in the grocery and marry a much older man, a Mr. Goodstein. At age 14 Golda ran away to live with Sheyna in Denver, where she met her future husband, a gentle, erudite sign painter named Morris Myerson, another émigré from Russia.

After an argument with Sheyna, Golda, now 16, moved out and was given shelter by two of Sheyna's friends. She got a job measuring skirt linings, and in later years found herself involuntarily glancing at hems.

Her father wrote to her that if she valued her mother's life she would come home, so she did, aged 18, to plunge into a confusion of enthusiasms: Socialism, teaching, public speaking, Zionism. When there were attacks on Jews in the Ukraine and in Poland, she helped organize a protest march in Milwaukee. Her home became a center for visitors from Palestine. "I knew that I was not going to be a parlor Zionist," she wrote.

She pressed her reluctant husband-to-be to go to Palestine, and when he agreed, in 1917, they were married. They left in 1921, on a trip that included a mutiny and near starvation. She had learned much about freedom in America, she loved her first adopted country, but she never knew a moment of homesickness for it.

Much later, in jest, she echoed her Israeli compatriots' complaint against Moses: "He dragged us 40 years through the desert to bring us to the one place in the Middle East where there was no oil." The only heavy industry in Palestine was the manufacture of chocolate, she recalled. "Why does it taste so sandy?" she asked, and was told that sand was the only natural resource.

The new immigrants—she, her husband, her sister Sheyna, with whom she had been reconciled, and Sheyna's children—had no one to help them. Many others found the struggle too much and left, and Mrs. Meir was to say later: "I have always felt sorry for those people, because, to my mind, the loss has always been theirs."

Golda and Morris Myerson applied to join Kibbutz Merhavia, whose name means "God's wide spaces," and were rejected because a majority of the members suspected that she would not be willing to do physical labor. Furious at this attitude, she persisted and was finally accepted. Afterward, she said jokingly that she was accepted only because of her phonograph and records.

On the kibbutz she worked herself to exhaustion picking almonds, planting trees, caring for chickens.

"The kibbutz made me an expert in growing chickens," she said. "Before that I was afraid to be in a room with even one chicken."

With her stints on kitchen duty, new amenities were introduced. She began using glasses in place of chipped cups, insisted on peeling the herring before serving, replaced herring with oatmeal at breakfast and distributed cookies twice a week instead of once. For Sabbath eve supper she improvised a tablecloth from a sheet and even put flowers on the table.

Her innovations were eventually appreciated: The kibbutz chose her as its representative to Histadrut, the General Federation of Labor. But her insistence on refinements also drew criticism. Recalling her old phonograph, she wrote later: "I even wonder sometimes whether it might not have been a relief for Merhavia to accept the dowry without the bride."

When her husband could bear communal life no longer, she agreed to leave the kibbutz. They moved briefly to Tel Aviv, then to Jerusalem, where Golda Myerson gave birth to a son, Menachem, and a daughter, Sarah, endowing them with the inalienable right to share the family's poverty. Mrs. Myerson spent hours each day doing the laundry for Menachem's nursery school to pay for his tuition. "Was this what it was all about?" she asked herself. "Poverty, drudgery and worry?"

In 1928 she became secretary of the women's labor council of Histadrut, which meant supervising the vocational training of immigrant girls. Her marriage was breaking up, and accepting the job, which required frequent travel, was tantamount to recognizing the breakup. She and the children moved to a tiny apartment in Tel Aviv, and for years she slept there on the living room couch. Her husband died in 1951; characteristically, she was away at the time.

She made frequent fund-raising trips, and a woman reproached her for not talking sentimentally enough to make women in the audiences cry; tears were useful in raising money. "Tears don't have to be elicited from anyone in the Zionist movement," she replied. "God knows there is always enough to cry about."

In 1934 she joined the executive committee of Histadrut, then a kind of shadow government for the eventual independent state of Israel. In 1938, while attending a conference in Evian-les-Bains on refugees as a "Jewish observer from Palestine," she raged inwardly at the complacent manner in which official representatives expressed sympathy for the plight of Germany's Jews, then explained that their countries could not offer refuge.

In the Balfour Declaration of 1917 the British government promised "the establishment in Palestine of a national home for the Jewish people." The Jewish population in fact nearly quintupled during the British mandate, mostly through immigration, up to May 1939, just before World War II broke out. At that time the British, fearing an Arab shift toward the Axis powers, issued a white paper severely restricting Jewish immigration. David Ben-Gurion, who was to play a vital role in securing Israeli independence, fixed the lines of Jewish opposition: "We shall fight Hitler as if there were no white paper and fight the white paper as if there were no Hitler."

Mrs. Myerson became a member of the War Economic Advisory Council set up by the British authorities in Palestine. When the war ended and the British kept Jewish survivors of concentration camps in European detention centers, she went to work for the clandestine entry into Palestine of Jewish immigrants and joined a hunger strike in sympathy with them. "There is no Zionism except the rescue of Jews," she said.

Years after Israel won independence, Mrs. Meir—she had since Hebraized her name, as did others—said that she did not know if Ernest Bevin, the British foreign secretary, who bitterly opposed Jewish immigration to Palestine, was insane or just anti-Semitic or both. "Those responsible for British policy cannot forgive us for being a nation without their approval," she said. "They cannot understand that the problem of the Jews of Europe was not created for the sole purpose of embarrassing the British government."

"We have many grievances against the government," she insisted in 1946. "But the chief accusation that we have is that the policy of the white paper forced us to sit here helpless at a time when we were convinced we could have saved hundreds of thousands, and if only tens of thousands, if only one Jew!"

When Zionist leaders in Palestine were arrested in 1946, she was one of the few left free.

Mrs. Meir began running things. She took over Zionist negotiations with the British and meanwhile kept in close touch with leaders of the armed Jewish resistance who opposed the British and fought Arab guerrillas.

Finally a United Nations Special Committee on Palestine visited the country, recommended partition and the establishment of a Jewish state, and the world organization voted approval, with the United States and the Soviet Union voting with the majority. Upon Arab refusal to accept the decision, Palestine's Jews realized that war lay ahead and that they needed arms and money. Though warned that she should not expect much help, Golda—few now bothered to use her second name—left for America and collected $50 million.

On her return she undertook delicate political negotiations with King Abdullah of Transjordan, grandfather of King Hussein of Jordan. Disguising herself as an Arab woman, she traveled to Amman, Abdullah's capital, to urge him to keep his promise to her not to join other Arab leaders in an attack on the Jews. He asked her not to hurry the proclamation of a state. "We have been waiting for 2,000 years," she replied. "Is that hurrying?"

On May 14, 1948, she was one of 25 signers of Israel's independence declaration. "After I signed, I cried," she said. "When I studied American history as a schoolgirl and I read about those who signed the Declaration of Independence, I couldn't imagine these were real people doing something real. And there I was sitting down and signing a declaration of independence."

By May 15 Israel was under attack from the armed forces of Egypt, Syria, Lebanon, Transjordan and Iraq. Bearing what was in effect Israel's first passport, Mrs. Meir was sent to the United States again to raise more money. At home, the new state confounded the expectations of its Arab enemies by holding off their attacks and establishing its authority.

Later that year Israel named Mrs. Meir as its first minister to the Soviet Union, an assignment for which she felt unqualified: Her Russian was practically forgotten and she knew little about diplomacy. She did know a lot about communal living, however, and when she took up her post she ran the embassy as a kibbutz, with everyone, including the envoy, taking turns at the chores.

When she turned up at Moscow's Central Synagogue, thousands of Russian Jews, defying the government's hostility, flocked to welcome her and express their solidarity with Israel. "If you had sent a broomstick to Moscow," she said later, "and said it represented the state of Israel, it would have received the same welcome."

Mrs. Meir left Moscow and entered the Israeli Parliament in 1949, serving until 1974. From 1949 to 1956, years of severe economic difficulty, she was minister of labor. The meat ration was 3.5 ounces a day—"just so that we didn't forget that there is meat in the world," said Mrs. Meir. When a man courted a woman he did not give flowers; flowers grew wild all over the place. He brought an onion instead.

When the cabinet was trying to deal with a series of assaults on women, a minister suggested barring women from the streets after dark. The minister of labor protested: "Men are attacking women, not the other way around. If there is going to be a curfew, let the men be locked up, not the women."

People often asked Mrs. Meir if she felt handicapped at being a woman minister. "I don't know," she would reply. "I've never tried to be a man."

She campaigned vigorously for money to house the tens of thousands of immigrants who were living in tent cities and overwhelming the young state's facilities. Levi Eshkol, then finance minister, had his priorities, and they were not hers. "You can't milk a house," he said. "But you can milk a cow. If you want money you can have it—but only for cows." She threatened to resign, but stayed on and got money, though not as much as she wanted, to provide homes for those willing to join the adventure of a Jewish state.

"The period since we won our independence has been the first for many, many centuries, during which the words *Jewish refugee* are no longer heard," she said later. "There is no such thing any more because the Jewish state is prepared to take every Jew, whether he is a skilled worker or not, whether he is old or not, whether he is sick or not. It doesn't make a particle of difference."

In 1956 she became foreign minister, succeeding Moshe Sharett, and served under Prime Minister Ben-Gurion. A man of strong ideas and powerful will—it was he who prevailed on Golda Myerson to change her name—he is said to have called her the only man in his cabinet.

She, Moshe Dayan and Shimon Peres flew in secret to France in 1956 to lay plans for collaborating in the attack on Egypt, which had nationalized the Suez Canal and closed the Strait of Tiran, the link between the Gulf of Aqaba and the Red Sea. When war came, Israel took less than 100 hours to capture the Gaza Strip and all of Sinai; France and Britain, however, after landing at the northern end of the Suez Canal Zone and driving southward under the pretext of separating the Egyptian and Israeli armies, were forced by United States and Soviet pressure to withdraw.

Israel, also pressed by the two superpowers, later pulled out of Sinai, and the United Nations sent a peacekeeping force to open the Strait of Tiran. This force remained until 1967, when it was withdrawn at the request of President Gamal Abdel Nasser of Egypt in a prelude to a new war that lasted only six days.

During subsequent negotiations at the United Nations, the Iraqi foreign minister at one point exclaimed from the rostrum of the General Assembly: "Mrs. Meir, go back to Milwaukee—that's where you belong!"

Mrs. Meir was an architect of Israel's policy of extending technical assistance to developing African nations, a policy that improved relations until the Arab oil embargo swept the Africans into line against Israel. Asked by Billy Graham, the evangelist, for the secret of Israeli success in Africa before the embargo, she replied: "We go there to teach, not to preach."

When Mr. Ben-Gurion gave up office and then split with Levi Eshkol, Israel's third prime minister, Mrs. Meir sided with Mr. Eshkol, becoming his strongest supporter. Though it was fashionable to say that hers was the stiffest backbone in the cabinet, she said: "I have never believed in inflexibility except when Israel is concerned.

"If we are criticized because we do not bow," she said, "because we cannot compromise on the question 'To be or not to be,' it is because we have decided that, come what may, we are and we will be."

As foreign minister she worked an 18-hour day. After two years her chief of cabinet suggested she take a vacation. "Why?" she said. "Do you think I'm tired?" "No," he said, "but I am." She replied, "So you take a vacation!"

But in 1965, after much illness and the exhaustion of years of unremitting labor, she resigned from the cabinet. "I won't go into a political nunnery," she assured Mr. Eshkol, refusing an offer to be deputy prime minister on the basis that it was better to be a full-time grandmother than a part-time minister. She moved out of the foreign minister's large residence and went back to cleaning, cooking, ironing and shopping. Bus drivers often would make unscheduled stops to let her off near her home or detour to take her right to the door.

Her party soon pressed her to be its secretary general, and she agreed.

In 1967, when Israel lived in the shadow of renewed war, Prime Minister Eshkol delivered a radio address to the nation, for which he was criticized because he sounded far from inspiring and stumbled over his words. Mrs. Meir defended him: "A leader who doesn't hesitate before he sends his nation into battle is not fit to be a leader." To young volunteers who rushed to Israel during the Six-Day War and were preparing to return home, Mrs. Meir said: "You were ready to die with us. Why don't you live with us?"

Israel had won a brilliant and overwhelming victory. As the cease-fire took effect, Mrs. Meir commented, "The only alternative to war is peace and the only road to peace is negotiations."

"There is nothing Israel wants so much as peace," she added. "With all the bleakness of the desert, the desert of hate around us is even more bleak."

"We have been obliged to become good soldiers, but not with joy," she said. "We are good farmers with joy. It's a wonderful thing to go down to a kibbutz deep in the Negev and remember what it was—sand and sky, maybe a well of brackish water—and to see it now green and lovely. To be good soldiers is our extreme necessity, but there is no joy in it."

At the same time she warned: "There cannot be quiet on one side of the border and shelling on the other. We will either have peace on both sides or trouble on both sides.

"I understand the Arabs wanting to wipe us out," she noted, "but do they really expect us to cooperate?"

Though insisting that the Arabs would eventually have to negotiate and recognize Israel's right to live, she reinforced a reputation for stubbornness, and later complained that "intransigent" had become her middle name. "Hitler took care of six million Jews," she said. "If we lose a war, that's the end forever—and we disappear from the earth. If one fails to understand this, then one fails to understand obstinacy. We intend to remain alive. Our neighbors want to see us dead. This is not a question that leaves much room for compromise." She called Israel's secret weapon "no alternative."

In Israel there was growing debate about how to reach an understanding—and peace—with the Arabs. Mrs. Meir noted that Israel had doves and hawks, but she had found no one who wanted to turn himself into a clay pigeon. When foreign powers pressed Israel to return to its pre-1967 boundaries, she retorted that the war had started along those lines.

Critics argued that she failed to understand the Palestinians or even to recognize them as a national entity, and that she was anything but sympathetic to their just desires for recognition and land. "Do the Arabs need another land?" she asked. "They already have fourteen. We have only one."

To the complaint that she was intransigent and refused to seize opportunities for negotiation, she insisted that the Arabs refused to speak to Israel.

Speaking to an audience in New York just after the 1967 war, Mrs. Meir said: "Is there anybody who can honestly bid the Israelis to go home before a real peace? Is there anyone who wants us to begin training our 10-year-olds for the next war? You say no. I am sure that every fair-minded person in the world will say no, but—forgive my impertinence—most important of all the Israelis say no."

She was a popular, effective speaker. From a news conference at the National Press Club in Washington:

> Q. Your grandson, Gideon Meir, age 7, says that you are the best gefilte-fish maker in Israel. What is your recipe?
>
> A. My grandson . . . I'm afraid he's not very objective about me. I'm not very objective about him, either.

On Mr. Eshkol's death in February 1969 the Labor party selected her as its candidate for prime minister. That was not exactly the retirement she had in mind—"Being 70 is not a sin," she said; "It's not a joy, either"—but she accepted and won Parliament's vote of confidence.

Pressing for a meeting with the Arabs, she proclaimed her readiness to go to any length except national suicide to secure peace. "If Nasser chooses

New York for negotiations, it's all right," she said. "If he wants to go to New Jersey, that's fine, too. If he says Geneva, we agree. I'm even prepared to go to Cairo—how about that!—to sit down at the table.

"Arab officials will have to overcome the shock of meeting us not on the battlefield but at the negotiating table," she added.

"Suppose we want to return territory we have taken," she noted. "To whom? We can't send it to Nasser by parcel post."

Upon the death of President Nasser in September 1970, Israeli officials saw a new opportunity for peace under Mr. Sadat, his successor. In 1972 President Nicolae Ceausescu of Rumania told Mrs. Meir that President Sadat was agreeable to a meeting, and when she urged that it be arranged, Mr. Ceausescu said he would be in touch; but she related later that she never heard from him again.

In January 1973 she heard from the Vatican, which has never recognized Israel, that Pope Paul VI was ready to receive her. "Before we went to the audience," she recalled, "I said to our people: 'Listen, what's going on here? Me, the daughter of Moshe Mabovitch the carpenter, going to meet the Pope of the Catholics?' So one of our people said to me, 'Just a moment, Golda, carpentry is a very respectable profession around here.' "

The Pope had hardly opened the conversation before the daughter of Moshe Mabovitch spoke her mind. "I didn't like the opening at all," she recalled. "His Holiness had said he found it hard to understand that the Jewish people, who should be merciful, behaved so fiercely in their own country. I can't stand it when we are talked to like that, so I said to the Pope: 'Your Holiness, do you know what my earliest memory is? A pogrom in Kiev. When we were merciful and when we had no homeland and when we were weak, we were led to the gas chambers.' "

She had decided to look the Pope in the eye, and not lower her eyes under any circumstances. "There were moments of tension," she said. "I felt that I was saying what I was saying to the man of the cross, who heads the church whose symbol is the cross, under which Jews were killed for generations."

Mrs. Meir knew many bitter moments and difficult meetings, few more galling than her encounter with Chancellor Bruno Kreisky of Austria, whose background was Jewish but who had acceded to an Arab request that an Austrian transit camp for Soviet Jewish immigrants to Israel be closed. She could not persuade him to change his mind, and she never forgave him.

The greatest crisis of her years as prime minister came with the war in October 1973. Although she felt that Egypt and Syria might be planning an attack, she accepted the reassurances of her military leaders and held off mobilizing the reserves. "I shall live with that terrible knowledge for the rest of my life," she wrote in her autobiography.

In the first days of the war, with Israeli forces overwhelmed by superior numbers and firepower, Mrs. Meir lived endless hours of apprehension and exhaustion. "I couldn't even cry when I was alone," she wrote later. Finally, when Egypt and Syria faced defeat, the Russians, as they had in 1967, demanded a cease-fire, to which the United Nations agreed.

During subsequent negotiations between the United States and Israel, Mrs. Meir came to have ambivalent feelings about the role of Henry A. Kissinger, the secretary of state. To force Israeli compliance with American wishes, the United States threatened economic retaliation and the negotiations were broken off.

By this time Mrs. Meir had handed over the government to Yitzhak Rabin, having told the party leadership: "It is beyond my strength to continue carrying this burden." When she left office, on June 4, 1974, she was 76 years old, but she was still not prepared to go into that political nunnery, so she went on speaking her mind.

During a talk at Princeton a student asked her, in a reference to Yasir Arafat, the Palestinian guerrilla leader: "What if Arafat offered to recognize Israel?" The prospect seemed so ludicrous that Mrs.

Meir, bowdlerizing, replied: "There's a saying in Yiddish, 'If my grandmother had had wheels, she would have been a carriage.' " When another student asked for details of the Soviet Union's presence in the Middle East in men and in missile bases, she replied: "It was too much before and it's too much now."

At the end of her life she was still feeling guilty about the years during which she had neglected her children and about her failure to devote herself to the kibbutz rather than to public life. "There is a type of woman who cannot remain at home," she once wrote. "In spite of the place her children and family fill in her life, her nature demands something more; she cannot divorce herself from the larger social life. She cannot let her children narrow her horizon. For such a woman there is no rest."

Golda Meir died in Jerusalem on Dec. 8, 1978. She was 80 years old and had suffered from leukemia for 12 years.

LUDWIG MIES VAN DER ROHE

1886–1969

By Alden Whitman

Ludwig Mies van der Rohe, a man without any academic architectural training, was one of the great artist-architect-philosophers of his age, acclaimed as a genius for his uncompromisingly spare design, his fastidiousness and his innovations.

Along with Frank Lloyd Wright and Le Corbusier, the German-born master builder who was universally known as Mies (pronounced "mees") fashioned scores of imposing structures expressing the spirit of the industrial 20th century.

"Architecture is the will of an epoch translated into space," he remarked in a talkative moment. Pressed to explain his own role as a model for others—a matter on which he was shy, as he was on most others—he said: "I have tried to make an architecture for a technological society. I have wanted to keep everything reasonable and clear—to have an architecture that anybody can do."

A building, he was convinced, should be "a clear and true statement of its times"—cathedrals for an age of pathos, glass-and-metal cages for an age of advanced industrialism.

He thought the George Washington Bridge in New York an outstanding example of a structure expressing its period, and he used to go to admire it whenever he visited the city.

"It is the most modern building in the city," he remarked in 1963.

He was fond of the bridge because he considered it beautifully proportioned and because it did not conceal its structure. Mies liked to see the steel, the brick, the concrete of buildings show themselves rather than be concealed by ornamentation. A 20th-century industry building had to be pithy, he believed.

Mies's stature rested not only on his lean yet sensuous business and residential buildings but also on the profound influence he exerted on his colleagues and on public taste. As the number of his structures multiplied in the years since World War II and as their stunning individuality became apparent, critical appreciation flowed to him in torrents, and his designs and models drew throngs to museums where they were exhibited. It became a status symbol to live in a Mies house, to work in a Mies building, or even to visit one.

The Mies name had already been established among architects long before he came to the United States in 1937. In 1919 and 1921 in Berlin he designed two steel skyscrapers sheathed in glass from street to roof. Although the buildings were never erected, the designs are now accepted as the originals of today's glass-and-metal skyscrapers.

In 1922 Mies introduced the concept of ribbon windows, uninterrupted bands of glass between the finished faces of concrete slabs, in a design for a German office building. That has since become the basis for many commercial structures.

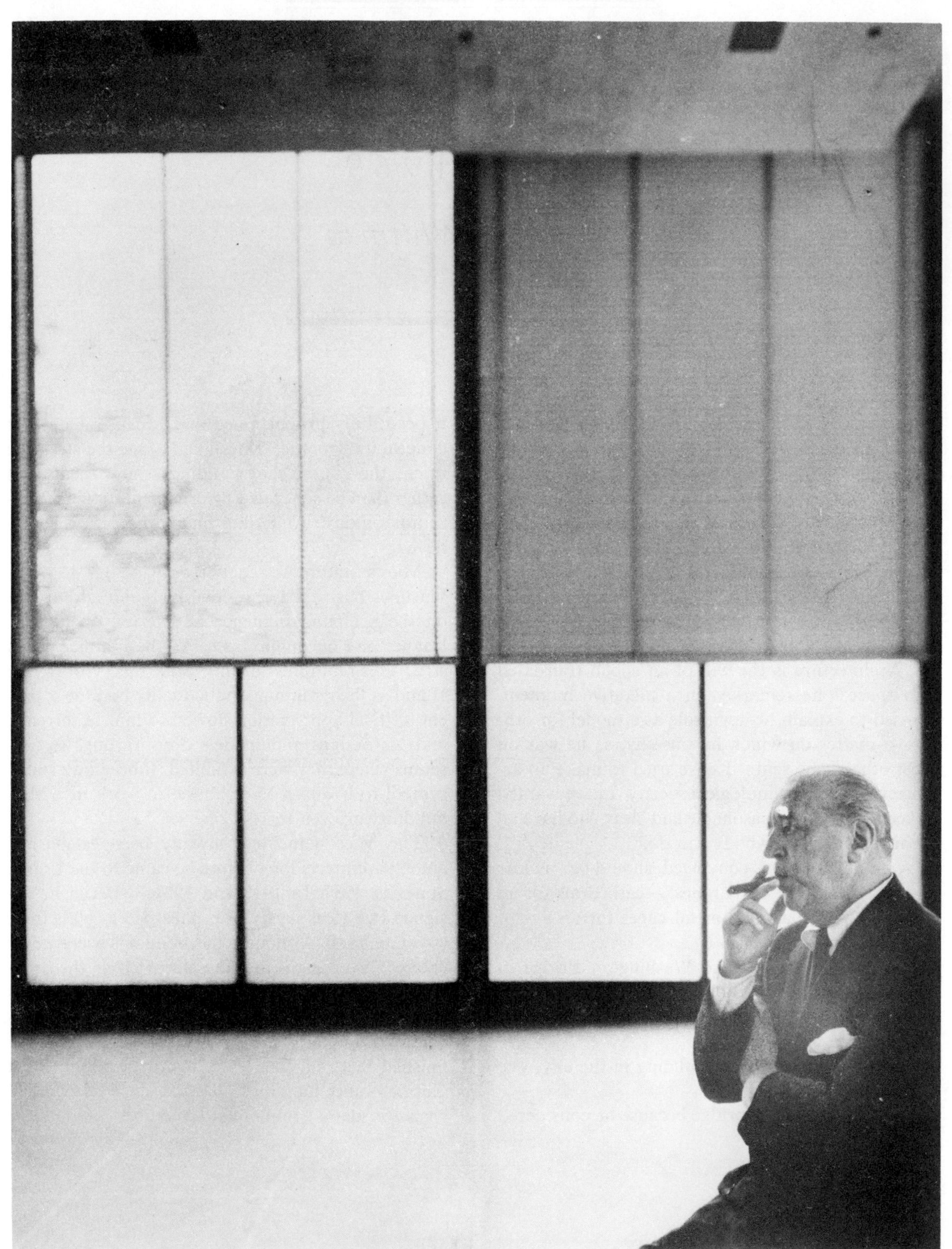

Hedrich-Blessing

Mies, in 1924, produced plans for a concrete villa that is now regarded as the forerunner of the California ranch house. He is also said to have foreshadowed the return of the inner patio of Roman times in an exhibition house built in 1931; to have started the idea of space dividers, the use of cabinets or screens instead of walls to break up interiors; and to have originated the glass house, with windows and glass sliding panels extending from floor to ceiling to permit outside greenery to form the visual boundaries of a room.

Apart from simplicity of form, what struck students of Mies's buildings was their painstaking craftsmanship, their attention to detail.

"God is in the details," Mies liked to say.

In this respect the buildings reflected the man, for Mies was fussy about himself. A large, lusty man with a massive head topping a 5-foot-10-inch frame, he dressed in exquisitely hand-stitched suits of conservative hue, dined extravagantly well on haute cuisine, sipped the correct wines from the proper goblets, and chain-smoked hand-rolled cigars.

For a man so modern in his conceptions, he had more than a touch of old-fashionedness. It showed up in such things as the gold chain across his waistcoat, to which was attached his pocket timepiece. Rather than live in a contemporary building or one of his own houses—he briefly contemplated moving to a Mies apartment but feared fellow tenants might badger him—he made his home in a high-ceilinged, five-room suite on the third floor of an old-fashioned apartment house on Chicago's North Side. The thick-walled rooms were large and they included, predictably, a full kitchen with an ancient gas range for his cook.

The apartment contained armless chairs and furniture of his own design as well as sofas and wing chairs—in which he preferred to sit. The walls were stark white; but the apartment had a glowing warmth, given off by the Klees, Braques and Schwitterses that dotted its walls. Paul Klee was a close friend, and Mies's collection of Klees was among the finest in private hands.

Mies's chairs were almost as well known as his buildings, and they were just as spare. He designed his first chair, known as the MR chair, in 1926. It had a caned seat and back and its frame was tubular steel. There followed the Barcelona chair, an elegant armless leather-and-steel design of which the legs formed an X; the Tugendhat chair, an armless affair of leather and steel that resembled a square S; and the Brno chair, with a steel frame and leather upholstery that looked like a curved S.

The bottoms of all these chairs were uniformly wide, a circumstance that puzzled furniture experts until one of them asked Mies for an explanation. It was simple, he said; he had designed them with his own comfort in mind.

Mies did not receive wide public recognition in the United States until he was over 50 years old. Up to 1937 he lived in Germany, where he was born, at Aachen, on March 27, 1886. Emigrating to Chicago, he had to wait for the postwar building boom before many of his designs were translated into actuality. At his death, examples of his work were in Chicago, Pittsburgh, Des Moines, Baltimore, Detroit, Newark, New York, Houston, Washington, São Paulo, Mexico City, Montreal, Toronto and Berlin. All his buildings were dissimilar, although the same basic principles were employed in each.

The principles centered in a gothic demand for order, logic and clarity.

"The long path through function to creative work has only a single goal," he said; "to create order out of the desperate confusion of our time."

One Mies structure, accounted among his outstanding ones, is the 38-story dark bronze and pinkish-gray glass Seagram Building on Park Avenue between 52d and 53d streets. The building, which was designed in association with Philip C. Johnson, has been called by appreciative critics the city's most tranquil tower and "the most beautiful curtain-wall building in America." It emphasizes pure line, fine materials and exact detailing outside and in. Special attention was paid to the room numbers, doorknobs, elevator buttons, bathroom fixtures and mail chutes, as well as the furniture.

The building's grace is enhanced by its being set in a half-acre fountained plaza of pink granite. It was begun in 1956 and completed two years later at a cost of $35 million. It was, at the time, the city's most costly office building.

Not everyone who gazed upon it or watched its extruded bronze aging was convinced of its beauty. Acerbic nonarchitectural critics pointed out that the tower rises 520 feet without setbacks and that it is unornamented. It is too spare, they said. One likened it to an upended glass coffin.

The Seagram Building ranked third in Mies's offhand list of his six favorites, chosen to illustrate his most notable concept—"less is more." (By this Delphic utterance he meant achieving the maximum effect with the minimum of means.)

First on the list was the Illinois Institute of Technology's Crown Hall. This is a single glass-walled room measuring 120 feet by 220 feet and spanned by four huge trusses. The structure appears to do no more than to enclose space, a feeling reinforced by its interior movable partitions. It was one of 20 buildings that Mies designed for the school's 100-acre campus on Chicago's South Side. Crown Hall is as good an example as any of Mies's "skin-and-bones architecture," a phrase that he once used to describe his point of view.

The Chicago Federal Center, Mies's largest complex of high- and low-rise buildings, was his second favorite. He considered its symmetry symbolic of his lifelong battle against disorder.

Another Chicago creation was fourth—two 26-story apartment house towers at 860 and 880 Lake Shore Drive that overlook Lake Michigan. The facades are all glass. Tenants had to accept the neutral gray curtains that were uniform throughout the buildings and that provided the only means of seeking privacy and excluding light. No other curtains or blinds were permitted lest they mar the external appearance. (He was also the architect of the Promontory Apartments in Chicago, in which he used brick and glass in an exposed concrete frame.)

Mies's fifth favorite was a project for a Chicago convention hall, a place for 50,000 people to gather in unobstructed space under a trussed roof 720 feet square. The project never materialized.

The final pet on the architect's list was the since-destroyed German Pavilion at the 1929 International Exposition at Barcelona. It was, one critic said, "a jewel-case structure employing the open planning first developed by Frank Lloyd Wright that combined the richness of bronze, chrome, steel and glass with free-standing walls."

In addition to the Seagram Building, the architect was represented in the New York area by the Pavilion and Colonnade apartments, both in Colonnade Park, Newark. He also devised a master plan for a 21-acre development in New Haven.

Mies's most recent building, the National Gallery in Berlin, opened in 1968. It is a templelike glass box set on top of a larger semibasement, and serves as a museum.

Although many accolades were bestowed on Mies for these and other works, there were also brickbats. "Unsparing," "grim," the work of "barren intellectualism" and "brutal in its destruction of individual possessions and the individual" were some of the terms his detractors used.

"Less is less," they said, turning his aphorism against him.

Ludwig Mies, who added the "van der Rohe" from his mother's name because of its sonority, learned the elements of architecture from his father, a German master mason and stonecutter, and from studying the medieval churches in Aachen.

At times, friends recalled, he would describe with unrestrained enthusiasm the quality of brick and stone, their texture, pattern and color.

"Now a brick, that's really something," he once said. "That's really building, not paper architecture."

For him the material was always the beginning. He used to talk of primitive building methods, where he saw the "wisdom of whole generations" stored in every stroke of an ax, every bite of a chisel.

His students in the United States and Germany had to learn the fundamentals of building before they could start to consider questions of design. He taught them how to build, first with wood, then stone, then brick and finally with concrete and steel.

"New materials are not necessarily superior," he would say. "Each material is only what we make it."

At Aachen, Mies attended trade school and became a draftsman's apprentice before setting off for Berlin at the age of 19 to become an apprentice to Bruno Paul, Germany's leading furniture designer. Two years later he built his first house, a wooden structure on a sloping site in suburban Berlin. Its style was 18th-century.

In 1909 Mies apprenticed himself to Peter Behrens, then the foremost progressive architect in Germany, who had taught Le Corbusier and Walter Gropius. Mies was put in charge of Behrens's German embassy in St. Petersburg, Russia.

Going to the Netherlands in 1912, Mies designed a house for Mrs. H. E. L. J. Kröller, owner of the renowned Kröller-Muller collection of modern paintings, near The Hague. He set up a full-scale canvas-and-wood mock-up on the site to assure perfection, but the house was never built.

Mies returned to Berlin in 1913 and opened his own office, but with the outbreak of the war in 1914 his life was dislocated. During four years in the German army, he built bridges and roads in the Balkans. After the war, with his own style coming into definition, he directed the architectural activities of the Novembergruppe, an organization formed to propagandize modern art, and became one of the few progressive architects of the time to employ brick.

Often he would go to the kilns to select one by one the bricks he wanted. He used them for the monument (now destroyed) to Karl Liebknecht and Rosa Luxemburg, the German Communist leaders; for suburban villas for wealthy businessmen; and for low-cost housing for the city of Berlin.

From 1926 to 1932 he was first vice president of the Deutscher Werkbund, formed to integrate art and industry in design. He directed the group's second exposition, the Weissenhof housing project erected in Stuttgart in 1927.

The peak achievements of Mies's European career were the German Barcelona pavilion and the Tugendhat house in 1930. A. James Speyer, a critic for *Art News,* extolled them both as "among the most important buildings of contemporary architecture and the most beautiful of our generation." The pavilion consisted of a rectangular slab roof supported by steel columns, beneath which free-standing planes of Roman travertine, marble, onyx and glass of various hues were placed to create the feeling of space beyond. The Tugendhat house permitted space to flow in a similar fashion.

In 1930 Mies took over direction of the Bauhaus, a laboratory of architecture and design in Dessau, Germany. It was closed three years later after the Nazis attacked the architect as "degenerate" and "un-German."

At the urging of a New York architect who was a close friend, Philip C. Johnson, Mies emigrated to the United States to head the School of Architecture at the Armour (now Illinois) Institute of Technology in Chicago. He retired from the post in 1958.

As a teacher Mies did not deliver formal lectures, but worked, seminar fashion, with groups of 10 or 12 students. His method of teaching, according to a former student, was "almost tacit." "He was never wildly physically active, and he did not do much talking," this student recalled, adding that Mies, sitting Buddha-like, would frequently puff through a whole cigar before commenting on a student sketch.

Abandoning the Beaux Arts system based on competition for prizes, Mies sternly told his students: "First you have to learn something; then you can go out and do it."

He was not one to tolerate self-expression among his students. One of them once asked him about it. Silently he handed the student a pencil and paper.

Then he told her to write her name. This done, he said: "That's for self-expression. Now we get to work."

Another former student thought of Mies as "a great teacher because he subjects himself to an extraordinary discipline in thinking and in his way of working, and because what he is teaching is very clear to him."

Mies himself was quite confident of his influence. "I don't know how many students we have had," he said a couple of years ago, "but you need only 10 to change the cultural climate if they are good."

Mies was well-to-do, but not wealthy. He received the usual architect's fee of 6 percent of the gross cost of a building, but he was not a very careful manager of his income, according to his friends. He was considered generous with his office staff and on spending for designs that were unlikely to see the light of day.

The architect received three noteworthy honors—the Presidential Freedom Medal and the gold medals of the Royal Institute of British Architects and of the American Institute of Architects. He was a member of the National Institute of Arts and Letters.

Mies van der Rohe died at 88 on Aug. 18, 1969, in Chicago.

AN EXQUISITE SENSE OF ORDER

ADA LOUISE HUXTABLE

THE GLASSY skyscrapers and sleek-walled buildings that are the pride of modern cities and the symbol of modern life owe more to Mies van der Rohe than to any other architect of our time. In an age of complexity and confusion, Mies knew exactly what he was doing, and what he did, essentially, was to give that age its characteristic look and style. Almost every important street of every major city today is lined with the offspring of the spare, elegant structures that were his personal contribution to the art of architecture.

Mies made the glittering, soaring, straight-lined tower of today's urban world peculiarly his own. Even more than Le Corbusier and Frank Lloyd Wright—with whom he completed the architectural triumvirate of form-givers for the 20th century—he left the stamp of his art and philosophy on much of the world's contemporary construction.

That art and philosophy were based exclusively on contemporary technology: the supporting metal skeleton frame, the non-load-bearing wall hung lightly from it, and the modern materials that made the traditional heavy masonry building obsolete. He used those materials—glass, steel and aluminum, as well as timeless marble and bronze—with an exquisite, demanding and even rigid sense of order, appropriateness and beauty. There is not a cheap, vulgar or fussy passage in anything he designed or built.

There is much that is cheap and vulgar in the legion of structures that derived from his work, however. Because he enunciated a set of rational principles that met modern building needs in terms of scale, engineering and production, the formula was promptly reduced to its lowest common denominator by commercial builders. For every Seagram Building, there are the uncountable crudities of numberless routine adaptations of a style superficially easy to "knock off."

But more important than speculative abuses is the fact that the reduction of much large-scale utilitarian building to simple, practical "Miesian" elements has resulted in a valid and handsome, genuinely vernacular architecture for our day.

Although it is also a day when architects are increasingly preoccupied with the total environment, Mies remained an artist committed to the design of the individual building. His lifelong interest was the creation of the most perfect product that an infallibly refined taste and progressive technology could produce. His singular aim was the beautiful and efficient framing of large, all-purpose spaces; some worked superbly, and some did not. But the strong, richly austere aesthetic that he established was an unparalleled expression of new materials and engineering techniques.

He succeeded in his objectives with consummate artistry and skill. The artistry is subtle, extremely sophisticated and not always easily discernible to the untrained eye, to which all plain, modern buildings tend to look alike. Ultimately, the excellence of these buildings rests on the same basis as that of any of the great monuments of the past; fine proportion, sensitive detail and expressive pertinence to their times.

In recent years, when modern architecture became a stylistic free-for-all of almost baroque exuberance, he never wavered from the stripped-down, severely disciplined style that expressed his own convictions and the doctrines of the architectural revolution that he helped pioneer.

"You can't invent a new architecture every Monday morning," he commented, cutting some well-publicized Monday-wonders down to Lilliputian size.

Today it has become fashionable for young architects to call the masterworks of Mies "irrelevant" to the immediate social problems of our time. But cities endure, and Mies's "relevance" is timeless.

Mies was large—in history, as an innovator and talent of Michelangelesque stature; and personally, as a calm, massive, craggy man with the tacit monumentality of his work. His buildings are large—soaring symbols for an age. Today, however, larger buildings are being built by smaller men. And surprisingly few of the inhabitants of a Mies-shaped world know how much they have gained, and lost.

VLADIMIR NABOKOV

1899–1977

By Alden Whitman

Mr. Nabokov was born in Russia in 1889 and settled in the United States in 1939, living here until 1959. With the publication of *Lolita* in 1958 he received popular recognition. His later works, combined with the publication of earlier novels in translation from the original Russian, saw him elevated to the first rank of world authors.

His writing often perplexed his readers.

"For some weeks now I have been floundering and traveling in the mind of that American genius, Vladimir Vladimirovitch Nabokov," wrote the critic Alfred Kazin on reading the writer's novel *Ada* in 1969. His remark echoed the attitude of many readers to the Russian-born author who became an adoptive American after many years of exile in Europe and who in 1959 took up residence in Switzerland.

These readers recognized Mr. Nabokov's technical brilliance and mastery of form, but were frequently baffled by his irrepressible sense of flippancy and his penchant for parody. Was he, it was asked, a gifted artificer entranced by fun and games, or was he a creative and profound artist?

The perplexity sprang in part from the fact that Mr. Nabokov possessed such a cultivated mind (he was Cambridge-educated and a Cornell professor) and had such a cosmopolitan upbringing ("I was a perfectly normal trilingual child") that he tended to emphasize the paradoxes and humor of life rather than its congruities and dolorousness. "Every artist," he once remarked, "sees the comic and cosmic side of things."

Indeed, his explosion to prominence was based on a paradox, the public reaction to his novel *Lolita,* which was published in the United States in 1958, when Nabokov was 59 years old. Intended as a metaphor for the eternal quest for innocence that is resolved in satiric terms, the book sold in the thousands as an erotic story of Dolores Haze, a 12-year-old nymphet (a term coined by the author) and Humbert Humbert, her middle-aged pursuer.

That the serious novel succeeded for salacious reasons of course amused its author, but it also cost him many hours of explanation. "My knowledge of nymphets is purely scholarly," he was obliged to say. Ironically, the royalties gave him long-sought freedom to devote himself wholly to writing.

Lolita, like most Nabokov stories, can be read on several levels: as a narrative, as an exercise in logodaedaly, as a search for meaning and truth, as a tantalizing flight of imagination, as an exploration of a dreamlike confusion of time and place, and as an elaborate spoof. "He is not the kind of novelist whom you sit down to with a Scotch or an apple," Anthony Burgess, the British critic, declared.

This dazzling multifariousness gave employment to many academic exegetes. In addition to a quarterly devoted to Nabokoviana, at least one full-dress

Horst Tappe/Camera Press

critical study has been produced, along with two books, one offering a "key" to *Lolita* and the other annotating that novel. And there are scores of glosses on his other works.

One book, Carl R. Proffer's *Keys to Lolita,* was seriously discussed as actually coming from Mr. Nabokov's pen because its pedantry was such that it could be read as a parody on pedantry and because the name Proffer, with its scholastic implications, seemed like one Mr. Nabokov might adopt as a pseudonym. But Mr. Proffer, it turned out, was a very serious Indiana University scholar.

Mr. Nabokov did employ pseudonyms. "My main pseudonym, Sirin, thrived from 1920 to 1940," he said in an interview for this article. "Occasionally I used the little silk mask of an additional pen name in order to deceive this or that captious critic—with most gratifying results ('At last a great writer!' cried my favorite Zoilus in 1939)."

While insisting on his underlying seriousness. Mr. Nabokov admitted to delight in humor and the necessity for it. "While I keep everything on the brink of parody," he explained, "there must be on the other hand an abyss of seriousness, and I must make my way along this narrow ridge between my own truth and the caricature of it."

He maintained that all writers worth anything are humorists. "Give me an example of a great writer who is not a humorist," he demanded. "The worst tragedian is O'Neill. He is probably the worst writer. Dostoyevsky's slapstick is wonderful, but in his tragedy he's a journalist.

"The writer creates his own kind of life. Seeing things in a singular, unique, extraordinary way sounds funny to the average person.

"Seeing things as if they were new is funny in itself. The unusual is funny in itself. A man slips and falls down. It is the contrary of gravity in both senses. That is a great pun, by the way."

In addition to its humor (much of it donnish to a degree, or Joycean), a Nabokov novel was a game, with the reader invited to figure out the illusive reality that the writer offered. "In a first-rate piece of fiction, the real clash is not between the characters," he contended, "but between the author and the world."

Ada (Mr. Nabokov pronounced it Ahdah) was such a novel, and to get the most out of it, a reader could benefit from some knowledge of the theory of matter and antimatter, John Milton, T. S. Eliot, Lord Byron, Jane Austen and the 17th-century English poet Andrew Marvell. Acquaintanceship with Russian and French was also helpful, not to mention an inkling of theological speculation about prelapsarianism.

Furthermore, a reader who knew something about butterflies could gain valuable insights into what Mr. Nabokov was trying to say, for the author, a distinguished and passionate lepidopterologist, put butterflies and moths into virtually everything he wrote. (As a butterfly expert, Mr. Nabokov discovered several species and subspecies, made scholarly contributions to scientific literature and served from 1942 to 1948 as a research fellow in entomology at Harvard's Museum of Comparative Zoology.)

In his later years, when he had become famous, Mr. Nabokov loved to make pronouncements—some plainly outrageous, some mystifying, some obviously designed to sustain his self-assessment that "I am a very funny man." In an interview for this article in the spring of 1969, for example, he pronounced merrily on the pronunciation of his name. After reciting in mock horror several variants that he considered vulgar, he said, twinkling: "My name, if you must know, is vla-DEE-mir, to rhyme with redeemer, na-BOAK-off. But only a Russian can say it with its true inflections."

In another utterance he offered a new English word for vulgarity—the Russian word *poshlost* (pronounced "PUSH-lost"), which means, he said, "corny trash, vulgar clichés, Philistinism in all its phases, imitations of imitations, bogus profundities, crude, moronic and dishonest pseudoliterature." Pressed for examples, he said: "*Poshlost* speaks in such concepts as 'America is no better than Russia' or 'We all share in Germany's guilt.' The flowers of *poshlost* bloom in such phrases and terms as 'the moment of truth,' 'charisma,' 'existential' (used seriously), 'dialogue' (as applied to political talks between nations) and 'vocabulary' (as applied to a dauber)."

A few of Mr. Nabokov's other declarations were:

"Of course everybody has his bête noire, his black pet. Mine is that airline ad: The snack served by the obsequious wench to a young couple—she eyeing the cucumber canapé, he admiring wistfully the hostess. And, of course, *Death in Venice* [a novella by Thomas Mann]."

"Many accepted authors simply do not exist for me. Brecht, Faulkner, Camus, many others, mean absolutely nothing to me. I must fight a suspicion of conspiracy against my brain when I blandly see accepted as 'great literature' by critics and fellow authors Lady Chatterley's copulations or the pretentious nonsense of Mr. [Ezra] Pound, that total fake."

"How can I talk about the novel when I don't know what a novel is? There are no novels, no writers, only individual books."

"I reject completely the vulgar, shabby, fundamentally medieval world of Freud, with its crankish quest for sexual symbols (something like searching for Baconian acrostics in Shakespeare's works) and its bitter little embryos spying from their natural nooks upon the love life of their parents."

"I don't fish, cook, dance, endorse books, sign declarations, eat oysters, get drunk, go to analysts, or take part in any demonstrations. I'm a mild old gentleman, very kind."

Six feet tall and sturdily built, Mr. Nabokov resembled an athlete (he was an excellent tennis player most of his life), yet when he donned his shell glasses he seemed like an avuncular professor. His manner was courtly, his green-and-amber eyes merry, his lips seemed always to be pursed for a joke or a jape. His voice was that of a skilled actor; he could project it to any emotion or range, so that his conversations had a quality of drama that transfixed listeners.

"I was born a cosmopolite, and my Russia is little more than the park of an ancestral estate in the latitude of Yukon," the writer said in his 1969 interview. Born April 23, 1899 (he shared Shakespeare's birthdate, he maintained), he was the son of a wealthy jurist and was brought up in a St. Petersburg townhouse and at a country estate by a series of nannies and governesses. He learned to speak and read English before he could read Russian.

As a youth he was handsome and talented, disciplined and competitive. He learned to box and to play tennis, to become an expert at chess problems and to collect butterflies. He also wrote, at 15, his first poem, after seeing a raindrop cause a cordate leaf to flutter.

In 1919 he inherited $2 million from an uncle, but the Bolshevik Revolution obliged the family to flee Russia for Germany with only a few jewels and clothing. Three years later the elder Nabokov was killed at an émigré political rally in Berlin.

The same year Mr. Nabokov was graduated from Trinity College, Cambridge ("I played soccer—the great love of my life") after studying French and Russian literature on a scholarship. Rejoining his family in Berlin, he made a modest living for a number of years by teaching boxing, tennis and languages; by constructing Russian crossword puzzles and by compiling a Russian grammar. Unlike many émigrés, Mr. Nabokov did not anguish over a lost life or engage in endless intrigues and interminable argument.

Meanwhile, he was determined to write (indeed, he could not help himself) as an outlet for his rich nostalgia for Russia, as a way to express his fantasies and inventions and emotions. He earned his living by day and wrote mostly at night, sometimes in the bathroom where the light disturbed no one. In this unorthodox fashion, pursued over 15 years, he created nine novels, nine plays and dozens of stories and plays in Russian, but was virtually unknown outside Russian circles.

Most of this output was later translated (in part by Mr. Nabokov himself) into English, including the novels *Mary; King, Queen, Knave; The Great Deed; The Luzhin Defense; Despair* and *Laughter in the Dark.*

Mr. Nabokov's life took a decisive turn in 1939, when he accepted an invitation to lecture on Slavic languages at Stanford. Staying on in the United States for 20 years, he became a citizen and found a new emotional homeland. "It had taken me some 40 years to invent Russia and Western Europe," he said, "and now I was faced with the task of inventing America."

Ultimately, he categorized himself as an American writer, telling this reporter in 1969: "An American writer means, in the present case, a writer who has been an American citizen for a quarter of a century. It means, moreover, that all my works first appear in America. It also means that America is the only country where I feel mentally and emotionally at home."

After Stanford, Mr. Nabokov taught at Wellesley from 1941 to 1948, first as a lecturer, then as a professor of literature. Simultaneously he was a working entomologist at Harvard, for which he discovered several species and subspecies of butterflies, including Nabokov's wood nymph. And, of course, he was writing—poems, essays, stories for *The New Yorker, Atlantic Monthly, Harper's, Partisan Review.*

He was introduced to the American literary scene by Edmund Wilson, the late critic, in whose home at Westport, Conn., he wrote his first poem in the United States. The two were intimate friends until the late 1950s, when, according to Mr. Nabokov, "a black cat came between us—Boris Pasternak's novel *Doctor Zhivago.*"

Mr. Nabokov called the book third-rate and clumsy while Mr. Wilson praised it. "He started the quarrel," Mr. Nabokov said, and it was exacerbated in 1963 when Mr. Nabokov published his annotated English translation of *Eugene Onegin,* Alexander Pushkin's romantic novel in verse form.

Mr. Wilson attacked the translation, hinting that Mr. Nabokov's Russian was faulty. Their donnish dispute raged in the *New York Review of Books* until their friendship was ruptured.

Mr. Nabokov's first novel written in English came out in 1941—*The Real Life of Sebastian Knight.* It was the life story of a gifted novelist, reconstructed, after his death, by a half brother. It was followed by *Bend Sinister* in 1947, a Kafkaesque novel about an intellectual's vain effort to maintain his integrity in a totalitarian environment; *Conclusive Evidence* (also known as *Speak, Memory*) in 1951, a vivid account of the writer's life in Russia; *Pnin* in 1957, about a Russian émigré's life in an American university; *Lolita* in 1958; *Pale Fire* in 1962, a parodistic novel written in the form of a 999-line poem with a lengthy commentary by a demented New England scholar who turns out to be the exiled king of a mythical country.

As he was writing novels in the 1940s and 1950s (plus poems and short stories), Mr. Nabokov continued to teach. He was at Cornell from 1949 to 1959 as professor of Russian literature, and he was a visiting lecturer at Harvard in the spring of 1952. Popular, provocative and tough with his students, he wrote out his lectures in advance, delivered them sonorously (with a bit of acting) and upset a number of cherished values. He didn't care for Cervantes, for example, and delighted in taking *Don Quixote* to pieces.

Summers he toured the United States in search of butterflies ("a passion and a madness"), stopping at motels and absorbing roadside culture. Many of his observations were incorporated in *Lolita,* and led to a charge that the book was intended as, among other things, a mockery of America. Discussing this in 1969, the writer said: "Poking fun at suburban genteelness or inventing a half-dozen grotesque motels does not mean sneering at America. Let us not make a mockery out of a mock-up."

Lolita was turned down as lewd by four publishers before G. P. Putnam's Sons issued it. Even then it was banned by several public libraries, and the *Chicago Tribune* refused to review it. Its critical reception was mixed; Orville Prescott of *The New York Times* termed the book "highbrow pornography," while Graham Greene acclaimed it as a distinguished novel. It has since come to be regarded as a classic, and was made into a movie by Stanley Kubrick with James Mason as Humbert and Sue Lyon in the title role.

With his royalties and $150,000 for screen rights, Mr. Nabokov went back to Europe for the first time in 20 years. He established himself in the Montreux-Palace Hotel, a marvelous Victorian and Edwardian pile on the shores of Lake Geneva in Switzerland, which he eventually made his home. "Sheer laziness" was one of the reasons he gave for remaining there; he also wanted to be near his only son, Dmitri (an opera singer in Italy), and a sister in Geneva.

At the Montreux-Palace, Mr. Nabokov had a warren of small rooms where he lived with his wife, Vera, who was his confidante, typist, chess partner, Scrabble adversary, butterfly-hunting companion and conversational jouster. Their dedication to each other was total.

Mr. Nabokov's writing habits were unusual. Although he might have the general conception of a novel or a story in his mind, he worked it out as one would a crossword puzzle. Sentences, bits and scenes were jotted down in longhand on 3-by-5-inch index cards, and the grand design filled out a section at a time, in no special order. An insomniac, he kept his cards under his pillow, to make use of wakeful moments at night.

"Writing for me has always been a blend of dejection and high spirits, a torture and a pastime," he once said. And the product often baffled critics and readers.

Ada, which was published in 1969, was an example. Sometimes called "the last of the mandarins," Mr. Nabokov wrote the best-selling novel as a family chronicle, he said, but it was so full of allusions, commentaries on incest (some of them quite obscure) and ruminations on the nature of time that interpretation of it varied with the critic. The author hardly dispelled the confusion when he described the novel in his 1969 interview by saying: "*Ada* is a leisurely, ample, old-fashioned family chronicle some 600 pages long. A childhood romance between closely related Van Veen and Ada Veen in an unspoiled part of New England develops into a lifelong obsession, with tragic interludes, reckless trysts and a rapturous end in the 10th decade of their cosmopolitan existence.

"The crucial chapter in *Ada* is the penultimate part of the book, entirely concerned with an exploration—a scholarly exploration—of the texture of time mainly by means of metaphors. The two leading characters die. Indeed, they die away to a built-in blurb, with a sort of *perdendosi* [a musical term meaning "to lose strength"] effect."

Vladimir Nabokov died of a viral infection on July 2, 1977, in the suite at the Montreux-Palace Hotel in Montreux, Switzerland, where he and his wife, Vera, had lived for 18 years. Mr. Nabokov was 78 years old.

A MEMOIR

HERBERT GOLD

NABOKOV WOULD be flabbergasted by the information that he was loved as a person. Whatever sins could he have committed to deserve such unjust affection? A declaration of feeling—should one be rude enough—would cause those deep Russian rumblings of laughter to gather in all his caverns and to come rolling out with desperate chortlings and running tears and final dabs with a handkerchief. Love, love, love, you say? *Poshlost:* Such avowals belonged for him in the realm of *poshlost,* a word he defined for me as covering the spectrum of feeling from the airline ad in which a young couple eye ecstatically the cucumber canapé ("he admiring wistfully the hostess") to *Death in Venice*. "You see the range," he added.

It might almost seem that he didn't need the love of friends, admirers, critics, the public. He was blessed with a wife who adored him, whom he adored, a critical partnership without question; he loved Vera and their son, and the double hunt for butterflies, and the perfect shaping of wit, rage and nostalgia in his books; he frankly admired the constant sparkling tricks of his own mind and imagination. He loved to work, his favorite form of play. He was not sweet and easy; he was never just folks.

Nevertheless, he somehow earned the love of those around him, even before *Lolita* catapulted him to fame. I first heard of him from a student at Wellesley in the early 1940s, when I was a freshman in college. She used words like *cute* and *delicious* about her Russian teacher. Then I read his marvelously perverse biography of Gogol, really a novel about Gogol, in which he played unfamiliar games, such as spelling Gogol's doctor's name differently each time he used it, telling us that this butcher was beneath contempt. I read his translation of *Three Russian Poets*, published as a good gray New Directions paper pamphlet, which introduced me to Pushkin and to a typical Nabokov reversal. In *Mozart and Salieri*, the legend that Salieri, a minor composer, poisoned Mozart out of jealousy is turned several degrees westward: Salieri poisoned him to save music, because he loved Mozart and understood him, because otherwise Mozart would write all the music necessary and destroy the living art.

Later I found *Lolita* in the green Olympia Press version and participated first in the shock of discovery of a masterpiece and then in the comedy of its difficulty in finding an American publisher. "I can't publish this," several said. Eventually one believed he could, and did.

Nabokov and I became friendly in 1958 when he brought me to Cornell to replace him after he decided to leave teaching. He guided me through interviews, flattered me to keep my spirits up and buttered up the committee for the fun of it; advised me on how much to drink in order to be a good fellow, but suggested I not be too good a fellow; got lost with me in the snow as we tried to find our way from his classroom to the house where, as usual temporary in all but his work, his family and his past, he and Vera lodged in the absence of some professor on sabbatical.

Ten years ago Nabokov allowed me an interview for the *Paris Review*, and also entertained me for two weeks while I wrote an article about him. The measure of my difficulty in summing him up is the title I gave the typescript of the article: "Vladimir Nabokov Is a Great American Writer, Born in Russia and Educated in England, Where He Studied French Literature Before Spending Fifteen Years in Germany. He Now Lives in Switzerland. 'I Travel Through Life in a Space Helmet,' Says Nabokov. 'Art Is Complex and Deceitful. I Had to Invent Both *Lolita* and America.' "

If used, this might have entered the competition for the longest title in literary history. Partly it came from the need to explain to the readers of the *Saturday Evening Post* who this man was—not a movie star, not an athlete, not a pop celebrity. But upon maturer thought the editors called the piece "Nabokov." If a San Francisco drive-in could advertise Lolitaburgers, the kindly old professor was well enough known. He was a new young writer whose first work had been printed more than 50 years earlier.

In Montreux he denied that he had called *Dr. Zhivago* "Dr. Van Cliburn" but lay back and roared when I reported that I treasured the copy he had annotated and inscribed and left as a good-bye present on my desk in his office in Goldwin Smith Hall at Cornell. He explained that, despite his wanderings, he was now one-third American, because of all the weight he had put on in the States—"good American flesh"—but that his loss of Russia was the permanent tragedy of his life. "I am not emotionally involved with Indian dances or pumpkin pie on the spiritual plane," he said, "but I am as American as April in Arizona." And lay back in his deck chair, beaming and chuckling and dabbing at his eyes.

During those weeks in Montreux I promised not to disturb him till his day's work was done. So he would telephone around 9 o'clock in the morning, when his early writing was over, to make plans for our swim, walk, lunch, dinner. He would wake me with: "You called for two whiskies, sir?" Or "Did you know the hawk moth can fly two or three hundred miles an hour?" and later explained that this was discovered by a pilot who found the moths outdistancing his plane. "He thought he was perhaps standing still or flying backwards."

As he carried himself with elephantine grace, he disported himself with an ingratiating mixture of buffoonery and elegance. He would begin a story, rolling his eyes at Vera, signaling in advance the sharp correction he expected; and then he would beam at her, grateful for her care and critical devotion; and finally he would proceed cajolingly through the thicket of the verbal drama between them, ending usually in a joke on everybody. He took his tricks seriously. When he assured me that he never wrote personal letters (my communications with him over the years had always come through the intermediary of Vera: "My husband asks me to tell you . . ."). I'm sure he meant for me to note: Never writes letters. I fell into the trap. When the article appeared, he penned by hand a communication to the editor of the *Post*: "not exactly . . ." His wife and his wit put a screen between Nabokov and his obsessions: butterflies, chess, the grace of ideas and the image of childhood; his enormous nostalgia for Russia, a paradigm of what all living creatures must lose; his passion for freedom, words, art.

In a garden of Montreux, near Lake Geneva, in the sight of peeling posters announcing a chamber music concert, he recollected arriving at the scene of the murder of his father at a public meeting in Berlin. Smoke, confusion and horror; and an acquaintance who showed his own flesh wound to the boy holding his dead father, saying, "I was hurt, too." Nabokov rumbled and hesitated as we paced: "He was a good man, not insensitive, just excited."

Probably one explanation for his extraordinary richness of style in English, besides his "totally normal trilingual childhood," was the gift (also burden) of total recall. He would fit phrases from novels or stories of mine into his own sentences, stare, and then fall back chortling that he had caught me: "You do not remember your own work." Despite the noise of so much playfulness, what he said of Gogol is true of himself, that he appeals "to that secret depth of the human soul where the shadows of other worlds pass like the shadows of nameless and soundless ships."

The man who announced that Russia is gone and the Soviet Union does not really exist knew that he was denying history. This did not concern him. The shadows of other worlds were his concern. He allowed as how the American government is one of his "hobbies" and he was writing a novel to be called *The Texture of Time*. Prophecy is the wit of the fool, he said: Human intelligence is much too important to bother with such trivial matters as predicting the future. In the mosaic of his books he suspiciously explored the capacity for goodness, the dreadful gulf between tenderness and virtue. With all his coolness and grandness, he adored the things of this world; he valued the past for its ability to happen in his mind right now; he loved intelligence, shapeliness, rhythm and a good laugh. He liked to joke at the expense of an enemy or, if none was at hand, a friend.

Philippe Halsman, who had just come to Montreux from photographing President Johnson, a jittery and insecure subject, said that Nabokov was a blessing for a photographer because he liked himself. He had no problem with masks. His own suited him perfectly. He did not consider his work prophetic or nostalgic but, rather, the memory of an imagined future. He had no problems with paradox either.

Within all this love for what he found in his space helmet, did he admire other writers? Of course. Proust, Joyce, Tolstoy, Gogol, H. G. Wells . . . And among the living? Of course, of course, and occasionally he named a few, as in his essay "On Inspiration," but in general: "Anonymous praise hurts nobody."

After spending those weeks with the Nabokovs at the Montreux-Palace Hotel, I saw butterflies everywhere, as had the great lepidopterist on our walks. He was persuasive; he trains one's eyes. Gradually the butterflies became nearly invisible again; one has other concerns than Nabokov's; but today, after hearing of his death, I find the air once more filled with his butterflies. Nabokov had the genius to make us see what he saw, not merely as fantasy but because it is really there; not merely because he longed for style, beauty and color, but because they really existed in his witty, shapely longing. And after his unique set of gifts to the world, certain butterflies in our consciousness can never be invisible again.

GEORGIA O'KEEFFE

1887–1986

By Edith Evans Asbury

As an artist, as a reclusive but overwhelming personality, and as a woman in what was for a long time a man's world, Georgia O'Keeffe was a key figure in the American 20th century. As much as anyone since Mary Cassatt, the American Impressionist painter who worked with Degas in France, she raised the American public's awareness of the fact that a woman could be the equal of any man in her chosen field.

As an interpreter and manipulator of natural forms, as a strong and individual colorist and as the lyric poet of her beloved New Mexico landscape, she left her mark on the history of American art and made it possible for other women to explore a new gamut of symbolic and ambiguous imagery.

Miss O'Keeffe was strong-willed, hardworking and whimsical. She would wrap herself in a blanket and wait, shivering, in the cold dark for a sunrise to paint; would climb a ladder to see the stars from a roof, and hop around in her stockings on an enormous canvas to add final touches before all the paint dried.

Miss O'Keeffe burst upon the art world in 1916, under auspices most likely to attract attention at the time: in a one-woman show of her paintings at the famous "291" gallery of her husband, Alfred Stieglitz, the world-renowned pioneer in photography and a sponsor of newly emerging modern art.

From then on, Miss O'Keeffe was in the spotlight, shifting from one audacious way of presenting a subject to another, and usually succeeding with each new experiment. Her colors dazzled, her erotic implications provoked and stimulated, her subjects astonished and amused.

She painted the skull of a horse with a bright pink Mexican artificial flower stuck in the eye socket. She painted other animal skulls, horns, pelvises and leg bones that gleamed white against brilliant skies, spanned valleys and touched mountaintops, all with serene disdain for conventional notions of perspective. She also painted New York skyscrapers, Canadian barns and crosses and oversized flowers and rocks.

The artist painted as she pleased, and sold virtually as often as she liked, for very good prices. She joined the elite, avant-garde, inner circle of modern American artists around Stieglitz, whom she married in 1924. Stieglitz took more than 500 photographs of her.

"He photographed me until I was crazy," Miss O'Keeffe said in later years. Others have called the pictures Stieglitz took of her the greatest love poem in the history of photography.

Her beauty aged well to another kind—weatherbeaten, leathery skin wrinkled over high cheekbones and around a firm mouth that spoke fearlessly and tolerated no bores. And long after Stieglitz had died, in 1946, after Miss O'Keeffe forsook New York for

Photograph by Philippe Halsman 1948 © Yvonne Halsman 1988

the mountains and deserts of New Mexico, she was discovered all over again and proclaimed a pioneering artist of great individuality, power and historic significance.

Miss O'Keeffe had never stopped painting, never stopped winning critical acclaim, never stopped being written about as an interesting "character." But her paintings were so diverse, so uniquely her own and so unrelated to trends or schools that they had not attracted much close attention from New York critics.

Then, in 1970, when she was 83 years old, a retrospective exhibition of her work was held at the Whitney Museum of American Art. The New York critics and collectors and a new generation of students, artists and aficionados made an astonishing discovery. The artist who had been joyously painting as she pleased had been a step ahead of everyone, all the time.

Strolling through the Whitney show, one could think Miss O'Keeffe had made some "very neat adaptations of various successful styles of the 1950s and 1960s in her own highly refined and slightly removed manner," wrote John Canaday, art critic of *The New York Times*. He described apparent similarities to Clyfford Still, Helen Frankenthaler, Barnett Newman, Ad Reinhardt and Andrew Wyeth.

But the paintings that seemed to reflect those styles were done by Miss O'Keeffe in 1920 or earlier, Mr. Canaday pointed out, "when her seeming models were either not yet born or were delighting their mothers with their first childish scrawls."

Despite the affinity of Miss O'Keeffe's work to paintings of other modern American artists, her paintings show surprisingly little evidence of the European influence seen in other American art. "She escaped the fate of remaining in thrall to a European model by taking possession of her American experience and making that the core of her artistic vision," Hilton Kramer wrote in *The Times* in 1976 in his review of her illustrated autobiography. Nevertheless, he declared, "her painting, though filled with vivid images of the places where she has lived, was anything but a product of the provinces."

Miss O'Keeffe's career, Mr. Kramer wrote, "is unlike almost any other in the history of modern art in America." It embraced virtually the whole history of modern art, from the early years of the century when Stieglitz exhibited the new art to a shocked New York, to its eventual acceptance as a part of our culture, according to Mr. Kramer. At the age of 89, when her book was published, Miss O'-Keeffe remained "a vital figure first of all as a painter of remarkable originality and power but also as a precious link with the first generation of American modernists," he wrote.

Georgia O'Keeffe was born on a wheat farm near Sun Prairie, Wis., on Nov. 15, 1887. Her father, Francis Calixtus O'Keeffe, was Irish; her mother was the former Ida Totto. Georgia was named for her maternal grandfather, Giorgio Totto, who came to the United States from Hungary, where he had gone from Italy.

When Miss O'Keeffe was 14 years old, the family moved to Williamsburg, Va. Three years later she graduated from Chatham Protestant Episcopal Institute in Virginia. She went immediately to Chicago, where she studied for a year at the Art Institute with John Vanderpoel. Both of her grandmothers had dabbled at painting, two of her four sisters painted and one taught art. The elder of her two brothers was an architect.

Miss O'Keeffe had decided in Sun Prairie that she was going to be an artist when she grew up, although, she wrote in her book, "I hadn't a desire to make anything like the pictures I had seen," and she did not have a very clear idea of what an artist would be.

For 10 discouraging years, she studied and painted, supporting herself by doing commercial art for advertising agencies and by teaching. She attended art classes at the Art Students League in New York in 1907–8, the University of Virginia Summer School in 1912 and Teachers College of Columbia University in 1916.

She was supervisor of art in the public schools of Amarillo, Tex., from 1912 to 1916, and taught summer classes at Columbia College in South Carolina and the University of Virginia. In 1916 she became head of the art department of West Texas Normal College.

Miss O'Keeffe's early pictures were imitative, but as she developed her technique, a ruggedly individual style began to assert itself. The results were out of step with the popular taste and accepted style of the early 1900s, but they encouraged her to concentrate boldly on expressing her own ideas.

"One day," Miss O'Keeffe recalled in later years, "I found myself saying to myself, 'I can't live where I want to. I can't even say what I want to.' I decided I was a very stupid fool not to at least paint as I wanted to."

A friend, Anita Pollitzer, showed a group of Miss O'Keeffe's drawings and watercolors to Stieglitz in 1916. Miss Pollitzer, later to become a champion of equal rights for women and chair of the National Woman's Party, had been a classmate of Miss O'Keeffe's at Columbia.

"At last, a woman on paper!" Stieglitz exclaimed when he saw the pictures. He hung them in his gallery, and the unknown Miss O'Keeffe created an immediate stir in the art world.

"Mabel Dodge Luhan brought strings of psychiatrists to look at them," Stieglitz recalled later. "The critics came. There was talk, talk, talk." Some of the talk hinted at erotic symbolism.

Miss O'Keeffe stormed up from Texas and upbraided Stieglitz for showing her work without her permission. His answer was to persuade her to move to New York, abandon her teaching and devote herself to painting. He presented one-woman shows of her work almost annually thereafter until 1946, the year of his death. He and Miss O'Keeffe had been married 21 years.

After moving to New York, Miss O'Keeffe divided her time between New York City and Lake George, N.Y. After 1929, she also spent a great deal of time in New Mexico. She made her permanent residence at Abiquiu after the death of her husband.

Stieglitz's vigilant and canny management was a major factor in her rise to fame and fortune. Miss O'Keeffe continued to wear the clothes she pleased and to paint as she pleased.

Spare and dark-skinned, she had dark hair drawn severely back and knotted into a bun in those years. No makeup softened the angularity of her face with its high cheekbones, but her large, luminous eyes betrayed inner fires. Her clothes were usually black, loose-fitting and shapeless, functional rather than fashionable.

Miss O'Keeffe's paintings hang in museums all over the United States—including, in New York, the Metropolitan, the Whitney and the Museum of Modern Art—and in most major private collections. But she retained a great deal of her prolific production.

Miss O'Keeffe was elected to membership in the National Institute of Arts and Letters, the American Academy of Arts and Letters and the American Academy of Arts and Sciences. She was awarded honorary degrees by several colleges and universities, including Mount Holyoke and Columbia in 1971 and Harvard in 1973.

Back in Abiquiu, she resumed a daily routine of work, now with the help of a young protégé, Juan Hamilton, a potter. He had knocked at her kitchen door asking for work and made his way up from man Friday to secretary. He supervised production of her book and assisted with and appeared in the television film about her in 1977. He traveled with her to New York and California and managed her business affairs. Their companionship was so close there were rumors of marriage.

Miss O'Keeffe traveled to New York to visit friends and see art exhibitions until poor eyesight and failing health kept her at home.

Miss O'Keeffe won numerous awards, including the Medal of Freedom, the nation's highest civilian award, in 1977; an award from Radcliffe College, for lifetime achievements by women, in 1983; and the National Medal of Arts in 1985.

Georgia O'Keeffe died in Santa Fe, New Mexico, on March 6, 1986. She was 98 years old.

J. ROBERT OPPENHEIMER

1904–1967

Starting precisely at 5:30 A.M., Mountain War Time, July 16, 1945, J. Robert Oppenheimer lived the remainder of his life in the blinding light and the crepuscular shadow of the world's first atomic event, for which he was largely responsible.

That sunlike flash illuminated him as a scientific genius, the technocrat of a new age for mankind. At the same time it led to his condemnation by the government when, in 1964, he was described as a security risk to his country and a man with "fundamental defects in his character." Publicly rehabilitated in 1963 by a singular government honor, this bafflingly complex man nonetheless never fully succeeded in dispelling doubts about his conduct during a crucial period of his life.

The perplexities centered on a story of attempted atomic espionage that he told army counterintelligence officers in 1943 and that he later repudiated as a fabrication. His sole explanation for what he called "a cock-and-bull story" was that he had been "an idiot." Misgivings also sprang from the manner in which he implicated a close friend in his asserted concoction.

A brilliant nuclear physicist, with a comprehensive grasp of his field, Dr. Oppenheimer was also a cultivated scholar, a humanist, a linguist of eight tongues and a brooding searcher for ultimate spiritual values. And, from the moment that the test bomb exploded at Alamogordo, N.M., he was haunted by the implications for man in the unleashing of the basic forces of the universe.

As he clung to one of the uprights in the desert control room that July morning and saw the mushroom cloud rising in the explosion, a passage from the Bhagavad-Gita, the Hindu sacred epic, flashed through his mind. He related it later as: "If the radiance of a thousand suns were to burst into the sky, that would be like the splendor of the Mighty One."

And as the black, then gray, atomic cloud pushed higher above Point Zero, another line—"I am become Death, the shatterer of worlds"—came to him from the same scripture.

Two years later, he was still beset by the moral consequences of the bomb, which, he told fellow physicists, had "dramatized so mercilessly the inhumanity and evil of modern war."

"In some sort of crude sense which no vulgarity, no humor, no overstatements can quite extinguish," he went on, "the physicists have known sin; and this is a knowledge which they cannot lose."

In later years, he seemed to indicate that "sin" was not to be taken personally. "I carry no weight on my conscience," he said in 1961 in reference to the atomic bombings of Hiroshima and Nagasaki.

"Scientists are not delinquents," he added. "Our work has changed the conditions in which men live, but the use made of those changes is the problem of governments, not of scientists."

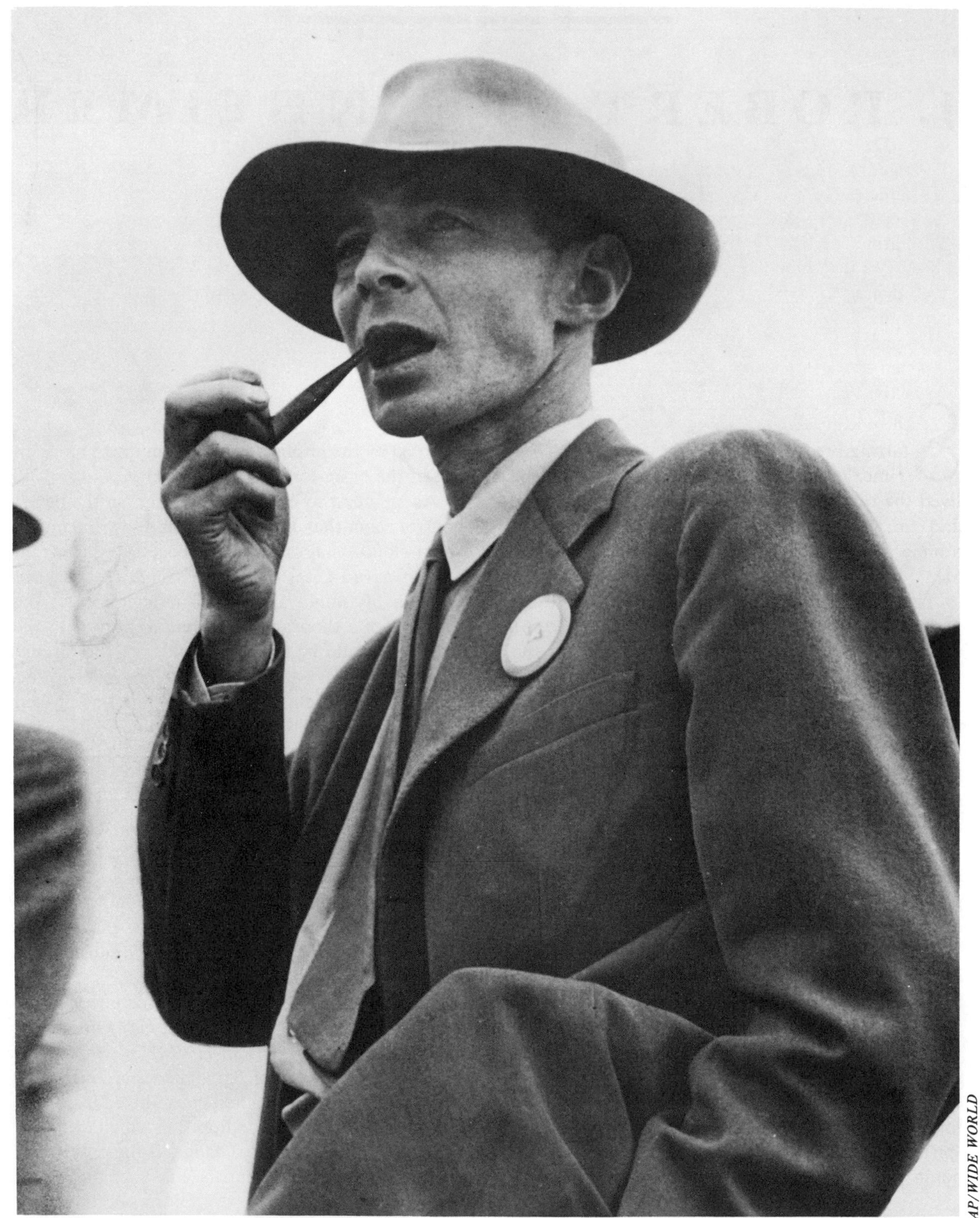

AP/WIDE WORLD

Dr. Oppenheimer on September 9, 1945, at the site of the first atomic explosion, Alamagordo, New Mexico

With the detonation of the first three atomic bombs and the immediate Allied victory in World War II, Dr. Oppenheimer, at the age of 41, reached the apogee of his career. Acclaimed as "the father of the atomic bomb," he was officially credited by the War Department with "achieving the implementation of atomic energy for military purposes." Secretary of War Henry L. Stimson led a chorus of national praise when he said of the scientist: "The development of the bomb itself has been largely due to his genius and the inspiration and leadership he has given to his colleagues."

Shortly thereafter, in 1946, Dr. Oppenheimer received a Presidential Citation and a Medal of Merit for his direction of the Los Alamos Laboratory, where the bomb had been developed.

In the years from 1945 to 1952, Dr. Oppenheimer was one of the foremost government advisers on key phases of United States atomic policy. He was the dominant author of the Acheson-Lilienthal Report (named for Secretary of State Dean Acheson and David Lilienthal, first chairman of the Atomic Energy Commission), which offered a plan for international control of atomic energy.

He was also the virtual author of the Baruch Plan, which was based on the Acheson-Lilienthal Report, calling for United Nations supervision of nuclear power. He was consultant to Bernard M. Baruch at the United Nations and to Frederick H. Osborn, Baruch's successor, in futile United Nations negotiations over the plan, which was balked by the Soviet Union.

Furthermore, from 1947 to 1952, Dr. Oppenheimer headed the Atomic Energy Commission's General Advisory Committee of top nuclear scientists, and for the following two years he was its consultant. He also served on the atomic committee of the Research and Development Board to advise the military, on the science advisory committee of the Office of Defense Mobilization and on study groups by the dozen. He had a desk in the president's executive offices, across the street from the White House.

This eminence ended abruptly in December 1953, when President Dwight D. Eisenhower ordered that a "blank wall be placed between Dr. Oppenheimer and any secret data" pending a security hearing. The following June he was stripped of his security clearance by the Atomic Energy Commission. It was never restored to him.

Up to 1954 Dr. Oppenheimer's big-brimmed brown porkpie hat, size 6⅞, was a frequent (and telltale) sight in Washington and the capitals of Western Europe, where he traveled to lecture or consult. (The trademark hat was also in evidence at Princeton, N.J., where he headed the Institute for Advanced Study, a research facility for some 200 postdoctoral fellows in many fields, from 1947 to 1966.) He was Oppy, Oppie or Opje to hundreds of persons who were captivated by his charm, eloquence and sharp, subtle humor and who were awed by the scope of his erudition, the incisiveness of his mind, the chill of his sarcasm and his arrogance toward those he thought were slow or shoddy thinkers.

Six feet tall and a bit stooped, he was as thin as the wisps from his chain-smoked cigarettes or pipes. Blue-eyed, with close-cropped hair (it was dark in 1943, gray by 1954 and white a few years later), he had a mobile, expressive face that became lined and haggard after his security hearings.

He was extremely fidgety when he sat, and he constantly shifted himself in his chair, bit his knuckles, scratched his head and crossed and uncrossed his legs. When he spoke on his feet, he paced and stalked, smoking incessantly and jerking a cigarette or pipe out of his mouth almost violently when he wanted to emphasize a word or phrase with a gesture.

He was an energetic man at parties, where he was usually the center of attention. He was gracious as a host and the maker of fine and potent martinis. He was full of droll stories.

What impressed people first about Dr. Oppenheimer was his intellect. "Robert is the only authentic genius I know," Mr. Lilienthal said of him.

Echoing this appraisal, Charles Lauritsen, a former colleague at the California Institute of Technology, once remarked: "The man was unbelievable! He always gave you the right answer before you formulated the question."

Knowledge came easily to Dr. Oppenheimer. As a young man he learned enough Dutch in six weeks to deliver a technical lecture while on a visit to the Netherlands. At the age of 30 he learned Sanskrit, and he used to enjoy passing notes in that language to other savants. On a train trip from San Francisco to the East Coast he read Edward Gibbon's seven-volume *The History of the Decline and Fall of the Roman Empire*. On another such trip he read the four volumes of Karl Marx's *Das Kapital* in German. On a short summer holiday in Corsica he read in French Marcel Proust's massive *A la recherche du temps perdu*, which he later said was one of the great experiences of his life.

This almost compulsive avidity for learning was not sterile, for he invaribly made some use of what he read. He was, moreover, an authority, if not an expert, in baroque and classical music, to which he liked to listen. In the words of a friend, Dr. Oppenheimer was "a culture hound."

Even as a child, J. Robert Oppenheimer was made much of for his ability to absorb knowledge. He was born in New York on April 22, 1904, the son of Julius and Ella Freedman (or Friedman) Oppenheimer. Julius Oppenheimer was a prosperous textile importer who had emigrated from Germany, and his wife was a Baltimore artist who died when her elder son was 10. (The younger son, Frank Friedman Oppenheimer, also became a physicist.)

The family lived in comfort, with a private art collection that included three Van Goghs. Robert was encouraged to delve into rocks after starting a collection at the age of 5, and he was admitted to the Mineralogical Club of New York when he was 11.

He was a shy, delicate boy (he was once thought to have tuberculosis) who was more concerned with his homework and with poetry and architecture than with mixing with other youngsters. After attending the Ethical Culture School ("It is characteristic that I don't remember any of my classmates," he said) he entered Harvard College in 1922, intending to become a chemist.

He was a solitary student with an astonishing appetite for work. "I had a real chance to learn," he said later. "I loved it. I almost came alive. I took more courses than I was supposed to, lived in the [library] stacks, just raided the place intellectually."

In addition to studying physics and other sciences, he learned Latin and Greek and was graduated summa cum laude in 1925, having completed four years' work in three.

From Harvard, Robert Oppenheimer went to the University of Cambridge, in England, where he worked in atomics under Lord Rutherford, the eminent physicist. Thence he went to the Georg-August-Universität in Göttingen, Germany, at the invitation of Dr. Max Born, also a celebrated scientist interested in the quantum theory of atomic systems. He received his doctorate there in 1927.

In 1927–28 he was a National Research Fellow at Harvard and Caltech, and the following year he was an International Education Board Fellow at the University of Leyden, in the Netherlands, and the Technische Hochschule in Zurich, Switzerland.

Returning to the United States in 1929, Dr. Oppenheimer joined the faculties of Caltech at Pasadena, Calif., and the University of California at Berkeley. He was attached to both schools until 1947 and rose to the rank of professor. He proved an outstanding teacher. Magnetic, lucid, always accessible, he developed hundreds of young physicists, some of whom were so devoted to him that they migrated with him back and forth from Berkeley to Pasadena and even copied his mannerisms.

Describing at his security hearings his ivory-tower life up to late 1936, he said: "I was not interested in and did not read about economics or politics. I was almost wholly divorced from the contemporary scene in this country. I never read a newspaper or a current magazine like *Time* or *Harper's*; I had no radio, no telephone; I learned of the stock market crash in the fall of 1929 only long after the event; the first time I ever voted was in the presidential election of 1936."

In this period and subsequently, Dr. Oppenheimer was noted more for his inspirational teaching and his overall grasp of nuclear physics than for any major discoveries or theories.

However, in the 1930s Dr. Oppenheimer greatly influenced American physics as leader of a dynamic school of theoreticians in California. His influence continued in his recent years at the Institute for Advanced Study. In the words of one Nobel laureate in physics: "No one in his age group has been as familiar with all aspects of current developments in theoretical physics."

One of his earliest contributions was in 1926–27 while he was working with Dr. Born, then a professor at Göttingen. Together they helped lay the foundations of modern theory for the quantum behavior of molecules.

In 1935 he and Melba Phillips made another basic contribution to quantum theory, discovering what is known as the Oppenheimer-Phillips process. It involves the breakup of deuterons in collisions that had been thought far too weak for such an effect.

The deuteron consists of a proton and neutron bound into a single particle. The two physicists found that, when a deuteron is fired into an atom even weakly, the neutron can be stripped off the proton and penetrate the nucleus of the atom. It had been assumed that, since the deuteron and nucleus are both positively charged, each would repel the other except in high-energy collisions.

Another theoretical study by Dr. Oppenheimer has figured prominently in recent efforts to explain the astronomical objects, known as quasars, that radiate light and radio waves of extraordinary intensity. One possibility is that the quasar is a cloud of material being drawn together by its own gravity.

In 1938–39 Dr. Oppenheimer, with Dr. George M. Volkoff and others, had analyzed such a "gravitational collapse" in terms of the general theory of relativity. Their calculations are now cited in efforts to explain the quasars.

Beginning in late 1936, Dr. Oppenheimer's life underwent a change of direction that involved him in numerous Communist, trade union and liberal causes to which he devoted time and money and that added to his circle of acquaintances many Communists and liberals, some of whom became intimate friends. These commitments and associations, which were to be recalled with sinister overtones at his security hearings, ended about 1940, according to the scientist, or, in the version of some others, they persisted until the end of 1942, when he was about to go to Los Alamos.

One precipitating factor in Dr. Oppenheimer's awakening to the world about him was a love affair, starting in 1936, with a woman Communist. (In 1940 he married the former Miss Katherine Puening, who had been a Communist during her marriage to Joseph Dalet, a Communist who died fighting for the Spanish Republican government.)

Apart from the influence exerted by his fiancée in 1936 there were other compelling elements in Dr. Oppenheimer's transformation from cloistered academician to social activist. He described them this way: "I had had a continuing smoldering fury about the treatment of Jews in Germany. I had relatives there, and was later to help in extricating them and bringing them to this country. I saw what the Depression was doing to my students; often they could get no jobs, or jobs which were wholly inadequate. And through them, I began to understand how deeply political and economic events could affect men's lives. I began to feel the need to participate more fully in the life of the community."

Dr. Oppenheimer's activism was far-ranging, but he consistently denied that he was ever a member of the Communist party ("I never accepted Communist dogma or theory") and no substantial evidence was ever adduced to refute him.

Dr. Arthur H. Compton, the Nobel Prize–winning scientist, brought Dr. Oppenheimer informally into the atomic project in 1941. Within a year he had convinced Dr. Compton and military authorities that, to build a bomb, it was essential to concentrate qualified scientists and their equipment in a single community under a unified command.

He also impressed Maj. Gen. Leslie R. Groves, in charge of the $2-billion Manhattan Engineer District, as the bomb project was code-named, who selected him for the post of director and who ordered him cleared for the job despite army counterintelligence qualms over his past associations. With General Groves, Dr. Oppenheimer selected the Los Alamos site for the laboratory.

"To recruit staff," he said later, "I traveled all over the country talking with people who had been working on one or another aspect of the atomic-energy enterprise, and people in radar work, for example, and underwater sound, telling them about the job, the place that we are going to, and enlisting their enthusiasm."

Dr. Oppenheimer's persuasiveness and his new-found qualities of leadership were such that he gathered a top-notch scientific staff that numbered nearly 4,000 by 1945 and that lived, often amid frustrations and under quasi-military rule, in the hastily built houses of Los Alamos. Among the staff were Dr. Enrico Fermi and Dr. Niels Bohr, two physicists of immense world standing.

In the two tension-filled years it took to construct the bombs, Dr. Oppenheimer displayed a special genius for administration, for handling the sensitive prima-donna scientific staff (often he spent as much time on personal as on professional problems) and for coordinating its work. He drove himself at breakneck speed, and at one time his weight dropped under the whiplash of the war to 115 pounds. But he always managed to surmount whatever problem arose, and it was for this enormous all-around task that he was acclaimed as "the father of the atomic bomb."

Dr. Oppenheimer's security troubles had their genesis while he was director at Los Alamos. Because a security-risk potential was imputed to him on account of past associations, Dr. Oppenheimer was dogged by army agents, his phone calls were monitored, his mail was opened and his every footstep was watched. In these circumstances his overnight visit with his former fiancée—by then no longer a Communist—on a trip to San Francisco in June 1943 aroused the counterintelligence corps.

The following August, for reasons that still remain obscure, Dr. Oppenheimer volunteered to a C.I.C. agent that the Russians had tried to get information about the Los Alamos project. George Eltenton, a Briton and a slight acquaintance of Dr. Oppenheimer, had asked a third party to get in touch with some project scientists. In three subsequent interrogations Dr. Oppenheimer embroidered this story, but he declined to name the third party who had approached him or to identify the scientists. (In one interrogation, however, he gave the C.I.C. a long list of persons he said were Communists or Communist sympathizers in the San Francisco area, and he offered to dig up information as to former Communists at Los Alamos.)

Finally, in December 1943, Dr. Oppenheimer, at General Groves's direct order, vouchsafed the third party's name as Prof. Haakon Chevalier, a French teacher at Berkeley and a longtime close and devoted friend of the Oppenheimer family. At the security hearings in 1954, the scientist recanted his espionage account as a "cock-and-bull story," saying only that he was "an idiot" to have told it. Dr. Oppenheimer never gave a further explanation.

There was some basis for Dr. Oppenheimer's original story, according to him and Professor Chevalier. The professor said that Mr. Eltenton had indeed approached him in late 1942 or early 1943 with a nebulous notion about getting scientific information and had been quickly rebuffed. Professor Chevalier said that he had recounted the episode to Dr. Oppenheimer and that both had dismissed the matter. This part of the incident was corroborated by Dr. Oppenheimer in his testimony at his security hearings.

(Just how much of Dr. Oppenheimer's spy-attempt story the C.I.C. believed is difficult to judge in light of the fact that neither Professor Chevalier nor Mr. Eltenton was interrogated until May 1946. Neither was prosecuted. Indeed, Professor Chevalier was an interpreter on the United States staff at the Nuremberg war crimes trial in 1945. Twenty years later he wrote *Oppenheimer: The Story of a Friendship*, in which he charged that Dr. Oppenheimer had betrayed him out of ambition for fame and to stay in the C.I.C.'s good graces.

(A C.I.C. operative who had questioned Dr. Oppenheimer in 1943 suggested to his army superiors that an unimpeachable assistant be assigned to the scientist. The operative's memo included this sentence: "It is the opinion of this office that subject's [Dr. Oppenheimer's] personal inclinations would be to protect his own future and reputation and the high degree of honor which would be his if his present work is successful, and, consequently, it is felt that he would lend every effort to cooperation with the government in any plan which would leave him in charge.")

With the end of World War II and Dr. Oppenheimer's return to full civilian life, he caused some disquiet in the scientific community by supporting the May-Johnson bill for military control of further atomic experiments. This was countered, however, when he later supported the McMahon bill, which created the Atomic Energy Commission, a civilian agency.

Another of the charges pressed against Dr. Oppenheimer in 1954 also had its origin at Los Alamos, and it involved the hydrogen, or fusion, bomb and his relations with Dr. Edward Teller over that superweapon, of which the Hungarian scientist was a vociferous proponent. At Los Alamos Dr. Teller was passed over for Dr. Hans Bethe as head of the important Theoretical Physics Division. Dr. Teller, meantime, worked on problems of fusion.

At the war's end, when most of the Los Alamos scientists returned to their campuses, hydrogen bomb work was generally suspended. In 1949, however, when the Soviet Union exploded its first fusion bomb, the United States considered pressing forward immediately with building and testing a fusion device. The matter came to the Atomic Energy Commission's General Advisory Committee, headed by Dr. Oppenheimer.

On the ground that manufacturing a hydrogen bomb was not technically feasible at the moment, the committee unanimously recommended that thermonuclear research be maintained at a theoretical level only. Dr. Oppenheimer, who also thought a hydrogen bomb morally dubious, played a leading role in this proposal, and it did not endear him to Dr. Teller.

In 1950 President Harry S Truman overruled Dr. Oppenheimer's committee and ordered work pushed on the fusion bomb. Dr. Teller was given his own laboratory and within a few months the hydrogen bomb was perfected with the aid of a technical (and still secret) device suggested by Dr. Teller.

It was charged at the security hearings that Dr. Oppenheimer was not sufficiently diligent himself in furthering the hydrogen bomb and that he influenced other scientists against participating in work on it. Dr. Teller testified that, apart from giving him a list of names, Dr. Oppenheimer had not assisted him "in the slightest" in recruiting scientists for the project.

Dr. Teller, moreover, went on record as being opposed to restoring Dr. Oppenheimer's security clearance, saying: "In a great number of cases I have seen Dr. Oppenheimer act—I understood that Dr. Oppenheimer acted—in a way which for me was exceedingly hard to understand. I thoroughly disagreed with him in numerous issues and his actions frankly appeared to me confused and complicated. To this extent I feel that I would like to see the vital interests of this country in hands which I understand better, and therefore trust more.

"In this very limited sense I would like to express a feeling that I would personally feel more secure if public matters would rest in other hands."

Dr. Oppenheimer, for his part, vigorously denied that he had been dilatory or neglectful in supporting the hydrogen bomb, once President Truman had acted. "I never urged anyone not to work on the hydrogen bomb project," he declared. He insisted, too, that his board had materially assisted Dr. Teller's work.

If Dr. Oppenheimer had stirred Dr. Teller's displeasure in 1949, he also aroused strong feelings in Dr. Edward U. Condon of the National Bureau of Standards for different reasons. In an appearance before an executive session of the House Un-American Activities Committee, Dr. Oppenheimer described a fellow atomic scientist as a former German Communist.

When quotations from the testimony were printed in the newspapers, Dr. Condon and a number of other scientists were shocked on the ground that Dr. Oppenheimer had acted as an informer. "It appears that he [Dr. Oppenheimer] is trying to buy personal immunity from attack by turning informer," Dr. Condon wrote.

Subsequently, Dr. Oppenheimer wrote a public letter in which he attested the atomic scientist's patriotism, but the incident perplexed a number of Dr. Oppenheimer's friends.

The security hearings for Dr. Oppenheimer were triggered late in 1953, when William L. Borden, former executive director of the Joint Congressional Committee on Atomic Energy, wrote an unsolicited letter to J. Edgar Hoover, director of the Federal Bureau of Investigation. Mr. Borden gave it as his opinion that the scientist had been "a hardened Communist" and that "more probably than not he has since been functioning as an espionage agent."

Mr. Hoover wasted little time in sending the letter and an F.B.I. report to the White House and other agencies. It was then that President Eisenhower cut Dr. Oppenheimer off from access to secret material. Lewis L. Strauss (pronounced "straws"), then chairman of the Atomic Energy Commission, gave Dr. Oppenheimer the option of resigning his consultantship with the commission or asking for a hearing. He chose a hearing.

The action against Dr. Oppenheimer dismayed the scientific community and many other Americans. He was widely pictured as a victim of McCarthyism who was being penalized for holding honest, if unpopular, opinions. The A.E.C., Mr. Strauss and the Eisenhower administration were accused of carrying out a witch-hunt in an attempt to account for Soviet atomic successes and to feed public hysteria about Communists.

The Personnel Security Board of the A.E.C., consisting of Gordon Gray, an educator, chairman; Thomas A. Morgan, a businessman; and Dr. Ward V. Evans, a chemist, held hearings in Washington from April 12 to May 6, 1954. They considered a long list of specific charges, one batch dealing with Dr. Oppenheimer's past associations, another with the Haakon Chevalier incident and another with the hydrogen bomb.

Dr. Oppenheimer testified in his own behalf, and 40 great names in American science and education offered evidence of his loyalty. However, by a vote of 2 to 1 (Dr. Evans dissented), the board declined to reinstate its consultant's security clearance.

After asserting as "a clear conclusion" that Dr. Oppenheimer was "a loyal citizen," the majority report said it had "been unable to arrive at the conclusion that it would be clearly consistent with the security interests of the United States to reinstate Dr. Oppenheimer's clearance. . . ."

The report listed the following as controlling its decision:

"1. We find that Dr. Oppenheimer's continuing conduct and associations have reflected a serious disregard for the requirements of the security system.

"2. We have found a susceptibility to influence which could have serious implications for the security interests of the country.

"3. We find his conduct in the hydrogen-bomb program sufficiently disturbing as to raise a doubt as to whether his future participation, if characterized by the same attitudes, in a government program relating to the national defense would be clearly consistent with the best interests of security.

"4. We have regretfully concluded that Dr. Oppenheimer has been less than candid in several instances in his testimony before this board."

On appeal to the commission, Dr. Oppenheimer lost by a vote of 4 to 1. After declaring that Dr. Oppenheimer had "fundamental defects in his character," the majority said that "his associations with persons known to him to be Communists have extended far beyond the limits of prudence and self-restraint."

With the commission ruling, Dr. Oppenheimer returned to Princeton and the institute he headed. There he lived in quiet obscurity until April 1962, when President John F. Kennedy invited him to a White House dinner of Nobel Prize winners.

In December 1963, as further evidence of a rapprochement, President Johnson handed Dr. Oppenheimer the highest award of the Atomic Energy Commission, the $50,000 tax-free Fermi Award, which is named for Dr. Enrico Fermi, the late distinguished nuclear pioneer.

In his acceptance remarks Dr. Oppenheimer adverted to his security hearings, saying: "I think it is just possible, Mr. President, that it has taken some charity and some courage for you to make this award today."

Dr. Oppenheimer was the author of several books: *Science and the Common Understanding* (1954); *The Open Mind* (1955); *Some Reflections on Science and Culture* (1960).

Ailing, he retired as director of the Institute for Advanced Study in early 1966. He was succeeded by Dr. Carl Kaysen of Harvard.

In addition to the Medal of Merit for his work in Los Alamos and an assortment of honorary doctorates, Dr. Oppenheimer was a fellow of the National Academy of Arts and Sciences, the American Physical Society and Britain's Royal Society. He was also a member of the National Academy of Sciences, the American Philosophical Society and several foreign academies.

Dr. Oppenheimer died at his home in Princeton on Feb. 18, 1967. He was 62, and had been suffering since early 1966 from cancer of the throat.

THE MEMORIAL SERVICE

MURRAY SCHUMACH

SIX HUNDRED persons at a memorial service for Dr. J. Robert Oppenheimer in Princeton, N.J., were told on February 25, 1967, that he had spurned an opportunity to work abroad as a scientist after the government had stripped him of his security clearance.

Instead, when the idea was suggested to him in the early 1950s, George F. Kennan said, he replied, with tears in his eyes: "Damn it, I happen to love this country."

The episode was disclosed here by Mr. Kennan, the former United States ambassador to the Soviet Union.

In the audience that paid homage today to the nuclear physicist were five Nobel laureates. Indicative of the scope of Dr. Oppenheimer's interests, there were Stephen Spender, the poet; John O'Hara, the novelist; George Balanchine, director of the New York City Ballet; Paul Nitze, secretary of the navy; Frederick Seitz, president of the National Academy of Sciences; Senator Clifford Case of New Jersey; Donald F. Hornig, President Johnson's scientific adviser, who represented the White House; Arthur M. Schlesinger Jr.; and Margot Einstein, daughter of Albert Einstein.

The Nobel laureates were Eugene Wigner, Julian Schwinger, I. I. Rabi, Tsung Dao Lee and Edwin McMillan.

Dr. McMillan's Nobel Prize came in chemistry, and the others won their awards in physics.

With visible emotion the speakers stressed what they called the injustice that had reduced the man who has been called "father of the atomic bomb" in 1945 to a security risk less than a decade later.

In the first row as the eulogies were delivered were members of the Oppenheimer family—his widow; their daughter, Katherine; their son, Peter, and his wife; and the scientist's brother, Frank, also a physicist.

The speakers were men who had known the slender, slightly stooped scientist as the chain-smoking director of Los Alamos, where the atomic bomb was developed, or as the fervent debater of nuclear theory at the Institute of Advanced Study here.

Dr. Hans A. Bethe, professor of physics at Cornell, recalled how, at Los Alamos, Dr. Oppenheimer had fought against enormous odds "for the free discussion among all qualified members of the laboratory."

And Henry DeWolf Smyth, who alone among the five members of the Atomic Energy Commission wanted Dr. Oppenheimer's security clearance restored in 1954, said: "Such a wrong can never be righted; such a blot on our history can never be erased."

He added, however, that "belatedly an attempt was made to set the record straight" when the Atomic Energy Commission gave to Dr. Oppenheimer the Enrico Fermi Award in 1963.

But it was Mr. Kennan, now on the staff of the Institute for Advanced Study, which Dr. Oppenheimer headed from 1947 until last year, who summed up the sense of injustice that marked this audience.

"In the dark days of the early 1950s," Mr. Kennan said, "when troubles crowded in upon him from many sides and when he found himself harassed by his position at the center of the controversy, I drew his attention to the fact that he would be welcome in a hundred academic centers abroad and asked him whether he had not thought of taking residence outside this country."

It was then, he said, that Dr. Oppenheimer spoke of his love of the United States.

To recall the scientist's deep love of music the program opened and closed with selections of which he had been fond. Even before the first opening remark by Dr. Carl Kaysen, who succeeded Dr. Oppenheimer as director of the institute last year, there was a recording of Stravinsky's "Requiem Canticles," which Dr. Oppenheimer had heard and applauded in this same hall last October when it was conducted by the composer.

And after Mr. Kennan had delivered his eulogy, the members of the Juilliard String Quartet performed the adagio and allegro movements of Beethoven's Quartet 14 in C sharp minor.

Then, as quietly as the hundreds had assembled, they left the hall.

PRESIDENT TO GIVE FERMI AWARD TO OPPENHEIMER AT WHITE HOUSE

JOHN W. FINNEY

PRESIDENT KENNEDY will present the $50,000 Enrico Fermi Award to Dr. J. Robert Oppenheimer at a White House ceremony on December 2, administration officials disclosed today.*

Presentation by the president will represent another step in the effort of the administration to clear the name of the prominent physicist who was declared a security risk nearly a decade ago during the Eisenhower administration.

The award, the highest honor conferred by the Atomic Energy Commission, has customarily been presented by the president. But in the case of Dr.

*The day this story appeared in *The Times*, Nov. 22, 1963, President Kennedy was assassinated in Dallas. The Fermi Award was later presented to Dr. Oppenheimer by President Johnson.

Oppenheimer, according to officials, there was some question whether to continue this White House custom.

The administration has not been insensitive to the possible political repercussions of giving an award to Dr. Oppenheimer. There was some hesitation, therefore, about the political desirability of having the president present the award personally at a public ceremony in the White House.

Ever since the commission announced in April that Dr. Oppenheimer would receive the award, the administration has been watching with particular interest the political reaction.

To the relief of the administration, the announcement was greeted with general silence in political quarters. There were a few critical Republican comments, but nothing indicating that the award would provoke a serious political attack on the administration.

Within the last two days the commission, on behalf of the White House, has sent out invitations to certain members of Congress to attend the December 2 ceremony. The original plan called for a noontime ceremony at the White House, followed by a luncheon at the Statler Hotel in honor of Dr. Oppenheimer. The commission informed congressmen today that the White House ceremony will be held late in the afternoon, followed by a reception at the National Academy of Sciences.

The award will come almost exactly ten years after President Dwight D. Eisenhower ordered that "a blank wall be placed between Dr. Oppenheimer and secret data" pending a security review. Six months later, the A.E.C. found Dr. Oppenheimer a security risk and ordered that his security clearance not be reinstated.

Even before the Eisenhower administration left office, a move was under way within the government to reverse the security decision or to take some action that would symbolically clear Dr. Oppenheimer's name.

The approach finally decided upon by the administration to vindicate Dr. Oppenheimer was to give him the award created in 1954 in honor of the late Dr. Enrico Fermi, the Italian-born scientist who directed the team that achieved the first self-sustained chain reaction in a nuclear reactor.

The award is being given to Dr. Oppenheimer "in recognition of his outstanding contributions to theoretical physics and his scientific and administrative leadership not only in the development of the atomic bomb, but also in establishing the groundwork for the many peaceful applications of atomic energy."

PABLO PICASSO

1881–1973

By Alden Whitman

There was Picasso the neoclassicist; Picasso the cubist; Picasso the surrealist; Picasso the modernist; Picasso the ceramist; Picasso the lithographer; Picasso the sculptor; Picasso the superb draftsman; Picasso the effervescent and exuberant; Picasso the saturnine and surly; Picasso the faithful and faithless lover; Picasso the cunning financial man; Picasso the publicity seeker; Picasso the smoldering Spaniard; Picasso the joker and performer of charades; Picasso the generous; Picasso the Scrooge; even Picasso the playwright.

A genius for the ages, a man who played wonderful yet sometimes outrageous changes with art, Pablo Picasso remains without doubt the most original, the most protean and the most forceful personality in the visual arts in the first three quarters of the 20th century. He took a prodigious gift and with it transformed the universe of art.

Henri Matisse and Georges Braque, two painters with assured stature in modern art and both his close friends, were also original; but both developed a style and stuck pretty much to it, whereas Picasso, with a feverish creativity and lavish talent lasting into old age, was a man of many styles whose artistic life revealed a continuous process of exploration. He created his own universe, investing it with his own human beings and his own forms of beasts and myths.

"For me, a picture is neither an end nor an achievement but rather a lucky chance and art experience," he once explained. "I try to represent what I have found, not what I am seeking. I do not seek—I find."

On another occasion, however, he saw his work in a different light. "Everything I do," he remarked at 76, "is only one step on a long road. It is a preliminary process that may be consummated much later. Therefore my works must be seen in relation to one another, keeping in mind what I have already done and what I will do."

For all his guises, or disguises, Picasso had an amazing fecundity of imagination that permitted him to metamorphize a mood or an idea into a work of art with bewildering quickness. He was, in André Malraux's phrase, "the archwizard of modern art," a man who, as a painter alone, produced well over 6,000 pictures. Some he splashed off in a few hours; others took weeks.

In 1969, his 88th year, he produced out of his volcanic energy a total of 165 paintings and 45 drawings, which were exhibited at the Palace of the Popes in Avignon, France. Crowding the walls of that venerable structure, the Picasso array drew exclamatory throngs and moved Emily Genauer, the critic, to say, "I think Picasso's new pictures are the fire of heaven."

Explaining the source of this energy, Picasso said as he neared 90, "Everyone is the age he has decided on, and I have decided to remain 30."

The painter was so much known for works that

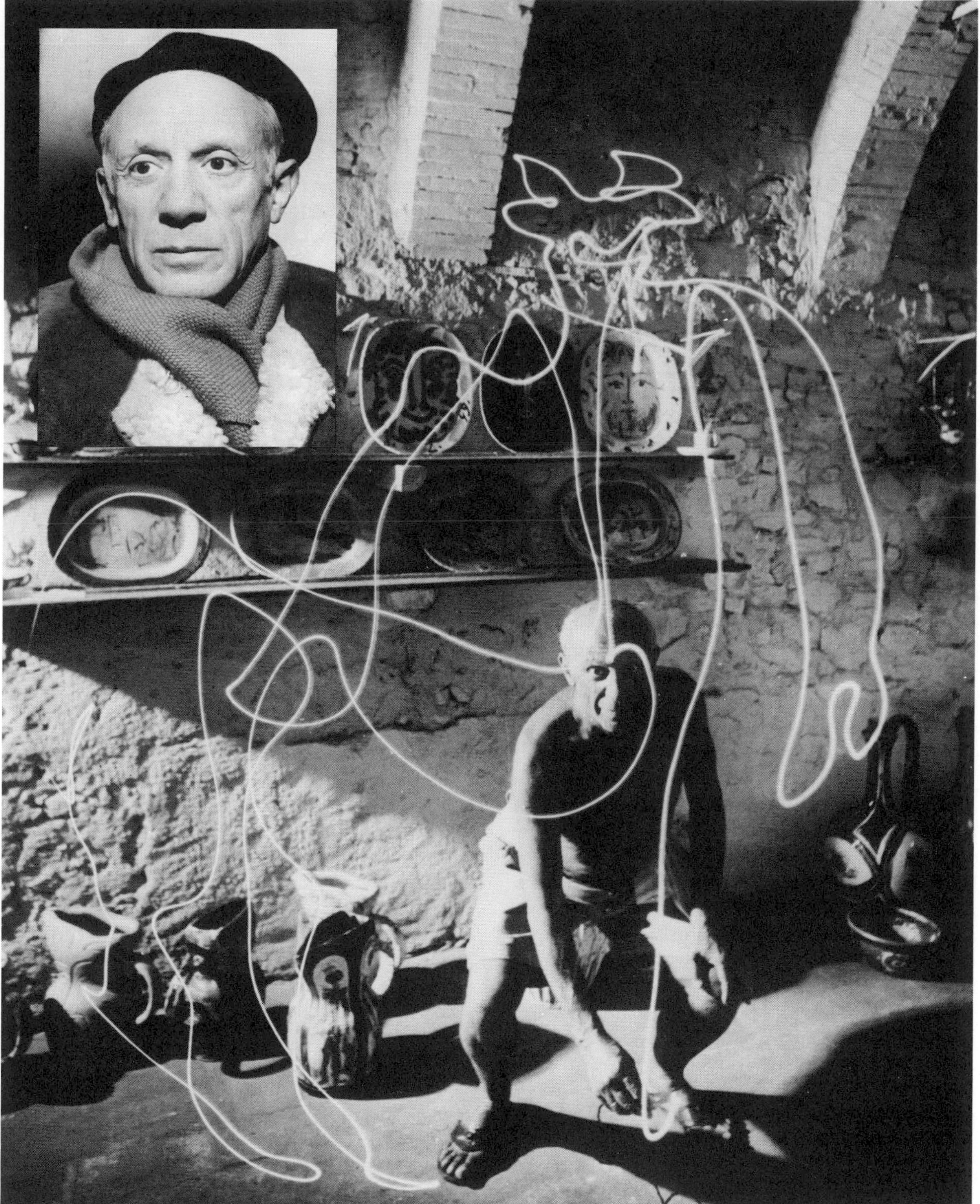

New York Times Photo

Gjon Mili, LIFE Magazine © TIME Inc.

blurred or obliterated conventional distinctions between beauty and ugliness and for depersonalized forms that he was accused of being an antihumanist. That appraisal disturbed him, for he regarded himself, with all his vagaries, as having created new insights into a seen and unseen world in which fragmentation of form was the basis for a new synthesis.

"What is art?" a visitor once asked him. "What is not?" he replied. And he substantiated this point once by combining a bicycle seat and a pair of handlebars to make a bull's head.

"Whatever the source of the emotion that drives me to create, I want to give it a form that has some connection with the visible world, even if it is only to wage war on that world," he explained to Françoise Gilot, who was one of his mistresses and herself a painter.

"Otherwise," he continued, "a painting is just an old grab bag for everyone to reach into and pull out what he himself has put in. I want my paintings to be able to defend themselves, to resist the invader, just as though there were razor blades on all surfaces so no one could touch them without cutting his hands. A painting isn't a market basket or a woman's handbag, full of combs, hairpins, lipstick, old love letters and keys to the garage.

"Valéry [Paul Valéry, the French poet] used to say, 'I write half the poem. The reader writes the other half.' That's all right for him, maybe, but I don't want there to be three or four thousand possibilities of interpreting my canvas. I want there to be only one and in that one to some extent the possibility of recognizing nature, even distorted nature, which is, after all, a kind of struggle between my interior life and the external world as it exists for most people.

"As I've often said, I don't try to express nature; rather, as the Chinese put it, to work like nature. And I want that internal surge—my creative dynamism—to propose itself to the viewer in the form of traditional painting violated."

In the long course of upending traditionalism, Picasso became a one-man history of modern art. In every phase of its turbulent (and often violent) development he was either a daring pioneer or a gifted practitioner. The sheer variousness of his creations reflected his probings of modern art for ways to communicate the multiplicity of its expressions; and so Picasso could not be categorized as belonging to this or that school, for he opened and tried virtually all of them.

In his peripateticism he worked in oils, watercolors, pastels, gouaches, pencil-and-ink drawings and aquatints; he etched, made lithographs, sculptured, fashioned ceramics, put together mosaics and constructed murals.

One of his masterpieces was *Guernica*, painted in 1937 and on loan for many years to the Museum of Modern Art in New York. An oil on canvas 11¼ feet high and 25½ feet long, it is a majestic, stirring indictment of the destructiveness of modern war. By contrast, another masterpiece was a simply and perfectly drawn white pigeon, *The Dove*, which was disseminated around the world as a symbol of peace. But masterpiece or something not so exalted, virtually all Picassos were interesting and provocative. Praised or reviled, his work never evoked quiet judgments.

The artist, however, held a different view. "There is no such thing as a bad Picasso," he said. "Some are less good than others."

Exhibitions of his work, especially in his later years, were surefire attractions. The mention of his name was sufficient to lure thousands, many of them only barely acquainted with any art, to museums and galleries and benefits. Reproductions and prints were nailed up in homes all over the Western world, a certain mark of the owner's claim to culture. Originals were widely dispersed, both in museums and in the hands of collectors wealthy enough to meet Picasso's prices. And they were steep. In 1965 he charged London's Tate Gallery $168,000 for *Les Trois Danseuses*, a painting he did in 1925. For a current painting, private collectors felt that $20,000 was a steal and $35,000 not too much.

For the last 50 years there has been no such thing

as a cheap Picasso. Indeed, Leo and Gertrude Stein and Ambroise Vollard, a Paris dealer, may have been the last to get a Picasso for $30, and that was in 1906 and 1907.

As Picasso's fame grew so did his income, until it got so that he could manufacture money by sketching a few lines on a piece of paper and tacking on his dramatic signature. He was probably the world's highest-paid pieceworker, and there were many years in which he garnered more than $1 million.

"I am rich enough to throw away a thousand dollars," he told a friend with some glee.

The artist, however, was canny about money, driving hard bargains with his dealers and keeping the bulk of his work off the market. He released for sale about 40 of his paintings a year out of a production of hundreds, so that the market for his work was never glutted. What he did not sell (and he said that many of these constituted the best from his palette) he squirreled away in bank vaults, studios, in a castle not far from the Riviera and in empty rooms in his villa near Cannes. Picasso did not exactly hide his collection, for on occasion he permitted special friends to see it, to photograph it and to publish the results.

Toward the close of his life he donated 800 to 900 of his finest early works to a Barcelona museum. Worth a multimillion-dollar fortune, his works represented his Spanish period and were given in memory of Jaime Sabartés, his longtime secretary. In 1971 he gave an early constructed sculpture, *Guitar*, to the Museum of Modern Art in New York.

Mostly, though, Picasso took a merchant's delight in acquiring his money. "Art is a salable commodity," he once observed. "If I want as much money as I can get for my art, it is because I know what I want to do with it." But just what that was only a few intimates knew. He is said to have owned a great deal of real estate in France and to have made some excellent stock investments.

Contrary to Miss Gilot's suggestion that Picasso was tightfisted, he gave large sums to the Republican side in the Spanish Civil War and then to refugee groups that cared for the defeated Republicans who had fled to France.

"He was a very generous man," Daniel-Henry Kahnweiler, his principal dealer since 1912, said of him. "He supported for many years more than a dozen indigent painters, most of whom would have been living in poverty but for his help. And whenever he was asked to help some charities, he always gave something."

He was, surprisingly, even open-handed in a quiet fashion with women of his past. One of these was Fernande Olivier, who was his mistress for a number of years until 1912 and whose book about her experiences with him was not flattering. However, when Picasso heard that her funds were running low, he saw to it that she was supplied with money.

Nonetheless, his generosity, like his temperament, could be fitful. Once, when the faking of Picassos was a small industry, a friend brought the painter a small work belonging to a poor artist for authentication so that it could be sold. "It's false," said Picasso.

From a different source the friend brought another Picasso, and then a third. "It's false," Picasso said each time.

"Now listen, Pablo," the friend said of the third painting. "I watched you paint this with my own eyes."

"I can paint false Picassos just as well as anybody," Picasso replied. And then he bought the first Picasso at four times the amount the poor artist had hoped it would fetch.

As for himself, Picasso, from the time he began to take in appreciable sums until his death, lived like an Okie, albeit one who never had to worry about where his next meal or his next pair of trousers was coming from. "I should like to live like a poor man with a lot of money," he had said in the days when he was desperately poor and burning some of his paintings for heat.

All his studios and homes—even the 18-room rambling La Californie at Cannes—were crammed and cluttered with junk—pebbles, rocks, pieces of glass, a hollow elephant's foot, a bird cage, African drums, wooden crocodiles, parts of old bicycles, ancient newspapers, broken crockery, bullfight posters, old hats, weird ceramics. Picasso was a compulsive collector of oddments, and he never threw any of them away, or permitted anyone to move any object once he had dropped it, tossed it or placed it somewhere.

To compound the chaos inside La Californie, the villa's lawn was home to clucking chickens, pigeons, at least one goat, dogs and children. They all disported among bronze owls, fountains and statuary scattered about the grounds. Freedom for animals and children was a cardinal belief.

In later years this villa became a weekend residence, while his main home was Notre Dame de Vie in nearby Mougins. He also owned two chateaus: Vauvenargues, in Provence, and Boigeloup, in Normandy.

Despite the disorganization with which he surrounded himself, Picasso was a most methodical man. When he drove to Cannes or to Arles he invariably followed the same route; and when he lived in Paris he walked or rode the same streets in a fixed order. When his Paris studio was at 7, rue des Grand-Augustins on the Left Bank, he almost always dined at La Brasserie Lipp on the Boulévard Saint-Germain and then cross the street to the Café Flore to join friends in a mineral water and conversation before going home.

One Picasso day was, in outline, much like the next. He arose late, usually around 10 or 11, devoted two or three hours to friends, conversation, business, letters and lunch; then, at 3 or 4, he would go to his studio to work in Trappist silence, often for 12 hours at a stretch, breaking off only for dinner around 10:30. Afterward, he sometimes worked until 2 or 3 in the morning.

When Miss Gilot was living with Picasso in Paris, she found that one of her most difficult tasks was to get him started on his day. "He always woke up submerged in pessimism, and there was a definite ritual to be followed, a litany that had to be repeated every day," she recalled in her book, *Life with Picasso*, published in 1964.

The rigamarole, as Miss Gilot recounts it, had largely to do with reassuring Picasso that his lamentations were falsely based. "Well, I do despair," he would say in Miss Gilot's reconstruction. "I'm pretty nearly desperate. I wonder, really, why I bother to get up. Why should I paint? Why should I continue to exist like this? A life like mine is unbearable."

Eventually, of course, Picasso permitted himself to be convinced that the world was not in conspiracy against him. Part of his maledicent mood could perhaps be traced to the physical aspects of his bedroom.

"At the far end was a high Louis XIII secretary," according to Miss Gilot, "and, along the left-hand wall, a chest of the same period, both completely covered with papers, books, magazines and mail that Pablo hadn't answered and never would, drawings piled up helter-skelter, and packages of cigarettes. Above the bed was a naked electric-light bulb. Behind the bed were drawings Pablo was particularly fond of, attached by clothespins to nails driven into the wall.

"The so-called more important letters, which he didn't answer either but kept before him as a permanent reminder and reproach, were pinned up, also with clothespins, onto wires that stretched from the electric-light wire to the stovepipe. There was almost no other furniture, except a Swedish chair in laminated wood."

By early afternoon, Picasso, amid the bustle of the household and friends who came to pay him court, was bubbly and sunny. He liked not so much to converse as to talk, and his monologues were usually witty. His agile mind leaped from subject to subject, and he had almost total recall.

He always had several projects in hand at the same time, and to each he seemed equally lavish with his talent. "Painting is my hobby," he said.

"When I am finished painting, I paint again for relaxation."

"He used no palette," Miss Gilot wrote of his working habits. "At his right [as he addressed his easel] was a small table covered with newspapers and three or four large cans filled with brushes standing in turpentine.

"Every time he took a brush he wiped it off on the newspapers, which were a jungle of colored smudges and slashes. Whenever he wanted pure color, he squeezed some from a tube onto the newspaper. At his feet and around the base of the easel were cans—mostly tomato cans of various sizes—that held gray and neutral tones and other colors that he had previously mixed.

"He stood before the canvas for three or four hours at a stretch. He made almost no superfluous gestures. I asked him if it didn't tire him to stand so long in one spot. He shook his head.

" 'No,' he said. 'That is why painters live so long. While I work I leave my body outside the door, the way Moslems take off their shoes before entering the mosque.'

"Occasionally he walked to the other end of the atelier and sat in a wicker armchair. He would cross his legs, plant one elbow on his knee and, resting his chin on his fist, would stay there studying the painting without speaking for as long as an hour.

"After that he would generally go back to work on the portrait. Sometimes he would say, 'I can't carry that plastic idea any further today,' and then begin to work on another painting. He always had several half-dry unfinished canvases to choose from.

"There was total silence in the atelier, broken only by Pablo's monologues or an occasional conversation; never an interruption from the world outside. When daylight began to fade from the canvas he switched on two spotlights and everything but the picture surface fell away into the shadows.

" 'There must be darkness everywhere except on the canvas, so that the painter becomes hypnotized by his own work and paints almost as though he were in a trance,' he said. 'He must stay as close as possible to his own inner world if he wants to transcend the limitations his reason is always trying to impose on him.' "

Mood was a vital ingredient of Picasso. Everything he saw, felt or did was for him an incomplete experience until it had been released and recorded. Once he was lunching on sole and happened to hold up the skeleton so that it caught his glance. He got up from the table and returned almost immediately with a tray of clay in which he made an imprint of the skeleton. After lunch he drew colorful designs around the filigree of the bones, and the eventual result was one of his most beautiful plates.

Here, as in other areas of art, when the inspiration was upon him he worked ceaselessly and with such concentration that he could, for example, paint a good-sized picture in three hours.

Just as intensely, Picasso loved to mime, to clown, to play charades, to joke. To amuse his friends (and himself) he would don a tuxedo, red socks and funny hats; or he would put on Chaplinesque garb and engage in horseplay.

He put on disguises, too, to romp with children, and they loved him for the ease with which he entered their fantasy world.

Picasso was a short, squat man with broad, muscular shoulders and arms. He was proud of his small hands and feet and of his hairy chest. In old age his body was firm and compact; and his cannonball head, which was almost bald, gleamed like bronze. Set into it were deep black eyes of such penetration and alertness that they became his hallmark.

Photographs from his younger years showed him a handsome man with jet-black hair. Apart from the absence of hair, the description of him by Miss Olivier, his first long-term mistress, could have applied to the artist of later years.

"Small, dark, thickset, unquiet, disquieting, with somber eyes, deep-set, piercing, strange, almost fixed," she wrote. "Awkward gestures, a woman's hands, ill-dressed, careless. A thick lock of hair, black and glossy, cut across his intelligent, obstinate forehead. Half Bohemian, half workman in his clothes; his hair, which was too long, brushing the collar of his worn-out coat."

Although at various times in his life Picasso dressed as a dandy, he was never comfortable in conventional clothes. He preferred corduroy or heavy velvet jackets, a T-shirt and heavy trousers made of a blanket type of wool. These, after he could afford them, were custom-made in odd designs. Sometimes he varied his getup by wearing a striped jersey pullover and sometimes he just walked around in shorts. It was all a matter of whim.

Although whim at times governed whom he would see and for how long, Picasso was generally a hospitable host in the Spanish manner. He had scores of close friends—Mr. Kahnweiler, Jean Cocteau, Paul Eluard and Louis Aragon among many others.

However, like most illustrious people, Picasso attracted gushing admirers and sycophants. Some called him "maestro" and fawned on him for the subsidiary fame that came from standing in his light. He was not above their company; and, indeed, he seemed to have relished some who gave him favorable publicity.

Women were one of Picasso's most persistent preoccupations. Apart from fleeting affairs, there were seven women significant in his personal and artistic life. He married two of them, but his relationships with the five others were well recognized and generally respected. Two of his companions bore three of his four children.

The artist's wives and mistresses served as his models, organized the domestic aspects of his household so far as that was possible, petted him, suffered his mercurial moods and greeted his friends.

In Picasso's early days in Paris, his mistress was Miss Olivier, a young painter and teacher, who lived, as he did, in the Bateau-Lavoir—a Montmartre building called that by the poet and painter Max Jacob because it swayed like a creaky Seine laundry boat.

"I met Picasso as I was coming home one stormy evening," Miss Olivier recalled. "He had a tiny kitten in his arms, which he laughingly offered me, at the same time blocking my path. I laughed with him. He invited me to his studio."

Their liaison lasted until 1912, when Picasso met Marcelle Humbert, the mistress of a sculptor friend. The two ran off together, and there followed a series of superb canvases expressing the artist's happiness. He called Miss Humbert "Eva" and signed two of his works "J'aime Eva." Miss Humbert died in 1914.

In Rome, early in 1917, he met Olga Khoklova, a ballerina with Sergei Diaghilev's Ballets Russes. He painted her in a Spanish mantilla, and he and Olga were married in 1918. Three years later a son, Paolo—Italian for Pablo or Paul—was born.

The marriage broke up in 1935, and Olga died in southern France 20 years later. The couple were never divorced. One reason, it is said, was that they had been married under a community property arrangement that would have obliged Picasso to divide his fortune with her.

At the time of the separation Picasso's mistress was his blond model, Marie-Thérèse Walter. In 1935 she bore him a daughter, Marie de la Concepcíon. A portrait of the girl, known as Maya, was one of Picasso's most fetching naturalist studies.

Dora Maar, a young Yugoslav photographer, was the painter's next mistress. Their companionship lasted until 1944.

The same year, when Picasso was 62, he began an 11-year liaison with Miss Gilot. Their children were Claude, born in 1947, and Paloma, born in 1949. In 1970 Miss Gilot was married to Dr. Jonas E. Salk, the polio vaccine developer.

Picasso's final attachment was to Jacqueline Roque, who became his mistress in 1955 and his wife in 1961, when she was 35 and he was 79. Miss Roque had a rather wry sense of her role in the painter's life. A member of a movie crew that was making a picture at their home asked her quite innocently who she was. "Me, I'm the new Egeria," she replied.

Amid the bohemian clutter in which he lived and thrived, despite the concomitant disarray of his personal affairs, Picasso maintained a strong, consistent and lasting emotional bond to the country of his birth. This bond influenced his painting and, after 1936 and the Spanish Civil War, propelled him for the first time into politics. His attachment to Spain was romantic and passionate; and the fact that he shunned Generalissimo Francisco Franco's Spain yet kept his Spanish citizenship was an expression of his umbilical feeling for the country.

There were two principal consequences of this bond: One was *Guernica* and the other was his membership in the French Communist party, which he joined in 1944. "Up to the time of the Spanish Civil War, Picasso was completely apolitical," Mr. Kahnweiler, his agent, recalled. "He did not even know the names of the different parties. The civil war changed all that."

Previously, Picasso's insurgency had been that of every artist against the constrictions of conventional life. But with the outbreak of conflict in his homeland, Picasso became instinctively an aroused partisan of the Republican government.

In January 1937 he began etching the two large plates of *Sueño y Mentira de Franco* ("The Dream and Lie of Franco"). These showed the rebel leader as a perpetrator of symbolic horrors—himself ultimately transformed into a centaur and gored to death by a bull. Countless copies of these etchings were dropped like propaganda leaflets over Franco territory.

But it took the bombing of the Basque town of Guernica y Luno on April 26, 1937, to drive Picasso to the heights of his genius. At 4:30 on that cloudless Monday afternoon, Germen airmen, who had been provided to Franco by Adolf Hitler, descended on Guernica, a town of no military importance, in a test of the joint effect of explosive and incendiary bombs on civilians. The carnage was enormous, and news of it appalled the civilized world.

At the time Picasso had been engaged by the Loyalist government to do a mural for its pavilion at a Paris fair later that year. The outrage at Guernica gave him his subject, and in a month of furious and volcanic work he completed his great and stunning painting.

The monochromatic mural, stark in black, gray and white, was retained by the artist in trust for the Spanish nation. It was to be given to the nation when it became a republic again.

Assessing the picture's searing impact on viewers over the years, Roland Penrose wrote: "It is the simplicity of *Guernica* that makes it a picture which can be readily understood. The forms are divested of all complications which would distract from their meaning. The flames that rise from the burning house and flicker on the dress of the fallen woman are described by signs as unmistakable as those used by primitive artists.

"The nail-studded hoof, the hand with deeply furrowed palm and the sun illuminated with an electric-light bulb are drawn with a childlike simplicity, startling in its directness."

Guernica was responsible for one of Picasso's most noteworthy ripostes. During the Nazi occupation of France in World War II, a German officer visited the artist's studio, where a large reproduction of the mural was on display.

"Ah, so it was you who did that," the German said.

"No," snapped Picasso. "You did it!"

Picasso painted two other major historical pictures, *The Korean Massacres* and *War and Peace*. The two large compositions are in an old chapel in Vallauris, France. Both were intended to arouse the conscience of mankind to the horrors of war.

Toward the close of World War II the artist joined the Communist party, and *L'Humanité*, the party daily, marked the occasion by publishing almost a full-page photograph of him. Although his decision seemed clearly motivated by the Spanish war and the ensuing world war, there were many who thought at first that the action was another of Picasso's caprices.

He responded to such charges with a statement published in *Les Lettres Françaises*, which said in part: "What do you think an artist is? An imbecile who has only his eyes if he is a painter, or his ears if a musician, or a lyre at every level of his heart if he is a poet, or, if he is merely a boxer, only his muscles?

"On the contrary, he is at the same time a political being, constantly alert to the heartrending, burning, or happy events in the world, molding himself in their likeness.

"How could it be possible to feel no interest in other people and, because of an ivory-tower indifference, detach yourself from the life they bring with such open hands?

"No, painting is not made to decorate apartments. It is an instrument of war, for attack and defense against the enemy."

But Picasso's brand of Communism was not Moscow's, at least in the Kremlin's Stalinist period. In 1948, his works were denounced by Vladimir Kemenov, a Soviet art critic, as an "apology for capitalistic esthetics that provokes the indignation of the simple people, if not the bourgeoisie."

"His pathology has created repugnant monstrosities," Mr. Kemenov went on. "In his *Guernica* he portrayed not the Spanish Republic but monsters. He treads the path of cosmopolitanism, of empty geometric forms. His every canvas deforms man—his body and his face."

Picasso was pained but unmoved by the attack. "I don't try to advise the Russians on economics. Why should they tell me how to paint?" he remarked to a friend.

About that time, according to one account, an orthodox Soviet painter said to Picasso on being introduced, "I have known of you for some time as a good Communist, but I'm afraid I don't like your painting." "I can say the same about you, comrade," Picasso shot back.

After Mr. Kemenov's appraisal, Moscow's attitude to the artist fluctuated. *The Dove* helped, quite unintentionally, to create a thaw.

One day in 1949 Matisse came to visit Picasso, bringing a white fantail pigeon for his friend's cote. Virtually on the spot, Picasso made a naturalistic lithograph of the newcomer; and Louis Aragon, the Communist poet and novelist, who saw it shortly afterward, realized its possibilities at once.

The lithograph, signed by the artist, was first used as a poster at a world peace conference. And from that introduction it flew around the world, reproduced in all sizes and in all media as a peace symbol.

Picasso got into Communist hot water again, however, in 1953. This time the attack came from his French comrades. The occasion was Stalin's death and a crayon portrait that the artist sketched. The imaginative likeness of Stalin as a young man stirred up the working-class members of the French party. Mr. Aragon, who had published it, felt obliged to recant in public, and Picasso was not amused.

"When you send a funeral wreath, the family customarily doesn't criticize your choice of flowers," he said.

Nevertheless, in 1954 Moscow appeared to relent, for it took out of hiding its 37 precious early Picassos (they had never been shown to the Soviet public) and lent them to a Paris exhibition. And two years later the Soviet Union marked the painter's 75th birthday by showing a large number of his pictures and ceramics to the public.

Picasso's distortions of reality, to which Mr. Kemenov objected, also baffled less political critics who were unaccustomed to the artist's private language and private mythology or who did not appreciate the aesthetics of plane and solid geometry and of Mercator-like projections of the human face and form.

The man who so largely created the special aesthetic of modern art was born on the night of Oct. 25, 1881, in Málaga, on Spain's south coast.

Picasso's father was José Ruiz, an Andalusian who taught for small pay in the local school of arts and crafts. His mother was Maria Picasso, a Majorcan. Pablo could draw as soon as he could grasp a pencil, but as a pupil in the ordinary sense he preferred looking at the clock to doing sums and reading. Save for art, he managed to avoid all but the rudiments of formal schooling. He was obstinate about this, as in other matters.

As a child, Picasso often accompanied his father to the bullfights. These made an indelible impression, for throughout his life bullring scenes and variations on them were a significant part of his work, recurring more persistently than any other single symbol. His first oil, painted when he was 9, was of the bullring.

In 1895 the family moved to Barcelona, where Pablo's father taught at the School of Fine Arts. By that time the youngster's talent was truly Mozartean, so obviously so that his father solemnly presented him with his own palette and brushes. This confidence was justified when Pablo, at 15, competed for admission to the art school. A month was ordinarily allowed, but he completed his picture, a male nude, in a single day and was admitted to classes in 1896.

He remained there for a year before going to Madrid for further study. During an illness he lived among the peasants of Catalonia, the poverty and barrenness of whose lives appalled him. From them and from the countryside, he said later, he learned "everything I know."

Late in 1898, the young artist dropped his father's name from the signature "P. Ruiz-Picasso" for reasons that have never been made clear. (His full baptismal name had been Pablo Diego José Francisco de Paula Nepomuceno Paria de los Remedios de la Santisima Trinidad Ruiz Picasso.)

Picasso paid his first visit to Paris in 1900 and after three more visits settled in Paris in 1904. On one of these visits he met Max Jacob, who was, next to Pierre Reverdy, his most appreciative friend until Jacob's death in a Nazi concentration camp. Picasso also became acquainted with Berthe Weill, the art dealer, who purchased some of his paintings, and Petrus Manach, another dealer, who was to support him briefly at the rate of $37.50 a month.

Meanwhile, Picasso's "blue" pictures had established him as an artist with a personal voice. This period, ending about 1904, was characterized by his use of the color blue to depict fatalistically the haunting melancholy of dying clowns, most of them in catatonic states, and agonized acrobats. *La Mort d'Arlequin* is one of the most widely known of these.

When the artist moved into the Bateau-Lavoir, his rickety and drafty studio became an important meeting and talking place for persons later to be famous in arts and letters. In addition to Mr. Jacob there were Guillaume Apollinaire, the poet; André Salmon, the writer; Matisse; Braque; Le Douanier Rousseau; Juan Gris, the Spanish painter; Cocteau; Dufy; Gertrude and Leo Stein; Utrillo; Lipschitz and Marcoussis. Apollinaire, Picasso's spiritual guide in those days, introduced him to the public with a long article in a Paris review in 1905.

One of Picasso's lifelong habits, painting at night, started during this time, and for the simple reason that his day was frequently absorbed by friends and visitors. It was also the time of his two-year "rose period," generally dated from 1904 to 1906, so-called because hues of that color dominated his pictures.

Near the rose period's close, he was taken up by the Steins, American expatriates in Paris. Leo and Gertrude did not so much discover the painter as popularize him. He, in turn, did a portrait of Gertrude with a face far from representational. When Miss Stein protested that she didn't look like that, Picasso replied, "But you will," and, indeed, in her old age Miss Stein came to resemble her picture.

The year 1907, the end of a very brief "Negroid" or "African period," was a milestone for the painter, for it marked the birth of cubism in an oil of five distorted nudes called *Les Demoiselles d'Avignon*.

With cubism, Picasso—along with Braque—rejected light and perspective, painting not what he saw but what he represented to himself through analysis. (The name "cubism" was coined afterward, and it was based on the cube forms into which Picasso and Braque tended to break up the external world.)

"When we painted as we did," Picasso said later,

"we had no intention of creating cubism, but only of expressing what was inside us.

"Cubism is neither a seed nor a fetus, but an art which is primarily concerned with form, and, once a form has been created, then it exists and goes on living its own life."

This was also the case when Picasso added a new dimension to cubism in 1911 or 1912 by inventing the collage by gluing a piece of imitation chair caning to a still life. Later he went on to an even less academic cubism, sometimes called rococo cubism.

These expressions in the cubist manner were not Picasso's total expression in the years from 1907 to 1917, for at the same time he was painting realistically.

His first substantial recognition came in this period through an exhibition in New York in 1911 and one in London in 1912. His pictures began to fetch high prices—almost $3,000 for *Acrobats* in 1914.

With the war and his marriage to a ballerina, Picasso was a costume designer and scenery painter for the Ballets Russes up to about 1925, all the while painting for himself, mostly in a neoclassic and romantic manner. *The Woman in White* is among the best-known of these naturalistic pictures.

With the advent of the surrealist movement in the middle 1920s, the artist's work turned to the grotesque. Some of his figures were endowed with several heads, displaced noses, mouths and eyes, overenlarged limbs. Turbulence and violence seemed to be at the bottom of his feelings.

Then, in 1929, Picasso returned somewhat abruptly to sculpture, of which he had done little for 15 years. But again it was not a full preoccupation, and he was soon attacking his easel, this time with variations within a distinctive generally surrealistic framework. One typical picture was *Young Woman with a Looking-glass*, painted in 1932.

With these and other pictures of a similar genre, the artist's renown and income reached new heights. Life was also quieter for him, especially after 1935, when Dora Maar helped put routine into his daily existence. She was also the model for a notable series of portraits in which the Mercator projection principle was applied to the human face.

Serenity, or as much of it as ever was possible for Picasso, persisted until the fall of Paris in 1940. He rejected an opportunity to escape to the United States, and instead remained in Paris throughout the war, painting industriously.

After the war, Picasso became enchanted by lithography, which he taught himself. In a short period he turned out more than 200 lithographs. He was at the same time painting, in Paris and in Antibes, and restlessly investigating pottery. Ceramics entranced him, and his work with clay created an industry for the town of Vallauris, not far from the Riviera. In a single year he made and decorated 600 figures and vessels, all different.

Even this concentration on one medium seemed not to diminish the intensity with which he, at the time, painted, sculptured and illustrated books.

His painting style, although it had moments of naturalism, contained wild reinventions of anatomy, but these were so idiosyncratic that surrealism or any other "ism" did not appear to apply. Picasso had isolated an idiom for himself.

Popular acclaim for Picasso seemed to mount with his age. In 1967, when he was 86, "Homage to Picasso," an exhibition of some of his works, drew throngs to museums here and abroad. His sculpture was given a special exhibition at the Museum of Modern Art in New York. One example of his sculpture, *Bust of Sylvette*, is a 60-ton, sandblasted work that rests in University Plaza, in downtown New York.

A Picasso play also attracted attention, not to say notoriety. It was *Desire Caught by the Tail*, which he had written in three days on a sickbed in 1941. It was produced privately in Paris three years later with a cast that included the playwright, Simone de Beauvoir, Valentine Hugo, Albert Camus, Raymond Queneau and Jean-Paul Sartre. The main prop was a big black box that served as a bed, bathtub and coffin for the two principal characters, Fat Anxiety and Thin Anxiety. The play's action was earthy.

When *Desire* was commercially staged in St. Tropez in 1967, it aroused protests even in that resort town's atmosphere of tolerance. The objection was that some of the characters were expected to urinate on stage. Although this did not take place, the play was thought overly suggestive.

Picasso wrote a second play, *The Four Girls*, in 1965, but it was not produced.

The painter did not venture to St. Tropez for his play, nor did he often leave his hilltop villa in his last years. He seemed to feel the world slipping away from him, especially when his old friends died one after another. He shut himself up, refusing to answer the telephone, for example.

But for the most part he painted. Rather than stand, he sat down, bending almost in half over his canvas. Age lines in his face underscored an intensity of purpose hardly abated by time. And as he painted his nostrils flared, his eyes widened, he frowned and all the while his hand was never still.

He was, in the words of a friend, "like a sturdy old oaken tub brimful of the wine of life."

"You would think," another friend said, "he is trying to do a few more centuries of work in what he has left to live."

The titan of 20th-century art died on April 8, 1973 at his hilltop villa of Notre Dame de Vie in Mougins, France. His death was attributed to pulmonary edema. With him when he died was his wife, the 47-year-old Jacqueline Roque.

PICASSO: Last of the Old Masters?

HILTON KRAMER

"AFTER A man's long work is over and the sound of his voice is still," Henry James once wrote, "those in whose regard he has held a high place find his image strangely simplified and summarized. The hand of death, in passing over it, has smoothed the folds, made it more typical and general. The figure retained by the memory is compressed and intensified; accidents have dropped away from it and shades have ceased to count; it stands, sharply, for a few estimated and cherished things, rather than, nebulously, for a swarm of possibilities. We cut the silhouette, in a word, out of the confusion of life, we save and fix the outline, and it is with his eye on this profiled distinction that the critic speaks."

Certainly, in the immediate aftermath of Picasso's death it is something akin to this "profiled distinction" that remains uppermost in our minds—the distinction of an achievement and a career that were of transfiguring importance in the art of this century. Yet in Picasso's case, so great was the achievement, so prodigious the career, so encompassing and inexhaustible the task of coming to terms with what it is he has left us, that the image of the artist—even in death—resists simplification and summary. The "swarm of possibilities," so many of which were brought to resplendent realization, still dizzies the mind, and the things we cherish are quite the reverse of "a few." In death, as in life, he defeats our commonplace expectations.

For Picasso's immense oeuvre—more immense, indeed, than many that have been left us by entire civilizations—looms like a continent still to be explored. What we know, mainly, are the legends and the folklore, the historic monuments and the picturesque views. In varying degrees, we have gained a certain mastery over the many languages employed; we have charted many of the vital routes and brought back a great many trophies. Yet so much remains to be discovered that it seems, at times, we are only at the beginning of our search.

The terms by which we pursue that search have changed, however. We no longer expect it to disclose the lineaments of a vital future. During the most creative years of Picasso's development, when he was astonishing friends and enemies alike with a succession of masterpieces, each of which carried the burden of a new idea and a new emotion, his art seemed poised on the very frontier of our culture. It seemed to initiate a new era, and to carry within it some radical repudiation of the past. Yet once its most radical work was accomplished, Picasso's art was more and more preoccupied with conducting a dialogue with the past. He came to be more and more concerned with conserving something that had been endangered by the very force of his own innovation.

His art has thus acquired, in the light of its own influence, an altered historical identity. It now stands revealed as having a deeper affinity with the art of the Old Masters than with that of the generation that now upholds the tattered banner of the avant-garde. It is not to Picasso but to Duchamp that this generation looks for its cues to the future—and with good reason, for it was Duchamp who broke, and broke decisively, that compact with the past that, however, unconsciously, still serves as one of the vital foundations of Picasso's achievement. Picasso's art extends and affirms the very tradition that Duchamp and his myriad disciples have shattered.

The creation of cubism will no doubt remain the single most important of Picasso's contributions to the art of this century. Even now, when artists are obliged to define their originality in terms of their distance from cubist form, it is cubism that looms as the dominant style of the age. And it is in cubism, especially Picasso's, that the Western pictorial tradition was given its most significant modern renewal. From the vantage point of the 1970s, the place of cubism in the classical tradition seems assured, and Picasso looks more like the last of the Old Masters than the first of those diehard innovators determined to destroy whatever may lie in the path of their own novelties.

Yet Picasso was himself a key figure in the creation of the very ethos that now seems so hostile to his own achievement. That appetite for innovation, which once carried him to the heights of his creative powers, proved to be a force far greater than any of the objects it produced. Along with his masterpieces, Picasso bequeathed to posterity an aesthetic momentum that made it increasingly difficult, if not indeed impossible, for the artists who followed him to pursue their work in quite the same way. He himself withdrew, long before the end of his productive life, from the very race he had done so much to initiate, and concentrated instead on refining what he had already established. Others, not so lucky, were obliged to carry on until overtaken by exhaustion.

We shall be a long time, then, coming to grips with Picasso's immense influence—his negative influence as well as his great creative influence—on the art of our time. It falls on the whole of our visual culture, on the very way we think about our aesthetic problems. It accounts for what we curse, and it accounts for what we praise; above all, it accounts for what we experience.

It is his own achievement that now needs to be distinguished and isolated from that influence. That he was one of the greatest artists who ever lived seems to me undeniable. That he was the last of the great masters seems to me more than likely. His death marks the end of a great tradition as well as a great oeuvre. Perhaps it will also serve as an impetus to a new understanding of that continent we have not yet fully discovered.

THE ORDEAL OF PICASSO'S HEIRS [1980]

DEBORAH TRUSTMAN

"EVERYBODY WHO loves Pablo comes to this house," says Jacqueline Picasso slowly. "Sometimes I dream that he loved me. Perhaps he did, perhaps he did not. It is thanks to me that Pablo still lives."

Seven years after Pablo Picasso's death, he dominates the thoughts of his heirs even more than he did in life; indeed, for some of them, he *is* their life.

Picasso died in 1973, at the age of 91, leaving no

will but an estate—land and houses as well as art works—valued at $260 million in 1976. Through most of his life, Picasso had hoarded his works and as he grew steadily richer and came to accept his own legendary status, he bought back many that had been sold earlier. An assortment of lawyers, art experts and court-appointed administrators is still busy sorting out the problems connected with apportioning thousands of paintings, graphics, sculptures and ceramics from all periods of his career.

Among the numerous problems, they have had to determine: Who were the legal heirs? Which works of art constituted the estate? To whom did they belong? How was the estate to be evaluated and divided? Who would coordinate the affairs of the estate? Would the works of art be sold? By whom? Where? How? Who owns reproduction rights? Who can sell them? How to pay the enormous estate taxes?

These dry questions cannot convey the underlying passions. Settling the huge estate was complicated by Picasso's tangled domestic history. Each of the children has had to piece together an image of the man from scattered fragments of memory, as Picasso himself imposed form on visual fragments. The family, in fact, resembles one of Picasso's cubist constructions—wives, mistresses, legitimate and illegitimate children (his youngest born 28 years after his oldest), and grandchildren—all strung on an axis like the backbone of a figure with unmatched parts. The axis is the long span of Picasso's life.

Picasso relished his former mistresses' continued dependence on him. He made a point of introducing his women to each other, enjoying the new lover's discomfort and the former one's misery. But he rarely discarded any totally. His first wife, in whom he effectively lost interest soon after their child was born, continued to live near him in the south of France until her death. He was capricious, self-involved, and the Picasso women and children never knew exactly where they stood with him; the turbulence and uncertainty he fostered among them did not abate after his death. When his heirs had to divide the estate, their old jealousies and suspicions erupted.

In 1918, Picasso married his first wife, Olga Khoklova, a dancer with the Ballet Russe, for which he was doing sets; he remained married to her, in name, until she died in 1955. Their son, Paolo, born in 1921, was Picasso's only legitimate child. Paolo, who died in 1975 from the effects of alcoholism, had three children, Pablito and Marina from his first marriage, Bernard from his second.

After Paolo, Picasso had three illegitimate children. Maya, the oldest, was born in 1935 to Marie-Thérèse Walter. Two more children—Claude, born in 1947, and Paloma, born in 1949—resulted from Picasso's liaison with Françoise Gilot, who lived with him for seven years. In 1952, the year before Françoise left Picasso, he met Jacqueline Roque, who was related to his ceramicist; nine years later she became his second wife and (after his death) continued to live in the Picasso villa in Mougins in the south of France.

Since Picasso's death, there have been three suicides among those who were close to him. His grandson Pablito committed suicide in 1973, his former mistress Marie-Thérèse Walter in 1977. (In 1986, Picasso's widow, Jacqueline Roque, killed herself in the house in Mougins.) Except for his widow, Jacqueline, his survivors hardly saw Picasso toward the end of his life. Friends recount that when Claude married for the first time, he called his father and asked him to meet his bride. Picasso agreed, but when Claude and his wife arrived at his father's house, the gatekeeper kept them out. Just then, a plumber arrived and was admitted, telling Claude, "You have to work for Picasso to see him."

At Picasso's death, his only legal heirs were Paolo and Jacqueline. Although Picasso had allowed Claude and Paloma to use his surname, he made no financial provision for them or for their half sister, Maya, who used her mother's maiden name until she married. In 1970, while Picasso was still living, Claude and Paloma sued to be recognized as heirs. They had the financial support of their mother, Françoise Gilot, and the suit attracted a great deal of publicity. According to Paloma, all they wanted at first was to be given works of art, but when their father refused this, they tried to have him declared mentally incompetent. They lost.

Eventually, however, a year after their father died, Claude and Paloma were declared legal heirs as a result of a 1972 change in French law that gave illegitimate children the right to a part of their father's estate. Maya sued soon after and also won. Paolo's two surviving children, one from each marriage—Marina, now 29, and 20-year-old Bernard—are each entitled to half of Paolo's legacy.

The heirs, then, have little in common except their marriage or blood ties to Picasso, but they have had to cooperate in settling the estate. "We are not close to each other," says the painter's daughter Paloma. "We never were a family, but in a way, we have become one now. At least we have all the problems of a family."

Picasso may have contemplated that leaving no will would force his often competitive heirs to confront one another; it was also in character for him to have created a situation that would consume them after his death. "Although he was a great artist," says Françoise Gilot, now Mrs. Jonas Salk, "morally, he had a dark side. He was sadistic, he enjoyed manipulating people."

Some friends and family insist that he left no will because he was a deeply superstitious man. "He was a Spaniard, an Andalusian," his daughter Maya says. "Where else in the world do people discuss the last days of their fathers, their aunts and their uncles? They do not talk about their family's lives, they talk about their deaths. They believe that death will happen to everybody but themselves. He did not make a will because he did not want to suggest that he might ever die. My father was terrified of dying."

As a result of the change in French law, not only Jacqueline but all the other heirs are now rich. Paloma, who says money isn't everything, wears a poncho made of sable pelts. Claude has two houses and two cars, and takes frequent vacations. Only Maya has not changed the way she lives. She has no plans to hang the pictures from her inheritance. "My apartment is too small, and, anyway, I don't want to worry about being robbed."

The widow's share amounts to roughly three tenths of the art in the estate, after taxes, or $52 million. The two grandchildren each have one fifth of the art, or $35 million; the three illegitimate children, one tenth, or $18 million apiece. But managing the estate and its proceeds consumes much of the heirs' time. Publicity is unrelenting. Each move Claude and Paloma made to establish their legal claims, every aspect of *l'affaire Picasso,* has been big news. But Paloma, for one, enjoys public attention and has used it to promote her many projects—acting in movies and designing fur coats, jewelry, sets and costumes for plays written and directed by her Argentine husband, Rafael López Sanchez.

Before the heirs divided the estate, the French government took its share. Estate taxes were paid in works of art, under the legal principle of the *dation en paiement,* which permits partial settlement by transfer of a single valuable work. Because the government saw an unprecedented opportunity to obtain an important selection of Picasso's work, under an expanded arrangement the entire tax—290 million francs, or just under 25 percent of the value of the estate—was paid in art. This will form the core of the Picasso Museum founded by the government and scheduled to open in Paris in 1982; most of it will come to New York as part of the Picasso exhibition, which will have its preview at the Museum of Modern Art on May 14.

After the government had taken its pick, each heir then selected a few specific works, so-called sentimental choices. Paloma, for instance, chose a group of dolls painted with her face; Claude picked a portrait of himself; Maya wanted statues of her mother, and Marina, a picture of her grandmother, Olga Khoklova. The rest of the works were divided into portions of equal value, and the heirs drew lots until each had his due percentage of the inheritance; they are now trading some of these works among themselves. According to William Rubin, director of paintings and sculpture at the Modern, "In one of their few unanimous acts, the heirs agreed to lend our Picasso show whatever works of art we wanted, regardless of whom they belonged to after the division."

Other problems remain: How to market that portion of the estate the heirs wish to sell? Will the heirs sell through a single dealer? Who owns the copyright, the *droit de reproduction* and the *droit moral* (inalienable legal rights giving the heirs control over the quality and nature of reproductions of an artist's work)?

The heirs take different views of the seriousness of the unresolved issues. "Everything is settled now," says Paloma. "When the exhibition opens at the Museum of Modern Art, we will be able to put our names on what we have donated." Maya, however, says, "Paloma and Claude are so American. They expect things to be finished quickly. But these things take time, they have their own momentum. I was supposed to go to Paris this week, but my daughter has chicken pox. I can't leave her. Business will have to wait."

"Maya feels that since she's the oldest child, she should be the head of the family," says Paloma. "She is very talented and charming, but she lives in Marseilles and refuses to come to Paris often enough to take care of the estate. Now she's worried that Claude and I are going to cheat her."

Considering the heirs' charged feelings toward one another, a lawyer involved with the case observes, "The issue is not how long it took to reach a settlement. The extraordinary thing was that it could be decided so quickly."

The initial problem, determining the estate's size, was perhaps the most difficult. It was necessary to decide which of the works in Picasso's bank vaults in Paris and in three houses on or near the Riviera—La Californie at Cannes, the chateau at Vauvenargues and the villa in Mougins—were *divulgué;* that is, exhibited, photographed, cataloged or otherwise made public, and so could be considered finished under French law. An unfinished work remains an artist's private possession. Once *divulgué,* however, it becomes part of the community property, half of which belongs to the artist's widow, and is not subject to estate taxes. The government had to establish which of Picasso's works had been legally completed before computing the taxable portion of the estate. The government also had to identify those works that were *divulgué* while Picasso was married to Olga Khoklova; these are part of his joint property with *her*—belonging after her death to Paolo, and, after Paolo died, to his children.

An expert appraiser, Maurice Rheims, spent five years cataloging the 1,885 paintings, 7,089 drawings, 3,222 ceramic works, 17,411 prints and 1,723 plates, 1,228 sculptures, 6,121 lithographs, 453 lithographic stones, 11 tapestries and eight rugs. After determining which were *divulgué,* he appraised each item. According to one lawyer, the valuations are generally conservative, about 50 percent below today's market values; the appraised value is based on what the estate might bring if sold at one time, not on what individual works could sell for. David Douglas Duncan was appointed to photograph each work. A few at a time, they were removed from the three houses and taken to bank vaults in Paris. The slow process was especially painful for Jacqueline, who had to continue living in an empty house that was once full of works of art.

All of the heirs accepted Rheims's inventory and valuations. "That was a miracle," sighs one of the lawyers. "Otherwise, each heir would have hired his own expert and the disagreements would have continued for decades." Of course, the government had tied up the estate so that the heirs had access to nothing until the tax question had been settled. Even so, the process was far from easy. Aside from the quantity of material, it was difficult to gain access to much of it. Jacqueline, recalls one lawyer, would make an appointment to see the appraisers, who would then come down from Paris only to find the house empty and locked. "You had to be prepared to wait three or four days," he says.

Dominique Bozo, the curator of the new Picasso

Museum, compiled a list of the 800 paintings he most wanted and compared his selections with the heirs' sentimental choices. The heirs drew up their own lists. Bozo reconciled conflicting claims and narrowed his final selection down to 225 paintings. He repeatedly sorted through photographs of all the works to cull the drawings, graphics, sculptures and 33 of the more than 100 notebooks Picasso kept during his career, including studies revealing the evolution of the cubist style in *Les Demoiselles d'Avignon.*

Bozo, a short, industrious man in his mid-40s, is a former curator at the Musée National d'Art Moderne and a highly regarded museologist. He has avoided too close an involvement with family intrigues. "I have no reason to include the heirs in the planning of the museum," he says. "What I took belonged to the government. Technically, the heirs were not even the donors of the works of art."

According to Claude's friends, he had hoped to be named director of the Picasso Museum and was disappointed when that did not happen. The museum, however, is a part of the French national system, and the director had to be a civil servant as well as a professional art historian.

Bozo works out of a tiny office in the Musée National d'Art Moderne while waiting for restorations to be completed on the Maison Salé, an 18th-century *hôtel particulier,* or private residence, which will house the Picasso Museum. Right now, all he has is a roomful of photographs. The inevitable delays of construction frustrate him; he can't wait to see his museum. "I used three criteria in choosing works for the museum. The first was that it was unique, a masterpiece. The second was that it helped make up a complete series of etchings or ceramics or drawings, which existed nowhere else. The third was that a work reinforced the particular strengths of the museum. For instance, we are particularly rich in Picasso's sculpture. No museum in the world can match our collection. This puts us in a strong bargaining position when it comes to lending works of art to other museums."

Bozo wants the new museum to expand beyond the *dation.* Jacqueline and the grandchildren have already donated Picasso's collection of works by other artists. "There will be other donations, too, but they will not be announced until after the museum is officially open," says Bozo. Some family members, aware of Bozo's ambitions for his museum, criticize the way he has handled the works of art so far, implying that he did not mount the collection carefully when it was shown to the public for the first time last year at the Grand Palais. "And he is not exhibiting the notebooks of studies for *Les Demoiselles d'Avignon* in New York," says Paloma. "He is afraid that there will be nothing left to show in his museum."

Bozo explains that the Grand Palais exhibition was mounted very quickly. "I, of course, knew about the MOMA exhibition," he says. "But I knew that the French people would never stand for having the *dation* shown first in America. We mounted the Grand Palais exhibition to let the public see what we had and to make it possible to lend it to New York. As for not wanting to bring the notebooks to the show, they would be out of place. They are too personal, too intimate."

All the heirs agree that Bozo chose the cream of Picasso's private collection. Nevertheless, some feel hurt that they were left out of the process of creating the museum. In truth, they are peripheral to the major monument to Picasso's memory. Except for Maya, who is glad that the curator has taken the problem out of her hands, the family continues to carp at Bozo. "The museum has not been very cooperative with the heirs," says one. "We were not shown the architect's plans for the Maison Salé. Unless he takes us into consideration, it might affect where we decide to donate our collections." These threats do not bother Bozo. "By and large," he says, "the works that the heirs have kept are not of museum quality, given this museum's criteria. I don't mean that some of them are not very great and important, but none is unique."

Bozo took many of Picasso's earlier and more

valuable works. Although each heir has important early pieces, most of what the family had to choose from was completed near the end of Picasso's career, when Picasso tended to put aside a piece as soon as he found its solution. When he was younger, he had more patience for details; the earlier works seem more finished.

Bozo is unhappy that the heirs—except for Jacqueline—are unwilling to relinquish their right to the royalties from reproductions of works of art in connection with the Picasso Museum and the upcoming MOMA exhibition. Of this, Paloma says, "Jacqueline knows nothing about art or the business of art. Well, maybe she's learned something from being around my father. But Claude and I feel better equipped to handle the business details."

Potential profits from authorized reproductions are enormous, and Claude has focused much of his attention on the rights inherited by the heirs. The *droit de reproduction* is an aspect of the copyright and can be sold or transferred. It is valuable because Picasso's images are very commercial and are widely reproduced. Whether an heir can transfer this right *individually* has not yet been clarified by French law. The legal concept of *droit moral* is important in a different way. It has to do with the moral right of an artist to control the reproduction and use of his work, to prevent distortion of the image, even after it has been sold. The *droit moral* is inherited by the artist's descendants. At the time of the interim settlement of the estate, Picasso's heirs agreed to act together to keep his work from being debased—for instance, by inaccurate reproductions.

For several years, Claude has been the president of SPADEM (Société de la Propriété Artistique et des Dessins et Modèles), an international organization formed to collect royalties on reproductions of artists' images and to police improper use of these images. All the heirs, except Marina, who recently changed her mind, have designated SPADEM their agent in these matters. The fee SPADEM charges depends on the purpose of the publication, its size, circulation and the number of works reproduced.

Royalties frequently are much greater than the $8,500 fee that the Museum of Modern Art paid for use of illustrations in its catalog and posters. Picasso is the most reproduced artist in the world. Last year, for instance, the estate entered into an agreement with a wallpaper manufacturer that netted it more than $100,000. The estate stood to make much more, but Claude, exercising the *droit moral* on behalf of the heirs, rejected half of the manufacturer's 30 designs because he said they distorted the original work; he sued the company to prevent their changing elements of the work.

In the past seven years, Claude has moved from wanting to exploit the estate himself—he once intended to make bronze editions of his father's unique metal sculptures, but the plan was dropped—to working to maintain its integrity. Recently, for example, he has begun playing a leading role in the negotiations between the heirs and the Spanish government over delivering *Guernica*, perhaps Picasso's most famous work, to the country of his birth.

Claude is short, with large black eyes and white teeth—"just like photographs of his father as a young man," says the *New York Times*'s chief art critic, Hilton Kramer. He talks rapidly, makes a point of keeping busy—"If I saw everybody who wanted to see me, I'd never sleep." He has become an able businessman, according to those who work with him. Even so, says a lawyer, "SPADEM is not enough to keep him engaged. He must find a real interest. He cannot go along being an heir forever." In the meantime, Claude does work hard at SPADEM. He enjoys the wheeling and dealing, but he is also ambivalent; he is aware that neither he nor SPADEM would be taken quite so seriously if he were not named Picasso. When the estate is completely settled, a friend says, Claude will move on: "He is interested in other things and he has the capacity to do anything he wants." Claude has tried journalism and shown talent at photography, but neither interests him now. "It's too difficult," he explains. "You have to rush around all the time; you have to hustle."

Now people hustle to see him. "He has changed since the inheritance," says another friend. "He used to be quiet, shy. His friends used to be artists. Now I don't know who they are. We had dinner recently. He came late, kept getting up to make phone calls and then he rushed away early for a meeting. It was strange; when he got married again, he didn't tell anybody about it."

At 22, while living in the United States, Claude married Sara Lee Schultz, an aspiring comedienne. They were divorced in 1973, and she is now suing him for some of his father's works that the couple acquired while they were married. Last November, Claude married another American woman, Sydney Russell, who had also been previously married and has a 10-year-old son. She is a paleontologist working at the Musée de l'Homme, the French anthropological museum.

"Claude was terribly hurt by his father," says Louise Leiris, whose gallery handled Picasso's paintings during World War II. "The separation was very difficult for him." Françoise Gilot left Picasso when Claude was 6 and Paloma 4. The children continued to spend school vacations with their father for the next 10 years, but after Françoise published her widely read book, *Life with Picasso*, the children were virtually banished from his company. "Being legally recognized was a big thing for Claude," says Paloma. Claude's need to connect with his father shows up in little ways: for example, like Picasso, Claude owns an Abyssinian cat.

Picasso was not what one would call a family man. "He would play with the children for a few minutes, then he forgot about them," says one of Picasso's lawyers. "He loved only one thing and that was his painting—not his women, not his children. Each woman thought she was the one and only Madame Picasso, but he lived for nothing but himself. It is true that he painted only the woman he was currently with, but that is because she was there, not because she was the center of his universe."

Claude does not talk about his father, only about his father's business; but the other children do. "It was easy for me," says his sister, Paloma. "A father is going to like a little girl, and anyway, I was the last child. It was much harder for Claude. There was some rivalry between father and son. My father was a difficult man. He was a baby all his life. You could not expect from him what you would from an ordinary father, so I stopped looking for it. I would have liked to ask him a lot of questions, but, on the other hand, I was spared a great deal of turmoil by not seeing him as I was growing up. People say that what has happened to me must hurt me terribly, but my mother [Françoise Gilot] was very strong, and we were lucky that way." More than the other heirs, Paloma seems to have come to terms with the problems and advantages of being a Picasso.

Paloma is short and sturdy with black hair, black eyes and bright red lipstick. Friends agree that she has her father's spirit and sense of humor.

"Paloma always did what she wanted," says Louise Leiris. "Unlike Claude, she inherited a kind of hardness, an immunity, from her mother. Nothing ever bothered her. She always was off in her own corner." With apartments in New York and Paris, Paloma spends a lot of time in the United States, but no matter where she is, she lives like a Spaniard—and like her father. She gets up at noon, eats supper at 11, and parties until 3.

Paloma blames Jacqueline for her estrangement from her father. "She excluded us. She tried to get everything, but she never was happy with what she had. Now all she has is her memory of my father. My father tried to legitimize us, but she fought against it. If you mentioned Claude or me, you never came back to the house. She told people to say terrible things about my mother and her book, but I know for a fact that Picasso never read the book. We were kicked out of the house as soon as we were old enough to be a threat to her. She insulated my father from the world, calling him *'Monseigneur'* and *'le roi d'Espagne.'* "

A friend of Jacqueline and Picasso says that Jacqueline did try to make Picasso believe that she was the only person who loved him and cared about him. Picasso enjoyed the adulatory world she built around him. Another friend says that Jacqueline paid more attention to Picaso than to Cathy, her daughter by a previous marriage. Jacqueline once said to a guest who was admiring the sunset, "How can you talk about the sunset when Picasso is here in the house?" Some observers even felt that in this way she manipulated him. However, in the opinion of the photographer David Douglas Duncan, who has had a long association with Picasso and his family, "There are many sides to this, but nobody pushed this guy around."

Paloma continues, "Now I can begin to deal with her. We have some portraits of her which we want to trade. I know that she will be unpleasant and difficult, but now I am old enough and it doesn't bother me. When I was 14, it was different. She would tell me how ugly I was."

One of the lawyers contradicts Paloma's assertion that Picasso never read her mother's book and feels that it was he who made the children choose between himself and their mother. "Of course he read it," the lawyer says. "It made him very angry, and he transferred this anger to the children." Indeed, Picasso sued, unsuccessfully, to bar the book's serialization in *Paris Match*.

Maya Widmaïer says she stopped seeing her father because "Spaniards lock their women up," but her estrangement from him—like that of Claude and Paloma—began about two years after he married Jacqueline. Maya says, "I was glad I left when I did. I was 20. I didn't have to sit around and adore him. But Claude and Paloma left their father when they were so young, what could they know of him? In a way, I feel like their mother. I was closer to Françoise, their mother, than I was to them."

Married at 23, Maya lives with her husband, a retired merchant marine captain, in a small, cluttered, comfortable apartment overlooking the marina in Marseilles. A portrait Picasso sketched of Maya on her 14th birthday hangs behind the sofa, next to a larger drawing of her by Françoise Gilot. There is a tiny Renoir on the opposite wall. Her apartment, however, is hardly dominated by her father's presence. Picasso's easel (a present from him), in the dining room, holds a bulletin board with drawings and photographs of her three children, whom Picasso never saw. Like Picasso's other children, Maya is short and stocky; her hair is blond and she has pale blue eyes. She talks quickly; her face is mobile and she laughs often. "What did the others tell you about me, that I am always joking?" she asks. (The heirs invariably ask for information about the others. Another extended-family trait they share is exchanging barbed remarks.)

According to Louise Leiris, Maya was the only child who called Picasso "Papa"; the others used "Father." Although he did not live with Marie-Thérèse Walter, Maya's mother, while Maya was growing up, he continued to see Marie-Thérèse regularly and spent a great deal of time with her even though he had other mistresses. "When I stopped seeing him," Maya says, "I still had a memory of him when he was alert and vital. He and my mother had a great love, an *amour fou.* They wrote to each other throughout their lives. The statue over his grave is of my mother. He had known her for years before they had me. I was not an accident. By the time he had Claude and Paloma, he was an old man. He could not play with them. They have had to invent their own image of him. I am the oldest now, *la mère Maya,* and I can't help it; I still consider them children."

Maya does have a vivid image of her father, but one that she has to reinforce constantly. She looks for concrete evidence to intensify her sense that he was her father. Maya emphasizes her similarities to him, their shared superstitions, shared ailments. She picks up a bronze cast of a hand from a shelf under a table. "This is his hand," she says, holding hers out next to it. The hands are identical, with broad, deeply creased palms, the same short fingers.

About her half brother Paolo, Maya says, "He saw much less of our father than I did. He lived with his mother. But it was very difficult for him. Imagine that your father is very rich and you will never make as much money as he does. In addition, he makes money out of nothing—a pencil and a piece of paper. When Paolo was 20, he began to drink. He stopped but started again when he was going through a divorce. After my father died, he was not drinking, but his body had already given out."

Maya continues: "It bothered my father very much that Paolo did nothing, but for Paolo, there was nothing he could do." Cars were the only thing that interested him, and, for a while, he was his father's chauffeur.

Picasso's grandson Bernard, Paolo's son by his second wife, Christine Pauplin, largely keeps to himself in Paris but is close to Claude and has begun to work with him on the administration of the estate. The estate negotiations have been going on for nearly half of his 20 years. A friend says, "He's very fragile. He doesn't know how to cope with all this money." Paloma explains, "He is so young. He cannot deal with people wanting to know him only because he is an heir to the Picasso estate. He doesn't know what he is himself yet."

Bernard's half sister, Marina, has been the least willing to cooperate with the family—perhaps because she had the least contact with Picasso, who disapproved of her mother, Emilyenne Lotte May, Paolo's first wife. After Paolo divorced her, he lost interest in the children of that marriage. At the time of her grandfather's death, Marina was working in a hospital for handicapped children. Marina and her brother, Pablito, already estranged from their father, were excluded from the funeral, as were Paloma, Claude and Maya. Distraught, Pablito drank poison. He suffered for three months before dying.

Marina now lives near Antibes on the Riviera with her two illegitimate children, Gael and Fleur. An acquaintance says she "looks just like a little bird, thin and frightened. She is totally dominated by her lawyer."

Marina's lawyer contested a preliminary arbitration dividing the estate and, according to Jan Krugier, an art dealer who represents Marina's interest in the estate, she was awarded a larger share to compensate for her long estrangement from her father and grandfather. After the government took its portion, Marina's representative, Krugier, was allowed to choose a number of works before the rest of the family drew lots. Thus, Krugier says, Marina got the pick of the remaining estate. Her share, like Bernard's, is more representative of Picasso's career than that of any other heir; the two of them have more early works than the other heirs because of the community property Picasso shared with Olga Khoklova, their grandmother.

With Krugier, Marina is planning a traveling exhibition of her legacy, which will open in Munich next February. For $22.5 million, she has sold reproduction rights to approximately a thousand works in her collection to a New York tax-shelter art-investment firm, Jackie Fine Arts. This firm will resell to investors reproduction rights to individual works, along with a lithographic plate of the work of art, called an "art master," from which impressions can be made. The investors can arrange to print and distribute limited runs of high-quality reproductions, which will be signed "From the collection of Marina Picasso." This kind of arrangement has become increasingly common in the art world and, recently, has drawn the attention of the Internal Revenue Service.

Some of the family are not happy with Marina's sale, which undermines Claude's efforts to have the heirs act together through SPADEM. Claude asserts: "There is no question that what she wants to do is illegal. The reproduction rights for the entire estate belong to the entire family. One part cannot be separated."

On the other hand, Marina and Jackie Fine Arts maintain that the *droit de reproduction* belongs to the owners of the specific works. Although French law, again, is not clearly defined on this point, they may be right. According to John Henry Merryman, a professor at the Stanford University Law School and author of a widely used casebook on art and the law: "Until they are separated, the reproduction right is attached to the work of art. Reproduction rights are regarded as property. The heir succeeds to the position of the ancestor [the original creator]. Thus, whatever rights Picasso had, the inheritor has." The heirs' lawyers are trying to settle this, but strong feelings persist.

Krugier, of course, sympathizes with his client: "Marina has lost both her father and her older brother, whom she adored. She lives all alone, very simply, devoting her life to her children. Her life is governed by the idea of duty. Marina is planning a foundation for retarded children—she has worked with them all her life—and she plans to use her proceeds from the sale of the reproduction rights to finance it." Claude says that he has heard of the foundation, but he has no idea whether Marina is serious.

Another major unresolved issue is the marketing of the works of art. "Picasso almost has to be treated as if he were a living artist," a dealer explains. "There is so much stuff that it has to be marketed very carefully over a long period of time. If too much were offered at once, it could cause prices to fall sharply. Right now the timing is perfect. The Museum of Modern Art show will create Picasso fever in New York. Every tourist will want to buy his own Picasso to take home with him."

In January, there were rumors that the family was meeting to decide on a plan and a dealer to handle the sales, but nothing was agreed upon. It is not clear that the heirs have any intention of selling anything. According to a Paris dealer, Paloma, Claude and Bernard are likely to work together on whatever they do, but Maya and, obviously, Marina will not go along with them. Nobody seems to know what Jacqueline will decide; she has isolated herself in a villa she rarely leaves.

"Try to see her," urges Dominique Bozo. "She is genuinely concerned with Picasso's memory."

"Of course you can come," says Jacqueline's voice on the telephone. "Mstislav Rostropovich and Galina Vishnevskaya were here yesterday and Vishnevskaya sang all night for me and for Pablo. I am always here."

It takes 20 minutes to drive from Nice to the Picasso villa in Mougins, near Cannes. The day is cold, overcast, but the fruit trees are flowering. The house is among the cypresses at the top of a steep, winding road. Its unmarked green gates are locked; barbed wire curls through the bars at the top. A servant opens the gates.

The villa, beyond the brilliant primroses blooming beside the driveway, is built of pale pink stone. Picasso's widow opens the door. She is small and trim and stands erect, wrapped in a black Spanish shawl. Her black hair, beginning to turn gray, curves smoothly around her face, which needs no makeup. In her mid-50s, she is still striking.

She nods a greeting and leads the way through a narrow hall. The inside walls of the house are also pale pink; the floor is stone. At the end of the hall hangs a large photograph of Picasso. A peach-colored rose is set in a vase in front of the picture.

Jacqueline goes into a sitting room, seats herself at a small round table and begins to talk, in a mixture of French and English. "I am an alphabet of languages. It was the snobbism of my time. I learned five languages at school. Pablo did not have time to teach me. Sometimes I dream that I see Pablo." She smiles, a slow, vague smile. Her cheeks are webbed with delicate wrinkles. "But maybe I dream, maybe I don't. Maybe he was here, maybe not."

About the inheritance—Bozo said she was very generous. "*Bozo a appris tout ici,*" she says sharply—"Bozo learned everything he knows about Picasso from me." Then she smiles again and stands. "Come, I will show you something." She offers her hand and leads the way. She tries four keys until she finds the right one. "I don't know why I lock the door. I am always here."

The door opens into a large room with a shallow arched ceiling. Coarse muslin curtains are drawn across the tall windows; Picasso hated to paint in daylight. The room was his studio; now it is his shrine. Paints and brushes are stacked on a worktable, a jar of olive oil ready to mix with the colors, a lamp clamped to the side of an easel, papers strewn on the floor. And on all the walls, paintings—portraits of Jacqueline: holding a cat, in a scarf, sitting cross-legged on a chair, wearing a Turkish jacket, smiling, sad, a cubist Jacqueline. She opens her arms and smiles. "Not bad?"

In the muted yellow light, the painted eyes are terrifying: they are Picasso's own eyes—black, obsessive. Jacqueline's are light brown, almost hazel. Picasso's eyes stare from Jacqueline's faces. His power—the force of his will—is overwhelming. There is also something destructive, brutal, about these portraits. They catch—and exploit—Jacqueline's terrible anxiety and self-effacement; Picasso was not merciful. Her smile is too fixed, too serene. Perhaps this room explains Jacqueline. Perhaps Picasso used her up and drained her; now all she has of herself is his image of her. "I come here every day to cry."

Jacqueline plays a Nathan Milstein recording of the Mendelssohn violin concerto and the music echoes in the stone vaults of the studio. She dances as she comes back to her chair. Then she begins to pose, putting on that smile like a costume. She crosses her legs and drapes her wrists over her ankles like the portrait hanging to her left; her fingernails are painted the same red as in the painting. She picks up two small panels leaning against the legs of an easel, nudes painted in rounded geometric forms. Jacqueline imitates one, standing with her arms hanging at her sides, glaring.

"Pablo and I were like this." Jacqueline clasps her hand, intertwining her fingers. "Maybe I dream, maybe I don't. It is the same thing." Everything she has, she says, will go to the chateau at Vauvenargues, where Picasso is buried; she is going to make it into a museum. Behind a chair lurks a bronze statue of the cat Jacqueline holds in one of the paintings. It is ready to pounce.

Abruptly, she shuts off the record player. "Come," she says and unlocks other rooms. The dining room: the long narrow table filled with papers, lawyers' letters: a display case holding a flock of swans Picasso made by bending tinfoil bottle caps—*"Cygnes d'amour,"* says Jacqueline; a Braque on the wall; and Picasso cutouts of himself and Jacqueline on easels at the far end of the room. "I have a lover," she smiles and begins talking in a low voice to a harlequin puppet, accepting the silk rose it holds in its hand—a token of love.

In the bedroom there is a copy of *Paris Match* featuring Picasso's 90th birthday and another jumble of papers. The shutters are closed. "I have not opened them since Picasso"—Jacqueline pauses—"died." The bed is half-made. It seems as if Jacqueline is only living on the surface of the house; it is really the house of a dead man. She insists on showing the rest of the villa, repeating over and over again, "It's a pretty house, isn't it?"

Jacqueline still looks like her portraits. She smiles at this, but then she frowns and shakes her head: "I've changed. Maybe, maybe not." She says she has too much to do to be a widow. She is a poet, she has always written; she writes, she says, what she is going to be.

On the way back to the villa's gates, past five barking Afghans in a kennel, Jacqueline says, "It is very difficult to live in this house. Maybe I am stupid, maybe not." She gets out of the car without saying good-bye and walks back up the driveway, wrapped in her black shawl.

The rest of the family does not live in houses haunted by Picasso's memory. They have been able to shield themselves from Picasso with lawyers and time and distance. Jacqueline has not. "She's burned out," said a friend. "She had to adapt herself totally to his life. He would not permit her to be sick, or to show that she was tired. But she's better now than she used to be."

The Picasso estate is largely settled. But there is so much art, and so much money—and so much bitterness and pain—that the remaining problems, and the problems *they* engender, may take years to work out. The heirs can live lavishly, whether they choose to sell works of art or to collect royalties. "But," says a friend who lives outside of Paris, "why shouldn't they get everything out of it that they can?" It is, perhaps, a kind of compensation for not having had much of the man while he was alive.

Says Paloma, "Living with my father, for us the main thing was to survive." Some survivors have done better than others. Paloma, with her tough sense of humor, knows how to work and how to have a good time. Claude and Bernard are running the affairs of a father and grandfather they hardly knew. A friend says Marina feels persecuted and lives in fear of her children's being kidnapped. Jacqueline locks herself into Mougins. Maya has her family, but her mother, Marie-Thérèse Walter, depressed since Picasso's death, committed suicide a few years ago. Paolo and Pablito are also dead.

The painter of *Guernica*, a testament to war's cruelty, has left behind his own casualties.

THE PICASSO RETROSPECTIVE: A New Measure of His Achievement

HILTON KRAMER

THE HISTORIC Picasso exhibition at the Museum of Modern Art in 1980 is clearly intended to overwhelm us, and—no question about it—it does. The legendary force, momentum and multiplicity of Picasso's gifts have not been exaggerated, after all. They are truly prodigious, and the art that resulted from this extraordinary endowment is, as promised, presented to us in this exhibition on a scale and with a discrimination never before lavished on Picasso or any other modern artist. That his art proves to be fully equal to this outsize scale—that, indeed, it requires this scale to be fully seen and understood—is but one of the many revelations this exhibition discloses to us for the first time.

Thus, though Picasso has long been the most famous of modern artists, and in New York one of the most frequently exhibited, this show nonetheless gives us a new measure of his achievement. Henceforth, Picasso will live for us as the artist we will have studied and lived with—and argued about, and at times even been a little sickened by—in this exhibition.

The artist who emerges from an initial contact with this immense survey of nearly 1,000 objects is, then, in some respects quite different from the artist we may have expected to see on our arrival—different, that is, from the artist we have carried around in our heads as a familiar fiction on the basis of many previous exhibitions and the words beyond number that have been written and spoken about him. He is at once larger and smaller than the Picasso of our dreams. His powers seem preternatural, his imagination gargantuan and his energy absolutely demonic; but his character, the character that is at first slowly but then more and more insistently disclosed to us in this immense oeuvre, looks—how is one to put it?—deficient in many human qualities, and even at times positively frightening and malevolent. It may shock the pious to hear this said, but it is worth remembering that Wagner—to choose but one example from many—presents us with a similar problem, and I think we shall fail to take this momentous exhibition, and the great artist it apotheosizes, with the seriousness they deserve if we do not face up to the implications of what it is we are actually looking at in this show.

Nietzsche said of Wagner, whom he greatly admired and greatly feared, that he was "by no means good-natured," and even spoke of Wagner's music—which affected Nietzsche so profoundly—as "a poison." This may now strike us as a characteristic example of Nietzschean hyperbole, but there is this to be said for it. It has the virtue of acknowledging what the rosy sentiments of our own culture tend so often to deny when it comes to judging aesthetic achievement: that even the greatest art may sometimes exert a spiritual force that is by no means uniformly beneficent or benign. It therefore behooves us to bear this possibility in mind in approaching an artist as central to the spirit of our culture as Picasso.

It is, in any case, in the very nature of Picasso's work to direct our attention to the man himself, for he is the most autobiographical of the great modern artists. From the bawdy drawings in which he recorded his youthful escapades in the brothels of Barcelona at the turn of the century to the geriatric rage of *The Kiss* of 1969 and the sardonic self-aggrandizement of the 1970 engraving called *Picasso's Stage*—one of the last and most revealing of the many self-analytical images we observe in this show—Picasso placed his life at the very center of his art. The point is so obvious that it would scarcely need making were it not for the fact that our preoccupation with "style" in Picasso—and in modernist art generally—has led us at times to discount, if not actually to dismiss, the expressive functions implicit in every nuance of style.

A keen appreciation of the well-known shifts of style—the celebrated "periods" into which Picasso's work divides itself—is absolutely essential, of course, to our understanding of his art, and it is one of the special glories of the present exhibition that it documents this amazing succession of styles with a clarity and precision never before equaled. One of the salutary effects of the very abundance of the exhibition, moreover, and of the care that has been taken to keep this abundance firmly focused on the main lines of development in Picasso's work, is that it takes us—to the extent that any single exhibition can—virtually inside the artist's mind, where year by year and sometimes even month by month we are able to observe its decisions, and the emotions and ideas governing those decisions, with an intimacy rarely accorded to outsiders.

Yet in any attempt to penetrate to the inner substance of Picasso's art—to search out its "soul," so to speak—the appreciation of style so vividly given us in this exhibition is little more than a beginning. This is one important reason why the exhibition needs to be seen more than once. Our first view may serve, then, as a form of reconnaissance, allowing us to chart the vast terrain of this art and identify its principal points of entry. When this vast terrain has been even provisionally encompassed, however, its salient features begin to acquire a unity of interest that is no longer usefully divisible into discrete "periods" or styles. For persisting throughout all these shifts of style is an attitude—a *Weltanschauung,* if you will—that is far more consistent and fundamental to Picasso's vision than the individual styles that give it voice. It is only when we have grasped what remains unchanging—almost fixed—in the sometimes frantic, sometimes serene, but always searching metamorphosis of style, that we begin to feel ourselves in touch with the inner life of the art itself.

Simply stated, this inner life of Picasso's art—the very crux of the spirit animating it through every change of form—centers on two all-consuming and, for Picasso, closely connected passions: making art and making love. The world that exists beyond the boundaries of the artist's studio and his bedroom, or seraglio, is quite conspicuously lacking in what philosophers call ontology. It lacks, in other words, reality or being. Picasso's world is thus largely confined to the aesthetic and the erotic—which, in his case, are all but inseparable—and with the scenarios of power and dominance that are endemic to these self-centered and self-glorifying interests when they acquire the force—as they so obviously did for him—of a transcendent, self-defining obsession.

This is not to deny that there are pictures and objects in this show—and beyond it, in the oeuvre as a whole—exploring other themes. Picasso lived a long time; he was a compulsive, curious and tireless worker; and his attention was often easily diverted by a great many transitory interests—some serious, but many not—especially in the long period following his association with the Ballets Russes during World War I when, let us remember, he still had more than half his life to live out. With few exceptions, however, most of these are little more than diversions—delightful, perhaps, but often trivial, too—from the central course of his work.

The towering exception is, of course, *Guernica*,

the painting that Picasso produced at breakneck speed in May and June of 1937 as a memorial to the victims on the Republican side of the Spanish Civil War. Yet even this extraordinary painting, which for many people has long enjoyed a special status—and not only among the artist's confirmed admirers but for those, too, who otherwise feel nothing but disgust for modernist painting and yet tend to exempt *Guernica* from their usual strictures because of its manifest political content—even this painting emerges in a somewhat altered perspective in the present exhibition.

At least it does for me. The element of rage that is such a palpable and powerful constituent of this work—and that is traditionally taken to be so transparently political in its inspiration—turns out to have been well established as one of the dominant sexual motifs in Picasso's work years before either the bombing of Guernica, or the civil war itself, loomed on the artist's horizon.

It makes its explosive debut in a ferociously erotic picture called *The Embrace*, painted in the summer of 1925. (This is one of the many works here from the artist's estate and now in the collection of the new Picasso Museum in Paris.) Thereafter it is never for very long absent from Picasso's work until the end of his life, but on the contrary, grows to absorb more and more of his creative energy. From the late 1920s onward, this theme of erotic rage is central to his art and assumes more and more violent forms. From this time, certainly, and rising to a crescendo in the 1930s, women are the special object of this rage (as they had, in earlier years, been the special object of his tenderness and *tristesse*), but it attaches itself to a great many other objects and motifs, too.

The *Crucifixion* drawings after Grünewald, done in 1932, for example, are consumed with it, and so are a great many works devoted to the themes of *Bathers, The Minotaur* and *The Bullfight,* which, like the *Crucifixion* series, now look quite unmistakably like surrogate scenarios for episodes of erotic combat.

In this altered context, the force of *Guernica* as a painting is not diminished, but its meaning emerges as somewhat changed. It is no longer quite as convincing as the strictly political avowal it has traditionally been taken to be. Its force is the force of something more personal and primitive. Its anger now seems to address its fury to human life itself—to the spectacle of all those unappeased and unappeasable appetites of the flesh and the spirit that, for want of other means of fulfillment or resolution, end in grotesque acts of violence.

The reputation earned by *Guernica* as the most celebrated political painting of the 20th century has given us, I think, a distorted view of Picasso's true interests, which were only marginally and intermittently social. His fractional career as a political artist is no cause for celebration, in any case. The organizers of the present exhibition have prudently spared us his ingratiating peace doves, which won Picasso great popularity on the political Left during the Cold War, and the benign portrait of Stalin he produced for the Communist party on the occasion of the tyrant's death isn't here either (though the latter is reproduced in the catalog). Only the *Massacre in Korea* that he obligingly turned out as a propaganda painting for the Communists in 1951 is here to represent this dishonorable episode when he betrayed his position as one of the leaders of the free culture of the West and lent his immense prestige to the support of a regime far worse than Franco's.

There is nothing more striking in this exhibition than the gulf of feeling that separates the rage and mockery—including some notable examples of self-mockery—of the later work from the almost serene absorption in matters of pure aesthetic analysis that we observe in the earlier years (from 1909, say, to 1915), when Picasso was producing the incredible succession of cubist masterworks that remain unrivaled in his oeuvre as his greatest achievement.

Picasso was 30 years old in 1909, and had already accomplished a great deal—enough, certainly, to assure him a permanent place in art history if he had done nothing more. But the leap that occurs in his work at that time, when the audacities already broached in *Les Demoiselles d'Avignon* are so painstakingly reexamined and so subtly and delicately developed into the classical language of cubism, places his art on another level altogether.

For the first time in Picasso's work we are made to feel that all worldly distraction is in abeyance and the pressures and inspiration of mind—of pure thought—are firmly in control. Cleverness has been eschewed, facility resisted and sensual impulse held in check. The hammering ego that creates such a din in the later work is not yet unleashed to wreak its havoc. An inspired detachment, wielding extraordinary powers of analysis, exerts a magisterial authority, and for a few magical years Picasso sustains his art on a plateau of Apollonian emotion that is like nothing else he had ever achieved before or would ever achieve again.

This, surely, was one of the sublime accomplishments of the human spirit, and for this reason those galleries that contain such an astonishing number of these great cubist paintings, drawings, collages and sculptures afford one of the most incomparable experiences that art can offer us. The beauty and power that is sustained in these works remains so breathtaking that familiarity breeds only a deeper admiration, and we return to them with a gratitude that it is not quite possible to feel to the same degree in any other section of this vast exhibition.

Had Picasso ended his career in 1915, he would therefore still count as one of the greatest artists of his time—less versatile and less prodigious perhaps, and certainly less overbearing than we now know him to have been, but unquestionably great all the same, and probably more appealing. But greatness in art comes in many forms and in many degrees, and Picasso's—even after the experience of this unprecedented exhibition—is by no means easy to place. If he does not finally, even in the face of this immense accomplishment, seem quite the equal of Cézanne—to go no further back in art history than that—it is unquestionably because of the character and spirit that his art reveals to us in the long aftermath of that early cubist achievement. Cézanne leaves us with nothing like the awful sense of spiritual debacle that we feel at the end of Picasso's career. The disarray of those last years remains terrifying to contemplate, and sends us hurrying back to the halcyon years of cubist splendor for a renewal of our faith in his genius and integrity.

GUERNICA'S QUIET DEPARTURE FOR SPAIN

GRACE GLUECK

IN DEEP secrecy and with no opportunity for farewells, *Guernica*, Picasso's monumental antiwar mural, on loan to the Museum of Modern Art for 42 years, left New York for a final home in Spain in Sept. 9, 1981.

Ending its refugee existence after years of dispute and agitation over its status, the painting, rolled up and crated and carefully guarded by Spanish officials, departed in the cargo hold of an Iberia airliner that took off at 7 P.M. on a regularly scheduled commercial flight.

In accordance with Picasso's wishes, the huge painting, more than 25 feet long, has been put on permanent exhibition in a specially restored annex of the Prado museum in Madrid.

The secrecy of *Guernica*'s going was dictated by "overriding security considerations," according to Richard Oldenburg, the museum's director, who expressed "regret" that the precautions would not allow the museum to "give advance notice to its public that the departure of *Guernica* was imminent."

Over the years there have been sporadic protests against the transfer to Spain of the painting, a political and aesthetic symbol of great significance, and it has been the subject of claims from various political, ethnic, artistic and other factions who wanted a say over its final disposition. In 1974 it was subjected to physical attack, when a young Iranian artist named Tony Shafrazi vandalized it with spray paint as it hung in its third-floor gallery at the Museum of Modern Art.

In a small private ceremony at the museum yesterday afternoon, Inigo Cavero, Spanish minister of culture, signed the formal transfer agreement in the presence of the Spanish ambassador to the United States, José Llado, and other Spanish officials, as well as William S. Paley, chairman of the museum; Blanchette Rockefeller, its president; and Mr. Oldenburg.

In a brief talk, Mr. Cavero said the painting would "enrich the national patrimony of Spain," and added that it "poses a demand for reconciliation obtained among all Spaniards within the democratic constitution whose first guarantor is His Majesty, King Juan Carlos."

He also thanked the museum "for the conservation of this work for so many years and for the attention and care with which they have shown it to millions of visitors."

The Spanish government has indemnified the museum against claims from any possible source that it might have acted imprudently in releasing the mural. It has also agreed that it has no claim to any other works in the museum's collection, and that it will pay all costs of crating and shipping for *Guernica* and the 62 preliminary studies and "postscripts" that accompany it.

The painting, of incalculable value, was at one time unofficially valued for insurance purposes at $40 million. It was originally commissioned by the Spanish Republic very early in the Spanish Civil War for its building at the 1937 Paris World's Fair. Picasso had not begun work on the project when news broke of the savage bombing by Generalissimo Francisco Franco's forces on April 26, 1937, of the Basque town for which the painting is named. Seizing on that as the theme of his work, the artist made the first sketches on May 1. The mural was installed in June, and on July 12 the Spanish Pavilion opened to the public. Sent to New York in 1939 on a tour for the benefit of the Spanish Refugee Relief Committee, *Guernica* was later included in the exhibition "Picasso: Forty Years of His Art," organized by the late Alfred H. Barr, Jr., then the director of the Museum of Modern Art.

When World War II broke out in Europe, Picasso suggested that *Guernica* and a number of his other works be held at the Museum of Modern Art on extended loan. Although the rest of the Picassos were eventually returned, the artist stipulated that *Guernica* and the numerous studies for it would ultimately go to his native Spain, and asked that the museum hold them until the death of Franco and "the reestablishment of public liberties" there. He entrusted his lawyer, Roland Dumas, with the decision as to when those conditions had been met.

It was Mr. Dumas's assent, given in writing last month, that actually triggered the painting's departure, although the museum had been hard-pressed recently by Spanish government officials, who wanted the painting in Spain for the centennial celebration of Picasso's birth on Oct. 25. "Last April, Spanish officials visited us at the museum and asked that we expedite transfer of the painting," Mr. Oldenburg said. "It was their first formal request, although we'd been having discussions before that. Following that, we hired Cyrus Vance as legal counsel to reexamine the question of *Guernica*'s transfer and make sure we were on proper ground."

A possible stumbling block to the dispatching of *Guernica* was resolved last June when four of the Picasso heirs, uncertain whether the time was ripe for the painting to go to Spain, came to an agreement after a meeting in Paris with Mr. Oldenburg and William Rubin, director of painting and sculpture at the Museum of Modern Art. The heirs did not claim ownership of the painting, but they held that under French law, which gives "moral rights" to an artist's survivors, they had a say in determining its fate.

Although the Spanish government demurred, it had participated in discussions with the heirs throughout last year. "But the question of how far 'moral rights' extended became academic after the heirs gave their assent," Mr. Oldenburg said.

In Madrid, Prado officials have restored a 17th-century pavilion near the main museum, called the Casón del Buen Retiro, where *Guernica* will hang. Thus, although separated from the main museum, the painting will join the Prado's matchless collection of works by Velázquez, Goya and other artists from earlier centuries in whose tradition Picasso placed himself. Prado officials hope that *Guernica* and its studies will eventually be joined there by other Picasso works.

It is understood that the picture, once installed in Madrid, will never be lent again, because the repeated rolling and unrolling of the canvas required for several European loans—made at Picasso's request and against the advice of the Museum of Modern Art—during the 1950s have already caused serious damage to the surface.

The painting's unceremonious departure gives little indication of the immense influence it has exercised on artists here, and its strong appeal for the museum's public. A tour de force of expressionistically distorted forms arranged in a powerful composition of blacks, whites and grays, it presents a horrifying scene of the brutalities of war. Yet Picasso did not mean it as a specific depiction of the events in the Basque town, according to Mr. Rubin, who had several discussions with the artist himself about *Guernica* and his intentions for it.

"The painting obviously has political implications, but he resented the idea that people would use it as a political football," Mr. Rubin said. "He has always resisted any specific political interpretation of it in terms of particular events. He called it *Guernica* and the original inspiration for the picture was his rage at the bombing of the town. But although inspired by that event, it was not a picture of it. Rather, it was a universalized image of violence and destruction. It deals with experiences that transcend any one event or nation."

Picasso had often been petitioned, especially by leftists during the Vietnam War, Mr. Rubin recalled, to take the painting away from the United States, but he remained resolute. Also during the Vietnam War the museum had received petitions asking for removal of a text by Mr. Barr that hung near the painting, which said that Picasso denied any specific political meaning for the picture. "I took a copy of the text to Picasso, but he said, 'Leave it up,' " Mr. Rubin added.

Citing the "direct and immediate effect" that the painting had had on American art, particularly that of the early Abstract Expressionists, Mr. Rubin said: "Everyone was influenced by it. The early work of Jackson Pollock, for example, was inconceivable without *Guernica*; he was engaged in a kind of mano à mano with Picasso. That aspect of it no longer functions, but it has the eternal characteristic of any great masterpiece, in that it inspires artists indirectly. It tells them something very important and profound about what it is to be an artist, and what the nature of that enterprise is."

The painting had "a big role in changing art and the life of art in America," Mr. Rubin concluded, "and I think it has a big role to play yet in Spain. It could be a symbol of a kind of national reconciliation, since it might be seen as the final act in the closing of the civil war. It's a homecoming for Picasso also; it would mark a change in attitude toward modern art. Spain is a country that, relative to other European nations, has felt less the effect of modernism. It could symbolically annihilate the last vestiges of parochialism in matters of art in Spain."

SPAIN SAYS *BIENVENIDA* TO *GUERNICA*

JAMES M. MARKHAM

SEPT. 10, 1981—At 10:08 A.M. the movers in blue overalls deposited the huge wooden crate—stamped with the admonition "Use No Hooks" in English—in the stone pavilion a block away from the Prado museum. Civil Guards with submachine guns looked on. A helicopter clattered overhead.

The 44-year odyssey of Pablo Picasso's *Guernica* was over, and, more or less as he had wanted, his masterpiece is finally at rest in his homeland's greatest museum—or an annex of it—and in a Spain where democratic freedoms have been restored.

Guernica's secretive departure last night from New York and its unspectacular arrival here this morning aboard a regular Iberia Air Lines flight prevented Culture Minister Inigo Cavero and other officials who accompanied the crated mural from making a big political splash.

Even so, newspapers and politicians hailed what is regularly and erroneously called "the return" of the *Guernica* to Spain—where it has never been before—as a symbol of the robustness of the country's young democratic institutions. "Welcome!!!" read the banner in the afternoon tabloid *Diario 16*, which in a front-page editorial proclaimed the painting "one of the major moments of the history of our people."

Inspired and outraged by the bombing of the Basque town of Guernica during the Spanish Civil War, Picasso painted the arresting mural in a burst of activity in Paris in 1937, under commission from the Republican government in Madrid. But, after Generalissimo Francisco Franco's victory, the exiled artist insisted that the painting should go to Spain only when the country once again allowed "public liberties."

Picasso's anti-Franco stand, coupled with the Franco regime's own refusal to admit real responsibility for Guernica, made the picture taboo in Spain. But in 1968, Franco's government, accepting that Picasso was a great Spaniard, made an attempt to recover the painting. Picasso refused, saying he would never let the painting go until democracy was restored.

This remained his wish at the artist's death in 1973. After the death of Franco in 1975, a determined effort was made to recover the painting. Legal problems, objections from some Picasso heirs, challenges to Spain's democratic credentials and some reluctance by the Museum of Modern Art in New York to let the work go, dragged the matter out. A turning point came when the Spanish found a 150,000-franc receipt for a payment of commission to Picasso by the Republican government.

Despite some protests, there has been general agreement the painting should be housed among Spain's national art treasures at the Prado (which, incidentally, already has the greatest collection of paintings depicting the horrors of war by Goya and Bosch). Apart from being an antiwar picture, its presence in Spain now is seen as a moral endorsement of the country's infant democracy.

There have been protests from Málaga, where Picasso was born, and from Guernica and other Basque cities, over the siting of the mural in Madrid. "We gave our blood, and they enjoy the painting," commented José Antonio Aspuru, a Basque politician, referring to the sacrifices of his people at Guernica in 1937.

To appease such regional anger—Barcelona with its fine Picasso Museum has in the past also claimed the painting—Mr. Cavero said it was possible that the *Guernica* might eventually travel around Spain. Curators at the Museum of Modern Art are known to have insisted that today's trip be the last by the faintly cracked and much-traveled canvas, though Mr. Cavero denied promising them that it would never be moved again.

The painting was inspired by the wholesale destruction of the historic town of Guernica on April 26, 1937, by the German Luftwaffe on Franco's orders. Guernica was well behind the battle line and the attack was later admitted to be the first experiment in blanket bombing.

Picasso's composition evolved through at least eight stages over two months. The final work, in desolate tones of black, gray and white, is a savage indictment of the horrors of war: the raw anguished pain of a mother with her dead child; the desperation of a person trapped in a burning house; a mutilated body; the savage suffering of a wounded horse; a bewildered bull and a sun that has been reduced to the feebleness of a light bulb in the holocaust.

Picasso never explained all the symbolism and preferred to let people work out their own interpretation of his basic message of man's inhumanity to man.

Just before the Guernica bombing, Picasso had been commissioned by the Republican government to do a large work for the Spanish pavilion in the Paris International Exhibition. Thus the tragedy of Guernica merely stimulated him more to show his anger over the Spanish Civil War in which he vigorously opposed the nationalist forces of Franco.

Mr. Cavero said that the painting and its accompanying preparatory drawings and so-called postscripts would be unveiled to the public at the centenary of Picasso's birth—Oct. 25—in the Casón del Buen Retiro, as the columned Prado annex is called. The *Guernica* will be protected by a clear, three-sided bulletproof shield, and visitors, watched by closed-circuit television, will have to pass through metal detectors.

In November, the painting will be the centerpiece of a major Picasso retrospective exhibition that will open here, giving Spaniards a chance to learn more about an artist who has been something of a prophet without honor in his homeland. "The magnitude of Picasso's love for Spain is comparable only to the ignorance in Spain about Picasso," quipped Rafael Fernández Quintanilla, a sophisticated, 60-year-old Spanish diplomat who conducted most of the negotiations that finally brought the painting to Madrid.

Differing somewhat from an account offered by officials of the Museum of Modern Art, Mr. Fernández Quintanilla and other informants close to the negotiations said that the breakthrough occurred in April, when a Spanish government delegation threatened to take the New York museum to court if it did not deliver the painting.

Until then, according to these same sources, the Museum of Modern Art had been worried by veiled threats by some of Picasso's heirs to resort to legal action under what French law terms "moral rights" to block the *Guernica*'s transfer.

Opposition to the transfer was led by Maya Picasso, daughter of the painter by Marie-Thérèse Walter, who argued that Spain had not become fully democratic. She was occasionally supported by Claude Picasso, a son of the artist by Françoise Gilot. Jacqueline Picasso, the artist's widow, firmly supported shifting the canvas to Spain, and reportedly told a friend today: "We have won."

Mr. Fernández Quintanilla said that, after its April demarche, the Spanish government insisted that the squabbling Picasso clan was the museum's problem, not its own. And he said that at a meeting in Paris in June, Richard Oldenburg, the museum's director, and William Rubin, director of painting and sculpture, warned four of the Picasso heirs that if they attempted to block the transfer, the Museum of Modern Art intended to roll up the canvas and store it in a vault pending the court claims against it.

Faced with the possibility of being blamed for depriving the world of seeing the *Guernica*, Maya and Claude Picasso reportedly backed off, though the heirs have not issued a joint statement endorsing the move. Mr. Fernández Quintanilla said he believed that the museum's hand was strengthened by an advisory from its lawyer, Cyrus R. Vance, saying that the Picasso heirs' legal case was extremely weak.

The Casón del Buen Retiro is only two blocks from the Cortes, or parliament, which was invaded last Feb. 23 by a band of rebel Civil Guards, detonating a coup d'etat. King Juan Carlos stopped the coup by rallying wavering commanders.

Ironically, only two days before, in Paris, Roland Dumas, a lawyer designated by Picasso, had handed Mr. Fernández Quintanilla a document giving his considered judgment that Spain had become a democracy consonant with the painter's wishes. "I didn't call him back for a second opinion," joked Mr. Fernández Quintanilla today.

FOR SPAIN, *GUERNICA* STIRS MEMORY AND AWE

JAMES M. MARKHAM

NOV. 1, 1981—The silence in the presence of Pablo Picasso's *Guernica* in the Prado annex is impressive. Spaniards are given to chattering and exclaiming in museums, but, confronted with the stark mural and its shrieking victims, they are hushed, as if in church. Old men take off their berets and hold them at their sides.

Some people may be intimidated, after setting off the buzzing metal detector, by the brown-uniformed policemen who look on as they edge up to the bulletproof glass. But it seems as if the painting itself silences.

"I do not understand much of these things," whispered Eusebio Olmedo, a 76-year-old retired railway man, who wore what looked like one of his best suits to come see the *Guernica* on the second day of its exposition to the public. "But I know that I like it."

The human devastation on the canvas—an evocation of the carpet-bombing of the Basque city of Guernica in 1937—reminded Mr. Olmedo very much of what he had witnessed when a bomb landed on his house in Madrid the same year. Like Guernica, he had been on the receiving end of Franco's warplanes in the civil war: "It landed, and there was a little girl who was killed right in front of me. I remember the whole side of the building was ripped down, but in the kitchen a glass of water was still standing on a table." Picasso's woman with a dead child in her arms had brought back this memory. "I like the picture," Mr. Olmedo said, "but it makes me think of sad things." And then he cried.

Blas Podadera, a stocky 56-year-old shopkeeper, said the mural made him think of his childhood in Málaga—Picasso's birthplace—when the civil war erupted. "I was so afraid of the bombing," he said, "that my parents took me out to a village in the countryside."

"I don't understand it, but I like it," said Mr. Podadera, almost transfixed by the painting. "It's like opera: Mozart, Wagner and that other one—Vivaldi. I put it on, I don't understand it, but I like it."

The big room in the Casón del Buen Retiro, as the annex is called, permits people to mill about without jostling before the great painting. But the protective glass-and-metal encasement around the *Guernica* seems to unsettle some visitors.

"I saw it in New York, and it was better, more alive," Dolores Vazquez, a 30-year-old doctor, said. "Here it seems cold. Now it is like you put someone in a coffin, and there are its ashes. All the force of its realism is lost, because this situation is unreal."

But first-time viewers seem untroubled by the glass cage. "This is a symbol of freedom, a renunciation of violence," Jesus Alejo Fernández Montes, a student, said. "It is a reason for celebration and happiness."

One of the policeman in brown said, "It is a chapter of our history that we hope never happens again."

Since the long-exiled *Guernica* finally came to Madrid on Sept. 10, Rafael Fernández Quintanilla, the witty diplomat who dealt with the Museum of Modern Art in New York and with Picasso's heirs, has felt free to disclose some of the secrets of his protracted negotiations.

One is an elaborate bluff. To demonstrate that the Spanish government had in fact paid Picasso to paint the mural in 1937 for the Paris International Exhibition, Mr. Fernández Quintanilla had to secure documents in the archives of the late Luis Araquistain, Spain's ambassador to France at the time. But Araquistain's son, poor and opportunistic, demanded $2 million for the archives, which Mr. Fernández Quintanilla rejected as outrageous.

He managed, however, to obtain from the son photocopies of the pertinent documents, which in 1979 he presented to Roland Dumas, the Paris lawyer named by Picasso to determine when "public liberties" had been reestablished in Spain, permitting delivery of the *Guernica* to the Prado.

"This changes everything," a startled Mr. Dumas told the Spanish envoy when he showed him the photocopies of the Araquistain documents. "You of course have the originals?" the lawyer asked casually. "Not all of them," replied Mr. Fernández Quintanilla, not lying but not telling the truth, either.

The existence of the papers—and the assumption that the government possessed them—was the turning point in the legal tussle. The Museum of Modern Art, which held the painting on "loan," determined that it had more to fear from a threatened suit by Spain than it did from a hypothetical suit by some of Picasso's heirs who opposed the transfer.

Early in 1981, as his government prepared for litigation, Mr. Fernández Quintanilla knew he was skating on thin ice; he didn't actually have the documents. Then—"almost miraculously"—Araquistain's son died. His widow was unaware of the huge sum he had been demanding, and settled for $50,000.

The next day in Paris, on Feb. 20, Mr. Dumas confirmed in writing to the ambassador that in his judgment the painting should go to Spain "without further delay." On Feb. 23, right-wing soldiers in Madrid staged a coup, which failed.

In the longer view of history, another bluffer was of course Picasso, who, having been paid 150,000 French francs for the execution of the *Guernica* in 1937, had a most tenuous legal claim to it afterward. "Picasso was worried that it would fall into Franco's hands," Mr. Fernández Quintanilla said, "but at the same time, he knew it would have been false if it had become part of his estate."

Mr. Fernández Quintanilla, who has related these and other tantalizing tales in *The Odyssey of the* Guernica, just published here, is half convinced that the *Guernica* is a magical object. "In Paris, in 1937, for example," the 60-year-old diplomat said, "Picasso picked up the painting from the exhibition because no one else picked it up. Araquistain had just resigned. If Picasso hadn't picked it up, it would have ended up in the hands of the Franco government, which probably would have stored it in some basement, or burned it. Certainly it would never have become as celebrated as it is today."

The mural's gypsy life is indeed associated with a long list of strange deaths and unexpected turns of fortune. The latest occurred shortly after the *Guernica* landed here—José Manuel Pita Andrade, director of the Prado, resigned.

Mr. Pita Andrade was already weary of struggling with the state bureaucracy for greater subsidies for his financially strapped museum and was angered by an administrative decision to raise entry fees to the Prado from $1 to $2. But he was furious when he was cut off completely from the *Guernica* negotiations and quit when he learned from the newspapers that the mural was en route to Madrid and his museum.

JACKIE ROBINSON

1919–1972

By Dave Anderson

For sociological impact, Jack Roosevelt Robinson was perhaps America's most significant athlete. As the first black player in major league baseball, he was a pioneer. His skill and accomplishments resulted in the acceptance of blacks in other major sports, notably professional football and professional basketball. In later years, while a prosperous New York businessman, he emerged as an influential member of the Republican party.

His dominant characteristic, as an athlete and as a black man, was a competitive flame. Outspoken, controversial, combative, he created critics as well as loyalists. But he never deviated from his opinions.

In his autobiography, *I Never Had It Made*, he recalled the scene in 1947 when he stood for the National Anthem at his debut with the Brooklyn Dodgers. He wrote: ". . . but as I write these words now I cannot stand and sing the National Anthem. I have learned that I remain a black in a white world."

Describing his struggle, he wrote: "I had to fight hard against loneliness, abuse and the knowledge that any mistake I made would be magnified because I was the only black man out there. Many people resented my impatience and honesty, but I never cared about acceptance as much as I cared about respect."

His belligerence flared throughout his career in baseball, business and politics.

"I was told that it would cost me some awards," he said last year. "But if I had to keep quiet to get an award, it wasn't worth it. Awards are great, but if I got one for being a nice kid, what good is it?"

To other black ballplayers, though, he was most often saluted as the first to run the gauntlet. Monte Irvin, who played for the New York Giants while Robinson was with the Dodgers, and who served as an assistant to the commissioner of baseball, said: "Jackie Robinson opened the door of baseball to all men. He was the first to get the opportunity, but if he had not done such a great job, the path would have been so much more difficult.

"Bill Russell says if it hadn't been for Jackie, he might not ever have become a professional basketball player. Jack was the trailblazer, and we are all deeply grateful. We say, thank you, Jackie; it was a job well done."

"He meant everything to a black ballplayer," said Elston Howard, the first black member of the New York Yankees. "I don't think the young players would go through what he did. He did it for all of us, for Willie Mays, Henry Aaron, Maury Wills, myself.

"Jack said he hoped someday to see a black manager in baseball. Now I hope some of the owners will

New York Times Photo *New York Times Photo*

Jackie Robinson stealing home
in the fourth inning
of the 1952 game against the Cubs

see how important that would be as the next step."*

After a versatile career as a clutch hitter and daring baserunner while playing first base, second base, third base and left field at various stages of his 10 seasons with the Brooklyn Dodgers, he was elected to baseball's Hall of Fame in 1962, his first year of eligibility for the Cooperstown, N.Y., shrine.

Despite his success, he minimized himself as an "instrument, a tool." He credited Branch Rickey, the Brooklyn Dodgers owner who broke professional baseball's color line. Mr. Rickey signed him for the 1946 season, which he spent with the Dodgers' leading farm, the Montreal Royals of the International League.

"I think the Rickey Experiment, as I call it, the original idea, would not have come about as successfully with anybody other than Mr. Rickey," he often said. "The most important results of it are that it produced understanding among whites and it gave black people the idea that if I could do it, they could do it, too, that blackness wasn't subservient to anything."

Among his disappointments was the fact that he never was afforded an opportunity to be a major-league manager.

"I had no future with the Dodgers because I was too closely identified with Branch Rickey," he once said. "After the club was taken over by Walter O'Malley, you couldn't even mention Mr. Rickey's name in front of him. I considered Mr. Rickey the greatest human being I had ever known."

Robinson kept baseball in perspective. Ebbets Field, the Brooklyn ballpark that was the stage for his drama, was leveled shortly after Mr. O'Malley moved the Dodger franchise to Los Angeles in 1958. Apartment houses replaced it. Years later, asked what he felt about Ebbets Field, he replied: "I don't feel anything. They need those apartments more than they need a monument to the memory of baseball. I've had my thrills."

He also had his heartbreak. His older son, Jackie Jr., died in 1971 at the age of 24 in an automobile accident on the Merritt Parkway, not far from the family's home in Stamford.

Three years earlier, Jackie Jr. had been arrested for heroin possession. His addiction had begun while he served in the army in Vietnam, where he was wounded. He was convicted and ordered to undergo treatment at the Daytop drug abuse center in Seymour, Conn. Cured, he worked at Daytop helping other addicts, until his fatal accident.

Robinson and his wife, Rachel, had two other children—David and Sharon.

"You don't know what it's like," Robinson said at the time, "to lose a son, find him, and lose him again. My problem was my inability to spend much time at home. I thought my family was secure, so I went running around everyplace else. I guess I had more of an effect on other people's kids than I did on my own."

With the Dodgers, he had other problems. His arrival in 1947 prompted racial insults from some opponents, an aborted strike by the St. Louis Cardinals, an alleged deliberate spiking by Enos Slaughter of the Cardinals and stiffness from a few teammates, notably Fred (Dixie) Walker, a popular star from Georgia.

"Dixie was very difficult at the start," Robinson acknowledged, "but he was the first guy on the ballclub to come to me with advice and help for my hitting. I knew why—if I helped the ballclub, it put money in his pocket. I knew he didn't like me any more in those few short months, but he did come forward."

As a rookie, Robinson had been warned by Mr. Rickey of the insults that would occur. He also was urged by Mr. Rickey to hold his temper. He complied. But the following season, as an established player, he began to argue with the umpires and duel

* Frank Robinson became the first black manager. He managed Cleveland in 1975 and later managed the San Francisco Giants and Baltimore Orioles. But the lack of blacks in the front office and in the managerial ranks still is a stain on major-league baseball.

verbally with opponents in the traditional give-and-take of baseball.

As the years passed, Robinson developed a close relationship with many teammates.

"After the game we went our separate ways," he explained. "But on the field, there was that understanding. No one can convince me that the things that happened on the ballclub didn't affect people. The old Dodgers were something special, but of my teammates, overall, there was nobody like Pee Wee Reese for me."

In Boston once, some Braves players were taunting Robinson during infield practice. Reese, the popular shortstop, who came from Louisville, moved to the rescue.

"Pee Wee walked over and put his arm on my shoulder, as if to say, 'This is my teammate, whether you like it or not,' " Robinson said. "Another time, all our white players got letters, saying if they don't do something, the whole team will be black and they'll lose their jobs. On the bus to the ballpark that night, Pee Wee brought it up and we discussed it. Pretty soon, we were all laughing about it."

In clubhouse debates, Robinson's voice had a sharp, angry tone that rose with his emotional involvement.

"Robinson," he once was told by Don Newcombe, a star pitcher, who was also black, "not only are you wrong, you're loud wrong."

As a competitor, Robinson was the Dodgers' leader. In his 10 seasons, they won six National League pennants—1947, 1949, 1952, 1953, 1955 and 1956. They lost another in the 1951 playoff with the New York Giants, and another to the Philadelphia Phillies on the last day of the 1950 season.

In 1949, when he batted .342 to win the league title and drove in 124 runs, he was voted the league's Most Valuable Player award. In 1947, he had been voted the Rookie of the Year.

"The only way to beat the Dodgers," said Warren Giles, then the president of the Cincinnati Reds, later the National League president, "is to keep Robinson off the bases."

He had a career batting average of .311. Primarily a line drive hitter, he accumulated only 137 home runs, with a high of 19 in both 1951 and 1952.

But on a team with such famous sluggers as Duke Snider, Gil Hodges and Roy Campanella, who was also black, he was the cleanup hitter, fourth in the batting order, a tribute to his ability to move along teammates on base.

But his personality flared best as a baserunner. He had a total of 197 stolen bases. He stole home 11 times, the most by any player in the post–World War II era.

"I think the most symbolic part of Jackie Robinson, ballplayer," he once reflected, "was making the pitcher believe he was going to the next base. I think he enjoyed that the most, too. I think my value to the Dodgers was disruption—making the pitcher concentrate on me instead of on my teammate who was at bat at the time."

In the 1955 World Series, he stole home against the New York Yankees in the opening game of Brooklyn's only World Series triumph.

Pigeon-toed and muscular, wearing No. 42, he ran aggressively, typical of his college football training as a star runner and passer at the University of California at Los Angeles in 1939 and 1940. He ranked second in the Pacific Coast Conference in total offense in 1940 with 875 yards—440 rushing and 435 passing.

Born in Cairo, Ga., on Jan. 31, 1919, he was soon taken to Pasadena, Calif., by his mother with her four other children after his father had deserted them. He developed into an all-round athlete, competing in basketball and track in addition to baseball and football. After attending U.C.L.A., he entered the army.

He was commissioned a second lieutenant. After his discharge, he joined the Kansas City Monarchs of the Negro National League as a shortstop.

"But if Mr. Rickey hadn't signed me, I wouldn't have played another year in the black league," he said. "It was too difficult. The travel was brutal. Financially, there was no reward. It took everything you made to live off."

If he had quit the black leagues without having

been signed by Mr. Rickey, what would he have done?

"I more than likely would have gone to coach baseball at Sam Houston College. My minister had gone down there to Texas as president of the college. That was about the only thing a black athlete had left then, a chance to coach somewhere at a small black college."

Instead, his presence turned the Dodgers into the favorite of black people throughout the nation.

"They picked up 20 million fans instantly," said Bill Russell, the famous center of the Boston Celtics who was professional basketball's first black coach. "But to most black people, Jackie was a man, not a ballplayer. He did more for baseball than baseball did for him. He was someone that young black athletes could look up to."

As the Dodgers toured the National League, they set attendance records. But the essence of Robinson's competitive fury occurred in a 1954 game at Ebbets Field with the rival Giants.

Sal Maglie, the Giants' ace who was known as "The Barber" because of his tendency to "shave" a batter's head with his fastball and sharp-breaking curve, was intimidating the Dodger hitters. In the Dodger dugout, Reese, the team captain, spoke to the 6-foot-195-pound Robinson.

"Jack," said Reese, "we got to do something about this."

Robinson soon was kneeling in the on-deck circle as the next Dodger batter. With him was Charlie DiGiovanna, the team's adult batboy, who was a confidant of the players.

"Let somebody else do it, Jack," DiGiovanna implored. "Everytime something comes up, they call on you."

Robinson agreed, but once in the batter's box, he changed his mind. Hoping to draw Maglie toward the first-base line, Robinson bunted. The ball was fielded by Whitey Lockman, the first baseman, but Maglie didn't move off the mound. Davey Williams, the second baseman, covered the base for Lockman's throw.

"Maglie wouldn't cover," Robinson recalled. "Williams got in the way. He had a chance to get out of the way but he just stood there right on the base. It was just too bad, but I knocked him over. He had a Giant uniform on. That's what happens."

In the collision, Williams suffered a spinal injury that virtually ended his career. Two innings later, Alvin Dark, the Giants' captain and shortstop, retaliated by trying to stretch a double into a third-base collision with Robinson.

Realizing that Dark hoped to avenge the Williams incident, Robinson stepped aside and tagged him in the face. But his grip on the ball wasn't secure. The ball bounced away. Dark was safe.

"I would've torn his face up," Robinson once recalled. "But as it turned out, I'm glad it didn't happen that way. I admired Al for what he did after I had run down Williams. I've always admired Al, despite his racial stands. I think he really believed that white people were put on this earth to take care of black people."

Ironically, after the 1956 season, Robinson was traded to the rival Giants, but he announced his retirement in *Look* magazine. Any chance of his changing his mind ended when Emil (Buzzy) Bavasi, then a Dodger vice president, implied that after Robinson had been paid for the bylined article, he would accept the Giants' offer.

"After Buzzy said that," Robinson later acknowledged, "there was no way I'd ever play again."

He joined Chock Full O'Nuts, the lunch-counter chain, as an executive. He later had a succession of executive posts with an insurance firm, a food-franchising firm and an interracial construction firm. He also was chairman of the board of the Freedom National Bank in Harlem and a member of the New York State Athletic Commission.

In politics Mr. Robinson remained outspoken. He supported Richard M. Nixon in the 1960 presidential election. When Mr. Nixon and Spiro T. Agnew formed the 1968 presidential ticket, however, he resigned from Governor Rockefeller's staff, where he was a special assistant for community affairs, to campaign for Hubert H. Humphrey, the Democratic nominee.

Mr. Robinson described Mr. Nixon's stand on civil rights in 1960 as "forthright" but denounced the Nixon-Agnew ticket as "racist."

Mr. Robinson's niche in American history is secure—his struggle predated the emergence of "the first black who" in many areas of American society. Even though he understandably needed a Branch Rickey to open the door for him, Branch Rickey needed a Jackie Robinson to lead other blacks through that door.

Mr. Robinson died of a heart attack at his home in Stamford, Conn., on Oct. 24, 1972. He was only 53 years old.

A HERO'S FUNERAL

STEVE CADY

JACKIE ROBINSON received a hero's burial in New York City on Oct. 28, 1972, mourned as a man of courage by those who knew him and solemnly saluted as a legend by strangers who never saw him play.

"Today we must balance the tears of sorrow with tears of joy," the Rev. Jesse L. Jackson of Chicago told a celebrity-laden congregation of 2,500 at the Riverside Church in his eulogy to major-league baseball's first black player.

Mr. Jackson, founder and president of People United to Save Humanity, noted that the body corrodes and fades away, but the deeds live on: "When Jackie took the field, something reminded us of our birthright to be free."

These words, delivered over a silver-blue coffin draped with red roses, accurately reflected the mood of what amounted to an outpouring of interracial respect that softened grief with pride and hope.

Sargent Shriver, Robert Finch, Governor Nelson Rockefeller, Mayor John Lindsay and hundreds of other dignitaries and sports figures attended the interdenominational services at the Gothic church with its 30-story tower overlooking Grant's Tomb and the Hudson River at Riverside Drive and 122d Street. Family mourners included Robinson's mother, his widow, Rachel, and their two children, Sharon and David.

Also in attendance were Bowie Kuhn, commissioner of baseball; Roy Wilkins, executive director of the National Association for the Advancement of Colored People; and A. Philip Randolph, labor union executive.

Later, tens of thousands of persons lined the streets of Harlem and Bedford-Stuyvesant in bright sunshine to watch a mile-long funeral cortege carry Robinson back to Brooklyn, the borough where he made baseball history 25 years ago as a second baseman for the Dodgers.

Robert Finch, the White House counselor, headed a 40-member delegation representing President Nixon.

Three daughters and the grandson of Branch Rickey, the late Dodger president who gave Robinson his chance to break the color barrier in major-league baseball, also were in the gathering.

So were such diverse celebrities as Joe Louis, Dick Gregory, Hank Aaron and Vida Blue. The services were conducted by the Rev. Ernest T. Campbell, with music by the 60-voice Canaan Baptist Choir.

Governor Rockefeller, whose family financed construction of the stone church, was an honorary pallbearer. Active pallbearers included five of Robinson's former Dodger teammates: Jim Gilliam, Don Newcombe, Ralph Branca, Pee Wee Reese and Joe Black. Roy Campanella, another teammate during Robinson's 10-year career with the Dodgers (1947–1956), attended in a wheelchair.

He was buried in Cypress Hills Cemetery, a few miles from the site of the old Ebbets Field. As one of "The Boys of Summer," the subject of Roger

Kahn's book, Robinson was the National League's rookie of the year in 1947 and most valuable player in 1949. He averaged .311 as a hitter in 10 seasons en route to a place in baseball's Hall of Fame. In those 10 years, the Dodgers won six pennants.

Before the services yesterday, Kahn looked at the swooping television cameras and harried V.I.P.-coordinators and confessed he had run out of words.

"How can you sum him up in two sentences?" said Kahn. "After you've done it four times in eight hours on television and radio, it becomes kind of mechanical. But I did have one good moment. Somebody asked me what Jackie Robinson had done for his race, and I said: 'His race was humanity, and he did a great deal for us.' "

In his eulogy, Mr. Jackson appeared at times to be rebutting any notions that Robinson was merely a pawn of the white establishment, that he was nothing more than the first black man to expose himself to American bigotry through baseball.

"Jackie was neither a puppet of God nor one of other men," he said. "Progress does not roll in on the wheels of inevitability. In order for an ideal to become a reality, there must be a person, a personality, to translate it. He had options. He didn't have to do what he did."

Even the children seemed to sense what Robinson meant to them.

"They made fun of him, teased him," said Floyd Branch, one of a number of youngsters excused from eighth-grade classes at Joan of Arc Junior High School on 93d Street so they could attend the services. "We talked about him in school, they said he meant history to the black people."

Across the street in the Union Theological Seminary, where the dignitaries began gathering two hours before the funeral, Wilson Woodbeck quietly explained why he was there.

"Jackie was a few years ahead of his time," said Woodbeck, public relations director for the National Association of Negro Musicians. "It's always time to do what's right, but the power structure does not always see it that way. Jackie carried so many burdens, took so much abuse. So many times, he lost sight of himself for others."

More celebrities crowded into the waiting rooms as Bayard Rustin, the civil rights leader, tried to smooth out the logistical problems. There were too many important people to count or keep track of: Willie Mays, Bill Russell, Hank Greenberg, Bill Veeck, Howard J. Samuels, Ernie Banks, Warren Giles, Ed Sullivan, Mike Burke, Peter O'Malley. Larry Doby, the American League's first black player (1948), was there. So were Carl Erskine, Gene Hermanski and Billy Loes, Dodger teammates.

"You know what Jackie would have said?" somebody asked. "He'd have said, 'We need some umpires in here to straighten this traffic out.' "

They did have umpires, like Tom Gorman, but not in uniform on this occasion.

The baseball men, from ex-players to league presidents and club presidents, waited for the signal to go over to the church and talked of Robinson's magic, of days like the one when Russ Meyer of the Chicago Cubs challenged him to steal home at Ebbets Field.

"Jackie was bouncing up and down on the basepath," somebody said, "and Meyer waved his arm toward the plate. Jackie took off and stole home."

Later, toward the end of his long eulogy, Mr. Jackson would bring tears and sobs from many in the church with another reference to baserunning.

"His feet danced on the basepaths," said the speaker, and a woman's voice in the congregation answered, "Yes, sir, that's right."

"But it was more than a game."

"Yes, it was."

"Jackie began playing a chess game, he was the black knight."

"Yes, sir, all right, go ahead."

"In his last dash, Jackie stole home and Jackie is safe."

"Yes, sir, you're right."

"His enemies can rest assured of that."

"Yes they can, hallelujah."

"Call me nigger, call me black boy, I don't care."

"Hallelujah!"

The eulogy was over and Roberta Flack, the pop recording artist, closed the musical part of the services by singing "I Told Jesus," a traditional Negro spiritual.

Then it was time for Robinson to go back to Brooklyn, a legend borne through the tenement-lined streets of Harlem and Bedford-Stuyvesant.

WHAT JACKIE ROBINSON MEANT TO AN OLD FRIEND

PEE WEE REESE*

IT WAS October, maybe November, in 1945 and I was on a navy transport ship coming back from overseas, from Guam. I'd played shortstop for the Brooklyn Dodgers for three seasons, then into the navy "for the duration," as they used to say during the war. Now I was finally coming home and somebody on board told me that the Dodgers had signed a black ballplayer. And that was the first time I can remember being aware of Jackie Robinson's arrival on the baseball scene.

Actually, I had heard of Jack before—as a football player at U.C.L.A. But now when his name came up in a baseball context, I didn't give it a whole lot of thought. You know, I reacted kind of instinctively to the news, something like "You've got to be kidding," because the color line was still keeping black players out of the major leagues.

But, except for that initial reaction, I didn't give it too much thought. I had been away for three years and was more concerned at the moment with getting myself back to work. Then I realized that Robinson could run and hit and play shortstop, and some of the guys started kidding me about my job. Welcome home, Pee Wee.

After that, it was more than a year before I saw him in a baseball uniform—a year that Jackie spent at Montreal in the International League and that I spent in Brooklyn with the Dodgers. Then in spring training in 1947, we had our camp in Santo Domingo in the Dominican Republic that year, and I finally got my first look at him. What was my first impression? That he was big, awfully big. And fast, awfully fast.

Anyway, Jack was there that year; and, once we realized he was there to stay, I began to realize that there were more problems facing him than I'd thought at first.

One thing I remember was the petition some guys passed around. But I wouldn't sign it. I wasn't trying to think of myself as being the Great White Father, really, I just wanted to play the game, especially after being in the navy for three years and needing the money, and it didn't matter to me whether he was black or green, he had a right to be there, too.

Then you'd hear a lot of insults from the opposing benches during games, guys calling him things like "nigger" and "watermelon-eater," trying to rile him. But that was when Jackie Robinson started to turn the tables: You saw how he stood there at the plate and dared them to hit him with the ball, and you began to put yourself in his shoes. You'd think of yourself trying to break into the black leagues, maybe, and what it would be like—and I know that I couldn't have done it.

In a word, he was winning respect.

That was the decisive thing about Jack: He had all kinds of class. That's the reason he was selected

*Pee Wee Reese spent his entire career in the major leagues with the Dodgers—15 years in Brooklyn and one in Los Angeles. He was the shortstop, the captain, the "little colonel" of the team, and he played alongside Jackie Robinson. Since retiring, he has been active as a baseball broadcaster. He is a member of the Baseball Hall of Fame.

by Branch Rickey, and that's the best way to remember him.

Playing alongside him for so many years—10 years, actually, until the Dodgers left town after the 1957 season—I realized his impact. For one thing, he was one of the best pressure players I ever saw and he became instrumental in those Dodger pennants because of it. The old saying applied to him perfectly—"When the going gets tough, the tough get going." And when the chips were down, he was at his best. So after a while, I didn't pay the slightest attention to his being black. At first, he'd been a big black guy who came into a white man's game. But after two or three years, with all that class and talent, he was just a great ballplayer alongside me.

He had a big impact on all the Dodgers, too. In Birmingham and some other southern towns, traveling up from Florida, it was rough. Even during the season, I remember we got to St. Louis for a series, and that might've been the last place in the league where the black players were segregated, where they stayed in one hotel in the black section and the other guys stayed in the regular hotel.

Jack got off the train one day there and said, "I'm going to the hotel with you." Roy Campanella and some of the other black guys told him not to do it, they said they were doing OK and so don't rock the boat. But Jackie joined us on the team bus, went right into the hotel and registered, and Campy and the others followed. That was Jack—he got the job done.

Finally, Jack had a big impact on me personally. We had many conversations about things, and I'd ask, "Do you think blacks and whites will ever get along smoothly?" And he'd say, "Yes, it'll work, give it some time."

I used to say to him later, "You know, I didn't particularly go out of my way just to be nice to you." And Jack would say, "Pee Wee, maybe that's what I appreciated most—that you didn't."

As a ballplayer? Super. Jack was super. For a guy his size, well over 6 feet and maybe 215 pounds, he had the quickness of a guy 5 foot 10. In a rundown, you couldn't run him down. I don't know how many bases he would have stolen if our club ran more. . . . He didn't have the greatest arm in the world, but making the double play, he'd straddle the bag and dare you to hit him.

For all that, he was a fun guy. Sure, he could be a little nasty at times, but who couldn't? I never saw him take a drink in my life. He was just a great friend, a great baseball player and a great influence on our lives—a lot greater than I ever could have guessed that day on the ship coming home from Guam when somebody told me the Dodgers had signed a black ballplayer.

DEATH OF AN UNCONQUERABLE MAN

RED SMITH

IN THE scene that doesn't fade, the Brooklyn Dodgers are tied with the Phillies in the bottom of the 12th inning. It is 6 P.M. on an October Sunday, but the gloom in Philadelphia's Shibe Park is only partly due to oncoming evening. The Dodgers, champions-elect in August, have frittered away a lead of 13½ games, and there is bitterness in the dusk of this last day of the 1951 baseball season. Two days ago, the New York Giants drew even with Brooklyn in the pennant race. Two hours ago, the numbers went up on the scoreboard: New York 3, Boston 2. The pennant belongs to the Giants unless the Dodgers can snatch it back.

With two out and the bases full of Phillies, Eddie Waitkus smashes a low, malevolent drive toward center field. The ball is a blur passing second base, difficult to follow in the half light, impossible to catch. Jackie Robinson catches it. He flings himself headlong at right angles to the flight of the ball, for an instant his body is suspended in midair, then somehow the outstretched glove intercepts the ball inches off the ground.

He falls heavily, the crash drives an elbow into his side, he collapses. But the Phillies are out, the score is still tied.

Now it is the 14th inning. It is too dark to play baseball, but the rules forbid turning on lights for a game begun at 2 o'clock. Pee Wee Reese pops up. So does Duke Snider. Robin Roberts throws a ball and a strike to Robinson. Jackie hits the next pitch upstairs in left field for the run that sets up baseball's most memorable playoff.

Of all the pictures left upon memory, the one that will always flash back first shows him stretched at full length in the insubstantial twilight, the unconquerable doing the impossible.

The word for Jackie Robinson is *unconquerable.* In *The Boys of Summer,* Roger Kahn sums it up: "In two seasons, 1962 and 1965, Maury Wills stole more bases than Robinson did in all of a 10-year career. Ted Williams' lifetime batting average, .344, is two points higher than Robinson's best for any season. Robinson never hit 20 home runs in a year, never batted in 125 runs. Stan Musial consistently scored more often. Having said those things, one has not said much because troops of people who were there believe that in his prime Jackie Robinson was a better ballplayer than any of the others."

The point is, he would not be defeated. Not by the other team and not by life.

Another picture comes back. Robinson has taken a lead off first basc and he crouches, facing the pitcher, feet fairly wide apart, knees bent, hands held well out from his sides to help him balance, teetering on the balls of his feet. Would he be running? His average was 20 stolen bases a year, and Bugs Baer wrote that "John McGraw demanded more than that from the baseball writers."

Yet he was the only baserunner of his time who could bring a game to a stop just by getting on base. When he walked to first, all other action ceased. For Robinson, television introduced the split screen so the viewer at home as well as the fan in the park could watch both the runner on first and the pitcher standing irresolute, wishing he didn't have to throw.

Jackie Robinson established the black man's right to play second base. He fought for the black man's right to a place in the white community, and he never lost sight of that goal. After he left baseball, almost everything he did was directed toward that goal. He was involved in the foundation of the Freedom National Banks. He tried to get an insurance company started with black capital, and when he died he was head of a construction company building housing for blacks. Years ago a friend, talking of the needs of blacks, said, "Good schooling comes first."

"No," Jackie said, "housing is the first thing. Unless he's got a home he wants to come back to, it doesn't matter what kind of school he goes to."

There was anger in him, and when he was a young man he tended to raise his falsetto voice. "But my demands were modest enough," he said, and he spoke the truth. The very last demand he made publicly was delivered in the mildest of terms during the World Series just concluded. There was a ceremony in Cincinnati saluting him for his work in drug addiction and in his response he mentioned a wish that he could look down to third base and see a black manager on the coaching line.

Seeing him in Cincinnati recalled the Dylan Thomas line that Roger Kahn borrowed for a title: "I see the Boys of Summer in their ruin." At 53 Jackie was sick of body, white of hair. He had survived one heart attack, he had diabetes and high blood pressure and he was going blind as a result of retinal bleeding in spite of efforts to cauterize the ruptured blood vessels with laser beams. With him were his wife, Rachel, their son, David, and daughter, Sharon. Everybody was remembering Jack Jr., an addict who beat the heroin habit and died at 24 in an auto accident.

"I've lost the sight in one eye," Jackie had told Kahn a day or so earlier, "but they think they can save the other. I've got nothing to complain about."

Unconquerable is the word.

ARTHUR RUBINSTEIN

1887–1982

In the pantheon of 20th-century pianists, Mr. Rubinstein's place is assured as one of the titans. With his remarkable technique, golden tone and musical logic, with the élan he brought to his interpretations, with his natural, unforced and unflurried style, he was unique—as, indeed, every great artist is. What Mr. Rubinstein offered, above all others, was the ability to transmit the joy of music.

"What good are vitamins?" Mr. Rubinstein demanded when he was asked, at the age of 75, to explain his youthful vivacity and fire. "Eat a lobster, eat a pound of caviar—live! If you are in love with a beautiful blonde with an empty face and no brains at all, don't be afraid. Marry her! Live!"

The great pianist conscientiously applied the prescription to himself, and everything he did was con brio. There was dash to his rich mode of life, just as there was to his making of sumptuous music.

From his earliest to his latest days he was the embodiment of the grand manner. Even at an age when most musical artists slow down, he was giving concerts on an average of one every three days; he was recording furiously out of his vast repertory; he was the life of innumerable parties and luncheons; he was the irrepressible talker and raconteur; he was, ineffably, Rubinstein.

The supreme and serious musician that most Americans knew was Rubinstein since 1937, the year of his historic reappearance at Carnegie Hall that marked a new dedication to his art. "It is said of me that when I was young I divided my time impartially among wine, women and song," he remarked afterward. "I deny this categorically. Ninety percent of my interests were women."

There was an element of exaggeration to this comment, but it was certainly true that the post-1937 Rubinstein was a mature artist. His special fusion of Romanticism and intellectualism caught the public fancy. Audiences could not hear enough of him; his concerts were standing room only; his recordings sold in the millions; he performed all over the world at fees of $6,000 and more a concert, then the highest fee for any artist before the public.

Rubinstein moved with confident ease through a repertory ("my musical valise") that started with Mozart, proceeded through Beethoven and the entire 19th century and wound up with such moderns as Hector Villa-Lobos, Igor Stravinsky and Karol Szymanowski. Chopin, however, was his specialty, and it was as a Chopinist that he was considered by many without peer.

As superb an interpreter of Chopin as he was, he counted himself also as a Mozart man. He returned to Mozart "on my knees" in late life.

Undeniably, part of the Rubinstein manner (and mystique) was his pianistic pedigree, which went back to many legendary 19th-century musicians. Rubinstein's first big-name enthusiast was Joseph

Sam Falk/The New York Times

Joachim, the violinist friend of Brahms. His early piano training came from Karl Heinrich Barth, a pupil of Franz Liszt, who had been taught by Carl Czerny, who had in turn been a pupil of Beethoven. Rubinstein, moreover, drew personally from such titans as Camille Saint-Saëns, Ignace Jan Paderewski, Eugene Ysaÿe, Claude Debussy, César Franck, Artur Schnabel and Vladimir de Pachmann.

In his youth Rubinstein tended to perform what he called "the crowd pleasers"—Tchaikovsky, Rachmaninoff and Liszt—and his piano belched fire. With maturity, however, he turned more and more to Chopin, his fellow Pole, whose compositions of delicate expression called for an artist who could make the piano breathe.

Rubinstein was so spontaneous and exuberant that he declined to think of his artistry as work. "I can play 10 hours," he remarked in his late 70s. "I don't feel that making art should be called work. Work is something disagreeable that you have to do."

That statement, like so many of Rubinstein's about himself, was true and not true; for this most gifted of pianists worked very hard by any other standards than his own to perfect and project his artistry, even if he liked to create the impression that it was all effortless, as it indeed sounded to audiences.

In a recording session for RCA Victor Records, in Webster Hall in New York, he would play and replay a piece until he was satisfied that it was his best; and before a concert he would practice, particularly passages that he thought he might have difficulty with. Nothing less than perfection was tolerated.

Practice for its own sake, however, was not Rubinstein's notion of how to extract music from the printed notes.

"I was born very, very lazy and I don't always practice very long," he said once. "But I must say, in my defense, that it is not so good, in a musical way, to overpractice. When you do, the music seems to come out of your pocket. If you play with a feeling of 'Oh, I know this,' you play without that little drop of fresh blood that is necessary—and the audience feels it."

On another occasion he explained his philosophy this way in his tumbling English: "At every concert I leave a lot to the moment. I must have the unexpected, the unforeseen. I want to risk, to dare. I want to be surprised by what comes out. I want to enjoy it more than the audience. That way the music can bloom anew. It's like making love. The act is always the same, but each time it's different."

One of the elements of freshness in a Rubinstein concert was also the evident happiness with which he played.

"Don't tell Hurok"—Sol Hurok, his impresario of many years—he admonished one interviewer, "but I'd play the piano for nothing, I enjoy it so much."

This was of the essence of the pianist's attitude toward life generally, which he expressed by saying: "Happiness is to live. It is the only happiness possible."

This total joie de vivre undoubtedly lent a special quality to Rubinstein's music ("Music is not a hobby, not even a passion with me; music is me") and lifted him above his contemporaries. Moreover, underneath his panache he possessed insight and a capacity for musical growth that markedly enriched the work of his later years. For example, he recorded the Schumann *Carnaval* at 65; and when he recorded the piece 10 years later "there was no question but that it was a better performance," in the opinion of Harold C. Schonberg, *The New York Times* music critic.

"His colleagues consider him a miracle, geriatric experts mumble when they talk about him and nobody will put up much of an argument when he is called the greatest living pianist," Mr. Schonberg wrote on Rubinstein's 75th birthday. He continued: "Vladimir Horowitz may have a more glittering technique, Rudolf Serkin may have a better way with German music, Rosalyn Tureck more of an affinity for Bach, Sviatoslav Richter for Prokofiev and Scriabin, and Claudio Arrau may have a bigger repertory.

"But no pianist has put everything together the way Rubinstein has. Others may be superior in specific things, but Rubinstein is the complete pianist."

To see and hear Rubinstein at a concert was to be in the presence of majesty. A 5-foot-8-inch figure resembling a cube on sticks in impeccable evening clothes strode briskly on stage and received the homage that his subjects' thunderous applause connoted. He bowed slightly from the waist, and his pearl-gray hair glistened in the stage lights and his blue eyes darted around the hall.

Before the applause subsided, he seated himself on the piano bench and carefully draped the tails of his coat over its back. Then he raised his face, masked in concentration, until his nose tilted upward at a 45-degree angle. His back was erect. He kneaded his fingers. He bowed his head for a moment as the last coughs died out and then he eased into the keyboard.

Sometimes in playing he seemed about to overwhelm the instrument as he rose off the bench; other times, when the music was lyrical, he moved his arms and hands in graceful symmetry. His eyes appeared fixed on a distant object.

"I like to look up over the piano," he explained, "so I can listen and follow the lines of the piece. Looking at your fingers for accuracy is too confusing. I'd rather miss a few notes than play by phrase instead of as a whole."

Rubinstein's sound, or tone, was elegant. One critic described it as "a firm, clear, colorful sonority that is one of the miracles of 20th-century pianism."

"He simply cannot produce an ugly, forced or jagged sound no matter how heavily he comes down on the keyboard," this observer continued. "As soon as his fingers touch the keys, one knows that the Old Master is at work; and the penetrating tone rolls out and fills the house."

The pianist himself did not know how to account for the distinctiveness of his tone. Contributing to it, however, was his physique, considered perfect for a pianist. His torso was short and muscular; his arms were long, his biceps those of a blacksmith and his fists like a longshoreman's. He would spread his spatulate fingers, whose tips were callused from years at the keyboard, to encompass the 12 notes from C to G—two more than normal. Moreover, his pinkies were nearly as long as his index fingers, and his elongate thumbs extended downward at an obtuse angle.

Another ingredient of Rubinstein was an unusually fine ear that, among other things, permitted him to spin music through his mind.

"At breakfast, I might pass a Brahms symphony in my head," he said. "Then I am called to the phone, and half an hour later I find it's been going on all the time and I'm in the third movement."

This phenomenon was the basis for a game Rubinstein's friends liked to play with him, in which they would randomly name musical excerpts that he would then play. He was seldom stumped.

"Rubinstein is the only pianist you could wake up at midnight and ask to play any of the 38 major piano concertos," according to Edouard van Remoortel, the conductor.

The pianist was usually labeled a Romantic, but that was an error, in the opinion of many critics. Mr. Schonberg, for example, wrote: "Rubinstein today is called—mistakenly—a Romanticist. And he is—in relation to the younger pianists, just as he was a classicist in relation to the older ones. Today's new style is represented by the young spit-and-polish pianists, who never hit a wrong note, who come to music with the utmost dedication and who all tend to sound alike."

If Rubinstein had not been a pianist, his friends were certain that he could have made an enjoyable living as a stand-up comedian and raconteur. A born extrovert, he loved to meet people, to act out his stories and to tell them in the eight languages in which he was fluent—English, Polish, Russian, French, German, Italian, Spanish and Portuguese. When he told a story, he performed all the roles with appropriate facial expressions and gestures—climbing atop a chair or table and beating time if the anecdote were about a conductor, or simpering coquettishly if it were about a young woman. Even lighting a cigar (he prudently laid in a big stock of Upmanns just before the United States' break with Cuba) was an act worth watching.

One of his stories concerned the time he and Albert Einstein played a violin-and-piano sonata. The physicist missed a cue in one passage and came in four beats late. They started again, and once more Einstein missed the cue. Rubinstein turned to his partner in mock exasperation and exclaimed, "For God's sakes, professor, can't you even count up to four?"

In another Rubinstein story, which he delighted to tell on himself, he was making a recording in Webster Hall when a porter in overalls carrying a pail and mop came up to the piano, watched silently and then asked, "Do you do this professionally?" Rubinstein always said that at this point he was for the only time in his life nonplussed.

In addition to a sensitive appreciation of the best in cigars, haute cuisine and wines, the pianist was a connoisseur of painting who was able to say, "I knew Picasso before he was Picasso and I was Rubinstein."

Apart from his Picassos, Rubinstein's collection was dominated by Vuillards, Chagalls and Dufys.

Rubinstein's start in life was much more modest than his eventual eminence. Born in Lodz, Poland, on Jan. 28, 1887, he was the youngest of seven children of Ignace Rubinstein, a textile producer, and Felicia Heyman Rubinstein. (Late in life, Rubinstein became vain about his age, and advanced his birthdate to 1889, according to those who knew him.)

He took piano lessons at the age of 3, and at 4 he was performing in public and flourishing a calling card that read "Artur the Great Piano Virtuoso." A little later, tired of being asked if he were a relative of the great Anton Rubinstein, he inscribed the words "No Relation" on the cards.

By the time he was 8 he had exhausted the teaching resources of the Warsaw Conservatory of Music and was sent to Berlin to perform for Joseph Joachim, the violinist. Impressed by the boy's precocity, the friend of Brahms and Schumann assumed responsibility for his study. He was the conductor at Rubinstein's Berlin debut at the age of 11.

There followed recitals in Dresden, Hamburg, Warsaw (where he played under the baton of Emil Mlynarski, his future father-in-law) and a visit to Paderewski in Switzerland.

Among Paderewski's guests was a Boston critic who brought Rubinstein to the attention of the Knabe Piano Company, which underwrote his first American tour in 1906. His showpiece was Saint-Saëns's Concerto No. 2 in G for Piano and Orchestra, which he performed at Carnegie Hall. The tour lasted 75 concerts and it was not a critical success. He returned to Europe disheartened.

He went back to school, so to speak, by playing in private for Paderewski. "I just played and listened, and he would tell me little things," Rubinstein recalled. He did not return to the concert stage until 1910. He lived in Paris, had a series of love affairs, became friends with artists and writers.

"I had, often, lobster and champagne, and often I had nothing," he said. "Once I spent two days on a park bench because I could not pay my hotel bill. But I also had wonderful chamber music with Ysaÿe and Thibaud and Casals."

Back as a performer, Rubinstein established himself in Europe as a top-ranking pianist. In the early part of World War I he gave recitals for the Allied cause. At that time he became so enraged with the German treatment of the Poles and the Belgians that he vowed never to appear in Germany, and he never thereafter did.

A turning point in Rubinstein's career came in 1916, when he made a tour of Spain. It was a grand success. Four concerts stretched to 125. And from there he went to South America.

"They loved me for my improvised way of playing," he recalled. "It was not really intentional with me, because I could not even then work out a conception and stick to it. But to them it was a relief from what they called 'the pedants.' "

Convinced that he would now be a hit in the United States, he reappeared in Carnegie Hall in 1919, but his reception was lukewarm. "When I played in the Latin countries they loved me because of my temperament," he said later. "But when I played in England and America, they felt that because they had paid their money they were entitled to hear all the notes. I dropped too many notes in those days, and they felt they were cheated."

Rebuffed but not chastened, he returned to Europe, where he divided his time between concerts and high living with the international set. He was as frequently sitting on the Riviera or palling around with Picasso, the Prince of Wales, an attractive woman or Ernest Hemingway as he was sitting before a concert grand.

The late 1920s were decisive for the pianist's later career. First, in 1928, he met 15-year-old Aniela Mlynarski, daughter of the Polish conductor. According to them both it was love at first sight, although they were not married until 1932. Second, Rubinstein began recording. Third, he began to take stock of himself as an artist. The result was the end of his days as a playboy and intensive study and practice—six, eight, nine hours a day. In the process he brought discipline to his abundant temperament and intelligence to his grand manner.

"I didn't want my kids to grow up thinking of their father as either a second-string pianist or as a has-been," he remarked.

Rubinstein's early recordings (now collectors' items) called renewed attention to him, and Mr. Hurok, his agent, persuaded him to have another go at the United States. When he made his reappearance at Carnegie Hall on Nov. 21, 1937, he was acclaimed as "a giant who had transformed his joie de vivre into the strongest alloy of his music." It was the start of the love affair between American music lovers and Rubinstein, which never thereafter abated.

In World War II he moved his family from Paris to Beverly Hills, Calif., where he ghosted at the piano for movie actors who played the roles of Schumann, Liszt, Brahms and others. The films were *I've Always Loved You* (1946), *Song of Love* (1947), *Night Song* (1947), *Carnegie Hall* (1947) and *Of Men and Music* (1950), in which he appeared as himself.

Meanwhile, Rubinstein toured the world—North Africa, China, Japan, Indonesia, Australia, Europe. In 1958 he returned to Warsaw after an absence of 20 years, and the audience cheered and applauded and brought him back from the wings 10 times after he played Chopin's "Polonaise" in A flat.

Rubinstein became an American citizen in 1946 and moved to New York in the 1950s.

As his career came to a halt, because of his extreme age and loss of sight, Rubinstein found time to concentrate on his autobiography, which he had promised to write for Alfred A. Knopf many years previously. In 1973 the first volume, *My Young Years,* was published, and was followed in 1980 by *My Many Years.* In his last years his constant companion was his secretary, Annabelle Whitestone.

His American audience had a chance to enjoy Rubinstein the man and the musician once more when he was interviewed on a 90-minute television special, as part of the Great Performances series, entitled "Rubinstein at 90."

The pianist's other honors included Commander of the Legion of Honor, officer of Portugal's Order of Santiago, Commander of the Chilean Republic and Commander of the Crown of Belgium's Order of Leopold I, and he wore Spain's Cross of Alfonso XII.

Mr. Rubinstein died quietly in his sleep at his home in Geneva, Switzerland, on Dec. 20, 1982. He was 95.

A NATURAL, BORN TO PLAY THE PIANO

HAROLD C. SCHONBERG

FROM THE very beginning, the career of Arthur Rubinstein followed a consecutive line, and the chances are that in essentials his piano playing changed very little during the years. Rubinstein used to tell reporters that he did not really start to practice until the 1930s; that he was a sloppy pianist before then, relying on personality and temperament. But his earliest recordings do not bear out that statement; and, in any case a few wrong notes, or even handfuls of wrong notes, have nothing to do with a pianist's spirit and imagination.

The fact is that Rubinstein never had to practice very much. He was a natural, born to play the piano. A natural pianist is one who seems to be born with tone and technique, whose fingers automatically resolve any patterns no matter how difficult. Other pianists have to work six or seven hours a day to keep their fingers loose, but for a natural pianist three or four readings are enough to put a piece of music in his mind for life. Rubinstein was one of those.

He gloried in playing the piano. He was an extrovert, an actor, a "ham," if you will. Certainly he was always cognizant of the impact he could make on an audience. But fortunately he had pure musical instincts, and allied to his undoubted theatricality was a mind that saw the architecture of a piece of music, the correct shape of a phrase, the nuances that lie beneath the printed note.

And then there was the fabulous Rubinstein tone: a large, golden sound that made one forget the piano was a percussive instrument. Like any great pianist's, his sound could not be duplicated, for part was muscular, part a projection of personality, part an ability to hear himself. He was one of those pianists—there are very few in any generation—for whom the instrument is an extension of self, welded to finger, arm and body, ears, brain and heart.

His repertory was huge. When musicians grow old, they almost invariably curtail their repertories to the pieces they know and love best. In this, Rubinstein was no exception. But it seemed that he loved almost everything—certainly the entire body of 19th-century music. As a Chopinist he was superb, and he played substantially that composer's entire oeuvre. The only important Chopin works he left unrecorded were the two books of études. But he also was supreme in Schumann, Liszt, Brahms, Franck and Mendelssohn, and he played Debussy and Ravel with complete conviction.

In his younger years he played everything from Beethoven on, and introduced many new works. Then, in the last years of his life, he had the courage to engage several large-scale works that for some reason he had never played in public—Schubert's enormous B-flat Sonata, for one; and several piano concertos by Mozart. For a man of his age, this took extreme courage. But Rubinstein had complete—and justified—confidence in himself.

Nobody in our time, it is safe to say, communicated the same degree of sheer joy in playing. Concert life has become very serious, and the younger musicians tend to be grave philosophers, interested primarily in the weightiest kind of music. Rubinstein's musical mind was as good as anybody's, but he never made a mystique out of music. He loved music, loved playing the piano and was eager to transmit that love. The analogy with love is fair. Rubinstein treated the piano like a beloved woman, and there was something actually sensuous in his approach to it.

Stylistically he has been called a Romantic, and it is true that his musical philosophy had many elements of Romanticism in it. But his was a Romanticism strongly tempered by classicism, in that he seldom exaggerated, in that the musical lines sang freely and unfussily and in that the overall conception was never cluttered by detail.

In short, he completely avoided the typical exaggerations of some of the Late Romantic pianists. Indeed, he had nothing but scorn for that kind of playing. Rubinstein represented the best of the old school and the best of the new. From the old school he took the idea of the piano's being a singing instrument. And he helped shape the new school of piano playing by his insistence on clarity, steady but supple rhythm and a strong, arched line.

Thus in addition to having a strong involvement with music (which the old pianists had), Rubinstein also had taste and an unerring feeling for proportion (which not all the old pianists had). He did not use music to bolster his ego. Quite the reverse. With all his flair, exuberance and temperament, he nevertheless did his best to transmit the message of the composer as purely and honestly as possible.

RUBINSTEIN'S RETURN TO WARSAW [1958]

A. M. ROSENTHAL

WARSAW AND Arthur Rubinstein met again after 20 years, and they brought tears to each other's eyes.

Rubinstein likes to say he always loved Warsaw concert audiences but always feared them, too. Krakow was gentle but Warsaw was different; Warsaw was harder, more sophisticated.

Only once had a Warsaw audience been known to stand to greet a musician and that was for the pianist who became president, Ignace Paderewski.

On June 11, 1958, however, the members of the audience stood for Rubinstein. They stood when he walked onto the stage under the great chandeliers of the Philharmonia Concert Hall. They rose again with a surge with the last chords of Chopin's "Polonaise." They stood and cheered and shouted and sang "May He Live a Hundred Years" and 10 times they brought him back from the wings.

This is not simply a story of a triumphal concert by a great pianist. It is a story of the reunion of a man and a city and of the emotions that swept them both.

Arthur Rubinstein was born in the shabby textile-manufacturing city of Lodz, in central Poland, 69 years ago. He is an American now, but a Polish writer said with a shrug, "He is the best so he is a Pole."

In the old days Rubinstein came back again and again to Poland from tours that made his one of the great names in music. But he never came back after 1938. There was World War II and occupation and the murder of his family in Lodz by the Germans.

("They wanted him to play in Lodz this time," said Mme. Aniela Rubinstein, his 49-year-old wife, "but he couldn't." That was too much. That he couldn't do.")

During the long, icy years after the war, Rubinstein felt he could not come back. But the pull of old friends and old memories never left him. After 1956 the Rubinsteins were able to see some of their friends and relatives abroad, and he felt that things had changed enough in Poland for him to come back.

The Rubinstein concerts—the three that had been scheduled grew to six, including a rehearsal at which 1,200 people showed up—meant a variety of things in Poland.

For the young musicians who crowded around him and for a whole new generation of music lovers it meant a chance to hear a man they had known only through records.

For musicians and writers who were Rubinstein's friends it was an almost painfully poignant link with youth and memories. They kissed him and hugged him and asked delightedly, "You really do remember me?"

For the Rubinsteins these days in Warsaw have been an experience both joyous and racking.

Friends and relatives unseen for two decades crowded into the couple's rooms all day long to talk, to cluck admiringly at their 11-year-old son and 13-year-old daughter or just to sit awhile, drink tea and look.

The sight of old friends brought Rubinstein to tears and so did the sight of Warsaw. It was not just stretches of wrecked streets, but the rebuilding of beloved squares and churches and other old and dear things.

"They asked me what I thought of Warsaw now," said Rubinstein before he left on June 12. "And I said, 'Divinely impractical!' Oh, Poles!"

A RUBINSTEIN SPECTACULAR [1975]

DONAL HENAHAN

The Program

NEW YORK PHILHARMONIC. Pension Fund Concert conducted by Daniel Barenboim with Arthur Rubinstein, piano soloist. At Avery Fisher Hall.

"Leonore" Overture No. 3. . . . Beethoven.
Piano Concerto No. 4 in G. . . . Beethoven.
Piano Concerto No. 1 in D minor. . . . Brahms.

GRANDPA AND Grandma, it is safe to predict, will gather their clan about them on some distant evening and tell how they heard Arthur Rubinstein at the age of 89 play the Beethoven Fourth and the Brahms First concertos back to back on one New York Philharmonic program on February 3, 1975. And how the puissant Arthur not only performed the mighty works note-perfectly but also played with overwhelming conviction, ardor and musical authority.

But of course the old folks will be embroidering what actually took place at Avery Fisher Hall. The performances were not quite note-perfect. Otherwise, however, let the legend-making talk stand. Mr. Rubinstein, never one to overlook a chance to challenge himself (since there are so few other pianists capable of it), rounded off his evening with nothing less than Brahms in D minor, arguably one of the two or three most punishing works in the Romantic repertory.

Has there ever been another performer such as this one? Leaving aside the gerontological phenomenon of a man who, as he pushes 90, still has the fingers for such a night's work, consider the purely musical miracle. Both the Beethoven and the Brahms existed on the highest plane as the pianist and the orchestra, sympathetically led by Daniel Barenboim, joined in going directly to the heart of the music.

Mr. Rubinstein's tone, while certainly less robust than in the past, was still cushioned and unsplintering even in the loudest double-handed attacks on the keyboard. For a night one could almost forget that Avery Fisher Hall is not a pianist's paradise. And the scales, rippled off with the familiar Rubinstein gift for phrasing beautifully even in bravura runs, were quite amazing.

But the miracle is not how accurately or fluently Mr. Rubinstein still plays, at what must be considered a fairly ripe old age, but the spirit that he conveys in his music-making. In a rather grubby period of history he continues to show us what it means to live in the world as it is and savor it.

Now and then, especially in the Beethoven first movement and in the cadenza (the longer of the two Beethoven wrote for this movement), Mr. Rubinstein found himself in the technical thickets and had to cut his way out. He did so, of course, with aplomb. And as the murderous pages of the Brahms flipped by, he seemed actually to gain power and facility, so that, arriving at the last movement's brief cadenza (marked *molto accelerando* at the end), the pianist was able to put on an outburst of power that capped the performance excitingly.

Still, what one will remember, probably, is the slow movements, each a communion between Mr. Rubinstein and his dearest friend—you or me, that is. In the Brahms he seemed to be saying "This, my dears, is what this movement has come to mean to me. Listen. Isn't it lovely?" And in the Beethoven he was the incomparable orator taming the growling orchestral mob with sweet, serene reason.

Finally, unable to appease the multitude with what seemed to be endless returns for bows, Mr. Rubinstein gave a solo encore, Chopin's Polonaise in A Flat (Op. 53). He might have gone on all night if someone had thought to break out the cigars and brandy.

THIS AGELESS HERO, RUBINSTEIN [1976]

DONAL HENAHAN

ONE DAY, in what we may only hope is the distant future, an archeologist sifting through the detritus of Western civilization may come upon certain puzzling artifacts. A pair of tennis sneakers, perhaps, with 4-inch platform soles. A goose-quill pen with a felt tip. A petrified senator holding a Pentagon budget request. Or, if Western civilization is lucky, some piano recordings made by Arthur Rubinstein when he was on the brink of 90 and still playing with astonishing vigor, virtuosity and panache. Like Heinrich Schliemann pondering the myths and legends of Homeric Troy, the excavator will have a mystery on his hands. Did such a hero really live in those benighted times?

We know the answer, of course. Rubinstein made his New York debut 70 years ago at Carnegie Hall, performing with the Philadelphia Orchestra on Jan. 8, 1906. But actually he has been playing in public for 85 years. Although he did not make his formal debut until he was 7 years old, he was performing for small audiences of family friends in his native city of Lodz, Poland, by the age of 4 and at 6 was appearing at charity concerts. He had taken to the piano unbidden and uncoerced, at 3, when his parents brought an old upright into their home so that two older sisters could take lessons.

The other day, while Rubinstein was stopping off in New York during a midwinter break in his concert schedule, I spent several exhilarating though eventually quite sobering hours with him in his suite at the Drake Hotel. The first minutes, as usual, were taken up in making sure the visitor had the most comfortable, the softest seat in the room. Rubinstein insisted on a plain, hard chair for himself. "All my life I have been sitting up straight, you know. Which reminds me of a story, a very funny story. . . ." (And off he goes. If you have questions to ask Rubinstein, you had better get them in early or it's no use.) "Not long ago in Boston, they gave me what is called the Agnon Award. You know who Agnon was? S. Y. Agnon, the old Hebrew poet who died a few years ago. He won a Nobel Prize and they named this award for him. Well, as it happened, I had been giving a concert in Jerusalem some years ago and a friend of mine brought Agnon back to see me. I said to him, 'Do you like music?' And he said, 'I don't know, this is the first time in my life that I go to a concert. But I *like* how you sit so straight at the piano.' "

You are never far from a good laugh when you are around Rubinstein, but his is not a mindless good humor. An Academy Award–winning documentary film about his career, made in 1968 but released here only last year, was titled *Love of Life,* and it is true, he says, that "I love life unconditionally." He shrugs impatiently. "But it is not that I walk around stupidly smiling [pantomime of a slack-jawed, grinning lout]."

Thomas Mann, hardly one to be impressed by a stupid smile, called Rubinstein "that civilized man," and a story of my own may illustrate his deep-grained civility. The city was Buffalo, where on a bitter midwinter's night four years ago I went to talk with Rubinstein on the occasion of his 85th birthday, the trip being necessary because his concert schedule at that time was to bring him no nearer to Manhattan. I arrived at his hotel in the evening at what I believed was the agreed-upon hour, called his room and found to my horror that Rubinstein had not been told of our date. A communications breakdown somewhere in his entourage, I later learned. Moreover, the voice on the phone instantly suggested itself as that of a man who had been aroused from sleep. He grasped finally that I was from a newspaper, but apparently thought it was a local one, and my attempts to explain did not penetrate. But he said, "Please, can you give me 15 minutes before coming up?"

When I arrived at his room, unexpected and, I am quite sure, unwanted, Rubinstein had gotten into a dark blue suit, with the rosette of a Commander of the Legion of Honor in a lapel, and was ready to receive me, all apologies. He had the flu, he said, and his wife had been calling him to tell him to cancel his tour. "But when I am at the piano, my sickness goes away and that makes me terribly happy. I won't cancel." Despite all, he managed to be vivacious and full of stories I had not heard before. Since then, I often have thought of Rubinstein in that Buffalo hotel room, trying to sleep off the flu, and at the mercy of whoever might pick up the house phone. And I try to imagine how gracious I would have been under similar circumstances. Not very, I'm afraid.

Grace under pressure is a gift not given to most people, and for a long time now Rubinstein has been graceful under the ultimate, inescapable pressure of being old. How did he get that way? And more puzzling, how does he stay that way?

To answer those questions with confidence, one would have to know exactly how to solve the old equation in which nature and nurture are both unknown factors. As far as he knows, Rubinstein does not come from particularly long-lived ancestors, although the pogroms and wars that swept over Poland in the last century or so seem to have made that question academic. His six brothers and sisters, for instance, disappeared along with six million other Jews during World War II. Physically and mentally, he has been a living refutation of the old wives' tale about the weakness of children born to older fathers: He was the seventh child, born when his father was past 40, a ripe age in the Poland of that day.

Until now, at least, he has suffered from almost none of the usual human infirmities. He has no arthritis or rheumatic aches, and subscribes to no fanatical health-food regimen. He arises at 8 or thereabouts, hungry for breakfast, but first does about 20 minutes of setting-up exercises. However, he gets his most strenuous exercise by playing the piano—which is perhaps exercise enough if you play as flamboyantly as Arthur Rubinstein. According to his wife and other intimates of long standing, he takes no pills of any kind other than vitamin C. For many years he has enjoyed the best wines and the most expensive cigars (two or three a day, only with coffee) and, in his sybaritic approach to daily existence, has long been the Winston Churchill of the piano. His adherence to the Pleasure Principle is no doubt rooted somehow in his genes and nurtured by a lifetime of adulation. But he also feels there is a pragmatic philosophical basis for his cheery temperament and open nature, and his ability to sustain a youthful outlook into what is, chronologically, very old age.

In fact, the civility and wholehearted humanism that his audiences sense and find so appealing is completely unsentimental in origin and grew out of Rubinstein's clear-eyed analysis, early on, of a hard world. He is a firm agnostic. "When I was a child, I looked and I did not see any god. I doubt if Moses saw him, really. All those little girls who saw the Virgin. All that, no, a lie." He laughs and waves one of the largest hands ever placed at the disposal of a great pianist. "They did not convince me. Jeanne d'Arc, a charming story. But not my idea of what is.

Look at those Irish people now, who produce such fine poetry—civilized, musical people, like you and me. But one side is Protestant and the other is Catholic, so they kill each other for it. The Arabs and the Israelis, what do they want of each other? The Arabs have Mohammed, Israel has another fellow, so they say, sorry, but we must kill you for that. So, long ago, I decided I did not see any god. We are put here on earth without being asked if we want to live, just like any animal but more unfortunate because we also have this brain." Rubinstein's voice has lost its rich timbre by this time and dropped to an enervated whisper. Then, jerking himself up straight, he brightens.

"I felt I was left alone in the world, *forced* to live." And here he launches into one of his favorite stories, about the time when he tried to hang himself. He made the attempt in Berlin at the age of 21 when his career had hit bottom. It was a gray day in 1908. He was out of money and being dunned by hotels and restaurants. He could not get concert engagements. He was not, for the moment, in love. So he tried to hang himself in his bathroom. Fortunately, the rope (his bathrobe belt) broke and sent him sprawling ("If I saw today such a scene on television, I would roar with laughter," he comments in his memoirs). And he found himself born again, looking at the world with an ecstasy that, 68 years later, he manages to sustain.

According to Max Wilcox, who has produced all of Rubinstein's recordings since 1959, the Beethoven sessions "went terribly well." Done in 1975 in London with Daniel Barenboim conducting the London Philharmonic, the five concertos were recorded in seven and a half sessions, a total of not quite 19 hours. "That would be very quick for anybody, but for someone who's nearly 90, well . . ." Wilcox pauses to think. "Has there ever been a reigning piano virtuoso at this age? I don't think so." Saint-Saëns, Isidor Philipp, Francis Planté and others played in public when they were approaching or even past 90, but apparently at nothing like Rubinstein's level.

For years Stephen Borell traveled with Rubinstein as his piano tuner and sometime page turner. He finds it easy to grow lyrical about both the artist and the man. "He has such a spirit, such a sense of humor, such a natural graciousness. And that tone. . . ." The Rubinstein tone, full and sonorous at any volume level, has been one of the distinctive features of his playing from the beginning, and piano experts have never given up trying to explain it. Borell knows all the theories—the thick pads of flesh at the fingertips, the arm-weighted stroke, the pliant wrists—but he has a close-up observation to offer, too.

"Sitting beside him and turning pages, I was able to watch what he does, and I discovered something surprising. You know the way he likes to rise off the piano bench, lift his hands high over the keys and bring them down with what you'd expect to be a terrible crash? Well, I noticed that, just before hitting the keys, he stops for a split second and then pushes on into them. It's done so fast you can barely see it, but that's what happens." Rubinstein enjoys the dramatic impact that he can provide with such high-handed tactics, but it is not done purely for the eyes, as you can prove by closing your own when he is about to strike. In fact, an almost imperceptible pause before pushing into the keys can act to cushion the tone, and if you have a piano handy you might even be able to check out Borell's theory for yourself. "The man doesn't just sit down at a strange piano and start playing," Borell goes on. "He experiments for a while to find out what its potential is, what its character is. Then he adjusts with incredible speed. That's typical of his whole approach to life, too." No man is a hero to his valet, as the saying goes, but Arthur Rubinstein is a hero to his piano tuner.

Everywhere he goes someone presses a new award or honorary degree upon him. In 1975 he was invited to take part in a symposium on "The Majesty of Man" at the Stanford University Medical Center, to discuss the mysteries of human creativity. His fellow panelists were scientists, including two Nobel

Prize winners, Linus Pauling and Joshua Lederberg. Poor innocent scientific souls. As anyone could have told them, Rubinstein does not appear on panels, he performs on them. According to a report in the *Stanford Observer,* the pianist waited until the others had carried on for a time about "how 1/10-volt nerve impulses travel at 250 miles per hour through the body," and then began to talk about "his concept of happiness and the importance of emotion." As the reporter noted with unconcealed glee, Rubinstein stole the show. Recalling the event now, Rubinstein chortles over how "they wanted to poke my brain and examine me—they seemed amazed I was still alive. Look, he still can walk and talk! By Jove, I tell you I had a good time. I wanted them to tell me in which part of the body the soul is located but they couldn't."

In 1975, for the first time in 16 years, Rubinstein went back to Poland, where he visited Lodz, an event that was documented in a film titled *The Comeback.* He had been quite apprehensive about returning after so many years, during which both his homeland and he had changed so much. But everything went well. "It is a very touching country, you know, a very proud little country. They have something in common with the Spaniards, a certain noble pride. A bit stupid, some practical people might say. They will go a thousand strong against an army of a million Russians, fighting with forks and spoons and I don't know what. They are already proud to know that, if they fall on the battlefield, there will be beautiful poems written in their honor. They have kept that, even now. They are the only ones who opposed Hitler from first to last."

Rubinstein seldom goes on for long without talking politics, especially international politics in relation to Israel, "where I have been playing for nothing, you know, for the last 30 years." He is outraged by the treatment Israel has received in the United Nations and has as little respect for that body as for all the other bodies that misgovern the people of the world—his people, all of them his personal friends. "Look here, the United Nations, if you will allow me to say it, is an assembly absolutely of rascals. It is supposed to be a gentlemen's club. So in this club they have had a Stalin, heh, heh, heh. A Mr. Kadar who has killed I don't know how many thousands of people in Hungary. The Czech fellow whom I would like to kick. And all those others who are not ripe for such a club, who don't know what it is all about. An absurdity, really."

Rubinstein, who was living in Paris with his wife and two children (subsequently two more arrived) when World War II broke out, picked up his family and moved to the United States, like so many European refugee artists, among them Mann, Bartók, Schoenberg, Hindemith and Stravinsky. And like so many of them, Rubinstein moved to California, where he settled in Beverly Hills in what was, by that time, his 32d home. He became a United States citizen in 1946 but now lives—when he is not making the international hotel circuit on his incessant tours—in homes in Marbella on Spain's Costa del Sol and in his prewar house on the Avenue Foch in Paris, close to the onetime home of Debussy.

Many of Rubinstein's old friends have deserted him by now and while the ranks have been filed by the multiplying millions of us who know him through his music-making, the absentee list is a glorious one.

Man and boy, Rubinstein has been close to virtually all the important artists and public figures of the century. He was, it is startling to realize, a protégé of Joseph Joachim, the man to whom Brahms dedicated his Violin Concerto, and of Paderewski, the only pianist ever to be the political leader of his country (one makes this statement in full recognition of the fact that Harry Truman, Richard Nixon and others have been known to sit at the instrument on occasion). He was befriended by Saint-Saëns, rubbed elbows and minds with Hemingway and Picasso ("I knew him before he was Picasso and I was Rubinstein") and championed the music of such friends as Stravinsky, Albéniz, Granados, Falla, Szymanowski, Ravel, Poulenc and Milhaud when these names were considered part of the accursed avant-garde. He even—yes, even this—knew Sol Hurok before Hurok was an impresario. Now, of course, the Great Sol is gone, too, and Rubinstein is lonelier for it.

"I met Hurok when I was 40, you know, and we were both struggling to begin. Chaliapin, who was my dear friend—my big brother almost, I adored him—invited me to his hotel here in New York for breakfast. This was in those for me very dark 1920s, you see. And there was a little man sitting in the corner. Chaliapin treated him terribly, told him to sit there, don't speak, things like that. I played 'Petrushka' on the piano and the little man—who, of course, was Hurok—thought it was fine."

At the time of meeting Hurok, Rubinstein was middle-aged and a notoriously erratic artist. Although he had made his New York debut in 1906 and had returned in 1919 for a second try at the brass ring on the American concert carousel, he had made something less than an unforgettable impression. Technically, he insists (although there are those who will dispute him on the basis of existing recordings), he was not first-class. So, after his marriage at 43 in 1932 to Aniela Mlynarski, he made up his mind to become a responsible fellow. He cloistered himself in an Alpine village and practiced 12 to 16 hours a day, trying to rebuild from the ground up a technique that could match his innate musicality and flair. "You see, before that I was a little too interested in other things at certain periods of my life. I adored literature. I enjoyed hearing intelligent people talk and that stopped me from wanting to practice." (As others remember it, and as Rubinstein documents it in his memoirs, the problem was not so much literature as women, wine and song, to revise slightly the traditional recipe for oats-sowing.)

"So, here was this little fellow Hurok, at that time putting on low-priced concerts here in the Hippodrome. Mischa Elman, the circus, horse shows, Galli-Curci, everything—oh, how it smelled. Hurok remembered me from Chaliapin's and came to see me. 'I have Titta Ruffo for a concert but he is able to sing only a few arias, so would you play two items on his program?' Yes, I would. As it happened, Ruffo was not in voice, but I was in voice and the audience made me give two encores in the middle of the concert. Hurok was very impressed. He thought my kind of personality was absolutely right for the country at that moment and so we made the career together, Hurok and I."

Hurok was a shrewd judge of performing chemistry and it is not hard to see now why Rubinstein has enjoyed such a large and fanatically devoted audience. Above all, he pays attention to a work's "line," its overall meaning and design and, as Sir Thomas Beecham once reminded an orchestra, "That's all the audience really cares about." Rubinstein himself remembers that "even in the days when the critics used to complain most about details, the line was there, it jolly well was there." However, the line must be supported by innumerable nuances of phrasing, accentuation, color changes and dynamic gradations or it will fail to please discerning listeners; and the fact is that musicians have been Rubinstein's most dedicated fans throughout his career. It is not given to every pianist to please both the finest musicians of his time and Sol Hurok's millions.

Mrs. Rubinstein, a lively blond woman who is 23 years younger than her husband, had joined the conversation by this time and put in, "We miss him very much, Hurok. He was so funny about that 'Artur' business." Rubinstein nodded and immediately slipped into his Sol Hurok impression, rumbling in the familiar tone of the Ukrainian immigrant showman: "Ah, my dear Artoooor." Hurok insisted on calling Rubinstein Artur for publicity purposes because he thought the name had more class than plain Arthur. "But I always signed my name in Spain as Arturo, in Slavic countries as Artur, and in America I want to be Arthur. It's silly to make a fuss and I feel guilty about it, but I always preferred that."

At the word *guilty,* Mrs. Rubinstein looks at her husband reproachfully. "This man, he is ridden with guilt. He feels guilty about the wars, about being a survivor when so many others are gone.

And he even feels guilty about not having played some great pieces of music." Rubinstein nodded glumly. "Yes, I will die with the feeling that there are at least a hundred works that I might have played—the Sixth Sonata of Prokofiev, for instance, also the First and Third concertos. But, you know, I really never wanted to play the last sonatas of Beethoven in public. I think these are private works, for the drawing room. The public pretends to love them but really it gets rather bored. The slow movement of Op. 111 is sublime but in the concert hall, unless it is played in an absolutely sublime way, I want to fall asleep."

Such Rubinstein attitudes as that have always gotten him in trouble with people who consider themselves more serious than he about music. But while he may be temperamentally in tune with much of the piano literature that these more somber souls admire, he has found much of it unsuited to his public needs. Until recent years, for instance, he played little Mozart and less Schubert, though when he got around to recording a Schubert sonata, he chose the greatest and most challenging of them all, the posthumous B-flat. He isn't very good at explaining why he favored Brahms or Chopin. "I always had the feeling that music is good to be heard but not too much spoken about. That's why I didn't write so much about music in my book. I find them pretty funny, actually, those little books that musicians write about how they play." He casts his astonishingly pliable face into the caricature of a philosopher-pedant and ponderously intones, "I was reading one day more of Schopenhauer, and then I played the Chaconne a little—ah, slower." A throwaway joke, delivered with the timing of the born comedian.

Despite a career-long addiction to the music of Beethoven, Brahms and Schumann, Rubinstein seems to have grown increasingly disturbed about the nation that produced them. He has not played in public on German soil since the beginning of World War I, when he became outraged at the treatment of the Belgians by the German invaders. For a while after the Holocaust of World War II, he even refused to get out of planes when they touched down in Germany for brief stopovers.

However, in 1963, he gave a special concert in the Netherlands, just across the German border, to which busloads of his German admirers were brought, simply to show that he clearly distinguishes the people of any country from the fools and scoundrels who rule them. He has faith in them, even now. "Why should I be cynical? My public is individuals, made up of people who love music. I hate all the *nations* in the world because can you ever really believe one word that their leaders say? Hypocrites! Russia, for instance—250 million Russians, and 240 million are slaves. Revolutions are always made by decent people, but right away . . ."

Because Rubinstein has never been able to treat music as one of the abstract sciences, his ideas about composers and their works seem to conflict at times or overlap into politics. Even Brahms, his beloved Brahms, can be annoyingly Prussian. "Do you know that Brahms broke off his friendship with a Viennese doctor, a great patron of the arts, because that doctor once invited Massenet to dinner? Massenet had come to Vienna to produce his opera *Werther.* Brahms said to his friend, 'How could you tolerate that dirt, that so-called music? You are no friend of mine.' He didn't even go to the doctor's funeral. I was absolutely furious when I read that. I spat blood, because I adore Brahms. But he was always rude, terribly rude, a vicious fellow, if you like. But what can you do about it? You know how rude he was to Clara Schumann at the close of her life? Last year I swallowed eight volumes of Max Kalbeck's biography of Brahms, absolutely, day by day. He tells those stories on Brahms." Rubinstein talks heatedly, not about some historical figure, but about a contemporary whose life became intertwined, through Joachim, with his own.

We have moved to the dining table by now, and Mrs. Rubinstein is revealing to me one of the possible answers to the mystery of her husband's physical and mental resilience—his eating habits. "For many years I have cooked for him. I am a professional cook, I love it. You know, this new fat-free French cuisine they are talking about, I like it very much because I have always done it. I take off all the grease, all the fats, and at the end I put in a little cream here and there."

The Rubinsteins laugh a lot, loudly and with gusto, and seem to enjoy each other's jokes enormously. "For 43 years, all my married life, I have cooked that way. He is a very easy fellow to feed. Good appetite. He loves chicken, so I have a million ways to cook it. He could eat it every day and not complain. He doesn't very much like red meat." Rubinstein drops his jaw, hunches over his plate and gives his imitation of your average American gourmand tearing at a bloody steak, complete with caveman growls and digestive sound effects. But then the winds of Rubinstein's moods change again. "You know," he says quietly, "I would like to continue writing—but no, it is too late now, I am too old, and my eyes . . ."

Mrs. Rubinstein winces, and the reason quickly becomes clear: Rubinstein is losing his sight. "Shall we tell?" Mrs. Rubinstein asks her husband. He smiles and shrugs. "Why not, after all," she goes on, "when it is really more wonderful that you play without . . ." And so the suspected but still startling facts come out.

"For the last six concerts I couldn't see the keys," Rubinstein says. The trouble, which has been growing increasingly more serious in the last few years and now affects both eyes, seems to date from a time when Rubinstein was hospitalized by an attack of shingles. A type of eye failure that is not helped by glasses, it is caused by a hardening of blood vessels in the eyeball. Rubinstein has been left with only dim peripheral vision. Moreover, as has become increasingly evident during our conversation, the hearing in his right ear is just about gone.

But Rubinstein's reservoir of good humor seems bottomless and his élan does not desert him even at this dark turn of events. "Of course, it is very bad for me, this thing of the eyes, because, next to music and my family, I love books the most. So my wife will have to read to me now. We are making plans for this new kind of life. Naturally, I regret this very much, but what can you do? I am getting old and these things happen to one at this time. I still will enjoy every day, and keep on playing if I can." Fortunately, he has a photographic memory in which are stored hundreds of pieces, including about 40 concertos.

Something has been nagging at my own memory during this discussion and, after leaving the Rubinsteins, I go home and look up my notes from a 1972 interview in Buffalo with the pianist. I find a few sentences that hadn't seemed important enough to include in the article I wrote then but that now leap out of the page. Rubinstein had been good-naturedly defending his flamboyant style of playing, his way of leaning back, gazing at the ceiling and lifting his hands high off the keyboard. "As you know, I was always the champion of wrong notes, but I don't care because I need the impact that I can get in this way," he had said. "I must confess, in fact, that my dream is to play whole pieces, maybe whole programs, without looking at the keys once."

The dream is now reality. Perhaps there will again be a few wrong notes? Perhaps. But Rosina Lhevinne, herself one of the famous pianists and teachers of her time, long ago had the last word on that. To a student who mentioned Rubinstein's occasional wrong notes, Lhevinne responded dreamily, "Ah, yes, but *what* wrong notes."

BERTRAND RUSSELL

1872–1970

By Alden Whitman

Three passions, simple but overwhelmingly strong, have governed my life: the longing for love, the search for knowledge and unbearable pity for the suffering of mankind."

In those words Bertrand Arthur William Russell, the third Earl Russell, described the motive forces of his extraordinarily long, provocative and complex life. But only one yearning, that for love, was fully satisfied, he said, and only when he was 80 and married his fourth wife, Edith Finch, then a 52-year-old American.

Of his search for knowledge, he reflected, "a little of this, but not much, I have achieved."

And as for pity: "Echoes of cries of pain reverberate in my heart. Children in famine, victims tortured by oppressors, helpless old people a hated burden for their sons and a whole world of loneliness, poverty and pain made a mockery of what human life should be. I long to alleviate this evil, but I cannot, and I too suffer."

Russell's self-assessment scanted his lifelong passionate skepticism, which provided the basis for his intellectual stature. Possessing a mind of dazzling brilliance, he made significant contributions to mathematics and philosophy for which, alone, he would have been renowned. Two works, *The Principles of Mathematics* and *Principia Mathematica,* both published before World War I, helped to determine the direction of modern philosophy. Russell's name, as a result, was linked with those of such titans of thought as Alfred North Whitehead and Ludwig Wittgenstein.

Largely for his role as a philosopher, Russell received the Nobel Prize for Literature in 1950. A year earlier, he had been named by King George VI to the Order of Merit, whose British membership is limited to 24 persons. These honors cast into strange relief the fact that in 1940 a New York State Supreme Court justice ruled him unfit to teach at City College.

Unlike some generative thinkers, Russell epitomized the philosopher as a public figure. He was the Voltaire of his time, but lacking in the Sage of Fernay's malice. From the beginning to the end of his active life, Russell engaged himself with faunlike zest in the great issues of the day—pacifism, rights for women, civil liberty, trial marriage, new methods of education, Communism, the nuclear peril and war and peace—for he was at bottom a moralist and a humanist. He set forth his views on moral and ethical matters in such limpidly written books as *Marriage and Morals, Education and the Social Order* and *Human Society in Ethics and Politics.*

He posed awkward questions and gave answers that some regarded as less than commonsensical. However, from his first imprisonment (as a pacifist in World War I) to his last huzza of dissent (as a Zola-like accuser of the United States for its involve-

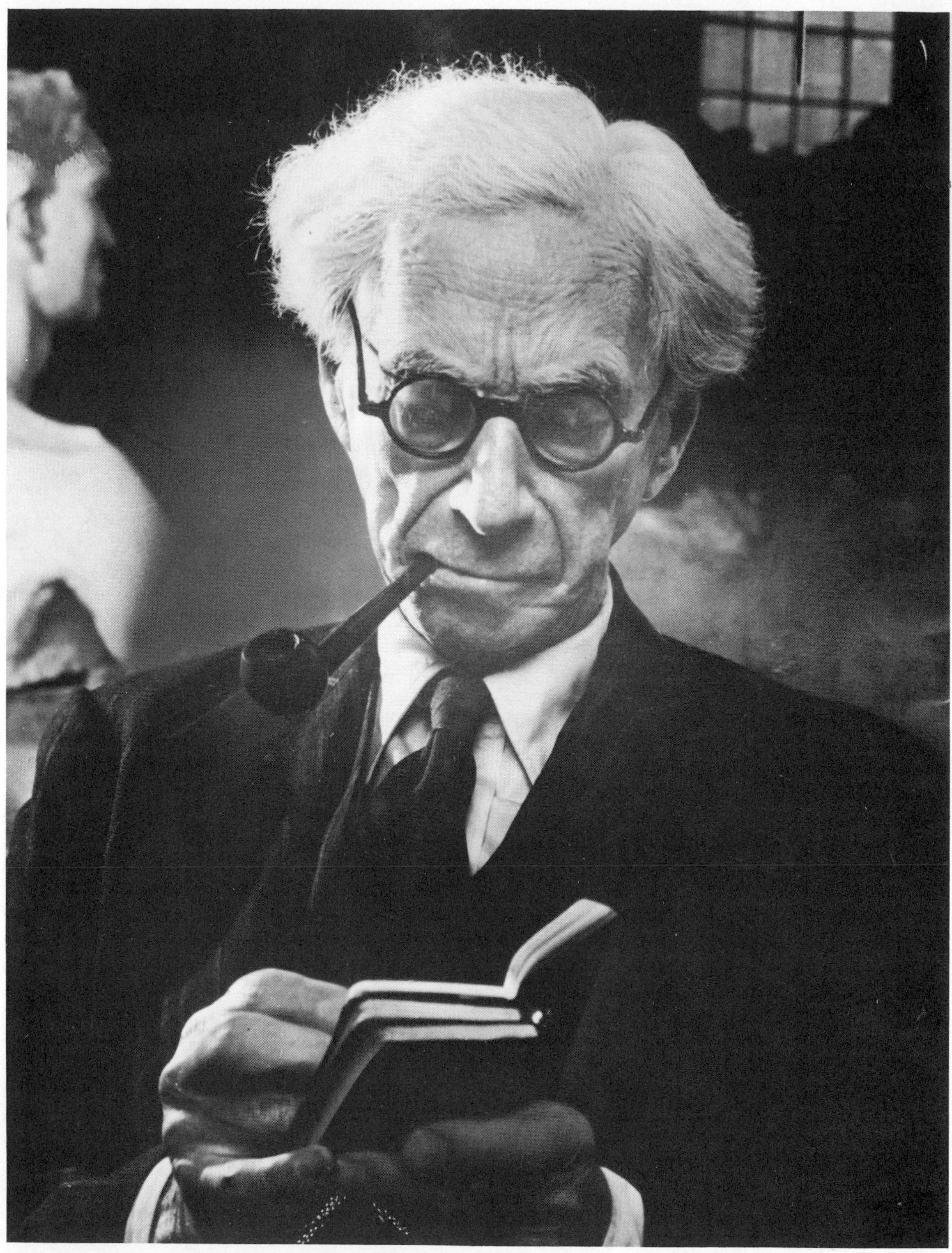

Ida Kar/Camera Press

ment in Vietnam), he scorned easy popularity and comfortable platitudes. He was, indeed, untamable, for he had a profound faith in the ultimate triumph of rationality, which he was certain he represented in an undidactic fashion.

"I don't think, taking it generally, that I have a dogmatic temperament," he insisted. "I am very skeptical about most things and I think that skepticism in me is deeper than positive statements. But, of course, if you get into propaganda you have to make positive statements."

His active involvement in causes (and the scores of positive declarations he made in their behalf) earned him a good deal of abuse and even ridicule. "England's wisest fool" was what his deriders said.

Some of the severest criticism was directed at Russell for his condemnation of United States policy in Vietnam and for his attempts to show this country guilty of crimes against humanity there. Oddly, the criticism came not only from war partisans but also from the Soviet Union, a professed ally of North Vietnam, which Russell believed lacked staunchness because it was under the thumb of the United States.

His vitriolic stand on Vietnam stemmed from concern over the possibility of a nuclear war. Although he had once suggested the threat of a preventive nuclear war to impose disarmament on the Soviet Union, his views sobered in the mid-1950s and through the Committee of 100 in Britain he strove to arouse mass opposition to atomic weaponry. For his part in a London demonstration in 1961 he went unrepentantly to jail. He was 89 at the time.

Later, at the height of the Cuban missile crisis in 1962, he dispatched letters to President John F. Kennedy and Premier Nikita S. Khrushchev, bidding them hold summit talks to avert war. Although he was curtly rebuffed by Mr. Kennedy, Russell was convinced that he had been instrumental in settling the dispute peacefully. *Unarmed Victory,* published in 1963, contained this correspondence as well as letters he addressed to U Thant, Jawaharlal Nehru and Zhou Enlai, among others, about the Chinese-Indian border conflict, for the settlement of which he also took some credit.

No Communist ("I dislike Communism because it is undemocratic and capitalism because it favors exploitation"), Russell was a relentless critic of the Soviet Union until after the death of Stalin in 1953. He then softened his attitude because he considered the post-Stalin leadership more amenable to world peace. But in the Vietnam conflict he was certain that the United States acted from sinister economic and political motives—a grasping for Southeast Asian raw materials and an itching for war with China.

Russell took the position that the United States, "the excessive power in the world," had escalated a war for which it bore "total responsibility." He compared American actions to the German occupation of Czechoslovakia, French terror in Algeria and Soviet suppression in Hungary.

"Whatever happens," he told a visitor in his wafer-thin voice in the spring of 1967, "I cannot be a silent witness to murder or torture. Anyone who is a partner in this is a despicable individual. I am sorry I cannot be moderate about it. . . .

"What I hope is that the Americans will arouse so much opposition that in their own minds they will start to think that it is not worth the trouble."

Convinced by data collected for him in Vietnam that the United States was committing war crimes, Russell organized and helped finance a mock trial of this country's leaders. The War Crimes Tribunal, presided over by Jean-Paul Sartre and Isaac Deutscher, met in Stockholm in May 1967, and issued a detailed indictment of United States military practices. Although the State Department discounted the testimony adduced by the tribunal, Russell was impressed by the evidence. The tribunal, in the end, caused only a minor stir, in part because the Communist press in Europe boycotted its proceedings.

Russell later denounced the Soviet invasion of Czechoslovakia. But he also criticized Czechoslovak leaders for what he termed compromising with the occupiers.

Because of the stridency of his views, some charged that Russell was senile and a dupe of one of his secretaries, Ralph Schoenman, who was also secretary of the Bertrand Russell Peace Foundation and active in the War Crimes Tribunal. Dispassionate reporters who traveled to Russell's home overlooking the winding Glaslyn River at Penrhyndeudraeth, Wales, found the frail philosopher very much alert. As to Mr. Schoenman, he said, "You know he is a rather rash young man, and I have to restrain him."

In December 1969, Russell disavowed any connection with Mr. Schoenman after the former secretary announced an investigation by the American branch of the Peace Foundation into alleged atrocities by American soldiers in Vietnam. Russell said Mr. Schoenman, an American, had not been his secretary for more than three years.

A gentle, even shy man, Russell was delightful as a conversationalist, companion and friend. He was capable of a pyrotechnical display of wit, erudition and curiosity, and he bubbled with anecdotes about the world's greats. Despite his title, he was "Bertie" to one and all. His charm, plus his assured position in the upper reaches of the British aristocracy, created for him a worldwide circle of friends. They were a heterogeneous lot, ranging over the years from Tennyson to Graham Greene to Mr. Sartre.

Friends included philosophers such as Whitehead and Wittgenstein; scientists such as Einstein, Niels Bohr and Max Born; writers such as P. G. Wodehouse, Joseph Conrad, D. H. Lawrence, E. M. Forster, T. S. Eliot, Ezra Pound, George Bernard Shaw, Maxim Gorky and H. G. Wells; and political figures such as Sidney and Beatrice Webb, Harold Laski, Lenin and Trotsky. They numbered in the hundreds, and Russell maintained a lively correspondence with them. Someone calculated, in fact, that he wrote one letter for every 30 hours of his life.

As a young man, gaunt and black-haired, Russell favored a flowing mustache and high starched collars. In his autumnal years, his spareness became frailty and, mustache discarded, he resembled a frost-famished sparrow. His glittering eyes and half smile, combined with a shock of white hair, gave him the appearance of a sage, at once remote and kindly. It was a visage cartoonists delighted to draw.

Although he wrote a book about the mysteries of relativity, he humorously admitted that he could not change a light bulb or understand the workings of an automobile engine. However, he had a reason for everything. William Jovanovich, the American publisher, recalled that as a Harvard student he ate in a cafeteria where the food was cheap and not very good.

"I would sit at a long public table where on many occasions also sat the philosopher Bertrand Russell," Mr. Jovanovich said. "One day I could not contain my curiosity. 'Mr. Russell,' I said, 'I know why I eat here. It is because I am poor. But why do you eat here?' 'Because,' he said, 'I am never interrupted.' "

In his last years Russell lived mostly on liquids—a food concentrate, soups, puddings, tea and seven double Red Hackle Scotches a day—because an intestinal kink had been discovered when he was in his 80s and surgery was inadvisable.

The philosopher's eccentricity, or, as he would have it, his independence of mind, was familial. He was born at Ravenscroft, Monmouthshire, on May 18, 1872. He was the youngest of three children of Lord Amberley and the former Katharine Stanley, daughter of Baron Stanley of Alderley. His paternal grandfather was John Russell, the first earl, who was twice prime minister and a leader in obtaining passage of the Reform Bill of 1832 that liberalized election to the House of Commons.

One of Bertrand's maternal uncles became a Roman Catholic and a bishop; another became a Moslem and made the pilgrimage to Mecca; a third was a combative agnostic. His mother campaigned for votes for women and was a friend of Mazzini, the Italian revolutionary. His father was a freethinker.

Together they shocked society by arranging a ménage à trois with the tutor of their elder son.

Bertrand's mother died when he was 2, and his father died about a year later. Lord Amberley left the guardianship of his sons (the third child, a daughter, had died) to the tutor and another man, both atheists. The guardianship was broken, however, by Lord John Russell and Bertrand was reared, after his grandfather's death in 1878, by Lady Russell, a woman of strict puritan moral views.

In the first volume of *The Autobiography of Bertrand Russell,* published in 1967, the philosopher candidly disclosed his mixed feelings for his grandmother. He felt that she was overly protective; on the other hand, he admired (and profited from) one of her favorite Bible texts: "Thou shalt not follow a multitude to do evil."

His childhood, as he recalled it, was a lonely one, for most of his companions were adults and he had a succession of German and Swiss governesses. He was rescued, however, by geometry.

"At the age of 11 I began Euclid, with my brother [seven years his senior] as my tutor," Russell wrote. "This was one of the great events of my life, as dazzling as first love. I had not imagined there was anything so delicious in the world. From that moment until Whitehead and I finished *Principia Mathematica,* when I was 38, mathematics was my chief interest and my chief source of happiness."

As an adolescent Russell read widely, advanced in mathematics and speculated about religion. At 17 he became convinced that there was no life after death, "but I still believed in God because the 'First Cause' argument appeared to be irrefutable," he wrote, adding: "At the age of 18, however, I read Mill's *Autobiography,* where I found a sentence to the effect that his father had taught him that the question 'Who made me?' cannot be answered since it immediately suggests the further question 'Who made God?' This led me to abandon the 'First Cause' argument and to become an atheist."

Russell's *Autobiography* recites in detail the painful intellectual struggle that he waged with himself over theology, in the course of which he wrote out in his journal, in Greek, the argumentation that led to his conclusions.

Entering Trinity College, Cambridge, at 18, Russell was soon in the company of its brightest minds—G. Lowes Dickinson, G. E. Moore, John Maynard Keynes, Lytton Strachey, Charles Sanger, Theodore Davies, John McTaggart and Whitehead. Among them he became less and less solemn while continuing his devotion to philosophy and mathematics. "What I most desired," he said, "was to find some reason for supposing mathematics true."

Graduating with highest honors, he married Alys Pearsall Smith, a pretty American Quaker five years his senior. The marriage lasted from 1894 to 1921, but it was terminated in fact in 1901. "I went out bicycling one afternoon and, suddenly, as I was riding along a country road, I realized that I no longer loved Alys," he recalled. Subsequently, Russell had several love affairs, including a celebrated liaison with the flamboyant Lady Ottoline Morrell and another with Lady Constance Malleson, the actress known professionally as Colette O'Niel. His second marriage, in 1921, was to Dora Winifred Black; his third, to Patricia Helen Spence, in 1936; and his fourth, to Edith Finch, took place 16 years later.

After Russell's first marriage he and his wife traveled on the Continent, where he studied economics and German social democracy, and thence to the United States, where he lectured on non-Euclidian geometry at Bryn Mawr College and the Johns Hopkins University. Meanwhile, he became a Fellow at Trinity.

The year 1900 was one of the most important of Russell's life. In July he attended an International Congress of Philosophy in Paris and met Giuseppe Peano, an originator of symbolic logic. Russell devoured Peano's works. Recounting his exhilaration, he wrote: "For years I had been endeavoring to analyze the fundamental notions of mathematics, such as order and cardinal numbers. Suddenly, in the space of a few weeks, I discovered what appeared to be definite answers to the problems which had baffled me for years. And in the course of discovering these answers, I was introducing a new mathematical technique, by which regions formerly abandoned to the vagueness of philosophers were conquered for the precision of exact formulae."

In October he sat down to write *The Principles of Mathematics,* putting down 200,000 words in three months. With its publication in 1902, he plunged into the eight-year task of elucidating the logical deduction of mathematics that became *Principia Mathematica.* Reducing abstractions to paper was a grueling intellectual task. "Every morning I would sit down before a blank sheet of paper," he said. "Throughout the day, with a brief interval for lunch, I would stare at the blank sheet. Often when evening came it was still blank."

As time went on and the agony of effort increased, Russell "often wondered whether I should ever come out of the other end of the tunnel in which I seemed to be." Several times he contemplated suicide, but he persevered. However, he said, "my intellect never quite recovered from the strain."

"I have been ever since definitely less capable of dealing with difficult abstractions than I was before," he said.

Principia Mathematica, one of the world's great rationalist works, cost Russell and Whitehead, his off-and-on collaborator, £50 each to publish. Despite its complexities, the book took the mystery out of mathematical knowledge and eliminated any connection that might have been supposed to exist between numbers and mysticism.

In the years when Russell was writing his philosophical works, he continued an interest in social problems by participating in the woman suffrage movement and in Fabian Society activities. But he was essentially a don until World War I transformed him into a political animal. In the second volume of his autobiography he said that he "underwent a process of rejuvenation" because of the war.

"It may seem curious that the war should rejuvenate anybody, but in fact it shook me out of my prejudices and made me think afresh on a number of fundamental questions," he wrote, adding: "It also provided me with a new kind of activity, for which I did not feel the staleness that beset me whenever I tried to return to mathematical logic. I have therefore got into the habit of thinking of myself as a nonsupernatural Faust for whom Mephistopheles was represented by the Great War."

A jingoist in the early stages of the Boer War, Russell later became an anti-imperialist; and in 1914 he was a pacifist, but not a pro-German. He joined the No Conscription Fellowship, delivered a series of rousing pacifist lectures and displayed energy and courage in helping conscientious objectors. He also wrote *War—The Offspring of Fear, Principles of Social Recognition* and *Justice in Wartime.*

"Of all the evils of war," he wrote, "the greatest is the purely spiritual evil: the hatred, the injustice, the repudiation of truth, the artificial conflict."

Russell was jailed for six months for his utterances. He passed his sentence writing and studying in a comfortable cell in Brixton Prison.

His pacifism alienated many of his friends, and in his loneliness he entered into an intense love affair with the actress Colette O'Niel. "Colette's love was a refuge to me, not from cruelty itself, which was unescapable, but from the agonizing pain of realizing that that is what men are," he recalled.

"I became for the first time deeply convinced that puritanism does not make for human happiness," he said. "I became convinced that most human beings are possessed by a profound unhappiness venting itself in destructive rages, and that only through the diffusion of instinctive joy can a good world be brought into being."

After the war Russell visited the Soviet Union and met Lenin, Trotsky and Gorky. He expressed sympathy for the aims espoused by the Communists, but he also voiced misgivings about Soviet methods. "For my part, the time I spent in Russia was one of increasing nightmare," he wrote in his autobiography. "Cruelty, poverty, suspicion, persecution, formed the very air we breathed. There was a hypocritical pretense of equality, and everybody was called 'tovarisch,' but it was amazing how differently this word could be pronounced according as the person addressed was Lenin or a lazy servant."

Although Russell was handsomely treated by his hosts, he found their system wanting in logic. In *The Practice and Theory of Bolshevism,* published in 1920, he concluded: "I am compelled to reject Bolshevism for two reasons. First, because the price mankind must pay to achieve Communism by Bolshevik methods is too terrible; and secondly, because, after paying the price, I do not believe the results would be what the Bolsheviks profess to desire."

Soviet leaders apparently never forgave him for his harsh judgment despite his favorable appraisal of Lenin.

In the 1920s, after Russell's second marriage, he and his wife established an experimental school, the Beacon Hill School, to promote progressive education. Of the children there, Russell wrote: "We allow them to be rude and use any language they like. If they want to call me or their teachers fools, they call us fools. There is no check on irreverence toward elders or betters."

The school's concepts had a wide influence in Britain and the United States, where they were the foundation for scores of similar institutions and practices.

In 1931 Russell became the third Earl Russell on the death of his brother, John Francis Stanley Russell, the second Earl. He took the honor lightly.

Two years later his wife, Dora, who had borne him two children, announced that her third child had been sired by another man. The couple's divorce suit was a nine days' wonder in the press. After the decree was granted, Russell married his secretary, and the couple had a child in 1937.

With the rise of Hitler, Russell opposed Nazi methods, but also opposed any steps that might lead to war. His attitude changed in 1939 after the German invasion of Czechoslovakia and Poland. In *Unarmed Victory,* he explained his shift from pacifism: "I had hoped until after the time of Munich that the Nazis might be persuaded into not invading other countries. Their invasions proved that this hope was in vain, and at the same time evidence accumulated as to the utterly horrible character of their internal regime.

"The two factors led me reluctantly to the conviction that war against the Nazis was necessary."

Meantime, in 1938, Russell began an extended visit to the United States, teaching first at the University of Chicago and then at the University of California at Los Angeles. He also gave a lecture series at Harvard and in 1940 he received an appointment to teach at tax-supported City College.

The step loosed a storm of protest from politicians now forgotten and from the Right Rev. William T. Manning, a bishop of the Episcopal Church in New York. The bishop charged that Russell was "a recognized propagandist against religion and morality and who specifically defends adultery." The registrar of New York County suggested that the philosopher be "tarred and feathered and run out of the country." A city councilman called him a "bum." Among other things that incensed critics was a sentence from *Education and the Social Order* that read: "I am sure that university life would be better, both intellectually and morally, if most university students had temporary, childless marriages."

Amid guffaws from the intellectual community, State Supreme Court Justice John E. McGeehan vacated the appointment on the ground that Russell was an alien and an advocate of sexual immorality. He said Russell would be occupying "a chair of indecency" at City College.

For a brief period Russell found himself taboo. "Owners of halls refused to let them if I was to lecture," he recalled in his autobiography (the third volume of which appeared late last year), "and if I had appeared anywhere in public, I should probably have been lynched by a Catholic mob, with the full approval of the police." Although he undoubtedly overstated the reaction to himself, Russell did have trouble earning money for a while.

A SAMPLING OF RUSSELL'S THOUGHTS

Following are excerpts from the writings of Lord Russell on a variety of topics:

"Philosophy, from the earliest times, has made greater claims, and achieved fewer results, than any other branch of learning. . . . The one and only condition, I believe, which is necessary in order to secure for philosophy in the near future an achievement surpassing all that has hitherto been accomplished by philosophers, is the creation of a school of men with scientific training and philosophical interests, unhampered by the traditions of the past, and not misled by the literary methods of those who copy the ancients in all except their merits."

—*Our Knowledge of the External World,* 1929

"Philosophy . . . is something intermediate between theology and science. Like theology, it consists of speculations on matters as to which definite knowledge has, so far, been unascertainable; but like science, it appeals to human reason rather than to authority, whether that of tradition or that of revelation. All *definite* knowledge . . . belongs to science; all *dogma* as to what surpasses definite knowledge belongs to theology. But between theology and science there is a No Man's Land, exposed to attack from both sides; this No Man's Land is philosophy."

—*A History of Western Philosophy,* 1945

"The world that I should wish to see would be one freed from the virulence of group hostilities and capable of realizing that happiness for all is to be derived rather from cooperation than from strife. I should wish to see a world in which education aimed at mental freedom rather than at imprisoning the minds of the young in a rigid armor of dogma calculated to protect them through life against the shafts of impartial evidence. The world needs open systems, whether old or new, that these can be derived."

—Preface to *Why I Am Not a Christian,* a collection of essays, 1957

"We ought to make the best we can of the world, and if it is not so good as we wish, after all it will still be better than what these others have made of it in all these ages. A good world needs knowledge, kindliness and courage; it does not need a regretful hankering after the past or a fettering of the free intelligence by the words uttered long ago by ignorant men."

—*Why I Am Not a Christian*

"I am sorry to say that at the moment I am so busy as to be convinced that life has no meaning whatever, and that being so, I do not see how I can answer your questions intelligently. I do not see that we can judge what would be the result of the discovery of truth, since none has hitherto been discovered."

—Letter to Will Durant, the historian, 1931

"To my mind, a man without bias cannot write interesting history—if indeed, such a man exists. I regard it as mere humbug to pretend to lack of bias."

—Volume II of *The Autobiography of Bertrand Russell,* 1968

"Physical science is . . . approaching the stage when it will be complete, and therefore uninteresting. . . . The total number of facts of geography required to determine the world's history is probably finite; theoretically they could all be written down in a big book to be kept at Somerset House with a calculating machine attached, which, by turning a handle, would enable the inquirer to find out the facts at other times than those recorded.

"It is difficult to imagine anything less interesting or more different from the passionate delights of incomplete discovery. It is like climbing a high mountain and finding nothing at the top except a restaurant where they sell ginger beer, surrounded by fog but equipped with wireless.

"Knowledge and love are both indefinitely extensive; therefore, however good a life may be, a better life can be imagined. Neither love without knowledge nor knowledge without love can produce a good life. . . . The opposite pole of love is pure benevolence."

—Essay entitled "What I Believe"

"I am in entire agreement with you about fox-hunting, which I abominate. I very much dislike cruelty to animals, but I am so occupied with antinuclear work that I do not feel I can take on anything else. Since a nuclear war would probably kill all animals, I feel that what I am doing is also fighting their cause."

—Letter in response to appeal for support in a campaign against blood sports in Britain in 1960

"I am practically well now but I came as near dying as one can without going over the edge—Pneumonia it was. I was delirious for three weeks, and I have no recollection of the time whatever, except a few dreams of Negroes singing in deserts, and of learned bodies that I thought I had to address. The Doctor said to me afterwards: 'When you were ill you behaved like a true philosopher; every time that you came to yourself you made a joke.' I never had a compliment that pleased me more."

—Letter to Jean Nicod, 1921

"I had a second visit from Wittgenstein [the philosopher], but it only lasted 36 hours, and it did not by any means suffice for him to give me a synopsis of all that he has done. . . . His theories are important and certainly very original. Whether they are true, I do not know; I devoutly hope they are not, as they make mathematics and logic almost incredibly difficult. . . . I find I can only understand Wittgenstein when I am in good health, which I am not at the present moment."

—Letters to George E. Moore, the philosopher, written in 1930

"You ask what are my 20 favorite words. . . . The list is as follows: 1. wind; 2. health; 3. golden; 4. begrime; 5. pilgrim; 6. quagmire; 7. diapason; 8. alabaster; 9. chrysoprase; 10. astrolabe; 11. apocalyptic; 12. ineluctable; 13. terraqueous; 14. inspissated; 15. incarnadine; 16. sublunary; 17. Chorasmian; 18. alembic; 19. fulminate; 20. ecstasy."

—Letter to a vocabulary-minded inquirer in 1958

"I have never been an absolute pacifist or an absolute anything else."

—Letter written in 1956

From this situation he was rescued by Dr. Albert C. Barnes, the inventor of Argyrol and the millionaire art collector and creator of the Barnes Foundation, who gave him a five-year appointment to lecture on philosophy at his foundation, in Merion, Pa. In the fall of 1940, Russell also gave the William James Lectures at Harvard. In the next four years he spoke at various institutions and put the finishing touches on his *History of Western Philosophy,* the main source of his income for many years.

Returning to Britain in 1944, he continued to write and lecture there. In 1948 he gave the first Reith Lecture for the British Broadcasting Corporation. His reputation then, as in former years, was mixed: He was thought to be wise, yet he was ridiculed for uttering his maxims oracularly. He was recognized as a brilliant logician but a deficient politician—as when he wanted to take advantage of Western atomic superiority to bring the Soviet Union to heel. In defending this view he expressed the belief that he was motivated by a desire for human freedom.

Russell was lecturing at Princeton in 1950 when he was awarded the Nobel Prize "in recognition of his many-sided and significant writings, in which he appeared as the champion of humanity and freedom of thought."

Einstein, also at Princeton, was among the first to offer his congratulations.

Since the middle 1950s, Russell devoted most of his seemingly inexhaustible energies to a drive against nuclear war. In taking his stand, he proposed that Britain be neutral in the East-West conflict. He urged the withdrawal of United States nuclear arms from British soil.

"For my part, both as a patriot and as a friend of humanity," he said, "I would wish to see Britain officially neutral. The patriotic argument is very obvious to me. No sensible man would wish to see his country obliterated. And as things stand, so long as Britain remains allied to America, there is a serious threat of extermination without the slightest advantage either to America or to the Western way of life."

In furtherance of his views Russell took part in an anti-nuclear demonstration in London and was arrested for breach of peace. The 89-year-old man was jailed for seven days in Brixton Prison after replying "No, I won't" to a magistrate's request that he pledge himself to good behavior.

Although some thought that Russell meddled in the Cuban missile crisis in 1962, the main point of his activity, as conveyed in letters to world leaders, appeared to be that no national objective justified a crisis that might lead to world destruction.

"If people could learn to view nuclear war as a common danger to our species," he wrote, "and not as a danger due solely to the wickedness of the oppressing group, it would be possible to negotiate agreements which would put an end to the common danger."

The philosopher's attitude toward the Vietnam conflict flowed from his desire to advance the cause of world peace, which he saw endangered by "United States imperialism." He believed that a rebuff for the United States, indeed a military defeat, would dampen war fires.

Russell had a rather pixieish sense of humor about himself and death, and in 1937 he composed his own obituary as he imagined it might appear in the *Times* of London. He disclosed his article in an interview in 1959. It read in part: "In his [Russell's] youth he did work of importance in mathematical logic, but his eccentric attitude toward the first world war revealed a lack of balanced judgment, which increasingly infected his later writings.

"His life, for all its waywardness, had a certain anachronistic consistency, reminiscent of that of the aristocratic rebels of the early 19th century. His principles were curious, but such as they were they governed his actions. In private life, he showed none of the acerbity which marred his writings but was a genial conversationalist, not devoid of human sympathy." Earl Russell died at home in Wales on Feb. 2, 1970. He was 97.

ANWAR EL-SADAT

1918–1981

THE ASSASSINATION IN CAIRO

WILLIAM E. FARRELL

ON OCT. 6, 1981, President Anwar el-Sadat of Egypt was shot and killed by a group of men in military uniforms who hurled hand grenades and fired rifles at him as he watched a military parade in Cairo commemorating the 1973 war against Israel.

Vice President Hosni Mubarak, in announcing Mr. Sadat's death, said Egypt's treaties and international commitments would be respected. He said the Speaker of Parliament, Sufi Abu Taleb, would serve as interim president pending an election within the next 60 days. [Mubarak eventually assumed the presidency.]

The assassins' bullets ended the life of a man who earned a reputation for innovation in foreign affairs, a reputation based in large part on his decision in November 1977 to journey to the camp of Egypt's foe, Israel, to make peace.

Regarded as an interim ruler when he came to power in 1970 on the death of Gamal Abdel Nasser, Mr. Sadat forged his own regime and ran Egypt single-handedly. He was bent on moving this impoverished country into the late 20th century, a drive that led him to abandon an alliance with the Soviet Union and embrace the West.

That rule ended abruptly and violently. As jet fighters roared overhead, the killers sprayed the reviewing stand with bullets while thousands of horrified people—officials, diplomats and journalists, including this correspondent—looked on.

Information gathered from a number of sources indicated that eight persons had been killed and 27 wounded in the attack. Later reports, all unconfirmed, put the toll at 11 dead and 38 wounded.

The authorities did not disclose the identity of the assassins. They were being interrogated and there were no clear indications whether the attack was to have been part of a coup attempt.

[In Washington, American officials said an army major, a lieutenant and four enlisted men had been involved in the attack. The major and two of the soldiers were killed and the others captured, the officials said.]

Those standing nearby at the Cairo parade grounds said six to eight soldiers riding in a truck towing an artillery piece had broken away from the line of march and walked purposefully toward the reviewing stand. Onlookers thought the procession was part of the pageant. Suddenly, a hand grenade exploded and staccato bursts of rifle fire erupted while French-made Mirage jets screeched overhead.

The 62-year-old leader was rushed to Maadi Military Hospital by helicopter and died several hours

Denis Cameron

Sadat in Cairo minutes before he was assassinated

AP/WIDE WORLD

later, according to an official in his office. He was said to have been struck by two bullets. A medical bulletin later said he might have been hit by as many as five bullets and shrapnel fragments.

The bulletin said he had no heartbeat when he arrived at the hospital. It attributed his death, at 2:40 P.M. Cairo time (8:40 A.M. New York time), to "violent nervous shock and internal bleeding in the chest cavity, where the left lung and major blood vessels below it were torn."

The death of Mr. Sadat raised serious questions about the direction the nation would take.

Mr. Mubarak, in his broadcast announcing Mr. Sadat's death seven hours after the assassination, indicated that Egypt would continue to respect the peace treaty with Israel.

"I hereby declare," he said, "in the name of the great soul passing away and in the name of the people, its constitutional institutions and its armed forces, that we are committed to all charters, treaties, and international obligations that Egypt has concluded."

Security police patrolled Cairo's streets, nearly empty except for some shoppers because of the holiday marking the 1973 war, and government buildings were being closely guarded.

Regular television programming was canceled after the announcement of Mr. Sadat's death and was replaced by readings from the Koran and film clips of his achievements—the 1973 war against Israel, which Mr. Sadat said restored Egyptian dignity after its defeat in 1967, the peace treaty with Israel and other milestones. No film of the attack on the reviewing stand at today's parade was shown on Egyptian television.

Within seconds of the attack, the reviewing stand was awash in blood. Bemedaled officials dived for cover. Screams and panic followed as guests tried to flee, tipping over chairs. Some were crushed underfoot. Others, shocked and stunned, stood riveted.

This correspondent saw one assailant, a stocky, dark-haired man, standing in a half crouch, firing a rifle into the stand used by Mr. Sadat, who was wearing black leather boots and military attire crossed by a green sash.

Some onlookers reported a short, fierce exchange of fire between the killers and Mr. Sadat's security men. Others said the attackers had been overcome by some of the thousands of military men in the area.

While spectators sought a way out, the reviewing stand for a few seconds was nearly empty. Flanked on each side by displays of sleek missiles, the stand was a blood-soaked horror.

Mr. Sadat was promptly carried away, but others felled by bullets remained writhing on the ground. A few did not move. One man, seriously wounded, was slumped over a railing separating Mr. Sadat and his party from the parade about 20 yards away.

Among those hit was reported to be Bishop Samuel, whom Mr. Sadat had named as one of five clerics to run the Coptic Christians' affairs after he deposed their Pope, Shenuda III. The bishop was later reported to have died.

Others said to have died were two presidential aides—Mohammed Rashwan, the official photographer, and Sayed Marei, a confidant. The Belgian ambassador, Claude Ruelle, was seriously wounded, and three American military officers were hurt.

Egypt's defense minister, Gen. Abdel Halim Abu Ghazala, who had opened the parade with a speech, stood in the midst of the carnage. His face was bleeding, his gold-braided uniform was blood-soaked. He waved away attempts to assist him and began issuing orders.

Soldiers wearing red berets and perfectly creased uniforms promptly joined hands to cordon off the scene of the attack, widening the circle as more soldiers arrived. Some of the soldiers were sobbing, a few screamed hysterically, others looked dumbfounded.

Overhead, the air show continued. Planes looped and swerved and dove and arced and sent colorful sprays of vapor over the pandemonium below. The roar of engines drowned out the screams and the clatter of chairs.

The parade ground, which had witnessed a joyful

procession of Egypt's most advanced arms as well as the colorful camel corps, with its turbaned soldiers, and the cavalry, with its sleek, elegant Arabian horses, was littered with little Egyptian souvenir flags dropped by panicked guests. As members of military bands scattered, the brilliant sun beamed off shiny yellow tubas and other brass instruments.

The Egyptian military establishment has long been regarded as the ingredient needed by any leader to remain in power. Diplomatic and military analysts said that Mr. Sadat had the support of the military and that it assured the stability of his regime and permitted him to take daring steps, such as the peace overture to Israel and, finally, the peace treaty. In the absence of information, it was hard to tell whether the assassins represented a disenchantment with Mr. Sadat within the military.

Speculation abounded. Some thought the attackers, who many felt must have known that they were on a suicide mission, might be Moslem fundamentalists opposed to the alliance with Israel and to Mr. Sadat's recent crackdown.

About a month ago, he ordered the arrest of some 1,500 Coptic and Moslem extremists, along with some of his political opponents. He said they had fomented sectarian strife and endangered his efforts to bring democracy to Egypt.

A devout Moslem, Mr. Sadat was harsh toward fundamentalist groups, such as the Moslem Brotherhood and the Islamic Association. He banned both groups, calling them illegal. He said that he would not tolerate mixing religion and politics and that these groups were using mosques to denounce him and his policies.

The published names of those arrested in the crackdown did not include those of military personnel. But there were unverifiable though persistent reports that some of those detained were in the armed forces.

After Mr. Sadat's helicopter had left the scene, diplomats rushed to their limousines. Soldiers cleared the grounds and drove away the stunned spectators. Ambulances wailed, women clutching their children raced away. And the air show above continued.

Early in the parade, a rocketlike object had been launched. It rained down Egyptian flags and portraits of Mr. Sadat hanging from tiny parachutes that were whipped by the wind. Most of them floated over a nearby housing development called Nasser City.

As the grounds were being cleared, one of the parachuted portraits was seen hanging from a flagpole on which it had become impaled in landing. The portrait of Mr. Sadat had been torn by the sharp tip of the Egyptian flag.

THE DARING ARAB PIONEER OF PEACE WITH ISRAEL

ERIC PACE

"SADAT! SADAT!" tens of thousands of Cairenes chanted at the grinning figure in the open limousine. "Sadat! The man of peace!"

It was the night of Nov. 21, 1977. President Anwar el-Sadat had just returned from his epochal journey to Jerusalem. Egypt's people were giving their frenzied approval to what his trip had achieved—an Egyptian-Israeli thaw that set the stage for the peace treaty of 1979.

What made Mr. Sadat into such a catalytic force in Middle Eastern history was a display of courage and flexibility that transformed what had seemed to be an average Arab officer-turned-potentate.

Unlike so many of his brother Arab leaders, he was willing to ignore past Arab-Israeli hatreds. Unlike them all, he was daring enough to do what had been unthinkable in the anguished world of Arab politics—to extend the hand of peace to the Israeli foe. Reversing Egypt's long-standing policy, he proclaimed his willingness to accept Israel's existence as a sovereign state.

Then, where so many Middle East negotiators had failed, he succeeded, along with Presidents Carter and Reagan and Prime Minister Menachem Begin of Israel, in keeping the improbable rapprochement alive.

In the process he earned himself, in addition to the Nobel Peace Prize, the admiration of Americans, Israelis and other supporters of a Middle East settlement. But he also drew outpourings of hatred from Palestinians and other Arabs who felt he was a traitor to their struggles against Israel. And he was unable to quash dissidence in his impoverished, seething homeland.

He often said he wanted to bequeath democratic institutions to his people, but in the weeks before his death he staged a dictatorial crackdown on militant Moslems and Coptic Christians as well as secular political opponents. And he claimed imperially—but hollowly, as it turned out—to have put an end to "lack of discipline in any way or form."

Eleven days before Mr. Sadat made his trip to Jerusalem, he said in Cairo that he was willing to go to "the ends of the earth," and even to the Israeli Parliament, in the cause of peace. The Israeli government made known that he was welcome in Jerusalem, and after complex negotiations he flew there, although a state of war still existed between the two nations.

His eyes were moist and his lips taut with suppressed emotion as he arrived, but his Arabic was firm and resonant when, hours later, he told the hushed Israeli Parliament, "If you want to live with us in this part of the world, in sincerity I tell you that we welcome you among us with all security and safety."

Praising Mr. Sadat's initiative, Prime Minister Begin said, "We, the Jews, know how to appreciate such courage."

Mr. Sadat's flexibility, he said later, stemmed from his solitary confinement as a political prisoner in cell 54 of Cairo Central Prison in 1947 and 1948. "My contemplation of life and human nature in that secluded place taught me that he who cannot change the very fabric of his thought will never, therefore, make any progress," he wrote in his memoirs, *In Search of Identity,* which appeared in 1978, eight years after he assumed the presidency.

His willingness to make such a change led to the treaty that, after many snags, he and Prime Minister Begin signed at the White House on March 26, 1979. Before reaching agreement, Mr. Sadat and Mr. Begin had drawn-out and sometimes acrimonious negotiations, for which they were the joint winners of the Nobel Peace Prize in 1978.

The treaty provided that Israel return to Egypt in phases the entire Sinai Peninsula, which the Israelis seized in the 1967 war. It also envisioned internal autonomy for the Palestinian Arabs of the West Bank of the Jordan River under continued Israeli control.

The Egyptian and Israeli governments were helped and prodded by the Nixon and Carter administrations, and Henry A. Kissinger, after many meetings with Mr. Sadat, wrote that the Egyptian leader "possessed that combination of insight and courage which marks a great statesman." The former secretary of state continued in his book, *White House Years*: "He had the boldness to go to a war no one thought he could sustain; the moderation to move to peace immediately afterward; and the wisdom to reverse attitudes hardened by decades."

In dealings with Israel and the United States, Mr. Sadat strove to create a harmonious mood that would make it difficult for others to disagree with him. His most audacious use of that technique was the Jerusalem visit.

That gesture and the treaty with Israel brought him hatred and vituperation from many Arab leaders. There was particular outrage because the treaty did not provide a timetable for full self-determination for the West Bank Palestinians that would lead eventually to an independent Palestinian state.

Self-determination was originally Mr. Sadat's

minimum demand; when he settled for less, he found himself virtually isolated in the Arab world. Saudi Arabia's leaders, with whom he had achieved warm relations, cut back their aid to the Egyptian armed forces and the economy, which Mr. Sadat had tried to strengthen by encouraging business.

The Saudi action made Egypt more dependent than ever on support from the United States, with which Mr. Sadat had also been careful to cultivate bonds of friendship. Under his predecessor, Gamal Abdel Nasser, Cairo's relations with the Americans, as with the Saudis, were hostile much of the time. Mr. Sadat won moral and political support from Washington as well as large-scale economic and military aid, and in 1975 he became the first Egyptian president to make a state visit to the United States. He returned again during the treaty negotiations, and President Carter went to Egypt, where throngs hailed him and his host.

Many of the 40 million Egyptians, having gone through four painful and expensive wars with Israel, were enthusiastic about the peace treaty. Throngs of well-wishers danced, waved signs and threw rose petals in celebration.

Under the treaty Israel's withdrawal of its civilian and military forces from Sinai was to be carried out in stages over three years. Two thirds of the area was to be handed back within nine months after the exchange of formal ratification documents. In return for the Israeli pullback, Mr. Sadat agreed to establish peace. After the nine-month withdrawal was finished, the two governments were to take up "normal and friendly relations" in the diplomatic, economic and cultural spheres, among others. The early withdrawals were completed, and the final phase is scheduled for next April.

"This is certainly one of the happiest moments of my life," Mr. Sadat, deeply moved, said at the signing ceremony. "In all the steps I took I was merely expressing the will of a nation. I am proud of my people and of belonging to them."

Another of Mr. Sadat's major shifts in policy was his departure from Nasser's long-standing pro-Soviet stance. In July 1972 he abruptly ordered the withdrawal of the 25,000 Soviet military specialists and advisers in Egypt. By so doing, he later wrote, "I wanted to tell the whole world that we are always our own masters."

The changes in the relationship with Washington and Moscow were made after Mr. Sadat concluded that the Arabs could not achieve a satisfactory end to their confrontation with Israel as long as they were allied closely with the Soviet Union while Israel had the all-out support of the United States.

He was able to make such sharp policy shifts in part because for much of his later tenure as president, his power did not seem to be seriously challenged at home. A career officer and longtime confidant of Nasser, he was named vice president in 1969, came out ahead in a brief power struggle after Nasser's death in 1970 and was formally made president by a rubber-stamp vote of members of the Arab Socialist Union, the only legal political organization. He consolidated and enlarged his power in the spring of 1971 when, with the aid of the army, he forestalled what he said was a coup and arrested his opponents.

Mr. Sadat was widely though not universally popular with the Egyptian people, with whom, in his highly emotional way, he felt a warm and almost mystic bond. In *In Search of Identity,* he proudly called himself "a peasant born and brought up on the banks of the Nile."

Early in his presidency, Mr. Sadat enhanced his popularity by eliminating many of the police-state controls that Nasser had relied on to keep himself in power in the years after the officers' revolt that brought down the monarchy in 1952.

In 1973 Mr. Sadat did much to build national self-respect when he ordered Egyptian troops to cross the Suez Canal; they managed to overrun the heavily fortified Israeli positions on the east bank within a few hours. That confidence lingered although the Israelis counterattacked, putting a large tank force on the west bank.

As an administrator, he concerned himself with

broad lines of policy and for the most part left execution to his subordinates. Though an emotional man, he could conceal his feelings and be devious. He repeatedly lied his way out of trouble when he was a young officer plotting a military revolt, and as president he pulled off a masterstroke of deception when he concealed his preparations for the 1973 war, which began with a surprise attack on Israel.

Mr. Sadat had many quirks. He disliked offices and rarely appeared at Abdin Palace, Cairo's equivalent of the White House, preferring to work in his modest villa and in government-owned rest houses around the country. He wore elegantly cut British-style suits, though even as president he liked to stroll around his native village in a long Arab shirt. He never learned to dance. He could be the high-toned statesman one minute, relishing his associations with other world leaders, and the humdrum homebody the next, always beginning the day with a dose of Eno's Fruit Salts, a British-made aid to digestion.

Mohammed Anwar el-Sadat was born Dec. 25, 1918, in Mit Abul Kom, a cluster of mud-brick buildings in Minufiya Province between Cairo and Alexandria. He was one of the 13 children of Mohammed el-Sadat, a government clerk, and his part-Sudanese wife, a heritage manifest in the boy's skin, darker than the average Egyptian's.

Minufiya lies in the fertile Nile Delta, its irrigated fields producing rich crops of flax and cotton. In those lush surroundings young Anwar's early years passed happily. He wrote later that he had especially relished the sunrise hour, "when I went out with scores of boys and men, young and old, taking our cattle and beasts of burden to the fields."

His first schooling was at the hands of a kindly Islamic cleric, Sheik Abdul-Hamid, who instilled in him a deep and lasting faith in Islam; as an adult Mr. Sadat bore a dark mark on his forehead, the result of repeatedly touching his head to the floor in prayer.

In 1925 the father was transferred to Cairo, and the family moved into a small house on the outskirts of the capital, not far from Kubba Palace, one of the residences of Egyptian kings. Anwar gave early evidence of the audacity he repeatedly showed in later life, stealing apricots from the royal orchard.

Though the elder Mr. Sadat rose to be a senior clerk, the family was poor, so poor that it could not afford to buy bakery bread. In his memoirs President Sadat said that his early experience of village life, with its "fraternity, cooperation and love," gave him the self-confidence to make his way in the big city: "It deepened my feeling of inner superiority, a feeling which has never left me and which, I came to realize, is an inner power independent of all material resources."

In time the proud schoolboy, like other idealistic Egyptians of his generation, came to have a burning political desire: He wanted his country freed of the control of Britain, which had maintained troops there and exercised sway in other ways since the decline of Ottoman Turkish power late in the 19th century.

Wanting to play a role in Egypt's future, Mr. Sadat decided to become an officer. Despite his family's lack of influence, he managed to gain admission to the Royal Military Academy, which was once a preserve of the aristocracy but had begun taking cadets from the middle and lower classes. Graduating in 1938, he was assigned to a signal corps installation near the capital. From that central location, as he later told it, he became active in the formation of an organization of officers who wanted to mount an armed revolt against the British presence.

When World War II broke out, Captain Sadat continued to regard Britain as the main enemy and took part in a clandestine attempt to fly a former Chief of Staff, Gen. Aziz el-Masri, out of the country after the Germans had sent a message asking him to proceed to Iraq to work against British interests there. The plane crashed, the attempt failed and Captain Sadat was arrested and interrogated but later was released for lack of evidence.

Undeterred, Captain Sadat made contact with two Nazi agents who passed the evenings watching the dancers at the Kit Kat, a leading Cairo nightclub. Their heavy spending brought them under surveillance, they were arrested and interrogated, and they implicated their contact. As a result a swarm of British and Egyptian detectives and intelligence officers searched Captain Sadat's home. His hidden cache of homemade explosives went undetected, but he was arrested and sent to a succession of jails. While in jail, he profited from the time by polishing his English and learning German.

In 1944 Captain Sadat went on a hunger strike and was transferred to a prison hospital, where he dodged his guard, jumped into a friend's car and escaped. He then grew a beard and lived as a fugitive for a year, helping for a time with work on a rest house being built for King Farouk, who was later to be ousted by the junta of which Captain Sadat was a part.

With the end of the war came the lifting of the martial-law regulations under which Captain Sadat had been detained, enabling him to resume his real identity in freedom. He also resumed plotting against the British and their Egyptian supporters. After a fellow conspirator assassinated Amin Osman Pasha, an aristocrat who favored the British presence, Captain Sadat was tried as a conspirator and acquitted in 1948.

He worked for a while in a Cairo publishing house and in 1950 got himself reinstated in the army. He was soon promoted, thanks to help from the dissident officers' clandestine network, the Free Officers Organization, which had been growing in size and power under the leadership of an old friend, Lieutenant Colonel Nasser. The colonel summoned Major Sadat to a rendezvous in Cairo on July 22, 1952, saying the long-awaited uprising, now focused on King Farouk, was to take place soon. When Nasser did not appear, the major took his wife to the movies. Arriving home late in the evening, they found a note from Nasser saying operations were beginning that night and directing Major Sadat to join the revolutionaries.

"My heart leapt," Mr. Sadat recalled in one of his books, *Revolt on the Nile.* "I tore off my civilian clothes and threw on my uniform. In five minutes I was at the wheel of my car."

At army headquarters, where the rebels had taken control, Nasser told him to take over the Cairo radio at dawn and to broadcast a proclamation announcing the coup. Major Sadat carried out that historic task after waiting for the daily reading from the Koran to be completed.

The revolution led to the exile of Farouk, the withdrawal of British troops from Egypt and, before long, the emergence of Nasser as strongman and president.

Although Mr. Sadat filled high posts during the Nasser era, his abilities were underestimated by many influential men in the Nasser entourage. For more than a decade he was given a succession of jobs that were highly visible but of secondary importance. He served as a member of the Revolutionary Command Council; secretary general of an Islamic congress; editor of two newspapers; minister of state in the cabinet; deputy chairman, chairman and speaker of the National Assembly and chairman of the Afro-Asian Solidarity Council.

When Nasser named Mr. Sadat vice president, it was widely thought that he got the job because it was largely ceremonial and had no real power, but supporters of Mr. Sadat have contended that Nasser chose him to be his successor. Nasser, at odds with many other longtime associates, retained warm relations with Mr. Sadat.

Upon Nasser's death of a heart attack, Mr. Sadat, as the only vice president, automatically became acting president under the constitution. In that office and in his first months as president he had to share power in a collective leadership with others; some colleagues supported him for the presidency because they thought he could be manipulated.

In those first weeks many Egyptians, especially students and young intellectuals, found it difficult to take him seriously. With his grin, his fancy suits and his frequent hollow-sounding vows to wage war on Israel, he did not seem to be a strong and purposeful leader.

He showed his strength of will when, after a few months, he moved to consolidate his power by dismissing and imprisoning two of the most powerful figures in the regime, Vice President Ali Sabry, who had close ties with Soviet officials, and Sharawy Gomaa, the interior minister, who controlled the secret police.

Mr. Sadat enhanced his popularity by displaying an intuitive sense of what the people wanted. He was doing what they wanted when he cut back the powers of the hated secret police, when he ousted the Soviet military experts and when he prepared for war with Israel. Nevertheless, Golda Meir, Israel's prime minister when he took office, correctly appraised him, she later wrote, as a "reasonable man who might soberly consider the benefits" of ending the confrontation with Israel.

Early in 1973 Mr. Sadat decided to go to war against Israel. He was being criticized by students and others as an ineffective leader, and he concluded that it was necessary to break the Egyptian-Israeli deadlock. "If we don't take our case into our own hands, there will be no movement," he said in an interview. "The time has come for a shock. The resumption of the battle is now inevitable."

After Moscow approved a limited Egyptian invasion of Sinai and after more Soviet arms arrived, Mr. Sadat ordered the attack on Oct. 6. Egyptian troops surged across the canal and Syrian troops struck Israel from their side. In the fighting that followed, the Syrians were thrown back and the Israelis counterattacked fiercely, encircling Suez and carving out a broad bridgehead west of the canal. Despite Israel's strong showing, Mr. Sadat, in his memoirs, maintained that "the Egyptian military performance was a landmark in world military history" and that "if the United States hadn't intervened in the war and fully supported Israel, the situation could have been far different."

The war spurred Washington to work to ease tensions in the Middle East; Mr. Sadat was soon visited by Mr. Kissinger. The two hit it off from the first and, Mr. Sadat wrote, began "a relationship of mutual understanding culminating and crystallizing in what we came to describe as a 'peace process.' " Before long Mr. Kissinger was able to work out a disengagement agreement between Egypt and Israel that allowed the Egyptians to take back a strip of Sinai. Mr. Sadat welcomed American participation and said later, "No one else except the United States can play this role of mediator between two sides that harbor intense hate for one another—a gulf of bad blood, violence and massacres."

The agreement, signed in January 1974, was followed by months of "shuttle diplomacy" by Mr. Kissinger and by a second limited Egyptian-Israeli accord in September 1975. Efforts toward a more comprehensive peace agreement bore no fruit in the next months, however, although the United States and the Soviet Union agreed on Oct. 1, 1977, on principles to govern a Geneva conference on the Middle East. Syria continued to resist such a conference.

At that point Mr. Sadat, not wanting to let Moscow and Damascus determine the pace of events, decided that a new approach was needed. Disregarding objections from his advisers, he made the trip to Jerusalem. He told the Israeli Parliament that Egypt's willingness to "welcome you among us" amounted to "a decisive historical change," but he continued to insist that the Israelis withdraw from occupied Arab land and recognize what he called the rights of the Palestinians. He claimed a newfound friendship with Mr. Begin and set in motion the first high-level Egyptian-Israeli peace talks.

When Mr. Sadat returned to Cairo, he told his people that "all barriers of doubt, mistrust and fear were shattered." But the negotiations bogged down over differences on the Palestinians and other issues; by January 1978 they were deadlocked, with Mr. Sadat denouncing the Israelis as stiff-necked. That deadlock prevailed until Mr. Sadat met with Mr. Begin and President Carter in September 1978 at the Camp David conference called by Mr. Carter. Two weeks of talks produced signed agreements on what was called "a framework for peace."

After further efforts Mr. Carter flew to Jerusalem and then to Cairo on March 13, 1979, with compromise proposals to break yet another deadlock, and Mr. Sadat approved them quickly in a meeting at a Cairo airport. Later that month Mr. Sadat and Mr. Begin signed the treaty, ending 30 years of Egyptian-Israeli confrontation. "Let us work together," Mr. Sadat said, paraphrasing the Prophet Isaiah, "until the day comes when they beat their swords into plowshares and their spears into pruning hooks."

In the hard-line Arab protest against the treaty, 17 Arab nations adopted political and economic sanctions against Mr. Sadat's government. Yet his isolation in the Arab world did not undercut his domestic support; he deftly reaped political profit from the isolation by underscoring the idea, widespread in Egypt, that other Arabs had grown wealthy while the Egyptians had borne the burden of the four wars.

His popularity benefited also from the fairly strong condition of the economy, which had seemed on the brink of disaster after Egypt's catastrophic defeat in the 1967 war. By late 1979 the economic growth rate had reached 9 percent a year and was one of the highest in the developing world, thanks largely to more than $1 billion a year in American aid.

President Sadat's relations with the Americans and the Israelis, despite some intense friction, remained relatively harmonious in the months after the signing of the treaty. That good will paid off when, as a gesture of friendship, Mr. Begin fulfilled one provision of the treaty ahead of time, returning a 580-square-mile tract of Sinai to Egypt on Nov. 15, 1979, instead of on Jan. 25, 1980, as scheduled. Yet no real progress was made in months of Egyptian-Israeli negotiations on home rule for the Palestinians in the West Bank and the Gaza Strip.

Early in 1980 Mr. Sadat held inconclusive talks with Mr. Begin at Aswan, in upper Egypt. Israeli forces withdrew from more of Sinai, leaving two thirds of the area evacuated. The Israeli-Egyptian border was declared open, and the two countries exchanged ambassadors. In March 1980 Mr. Sadat drew new criticism at home and in unfriendly Arab capitals when the deposed Shah of Iran, who was ill, moved to Cairo, accepting a long-standing invitation.

As the new decade got under way, President Sadat seemed confident of his policies, but events seemed to have taken a somewhat unfavorable turn. Cairo's isolation in the Arab world and elsewhere in the third world was galling, and the almost total reliance on Washington for food, aid and weapons was a source of concern. Inflation was running at a rate of 30 percent a year, there were signs of increasing repression, and Israel's policy of multiplying settlements on the occupied West Bank intensified pessimism.

In April 1980 President Sadat visited Washington to discuss the Israeli settlements with President Carter. From there he denounced the Israeli policy as "unfounded, ill-conceived and illegal."

In the final months of Mr. Sadat's life, as his intricate and sometimes stormy dialogue with Israel continued, there were repeated expressions of internal opposition to his rule. They continued, and mounted, despite his general popularity and his continued use of such means as government food subsidies to dampen discontent.

Early in 1981 Egypt's leftist National Unionist Progressive Party publicly denounced Mr. Sadat's policies toward Israel. "This so-called normalization with the Israeli enemy was done at the expense of the Arabs and was opposed by a growing number of Egyptians," a party statement said.

In June of 1981 a government prosecutor said a former Egyptian Chief of Staff, Lieut. Gen. Saad Eddin el-Shazli, and 18 other Egyptian dissidents living abroad had plotted to overthrow Mr. Sadat. They were said to have been given $2.8 million by Libya at Syria's urging. And the head of the Egyptian Bar Association complained that Mr. Sadat's regime was trying to dismember the association's leadership because it had opposed the peace treaty with Israel.

Yet Mr. Sadat continued to give much of his attention to foreign affairs. In June he met inconclusively with Mr. Begin, for the first time in 17 months. In the meeting in an abandoned restaurant at Sharm el Sheik in Sinai, the Israeli leader rejected Mr. Sadat's appeal to halt Israeli attacks on Palestinian guerrilla bases in Lebanon.

A few days later Mr. Sadat was denouncing Israel for its bombing of an Iraqi nuclear reactor, which he called an "unlawful, provocative" act. It was embarrassing to him because Mr. Begin had told him nothing about it.

On Aug. 3 Egypt and Israel signed an agreement establishing a 2,500-member international peacekeeping force in Sinai to police their peace treaty. On Aug. 5 and 6 Mr. Sadat held friendly but inconclusive talks with President Reagan in Washington. And on Aug. 25 and 26 he and Mr. Begin met yet again, this time in the Egyptian port of Alexandria, to try to resolve problems that had delayed normalization of relations.

But then Mr. Sadat turned his full attention to internal affairs, evidently acting in response to information about the extent of dissidence in his perennially unstable land. Citing Moslem and other opposition to his regime, he departed markedly from the largely velvet-glove treatment of opponents that had characterized his 11 years of rule.

He cracked down hard, detaining 1,600 opponents, mostly Moslem militants, partly in response to bloody rioting in June between Moslems and members of Egypt's Coptic Christian minority. After a hastily called referendum, his government reported that 99.45 percent of the voters endorsed its measures to curb secular as well as religious dissidence. Moslem dissidents resented the rapprochement with Israel and wanted a more Islamic cast to Egypt's government.

At a news conference on Sept. 9, 1981, Mr. Sadat made a wry reference to his country's heritage of violence and to the opposition to his rule. To a foreign reporter who asked an impertinent question, he said, "In other times I would have shot you, but it is democracy I am really suffering from as much as I am suffering from the opposition."

Also in September, Mr. Sadat accused a dozen former Egyptian officials of "conniving" with the Soviet Union to destabilize his government. He ordered the expulsion of more than 1,000 Soviet citizens, including the Soviet ambassador, Vladimir P. Polyakov.

The government-supervised Egyptian press reported that Egyptian intelligence had uncovered antigovernment plotting by Soviet agents in league with Egyptian religious extremists, leftists, Nasserites, educators, journalists and others.

Later in the month—even as officials of Egypt, Israel and the United States held talks in Cairo seeking a plan for self-rule for Palestinians—Mr. Sadat's government took further action to quell dissidence. Among other measures, uniformed guards in university campuses were reinforced. A sweeping investigation of the bureaucracy was decreed.

In a widely quoted speech, Mr. Sadat asserted, in what proved to be a display of overconfidence, that all of Egypt's internal indiscipline had come to a halt.

"Lack of discipline in any way or form," he said, in a two-hour televised address, "in the streets, in the government, in the university, in the secondary schools, in the factory, in the public sector, in the private sector, this all has ended, it has ended."

In Israel, however, a longtime observer of Mr. Sadat was already speaking of the possibility that his work might be snuffed out. The Israeli Chief of Staff, Lieut. Gen. Raphael Eitan, said bleakly, "There are troubles in Egypt, and it is possible that President Sadat will go and everything will come to an end."

Mr. Sadat was divorced from his first wife, who was from his native village; they had three daughters. His second wife, Jihan, has played a strong role in public affairs, particularly concerning the condition of women and children. The four children of his second marriage are a son, Gamal, named for Nasser, and three daughters—Lubna, Noha and Jihan.

ANWAR EL-SADAT: OFTEN OUTSPOKEN ON WAR AND PEACE IN THE MIDEAST

"In Egypt, personalities have always been more important than political programs."

—*Revolt on the Nile, 1957*

"Don't ask me to make diplomatic relations with them. Never. Never. Leave it to the coming generations to decide that, not me."

—On Israel in 1970, a few months before he became president

"The situation here—mark my words—will be worse than Vietnam."

—In a magazine interview, July 1973

"We have always felt the sympathy of the world, but we would prefer the respect of the world to sympathy without respect."

—In a speech to the People's Assembly after the first attack of the Yom Kippur War, Oct. 6, 1973

"Let every girl, let every woman, let every mother here—and there in my country—know we shall solve all our problems through negotiations around the table rather than starting war."

—During his visit to Israel, Nov. 1977

"I have a great ally in Israel that I depend upon. Do you know who? The Israeli mother."

—Commenting on the vote of approval by Israel's Parliament of the peace treaty between Egypt and Israel, March 22, 1979

"In all the steps I took I was not performing a personal mission. I was merely expressing the will of a nation. I am proud of my people and of belonging to them.

"Today a new dawn is emerging out of the darkness of the past.

"Let us work together until the day comes when they beat their swords into plowshares and their spears into pruning hooks."

—At the peace treaty signing between Egypt and Israel at the White House, March 26, 1979

"There will be no barriers between our peoples, no more anxiety or insecurity, no more suffering or suspicion."

—Meeting with Menachem Begin at Beersheba, May 27, 1979

"It is democracy I am really suffering from as much as I am suffering from the opposition."

—Speaking to foreign journalists of unrest in Egypt, Sept. 9, 1981

SADAT IN ISRAEL

WILLIAM E. FARRELL

THE LEADERS of Egypt and Israel, two nations that have fought four wars in 29 years, met on Israeli soil on Nov. 19, 1977.

At 8:03 P.M. [1:03 P.M., New York time], President Anwar el-Sadat of Egypt stepped aground at Ben-Gurion International Airport, creating Middle East history as the first Arab leader to visit Israel since its founding in 1948.

He was greeted by Prime Minister Menachem Begin and President Ephraim Katzir, who had lauded Mr. Sadat in recent days for his bold move in deciding to come to Israel despite the growing antipathy and violence in the Arab world caused by Mr. Sadat's tacit recognition of Israel's existence.

Mr. Sadat greeted Mr. Begin by saying, "Thank you." Mr. Begin responded, "It's wonderful to have you. Thank you for coming."

Then, as Mr. Sadat walked from his airliner to a waiting limousine, he shook hands with people whose very names recalled the years of conflict that have marked relations between Israel and the Arab world, among them Moshe Dayan, Golda Meir, former Prime Minister Yitzhak Rabin and Gen. Ariel Sharon.

After his arrival at the King David Hotel, President Sadat met for a half hour with Mr. Begin, Mr. Dayan and Deputy Prime Minister Yigael Yadin for what was described as a courtesy call.

"I have already had a private discussion with him," Mr. Begin said to reporters, referring to the Egyptian leader, "and I can say that we like each other."

Mr. Sadat and an entourage of Egyptian officials and reporters had flown from the Abu Suweir air base in Egypt, directly to Ben-Gurion International Airport. The plane, emblazoned with Egypt's flag and the words "Arab Republic of Egypt," taxied up to a red carpet on the tarmac. Three minutes later the Egyptian leader emerged onto an airport ramp of El Al, Israel's airline, and was greeted by a fanfare of trumpets.

Mr. Sadat was visibly moved as he stood on the platform, his eyes moist, his mouth tight.

Reporters traveling on the president's plane said he had told them, without elaborating, that he had come with specific proposals for cessation of the decades of Arab-Jewish hostilities and that he hoped to return to Egypt secure in the knowledge that peace talks were much closer.

A few minutes after his arrival an Israeli band struck up the Egyptian national anthem, which was followed by the Israeli anthem. Cannons boomed in salute.

Mr. Sadat then reviewed a 72-member Israeli honor guard, made up from all branches of the Israeli armed services. At one point, the Egyptian president, dressed in civilian clothes, saluted the guard.

As he walked with Mr. Begin and Mr. Katzir, the Egyptian leader was applauded by Israeli dignitaries and other officials, who were as stunned as their fellow countrymen in recent days as the Egyptian's declaration that he would come to Israel came to fruition.

Mr. Sadat shook hands and smiled his way down a long reception line in a bizarre state ceremony, with full fanfare and panoply, being given for the leader of a country with which Israel is in a state of war.

At one point, Mr. Sadat asked if Ariel Sharon was there. He was, and Mr. Sadat gave a warm handshake to the former general, who was a hero in the 1973 war for his successful crossing to the western bank of the Suez Canal.

At another point, Mr. Sadat stopped and had a special greeting for Golda Meir, the former prime minister.

"I have wanted to meet you for a long time," Mr.

Sadat said. Mrs. Meir replied, "Mr. President, so have I waited a long time to meet you."

Mr. Sadat bent over and kissed her on the cheek.

Theaters canceled performances, shops were shuttered and hundreds of thousands of Israelis sat glued to television sets to watch proceedings that were unthinkable two weeks before.

While the overwhelming response here to the Sadat visit was positive, some extremists in the occupied territories tried to get Palestinians to call a general strike. But the call, by the Palestine Liberation Organization, fizzled.

After the airport welcome and exchange of greetings, Mr. Sadat, accompanied by President Katzir, entered a limousine for the drive to Jerusalem, where he and his retinue will stay at the King David Hotel.

The hotel, with a view of the walled Old City captured by Israel from Jordan in 1967, was sealed by security officials, who have barred all outsiders from entering the lobby.

Extraordinary security measures attended the Sadat visit. Thousands of Israeli soldiers, policemen and security officials will be on constant alert during the visit.

At the airport, where more than 1,000 foreign and local reporters gathered to watch the momentous landing, Egyptian flags fluttered and Israeli border police carried the Arab emblem.

Among the people Mr. Sadat greeted were dignitaries from the Israeli-occupied West Bank of the Jordan, which Israel captured during the 1967 war.

Mr. Sadat's arrival time was arranged, at his request, so that it would not conflict with the Jewish Sabbath, which ended at sundown. As his plane flew low over Tel Aviv hundreds of bystanders in the streets applauded.

Along the route from the airport to Jerusalem, thousands of Israelis waited, threaded among hundreds and hundreds of security men, to see the historic procession wind its way through the serpentine roads of the Judean Hills.

One hour and ten minutes after the landing of the Egyptian plane, the first of the Arab entourage arrived in Jerusalem. Thousands cheered the procession as it moved through the streets of the city that is sacred to Moslems, Jews and Christians.

Tomorrow morning, Mr. Sadat will pray at Al Aksa Mosque, a sacred shrine, in the ancient walled city. He will take part with his Arab co-religionists in Id al-Adha, or the Feast of Sacrifices.

Afterward, he will visit a Christian shrine, the Church of the Holy Sepulcher. He is then scheduled to visit Yad Vashem, Israel's intensely emotional memorial to the six million Jews killed by Germans during World War II.

Later in the day, Mr. Sadat will address the Israeli parliament, and he is also expected to have private meetings with Mr. Begin.

The visit had a tremendous impact on Israelis. At a soccer game the day of Sadat's arrival, a peanut vendor shouted, "Sadat shalom," a play on the traditional Jewish Sabbath greeting of "Shabbat Shalom," or "Peaceful Sabbath."

As Mr. Sadat moved about on his epochal trip, he was girded by two rings—one of security men, the other of reporters craning for every utterance of the meetings between him and Mr. Begin.

It was the most dramatic Middle East encounter since Jan. 3, 1919, when Dr. Chaim Weizmann, who became Israel's first president, met with Emir Faisal, who became king of Iraq. The accord between the two so long ago was never put into effect.

Mr. Begin has let it be known he would like to visit Cairo. The other day, he said he wanted to see the Pyramids because "after all, we helped to build them."

Mr. Sadat's arrival on Israeli soil capped 10 frenetic days during which the Egyptian president's remarks to his parliament that he would go to Israel's Parliament in his quest for Middle East peace moved from rhetoric to reality.

Even by the evanescent standards of the Middle East, the presence of a major Arab leader walking on Israeli soil so soon after making such an utterance—in itself unprecedented—was dizzying.

Whether the Sadat visit will mean substantive progress toward the convening of a Middle East peace conference at Geneva to settle the protracted and bitter Arab-Israeli impasse is not known.

But the consensus among politicians, statesmen and analysts is that Mr. Sadat's visit has ineradicably altered the Middle East scene and, depending upon one's view, has in greater or lesser measure eased Israel's status as a pariah among its Arab neighbors.

Unquestionably, the days of the Sadat visit were filled with expectation and excitement. And hundreds of thousands of Israelis, weary of war and the achingly stringent demands the military has placed on them in personal and economic terms, expressed the hope that the elusive Middle East peace might be nearer.

For now, the Sadat visit has carried the nation along on a wave of euphoria that must ultimately dissipate into a more sober reality. Whether it will subside into another round of despair and a sense of hopelessness depends in good measure on what it is Mr. Sadat tells the Israeli parliament tomorrow and on the outcome of his talks with Mr. Begin.

Many Israelis have tried to balance the euphoric feeling with sober examinations of the grim realities of Middle East politics. But after 29 years of war and tension—which began the day Israel was born in 1948—the tendency to surrender to hopefulness was very strong.

The streets of Jerusalem and Tel Aviv were strange sights in the last few days. Taxis sported little Egyptian flags on their antennas; the stately King David Hotel flew the banners of both Israel and Egypt.

Visiting Egyptian reporters were hunted down by their Israeli counterparts for interviews today, and both Egyptians and Israelis made sometimes faltering, sometimes shy attempts to bridge a gap that existed before some of them were born.

"The Egyptians have taken over the city bloodlessly," said Mayor Teddy Kollek of Jerusalem after a survey of the city he had run for years and of which there is no stronger booster.

Peddlers and hucksters and anglers out for a fast buck dotted the landscape today. But no one minded. In fact, their wares, ranging from amusing to shoddy, moved briskly.

There were T-shirts emblazoned with pictures of Mr. Sadat and Mr. Begin and captioned in English: "All you need is love."

One line of artifacts noted the common religious bonds of Moslems and Jews, proclaiming: "We are the sons of one father—Abraham."

Mr. Sadat and Mr. Begin will make some more history tomorrow when the Israeli parliament—a disparate and often raucous body that is expected to be, for a change, on its best behavior—convenes to hear what the Egyptian leader who traveled so far—not only in miles—has to say.

While the speeches of Mr. Begin and Mr. Sadat are billed as delineations of each side's position, there is speculation that the historic occasion could produce concessions that could shorten the long road leading to Geneva and to a yearned-for peace.

SADAT AT THE KNESSET

WILLIAM E. FARRELL

A FORMER legislator roamed the halls of the Israeli parliament on Nov. 21, 1977, conducting the most extraordinary bout of lobbying ever seen in that raucous and unpredictable body.

President Anwar el-Sadat of Egypt met with the disparate and often combative political factions that make up Israel's parliament. His message, which became almost incantatory with each repetition, was: "Let's fight no more wars; let's solve the very real differences between Arabs and Jews at a table, not on a battlefield."

A former speaker of the Egyptian parliament, Mr. Sadat seemed at ease, lapsing easily into the camaraderie of politicians who, whatever their political stripe or nationality, have such things as smoke-filled rooms and horse-trading and compromise and ambition in common.

Even when some of the Israelis were saying things that the Egyptian leader totally disagreed with, he displayed the mien of the consummate political operative. He basked almost shyly in the praise of those who lauded his bold move to come to a country with which he is at war.

And when each had finished his presentation depending upon his place in the political spectrum—Communist, right-wing hawk, left-wing dove, middle-of-the-road moderate—Mr. Sadat easily regained center stage by saying, about the 1973 conflict, "The October war is the last forever." Each time he was applauded.

By the time he greeted the Labor party bloc, the once predominant political entity and now the leading opposition party, he was relaxed enough to fish out a pipe and puff contentedly while some of the Laborites succumbed to that political hazard—long-windedness.

Of all the meetings, which had been scheduled at the Egyptian leader's request, he felt most at ease with the Labor members. And of all the Laborites, it was evident that the one he liked the most was Golda Meir, the former prime minister.

And it certainly seemed as though Mrs. Meir liked Mr. Sadat. The two old foes, who once sat in war rooms each plotting the other's defeat, sat beside each other—Mr. Sadat wreathed in pipe smoke, Mrs. Meir clutching her ever-present cigarette.

Direct contact is infinitely preferable to contact through intermediaries, the 79-year-old Mrs. Meir said.

"When you sit here and I look at you and I heard you last night it's not the same," she said. "I believe in your sincere desire for peace."

Then with directness, even bluntness, she turned to the alternately smiling and somber Egyptian and said: "Let us at least conclude one thing, the beginning that you made with such courage and with such hope for peace, let us decide one thing, it must go on, face to face, between us and between you so that even an old lady like I am will live to see the day."

At this point, Mr. Sadat roared with laughter as Mrs. Meir neatly pinioned him with one of his own epithets.

"You always called me an old lady, Mr. President," she said, and the laughter spread. "I want to live to see that day of peace between you and us." Mrs. Meir then presented Mr. Sadat—"as a grandmother to a grandfather"—with a gift for a newborn granddaughter.

After the lobbying, Mr. Sadat joined Prime Minister Menachem Begin at a news conference attended by many of the nearly 4,000 reporters who had come to Israel for the visit.

At the airport, in the last round of ceremonies, Mr. Sadat greeted members of the diplomatic corps and then government officials. In the Israeli line, the decorousness was shattered a couple of times, reflecting some of the warmth that had crept into the contacts the Egyptian had made.

"Ah, Moshe," he said to Foreign Minister Moshe Dayan.

"Oh, Mr. Jerusalem," Mr. Sadat said as he clasped the hand of Mayor Teddy Kollek, who accompanied him on his tour of Jerusalem yesterday.

Mr. Sadat listened, as he had on his arrival, to the Egyptian national anthem played by an Israeli band, then inspected the honor guard and saluted the two nations' flags.

As he strode down the red carpet to his plane for the trip home—the psychological distance to Egypt shortened by the man who governs it—Mr. Sadat turned and said, "Thanks for everything, thanks for everything."

A few minutes later, as exhausted security men sighed with relief, the final anomaly of the day appeared in the shimmering afternoon sky. Mr. Sadat's plane, bearing the insignia "Arab Republic of Egypt," zoomed off to join an honor escort of four Israeli Kfir fighters.

THE SIGNING OF THE PEACE TREATY

BERNARD GWERTZMAN

AFTER CONFRONTING each other for nearly 31 years as hostile neighbors, Egypt and Israel signed a formal treaty at the White House on March 27, 1979, to establish peace and "normal and friendly relations."

On a chilly early spring day, about 1,500 invited guests and millions more watching television saw President Anwar el-Sadat of Egypt and Prime Minister Menachem Begin of Israel put their signatures on the Arabic, Hebrew and English versions of the first peace treaty between Israel and an Arab country.

President Carter, who was credited by both leaders for having made the agreement possible, signed, as a witness, for the United States. In a somber speech he said, "Peace has come."

"We have won, at last, the first step of peace—a first step on a long and difficult road," he added.

At the signing ceremony, all three leaders offered prayers that the treaty would bring true peace to the Middle East and end the enmity that has erupted into war four times since Israel declared its independence on May 14, 1948.

By coincidence, they all referred to the words of the Prophet Isaiah.

"Let us work together until the day comes when they beat their swords into plowshares and their spears into pruning hooks," Mr. Sadat said in his paraphrase of the biblical text.

Mr. Begin, who gave the longest and most emotional of the addresses, exclaimed: "No more war, no more bloodshed, no more bereavement, peace unto you, shalom, saalam, forever."

Shalom and *salaam* are the Hebrew and Arabic words for "peace."

The Israeli leader, noted for oratorical skill, provided a dash of humor when in the course of his speech he seconded Mr. Sadat's remark that Mr. Carter was "the unknown soldier of the peacemaking effort." Mr. Begin said, pausing, "I agree, but as usual with an amendment"—that Mr. Carter was not completely unknown and that his peace effort would "be remembered and recorded by generations to come."

Since Mr. Begin was known through the negotiations as a stickler for details, much to the American side's annoyance, Mr. Carter seemed to explode with laughter at Mr. Begin's reference to "an amendment."

Minutes later, Mr. Begin was deeply somber as he put on the yarmulke (Jewish skullcap) and quoted in Hebrew from Psalm 126.

The signing was followed by an outdoor dinner on the South Lawn at the White House for 1,300 guests.

The treaty was the result of months of grueling, often frustrating negotiations that finally were concluded early this morning when a final compromise was reached on the last remaining issue—a timetable for Israel to give up Sinai oil fields.

Under the treaty, Israel will withdraw its military forces and civilians from the Sinai Peninsula in stages over three years. Two thirds of the area will be returned within nine months, after formal ratification documents are exchanged. The ratification process is expected to begin in about two weeks.

In return for Israel's withdrawal, Egypt has agreed to end the state of war and to establish peace. After the initial nine-month withdrawal is completed, Egypt and Israel will establish "normal and friendly relations" in many fields, including diplomatic, cultural and economic relations.

The outline for the peace treaty was achieved in September 1978 when Mr. Carter, Mr. Sadat and Mr. Begin met at Camp David, Md., for 13 days. In addition to the treaty, they also agreed on the framework for an accord to provide self-rule to the more than one million Palestinians living in the Israeli-occupied areas of the West Bank of the Jordan and the Gaza Strip.

The Camp David accords were opposed by most countries in the Arab world for two reasons. The Arabs regarded the decision by Mr. Sadat to sign a peace treaty with Israel as a betrayal of the Arab cause, since it suggested that Egypt would no longer be willing to go to war against Israel to help Syria, Jordan, and the Palestinians regain territory.

Arabs also viewed the self-rule agreement for Palestinians as insufficient because it did not guarantee the creation of a Palestinian state.

As a result of that opposition, the signing was greeted by criticism throughout the Arab world. Echoes of that were heard in Washington, where about a thousand Arabs demonstrated in Lafayette Park, several hundred yards from the signing ceremony. Their anti-Sadat chants could be heard at the White House.

"We must not minimize the obstacles that still lie ahead," Mr. Carter said. "Differences still separate the signatories to this treaty from each other and also from some of their neighbors who fear what they have just done.

"To overcome these differences, to dispel those fears, we must rededicate ourselves to the goal of a broader peace with justice for all who have lived in a state of conflict in the Middle East.

"We have no illusions—we have hopes, dreams, prayers, yes—but no illusions."

Mr. Carter read out a long passage that turned on a metaphor of peace being waged like war. It was later disclosed by the White House that the section was quoted from an essay written by the Rev. Walker L. Knight in the *House Missions* magazine of the Southern Baptist Convention.

At the end of the ceremony Mr. Carter, Mr. Sadat and Mr. Begin grasped each other in a three-way handclasp. Despite the show of cordiality, there were signs that differences between Egypt and Israel were far from over.

In his speech, Mr. Sadat never referred to Mr. Begin, whom he reportedly does not like personally. By contrast, Mr. Sadat praised Mr. Carter as "the man who performed the miracle."

"Without any exaggeration, what he did constitutes one of the greatest achievements of our time," President Sadat said.

In the printed text of his speech, Mr. Sadat made a strong appeal to Mr. Carter to lend "support and backing" to the Palestinians and reassure them that they would be able "to take the first step on the road to self-determination and statehood."

The following was in the text of Mr. Sadat's address, but he did not read it publicly: "No one is more entitled to your support and backing than the Palestinian people. A grave injustice was inflicted upon them in the past. They need a reassurance that they will be able to take the first step on the road to self-determination and statehood.

"A dialogue between the United States and the representatives of the Palestinian people will be a very helpful development. On the other hand, we must be certain that the provisions of the Camp David framework on the establishment of a self-governing authority with full autonomy are carried out. There must be a genuine transfer of authority to the Palestinians in their land. Without that, the problem will remain unsolved."

The remarks about the Palestinians would have been provocative to Mr. Begin, who has declared he will never permit a Palestinian state to be established. He has called the Palestine Liberation Organization the most "barbaric" group since the Nazis.

Later, Mohammed Hakki, the Egyptian embassy's spokesman, said that the section on the Palestinians, which was on page seven of the printed text, had been "inadvertently" omitted because Mr. Sadat had turned two pages, instead of one, and accidentally skipped that portion.

Mr. Begin's speech seemed highly charged with personal emotions, especially in two separate allusions to Jerusalem. These amounted to a reassertion of the Israeli stand on Jerusalem, in a context that was likely to prove embarrassing to Mr. Sadat.

The Israeli prime minister said that it was "the

third greatest day in my life." The first, he said, was the day of Israel's independence, May 14, 1948, and the second "was when Jerusalem became one city and our brave, perhaps most hardened soldiers, the parachutists, embraced with tears and kissed the ancient stones of the remnants of the wall destined to protect the chosen place of God's glory."

This was a reference to Israel's capture of East Jerusalem from Jordan in the 1967 war and Israel's subsequent annexation of that part of the city to become part of Israeli Jerusalem.

A major point of difference between Israel and the Arabs is the future of Jerusalem, with the Arabs, including Egypt, insisting that Israel must relinquish control over the eastern sector, and Israel's declarations that it will never yield it.

The peace treaty negotiations went through a series of ups and downs and surprises.

They began in October 1978 in Washington with expectations of an early conclusion. Although the basic treaty text was approved by both Egypt and Israel by early December, three months more were needed to obtain agreements on differing interpretations of the treaty—the subject of a separate document of "agreed minutes"—and over issues such as when ambassadors would be exchanged and target dates for beginning and concluding the Palestinian self-rule negotiations.

Mr. Carter finally resolved most of the questions during a weeklong trip to the Middle East earlier in March 1979.

Even though both governments approved the treaty, it was not completed until late the night before the signing, when Mr. Begin and Mr. Sadat agreed that the Sinai oil field would be returned to Egypt seven months after the treaty was ratified, instead of the nine months Israel had preferred and the six months Egypt had earlier asked.

In addition, Mr. Begin agreed to turn over the El Arish area within two months instead of the three months originally proposed by Israel.

An arrangement was also made to insure Israel a right to buy oil from the fields without interruption.

Even in last-minute final drafting, differences arose over whether to call a body of water the Gulf of Aqaba or the Gulf of Eilat. The Arabic and English texts refer to it as Aqaba, the name of the Jordanian port by that name. The Hebrew version calls it Eilat, after the Israeli port adjacent to Aqaba.

The White House made public the texts of all the documents included in the peace treaty package. These include the actual preamble, nine articles, three annexes and one appendix that comprise the actual treaty text. In addition, there is a document of "agreed minutes" covering differing interpretations of the treaty.

A letter signed by Mr. Begin and Mr. Sadat and covering the controversial "linkage" question of when negotiations on the Palestinian self-rule questions would begin—one month after ratification of the treaty—and when the negotiations would conclude—about a year afterward—was also released, as were certain clarification letters from Mr. Carter and maps.

THE PROPHET WHO FAILED TO SEE SOME FATEFUL SIGNS

HENRY TANNER

FEW WHO watched him over the years ever thought Anwar el-Sadat would become a tragic figure. There were moments when strain and loneliness broke through his usual expression of bonhomie. But most of the time, the descriptions of him that came to mind were slightly dismissive—intelligent, cunning, mercurial, debonair, well-tailored, vain, vindictive. There were times when it was difficult to take him entirely seriously. But at his assassination, the tragedy of the man was there for all to see.

He died of shots fired by soldiers, whom he used to address as "my sons." He was killed as he rose to salute his assassins, thinking they were putting on a special display for him. His funeral was held in a military area well away from the mass of ordinary Egyptians whose name he had invoked so many times.

The Cairenes who had poured out by the hundreds of thousands to applaud him showed few signs of grief. If most were saddened, many seemed indifferent. Some were afraid of the future. It seemed no exaggeration when an Egyptian reporter who had admired him said, "Sadat died a man alone."

What went wrong for Mohammed Anwar el-Sadat? What is his legacy? How much of it will be lasting?

Most foreigners in Cairo are convinced that President Sadat's successors want to continue his foreign policy. Even in the long term, they believe the changes will be in accents more than basics. Mr. Sadat was a man of broad concepts, not detailed policies, and at least two of these concepts changed the history of the Middle East.

Early in his presidency he concluded that the Arabs could not hope to win back the territories they lost to Israel in 1967 and achieve an acceptable settlement so long as the United States was the exclusive friend of Israel and the Arabs relied on the Soviet Union. He ended that polarization.

With President Sadat gone and the Israelis talking to Moscow for the first time in years, the Soviet Union may once more gain a diplomatic role in the area, but the old superpower lineup will not be restored.

The other permanent change was triggered by President Sadat's trip to Jerusalem and the peace treaty that flowed from it. The Israelis may find Hosni Mubarak more difficult to deal with than Mr. Sadat. But the precedent of an Arab leader recognizing Israel and negotiating with it has been set and moderate Arabs elsewhere may take it up sooner or later.

Egyptians had hoped that peace with Israel and friendship with the United States would also bring improved living conditions—bread, cars, apartments, television sets, good wages and jobs for all. These Mr. Sadat could not deliver.

The tragedy of his presidency is the failure of his policies at home. He started out as a man who ended political oppression. After a generation of one-party rule, he permitted three parties to be formed and to express their views, albeit carefully, within a national consensus.

He ended many of the police state aspects of the Nasser regime. For a time, Egyptians no longer had to fear the police knock on the door at dawn. They spoke freely without looking over their shoulders, even when they had unkind words to say about their president. A relatively permissive one-man ruler then, Mr. Sadat had genuine personal popularity.

He spoke often of wanting to set up permanent institutions. He had the wisdom to pick a successor, and the succession procedures he decided upon are being applied now.

He broke 20 years of state control over the economy and opened the way for an enormous influx of Western capital, technology and aid.

But he also turned loose the speculators and profiteers. There was little effective planning. Much of the construction in Cairo has been speculative and completely uninhibited by zoning laws. Almost no new housing has been built for the poor.

A small, wealthy middle class has been created, consisting of those who managed to insert themselves into his "open door" policy with the West. But overall, the economy remains a shambles. The rich have been getting richer, and the very poor, who are the majority of Egypt's 43 million people, are getting poorer.

Mr. Sadat's regime began to change as internal difficulties piled up and prosaic day-to-day aggravations took the place of the grand international initiatives he had relished. Having revoked many of the repressive practices of his predecessors, he introduced repressive measures of his own. A "law of shame" was proclaimed under which citizens were jailed on such vague charges as "violation of national unity." The political parties he created lost most of their freedom of action, and almost total conformity was imposed once again on the newspapers.

Mr. Sadat had never been one to accept personal criticism easily. Now he turned with vindictiveness on those who dared to cross him. The last major political act of his life was the crackdown against dissidents in early September 1981. The main targets were Moslem fundamentalists. More than a thousand of them, ranging from bearded young extremists to influential preachers, were jailed. Other victims were academics, lawyers, politicians and journalists.

Many Moslem and Coptic Christian associations were closed, 65 journalists were transferred to government service, several foreign correspondents were expelled. The head of the Coptic Christian Church, Shenuda III, was banished to his monastery in the western desert. For the next few weeks, President Sadat went on television every few days, threatening new crackdowns and denouncing at length criticism by American journalists of whom his Egyptian audiences had never heard.

The impression was created that the president was out of control. Many Egyptians now say that the September crisis was of Mr. Sadat's making, and that he had made his person the focal point of all tension in the country—between Moslems and Copts, left and right, Egyptian nationalists and pan-Arabists.

Egyptians commenting on the absence of any outpouring of public grief for the slain president said his popularity had been waning gradually and took a catastrophic dive in September. He was liked, even loved, as long as he seemed to reduce internal tensions and ruled without instilling fear; people turned away from him when he revived political repression.

"He has humiliated or ridiculed every religious, political and professional group in the country," said a journalist who had long supported him. "If he had been killed half a year ago, we would have wept. And if he had lived through April [when Israel is to withdraw from the rest of Sinai], perhaps we would have wept again."

There is little doubt that Mr. Sadat was killed by Moslem extremists, although the world will perhaps never know whether the mass arrests in September triggered the assassination or whether it had been planned earlier.

Moslem underground organizations in the poor neighborhoods of Egyptian cities and towns have been arming for years. The September crackdown obviously did not eliminate their power. The threat of large-scale violence by Moslem extremists is perhaps the most dangerous legacy that Mr. Sadat is leaving his successor.

MARGARET SANGER

1883–1966

As the originator of the phrase *birth control* and as its best-known advocate, Margaret Sanger survived federal indictments, a brief jail term, numerous lawsuits, hundreds of street-corner rallies and raids on her clinics to live to see much of the world accept her view that family planning is a basic human right.

The dynamic, titian-haired woman whose Irish ancestry also endowed her with unfailing charm and persuasive wit was first and foremost a feminist. She sought to create equality between the sexes by freeing women from what she saw as sexual servitude.

An active worker for the Socialist party, she included among her friends radicals of all shades—John Reed, Mabel Dodge Luhan, Bill Haywood, Emma Goldman, Alexander Berkman and Jessie Ashley.

The phrase *birth control* first appeared in 1914 in her magazine, *Woman Rebel,* which bore the slogan "No Gods; No Masters!" on its masthead.

In her days on the barricades of the birth control movement, Mrs. Sanger presented a figure not easy to forget. Many a policeman escorting her to the station had his ears wilted by Irish invective.

Trained in the methods of public demonstrations, she also could call attention to herself and her cause in more restrained environments.

Lawrence Lader, one of Mrs. Sanger's biographers, told of meetings called by a wealthy birth control advocate to discuss the movement. When her guests were deep in discussion of the problem, she would "telephone Margaret.

"Wearing a simple black dress (the more radical the ideas the more conservative you must be in your dress) Mrs. Sanger would arrive in the doorway.

"And now here is the woman who can answer all your questions. With it was a dramatic entrance that led easily into a short talk on birth control and often won new converts."

Mrs. Sanger was the daughter of Michael Hennessy Higgins, a tombstone cutter in Corning, N.Y., who was described as "a philosopher, a rebel and an artist." Mr. Higgins specialized in chiseling angels and saints out of stone. His wife—Mrs. Sanger's tubercular mother—was Anne Purcell Higgins, who died at 48 after bearing 11 children.

Mrs. Sanger herself was afflicted with incipient tuberculosis in 1903, the year after her marriage to Mr. Sanger, an artist and architect. The Sangers moved to Saranac, N.Y., in the Adirondacks, from a New York City apartment that had been a gathering place for Socialists.

"Almost without knowing it you became a 'comrade,' " Mrs. Sanger later wrote her husband of this period of their lives.

The Sanger living room had become a place where liberals, anarchists, Socialists and Wobblies

Courtesy Planned Parenthood of America

New York Times Photo

(members of the Industrial Workers of the World) could meet.

"My own personal feelings drew me toward the individualist, anarchist philosophy . . . but it seemed necessary to approach the idea by way of Socialism," she later wrote.

Trained as a nurse, she was educated at Claverack College in New York. She also studied at White Plains Hospital and Manhattan Eye and Ear Hospital.

Mrs. Sanger's life work began shortly after she returned to New York in 1912. It resulted from her job as a nurse for maternity cases, principally on the Lower East Side. Many of her patients were wives of small shopkeepers, truck drivers and pushcart vendors. Others were from a lower stratum of society.

"These submerged, untouched classes were beyond the scope of organized charity or religion," she wrote. "No labor union, no church, not even the Salvation Army reached them."

The young nurse saw them, weary and old at 35, resorting to self-induced abortions, which were frequently the cause of their deaths.

Mrs. Sanger nursed one mother, close to death after a self-inflicted abortion, back to health, and heard the woman plead with a doctor for protection against another pregnancy.

"Tell Jake to sleep on the roof," the physician said.

The mother died six months later during a second abortion.

Mrs. Sanger soon renounced nursing forever.

"I came to a sudden realization that my work as a nurse and my activities in social service were entirely palliative and consequently futile and useless to relieve the misery I saw all about me."

For nearly a year the ex-nurse read every scrap of material available on contraception. In 1913, she went to France and Scotland to study birth control conditions, returning the following year.

Her magazine, *Woman Rebel,* was the spearhead of her movement. In an early issue she specified seven circumstances in which birth control should be practiced: when either spouse has a transmittable disease; when the wife suffers a temporary infection of lungs, heart or kidneys, the cure of which might be retarded in pregnancy; when a woman is physically unfit; when parents have subnormal children; if the man and woman are adolescents; if their income is inadequate; and during the first year of marriage.

The articles did not violate New York's Comstock Law, which made it a crime to offer contraceptive information. Nevertheless, most of the issues of the *Woman Rebel* were banned by the New York post office.

In August 1914 Mrs. Sanger was indicted on nine counts of sending birth control information through the mails and was made liable to a prison term of 45 years.

She stood virtually alone. Even progressive women, Socialists and physicians offered her no assistance. Fighters for women's suffrage seemed more concerned with the vote than with Mrs. Sanger's immediate problem.

On the eve of her trial, Mrs. Sanger fled to Europe without the court's permission. There, she met H. G. Wells and became a friend of Havelock Ellis, the author of the pioneer study *Psychology of Sex.*

During her absence, Anthony Comstock, secretary of the New York Society for the Suppression of Vice, went to Mrs. Sanger's home, represented himself to Mr. Sanger as an impoverished father in search of aid and bought a birth control pamphlet from Mr. Sanger. For this sale, Mr. Sanger served a month in jail.

The indictment was quashed in 1916, shortly after Mrs. Sanger returned to this country. But she found that the indictment had aroused worldwide interest in the birth control movement and she decided to take a step beyond the propagandizing then carried on by the National Birth Control League.

Mrs. Sanger and a sister, Mrs. Ethel Byrne, a trained nurse, opened a birth control clinic on Oct. 16, 1916, in the Brownsville section of Brooklyn.

The clinic, at 46 Amboy Street, was the first birth control clinic in the United States.

The legislative approach, Mrs. Sanger wrote, "seemed a slow and tortuous method of making clinics legal; we stood a better and quicker chance of securing a favorable judicial interpretation through challenging the law directly."

Mrs. Sanger served 30 days in jail, but the case laid the groundwork for subsequent court rulings enabling physicians to give contraceptive advice "for the prevention or cure of disease."

Her sister went on an eight-day hunger strike in Brooklyn's Raymond Street Jail after her own arrest.

Despite her continued legal harassment, Mrs. Sanger's work was increasingly accepted. In 1937, a year after the Comstock Law was reinterpreted to provide for distribution of contraceptive information, the American Medical Association adopted a report that recognized birth control as part of legitimate medical practice.

In addition, she was the author of a number of books on birth control, including *What Every Girl Should Know.*

Mrs. Sanger's often picturesque struggles with the police and her differences with the Roman Catholic hierarchy furnished the birth control movement with ample publicity. On Nov. 14, 1921, when Mrs. Sanger arrived at Town Hall on West 43d Street to take part in a discussion called "Birth Control: Is It Moral?" she found the police closing the meeting.

In the angry pulling, shoving and shouting that followed, Mrs. Sanger left the platform with two policemen. A disorderly conduct charge against her was dismissed the next day. *The New York Times* account of the interrupted meeting stated that the police intervention was "brought about at the instance of Archbishop Patrick J. Hayes of this Roman Catholic Archdiocese."

Fifteen years later Town Hall was the scene of a ceremony in which the Town Hall Club gave Mrs. Sanger its annual Award of Honor for the most conspicuous contribution of the year to the enlargement and enrichment of life.

She and her adherents won a notable victory when, on Jan. 6, 1936, in the famous case of *The United States* v. *One Package,* United States District Court Judge Grover Moscowitz decided that Dr. Hannah Stone, a physician, could legally receive a contraceptive device sent to her by a physician in Japan. Subsequent interpretations of his decision greatly broadened the scope of the circulation of birth control devices and information about artificial birth control.

During one of Mrs. Sanger's visits to Europe the National Birth Control League was reorganized under the leadership of Mary Ware Dennett and Clara Stillman. Mrs. Sanger retained control of the New York State Birth Control League and later became the president of Planned Parenthood.

Mrs. Sanger's American Birth Control League, established in 1921, became the Planned Parenthood Federation of America in 1946 and led to the establishment of more than 250 Planned Parenthood centers in 150 cities throughout the country. The movement is now worldwide, with 38 member organizations and projects in 88 countries.*

"It was she who convinced America and the world that control of conception is a basic human right and like other human rights must be equally available to all," said Dr. Alan F. Guttmacher, president of the Planned Parenthood World-Wide Association.

On a visit to Japan, Mrs. Sanger was received with great cordiality by members of the Japanese government. She was the first woman to address the Japanese Diet. She was also warmly received by Jawalharlal Nehru of India. Her views on birth con-

* Planned Parenthood in 1987 had 187 affiliates in 43 states and the District of Columbia. It operates the International Family Planning Program from its headquarters in New York. The program operates in 41 foreign countries. The organization has 17,000 staff members and volunteers nationwide offering medical, educational and counseling services.

trol were widely circulated throughout the Far East and in Africa.

Mrs. Sanger was heard from in firm tones when, in September 1958, a controversy arose in New York over the refusal of Dr. Morris A. Jacobs, the city's commissioner of hospitals, to sanction birth control therapy in the hospitals.

Interviewed by telephone in her home in Tucson, Mrs. Sanger called the policy upheld by Dr. Jacobs "disgraceful." Mrs. Sanger was then nearing her 75th year and was still active as president of the International Planned Parenthood Federation.

From her Arizona home Mrs. Sanger kept up her fire of statements and letters to newspapers in behalf of birth control. Her disagreement with the Roman Catholic Church led her to say in 1960 that if Senator John F. Kennedy was elected president she would leave the United States. She opposed Mr. Kennedy because of his religion.

In an interview some weeks later Mrs. Sanger said that she had been informed that Senator and Mrs. Kennedy were both "sympathetic and understanding toward the problem of world population. I will wait out the first year of Senator Kennedy's administration and see what happens."

During her long career many institutions honored her for her work. The degree of Doctor of Letters was conferred upon her by Smith College in 1949.

Mr. and Mrs. Sanger were divorced in 1921 after having been separated for several years.

In 1922, Mrs. Sanger was married to J. Noah H. Slee, owner of the Three-in-One Oil manufacturing concern. The industrialist, who died in 1941, contributed large sums to the birth control movement. During her marriage to Mr. Slee, she continued to use the name of Margaret Sanger. Mrs. Sanger died in Tucson, Ariz., on Sept. 6, 1966. She was 82.

JEAN-PAUL SARTRE

1905–1980

By Alden Whitman

Jean-Paul Sartre's existentialist philosophy influenced two generations of writers and thinkers throughout the world.

Long regarded as one of France's reigning intellectuals, Mr. Sartre contributed profoundly to the social consciousness of the post–World War II generation through his leftward political commitments, which took him away from his desk and into the streets. He had ideas on virtually every subject, which were developed in novels, plays, biographies, essays and tracts.

Mr. Sartre's points of view were less heeded—although still respected—in the 1970s as he became a maverick political outsider on the extreme left. His last substantial work was a biography of the 19th-century French novelist Gustave Flaubert. Mr. Sartre completed just three of the four volumes he had planned, and while he used the biography to elaborate his own notions of psychology, society, letters and life, the work provoked only limited interest in literary circles.

Although he was once closely allied with the Communist party, Mr. Sartre was for the last 15 or so years an independent revolutionary who spoke more in the accents of Maoism than of Soviet Communism. As an intellectual and a public figure—a man the police disliked to arrest—he used his prestige to defend the rights of ultraleftist groups to express themselves, and in 1973 he became titular editor of *Libération,* a radical Paris daily. In addition he lent his name to manifestos and open letters in favor of repressed groups in Greece, Chile and Spain. He was a rebel with a thousand causes, a modern Don Quixote.

Mr. Sartre was scarcely less well known as a writer and thinker than Simone de Beauvoir, his staunch and close companion of many years. Their relationship persisted through numerous phases, but their basic attachment to each other, their fortification of each other, was never seriously doubted.

In the mid-1950s Mr. Sartre, with Albert Camus and a few others, was an iridescent intellectual leader, virtually a cult object. But he later became more of an ancestor figure whose generative conceptions had lost their force.

It was fashionable to say that his lasting contribution would be his plays, implying that his essays and novels would not survive. As a philosopher he was increasingly criticized for his unsystematic approach and for the retractions in his later writing. Nonetheless, few denied him respect for his continued attempts to live his ideas, often at the cost of ridicule.

"I have put myself on the line in various actions," Mr. Sartre said several years ago. He had in mind his activity against the Gaullist regime and his sometimes lonely protests against the American involvement in Vietnam. In 1966 and 1967, for example, he

AGIP/Pictorial Parade

Copyright by Gisela Freund

was a principal in the International War Crimes Tribunal, a private group that condemned the United States role in Indochina long before it was widely rejected in the West.

Much earlier in his career as a free-wheeling leftist, during the Nazi occupation of France, Mr. Sartre had, he said, "indeed worked with the Communists, as did all Resistants who were anti-Fascist." His support lasted until the Hungarian uprising of 1956 and the intervention by Russian troops. "The French Communist party supported the invasion of Hungary, so I broke with it," he explained. After backing the Algerian nationalists in their struggles with France, he moved steadily more leftward, and after the French demonstrations and street fighting of May 1968 he was an active militant.

Among other things, he permitted himself to be arrested—these arrests did not result in jail terms—for ultraleftist causes; his voice became more strident, and he lectured his fellow thinkers about class warfare: "The task of the intellectual is not to decide where there are battles but to join them wherever and whenever the people wage them. Commitment is an act, not a word."

His sense of commitment precluded homage. For this reason he rejected the Nobel Prize in Literature, awarded him in 1964, on the ground that he did not wish to be "transformed into an institution." He also turned down the Legion of Honor for its bourgeois connotations.

Mr. Sartre's philosophical views developed and shifted. In *The Words,* the caustically ironic story of his youth, published in the mid-1960s, he criticized the social, philosophical and literary ideas with which he had been raised and he called into question the presuppositions of his early works. Commenting on his autobiographical novel *Nausea* and his philosophical work *Being and Nothingness,* he said that an attitude of aristocratic idealism lay behind their composition, which he now rejected. The core of his existentialism, however, was not condemned. Roughly expressed, this suggests that "man makes himself" despite his "contingency" in an "absurd world."

His existentialism, which was nonreligious despite the clerical origins of the philosophy, seemed to express a widespread disillusionment with fixed ideas amid the revolutionary changes that flowed from World War II and the chaotic breakup of colonial empires. Out of this existentialism came such diverse manifestations as the antinovel and the antihero, the New Wave cinema and the notion of man's anguished consciousness. Also implicit in it was a call to action, in which man could vindicate his freedom and assume some control of his destiny.

This was a far different set of values from those into which Jean-Paul Sartre was born in Paris on June 21, 1905. His father, Jean-Baptiste, was a naval officer who died shortly after his son's birth. His mother, Anne-Marie Schweitzer, was a first cousin of Albert Schweitzer, the theologian and jungle physician.

In *The Words,* Mr. Sartre recalled that until 1919, when she remarried, his mother and he lived with her parents, Charles and Louise Schweitzer, mostly in Paris. The grandparental home was, he said, a "hothouse" of bourgeois hypocrisy, where role playing was taken seriously and he became an imposter, too. His father's death, he went on, not only meant that the son grew up with the "incredible flippancy" of a person without a superego, but also led to his inheriting a mid-19th-century concept of society and literature.

As Mr. Sartre described himself, he was an ugly "toad" of a boy, without friends his age. It was demanded of him by his doting, authoritarian grandfather that he be a prodigy; and by pretending to read, he actually learned to read before he was 4. By plagiarizing, he learned in a few years how to write stories, a process that hastened his retreat from life into words, which he came to regard as "the quintessence of things," more real than the objects they denoted.

With his increasing erudition, the young Sartre grew in cynicism about all religion, but he clung to one of his grandfather's Lutheran concepts, the Holy Spirit. This was a divine muse that inspired a literary "elect," of whom he once thought himself one.

As an overprotected child, the boy was tutored at home for some years, and once in school he was slowed at first by faulty spelling and a difficulty in getting "used to democracy." Shortly, though, he became without effort a very good student, and he had no trouble entering the elite Ecole Normale Supérieure when he was 20.

There he began his lifelong companionship with Simone de Beauvoir, a fellow student, with an agreement pledging mutual loyalty in times of need but allowing "contingent loves." Among his other student friends were Albert Camus and Raymond Aron, the political observer, with both of whom Mr. Sartre broke after the war.

After taking his *agrégation*—a degree slightly higher than a Doctor of Philosophy—he went to Germany in 1933 to study under Edmund Husserl and Martin Heidegger, two of the most influential European philosophers, interested in the nature of being and reality and the mysteries of perception.

Existentialism has a mixed parentage and there are several versions of it. Mr. Sartre's ideas were summed up by Frank Kappler, an American writer who, after quoting Mr. Sartre's famous formula—"Existence precedes essence"—wrote: "Man comes into a totally opaque, undifferentiated, meaningless universe. By the power of his mysterious consciousness, which Sartre calls unmeant, man makes of the universe a habitable world. Whatever meaning and value the world has comes from his existential choice. These choices differ from one to another.

"Each lives in his own world, or, as Sartre also says, each creates his own situation. Frequently this existential choice is buried in a lower level of consciousness. But to become truly alive, one must become aware of oneself as an 'I'—that is, a true existential subject, who must bear alone the responsibility for his own situation."

And in this predicament, Mr. Sartre believed, one can choose an "inauthentic existence," or one can commit oneself by a resolute act of free choice to a positive role in human affairs. Most of these ideas are elaborated in *Being and Nothingness,* which he wrote during the Nazi occupation of France. In 1938, he had published *Nausea,* a novel in which a character named Antoine Roquentin, living in Bouville (or Mudville), is seized with the horrors of existentialism while meditating in a public park.

The novel, which still makes instructive reading, ends when Roquentin decides that if he can only create something, a novel perhaps, his creativity could mean engagement. The central character was almost certainly Mr. Sartre himself, an impression heightened by the book's original English title, *The Diary of Antoine Roquentin.*

By the end of World War II, Mr. Sartre was well known in France both for his writings and for his activity in the Resistance. His philosophy suited many of the younger generation of students, who had been knocked about by the war physically and spiritually, for they saw in existentialism an opportunity for salvation through commitment to a "new" French culture.

Mr. Sartre and his disciples at first gathered at the Café de Flore near the Place St.-Germain des Prés on Paris's Left Bank. Little was available at the Flore then except tasteless tea, but the ferment of discussion was stimulation enough. And as the group grew, it and a crowd of gawkers moved to the more roomy Café Pont-Royal.

After doing two plays during the war, including *No Exit,* Mr. Sartre busied himself with the theater in a number of dramas of ideas. These included *The Respectful Prostitute,* an indictment of racism in America; *The Victors,* about an ordeal of conscience among Resistance fighters; *The Devil and the Good Lord,* in which a group of peasants who accept the kindness of a tyrant discover that complacency is futile so long as others are oppressed; and *The Condemned of Altona,* about a former Nazi who is tormented by the significance history may place on his acts.

In addition to his plays Mr. Sartre was writing biographies of Baudelaire, the 19th-century poet, and Jean Genet. Mr. Genet, a man with a long criminal record who wrote exceedingly well, was celebrated as an antihero—an orphan, judged delinquent by society, who had decided to play the role assigned to him.

Parts of these and other of his writings were published in *Les Temps Modernes,* his monthly review founded in 1945. The periodical, once quite influential, has declined in importance.

Mr. Sartre was a short, wall-eyed man who always seemed in a fury of creativity. Relaxing from his desk, he was attentive, natural and full of good humor. This was in keeping with his view that life was a game board on which he created both the game and the rules. He had, he once said, "incredible levity."

He lived simply, with few possessions other than his books, in a small apartment on the Left Bank. His gradual loss of sight—he was virtually blind at his death—and failing health forced him to curtail his public appearances. On March 20, 1980, Mr. Sartre was admitted to Proussais Hospital, where he died on April 15.

During his last years he continued to speak out on political and social issues. In 1977, opposing the emerging trend of Eurocommunism independent of the Soviet Union, he accused the Italian Communist party of collaborating with the Christian Democratic party in a program of patronage and repression.

Life/Situations, a collection of his essays, was published in translation in the United States in the same year. In one of these, "Self-Portrait at 70," he writes amusingly of his careless way with money, his fondness for music and the changes he had to make in his life when he could no longer see to read.

Although Mr. Sartre betrayed a certain amiability, he remained until the end an angry man. "As far as the state of French politics goes, I don't see a lot I can do," he wrote. "It's so rotten what's happening in France now! And there's no hope in the immediate future; no party offers any hope at all."

On death, he commented in a book of photographs in 1978: "I think of death only with tranquillity, as an end. I refuse to let death hamper life. Death must enter life only to define it."

IGOR STRAVINSKY

1882–1971

By Donal Henahan

During World War I, Igor Stravinsky was asked by a guard at the French border to declare his profession. "An inventor of music," he said.

It was a typical Stravinsky remark: flat, self-assured, flagrantly antiromantic. The composer who revolutionized the music of his time was a dapper little man who prided himself on keeping "banker's hours" at his worktable. Let others wait for artistic inspiration; what inspired Igor Stravinsky, he said, were the "exact requirements" of the next work.

Between the early pieces, written under the eye of his only teacher, Nikolai Rimsky-Korsakov, and the compositions of Stravinsky's old age, there were more than 100 works: symphonies, concertos, chamber pieces, songs, piano sonatas, operas and, above all, ballets.

The influence of these works was profound. As early as 1913, Claude Debussy was praising Stravinsky for having "enlarged the boundaries of the permissible" in music. Forty years later, the tribute of Lincoln Kirstein, director of the New York City Ballet, was remarkably similar: "Sounds he has found or invented, however strange or forbidding at the outset, have become domesticated in our ears."

Aaron Copland estimated that Stravinsky's work had influenced three generations of American composers; a decade later Copland revised the estimate to four generations, and added European composers as well. In 1965 the American Musicological Society voted Stravinsky the composer born after 1870 who was most likely to be honored in the future.

He was not unanimously honored during his lifetime. Three colorful works of his young manhood—*L'Oiseau de Feu* ("The Firebird"), *Petrushka* and *Le Sacre du Printemps* ("The Rite of Spring")—were generally admitted to be masterpieces.

But about his conversion to the austerities of neoclassicism in the 1920s, and his even more startling conversion to a cryptic serial style in the 1950s, there was critical disagreement. To some, his later works were thin and bloodless; to others, they showed a mastery only hinted at in the vivid early pieces.

To all, Stravinsky the man was a figure of fascination. The contradictions were dazzling. The composer marched through a long career with the self-assurance of a Wagner, yet was so nervous when performing in public that he thrice forgot his own piano concerto.

He once refused to compose a liturgical ballet for his earliest patron, Serge Diaghilev, "both because I disapproved of the idea of presenting the mass as a ballet spectacle and because Diaghilev wanted me to compose it and 'Les Noces' for the same price."

His Charles Eliot Norton lectures at Harvard in 1939–40 were dignified papers, delivered in French, on the high seriousness of the artist's calling. Three

Camera Press

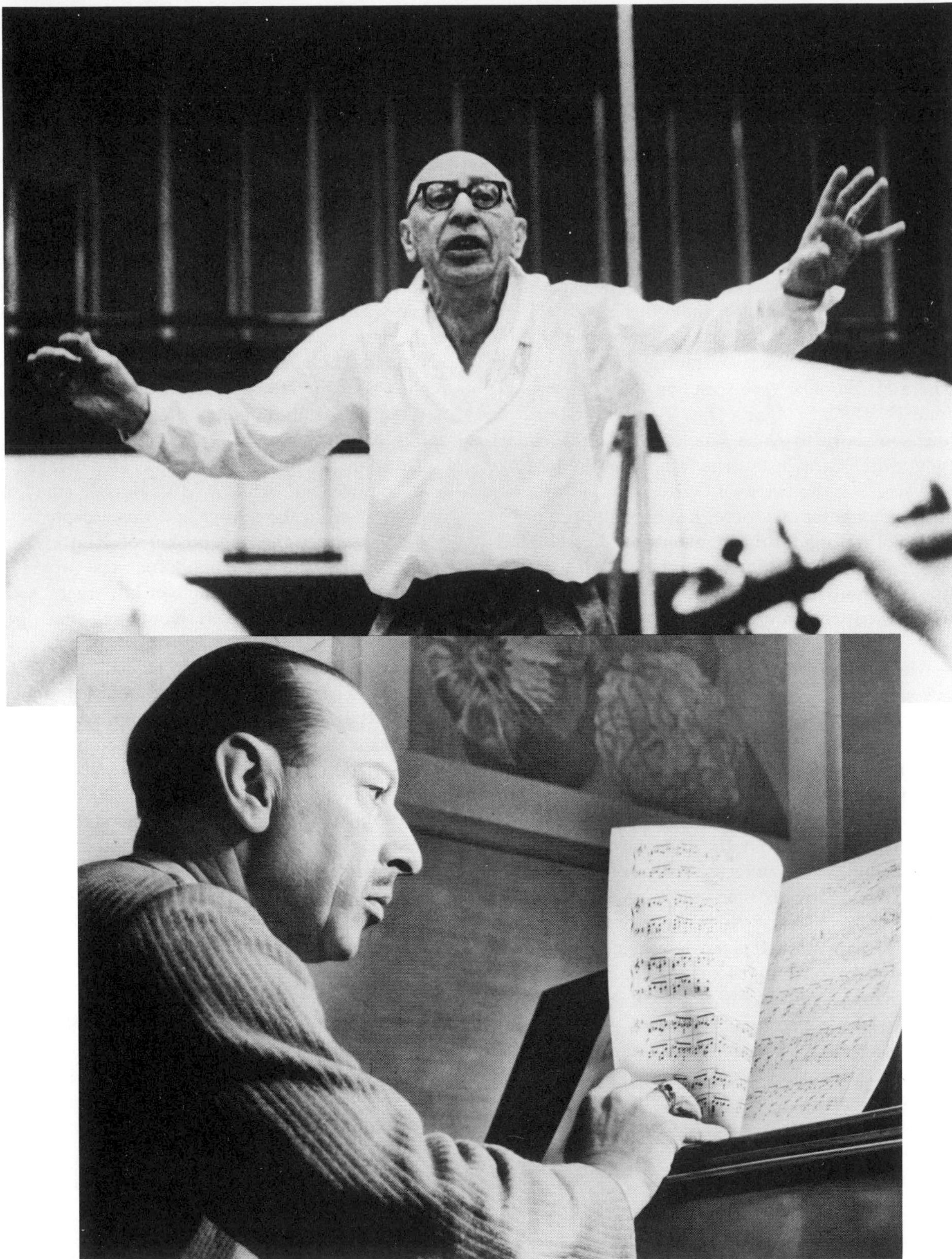

AP/WIDE WORLD

years later he wrote a polka for an elephant in the Ringling Brothers and Barnum & Bailey Circus.

He had many friends—Claude Debussy, Maurice Ravel, Pablo Picasso, Vaslav Nijinsky, André Gide, Jean Cocteau—and many homes: Russia until 1914; Switzerland (1914–20), France (1920–39) and the United States (1939 until his death). In every home he was restless at night unless a light burned outside his bedroom. That was how he slept, he explained, as a boy in St. Petersburg (now Leningrad).

Igor Feodorovich Stravinsky was born in a suburb of St. Petersburg—Oranienbaum, a village where his parents were spending the summer—on June 17, 1882, St. Igor's Day. He was the third of four sons born to Anna Kholodovsky and Feodor Ignatievitch Stravinsky. His father was the leading bass singer at the Imperial Opera in St. Petersburg.

The composer once described his childhood as "a period of waiting for the moment when I could send everyone and everything connected with it to hell." For his family he felt only "duties." At school he made few friends and proved only a mediocre student.

Music was a bright spot. At the age of 2 he surprised his parents by humming from memory a folk tune he had heard some women singing.

He dated his career as a composer from the afternoon a few years later when he tried to duplicate on one of the two grand pianos in the family's drawing room the blare of a marine band playing outside.

"I tried to pick out the intervals I had heard . . . but found other intervals in the process I liked better, which already made me a composer," Stravinsky said.

At 9, Igor started piano lessons and proved a good student, but no prodigy. Nevertheless, his interest in music grew. An uncle—"the only one in the family who believed I had any talent"—encouraged him. As a teenager he haunted his father's rehearsals at the Maryinsky Theater.

To his parents, the boy's interest in music was "mere amateurism, to be encouraged up to a point, without taking into consideration the degree to which my aptitudes might be developed." They agreed to let him study harmony with a private teacher—on the condition that he also study law at the University of St. Petersburg.

In four years at the university, Stravinsky recalled, "I probably did not hear more than 50 lectures." For by this time he had taken the first step toward becoming a composer.

One of his classmates was a son of the great Russian composer Rimsky-Korsakov. In 1902 Stravinsky visited the elder man, gave him some of his early piano pieces for criticism and asked to become his pupil. The composer looked at the scores and replied noncommittally that the young man would need more technical preparation before he could accept him as a student.

Crestfallen at first, Stravinsky decided to take this as encouragement. After a year's outside study, he applied again to the master and was accepted.

It was under the supervision of Rimsky-Korsakov that Stravinsky's first orchestral works—a symphony, a suite ("Le Faune et la Bergère"), the Scherzo Fantastique—were composed and performed.

In 1908, a few days after he had mailed his teacher the score of a new orchestral piece, "Fireworks," the package was returned to the young composer with the note "Not delivered on account of death of addressee." Stravinsky's formal education was over.

Later that year Stravinsky met Serge Diaghilev, then assembling a company of Russian dancers for a season in Paris. Impressed with the composer's first work, Diaghilev had a job for him: to orchestrate two piano pieces by Chopin for the ballet *Les Sylphides.* The commission was gratefully accepted—Stravinsky now had a wife and two children—and impressively fulfilled.

A year later there was a more important Diaghilev commission: a ballet on a Russian folk tale, *The Firebird,* for the Russian Ballet's second season at the Paris Opera House. Somewhat apprehensively—"I was still unaware of my own capabilities"—Stravinsky set to work.

The flashing, vigorous *Firebird* was a great success: so great a success that Stravinsky, in his later years, thought of it as an albatross around his neck. Arranged as an orchestral suite, it was played all over the world; the composer was asked to conduct it everywhere; it was the work the man in the street most associated with the name Stravinsky. (On a train the composer met a man who called him "Mister Fireberg.") The irony was that because Russia had no international copyright protection, *The Firebird* brought him few royalties.

The next Stravinsky-Diaghilev production was *Petrushka* (1911), a brash, colorful ballet about puppets come to life. To signify the insolence of one of the puppets, Stravinsky put some of the music in two keys at once. The combination of an F sharp major arpeggio (all black notes on the piano) and a C major arpeggio (all white notes) was to be known ever afterward as "the *Petrushka* chord": it was the first important use of bitonality in modern music.

The ballet, with Nijinsky in the title role, was another popular success. More important, said the composer, "It gave me absolute conviction of my ear."

While completing *The Firebird,* Stravinsky had a daydream about a pagan ritual in which a young girl danced herself to death. This was the genesis of *The Rite of Spring,* a revolutionary work whose premiere on May 29, 1913, caused one of the noisiest scandals in the history of music.

An open dress rehearsal had gone quietly, but protests against the music—barbarous, erotic, unlike anything Paris had ever heard—began almost as soon as the curtain went up on opening night.

Soon the Théâtre des Champs-Elysées was in an uproar. Stravinsky hurried backstage to find Diaghilev flicking the house lights in an attempt to restore order, and Nijinsky, the choreographer, bawling counts at the dancers from the wings.

Stravinsky was furious; Diaghilev, who knew the value of publicity, said afterward that the crowd's reaction had been "exactly what I wanted." Less than a year later, Pierre Monteux conducted a concert version of the score in Paris and Stravinsky received a hero's ovation.

World War I separated the composer permanently from his homeland (he did not see Russia again until a tour in 1962) and temporarily from Diaghilev. It also marked the start of a new style for Stravinsky—a leaner, more astringent, less colorful musical idiom that critics were to label "neoclassical."

An early work in the new manner was *Histoire du Soldat* ("The Soldier's Tale"), written in 1918. This was a jazzy theater piece with only seven instrumentalists. The economy of orchestration was less a matter of aesthetic choice than of practical necessity—Stravinsky and his collaborators, down on their luck in Switzerland, wanted a work that would tour cheaply—but the composer found austerity to his liking.

In the years that followed Stravinsky's postwar move to Paris, the "Apollonian principles" (as he liked to call them) of order and restraint replaced the Dionysian ecstasy of the big early works.

"One is tired of being saturated with timbres," he decided. "One wants no more of this overfeeding."

Les Noces (1923), a throbbing Russian wedding cantata, seemed a throwback to the Dionysian style. Actually, most of it had been composed before the war and could be seen, in retrospect, as part of the transition from opulence to severity.

Representative of another aspect of the new style was *Pulcinella* (1920), a ballet composed at Diaghilev's suggestion. This work employed themes attributed to the 18th-century composer Giovanni Battista Pergolesi, with contemporary glosses by Stravinsky. The composer called it "my discovery of the past."

Stravinsky now looked to the past for his models; the trick, he said, would be "to make use of academic forms . . . without becoming academic."

A piano concerto composed for his first American tour, in 1925, evoked Bach and the baroque. *Oedipus Rex* (1926) suggested a Handel oratorio. *Le Baiser de la Fée* (1928) was an explicit tribute to Tchaikovsky.

Apollon Musagète (1928) was a ballet scored for strings alone. *Capriccio* for piano and orchestra

(1929) reminded some of an up-to-date Carl Maria von Weber. *Perséphone* (1933) wore the pastels of the impressionists.

The forms had been used by others. The contents were unquestionably new and unquestionably Stravinsky's—complicated, tic-like rhythms; harmonies no less audacious for being uttered in a moderate tone of voice. During this period the composer was often accused of antiquarianism, but no one ever called him old-fashioned.

In his middle years, Stravinsky turned more and more to purely instrumental music, including the Dumbarton Oaks Concerto for chamber orchestra (1938), the Symphony in C (1940), the Symphony in Three Movements (1946).

His dogged productivity did not lessen with increasing age. Having moved to the United States in 1939, Stravinsky arranged "The Star-Spangled Banner" for a performance in Boston—and brought in the police, who almost arrested him for tampering with the National Anthem.

Then he moved to Los Angeles, where he composed the rest of his works. *Danses Concertantes* (1942), a chamber piece, was commissioned by the Werner Janssen Symphony Orchestra of that city. *Orpheus* (1948) was a ballet choreographed by an old friend, George Balanchine.

As a young man Stravinsky had written two operas: *The Emperor's Nightingale* (1908–14) and *Mavra* (1922). After World War II he began a third. *The Rake's Progress,* with libretto by W. H. Auden and Chester Kallman, was a deliberate re-creation of Mozartean 18th-century style. First performed in 1951, it received the composer's usual mixed reviews.

"You never see the change when you are driving along," Stravinsky told an interviewer in 1948. "A little curve in the road and suddenly you are proceeding east. . . ."

Donning the monk's cloth of neoclassicism had been such a change for the composer; an even more unexpected one was to come.

For years Stravinsky and Arnold Schönberg were thought to divide the world of contemporary music between them. Stravinsky was head of the tonal camp: those whose works, dissonant or not, inhabited a universe of harmonic gravity, the world of "key."

Schönberg and his disciples belonged to the 12-tone camp: a world where all notes of the scale were in free fall, none having more harmonic weight or status than another. It was a style of composition, Stravinsky had said, "essentially different" from his own.

Soon after *The Rake's Progress,* however, Stravinsky himself became a 12-tone composer—more precisely, a "serial" composer, who based each work on a series of notes stated as a "tone row" in the opening measures.

Robert Craft, a young musician whom Stravinsky had hired as an assistant in 1947, unquestionably had much to do with the composer's conversion to serialism. It is also apparent that Stravinsky, to whom obstacles were inspirations, was attracted by what he called the "dogmatism" of the row.

Whatever the reason, the tone row was the spine of his last works, among them *Agon,* a ballet (1957); "Movements" for piano and orchestra (1960); and *Abraham and Isaac,* a "sacred ballad" (1964). The change kept him a controversial composer to the last.

This did not bother Stravinsky. "I don't mind my music going on trial," he wrote in 1957. "If I'm to keep my position as a promising young composer I must accept that."

What Stravinsky could not accept was "the professional ignoramus, the journalist-reviewer pest." His battles with music critics became legendary.

At first he was above battling. In 1929 he stated grandly that his music "was not to be discussed or criticized.

"One does not criticize somebody or something that is in a functional state. The nose is not manufactured. The nose *is.* Thus also my art," he said.

Thirty years later he was naming the "pests." Winthrop Sargeant, music critic for the *New Yorker* magazine, was, to Stravinsky, "W. S. Deaf." Paul Henry Lang's unfavorable review of Stravinsky's ballet *The Flood* (1962), composed for television, brought a telegram from the composer to the *New York Herald Tribune* accusing the critic of "gratuitous malice."

But Stravinsky's scorn was not reserved for writers only. He disliked showy performers and conductors ("Stokowski's Bach? Bach's Stokowski would be more like it"). The dislike turned to loathing when the performer was caught mis-"interpreting" (a word the meticulous composer considered a personal affront) one of his pieces.

To show musicians exactly how his compositions were to be performed, especially as to their tempos, Stravinsky made piano-roll transcriptions of his works for the Pleyel Company in the early 1920s. For the same purpose, he signed an exclusive contract with Columbia Records in 1928. Well before his death, Stravinsky and his assistant, Mr. Craft, had recorded nearly all his works for Columbia.

During the 1920s Stravinsky also began to conduct and perform his works in public. Never a virtuoso pianist and scarcely trained at all in conducting, he suffered acute stage fright before his first appearances and seldom performed without a score.

Stravinsky was a small, wiry man (5 feet 3 inches, 120 pounds) whose morning regimen, until he was 67, started with a set of "Hungarian calisthenics" (including walking on his hands). A renowned hypochondriac, according to his friends, the composer would visit his Los Angeles doctor almost every day—and then hike two miles home.

Stravinsky's remarkable face—long-lobed ears, hooded eyes, large nose, small mustache, full lips—tempted portraits from many artists. A straightforward Picasso sketch of the composer once caused a furor at the Italian border. A guard refused to let it out of the country on the suspicion that it was not a portrait at all but a mysterious, and probably subversive, "plan." "It is a plan of my face," Stravinsky protested. But the sketch had to leave the country in a diplomatic pouch from the British embassy.

To Stravinsky, composing music was a process of solving musical problems: problems that he insisted on defining before he started to work.

Before writing *Apollon Musagète,* for example, he wrote to Elizabeth Sprague Coolidge, who had commissioned the ballet, for the exact dimensions of the hall in which it would be performed, the number of seats in the hall, even the direction in which the orchestra would be facing.

"The more constraints one imposes, the more one frees one's self," he would say. "And the arbitrariness of the constraint serves only to obtain precision of execution."

He worked like a craftsman in a room that looked like a laboratory, organized down to the very labels on the gum erasers and the pens for different-colored inks. He worked almost every day, behind closed doors ("I have never been able to compose unless sure that no one would hear me"). Unlike many composers, he worked directly at the piano.

Some took this to indicate that Stravinsky's "ear" was not as acute as one might have expected. He defended the practice: "Fingers are not to be despised . . . [they] often give birth to subconscious ideas that might otherwise never come to life. . . . I think it is a thousand times better to compose in direct contact with the physical medium of sound than to work in the abstract medium produced by one's imagination."

"Our Igor," Diaghilev used to sigh. "Always money, money, money." It was a frequent criticism of the composer that he not only worked like a businessman but also charged like one.

Stravinsky coolly agreed that he had never "regarded poverty as attractive" and that his ambition was "to earn every penny that my art would enable me to extract" from a society that had let Mozart and Bartók die in poverty.

Most of his works were written on commission—"The trick," he once wrote, "is to compose what one wants to compose and get it commissioned afterwards"—and the fees were handsome. But they did not affect his artistic independence.

Many of Stravinsky's works, especially during his last years, were based on religious themes—*Symphony of Psalms* (1930), *Canticum Sacrum* (1956), *Threni* (1958) and others.

To write good church music, the composer maintained, one had to believe, literally, in what the church stood for: "the Person of the Lord, the Person of the Devil and the Miracles of the Church."

He was himself such a believer. Born into the Russian Orthodox Church, he left it in 1910. Later he discovered "the necessity of religious belief" and was a regular communicant from 1926 to 1939.

Thereafter his churchgoing lapsed a bit. But to the end he considered himself staunchly Russian Orthodox, tempted at times by Roman Catholicism—he wrote a Roman Catholic mass in 1948—but remaining with the faith of his fathers "for linguistic reasons."

Words fascinated Stravinsky. Besides Russian he could hold forth, and make puns, in French, German and English.

"When I work with words in music, my musical saliva is set in motion by the sounds and rhythms of the syllables," he said.

Stravinsky wrote his own librettos for two works—*Renard* (1915) and *Les Noces*—and wrote several books as well.

Chronicles of My Life (1936) and *Poetics of Music* (1948), the latter his Harvard lectures, expounded Stravinsky's ideas about music with dry, episcopal confidence: "Music is by its very nature essentially powerless to express anything at all. . . . The sensation produced by music is that evoked by contemplation of the interplay of architectural forms. . . . The more art is controlled, limited, worked over, the more it is free."

No less controversial but far more lively were the books written with the help of Mr. Craft: *Conversations with Igor Stravinsky* (1958), *Memories and Commentaries* (1959), *Expositions and Developments* (1962), *Dialogues and a Diary* (1963), *Themes and Episodes* (1966) and *Retrospections and Conclusions* (1969).

These "disguised monologues" combined contradictory recollections of the past, domestic trivia, name-dropping anecdotage, gratuitous insults, handsome compliments, bad puns and stunning insights into life, art and self. They were a portrait of the composer that few artists would have dared paint, and Stravinsky was proud of them.

Stravinsky married twice. His first wife, Catherine Nossenko ("my dearest friend and playmate"), was his first cousin. Married in 1906, they had four children: Theodore, Ludmilla, Sviatoslav Soulima and Maria Milena. Ludmilla died in 1938 and Mrs. Stravinsky in 1939, both of tuberculosis.

In 1940 Stravinsky married Vera de Bossett, a painter.

The man whose *Le Sacre du Printemps* exploded in the face of the music world in 1913 and blew it into the 20th century died of heart failure on April 6, 1971, in his apartment in New York City. He was 88 years old.

Stravinsky's power as a detonating force and his position as this century's most significant composer were summed up by Pierre Boulez: "The death of Stravinsky means the final disappearance of a musical generation which gave music its basic shock at the beginning of this century and which brought about the real departure from Romanticism.

"Something radically new, even foreign to Western tradition, had to be found for music to survive, and to enter our contemporary era. The glory of Stravinsky was to have belonged to this extremely gifted generation and to be one of the most creative of them all."

George Balanchine, head of the New York City Ballet and a fellow Russian and longtime friend, said: "I feel he is still with us. He has left us the treasures of his genius, which will live with us forever. We must have done 20 ballets together, and I hope to do more."

STRAVINSKY'S BURIAL IN VENICE

IN GOLDEN sunshine, Igor Stravinsky was buried on April 15, 1971, in the cemetery on the island of San Michele, close to his friend and early patron, Sergei Diaghilev.

The Russian-born composer, who died in New York on Friday at the age of 88, had asked to be interred in the Russian corner of the cemetery. His flower-bedecked coffin was transported to the cemetery by gondola.

Stravinsky had long been fond of Venice, where several of his works, including *The Rake's Progress,* were first performed. Diaghilev, the ballet impresario and choreographer who produced the first performance of *Le Sacre du Printemps* in 1913, died in 1929.

The composer's burial today was preceded by religious services in the Gothic Church of San Giovanni e Paolo, traditional site of the obsequies of the doges of Venice.

Mrs. Vera Stravinsky, the widow, and his children by his first marriage heard the mayor of Venice, Giorgio Longo, deliver a short address quoting Stravinsky and Ezra Pound in words of affection and praise for the city.

The poet was present in the church, as was Nicolas Nabokov, the composer, who accompanied Mrs. Stravinsky, Eugene Berman, stage designer, Peggy Guggenheim, and representatives of the Italian and Austrian music worlds.

Robert Craft directed the orchestra of Venice's Le Fenice Theater and the chorus of the Italian radio in Stravinsky's *Requiem Canticles,* following which the Archimandrite of the Greek Orthodox Church, Cheruin Malissianos, performed the religious ceremony, intoning benedictions and burning incense before the coffin.

From the church, a small procession of family and floral tributes crossed the square dominated by Verrocchio's Colleoni Monument and embarked by gondola to the island cemetery of San Michele.

THE SYMBOL OF THE AVANT-GARDE

HAROLD C. SCHONBERG

WHEN THE history of 20th-century music comes to be written, Igor Stravinsky will occupy the most prominent position in the period from about 1910 to the beginning of World War II. More than any other composer, he put his mark on an entire generation. He was a shaper, a seminal force, a creator who was the symbol of the musical avant-garde not only in the public eye but also—much more important—in the estimation of his fellow musicians.

The strange thing is that Stravinsky never was a composer especially popular with the public. It irritated him that his only works that achieved real international popularity were the early *Firebird* (1910) and *Petrushka* (1911). It is true that other Stravinsky works have been a strong part of the repertory. One thinks of the *Symphony of Psalms, Oedipus Rex, Histoire du Soldat, Le Sacre du Printemps.* But in any popularity poll Stravinsky would be far down were it not for his first two ballets.

His music has been called dry, cerebral, intellectual; and this too irritated the composer. He would acidly ask what was wrong with having a brain.

But the fact remains that the influence of Stravinsky was nevertheless all-embracing, and that is a testimonial to his musical strength. No weak composer, no mere technician could have so stimulated the creative processes of virtually every living composer of his time.

After *Petrushka,* with its famous bitonal combination of F sharp against C major, virtually every

European composer started experimenting with polytonality. And after *Le Sacre du Printemps,* every composer for years was playing with ostinatos (a recurrent rhythmic figure in the bass), block harmonies, atonality and planes of sound. The great figures—Bartók, Prokofiev, Copland, everybody—all were hypnotized by Stravinsky's ideas. Only the Viennese atonalists headed by Arnold Schönberg held aloof.

Stravinsky above all was a rhythmic innovator. It was he who introduced the kind of eccentric rhythm that nevertheless had a rhythmic unity that covered an entire work. It is significant that the world of ballet was never far away, and many consider him one of the two greatest composers of ballet music, Tchaikovsky being the other. Stravinsky's music, in conjunction with George Balanchine's choreography, seemed naturally to fall into place, its rhythms "made" for dancers.

Stravinsky was never interested in melody; and, indeed, could not be classified as an important melodist, even on his own terms. What he worked for, during the greater part of his career, was pointed development, exquisite workmanship, stripped-down orchestrations and music that was above all logical and clear. Musicians responded enthusiastically to this kind of sheer compositional logic. And if the public was less impressed, it nevertheless took the word of the professionals that Stravinsky was their leader.

Of course there was much more to Stravinsky's music than mere craft. A score like the *Symphony of Psalms* or *Oedipus Rex* created a world of its own, as much as cubism or the poetry of the symbolists created its own world. Not only did the strong individual mind of the composer of the *Symphony of Psalms* come through. By purging the dross, Stravinsky got down to the essentials: the essentials of religious experience, of the dance, of sonata form (in such a work as the Symphony in Three Movements), of the baroque (in the Violin Concerto), and so on.

There was much talk in musical circles when Stravinsky started writing serial music. He and Schönberg were almost neighbors, both living in Los Angeles. But there was little contact between the two. Schönberg was on record as thinking little of Stravinsky's music. Stravinsky maintained that he had a much higher regard for Schönberg's, although many who knew him indicate that the regard came after Schönberg's death and virtual canonization.

In any case, Stravinsky, always of the avant-garde, wholeheartedly embraced serial structure. None of his serial works, however, have entered the repertory. In New York they were presented at special concerts honoring the composer, and have not been heard again.

But it is not on his serial music that Stravinsky's reputation will live or die. Long before he started composing serial music, he had a secure place in musical history because of his extraordinary power, imagination, craft and style. Like Picasso, Frank Lloyd Wright, Brancusi and a small handful of other creators, he was an important figure in helping shape a period.

JOSIP BROZ TITO

1892–1980

By Raymond H. Anderson

Throughout his long and extraordinary life, Josip Broz Tito was known as a man of stubborn courage, ready to fight and intrigue, endure hardship and risk death for his beliefs. In the tradition of the Balkans, he was proud, strong-willed, unbending before an opponent, ruthless to an enemy—and a bit vain.

The peasant's son and wartime guerrilla leader who was to become president relished power. He used it with the confident air of a king born to the throne, not an insecure usurper. Tito lived like a monarch, with many palaces, a personal island, his own train and an awed retinue. But he proclaimed, to his last days, that Communism was his goal for Yugoslavia.

In striving toward that goal, he did not allow power to turn him into an ascetic ideologue like Lenin, a suspicious tyrant like Stalin or a know-it-all like Nikita S. Khrushchev.

Tito's pride put him in conflict with Stalin when the Kremlin leader attempted to dominate postwar Yugoslavia. The outcome was a historic rift in Communism in 1948. Adrift between East and West, Tito worked with other third world leaders in the 1950s to develop the movement of "nonalignment" and he was to stay at its forefront.

Unlike others who rose to power on the Communist wave after World War II, Tito did not long demand that his people suffer and sacrifice for a distant vision of a better life. After an initial Soviet-influenced bleak period, Tito moved toward radical improvement of life in the country. Yugoslavia gradually became a bright spot amid the general grayness of Eastern Europe.

As a boy in his home village in Croatia, a wandering metalworker before World War I, and a Communist conspirator in the 1920s and 1930s, Tito was drawn to smart clothes, fine food and other touches of stylish living. As a wartime guerrilla leader he often slept in caves or forests and had too little to eat.

In his later years as prime minister and then president, Tito loved imperial uniforms with white gloves and gold braid, black-tie dinners and luxury automobiles. He took pleasure, even in his 80s, in getting behind the steering wheel of a convertible, smoking large cigars, sipping Chivas Regal and dancing with beautiful women.

In 1941, at the age of 49, Tito went into the mountains of Bosnia and Montenegro to organize and lead outnumbered and ill-equipped guerrillas in battle against Germans, Italians and their collaborators, with little help from anyone, including the Russians on whose behalf he went to war.

After victory and the creation of a Communist state in Yugoslavia, Tito was his own man and stood up to pressure, threats and abuse from Stalin. For his defiance, Tito won admiration at home and abroad, even from some of his foes.

Cast out of the Soviet bloc in 1948 for "boundless

New York Times Photo

ambition, arrogance and conceit" in refusing to submit to Stalin's dictates, Yugoslavia under Tito advanced for more than three decades along a path between the Soviet bloc of the East and the capitalist powers of the West. Tito rarely, if ever, compromised with either. He sometimes exasperated both.

What emerged in Yugoslavia was to become known as Titoism, a brand of Communism with free-market forces, consumerism, Western publications at the newsstands (including magazines with nude centerfolds), a decision-sharing role for employees (called workers' self-management) and, importantly, freedom for virtually all citizens to travel abroad and to return at will.

In many ways, Tito seemed to typify the general Yugoslav approach to life—make it a pleasurable experience but do not compromise on honor or principle. As car ownership multiplied in Yugoslavia, for example, the highway death rate rose to appalling levels. Yugoslavs tended to pass on hills and curves and found it unmanly to yield to oncoming vehicles. In a sense, Tito met Stalin on a curve and refused to yield.

At intervals over the decades, strains and conflict developed as Tito endeavored to forge a nation out of diverse and rival peoples like Serbs and Croats, Slovenes and Macedonians, Albanians and Montenegrins—Eastern Orthodox, Roman Catholic and Islamic. All the while, the shadow of the disapproving Kremlin hung over the country, interfering with Yugoslavia's efforts for unity and perhaps menacing its very existence.

Spurring separatist tendencies was the absence of a single unifying language. The dominant tongue was Serbo-Croatian, as it was known in Serbia, or Croato-Serbian, as it was called in Croatia. Other languages were Slovenian, Albanian, Macedonian and various minority tongues like Hungarian, Rumanian and German. Moreover, the country was divided by two alphabets—Latin in Croatia and Slovenia and other areas with a Catholic tradition; Cyrillic in Serbia, Macedonia, Montenegro and other areas with an Eastern Orthodox tradition.

For several decades, Tito had to look beyond his own death, to a Yugoslavia under secessionist threat from within and Soviet inducements and coercion from without to return to Moscow's fold. Many of Tito's actions, decisions and policies were intended to bolster Yugoslavia internally against the separatists and externally against the Soviet Union.

As part of the objective of safeguarding Yugoslav independence, Tito strove to weld a strong third world movement, nonaligned with either the Soviet or the Western bloc. Various third world conferences were held but the results were largely inconclusive. In striving to organize the third world, Tito became a frequent traveler and a host to presidents, kings and prime ministers.

In 1979, at the age of 87, Tito flew to Havana to lead a fight at a third world conference against efforts by Fidel Castro, the Cuban leader, to orient the movement toward the Soviet Union.

Despite controversy over Yugoslav repression of dissenters, Tito succeeded for many years in retaining the friendship and support of the United States. But at times, the precarious balance between Washington and Moscow seemed endangered as Tito denounced "imperialists" and accused the United States of aiding Yugoslavia's foes abroad.

In 1971, Yugoslavia was jolted to its foundations by a secessionist upheaval in the republic of Croatia, mainly among students, professors, writers and other intellectuals. Tito's answer was suppression of secessionists and purges of the Croatian leadership, opening the way to a nationwide retightening of controls by the Communist party.

In 1972, after a running gun battle in the mountains between armed Croatian infiltrators and Yugoslav troops, Tito's drive to reimpose full party control gained swift momentum. "Liberal" officials were ousted in Serbia, Slovenia and elsewhere. Professors at Belgrade University and other schools were removed as "anarcho-liberal elements." Some newspaper editors and film directors were also ousted, mainly persons identified with the United States or who spoke out openly in opposition to strict party controls over social, political and economic life.

Tito seemed to be the main unifying force in the country. The mystique of his wartime leadership remained a powerful influence. His was virtually the only voice in Yugoslavia to which all listened, whether in agreement, awe or fright.

Although Titoism involved a mixed economy with widespread private enterprise in commerce, public services and agriculture, with brash Western-style advertising in the press and broadcasting, Tito took pains to disclaim that this was a concession to capitalism.

Reacting angrily to suggestions that Yugoslavia was moving down the road to capitalism, Tito declared in a speech in 1972: "The class enemy has not been eliminated. He lives, he acts, he undermines our society and hinders social progress. We are submerged by the West with theories, concepts and conceptions of all kinds. And all are negative.

"Our society has real democracy, where people speak freely. And they freely give vent to their initiatives. But it is clear that there must be no democracy for those who act from an antisocialist position."

He went on to threaten a purge, a "progressive selection from top to bottom" among the million members of the Yugoslav League of Communists, as the party had been renamed to make it seem more democratic, and added: "They say in the West that Yugoslavia is gradually adopting a Western regime. That is what our class enemies want, but they are mistaken if they imagine that we will deviate from our dedication to socialism."

Josip Broz was born in May 1892 in the village of Kumrovec in Croatia, then under the Austro-Hungarian Empire. (The birth was registered as May 7 but was celebrated on May 25.) Josip was the seventh of 15 children of Franjo and Marija Broz. He adopted the name Tito, common in his home region, in the 1930s for conspiratorial cover.

His father, a Croatian, had met Tito's Slovenian mother while illicitly cutting firewood. The father had a 15-acre farm and a comfortable house and dealt in horses, cattle and hay. But life was hard and uncertain for the family because much of the father's income was spent in neighborhood inns.

Josip, as was the rural custom at the time, left school at 12 to start work. It was his father's ambition to send the boy to America to make his fortune, but there was no money for passage. Josip's first job was for an uncle, tending cattle. At 15, he went to work at a restaurant in Sisak, a small industrial town southeast of Zagreb. But he did not take to the life of a waiter and soon agreed to apprenticeship for three years with a locksmith and metalworker who repaired machinery and did fancy ironwork. A railing that Josip helped make is still part of the staircase in the Sisak District Court.

While learning his trade as metalworker, the boy began to read widely—history, fiction, travel and adventure, from Sherlock Holmes to Edward Bellamy and Upton Sinclair. He was introduced by fellow workers to Socialist ideas and soon joined the metalworkers' union and the Social-Democratic Party.

His apprenticeship over, he took to the road at the age of 18 in the old tradition of wandering journeymen, working in Zagreb, Ljubljana, Trieste, Pilsen, Mannheim, Munich and other places along the way. In 1913 at the age of 21, when the young Broz was called to service in the Austro-Hungarian armed forces, he was a skilled mechanic at the Daimler plant in Wiener Neustadt, near Vienna. He had shed his village ways and had become an urbane, well-attired man of the world, with fluent knowledge of German.

During the war, he fought in a Croatian regiment, where the spirit was as indifferent as in *The Good Soldier Švejk,* depicting Czechs serving the Austro-Hungarians. Broz was on the Russian front in 1915 when Circassian horsemen galloped up and leaped into the trenches with lances and sabers. He suffered a lance wound in the back, fell unconscious and was taken alive only when Russian soldiers intervened to stop the Circassians from slaughtering the wounded.

A prisoner in the depths of Russia, Broz volunteered to work and was moved from village to village to jobs as a mechanic, becoming fluent in Russian. He was working in the Urals in 1917 when the Czar was deposed and the Bolsheviks were intriguing to take power. From the outset, the sympathies of the young Broz were with the Bolsheviks. Escaping, he made his way to Petrograd, now Leningrad, and took part in street fighting.

Broz was arrested as a fugitive prisoner of war and sent to Siberia. He escaped again and joined the Red Guard at Omsk. In the civil war that followed the revolution, Broz had to flee and found refuge with Kazakh tribesmen. Later, he returned to Omsk, married a young Russian, went with her to Petrograd, and from there back to what had become the Kingdom of Serbs, Croats and Slovenes, later the Kingdom of Yugoslavia, and then, under Tito, the Socialist Federal Republic of Yugoslavia. He was, in reality, a Moscow agent.

Broz joined the Communist party in Zagreb and promptly helped organize a metalworkers' strike. He was a respected and active party worker, with a sense of humor and an ability to express political abstractions in simple terms, never falling into ideological fetishism. He once said that Marxism was "nine tenths action and one tenth theory."

For seven years, Broz worked at his trade in various cities, all the while organizing union activity, agitating and stirring up political unrest. Despite a drive against radicals, he managed to avoid prosecution until 1927, when he was sentenced to seven months in jail for distributing Communist literature.

While at liberty on appeal, he took his first major party office, becoming a member of the party committee for the Zagreb region. Thereafter, he led the clandestine life of a revolutionary. He was arrested again, this time for belonging to a banned party.

Broz turned the trial in Zagreb into a propaganda spectacle, fencing with the court and proclaiming his Communist beliefs. When he was sentenced to five years in prison, he turned to the courtroom crowd and shouted "Long live the Communist party! Long live the Third International!"

Broz spent most of the term in a former monastery, where his main duty was to take care of the prison's power plant. He organized a party unit among the prisoners and he read widely—Shakespeare, John Stuart Mill, Greek philosophy, Marx and Engels. "It was," he recalled, "just like being at a university."

Leaving prison in 1934 without bitterness, he remarked: "It was only natural that when they caught me they should shut me up. I would have done the same thing in their place."

After his release, Broz, traveling in disguise and with various aliases and false documents, made his way to Moscow to work for the Comintern, as the Third International was called. There, living in the old Lux Hotel, he met leaders of the Communist movement—Georgi Dimitrov of Bulgaria, Otto Kusinen of Finland, Palmiro Togliatti of Italy and others. Now using the party name Tito, he earned a reputation for reliability. He narrowly survived Stalin's purges of the 1930s but the fear and disillusionment of the Moscow years never left him.

Tito escaped the terror with an assignment from the Comintern to slip into Yugoslavia, under an alias, as organizing secretary of the Yugoslav Communist party. In 1937, after Milan Gorkic, the party's leader, fell victim to Stalin's secret police, Tito was named secretary general to succeed him.

Living clandestinely a few jumps ahead of the police, Tito managed to settle many of his small party's disputes through both toughness and common sense. He became skilled in the art of disguise and using false names not only in Yugoslavia but also on many trips abroad, especially while recruiting for the International Brigade in the Spanish Civil War.

Yugoslavia in the 1930s was a hard land, with widespread illiteracy, unemployment and misery. Tito told later of his feelings when he made a clandestine visit to his home village: "I thought of the day when Kumrovec and thousands of other towns and villages all over Yugoslavia would rouse themselves from backwardness, when young people would at last have a chance in life, a chance to live in peace and happiness and to bring up their families. I did not know when that would happen. But I knew very well that it was worth making every effort and sacrifice to insure that it did happen."

Like Lenin in Russia, he believed that the answer for Yugoslavia was industrialization in a Socialist society.

Building the underground party to a membership of 12,000, Tito created a leadership under his control, choosing men noted for courage and common sense. Among them were Aleksandr Rankovic and Milovan Djilas, both of whom in the postwar years fell out with Tito and lost their posts, but not their lives.

In August 1939, the Yugoslav Communist party bore up under the shock of Stalin's pact with Hitler. When Germany invaded Poland on Sept. 1 and found itself in war with France and Britain, the Yugoslavs, like the Russians, denounced the war as "imperialist." Even Hitler's ruthless assault on Yugoslavia in April 1941 evoked no initial resistance from the Yugoslav Communists, who were mindful of Moscow's tactics of delaying a war with Germany as long as possible. Tito did issue a proclamation blaming the "Serb ruling class" for Yugoslavia's defeat by the invaders.

But when the Germans attacked the Soviet Union on June 22, 1941, the Yugoslav Communists stirred into action, prompted by radioed instructions from Moscow to take diversionary action against the Germans.

Tito had slipped out of Zagreb, where Croatians had set up an independent state. He first went into hiding in Belgrade and then sought refuge in the mountains to form guerrilla units and fight the occupation forces of Germany, Italy, Hungary and Bulgaria, which had sliced up Yugoslavia like a cake.

From the very start of their guerrilla activity, Tito and his colleagues saw the war not only as a struggle against the occupiers but also as an opportunity "to seize power and to seize it in such a way that the bourgeoisie would never regain it." As guerrilla commander, Tito urged a unified struggle by all the peoples of the country, Serbs and Croats, Slovenes and Macedonians, Montenegrins and Albanians.

This appeal for a common struggle found a wide response, causing many to quit the Croatian Ustashi forces or the Serbian Chetnik movement and join the guerrillas.

The Ustashi represented the separatist state in Croatia. The Chetniks were backers of the Serbian royal government. After the capitulation of Yugoslavia to the Axis invaders in April 1941, Col. Draja Mihailovich, a staff officer of the royal army, went into the Serbian hills and formed a guerrilla group known as the Chetniks, an old name for Serbs who resisted the long domination by Turks.

The Chetniks sought to save Serbs who were being slain in Croatia. The Chetnik movement received the backing of the royal Yugoslav government in exile and of the British and Soviet governments. The Soviet attitude toward the Chetniks was especially galling to Tito. For almost three years, the Chetnik resistance was played up in the Allied press and, to Tito's vexation, his own guerrilla raids were initially attributed to the Chetniks.

The priority of the Chetniks was saving the Serbs. They disapproved of ineffectual sabotage and guerrilla raids that did little but provoke enemy reprisals against civilians. The Chetniks, as backers of the royal government, despised and feared the Partisans, as Tito's guerrillas were called, with their Red Star emblems and proletarian divisions.

Gradually, the Allies began to hear of the Partisan warfare under some unknown figure called Tito and they puzzled over his true identity—perhaps he was a Russian, or the name might be a cover for a committee or, according to one rumor, Tito might be a woman.

The Partisans fought alone, aided by some captured equipment but with little food or medicine. The Russians made promises, but they had their own problems and sent no aid until late in the war.

In 1942, Tito formed a national liberation committee that was to develop ultimately into the Communist government of postwar Yugoslavia. Later, to give himself greater standing with wartime leaders like Stalin and Churchill, Tito took the rank of marshal.

With the surrender of Italy in 1943, the Partisans were enormously strengthened by their capture of equipment and arms from Italian troops along the coast. As the territory under Partisan control expanded, the British and Americans parachuted in liaison teams to find out what the Partisans were doing and to oversee aid and supply efforts.

On May 25, 1944, Tito barely escaped capture by a German airborne force that descended near his headquarters cave at Drvar. Tito went to Italy, where, wearing his new marshal's uniform, he later met with Churchill. Soon after, he slipped away to Moscow to consult Stalin.

The talks with Stalin took place in what Tito later called "a very painful atmosphere."

When the war in Europe ended in 1945, Yugoslavia was a devastated land. Its small industry was in ruins, railroads were destroyed, cities bombed and many farm areas lifeless. The country was torn by bitter memories of atrocities committed by Yugoslavs against Yugoslavs.

Tito's Marxist policies alienated many, especially the middle class. He angered Croats, and Catholics around the world, by ordering the arrest of Archbishop Aloysius Stepinac and having him tried for supporting the wartime state of Croatia. The archbishop was sentenced to 16 years in prison but was freed subject to residence restrictions in 1951.

General Mihailovich, the Chetnik commander, was captured, tried as a traitor and shot along with fellow officers. Terror was felt throughout the nation. Many opponents of Tito and Communism were simply shot without trial.

In 1946 the Yugoslavs infuriated the United States by downing two transport planes that were taking a shortcut, killing five.

In his first years of rule, Tito, as prime minister and minister of defense, sought to transplant the Soviet economic and political system to Yugoslavia. Industry, trade and banking were nationalized. Collectivization of agriculture was tried, but abandoned under peasant resistance.

Tito turned to the Soviet Union for development assistance. According to Yugoslavs, the Russians were willing to help establish light industry but balked at larger projects. They wanted to centralize heavy industry in the Soviet Union while making use of Yugoslavia's raw materials.

Yugoslav bitterness over this, combined with other differences and resentments—over Trieste, Greece, a Balkan federation with Bulgaria, Tito's economic plan, and Soviet manipulation in Yugoslavia—all led to the dramatic break between Tito and Stalin. On June 28, 1948, the Cominform, successor to the Comintern, read the "Tito clique" out of the world Communist movement.

The break, the first in the monolithic facade of Communism, shook and bewildered the world. Some people suspected that it was a Soviet trick to win Western military equipment and economic aid for Yugoslavia.

Under threat of invasion from the Soviet bloc and weakened by economic problems, Tito turned to the United States. After heated and anguished debate, Washington gave him more than $1 billion in various forms of aid. Tito expressed gratitude but took a position of neutralism between the blocs.

Tito took the post of president in 1953, and after the death of Stalin in March 1953 relations with Moscow began to improve. In 1955, Nikita S. Khrushchev, the new Soviet party leader, and Prime Minister Nikolai A. Bulganin went to Belgrade, hats in hand, to apologize for 1948 and to entice Yugoslavia back into the Soviet camp. Tito could barely conceal his contempt.

Relations with Moscow worsened again in the years after the Russians crushed the Hungarian revolution in 1956 and later executed Imre Nagy after having lured him from asylum in the Yugoslav embassy in Budapest.

There were alternate freezes and thaws in ties between Belgrade and Moscow. The ties warmed in 1963 when Khrushchev paid another visit and spoke warmly of Tito's worker self-management councils.

In 1968, a mood of crisis developed again in Yugoslavia when the Russians and their allies invaded Czechoslovakia to suppress the liberal movement in Communist rule. When Moscow made threatening gestures toward independent-minded Rumania and Yugoslavia, Tito mobilized the armed forces, called up the militia and made it clear that Yugoslavia, unlike Czechoslovakia, would resist an invasion. The Russians backed off.

Tito worried about Soviet pressures on Yugoslavia after his death and sought to head them off by inviting Leonid I. Brezhnev, the Soviet leader, to Belgrade in 1971 and then going to see the Russian in Moscow in 1972. Tito returned to Belgrade with an Order of Lenin.

He formed a rotating presidency, representing the various republics in succession, to take power after his death. In 1974 he was made "President for Life."

A new constitution was adopted in 1974, "restoring to the working class its rightful leadership role." Elected representatives were to retain their regular jobs and perform public duties in their spare time. This was to prevent the rise of a class of dreaded "technocrats and bureaucrats."

Despite gains over the years, the economy as a whole suffered distortions and weaknesses from a crash effort to transform the rural land into an industrial society.

As he advanced into his 80s, Tito dyed his hair, took long rests and, at intervals, demonstrated to the nation his vigor by going hunting and shooting a bear.

He tended plants at his island retreat in the Adriatic, dabbled in photography and made things in a machine shop, perhaps indulging nostalgia for his youth.

Tito and his Russian wife were divorced in the late 1930s. A son from that marriage, Zarko, was wounded in the Red Army and was later allowed to join his father. In 1940, in an obscure episode, Tito married, or lived with, a Slovenian revolutionary, Herta Has, and left her after the war. A son, Miso, was born of that relationship.

In 1952, when Tito was 60 years old, it was announced that he had married a strong-willed and beautiful Serb who had served in the Partisans, Jovanka Budisavljevic, 28. She became his constant companion, traveling with him around the world, acting as hostess to dignitaries and watching alertly over her aging husband.

The marriage broke apart mysteriously in 1977 when Jovanka was detected, it was rumored, engaging in political intrigue with Serbian generals. There were later reports that Tito had taken up with an opera singer or a masseuse. The reports were never confirmed.

Tito fell seriously ill in January 1980. His left leg was amputated that month, and in the following months he suffered a series of ailments accompanying the failure of his vital organs. He died in Belgrade on May 4, 1980, at the age of 87. In Washington, President Carter called Marshal Tito "a towering figure on the world stage."

THE FIGHTER-SURVIVOR WHO UNIFIED A COUNTRY

DAVID BINDER

HE WAS the metalworker from the village of Kumrovec, the drill sergeant from World War I, the Partisan commander from World War II and, finally, the father of his country: Josip Broz Tito.

His 87 years spanned the collapse of the European monarchs—one of whom, Francis Joseph, he served as a soldier—and the rise of new governments and nations—one of which, the Federal Republic of Yugoslavia, he fostered.

Above all he was a fighter and a survivor, with a price on his head as an illegal Communist party organizer in prewar Yugoslavia, a reward posted by Hitler for his capture dead or alive during World War II and anathema pronounced upon him by Stalin in 1948.

Marshal Tito dealt with many of the great and powerful—Churchill, de Gaulle, Khrushchev, Nehru, Nasser—and lived on to deal with their lesser successors. He was the last survivor of the generation of leaders that emerged from World War II.

His closest wartime comrades had fallen by the way: Edvard Kardelj died in 1979; Aleksandr Rankovic was dismissed from his posts 14 years ago and was living in sad retirement; Milovan Djilas, the classic dissident since 1954, was in a kind of internal exile in Belgrade. In the end there were no heirs apparent.

After the death of Mr. Kardelj a Yugoslav official who had fought in the war as a young man remarked: "After Tito we have to jump two generations for the next leaders. That is the problem."

Did President Tito live too long?

At a time when Soviet tanks were on the move in Afghanistan, raising uncertainties again along the perimeter of the Soviet bloc, few in Yugoslavia wanted him to go.

His legacy for the six Yugoslav republics, with their three religious faiths and their welter of languages, was the simple slogan of his Partisan brigades: brotherhood and unity. This and the trust embodied in his arming of every able-bodied man in a country with a terrible history of ethnic rivalries was his prescription for continued independence.

In politics Marshal Tito was more innovator than inventor. The one-time mechanic for the Daimler auto factory in Vienna was a lifelong tinkerer. As a young man he had witnessed not only the collapse of the Austro-Hungarian Empire but also, firsthand, the birth of the vigorous Soviet Union. In 1920 he returned from Russia to the newly created kingdom of Yugoslavia, a fragile entity seemingly foredoomed because one nationality, the Serbs, was in a position to dominate a nation of several nationalities.

Part Croat and part Slovene, Marshal Tito appears to have developed a vision in the mid-1920s of a Yugoslavia that could work and survive by virtue of giving each nationality and each region an equal stake. It was a vision of a Socialist Yugoslavia, and in the next five decades he never lost sight of it.

In 1937 he took over the Yugoslav Communist party, riddled by factionalism and decimated by Stalin's purges, and immediately set out to put his ideas into practice. Finding "whole regions with no party organization," he made it a cardinal point to spread his own organization throughout the country. When the Germans invaded in 1941 his was the only political movement functioning in all the provinces and the only one to promote a "united Yugoslavia."

He had brought something more back from his years as an official of the Comintern in Moscow: the determination not to accept bribes or subsidies from the Russians and become their vassal. He also said that the party leadership should "be at home among the people to share the rough and the smooth with them." This made him more independent than the "Muscovite" European Communists who spent World War II in the Soviet capital. In this sense he had already begun to defy Soviet suzerainty 10 years before he defied Stalin.

Marshal Tito learned early that loneliness was the only real companion of power. His first wife abandoned him during a five-year prison term for Communist agitation, and he left his second and third wives. He chose as party lieutenants men 10 to 15 years his junior, who called him Stari (Old Man) even when he was in his late 40s. He started the Communist uprising alone, with no help from the Russians or anyone else, when the old Yugoslavia was torn to pieces by German, Italian and Bulgarian invaders and by quislings. His Yugoslavia later stood alone against Stalin's monolithic "Socialist camp."

The logic of the break with the Soviet bloc in

1948, and Yugoslavia's vulnerability by virtue of its small size and location, led Tito the tinkerer to seek new instruments for guaranteeing his country's external and internal security. Domestically he favored Mr. Kardelj's proposals of decentralization, the principle of "workers' self-management" and, ultimately, a market economy. Externally he sought conciliation with the West and reconciliation with the East. When neither East nor West would offer sufficient agreement, he developed the policy of nonalignment between the two great blocs and found support in the third world.

Nonalignment abroad and self-management at home, innovations more than inventions, were introduced, essentially, to keep Yugoslavia going. In Marshal Tito's later years he had the satisfaction of winning apologies, acceptance and even a measure of emulation from his former enemies and critics in the Communist world.

He had his faults. He could be ruthless toward real or supposed foes, but he did not have a permanent vindictive streak. He surrounded himself with royal trappings and in many ways lived like a king for his last three decades, but he remained Comrade Tito to his subordinates and never lost the ability to talk with ordinary people. He was unintellectual, sometimes anti-intellectual, but he learned to tolerate great freedom in the arts.

Marshal Tito's countrymen sometimes called him the "first and only Yugoslav." Yet in the end he could be fairly certain that even if they considered themselves Serbs or Bosnians or Macedonians at home, they would all become Yugoslavs if attacked.

HARRY S TRUMAN

1884–1972

By Alden Whitman

At 7:09 P.M. on April 12, 1945, Harry S Truman, the vice president of the United States, was elevated by the sudden death of Franklin D. Roosevelt to the presidency of the United States. He was a month short of his 61st birthday, and he had been vice president for only 83 days when Chief Justice Harlan F. Stone administered the oath in the White House Cabinet Room.

It was the third time since 1900 that a president had died in office, but it was the first wartime accession. For Truman, a hitherto minor national figure with a pedestrian background as a senator from Missouri, the awesome moment came without his having intimate knowledge of the nation's tremendously intricate war and foreign policies. These he had to become acquainted with and to deal with instantly, for on him alone, a former haberdasher and a politician of unspectacular scale, devolved the executive power of one of the world's mightiest nations.

"But now the lightning had struck, and events beyond anyone's control had taken command," Truman wrote later.

These events, over which he presided and on which he placed his indelible imprint, were among the most momentous in national and world history, for they took place in the shadow and the hope of the Atomic Age, whose beginning coincided with Truman's accession. And during his eight years in office, the outlines of the Cold War were fashioned.

In war-ravaged Europe in those years, Truman and the United States established peace, held back Soviet expansion and built economic and political stability through the Truman Doctrine, the Marshall Plan and the North Atlantic Treaty Organization. In the Mideast he recognized the state of Israel. In the Far East the president imposed peace and constitutional democracy on the Japanese enemy, tried valiantly to save China from Communism and chose to wage war in Korea to halt aggression. In the United States, Truman led the nation's conversion from war to peace, while maintaining a stable and prosperous economy.

The drama and significance of these accomplishments were, of course, not readily predictable when Truman took office April 12, 1945, as the 33d president, but there was an element of theatricality in the way he was notified that the burden had fallen on him.

Two hours before Truman stood, Bible in hand, before the Chief Justice that misty Thursday, he had entered the office of Speaker Sam Rayburn in the House wing of the Capitol for a chat. Writing to his mother and sister a few days later, he said: ". . . as soon as I came into the room Sam told me that Steve Early, the president's confidential press secretary, wanted to talk with me. I called the White House, and Steve told me to come to the White House 'as *quickly* and as quietly' as I could.

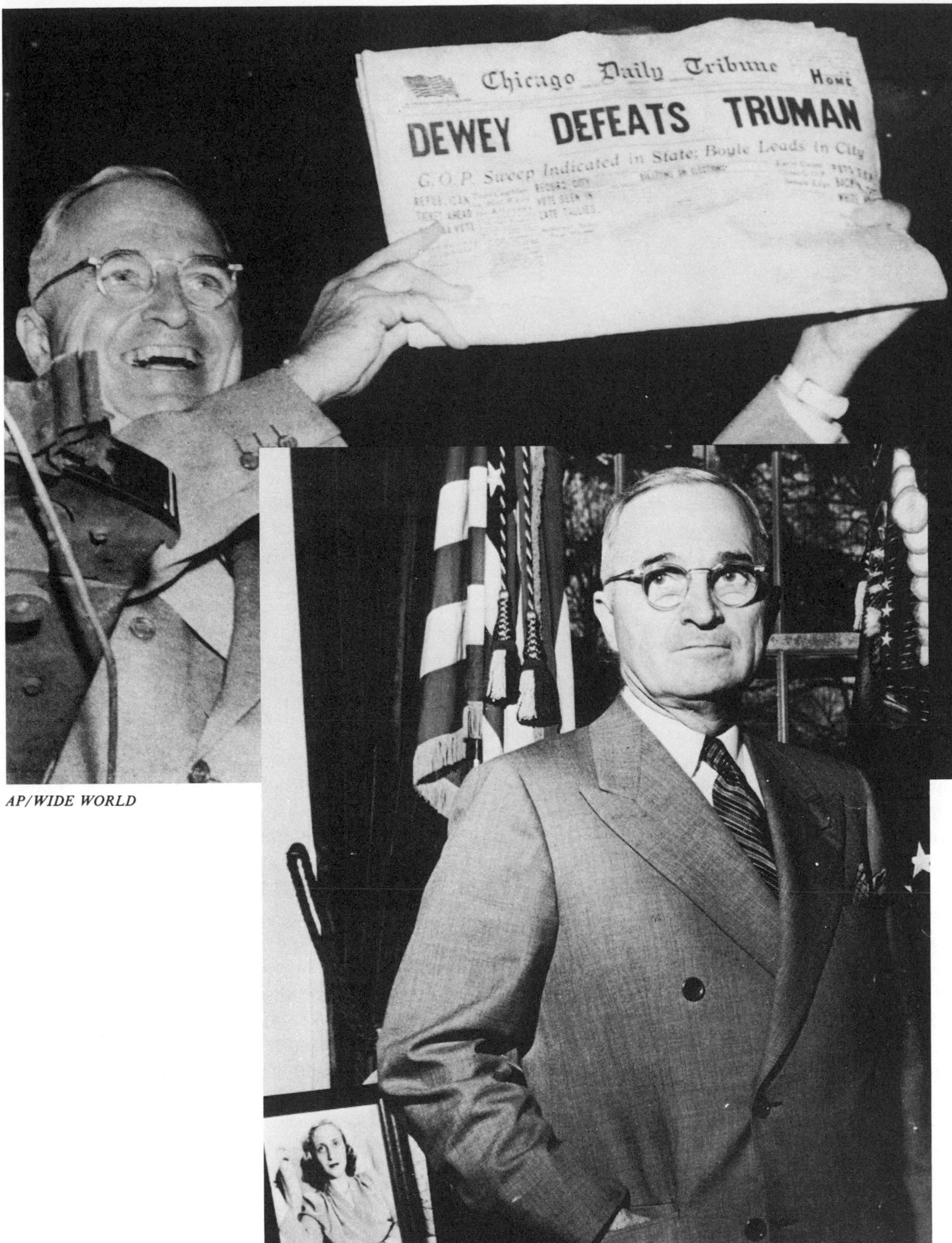
Chicago Daily Tribune
HOME
DEWEY DEFEATS TRUMAN
G.O.P. Sweep Indicated in State; Boyle Leads in City

AP/WIDE WORLD

George Tames/The New York Times

"I ran all the way to my office in the Senate by way of the unfrequented corridors in the Capitol, told my office force that I'd been summoned to the White House and to say nothing about it. . . ."

He arrived there at 5:25 P.M. and was taken by elevator to Mrs. Franklin D. Roosevelt's study on the second floor. As he emerged, Mrs. Roosevelt stepped forward and put her arm across his shoulders.

"Harry," she said quietly, "the president is dead."

For a minute Truman was too stunned to speak. Then, fighting off tears, he asked, "Is there anything I can do for you?"

With her characteristic empathy, Mrs. Roosevelt replied, "Is there anything *we* can do for *you?* For you are the one in trouble now."

In the next hour and a half Truman learned the details of Roosevelt's death at Warm Springs, Ga., gathered his composure and prepared to take the oath in the presence of congressional leaders; cabinet members; his wife, Bess; and their daughter, Margaret.

The person on whom the executive power of the United States was so abruptly thrust was, in appearance, not distinctive. He stood 5 feet 8 inches tall. He had broad, square shoulders; an erect carriage; a round, apple-cheeked face; a long, sharp nose; deep blue eyes that peered through steel-rimmed glasses; and thin, gray-white hair that was neatly parted and carefully brushed.

Apart from the plain eyeglasses, the most catching feature of Truman's face were his thin lips, which could be clamped in grimness or parted, over even teeth, in an engaging smile.

Dressed in a conservative double-breasted suit, with a 35th Infantry Division insigne in the left lapel and a white handkerchief peeping out of the breast pocket, Truman looked neat and plain. His only jewelry was a double-band gold Masonic ring on the little finger of his left hand. Aside from his speech—its flat, clipped, slightly nasal quality pegged him as a midwesterner—he seemed a typical small-city businessman, pleasant and substantial, more at home on Main Street than on Pennsylvania Avenue.

Certainly he could not have been typecast as a senator. He was not an orator, nor even a frequent speaker, in his 10 years as a Democratic senator from Missouri. But when he did speak, he was listened to closely, for his remarks were coherent, forceful and usually brief.

He was industrious on Senate committees, and he served with distinction and fairness as chairman of the Special Committee to Investigate the National Defense Program. He was popular ("Harry" to everyone) and a member of the Senate's inner circle. He was known for his informal geniality, his homely language and also, on occasion, for his irascibility and brusqueness.

Unlike most of his fellow legislators, Truman did not have a college degree or a fixed profession. His formal education had ended with high school, and he had been in business from time to time, but mostly he had been in politics. He was a county official from 1922 until his election to the Senate in 1934.

An inquisitive and retentive mind helped to compensate for Truman's lack of schooling, and he employed it in prodigious, if haphazard, reading, especially in American political history.

Although he had been Roosevelt's choice as a ticket mate in 1944, and although the two men were on good terms, Truman was not, even as vice president, a White House intimate, closely informed on the progress of the war. He had supported Roosevelt at home and abroad, but his personal inclinations were more conservative.

His private attitude toward Roosevelt was astringent, according to Margaret Truman Daniel's *Harry S Truman*, published this year. His daughter's book quoted a desk-pad memo of 1948 that said: "I don't believe the USA wants any more fakers—Teddy and Franklin are enough. So I'm going to make a common-sense, intellectually honest campaign."

From the very first, Truman had to exercise his new authority from minute to minute, while his advisers briefed him as swiftly as they could. "I did more reading than I ever thought I could," he said after his first full day in office. But he was aware of his inadequacies.

"Boys," he told a group of reporters in those first days, "if you ever pray, pray for me now. . . . I've got the most terribly responsible job a man ever had."

Truman's first decision was routine. The question: Should the San Francisco conference on the United Nations meet April 25, as scheduled? "I did not hesitate a second" in giving an affirmative response, he recalled.

His second decision—to meet with the cabinet and ask its members to stay on—was also easy. But most of the judgments that followed (including cabinet dismissals) were not.

"I felt as if I had lived five lifetimes in those first days as president," he said of his "mighty leap" into the White House and global politics.

In creating and carrying out his policies, Truman built a reputation for decisiveness and courage. He did not fret once his mind was made up.

"I made it clear [to the first cabinet session] that I would be president in my own right," Truman said, "and that I would assume full responsibility for such decisions as had to be made."

Expressing the same thought, a sign on his desk read: "The buck stops here."

With the war in Europe near its triumphant end, Truman had immediately to deal with Soviet intentions to impose Communist regimes in Eastern Europe and possibly to exploit the economic breakdown in Western Europe. Simultaneously he had to seek military and political solutions in the war against Japan. Both situations involved Soviet-American relations, and both gave initial shape to decades of strife and conflict between the world's two major powers.

Whereas Roosevelt tended to be flexible in coping with the Russians, Truman held sterner views. "If we see that Germany is winning the war, we ought to help Russia; and if that Russia is winning, we ought to help Germany, and in that way let them kill as many as possible. . . ." he said as a senator in 1941. This basic attitude prepared him to adopt, from the start of his presidency, a firm policy.

The Polish question epitomized his approach. This thorny matter arose from the Yalta agreements of February 1945, when the Red Army had driven the Nazis from the plains of Poland. The accord, calling for a broadly based Polish regime and eventual free elections, was fuzzily worded. The Russians took it to mean a pro-Moscow government; Truman read it to require a Western style of government.

"I was not afraid of the Russians and . . . I intended to be firm," he said. "I would be fair, of course, and anyway the Russians needed us more than we needed them."

Determined to push his point on Poland as a symbol of Soviet-American relations, Truman had his first personal exchange, tart and brusque, with Vyacheslav M. Molotov, the Soviet foreign minister, in Washington on April 22 and 23, 1945. The president used "words of one syllable" to convey his insistence that Poland be "free and independent."

"I have never been talked to like that in my life," Molotov complained.

"Carry out your agreements, and you won't get talked to like that," his host retorted.

After much pulling and hauling, Poland got a regime that the United States recognized, but not before Truman's dislike of Russian diplomatic infighting had hardened.

"Force is the only thing the Russians understand," he concluded, and force in one guise or another was to underlie his subsequent dealings with Moscow and the Communist bloc.

Even so, Truman got along rather well with Josef Stalin, the Soviet dictator, whom he met for the first time at the Potsdam Conference in July 1945. "I liked him a lot," Truman said, adding that, of course, "Uncle Joe" (as he called Stalin behind his back) "didn't mean what he said" and consistently broke his word.

In the foreground of Truman's dealings with Stalin at Potsdam and afterward was the atomic bomb project. Started in the deepest secrecy in the early days of World War II, it was on the verge of producing its first explosive when Truman became president.

Although project scientists, some people in the military and a few civilians were aware of the incalculable world importance of an atomic bomb, the president himself had been told nothing. Not only had the project been kept secret from him as a senator and as vice president, but also the immense scientific, military, civilian and moral implications of atomic fission had not been presented to him.

Thus Truman was unprepared when Secretary of War Henry L. Stimson explained the atomic project to him on April 25, 1945—13 days after he had become president—and told him of the then presumed fantastic power of an atomic bomb. Apart from its staggering military potential, what impressed the president almost immediately were its implications for American diplomacy and world peace.

"If it explodes, as I think it will, I'll certainly have a hammer on those boys," he said, alluding to the Russians.

At the same time it was assumed by Truman and Stimson and virtually everyone connected with the atomic project that the bomb would be employed as a matter of course to shorten the Japanese war. The moral implications of its use and the total effect of atomics on United States–Soviet relations, later topics of vigorous debate, were not then publicly raised or widely appreciated.

Nevertheless, once an atomic device was tested and its destructiveness was confirmed, Truman said in an interview in 1966 for this article that he had given the matter of actually using the bomb "long and careful thought."

"I did not like the weapon," he said, "but I had no qualms, if in the long run millions of lives could be saved."

Responding to his critics—and there were many in after years—he took the responsibility for the atomic havoc inflicted on Hiroshima and Nagasaki. The bombs, he maintained, did shorten the war and did save millions of American and Japanese battlefield casualties.

With the unconditional surrender of Germany on May 8, 1945, a meeting of Truman, Stalin and Winston Churchill, the British prime minister, became necessary to consider Europe's problems and to prepare, in accordance with Yalta, for Soviet entry into the Pacific war. Twice delayed by Truman pending the plutonium bomb test at Alamogordo, N.M., the conference at Potsdam began July 17—the day Truman learned the bomb was a success—and lasted through Aug. 1. It was the president's only meeting with Stalin and his first with Churchill, with whom he formed a lasting friendship.

For all the popular hope that was invested in Potsdam and for all the grinding hours that the statesmen and their aides conferred, few European disputes were settled. Stalin pledged, however, to invade Japanese-held Manchuria early in August, and he subscribed to a surrender appeal to Japan that implied she could retain a constitutional emperor.

Amid the Potsdam wrangles, Truman, by arrangement with Churchill, offhandedly informed Stalin of the bomb, but not that it was atomic.

"On July 24 I casually mentioned to Stalin that we had a new weapon of unusual destructive force," Truman recalled. "The Russian premier showed no special interest. All he said was that he was glad to hear it and hoped we would make 'good use of it against the Japanese.' "

Tottering since June, Japan surrendered Aug. 14, 1945, after the atomic bomb toll at Hiroshima and Nagasaki had exceeded a total of 100,000 lives and after the Russians had stormed into Manchuria. The victory was sealed on the battleship *Missouri*, in Tokyo Harbor, when Gen. Douglas MacArthur, the United States commander, accepted the capitulation of the Japanese. The global war, in which the United States had been engaged since 1941, was ended, and a new and different era was emerging.

In the war's course the United States created an industrial plant of unrivaled productivity, with a gross national product that soared from $101 billion in 1941 to $125 billion in 1945. Its citizens, meanwhile, accumulated millions in unspent cash. How to handle this new affluence without touching off perilous inflation was the major concern of reconversion.

The Truman program, given to Congress on Sept. 6, 1945, called for full employment, increased minimum wages, private and public housing programs, a national health program, aid to education, Negro job rights, higher farm prices and continuation of key wartime economic controls.

A president generally friendly to labor (he vetoed the Taft-Hartley bill in 1947), Truman stoutly refused what he considered exorbitant pay goals. In April 1946 he seized the coal mines when John L. Lewis's 400,000 miners struck for more money. And in another strike that November, Lewis and his union were fined.

The contest between Truman and Lewis, both stubborn men, captured the headlines, with Lewis insisting that mine seizure by troops was a hollow gesture, because "you can't mine coal with bayonets," and with Truman appealing to the miners' patriotism. It was Lewis who yielded, as did the railway unions when the president seized the carriers in May 1946 to avert a walkout.

If Truman turned out to be not a pet of labor, neither was he a darling of business and industry. He lifted price and profit controls gingerly, vetoed a $4-billion budget cut in 1947, seized steel plants in the labor-and-price dispute in 1952 and increased the federal budget.

Fair Deal programs met a mixed reaction in Congress, especially after the midterm elections of 1946 gave the Republicans a majority in both the House and the Senate. Truman proposals for broadening civil rights and for Medicare were shunned. In both areas he was in advance of his time, but he lived to see himself vindicated.

In 1965, when Congress passed the Medicare bill, President Johnson journeyed to Missouri to sign the measure in Truman's presence. The Civil Rights Act of 1964 reflected many of Truman's aspirations for Negro equality.

President Truman fared better on unification of the armed forces into a Department of Defense and on establishment of an Atomic Energy Commission. On taxes, price controls and union regulation, his relations with Congress were not uniformly smooth.

"I discovered that being president is like riding a tiger," he remarked afterward. "A man has to keep on riding or be swallowed."

Truman's individuality was also reflected in cabinet changes. The Roosevelt cabinet, save for James V. Forrestal as secretary of defense, was dismembered by 1948. Some departures were summary, as with Treasury Secretary Henry Morgenthau, Jr., and Commerce Secretary Henry A. Wallace.

Wallace was discharged in the fall of 1946 in an uproar over a speech that seemed to contradict the president's hard Soviet policy. Wallace had thought his remarks were approved by the White House, but it turned out that Truman had only glanced at the text.

Other appointments brought Gen. George C. Marshall, whom Truman revered, into the cabinet as secretary of state and secretary of defense; Dean Acheson, whose intellect Truman admired, as secretary of state; and John C. Snyder, whose financial acumen the president respected, as Treasury secretary. James F. Byrnes served briefly as secretary of state and was dropped in a personality clash.

Truman's foreign program was to combat Communist expansion and to strengthen what he called the free world. Supported by Senator Arthur H. Vandenberg and other leading Republicans, this policy became bipartisan in its major aspects. Backed by American economic and atomic power, it was remarkably successful. In China, however, the Nationalist government collapsed despite American exertions, and the Communists took over in 1949.

But in the Middle East the Soviet Union was obliged to withdraw from Iran. In Yugoslavia a non-

Stalinist regime developed. There was outstanding success in Europe, thanks to the Truman Doctrine, inaugurated in 1947.

In that year Britain, for lack of money, had to halt her subventions to Greece and Turkey, nations under heavy Communist pressure. With great dispatch, Truman convinced Congress it should extend cash help. This historic action, he said later, was "the turning point" in damming Soviet expansion in Europe, because it "put the world on notice that it would be our policy to support the cause of freedom wherever it was threatened."

The president's doughty action kept Greece and Turkey in the Western orbit, and the Truman Doctrine was the logical base for the Marshall Plan, enunciated by Secretary of State Marshall in the summer of 1947. Under it, the United States invited all European nations to cooperate in their economic recovery, with billions of dollars in American backing.

Western Europe, on the brink of economic disaster, responded favorably, achieving stability and eventually a new prosperity. The Marshall Plan, or the European Recovery Plan as it was formally named, "helped save Europe from economic disaster and lifted it from the shadow of enslavement by Russian Communism," Truman said.

Truman's leadership of the non-Communist world was reflected in vigorous support of the United Nations. Through its mechanism he hoped to keep world peace by positive actions, as well as by thwarting Soviet power plays and intrigues. Moscow, for its part, appeared bent on troublemaking both in the United Nations and out of it.

The Soviet strategy of trying to humble the United States had a crucial test in 1948, when the Russians blockaded Berlin by land in an effort to force the United States to quit the city. Truman resisted, and under his direction an American airlift was organized to fly food and medicines into that beleaguered city. The airlift, in which hundreds of planes participated over many months, forced the Russians to back down.

Soviet-American clashes intruded into domestic politics, especially after the Soviet Union exploded its first atomic device in 1949. A vocal segment of public opinion asserted that the Russians could only have mastered atomics by stealing American secrets. Outcries led to heated charges of Communist infiltration in high government places. In time a loyalty-security program was set up for government employees and defense workers.

But disquiet, fear and suspicion spread in the land. In vain Truman sought to establish calm and a sense of perspective that could be gained through judicial proceedings against suspected spies and disloyal persons.

As Truman's first term came to a close, he was accounted successful in foreign affairs and beset by trouble in domestic ones.

He had won recognition as a person in his own right, but there was dispute over the degree to which the country liked what he had become—dogged, scrappy, "right in the big things, but wrong in the small ones," as House Speaker Sam Rayburn phrased it.

"My first memory is that of chasing a frog around the backyard in Cass County, Missouri. Grandmother Young watched the performance and thought it very funny that a 2-year-old could slap his knee and laugh so loudly at a jumping frog."

Harry S Truman was 68 when he wrote that recollection of his carefree farm childhood, so secure in strong, affectionate family bonds.

A product of the Middle Border and of hardy farming stock with frontier traditions, Truman was born at 4 P.M. May 8, 1884, in a small frame house at Lamar, Mo. He was the firstborn of John Anderson Truman and Mary Ellen Young Truman. The initial "S" was a compromise between Shippe and Solomon, both kinsman's names.

Within the year the family moved to a farm near Harrisonville, Mo., where another son, Vivian, was born in 1886. A year later the Trumans were living on a Jackson County farm, near what was to be Grandview. There, Mary Jane, the third child, was born.

"Those were wonderful days and great adventures," Truman said of his growing up on 600 stretching acres. "My father bought me a beautiful black Shetland pony and the grandest saddle to ride him with I ever saw." When Harry was 6, the family moved once more, to Independence, a Kansas City suburb, but John Truman remained a farmer and took up the buying and selling of cattle, sheep and hogs.

It was in Independence that Harry, whose mother had taught him his letters by 5, went to school. He made friends, one in particular. "She had golden curls . . . and the most beautiful blue eyes," he said of Bess Wallace, the childhood sweetheart who was to become his wife. Harry was a shy boy with weak eyes, who wore glasses from the age of 8. Shunning rough-and-tumble sports, he read fast and furiously. By 14 he "had read all the books in the Independence Public Library, and our big old Bible three times through."

Poor eyesight barred him from the United States Military Academy (to which he had an appointment) when he was graduated from high school in 1901; and, since the family lacked the money to send him to college, he turned to a variety of jobs. He worked as a drugstore clerk, as a timekeeper on a railroad construction project, in a mailroom, in a bank. He speculated in zinc and oil. And he toiled on the family farm. Meantime, he joined Battery B of the National Guard in 1905 and became a member of the Masonic Order in 1909.

When the United States entered World War I, Truman, then 32, was a farmer. He left the soil to help organize the 129th Field Artillery, and he became commander of its Battery D. He led it into action at St. Mihiel, in the Meuse-Argonne offensive in France, and again at Verdun, gaining the respect and affection of his men. (At convivial reunions later, "Captain Harry" used to play the piano—he had learned as a youth, at his mother's insistence—while his comrades sang.)

Mustered out in 1919, he returned to Independence and married Miss Wallace on June 28. Then 35 and without a firm station in civilian life, he opened a haberdashery shop in Kansas City in association with Edward Jacobson, an army buddy. At the start, business was excellent, but the postwar depression changed all that, and Truman & Jacobson was obliged to close. Jacobson went through bankruptcy proceedings; Truman did not, and he was still paying off his creditors (the total debt was $28,000) 10 years later when he was a senator.

Truman's entry into politics was fortuitous. It occurred in 1921, when James Pendergast, an army friend, introduced Truman to his father, Mike Pendergast, who, with his brother, Thomas J., ran Democratic politics in western Missouri. A veteran, a Baptist, a Mason, the personable Truman was adjudged a likely officeholder, and in 1922 he was elected a judge of the Jackson County Court. The post, a nonjudicial one, had jurisdiction over the building and upkeep of the county roads and public buildings.

Truman was conscientious, vigorous and industrious, both as a campaigner and as an administrator. He was defeated, however, in 1924. But in 1926 and again in 1930 he was elected presiding judge, both times with the help of the Pendergast organization. In 1934 Truman wanted to run for the House of Representatives, but the Pendergasts put him up for the Senate instead. Running on a pro-Roosevelt program in a strenuous campaign, he won with a majority of more than 250,000 votes. His record of probity as a county official and his Masonic connections helped him.

Although Truman never disavowed his close friendship with Thomas Pendergast, the leader of the party machine, he made it clear in the Senate and elsewhere that he was not "Pendergast's messenger boy." There was never any tarnish on his reputation for personal integrity.

Truman was nearly 51 when he took his Senate

seat. But "I was as timid as a country boy arriving on the campus of a great university for his first year," he recalled. "I had a prayer in my heart for wisdom to serve the people acceptably."

The years Truman spent in the Senate he recalled as "the happiest 10 years of my life." He found his fellow senators "some of the finest men I have ever known," and he used the word *cherish* to describe his friendship for them. He was a member of two important committees—Appropriations and Interstate Commerce—to whose work he devoted himself with diligence. He read voluminously from the Library of Congress, but he spoke seldom on the Senate floor, and then simply, briefly, without ostentation. His voting record was New Deal, which earned him the opposition of the big Missouri papers.

When Truman was sworn for his second term in 1941, the nation was preparing for war, and the letting of defense contracts was surrounded with rumors of favoritism and influence. Deeply concerned, Truman got into his automobile for a 30,000-mile tour of major defense plants and projects.

"The trip was an eye-opener, and I came back to Washington convinced that something needed to be done fast," he said. "I had seen at first hand that grounds existed for a good many of the rumors . . . concerning the letting of contracts and the concentration of defense industries in big cities."

The result was the Special Committee to Investigate the National Defense Program, soon shortened to the Truman Committee after the name of its chairman. It saved the country many millions of dollars by curbing waste and discouraging graft. And it made Truman a minor national figure, conspicuous for his firmness and his fairness.

Truman prepared his investigation by making a thorough study of similar committees in the past, especially of the records of the Joint Committee on the Conduct of the War Between the States. Defining his approach, the senator said: "The thing to do is to dig up the stuff now and correct it. If we run the war program efficiently, there won't be an opportunity to undertake a lot of investigations after the war and cause a wave of revulsion that will start off the country on the downhill road to unpreparedness and put us in another war in 20 years."

The committee got under way slowly, with $15,000 appropriated for its tasks. Truman invested $9,000 of this in the salary of Hugh Fulton, the group's investigator and counsel. The committee quickly turned up disquieting evidence of waste in military camp construction and equipment. And once its first reports—sober, factual and damning—were issued, more money for its operations was forthcoming.

The dollar-a-year man came under its scrutiny, and the committee was able to produce evidence that between June 1, 1940, and April 30, 1941, army and navy contracts totaling almost $3 billion had gone to 65 companies whose officials or former officials were serving in Washington and elsewhere as unpaid advisers to federal agencies.

Truman also inquired into aluminum production, the automobile industry, the aviation program, copper, lead, zinc and steel; into labor, plant financing, defense housing, lobbying, ordnance plants, small business and government contracts. Scarcely any aspect of procurement escaped his attention. The committee's hearings were orderly, remarkably free of partisanship, but they produced news and, more important, correction of the abuses that the senators had brought to light.

Truman was as unsparing of industrialists as he was of union leaders. He criticized William S. Knudsen, director of the Office of Production Management, for "bungling"; he was just as harsh with Sidney Hillman, the union leader, who was associate director of the office.

The senator was himself a zestful investigator and a keen questioner. He said later that the committee's watchdog role "was responsible for savings not only in dollars and precious time but in actual lives" on the battlefield.

In the course of the committee's work, Truman

was in touch with President Roosevelt, but there was no immediate serious thought of him as vice presidential material. When early in 1944 some friends mentioned the possibility to him, Truman "brushed it aside."

"I was doing the job I wanted to do; it was the one I liked, and I had no desire to interrupt my career in the Senate," he said.

Indeed, Truman had so far removed himself from consideration that he had agreed in July, on the eve of the Democratic convention in Chicago, to nominate James F. Byrnes for vice president, after Byrnes told him that Roosevelt had given him the nod. Meantime Roosevelt had decided to drop Vice President Henry A. Wallace and also, it turned out, to pass over Byrnes.

The choice fell on Truman. He was not so closely identified with labor as Wallace, although he was acceptable, nor was he a southern conservative, as was Byrnes. He was without fierce enemies, had an excellent reputation, was moderate on civil rights and was a midwesterner. Truman, however, was almost the last to know of Roosevelt's decision.

"On Tuesday evening of convention week," he recalled, "National Chairman Bob Hannegan came to see me and told me unequivocally that President Roosevelt wanted me to run with him on the ticket. This astonished me greatly, but I was still not convinced. Even when Hannegan showed me a longhand note written on a scratch pad from the president's desk which said, 'Bob, it's Truman, F.D.R.,' I still could not be sure that this was Roosevelt's intent."

It took a long-distance call to Roosevelt, then on the West Coast, to convince Truman.

"Bob," Roosevelt said, "have you got that fellow lined up yet?"

"No," Hannegan replied. "He's the contrariest Missouri mule I've ever dealt with."

"Well, you tell him," Truman heard the president say, "if he wants to break up the Democratic party in the middle of a war, that's his responsibility."

"I was completely stunned," Truman remarked afterward. After walking around the hotel room, he said, "Well, if that is the situation, I'll have to say yes, but why the hell didn't he tell me in the first place?"

Following the nomination, Truman stumped the nation for Roosevelt and himself; for the president campaigned almost not at all. The Roosevelt-Truman slate won with ease over Gov. Thomas E. Dewey of New York and Senator John W. Bricker of Ohio, the Republican choices for president and vice president. The popular vote was 25,602,555 to 22,006,278, and the Electoral College tally was 432 to 99.

On Jan. 20, 1945, a snowy Saturday, Harry S Truman stood on the South Portico of the White House and was inaugurated. The man he was about to displace, Vice President Henry A. Wallace, administered the oath.

THE GLORIOUS COMEBACK OF 1948

"A GONE goose" was how Clare Boothe Luce described Harry S Truman in 1948. With that Republican assessment of the president's chances for election on his own, many Democrats agreed—Frank Hague of Jersey City and Mayor William O'Dwyer of New York among them. Truman had his own views.

"There was no doubt of the course I had to take," he said. "I felt it my duty to get into the fight and help stem the tide of reaction, if I could, until the basic aims of the New Deal and the Fair Deal could be adopted, tried and proved."

The Republicans' exultancy and the Democrats' pessimism seemed well founded. Early in 1948 Truman, who had always opposed discrimination, submitted to Congress a series of moderate civil rights proposals that included antilynching and antisegregation measures. Southern Democrats were disconcerted. They organized a States Rights party, with Senator J. Strom Thurmond of South Carolina as its presidential candidate, to sunder the Democrats' traditional Solid South.

At the other end of the political spectrum, pacifist and leftist groups, alarmed over the Cold War with the Soviet Union, and dissident labor groups rallied around Henry A. Wallace and formed a Progressive party to challenge the Democrats in the big northern and western cities.

Added to those seemingly fatal Democratic rifts was a generalized voter discontent over inflation, high taxes and the presence of Truman's Missouri friends in the White House and in preferred administrative jobs.

Furthermore, some sophisticates thought ill of a president who relaxed at Key West, Fla., in brightly hued sports shirts, whose words lacked scholarly elegance and who was inclined to be snappish with his Republican Congress.

Truman himself conceded the dismal outlook for his fortunes. "Almost unanimously the polls taken before the 1948 Democratic convention showed my popularity with the American people to have hit an all-time low," he said.

He was convinced nonetheless that this "resulted from the efforts made by the American press to misrepresent me and to make my program, policies and staff appear in the worst possible light." His complaint had some merit; most publishers were staunchly Republican, and frequently their news columns gave more space to Truman's opponents than to his defenders.

"I knew I had to do something," the president recalled, and that "something" was to "go directly to the people in all parts of the country with a personal message."

The consequence was a "nonpolitical" train trip in May to the West Coast and back. On it Truman delivered 76 speeches, many at whistle-stops, and the bulk of them extemporaneously. They were plain, earnest talks that expounded his domestic and foreign program, and they created a favorable impression. Indeed, even those Democrats who were considering drafting Gen. Dwight D. Eisenhower, because of his aura as a war leader, now warmed up to Truman.

He was thereupon nominated with ease, and selected to run with him was Senator Alben W. Barkley of the border state of Kentucky.

Earlier, expectant Republicans had chosen Gov. Thomas E. Dewey of New York as their presidential candidate and Gov. Earl Warren of California as his ticket mate. Their platform emphasized that "it is time for a change," and it pledged action to halt rising prices, meet the housing shortage, promote civil rights and aid education. The party exuded confidence; the campaign appeared to be little more than a formal prelude to inauguration.

Truman, however, took the offensive, starting with his acceptance speech before the Democratic convention. It was a rousing talk given from notes, and it foreshadowed his campaign strategy and his style.

"I made a tough, fighting speech," he recalled. "I recited the benefits that had been won by the Democratic administrations for the people."

He singled out farmers and workers, telling them that "if they don't do their duty by the Democratic party, they are the most ungrateful people in the world."

Then, to use his words, he "tore into the 80th Congress" and the Republican party, building to his climax—an announcement that he would recall the Congress into special summer session to enact the recently adopted Republican platform.

It was a masterly tactic, for the special session accomplished nothing. Its Republican leaders were awaiting what seemed to them an assured Dewey victory in November, and they had no desire to give Truman credit for legislation that might better go to Dewey. In the meantime Truman took himself to the country.

"I am going to fight hard; I am going to give them

hell," he assured Barkley as he prepared to denounce again and again "that no-good, do-nothing 80th Congress."

His campaign covered 31,700 miles, and it included 256 speeches—16 in one day once. More than 12 million people turned out to see him. "I simply told the people in my own language," he said later, "that they had better wake up to the fact that it was their fight."

He appealed to farmers not to jeopardize their prosperity. To labor he vowed a fight to repeal the Taft-Hartley Act. To Negroes he promised more civil rights. And to everyone he said he would carry on his domestic program "for the benefit of all the people."

The response, mild at first, grew in late September and October, and at the end, wherever he appeared, the crowds were large and friendly, and there were yells of "Give 'em hell, Harry," and the throngs applauded and cheered when he did just that. Owing to bipartisanship, however, foreign policy was not an active issue; the concentration was on domestic affairs.

Dewey, for his part, was speaking in polished and euphonious generalities, virtually ignoring his opponent. He pleaded for "unity" among the voters, much like a man who had already won an election. The polls and the commentators all predicted he would win, and he did not see how he could lose.

But Truman sensed something else. A homespun man without guile, he believed that he had touched the common man with simple, hortatory speeches, whose theme was "Help me."

On election eve, Truman was in Missouri. He took a Turkish bath, ate a ham sandwich, drank a glass of milk and went to bed. He awoke twice during the night, both times to listen to Hans von Kaltenborn's clipped, slightly Teutonic-voiced radio analyses of the returns. These showed Truman ahead in the popular vote—but he couldn't possibly win, the commentator insisted. (For years afterward Truman delighted in imitating Kaltenborn's remarks that night, just as he enjoyed poking fun at the *Chicago Tribune*, which "elected" Dewey in its early-edition headline.)

At 6 A.M. on Nov. 3, when the California vote came in, Truman was elected in what many experts called a stunning upset. The tally gave him 24,105,695 votes to Dewey's 21,969,170; in the Electoral College the vote was Truman, 303; Dewey, 189, and Thurmond, 39. Wallace received no electoral votes, though his popular vote, a little more than a million, equaled Thurmond's.

"I was happy and pleased," the president said, not only for himself but also for the Democratic Congress that was elected with him.

The president opened his new term with characteristic audacity, by using his Inaugural Address on Jan. 20, 1949, to call for fulfillment of his domestic plans and to urge reinforcement of the Western alliance against Soviet power.

But the high spot of his foreign program was a proposal that the United States share its tremendous scientific and industrial experience with nations emerging from colonialism into freedom. He summed up the plan (quickly shortened to Point Four, because it was the fourth point in the foreign program) in these words: "I believe we should make available to peace-loving people the benefits of our store of technical knowledge, in order to help them realize their aspirations for a better life."

Point Four captured the imagination of the peoples of the underdeveloped world, and more than 34 nations eventually signed up for technical assistance. By 1953 Truman was able to report that the program "had relieved famine measurably in many portions of the world, had reduced the incidence of diseases that keep many areas poverty-stricken, and had set many nations on the path of rising living standards by their own efforts and by the work of their own nationals."

Truman detailed his domestic proposals in a State of the Union message. These included controls on prices, credit, wages and rents to fight inflation; priorities and allocations of essential materials; new civil rights laws; a 75-cent-an-hour basic wage;

health insurance; expanded Social Security; low-cost housing and a tax increase.

"Every segment of our population and every individual has the right to expect from our government a fair deal," he declared. The "fair deal" phrase was picked up and became the shorthand name for his program.

Meanwhile the president was confronted with a fearful and insecure Europe, uncertain anew of the extent of Soviet bellicosity after the Communist takeover of Czechoslovakia in 1948. The response Truman framed was military: the mutual security system of the North Atlantic Treaty Organization. The treaty, embracing Western Europe and the United States, was signed April 4, 1949, and ratified Aug. 14 by the Senate.

The pact, which placed this country's allies under its military umbrella, was a milestone in American foreign relations, for it dramatized United States determination to block any Soviet westward thrust by force of arms.

To head the NATO command, Truman had one man in mind—Dwight D. Eisenhower, whose organizational skills the president admired. With the general in charge, NATO quickly shaped common defense measures for Europe, and by early 1950 its nations were receiving the first of many hundreds of shipments of American arms. Military might was reinforcing the economic recovery fostered through the Marshall Plan and the Truman Doctrine.

Domestically business slumped in 1949, swelling the jobless rolls to 3.7 million and creating a federal deficit of $3.7 billion. Despite vigorous prodding from the White House, Congress was not, on the whole, responsive to appeals for social legislation or economic pump-priming; nor did it repeal the Taft-Hartley Act, as Truman had urged. Much of its mind, instead, was on the loyalty of federal employees, a question raised acutely by the Soviet explosion of an atomic device in 1949 and by revelations in the Alger Hiss case.

A former high State Department officer, Hiss was convicted of perjury in 1949. Testimony at his trial alleged that he had been involved in giving classified information to Soviet agents. This, and similar charges involving other former and current federal employees, aroused demands for a finer screening of government workers and for restraint of Communist and leftist groups.

Although Truman objected pungently to what he termed "the witch-hunting tactics" of congressional inquiries, and although he stoutly defended witness invocations of the Fifth Amendment, he did tighten loyalty-security procedures in an effort to bar Communists and subversives from federal jobs.

Nonetheless, he was never entirely convinced that these programs were in the American tradition, because, he argued, virtually any such program gave "government officials vast powers to harass all of our citizens in the exercise of their right of free speech."

"There is no more fundamental axiom of American freedom," he declared at the time, "than the familiar statement: 'In a free country, we punish men for the crimes they commit but never for the opinions they have.' "

It was in that vein that the president vetoed the Internal Security Act of 1950—a law designed to curb and punish "subversive" political expression. It was a courageous move, but an ineffective one, for Congress overrode the veto within 24 hours.

Internal security problems preoccupied legislators and the public for the remainder of Truman's term, becoming acute when Sen. Joseph R. McCarthy, Republican of Wisconsin, began to accuse the state department of harboring Communists and to charge that the administration was "soft" on party members and sympathizers.

Truman, of course, was not "soft" on Communists, but neither was he "soft" on McCarthy, whom he scorned as a demagogue. He was especially bitter about McCarthy's attacks on Marshall and the imputation that the general, who had headed a mission to China, was responsible for the Nationalist debacle there. Later the president condemned Eisenhower for his failure, in 1952, to disavow McCarthy publicly for having criticized Marshall.

Beset on the home front, Truman was soon fatefully involved again in the Far East. As one result of the peace settlement there, Japan was obliged to give up her 40-year suzerainty over Korea. The peninsula was divided for occupation purposes between the United States and the Soviet Union, with American forces supervising the area south of the 38th Parallel.

Shortly, however, a Communist regime was established in the Soviet zone, and it became North Korea. In the American zone a government headed by Syngman Rhee had been set up in 1948, after elections watched over by a United Nations commission. To this new republic the United States extended military and economic aid.

Nonetheless, pockets of discontent persisted in South Korea, and these were exploited by Communists in the north. By 1950 it seemed to North Korea that the Republic of Korea could be readily obliterated and the peninsula united in a single Communist regime.

Throughout the spring Central Intelligence Agency reports indicated to Truman that the North Koreans might attack, but these reports, the president noted later, were vague on timing. Besides, he said, "these same reports also told me repeatedly that there were any number of other spots in the world where the Russians 'possessed the capability' to attack." Moreover, at that time, America's first-line defense perimeter did not include Korea, as Secretary of State Dean Acheson had made clear.

So it was that on Saturday, June 24, 1950, the president was in Independence, Mo., on a family visit. "It was a little about 10 in the evening, and we were sitting in the library of our home on North Delaware Street, when the telephone rang," he recalled. "It was the secretary of state calling from his home in Maryland. 'Mr. President,' said Dean Acheson, 'I have very serious news. The North Koreans have invaded South Korea.' "

Truman's reaction was swift: to request an immediate special meeting of the United Nations Security Council and to seek from it a declaration that the invasion was an act of aggression under the United Nations charter.

The next day Truman flew back to Washington for a Blair House conference with his diplomatic and military advisers. As they were meeting, the Security Council (which the Soviet Union was boycotting at the moment) approved, 9 to 0, a resolution ordering the North Koreans to halt their invasion and to withdraw their forces. (Yugoslavia abstained on the roll call.)

"As we continued our discussion," Truman wrote later, "I stated that I did not expect the North Koreans to pay any attention to the United Nations. This, I said, would mean that the United Nations would have to apply force if it wanted its order obeyed.

"Gen. [Omar] Bradley said we would have to draw the line somewhere. Russia, he thought, was not yet ready for war, but in Korea they were obviously testing us, and the line ought to be drawn now.

"I said most emphatically I thought the line would have to be drawn."

With North Korean forces rapidly penetrating southward, the president ordered Gen. Douglas MacArthur, in Tokyo, to use American air and naval forces to aid the South Koreans. Simultaneously, with United States backing, the Security Council called on all members of the United Nations to help South Korea.

Within the next few days, under nominal United Nations command, American ground troops entered the conflict. This decision to intervene, Truman said later, "was probably the most important of all" that he made in his years of office.

In succeeding weeks Truman was immersed in the conflict and its incessant demands for decisions that only he could make. From the start, he did not regard the United Nations effort as a war but rather as a "police action" to punish aggression, as an armed struggle with clearly limited objectives.

"Every decision I made in connection with the

Korean conflict," he said, "had this one aim in mind: to prevent a third world war. . . . This meant that we should not do anything that would provide the excuse to the Soviets and plunge the free nations into full-scale, all-out war."

On the battleground itself, the North Koreans pushed the battered South Koreans and American forces into a pocket, and disaster seemed imminent until MacArthur, in a brilliant maneuver, landed troops at Inchon, behind the North Korean lines. Slowly the American forces regained the initiative. In October American troops were sweeping up the neck of the peninsula, deep into North Korea.

In Washington, Truman asked Congress to remove limitations on the size of the armed forces, authorize priorities and allocation of materials to prevent hoarding, raise taxes, restrict consumer credit and add $10 billion for armaments. The proposals, most of which were adopted, gave rise to grumbling later on, in 1952, when the conflict became stalemated.

Early in the conflict there were two developments that, as they matured, deeply affected the fighting and brought Truman into collision with MacArthur. These were indications that the Communist People's Republic of China might intervene in North Korea and that the general was not hewing to the Truman policy that called for a neutral Taiwan.

(MacArthur doubted the likelihood of Red Chinese intervention, and he wanted to bring Chiang Kai-shek into the fighting. His public disagreement with Truman on that point almost cost him his command in August 1950.)

Truman decided that the best way to handle his differences with MacArthur was in a face-to-face talk. "Events since June had shown me that MacArthur had lost some of his contacts with the country and its people in the many years of his absence," the president wrote. "He had been in the Orient for nearly 14 years then. . . . I had made efforts through [W. Averell] Harriman and others to let him see the worldwide picture as we saw it in Washington, but I felt that we had little success. I thought he might adjust more easily if he heard it from me directly."

The two men met for the first time on Wake Island in the Pacific on Oct. 15, 1950. The general was optimistic: The Chinese Communists would not enter Korea and the fighting would end by Thanksgiving, he predicted. Truman was pleased, and again he emphasized that the "police action" had strictly limited objectives, a prime one being the containment of the fighting to Korea.

Strategists differ as to what prompted the action, but on Oct. 25 the Chinese did enter the conflict, sending thousands of "volunteers" across the Yalu River into North Korea. Thus reinforced, the Communist forces eventually beat back the American and United Nations troops to the 38th Parallel, where a front was established that lasted until the truce of 1953.

Truman's policy in the face of the Chinese intervention was to continue to confine the fighting to Korea, to avoid escalation, a policy in which other members of the United Nations concurred. MacArthur, on the other hand, wanted to strike directly at the Chinese by air action in Manchuria across the Yalu River.

Matters came to a head in March 1951, when MacArthur wrote to Representative Joseph W. Martin, Jr., the House Republican leader, criticizing the president's policy. Truman believed that he had no choice but to relieve the general of his command.

"If there is one basic element in our Constitution, it is civilian control of the military," he explained. "Policies are to be made by elected political officials, not by generals or admirals. Yet time and again General MacArthur had shown that he was unwilling to accept the policies of the administration. By his repeated public statements, he was not only confusing our allies . . . but, in fact, was also setting his policy against the president's."

Amid mounting public speculation, Truman acted dramatically on April 10, 1951. In a concise order he discharged MacArthur for insubordination. To the American public, MacArthur was an almost legendary figure as a result of his Pacific war exploits—a general with superb aplomb who had turned the tide against Japan—and it was difficult at first to accept the possibility that he had overstepped the bounds of his role in Korea. It seemed logical, after all, for a general to want to win a clear-cut victory, and it was obvious to many that it must be frustrating for him to be forbidden the means to do it.

Realizing this, the president went on the radio to explain his action. The United States and the United Nations, he said, could not permit the Korean conflict to become a general war. Bringing China into that conflict directly, he warned, might unleash a third world war.

"That war can come if the Communist leaders want it to come," he said. "But this nation and its allies will not be responsible for its coming."

The deposed MacArthur returned to the United States, and to triumphal adulation. It appeared for a time that Truman, the commander in chief, was about to be outflanked by MacArthur, the dismissed general. Senate hearings were called in an air of expectancy, but after a few weeks the furor subsided, and the validity of Truman's step was generally accepted.

In the midst of the Korean conflict there was a crude attempt to assassinate the president. It occurred Nov. 1, 1950, when the Trumans were living in Blair House while the White House was under repair.

On the street below the president's window, guards kept vigil. At 2 P.M., as Truman was napping, a taxicab stopped nearby, and two men got out and walked toward Blair House. Suddenly one drew a pistol and fired at a guard. The other ran toward the front door of Blair House.

The guards sprang into action, and when the shooting ceased in a few minutes, Griselio Torresola, a Puerto Rican extremist, lay dead, and Leslie Coffelt, a guard, was mortally wounded.

The second would-be assassin, Oscar Collazo, was shot in the chest. He was subsequently convicted of murder and sentenced to die, but in 1952 the president commuted the penalty to life imprisonment.

Truman's second term, like his first, was marked by greater harmony on foreign policy—especially economic and military aid to Europe—than on domestic affairs. He found Congress reasonably willing to spend on foreign aid but reluctant to provide for social welfare, housing and education. This, in part, stemmed from home-front discontent over dislocations—taxes and a rise in living costs—caused by the Korean fighting.

Truman strove to keep the economy stable, a determination that he dramatized by seizing the steel industry on April 8, 1952, to avert a strike and a price rise in that basic commodity. Invoking his Korean conflict emergency powers, he put the industry under government operation. The stunning move aroused the ire of the business community, but the president was prepared with an explanation.

"If we give in to the steel companies on this issue," he said, "you could just say good-bye to stabilization. If we knuckled under to the steel industry, the lid would be off, prices would start jumping all around us—not just the prices of things using steel but prices of many other things we buy, including milk and groceries and meat."

The steel companies challenged the seizure and were upheld by the Supreme Court on the ground the president had exceeded his authority. He was obliged to approve a price rise. He always insisted, however, that the seizure was justified and legal.

As far back as 1949 Truman had decided not to run for election in 1952, and as that year drew near, he cast about for a suitable candidate. Once, in 1945, he had impulsively told Eisenhower he would back him in 1948, but by 1952 the general had been courted by the Republicans.

Truman's initial choice for 1952 was Chief Justice Fred M. Vinson, but the latter declined on grounds of health in the fall of 1951. The president then turned to Gov. Adlai E. Stevenson of Illinois, who had been elected in 1948 by an impressively large vote. Stevenson rejected Truman's proffer at least twice. Then, after almost six months of uncertainty, he decided to seek the nomination.

Truman, always a loyal party man, helped him get the nomination and stumped for him vigorously. The president, however, did not like Stevenson's campaign tactics, and he was not greatly astonished when Eisenhower won.

Afterward Truman made elaborate arrangements to acquaint the president-elect with pending problems, but the White House meeting was stiff and unproductive. Truman felt that the general was still smarting from the partisanship of the campaign.

Truman's intimates and advisers, who had watched him mature in office, praised him above all for his forthrightness. He himself, reviewing his actions in December 1952, said: "The presidents who have done things, who were not afraid to act, have been the most abused . . . and I have topped them all in the amount of abuse I have received."

If he had to do it all over again, he went on, he would not change anything.

On another occasion, he was more poignant. He said: "I have tried my best to give the nation everything I had in me. There are probably a million people who could have done the job better than I did, but I had the job, and I always quote an epitaph on a tombstone in a cemetery in Tombstone, Arizona: 'Here lies Jack Williams. He done his damndest.' "

The pomp of the presidency, the incessant blaring of "Hail to the Chief," the constant pressure at the center of attention left remarkably few imprints on Harry S Truman. He escaped, he once said, acquiring an " 'importance' complex"; so when he returned to his 14-room Victorian home in Independence, Mo., to live until his death, he was still a man of simple tastes and uninflated ambitions. He was prepared to make an easy transition to private life.

He quickly discovered, however, that a former president is a considerable object of curiosity and that he could not just become Citizen Truman. Visitors came to gape at his stately white house and to finger the iron picket fence that surrounded it; to watch him take his customary early-morning stroll; to look as he ate luncheon in Kansas City; to visit the nearby Harry S Truman Library in hope of catching a glimpse of him. He was sought out to run for the Senate, to speak at Democratic party rallies, to receive plaques and scrolls and degrees, to endorse candidates, to write of his experiences.

"When you're elected president, you're elected for life," he mused to one visitor. He was nearing 82 at the time, and he sat in front of a stack of letters that asked his autograph or a signed picture or an inscription in his books.

His was a busy retirement, and until the frailties of age intervened, he seldom spent a day of complete inactivity. When he was in Independence, he worked in his library office every weekday, starting at 8 o'clock in the morning, and sometimes on Saturday and Sunday. He took short trips, especially between 1953 and 1964, and wherever he went crowds sprang up to greet him. They called him "Harry" for the most part, sometimes "Mr. President." Whatever the appellation, it was uttered with affection, for however much Truman had been criticized in the White House, he was much admired as a person, and this esteem grew in his retirement.

Among the qualities that endeared Truman to the public was his strong sense of family. He was extraordinarily close to his mother, Martha Ellen. Even in his busiest years in Washington he wrote her a weekly letter in his clear and angular hand. "Dear Mamma and Mary," these letters began (the "Mary" was his younger sister, who lived with his mother in Missouri), and in unaffected sentences they recounted his activities, news of his wife and daughter, and family chitchat.

His mother was a cover-to-cover reader of the *Congressional Record,* with fixed likes and dislikes of members of Congress. In 1947, just before her death at the age of 94, she discussed political figures with her son, mentioning her distaste for Sen. Robert A. Taft, the Ohio Republican.

"Is Taft going to be nominated?" she asked.

"He might be," Truman replied.

"Harry, are you going to run?"

"I don't know, Mamma."

"Don't you think it's about time you made up your mind?" Mrs. Truman said, as if talking to a small boy. Her death in July 1947 overwhelmed her son.

Truman's hearty and unabashed affection for his wife, Bess, charmed most Americans. He was accustomed to confide in Mrs. Truman, for whose judgment he had enormous respect. They talked over each day's events, with Mrs. Truman offering her comments, political and personal. Except at campaign time, Mrs. Truman remained in the political background. Her husband wanted it that way, for he was convinced that womanhood was a state apart and that Bess was not fair political game.

The quickest way to arouse Truman's ire was to cast a slur on his wife. On the ground that they had maligned her, two members of Congress were barred from the White House, as was Clare Boothe Luce, the wife of the publisher Henry Luce. According to Harry Vaughan, the president's aide and confidant, Mr. Luce inquired about the ban.

"Mr. Luce," the president replied, according to Vaughan, "you've asked a fair question, and I'll give you a fair answer.

"I've been in politics 35 years, and everything that could be said about a human being has been said about me. But my wife has never been in politics. She has always conducted herself in a circumspect manner, and no one has a right to make derogatory remarks about her. Now, your wife has said many unkind and untrue things about Mrs. Truman. And as long as I am in residence here, she'll not be a guest in the White House."

In Truman's retirement "The Boss" or "The Boss Lady" (as he referred to his wife) also remained out of the spotlight. Nonetheless, she exercised a veto over his tendency to be too active and too gregarious. Her tug at his sleeve was sufficient to bring an end to a conversation or to quiet him down.

Of his daughter, Margaret, Truman was aggressively proud. At one point when her father was in the White House Miss Truman made her bow in Washington as a professional singer. Paul Hume, music critic of the *Washington Post*, reviewed her voice unenthusiastically. Truman read the notice, reached for his pen and dashed off a salty note in which he promised to punch the critic in the nose. Margaret was embarrassed, and Truman apologized for his outburst, but the episode added to his luster as a family man.

The former president had four grandchildren—Clifton, William, Harrison and Thomas, sons of Miss Truman's marriage in April 1956, to Clifton Daniel, a foreign correspondent for *The New York Times*, and later its managing editor. Truman proved to be a doting grandfather, visiting the children and their parents frequently in New York and being host to them in Missouri.

Interest in the welfare of young people occupied much of his attention as a private citizen. Before he left the White House he had decided, he said, that "the rest of my life was to be spent in large measure teaching young people the meaning of democracy as exemplified in the Republic of the United States."

For several years he was what he called "a kind of roving teacher." He would talk or lecture at colleges and universities and then reply to students' questions. "To me," he said, "there is nothing more rewarding than to stand before young people and find them so vitally interested in everything pertaining to the affairs of the country and the world." His aim was to pass along both his experiences in government and his fund of information on American political history.

He strove to encourage study of the presidency. He helped set up the Harry S Truman Library Institute for National and International Affairs, to which he contributed his lecture fees and other monies. The institute is designed to help young scholars who are investigating the presidency and the Truman years. "The library," he told one visitor with pride, "aims to be a storehouse for the history of the presidency, and I want to see it used that way."

Besides talking to older students, Truman took great delight in chatting with groups of schoolchildren who visited the library after it was opened in 1957. Once or twice a week, as long as he was at the library, the former president talked to these groups. Standing at a lectern, he was a relaxed and informal schoolteacher as he solicited and answered questions from the floor. Aides, anxious about his health, tried to restrain him, but he enjoyed the sessions so much that they gave up.

The library was very much the focus of the former president's life. Built by private subscription, it was given to the government and administered by the National Archives and Records Service. In addition to museumlike exhibits dealing with Truman's life and the presidency, it houses Truman's public and private papers and a large collection of books. His office in the library occupied one wing of the horseshoe-shaped structure.

When he returned to Independence in 1953, he was restless without a fixed daily routine. Most days he would go to a temporary office in Kansas City, 10 miles away, but by noon he was eager for companionship. Tom Evans, a businessman and a friend of 40 years, took to inviting him to lunch at the 822 Club in the Kansas City Club, where, after the dishes were cleared, there followed a few hours of poker (being too inquisitive, Truman was not a good player), a nap and the return to Independence. He was bored. Apart from walking, he had no athletic diversions. He shunned household chores. Despite his years as a farmer, he disliked to garden or mow the lawn.

In the early days of his retirement, his wife, perhaps to tease him, pressed him to do something about the lawn, but he devised a canny plan.

"So I waited until Sunday morning," he recalled, "just as our neighbors were beginning to pass on their way to church, and I took out the lawn mower and started to cut the grass. Mrs. Truman, preparing to leave for church, was horrified to see me cutting the lawn.

" 'What are you doing on Sunday?' she asked.

" 'I'm doing what you asked me to do,' I replied.

"Meanwhile the neighbors continued to pass by the house. Their glances were not lost on Mrs. Truman. She never asked me to mow the lawn again."

Being aware of Truman's hopes for a library dating from the White House years, Evans and a few other close friends stepped up fund-raising for the project. Land was given by Independence, and the completed building was dedicated with a speech by Chief Justice Earl Warren, whom Truman held in high esteem. Thereafter the former president organized his time around the library, where he worked and received visitors with warmth and in simple dignity.

There, in a book-lined office, he worked behind a trinket-strewn desk. Facing him on one wall were paintings of Andrew Jackson and Sam Rayburn. The presidential flag stood in a standard beside a leather couch. Over the bookcases on other walls were pictures of his wife, his daughter, his grandchildren and his ancestors.

In one bookcase was a thumbed four-volume set of *Great Men and Famous Women*, which had been published in 1894. It was a reminder of his youth and his first vision of the world beyond Jackson County, Mo.; for from these biographies Truman had drawn his early inspiration and his first criteria of public greatness.

Shortly after leaving the presidency, Truman sold the rights to his memoirs for $600,000. The two volumes—*Year of Decisions* and *Years of Trial and Hope*—took about two years to prepare. The books, which were best-sellers, were published by Doubleday. He also wrote *Mr. Citizen*, published in 1960 by Bernard Geis Associates. It was a collection of articles on his role as a private citizen that included a suggestion that former presidents sit in Congress, with a voice but no vote.

Truman's views on public issues were much sought after, and he became the master of the walking news conference. These took place mostly in large cities, when reporters accompanied him on his 120-paces-a-minute pre-breakfast hikes. He was a familiar sight in New York as, walking stick in hand, he strode the Upper East Side at the head of a covey of panting newsmen. He could usually be depended upon for a peppery remark or two about current politics.

From time to time Truman also wrote on public issues for the North American Newspaper Alliance. His articles were reflective statements in which he concerned himself with principles rather than with personalities. In the same vein, he appeared on a television series, "Years of Decision," that dealt with world events. His written and televised remarks displayed a strong sense of history and his desire to expound it without flourish.

(His version of postwar events and of his presidency was strongly challenged by some historians who believed that his hard-line anti-Sovietism, which set the tone of the Cold War, was a serious misreading of Russian and Chinese ambitions. In this view, a policy of peaceful coexistence might have been evolved between 1945 and 1953, had Truman exhibited more flexibility in his world outlook. These historians argued that his division of the globe between the free and the Communist worlds was ultimately counterproductive.)

As much as the former president liked the comfortable outlines of life in Independence and the tree-shaded quiet of its residential area, he was also drawn to occasional travel. He preferred casual trips similar to the one that he and his wife took in 1953, when they drove from Missouri to Washington and New York. More often, though, because of the crowds he collected, he was obliged to travel by train and plane. He used the train as often as he could, because his wife and his family abhorred air travel.

In 1956 the Trumans visited Western Europe for seven weeks and were received by Queen Elizabeth II in Britain and King Baudouin in Belgium. There was also a private audience with Pope Pius XII and an honorary degree at Oxford. But the former president didn't really enjoy himself, he confessed later, because the trip was too ceremonial.

Out of office, Truman was not out of Democratic politics, for he was a lifelong politicker. But his force in party councils diminished over the years. He handpicked Gov. Adlai E. Stevenson of Illinois to head the ticket in 1952. Afterward he was critical of the candidate, asserting that Stevenson "didn't understand people" and had "conducted a campaign that was not in support of the Democratic program of President Roosevelt and myself." In 1956 he backed W. Averell Harriman of New York for the nomination, but he stumped for Stevenson when the latter again carried the convention.

"I was just as unsparing of myself as if I were campaigning for myself," Truman said. He took especial pride in his party loyalty. "This is the way I think a man must act in politics," he said. "He must close ranks and forget personalities."

He exemplified this in 1960. After boycotting the Democratic convention on the ground that it had been rigged to produce the nomination of John F. Kennedy, he made his peace with Kennedy and campaigned for him. He was far happier with the nomination in 1964 of Lyndon B. Johnson, whose legislative and executive skills he esteemed. And he backed Hubert H. Humphrey in 1968.

Truman lived to witness the realization of at least four programs close to his heart. They were Medicare, low-income housing, broadened civil rights and a peace center in Israel. Medicare, which he proposed in principle in 1945, was enacted in 1965, and the bill was signed in his presence. He was acclaimed by President Johnson as "the real daddy of Medicare" when he received his government enrollment card.

In the crucial confrontations of clashing national ambitions in the postwar years, Truman acted, according to his lights, to preserve peace and to uphold freedom. This aspect of his career was recognized in 1966, when the Harry S Truman Center for the Advancement of Peace was set up by private subscription at Hebrew University in Jerusalem. On his doctor's advice, Truman did not attend the ceremonies in Israel in July, but he sent a vigorous call for a "fresh start" on solving the world's peace problems.

"When it is time to close the book of my life," he said earlier, "I will be comforted by the hope that this center will become a major source of light and reason toward the achievement of eternal peace."

A VIGOROUS AND DECISIVE LEADER*

DEAN ACHESON

ON AN April morning in 1945, advisers of a new president of the United States, working on a statement for him, were having a hard time. Answering their appeal for reinforcement, he recalled having met one of the assistant secretaries across the street in the State Department who might be helpful. In minutes I had joined the puzzled group.

A first question revealed that they had no idea what the new president would like to say. When we put the question to him, he had no doubt whatever what he wanted to say, and said it briefly and strongly. I scribbled notes as he spoke and soon produced a draft that, with a little joint editing, was typed and given to him. He was genuinely surprised. "That's just what I said. Will that do?" he asked us.

Over the next seven years, I saw a good deal of Mr. Truman and watched him grow into a president of commanding power. Yet the endearing qualities we saw that morning in the White House never left him. He had clear ideas on all occasions and he stated them well—but never as authoritative revelations of truth. His ideas were put forward for discussion and criticism by others, just as their ideas were submitted to him. He welcomed, and was never irritated by, the views of others, no matter how far they differed from his own initial impressions. Yet he never forgot that responsibility for decision was his.

Like Abraham Lincoln, he sought advice, but his vote was the only one that counted. Gen. George C. Marshall used to say that the capacity for decision was the rarest gift of God to man, and that Harry S Truman had it abundantly. He had something added to it that made him even more special: a high batting average in the soundness of his decisions. Whether this came from wisdom, experience or luck, or, as I believe, from all three together, the result was an uncommon blessing and benefit to the country.

A tendency that President Truman had to combat was to decide too quickly. He knew this, and learned to ask us at the outset of a discussion how much time he had in which to make his decision.

Within that limit he would listen to discussion and read documents—he was a voracious reader, not a one-page man—until he had mastered the subject, or until the subject was ready for decision.

It was not always easy for him to wait. On April 5, 1951, Mr. Joseph Martin, the minority leader of the House of Representatives, read in the House a letter from Gen. Douglas MacArthur that was bitterly critical of the conduct of the war in Korea—the "there is no substitute for victory" letter. On April 6 the president summoned General Marshall, the secretary of defense; Gen. Omar Bradley, the chairman of the Joint Chiefs of Staff; Mr. Averell Harriman, his special assistant, and me to meet and consider the situation.

Despite Mr. Truman's well-deserved peppery reputation, he gave very little outward sign of inward stress. Only a slight flaring and whitening of the nostrils, a tightening of the mouth, the increased staccato quality of his speech and a jerky, emphatic

* This essay on former President Harry S Truman was written for *Life* magazine by the late Dean Acheson in 1964 and was twice updated, the last time in 1970. It was made available to *The New York Times* by *Life,* whose final issue went to press before Mr. Truman's death.

A SELECTION OF QUOTATIONS OF

"I have issued a proclamation setting aside Sunday as a day of prayer. After the two-days' celebration [of Japan's unconditional surrender] I think we will need the prayer."

—Aug. 16, 1945. Press conference two days after the Japanese surrender

"Whenever the press quits abusing me, I know I'm in the wrong pew."

—April 17, 1948. Washington

"Never in history has society been confronted with a power so full of promise for the future of man and for the peace of the world. . . . We can use the knowledge we have won, not for the devastation of war, but for the future welfare of humanity."

—Oct. 3, 1945. In the atomic bomb message to Congress

"It all seems to have been in vain. Memories are short and appetites for power and glory are insatiable. Old tyrants depart. New ones take their place. Old allies become the foe. The recent enemy becomes the friend. It is all very baffling and trying, [but] we cannot lose hope, we cannot despair. For it is all too obvious that if we do not abolish war on this earth, then surely, one day, war will abolish us from the earth."

—Jan. 25, 1966. Independence, Mo.

"My father was not a failure. After all, he was the father of a president of the United States."

—To a reporter who remarked that John Anderson Truman had been a failure; from *Mr. Citizen*, 1960

"McCarthyism . . . the meaning of the word is the corruption of truth, the abandonment of our historical devotion to fair play. It is the abandonment of 'due process' of law. It is the use of the big lie and the unfounded accusation against any citizen in the name of Americanism and security. . . .

"My friends, this is not a partisan matter. This horrible cancer is eating at the vitals of America and it can destroy the great edifice of freedom."

—Radio and television address, Nov. 17, 1953. Kansas City, Mo.

"I have said many a time that I think the Un-American Activities Committee in the House of Representatives was the most un-American thing in America."

—April 29, 1959. Lecture series, Columbia University

"I am getting ready to see Stalin & Churchill; and it is a chore. I have to take my tuxedo, tails . . . preacher coat, high hat, low hat and hard hat."

—Letter to his mother, July 3, 1945, shortly before the Potsdam Conference

FORMER PRESIDENT HARRY S TRUMAN

"I believe that it must be the policy of the United States to support free peoples who are resisting attempted subjugation by armed minorities or any outside pressures.

"I believe that we must assist free peoples to work out their own destinies in their own way.

"I believe that our help should be primarily through economic and financial aid which is essential to economic stability and orderly political processes."

—Special message to the Congress on Greece and Turkey: The Truman Doctrine, March 12, 1947. Public Papers

". . . I have never deliberately given anybody hell. I just tell the truth on the opposition—and they think it's hell."

—In reply to a question on why people in political audiences always called out "Give 'em hell, Harry"; from *Mr. Citizen*

". . . [T]he president gets a lot of hot potatoes from every direction . . . and a man who can't handle them has no business in that job. That makes me think of a saying that I used to hear from my old friend and colleague on the Jackson County Court. He said, 'Harry, if you can't stand the heat you better get out of the kitchen.' I'll say that is absolutely true."

—Remarks at the Wright Memorial Dinner of the Aero Club of Washington, Dec. 17, 1952

"I believe in the brotherhood of man, not merely the brotherhood of white men but the brotherhood of all men before the law. . . . In giving the Negro the rights which are theirs we are only acting in accord with our ideals of a true democracy."

—Speech, June 15, 1940, at Sedalia, Mo., in campaign for reelection to the United States Senate, as quoted in *Harry S Truman*

Some of the presidents were great and some of them weren't. I can say that, because I wasn't one of the great presidents, but I had a good time trying to be one, I can tell you that."

—April 27, 1959. Lecture series, Columbia University

"There is no conversation so sweet as that of former political enemies. The way I look at it, I have been blessed in both enemies and friends."

—From *Mr. Citizen*

chopping with his right hand showed how strictly he was holding himself in control.

Early in the discussion the president agreed with our suggestion that he should reserve decision upon his action until he had the benefit of the recommendation of the Chiefs of Staff. General Bradley told us that he would need a couple of days to convene them, since one or more of the chiefs was overseas. Although we discussed the problem created by General MacArthur's public message at considerable length—and the press and public did likewise—the president did not disclose his thoughts.

On Sunday, April 8, he summoned me to Blair House for further talk and told me that he would be prepared to make his decision on the following day. Again I recognized the signs of nervous tension. I agreed that quick resolution was most desirable because of mounting speculation, and proper because then all views would be in. As he started to speak again, I urged that the less said before Monday the better.

When we met on Monday, April 9, the president was calm and relaxed, the tension wholly gone. He asked for our considered advice and listened without interruption while his advisers, civil and military, gave their unanimous opinion that General MacArthur should be relieved.

The president said to us that day that he had come to this same conclusion some two weeks before, at the time of MacArthur's undercutting of a proposed presidential move. My own views had been the same. But a general conclusion is different from a final determination. The president's self-discipline in making his decision created a solidly unified administration through what might have been a most critical period and certainly was a trying one.

Early we saw emerging in our chief a vigorous, decisive and self-disciplined character. Soon we saw added a strong sense of orderly procedure and a simple fairness. Mr. Truman never doubted that he must act through the great departments of government and with the advice of their heads. They furnished his instruments and his advisers—whomever else he might choose to consult. He also never doubted another rule, so simple that one is always amazed how rarely it is observed in high places: that officials importantly affected by a decision should be present and be heard when the decision is being discussed. When we add to this another practice of Mr. Truman's—making his decision in writing and communicating it to all concerned—the result was a trusted and respected leader and administrator.

Other presidents before and since Mr. Truman have multiplied confusion and doubt by neglecting these simple principles of orderliness and fairness. Evidence bearing on a decision comes in piecemeal if a president talks separately with several people, and each is left with a different idea of the president's decision (or whether there is one), and of the hearer's authority and responsibility in carrying it out.

Mr. Truman's natural modesty survived even the corrupting adulation that normally seeps through every opening of the White House. I say "modesty" not "humility," a detestable word that suggests the oily hypocrisy of Uriah Heep. The president's modesty came from a candid understanding of his own capacities and limitations, which left him at peace with himself. After some of us had seen him off on a vacation, he could write without the slightest self-consciousness, "I'm still a farm boy and when the Secretary of State of the greatest Republic comes to the airport to see me off on a vacation, I can't help but swell up a little bit." Awareness that he was not an intellectual did not result in self-distrust. The conviction that views opposing or critical of his own might be sound held his irritation in check and made dissent and criticism possible.

Two illustrations of his generosity to opposition and criticism jump to mind. On one occasion he cut me short in discussing an important presidential appointment, saying that he had already made up his mind and committed himself. When I continued to expostulate that he had not heard all the considerations, he insisted that he had committed himself, which, he said, ended the matter. Deciding to risk all, I suggested that it did not end the matter, since on the East Front of the Capitol I had heard him commit himself to "faithfully perform the duties of the office of the President of the United States," which surely required full hearing of the facts before making a decision.

For a moment the famous Truman temper rose with his flush. Then he said calmly, "Go ahead. You're quite right." His final decision was the opposite of his "commitment."

On another occasion a note came to me from one of his staff saying that it had been brought to the president's attention that a certain Foreign Service officer had been stationed for some months in a "hardship post" in Africa, and that the president would like to have him transferred to a more healthy one. A cabinet officer does well to maintain a healthy skepticism of the degree of presidential involvement in communications of this sort. Accordingly, I took the note with me on my next appointment at the White House and at the end of our business laid it before the president. If it was a correct transmission of an instruction of his, I said, it would, of course, be obeyed. In that case the president might wish to give his staff more continuing supervision of the assignment of Foreign Service officers, which often presented perplexing problems. For instance, the officer concerned here had only begun his service at the Africa post; if he were withdrawn, some other officer would have to replace him. Perhaps the White House staff might be the place to lodge the responsibility of choosing him.

Mr. Truman gave me a long amused look, then tore up the note. "Is that an adequate answer?" he asked. It was. I never asked for or received more.

Any portrait of Mr. Truman that left out the quality of tenderness would be grossly distorting. His well of affection was very deep and he constantly drew from it. All of us benefited from his thoughts of us. Absent on a mission at a time when one of our children was critically ill, I was called by the president on the telephone every day with a bulletin that he had personally obtained from my wife.

In summing up our thoughts of this man we must say, first, that he was deeply indebted to his ancestors who, like Sir Winston Churchill's, bequeathed him the priceless legacy of vitality, the foundation upon which he developed the decisiveness and strength "to withstand in the evil day, and having done all, to stand." For this made him a strong man. Second, he used to the full his education. Not formal education, for by today's standards he had little of that; but all the influence from individuals and experience of life that disciplined his ebullient nature and molded it, and from which in some mysterious way he distilled judgment. In this manner he made himself what the Greeks called a "just" man.

Finally, from the depths of a sweet and tender nature he was able to give, and by giving to inspire, affection. This added real devotion to mere sense of duty in those who served him, and elevated him to that small, high company of beloved leaders.

A MAN WHO "DONE HIS DAMNDEST"

CABELL PHILLIPS*

ON THE day after Franklin Roosevelt's death in April 1945, the shaken new president, Harry Truman, said to a group of reporters, "If you fellows know how to pray, pray for me now." The plea was typical of the plainspoken, essentially modest man who occupied the White House during eight tumultuous years in the nation's history, and who died last week in Kansas City at the age of 88.

Harry Truman worked less to ingratiate himself with people but succeeded better at it than any im-

* Mr. Phillips, a former member of the Washington staff of the *Times,* is author of *The Truman Presidency*, published by Macmillan in 1966.

portant public figure I have ever known. He did it, I think, because he was so utterly honest with and about himself, so free of what we call "side" or "put on."

He wasn't above cutting a corner or trimming the truth to gain a political or policy objective. He would go to almost any lengths to save the face of a friend. But neither as a public nor as a private figure did he ever pretend to be anything but what he was, and it mattered precious little to him whether anyone liked what he was or not.

What he was grated unpleasantly on some sensitive nerves—his brashness, his minor crudities of speech and manner, the fact that he did not adorn the great office of president with what they considered the requisite style and grace. He was the sort who synthesized the awesome responsibilities of his office not in resonant phrases that would look good in bronze, but with a simple, homespun aphorism: Tapping his desk and looking solemn as a preacher he would say, "The buck stops here."

There was eloquence and deep sincerity in the way he said it that made anything you might add redundant.

I once wrote a book about Mr. Truman, and something I said then is relevant in this context: "Harry Truman was and remains an ordinary man . . . who must make do without any special endowments of genius, intellect or charm. His strength lay in his ability to do the best he could with what he had and not despair over what he did not have. . . . He never suffered the illusion that he was another Roosevelt or Churchill, neither did he agonize over whether he was their inferior. Destiny linked his life to theirs in an apocalyptic enterprise and each rode it out to greatness according to his own fashion."

The most cynical and skeptical audience a president has to face is the Washington press corps. There is a congenital distrust between them, a built-in competitiveness that more often than not degenerates into mutual hostility.

No president of the last 50 years was so widely and warmly liked by the reporters as Mr. Truman. He "used" the press occasionally, as most presidents have done, to test the wind. But he never tried to con them with flattery and devious favoritism. He was reasonably accessible to reporters, enjoyed having them along on trips and liked to play practical jokes on them or take them for their expense accounts in after-hours poker sessions.

They felt that he leveled with them. On his frequent visits to Washington after 1952, as many reporters as politicians dropped into his suite at the Mayflower on an afternoon for a friendly chat and a toast of "bourbon 'n' branch."

Since Mr. Truman never constructed any false images of himself, he enjoyed a large dividend of self-confidence. Call it cockiness: That was its outer manifestation much of the time. Whatever it was, it gave him an immense capacity for making up his mind to do what had to be done and then putting it behind him—whether it was a bit of legislative strategy, or the dropping of the atom bomb. Many people think this was one of his strongest attributes as president.

I ran into an example of this quality in 1959. I went to Independence to write an article about him on the approach of his 75th birthday. Routinely, I asked him to recall the half dozen most difficult decisions he had had to make as president. When he finished I remarked that he had failed to mention the dismissal of Gen. Douglas MacArthur during the Korean War.

"That must have taken a bit of courage," I said.

"Courage had nothing to do with it," he snapped, his eyes flashing through the thick glasses. "He was insubordinate and I fired him, and that's all there was to it. Sure, I knew there would be a lot of stink about it. But it was the right thing to do and I did it, and I've never lost any sleep over it since."

Did those qualities add up to greatness? Was Harry Truman a "great" president? There is no firm definition of the term, but many competent scholars have given him that accolade. The late Prof. Clinton Rossiter, of Cornell, said of him some years ago: "I am ready to hazard an opinion, to which I did not come easily or lightly, that Harry Truman will eventually win a place as president, if not as a hero, alongside Jefferson and Theodore Roosevelt."

One measure of greatness, certainly, is the extent to which a president uses the great potentialities of his office to advance the national interest. By this yardstick, Mr. Truman must be rated among the best. True, his tenure was turbulent and bedeviled by partisan strife; he could never be certain that his own party might not desert him in a showdown. But few presidents have fought harder, or against greater odds, than Mr. Truman for the programs and the values he believed in.

His net gains on the domestic front were, in the end, relatively modest, but in the area of foreign policy they were monumental. His was the era of the Cold War and of the atom. His two terms in office were overshadowed by a danger no other president has ever had to face: the grinding rebalancing of world power between two hostile and incompatible forces, each capable of destroying the other.

President Truman met that danger with bold and imaginative—albeit to some persons, controversial—countermeasures. The Truman Doctrine, the European recovery program, NATO, the Berlin airlift, the Korean intervention—these were landmarks along the road to national maturity. They have profoundly affected the destiny of the American people and of the world.

Some revisionist historians now hold these measures to have been ill chosen and wrongly conceived; that they advanced rather than retarded the Cold War. They may be right. It is hard to argue with 20/20 hindsight. But these events ought to be judged in the context of their time; in terms of the stresses felt and the wisdom at hand when they occurred. Those years from 1947 to 1952 were full of anxiety and uncertainty. Most people at the time thought Mr. Truman's decisions were the right ones. Some, myself included, still think so.

One day in April 1952, at his 300th press conference as president (to explain his decision not to seek renomination), Mr. Truman said to many of the same reporters whom he had asked eight years previously to pray for him: "I have tried my best to give the nation everything I have in me. There are a great many people—I suppose a million in this country—who could have done the job better than I did. But I had the job and I had to do it.

"I always remember an epitaph which is in the cemetery at Tombstone, Arizona. It says: 'Here lies Jack Williams. He done his damndest.' I think that is the greatest epitaph a man can have—when he gives everything that is in him to do the job he has before him. That is all you can ask of him and that is what I have tried to do."

TRUMAN AND THE BOMB

LESTER BERNSTEIN

THE DAY Harry S Truman may have saved my life is not one I've thought about very often over the years, but it deserves some reflection in this centennial year of his birth. The day was August 6, 1945. I was a G.I. who had weathered the war in Europe and now awaited my place in the storming of Japan's home islands. On Truman's orders, the first atomic bomb ever wielded in war exploded over Hiroshima. For Americans in uniform and those who waited for them to come home, outrageous as this may appear from the moral heights of hindsight, it was a sunburst of deliverance.

Shock waves have reverberated ever since. No decision by any American president has thrown so long a shadow or stirred so stubborn a controversy. Today I know much more about Truman's decision, and for reasons that are not entirely selfish, I still think it was for the best.

The fateful decision has been viewed increasingly through a mist of might-have-beens. Was the bomb really needed to force Japan's surrender? The United States Strategic Bomb Survey in 1946 conjectured that Japan could have fallen no later than Dec. 1, 1945, without either the bomb or an invasion. Deciphered intercepts in the summer of 1945 reflected Tokyo's maneuvering for a mediated end to the war; might the Japanese have given up earlier than August if the demand for unconditional surrender had been softened to assure survival of the emperor? And if the bomb had to be used at all, wouldn't a demonstration in an uninhabited area have done the job?

Those who write history have the gift of revision; those who make it get only one chance. Truman had to deal with the realities confronting him in the summer of 1945. His Joint Chiefs told him it would take an invasion to topple Japan by conventional means. They projected possible American deaths at upward of 250,000 against an army of two million supported by thousands of kamikaze planes. The fanatical defenders of Okinawa alone had just exacted 45,000 American casualties. As for diplomacy, the Japanese never advanced any peace feeler; their efforts to find mediation suggested they hoped to retain some of their territorial gains. Unconditional surrender, already imposed on Germany and reaffirmed as a goal by the new president to a cheering Congress, had become an article of faith through years of sacrifice.

The possibility of using the bomb only to stage a demonstration was explored by the "Interim Committee" of eight distinguished civilians who advised Truman on atomic issues, including far-ranging ones of postwar international control. They asked their own advisory panel of four scientists whether such a demonstration could be effectively devised. The four—J. Robert Oppenheimer, Arthur H. Compton, Ernest O. Lawrence and Enrico Fermi—reported: "We can propose no technical demonstration likely to bring an end to the war; we can see no acceptable alternative to direct military use."

The reasoning of Truman's advisers, and finally his own, was that using the bomb without warning against a military installation in a populated area would shock the Japanese into surrender, thereby saving far more lives than it would cost. Given the military opportunity, the decision had an inevitability implicit in the monumental effort in which an army of 120,000 scientists and technicians spent three years and a then staggering $2 billion to build a bomb.

The moral stigma of the two atomic bombs Truman dropped has overshadowed the swift victory they won. In a curious way, that stigma seems misapplied to the bomb that destroyed Hiroshima or even to the one that fell three days later on Nagasaki, which was somewhat harder to justify militarily. Were those bombs really different, morally, from the indiscriminate horror that inflicted even greater civilian casualties in the firebombing of Tokyo or Dresden?

What makes nuclear weapons different in kind, not just in degree, is the threat of human extinction. That unique and ultimate immorality was not born at Hiroshima. Its birthday was July 16, 1945, at Alamogordo, N.M., where the sky blazed with the first atomic explosion, a sterile test blast that killed no one. If atomic bombs had never fallen on Japan, the genie would still have been out of the bottle. The nuclear arms race and proliferation would not have been far behind—but the temptation to use the bomb would have been harder to resist.

What the bombs over Hiroshima and Nagasaki did accomplish, apart from ending the war, was a kind of inoculation of fright and revulsion, the stuff that deterrence is made of. So far, for a remarkable 39 years full of war and crisis, it has made nations and governments shrink from using the bomb again. That is no small accomplishment.

THE TRUMAN CORRESPONDENCE

EDWIN McDOWELL

ALMOST 1,300 letters from Harry S Truman to his wife, Bess, spanning a half century from the time he was a struggling 26-year-old farmer until six years after he left the presidency in 1953, were made public in March of 1983.

Some of the letters, held by the Harry S Truman Library in Independence, Mo., include frank descriptions of such world leaders as Stalin and shed new light on political and diplomatic history.

Others, from a young farmer and soldier to the small-town girl he would marry, portray something of life and love in an earlier generation.

Several contain what would "practically amount these days to secrets of state," according to Robert H. Ferrell, a Truman scholar who has been examining and collating the letters.

Scholars, who according to Mr. Ferrell had generally believed that Mrs. Truman burned her husband's letters after he became president, had no idea until recently that such a large cache existed.

The most important discovery in the letters examined so far, Mr. Ferrell said, is proof that President Truman wanted the Soviet Union to enter the war against Japan. In a letter dated July 18, 1945, written from Berlin at the time of the Potsdam Conference with the Soviet Union's Stalin and Britain's Winston Churchill, Truman assured his wife, "I've gotten what I came for—Stalin goes to war August 15th with no strings on it . . . I'll say that we'll end the war a year sooner now, and think of the kids who won't be killed! That is the important thing."

In another letter, written in 1947 at the dawn of the Cold War, Truman said he was afraid Italy might go Communist in the elections and he feared the Russians might attack Western Europe.

"This may be the frankest and most important presidential correspondence of this century," Mr. Ferrell said. "It is also a wonderful 19th-century love story talking to the 20th century."

President Truman's letters from the Potsdam Conference, held near Berlin from July 17 to Aug. 2, 1945, indicate that his initial impression of Stalin was favorable. On July 29, in a letter saying that Stalin and his foreign minister, Vyacheslav M. Molotov, were coming to see him that morning, the president added: "I like Stalin. He is straightforward, knows what he wants and will compromise when he can't get it. His foreign minister isn't so forthright."

The Potsdam meeting, the last of the Big Three summit conferences, was the first attended by Truman and marked his diplomatic baptism by fire with his Soviet and British counterparts. It was called to clarify and carry out agreements made at Yalta in February 1945, before President Roosevelt's death.

On several occasions, Truman refers to Stalin as "Uncle Joe," an appellation the president's political opponents would eventually use against him as the Potsdam agreements were consistently breached in the gathering postwar chill.

But the letters to his wife written during that conference indicate that while the 33d president liked Stalin personally, he applied to the Russian leader and to Churchill the same "Give 'em hell" techniques that captivated his political friends at home and repelled his political enemies. "We had a tough meeting yesterday. I reared up on my hind legs and told 'em where to get off and they got off," he wrote to his wife on July 20. Five days later he told her, "We have been going at it hammer and tongs in the last few days," adding that Stalin "seems to like it when I hit him with a hammer."

The Russians actually declared war on Japan Aug. 8, earlier than Truman had said. But that was two days after the atomic bomb destroyed Hiroshima and six days before Japan surrendered.

"Truman always said that his main purpose at Potsdam was to get Russia into the war," said Mr.

Ferrell, a professor of history at Indiana University and author of several books about Truman, who died in 1972. "But a lot of historians say he was there to keep Russia out, because it looked like the U.S. could end the war itself. The day before the conference opened on July 17, the U.S. tested a plutonium bomb. So unless he lied to Bess, he really wanted the Russians in."

Just as Truman was later to say he had no regrets about ordering the atomic bombing of Japan, he apparently suffered few qualms about what befell Nazi Germany. Describing prostrate Berlin and its residents to his wife in 1945, he said: "This is a hell of a place—ruined, dirty, smelly, forlorn people, bedraggled, hangdog look about them. You never saw as completely ruined a city. But they did it."

Most of the letters were found squirreled in a dozen or more locations in the Truman house at 219 Delaware in Independence, but they have been in the Truman Library for many months, according to Dr. Ben Zobrist, the library director. In the fall of 1979, after her mother's death at age 97, Margaret Truman Daniel, the owner and donor, signed the agreement giving the letters to the people of the United States.

Library personnel have meanwhile been arranging the letters chronologically, indexing them and copying the letters and the envelopes they were mailed in. All the material had to be reviewed to insure there were no state secrets or anything highly embarrassing to living individuals. The letters were formally opened to the public last Monday.

In the July 25 letter from Berlin—like much of the correspondence, it was delivered to Independence through regular post office mail—the president also referred to Drew Pearson, an influential syndicated columnist of the time and a longtime Truman antagonist. "If that so and so ever says anything to your or Margaret's detriment," he warned, "I shall give him a little Western direct action that he'll long remember. I don't care what he says about me but I can get hotter than a depot stove when he mentions my family."

The letters, all written in the same bold hand as the Truman diaries, contain an estimated 500,000 words. They cover Truman's 11 years as a farmer, the year he served as an artillery officer in France in World War I, and his careers as haberdasher, county judge and two-term United States senator as well as almost eight years in the White House.

"He had a rule of writing Bess every day when they were apart," Professor Ferrell said. They were apart whenever Mr. Truman had to be away on official business, or, he said, whenever Mrs. Truman returned from Washington to her beloved Independence.

The letters disclose much about courtship in the early years of this century, a courtship whose progression is marked by the increasingly familiar manner in which the future president addressed the young woman who was to become his wife. His letters begin "Dear Bessie" and are signed "Harry S Truman." Soon they begin "My Dear Bessie" and are signed "Harry S." Finally they begin "Dear Bess" and are signed "Harry." What never flags through all those decades is Truman's eagerness for letters from her.

For example, in letters written starting in 1910, nine years before their marriage, Truman hints, cajoles and pleads for her to write to him: "I sure do like to hear from you." "Please don't wait so long to write as I do enjoy your letters even if you do call them notes." "I should be just as pleased to get a letter from you on wrapping paper as [on] the finest stationery built."

Those were not just the temporary sentiments of a heartsick swain. Thirty-five years later, the day after the Potsdam Conference convened, the opening sentence of his letter declared: "I've only had one letter from you since I left home. I look carefully through every pouch that comes—but so far not much luck." If Mrs. Truman's letters to Mr. Truman exist, said Professor Ferrell, scholars do not know about them.

In addition to shedding light on diplomatic and political history, the Truman letters are certain to throw additional light on the Truman personality and on the mores of the time. To the future president, farm life meant hard work and an existence that "as an everyday affair is not generally exciting." Yet he managed to retain a sense of humor even while recuperating from a broken leg, caused when a 400-pound calf brushed against him when he was setting fence posts. "I have the sincere satisfaction of knowing that he will some day grace a platter—perhaps my very own," he wrote to his intended.

Many of those early letters were addressed to Elizabeth Virginia Wallace of Independence from nearby Grandview, the Truman family farm to which young Harry returned in 1906 after four years as a bank clerk in Kansas City. He had met Bess in Independence in 1890 when he was 6 and she 5, and they attended school together until 1901. "I thought she was the most beautiful and the sweetest person on earth," Truman was to write years later.

But during those years they pursued other interests. Their courtship began in 1910 when Harry, visiting an aunt in Independence, walked across the street to return a cake plate to Mrs. Wallace. Bess opened the door, to the house and also to their eventual courtship.

The Truman letters reveal a blend of naïveté and obstinacy, tenderness and toughness, plus a touch of the pedant. A voracious reader in his early years—he once boasted of having read many of the 2,000 books in the public library—he told Bess that he regarded Mark Twain as "my patron saint in literature," and said "I would rather read Mark Twain or John Kendrick Bangs than all the Shakespeare and Miltons in Christendom."

He told her that he loved music ("I can even appreciate Chopin when he is played on the piano") but he pointedly excluded opera. When it comes to "a lot of would-be actors and actresses running around over the stage and spouting song and hugging and killing each other promiscuously, why I had rather go to the Orpheum," he wrote.

Truman wrote wryly about the 10-party-line telephones of his day. "If someone would invent a contraption to shut out the other nine when a person wanted to use the tenth he would be richer and more famous than Edison," he wrote.

Another time he opined that if someone would invent a fork with a spring—"so you could press it and spear a biscuit at arm's length without having to reach over and incommode your neighbor—well he'd just simply be elected president, that's all." The early letters give no hint that Truman, busy tilling soil, sowing crops and feeding livestock, ever imagined that he would be elected president or that he would do anything but what he was doing. "I never expect to be rich," he wrote in 1911, "but if I can't make what I get myself without waiting for someone to leave it to me I hope somebody will knock me on the head and put me out of danger."

In one of his more descriptive letters, Truman told of a party where a widow taught him a hoedown. "It goes something like this," he wrote. " 'Swing the girl with the pretty brown hair and now the one with the face so fair. Swing the gal with a lantern jaw and now the one from Arkansas. Balance and turn and left and right and all promenade.' Then you do it over. You can get most gloriously dizzy and it's a lot cheaper than booze."

Unlike many of his coreligionists, young Harry Truman not only approved of dancing and going to shows, but he told Bess he enjoyed them and liked playing cards besides. "So you see I am not very strong as a Baptist," he said soon after he began writing to her. "Anyhow I don't think any church on earth will take you to heaven if you're not real anyway. I believe in people living what they believe and talking afterwards, don't you?"

His penchant for cards was to last a lifetime. In a letter from Berlin he told Bess that he bought her a Belgian lace luncheon set. "I'm not going to tell you what it cost," he wrote, "you'd probably have a receiver appointed for me and officially take over the strongbox. But I came out a few dollars to the good in the game of chance on the boat, so it's invested in a luxury for you."

Apparently, however, he had a much more limited capacity for drink than for cards. During the Potsdam Conference he wrote to his wife: "Uncle Joe gave his dinner last night. There were at least 25 toasts—so much getting up and down that there was practically no time to eat or drink either—a very good thing."

Following are excerpts from letters written by Harry S Truman to Elizabeth Virginia Wallace in 1911. He was recovering from a broken leg suffered while working at his grandmother's farm in Grandview, Mo. Miss Wallace was living 10 miles away in Independence.

April 24, 1911
Dear Bessie:
To think that I have had some really respectable falls and came off without a scratch and then have a sucking calf knock me down and actually break my leg. Tis indeed a disgrace. But perhaps I can live it down.

I had thirteen callers yesterday and the telephone bell is almost worn out. I really didn't know I had so many friends. It does me good to find it out even if I do have to stay penned up.

Your letter did me lots of good so please send another when you have time. I hope your incubator behaved well. Mamma has 112 young chickens and more coming every day. Write when you can to

Yours sincerely,
Harry

April 27, 1911
Dear Bessie:
My pleasure is not to be expressed in words for the nice long letter you sent me so soon. Of course, now I have nothing else to do but write and read, and I certainly appreciate the fact that you wrote so promptly because you I know are busy.

I shall be worse spoiled than an only child when I get well. Papa buys me candy and fruit as if I were a two-year-old and Mamma spends half her time making me comfortable and making my favorite pies. You really don't know how much you're thought of until you get knocked out. I shall try and keep my head though.

Write when you can soon to

Yours sincerely,
Harry

May 3, 1911
Dear Bessie:
I don't care what kind of paper you write on. I should be just as pleased to get a letter from you on wrapping paper as the finest stationery built.

I am sorry to hear of your chickens dying. Mamma has lost quite a number though. She says it is the cold damp weather more than anything else. She is going to dip them as soon as the weather will permit and then she says they'll be all right.

I had a letter from Nellie saying she was going to quit teaching in Independence and go down to Sugar Creek. They offered her a larger salary. I told her not to fall in love with a Bohunk but if she ran across a Standard Oil Magnate to nab him.

I have been reading David Copperfield and really found out that I couldn't appreciate Dickens before. I have only read Oliver Twist and Tale of Two Cities. I do think that Mr. Micawber is the killingest person I have run across in any book anywhere. He is exactly true to life. I know a half dozen of him right here in Grandview. They are always waiting for something to turn up or for something to die and leave them something.

I guess you'll have a good time with your bridge club. Speaking of people crying at plays, I don't think there is anything funnier. That is the only way I enjoy a tragedy is to laugh at those who cry. Uncle Harrison says he'd rather go to the Orpheum and laugh all evening than sit and grate the enamel off his false teeth to see Mansfield or Sothern or any other big gun. He is very near right I think. Well I hope you'll consider this worth an answer as I'll be glad to get one.

May 9, 1911
Dear Bessie:
You may be very very sure that your letters cannot possibly come too often or too regular for me. They are the most pleasant and

Speaking of that ——— calf. It had the impudence to come up and look at me through the window a day or two ago and then kick up and bawl, as much as to say, "See what he got for monkeying with the bandwagon." He had three or four more calves of his own age with him. I have the sincere satisfaction of knowing that he will some day grace a platter—perhaps my very own.

Mamma gave me her prescription for dipping chickens and it's a dinger I tell you. She takes a twist of tobacco and steeps it in hot water as if you were making tea. Put in cold water enough to cover the hen and make it the right temperature. Then she puts in a tablespoon full of melted grease. She says she puts her hand over the chicken's bill and eyes and then souses him good. Will make chickens healthy although I wouldn't fancy the job of dipping them.

My opinion of Dickens is not so rosy as it was. Lorna Doone is a fine story but written in such a style that it takes about 700 pages to tell what might be told in 250 with ease. I have nothing to do but read and so I waded through it.

I stood up on one foot yesterday and this morning but was mighty glad to get back in bed. The doctor is going to bring me some crutches the last of the week and then it won't be long till I can hop around.

I hope your chickens will continue to live and that Mamma's strenuous dip will do you some good.

Keep on writing oftener and more regularly and please me more and more.

Following are excerpts from letters written by President Truman to Bess Truman while he was at the Potsdam Conference:

Berlin, July 18, '45
Dear Bess:
I've only had one letter from you since I left home. I look carefully through every pouch that comes—but so far not much luck. I had to dictate you one yesterday in order to get it off in the pouch. I told you about Churchill's call and Stalin's calling and staying to lunch.

The first session was yesterday in one of the Kaiser's palaces. I have a private suite in it that is really palatial. The conference room is about 40 × 60 and we sit at a large round table—fifteen of us. I have four and they each have four, then behind me are seven or eight more helpers. Stalin moved to make me the presiding officer as soon as we sat down and Churchill agreed.

It makes presiding over the Senate seem tame. The boys say I gave them an earful. I hope so. Adm. Leahy said he'd never seen an abler job and Byrnes and my fellows seemed to be walking on air. I was so scared I didn't know whether things were going according to Hoyle or not. Anyway a start has been made and I've gotten what I came for—Stalin goes to war August 15th with no strings on it. He wanted a Chinese settlement—and it is practically made—in a better form than I expected. Soong did better than I asked him. I'll say that we'll end the war a year sooner now, and think of the kids who won't be killed! That is the important thing.

Wish you and Margie were here. But it is a forlorn place and would only make you sad.

Please write and tell the young lady her dad can still read.

Berlin, July 20, '45
Dear Bess:
It was an experience to talk to you from my desk here in Berlin night before last. It sure made me homesick. This is a hell of a place—ruined, dirty, smelly, forlorn people, bedraggled, hangdog look about them. You never saw as completely ruined a city. But they did it. I am most comfortably fixed and the palace where we meet is one of two intact palaces left standing.

We had a tough meeting yesterday. I reared up on my hind legs and told 'em where to get off and they got off. I have to make it perfectly plain to them at least once a day that so far as this President is concerned Santa Claus is dead and that my first interest is U.S.A., then I want the Jap War won and I want 'em both in it. Then I want peace—world peace and will do what can be done by us to get it. But certainly am not going to set up another [word intelligible] here in Europe, pay reparations, feed the world and get nothing for it but a nose thumbing. They are beginning to awake to the fact that I mean business.

It was my turn to feed 'em at a formal dinner last night. Had Churchill on my right, Stalin on my left. We toasted the British King, the Soviet President, the U.S. Pres., the two honor guests, the foreign ministers, one at a time etc. etc. ad lib. Stalin felt so friendly that he toasted the pianist when he played a Tskowsky (you spell it) piece especially for him. The old man loves music. He told me he'd import the greatest Russian pianist for me tomorrow. Our boy was good. His name is List and he played Chopin, Von Weber, Schubert and all of them.

The Ambassadors and Jim Byrnes said the party was a success. Anyway they left in a happy frame of mind. I gave each of them a fine clock, specially made for them and a set of that good navy luggage. Well I'm hoping to get done in a week. I'm sick of the whole business—but we'll bring home the bacon.

Berlin, 7/22/45
Dear Bess:
The letter came last night while I was at Joe's dinner. Was I glad to get it! No your taste in hats is *not* screwy. If you ever cultivate the same sort of yen for crazy hats that the two you gave those Paris one's [sic] to, hope I'll refuse to go to church with you. I'd say that is a dire threat. Your hats suit me and theirs do not.

I can't get Chanel #5. Padre says there is none to be had—not even on the black market & his home station is in Paris. But I managed to get some other kind for $6.00 an ounce at the American P.X. They said it is equal to #5 and sells for $35.00 an ounce at home. So if you don't like it a profit can be made on it.

I seem to have Joe & Winnie talking to themselves and both are being exceedingly careful with me. Uncle Joe gave his dinner last night. There were at least 25 toasts—so much getting up and down that there was practically no time to eat or drink either—a very good thing. Being the super-duper guest I pulled out at 11 o'clock after a lovely piano and violin concert. The two men play the piano, the two women the violin. I never heard any better ones. Chopin, Tschiakowsky [sic], Listz [sic]; Hungarian Rhapsody, Russian, Ukrainian and Polish folk dances—it was real music. Since I'd had America's No. 1 pianist to play for Uncle Joe at my dinner he had to go me one better.

He talked to me confidentially at the dinner and I believe things will be all right in most instances. Some things we won't and can't agree on—but I have already what I came for. Hope I can break it off in a few days.

Lots & lots of love. Kiss the baby.

Berlin, July 25, '45
Dear Bess:
We have been going at it hammer and tongs in the last few days and it looks as if we may finish up Sunday. I hope so at any rate. I told them yesterday that I intend to head for Washington at the earliest possible moment and that when we came to an impasse I would leave.

We have accomplished a very great deal in spite of all the talk. There are some things we can't agree to. Russia and Poland have gobbled up a big hunk of Germany and want Britain and us to agree. I have flatly refused. We have unalterably opposed the recognition of police governments in Germany Axis countries. I told Stalin that until we had free access to those countries and our nationals had their property rights restored, so far as we were concerned there'd never be recognition. He seems to like it when I hit him with a hammer.

Berlin, July 29 '45
Dear Bess:
It made me terribly homesick when I talked to you yesterday morning. It seemed as if you were just around the corner, if 6,000 miles can be just around the corner. I spent the day after the call trying to think up reasons why I should bust up the Conference and go home.

Stalin and Molotov are coming to see me at 11 o'clock this morning and I am going to try to straighten it out.

I like Stalin. He is straightforward, knows what he wants and will compromise when he can't get it. His foreign minister isn't so forthright.

Pray for me and keep your fingers crossed too. If I come out of this one whole there'll be nothing to worry over until the end of the Jap War. Kiss Margie. Lots of love to you.

Berlin, July 31, 1945
Dear Bess:
We have been going great guns the last day or two and while the Conference was at a standstill because of Uncle Joe's indisposition, the able Mr. Byrnes, Molotov and Attlee and Bevin all worked and accomplished a great deal. I rather think Mr. Stalin is stalling because he is not so happy over the English elections. He doesn't know it but I have an ace in the hole and another one showing—so unless he has threes or two pair (and I know he has not) we are sitting all right.

I'll sure be glad to see you and the White House and be where I can at least go to bed without being watched.

Kiss my baby. Lots & lots of love,

Harry

EARL WARREN

1891–1974

By Alden Whitman

Presiding over the Supreme Court for 16 years—from 1953 to 1969—Earl Warren championed the Constitution as the vigorous protector of the individual rights and the equality of all Americans.

Reflecting the dynamics of social change in the nation (and profoundly affecting them) Mr. Warren's Court, amid much dispute, elaborated a doctrine of fairness in such areas as criminal justice, voting rights, legislative districting, employment, housing, transportation and education. In so doing, the Chief Justice of the United States contributed greatly to a reshaping of the country's social and political institutions.

"I would like the Court to be remembered as the people's court," he remarked on his retirement, expressing his strong sense of indignation over wrongs done to obscure citizens in the government's name. This was a quite different attitude from his earlier law-and-order views as a California prosecutor; but Mr. Warren had become more liberal with age and perspective. "On the Court I saw [things] in a different light," he once explained.

The impact of the Warren Court was cumulative, and Mr. Warren's stature grew perceptibly over 16 years. The parts that constituted the whole were embodied in a series of decisions that had the collective effect of reinforcing popular liberties. Among these were rulings that:

Outlawed school segregation.

Enunciated the one-man, one-vote doctrine.

Made most of the Bill of Rights binding on the states.

Curbed wiretapping.

Upheld the right to be secure against "unreasonable" searches and seizures.

Buttressed the right to counsel.

Underscored the right to a jury trial.

Barred racial discrimination in voting, in marriage laws, in the use of public parks, airports and bus terminals and in housing sales and rentals.

Extended the boundaries of free speech.

Ruled out compulsory religious exercises in public schools.

Restored freedom of foreign travel.

Knocked out the application of both the Smith and the McCarran Acts—both designed to curb "subversive" activities.

Held that federal prisoners could sue the government for injuries sustained in jail.

Said that wages could not be garnished without a hearing.

Liberalized residency requirements for welfare recipients.

Sustained the right to disseminate and receive birth control information.

George Tames/The New York Times

Although Mr. Warren did not write the opinions in all these cases, he bore the brunt of the criticism that many of them aroused. This criticism came from policemen and prosecutors; politicians; white supremacists; conservatives; and, indirectly, from the Nixon White House. The cry from the Nixon administration that the Warren Court "coddled criminals" and fostered "permissiveness" misled many people, according to Mr. Warren.

In an interview Mr. Warren bristled visibly as he recalled charges that he had been "soft" on crime. "I wasn't 'softer' on crime than I ever was," he declared. "All we did on the Court was to apply the Constitution, which says that any defendant is entitled to due process and to certain basic rights."

Some critics of Mr. Warren wanted him removed, and at one time there was a spate of billboard and bumper signs that said "Impeach Earl Warren."

Of the signs, Mr. Warren said, "It was kind of an honor to be accused by the John Birch Society [the right-wing group that opposed him strenuously]. It was a little rough on my wife, but it never bothered me."

Although impeachment was clearly a minority movement (there was never even a House resolution), there were conservatives, some lawyers among them, who agreed with President Eisenhower when he called the Warren appointment "the biggest damned-fool mistake I ever made."

He was alluding to the Court's desegregation decisions, which provoked lawless dissension among many southern whites, before they became reconciled to laws fostering racial equality.

Many observers believed that the desegregation rulings, starting with *Brown* v. *Board of Education of Topeka* in 1954, were the Warren Court's most important because they led to a readjustment of long-standing racial imbalances in the country. Mr. Warren himself, however, regarded the redistricting cases as the most significant. He expressed his feelings this way: "If everyone in this country has an opportunity to participate in his government on equal terms with everyone else, and can share in electing representatives who will be truly representative of the entire community and not some special interest, then most of the problems that we are confronted with would be solved through the political process rather than through the courts."

If the one-man, one-vote principle had been in effect much earlier in our history, according to Mr. Warren, "our Court would not have been compelled to decide big cases just on the bare bones of the Constitution, on the bare bones of the Civil War Amendments."

If the 15th Amendment, assuring the right to vote regardless of race, had been translated into legislation giving the black man the right to vote, "by this time racial problems should have been solved by the political process," he said, adding: "If *Baker* v. *Carr* [the leading redistricting case] had been in existence 50 years ago, we would have saved ourself acute racial troubles. But as it was, the Court just had to decide."

The essence of Mr. Warren's (and the Court's) position on one man, one vote—a doctrine that transformed the political map of the nation—was set forth in *Reynolds* v. *Sims.* At issue was whether factors other than equal representation of voters could be considered in electing state legislators. Assuming that members of one house would be elected from districts of equal populations, could members of the other house represent geographical areas of varying densities in order to assure a voice to sparsely settled localities and minority interests?

Because to do so would give some persons more influence than others, Mr. Warren replied with a firm no.

"Legislators represent people, not trees or acres," he wrote. "Legislators are elected by voters, not farms or cities or economic interests."

He saw no reason, he added, why "history alone, nor economic or other sorts of group interests" could justify giving "one person a greater voice in government than any other person."

"The overriding objective," he remarked, "must be substantial equality among the various districts, so that the vote of any citizen is approximately equal in weight to that of any other citizen in the state."

As a result of this and other rulings—and sometimes prodded by lower courts—states redrew their legislative districts, and many reviewed congressional boundaries.

Ranking just below redistricting in Mr. Warren's estimation came the school desegregation rulings that started with the Brown case in 1954. This historic decision was one of 45 in which the Warren Court overruled prior Supreme Court holdings and set in motion profound changes in the country's racial relations.

Mr. Warren's handling of the Brown case to achieve unanimity inside the Court illustrated the qualities that made him, in the minds of many lawyers, an outstanding chief justice. Describing what happened, he said: "Ordinarily, the justices, at our Friday conferences, stated their positions, offered debate and then voted. But in *Brown* we were all conscious of the case, so I held off a vote from conference to conference while we discussed it. If you'll remember, *Brown* was argued in the fall of 1953, and I did not call for a vote until the middle of the following February, when I was certain we would be unanimous. We took one vote, and that was it.

"I assigned myself to write the decision, for it seemed to me that something so important ought to issue over the name of the Chief Justice of the United States. In drafting it, I sought to use low-key, unemotional language and to keep it short enough so that it could be published in full in every newspaper in the country. I kept the text secret (it was locked in my safe) until I read from the bench."

Speaking for the Court, Mr. Warren brushed aside the "separate but equal" doctrine of *Plessy* v. *Ferguson* that had been in effect for 58 years. Basing himself on the 14th Amendment's declaration that no person should be denied the equal protection of the laws, he wrote of black schoolchildren: "To separate them from others because of their race generates a feeling of inferiority as to their status in the community that may affect their hearts and minds in a way unlikely to be undone."

This led him to declare: "We conclude that in the field of public education the doctrine of 'separate but equal' has no place. Separate educational facilities are inherently unequal."

The Brown ruling touched off a series of acts of defiance in the South and generated serious tensions in other parts of the country. These had largely subsided by 1973, although strong undercurrents of white supremacy were still evident in disputes over the busing of schoolchildren and other racial matters. The moral authority of the Court, which had been severely tested, survived.

From the Brown decision flowed a score or more of holdings by the Court and by inferior courts that collectively struck down racial inequalities in most areas of public life. As a result, parks, swimming pools, bus terminals and housing were desegregated. A hundred years after the Civil War blacks began to achieve full citizenship.

Ranking third in importance to Mr. Warren was a group of criminal cases that expanded protection for the rights of the accused. In the view of many lawyers (and of Mr. Warren) these decisions were often misunderstood as permitting the "coddling of criminals," whereas these lawyers contended that the rulings did little more than make specific the words of the Constitution.

"I think one of the most important cases we had was the Gideon case," Mr. Warren remarked after his retirement. "That was the case that interpreted the Constitution to say it meant just exactly what it said, that a man was entitled to counsel in a criminal proceeding."

Continuing his analysis, he said: "Before the case, in many places throughout the country a man was afforded counsel if he couldn't pay for it only if he was charged with a capital offense, and of course that means that hundreds of thousands of men every year were arrested and tried and perhaps had no legal advice at all. The Gideon case made it a living thing that every man charged with a serious offense was entitled to counsel at his trial.

"Then also I think the case of Escobedo was a very important case, because in that case it was determined that when a man was in jail and asked for his lawyer and his lawyer was available, he was entitled to have him there.

"Then we come to the Miranda case, and the question arises: If he's entitled to a lawyer when his lawyer is present, when is he first entitled to a lawyer?

"*Miranda* simply said that when the law puts upon a man by putting him in restraint and taking him away from his home and his family and his friends and starts to put him behind bars, that then he's in the toils of the law in a criminal case and is entitled to have representation of counsel."

Mr. Warren's explication, his reducing of legalisms to comprehensible language, was, according to his colleagues, typical of the way he presented cases in the Court's conferences and typical also of the language of his opinions. This scanting of law book language led some scholars to doubt his learning, but he contended that "expressing the concepts of the Constitution in common language was part of my idea of the Court as a people's court."

The chief justice was at pains to deny that the Court's criminal justice decisions had hampered legal law enforcement. "It is always easier to obtain a conviction if you are permitted to use excesses that are prohibited by the Constitution," he said. "I'm not softer on crime than I was as a California prosecutor, but a lot of things change in 50 years," he went on. "The third degree called for some restraints so that innocent people were not convicted, and all we did was to keep up with the times."

Actually, Mr. Warren's votes in the criminal cases illustrated the phenomenon of a man growing more liberal with age. He was, in succession, a crime-busting district attorney, a law-and-order state attorney general, a progressive governor and a libertarian chief justice. His views changed, he once said, because he saw things "in a different light." He once remarked, "No man can sit on the Court over 16 years and remain parochial, for he must look out over all the United States.

"I do not see how a man could be on the Court and not change his views substantially over a period of years," he said.

One example was his vote early in his term to uphold a gambling conviction that was based on the placing of wiretapping devices in a bookie's bedroom. Mr. Warren agonized, believing that prosecutors should not be allowed to use the fruits of such practices, but he could not bring himself to encroach on a state's law enforcement prerogatives. His attitude shifted markedly with later cases.

Starting with the Mapp case in 1961, the Court made the Bill of Rights' curb on unreasonable search and seizure fully binding on state and local policemen. After this ruling, the Court went on to apply most of the Bill of Rights to the states.

"This was a most significant development," Justice William J. Brennan, Jr., said. "Ultimately, all but three or four of the Bill's guarantees were laid on the states.

"Warren was not the chief architect of this development, in which [Justice Hugo L.] Black and [Justice William O.] Douglas were leaders, but the Chief helped to make a consensus among several of us."

By the early 1960s Mr. Warren was clearly demonstrating an ability to give the Court cohesion and direction. This leadership was buttressed by the appointment of several liberal justices who tended to see things his way. Thus the familiar "Warren majority" of the chief justice and Justices Arthur J. Goldberg, Black, Brennan and Douglas was bolstered by Thurgood Marshall and Abe Fortas.

A mild and genial man, Mr. Warren got along well with his colleagues on the bench, all men of strong personalities. According to both Justices Brennan and Douglas, the members of the Court often engaged in vigorous disagreements over issues, but their personal relations were always cordial. One justice recalled, however, at least one personal clash between Mr. Warren and Justice Felix Frankfurter, who had the habit of lobbying his colleagues.

Mr. Warren acknowledged that Mr. Frankfurter had sometimes been prickly and long-winded, but in retrospect he laughed about the justice's traits.

According to Mr. Brennan, "It was incredible how efficiently the Chief would conduct the Friday conferences, leading the discussion of every case on the agenda, with a knowledge of each case at his fingertips."

More than many chief justices, Mr. Warren removed himself from partisanship and political activity, but in one instance he felt obliged to take on, albeit reluctantly, an extrajudicial task. That was the chairmanship of the so-called Warren Commission, which investigated the assassination of President Kennedy in November 1963, and concluded that Lee Harvey Oswald, acting alone, had shot the president.

In taking the post, Mr. Warren yielded to the importunings of President Johnson. The 10 months of the commission's work were "the unhappiest time of my life," he said, adding that "to review the terrible happenings of that assassination every day [was] a traumatic experience.

"The only reason I undertook the commission was the gravity of the situation," he recalled. "There was no way of holding a trial, for Oswald was dead and the country needed to have the facts of the killing brought out. But it isn't a good thing for a justice to undertake such duties."

Although many disputed or disbelieved the commission's findings, Mr. Warren was unshaken, asserting, "No one has produced any facts that are contrary to the commission's conclusions."

Mr. Warren's path to the Court began in Los Angeles, where he was born March 19, 1891, the son of Methias H. (Matt) Warren and Crystal Hernlund Warren. His mother was a native of Sweden and his father was born in Norway. The elder Warren was a car repairman and inspector for the Southern Pacific Railroad.

The family moved to Bakersfield, where, after a number of years, Matt Warren grew more and more eccentric and stopped living with his family. He was bludgeoned to death in 1938, and the case was never solved.

His son attended public schools in Bakersfield, played the cornet in bands and orchestras (he joined the musicians' union in the process) and worked at odd jobs—railroad call boy, freight hustler, truck driver—to meet expenses. He went to the University of California, getting a Bachelor of Letters degree in 1912 and a doctorate in jurisprudence in 1914.

He practiced law for several years, served as an infantry first lieutenant in World War I and began his public career as deputy city attorney for Oakland, Calif. Then he became a deputy district attorney for Alameda County, which embraces the cities of Oakland, Alameda and Berkeley in the San Francisco Bay area. His career in both posts was unspectacular, but in the 13 years he served as the county's district attorney, from 1925 to 1938, he emerged as a racket-busting prosecutor.

Even so, Mr. Warren was not thought of as brilliant, merely thorough. None of the convictions he obtained, for example, was upset on appeal. Although he was proud of his legal footwork, he said later that he had got no personal satisfaction from the convictions.

"Although I fought vigorously in the cases I prosecuted," he remarked, "I invariably felt nauseated when the jury brought in a verdict of guilty."

In his years as a district attorney, Mr. Warren made many friends in the state. Standing a little over 6 feet and weighing 215 pounds, he had a hearty handshake and an easy manner.

"Hello, there," he would say. "How ARE you? Glad to SEE you!"

He joined the ritual organizations, including the whites-only Order of Elks. In those days, he said later, he accepted without thought the prevailing racial attitudes.

Mr. Warren had been his party's state chairman from 1934 to 1936, and was Republican national committeeman when he ran for California attorney general in 1938 at the age of 47. He cross-filed and won three nominations—his party's, the Democratic and the Progressive. He won election in an otherwise Democratic year.

In four years as attorney general, he kept in the public eye with an occasional raid on gambling dens, but most of his work was administrative. Nonetheless, he appeared frequently around the state, usually with his wife, the former Mrs. Nina Palmquist Meyers, a widow, whom he had married in 1925. With her son, James, whom Mr. Warren adopted, and the couple's five children—Virginia, Earl Jr., Dorothy, Nina Elizabeth and Robert—the family was attractive, and Mr. Warren was not averse to showing it off. "How can you beat a man with a family like that?" asked one California politician.

In 1942 Mr. Warren ran for governor and won by defeating the favored Democratic nominee, Governor Culbert L. Olson. He proved an amiable and popular governor but not a governmental leader of great distinction or a political leader of great power. Nonetheless, when he sought reelection in 1946 he cross-filed in the primaries and won both the Republican and Democratic designations. The election was a formality.

In 1950 he was again his party's choice, but this time he faced James Roosevelt, the son of the late President Franklin D. Roosevelt. The Roosevelt name, however, carried no magic and Mr. Warren won by a million votes.

In between, in 1948, he was selected for geopolitical reasons to run for the vice presidency with Gov. Thomas E. Dewey of New York. They lost to Harry S Truman and Alben W. Barkley after having convinced many journalists and pundits that they would surely triumph. Again in 1952 Mr. Warren made a national bid as a contender for his party's presidential nomination. He actually had little hope of getting it over the popular Dwight D. Eisenhower, but in the general's contest with Sen. Robert A. Taft of Ohio he sided with General Eisenhower at a crucial moment in the convention, thus accumulating a political due bill.

Up to this point, Mr. Warren's career reflected some of the same qualities he demonstrated later on the Court—a capacity for hard work, a disarming affability and an ideological progression from right to left.

As a young prosecutor, he made himself indispensable by frequently working until midnight and by mastering his and other assistants' cases so that as they departed for private practice, it became automatic for the district attorney to turn more responsibility over to him.

When he became a top official himself, he was a taskmaster who assumed that his subordinates would toil long hours, and who rarely expressed gratitude for it.

With all of his ambition, there was an openness about Mr. Warren that permitted him to move smoothly toward his own goals, without making those whom he might be passing—or using—feel threatened.

He was a big, fair-haired man, called Pinky in his youth, who loved spectator sports and outdoor life, and whose suits were always double-breasted blue serge. He could call hundreds of people by name, but he had few close friends, preferring to spend free time with his family.

In his early years, Mr. Warren was instinctively attracted to the kind of conservative thinking that made him a favorite of California's regular Republicans.

One February morning in 1935, he stomped grumpily into his office, where a young assistant was working at a desk with open law books spread around him. Mr. Warren began to slam the books shut, muttering, "Throw them away—forget them. They're no good now, contracts don't mean anything anymore." He had just learned of the Supreme Court's decision upholding the law taking the United States off the gold standard.

When he later ran for attorney general, he favored a bill to make schoolchildren salute the flag. He also proclaimed that the Communist party "should not be entitled to legal recognition in the political life of America," and he opposed a pardon for Tom Mooney, the trade union radical.

Early in his term as governor he supported the wartime federal order moving all persons of Japanese ancestry from the West Coast into concentration camps inland. In 1943 he opposed the return of the internees. In a governors' conference speech, he warned that "if the Japs are released, no one will be able to tell a saboteur from any other Jap."

From there he moved on to a proposal that, when he made it in 1945, was so far to the left that it was denounced as socialistic. It was compulsory health insurance for all citizens of California, to be financed by a 3 percent payroll tax.

In this, he proved to be too far ahead of his time. The American Medical Association mounted an attack against his proposal, and it was rejected by the legislature.

Mr. Warren's opportunity for a Court seat came in 1953 when Chief Justice Fred M. Vinson, a lackluster jurist, died, and President Eisenhower nominated the Californian. There were complaints at the time that it was a political deal, but it later appeared that it was not quite that pat.

General Eisenhower said in his memoirs that he had mentioned the possibility of a Supreme Court seat to Mr. Warren, but that he had not considered that the first vacancy might be the chief justice's seat.

When it occurred, General Eisenhower was said to have offered it first to John Foster Dulles, who preferred to remain secretary of state. Next Mr. Dewey turned it down, as he wished to retire.

General Eisenhower felt that judicial experience was needed, and he considered elevating one of the associate justices. But dissension within the Court and the dearth of distinguished Republicans there made that impracticable. Nevertheless, General Eisenhower was reported to have suggested that Mr. Warren wait until an associate justice's seat opened up.

Mr. Warren reportedly replied that for him it would be chief justice or nothing. On Sept. 30, 1953, the administration let it be known that the president would give Mr. Warren a recess appointment, making him the 14th chief justice of the United States. He was sworn in on Oct. 5.

There was some criticism as Mr. Warren began to preside over the Court though the nomination did not reach Congress until early the next year. At the Senate hearings, he declined an invitation to appear, even though more than 200 objections to his nomination had been filed.

Several spokesmen for right-wing groups testified against him. Charges were made that he had allowed crime and corruption to flourish in California, that he "had a 100 percent record of following the Marxist line," and that he had no experience for the job. He was nonetheless confirmed by a voice vote on March 1, 1954.

Later, many Warren admirers and critics termed the nomination the most momentous act of the Eisenhower presidency. To President Eisenhower, who evidently took Mr. Warren at face value as a rather bland, unexceptional individual, his performance was surprising, and, judging by the "damned-fool mistake" comment, apparently it was not a pleasant surprise.

As two figures in the traditionally fratricidal Republican party, Mr. Warren and Richard M. Nixon never enjoyed warm relations. The events of the 1952 convention did most to cool them off. Senator Nixon, a delegate pledged to vote for Mr. Warren, was never quite able to conceal his own national ambitions, or his preference for General Eisenhower. After the general won the nomination and picked Mr. Nixon as his running mate, hostility between Mr. Warren and Mr. Nixon was widely rumored.

But the destinies of the two men were not so easily severed. In 1968, when Mr. Nixon was elected president, one of his most effective campaign issues was to accuse the Warren Court of going "too far in weakening the peace forces as against the criminal forces in this country."

After his election, in mutual gestures of reconciliation, Mr. Warren administered the presidential oath to Mr. Nixon, and the president subsequently delivered a speech in the Supreme Court on the day Mr. Warren retired. Mr. Nixon praised Mr. Warren's example of dignity, fairness and integrity in bringing "continuity and change" to the law.

In his earlier years several incidents demonstrated that behind Mr. Warren's benign exterior was a man who was deeply sensitive to personal slights or hints of disloyalty. As late as 1957 he was still sufficiently piqued at Mr. Nixon to inform the American Bar Association that he would refuse an invitation to attend its convention if Vice President Nixon were also invited. The A.B.A. chose not to invite Mr. Nixon.

Internal doubts or gropings for consistency were rarely discernible in Mr. Warren's makeup. He was a man of intense emotions, which sometimes led him to judicial positions that clashed with other doctrines that he espoused.

In his opinions on Communism and political speech and association, he made it clear that the values of free speech overwhelmingly outweighed the interest in "social order" asserted by the government.

But he was the kind of old-fashioned moralist who once told a man he had just met on an airplane that if a smut peddler were to sell pornography to one of his daughters, he would throttle him with his bare hands.

So in the area of obscenity, the chief justice stood out from the trend of decisions that during his tenure turned the United States from one of the most Puritan to one of the most permissive nations in writing about sex. It was the only issue upon which he resisted a long-term judicial movement toward greater individual liberty.

Thus when the Court majority held in 1964 that erotic material could not be suppressed by local officials unless it was objectionable under a national standard, the chief justice dissented. He felt that each locality should be free to ban material that violated the values of that community.

At the same time he was leading the Court in laying down rigid police procedures that would have to be obeyed in every community.

In a stand similar to his position on obscenity, Mr. Warren dissented alone when the Supreme Court ruled in 1968 that gamblers could invoke the Fifth Amendment's privilege against self-incrimination to avoid buying a federal tax stamp. The Court was applying the principle of a 1965 decision that allowed Communist party members to refuse to register.

Mr. Warren had joined the 1965 ruling, but he saw a difference in 1968, in that gambling and not political expression was at stake. The Fifth Amendment makes no distinction in the nature of the charge that allows a suspect to refuse to answer, but Mr. Warren's aversion to gambling permitted him to find such a distinction.

The Court's "antipolice" image grew out of decisions limiting the kind of police activities that fell hardest upon the nonwhite, poor and ignorant. Thus the Warren majority cracked down on techniques of interrogation, identification, dragnet arrest and searching that were most frequently abused in the slums.

But police techniques most commonly used against organized crime survived the Warren era virtually unscathed. The majority found that the Constitution would permit the use of informers, police spies, surveillance and court-approved wiretapping.

One notable exception to this pattern came in 1968, when a political backlash was building up against the Court's restrictions on the police, and even some liberals were beginning to wonder if the Court had not been too rigid in ruling out all evidence obtained in violation of the Supreme Court's procedural rules.

In *Terry* v. *Ohio,* a ruling that quickly came to be known as the "stop and frisk" decision, Mr. Warren wrote an 8-to-1 opinion that gave the police the authority to search dangerous-looking persons "on suspicion" for weapons. It was clear that this power might be used in a discriminatory manner against the poor and powerless, but the Court was faced with the fear that without it the police in urban slums faced great dangers from an armed population.

In an opinion that reflected the painful tensions between the rising crime problem and the Court's concern for minorities, Mr. Warren wrote: "The wholesale harassment by certain elements of the police community, of which minority groups, particularly Negroes, frequently complain, will not be stopped by the exclusion of any evidence from any criminal trial.

"Yet a rigid and unthinking application of the exclusionary rule, in futile protest against practices which it can never be used effectively to control, may exact a high toll in human injury and frustration of efforts to prevent crime."

He then declared, with obvious reluctance, that weapons seized by "frisking" could be used in evidence—a decision that civil libertarians lamented as a serious breach in the Fourth Amendment's shield against unreasonable searches and seizures.

It was Mr. Warren's tendency to interpret the Constitution in terms of the result he found desirable that drew the most criticism. The result, critics said, was to transform the Supreme Court into a perpetual constitutional convention, updating the Constitution to square with the liberal majority's concept of what the law ought to be.

The late Justice John M. Harlan, dissenting in the 1964 *Reynolds* v. *Sims* case, put it as follows: "These decisions give support to a current mistaken view of the Constitution and the constitutional function of this Court. This view, in a nutshell, is that every major social ill in this country can find its cure in some constitutional 'principle,' and that this Court should 'take the lead' in promoting reform when other branches of government fail to act. The Constitution is not a panacea for every blot upon the public welfare, nor should this Court, ordained as a judicial body, be thought of as a general haven for reform movements."

Philip B. Kurland, of the University of Chicago Law School, complained that the Court leaped to its conclusions, without adequately explaining or justifying them.

"The judicial process, as demonstrated by the Warren Court, is coming closer and closer to the legislative process," he wrote. He added the charge that "the Court has not been honest in the means that it has used to support its judgments."

Mr. Warren's admirers answered that a half century had passed since Charles Evans Hughes had conceded that the Constitution is what the judges say it is, and that the Supreme Court must, because it is supreme, "make" law. At a time of great social upheaval, sensitive issues were being placed before the Court, and it was argued that the justices' duty was to decide those issues.

For Mr. Warren, the outcome almost always reflected idealism, fairness and equality—and the decisions made him a revered figure to many Americans and people around the world.

One of the secrets of his success had always been that he was more effective at whatever he did than a superficial look made him appear to be. This was equally true of his performance as a justice.

His opinions did not mark him as a great jurist, as Anthony Lewis, a critic and admirer, once observed: "A Warren opinion, characteristically, is a world made new—a bland, square presentation of the particular problem in that case almost as if it were unencumbered by precedents or conflicting theories, as it inevitably must be. Often, the framework of the argument was ethical rather than legal, in the sense that one expects the law to be analytical. Chief Justice Warren's opinions are difficult to analyze because they are likely to be unanalytical."

But Mr. Warren's years as a trial lawyer had made him aware of the extent to which the facts of a case reveal its real meaning. In his relentless, polite way he often drew out, during Court arguments, facts that laid bare cases that had been obscured by murky constitutional principles.

Mr. Warren developed the outside-the-record

disclosure to a high art. In his questioning of counsel, he often brought out facts crucial to a decision he wanted the Court to reach. He would cheerfully permit the facts to be added to the record in the form of a letter or statement, and the subsequent decision frequently leaned heavily upon the new information.

As chief justice, Mr. Warren was a far more insular figure than his successor, Warren E. Burger. He severed his connections with the organized bar, refused to accept awards and made few speeches. His view was that the Supreme Court spoke solely through its opinions, and he kept himself—and his law clerks and subordinates—at arm's length from the press.

In June 1968, Mr. Warren was stunned by the assassination of Robert F. Kennedy. He later told an old friend of reading with astonishment that a few hours before the assassination, people stood two and three deep along the highway into Los Angeles from the airport. He had seen many politicians travel that route, and he knew that no such assemblage had ever greeted a candidate before. He took it as a sign that the nation was reaching out for younger leaders and new ideas.

On June 13, he wrote President Johnson and tendered his resignation "at your pleasure." A few days later, in his first public news conference as chief justice, he explained that "at the age of 77, this was a good time to retire." He added, "I do believe we are coming into a new era as far as American life is concerned—probably so far as the entire world is concerned."

Mr. Johnson accepted the resignation, effective when Mr. Warren's successor would be confirmed. Then he nominated Mr. Fortas, a justice closely associated with the doctrines of the Warren Court.

Mr. Warren insisted later that this arrangement was necessary because "there always ought to be a chief justice of the United States," but to some others it appeared that Mr. Warren, in collusion with Mr. Johnson, was offering the Court's critics a Hobson's choice—take Abe Fortas as chief justice or continue to suffer Earl Warren.

In an attack that focused upon the rulings of the Warren Court as well as upon Mr. Fortas, a coalition of Republicans and conservative Democrats blocked Senate action on the nomination, and it was withdrawn.

Mr. Warren then announced that he would retire at the end of the Court's term in June 1969.

A final sour note was the disclosure in May that Mr. Fortas had accepted and later returned a $20,000 fee from a foundation created by the financier Louis E. Wolfson. Mr. Warren was drawn into the matter when Attorney General John N. Mitchell came secretly to the Court and delivered documents bearing on the case.

It was later known that Mr. Mitchell gave Mr. Warren documents showing that Justice Fortas had been promised $20,000 a year for his life and the life of his wife, but it was never disclosed what Mr. Mitchell said to the chief justice, or what he and his colleagues on the Court did.

Mr. Fortas resigned a few days later, becoming the first member of the Supreme Court to quit under fire. This gave President Nixon another early vacancy to fill in his campaign to change the direction of the Court.

But if the tide of events was running against the Warren Court at the end of his tenure, Mr. Warren's actions did not reveal it. In the week before he stepped down, he wrote an opinion that went beyond precedent for asserting judicial supremacy, as he ruled for the Court that the House of Representatives had illegally excluded the maverick black congressman, Adam Clayton Powell, Jr.

His decision overturned a lower court holding, written by Mr. Burger, that the courts should stay out of such congressional squabbles.

On Mr. Warren's last day on the bench, June 23, the Court handed down three decisions, with the chief justice in the majority in each. All three were criminal cases, and in each the Court broke new legal ground in enlarging the rights of the accused.

Mr. Warren had often mentioned his desire to return to California, but he proved to be as susceptible to Potomac fever as others, and he stayed on in Washington after his retirement. He moved into a smaller office in the Supreme Court building, and kept his apartment at the Sheraton Park.

He spent much time fishing, hunting and attending football and baseball games. He was greatly in demand on the banquet circuit, where he accepted awards. He demonstrated his political touch by telling several organizations that their award was the first he had accepted since ascending the bench.

Supreme Court justices who retire and publish usually produce weighty legal articles, analyzing where the Supreme Court has gone or is going, but Mr. Warren wrote a book appropriate for a high school civics text.

It declared fidelity to the Bill of Rights to be the highest duty of the citizen, and concluded with a homily that expressed the sweep of his hopes for American society: "Where there is injustice, we should correct it; where there is poverty, we should eliminate it; where there is corruption, we should stamp it out; where there is violence, we should punish it; where there is neglect, we should provide care; where there is war, we should restore peace; and wherever corrections are achieved we should add them permanently to our storehouse of treasure."

A TALK WITH EARL WARREN ON CRIME, THE COURT, THE COUNTRY [1969]

ANTHONY LEWIS

Crime

Mr. Chief Justice, what do you think are the reasons for the amount of crime that so deeply disturbs the United States today? Where do we look for solutions—to the courts, to the police, to general social reform?

WARREN: Well, of course there is no simple answer to that, but I believe that in the main it demonstrates that we have a disrupted society.

One thing that I think is really basic to our whole situation is that the people who are now, let's say, 30 years of age in the United States have never known anything but war conditions in our country and in the world. From the time they could learn to talk they have learned that we are in the war business, and young people are taught to kill and to recognize violence as a part of life.

Many hundreds of thousands, even millions of our young people have been thrust into actual warfare, have seen violence and all of the degradation that it brings about, and it has no horrors to them as it would to someone who had never been influenced by that kind of life. I think that that's had a great effect on our people.

Then also we have people in our big cities who are living in ghettos, without any employment of any kind. They are ignorant, they have had no schooling, they have no skills with which to compete in the economic market, they are easy prey to all kinds of bad influences in the community.

I think one of the things that must be done in order to eliminate much of that is to improve the condition of our cities. We must get rid of the ghettos, we must see that every youngster who comes into being in our country is afforded a decent education and is given some skill through which he can compete in the market.

Then, I think, he must not only have that skill but he must have the opportunity to get a job, he must be able to join a union. We must eliminate the discrimination that is so prevalent in many places if we are to have a society that in general will accommodate itself to the law.

You are saying in effect that the causes of crime are deep.

WARREN: Very deep, indeed.

Why do you think it is that the public and a

number of politicians seem to blame crime rather on judges?

WARREN: Someone always has to be a scapegoat when there is crime, and the only people who cannot talk back, who cannot argue their case, are the courts. The police can take their case to the public. The prosecutors can take their case to the public. The only people who cannot talk back but must do their job day by day are the courts. I don't mean by that, that the courts are faultless, but I mean that they are defenseless when it comes to entering into a debate as to who is the cause for crime.

What do you say to the complaint widely heard from the police, and even I think it is fair to say from the present attorney general of the United States, that the Miranda *rule—whatever its base—just makes it too difficult to deal with criminals?*

WARREN: That same argument could of course be applied to almost any rule that keeps the law enforcement agencies of the state from excesses. It is always easier to obtain a conviction if you are permitted to use excesses that are prohibited by the Constitution, and thereby avoid the necessity of going out and convicting a man on independent evidence.

It would be easy to let anyone come and crash into your home at any time and search it and see if you possibly were committing any crime, but the Constitution says that you can't do that. Of course, that makes it more difficult to convict people; but there are certain things that an ordered society must honor in the rights of individuals—and things that cannot be countenanced in a decent society.

There is a more general concern about American criminal law, I think expressed by your successor, namely that our criminal law system has become too complicated, that the trial and appeal of cases goes on for years. There is a contrast, for example, with the situation in Britain, where ordinarily the whole conduct of the criminal law is short and swift and therefore has more impact on the potential criminal. What do you think about that?

WARREN: That's not new doctrine of any kind. That's been bruited around since long before I was a district attorney 40-odd years ago. It is true in a sense that our whole society is more complex, our whole governmental system is complex. Here in England you have a small compact nation that in size is only half the size of my state of California, and as a consequence they can have a unitary system that will operate efficiently and smoothly and go right through to a quick conclusion.

They are not hampered by a federal system such as we have, where for instance they can go through the state courts and then after that they have a right to come to the federal system or to the Supreme Court on constitutional and federal questions.

Now I wouldn't defend everything that exists in our federal judicial system. We have great ills, and I think that many of them can be improved if not eliminated. I want to refer first to the great backlogs that we have in our courts today, whether it's in state courts or in federal courts. I found recently that in Brooklyn, in the eastern district of New York, in the federal court the average length of time between indictment and trial in a criminal case was 22 and 2/10ths months. Now you add to that the time between arrest and indictment and you'll find that you have a solid two years of delay there before a man has a jury trial. Now, if a man is innocent that is a practical destruction of his life, and if he is guilty and is out on bail during that period committing other crimes it's a great injustice to society.

Those things must be changed, they can be changed, and I think so far as the courts' responsibility is concerned it is largely one of administration. The answer to it isn't just putting on more new judges. When you have a bad system, even though new judges come in with great vigor and earnestness and a desire to make the system work properly, they find out that they cannot do what they had hoped to do, and they gradually fall into the same pattern as the others.

You wouldn't want to see us abandon our fed-

eral system—the whole complicated relationship between the states and the federal government that you spoke of?

WARREN: No, in no sense. It is just one of those situations that does make our system more complicated and more time-consuming, but it does afford us certain protections against the centralization of power that, it seems to me, are just basic to our way of life.

That may strike some as ironic, since you and your Court were always accused of destroying states' rights and state powers.

WARREN: I could argue that, but I don't think there is any necessity. If anybody could show me anything that we have done in the time that I have been on the Court other than to insist that a man is entitled to counsel at all times after he has been put upon by the government in a criminal case, and entitled to fair treatment, to due process in the trial of his case, I would concede that we had perhaps done something wrong. I can't think of any such thing.

Remembering your years as a district attorney and state attorney general, what do you think has changed about the problem of crime? Why does it seem to be growing so much worse?

WARREN: People are prone to forget that we have had enormous crime problems in other eras. I can refer particularly to the era in which I was a district attorney, from 1925 until 1938. If you will remember, most of those years were years of the Prohibition era, and in it we had the bootlegging, the hijacking, the rum-running and all of the crimes that surrounded that liquor business, and particularly the gang murders that that involved.

To my mind, that was about as badly criminalized an era as we have had, and the public was contributing to it through their refusal to obey the Prohibition laws. We have situations that are comparable to that at the present time, but it is a different kind of crime that is dominating the situation. Now the things that people are terribly concerned about are the robberies and the burglaries and the muggings and the rapes and all these other individual crimes that largely emanate from the slums in our cities. The public is very much aroused about these, but even at the present time it is not aroused about organized crime. Where do we find the people crusading against organized crime, the crime in which there is a big business, the narcotics business for instance?

Are you saying that the public on the whole disregards the big crime, the organizations that rake in millions from narcotics and gambling particularly?

WARREN: I am. And furthermore I will say that that kind of crime cannot exist and flourish in any community unless there is corruption in some form, in some segment of law enforcement. It might be the police, it might be the prosecutor, it might even be contributed to by the courts.

How do you feel about the use of wiretapping by law enforcement officials on the ground that it is necessary to fight criminals at their own level?

WARREN: I think that any invasion of the privacy of the home or of business that is not within the limitations of the Constitution is destructive of our security in this nation. While of course there have to be searches and seizures under given circumstances, they must under the Constitution be reasonable and the courts must determine what is reasonable. The indiscriminate use of wiretapping is an outrageous violation of the privacy of individuals and can lead to the grossest kind of abuse.

The prosecutor under our system is not paid to convict people. He's there to protect the rights of people in our community and to see that when there is a violation of the law, it is vindicated by trial and prosecution under fair judicial standards.

The Court

Mr. Chief Justice, you have said that the reapportionment cases were the most important decided by the Court during your 16 years. It was predicted by some people that those decisions would not be accepted by the country and would lead the Court into great difficulties—the political thicket. Why do you think that did not in fact happen?

WARREN: I think it did not happen largely because almost everyone recognizes that ours is a representative form of government, and if it is to be representative it must have fair representation, and by fair representation we mean that everyone should have an equal voice. There had been such a departure from that standard for so many years, with no remedy of any kind available, that the nation was ready for the decision.

While those who were in office did not acquiesce, there was general recognition of the principle that your vote should be as good as mine and mine as good as anybody else's. It is consistent with our institutions and, I think, with the intention of the Founding Fathers, and I also believe that it will be conducive to better government. I say that because I believe in government by the people and I believe in the wisdom of the people when they are thoroughly informed and everyone participates.

As governor of California, you defended that state's apportionment system, which gave grossly unequal representation to people in different parts of the state. Why did you take a different view as chief justice?

WARREN: Because on the Court I saw it in a different light. Politics has been said to be the art of the possible, and in it we accomplish what we can accomplish by compromise and by getting agreement with people. We look at a problem from that standpoint, not perhaps from a standpoint of exact principle, because politics is not an exact science.

But when we come to the Court and we face a similar problem where the question of constitutionality is raised, we then test it by constitutional principles; if it violates the constitutional principles, we no longer can compromise, we no longer can change to bring people into agreement, we have to decide the matter according to the principle as we see it.

Now in California, when I was governor, we did have a malapportioned legislature. Los Angeles County with a million people had one state senator, and so did a mountain district with somewhere between 50,000 and 100,000 people.

That was not equal representation by any manner of means, but our system was getting along and the people were having an opportunity to vote upon it. There was no question of constitutionality raised. At that time I didn't reflect seriously on the constitutionality of it, and I went along with the thought that we were doing pretty well and we would leave well enough alone.

Now, when I got to the Court, I found what was happening in some of these other states—Tennessee, for instance, where the matter first arose under *Baker* v. *Carr,* and other states where they had a constitutional provision that the representation must be equal. They had had terribly malapportioned legislatures for over 60 years, and those who were in office and had sole control of whether there should be a reapportionment absolutely refused to permit any change of any kind because it would affect their possibilities for election. When we ran across that and applied the constitutional provision, we found that it was not fair representation and we so held.

Also I think we'll find that when men go on the Supreme Court that the empirical views that they've had in certain fields do change. I don't see how a man could be on the Court and not change his views substantially over a period of years.

I think you said to me that he comes to realize that he has the last word.

WARREN: That's right. It is purely a matter of principle with him and not a question of accommodation.

Can you remember any specific area in which you felt your own views changing on the Court aside from reapportionment? I remember one case, Irvine *v.* California, *that was decided soon after you came on the bench and that involved eavesdropping in a gambler's home in California. The conviction was upheld despite the use of this eavesdropping evidence, and you were with the majority. I would be fairly certain myself that in more recent years you would not have voted to sustain that conviction. Can you tell us anything about that?*

WARREN: Yes, I was shocked by the Irvine case. I thought it was a terrible abuse of power on the part of the police, a shocking invasion of privacy. If you will remember, I joined Justice Jackson in an opinion which suggested, because of that violation of privacy, that the federal government should investigate it as a violation of civil rights.

But just a few years before that we had had the case—not we, I wasn't on the Court at that time—the Court had had the case of *Wolf* v. *Colorado* in which it had held that an illegal search was a violation of the Constitution but that it was within the power of the states to remedy this situation. The federal government, the Court, withheld its hand in that field. That having been a very recent case and a majority of the Court having agreed not to overrule it at that particular moment, and I being a new justice on the Court still groping around in the field of due process, I went along with that opinion, shocked as I was at the conduct of the police.

That leads me to ask you something else. On reflection now, after the 16 years, how free should a Supreme Court justice be to overrule a prior decision in a situation like that, where he is shocked? What are the pressures on you to stick with the past decision?

WARREN: I don't believe that there is any simple answer that I could give to it. I would say that I have been in dissent on a few constitutional cases in my career on the Court, and where I have been and the majority has held one way, normally I have gone along with it until and unless some flagrant thing developed to reaffirm my view that I was right in the first instance. If there was no new element in it, I would be inclined to go along and I've done that in a number of cases and I think that is the right approach.

But at the same time we have always had the view that in constitutional cases *stare decisis* is not absolute, that constitutional questions are always open for reexamination, and I believe that too. It's a combination of those two things that I've just talked about that I would say one must judge it by.

I suppose it is inevitably the case that the arrival of a new justice or justices on the Court may reopen a question because men have different views.

WARREN: Oh yes, oh yes, without doubt. In fact, even men of the same Court are entitled to change their minds when they are confronted by new conditions and have done so.

Do you think the constitutional decisions of the Warren Court in the three great areas of reapportionment, race and the criminal law—the sweep of those decisions, their general tendency—will last?

WARREN: In all three of those areas, of course, I believe that our decisions are consistent with the principles of the Constitution and that they were but implementations of those principles to be in accordance with the conditions of American life that confront us. I would, of course, believe that the decisions should stand, but I would not predict.

Different men see things in different ways, and it might be that others will see them differently. That is for those who are on the Court and have the keeping of the Court in their hands to determine in accordance with the Constitution. But I believe the decisions are wholesome, in the best interests of society according to constitutional principles, and in keeping with the life of our nation. Naturally I would hope that they would remain.

How much pressure does a Supreme Court justice feel from the outside world? You came in as governor of California, appointed by President Eisenhower, with certain relationships with the Republican party, although you were, of course, a very independent politician. Does all that drop off when you go on the Court? Do you still feel that you need the approval of people you have related to?

WARREN: To be on the Supreme Court is an entirely different kind of life, an entirely different responsibility. I think my change from being governor of California to Chief Justice of the United States was almost a traumatic thing for me; but change you must if you are to do your duty on the Supreme Court.

In the first place I felt it necessary to divorce myself from every political activity of every kind and to try to bring myself to act in as nonpartisan a way as it is possible for a human being to do. I tried also to eliminate every influence from personal contacts that could be brought to bear upon me. As you know I secluded myself from the press.

I also adopted the practice of not reading my fan mail, whether it was good or bad, because I had the idea that if you were going to believe the good things that were said about you, you'd probably have to put some thought to the accuracy of those who were against you also.

In other words, I led pretty much of a monastic life on the Court, contrary to what I had been before—because I had visited with and exchanged views with people in every part of my state and I loved to discuss matters with newspaper people.

There is no pressure on the Court from individuals, because I think practically every American realizes that it would be improper for him to try to influence a member of the Supreme Court by any contact with him on a given case, and so the only pressure comes from the pressure of these problems that you are daily confronted with.

What about your relationships with your colleagues? It must be difficult at times living in that secluded way with just eight other people.

WARREN: There is no more intimate association, other than that of man and wife, I should say, than the association that we have on the Supreme Court of the United States. It can be a very agreeable and stimulating association, or it could be a bedlam and almost hell for a person.

But I want to say that during my term on the Court our relationships have been as fine as any that I could conceive of with eight other men.

It's true that we write differently and sometimes critically and sometimes with a little feeling, but that has not been carried over to our personal relationship. I can say, after 16 years and my association with—how many?—about 16 different justices, that I have had nothing but admiration and affection for each one of them. I believe they were trying as hard as I was to be independent and to vote their convictions and their willingness to live with their convictions, and you can't ask more of people.

As you look back at the 16 years, is there one day that stands out in your memory as a particularly happy day?

WARREN: I do not think at the moment of any day that was particularly joyful. Almost every day on the Court is a great day of responsibility. It doesn't lend itself to levity, and even when some very important cases are decided in conformity with one's views one must have a great feeling of responsibility and wonderment as to what the consequences may be. There is no exuberance, but there may be real satisfaction.

I didn't mean to suggest only exuberance; I think satisfaction is better. I remember the day that you delivered the opinions in Reynolds *v.* Sims, *for example, laying down the rule of one man, one vote, and I had very much a feeling of history that particular day. I wonder whether you felt it.*

WARREN: Yes, I did. I think *Baker* v. *Carr* was the most important case that we decided in my time, because that gave to the courts the power to determine whether or not we were to have fair representation in our governmental system, and *Reynolds* v. *Sims* was merely the application of that principle.

It was a case in which I derived real satisfaction, although I was thoroughly cognizant of the controversy that it was going to start. As a matter of fact, people in California have said to me since, "Why on earth did you have to take that case of *Reynolds* v. *Sims?*" While I didn't respond to them in this manner, my real reason for it was because I had viewed the matter in a different way when I was governor, and when I had to face it on the Court, I just thought that as long as I had to face it I would face it directly myself.

You mean you assigned the opinion to yourself.

WARREN: Yes.

How important do you think that function is—the function of assigning opinions? Does it give the chief justice a very different weight on the Court from his colleagues?

WARREN: No—I don't think it gives him any additional weight. But I do believe that if it wasn't done with regard to fairness, it could well lead to great disruption in the Court.

During all the years I was there I never had any of the justices urge me to give them opinions to write, nor did I ever have anyone object to any opinion that I assigned to him or to anybody else. I did try very hard to see that we had an equal work load, that we weren't all writing in one field where one person would be considered the expert. Everybody, regardless of length of time they were on the Court, had a fair opportunity to write important cases.

There wasn't any of the backbiting that one senses in Mason's biography of Chief Justice Stone?

WARREN: Never one, never one shred of that—never have I had one indication of that in all the time I have been on the Court.

There were a lot of peppery exchanges between you and Justice Frankfurter over the decision of cases. Did that affect your relationship at all?

WARREN: No, no, no. I've been in dissent with Justice Black, too, recently where Black has been very, very incisive in his remarks, but that makes no difference at all.

No, Justice Frankfurter by nature was a very decisive fellow in his speech. Sometimes he could raise hackles, you know, but he was a delightful companion, and our relations throughout the years I was there were always very friendly as they have been with all of the rest of the justices.

Mr. Chief Justice, do you have thoughts about American lawyers and the American bar and how they have changed? Have the law schools been turning out better lawyers, or what do you think of our legal profession?

WARREN: I think the products of the law schools these days are infinitely better than they were in my day. I have a lot of contacts, as you can imagine, with youngsters out of law school, having had three or four law clerks each year. I deal with them on an intimate basis, and I come to know them almost like you would know a son, and when they leave me I feel almost like I used to feel when one of my boys would leave home to go to college. You just feel a sense of loss.

They are great people, and they couldn't have been as good as they were without having much better instruction, much more comprehensive instruction than we had when I was in law school. And you have to bear in mind also that the law now is infinitely more complex and voluminous than it was when I was admitted to practice in 1914.

Over the years various people have charged that the law clerks play a secret, powerful role on the Supreme Court. What do you think of that?

WARREN: I remember when President Eisenhower appointed Lloyd Wright, the former president of the American Bar Association, to head up a commission on subversion, and he reported that great possibilities for subversion stemmed from these young law clerks who were just out of the law school. He referred to them as a group of young radicals and proposed in his commission report that all of them be given complete F.B.I. investigations and that they be confirmed by the Senate before they could be employed by the Supreme Court.

Now, the fact was that at that particular time our law clerks were more conservative than any young lawyers that I had ever seen. They were in that phase; at that time law schools were very, very conservative.

Since then, I want to say, the law clerks have become far more interested in public affairs, interested in the defense of people, interested in teaching and law schools, interested in constitutional questions.

Really they are a rare lot, and I think they are a great institution. The Court uses them normally only for one year, because it doesn't want to build up a bureaucracy. We bring new young men right out of the law school, and it's great for them, it's wonderful for the Court. We get great help from them, and I think that they can be a real force in our profession throughout the country.

If the law clerks have become less conservative, have the law schools also?

WARREN: You know now that the big law firms in

New York, Chicago, San Francisco and Los Angeles are recruiting young men just like universities recruit football players. They go out and pay their way back to New York—you know, to visit with their office, show them the theaters and so forth, let them mix with their elders in their offices and invite them to come to the firm.

They tell me that in New York some firms are up to $17,000 a year now right out of the law school, and the graduates are not beating a path to their door either. The firms are having difficulty in getting them because a lot of these boys work for the Peace Corps, they work in the Poverty Program, they go to work in district attorneys' offices, in public defenders' offices and in the federal and state governments, and for Ralph Nader.

In other words, we'll put it they are interested in public causes where 15 years ago, or even 10 or 12 years ago, it was very difficult to get young lawyers to be interested in public causes.

I have only one real quarrel with the law schools—I don't know one in the country where they give an adequate course on the responsibilities of lawyers to the cause of justice, or where they give a comprehensive course on the reciprocal responsibilities of court and lawyers to the administration of justice, and I think that that has kept our bar from being alert to many of these problems that have confronted our courts.

The Court has suffered from that fact, too, because the great debate on important issues has never been developed as it should be. Take this proposal of Senator Dirksen's, that came through the Council of State Governments, for a new constitutional court of 50 members, the chief justices of every state of the Union to constitute a court above the Supreme Court of the United States—and then the other constitutional amendment on reapportionment. Those things went through legislature after legislature till almost two-thirds of them passed some kind of resolution on them, and there was no debate of any kind on the part of the bar in the country. To think of coming that close to a constitutional amendment on important subjects of that kind without the bar taking an interest is almost a frightening thing.

Perhaps you are saying that the organized bar in the United States has not improved quite so much as the law schools have improved.

WARREN: That is true. The American Bar Association for many years, particularly during the McCarthy era, never had a kind word to say for the Supreme Court. Everything was critical.

There have been some splendid men in recent years as president of the American bar. Last year Mr. William Gossett was the president, and he was a very enlightened person and has done a great deal to improve the situation, it seems to me. Mr. Bernard Segal, who's the new president of the American bar, is also a very enlightened, forward-looking man, and I'm sure he will make a real contribution to the work of the bar.

The Country

Mr. Chief Justice, is there a day that you remember as the most unhappy of your years in Washington?

WARREN: That is not a difficult question to answer. The saddest day I remember, the saddest week I remember, the saddest year I remember all started one Friday afternoon when we were in conference and I received a note from my secretary, Mrs. Margaret McHugh, to the effect that President Kennedy had been shot.

We immediately adjourned, and by the time I was back in my office Mrs. McHugh informed me that it had just come over the radio that the president was dead. And that and the following week were the saddest days I've ever seen not only during my 16 years but, I think, the saddest I've ever seen in any community in my life.

It was only a day or two after he was buried that President Johnson sent the solicitor general [Archibald Cox] and the deputy attorney general [Nicholas deB. Katzenbach] to see me to ask if I would head a commission to investigate the facts of the Kennedy assassination. I told them that I wished they would tell the president I thought I could not do that, because the Court did not look with favor upon extracurricular commissions of that kind. I myself had expressed an aversion to it, and I thought it would be much better if he would get someone else, and I proposed a couple of names to them.

I thought that was the end of it. But in about an hour I received a message from the president asking if I could visit him at his office. I did so, and he told me of the wild stories that were going around the world and of what this might mean internally if there was not a thorough probe of the facts and some conclusion reached as to who was responsible for the assassination.

He told me that he had conferred with the leaders of both parties in the Congress and that he was going to set up a commission to explore the facts, and he said they would all serve if I would be the chairman of it. He thought that no less a personage than the Chief Justice of the United States, the chief judicial officer of the nation, should head it up. He told me it was of paramount importance; I remember him saying, "You served the country in uniform, and this will be a more important service than anything you could do in a uniform." And so I said, "Mr. President, in spite of my feelings about the matter, if you consider it of that importance, of course, I will do it."

I spent 10 months on that. I think that, too, was the unhappiest year of my life, because I spent at least half of each day and night on that—the rest on my Court work—and to review the terrible happenings of that assassination every day for 10 months is a traumatic experience.

Those days were the unhappiest days I have ever spent in the public service.

And you didn't get much in the way of applause for doing the job, did you?

WARREN: No, that is very true. But up to the present time no one has produced any facts that are contrary to the findings of that commission. A great many people have written to the effect that it might have been this, it might have been that, and some inferences could be drawn other than those that the commission drew. But there has been no confrontation of the facts at all to discredit anything that is in that report.

You are now in retirement, Mr. Chief Justice. How do you think you will like it, a person who's been as active and as engaged in issues as you have been?

WARREN: I'm not so sure how I will like it when I get back to Washington, in my new office in the Court, and the term opens and others all are working and I am not. I haven't felt the strain at all up to the present time because I remained on the Court until the end of the term, and I have been traveling since then.

I can say that I want to cure the problem by doing something that is worthwhile in three fields that I have been interested in. How much time I can or will give to each of them I don't know, but I hope in the aggregate that I will fill my days as I have in the past.

I am interested, of course, in peace, in our country being a leader in the movement for peace around the world. I am interested naturally in court administration; I think there is much to be done, and I have offered my services to the new federal judicial center, which I have worked to have established for many years. And then I am interested in the conservation of our environment, and there is so much to be done in that field that I may find some little niche where I can be of help.

In general, are you optimistic for the United States, or do you think that with all the troubles we've been having we are in a period of some kind of moral decay?

WARREN: I am optimistic, of course, about the United States. For many years I have been at odds with those people who feel that we are living in a mature society, that the society is starting to disintegrate and that the institutions based on that society are themselves deteriorating and becoming degraded. I do not believe that.

I believe that this is a young nation, that we haven't yet reached our potential in any sense of the word. I believe that our forms of government are still on trial, that we are still going through the growing process, that we are learning from day to day.

And I think that many of the problems we have today are the result of more active conscience than they are of degradation or of decadence rather than degradation. I have been in the public service now for 52 years, and when I first went into the service of my state 50 years ago I found moral standards in government far below what they are today.

The standards of government today are head and shoulders over what they were in those days, and I am speaking now of local government, of state government and of federal government as well. There are a lot of things brought to light today that create real scandal, that in those days would never have been mentioned—they would just be overlooked.

So I think there is improvement. I think in spite of the travail we are going through now that we will emerge a better nation and a stronger nation, because I believe the things that we are learning will convince us that our system, being a pluralistic system, must also be a system of equality.

Do you take seriously the warning that President Eisenhower gave in his final speech, against what he termed the military-industrial complex?

WARREN: Yes, I do, and I wish that General Eisenhower had said that before the day he left the White House. I think there is a great danger. One can find the industrial world linked with the military today in almost every request of the military.

I received something of a shock about six months ago when I read an article in one of the Sunday papers that was an interview with the top executives of the 10 largest defense contractors in the country, and each one of them said their companies were not expecting any decrease in their military contracts even if the war in Vietnam ended tomorrow.

It seems to me that the armed forces are always interested in improving their forces to the point of perfection as they see it, and with the alliance of the business world this becomes almost impossible to resist.

I also have some concern about bringing our universities and colleges into that same complex. You will find that a major portion of the budgets of our great universities these days is in the field of research for military purposes, and many have expanded to such an extent that it would be very undesirable from their standpoint to cut back to the size they were before.

I take it from what you said right at the beginning of this talk that you regard the ending of violence as vital for the future of the United States, and specifically the end of the war in Vietnam.

WARREN: I do indeed. I don't believe that we can continue to be in war, and continue to teach our young people that war is an essential part of their lives, and still expect our young people to grow up normal and quiescent.

TENNESSEE WILLIAMS

1911–1983

By Mel Gussow

Author of more than 24 full-length plays, including *The Glass Menagerie*, *A Streetcar Named Desire*, *Cat on a Hot Tin Roof*—the latter two won Pulitzer Prizes—and *The Night of the Iguana*, Tennessee Williams had a profound effect on the American theater and on American playwrights and actors. He wrote with deep sympathy and expansive humor about outcasts in our society. Though his images were often violent, he was a poet of the human heart.

His works, which are among the most popular plays of our time, continue to provide a rich reservoir of acting challenges. Among the actors celebrated in Williams roles were Laurette Taylor in *The Glass Menagerie*, Marlon Brando and Jessica Tandy in *A Streetcar Named Desire* (and Vivien Leigh in the movie version) and Burl Ives in *Cat on a Hot Tin Roof*.

The Glass Menagerie, his first success, was his "memory play." Many of his other plays were his nightmares. Although seldom intentionally autobiographical, the plays were almost all intensely personal—torn from his own private anguishes and anxieties.

He once described his sister's room in the family home in St. Louis, with her collection of glass figures, as representing "all the softest emotions that belong to recollection of things past." But, he remembered, outside the room was an alley in which, nightly, dogs destroyed cats.

Mr. Williams's work, which was unequaled in passion and imagination by any of his contemporaries' works, was a barrage of conflicts, of the blackest horrors offset by purity. Perhaps his greatest character, Blanche Du Bois, the heroine of *Streetcar*, has been described as a tigress and a moth, and, as Mr. Williams created her, there was no contradiction.

His basic premise, he said, was "the need for understanding and tenderness and fortitude among individuals trapped by circumstance."

Just as his work reflected his life, his life reflected his work. A monumental hypochondriac, he became obsessed with sickness, failure and death. Several times he thought he was losing his sight, and he had four eye operations for cataracts. Constantly he thought his heart would stop beating. In desperation, he drank and took pills immoderately.

He was a man of great shyness, but with friends he showed great openness, which often worked to his disadvantage. He was extremely vulnerable to demands—from directors, actresses, the public, his critics, admirers and detractors.

He feigned lack of interest in reviews, but he was deeply disturbed by them. Unfavorable ones could devastate him. Favorable ones might corrupt him. The most successful serious playwright of his time, he did not write for success but, as one friend said, as a "biological necessity."

Success struck him suddenly in 1945, with the

Martha Swope

Broadway premiere of *The Glass Menagerie*, and it frightened him much more than his failure.

He was born Thomas Lanier Williams in Columbus, Miss., on March 26, 1911.

His mother, the former Edwina Dakin, was the puritanical daughter of an Episcopal rector. His father, Cornelius Coffin Williams, was a violent and aggressive traveling salesman who later settled down in St. Louis as manager of a show company. There was an older daughter, Rose (memorialized as Laura in *The Glass Menagerie*), and in 1919 another son was born, Walter Dakin.

"It was just a wrong marriage," the playwright wrote.

The familial conflict is made clear by instances from the son's art. His mother was the model for the foolish but indomitable Amanda Wingfield in *The Glass Menagerie*, his father for the blustering, brutish Big Daddy in *Cat on a Hot Tin Roof*.

While his father traveled, Tom was mostly brought up, and overprotected, by his mother—particularly after he contracted diphtheria at the age of 5. By the time the family moved to St. Louis, the pattern was clear. Young Tom retreated into himself. He made up and told stories, many of them scary.

In the fall of 1929 he went off to the University of Missouri to study journalism. When his childhood girlfriend, Hazel Kramer, also decided to enroll at Missouri, his father said he would withdraw him, and succeeded in breaking up the incipient romance. It was his only known romantic relationship with a woman.

In a state of depression, Tom dropped out of school and, at his father's instigation, took a job as a clerk in a shoe company. It was, he recalled, "living death."

To survive, every day after work he retreated to his room and wrote—stories, poems, plays—through the night.

The strain finally led to a nervous breakdown. Sent to Memphis to recuperate, the young Mr. Williams joined a local theater group.

Back in St. Louis, he became friendly with a group of poets at Washington University, particularly Clark Mills McBurney, who, among other things, introduced Mr. Williams to the poems of Hart Crane. Crane became his idol.

In 1937, Mr. Williams reenrolled as a student, this time at the University of Iowa. There and in St. Louis he wrote an enormous, and uncounted, number of plays, some of which were produced on campus. In 1938, nine years after he had entered college, he graduated.

Success seemed paired with tragedy. His sister lost her mind. The family allowed—with subsequent recriminations—a prefrontal lobotomy to be performed, and Rose spent much of her life in a sanitarium.

At 28, Thomas Williams left home for New Orleans, where he changed his style of living, as well as his name.

He offered several reasons for the name change. It was a reaction against his early inferior work, published under his real name. It was a college nickname. It was because his father was from Tennessee. It was distinctive.

In New Orleans he discovered new netherworlds, soaking up the milieu that would appear in *A Streetcar Named Desire*.

He wrote stories, some of which later became plays, and entered a Group Theater playwriting contest. He won $100 and was solicited by the agent Audrey Wood, who became his friend and adviser.

Battle of Angels, a play he wrote during a visit of several months to St. Louis, opened in Boston in 1940 and was a disaster. It closed in two weeks and did not come to New York.

Mr. Williams, however, brought it back in a revised version in 1957 as *Orpheus Descending* and as the Marlon Brando–Anna Magnani movie, *The Fugitive Kind*, and in 1973 it was presented at the Circle Repertory Company.

To his amazement, Audrey Wood got him a job in Hollywood writing scripts for Metro-Goldwyn-Mayer at $250 a week for six months. He wrote a

Lana Turner picture, worked briefly on a Margaret O'Brien picture and, disdainfully, began writing an original screenplay, which was rejected.

Still under contract, in a house at Malibu, he began turning the screenplay into a play titled *The Gentleman Caller*, which slowly evolved into *The Glass Menagerie*. On March 31, 1945, five days after its author became 34, it opened on Broadway and changed Mr. Williams's life, and the American theater.

He was inundated with success—the play won the New York Drama Critics' Circle award—and he fought to keep afloat.

"Once you fully apprehend the vacuity of a life without struggle," he wrote, "you are equipped with the basic means of salvation." His art was his salvation. Apprehending, he wrote his second masterpiece, *A Streetcar Named Desire*.

Opening in December 1947, *Streetcar* was an even bigger hit than *The Glass Menagerie*. It won Mr. Williams his second Drama Critics' award and his first Pulitzer Prize.

For many years after *Streetcar*, almost every other season there was another Williams play on Broadway (and a one-act play somewhere else). Soon there was a continual flow from the stage to the screen. And he never stopped revising his finished work. For more than 35 years, the stream was unabated. He produced an enormous body of work, including more than two dozen full-length plays, all of them produced—a record unequaled by any of his contemporaries.

There were successes and failures, and often great disagreement over which was which. In 1948 there was *Summer and Smoke*, which he wrote on Nantucket while sharing his house with his friend Carson McCullers (at his encouragement she was dramatizing *The Member of the Wedding*). *Summer and Smoke* failed on Broadway, was a huge success in a revival Off Broadway and made a star of Geraldine Page, one of many magnificent leading ladies in Mr. Williams's works (among the others: Laurette Taylor, Jessica Tandy, Vivien Leigh, Maureen Stapleton, Anna Magnani).

There followed *The Rose Tattoo*, *Camino Real* (a flop in 1953, but revived as a classic at Lincoln Center in 1970), *Cat on a Hot Tin Roof* (his third Drama Critics' prize, his second Pulitzer), *Orpheus Descending*, *Garden District*, *Sweet Bird of Youth*. Most of these plays have been seen again in major revivals.

In addition to the plays, he wrote two novels, *The Roman Spring of Mrs. Stone* and *Moise and the World of Reason*; short stories, such as "One Arm" and "Hard Candy"; a book of poetry, *In the Winter of Cities*; the film *Baby Doll* and his *Memoirs*. In his *Memoirs*, for the first time he wrote in detail about his homosexuality but, as usual, he was restrained in dealing with his creative life, explaining that his art was "private."

As he became more and more successful, Mr. Williams lost his look of boyish innocence and became somewhat portly and seedy.

Gradually he found it more and more difficult to write. The turning point, as he saw it, was 1955, and after *Cat on a Hot Tin Roof* there was a noticeable decline in his work. To keep going, he began relying on a ritualistic combination of ingredients—strong coffee, cigarettes, drugs and alcohol.

In the late 1950s, Mr. Williams undertook psychoanalysis, explaining, "If I am no longer disturbed myself, I will deal less with violent material." His first postanalysis work was the 1960 *Period of Adjustment*, a comedy that by common critical agreement was one of the slightest of his works.

He went back to his nightmares and reached further out for subject matter. In terms of subject and theme, he was a pioneer.

The Night of the Iguana, which won a fourth Drama Critics' award for Mr. Williams in 1961, was considered a return to his earlier important work. As it turned out, it was his last major success.

After *Iguana*, Mr. Williams went searching and

seemed to fall apart. But at the same time he discovered religion. In 1968 he was converted to Roman Catholicism. And his last plays, though still dealing with grotesques, also dealt with salvation.

The Milk Train Doesn't Stop Here Anymore, which failed in successive years on Broadway and as an Elizabeth Taylor–Richard Burton movie entitled *Boom!,* was an allegory about a Christlike young man and a dying dowager. His next three plays, *Slapstick Tragedy*, *The Seven Descents of Myrtle* and *In a Bar in a Tokyo Hotel*, also had minuscule runs.

Recovering from an illness, he plunged back to work, writing and rewriting.

In the 1970s he was, characteristically, prolific, but success continued to elude him. *Small Craft Warning* had a comfortable run Off Broadway in 1972, and at one point, the author himself made his professional debut as an actor in his own play, assuming a small role.

Out Cry was a quick failure on Broadway in 1973 and *The Red Devil Battery Sign* closed in Boston, although it was subsequently presented in London. *Vieux Carré* had a brief Broadway run in 1979. Of his later plays, his most popular was the poignant *A Lovely Sunday at Creve Coeur* in 1979.

His last Broadway play was *Clothes for a Summer Hotel,* a drama about Scott and Zelda Fitzgerald that proved to be one of his biggest failures. Though wounded by the critical reception, he continued writing, in his last years working with noncommercial institutional theaters.

Something Cloudy, Something Clear was produced Off Off Broadway at the Jean Cocteau Theater in 1981, and last year his final play, *A House Not Meant to Stand*, had its premiere at the Goodman Theater of Chicago. That play, subsequently presented at the New World Festival of the Arts in Miami, deals with the physical and emotional disintegration of an older married couple in Mississippi.

In his later years, Mr. Williams divided his time between his apartment in New York at the Elysée and his house in Key West. He also kept an apartment in the French Quarter of New Orleans, the scene of *A Streetcar Named Desire*. Mr. Williams died in his apartment in New York on Feb. 25, 1983. He was 71 years old.

"I always felt like Tennessee and I were compatriots," said Marlon Brando. "He told the truth as best he perceived it, and never turned away from things that beset or frightened him. We are all diminished by his death."

MR. WILLIAMS'S REPORT ON LIFE IN NEW ORLEANS [1947]

BROOKS ATKINSON

BY COMMON consent, the finest new play on the boards just now [December 1947] is Tennessee Williams's *A Streetcar Named Desire.* As a tribute to the good taste of this community, it is also a smash hit. This combination of fine quality and commercial success is an interesting phenomenon. For if the literal facts of the story could be considered apart from Mr. Williams's imaginative style of writing, *Streetcar* might be clattering through an empty theater. It is not a popular play, designed to attract and entertain the public. It cannot be dropped into any of the theater's familiar categories. It has no plot, at least in the familiar usage of that word. It is almost unbearably tragic.

After attending a play of painful character, theatergoers frequently ask in self-defense: "What's the good of harrowing people like that?" No one can answer that sort of question. The usual motives for self-expression do not obtain in this instance. There is no purpose in *Streetcar.* It solves no problems; it arrives at no general moral conclusions. It is the rueful character portrait of one person, Blanche Du

THE VOICE OF TENNESSEE WILLIAMS

Two speeches of Blanche Du Bois from *A Streetcar Named Desire*:*

Having great wealth sometimes makes people lonely! A cultivated woman, a woman of intelligence and breeding, can enrich a man's life—immeasurably! I have those things to offer, and this doesn't take them away. Physical beauty is passing. A transitory possession. But beauty of the mind and richness of the spirit and tenderness of the heart—and I have all of those things—aren't taken away, but grow! Increase with the years! How strange that I should be called a destitute woman! When I have all of these treasures locked in my heart. *(A choked sob comes from her.)* I think of myself as a very, very rich woman! But I have been foolish—casting my pearls before swine!

. . . some things are not forgivable. Deliberate cruelty is not forgivable. It is the one unforgivable thing in my opinion and it is the one thing of which I have never, never been guilty.

Tom Wingfield's final soliloquy from *The Glass Menagerie*:**

I didn't go to the moon, I went much further—for time is the longest distance between two places—

Not long after that I was fired for writing a poem on the lid of a shoebox.

I left Saint Louis. I descended the steps of this fire escape for a last time and followed, from then on, in my father's footsteps, attempting to find in motion what was lost in space—

I traveled around a great deal. The cities swept about me like dead leaves, leaves that were brightly colored but torn away from the branches.

I would have stopped, but I was pursued by something.

It always came upon me unawares, taking me altogether by surprise. Perhaps it was a familiar bit of music. Perhaps it was only a piece of transparent glass—

Perhaps I am walking along a street at night, in some strange city, before I have found companions. I pass the lighted window of a shop where perfume is sold. The window is filled with pieces of colored glass, tiny transparent bottles in delicate colors, like bits of a shattered rainbow.

Then all at once my sister touches my shoulder. I turn around and look into her eyes . . .

Oh, Laura, Laura, I tried to leave you behind me, but I am more faithful than I intended to be!

I reach for a cigarette, I cross the street, I run into the movies or a bar, I buy a drink, I speak to the nearest stranger—anything that can blow your candles out! . . .

—for nowadays the world is lit by lightning! Blow out your candles, Laura—and so goodbye . . .

From the foreword to *The Rose Tattoo*, 1950:

Time rushes toward us with its hospital tray of infinitely varied narcotics, even while it is preparing us for its inevitably fatal operation.

Maggie's final words in *Cat on a Hot Tin Roof*, 1955:

Nothing's more determined than a cat on a tin roof—is there? Is there, baby?

Bois of Mississippi and New Orleans. Since she is created on the stage as a distinct individual, experiences identical with hers can never be repeated. She and the play that is woven about her are unique. For Mr. Williams is not writing of representative men and women; he is not a social author absorbed in the great issues of his time, and, unlike timely plays, *Streetcar* does not acquire stature or excitement from the world outside the theater.

These negative comments are introduced to establish some perspective by which *Streetcar* may be appreciated as a work of art. As a matter of fact, people do appreciate it thoroughly. They come away from it profoundly moved and also in some curious way elated. For they have been sitting all evening in the presence of truth, and that is a rare and wonderful experience. Out of nothing more esoteric than interest in human beings, Mr. Williams has looked steadily and wholly into the private agony of one lost person. He supplies dramatic conflict by introducing Blanche to an alien environment that brutally wears on her nerves. But he takes no sides in the conflict. He knows how right all the characters are—how right she is in trying to protect herself against the disaster that is overtaking her, and how right the other characters are in protecting their independence, for her terrible needs cannot be fulfilled. There is no solution except the painful one Mr. Williams provides in his last scene.

For Blanche is not just a withered remnant of southern gentility. She is in flight from a world she could not control and which has done frightful things to her. She has stood by during a long siege of deaths in the family, each death having robbed her of strength and plunged her further into loneliness. Her marriage to an attractive boy who looked to her for spiritual security was doomed from the start; and even if she had been a superwoman she could not have saved it.

By the time we see her in the play she is hysterical from a long and shattering ordeal. In the wildness of her dilemma she clings desperately to illusions of refinement—pretty clothes that soothe her ego, perfumes and ostentatious jewelry, artifices of manners, forms and symbols of respectability. Since she does not believe in herself, she tries to create a false world in which she can hide. But she is living with normal people who find her out and condemn her by normal standards. There is no hope for Blanche. Even if her wildest dreams came true, even if the rich man who has become her obsession did rescue her, she would still be lost. She will always have to flee reality.

Although Mr. Williams does not write verse or escape into mysticism or grandeur, he is a poet. There is no fancy writing in *Streetcar.* He is a poet because he is aware of people and of life. His perceptions are quick. Out of a few characters he can evoke the sense of life as a wide, endlessly flowing pattern of human needs and aspirations. Although *Streetcar* is specific about its characters and episodes, it is not self-contained. The scenes of present time, set in a New Orleans tenement, have roots in the past, and you know that Mr. Williams's characters are going on for years into some mysterious future that will always be haunted by the wounding things we see on the stage. For he is merely recording a few lacerating weeks torn out of time. He is an incomparably beautiful writer, not because the words are lustrous, but because the dialogue is revealing and sets up overtones. Although he has confined truth to one small and fortuitous example, it seems to have the full dimensions of life on the stage. It almost seems not to have been written but to be happening.

Streetcar deserves the devotion of the theater's most skillful craftsmen; and, not entirely by accident, it has acquired them. Elia Kazan, who brilliantly directed *All My Sons* last season, is versatile enough to direct *Streetcar* brilliantly also. He has woven the tenderness and the brutality into a single strand of spontaneous motion. Confronted with the task of relating the vivid reality of *Streetcar* to its background in the city and to its awareness of life in general, Jo Mielziner has designed a memorable, poetic setting with a deep range of tones.

The acting cannot be praised too highly. Marlon Brando's braggart, sullen, caustic brother-in-law,

Karl Malden's dull-witted, commonplace suitor, Kim Hunter's affectionate, levelheaded sister are vivid character portraits done with freshness and definition. As Blanche Du Bois, Jessica Tandy has one of the longest and most exacting parts on record. She plays it with an insight as vibrant and pitiless as Mr. Williams's writing, for she catches on the wing the terror, the bogus refinement, the intellectual alertness and the madness that can hardly be distinguished from logic and fastidiousness. Miss Tandy acts a magnificent part magnificently.

It is no reflection on the director and the actors to observe that Mr. Williams has put into his script everything vital we see on the stage. A workman as well as an artist, he has not only imagined the whole drama but set it down on paper where it can be read. The script is a remarkably finished job: it describes the characters at full length, it foresees the performance, the impact of the various people on each other, the contrasts in tone of their temperaments and motives.

In comparison with *The Glass Menagerie, Streetcar* is a more coherent and lucid drama without loose ends, and the mood is more firmly established. *Summer and Smoke,* which has not yet been produced in New York, has wider range and divides the main interest between two principal characters. If it is staged and acted as brilliantly as the performance of *Streetcar,* it ought to supply the third item in a notable trilogy. For there is considerable uniformity in the choice of characters and in the attitude toward life. That uniformity may limit the range of Mr. Williams's career as a playwright; so far, he has succeeded best with people who are much alike in spirit. In the meantime, he has brought into the theater the gifts of a poetic writer and a play that is conspicuously less mortal than most.

A PLAYWRIGHT WHOSE GREATEST ACT WAS HIS FIRST

FRANK RICH

IT SEEMS only too ironic that the last Tennessee Williams play to be seen on Broadway, *Clothes for a Summer Hotel* in 1980, was an attempt to exhume the ghost of F. Scott Fitzgerald. For what writer more than Mr. Williams exemplified Fitzgerald's notion that there are no second acts to American lives?

During the first half of his career, Mr. Williams produced a body of work that did and still does give our theater one of its few claims to greatness. Though Mr. Williams continued to write prolifically for the rest of his life, the second act of his career cannot be said to have happened.

Yet the sad fall, while tragic, in no way diminishes the glory of what came before. Such is the timeless power of Mr. Williams's major plays that he remains the most important and influential American playwright after Eugene O'Neill. He wrote at least two masterpieces, *The Glass Menagerie* and *A Streetcar Named Desire*, as well as at least five other works, not all of them universally beloved, that are a permanent part of the international theatrical repertoire: *Cat on a Hot Tin Roof*, *The Rose Tattoo*, *Summer and Smoke*, *Sweet Bird of Youth* and *The Night of the Iguana*. There are shafts of light in many of the lesser plays, too, though they dimmed considerably as Mr. Williams's decline accelerated in the 1960s and 1970s.

What Mr. Williams created at the height of his powers were vulnerable, lost, tortured people struggling for dignity, compassion and at least a measure of salvation in a world of almost apocalyptic cruelty. If that world was grotesque and nightmarish, it was nonetheless, as the famous Williams phrase had it, "lit by lightning."

That lightning was provided by Mr. Williams's

extraordinarily fecund and lyrical poetry, his mastery of dramatic moments and effects, and his ability to raise lowly characters to almost mythic size. If there is any literate person who has not encountered Amanda and Laura Wingfield, Blanche Du Bois and Stanley Kowalski or Maggie and Big Daddy, his life is the poorer for it.

It is no coincidence that Mr. Williams's characters provided career high points for a remarkable array of actors, most (though not all) of them women: Laurette Taylor, Jessica Tandy, Maureen Stapleton, Barbara Bel Geddes, Geraldine Page, Marlon Brando and Burl Ives, among many others. The film versions of the plays performed the same service for such stars as Vivien Leigh, Paul Newman and Elizabeth Taylor.

The idiom of Mr. Williams's works is indelibly linked to the decaying post–Civil War South, but his themes belong to no particular placc or time. Mr. Williams's characters live in terrifying fear of death; they are torn between aspirations of the soul and hungers of the body; they hope against hope that strangers will be kind.

Though Mr. Williams's use of homosexuality and nymphomania was once considered shocking, we see now that the sexual and neurotic components of his people are highly theatrical expressions of the ontological chaos that is man's universal plight. And even so, not all Mr. Williams's plays were psychosexual hothouses. The tone of *Menagerie* and *Iguana* is elegiac. There is humor in most of the plays, as well as an outright comedy in the 1960 *Period of Adjustment*.

The daring theatrical innovations and psychological liberation that mark Mr. Williams's breakthrough plays were built on foundations laid by O'Neill and, of course, Freud. In turn, Mr. Williams has exerted an enormous influence on the generation of writers that followed him. Hardly a month goes by without the production of a new American play that is written in the patented Williams style sometimes referred to, for lack of a better term, as "poetic realism." Echoes of his voice can be heard in the works of Edward Albee and Lanford Wilson, to name just his two most prominent successors.

It took time for audiences to catch up with some of Mr. Williams's major plays, which often found second and enhanced lives in revised versions and revivals. Already there is a small critical community that champions the plays that were received poorly by critics and audiences over the past two decades.

In these works—among them, *The Milk Train Doesn't Stop Here Anymore*, *Slapstick Tragedy* and *The Seven Descents of Myrtle*—Mr. Williams indulged in explicit metaphysical symbolism and allegory; he experimented with surrealism, mysticism and the new techniques of the theater of the absurd. Though it would be worth looking at some of these plays in better productions than they originally received—especially the autobiographical *Vieux Carré* of 1977—they are unlikely to be rescued. Poorly crafted and sometimes self-parodying, they have more to do with the personal tragedies of Mr. Williams's declining years than with the grandeur of his talent.

Though he wrote an autobiography (*Memoirs*) and granted many interviews, not all of Mr. Williams's own explications of his work and life can be taken at face value. But, along with his great plays, a fitting epitaph may be contained in the published afterword to *Camino Real* (1953).

"My own creed as a playwright," Mr. Williams wrote, "is fairly close to that expressed by the painter in Shaw's play *The Doctor's Dilemma*: 'I believe in Michelangelo, Velasquez and Rembrandt; in the might of design, the mystery of color, the redemption of all things by beauty everlasting and the message of art that has made these hands blessed. Amen.' "

POET AND PURITAN [1970]

HAROLD CLURMAN

WE ARE in the habit of judging our playwrights piecemeal. As with cars, we think in seasonal models. Last year's issue was a triumph, this year's is a bust. When several flops follow one another, we pronounce the erstwhile wonder "finished," or "dead." We may even question whether the golden boy's glitter was really as bright as we had once believed it to be. Racine's tart reply to his contemporary detractors, "The critics have vanished, the plays remain," applies here.

Tennessee Williams is a dramatist of lost souls. His work describes a long laceration. No American playwright is altogether a pessimist. The conclusion of *Camino Real*, "the violets in the mountains have broken through the rocks," simply means that idealism will ultimately smash the battlements of villainy in which we are immured. But this thought only marks a pause along the road. Williams's path leads to no final statement. He has no doctrine, unless it be the need for compassion. He traces a chart of the fevers that he has experienced in looking at the world outside and within himself.

The picture is muted and tender in the fragmented memories of *The Glass Menagerie*. Because of its gentle qualities, many folk prefer this play to all the others. It is the seedbed of his future work. Amanda, the mother, establishes the tone of a life gone by. She is a fading personality, the idealist become foolish for want of a foundation in the present. She remains wistfully hopeful as she recalls a time of greater stability and grace. Here too we find her daughter, Laura, an injured girl withdrawn from life because of the visible handicap of her lameness. She consoles herself with playthings that will not endure. The memorable Gentleman Caller is the first example of Williams's ability to depict the average uneducated "good guy" with both truthfulness and sympathy. And there is her son, Tom, oppressed by the lack of vitality in the meager maternal nest. He is eager to escape it and explore long distances. "I seem dreamy," he says, "but inside—well, I'm boiling."

Amanda is a puritan. She shies away from instinct. "It belongs to animals," she says. What people like herself want are "superior things! Things of the mind and the spirit." This note is struck again and again, developed at length and more eloquently by Blanche in *A Streetcar Named Desire* and by Alma in *Summer and Smoke*. The yearning to transcend the senses is sometimes viewed as comic or pathetic but is never extinguished. It finds its purest expression in Hannah Jelke, the poet's daughter in *The Night of the Iguana*.

The puritan seeks God as do all good poets, Williams intimates in *Suddenly Last Summer*, and Williams is both poet and puritan. The world he has entered on his long journey is grotesquely harsh, depleted of sacred values; even where they *seem* to obtain, they exist only in travesty. Specifically, Williams's milieu is usually the tense and still unreconstructed South, but that is only a locale typical of an environment we all inhabit.

Blanche Du Bois, Williams's most representative character, has been exiled through the loss of the ancestral site into a society in which she can no longer be "a young *lady,*" that is, a whole person. The world she now finds herself in is self-sufficiently and complacently brutal. It is a world in which "superior things of mind and spirit" are scorned. Innocently and achingly, she depends on the "kindness of strangers." But most of these strangers are the devil's surrogates. They spell death. Bearing flowers, death haunts Williams and terrifies him.

The opposite of death is desire—the will to live, the need for the most intimate contact with those outside us. It inspires us with a sense of beauty. Blanche gives herself to desire in ignorance, confusion, dismay. She does not know that desire and beauty, through their simulacra, frequently lead to an impasse, to destruction, to death.

With only a few exceptions, Williams characters are lost souls because they are torn between the God-seeking impulse and the pull of desire. In the shambles of our civilization, desire has been debased into raw carnality. Sex without the blessedness of love is death-dealing corruption. In this corrupt atmosphere—always captivatingly colorful in Williams, even to the very names of the vicinities in which his dramas take place—his men and women are destroyed by the poisons that emanate from it. The lacerations they suffer are the result of their bodies and souls being at odds. The sharpness of this division is a characteristic of puritan consciousness. Unity of spirit is achieved only by the chaste Hannah in *Iguana* and the impassioned and therefore utterly loyal Rosa in *The Rose Tattoo*, in which sex becomes glorified through its pure flame. But Rosa is a Sicilian—a foreigner to our way of life.

When we speak of the world and of society, we imply a realm beyond the strictly personal. Sex, it is commonly held, is Williams's major theme. This, I believe, is only partly true; when this preoccupation with sex in Williams is insisted upon as the determining ingredient, such insistence leads to a falsification. Williams is also very much a social playwright. Sex being a central factor in existence, it becomes the arena in Williams's plays where the social battles as well as the battle of angels rage.

It is in a fatal incapacity to integrate the conflict of body and soul, or, to put it more concretely, the struggle between power and love, egotistical acquisitiveness and social generosity, that we find the thematic core of Williams's work. The tension in these forces creates a split in the social order as well as in the individual personality. It causes his people to grope, trembling and bewildered, between that light and shadow to which he repeatedly refers. It also gives rise to personal self-deception and public hypocrisy.

The duality in Williams assumes many guises. It is merely a sidelight on his character, but those who have worked with him (myself among them) have noted that he wavers even in the judgment of his own creations and more especially in the matter of their performances. He may say, for instance, that Stanley Kowalski in *Streetcar* points to America's future. This may mean that he fears that the gorillas will inherit our earth or, on the contrary, that he prefers the primitive drive of such folk to the palsied sensibilities of the super-aesthetes.

He will praise totally diverse interpretations of his plays and tell various producing companies in turn that they alone have done his plays as he envisioned them. This is not merely professional politesse but a sign of an inner uncertainty.

The doppelgänger or second self ascribed to Alma in *Summer and Smoke* is his own. The accusatory ferocity in regard to our society, which becomes a debilitating fixation in his later plays, alternates with a certain calm or balance in *The Night of the Iguana* or even takes the form of good-natured comedy in his *Period of Adjustment*.

There is a salutary humor in all his work. It is quizzical and given to grass-roots laughter. His violence too is softened by the colorfulness and musicality that bathe his plays in glamour. "A kind of lyricism," a stage direction in *Streetcar* reads, "gracefully attenuates the atmosphere of decay." There is magic in Williams's realism.

In the illusionist sense of theatricality, he has no match in American dramatic writing. The rhythms of his colloquial speech are seductive. His dialogue excels in euphony and ease. It has a fragrance like that of a tropical flower planted in a northern soil. The diction is at once limpid and elusive, achieving both mystery and suspense.

Williams writes rich roles for actors. They are gratifying because they represent people who mirror some of his own ambivalence, assertive and tremulously vulnerable, staunch and retreating. His particular nature has enabled him to fashion several of the most perceptive and touching portraits of women our drama has produced. He is one of the few dramatists among us who writes genuine love scenes.

He is no intellectual. Some of his views and sentiments—as in *Camino Real*—are couched in terms that betray an almost adolescent sentimentality. His weaknesses, however, should not dim for us his mastery of stage poetics, his immense gift for theatrical effect and, above all, his vital contribution to the understanding of formerly undisclosed phases of American life.

Through his fascination with sin and his affinity with sinners, Williams, even more than O'Neill, has opened our eyes and hearts to the victims of our savagely mechanized society, the company of the "somehow unfit," the fragile, the frightened, the different, the odd and the lonely, whom we have so long sought to avoid thinking about and recognizing as our kin.

Williams is nothing if not honest. He has acknowledged the tension induced by the dichotomy of his spirit, which has led him to the verge of permanent breakdown. He dramatized this state bewilderingly in his 1969 play *In the Bar of a Tokyo Hotel* and in the unjustly neglected *The Gnädige Fräulein*—part of his 1966 *Slapstick Tragedy*—where the romantic dreamer in the entertainment business, the leeches of publicity, the callous public, the profiteer and exploiters of talent are symbolized with originality and wit.

ZHOU ENLAI

1898–1976

By Alden Whitman

Among statesmen of the second half of the 20th century, Zhou Enlai, prime minister of China for 26 years, was notable for his grasp of world affairs, his skill as a negotiator and his ability to weather the turmoil of Chinese politics.

Prime minister since the proclamation of the Communist government in 1949 (and concurrently foreign minister until 1958), Zhou was also credited with exercising pragmatism in running the machinery of government. Although he was at times under political attack, he was counted as one of the two or three most powerful men in the Chinese Communist movement. Some policies with which he was associated failed, yet he proved resourceful enough to retain membership in the highest party councils.

One explanation was Zhou's loyalty to Mao Zedong, the supreme revolutionary symbol of China. Another was that Zhou was a tested veteran of the Long March, the anabasis of 1934–35, in which the Communists established a secure base in Yanan against great odds. A third was that, in the intraparty struggles that marked the Great Leap Forward of 1958–59 and the Great Proletarian Cultural Revolution of 1966–76, he was able to keep the state apparatus functioning.

Many China watchers remarked Zhou's agility in adapting to prevailing situations. When the military was powerful, he appeared to go along; and when Mao displayed strength, as he did in the Cultural Revolution, he also went along. Discussing this reedlike flexibility, Chester A. Ronning, the Canadian diplomat who was a friend and observer for many years, summed up a common view of many Sinologists by saying: "Zhou was a long-range man. He strove to preserve and maintain the Chinese revolution for years to come. He measured time by the centuries, not by lifespans."

On the world stage, Zhou—the name is pronounced "jo"—became visible to millions of Americans in February 1972, when they watched him on television acting as host to President Nixon during Nixon's historic journey to China. Erect in his military posture, trim in a well-tailored gray tunic and trousers, Zhou, whose dark face was dominated by brown eyes and black eyebrows, was witnessed as a relaxed and evidently tireless banqueter.

Off camera, he was reported to have been a supple negotiator of an easing of Chinese-American tensions. These talks paved the way for a substantial increase in commercial and cultural relations between the two nations as well as for limited diplomatic ties. Zhou, however, did not succeed in persuading the United States to terminate relations with the Chinese Nationalist regime on Taiwan.

Zhou's skill in negotiation was well regarded even by those who differed with him or sat on the other side of the table. General of the Army George C. Marshall, who dealt with him on a post–World War

Audrey Topping/The New York Times

II mission to China, expressed esteem. And Dag Hammarskjöld, the late secretary general of the United Nations, once said that Zhou had "the most superior brain I have so far met in the field of foreign politics."

As China's principal face to the world, Zhou attended the Geneva conference on Vietnam in 1954 and the Bandung, Indonesia, meeting of the third-world countries the following year. Later he traveled widely in Asia, Africa and Eastern Europe in search of goodwill and wider influence for Beijing, although not always successfully. He negotiated diplomatic recognition with Japan. He played an important role, moreover, in the delicate dealings with the Soviet Union, whose relationship with China was exceedingly tense from 1960 onward. With patience and adroitness he brought China out of her virtual diplomatic isolation in 1949 into the ranks of the great powers, a process culminating in China's admission to the United Nations in 1971.

In constructing an intricate network of alliances, pacts and understandings, Zhou met leaders of scores of countries and succeeded in raising the number that recognized Beijing to over 100, compared with slightly over 50 as late as 1970. His attention to foreign affairs was the most visible part of his work, and his seeming tirelessness—playing host to 12-course banquets, giving foreign journalists interviews that sometimes began after midnight and lasted until first light, traveling around the country with visiting presidents and prime ministers—became his international trademark.

Foreigners who met him were struck, above all, by his combination—rare among Chinese leaders—of toughness and sophistication. He was always immaculate, his tunic creaseless and shoes gleaming. His right arm was permanently crooked as a result of a riding accident in the 1930s, but his handshake was vigorous.

He remembered enough English and French from his student days, which he spent in England and France as well as Germany, to correct his interpreters.

He did not smoke, drank lightly and was often coatless in cold weather. In a rare personal disclosure, he conceded that he had not had a holiday in 50 years.

He could speak angrily to subordinates who fell short of his standards, but also took care to know about their wives and families. He also had a penetrating sense of humor, sometimes exercised at his aides' expense, as when he exposed the frayed sleeve of his undershirt to a visiting prime minister as an example of the poor quality of Chinese exports, to the evident embarrassment of the Chinese trade minister, who sat nearby.

Just as Zhou, as the helmsman of China's foreign relations, suffered moments of unstable sailing, so did Zhou, as the party politician. In the Cultural Revolution he weathered the wrath of the young Red Guards and managed, amid the countrywide upheaval, to retain his standing near the pinnacle of party power. And in 1974, in a campaign to "criticize Confucius"—to attack some modes of traditional thought—some China watchers sensed instances of veiled references to Zhou.

One of Zhou's most difficult moments was the Lin Biao affair of 1970–71. This affair, the full scope of which is still unclear to outsiders, involved the reported death in a plane crash in 1971 of Lin, minister of defense and Mao's designated heir. The official version maintained that Lin sought to oust Mao in a coup and fled toward the Soviet Union after its failure. In recent years Beijing has been at pains to assert that Lin had harbored traitorous designs for some time and was not responsible for military successes except when he was acting under Mao's orders.

Some American specialists believed that the basic division between Lin and Mao was over the orientation of foreign policy, with Lin favoring some sort of détente with the Soviet Union and Mao, who harbored bitter feelings about Moscow, desiring to explore the possibilities of eased relations with the United States. In this situation, Zhou, the loyalist, threw his weight in the party to Mao, thus facilitating Lin's disgrace.

Other Sinologists, including O. Edmund Clubb, saw Zhou's role differently. "Mao's governing urge," Mr. Clubb said, "was to remain the supreme hero of the Chinese Revolution. Lin, who had been designated Mao's successor in 1969, grew impatient, all the more because it was never defined as to which of Mao's roles he would succeed—party chairman, philosopher, final arbiter of policy. In a 1970 intraparty debate over abolishing the post of chief of state, Lin opposed Mao, and Mao, in his suspicious fashion, supposed that Lin yearned for the post.

"Zhou sided with Mao in this power struggle not only out of loyalty, but also because he regarded Lin and his army power base as a threat to the day-to-day functioning of his [Zhou's] bureaucracy."

Many China observers, including those like Mr. Ronning who had firsthand experience with Zhou, believed that the prime minister was more fired by ambition for China than for himself. His overriding desire, according to Mr. Ronning and others, was the establishment of his country as a great power. In this context, it was said, he realized China's economic weaknesses, chiefly the modesty of her industrial development and her comparative political feebleness in the Pacific basin.

As a pragmatist and a moderate, Zhou, this reading suggested, was content to let Mao retain his oracular leadership while pressing for such practical steps as he could. He had gone along with Mao in backing revolution in such countries as Indonesia—a coup that failed disastrously—and in preaching it in Africa, the specialists said, and had bided his time. When the moment seemed ripe in 1970, he advanced the merits of an opening to the East—an accommodation with the United States and Japan, which might also put a spoke in the Soviet wheel. Both countries, it was argued, could help China economically through trade.

Although Mao had often hurled invective against United States "imperialism" and was a vigorous opponent of American involvement in Southeast Asia, it was agreed in August and September 1970 to feel out the United States, with which there had been some liaison over the years through ambassadorial meetings in Warsaw. Thus it was that in December 1970 Mao indicated in an interview with Edgar Snow, the American journalist, that President Nixon would be welcomed in Beijing.

The United States, it was contended, would respond not only in the interest of a more stable Asia but also because a Nixon visit could strengthen its hand with the Soviet Union. The Beijing sessions of early 1972, conducted largely by Zhou, lightened the atmosphere between the two nations, but fell far short of establishing diplomatic relations. Even so, Zhou was credited with helping to relax tensions and with opening the door to significant commercial and cultural interchanges.

In September 1972 Zhou was host to Kakuei Tanaka, the Japanese prime minister, on a visit to Beijing that produced diplomatic recognition, the prospect of greatly increased trade and a Chinese assurance of military aid under certain unspecified conditions. By promoting the Japanese relationship, Zhou seemed to have blocked any Soviet strategy of encirclement.

Without conceding any ideological points, Zhou appeared to strive for normal state-to-state relations with the Soviet Union. Trade between the countries picked up after 1969.

Until late 1974 Beijing had publicly expressed fears of an armed Soviet attack as talks over border problems took a desultory course. But in October 1974 China let it be known that she no longer expected a major military confrontation. Zhou's role in this shift was unclear, since he was reported ill when it occurred.

In all, China seemed to have achieved a delicate balance. Her foreign relations, with some exceptions, such as India, were accounted in good shape. There was a measure of domestic quiet. And the country could now build a more industrial economy as the underlying basis for its power role in the world. In bringing China to this point, Zhou was widely regarded as the master organizer. "One of the great political figures of modern China" was the characterization of Donald W. Klein of Columbia University's East Asian Institute.

Zhou's life bridged traditional and revolutionary China. He was born in the waning years of the Manchu Dynasty, in 1898—the month and day are unclear—in Jiangsu Province. His family was of the gentry and well-to-do. Both his parents were versed in the Chinese classics. His mother died in his boyhood, and his father, a minor bureaucrat fond of rice wine, was thought ineffectual by members of the Zhou family. It was agreed that the youth would be reared by an uncle in Shanghai.

Zhou's attachment to his extended family was in the traditional manner. In 1939, for example, he made a special trip to the ancestral home in Shaoxing, southwest of Shanghai, to pay his respects—by bowing three times—to the then head of the clan. And when his father died in 1942, the son saw to it that the obituary notice in the Communist party paper conformed to ancient custom, quite contrary to general party practice.

When Zhou was 10, still another uncle undertook his upbringing, and took him to live in Shenyang, formerly Mukden, where he passed his elementary school years. At home and in class he became acquainted with the writings of Chinese reformers and Western political thinkers. He also learned some English.

From 1913 to 1917 Zhou was at the Nankai Middle School in Tianjin, where his nationalist feelings were further fortified.

With the crumbling of the Manchu Dynasty and the concomitant rise of foreign influence in Chinese internal affairs, the spirit of reform and nationalism had grown during the 19th century, especially among the country's educated elite. One expression of the nationalist movement's force was the Boxer Rebellion, which was crushed by foreign (mostly European and American) troops in 1900 and which cost the Chinese people additional losses in pride and sovereignty.

Ultimately, in 1911, the crumbling Manchu rule was overthrown, and the long and often chaotic and halting process of establishing a new China began. Lacking strong, coherent leadership, the country was initially divided by the contentious aspirations of various provincial generals and warlords; it took more than 10 years for a significant national authority to emerge under Dr. Sun Yat-sen.

Meantime, Zhou was making his mark at the Nankai school as a writer and editor of the student journal. His articles stressed China's need for unification and industrialization, as well as the importance of enrolling youth in the political and social process. Completing four years at Nankai and in search of new knowledge, Zhou went to Tokyo, then a center for many Chinese students with nationalist leanings. In two years in Japan, the young man was introduced to socialism through the writings of Kawakami Hajime and audited courses in social science. And in constant discussions with his fellow students his nationalist fervor mounted. In one such conversation, Zhou reportedly said: "You cannot salvage the situation with strong leadership alone. You have to have strong followers to support the leadership. You have to start with a thorough reeducation of the younger generation—of the students, the workers and even the peasants. You have to have them all with you before you can push a revolution to a successful conclusion."

The transition from talk to action came in the May Fourth Movement, which grew out of a violent student demonstration in Beijing on May 4, 1919. The protest was against a decision at the Paris Peace Conference (ending World War I) that awarded Germany's economic concession in the Shandong Peninsula to Japan.

The movement took Zhou back to Tianjin, where he was named editor of *Juewu* (*The Awakening*), an organ of the strongly nationalist Awakening Society. This society and others like it in other parts of China were the taproots of the Chinese Communist party, organized in mid-1921.

Some nationalists, Mao and Zhou among them,

were deeply influenced by the Bolshevik Revolution of 1917 in Russia, articles about which appeared from time to time in the student press. Zhou's link with the Communists was not immediate, however, although the drift of his thinking shifted leftward.

After spending a few months in jail for his agitational activities, Zhou left China in mid-1920 for France. The object was further study, but he spent much of his four years in Europe in organizing other Chinese students and in absorbing Marxist thought. Sometime in this period he joined the Chinese Communist Youth Corps, a training ground for potential party members, and then the party itself, of which he became a leading member.

By the time of his return to China in 1924, Zhou was also an active member of the Kuomintang, the Nationalist Party of Dr. Sun, who was consolidating his authority in South China. In Canton, Zhou quickly rose to high posts in both the Kuomintang and the Communist party, then cooperating with each other and then both receiving help from Soviet military men and Comintern emissaries.

Owing to his organizing adeptness and his political savvy, Zhou was named secretary to the party's Guangdong Regional Council and head of its Military Committee. And of perhaps greater immediate importance was his work in the political department of the Whampoa Military Academy, commanded by Chiang Kai-shek. Zhou was the dominant person in the political department, directing the political education of the cadets for two years. His stature rose with his front-line success as a political officer in a campaign against a Guangdong warlord, the first of his many battlefield experiences.

After Dr. Sun's death in 1925, tensions between the right and left wings of the Kuomintang sharpened, and the united front between Chiang, representing the bankers and merchants, and the Communists, speaking for many intellectuals and workers, began to dissolve. The Communists, the weaker of the two groups, were set back, and Zhou, among others, lost his Whampoa post. An open break, however, was avoided in 1926 at the insistence of the Comintern, which believed it still possible to manipulate Chiang and the Kuomintang as the vehicles of revolution.

Indeed, the Communists cooperated in the expedition that captured Shanghai in early 1927. Almost immediately, however, Chiang turned on the Communists, and in a coup staged on April 12, 1927, arrested and shot hundreds of Communists and their associates. Zhou barely escaped with his life, as did Mao. Zhou's role in the capture of Shanghai and his flight were immortalized in André Malraux's *Man's Fate,* in which Zhou, thinly disguised, is the novel's principal character.

In the Communist party congress that met in Wuhan shortly after the Shanghai disaster, Zhou was elected to the Central Committee and then to its Politburo, a group that did not then include Mao. In the brief but celebrated Nanchang Uprising of August 1927, he was a member of the city's Revolutionary Committee. But this revolt also fizzled, and Zhou went underground.

He emerged in Moscow in the summer of 1928 for a congress of his shattered party, becoming second in rank to Li Lisan, de facto chief of the party. And at the Comintern meeting that September he was elected a candidate member of its executive committee. Returning to Shanghai, he lived a shadowy existence, trying to reconstitute the party on "the proletarian base" proposed by the Comintern and by Stalin.

Meanwhile, Mao and some party associates were becoming convinced of the crucial importance of the peasantry to the revolution, a point of view Mao developed from 1927 onward. It differed fundamentally with the Comintern position, which argued for a revolution based on the working class. This difference was the nub of the often-fierce doctrinal dispute between Mao and Soviet Communists, a quarrel that was exacerbated as Mao's theory and tactics proved correct for China. Organizing the countryside and surrounding and capturing the cities, the essence of Maoist tactics, proceeded from the assumption that the exploited peasantry, the bulk of the country's millions, were the ones who had nothing to lose but their chains.

Mao created a peasant and guerrilla base at the remote town of Jinggangshan, shifting later to Jiangxi Province, where a soviet republic was set up in 1931. Zhou, who had been adhering to the Moscow policy with rising doubts, finally joined Mao in the Jiangxi fastness in 1931 and was elected a member of the soviet's Central Executive Committee. The election attested his consummate ability to adapt to political reality at the right time.

During the growth of the Jiangxi soviet in the face of at least four Chiang "bandit suppression" campaigns against it, Mao's stature in the party shrank temporarily in a complex argument over the nature of guerrillaism. He was, in fact, replaced as political officer for the military by Zhou, who also became a vice chairman of the Central Revolutionary Military Council, whose chief was Zhu De.

The Communists' position in Jiangxi was considered firm until 1934, when Chiang imported Hans von Seekt, a German general, to supervise yet another "bandit" campaign. He decided on a tactic of encirclement. In this situation, Zhou, according to a Western biographer, "worked feverishly to strengthen the Red Army." The biographer adds: "Much of his work took the form of exhortations in various party and Red Army journals to rally every available force to the defense of the soviet base."

But as von Seekt's ring tightened, the Communist leaders agreed on a breakout to the northwest, and army units left Jiangxi in October 1934 on the start of what came to be called the Long March, a year's trek to the caves of Yanan. Zhou and Mao actively collaborated both in the decision to march and in the day-to-day planning along the way. It was Zhou's soft persuasion and iron discipline that helped bring the Communist forces through the epic migration.

Along the way to Yanan, at Zunyi, in Guizhou Province, the Red Army paused for a political reassessment, in the course of which Mao asserted his supremacy as party leader. Although Zhou slipped from chairman (the post was given to Mao) to vice chairman of the party's Military Affairs Committee, the two men worked in harmony. The conference—its details are still murky—not only put Mao's imprint on the Chinese Revolution, but also consolidated behind Mao the important intellectual and nationalist forces represented by Zhou.

In the last stages of the Long March, Zhou was seriously ill and had to be carried on a litter, but he retained his authority as a senior commander. He was still a commander in 1936 when Edgar Snow interviewed him in Yanan. "Like many Red leaders [Zhou] was as much a legend as a man," Snow wrote later, continuing: "Slender and of medium height, with a slight wiry frame, he was boyish in appearance despite his long black beard, and had large, warm, deep-set eyes. A certain magnetism about him seemed to derive from a combination of personal charm and assurance of command. . . . Zhou left me with an impression of a cool, logical, empirical mind."

After 1936, when the Red Army position in Shaanxi was secure, Zhou relinquished his military role for that of a diplomat, a step facilitated by restiveness in northern China over Japanese aggression and a renewed general sentiment for a domestic peace that would permit a united front against the invader.

Some of Chiang's generals in North China, notably Zhang Xueliang and Yang Huzheng, felt that they should make common cause with the Communists against the Japanese, a sentiment that Zhou assiduously cultivated in secret talks with them. Alarmed, Chiang went to Xian in December 1936 and was kidnapped by his dissident generals, who reportedly threatened his life. After complex negotiations, with Zhou as the Communist spokesman, Chiang was released on Dec. 25 after agreeing to cease military operations against the Communists and to battle the Japanese.

In the next year, Chiang's party, the Kuomintang, and the Communists edged gingerly toward a united front, a process that was speeded in the summer of 1937, when the war of resistance to Japan became a reality. Zhou's role was that of the Communist party's liaison officer to Chiang's government. Indeed, he was reinstated as a Kuomintang member and was on the presidium of its party congress in 1938.

Harmony between Chiang and the Communists, a fragile state at best, was often on the verge of rupture, and by 1941 the united front was moribund. The Japanese attack on Pearl Harbor, which brought the United States into the war in December 1941, revived Kuomintang-Communist cooperation. Under American pressure, Chiang seemed to yield. Zhou was almost constantly in Chongqing, the wartime Chinese capital, until mid-1943. Not only did he confer with Chiang in this period, but he also circulated among foreign diplomats and journalists, making a favorable impression for his savoir faire and his devotion to nationalism.

He seemed to place the defeat of Japan above petty considerations. At one point, in fact, he conveyed to Gen. Joseph Stilwell, the American commander who was trying to piece together an effective war effort against Japan, this message: "I would serve under General Stilwell and I would obey."

Despite Chiang's tepidity, the Communists, through Zhou and others, pressed, in 1944, for a national coalition government. With Maj. Gen. Patrick J. Hurley, an American diplomat who was then trying to bring the two sides together, Zhou engaged again in talks with Chiang. These were fruitless, as was another round of conversations in Chongqing in January 1945.

With the end of World War II in August 1945, there was renewed pressure from within China and from the United States to patch together an all-party government. Mao himself went to Chongqing to join Zhou in dealings with Chiang. Chiang proved obdurate, although the Communists moderated their terms. Finally, Washington dispatched General Marshall to Chongqing to strive for an accord. His impression of Zhou was a happy one, and the two came to consider themselves friends.

Amiable relations, however, could not bridge the growing chasm between Chiang and the Communists, especially since Chiang believed he might ultimately best his longtime enemies. Marshall was able to arrange several temporary truces, but by 1947 his mission had failed and civil war raged in China. At first Chiang seemed to have the upper hand, forcing the Communists to evacuate their Yanan base. But in 1948–49, the Nationalists suffered one defeat after another. Zhou was ill during much of this time, but he was consulted on major strategic decisions.

Recovering by the time the Communists triumphed in mid-1949, Zhou applied himself to the two tremendous tasks that were to occupy the remainder of his life: that of chief diplomat in China's foreign relations and that of administering the vast state bureaucracy.

Professor Klein's profile contains this outline of Zhou's activities in those years: "In the earliest days of [the new regime] Zhou established himself as the ubiquitous political figure. It is difficult to overstate the extraordinary pace and variety of his activities. For example, he apparently attended the overwhelming majority of the 34 meetings of the Central People's Government Council and the 224 meetings of the Government Administration Council (the Cabinet) between 1949 and 1954. His innumerable reports before these two bodies would fill many volumes, and many more would be required for still other addresses."

As foreign minister, Zhou enunciated to the world that henceforth China was the sovereign in her own house and expected nothing less than absolute equality among other nations—a position he persistently adhered to until other nations, at first hostile, accepted those principles.

At the outset China was virtually a pariah except among other Communist states, obliging her to make relations with the Soviet Union a cornerstone of policy. With Mao, Zhou negotiated the key 1950 treaty of friendship with the Soviet Union and an ancillary accord that provided for the return of Dalian to China and $300 million in credit.

One of the tense points of Chinese-Soviet relations even in 1950 was that it was China that went cap in hand to Moscow. Indeed, no significant Soviet leader visited Beijing until after the death of Stalin in 1953; nor was Mao recognized by Moscow as the great revolutionary leader he believed himself to be.

Zhou's efforts to gain non-Communist friends for China suffered a serious setback with the Korean conflict in 1950. The Chinese backed the North with matériel and men, a step that led to serious American battlefield reverses and a truce in July 1953, the intricate details of which Zhou helped to work out.

While one war raged in Korea, another was being fought in Vietnam. The French were decisively beaten by Communist-led forces at the historic battle of Dien Bien Phu, leading to the Geneva conference of 1954. Zhou headed the Chinese delegation to that meeting, blossoming for the first time as a world statesman.

Sitting as an equal for the first time with diplomats of the great powers—the United States, the Soviet Union, Britain and France—Zhou chose the conference as the occasion for an approach to John Foster Dulles, the American secretary of state. Dulles's refusal to shake Zhou's extended hand in a room outside the conference chamber was taken as an unforgiveable affront by Zhou, who mentioned it frequently in later years.

At the conference, he demanded an end to colonial rule in Asia, saying: "We hold that interference in the internal affairs of the Asian nations should be stopped, all foreign military bases in Asia be removed, foreign armed forces in Asia be withdrawn, the remilitarization of Japan prevented and all economic blockades be abolished."

He also accused the United States of "creating an aggressive bloc" in Asia, using the island of Taiwan as one base.

The Geneva accord, which the United States did not sign and subsequently did not observe, called for a temporary division of Vietnam and elections in 1956 to determine a unified national government. In later years Zhou expressed deep regret that he had signed the agreement, for he had come to feel that Ho Chi Minh's nationalists had been obliged by the Chinese to make too many concessions and had been swindled.

Zhou was also disturbed because, in 1954, the United States sponsored the Southeast Asia Treaty Organization and signed a mutual security pact with the Chiang regime on Taiwan. Both actions seemed to Zhou directed against China.

Partly in reaction to these developments, Zhou led a delegation to the 29-nation African-Asian (Bandung) Conference in early 1955. At this meeting in Indonesia, Zhou's performance was again impressive.

Zhou exploited the Bandung meeting in several ways: by saying that China would "strive for the liberation of Taiwan by peaceful means so far as it is possible"; by inviting Asian heads of state to Beijing; and by embarking on a spectacular tour of Asia.

Meanwhile, Chinese-Soviet relations were outwardly correct. Zhou did make some references to "great-power chauvinism," and Soviet leaders did criticize the Great Leap Forward, China's 1958 attempt to spur the pace of industrialization. Despite these differences, Zhou went to Moscow in 1959 and negotiated expanded economic and technical aid that was supposed to carry through to 1967. A year and a half after the accord was signed, Soviet aid and technicians were abruptly withdrawn, leading to open bitterness between the two countries.

The strife had many manifestations on both a state and a party level, not the least dramatic of which was Zhou's walkout at the 22d Congress of the Soviet Communist Party in 1961. The incident arose over Soviet remarks critical of Maoism, part of the war of epithets that has symbolized the doctrinal division of world Communism.

Also in the foreign field, China's relations with India suffered a fracture, ostensibly over the Chinese-Indian border. There were armed clashes in 1962, which left a residue of ill will for many years. This coldness was further intensified in March 1972, when China sided with Pakistan in the fighting over Bangladesh, in which India sided with the Bengalis.

During most of this time, from about 1958 to 1965, Mao's authority in the party and state was muted, and it was Zhou who articulated the policy of "taking agriculture as the foundation and industry as the leading factor" when the Great Leap Forward had clearly faltered by 1962.

Although Zhou had relinquished the post of foreign minister in 1958 to Chen Yi, he was still his country's chief traveling salesman, a fact dramatized by their 11-nation tour of Africa in 1963–64. The trip was regarded as an effort not only to counter Soviet influence but also to gain support for a second Bandung Conference in 1965.

On the journey, Zhou spoke of the revolutionary potential in the emerging African nations, espousing an anti-imperialist position that depicted both the United States and the Soviet Union as "imperialist countries." Most of the leaders of the former colonial territories proved unreceptive, apart from those of Mali, Guinea and Tanzania.

Shortly before the conference was scheduled to convene in Algiers, a Communist-led coup in Indonesia was crushed, an event that cost Beijing its chief non-Communist ally. Then President Ahmed Ben Bella of Algeria, who was sympathetic to China, was deposed. Beijing, which had looked forward to dominating the meeting, was suddenly confronted with the virtual certainty of a diplomatic setback, and arranged to have the sessions postponed indefinitely. In the preparation for the conference, it appeared, either Mao or Zhou seriously misread the temper of the African leaders.

Most specialists who professed acquaintanceship with Zhou contended that it was Mao who had wanted to ignite revolutionary fervor in Africa. Zhou, in this version, was more sophisticated than Mao, who had never traveled widely; but he trimmed his sails and followed the party line.

Having been reaffirmed as prime minister in 1965, Zhou was on hand when the Great Proletarian Cultural Revolution began in the middle of 1966, an event that coincided with Mao's reemergence as supreme political leader. The turmoil of the Cultural Revolution, which persisted for 10 years, involved a power struggle and an ideological dispute over how to restructure Chinese society. One of its first evidences was the isolation and disgrace of Liu Shaoqi, the chief of state. A fundamental difference between Liu and Mao (and Zhou) was over material incentives—whether pay or politics should motivate social change. Another difference was over the role of the bureaucracy—how elitist it should be.

In the early stages of the upheaval Mao called upon the nation's youth to criticize their elders, and for a time the Red Guards seemed to have thrown China into a state of chaos. Zhou himself was under attack by extremist factions of the Red Guards, and a number of his subordinates lost their posts. The domestic revolution (and its renewal of élan) paralleled a withdrawal in foreign affairs, but throughout this period Zhou continued to make his mark as the administrator of the government.

After the Ninth Congress of the party in 1969, which signaled the winding up of the Cultural Revolution, Zhou's activities intensified as he began to remend China's fences abroad and to get the economy rolling again.

Beginning in 1973, Zhou tapered his activity in the day-to-day affairs of his office. Some observers ascribed this to the possibility that he was under attack in an apparent revival of the Cultural Revolution conducted in the guise of criticizing Confucius and Lin Biao. Zhou was said to harbor Confucian, or outmoded, thoughts. There did indeed seem to be veiled allusions to the premier, but he was never singled out by name.

On the other hand, Zhou told visitors that he was getting old, and in July 1974, on the occasion of his meeting with Senator Henry M. Jackson, Democrat of Washington State, it was officially announced that he was in a hospital. He continued to meet visiting dignitaries there until September 1975, but the imminence of his death became unmistakable in December, when he failed to meet with President Ford despite his personal involvement in Chinese-American rapprochement from the beginning.

Officially, Zhou is known to have left the hospital only three times. In January 1975 he attended the funeral of a deputy prime minister, Li Fujun, and in the same week he delivered the main speech at the National People's Congress, China's parliament, when he declared it to be the nation's goal to become "a powerful, modern socialist nation by the end of the century."

Three months before, he appeared for the last time before a large foreign audience, receiving a huge ovation as he led Chinese leaders into the Great Hall of the People for a celebration of the 25th anniversary of the People's Republic.

During his months in the hospital his public duties, and much if not all of his power, devolved on the principal deputy prime minister, Deng Xiaoping, a diminutive figure in his early 70s who had been purged during the early stages of the Cultural Revolution but returned under Zhou's aegis in April 1973. Deng, whose organizational skills are said to be second only to his mentor's, moved swiftly to center stage after Zhou fell ill, adding the posts of deputy chairman of the party and chief of staff of the 2.8-million-man People's Liberation Army to his governmental position. With Zhou's death he stands second in importance to Mao and becomes the leading candidate to succeed him.

Although details of Zhou's private life were obscure, he was known to be devoted to his wife, Deng Yingchao. The couple, who had no children, met while they were students and married in 1925 while working in the Communist underground in Shanghai. Although Zhou's wife never achieved the political prominence of Chairman Mao's wife, Jiang Qing, she is a member of the Communist party's Central Committee and devotes much of her energy to ending the traditional subordination of Chinese women.

Miss Deng told visitors that she saw too little of her husband, who maintained a 20-hour-a-day schedule until he fell ill.

"I have given up trying to get him to sleep more," she would say, referring to his habit of working through the night, sleeping from 9 A.M. to noon, and getting what other rest he could by catnapping in his limousine.

Zhou's long and delicate foreign initiatives bore fruit in China's admission to the United Nations in 1971 and in Mr. Nixon's dramatic visit to Beijing and other cities in 1972. Although Zhou succeeded in creating conditions for a détente with the United States, he did not solve the thorny problem of Taiwan. He wanted explicit United States recognition of Beijing's sovereignty over that island. Nor was he able to resolve the border issue with the Soviet Union, although talks were kept alive, if only barely.

Internally, after the Lin Biao incident of 1971, a fragile political harmony seemed to prevail. Shifts in the leadership continued, but without the interruptions of production that had characterized the Cultural Revolution and without ostentatious purges.

If China's door is now partly open and if China is indeed on the road to acquiring the industrial and technological substance of a great world power, much of the credit must go to the foresighted and adaptable Zhou, his country's man for all weather.

Zhou died of cancer in Beijing on Jan. 8, 1976. He was 78 years old.

The announcement was made by the official New China News Agency at 4 A.M. on Jan. 9, a delay of some 18 hours. It said that Mr. Zhou had died of cancer. The agency said he became ill in 1972, but had continued at his work.

It described his death as a "gigantic" loss to the Communist party, the army and the people as well as the cause of international Communism.

Hours after the prime minister's death was announced, there was not a flicker of public reaction in the darkened, freezing streets of the capital as early morning joggers paced the pavements and blue-clad residents waited for buses.

In Tian An Men, scene of China's greatest parades, public security men chatted amiably, thumping their hands together to keep out the cold.

Asked whether he was aware that Mr. Zhou had died, one pedestrian stared back in disbelief.

There was no sign of abnormal activity around the red-walled compound of Zhongnanhai, where Mr. Zhou lived. The flagpole outside was bare.

The only sign of emotion was in the voices of Chinese operators on the international telephone exchange, who had clearly heard of the death.

Early-morning restaurants opened as usual to serve workers, crowds lined up for their trains at the railroad station and in the markets old women laid out their vegetables for sale.

A MEMOIR OF ZHOU: HIS MIND UNFETTERED, HIS HEART WITH MAO

HARRISON E. SALISBURY

NOTHING WAS more typical of Zhou Enlai than his open, almost boyish delight in engaging Henry Kissinger in a diplomatic duel of wits.

Mr. Zhou, at least in his last years, hardly sought to conceal the fact that few diplomatic exchanges really tested his skill. Mr. Kissinger was the great exception. Both men prided themselves on their intelligence, sophistication, and verbal and mental dexterity.

Two days before one of his last meetings with Mr. Kissinger, Mr. Zhou spent the evening with a group of Americans, questioning them about issues to be discussed with his American counterpart. Every so often he would grin with delight and clap his hands.

"Oh, that's very good," he would say. "That's something I can use with Kissinger."

This was Zhou Enlai's style. There was more champagne in his personality than there was maotai, the deadly 140-proof Chinese liquor. He bubbled.

One of his more spectacular displays occurred in 1954, when he paused in Moscow on his way back to Beijing after participating in the Geneva discussions on Indochina. It was his initial appearance on the international diplomatic stage after the Chinese Communists came to power in October 1949.

Mr. Zhou was given a great diplomatic reception by his Soviet hosts. In an inner room, Mr. Zhou sat down to dinner with the post-Stalin Politburo then headed by Georgi Malenkov and including Nikita Khrushchev, Nikolai Bulganin and Anastas Mikoyan. Also present were the chief diplomats of non-Communist countries that had diplomatic relations with China—the British, Swedish and Indian ambassadors among others.

As two Western correspondents craned their necks at the door, they saw Mr. Zhou, going from guest to guest offering toasts. But, to their surprise, he was speaking in English, a language understood by the reporters, by the Western diplomats but by none of the Russians.

When Mr. Zhou came to Mr. Mikoyan, the Armenian said in a surly tone, in Russian, "Why don't you speak Russian, Zhou? You know Russian perfectly well."

Mr. Zhou responded in English: "It's time for you to learn to speak Chinese, Mikoyan."

Mr. Mikoyan said, "Chinese is a very hard language."

"Never mind," Mr. Zhou said gaily. "Come around to our embassy in the morning. We'll be glad to give you lessons."

Mr. Zhou's sarcastic remarks were the first public symptom of what later became only too well known, the bad blood between the Chinese Communists and their Soviet allies.

Mr. Zhou loved talk—witty, sarcastic, difficult, mind-expanding. American correspondents who spent wartime years in the Chinese Nationalist capital of Chongqing were well aware of this. Mr. Zhou was there as the Communist regime's representative and spent almost every evening in conversation, particularly with Americans.

In later years he made no secret that these were the years he most enjoyed. Beginning in 1971, and continuing until his illness compelled him to give up the custom, he spent evening after evening in Beijing in conversation—gay, humorous but often extraordinarily serious—with one group of Americans after another. He seemed unable to get enough of it. Again and again he would say as talk became more and more freewheeling: "This is good. This is like it used to be in the old days."

By the old days he meant the wartime days, in Chongqing or in Yanan, where so many Americans first met him.

Mr. Zhou's energy in 1971 and 1972 seemed inexhaustible, but to many it also seemed he was racing against time, as though there were not enough hours in the day or night, or days in the week, or weeks in the month for him to accomplish the tasks ahead of him.

It was not all fireworks. Mr. Zhou knew what he wanted to know. He briefed himself on the United States, on its politics, on the world. It was as though he had to soak in everything that had happened in the West during the long years in which China was cut off.

How did Mr. Zhou and his extraordinary style fit in with the People's Republic of China, with Mao Zedong and his famous Red Book, with the Cultural Revolution, with the peasant mass of China, with the intrigues, the rivalries for position, the phenomena of Lin Biao and Liu Shaoqi?

None who knew Mr. Zhou, even those who knew China well, could entirely understand this. But Mr. Zhou always made one thing clear—his total and utter dedication to Chairman Mao. Again and again he said of the chairman with a sincerity that could not be doubted: "He taught us all we know."

There was no way in which Mr. Zhou's sophistication could be integrated into the kind of egalitarianism represented by the May 7 schools, the hard labor of peasant agriculture and the new training in the thought of Chairman Mao. Mr. Zhou never affected the manners of the peasant cadres of the party. He presented himself as he was, urbane, intelligent, intellectual. But no one was left in doubt that inside was steel.

He displayed that during the first year of the Cultural Revolution. In the late summer of 1966, Mr. Zhou was besieged in the People's Palace on Tian An Men by a million, and possibly more, Red Guards. There was no force to aid Mr. Zhou. Both Chairman Mao and Lin Biao, then army chief, were out of town, presumably by coincidence. For 48 hours, Mr. Zhou debated with the vehement Red Guards, who regarded him as a cosmopolitan traitor to the revolution. After 48 hours he won the argument. The throng dispersed and Mr. Zhou was freed. It may have been the greatest trial of his long career. But it was hardly the first. Mr. Zhou had fought his way up as a revolutionary leader of Communist army troops. The contrast between Chairman Mao's personality and Mr. Zhou's could hardly have been more complete, but at some point the two made an alliance that was not broken by years, rivalry or policy.

How did Mr. Zhou make it work? An acute sense of realism is surely one answer. He was always prepared to measure China, as well as her adversaries, realistically. When well-meaning American sympathizers sought to place on Washington the blame for the long years of antagonism, he gently but firmly rebuked them. China, too, he insisted, had displayed its share of hostility. It was a typical example of Zhou Enlai's pragmatism, and the breadth of his views.

THE BELOVED ENIGMA

JOHN F. BURNS

FORMER VICE President Walter F. Mondale was the host at a dinner in January 1986 at one of Beijing's new Western-style hotels. He was to visit Deng Xiaoping the next morning, and he was eager to share what a Chinese guest at the table thought of the outspoken man who has set China on an ambitious course of modernization.

The guest, a fashion designer, spoke enthusiastically of the new freedoms opened up by Mr. Deng. But the leader she admired most, she said, was Zhou Enlai, prime minister for more than 26 years after the founding of the Communist state in 1949.

"I loved him," she told Mr. Mondale, with none of the reserve Chinese often show when speaking of their feelings. "He was so mild. He tried to protect everybody."

The young woman paused, then added: "But he compromised so much. Perhaps he should have stood up more often and said, 'This is wrong!' If he had done that, perhaps we wouldn't have suffered so much."

Ten years after Zhou's death, on Jan. 8, 1976, he remained the most widely loved of China's 20th-century leaders.

Sun Yat-sen, founder of the republic that followed the collapse of the Manchu dynasty in 1911, has widespread respect. Mao Zedong, the dominant figure in the Communist government until his death in September 1976, is regarded with an awe tempered by recognition of the pain inflicted in his name. But for Zhou, who was 78 years old when he died of cancer, feelings are unstinting.

Many Chinese still speak of him as "our prime minister," using a possessive almost never employed when speaking of Mao, or even of Mr. Deng, who has gained enormous popularity of his own. Photographs of Zhou are common in the cramped two-room apartments in which many Chinese live.

Although Zhou's ashes were scattered over the mountains and rivers of China at his request, the commemorative room Mr. Deng directed to be set aside for him in Mao's mausoleum in Beijing draws large crowds, frequently more animated than those that file past Mao's bier.

Abroad, too, Zhou has achieved a lasting stature. Former Secretary of State Henry A. Kissinger, whose talks with the Chinese leader laid the foundation for the reconciliation between Washington and Beijing, found him "one of the two or three most impressive men" he had ever met—"urbane, infinitely patient, extraordinarily intelligent, subtle."

Even hardened Western reporters remember him for small acts of courtesy and consideration. An American television producer who came here in the early 1970s was aghast when her expensive jade bracelet fell to the floor and shattered as she held out her hand to greet Zhou at a banquet in the Great Hall of the People. The prime minister immediately beckoned an aide to collect the pieces and had the bracelet returned to the producer's hotel before noon the next day—immaculately bound with a series of solid gold rings.

Yet for all the affection, Zhou remains something of an enigma. The question that puzzles many Chinese was captured by the fashion designer's dinner table remarks—whether Zhou can be excused for the worst sufferings that millions of people here underwent in the first quarter century of Communist rule, when his authority was exceeded by only one or two men, and toward the end by only one man, Mao.

The standard answer is that he was an alleviating influence within the Communist party hierarchy, a leader who went along with Mao's excesses in the Great Leap Forward of 1958 to 1960 and the Cultural Revolution of 1966 to 1976 so as to be able to limit the human cost and rebuild something saner when the madness was spent. It was the interpretation shared by virtually every Western biographer, including the most recent, the English scholar and journalist Dick Wilson.

In his book *Zhou*, published in 1985, Mr. Wilson says this of Zhou's performance during the Cultural Revolution, when tens of thousands were hounded to their deaths: "Zhou had two choices. He could make a stand and demand that Mao call off the campaign or bring the Red Guards to heel."

He continued: "But this would have ended Zhou's usefulness to Mao. He would have been hounded out of his position of influence, removed from control of the government.

"The other possibility," Mr. Wilson wrote, "was to go on pretending to support the movement, while endeavoring to deflect its successes, blunt its mischief and stanch the wounds it was inflicting."

The explanation is one that is accepted by many Chinese, including those who survived beatings and other suffering. Among these is Mr. Deng, who was driven from high office in 1966 and humiliated. At the time Zhou was one of those who condemned Mr. Deng as a "capitalist roader," but it was the prime minister who interceded with Mao in 1973 to have him returned to Beijing.

These days, Mr. Deng rationalizes Zhou's personal role in the suffering, saying he was "sometimes forced to act against his conscience in order to minimize the damage" wrought by Mao.

It is a view that excuses much in Zhou's career. At the outset of the Communist period there was his involvement in the execution of millions of landlords and other remnants of the old bourgeoisie. Later there was his almost matter-of-fact reaction to the killing and mistreatment of several of his ministers by the Red Guards. More than once he responded by wondering aloud as to how he would "explain" the mistreatment to the party's Central Committee.

Against this, there is a mountain of evidence showing him as a voice for restraint. Under Mr. Deng, a wealth of previously unpublished speeches, memorandums and telegrams offered by Zhou have been published, some in a second volume of the prime minister's works, others in a newly published Chinese biography.

The picture these present is one of Zhou in very much the mold now being filled by Mr. Deng—the resolute Communist, but a fair and in the end compassionate one.

The new material shows Zhou telephoning Mao from a rural settlement in the aftermath of the Great Leap Forward in 1961, appealing for a breathing space to allow the peasants to "revive their physical strength"—when villagers in some areas were eating tree bark to survive.

The documents show Zhou by the mid-1950s appealing for fair treatment of scholars and other survivors of the pre-1949 elite, arguing that all but a few of them were eager to assist the Communists in reconstruction. And in the Cultural Revolution, they show him working to protect as many officials, intellectuals and others as he could from abuse by Mao's followers.

Without question, the image has been manicured to remove a side of Zhou that would not have identified so easily with the enormous changes being introduced by Mr. Deng.

It is hard to imagine the man who sided with Mao in the climactic struggle between the party's ideological and pragmatic wings in the 1960s aligning himself unreservedly with the dismantling of collective agriculture, with the wholesale importation of foreign influences and with the extraordinary license currently granted to small-scale private enterprise.

Still, Mr. Deng has a strong argument in the support he has received from Zhou's widow, Deng Yingchao, who retired from the Politburo in September 1985 at the age of 81. Miss Deng, who is not related to Deng Xiaoping, has worked energetically for the current leader's program.

So, too, has the man who was the closest thing to a family that the Zhous ever had—Li Peng, a 57-year-old deputy prime minister, whose boyhood in the 1930s and 1940s was spent as a foster son of the Zhous in the Communist sanctuary of Yanan. Mr. Li was elevated to the Politburo in the shuffle that brought Miss Deng's retirement, insuring a continuing "Zhou connection" at the pinnacle of power.

INDEX

DATE			
DEC. 1 8 1990			
FEB 2 6 1991			